POCKET

P9-CRL-735

Dictionary

OF CANADIAN

LAW

Second Edition

Daphne A. Dukelow, B.Sc., LL.B., LL.M.
Betsy Nuse, B.A. (Hon.)

 CARSWELL

Canadian Cataloguing in Publication Data

Dukelow, Daphne A., 1948-
Pocket dictionary of Canadian law

2nd ed.
ISBN 0-459-55324-0

1. Law — Canada — Dictionaries.   I. Nuse, Betsy,
1947-   . II. Title.

KE183.D84 1995   349.71′03   C95-932059-8
KF156.D84 1995

CARSWELL
Thomson Professional Publishing

One Corporate Plaza,   **Customer Service:**
2075 Kennedy Road,   Toronto 1-416-609-3800
Scarborough, Ontario   Elsewhere in Canada/U.S. 1-800-387-5164
M1T 3V4   Fax 1-416-298-5094

Preface

We have adapted this first edition of The Pocket Dictionary of Canadian Law from Carswell's comprehensive Dictionary of Canadian Law for a more general audience. Like its larger parent, this work was created largely from primary, Canadian sources: a term bank of definitions from federal and provincial statutes and regulations and a library of basic Canadian legal textbooks.

To create a more compact and concise reference work, we have selected more frequently encountered legal terms with the most general definitions of those terms, intending in this way to highlight the most current information with the widest appeal.

We hope that The Pocket Dictionary of Canadian Law will be be useful to any group or person whose life or work touches on legal issues.

Our thanks to the editorial staff of Carswell for the opportunity to work on this project and to our good friends for their encouragement and support.

Daphne Dukelow
Betsy Nuse

Galiano, B.C.
August, 1991

Preface to the Second Edition

The most important change in this edition of the Pocket Dictionary is the inclusion of definitions taken from Canadian case law. We have added terms and definitions relevant to the Canadian Charter of Rights and Freedoms. Again, we have emphasized terms in current use or likely to be encountered in current materials.

I wish to thank Leanne Berry and Catherine Campbell of Carswell for their assistance in preparation of this edition of the Pocket Dictionary.

Daphne A. Dukelow

Vancouver, B.C.
August, 1991

How to Use This Dictionary

Definitions in this dictionary are based largely on primary, Canadian sources: case law, a term bank of definitions from the statutes of Canada, all provinces and the Northwest Territories and Ontario and federal regulations and a library of basic Canadian legal textbooks.

In general, material is presented not historically but by frequency of use in the sources considered. Some historical terms have been included, e.g. "capital murder", "non-capital murder" and any term which appeared in an earlier statute revision if this was the only definition available to us at the time.

Where materials have been rewritten, we have attempted to remove sexual and racial bias, but material quoted verbatim has not been edited in this way.

Alphabetization

1. This dictionary is alphabetized absolutely by letter. Thus, the term "capitalisation" will be found after the term "capital" but before the term "capital property".
2. Abbreviations are integrated into the main work in the alphabetical order described above, rather than listed separately.
3. Homographs are ordered by function: first verbs, then nouns, adjectives, adverbs, abbreviations. Thus, the entry for "charge" used as a verb precedes the entry for "charge" used as a noun.

Elements of Each Entry

1. HEADWORD/HEADWORDS
(a) The word or phrase is presently in boldface, upper case letters.
(b) Variant spellings follow the most common spelling, in order of the frequency of their use.

2. FUNCTIONAL LABEL

(a) This identifies the grammatical part of speech or function (e.g. use as an abbreviation) of the headword/headwords. See the Table of Abbreviations Used in This Dictionary (on p. xi) for the abbreviations used here.

(b) A headword entered for cross-reference purposes only is assigned a functional label only to distinguish it from any homograph.

3. ETYMOLOGY

(a) Presented in square brackets, these characters show the language of origin of a word or phrase which is or was originally in a language other than English. See the Table of Abbreviations Used in This Dictionary (on p. xi) for the abbreviations used here.

(b) Where the word or phrase has adopted a more general meaning over time, a literal translation from the original language may be offered inside the brackets.

(c) A headword entered for cross-reference purposes only is assigned no etymological label.

4. DEFINITIONS

Multiple definitions are numbered. The most common or general definition is given first, less general or common definitions follow, ranked by frequency of use. In entries where case law is used, definitions are ranked from general to specific and also, where necessary, by the currency and weight of the authority.

5. CITATION OF AUTHORITY

(a) Where no authority is cited, the definition is derived from multiple sources.

(b) Specific citations of case law are complete and include pinpoint page reference from one law report. Most frequently, decisions have been quoted verbatim; such definitions are enclosed by quotation marks. Those definitions from case law which have been paraphrased or summarized do not contain quotation marks.

(c) Specific citations of legislation provide the chapter and section numbers. In most cases, legislation has been quoted verbatim, but occasionally minor editing has been done in the interest of clarity. Since this editing has been done and in some cases only the latest statute law revision has been used, those wishing to cite exactly are urged to refer to the original statutes.

(d) Specific citations of textual material provide exact page references. Since all textual material has been paraphrased or rewritten, those wishing to cite exactly are urged to refer to the original text.

(e) A general topical citation (italicized) limits a definition to a particular area of law.

(f) A general geographical citation (in ordinary type) limits a definition to a particular region or jurisdiction.

6. CROSS-REFERENCES

These refer the reader to more narrow or specific applications of the word or phrase or to related terms.

In the interest of saving space, the character "~" has been used to represent the headword/headwords in the cross-references which follow it.

ILLUSTRATION

HEADWORD —— **ASSIGNOR.** *n.* 1. One who makes a —— DEFINITIONS
transfer. 2. A corporation making an
assignment of book debts. *Corporation
Securities Registration acts.* 3. Any person
making an assignment of book debts.
Assignment of Book Debts acts.

ASSISE. *var.* **ASSIZE.** *n.* The trial of a civil —— VARIANT SPELLING
action before a travelling judge.

FUNCTIONAL —— **ASSN.** *abbr.* Association. —— ABBREVIATION
LABEL

ASSUME. *v* To take on a debt or
obligation.

ASSUMPSIT. [L. one promised] A form of —— ETYMOLOGY WITH TRANSLATION
action to recover damages for breach of a
simple contract.

ASSUMPTION AGREEMENT. An
arrangement by which a purchaser in a new
subdivision contracts directly with a
mortgagee to make mortgage payments so

that the developer is released from the covenant with the mortgage lender. D.J. Donahue & P.D. Quinn, *Real Estate Practice in Ontario*, 4th ed. (Toronto: Butterworths, 1990) at 231.

CITATION OF AUTHORITY text

ASSUMPTION OF RISK. See VOLUNTARY ~.

HEADWORD USED AS CROSS-REFERENCE

ASSURANCE. *n.* 1. A transfer, deed or instrument, other than a will, by which land may be conveyed or transferred. *Limitation of Actions acts.* 2. Insurance. See RE ~.

general topical

ASSURANCE FUND. A fund established under a statute to indemnify certain persons against loss. See LAND TITLES ~.

ATOMIC ENERGY. All energy of whatever type derived from or created by the transmutation of atoms. *Atomic Energy Control Act*, R.S.C. 1985, c. A-16, s. 2.

statute

ATTACHMENT OF WAGES. "... [A] continuous deduction or diversion of wages at source by an employer.... [which] originates by court order,..." *Ruthven v. Ruthven* (1984), 38 R.F.L. (2d) 102 at 106 (Ont. Co. Ct.). Dandie Co. Ct. J. See GARNISHMENT.

case law

CHARGE. *v.* 1. To give instructions to a jury. 2. To take proceedings or lay an information against a person believed to have committed an offence. 3. To lay a duty upon a person. 4. To impose a tax. 5. To purchase on credit.

CHARGE. *n.* 1. An instrument creating security against property for payment of a debt or obligation. 2. The amount required, as the price of a thing or service sold or supplied. 3. A judge's instruction to a jury. 4. A price or rate. See CARRYING ~; CESSATION OF ~; CHARGES; EQUITABLE ~; FIXED ~; FLOATING ~; SPECIFIC ~.

HOMOGRAPH

CROSS-REFERENCES

Table of Abbreviations Used in This Dictionary

abbr.	abbreviation	pl.	plural
adj.	adjective	pref.	prefix
adv.	adverb	prep.	preposition
AS.	Anglo-Saxon	suff.	suffix
conj.	conjunction	symbol	symbol
Fr.	French	var.	variant spelling
L.	Latin	v.	verb
n.	noun		

A

AB. *abbr*. Abridgment.

ABANDON. *v*. 1. Includes (a) a wilful omission to take charge of a child by a person who is under a legal duty to do so, and (b) dealing with a child in a manner that is likely to leave that child exposed to risk without protection. *Criminal Code*, R.S.C. 1985, c. C-46, s. 214. 2. ". . . [A]bandon [as used in the Adoption Act, R.S.B.C. 1979, c. 4, s. 8] means: 'To desert, surrender, forsake, or cede. To relinquish or give up with intent of never again resuming one's right or interest . . . to relinquish all connection with or concern in . . . ' This definition illustrates that both physical and mental components are involved in the definition of abandonment." *B.C. Birth Registration No. 77-09-010612, Re* (1989), 64 D.L.R. (4th) 432 at 436 (B.C. S.C.), Melnick L.J.S.C.

ABATE. *v*. To break down, destroy or remove; to lower the price.

ABATEMENT. *n*. Termination, reduction, destruction. See PLEA IN ~.

ABATEMENT OF NUISANCE. Removing or putting an end to nuisance.

ABDICATE. *v*. To refuse or renounce a thing.

ABDICATION. *n*. Where a person in office voluntarily renounces it or gives it up.

ABDUCTION. *n*. 1. Take or cause to be taken away a person under 16 years of age from the possession of and against the will of the parent or guardian who has lawful charge of that person. *Criminal Code*, R.S.C. 1985, c. C-46, s. 280. 2. Unlawfully taking, enticing away, concealing, detaining, receiving or harbouring a person under 14 years of age with intent to deprive a parent or guardian of the possession of that person. *Criminal Code*, R.S.C. 1985, c. C-46, ss. 281-283. 3. Forcibly stealing or carrying away any person. See CHILD ~.

ABET. *v*. ". . . [T]o instigate, promote, procure or encourage the commission of an offence." *R. v. Stevenson* (1984), 11 C.C.C. (3d) 442 at 449, 62 N.S.R. (2d) 193, 136 A.P.R. 193 (C.A.), the court per Macdonald J.A. See AID AND ABET.

ABEYANCE. *n*. 1. Lapse of an inheritance because it has no present owner. 2. In expectation.

ABIDE. *v*. ". . . [T]o accept without dispute or appeal any such order, and to fulfil or carry out such order if made." *Paulson v. Murray* (1922), 68 D.L.R. 643 at 644, 32 Man. R. 327, [1922] 2 W.W.R. 654 (K.B.), Dysart J.

ABILITY. *n*. Capacity to perform an act; skill.

AB INITIO. [L.] From the beginning.

ABODE. *n*. Residence. *R. v. Braithwaite*, [1918] 2 K.B. 319 at 330, [1918-19] All E.R. Rep. 1145 (U.K. C.A.), Scrutton L.J.

ABOLISH. *v*. To do away with.

ABOLITION. *n*. Doing away with something; destruction of thing.

ABORIGINAL PERSON. An original, a native or an indigenous person. *Canadian Cultural Property Export Control List*, C.R.C., c. 448, s. 1.

ABORIGINAL RIGHTS. 1. ". . . [R]ights arising from ancient occupation or use of land, to hunt, fish, take game animals, wood, berries and other foods and materials for sustenance and generally to use the lands in the manner they say their ancestors used them." *Delgamuukw v. British Columbia* (1991), 79 D.L.R. (4th) 185 at 209, [1991] 3 W.W.R. 97 (B.C. S.C.), McEachern C.J.B.C. 2. ". . . [T]he right of Indians to continue to live on their lands as their forefathers lived. It is nothing more and nothing less than that." *Ontario (Attorney General) v. Bear Island Foundation* (1984), [1985] 1 C.N.L.R. 1 at 34, 49 O.R. (2d) 353, 15 D.L.R. (4th) 321 (H.C.), Steele J.

ABORIGINAL TITLE. ". . . [A] legal right derived from the Indians' historic occupation and possession of their tribal lands." *Calder v. Attorney General of British Columbia*, [1973] S.C.R. 313, cited in *Guerin v. R.*, [1985] 1 C.N.L.R. 120 at 132 (S.C.C.), Dickson J.

ABORIGINE. *n.* The first, original or indigenous inhabitants of a country.

ABORTION. *n.* 1. Miscarriage or the premature expulsion of the fetus. 2. The interruption of a pregnancy.

ABOVE PAR. At a premium, at a price above face or nominal value.

ABR. *abbr.* Abridgment.

ABRIDGE. *v.* To shorten.

ABRIDGMENT. *n.* 1. Of law, a digest. 2. Of time, shortening. 3. *The Canadian Abridgment*.

ABROAD. *adv.* 1. Outside the country. 2. At large, out of doors.

ABROGATE. *v.* To annul or cancel.

ABROGATION. *n.* Annulment; repeal of a law.

ABSCOND. *v.* ". . . One who absconds from a particular place not only leaves but leaves it with the purpose of frustrating or rendering more difficult, by his absence, the effective application of the laws current in the jurisdiction whence he absconds." *Carolus v. Minister of National Revenue*, [1976] C.T.C. 608 at 610 (Fed. T.D.), Mahoney J.

ABSCONDING DEBTOR. A debtor who hides to avoid arrest or service, or simply is not in the province. C.R.B. Dunlop, *Creditor-Debtor Law in Canada* (Toronto: Carswell, 1981) at 206.

ABSENCE. *n.* 1. Non-existence; want; lack. 2. Not being present. *R. v. Brunet* (1918), 57 S.C.R. 83 at 91, 92, 95, 30 C.C.C. 16, 42 D.L.R. 405, Anglin J. See LEAVE OF ~.

ABSENTEE. *n.* Within the meaning of this Act means a person who, having had his or her usual place of residence or domicile in Ontario, has disappeared, whose whereabouts is unknown and as to whom there is no knowledge as to whether he or she is alive or dead. *Absentees Act*, R.S.O. 1990, c. A.3, s. 1.

ABSENTEEISM. *n.* 1. Absence from work. 2. When employees absent themselves from work for insufficient reasons.

ABSOLUTE. *adj.* 1. Unconditional. *R. v. Helliwell* (1914), 18 D.L.R. 550 at 552, 5 O.W.N. 936, 23 C.C.C. 146, 30 O.L.R. 594 (C.A.), the court per Meredith C.J.O. 2. Unqualified. *Bank of Montreal v. Brett* (1984), 53 B.C.L.R. 346 at 348-49 (S.C.), McLachlin J. 3. Complete. See DECREE ~; RULE ~.

ABSOLUTE ASSIGNMENT. Transfer of an entire thing. *Emmerson v. Clark* (1921), 62 D.L.R. 266 at 273-74, 49 N.B.R. 1 (C.A.), the court per McKeown C.J.

ABSOLUTE DISCHARGE. A sentence by which accused is discharged although the charge is proven or a plea of guilty entered.

ABSOLUTE INTEREST. Complete and full ownership.

ABSOLUTE LIABILITY. 1. Liability regardless of intention or negligence. 2. An offence for which an accused is criminally liable even though the accused acted under a reasonable mistake of fact. *R. v. Metro News Ltd.* (1986), 23 C.R.R. 77 at 89, 16 O.A.C. 319, 56 O.R. (2d) 321, 53 C.R. (3d) 289, 29 C.C.C. (3d) 35, 32 D.L.R. (4th) 321 (C.A.), the court per Martin J.A.

ABSOLUTELY. *adv.* Unconditionally.

ABSOLUTE PRIVILEGE. Exemption from censure granted to (a) a defamatory statement made by an executive officer acting in the course of duty, (b) matters relating to the affairs of state, (c) statements by members of Parliament during the course of its proceedings by it or any of its constituent bodies, or (d) any communication made in the course of, or incidental to, judicial and quasi-judicial proceedings. R.E. Brown, *The Law of Defamation in Canada* (Toronto: Carswell, 1987) at 11.

ABSOLUTE RESPONSIBILITY. Criminal liability regardless of fault. D. Stuart, *Canadian Criminal Law: A Treatise*, 2d ed. (Toronto: Carswell, 1987) at 157.

ABSQUE HOC. [L.] Without this.

ABSTENTION. *n.* Refusal to vote or debate.

ABSTRACT. *v.* To abridge; to remove.

ABSTRACT. *n.* Abridgment.

ABSTRACT. *adj.* Having no basis in fact. Robert J. Sharpe, ed., *Charter Litigation* (Toronto: Butterworths, 1987) at 335.

ABSTRACT BOOK. Record in which each parcel of land is assigned a separate page on which details describing the document affecting title are inscribed. B.J. Reiter, B.N. McLellan & P.M. Perell, *Real Estate Law*, 4th ed. (Toronto: Emond Montgomery, 1992) at 389.

ABSTRACT OF TITLE. History of the title to land which shows any conveyance of the land or any interest in the land in chronological order.

ABSURDITY. *n.* "... [I]n relation to the construction of statutes refers to disharmony between the parts of a statute or between a part and the whole, or inconsistency between the statute taken as a whole and a particular result of its application...." *Carfrae Estates Ltd. v. Gamble* (1979), 97 D.L.R. (3d) 162 at 164, 24 O.R. (2d) 113 (Div. Ct.), Reid J.

ABUSE. *v.* 1. To make improper or excessive use of. 2. "... [T]o cause unnecessarily substantial suffering to any animal." *R. v. Linder*, [1950] 1 W.W.R. 1035 at 1037, 10 C.R. 44, 97 C.C.C. 174 (B.C. C.A.), Bird, J.A.

ABUSE. *n.* 1. Misuse; maltreatment. 2. Condition of (a) physical harm wherein a child suffers physical injury but does not include reasonable punishment administered by a parent or guardian; (b) malnutrition or mental ill-health of a degree that if not immediately remedied could seriously impair growth and development or result in permanent injury or death; or (c) sexual molestation. 3. A state or condition of being physically harmed, sexually molested or sexually exploited. *Child and Family Services Act*, R.S.O. 1990, c. C.11, s. 79(1). See CHILD ~; DRUG ~.

ABUSE OF DISCRETION. Occurs when the possessor of power is not acting within the power as measured by the objects and purposes of that power. *R. v. Van Vliet* (1988), 38 C.R.R. 133 at 155, 45 C.C.C. (3d) 481, 10 M.V.R. (2d) 190 (B.C. C.A.), Southin J.A. See ABUSE OF POWER.

ABUSE OF POWER. "A municipality must exercise its powers in accordance with the purposes sought by the Legislature. It vitiates its acts and decisions if it abuses its discretionary power. A municipal act committed for unreasonable or reprehensible purposes, or purposes not covered by legislation is void. This illegality results not from the breach of specific provisions but from limitations imposed by the Courts on the discretionary power of government, and affects the substance of the act which must be assessed. The Court will accordingly determine whether the act is fraudulent, discriminatory, unjust or affected by bad faith, in which case it will be treated as an abuse of power." *Immeubles Port Louis Ltée c. Lafontaine (Village)* (1991), 5 M.P.L.R. (2d) 1 at 61, [1991] 1 S.C.R. 326, 78 D.L.R. (4th) 175, 121 N.R. 323, 38 Q.A.C. 253, the court per Gonthier J. See ABUSE OF DISCRETION.

ABUSE OF PROCESS. 1. ". . . [I]n *R. v. D. (T.C.)* (1987), 38 C.C.C. (3d) 434 at 447 . . . (Ont. C.A.), [it was] held that the onus of establishing that an abuse of process has occurred is on the respondent who must establish, on a balance of probabilities, that the Crown has acted in an oppressive or vexatious manner or that the prosecution is offensive to the principles of fundamental justice and fair play." *R. v. Miles of Music Ltd.* (1989), 24 C.P.R. (3d) 301 at 309, 31 O.A.C. 380, 69 C.R. (3d) 361, 48 C.C.C. (3d) 96 (C.A.), Krever J.A. 2. ". . . [T]he unreasonable multiplication of proceedings . . ." *General Foods Ltd. v. Struthers Scientific & International Corp.* (1971), 4 C.P.R. (2d) 97 at 105, [1974] S.C.R. 98, 23 D.L.R. (3d) 313, the court per Pigeon J. 3. ". . . [F]rivolous and vexatious, or if the process . . . is in fact being used for an ulterior or improper purpose, or if the process is being used in such a way as to be in itself an abuse . . ." *Canada Metal Co. v. Heap* (1975), 7 O.R. (2d) 185 at 192 (C.A.). 4. "The essence of the tort of abuse of process is the misuse or perversion of the court's process for an extraneous or ulterior purpose. There must be a purpose other than that which the process was designed to serve . . ." *D.K. Investments Ltd. v. S.W.S. Investments Ltd.* (1984), 59 B.C.L.R. 333 (S.C.), Finch J., affirmed (1986), 6 B.C.L.R. (2d) 291 (C.A.).

ABUT. *v.* To border upon.

A.C. *abbr.* Law Reports, Appeal Cases, 1891.

A/C. *abbr.* Account.

ACCEDE. *v.* To consent; to agree.

ACCELERATION. *n.* "The doctrine of acceleration is that all interests which fail or are undisposed of are captured by a residuary gift or go on an intestacy, but that a testator is presumed to have intended an acceleration of subsequent interests where a life interest fails in consequence of the donee being prevented by law from taking." *Kebty-Fletcher's Will Trusts, Re* (1967), (*sub nom. Public Trustee v. Swan*) [1967] 3 All E.R. 1076 at 1080 (U.K. Ch.), Stamp J.

ACCELERATION CLAUSE. A clause in a contract which makes several periodic payments become due immediately upon default of the payor or permits a lender to call for payment of money due.

ACCEPTANCE. *n.* 1. Signification by an offeree of willingness to enter into a contract with an offeror on the offeror's terms. G.H.L. Fridman, *The Law of Contract in Canada*, 2d ed. (Toronto: Carswell, 1986) at 41. 2. Of a bill, the signification by the drawee of assent to the drawer's order to pay the bill. E.L.G. Tyler & N.E. Palmer, eds., *Crossley Vaines' Personal Property*, 5th ed. (London: Butterworths, 1973) at 235. 3. An acceptance completed by delivery or notification. *Bills of Exchange Act*, R.S.C. 1985, c. B-4, s. 2. 4. In sale of goods, involves taking possession of the goods by the buyer. See BANKER'S ~; BLANK ~; CONDITIONAL ~; QUALIFIED ~.

ACCEPTANCE OF SERVICE. To endorse on the back of a document or a copy of it acknowledgement that the document was duly served.

ACCESS. *n.* 1. Either the opportunity to examine an original record or the provision of a copy, at the option of the Government. *Freedom of Information Act*, R.S.N.S. 1989, c. 180, s. 2. 2. ". . . [I]mplies that the custody of a child has been awarded to another person. Kay J., in Evershed v. Evershed (1882) 46 L.T. 690 at 691 (Ch.), stated at p. 691: 'The meaning of access is clear; it is that someone is to have leave to see children in custody of someone else . . .' " *Glasgow v. Glasgow* (1982), 51

N.S.R. (2d) 13 at 24, 67 A.P.R. 473, 102 A.P.R. 13 (Fam. Ct.), Niedermayer Fam. Ct. J. 3. ". . . '[R]ights to visit' . . ." *W. (E.C.) v. H. (P.J.J.)* (1982), 26 R.F.L. (2d) 164 at 177, [1982] 2 W.W.R. 313, 13 Man. R. (2d) 259, 131 D.L.R. (3d) 630 (C.A.), Matas J.A. (dissenting). 4. An exit from or an entrance to a highway. *Highways Protection Act*, R.S.M. 1987, c. H50, s. 1.

ACCESSION. *n.* Something belonging to one person which becomes the property of a second person because it was added to or incorporated with the second person's thing.

ACCESSION OF THE SOVEREIGN. The heir at once becomes the sovereign when a sovereign dies.

ACCESSIONS. *n.* Goods that are installed in or affixed to other goods.

ACCESSORY. *n.* 1. Anything joined to another; thing incident to another. 2. One who is not the chief actor in an offence but who is in some way concerned in it either before the act was committed, or at its commission, or soon after the initial and main act has been committed. *R. v. Smith* (1876), 38 U.C.Q.B. 218 at 227 (C.A.), Harrison C.J.

ACCESSORY AFTER THE FACT. One who knowing that a person other than his or her spouse has been a party to an offence receives, comforts or assists that person for the purposes of enabling that person to escape. *Criminal Code*, R.S.C. 1985, c. C-46, s. 23.

ACCESSORY BEFORE THE FACT. At common law, one who counsels or procures another to commit an offence but who is not present or active when it is committed. *R. v. Berryman* (1990), 78 C.R. (3d) 376 at 383, 48 B.C.L.R. (2d) 105, 57 C.C.C. (3d) 375 (C.A.), the court per Wood J.A.

ACCESS RIGHT. A right, granted in an order or agreement, of access to or visitation of a child. *Family Orders acts.*

ACCIDENT. *n.* ". . . [T]he expression 'accident' is used in the popular and ordinary sense of the word as denoting an unlooked-for mishap or an untoward event which is not expected or designed." *Fenton v. Thorley & Co. Ltd.*, [1903] A.C. 443 at 448, Macnaghten L.J. See AIRCRAFT ~; ENVIRONMENTAL ~; FATAL ~; INDUSTRIAL ~; INEVITABLE ~; NON-INDUSTRIAL ~.

ACCIDENTAL. *adj.* ". . . [I]ndicating an unlooked for mishap or an untoward event which is not expected or designed; or as an event which takes place out of the usual course of events without the foresight of expectation of the person injured; or as an injury happening by chance unexpectedly, or not as expected. . . ." *Voison v. Royal Insurance Co. of Canada* (1988), 33 C.C.L.I. 1 at 6, 66 O.R. (2d) 45, 53 D.L.R. (4th) 299, [1988] I.L.R. 1-2358, 29 O.A.C. 227 (C.A.), the court per Robins J.A.

ACCLAMATION. *n.* Occurs when only the number of candidates required to fill an office is nominated. The candidate(s) is (are) elected. I.M. Rogers, *The Law of Canadian Municipal Corporations*, 2d ed. (Toronto: Carswell, 1971) at 123.

ACCOMMODATION. *n.* Sleeping facilities provided on a commercial basis to the general public.

ACCOMMODATION BILL. A bill accepted or endorsed without value to accommodate a party to the bill. The party who accommodates thus is in fact a surety for a principal debtor who may or may not be a party to the bill. I.F.G. Baxter, *The Law of Banking*, 3d ed. (Toronto: Carswell, 1981) at 116.

ACCOMMODATION PARTY. A party who signs a bill without receiving value, lending his or her name to another. I.F.G. Baxter, *The Law of Banking*, 3d ed. (Toronto: Carswell, 1981) at 116.

ACCOMPLICE. *n.* 1. ". . . What is necessary to become an accomplice is a participation in the crime involved, and not necessarily the actual commission of it. . . ." *R. v. Morris* (1979), 10 C.R. (3d) 259 at 281, [1979] 2 S.C.R. 1041, 26 N.B.R. (2d) 273, 55 A.P.R. 273, 27 N.R. 313, 47 C.C.C. (2d) 257, 99 D.L.R. (3d) 420, Spence J. (dissenting) (Laskin C.J.C., Dickson and Estey JJ. concurring). 2, "One who is concerned with another or others in committing or attempting to commit any criminal offence. . . ." *R. v. Morrison* (1917), 51 N.S.R. 253 at 270, 29 C.C.C. 6, 38 D.L.R. 568 (C.A.), Chisholm J.

ACCORD. *v.* To agree.

ACCORD. *n.* Agreement by which an obligation in contract or tort is discharged. *Coulter Electronics of Canada Ltd. v. Motorways (1985) Ltd.* (1990), 42 C.P.C. (2d) 90 at 93, 65 Man. R. (2d) 45 (C.A.), O'Sullivan, Philp and Helper JJ.A.

ACCORD AND SATISFACTION. "Accord and satisfaction is the purchase of a release from an obligation whether arising under contract or tort by means of any valuable consideration, not being the actual performance of the obligation itself. The accord is the agreement by which the obligation is discharged. The satisfaction is the consideration which makes the agreement operative." *Coulter Electronics of Canada Ltd. v. Motorways (1985) Ltd.* (1990), 42 C.P.C. (2d) 90 at 93, 65 Man. R. (2d) 45 (C.A.), O'Sullivan, Philp and Helper JJ.A.

ACCOUNT. *n.* 1. Settlement of debits and credits between parties. 2. Any monetary obligation not evidenced by any chattel paper, instrument or securities, whether or not it has been earned by performance. 3. An account with a bank. See ~S; BANK ~; CAPITAL ~; CASH ~; CHARGE ~; DUTY TO ~; EXPENSE ~; HOLD BACK ~; MARGIN ~; PASS AN ~.

ACCOUNTABLE. *adj.* Liable; responsible.

ACCOUNTING. *n.* ". . . [T]he art of recording, classifying, and summarizing, in a significant manner and in terms of money, transactions and events which are, in part at least, of a financial character and interpreting the results thereof." *Toromont Industrial Holdings Ltd. v. Thorne, Gunn, Helliwell & Christenson* (1975), 23 C.P.R. (2d) 59 at 74, 10 O.R. (2d) 65, 62 D.L.R. (3d) 225 (H.C.), Holland J. See ACTION FOR ~; CURRENT VALUE ~.

ACCOUNTING PERIOD. Usually a year; fiscal year; period in respect of which financial statements are prepared.

ACCOUNTS. *n.* The statement of profit and loss and the balance sheet. See ACCOUNT; BOOK ~S; PUBLIC ~S; TERRITORIAL ~S.

ACCOUNTS RECEIVABLE. The amounts which are owing by customers to a business for goods shipped to them. S.M. Beck *et al.*, *Cases and Materials on Partnerships and Canadian Business Corporations* (Toronto: Carswell, 1983) at 777.

ACCOUNT STATED. ". . . I agree with the observation of Patterson, J.A., in Watson v. Severn, 6 A.R. 559, at p. 565 . . . 'An account stated is a settlement of accounts, in which both parties or their agents agree upon the amount due from the one to the other:' Bates v. Townley, 2 Exch. 152 . . ." *Robb v. Murray* (1889), 16 O.A.R. 503 at 506 (C.A.), the court per Osler J.A.

ACCRETION. *n.* 1. ". . . [T]he increase which land bordering on a river or on the sea undergoes through the silting up of soil, sand or other substance, or the permanent retiral of the waters. This increase must be formed by a process so slow and gradual as to be . . . imperceptible, by which is meant that the addition cannot be observed in its actual progress from moment to moment or from hour to hour, although, after a certain period, it can be observed that there has been a fresh addition to the shore line. The increase must also result from the action of the water and not from some unusual or unnatural action by which a considerable quantity of soil is suddenly swept from the land of one man and deposited on, or annexed to, the land of another." *Clarke v. Edmonton (City)*, [1930] S.C.R. 137 at 144, [1949] 4

D.L.R. 1010, the court per Lamont J. 2. Something which the mortgagor adds to property to improve its value for the mortgagee's benefit. W.B. Rayner & R.H. McLaren, *Falconbridge on Mortgages*, 4th ed. (Toronto: Canada Law Book, 1977) at 19.

ACCRUAL. *n.* Gradual vesting of a right in a person, without active intervention.

ACCRUE. *v.* ". . . [T]o fall (to any one) as a natural growth, to arise as a natural growth." *Hockin v. Bank of British Columbia* (1989), 36 B.C.L.R. (2d) 220 at 226 (S.C.), Spencer J.

ACCRUED. *adj.* Vested.

ACCRUED DIVIDEND. A dividend declared but not yet paid.

ACCRUED RIGHT. ". . . [A] right which has come into existence. . . . one that may be enjoyed at a period of time that is current or past, . . ." *Chafe v. Power* (1980), 117 D.L.R. (3d) 117 at 122, 125 (Nfld. T.D.), Goodridge J.

ACCRUING. *adj.* ". . . [N]ecessarily, or inevitably, not possibly or even probably, arising in due course. . . . the events giving rise to it or the condition upon which it depends for its existence, must have been so set in train or engaged as inevitably to give rise in due course to the right and its corresponding duty." *Scott v. College of Physicians & Surgeons (Saskatchewan)* (1992), 95 D.L.R. (4th) 706 at 719, [1993] 1 W.W.R. 533, 100 Sask. R. 291, 18 W.A.C. 291 (C.A.), the court per Cameron J.A.

ACCRUING RIGHT. ". . . [A] vested (or possibly contingent) one that may only be enjoyed at a future time." *Chafe v. Power* (1980), 117 D.L.R. (3d) 117 at 125 (Nfld. T.D.), Goodridge J.

ACCT. *abbr.* account.

ACCUMULATED DIVIDEND. A dividend due but not yet paid.

ACCUMULATED PROFITS. Profits which have not been distributed.

ACCUMULATION. *n.* 1. Adding of dividends, rents, and other incomes to capital. 2. Income from property is separated from the ownership of the property either to be an accretion to or to form the capital of any fund, or to be a restriction on and postponement of beneficial enjoyment of that property. In most jurisdictions, there is a statutory provision which limits provisions directing accumulation of income. T. Sheard, R. Hull & M.M.K. Fitzpatrick, *Canadian Forms of Wills*, 4th ed. (Toronto: Carswell, 1992) at 227-28.

ACCUMULATION TRUST. A trust requiring the trustee to accumulate specified income. D.M.W. Waters, *The Law of Trusts in Canada*, 2d ed. (Toronto: Carswell, 1984) at 491.

ACCUMULATIVE DIVIDEND. A dividend which accumulates from year to year if not paid.

ACCUSATION. *n.* A charge that a person has committed a crime.

ACCUSE. *v.* To charge with a crime or fault. *R. v. Kempel* (1900), 31 O.R. 631 at 633 (C.A.).

ACCUSED. *n.* One charged with a crime. *R. v. Kempel* (1900), 31 O.R. 631 at 633 (C.A.).

AC ETIAM. [L.] And also.

ACKNOWLEDGE. *v.* To admit; to accept responsibility.

ACKNOWLEDGEMENT. *n.* An admission that some claim or liability exists or that one owes a debt.

A COELO USQUE AD CENTRUM. [L.] From the heavens down to the centre of the earth.

ACQUIESCENCE. *n.* Occurs when a person knows his or her own rights and that they have been infringed, but, either at the time of infringement or after, by his or her conduct leads the person responsible for the infringement to believe that those rights were waived and abandoned. See DOCTRINE OF ~.

ACQUIRE. *v.* 1. ". . . [O]btaining or getting by paying or compensating therefor." *Felker v. McGuigan Construction Co.* (1909), 1 O.W.N. 946 at

ACQUISITION

948, 16 O.W.R. 417 (C.A.), Moss C.J.O. (Garrow and Meredith JJ.A. concurring). 2. "... Capable of being read as meaning, 'to get without payment or other consideration, as by way of gift', ..." *Felker v. McGuigan Construction Co.* (1909), 1 O.W.N. 946 at 948, 16 O.W.R. 417 (C.A.), Moss C.J.O. (Garrow and Meredith JJ.A. concurring).

ACQUISITION. *n.* Includes every action or method by which land or a right, interest or estate in it may be obtained.

ACQUIT. *v.* To find not guilty. 2. Originally, to free from pecuniary liability.

ACQUITTAL. *n.* A finding of "not guilty".

ACQUITTANCE. *n.* A written acknowledgement that a debt was paid.

ACQUITTED. *adj.* Absolved; found free from guilt.

ACT. *v.* 1. To perform; to carry out functions. 2. To carry out a function or fill an office on a temporary basis.

ACT. *n.* 1. A statute. *R. v. Thompson*, [1931] 2 D.L.R. 282 at 285, [1931] 1 W.W.R. 26, 39 Man. R. 277, 55 C.C.C. 33 (C.A.), Dennistoun J.A. (Trueman and Robson JJ.A. concurring). 2. An act (a) of commission, or, (b) in certain particular cases, of omission, (c) by a human being, (d) that is voluntary, and, (e) has caused consequences, if consequences are included in the definition of the offence. D. Stuart, *Canadian Criminal Law: A Treatise*, 2d ed. (Toronto: Carswell, 1987) at 66. See ADMINISTRATIVE ~; AUTHENTIC ~; BRITISH NORTH AMERICA ~, 1867; BULK SALES ~; CAMPBELL'S (LORD) ~; CANADA ~, 1982; COLONIAL LAWS VALIDITY ~, 1865; CONSOLIDATION ~; CONSTITUTION ~, 1867; CORPORATE ~; DELIBERATE ~; DUTY TO ~ FAIRLY; FEDERAL ~; JUDICIAL ~; LEGISLATIVE ~; LOCAL ~; MARRIED WOMEN'S PROPERTY ~; MORTMAIN ~; NOTARIAL ~; OVERT ~; PIRATICAL ~S; REGISTRY ~ SYSTEM;

REVENUE ~; SPECIAL ~; UNLAWFUL ~; WRONGFUL ~.

ACT FAIRLY. "In general it means a duty to observe the rudiments of natural justice for a limited purpose in the exercise of functions that are not analytically judicial but administrative." *Nicholson v. Haldimand-Norfolk (Regional Municipality) Commissioners of Police* (1978), 88 D.L.R. (3d) 671 at 680, [1979] 1 S.C.R. 311, 78 C.L.L.C. 14,161, 23 N.R. 410, Laskin C.J.C. See FAIRNESS.

ACTIO. [L.] Action.

ACTIO IN PERSONAM. [L.] "... [W]here the subject matter of the proceeding is the personal rights of the litigants and where the judgment affects only the immediate parties to the action...." *Works v. Holt* (1976), 22 R.F.L. 1 at 5 (Ont. Prov. Ct.), Beaulieu Prov. J.

ACTIO IN REM. [L.] "... [W]here the subject matter touches questions of status of the person or some thing and where the judgment binds all the world...." *Works v. Holt* (1976), 22 R.F.L. 1 at 5 (Ont. Prov. Ct.), Beaulieu Prov. J.

ACTIO MIXTA. [L.] See MIXED ACTION.

ACTION. *n.* 1. One party (the plaintiff) suit against another party (the defendant) for the protection or enforcement of a right, the prevention or redress of a wrong, or the punishment of an offence. 2. A civil proceeding in the court, commenced in such a manner as is prescribed in the rules, and without limiting the generality of the foregoing, includes set-off, counterclaim and garnishment, interpleader, and third party proceedings. See AFFIRMATIVE ~; CAUSE OF ~; CAUSE OF ~ ESTOPPEL; CHOSE IN ~; CIVIL ~; CLASS ~; CONSOLIDATION OF ~S; CROSS-~; DERIVATIVE ~; DISCIPLINARY ~; FORMS OF ~; INDUSTRIAL ~; LIMITATION OF ~; NOTICE OF ~; PERSONAL ~; REAL ~; RELATOR ~; REPRESENTATIVE ~; RIGHT OF ~;

SCIENTER ~; VEXATIOUS ~.

ACTIONABLE. *adj.* Capable of sustaining or giving rise to an action.

ACTIONEM NON. [L.] A statement by a defendant in pleadings that a plaintiff should not have brought the action against the defendant.

ACTION EX DELICTO. An action to remedy a tort.

ACTION FOR ACCOUNTING. A cause of action which a debtor may have against a security holder who has seized and sold assets or a beneficiary may have against a trustee or other person acting in a fiduciary capacity to make known what has been done with property and to adjust and settle accounts between them.

ACTION FOR DETINUE. A claim for damages caused by the improper withholding from the plaintiff of a chattel. D.M.W. Waters, *The Law of Trusts in Canada*, 2d ed. (Toronto: Carswell, 1984) at 1035.

ACTION FOR MONEY HAD AND RECEIVED. An action to recover money a defendant has received and which for reasons of equity the defendant should not retain.

ACTION FOR RECOVERY OF LAND. See EJECTMENT.

ACTION FOR REPLEVIN. An action in which a plaintiff seeks to recover possession of a chattel. D.M.W. Waters, *The Law of Trusts in Canada*, 2d ed. (Toronto: Carswell, 1984) at 1035-36.

ACTION FOR SALE. A mortgagee may choose to sue for an order requiring the sale of the property instead of foreclosure. W.B. Rayner & R.H. McLaren, *Falconbridge on Mortgages*, 4th ed. (Toronto: Canada Law Book, 1977) at 510.

ACTION IN PERSONAM. An action brought against a person for recovery of damages or other relief.

ACTION IN REM. ". . . [A] proceeding to determine the status or condition of the thing itself, and a judgment is a decision as to the disposition of the thing." *Fry v. Botsworth* (1902), 9 B.C.R. 234 at 239 (C.A.), Irving J.A.

ACTION OF CONTRACT. An action arising on a breach of contract.

ACTION OF EJECTMENT. An action to recover possession of land. W.B. Rayner & R.H. McLaren, *Falconbridge on Mortgages*, 4th ed. (Toronto: Canada Law Book, 1977) at 411-12. See EJECTMENT.

ACTIO. NON. *abbr.* Actionem non.

ACTION ON THE CASE. 1. ". . . [S]hould in the context of a modern statute be viewed somewhat as a residual category of action, . . ." *Peel (Regional Municipality) v. Canada* (1986), 7 F.T.R. 213 at 227, [1987] 3 F.C. 103, Strayer J. 2. An action brought to recover damages for injury or loss resulting indirectly or consequentially from the act complained of. *Burd v. Macaulay* (1924), 20 Alta. L.R. 352 at 356, 358, [1924] 2 W.W.R. 393, [1924] 2 D.L.R. 815 (C.A.), the court per Stuart J.A.

ACTION TO REDEEM. An action which may be brought by anyone with any interest in the equity of redemption, or who is liable for a mortgage debt and is sued for it. W.B. Rayner & R.H. McLaren, *Falconbridge on Mortgages*, 4th ed. (Toronto: Canada Law Book, 1977) at 554.

ACTIO PER QUOD CONSORTIUM AMISIT. [L.] The right of action of a husband against a defendant who has imprisoned, taken away or done physical harm to his wife so that he is deprived of her services or society. K.D. Cooper-Stephenson & I.B. Saunders, *Personal Injury Damages in Canada* (Toronto: Carswell, 1981) at 485.

ACTIO PER QUOD SERVITIUM AMISIT. [L.] "The action per quod [servitium amisit] is born of the relationship of master and servant, and though of very early origin in my opinion still persists in the common law provinces of Canada in one form or another. The action recognizes the right in the master to recover damages as against a wrongdoer who has injured his servant and thus deprived the master of his services." *R. v. Buchinsky* (1983), 24 C.C.L.T. 266 at 271, [1983] 5 W.W.R. 577, 145 D.L.R. (3d) 1, 47 N.R. 208, 22 Man. R. (2d) 121, Ritchie J. (Estey, Lamer and Wilson JJ. concurring).

ACTIVE DUTY. Something which requires a trustee to carry out an activity such as making a maintenance payment, ensuring that an investment policy balances between income return and capital growth in the interest of both the one holding the remainder and the life tenant, keeping accurate accounts and retaining and instructing solicitors to the trust. D.M.W. Waters, *The Law of Trusts in Canada*, 2d ed. (Toronto: Carswell, 1984) at 28. See ACTIVE TRUST.

ACTIVE TRUST. A trust which requires a trustee to carry out duties connected with it other than simply handing over the trust property to the beneficiary when required to do so. See ACTIVE DUTY. Compare BARE TRUST.

ACT OF BANKRUPTCY. An act which entitles another person to have a receiving order made against a debtor.

ACT OF GOD. ". . . [A]mounts to an interference in the course of nature so unexpected that any consequence arising from it is to be regarded as too remote to be foundation for successful legal action." *Tomchak v. Ste. Anne (Rural Municipality)* (1962), 39 W.W.R. 186 at 188, 33 D.L.R. (2d) 481 (Man. C.A.), Monnin J.A. (Miller C.J.M., Schultz and Guy JJ.A. concurring; Freedman J.A. concurring in the result).

ACT OF GOD CLAUSE. ". . . [G]enerally operates to discharge a contracting party when a supervening, sometimes supernatural, event, beyond the control of either party, makes performance impossible. The common thread is that of the unexpected, something beyond reasonable human foresight and skill." *Atlantic Paper Stock Ltd. v. St. Ann-Nackawic Pulp & Paper Co.* (1975), 10 N.B.R. (2d) 513 at 516, [1976] 1 S.C.R. 580, 4 N.R.

539, 56 D.L.R. (3d) 409, the court per Dickson J. See FORCE MAJEURE CLAUSE.

ACT OF PARLIAMENT. A statute.

ACT OF STATE. 1. "In the broad sense of the term, many lawful acts of the executive government, and many instances of the exercise of the prerogative of the Crown, might be designated 'acts of state;' . . ." *Baird v. Walker* (1891), 11 C.L.T. 223 at 226 (Nfld. S.C.), the court per Pinsent J., appeal dismissed (*sub nom. Walker v. Baird*) [1892] A.C. 491, C.R. [10] A.C. 262. 2. ". . . [T]here is a narrower sense, and that in which the term is more technically if not exclusively employed, which related to acts done or adopted by the ruling powers of independent states, in their political and sovereign capacity, particularly 'an act injurious to the person or to the property of some person who is not at the time of that act a subject of Mer Majesty; which act is done by any representative of Her Majesty's authority, civil or military, and is either previously sanctioned or subsequently ratified by Her Majesty:' Stephen's History of the Criminal Law, p. 61." *Baird v. Walker* (1891), 11 C.L.T. 223 at 226 (Nfld. S.C.), the court per Pinsent J., appeal dismissed (*sub nom. Walker v. Baird*) [1892] A.C. 491, C.R. [10] A.C. 262.

ACT OF THE LAW. The creation, transfer or extinction of a right by operation of the law itself, in no way dependent on the consent of any concerned party.

ACTUAL. *adj.* Real, in opposition to constructive, as in actual possession or actual occupation.

ACTUAL AUTHORITY. ". . . [A] legal relationship between principal and agent created by a consensual agreement to which they alone are parties. . . ." *Freeman & Lockyer v. Bockhurst Park Properties*, [1964] 2 Q.B. 480 at 502-3 (C.A.), Diplock L.J.

ACTUAL NOTICE. 1. ". . . [A]ctual knowledge of the very fact required to be established, whereas constructive notice means knowledge of other facts which put a person on inquiry to discover the fact required to be established." *Stoimenov v. Stoimenov* (1985), 35 R.P.R. 150 at 158, 44 R.F.L. (2d) 14, 7 O.A.C. 220 (C.A.), the court per Tarnopolsky J.A. 2. "The classic distinction ... is that of Strong J. in Rose v. Peterkin (1885), 13 S.C.R. 677 at 694: 'What such actual and direct notice is may well be ascertained very shortly by defining constructive notice, and then taking actual notice to be knowledge, not presumed as in the case of constructive notice, but shown to be actually brought home to the party to be charged with it, either by proof of his own admission or by the evidence of witnesses who are able to establish that the very fact, of which notice is to be established, not something which would have led to the discovery of the fact if an inquiry had been pursued, was brought to his knowledge.' " *Stoimenov v. Stoimenov* (1985), 35 R.P.R. 150 at 158, 44 R.F.L. (2d) 14, 7 O.A.C. 220 (C.A.), the court per Tarnopolsky J.A. See CONSTRUCTIVE NOTICE.

ACTUAL POSSESSION. Physical possession of goods or land.

ACTUAL RESIDENCE. Physical presence. *Giradin v. Giradin* (1974), 15 R.F.L. 16 at 22, [1974] 2 W.W.R. 180, 42 D.L.R. (3d) 294 (Sask. Q.B.), Disbery J.

ACTUAL VALUE. 1. "... [C]ash market value ..." *Canadian National Fire Insurance Co. v. Colonsay Hotel Co.*, [1923] 3 D.L.R. 1001 at 1004, [1923] S.C.R. 688, [1923] 2 W.W.R. 1170, Idington J. 2. "... [E]xchangeable value – the price which the subject will bring when exposed to the test of competition." *Lord Advocate v. Earl of Home* (1881), 28 Sc. L.R. 289 at 293, Lord MacLaren, cited with approval in *Montreal Island Power Co. v. Laval-des-Rapides (Ville)*, [1935] S.C.R. 304 at 305, [1936] 1 D.L.R 621, Duff C.J.

ACTUARIAL TABLE. Statistical data organized to show average life expectancies of persons.

ACTUARY. *n.* A Fellow of the Canadian Institute of Actuaries.

ACTUS REUS. [L.] 1. "... [T]he use of the expression 'actus reus' ... is liable to mislead, since it suggests that some positive act on the part of the accused is needed to make him guilty of a crime and that a failure or omission to act is insufficient to give rise to criminal liability unless some express provision in the statute that creates the offence so provides." *R. v. Miller*, [1983] 1 All E.R. 978 at 979 (H.L.), Diplock L.J. 2. A voluntary act of commission or of omission, in certain cases only, by a human being which caused consequences if consequences are part of the definition of the offence. D. Stuart, *Canadian Criminal Law: A Treatise*, 2d ed. (Toronto: Carswell, 1987) at 66.

ACT WITHIN SCOPE OF EMPLOYMENT. To carry out assigned duties, functions or activities contemplated.

A.C.W.S. *abbr.* All Canada Weekly Summaries.

A.D. *abbr.* Anno Domini.

ADDENDUM. *n.* Something added.

ADDICT. *n.* 1. Any person addicted to the improper use of cocaine, opium, or their derivatives, or any other narcotic drug which for the time being is included in the schedule to the Narcotic Control Act (Canada). 2. A person who is addicted to a substance other than alcohol. *Alcoholism and Drug Addiction Research Foundation Act*, R.S.O. 1990, c. A.16, s. 1.

ADDICTION. *n.* 1. The suffering from a disorder or disability of mind, as evidenced by a person being so given over to the use of alcohol or drugs that he is unable to control himself, or is incapable of managing his affairs, or places his family in danger or severe distress, or the use of drugs or intoxicating liquor to such an extent as to render the user dangerous to himself or others. *Mental Health Act*, R.S.M. 1987, c. M110, s. 1. 2. Addiction to a substance other than alcohol. *Alcoholism and Drug Addiction Research Foundation Act*, R.S.O. 1990,

c. A.16, s. 1.

ADDRESS FOR SERVICE. The address which a party gives to other parties and to the court for use in delivering documents or serving process during the course of proceedings.

ADDUCE. *v.* To present; to lead, in connection with evidence, to bring forward.

ADEMPTION. *n.* 1. ". . . [T]he taking away of the benefit by the act of the testator. . . ." *Re Tracy* (1913), 5 O.W.N. 530 at 531, 25 O.W.R. 413 (H.C.), Boyd C. 2. What occurs when a testator dies and the subject matter of a gift was converted into something else or destroyed by the testator's act or by duly appointed authority. T. Sheard, R. Hull & M.M.K. Fitzpatrick, *Canadian Forms of Wills*, 4th ed. (Toronto: Carswell, 1982) at 168.

ADEMPTION BY ADVANCEMENT. When a testator provides in a will for a child or another person to whom that testator stands *in loco parentis* and after that advances to that child or person a sum of money, it is presumed that the testator did not intend to provide a double portion to that child or person at the expense of other children. T. Sheard, R. Hull & M.M.K. Fitzpatrick, *Canadian Forms of Wills*, 4th ed. (Toronto: Carswell, 1982) at 170.

ADEQUATE. *adj.* Sufficient; suitable.

ADEQUATE CONSIDERATION. Sufficient consideration; reasonable value for what is received.

ADEQUATE NOTICE. Reasonably sufficient notice.

ADEQUATE VALUABLE CONSIDERATION. A consideration of fair and reasonable money value with relation to that of the property conveyed, assigned or transferred or a consideration of fair and reasonable money value with relation to the known or reasonably to be anticipated benefits of the contract, dealing or transaction. *Bankruptcy Act*, R.S.C. 1985, c. B-3, s.

97(2).

AD HOC. [L.] 1. For a particular purpose. 2. Appointed specially for a specified short period of time or until the occurrence of a stated event. *Formal Documents Regulations*, C.R.C., c. 1331, s. 2.

AD IDEM. [L. at the same point] Said when parties agree.

ADJECTIVE LAW. Law which relates to practice and procedure.

ADJOINING. *adj.* 1. Touching; coterminous. 2. "The word 'adjoining' is different from the word 'adjacent'. 'Adjoining' as its derivation implies, signifies being joint together; 'adjacent' is simply lying near." *Bowker & Richards, Re* (1905), 1 W.L.R. 194 at 196 (B.C. S.C.), Irving J. 3. "The word 'adjoining' as applied to parcels of land, does not necessarily imply that the parcels are to be in physical contact with each other; . . ." *McKenzie v. Miniota School District*, [1931] 2 W.W.R. 105 at 106, [1931] 2 D.L.R. 695 (Man. K.B.), Dysart J.

ADJOURN. *v.* To postpone; to recess.

ADJOURNMENT. *n.* 1. Postponement or putting off business to another time or place. 2. Of Parliament, an interruption during the course of one and the same session. A. Fraser, W.A. Dawson & J. Holtby, eds., *Beauchesne's Rules and Forms of the House of Commons of Canada*, 6th ed. (Toronto: Carswell, 1989) at 66.

ADJUDGE. *v.* ". . . [T]o pronounce judicially . . ." *R. v. Morris* (1979), 91 D.L.R. (3d) 161 at 182, [1979] 1 S.C.R. 405, 23 N.R. 109, 6 C.R. (3d) 36, 43 C.C.C. (2d) 129, Pratte J.

ADJUDICATE. *v.* To determine; to decide after a hearing.

ADJUDICATION. *n.* The decision or judgment of a court.

ADJUDICATIVE FACTS. ". . . [T]wo categories of facts in constitutional litigation: 'adjudicative facts' and 'legislative facts'. . . . Adjudicative facts are those that concern the immediate parties: . . ." *Danson v. Ontario (Attorney General)* (1990), 50

C.R.R. 59 at 69, 43 C.P.C. (2d) 165, 73 D.L.R. (4th) 686, [1990] 2 S.C.R. 1086, 41 O.A.C. 250, 74 O.R. (2d) 763n, 112 N.R. 362, the court per Sopinka J.

ADJUDICATOR. *n.* A person who hears and determines a reference to adjudication.

ADJUNCT. *adj.* Additional.

ADJUST. *v.* To determine amount to be paid by insurer to insured when loss occurs.

ADJUSTER. *n.* A person who, (a) on behalf of an insurer or an insured, for compensation, directly or indirectly solicits the right to negotiate the settlement of or investigate a loss or claim under a contract or a fidelity, surety or guaranty bond issued by an insurer, or investigates, adjusts or settles any such loss or claim, or (b) holds himself, herself or itself out as an adjuster, investigator, consultant or adviser with respect to the settlement of such losses or claims, but does not include, (c) a barrister or solicitor acting in the usual course of the practice of law, (d) a trustee or agent of the property insured, (e) a salaried employee of a licensed insurer while acting on behalf of such insurer in the adjustment of losses, (f) a person who is employed as an appraiser, engineer or other expert solely for the purpose of giving expert advice or evidence, or (g) a person who acts as an adjuster of marine losses only. See CLAIMS ~.

ADJUSTMENT. *n.* Settlement and ascertainment of the amount of indemnity which an insured may receive under a policy. See COST-OF-LIVING ~.

AD LIB. *abbr.* Ad libitum.

AD LIBITUM. [L.] At pleasure.

AD LITEM. [L.] For a suit; for the purposes of a suit. See GUARDIAN ~.

ADM. CT. *abbr.* Admiralty Court.

ADMINISTER. *v.* 1. To manage; to control. 2. Includes prescribe, give, sell, furnish, distribute or deliver. *Food and Drug Regulations*, C.R.C., c. 870, c. G.04.001.

ADMINISTERING. *adj.* Acting as guardian or custodian or trustee or executor or administrator of the estate of a person or a deceased person. *Public Trustee Act*, R.S.N.S. 1989, c. 379, s. 2.

ADMINISTRATION. *n.* 1. "There is nothing in the words 'administration' and 'administrative' which excludes the proprietary or business decisions of governmental organizations. On the contrary, the words are fully broad enough to encompass all conduct engaged in by a governmental authority in furtherance of governmental policy – business or otherwise." *B.C. Developmment Corp. v. Friedmann*, [1984] 2 S.C.R. 447. 2. "... [T]he winding-up and distribution of the estate of a deceased person, ..." *Flynn v. Capital Trust Corp.* (1921), 51 O.L.R. 424 at 425, 62 D.L.R. 427 (H.C.), Middleton J. 3. Letters of administration of the property of deceased persons, whether with or without the will annexed and whether granted for general, special or limited purposes. See ANCILLARY ~; GRANT OF ~; GRANT OF ~ WITH WILL ANNEXED; LETTERS OF ~; LETTERS OF ~ WITH WILL ANNEXED; LIMITED ~.

ADMINISTRATION OF JUSTICE. (a) "[Di Iorio v. Montreal Jail (1976), 33 C.C.C. (2d) 289] establishes that the police, criminal investigations, prosecutions, corrections, and the court system, all comprise part of the 'administration of justice' [as found in the Constitution Act, 1867 (30 & 31 Vict.), c. 3]." *MacKeigan v. Hickman* (1989), 61 D.L.R. (4th) 688 at 724, 99 N.R. 227n, 50 C.C.C. (3d) 449 (S.C.C.), McLachlin J. (L'Heureux-Dubé and Gonthier JJ. concurring). (b) "Since Keable No. 1 [Quebec (Attorney General) v. Canada (Attorney General)] (1978), [1979] 1 S.C.R. 218 ... and [Putnam v. Alberta (Attorney General) (1981), 37 N.R. 1], then it is clear that the boundaries of the 'administration of justice' do not include the discipline, organization and management of the R.C.M.P. In my dissent in Putnam I sought to make clear, however, that the 'administration of justice' does include the organization and management of police forces created by provincial legislation." *Robinson v. British Columbia* (1987) (*sub nom. O'Hara v. British Columbia*) 38 C.C.C. (3d) 233 at 243-44, [1988] 1 W.W.R. 216, 80 N.R. 127, 45 D.L.R. (4th) 527, 189 B.C.L.R. (2d) 273, [1987] 2 S.C.R. 591, Dickson C.J.C. (Beetz, McIntyre, Lamer, Wilson, Le Dain, La Forest and L'Heureux-Dubé JJ. concurring). (c) "... [I]nclude but are not limited to, the constitution, maintenance and organization of provincial Courts of civil and criminal jurisdiction and they include procedure in civil matters...." *Di Iorio v. Montreal Jail* (1977), 73 D.L.R. (3d) 491 at 527, [1978] 1 S.C.R. 152, 35 C.R.N.S. 57, 8 N.R. 361, Dickson J. (Martland, Judson, Ritchie and Spence JJ. concurring).

ADMINISTRATIVE. *adj.* 1. "... [I]t is reasonable to interpret 'administrative' as describing those functions of Government which are not performed by the Legislative Assembly and the Courts. Broadly speaking, it describes that part of Government which administers the law and governmental policy." *Ontario (Ombudsman) v. Ontario (Health Disciplines Board)* (1979), 26 O.R. (2d) 105 at 148 (C.A.). 2. That which concerns ministerial or executive action, used in contradistinction to judicial, quasi-judicial or legislative.

ADMINISTRATIVE ACT. To adopt a policy, to make and issue a specific direction, and to apply a general rule to a particular case. S.A. DeSmith, *Judicial Review of Administrative Action*, 4th ed. by J.M. Evans (London: Stevens, 1980) at 71.

ADMINISTRATIVE DISCRETION. In the work of an administrative agency, consideration not entirely susceptible of proof or disproof in relation to which the agency must make decisions.

ADMINISTRATIVE LAW. 1. Law relating to public administration. 2. The law which relates to the organization, duties and quasi-judicial and judicial powers of the executive, to proceedings before tribunals and to the making of subordinate legislation.

ADMINISTRATIVE TRIBUNAL. A person or body before whom a matter is heard, contrasted with a court.

ADMINISTRATOR. *n.* 1. "... [T]he person to whom the property of a person dying intestate is committed for administration and whose duties with respect thereto correspond with those of an executor." *Minister of National Revenue v. Parsons* (1983), 4 Admin L.R. 64 at 79, [1983] C.T.C. 321, 83 D.T.C. 5329 (Fed. T.D.), Cattanach J. 2. A person appointed to administer a plan, fund, facility or organization. See LITIGATION ~.

ADMINISTRATOR AD LITEM. An administrator for the purposes of litigation.

ADMINISTRATOR DE SON TORT. A person who is neither an executor nor an administrator but is either involved with the deceased's personal property or does other things characteristic of an executor.

ADMINISTRATOR WITH WILL ANNEXED. An administrator appointed to administer a testator's estate where the executors named in the will refuse or are unable to act.

ADMINISTRATRIX. *n.* A woman appointed to administer the estate of a person who died without appointing an executor in a will or without leaving a will.

ADMIN. L.J. *abbr.* Administrative Law Journal.

ADMIN. L.R. *abbr.* Administrative Law Reports, 1983-.

ADMIRALTY COURT. The Federal Court. *Canada Shipping Act*, R.S.C. 1985, c. S-9, s. 2.

ADMIRALTY LAW. Maritime law.

ADMIRALTY PROCEEDING. The Federal Court Act sets out the maritime or Admiralty jurisdiction of the Federal Court. See CANADIAN MARITIME LAW.

ADMISSIBLE EVIDENCE. Relevant evidence not otherwise excluded.

ADMISSION. *n.* 1. Excludes confession. *R. v. Rothman* (1981), 20 C.R. (3d) 97 at 122, [1981] 1 S.C.R. 640, 59 C.C.C. (2d) 30, 121 D.L.R.·(3d) 578, 35 N.R. 485, Estey J. (dissenting) (Laskin C.J.C. concurring). 2. Facts admitted by the opposite party in civil proceeding or allegations made by the plaintiff and not disputed by the defendant. 3. ". . . [A]s used in s. 9(1)(a) [of the Divorce Act, S.C. 1967-68, c. 24] means a voluntary statement against interest. It does not refer to a sworn statement in court of a compellable witness." *Veysey v. Veysey* (1970), 3 N.B.R. (2d) 415 at 416, 8 R.F.L. 123, 16 D.L.R. (3d) 239 (C.A.), the court per Limerick J.A. 4. Entry to any place of entertainment. 5. Entry or landing. *Immigration Act*, R.S.C. 1985, c. I-2, s. 2. 6. Call to the bar. See FORMAL ~; SOLEMN ~.

ADMISSION OF SERVICE. Acknowledgement that a true copy of the document was received.

ADOPT. *v.* To accept a contract as binding; to select; to choose.

ADOPTION. *n.* 1. ". . . [I]n its popular sense it means the act by which a person adopts as his own the child of another or, in other terms, the acceptance by a person of a child of other parents to be the same as his own child." *Anderson v. Minister of National Revenue*, [1947] 4 D.L.R. 262 at 280, [1947] Ex C.R. 389, [1947] C.T.C. 223, Angers J. 2. ". . . '[A]doption' bears the meaning 'putting into operation' or 'passing' when used in s. 240 [of the Municipal Act, R.S.B.C. 1960, c. 255] with reference to a resolution . . ." *Winter v. Surrey (District)* (1976), 72 D.L.R. (3d) 273 at 274 (B.C. S.C.), Legg J.

ADOPTION BY REFERENCE. Incorporation of a separate statement, statute, by-law, etc. into the original statement, statute, by-law, etc. by referring to it.

ADOPTION OF CONTRACT. Acceptance of a contract as binding.

ADS. *abbr.* [L. ad sectam] At the suit of. Used when the defendant's name is put first in the title of a proceeding.

AD SECTAM. [L. at the suit of] Used in its abbreviated form ads. or ats. when the defendant's name is put first in the title of a proceeding.

AD TESTIFICANDUM. [L.] For the purpose of testifying.

ADULT. *n.* 1. One who is neither a young person nor a child. 2. A person who is no longer required by law in the province in which he resides to attend school. *National Training Act*, R.S.C. 1985, c. N-19, s. 2.

ADULTERATION. *n.* Mixing into any substance intended for sale an ingredient which is either dangerous to health or which turns the substance into something other than what it is represented to be.

ADULTERY. *n.* Voluntary sexual intercourse between a spouse and any person other than his wife or her husband while the marriage exists.

A. DU N. *abbr.* Annales du notariat et de l'enregistrement.

ADV. *abbr.* [L.] Adversus.

AD VALOREM. [L.] According to their value, used in reference to customs or duties.

ADVANCE. *v.* 1. To pay. *Foster v. Minister of National Revenue*, [1971] C.T.C. 335 at 339, 71 D.T.C. 5207 (Ex. Ct.), Jackett P. 2. Pay before due. *Bronester Ltd. v. Priddle*, [1961] 3 All E.R. 471 at 475 (C.A.), Holroyd Pearce L.J. 3. Includes lend and give.

ADVANCE. *n.* 1. Payment made before due. 2. ". . . [A]dvances of money either by way of loan or payment at the request of the legatee. . . ." *Hauck v. Schmaltz*, [1935] S.C.R. 478 at 482, [1935] 3 D.L.R. 691, the court per Lamont J.

ADVANCEMENT. *n.* 1. Promotion. 2. A single outlay for a defined purpose. 3. Paying to a beneficiary part of the capital of a gift before the actual time when the capital falls into the beneficiary's hands. D.M.W. Waters, *The Law of Trusts in Canada*, 2d ed.

(Toronto: Carswell, 1984) at 930. 4. An equitable doctrine in which, when a purchase or investment is made by a person in loco parentis in the name of a child or by a spouse in the name of a spouse, the presumption is that the purchase or investment was intended as an advancement for the benefit of the child or spouse. This rebuts the ordinary presumption of a resulting trust in favour of the person who paid the money. See ADEMPTION BY ~; PRESUMPTION OF ~.

ADVANCE POLLING DAY. The day preceding ordinary polling day.

ADVANTAGE. See NO MAN CAN TAKE ~ OF HIS OWN WRONG.

ADVENTURE. *n.* A hazardous enterprise.

ADVENTURE IN THE NATURE OF TRADE. An adventure is in the nature of trade when it has none of the essential characteristics of an investment, but is a mere speculation if the purpose is not to earn income, but to turn to profit on prompt realization. *M.N.R. v. Sissons*, [1969] S.C.R. 507, [1969] C.T.C. 184, 69 D.T.C. 5152.

ADVERSARIAL SYSTEM. A system by which disputes between opposing parties are resolved by an impartial arbiter after hearing evidence and argument presented by both parties.

ADVERSARY. *n.* A party opposed to another in interest; a litigant.

ADVERSARY SYSTEM. "Procedure in our Courts is based on the adversary system, that is to say each party must present the evidence on which it seeks to rely and attempt to refute the other party's evidence by cross-examination of its witnesses or rebuttal proof. . . ." *Canadians for the Abolition of the Seal Hunt v. Canada (Minister of Fisheries & the Environment)* (1980), 20 C.P.C. 151 at 162, [1981] 1 F.C. 733, 10 C.E.L.R. 1, 111 D.L.R. (3d) 222 (T.D.), Walsh J. See ADVERSARIAL SYSTEM.

ADVERSE. *adj.* Opposed in interest; unfavourable; hostile.

ADVERSE EFFECT DISCRIMINA- **TION.** ". . . [A]rises where an employer for genuine business reasons adopts a rule or standard which is on its face neutral, and which will apply equally to all employees, but which has a discriminatory effect upon a prohibited ground on one employee or group of employees in that it imposes because of some special characteristic of the employee or group, obligations, penalties, or restrictive conditions not imposed on other members of the workforce. . . ." *Ontario (Human Rights Commission) v. Simpsons-Sears Ltd.* (1985), 9 C.C.E.L. 185 at 199, [1985] 2 S.C.R. 536, 52 O.R. (2d) 799, 17 Admin L.R. 89, 86 C.L.L.C. 17,002, 64 N.R. 161, 7 C.H.R.R. D/3102, 23 D.L.R. (4th) 321, 12 O.A.C. 241, the court per McIntyre J.

ADVERSE IN INTEREST. Parties not necessarily opposite, i.e., two defendants whose interests are opposed.

ADVERSE PARTY. The opposite party.

ADVERSE POSSESSION. 1. "The essentials to be established in a case of adverse possession are that the claimant be in possession and that the true owner be out of possession. . . ." *Lutz v. Kawa* (1980), 15 R.P.R. 40 at 54, 112 D.L.R. (3d) 271, 23 A.R. 9 (C.A.), the court per Laycraft J.A. 2. "In order for possession to extinguish true title the adverse claimant must prove that the possession was open, notorious and continuous, to the exclusion of the owner for the full statutory period. Acts of possession which are simply equivocal, or occasional will not be enough to displace paper title." *Burke Estate v. Nova Scotia (Attorney General)* (1991), 107 N.S.R. (2d) 91 at 103, 290 A.P.R. 91 (T.D.), Saunders J.

ADVERSE WITNESS. A witness who has a hostile mind to the party who is examining her or him.

ADVERSUS. [L.] Against, abbreviated v.

ADVERTISE. *v.* To make any representation to the public by any means whatever for the purpose of promoting directly or indirectly the sale of a product.

ADVERTISEMENT. *n.* Any representation by any means whatever for the purpose of promoting directly or indirectly the sale or disposal of any product.

ADVICE. *n.* ". . . [I]n ordinary parlance means primarily the expression of counsel or opinion, favourable or unfavourable, as to action, but it may, chiefly in commercial usage, signify information or intelligence . . ." *J.R. Moodie Co. v. Minister of National Revenue*, [1950] 2 D.L.R. 145 at 148, [1950] C.T.C. 61 (S.C.C.), Rand J. (Rinfret C.J.C. concurring).

ADVISEMENT. *n.* Deliberation.

ADVISORY COMMITTEE. A committee established under a statute to provide advice, usually to the government of the day.

ADVISORY OPINION. An answer to a hypothetical question put to a court.

ADVOCACY. *n.* The act of pleading for, supporting a position or viewpoint.

ADVOCATE. *n.* 1. The supporter of a cause who assists a client with advice and pleads for the client. 2. A barrister and solicitor. 3. An advocate or a notary and, in another Canadian province, a barrister or a solicitor. *An Act to Amend the Taxation Act and Other Fiscal Legislation*, S.Q. 1985, c. 25, s. 17. 4. A person entered on the Roll. *Barreau du Québec Act*, R.S.Q. 1977, c. B-1, s. 1.

ADVOCATE. *n.* The periodical, Advocate.

ADVOCATES' Q. *abbr.* The Advocates' Quarterly.

ADVOCATES' SOC. J. *abbr.* The Advocates' Society Journal.

ADVOCATE (TOR.) *abbr.* The Advocate, published by the Student Law Society, Faculty of Law, University of Toronto.

ADVOCATE (VAN.) *abbr.* The Advocate, published by the Vancouver Bar Association.

ADVOW. *v.* To maintain or justify an act.

AEQUITAS EST QUASI EQUALITAS. [L.] Equity is, in a manner of speaking, equality.

AEQUITAS NUNQUAM CONTRAVENIT LEGIS. [L.] Equity never contravenes the common law.

AERODROME. *n.* Any area of land, water (including the frozen surface thereof) or other supporting surface used, designed, prepared, equipped or set apart for use either in whole or in part for the arrival, departure, movement or servicing of aircraft and includes any buildings, installations and equipment situated thereon or associated therewith. *Aeronautics Act*, R.S.C. 1985 (1st Supp.), c. 33, s. 3.

AERONAUTICS. *n.* 1. ". . . [A]ir transportation as a whole." *Bensol Customs Brokers v. Air Canada* (1979), 99 D.L.R. (3d) 623 at 630, [1979] 2 F.C. 575 (T.D.), Le Dain J. 2. ". . . [A]s used in this section [Federal Court Act, R.S.C. 1970, c. 10, s. 23], certainly includes the control and regulation of air navigation over Canada, and regulation and control of aerodromes and air stations as well as the investigation of air accidents, such as used in the Aeronautics Act, R.S.C. 1970, c. A-3." *Canadian Fur Co. v. KLM Royal Dutch Airlines* (1974), 52 D.L.R. (3d) 128 at 133, [1974] 2 F.C. 944 (T.D.), Addy J.

AFFAIRS. *n.* 1. That which concerns a person in trade or property. 2. The relationships among a body corporate, its affiliates and the shareholders, directors and officers of those bodies corporate but does not include the business carried on by those bodies corporate.

AFFECT. *v.* ". . . '[T]o act upon or have an effect upon' . . ." *Desjarlais v. Piapot Band, No. 75* (1989), [1990] 1 C.N.L.R. 39 at 41, [1989] 3 F.C. 605, 12 C.H.R.R. C/466 (C.A.), Desjardins J.A.

AFFECTION. See NATURAL ~.

AFFIANT. *n.* A person who makes an affidavit.

AFFIDAVIT. *n.* 1. A written statement supported by the oath of the deponent or by a solemn affirmation, administered and attested by any person authorized by law to administer oaths. 2. Includes a statutory declaration. Various statutes. 3. An affirmation when made by a person entitled to affirm. Various statutes. See COMMISSIONER FOR TAKING ~S; CROSS-EXAMINATION ON ~.

AFFIDAVIT OF DOCUMENTS. A descriptive listing of the documents which a party to an action possesses, controls or has in their power.

AFFIDAVIT OF MERITS. An affidavit which a defendant files and which responds to a specially endorsed writ.

AFFIDAVIT OF SERVICE. An affidavit certifying that a document has been served on a party to a proceeding.

AFFILIATION. *n.* 1. The establishment of a bond between two or more organizations. 2. A process through which a child's parentage is determined. *Kirkpatrick v. Maroughan*, [1927] 3 D.L.R. 546 at 548, 60 O.L.R. 495 (C.A.), Middleton J.A.

AFFILIATION ORDER. ". . . There are two parts to the order; in some jurisdictions, such as Nova Scotia, there are two distinct orders. The first part of the one order or the first of two orders establishes the respondent's paternity while the second directs the payment of maintenance for the child. Maintenance can be directed if, and only if, paternity is established." *Works v. Holt* (1976), 22 R.F.L. 1 at 11 (Ont. Prov. Ct.), Beaulieu Prov. J.

AFFILIATION PROCEEDING. An application or action to determine paternity of a child.

AFFINITY. *n.* Relationship through marriage.

AFFIRM. *v.* 1. To promise in solemn form to tell the truth while giving evidence or when making an affidavit. 2. To confirm a lower court's decision. 3. When a party who is entitled to void a contract but chooses not to avoid the contract, to carry it out or act as though bound by it, the party is said to affirm the contract.

AFFIRMANT. *n.* One who solemnly affirms.

AFFIRMATION. *n.* A solemn declaration with no oath. A person who objects to taking an oath may affirm, and the affirmation has the same effect as an oath. See OATH OR ~ OF CITIZENSHIP.

AFFIRMATIVE. *adj.* Asserting positively.

AFFIRMATIVE ACTION. "Affirmative action has been defined by Laycraft J.A. (as he then was) and adopted by the Supreme Court of Canada [in] Athabasca Tribal Council v. Amoco Can. Petroleum Co., [1981] 1 S.C.R. 699 . . . : 'Terms and conditions imposed for the benefit of groups suffering from economic and social disadvantages, usually as a result of past discrimination, and designed to assist them to achieve equality with other segments of the population are referred to as "affirmative action" programs.' " *Shewchuk v. Ricard* (1986), 24 C.R.R. 45 at 52, 2 B.C.L.R. (2d) 324, [1986] 4 W.W.R. 289, 1 R.F.L. (3d) 337, 28 D.L.R. (4th) 429 (C.A.), Nemetz C.J.B.C.

AFFIRMATIVE DEFENCE. Equivalent to a plea in confession and avoidance. Pleading a limitation period is an example. The defendant first admits relevant allegations made by the plaintiff and then sets out facts which avoid the result for which the plaintiff is arguing. Watson & Williams, *Canadian Civil Procedure*, 2d ed. (Toronto: Butterworths, 1977) at 1-5, 6-2 and 6-101.

AFFIRMATIVE PREGNANT. An assertion implying a negation in favour of the adverse party.

AFFIXED. *adj.* As applied to goods means erected upon or affixed or annexed to land in such manner and under such circumstances as to constitute them fixtures. *Conditional Sales acts.*

AFFRAY. *n.* The act of fighting in

any public street or highway, or fighting to the alarm of the public in any other place to which the public have access. *Criminal Code*, R.S.C. 1927, c. 36, s. 100.

AFFREIGHTMENT. *n*. A contract in which a shipowner agrees to carry goods in exchange for a reward.

AFORESAID. *adj*. Mentioned previously.

AFORETHOUGHT. *adj*. Considered or thought of previously. See MALICE ~.

A FORTIORI. [L.] 1. By so much stronger reason. 2. Much more.

AFTER-MARKET. *n*. The market in a security once it has been sold initially by the issuer.

A.G. *abbr*. Attorney General.

AGAINST INTEREST. Used to describe a statement or admission which is adverse to the position or interest of the person making the statement or admission.

AGE. *n*. "... [I]ndicia of maturity, reflecting a length of time which a being or thing has been in existence...." *R. v. Panarctic Oils Ltd.* (1982), 12 C.E.L.R. 78 at 92 (N.W.T. Terr. Ct.), Bourassa Terr. Ct. J. See FULL ~; LEGAL ~; NON-~.

AGENCY. *n*. 1. A relationship existing between two persons. One, called the agent, is legally considered to represent the other, called the principal, in a way which affects the principal's legal position in relation to third parties. G.H.L. Fridman, *The Law of Agency*, 6th ed. (London: Butterworths, 1990) at 9. 2. "... [A] local place of business from which an agent acts for his principal, ..." *Minister of National Revenue v. Panther Oil & Grease Manufacturing Co.*, [1961] C.T.C. 363 at 378, 61 D.T.C. 1222 (Ex. Ct.), Thorson P. See CLEARING ~; EMPLOYMENT ~; EXPRESS ~; LAW OF ~.

AGENDA. *n*. A schedule or list of the business items to be considered at a meeting.

AGENT. *n*. 1. One who acts for another whether for any form of remuneration or not. 2. A person who, for another or others, for compensation, gain or reward, or hope or promise thereof, either alone or through one or more officials or salesmen, trades in real estate. 3. A person who for compensation solicits insurance on behalf of any insurer or transmits for another person, an application for or a policy of insurance to or from such insurer or offers to act or assumes to act in the negotiation of such insurance or in negotiating the continuance or renewal of insurance contracts. See BARGAINING ~; CROWN ~; DEL CREDERE ~; EXCLUSIVE ~; MERCANTILE ~; PARLIAMENTARY ~; PATENT ~; SPECIAL ~.

AGENT-GENERAL. *n*. The representative of a province in another country.

AGENT PROVOCATEUR. "... [O]ne who ... provides the opportunity for a person to commit a crime that of his own volition and intent and without encouragement he intended to commit when opportunity presented itself, ..." *R. v. Shipley*, [1970] 2 O.R. 411 at 414 (Co. Ct.), McAndrew Co. Ct. J.

AGE OF CONSENT. The age at which a person may marry without parental approval.

AGE OF CRIMINAL RESPONSIBILITY. The age at which a child may be held responsible for a criminal act.

AGE OF MAJORITY. 18 or 19 years of age; traditionally was 21 years of age; the age at which a person has full rights and responsibilities in legal matters.

AGGRAVATED ASSAULT. Wounding, maiming, disfiguring or endangering the life of the complainant. *Criminal Code*, R.S.C. 1985, c. C-46, s. 268.

AGGRAVATED DAMAGES. "... [A]warded to compensate for aggravated damage.... take account of intangible injuries and by definition will generally augment damages assessed under the general rules relating to the assessment of damages. . . ." *Vorvis v. Insurance Corp. of B.C.*, [1989] 1 S.C.R. 1085 at 1099, McIntyre J.

AGGRAVATED SEXUAL ASSAULT. Wounding, maiming, disfiguring or endangering the life of the complainant in committing a sexual assault. *Criminal Code*, R.S.C. 1985, c. C-46, s. 273.

AGGRAVATION. *n.* Increasing the enormity of a wrong.

AGGREGATE. *n.* 1. Collection of people, parts or things in order to form a whole. 2. ". . . [I]mplies a plurality of units whose total amount it represents." *Minister of National Revenue v. Imperial Oil Ltd.*, [1960] C.T.C. 275 at 297, [1960] S.C.R. 735, 60 D.T.C. 1219, 25 D.L.R. (2d) 321, Ritchie J. (Kerwin C.J.C., Judson and Martland JJ. concurring). See CORPORATION ~.

AGGREGATION. *n.* Adding together all property passing at death in a single estate to ascertain succession.

AGGRIEVED. *adj.* 1. ". . . [A] party is aggrieved or may be aggrieved [under the Ombudsman Act, R.S.B.C. 1979, c. 306, s. 10] whenever he genuinely suffers, or is seriously threatened with, any form of harm prejudicial to his interests, whether or not a legal right is called into question." *British Columbia Development Corp. v. British Columbia (Ombudsman)* (1984), 11 Admin L.R. 113 at 136, [1984] 2 S.C.R. 447, [1985] 1 W.W.R. 193, 55 N.R. 298, 14 D.L.R. (4th) 129, the court per Dickson J. 2. ". . . [W]ronged . . ." *Friends of Toronto Parkland v. Toronto (City)* (1991), 6 O.R. (3d) 196 at 205, 86 D.L.R. (4th) 669, 8 M.P.L.R. (2d) 127 (Div. Ct.), O'Driscoll, Hartt and O'Brien JJ.

AGREE. *v.* To concur; to make an agreement.

AGREED. *adj.* Settled.

AGREED STATEMENT OF FACTS. A statement of facts relating to evidence to which the parties agree and on which the case will be decided. P.K. McWilliams, *Canadian Criminal Evidence*, 3d ed. (Aurora: Canada Law Book, 1988) at 1-13.

AGREEMENT. *n.* 1. Two or more persons together express a common intention in order to alter their duties and rights. 2. A contract. 3. A collective agreement. 4. ". . . [I]n its more proper and correct sense, as signifying a mutual contract on consideration between two or more parties. . . ." *Wain v. Walters* (1804), 5 East 10 at 16-17, Lord Ellenborough C.J. 5. ". . . used, as synonymous to promise or undertaking, . . ." *Wain v. Walters* (1804), 5 East 10 at 16-17, Lord Ellenborough C.J. See ARBITRATION ~; ASSUMPTION ~; COHABITATION ~; COLLECTIVE ~; COLLECTIVE BARGAINING ~; CUSTODY ~; LISTING ~; LOAN ~; MARY CARTER ~; MEMORANDUM OF ~; PAROL ~; PATERNITY ~; PRICE MAINTENANCE ~; SECURITY ~; SEPARATION ~; TENANCY ~.

AGREEMENT FOR SALE. A contract for the sale of an interest in land under which the purchaser agrees to pay the purchase price over a period of time, in the manner stated in the contract, and on payment of which the vendor is obliged to convey the interest in land to the purchaser, but does not include a contract under which (a) the purchase price is payable in less than 6 months from the time the contract was entered into, and (b) the purchaser is not, during the 6 month period, entitled to possession of the land that is the subject-matter of the contract. British Columbia statutes.

AGREEMENT TO SELL. A contract of sale in writing under which (i) an interest in goods may be transferred to a purchaser (A) at a time in the future, or (B) subject to some condition to be fulfilled.

AID. *v.* ". . . [T]o assist or help." *R. v. Stevenson* (1984), 11 C.C.C. (3d) 443 at 449, 62 N.S.R. (2d) 193, 136 A.P.R. 193 (C.A.), the court per Macdonald J.A.

AID. *n.* See LEGAL ~.

AID AND ABET. 1. "Mere presence at the scene of a crime is not sufficient to ground culpability. Something more is needed: encouragement of the principal offender; an act which facilitates the commission of the offence, such as keeping watch or enticing the victim away, or an act which tends to prevent or hinder interference with accomplishment of the criminal act, such as preventing the intended victim from escaping or being ready to assist the prime culprit. . . . Presence at the commission of an offence can be evidence of aiding and abetting [Criminal Code, R.S.C. 1970, c. C-34, s. 21(1)(b)] if accompanied by other factors, such as prior knowledge of the principal offender's intention to commit the offence or attendance for the purpose of encouragement." *R. v. Dunlop* (1979), 99 D.L.R. (3d) 301 at 313, 317, [1979] 2 S.C.R. 881, [1979] 4 W.W.R. 599, 47 C.C.C. (2d) 93, 8 C.R. (3d) 349, 12 C.R. (3d) 330, 27 N.R. 153, Dickson J. (Laskin C.J.C., Spence and Estey JJ. concurring). 2. "An accused who is present at the scene of an offence and who carries out no overt acts to aid or encourage the commission of the offence may none the less be convicted as a party if his purpose in failing to act was to aid in the commission of the offence. . . . The authorities to which I have referred support the conclusion that where the accused had a duty to prevent the commission of an offence, or where he was in a position to have control over the acts of the offender and failed to prevent the commission of the offence, he will be guilty as an aider and abettor." *R. v. Nixon* (1990), 57 C.C.C. (3d) 97 at 109, 114, 47 B.C.L.R. (2d) 222, 78 C.R. (3d) 349, [1990] 6 W.W.R. 253 (C.A.), the court per Legg J.A.

AIRPORT. *n.* An aerodrome in respect of which a Canadian aviation document is in force. *Aeronautics Act*, R.S.C. 1985 (1st Supp.), c. 33, s. 3.

ALDERMAN. *n.* A member of a council of a municipality other than the mayor.

ALEATORY CONTRACT. A contract which depends on an uncertain event or contingency. R. Colinvaux, *The Law of Insurance*, 5th ed. (London: Sweet & Maxwell, 1984) at 3.

ALIAS. *n.* A name by which a person is known.

ALIAS WRIT. A replacement for an earlier writ which has been lost or has become ineffectual.

ALIBI. *n.* 1. ". . . [P]roof of the absence of the accused at the time a crime is supposed to be committed, satisfactory proof that he is in some place else at the time." *R. v. Haynes* (1914), 22 D.L.R. 227 at 230, 48 N.S.R. 133, 23 C.C.C. 101 (C.A.), Townshend C.J. 2. ". . . [N]ot confined to the situation where the accused claims to have been elsewhere when the actual offence was committed. It may refer to a separate and particular ingredient of an offence, or it may refer to a claim to have been elsewhere when any particular event is alleged to have taken place." *R. v. O'Neill* (1973), 6 N.B.R. (2d) 656 at 662, 22 C.R.N.S. 359 (C.A.), the court per Limerick J.A.

ALIEN. *v.* To transfer; to convey.

ALIEN. *n.* 1. At common law, the subject of a foreign government who was not born within the allegiance of the Crown. 2. A person who is not a Canadian citizen, Commonwealth citizen, British subject or citizen of the Republic of Ireland. *Canadian Citizenship Act*, R.S.C. 1970, c. C-19, s. 2.

ALIENABILITY. *n.* The quality of being transferable.

ALIENATE. *v.* " '. . . [H]as a technical legal meaning, and any transfer of real estate, short of a conveyance of the title, is not an alienation of the estate. No matter in what form the sale may be made, unless the title is conveyed to the purchaser, the estate is not alienated:' Masters v. Madison County Mututal Ins. Co. (1852), 11 Barb 624." *Meek v. Parsons* (1900), 31 O.R. 529 at 533 (Div. Ct.), Armour C.J.

ALIENATION. *n.* ". . . [B]ased on a voluntary transfer of the right of ownership. . . ." *Syndicat national des employés de la comm. scolaire régionale de l'Outaouais v. Union des employés de service, Local 298* (1988), 89 C.L.L.C. 14,045 at 12,399, 35 Admin. L.R. 153, 95 N.R. 161, 24 Q.A.C. 244, [1988] 2 S.C.R. 1048, Beetz J. See RESTRAINT ON ~.

ALIENEE. *n.* One to whom property is transferred.

ALIENI JURIS. [L.] Under the power of someone else, as opposed to sui juris.

ALIENOR. *n.* A person who transfers property.

ALIMENTARY. *adj.* Protective.

ALIMONY. *n.* 1. ". . . [O]riginally the word 'alimony' was limited to payments made by a husband to his wife up and until their marriage was dissolved and that any payments made or ordered to be paid thereafter were strictly called 'maintenance'." *Rystrom v. Rystrom* (1954), 14 W.W.R. (N.S.) 118 at 119, [1955] 2 D.L.R. 345 (Sask. C.A.), the court per Gordon J.A. 2. Includes a sum made payable for the maintenance of a wife, former wife, husband, former husband or a child pursuant to a judgment of divorce, nullity of marriage or judicial separation. *Maintenance Orders Enforcement acts.*

ALIQUOT. *adj.* A part of a whole obtained by dividing the whole evenly leaving no remainder. *Pinewood Aggregates Ltd. v. Ontario (Director of Titles)*, [1964] 1 O.R. 83 at 85, 41 D.L.R. (2d) 178 (H.C.), Hughes J.

ALITER. [L.] Otherwise.

ALIUNDE. [L.] From some other place or person.

ALLEGATION. *n.* Assertion.

ALLEGE. *v.* To state, to assert positively. *R. v. O'Malley*, [1924] 3 D.L.R. 430 at 432, 2 W.W.R. 652 (Alta. C.A.), the court per Stuart J.A.

ALLEGIANCE. *n.* Obedience owed to the sovereign or government. See OATH OF ~.

ALL E.R. *abbr.* All England Law Reports.

ALL FOURS. A phrase to describe cases which agree in all their circumstances.

ALLOCATION. *n.* Appropriation or assignment of funds to particular purposes or people.

ALLODIAL LANDS. *var.* **ALODIAL LANDS.** Lands held absolutely and not the estate of any lord or superior.

ALLOT. *v.* 1. To indicate that something should belong solely to a specific person. 2. To appropriate shares to those who applied for them.

ALLOTMENT. *n.* 1. "As applied to a fixed quantity of anything or a fixed number of shares, the word 'allotment' can mean nothing more than to give, to assign, to set apart, to appropriate. . . ." *Nelson Coke & Gas Co. v. Pellatt* (1902), 4 O.L.R. 481 at 489 (C.A.), McLellan J.A. 2. Distribution of land. 3. The portion of land distributed. 4. ". . . [T]he acceptance by the company of the offer to take shares." *Re Florence Land, etc. Co., Nicol's Case* (1885), 29 CH. D. 421 at 426, Chitty J.

ALLOW. *v.* To permit; to admit something is valid.

ALLOWANCE. *n.* 1. A limited predetermined sum of money paid to enable the recipient to provide for certain kinds of expenses; its amount is determined in advance and, once paid, it is at the complete disposition of the recipient who is not required to account for it. *The Queen v. Pascoe*, [1975] C.T.C. 58, 75 D.T.C. 5427 (Fed. C.A.). 2. Any discount, rebate, price concession or other advantage that is or purports to be offered or granted for advertising or display purposes and is collateral to a sale or sales of products but is not applied directly to the selling price. *Competition Act*, R.S.C. 1985, c. C-34, s. 51. See CAPITAL COST ~.

ALLUREMENT. *n.* An object which attracts. J.V. DiCastri, *Occupiers' Liability* (Vancouver: Burroughs/Carswell, 1980) at 111.

ALLUVION. *n.* An addition to existing land formed when sand and earth wash up from the sea or a river.

ALTA. L.R. *abbr.* Alberta Law Reports, 1908-1932.

ALTA. L.R.B.R. *abbr.* Alberta Labour Relations Board Reports.

ALTA. L. REV. *abbr.* Alberta Law Review.

ALTA. L.R. (2d). *abbr.* Alberta Law Reports, Second Series, 1977-.

ALTER EGO. [L.] Second self.

ALTERNATIVE. *n.* One of several possibilities.

ALTERNATIVE DISPUTE RESOLUTION. A term for processes such as arbitration, conciliation, mediation and settlement, designed to settle disputes without formal trials.

ALTERNATIVE LIABILITY. "... [I]f an injured party cannot identify which of two or more defendants caused an injury, the burden of proof may shift to the defendants to show that they were not responsible for the harm...." *Valleyview Hotel Ltd. v. Montreal Trust Co.* (1985), 33 C.C.L.T. 282 at 286, 39 Sask. R. 229 (C.A.), the court per Tallis J.A.

ALTERNATIVE PLEADING. A pleading which combines a traverse with a confession· and avoidance. These are set up as alternatives to each other. Watson & Williams, *Canadian Civil Procedure*, 2d ed. (Toronto: Butterworth's, 1977) at 1-5, 6-2 and 6-101.

AMALGAMATED COMPANY. A company that results from an amalgamation.

AMALGAMATION. *n.* A term describing various ways the interests of two or more companies may unite. H. Sutherland, D.B. Horsley & J.M. Edmiston, eds., *Fraser's Handbook on Canadian Company Law*, 7th ed. (Toronto: Carswell, 1985) at 513.

AMBASSADOR. *n.* A diplomatic agent representing a foreign government. J.G. McLeod, *The Conflict of Laws* (Calgary: Carswell, 1983) at 76.

AMBIGUITY. *n.* 1. Doubtfulness. 2.

"[Occurs when] ... one expression is capable of two meanings." *Westholme Lumber Co. v. St. James Ltd.* (1915), 21 D.L.R. 549 at 555, 8 W.W.R. 122, 21 B.C.R. 100, 30 W.L.R. 781 (C.A.), Irving J.A. (MacDonald C.J.A. concurring). See LATENT ~; PATENT ~.

AMBIGUOUS. *adj.* "[A word is ambiguous if] no meaning it reasonably has could effect the legislative intent, or if the legislative intent could not be ascertained ..." *Xerox of Canada Ltd. v. Ontario Regional Assessment Commissioner, Region No. 10* (1980), (*sub nom. Ontario Regional Assessment Commissioner, Region No. 10 v. Xerox of Canada Ltd.*) 11 O.M.B.R. 238 at 244, 30 O.R. (2d) 90, 17 R.P.R. 72, 115 D.L.R. (3d) 428 (C.A.), Jessup J.A.

AMBIT. *n.* Limit; the bounds encompassing any thing.

AMELIORATING WASTE. Acts which improve an inheritance, even though they technically amount to waste. R. Megarry & H.W.R. Wade, *The Law of Real Property*, 5th ed. (London: Stevens, 1984) at 96.

AMENABLE. *adj.* Capable of being led; tractable; responsible or subject to.

AMEND. *v.* 1. "... [T]o change in any way for the better. It includes removing anything that is erroneous or faulty and substituting something else in the place of what is removed ..." *Kucy v. McCallum*, [1944] 2 D.L.R. 101 at 112, 1 W.W.R. 361, 25 C.B.R. 128 (Alta. C.A.), Ewing J.A. (dissenting). 2. "[In the Judicature Act, R.S.O. 1970, c. 228, s. 114(10)] ... would include a change in form not involving a change in substance ..." *Johannes v. Johannes* (1981), 24 R.F.L. (2d) 412 at 419, 34 O.R. (2d) 548, 127 D.L.R. (3d) 88 (Div. Ct.), the court per Morden J.A. 3. "... [H]as several judicial meanings. It has been held to mean 'to annul or remove that which is faulty and substitute that which will improve.' And also, 'to substitute something in place of what is removed.' ..." *Elizabeth Shoe Co. v. Racine*, [1951] Que. K.B. 624 at 625, Barclay J.A. (Casey J.A. concurring).

AMENDING CLAUSE. Amending procedures for the Constitution absent from the B.N.A. Act but supplied by the Constitution Act, 1982.

AMENDING FORMULA. See DOMESTIC ~.

AMENDMENT. *n.* "[As] contemplated by No. 1 of section 92 [Constitution Act, 1867 (30 & 31 Vict.) c. 3] . . . was intended . . . to alter certain details of structure or machinery deemed necessary for the efficient operation of the constitution, the essential design and purpose being preserved." *Reference re Initiative & Referendum Act (Man.)* (1916), [1917] 1 W.W.R. 1012 at 1029, 27 Man. R. 1, 32 D.L.R. 148 (C.A.), Perdue J.A. See ARTICLES OF ~.

AMENDS. *n.* Satisfaction.

AMENITY. *n.* A feature adding to enjoyment of property. See LOSS OF AMENITIES.

AMMUNITION. *n.* An explosive of any class when enclosed in a case or contrivance or otherwise adapted or prepared so as to form a cartridge or charge for small arms, cannon, any other weapon or blasting, or so as to form any safety or other fuse for blasting or shells or so as to form any tube for firing explosives or so as to form a percussive cap, detonator, shell, torpedo, war rocket or other contrivance other than a firework.

AMNESTY. *n.* A government grant of general pardon for past offences.

AMORTIZATION. *var.* **AMORTISATION.** *n.* 1. Reduction of the amount owing under a mortgage or debt by instalment payments. 2. Of a blended payment mortgage, the period of time needed to pay all the principal and interest, assuming fixed monthly payments. D.J. Donahue & P.D. Quinn, *Real Estate Practice in Ontario*, 4th ed. (Toronto: Butterworths, 1990) at 227.

AMORTIZED VALUE. When used in relation to the value of a redeemable security at any date after purchase, means a value so determined that, if the security were purchased at that date and at that value, the yield would be the same as the yield would be with reference to the original purchase price.

AMOTION. *n.* Removal from office.

AMOUNT. *n.* 1. Money expressed in terms of the quantity of money. 2. Rights or things expressed in terms of the money value of the rights or things.

AMOVE. *v.* To remove from a position or place.

ANCESTOR. *n.* One from whom a person is descended; progenitor.

ANCESTRY. *n.* ". . . [F]amily descent . . . determined through the lineage of one's parents through their parents, and so on." *Cousens v. Canada (Nurses Assn.)*, [1981] 2 C.H.R.R. D/365 at D/367 (Ont. Bd. of Inquiry), Ratushny.

ANCILLARY. *adj.* 1. ". . . [A]uxiliary or subordinate . . ." *Whynot v. Giffin* (1984), 40 C.P.C. 344 at 350, 62 N.S.R. (2d) 112, 136 A.P.R. 112, 7 D.L.R. (4th) 68 (C.A.), the court per Macdonald J.A. 2. ". . . [S]omething grafted on to the primary matter. . . ." *Gwyn v. Mellen* (1978), 90 D.L.R. (3d) 195 at 201, 7 R.F.L. (2d) 106 (B.C. S.C.), McKenzie J. 3. ". . . [I]n the constitutional sense. In Re Fisheries Act, 1914; A.-G. Can. v. A.-G. B.C., [1930] 1 D.L.R. 194, [1930] A.C. 111, [1929] 3 W.W.R. 449, it was said that ancillary legislation is that which is necessarily incidental to effective legislation." *Cook v. Cook* (1981), 120 D.L.R. (3d) 216 at 228, 30 Nfld. & P.E.I.R. 42, 84 A.P.R. 42 (Nfld. T.D.), Goodridge J.

ANCILLARY ADMINISTRATION. Administration of a portion of an estate in a second jurisdiction where property of the deceased is located or where the deceased had a cause of action.

ANCILLARY RELIEF. Auxiliary relief.

ANIMAL. *n.* Any living being of the animal kingdom other than a human being. *Veterinary acts.* See DANGEROUS ~; DOMESTIC ~.

ANIMALS DOMITAE NATURAE. [L.] ". . . [A]nimals which are generally tame, living in association with man, ... subject of absolute ownership with all the rights, duties, privileges and obligations that legal relationship entails." *Diversified Holdings Ltd. v. R.* (1982), 133 D.L.R. (3d) 712 at 716, [1982] 3 W.W.R. 516, 35 B.C.L.R. 349, 20 C.C.L.T. 202 (S.C.), Wallace J.

ANIMALS FERAE NATURAE. [L.] "... [A]nimals which under normal circumstances are usually found at liberty, ... are not the subject of absolute ownership, although a qualified property in such animals might be acquired by taking or taming them or while they are on one's estate...." *Diversified Holdings Ltd. v. R.* (1982), 133 D.L.R. (3d) 712 at 716-17, [1982] 3 W.W.R. 516, 35 B.C.L.R. 349, 20 C.C.L.T. 202 (S.C.), Wallace J.

ANIMALS MANSUETAE NATURAE. [L.] Animals which are harmless by nature. See DANGEROUS ANIMAL.

ANIMO. *adv.* [L.] With intention.

ANIMUS. *n.* [L.] Intent; intention.

ANIMUS CONTRAHENDI. [L.] Intention that the language or conduct of parties should result in a contract. G.H.L. Fridman, *The Law of Contract in Canada*, 2d ed. (Toronto: Carswell, 1986) at 25.

ANN. AIR & SPACE L. *abbr.* Annals of Air and Space Law (Annales de droit aérien et spatial).

ANN. AIR & SP. L. *abbr.* Annals of Air and Space Law (Annales de droit aérien et spatial).

ANN. CAN. D. DE LA PERSONNE. *abbr.* Annuaire canadien des droits de la personne (Canadian Human Rights Yearbook).

ANN. CAN. D. INT. *abbr.* Annuaire canadien de droit international (Canadian Yearbook of International Law).

ANN. D. AÉRIEN & SPATIAL *abbr.* Annales de droit aérien et spatial (Annals of Air and Space Law).

ANNEX. *v.* To add to.

ANNEXATION. *n.* 1. Adding land to a municipality or nation. 2. Incorporation of a municipality into another municipality.

ANNO DOMINI. [L.] In the year of the Lord.

ANNO REGNI. [L.] In the year of the reign.

ANNOTATION. *n.* Description; explanation; comment.

ANNUAL. *adj.* 1. "... [T]he word 'annual' [in s. 3 of the Income War Tax Act, R.S.C. 1927, c. 97] as applied to profit or gain or gratuity does not mean that the profit or gain or gratuity must necessarily be of a recurring nature from year to year, but rather that it is the profit or gain or gratuity of or in or during the year in respect of which the assessment is made." *Consolidated Textiles Ltd. v. Minister of National Revenue,* [1947] 2 D.L.R. 172 at 175, [1947] C.T.C. 63, [1947] Ex. C.R. 77, 3 D.T.C. 958, Thorson P. 2." ... [I]nfers the quality of being recurrent or being capable of recurrence." *Lucas v. Minister of National Revenue* (1987), [1988] 13 F.T.R. 77 at 79, 87 D.T.C. 5277, [1987] 2 C.T.C. 23, Cullen J.

ANNUALLY. *adv.* Yearly.

ANNUITANT. *n.* A person in receipt of, or entitled to the receipt of, an annuity.

ANNUITY. *n.* 1. Includes an amount payable on a periodic basis, whether payable at intervals longer or shorter than a year and whether payable under a contract, will or trust or otherwise. *Income Tax Act,* R.S.C. 1952, c. 148, s. 248. 2. "... [U]sual purpose is simply to provide, by the deposit either of a lump sum or of payments over a period of years, a sum of money sufficient, with accumulated interest, to provide an annuity to commence in one's later years, either for the life of the annuitant or for a fixed term of years. The sum repayable on death if the annuitant dies before he has reached the age when the annuity has commenced or before the stipulated number of annual payments have been made is nothing more than a refunding of moneys deposited for a defined purpose, when that purpose has wholly or partially failed owing to the death of the annuitant." *Gray v. Kerslake* (1957), 11 D.L.R. (2d) 225 at 234, [1958] S.C.R. 3, Locke J. 3. ". . . [S]tated sums of money payable at regular intervals . . . derived from a fund or source in which the annuitant has no further property beyond the right to claim payment. Under the annuity contract, the issuer obligates himself to make those payments in return for the premium which he has extracted." *Rektor, Re* (1983), 3 P.P.S.A.C. 32 at 34, 47 C.B.R. (N.S.) 267 (Ont. S.C.), Smith J. 4. ". . . [T]he annuity income – the annual amount to be paid under the annuity contract. . . ." *Minister of National Revenue v. E.*, [1950] Ex. C.R. 509 at 514, [1950] C.T.C. 345, Cameron J. See DEFERRED ~; LIFE ~.

ANNUITY CONTRACT. A contract that provides for payment of an income for a specified period or for life and under which the sole benefit stated to be payable by reason of death does not exceed the sum of the amounts paid as consideration for the contract together with interest.

ANNUL. *v.* To deprive of effectiveness or operation.

ANNULMENT. *n.* Making void; depriving of effectiveness or operation.

ANON. *abbr.* Anonymous.

ANONYMOUS. *n.* A nameless person.

ANONYMOUS. *adj.* Nameless.

ANSWER. *n.* What is delivered by a respondent who wishes to oppose the claim in a petition. G.D. Watson & C. Perkins, eds., *Holmested & Watson: Ontario Civil Procedure* (Toronto: Carswell, 1984) at 69-6. See FULL ~ AND DEFENCE.

ANTE. [L.] Before.

ANTECEDENT. *n.* Some time prior.

ANTECEDENT. *adj.* Prior in time.

ANTICIPATION. *n.* Taking or doing something before the chosen time.

ANTICIPATORY BREACH. ". . .

[A] party is in breach from the moment that his actual breach becomes inevitable. Since the reason for the rule is that a party is allowed to anticipate an inevitable event and is not obliged to wait til it happens, it must follow that the breach which he anticipates is of just the same character as the breach which would actually have occurred if he had waited." *Universal Cargo Carriers Corporation v. Citati*, [1957] 2 Q.B. 401 at 436 (C.A.), Lord Devlin.

ANTICIPATORY CREDIT. Permitting an exporter to draw on credit prior to shipment by tender of particular documents. I.F.G. Baxter, *The Law of Banking*, 3d ed. (Toronto: Carswell, 1981) at 156.

ANTITRUST LAW. A law of a foreign jurisdiction of a kind commonly known as an antitrust law, and includes a law having directly or indirectly as a purpose the preservation or enhancement of competition between business enterprises or the prevention or repression of monopolies or restrictive practices in trade or commerce. *Foreign Extraterritorial Measures Act*, R.S.C. 1985, c. F-29, s. 2.

ANTON PILLER ORDER. An ex parte order for seizure, inspection or preservation of documents which is properly granted where a plaintiff has an extremely strong prima facie case, damage potential is serious and there is clear evidence that the defendant possesses incriminating documents or property and may dispose of it before motion on notice can be made. P.V. Baker & P. St. J. Langan, eds., *Snell's Equity*, 29th ed. (London: Sweet and Maxwell, 1990) at 673.

A., N.W.T. & Y. TAX R. *abbr.* Alberta, N.W.T. & Yukon Tax Reports.

APP. *abbr.* Appeal.

APPARENT. *adj.* Readily perceived.

APPARENT AUTHORITY. ". . . [A] legal relationship between the principal and the contractor created by a representation, made by the principal to the contractor, intended to be and in fact acted upon by the contractor, that the agent has authority to enter on behalf of the principal into a contract of a kind within the scope of the 'apparent' authority, so as to render the principal liable to perform any obligations imposed upon him by such contract. To the relationship so created the agent is a stranger. He need not be (although he generally is) aware of the existence of the representation but he must not purport to make the agreement as principal himself. . . ." *Freeman & Lockyer v. Buckhurst Park Properties (Mangal) Ltd.*, [1964] 2 Q.B. 480 at 502 (C.A.), Diplock L.J.

APP. CAS. *abbr*. Law Reports, Appeal Cases, 1875-1890.

APPEAL. *n*. 1. Examination by a higher court of the decision of an inferior court. 2. "In every appeal, under our system of justice, there must be a rehearing. The question that may arise in each case is whether the rehearing is based on a record created, in whole or in part, in the Court of Appeal. Some appeals are ordinarily reheard on a record created in the inferior Court . . . In some appeals, the rehearing is based entirely on evidence taken in the Court of Appeal; or, as it is sometimes put, the appeal is by way of a trial de novo . . . There can also be appeals where the rehearing is based on evidence taken by the inferior tribunal plus evidence adduced in the Court of Appeal." *Srivastava v. Canada (Minister of Manpower & Immigration)*, 36 D.L.R. (3d) 688 at 697, [1973] 1 F.C. 138 (C.A.), the court per Jackett C.J.A. 3. Proceeding to set aside or vary any judgment of the court appealed from. *Supreme Court Act*, R.S.C. 1985, c. S-26, s. 2. See COURT OF ~, CROSS-~; FEDERAL COURT – ~ DIVISION; FEDERAL COURT OF ~; NOTICE OF ~; RIGHT OF ~.

APPEAL BOARD. A board established under a statute to hear appeals from administrative decisions or from decisions of first level tribunals.

APPEAL COURT. In this section, means (a) in relation to each of the Provinces of Ontario, Quebec, New Brunswick, British Columbia, Manitoba, Saskatchewan, Alberta and Newfoundland, the Court of Appeal of the Province; and (b) in relation to the Province of Nova Scotia, the Appeal Division of the Supreme Court. *Judges Act*, R.S.C. 1985, c. J-1, s. 24(6). See COURT MARTIAL ~.

APPEARANCE. *n*. A document filed in court which indicates that a person will participate in proceedings or will defend. See CONDITIONAL ~.

APPEARANCE NOTICE. A document which requires people to appear in court to answer charges against them.

APPELLANT. *n*. The party bringing an appeal.

APPELLATE. *adj*. Appealed to.

APPELLATE COURT. In respect of an appeal from a court, means the court exercising appellate jurisdiction with respect to that appeal. See APPEAL.

APPELLATE JURISDICTION. A superior court's power to review the decision of a lower court.

APPLICANT. *n*. 1. A person who applies or on whose behalf an application is made for assistance, a benefit, a loan or grant. 2. A person applying for a licence, registration, permit or passport. 3. One who brings an application or petition.

APPLICATION. *n*. 1. A request. 2. A motion to a judge or court. 3. The commencement of proceedings before a court of tribunal. See SUMMARY ~.

APPLY. *v*. To request; to make application; to bring a motion to a court.

APPOINT. *v*. To select; to designate; to assign an office or duty.

APPOINTED DAY. A day designated for a particular purpose.

APPOINTEE. *n*. A person chosen for some purpose.

APPOINTMENT. *n*. 1. Designation of a person to fill an office. 2. An appointment made in the exercise of a power to appoint property among several objects. *Power of Appointment Act*, R.S.B.C. 1979, c. 333, s. 1. 3. As used in the Public Service Employment Act, R.S.C. 1970, c. P-32, s. 2, means assignment. *Lucas v. Public Service Commission Appeal Board* (1987), 40 D.L.R. (4th) 365 at 372 (Fed. C.A.), the court per Heald J.A. See POWER OF ~.

APPOINTOR. *n.* One given a power; a person who names someone else for an office.

APPORTIONMENT. *n.* A division of a whole into proportional parts according to the claimants' rights.

APPRAISAL. *n.* Valuation.

APPRAISAL REMEDY. "... [T]he statutory right granted to minority shareholders [Canada Business Corporations Act, S.C. 1974-75-76, c. 33, s. 184], even where 'oppression' as such is not in issue, to oblige either the majority or the corporation to purchase the shares of those minority shareholders who dissent from some basic change imposed by the majority. That purchase is at an appraised value effected by an independent outside instrumentality; ..." *Domglas Inc. v. Jarislowsky, Fraser & Co.* (1980), 13 B.L.R. 135 at 161, [1980] C.S. 925 (Que.), Greenberg J.

APPRAISAL RIGHT. See APPRAISAL REMEDY.

APPRAISE. *v.* To estimate or set the value of a thing.

APPRAISER. *n.* 1. "In determining whether the proceeding ... is a valuation or an arbitration, ... Generally speaking, if the person to whom a reference is made is intended to use his skill and knowledge of the particular subject without taking any evidence or hearing the parties, he is not prima facie an arbitrator, he is a valuer or appraiser." *Pfeil v. Simcoe & Erie General Insurance Co.*, [1986] 2 W.W.R. 710 at 715, 45 Sask. R. 241, 24 D.L.R. (4th) 752, [1986] I.L.R. 1-2055 (C.A.), the court per Vancise J.A. 2. A person appointed to engage in valuations. 3. A property valuator.

APPRECIATE. *v.* "The verb 'know' has a positive connotation requiring a bare awareness, the act of receiving information without more. The act of appreciating, on the other hand, is a second stage in a mental process requiring the analysis of knowledge or experience in one manner or another. It is therefore clear on the plain meaning of the section [Criminal Code, R.S.C. 1970, c. C-34, s. 16] that Parliament intended that for a person to be insane within the statutory definition, he must be incapable, firstly, of appreciating in the analytical sense the nature and quality of the act or of knowing in the positive sense that his act was wrong." *R. v. Kjeldsen* (1981), 24 C.R. (3d) 289 at 295, [1981] 2 S.C.R. 617, [1982] 1 W.W.R. 577, 17 Alta. L.R. (2d) 97, 28 C.R. (3d) 81, 39 N.R. 376, 64 C.C.C. (2d) 161, 131 D.L.R. (3d) 121, 34 A.R. 576, the court per McIntyre J.

APPRECIATION. *n.* 1. Growth in value. *Waters v. Waters* (1986), 4 R.F.L. (3d) 283 at 293, 44 Man. R. (2d) 109 (C.A.), Twaddle J.A. (Huband J.A. concurring). 2. An increase in an asset's value strictly due to inflation or market fluctuations. A. Bissett-Johnson & W.M. Holland, eds., *Matrimonial Property Law in Canada* (Toronto: Carswell, 1980) at M-6.

APPREHEND. *v.* "... [A]s used in s. 12 of the Act [Child Welfare Act, 1954 (Ont.), c. 8] contemplates a physical possession and custody of the child and taking him to place of safety and detaining him there until he can be brought before a Judge." *Blackmore, Re* (1958), 120 C.C.C. 19 at 23 (Ont. C.A.); Laidlaw J.A.

APPREHENSION. *n.* 1. Capturing a person on a criminal charge. 2. The act of taking a child into custody. See REASONABLE ~ OF BIAS.

APPREHENSIVE. *adj.* "... [S]uspicious, or fearful of something." *Golding v. Waterhouse* (1876), 16 N.B.R. 313 at 319 (C.A.), Allen C.J. (Duff and Fisher JJ.A. concurring).

APPRENDRE. *n.* [Fr.] A profit or fee to be received or taken.

APPRENTICE. *n.* 1. A person who is at least sixteen years of age and who has entered into a contract under which he or she is to receive, from or through an employer, training and instruction in a trade. 2. A person who works as assistant to a journeyman with a view to qualify as a journeyman. See PRE-~.

APPROPRIATE. *v.* 1. ". . . [T]o take it with a view to using it as one's own, to become indeed the owner in fact whatever the legality of the relationship is." *R. v. Dalzell* (1982), 3 C.C.C. (3d) 232 at 243, 54 N.S.R. (2d) 239, 111 A.P.R. 239 (Co. Ct.), O'Hearn Co. Ct. J. 2. To earmark for a purpose.

APPROPRIATE. *adj.* ". . . [E]mbraces a concept of suitableness, proper, and fitting to a particular situation. . . . Appropriate is the equivalent of 'convenable' in the sense of being the correct or suitable remedy or reparation; . . ." *Kodellas v. Saskatchewan (Human Rights Commission)* (1989), 89 C.L.L.C. 17,027 at 16,303, [1989] 5 W.W.R. 1, 10 C.H.R.R. D/6305, 60 D.L.R. (4th) 143, 77 Sask. R. 94 (C.A.), Vancise J.A.

APPROPRIATION. *n.* 1. Means by which Parliament or a legislature regulates the expenditure of public money voted to be applied to particular purposes. 2. Any authority of Parliament to pay money out of the Consolidated Revenue Fund. *Financial Administration Act*, R.S.C. 1985, c. F-11, s. 2. 3. Any authority of a legislature to pay money out of the Consolidated Fund. 4. An authorization contained in any Ordinance to make a disbursement from the Revenue Fund and, unless the context requires otherwise, includes a statutory appropriation. *Financial Administration Act*, S.N.W.T. 1982, c. 2, s. 2.

APPROPRIATION BILL. A bill ordered to be brought in by the House when it concurs with the Estimates. A. Fraser, W.A. Dawson & J. Holtby, eds., *Beauchesne's Rules and Forms of the House of Commons of Canada*, 6th ed. (Toronto: Carswell, 1989) at 263.

APPROVAL. *n.* Confirmation; acceptance; ratification. See SALE ON ~.

APPROVE. *v.* To confirm, accept, ratify.

APPROVED. *adj.* Authorized, directed or ratified.

APPURTENANCE. *n.* One thing which belongs to another thing.

APPURTENANT. *adj.* 1. Belonging or pertaining to. 2. ". . . '[A]nnexed'. . . ." *Moreau Estate v. Regnier*, [1986] 4 W.W.R. 548 at 551 (Man. Q.B.), Hansen J. 3. That which an act of parties attaches to land. R. Megarry & H.W.R. Wade, *The Law of Real Property*, 5th ed. (London: Stevens, 1984) at cxxiii.

A.P.R. *abbr.* Atlantic Provinces Reports, 1975.

A PRIORI. [L.] From cause to effect.

APTITUDE. *n.* ". . . '[N]atural or acquired abilities for performing a task' . . ." *Brossard (Town) v. Quebec (Commission des droits de la personne)* (1989), 10 C.H.R.R. D/5515 at D/5530, 88 C.L.L.C. 17,031, [1988] 2 S.C.R. 297, 88 N.R. 321, 18 Q.A.C. 164, 53 D.L.R. (4th) 609, Beetz J. (McIntyre, Lamer and La Forest JJ. concurring).

APT WORDS. Words which produce the intended legal effect. *Holloway v. Miner* (1916), 10 W.W.R. 995 at 999 (Man. K.B.), Curran J.

A.R. *abbr.* 1. Anno Regni. 2. Alberta Reports, 1977-.

ARABLE. *adj.* Suitable for purposes of cultivation.

ARABLE LAND. 1. Land which is suitable for cultivation. 2. "The test of arable land, in my opinion, is: Can it reasonably be cultivated, and, if so, is the soil of such a quality that it will, when cultivated, produce a reasonable crop of grain – not necessarily wheat – in an ordinary season? . . ." *Mutual Life Assurance Co. v. Armstrong*, [1924] 3 W.W.R. 659 at 664, 19 Sask. L.R. 90, [1924] 4 D.L.R. 1144 (C.A.), Lamont J.A. (Haultain C.J.S. concurring).

ARB. *abbr.* Arbitrator.

ARB. BD. *abbr.* Arbitration Board.

ARBITER. *n.* Referee; arbitrator.

ARBITRABILITY. *n.* The capability of matter to be determined by an arbitrator or referee.

ARBITRAGE. *n.* The act of purchasing in one place, where a thing is cheaper, and selling somewhere else simultaneously.

ARBITRAL AWARD. An award made by a board or an arbitrator appointed in respect of a dispute.

ARBITRAL TRIBUNAL. A sole arbitrator or a panel of arbitrators.

ARBITRAMENT. *n.* The award or decision of arbitrators upon a matter of dispute.

ARBITRAMENT AND AWARD. When parties had submitted a question to an arbitrator and received an award, they could successfully plead this in an action for damages as a good defence to the action.

ARBITRARILY. *adv.* Capriciously; without limits of power.

ARBITRARILY DETAINED. Detained without proper procedures having been followed.

ARBITRARILY IMPRISONED. Imprisoned without proper procedures having been followed.

ARBITRARY. *adj.* 1. "... A discretion if arbitrary if there are no criteria express or implied, which govern its exercise." *R. v. Hufsky* (1988), 84 N.R. 365 at 377 (S.C.C.), Le Dain J. 2. "... [C]apricious, despotic or unjustifiable." *R. v. Cayer*, [1988] 28 O.A.C. 105 at 114, 6 M.V.R. (2d) 1 (C.A.), Howland C.J.O., Martin and Griffiths JJ.A.

ARBITRARY PUNISHMENT. Punishment ordered at a judge's discretion.

ARBITRATION. *n.* 1. "The common law has ... developed two concepts which it regards as characteristic of arbitration: the existence of a dispute and the duty or intent of the parties, as the case may be, to submit that dispute to arbitration." *Zittrer c. Sport Masks Inc.* (1988), 38 B.L.R. 221 at 284, 83 N.R. 322, [1988] 1 S.C.R. 564, 13 Q.A.C. 241, L'Heureux-Dubé J. (Lamer, Wilson and Le Dain JJ. concurring). 2. The determination of a dispute by an arbitrator. 3. A procedure to determine an interest dispute. See COMMERCIAL ~; COMPULSORY ~; GRIEVANCE ~; INTEREST ~; LABOUR ~. ~.

ARBITRATION AGREEMENT. An agreement by the parties to submit to arbitration all or certain disputes which have arisen or which may arise between them in respect of a defined legal relationship, whether contractual or not. An arbitration agreement may be in the form of an arbitration clause in a contract or in the form of a separate agreement.

ARBITRATION BOARD. A board constituted by or pursuant to a collective agreement or by agreement between the parties of a collective agreement.

ARBITRATION CLAUSE. The clause in a contract providing for submission of disputes under contract to arbitration for resolution.

ARBITRATOR. *n.* 1. A person who decides disputes on the basis of evidence which the parties adduce. D.J.M. Brown & D.M. Beatty, *Canadian Labour Arbitration*, 3d ed. (Aurora: Canada Law Book, 1988-) at 1-11. 2. "... [A] person appointed under an agreement which contemplates such an appointment for the purpose of resolving a dispute between the parties to the agreement, ..." *Concord Pacific Developments Ltd. v. British Columbia Pavilion Corp.* (1991), 60 B.C.L.R. (2d) 121 at 132, 85 D.L.R. (4th) 402 (C.A.), Lambert J.A. 3. Includes umpire and referee in the nature of an arbitrator.

ARCHITECT. *n.* A person who is engaged for hire, gain or hope of reward in (i) the planning, designing or supervision of, or (ii) the supplying of plans, drawings or specifications for, the erection, construction, enlargement or alteration of buildings for other persons, but does not include a person employed by a registered architect as a draftsman, student clerk of works, superintendent or in any other similar capacity, nor a superintendent of buildings paid by the owner thereof and acting under the directions and control of a registered architect.

ARCHITECT'S CERTIFICATE. A certificate of completion required by a building contract.

ARCHIVES. *n*. 1. A place where old records are kept. 2. The body of documents of all kinds, regardless of date, created or received by a person or body in meeting requirements or carrying on activities, preserved for their general information value. *Archives Act*, S.Q. 1983, c. 38, s. 2.

ARCHIVIST. *n*. One who maintains archives.

AREA. *n*. 1. A district designated for a particular purpose. 2. A city, town, village, county, municipal district or improvement district. 3. A polling district or districts, or a part of a polling district or districts. See COMMON ~S.

AREA TAX. Any tax that is levied on the owners of real property and that is computed by applying a rate to all or part of the assessed dimension of real property and includes any tax levied on the owners of real property that is in the nature of a local improvement tax, a development tax or a redevelopment tax but does not include a tax in respect of mineral rights. *Municipal Grants Act*, R.S.C. 1985, c. M-13, s. 2.

ARGUENDO. [L.] While arguing.

ARGUMENT. *n*. A method of establishing belief by using a course of reasoning.

ARGUMENTATIVE. *adj*. 1. In describing a pleading, containing not only allegations of fact but arguments as to how those facts bear on the disputed matter. 2. In the old common law pleading, described a pleading in which a material fact was stated by inference only.

ARMED. *adj*. "Being 'armed' with an offensive weapon and 'using an offensive weapon' are not synonymous. A person is 'armed' with an offensive weapon if he is equipped with it; see R. v. Sloan (1974), 19 C.C.C. (2d) 190

at 192 (B.C. C.A.)." *R. v. Langevin (No. 1)* (1979), 10 C.R. (3d) 193 at 200, 47 C.C.C. (2d) 138 (Ont. C.A.), the court per Martin J.A.

ARM'S   LENGTH.   *var.* **ARM'SLENGTH**. See AT ~.

ARMY. *n*. The military force of a country intended to operate on land.

AROSE. *v*. ". . . [A] cause of action arises for purposes of a limitation period when the material facts on which it is based have been discovered or ought to have been discovered by the plaintiff by the exercise of reasonable diligence, . . ." *Central & Eastern Trust Co. v. Rafuse* (1986), 37 C.C.L.T. 117 at 180, 42 R.P.R. 161, 34 B.L.R. 187, [1986] 2 S.C.R. 147, 31 D.L.R. (4th) 481, 75 N.S.R. (2d) 109, 186 A.P.R. 109, 69 N.R. 321, the court per Le Dain J.

ARRAIGN. *v*. To bring a prisoner to the bar of a court to answer a charge.

ARRAIGNMENT. *n*. Calling a prisoner by name, reading the indictment, demanding of the prisoner whether he or she is guilty or not guilty, and entering the prisoner's plea.

ARRANGEMENT. *n*. With respect to a corporation, includes, (a) a reorganization of the shares of any class or series of the corporation or of the stated capital of any such class or series; (b) the addition to or removal from the articles of the corporation of any provision or the change of any such provision; (c) an amalgamation of the corporation with another corporation; (d) an amalgamation of a body corporate with a corporation that results in an amalgamated corporation; (e) a transfer of all or substantially all the property of the corporation to another body corporate in exchange for securities, money or other property of the body corporate; (f) an exchange of securities of the corporation held by security holders for other securities, money or other property of the corporation or securities, money or other property of another body corporate that is not a take-over bid as defined in the Securities Act; (g) a liquidation or dissolution of the corporation; (h) any other reorganization or scheme involving the business or affairs of the corporation or of any or all of the holders of its securities or of any options or rights to acquire any of its securities that is, at law, an arrangement; and (i) any combination of the foregoing.

ARREARS. *n.* ". . . [S]omething which is behind in payment, or which remains unpaid, . . ." *Corbett c. Taylor* (1864), 23 U.C.Q.B. 454 at 455 (C.A.), the court per Draper C.J.

ARREARS OF TAX. Tax unpaid and outstanding after the expiry of the year in which they were imposed, and includes penalties for default in payment.

ARREST. *n.* 1. ". . . [I]n general an arrest is effected by the compulsory restraint of a person either by actual seizure or by the touching of his body with a view to his detention. The person being arrested must be informed that he is being arrested and the reasons therefor. Until it has been made clear to the person that he is under arrest, the arrest is not complete in law: . . ." *R. v. Delong* (1989), 47 C.C.C. (3d) 402 at 417 (Ont. C.A.), the court per Griffiths J.A. 2. "To constitute an arrest it is not necessary to touch the person arrested if he acquiesces in the situation by acknowledging that he is deprived of his liberty: . . ." *Kozak v. Beatty* (1957), 7 D.L.R. (2d) 88 at 93, 20 W.W.R. 497, 118 C.C.C. 72 (Sask. C.A.), Martin J.A. 3. "The best expressed view of the matter that I have found is a note to Nicholl v. Darley (1828), 2 Y. & J. 399 [(U.K.)], at p. 405, (Philad. ed., 1869) viz.: 'The distinction seems to be, that if the party does not acquiesce, there must be an actual touching of his person by the officer, to constitute an arrest; and any touching of the person by the officer, in the execution of a writ, will be an arrest. But if the party submits and comes within the power of the officer, who thereupon abstains from interference with his person, this is such a conclusive confession of arrest as is equivalent in law to an arrest.' " *Higgins v. MacDonald*, [1928] 4 D.L.R. 241 at 243, [1928] 3 W.W.R.

115, 50 C.C.C. 353, 50 B.C.R. 150 (C.A.), Martin J.A. 4. An admiralty action brought against a ship. J.G. McLeod, *The Conflict of Laws* (Calgary: Carswell, 1983) at 111. 5. Seizure of property under a warrant of the Federal Court. D. Sgayias *et al.*, *Federal Court Practice 1988* (Toronto: Carswell, 1987) at 535. See FALSE ~.

ARSON. *n.* (1) Wilfully setting fire to (a) a building or structure, whether completed or not; (b) a stack of vegetable produce or of mineral or vegetable fuel; (c) a mine; (d) a well of combustible substance; (e) a vessel or aircraft, whether completed or not; (f) timber or materials placed in a shipyard for building, repairing or fitting out a ship; (g) military or public stores or munitions of war; (h) a crop, whether standing or cut down; or (i) any wood, forest, or natural growth, or any lumber, timber, log, float, boom, dam or slide. (2) Wilfully and for a fraudulent purpose setting fire to property not mentioned in subsection (1). *Criminal Code*, R.S.C. 1985, c. C-46, s. 433.

ARTICLED CLERK. A student-at-law bound by contract in writing to service with a member of the Law Society, who has filed articles of clerkship in accordance with the governing legislation.

ARTICLED STUDENT. 1. Any person validly holding a certificate of admission to the training period prescribed by by-law of the General Council. *Barreau du Québec Act*, R.S.Q. 1977, c. B-1, s. 1. 2. A person enrolled in the Bar Admission Course during the time he is not in attendance at the teaching period thereof. *Legal Aid Act*, R.R.O. 1980, Reg. 575, s. 1.

ARTICLES. *n.* 1. Clauses contained in a document. 2. The document itself. 3. An agreement respecting training and service between a member of the Association and a student. *Surveyors acts.* 4. The original or restated articles of incorporation, articles of amendment, articles of amalgamation, articles of continuance, articles of reorganization, articles of arrangement, articles of dissolution, articles of revival, a statute, letters patent, a memorandum of association, certificate of incorporation, a special act and any other instrument by which a corporation is incorporated or which evidences the corporate existence of a body corporate continued as a corporation under this Act and includes any amendments thereto. *Corporation acts.*

ARTICLES OF AMENDMENT. A document which changes the capital structure or the constitution of a company and is ordinarily authorized by a special resolution of the shareholders. H. Sutherland, D.B. Horsley & J.M. Edmiston, eds., *Fraser's Handbook on Canadian Company Law,* 7th ed. (Toronto: Carswell, 1985) at 453.

ARTICLES OF ASSOCIATION. Contain the internal regulations of a corporation. One of the incorporating documents in some jurisdictions. S.M. Beck *et al., Cases and Materials on Partnerships and Canadian Business Corporations* (Toronto: Carswell, 1983) at 159.

ARTICLES OF CONTINUANCE. A document which permits a body corporate incorporated in one jurisdiction to be reconstituted in another.

ARTICLES OF INCORPORATION. 1. Incorporation takes place when these articles are delivered to the appropriate Director and a certificate of incorporation is issued. H. Sutherland, D.B. Horsley & J.M. Edmiston, eds., *Fraser's Handbook on Canadian Company Law,* 7th ed. (Toronto: Carswell, 1985) at 3. 2. The original or restated articles of incorporation, articles of amalgamation, letters patent, supplementary letters patent, a special Act and any other instrument by which a corporation is incorporated, and includes any amendments thereto. 3. Correspond to memorandum of association in those jurisdictions using that method of incorporation. S.M. Beck *et al., Cases and Materials on Partnerships and Canadian Business Corporations* (Toronto: Carswell, 1983) at 159.

ARTICLES OF WAR. A code of laws which regulates armed forces.

ARTICULATED VEHICLE. A vehicle which can be divided into more than one part.

ARTIFICE. *n.* Contrivance or device; used to refer to fraud or deceit.

ARTIFICIAL PERSON. A body corporate or other body given the status of a person by law.

A RUBRO AD NIGRUM. [L. from the red to the black] To deduce the meaning of a statute (formerly printed in black) from its title (formerly printed in red).

AS AGAINST. To contrast the positions of two people by referring to a different relationship between one of them and a third person.

AS BETWEEN. To contrast the positions of two people by referring to a different relationship between one of them and a third person.

ASCENDANT. *n.* The ancestor of a family.

ASCERTAIN. *v.* To decide upon. *Stinson v. College of Physicians & Surgeons (Ontario)* (1913), 27 O.L.R. 565 at 581, 10 D.L.R. 699 (C.A.), Riddell J.A.

ASCERTAINED GOODS. ". . . [D]efined by Atkin L.J. In re Waite, [1927] 1 Ch. 606 in these words: 'Ascertained' probably means identified in accordance with the agreement after the time a contract of sale is made . . .' " *George Eddy Co. v. Noble Corey & Son* (1951), 28 M.P.R. 140 at 154, [1951] 4 D.L.R. 90 (N.B. C.A.), Michaud C.J.K.B.D.

ASPECT. See DOUBLE ~ DOCTRINE.

ASSASSINATION. *n.* Murder of a public figure for political motives.

ASSAULT. *n.* 1. Applying force intentionally to another person, directly or indirectly, without their consent; attempting or threatening, by an act or gesture, to apply force to another person if he has or causes the other person to believe upon reasonable grounds that he has, present ability to effect his purpose; or accosting or impeding another person or begging while openly wearing or carrying a weapon or imitation thereof. *Criminal Code*, R.S.C. 1985, c. C-46, s. 265(1). 2. In tort law, intentionally causing another person to fear imminent contact of a harmful or offensive nature. J.G. Fleming, *The Law of Torts*, 8th ed. (Sydney: Law Book, 1992) at 25. See AGGRAVATED ~; COMMON ~; INDECENT ~.

ASSAULT AND BATTERY. The actual carrying out of the threatened harmful or offensive contact. J.G. Fleming, *The Law of Torts*, 8th ed. (Sydney: Law Book, 1992) at 25.

ASSEMBLY. *n.* 1. A meeting of persons. 2. The Legislative Assembly of a province. 3. The House of Assembly of a province. See FREEDOM OF ~; LEGISLATIVE ~; UNLAWFUL ~.

ASSENT. *v.* 1. To agree to, concur in or recognize a matter. 2. ". . . [T]o be valid, must be given by a majority of eligible band members in attendance at a meeting called for the purpose of giving or withholding assent." *Cardinal v. R.*, [1982] 3 C.N.L.R. 3 at 9, [1982] 3 W.W.R. 673, 41 N.R. 300, 133 D.L.R. (3d) 513, [1982] 1 S.C.R. 508, the court per Estey J.

ASSENT. *n.* See MUTUALITY OF ~; ROYAL ~.

ASSERTION. *n.* ". . . [S]tatement, tale or news is an expression which, taken as a whole and understood in context, conveys an assertion of fact or facts and not merely the expression of opinion. . . . Expression which makes a statement susceptible of proof and disproof is an assertion of fact; . . ." *R. v. Zundel* (1992), 75 C.C.C. (3d) 449 at 492, 95 D.L.R. (4th) 202, [1992] 2 S.C.R. 731, 140 N.R. 1, 56 O.A.C. 161, 16 C.R. (4th) 1, 10 C.R.R. (2d) 193, Cory and Iacobucci JJ. (dissenting) (Gonthier J. concurring). See OPINION.

ASSESS. *v.* 1. ". . . '[I]mpose a liability to be taxed' . . ." *Ottawa (City) v. Nantel* (1921), 51 O.L.R. 269 at 274, 69 D.L.R. 727 (C.A.), Latchford J.A. 2. "As used in Section 46(1) [of the Income Tax Act, R.S.C. 1952, c. 148]

. . . roughly equivalent to 'ascertain and fix' and it seems to have two possible senses in one of which the mere acts of ascertaining and calculating only are included, and the other that of computing and stating the tax in the manner prescribed by the statute." *Scott v. Minister of National Revenue*, [1960] C.T.C. 402 at 415, [1961] Ex. C.R. 120, 60 D.T.C. 1273, Thurlow J. 3. ". . . [T]o consider and determine the whole amount necessary to be raised by rate. . . ." *Nova Scotia Car Works Ltd. v. Halifax (City)* (1913), 47 S.C.R. 406 at 414, 12 E.L.R. 282, 11 D.L.R. 55, Fitzpatrick C.J. 4. To value property for tax purposes.

ASSESS. *abbr.* Assessment.

ASSESSED COSTS. Costs which have been assessed by an assessment officer; taxed costs.

ASSESSED VALUE. The value established for any real property by an assessment authority for the purpose of computing a real property tax. *Municipal Grants Act*, R.S.C. 1985, c. M-13, s. 2.

ASSESSING AUTHORITY. A local authority, school board or other authority having power to assess and levy rates, charges or taxes on land or in respect of the ownership of land.

ASSESSMENT. *n.* 1. Valuation of property for taxation purposes. 2. The determination of an amount payable. 3. "In Income Tax Comm'rs for London v. Gibbs, [1942] A.C. 402 at p. 406, Viscount Simon L.C., in reference to the word 'assessment' said: 'The word "assessment" is used in our income tax code in more than one sense. Sometimes, by "assessment" is meant the fixing of the sum taken to represent the actual profit for the purpose of charging tax on it, but in another context the "assessment" may mean the actual sum in tax which the taxpayer is liable to pay on his profits.' That the latter meaning attached to the word 'assessment' under the [Income War Tax Act, R.S.C. 1927, c. 97] as it stood before the enactment of Part VIII . . . is clear. . . ." *Okalta Oils Ltd. v. Minister of National Revenue*, [1955] 5 D.L.R.

614 at 615, [1955] S.C.R. 824, [1955] C.T.C. 271, 55 D.T.C. 1176, Fauteux J. See CERTIFICATE OF ~; ENVIRONMENTAL ~.

ASSESSMENT AUTHORITY. An authority that has power by or under an Act of Parliament or the legislature of a province to establish the assessed dimension or assessed value of real property. *Municipal Grants Act*, R.S.C. 1985, c. M-13, s. 2.

ASSESSMENT OF COSTS. Calculation of the procedural costs to which a party is entitled, formerly taxation of costs.

ASSESSMENT OFFICER. Taxing officer; officer of the court who carries out assessments of costs.

ASSESS O. *abbr.* Assessment Officer.

ASSESSOR. *n.* 1. The official who evaluates property for tax purposes. 2. A specialist who assists the court in determining a matter. D. Sgayias *et al.*, *Federal Court Practice 1988* (Toronto: Carswell, 1987) at 494.

ASSET. *n.* 1. Any real or personal property or legal or equitable interest therein including money, accounts receivable or inventory. 2. "... [I]nclude[s] only such properties of the debtor as are available for the payment of this debt ..." *Sandberg v. Meurer* (1948), [1949] 1 D.L.R. 422 at 427, [1949] C.T.C. 35, [1949] 1 W.W.R. 117, 56 Man. R. 391 (C.A.), Adamson J.A. (MacPherson C.J.M., Richards and Coyne JJ.A. concurring). See BUSINESS ~; CAPITAL ~S; CURRENT ~S; FAMILY ~; FIXED ~; LIQUID ~S; WASTING ~.

ASSIGN. *v.* 1. To transfer property. 2. For a person to execute and perform every necessary or suitable deed or act for assigning, surrendering or otherwise transferring land of which that person is possessed, either for the whole estate or for any less estate. *Trustee acts*.

ASSIGN. *n.* 1. A person to whom something is transferred or given. *Quaal Estate, Re*, [1920] 2 W.W.R. 271 at 272, 51 D.L.R. 720 (Sask. K.B.),

Embury J. 2. "... [A]nyone to whom an assignment is made ..." *National Trust Co. v. Mead* (1990), 12 R.P.R. (2d) 165 at 177, [1990] 2 S.C.R. 410, [1990] 5 W.W.R. 459, 71 D.L.R. (4th) 488, 112 N.R. 1, 87 Sask. R. 161, Wilson J. (Lamer C.J.C., La Forest, L'Heureux-Dubé, Gonthier and Cory JJ. concurring).

ASSIGNEE. *n.* 1. The person to whom property is transferred. *Minister of National Revenue v. Parsons* (1983), 4 Admin L.R. 64 at 79, [1983] C.T.C. 321, 83 D.T.C. 5329 (Fed. T.D.), Cattanach J. 2. Includes any person in whom the right or benefit concerned has become vested, as a result of any assignment or series of assignments. *Consumer Protection acts*. 3. Any person to whom an assignment of book debts is made. *Assignment of Book Debts acts*.

ASSIGNMENT. *n.* 1. "... [P]roperty is transferred to another...." *Minister of National Revenue v. Parsons* (1983), 4 Admin L.R. 64 at 79, [1983] C.T.C. 321, 83 D.T.C. 5329 (Fed. T.D.), Cattanach J. 2. "[In s. 205(1)(b) of the Canada Shipping Act, R.S.C. 1970, c. S-9] ... a transfer of a right from one person to another...." *Makar v. "Rivtow Lion" (The)* (1982), (*sub nom. Makar v. Rivtow Straits Ltd.*) 82 C.L.L.C. 14,209 at 364, 43 N.R. 245, 140 D.L.R. (3d) 6 (Fed. C.A.), Thurlow C.J.A. (Verchere D.J.A. concurring). 3. Act of assigning, or the document by which a thing is assigned. 4. A transfer by a tenant of the full term remaining under the tenant's lease. W.B. Rayner & R.H. McLaren, *Falconbridge on Mortgages*, 4th ed. (Toronto: Canada Law Book, 1977) at 100. 5. Includes every legal and equitable assignment, whether absolute or by way of security, and every mortgage or other charge upon book debts. *Assignment of Book Debts acts*. 6. An assignment filed with the official receiver. *Bankruptcy Act*, R.S.C. 1985, c. B-3, s. 2. 7. "... As between mortgagors, an assignment would be an agreement between the original mortgagor and his purchaser by which the latter would assume the mortgage debt in exchange for valuable consideration. . . ." *National Trust Co. v. Mead* (1990), 12 R.P.R. (2d) 165 at 177, [1990] 2 S.C.R. 410, [1990] 5 W.W.R. 459, 71 D.L.R. (4th) 488, 112 N.R. 1, 87 Sask. R. 161, Wilson J. (Lamer C.J.C., La Forest, L'Heureux-Dubé, Gonthier and Cory JJ. concurring). See ABSOLUTE ~.

ASSIGNOR. *n.* 1. One who makes a transfer. 2. A corporation making an assignment of book debts. *Corporation Securities Registration acts.* 3. Any person making an assignment of book debts. *Assignment of Book Debts acts.*

ASSISE. *var.* **ASSIZE.** *n.* The trial of a civil action before a travelling judge.

ASSISTANCE. *n.* 1. Aid in any form to or in respect of persons in need for the purpose of providing or providing for all or any of the following: (a) food, shelter, clothing, fuel, utilities, household supplies and personal requirements (hereinafter referred to as "basic requirements"); (b) prescribed items incidental to carrying on a trade or other employment and other prescribed special needs of any kind; (c) care in a home for special care; (d) travel and transportation; (e) funerals and burials; (f) health care services; (g) prescribed welfare services purchased by or at the request of a provincially approved agency; and (h) comfort allowances and other prescribed needs of residents or patients in hospitals or other prescribed institutions. *Canada Assistance Plan,* R.S.C. 1985, c. C-1, s. 2. 2. Old age assistance provided under provincial law to the persons and under the conditions specified in this Act and the regulations. *Old Age Assistance Act,* R.S.C. 1970, c. O-5, s. 2. See CANADA ~ PLAN; FINANCIAL ~; GOVERNMENT ~; INCOME ~; IN NEED OF ~; MUNICIPAL ~; SOCIAL ~; STUDENT FINANCIAL ~; WRIT OF ~.

ASSIZE. *n.* ". . . [A] sitting of a Judge of the Supreme Court with a jury." *Imperial Bank v. Alley,* [1926] 3 D.L.R. 86 at 90, 59 O.L.R. 1 (C.A.), the court per Orde J.A. See ASSISE.

ASSN. *abbr.* Association.

ASSOCIATE. *n.* 1. ". . . [M]ay include the [partner] . . . may also signify a mere companion or companionship." *Derby Development Corp. v. Minister of National Revenue,* [1963] C.T.C. 269 at 279 (Ex. Ct.), Kearney J. 2. Where used to indicate a relationship with any person or company means, (i) any company of which such person or company beneficially owns, directly or indirectly, voting securities carrying more than 10 per cent of the voting rights attached to all voting securities of the company for the time being outstanding, (ii) any partner of that person or company, (iii) any trust or estate in which such person or company has a substantial beneficial interest or as to which such person or company serves as trustee or in a similar capacity, (iv) the spouse or any parent, son or daughter, brother or sister of that person, or (v) any relative of such person or of that person's spouse who has the same home as such person.

ASSOCIATION. *n.* See ARTICLES OF ~; BUSINESS OR TRADE ~; BUSINESS, PROFESSIONAL OR TRADE ~; CANADIAN PAYMENTS ~; CANADIAN STANDARDS ~; CONSTITUENCY ~; COOPERATIVE ~; EMPLOYERS' ~; FREEDOM OF ~; LLOYD'S ~; MEMORANDUM OF ~; RIGHT OF ~; UNINCORPORATED ~.

ASSUME. *v.* 1. To take on a debt or obligation. *Thompson v. Warwick* (1894), 21 O.A.R. 637 at 644 (C.A.), MacLennan J.A. 2. To take for granted. *Gillespie v. R.,* [1983] 1 W.W.R. 641 at 647, 82 D.T.C. 6334, [1982] C.T.C. 378, 45 N.R. 77, 141 D.L.R. (3d) 725 (Fed. C.A.), the court per Thurlow C.J.F.C.

ASSUMPSIT. [L. one promised] A form of action to recover damages for breach of a simple contract.

ASSUMPTION AGREEMENT. An arrangement by which a purchaser in a new subdivision contracts directly with a mortgagee to make mortgage payments so that the developer in released from the covenant with the mortgage lender. D.J. Donahue & P.D. Quinn,

Real Estate Practice in Ontario, 4th ed. (Toronto: Butterworths, 1990) at 231.

ASSUMPTION OF RISK. See VOLUNTARY ~.

ASSURANCE. *n.* 1. A transfer, deed or instrument, other than a will, by which land may be conveyed or transferred. *Limitation of Actions acts.* 2. Includes a gift, conveyance, appointment, lease, transfer, settlement, mortgage, charge, encumbrance, devise, bequest and every other assurance by deed, will or other instrument. *Mortmain and Charitable Uses Act*, R.S.O. 1980, c. 297, s. 1. 3. Insurance.

ASSURANCE FUND. A fund established under a statute to indemnify certain persons against loss.

ASSURE. *v.* To make certain; to insure.

ASSURED. *n.* One who is indemnified against particular events.

ASSURER. *n.* Indemnifier; insurer.

ASYLUM. *n.* 1. A sanctuary. 2. A place for the treatment of the mentally ill.

AT ARM'S LENGTH. Parties are said to be at arm's length when they are not under the control or influence of each other.

AT LARGE. 1. "... [L]eft unattended." *Thompson v. Grand Trunk Railway* (1895), 22 O.A.R. 453 at 461 (C.A.), the court per Osler J.A. 2. "[Refers to animals] ... which are away from home." *Hupp v. Canadian Pacific Railway* (1914), 16 D.L.R. 343 at 347, 6 W.W.R. 385, 27 W.L.R. 398, 17 C.R.C. 66, 20 B.C.R. 49 (C.A.), Galliher J.A. 3. "Damages in libel actions are 'at large' and rest upon a consideration of the injury to the plaintiff, the conduct of the defendant and the plaintiff and, in some cases, the deterrent effect sought to be accomplished. Except to the extent that they are intended to be a deterrent, they are compensatory and not punitive." *Munro v. Toronto Sun Publishing Corp.* (1982), 21 C.C.L.T. 261 at 294, 39 O.R. (2d) 100 (H.C.), J. Holland

J. 4. "[In Criminal Code, R.S.C. 1970, c. C-34, s. 133(1)(b)] ... has been defined, sensibly I think, in Joliffe v. Dean (1954), 54 S.R. (N.S.W.) 157 ... as free or at liberty...." *R. v. MacCaud* (1975), 22 C.C.C. (2d) 445 at 446 (Ont. C.A.), Donohue J. See DAMAGES ~.

AT LEAST. 1. "... '[N]ot less than' ..." *R. v. Robinson* (1951), 12 C.R. 101 at 108, [1951] S.C.R. 522, 100 C.C.C. 1, Locke J. (Rand and Kellock JJ. concurring). 2. "... '[A]s much as'." *R. v. Robinson* (1951), 12 C.R. 101 at 108, [1951] S.C.R. 522, 100 C.C.C. 1, Locke J. (Rand and Kellock JJ. concurring). 3. "... [W]hen the term 'at least' is used in reference to the days between two events, that means 'clear days.' ... when the term 'at least' is used in reference to the period between two events, whether that period is expressed in years, months, weeks, hours or minutes ... the same effect must be given to those words as is given to them when the period is expressed in days. There can be no basis for anything but a consistent interpretation of such words." *R. v. Davis*, [1978] 1 W.W.R. 381 at 384, 35 C.C.C. (2d) 224 (Sask. C.A.), the court per Culliton C.J.S.

AT PAR. Of stocks or bonds, sold or issued at face value.

ATS. *abbr.* At the suit of. Used when the defendant's name is put first in the title of a proceeding.

AT SIGHT. In reference to bills of exchange, payable on demand.

ATTACH. *v.* To take or apprehend; to take goods as well as persons. See ATTACHMENT.

ATTACHE. *n.* [Fr.] A person associated with an embassy.

ATTACHED. *adj.* 1. "... [P]laced ... with 'some kind of permanency' ..." *Boomars Plumbing & Heating Ltd. v. Marogna Brothers Enterprises Ltd.* (1988), 51 D.L.R. (4th) 13 at 24, 50 R.P.R. 81, 27 B.C.L.R. (2d) 305, [1988] 6 W.W.R. 289 (C.A.), the court per Esson J.A. 2. "... '[T]o lay hold of person or property by virtue of some process of law.' ..." *Barnard v. Walkem* (1880), 1 B.C.R. (Pt. 1) 120 at 127 (C.A.), Begbie C.J.

ATTACHMENT. *n.* 1. Arresting a person under an order of committal. 2. "Garnishee proceedings . . . stop orders and a writ of attachment against the goods of an absconding debtor. . . . appointment of a receiver under judicial process, that is by order of the Court. . . ." *W.C. Fast Enterprises Ltd. v. All-Power Sports (1973) Ltd.* (1981), 123 D.L.R. (3d) 27 at 38, 16 Alta. L.R. (2d) 47 (C.A.), the court per McGillivray C.J.A. 3. "The security interest is said to have attached [as found in s. 12(1) of the Personal Property Security Act, R.S.O. 1980, c. 375] when all events necessary for the creation of that interest have taken place. At that time, the rights of the debtor in the collateral assets are restricted and effected by the rights of the secured party . . . Attachment defines the commencement of the relationship betweeen the debtor and the secured party . . ." *Royal Trust Corporation of Canada v. No. 7 Honda Sales Ltd.* (1987), 7 P.P.S.A.C. 51 at 55-6 (Ont. Dist. Ct.), Kane Dist. Ct. J.

ATTACHMENT OF DEBTS. Where judgment for the payment of money is obtained against a person to whom another person owes money, an order is made that all debts owing or accruing from that person (called the garnishee) to the judgment debtor be applied to the judgment debt.

ATTACHMENT OF WAGES. ". . . [A] continuous deduction or diversion of wages at source by an employer. . . . [which] originates by court order, . . ." *Ruthven v. Ruthven* (1984), 38 R.F.L. (2d) 102 at 106 (Ont. Co. Ct.), Dandie Co. Ct. J. See GARNISHMENT.

ATTAINDER. *n.* Formerly, when judgment of outlawry or death was made against a person convicted of felony or treason, the principal consequences were the forfeiture and escheat of the convict's lands and the corruption of the convict's blood so that the convict was not able to hold or inherit land or transmit a title by descent to any other person.

ATTAINT. *adj.* Describing a person under attainder.

ATTEMPT. *n.* Having an intent to commit an offence, and doing or omitting to do anything for the purpose of carrying out the intention whether or not it was possible under the circumstances to commit the offence. *Criminal Code*, R.S.C. 1985, c. C-46, s. 24(1).

ATTEND. *v.* ". . . '[T]o be present' or 'go regularly to' . . ." *Howell v. Ontario (Minister of Community and Social Services)* (1987), 17 O.A.C. 349 at 353 (Div. Ct.), the court per Griffiths J. See ATTENDANCE.

ATTENDANCE. *n.* ". . . [A]ttendance in court necessarily involves making one's presence known to the presiding judge. One does not comply merely by being physically present...." *R. v.* Anderson (1983), 37 C.R. (3d) 67 at 73, 29 Alta. L.R. (2d) 66, 49 A.R. 122, 9 C.C.C. (3d) 539 (C.A.), Kerans J.A. (Moir J.A. concurring). See AVERAGE ~.

ATTENDANCE MONEY. 1. Conduct money. 2. Reimbursement paid to a witness for reasonable expenses incurred while going to, staying at and returning from the place where a discovery or trial is held.

ATTENDANT. *adj.* Accompanying.

ATTEST. *v.* To witness an event or act.

ATTESTATION. *n.* 1. Witnessing a written instrument and signing it as a witness. 2. ". . . [C]onsists, at the very least, of witnessing the execution of an instrument. . . ." *Cameron, Re* (1984), 63 N.S.R. (2d) 103 at 107, 141 A.P.R. 103 (S.C.), Hallett J.

ATTESTATION CLAUSE. The witness to the execution of a written instrument signs this sentence, stating that he or she has witnessed it.

ATTESTING WITNESS. A person who has seen someone else sign a written document or execute a deed.

ATTORN. *v.* To turn over; to agree to recognize a new owner as landlord.

ATTORNEY. *n.* 1. A person appointed to act in place of or to represent another. 2. Lawyer. 3. Patent agent. 4. The donee of a power of attorney or where a power of attorney is given to two or more persons, whether jointly or severally or both, means any one or more of such persons. *Powers of Attorney Act,* R.S.O. 1990, c. P.20, s. 1. See CROWN ~; POWER OF ~.

ATTORNEY GENERAL. *var.* **ATTORNEY-GENERAL.** 1. The principal law officer of the Crown, a Minister of the Crown. 2. ". . . [T]he Crown has the capacity to be a party to any suit. It exercises that capacity through its recognized officers and, in Quebec (art. 81 C.C.P.), as well as in all other provinces, that officer is the Attorney-General (c. 16 of R.S.Q. 1927)." *People's Holding Co. v. Quebec (Attorney General),* [1931] S.C.R. 452 at 456, [1931] 4 D.L.R. 317, the court per Rinfret J. 3. ". . . '[T]he chief law officer of the provincial Crown. He is the legal representative of the province." *Lavoie v. Nova Scotia (Attorney General)* (1989), 58 D.L.R. (4th) 293 at 316, 91 N.S.R. (2d) 184, 233 A.P.R. 184 (C.A.), the court per Clarke C.J.N.S.

ATTORNMENT. *n.* Agreement to become a new owner's tenant or a mortgagee's tenant. See BAILMENT BY ~.

ATTRIBUTION. *n.* To assign income or property to another person for certain purposes.

AUCTION. *n.* Public sale of property to the highest bidder.

AUCTIONEER. *n.* 1. ". . . [A] person who sells property of any kind by public auction. . . ." *Merritt v. Toronto (City)* (1895), 22 O.A.R. 205 at 213 (C.A.), MacLennan J.A. (Hagarty C.J.O. and Burton J.A. concurring). 2. An individual who conducts the bidding at a sale by auction of any property.

AUDI ALTERAM PARTEM. [L. hear the other side] 1. ". . . [P]arties must be made aware of the case being made against them and [be] given an opportunity to answer it . . ." *Canadian Cable Television Assn. v. American College Sports Collective of Canada Inc.* (1991), 4 Admin L.R. (2d) 61 at 72, 81 D.L.R. (4th) 376, 36 C.P.R. (3d) 455, 129 N.R. 296, [1991] 3 F.C. 626 (C.A.), the court per MacGuigan J.A. 2. "The broad scope of the rule in Canada is demonstrated in L'Alliance des Professeurs case . . . [[1953] 2 S.C.R. 140] where Rand J. said at p. 161: 'Audi alteram partem is a pervading principle of our law, and is peculiarly applicable to the interpretation of statutes which delegate judicial action in any form to inferior tribunals: in making decisions of a judicial nature they must hear both sides, and there is nothing in the statute here qualifying the application of that principle.'" *Downing v. Graydon* (1978), 9 C.C.E.L. 260 at 264, 21 O.R. (2d) 292, 78 C.L.L.C. 14,183, 92 D.L.R. (3d) 355 (C.A.), Blair J.A. 3. ". . . [T]he audi alteram partem rule . . . is one of the basic requirements of procedural fairness. According to that rule, a party to a decision must have an opportunity to be heard and, in particular, the decision-maker cannot hear evidence in the absence of a party whose conduct is under scrutiny. (See Kane v. University of British Columbia, [1980] 1 S.C.R. 1105 . . .)...." *Ontario (Attorney General) v. Grady* (1988), 34 C.R.R. 289 at 317 (Ont. H.C.), Callaghan A.C.J.H.C.

AUDIENCE. *n.* Interview; hearing. See PRE ~.

AUDIT. *n.* 1. ". . . [A]n examination of books of account and supporting evidence to determine the reliability of the information recorded." *Toromont Industrial Holdings Ltd. v. Thorne, Gunn, Helliwell & Christenson* (1975), 23 C.P.R. (2d) 59 at 74, 10 O.R. (2d) 65, 62 D.L.R. (3d) 225 (H.C.), Holland J. 2. (i) An independent examination of records for the purpose of expressing an opinion, or (ii) the preparation of a report or certificate or the expression of an opinion as to whether financial information is presented fairly. Alberta statutes.

AUDIT COMMITTEE. A committee of the board of directors of a corporation who nominate auditors and work with them.

AUDITOR. *n.* 1. One who reviews and verifies accounts. 2. A person who is a member in good standing of any corporation, association or institute of professional accountants, and includes a firm every partner of which is such a person. 3. ". . . [A] person whose position is an independent one, whose duty it is to discover and point out the errors or mistakes of the directors if any, the gains and losses of the company, – to shew in fact, exactly the true state of the accounts; so that he stands, as it were, between the directors and the shareholders as an independent investigator of all business transactions, in which the directors, as the managers of the affairs of the company, have been engaged . . ." *Ontario Forge & Bolt Co., Re* (1896), 27 O.R. 230 at 232 (H.C.), Robertson J. See PROVINCIAL ~.

AUDITOR GENERAL OF CANADA. 1. The officer appointed pursuant to subsection 3(1) of the Auditor General Act. *Financial Administration Act*, R.S.C. 1985, c. F-11, s. 2. 2. The federal official who examines Canada's public accounts, including those relating to public property, Crown corporations and the Consolidated Revenue Fund.

AUTHENTIC. *adj.* Original; genuine.

AUTHENTIC ACT. Something executed before a notary or another duly authorized public official.

AUTHENTICATION. *n.* 1. An attestation made by an officer certifying that a record is in proper form and that the officer is the proper person to so certify. 2. A municipal corporation's signing and sealing of a by-law. I.M. Rogers, *The Law of Canadian Municipal Corporations*, 2d ed. (Toronto: Carswell, 1971-) at 446.

AUTHENTICITY. *n.* 1. Proven of an original when it was written, printed, executed or signed as it claims to have been (Ontario, Rules of Civil Proce-

dure, r. 51.01(a)). G.D. Watson & C. Perkins, eds., *Holmested & Watson: Ontario Civil Procedure* (Toronto: Carswell, 1984) at 51-3. 2. Proven of a copy when it is a true copy of the original (Ontario, Rules of Civil Procedure, r. 51.01(b)). G.D. Watson & C. Perkins, eds., *Holmested & Watson: Ontario Civil Procedure* (Toronto: Carswell, 1984) at 51-3. 3. Proven of the copy of a letter, telecommunication or telegram when the original was sent as claimed and received by the addressee (Ontario, Rules of Civil Procedure, r. 51.01(c)). G.D. Watson & C. Perkins, eds., *Holmested & Watson: Ontario Civil Procedure* (Toronto: Carswell, 1984) at 51-3.

AUTHORITY. *n.* 1. A statute, case or text cited in support of a legal opinion or argument. 2. A legal power given by one person to another to do some act. 3. A person authorized to exercise a statutory power. *Administrative Procedures Act*, R.S.A. 1980, c. A-2, s. 1. 4. Body given powers by statute to oversee or carry out a government function. 5. ". . . '[J]urisdiction' . . ." *Toronto (City) v. Morson* (1916), 37 O.L.R. 369 at 376, 28 D.L.R. 188 (C.A.), Masten J.A. See ACTUAL ~; APPARENT ~; ASSESSING ~; ASSESSMENT ~; BINDING ~; CITATION OF AUTHORITIES; COMPETENT ~; CUSTOMARY ~; EXPROPRIATING ~; IMPLIED ~; LICENSING ~; LOCAL ~; OSTENSIBLE ~; PERSUASIVE ~; USUAL OR CUSTOMARY ~.

AUTHORIZATION. *n.* Licence; certificate; registration.

AUTHORIZE. *v.* 1. To empower. 2. ". . . [D]efined by the jurisprudence as meaning 'sanction, approve, and countenance' . . . And it has been said in C.B.S. Inc. et al. v. Ames Records & Tapes Ltd., [1981] 2 W.L.R. 973 at pp. 987-8 (Ch. D.): ' . . . indifference, exhibited by acts of commission or omission, may reach a degree from which authorisation or permission may be inferred. . . .' " *Apple Computer Inc. v. Mackintosh Computers Ltd.* (1986), 10 C.P.R. (3d) 1 at 46, 8 C.I.P.R. 153, 3

F.T.R. 118, [1987] 1 F.C. 173, 28 D.L.R. (4th) 178, Reed J.

AUTHORIZED. *adj.* 1. Properly empowered to perform any specified duty or to do any specified act. 2. "A work is authorized by statute whether the statute is mandatory or permissive, if the work is carried out in accordance with the statute." *Tock v. St. John's (City) Metropolitan Area Board* (1989), 1 C.C.L.T. (2d) 113 at 154, 47 M.P.L.R. 113, [1989] 2 S.C.R. 1181, 64 D.L.R. (4th) 620, 104 N.R. 241, 82 Nfld. & P.E.I.R. 181, 257 A.P.R. 181, Sopinka J.

AUTHORIZED CAPITAL. The total amount of capital which, by its incorporating documents, a company is authorized to issue.

AUTHORIZED INVESTMENT. A security in which a trust permits its trustee to invest funds.

AUTHORIZED PERSON. 1. A person authorized by legislation to perform a specified function under it. 2. An owner or occupier of premises, forest land or land used for agricultural purposes and an agent of an owner or occupier thereof. *Trespass Act*, S.N.B. 1983, c. T-11.2, s. 1.

AUTOGRAPH. *n.* 1. The handwriting of a person. 2. The signature of a person.

AUTOMATIC RENEWAL. Extension of an agreement from year to year or period of time to period of time when no notice of termination is given by either party.

AUTOMATIC WEAPON. Any firearm that is capable of firing bullets in rapid succession during one pressure of the trigger. *An Act respecting hunting and fishing rights in the James Bay and New Québec territories*, S.Q. 1978, c. 92, s. 18.

AUTOMATISM. *n.* "... [A]s it is employed in the defence of non-insane automatism, has in my opinion been satisfactorily defined by Mr. Justice Lacourciere of the Court of Appeal of Ontario in the case of R. v. K. (1970), 3 C.C.C. (2d) 84 ... : 'Automatism is a

term used to describe unconscious, involuntary behavior, the state of the person who, though capable of action, is not conscious of what he is doing. It means an unconscious, involuntary act, where the mind does not go with what is being done.' " *Rabey v. R.* (1980), 54 C.C.C. (2d) 1 at 6 (S.C.C.), Ritchie J.

AUTOMOBILE. *n.* Any vehicle propelled by any power other than muscular force and adapted for transportation on the public highways but not on rails.

AUTOMOBILE INSURANCE. Insurance (a) against liability arising out of, (i) bodily injury to or the death of a person, or (ii) loss of or damage to property, caused by an automobile or the use or operation thereof; or (b) against loss of or damage to an automobile and the loss of use thereof, and includes insurance otherwise coming within the class of accident insurance where the accident is caused by an automobile or the use or operation thereof, whether liability exists or not, if the contract also includes insurance described in clause (a). *Insurance acts*.

AUTOPSY. *n.* 1. Necropsy; postmortem. F.A. Jaffe, *A Guide to Pathological Evidence*, 3d ed. (Toronto: Carswell, 1991) at 1. 2. The dissection of a body for the purpose of examining organs and tissues to determine the cause of death or manner of death or the identity of the deceased and may include chemical, histological, microbiological or serological tests and other laboratory investigations. *Fatality Inquiries Act*, R.S.A. 1980, c. F-6, s. 1.

AUTRE. *adj.* [Fr.] Another.

AUTREFOIS ACQUIT. [Fr. formerly acquitted] An accused may not be prosecuted when he or she has been tried for and acquitted of the same offence. *R. v. Wright* (1965), 45 C.R. 38 at 39, [1965] 2 O.R. 337, [1965] 3 C.C.C. 160, 50 D.L.R. (2d) 498 (C.A.), Porter C.J.O.

AUTREFOIS CONVICT. [Fr. formerly convicted] "... [A]n absolutely effective plea in bar to the second information, if the accused has been ... convicted and it was attempted again to prosecute them for the same offence." *R. v. Ecker*, [1929] 3 D.L.R. 760 at 761, 64 O.L.R. 1, 51 C.C.C. 409 (C.A.), Latchford C.J.

AUTRE VIE. [Fr.] The life of another (period of time).

AVAILABLE. *adj.* "... [D]oes not mean 'existing.' It means 'in such condition as that it can be taken advantage of.' " *Devitt v. Mutual Life Insurance Co.* (1915), 33 O.L.R. 473 at 478, 22 D.L.R. 183 (C.A.), Riddell J.A. (Falconbridge C.J.K.B. concurring).

AVAILABLE MARKET. A particular situation of trade, area and goods in which there is enough demand that, if a purchaser defaults, the goods in question can readily be sold. G.H.L. Fridman, *Sale of Goods in Canada*, 3d ed. (Toronto: Carswell, 1986) at 359.

AVAILS. *n.* Proceeds; profits.

AVER. *v.* To allege.

AVERAGE. *n.* 1. A medium. 2. Loss or damage to goods on board a ship. See RACE ~.

AVERMENT. *n.* 1. Allegation. *R. v. Bellman*, [1938] 3 D.L.R. 548 at 551, 70 C.C.C. 171, 13 M.P.R. 37 (N.B. C.A.), Baxter C.J. 2. In a pleading, affirmation of any matter.

AVOID. *v.* To make a transaction void.

AVOIDANCE. *n.* Avoiding, setting aside or vacating. See CONFESSION AND ~; TAX ~.

AVOW. *v.* To maintain or justify an act.

AVULSION. *n.* Land which current or flood tears off from property to which it originally belonged and adds to the property of another or land joined to another's property when a river changes its course.

AWARD. *n.* 1. Judgment. 2. Instrument which embodies an arbitrator's decision. 3. A pension, allowance, bonus or grant payable under this Act. *Pension Act*, R.S.C. 1985, c. P-6, s. 2. 4. Includes umpirage and a certificate in the nature of an award. *Arbitration acts*. See ARBITRAL ~; ARBITRAMENT AND ~.

A.W.L.D. *abbr.* Alberta Weekly Law Digest.

AXIOM. *n.* A truth which is indisputable.

B

B. *abbr.* Baron.

BACHELOR. *n.* 1. The first degree in a university. 2. A never married man.

BACK. *v.* To countersign; to endorse.

BACK A WARRANT. For one justice to endorse a warrant issued by the justice of another district or jurisdiction permitting it be executed in the first justice's jurisdiction. *R. v. Solloway Mills & Co.* (1930), 65 O.L.R. 677 at 679, 54 C.C.C. 214 (C.A.), the court per Hodgins J.A.

BACK-BOND. *var.* **BACKBOND.** *n.* A bond of indemnity which one gives to a surety.

BACKSHEET. *n.* A page attached to the back and facing in the opposite direction to other pages of a document filed in a court proceeding; gives the title of the proceeding and other information.

BAD. *adj.* In pleadings, unsound.

BAD DEBT. A debt which is irrecoverable.

BAD FAITH. Concerning the exercise of statutory powers, dishonesty and malice. S.A. DeSmith, *Judicial Review of Administrative Action*, 4th ed. by J.M. Evans (London: Stevens, 1980) at 335.

BADGE. *n.* ". . . [H]ad its origin in heraldry as meaning a distinctive device worn by the adherents of the lord. The badge is not comprised of the arms of the lord, which are exclusive to him, but usually it utilizes the crest. In Scotland the badge worn by a clansman is the crest of the chief within a belt and buckle with the chief's motto inscribed on the belt." *Insurance Corp. of British Columbia c. Canada (Registrar of Trade Marks)* (1978), 44 C.P.R. (2d) 1 at 7, [1980] 1 F.C. 669 (T.D.), Cattanach J.

BADGES OF FRAUD. "(1) [S]ecrecy[,] (2) generality of conveyance[,] (3) continuance in possession by debtor[, and] (4) some benefit retained under the settlement to the settlor." *Re Dougmor Realty Hldg. Ltd.; Fisher v. Wilgorn Invt. Ltd.*, [1967] 1 O.R. 66 (Ont. H.C.).

BAD TITLE. 1. Unmarketable title. 2. One which conveys no or a very limited interest to the purchaser and a purchaser cannot be forced to accept.

BAIL. *v.* To free a person arrested or imprisoned after a particular day and place to appear are set and security is taken.

BAIL. *n.* 1. Security given by the persons into whose hands an accused is delivered. They bind themselves or become bail for the person's due appearance when required and, if they fear the person's escape, they have the legal power to deliver that person to prison. 2. ". . . [P]roperly the contract whereby the man is bailed (i.e. delivered) to his sureties but it is also applied to the sureties themselves. . . ." *R. v. Sandhu* (1984), 38 C.R. (3d) 56 at 63 (Qué. S.C.), Boilard J. 3. In any Admiralty proceeding, that which may be taken to answer any judgment so that the Court may release property under arrest. D. Sgayias *et al.*, *Federal Court Practice 1988* (Toronto: Carswell, 1987) at 539. See JUSTIFY ~.

BAIL-BOND. *n.* An instrument executed by sureties.

BAILEE. *n.* A person to whom goods are entrusted for a specific purpose with no intention of transferring the ownership.

BAILIFF. *n.* 1. A sheriff's officer or person employed by a sheriff to make arrests, carry out executions, and serve writs. 2. A person who, for remuneration, acts or assists a person to act, or represents a person that she or he is acting or is available to act, on behalf of another person in repossessing, seizing or distraining any chattel, or in evicting a person from property.

BAILIWICK. *n.* Geographic jurisdiction of a sheriff or bailiff.

BAILMENT. *n.* "... [T]he delivery of personal chattels on trust, usually on a contract, express or implied, that the trust shall be executed and the chattels delivered in either their original or an altered form as soon as the time for which they were bailed has elapsed ... the legal relationship of bailor and bailee can exist independently of a contract. It is created by the voluntary taking into custody of good[s] which are the property of another...." *Punch v. Savoy's Jewellers Ltd.* (1986), 33 B.L.R. 147 at 154, 54 O.R. (2d) 383, 35 C.C.L.T. 217, 14 O.A.C. 4, 26 D.L.R. (4th) 546 (C.A.), the court per Cory J.A. See GRATUITOUS ~.

BAILMENT BY ATTORNMENT. Occurs when, with the bailor's consent, a bailee delivers the goods to another person to hold, making that person bailee of the bailor. E.L.G. Tyler & N.E. Palmer, eds., *Crossley Vaines' Personal Property*, 5th ed. (London: Butterworths, 1973) at 84.

BAILOR. *n.* A person who entrusts something to another person for a specific purpose.

BAIT. *v.* To set one animal against another which is tied or contained.

BAIT AND SWITCH. To attract customers by advertising goods at a low price in hopes of selling them goods at a higher price.

BALANCE. *n.* The difference between the total debit entries and total credit entries in an account; the remainder.

BALANCE OF PROBABILITIES. Greater likelihood. K.D. Cooper-Stephenson & I.B. Saunders, *Personal Injury Damages in Canada* (Toronto: Carswell, 1981) at 102.

BALANCE OF TRADE. The difference between the value of the imports into and exports from a country.

BALANCE-SHEET. *n.* A statement showing the assets and liabilities of a business.

BALLISTICS. *n.* The science of the behaviour of projectiles. F.A. Jaffe, *A Guide to Pathological Evidence*, 3d ed. (Toronto: Carswell, 1991) at 213.

BALLOON PAYMENT. A large, final payment of principal due because a mortgage loan is for a short term and is not fully amortized. D.J. Donahue & P.D. Quinn, *Real Estate Practice in Ontario*, 4th ed. (Toronto: Butterworths, 1990) at 227.

BALLOT. *n.* 1. The paper by which a voter casts his vote at an election. *Elections Act*, R.S.M. 1987, c. E30, s. 1. 2. The portion of a ballot paper which has been marked by an elector, detached from the counterfoil, and deposited in the ballot box.

BAN. *v.* 1. To exclude. 2. To expel. 3. To prevent.

BAN. *n.* A proclamation or public notice which publicizes an intended marriage.

BANC. *n.* A bench or seat of justice.

BANCO. *n.* A bench or seat of justice.

BAND. *n.* 1. A body of Indians (a) for whose use and benefit in common, lands, the legal title to which is vested in Her Majesty, have been set apart before, on or after September 4, 1951, (b) for whose use and benefit in common, moneys are held by Her Majesty, or (c) declared by the Governor in Council to be a band for the purposes of this Act. *Indian Act*, R.S.C. 1985, c. I-5, s. 2. 2. With reference to a reserve or surrendered lands, means the band for whose use and benefit the reserve or the surrendered lands were set apart. *Indian Act*, R.S.C. 1985, c. I-5, s. 2.

BAND COUNCIL. The council of the band as defined in the *Indian Act* (Canada).

BAND COUNCILLOR. A councillor of a band within the meaning of the *Indian Act* (Canada).

BANDIT. *n.* An outlaw; a person who is put under the ban by law.

BANISHMENT. *n.* Expulsion from a nation; loss of nationality.

BANK. *n.* A bank to which the Bank Act applies. *Interpretation Act*, R.S.C. 1985, c. I-21, s. 35. See CHARTERED ~; FEDERAL BUSINESS DEVELOPMENT ~.

BANK ACCOUNT. "[Both a] ... debt, ... [and] property, ..." *Ontario (Securities Commission) v. Greymac Credit Corp.* (1986), 34 B.L.R. 29 at 45, 23 E.T.R. 81, 30 D.L.R. (4th) 1, 55 O.R. (2d) 673, 17 O.A.C. 88 (C.A.), the court per Morden J.A. See JOINT ~.

BANK-BOOK. *n.* "... [E]vidence of a debt...." *Cusack v. Day*, [1925] 2 W.W.R. 715 at 722, 3 D.L.R. 1028, 36 B.C.R. 106 (C.A.), MacDonald J.A. See BANK PASS BOOK.

BANK DEPOSIT. Money which a depositor loans to the bank and which the bank must repay according to the contract. I.F.G. Baxter, *The Law of Banking*, 3d ed. (Toronto: Carswell, 1981) at 2.

BANKER. *n.* 1. "... [A] person or corporation who carries on the business of banking, and to whom members of the public have access for the purpose of depositing money, opening accounts, drawing cheques, borrowing money, and a variety of other services such as are offered by banks." *655 Developments Ltd. v. Chester Dawe Ltd.* (1992), 42 C.P.R. (3d) 500 at 515, 97 Nfld. & P.E.I.R. 247, 308 A.P.R. 246

(Nfld. T.D.), Wells J. 2. "... '[A] dealer in credit.' " *Reference re Alberta Legislation*, [1938] S.C.R. 100 at 116, [1938] 2 D.L.R. 81, Duff C.J. (Davis J. concurring).

BANKER'S ACCEPTANCE. A draft drawn on and accepted by a bank used to pay for goods sold in import-export transactions and as a source of financing in trade.

BANKING. *n.* 1. Taking money on deposit from the public, issuing, paying and collecting cheques and related activities. I.F.G. Baxter, *The Law of Banking*, 3d ed. (Toronto: Carswell, 1981) at 197. 2. "The legislative authority conferred by these words [s. 91.15 of the Constitution Act, 1867 (30 & 31 Vict.), s. 3] is not confined to the mere constitution of corporate bodies with the privilege of carrying on the business of bankers. It extends to the issue of paper currency...." *Tennant v. Union Bank of Canada*, [1894] A.C. 31 at 46 (P.C.), Lord Watson.

BANKING BUSINESS. "... [I]ssuing letters of credit ... lending money; and ... accepting term deposits ... are within what, in common knowledge, would be considered the hard core of banking." *R. v. Milelli* (1989), 45 B.L.R. 209 at 215, 51 C.C.C. (3d) 165, 35 O.A.C. 241 (C.A.), the court per Finlayson J.A.

BANK-NOTE. *n.* 1. Includes any negotiable instrument (a) issued by or on behalf of a person carrying on the business of banking in or out of Canada, and (b) issued under the authority of Parliament or under the lawful authority of the government of a state other than Canada, intended to be used as money or as the equivalent of money, immediately on issue or at some time subsequent thereto, and includes bank bills and bank post bills. *Criminal Code*, R.S.C. 1985, c. C-46, s. 2. 2. "... [A]n instrument which is a promissory note payable to bearer on demand." *R. v. Brown* (1854), 8 N.B.R. 13 at 15 (C.A.), the court per Carter C.J.

BANK OF CANADA. The federal body which devises and carries out monetary policy and is the fiscal agent of the government of Canada. By the Bank of Canada Act, this is the only body authorized to issue notes for circulation in Canada.

BANK OF CANADA RATE. The rate of interest set by the Bank of Canada for loans by the Bank of Canada to the chartered banks, as published by the Bank of Canada.

BANK PASS BOOK. A record of the credits and debits in a customer's account. I.F.G. Baxter, *The Law of Banking*, 3d ed. (Toronto: Carswell, 1981) at 37.

BANK RATE. The bank rate established by the Bank of Canada as the minimum rate at which the Bank of Canada makes short-term advances to banks listed in Schedule I to the Bank Act. *Courts of Justice Act*, R.S.O. 1990, c. C.43, s. 127(1).

BANKRUPT. *n.* A person who has made an assignment or against whom a receiving order has been made. *Bankruptcy Act*, R.S.C. 1985, c. B-3, s. 2.

BANKRUPT. *adj.* The legal status of a person who has made an assignment or against whom a receiving order has been made. *Bankruptcy Act*, R.S.C. 1985, c. B-3, s. 2.

BANKRUPTCY. *n.* 1. The state of being bankrupt or the fact of becoming bankrupt. *Bankruptcy Act*, R.S.C. 1985, c. B-3, s. 2. 2. The legal status consisting of the vesting of a debtor's assets in a trustee. The trustee is required to realize the assets and distribute the proceeds rateably among the debtor's creditors. When bankruptcy is ended, the debtor is discharged, and, with certain exceptions, any unpaid debts are cancelled. P.W. Hogg, *Constitutional Law of Canada*, 3d ed. (Toronto: Carswell, 1992) at 633. See ACT OF ~; CLAIM PROVABLE IN ~; TRUSTEE IN ~.

BANKRUPTCY AND INSOLVENCY. 1. A federal head of power. *Constitution Act, 1867* (U.K.), 30 & 31 Vict., c. 3, s. 91(21). 2. "... [I]t is a feature common to all the systems of bankruptcy and insolvency to which reference has been made, that the enactments are designed to secure that in the case of an insolvent person his assets shall be rateably distributed amongst his creditors whether he is willing that they shall be so distributed or not...." *Reference re Assignments & Preferences Act (Ont.), s. 9*, [1894] A.C. 189 at 201, 70 L.T. 538, 63 L.J.P.C. 59 (Ont. P.C.), the board per Lord Chancellor.

BANNER. *v.* To carry picket signs on the picket line.

BANNS. *n.* (pl.) A proclamation or public notice which publicizes an intended marriage.

BAR. *n.* 1. A barrier which separates the judge's bench and the front row of counsel's seats from the rest of the court; Queen's counsel are the only counsel allowed within the bar. 2. Obstacle; barrier. 3. The Corporation professionelle des avocats du Québec constituted by section 3. *Barreau du Québec Act*, R.S.Q. 1977, c. B-1, s. 1. See CALL TO THE ~; OUTER ~.

BARE LICENSEE. "... [A] person merely permitted by the owner to enter without there being any obligation so to permit and with the right in the owner to revoke the permission at any time." *Musselman v. Zimmerman* (1922), 66 D.L.R. 350 at 351, [1922] 2 W.W.R. 640, 18 Alta. L.R. 104 (C.A.), Stuart J.A. (Scott C.J., Beck and Clarke JJ.A. concurring).

BARE TRUST. "[A trust under the terms of which] ... a trustee's only duty is to hold the legal estate until called upon by the beneficiary to convey...." *Creasor v. Wall* (1982), 25 R.P.R. 1 at 16, 38 O.R. (2d) 35 (H.C.), White J. Compare ACTIVE DUTY; ACTIVE TRUST.

BARGAIN. *v.* To contract; to enter into an agreement; to negotiate an agreement.

BARGAIN. *n.* Contract; agreement. See CATCHING ~; PLEA ~.

BARGAIN AND SALE. A contract for the sale of chattels, of an estate or of any interest in land followed by payment of the price agreed.

BARGAIN COLLECTIVELY. To negotiate in good faith with a view to entering into, renewing or revising a collective agreement.

BARGAINING. *n.* "... '[N]egotiating.' " *Bloedel, Stewart & Welch Ltd. v. Stuart* (1942), 58 B.C.R. 351 at 356, [1943] 1 W.W.R. 128, [1943] 1 D.L.R. 183 (C.A.), Sloan J.A. See BLUE-SKY ~; COLLECTIVE ~.

BARGAINING AGENCY. See EMPLOYEE ~; EMPLOYER ~.

BARGAINING AGENT. A trade union employee organization or other organization that acts on behalf of employees or other groups of workers or has exclusive bargaining rights in collective bargaining or acts as a party to a collective agreement or to a recognition agreement with their employer or an employers' organization.

BARGAINING COLLECTIVELY. Negotiating in good faith with a view to the conclusion of a collective bargaining agreement, or a renewal or revision of a bargaining agreement, the embodiment in writing or writings of the terms of agreement arrived at in negotiations or required to be inserted in a collective bargaining agreement by this Act, the execution by or on behalf of the parties of such agreement, and the negotiating from time to time for the settlement of disputes and grievances of employees covered by the agreement or represented by a trade union representing the majority of employees in an appropriate unit. *The Trade Union Act*, R.S.S. 1978, c. T-17, s. 2.

BARGAINING RIGHT. "... [O]nly entitle[s] a union to be recognized as the exclusive bargaining agent for a particular group of employees...." *Metropolitan Toronto Apartment Builders Association*, [1978] O.L.R.B. Rep. Nov. 1022 at 1034. See EXCLUSIVE ~.

BARGAINING UNIT. 1. A unit of employees appropriate for collective bargaining. 2. A group of employees usually designated by class of employee, geographical location, work performed, or by a combination of these concepts. D.J.M. Brown & D.M. Beatty, *Canadian Labour Arbitration*, 3d ed. (Aurora: Canada Law Book, 1988-) at 5-4. 3. "... [F]or the purpose of s. 57 [Labour Relations Act, R.S.O. 1980, c. 228], is a unit consisting only of those of the employer's employees whom the trade union is entitled to represent." *Snow v. S.M.W., Loc. 285*, [1984] O.L.R.B. Rep. 1004 at 1010, Gray (Vice-Chair), Bell and Kobryn (Members).

BARGAINING UNIT WORK. Tasks usually performed by a member of a bargaining unit. D.J.M. Brown & D.M. Beatty, *Canadian Labour Arbitration*, 3d ed. (Aurora: Canada Law Book, 1988-) at 5-11.

BARGAINOR. *n.* The person who transfers the subject matter of a bargain and sale.

BAR OF DOWER. Giving up of dower.

BARON. *n.* The former title of judges of certain courts.

BARRED. See STATUTE ~.

BARRING. *conj.* or *prep.* "... '[I]n the absence of'." *Price v. Williams* (1990), 46 C.C.L.I. 161 at 164, [1990] I.L.R. 1-2681 (B.C. C.A.), the court per Hinds J.A.

BARRISTER. *n.* Usually refers to a lawyer who appears as an advocate in court.

BARRISTER AND SOLICITOR. 1. "1) He is permitted to practice law in the province upon obtaining an annual certificate issued to him pursuant to the rules of the society ... 2) He is entitled to vote at an election of benchers ... 3) He is eligible to become a bencher ... 4) He is eligible to become an officer of the society ..." *Maurice v. Priel* (1987), 60 Sask. R. 241 at 245-6, [1988] 1 W.W.R. 491, 46 D.L.R. (4th) 416 (C.A.), Bayda C.J.S. (Brownridge J.A. concurring). 2. A member of the Law Society other than an honorary member or a student member thereof.

Legal Aid Act, R.S.O. 1990, c. L.9, s. 1.

BASE. *adj.* Inferior; impure.

BASE PURPOSE. "... [D]efined as meaning to vilify sex and to treat it as something 'less than beautiful' or to write in a manner calculated to serve aphrodisiac purposes: ..." *R. v. Ariadne Developments Ltd.* (1974), 19 C.C.C. (2d) 49 at 54 (N.S. C.A.), the court per MacDonald J.A.

BASIC NECESSITIES. Things, goods and services that are essential to a person's health and well-being, including food, clothing, shelter, household and personal requirements, medical, hospital, optical, dental and other remedial treatment, care and attention, and an adequate funeral on death.

BASIC WAGE. Minimum wage.

BASIS. See CASH ~; COOPERATIVE ~.

BASKET CLAUSE. Clause intended to ensure that the document covers a larger number of persons or instances than are actually specified in the document.

BASTARD. *n.* A person born to unmarried parents.

BATTERY. *n.* "... [T]he intentional infliction of unlawful force on another person." *Norberg v. Wynrib* (1992), 12 C.C.L.T. (2d) 1 at 16, [1992] 4 W.W.R. 577, 68 B.C.L.R. (2d) 29, 138 N.R. 81, 9 B.C.A.C. 1, 19 W.A.C. 1, 92 D.L.R. (4th) 449, [1992] 2 S.C.R. 226, La Forest J. (Gonthier and Cory JJ. concurring). See ASSAULT AND ~.

BAWDY HOUSE. *var.* **BAWDY-HOUSE.** *n.* A brothel. *Singleton v. Ellison*, [1895] 1 Q.B. 607, Wills J. See COMMON ~.

B.C. BR. LECT. *abbr.* Canadian Bar Association, British Columbia Branch Lectures.

B.C. CORPS. L.G. *abbr.* British Columbia Corporations Law Guide.

B.C.L.N. *abbr.* British Columbia Law Notes.

B.C.L.R. *abbr.* British Columbia Law Reports, 1977-1988.

B.C.L.R.B. DEC. *abbr.* British Columbia Labour Relations Board Decisions.

B.C.L.R. (2d). *abbr.* British Columbia Law Reports (Second Series) 1988-.

B.C.R. *abbr.* 1. British Columbia Reports, 1867-1947. 2. B.C. Rail Ltd.

B.C.T.R. *abbr.* British Columbia Tax Reports.

B.C.W.L.D. *abbr.* British Columbia Weekly Law Digest.

BD. *abbr.* Board.

BEAR. *n.* One who expects a fall in the price of shares.

BEARER. *n.* 1. The person in possession of a bill or note that is payable to bearer. *Bills of Exchange Act*, R.S.C. 1985, c. B-4, s. 2. 2. The person in possession of a security payable to bearer or endorsed in blank. See FUR-~.

BEARER FORM. When applied to a security means a security that is payable to bearer according to its terms and not by reason of any endorsement. *Business Corporations Act*, R.S.O. 1990, c. B.16, s. 53.

BECAUSE OF HANDICAP. For the reason that the person has or has had, or is believed to have or have had, (a) any degree of physical disability, infirmity, malformation or disfigurement that is caused by bodily injury, birth defect or illness and, without limiting the generality of the foregoing, including diabetes mellitus, epilepsy, any degree of paralysis, amputation, lack of physical coordination, blindness or visual impediment, deafness or hearing impediment, muteness or speech impediment, or physical reliance on a dog guide or on a wheelchair or other remedial appliance or device, (b) a condition of mental retardation or impairment, (c) a learning disability, or a dysfunction in one or more of the processes involved in understanding or using symbols or spoken language, (d) a mental disorder, or (e) an injury or disability for which benefits were claimed or received under the

Workers's Compensation Act. *Human Rights Code*, R.S.O. 1990, c. H.19, s. 10(1).

BECOME. *v.* "... [T]o come into being, ..." *R. v. Guaranty Properties Ltd.* (1990), 48 B.L.R. 197 at 209, 109 N.R. 284, 90 D.T.C. 6363, [1990] 2 C.T.C. 94, [1990] 3 F.C. 337, 37 F.T.R. 239n (C.A.), the court per Mac-Guigan J.A.

BEGIN. See RIGHT TO ~.

BEHAVIOUR. See MIS~.

BEING. See IN ~.

BELIEF. *n.* "... [M]ore than acceptance, and involves knowledge, probably knowledge of consequences. ..." *R. v. Budin* (1981), 20 C.R. (3d) 86 at 96, 32 O.R. (2d) 1, 58 C.C.C. (2d) 352, 120 D.L.R. (3d) 536 (C.A.), Brooke J.A. (concurring).

BELONG. *v.* 1. To be the property of, to be owned. 2. "... [B]roader than legal ownership." *Agnew v. Ontario Regional Assessment Commissioner, Region No. 7* (1990), 1 M.P.L.R. (2d) 138 at 140, 74 D.L.R. (4th) 154 (Ont. Gen. Div.), Philp J.

BELOW PAR. At a price lower than face or nominal value; at a discount.

BENCH. *n.* 1. The judge's seat in a court. 2. A single judge. 3. Judges collectively. See QUEEN'S ~.

BENCHER. *n.* An elected governing official of a provincial law society.

BENCH WARRANT. A court-issued warrant to arrest a person.

BENEFICIAL INTEREST. 1. "... [E]quitable and not a legal interest. ..." *Vancouver A & W Drive-Ins Ltd. v. United Food Services Ltd.* (1980), 13 B.L.R. 89 at 102, 10 E.T.R. 34, 38 B.C.L.R. 30 (S.C.), Fulton J. 2. The interest of a beneficiary or beneficial owner. 3. An interest arising out of the beneficial ownership of securities. 4. Includes ownership through a trustee, legal representative, agent or other intermediary.

BENEFICIAL OWNER. "... [T]he real owner of property even though it is in someone else's name." *Csak v.*

Aumon (1990), 69 D.L.R. (4th) 567 at 570 (Ont. H.C.), Lane J.

BENEFICIAL OWNERSHIP. Includes ownership through a trustee, legal representative, agent or other intermediary.

BENEFICIARY. *n.* 1. A person designated or appointed as one to whom or for whose benefit insurance money is to be payable. 2. A person entitled to benefit from a trust or will. 3. A person entitled to receive benefits under a statutory scheme. See IRREVOCABLE ~.

BENEFIT. *n.* 1. A pension; a monetary amount paid under a pension or other plan. 2. A drug or other good or service that is supplied to an eligible person. 3. Compensation or an indemnity paid in money, financial assistance or services. See CONDITIONAL ~; DEATH ~.

BENEFIT PLAN. See DEFINED ~; EMPLOYEE ~.

BENEFIT SOCIETY. See FRATERNAL ~.

BENEVOLENT. *adj.* Charitable; conferring benefits; philanthropic.

BENEVOLENT PURPOSE. A charitable, educational, religious, or welfare purpose or other purpose to the public advantage or benefit.

BEQUEATH. *v.* To leave through a will.

BEQUEST. *n.* Personal property given by will. See RESIDUARY ~; SPECIFIC ~.

BEST EFFORTS. "... [T]aking, in good faith, all reasonable steps to achieve the objective, carrying the process to its logical conclusion, and 'leaving no stone unturned' ..." *Bruce v. Waterloo Swim Club* (1990), 31 C.C.E.L. 321 at 336, 73 O.R. (2d) 709 (H.C.), Lane J.

BEST EVIDENCE RULE. Wherever possible, the original of a document must be produced. P.K. McWilliams, *Canadian Criminal Evidence*, 3d ed. (Aurora: Canada Law Book, 1988) at 6-1.

BESTIALITY. *n.* The act of a human being having sexual intercourse with an animal.

BEST INTERESTS OF THE CHILD. "... [T]he physical comfort and material advantages that may be available in the home of one contender or the other. The welfare of the child must be decided on a consideration of these and all other relevant factors, including the general psychological, spiritual and emotional welfare of the child...." *King v. Low* (1985), 16 D.L.R. (4th) 576 at 587, [1985] 1 S.C.R. 87, the court per McIntyre J.

BET. *n.* 1. A bet that is placed on any contingency or event that is to take place in or out of Canada, and without restricting the generality of the foregoing, includes a bet that is placed on any contingency relating to a horse-race, fight, match or sporting event that is to take place in or out of Canada. *Criminal Code*, R.S.C. 1985, c. C-46, s. 197. 2. A bet placed under the system known as pari-mutuel wagering.

BETTER BUSINESS BUREAU. An organization which provides information to consumers regarding local businesses.

BETTER EQUITY. When one claimant should have priority over the others because of notice, priority in time or some other reason.

BETTERMENT. *n.* Increasing property value.

BETTING. *n.* A wagering contract under which financial consideration is made payable as the result of a contingency.

BETTING HOUSE. See COMMON ~.

BEYOND A REASONABLE DOUBT. The standard of proof required in criminal cases. "... The burden cast upon the Crown is to prove all essential ingredients of the crime charged beyond a reasonable doubt, viz. 'outside the limit or sphere of' or 'past' a reasonable doubt...." *R. v. Lachance* (1962), 39 C.R. 127 at 130, [1963] 2 C.C.C. 14 (Ont. C.A.), Porter

C.J.O., Roach, Aylesworth, Schroeder and Kelly JJ.A.

BEYOND SEAS. 1. "... [O]utside the jurisdiction." *Schacht v. Schacht* (1982), 30 C.P.C. 52 at 54, [1982] 5 W.W.R. 189 (B.C. C.A.), the court per Hutcheon J.A. 2. Does not include any part of Canada, or of the British dominions in North America, or of the United States of America in North America. *Limitation of Actions Act*, R.S.N.B. 1973, c. L-8, s. 1.

B.F.L.R. *abbr.* Banking & Finance Law Review.

BFOR. *abbr.* Bona fide occupational requirement.

BIAS. *n.* 1. "... [C]overs a spectrum of disqualification ranging from partiality on one hand, to the extreme of corruption on the other...." *Calgary General Hospital c. U.N.A., Local 1* (1983), 6 Admin. L.R. 80 at 85, 29 Alta. L.R. (2d) 3, 84 C.L.L.C. 14,032, 50 A.R. 250, 5 D.L.R. (4th) 54 (C.A.), the court per Stevenson J.A. 2. "Bias may be of two kinds. It may arise from an interest in the proceedings.... Sometimes it is a direct pecuniary or proprietary interest in the subject-matter of the proceedings. A person possessing such an interest is disqualified from sitting as a judge thereon. Sometimes the interest is not financial but arises from a connection with the case or with the parties of such a character as to indicate a real likelihood of bias.... the second kind of bias – namely actual bias in fact." *Gooliah v. R.* (1967), (*sub nom. Gooliah, Re*) 63 D.L.R. (2d) 224 at 227-8, 59 W.W.R. 705 (Man. C.A.), Freedman J.A. See REASONABLE APPREHENSION OF ~.

BI-CAMERAL. *adj.* Having two chambers: in Canada, refers to the two houses of Parliament, the House of Commons and the Senate.

BID. *v.* To make an offer at an auction.

BID. *n.* 1. "... [T]he submission of a tender, ..." *Ron Engineering & Construction (Eastern) Ltd. 'v. Ontario* (1981), 13 B.L.R. 72 at 122-23, 119

D.L.R. (3d) 267, 35 N.R. 40, [1981] 1 S.C.R. 111, Estey J. 2. "[In the Combines Investigation Act, R.S.C. 1970, c. C-23, s. 32.2(1)(b)] ... must be interpreted to be an offer which may be accepted by the offeree binding the offeror ..." *R. v. Coastal Glass & Aluminum Ltd.* (1984), 8 C.P.R. (3d) 46 at 59, 17 C.C.C. (3d) 313 (B.C. S.C.), Lander J. 3. A take over bid or an issuer bid. *Securities acts.* See ISSUER ~; TAKE OVER ~.

BID BOND. A bond given to guarantee entry into a contract. *Government Contracts Regulations*, C.R.C., c. 701, s. 2.

BIDDER. *n.* At an auction, a person who makes an offer.

BIDDING. *n.* Quoting cost or price for a contract in response to a request or call for bids or tenders.

BIGAMY. *n.* Every one commits bigamy who (a) in Canada, (i) being married, goes through a form of marriage with another person, (ii) knowing that another person is married, goes through a form of marriage with that person, or (iii) on the same day or simultaneously, goes through a form of marriage with more than one person; or (b) being a Canadian citizen resident in Canada leaves Canada with intent to do anything mentioned in subparagraphs (a)(i) to (iii) and, pursuant thereto, does outside Canada anything mentioned in those subparagraphs in circumstances mentioned therein. *Criminal Code*, R.S.C. 1985, c. C-46, s. 290(1).

BILATERAL. *adj.* Involving two agreeing parties.

BILATERAL CONTRACT. A contract in which each of the two parties is bound to fulfil obligations towards the other.

BILL. *n.* 1. Writing; a letter. 2. An account. 3. In parliamentary practice, the first stage in the enactment of a statute. 4. An order. 5. A bill of exchange. *Bills of Exchange Act*, R.S.C. 1985, c. B-4, s. 2. See ~; ACCOMMODATION ~; APPROPRIATION ~; EXCHEQUER ~; FOREIGN ~; GOVERNMENT ~; INLAND ~; MONEY ~; PRIVATE ~; PRIVATE MEMBER'S ~; PUBLIC ~; TREASURY ~; TRUE ~.

BILL OF COSTS. A document setting out the claim for legal fees and disbursements in a proceeding.

BILL OF EXCHANGE. An unconditional order in writing, addressed by one person to another, signed by the person giving it, requiring the person to whom it is addressed to pay, on demand or at a fixed or determinable future time, a sum certain in money to or to the order of a specified person or to bearer. *Bills of Exchange Act*, R.S.C. 1985, c. B-4, s. 16(1).

BILL OF INDICTMENT. The printed or written accusation of crime made against one or more people. S. Mitchell, P.J. Richardson & D.A. Thomas, eds., *Archibold Pleading, Evidence and Practice in Criminal Cases*, 43d ed. (London: Sweet & Maxwell, 1988) at 2.

BILL OF LADING. Includes all receipts for goods, wares and merchandise accompanied by an undertaking (a) to move the goods, wares and merchandise from the place where they were received to some other place, by any means whatever, or (b) to deliver at a place other than the place where the goods, wares and merchandise were received a like quantity of goods, wares and merchandise of the same or a similar grade or kind. *Bank Act*, R.S.C. 1985, c. B-1, s. 2.

BILL OF RIGHTS. 1. The Canadian Bill of Rights. 2. The English Statute 1688, 1 Will. & Mary, sess. 2, c. 2. 3. The first 10 amendments to the U.S. Constitution. See CANADIAN ~.

BILL OF SALE. A document in writing in conformity with this Act evidencing a sale or mortgage of chattels but does not include a bill of lading, a warehouse receipt, a warrant or order for the delivery of goods, or any other document used in the ordinary course of business as proof of the possession or control of goods or authorizing or purporting to authorize the possessor of the document to transfer either by endorsement or delivery or to receive goods thereby represented. *Bills of Sale acts.*

BIND. *v.* To obligate; to secure payment.

BINDER. *n.* A written memorandum providing temporary insurance coverage until a policy is issued. *Kline Brothers & Co. v. Dominion Fire Insurance Co.* (1913), 47 S.C.R. 252 at 255, 9 D.L.R. 231, Fitzpatrick C.J. (Davies, Idington, Duff and Brodeur JJ. concurring).

BINDING AUTHORITY. Compelling authority; a decision of a higher court which a lower court must follow.

BIND OVER. To enter into a bond before the court to keep the peace and be of good behaviour.

BIPARTITE. *adj.* Having two parts.

BIRTH. *n.* The complete expulsion or extraction from its mother, irrespective of the duration of pregnancy, of a product of conception in which, after such expulsion or extraction, there is breathing, beating of the heart, pulsation of the umbilical cord, or unmistakable movement of voluntary muscle, whether or not the umbilical cord has been cut or the placenta is attached. *Vital Statistics acts.*

BLACK LIST. 1. A list of persons with whom those compiling the list advise that no one should have dealings of a certain type. 2. ". . . [H]istorically described the practice utilized by employers to identify and boycott unwanted employees, particularly trade-union activists and supporters." *Pacific Gillnetters Assn. v. U.F.A.W., British Columbia Provincial Council,* [1979] 1 Can. L.R.B.R. 506 at 518 (B.C.), Germaine (Vice-Chair), Fritz and Smith (Members).

BLACKMAIL. *n.* Menacing and making unwarranted demands. See EXTORTION.

BLACK MARKETING. Unauthorized dealing in or offering rationed, prohibited or restricted goods or services.

BLANK ACCEPTANCE. An accep-

tance written across a bill before it is filled out.

BLANK ENDORSEMENT. An endorsement written on the back of a bill of exchange before the bill is filled out.

BLANKET MORTGAGE. A second mortgage, granted when the first mortgage is small and at a low interest rate, whose principal includes the whole principal of the first mortgage even though the whole amount is not immediately advanced. The second mortgagee must make payments under the first mortgage as long as the second mortgage is valid. If the first mortgage matures, the mortgagee must pay it off and obtain a discharge so that the second mortgage becomes a first mortgage. D.J. Donahue & P.D. Quinn, *Real Estate Practice in Ontario,* 4th ed. (Toronto: Butterworths, 1990) at 226.

BLASPHEMY. *n.* ". . . [T]he profane speaking of God or sacred things . . . It may also bear the meaning of evil speaking or defamation, . . ." *Ralston v. Fomich* (1992), 66 B.C.L.R. (2d) 166 at 168, [1992] 4 W.W.R. 284 (S.C.), Spencer J.

BLDG. *abbr.* Building.

BLEND. *v.* Of payment of principal and interest, to mix so that they are indistinguishable and inseparable. W.B. Rayner & R.H. McLaren, *Falconbridge on Mortgages,* 4th ed. (Toronto: Canada Law Book, 1977) at 665.

BLENDED. *adj.* 1. Describes a combined payment of principal money with interest. W.B. Rayner & R.H. McLaren, *Falconbridge on Mortgages,* 4th ed. (Toronto: Canada Law Book, 1977) at 662. 2. ". . . '[M]ixed so as to be inseparable and indistinguishable.' " *Kilgoran Hotels Ltd. v. Samek,* [1968] S.C.R. 3 at 5, 65 D.L.R. (2d) 534, the court per Hall J.

BLENDED FUND. A mixed fund obtained from different sources.

BLENDED PAYMENT. A periodic payment on a loan, a definite amount of which is applied first towards interest and the rest of which is applied to reducing the principal.

BLIND TRUST. A trust in which an office holder transfers all personal wealth to a trustee to invest, reinvest and manage in a normal way according to the powers given to the trustee by an instrument. At no time may the trustee give any account to the settlor or office holder of the actual assets held. D.M.W. Waters, *The Law of Trusts in Canada*, 2d ed. (Toronto: Carswell, 1984) at 438.

BLOOD RELATIONSHIP. "... [D]escribed the relationship existing between two or more persons who stand in lawful descent from a common ancestor ..." *Army & Navy Department Store Ltd. v. Minister of National Revenues*, [1953] C.T.C. 293 at 300, [1953] 2 S.C.R. 496, [1954] 1 D.L.R. 177, 53 D.T.C. 1185, Locke J. (Taschereau and Fauteux JJ. concurring).

B.L.R. *abbr.* Business Law Reports, 1977–.

BLUE CHIP. Highest quality securities.

BLUE-SKY BARGAINING. Proposals by negotiators which are so unreasonable that there is no chance of their acceptance.

BLUE-SKY LAW. A law to protect investors from fraud in connection with sales of securities.

B.N.A. ACT(S). *abbr.* British North America Act(s).

BOARD. *n.* 1. A body of persons to which certain powers are delegated or assigned or who are elected for certain purposes. 2. The governing body of an institution. 3. The board of directors of a corporation. 4. "... [A] succession of meals obtained from day to day, or from week to week, or from month to month, &c...." *R. v. McQuarrie* (1862), 22 U.C.Q.B. 600 at 601, the court per Draper C.J. See APPEAL ~; ARBITRATION ~; CANADIAN WHEAT ~; CONCILIATION ~; FEDERAL ~ COMMISSION OR OTHER TRIBUNAL; LOCAL ~.

BOAT. *n.* 1. Includes any vessel used

or designed to be used in navigation of water. 2. "... [A]ny craft afloat, which carries goods or passengers...." *R. v. Conrad*, [1938] 2 D.L.R. 541 at 543, 12 M.P.R. 588, 70 C.C.C. 100 (N.S.T.D.), the court per Chisholm C.J.

BODILY HARM. Any hurt or injury to the complainant that interferes with the health or comfort of the complainant and that is more than merely transient or trifling in nature. *Criminal Code*, R.S.C. 1985, c. C-46, s. 267(2). See GRIEVOUS ~; SERIOUS ~.

BODY. *n.* 1. The main section of any document or instrument. 2. In writs, a person.

BODY CORPORATE. 1. A company or other body corporate with or without share capital wherever or however incorporated. 2. Any incorporated corporation, incorporated association, incorporated syndicate or other incorporated organization wheresoever incorporated.

BODY POLITIC. A nation; a corporation.

BOILERPLATE. *n.* Standard clauses used in legal documents of a particular kind.

BONA. *n.* [L.] Goods; property.

BONA. *adj.* [L.] Good.

BONA FIDE. [L. in good faith] "... '[H]onestly', 'genuinely' or 'in good faith': ..." *Extendicare Health Services Inc. v. Canada (Minister of National Health & Welfare)* (1987), 14 C.E.R. 282 at 286, 87 D.T.C. 5404, 15 F.T.R. 187, [1987] 3 F.C. 622, [1987] 2 C.T.C. 179, Can S.T.R. 80-127, Jerome A.C.J.

BONA FIDE OCCUPATIONAL QUALIFICATION. "... [M]ust be imposed honestly, in good faith, and in the sincerely held belief that such limitation is imposed in the interests of the adequate performance of the work involved with all reasonable dispatch, safety and economy, and not for ulterior or extraneous reasons ... it must be related in an objective sense to the performance of the employment concerned, in that it is reasonably necessary to assure the efficient and economical performance of the job without endangering the employee, his fellow employees and the general public." *Ontario (Human Rights Commission) v. Etobicoke (Borough)*, [1982] 1 S.C.R. 202 at 208, 40 N.R. 159, 82 C.L.L.C. 17,005, 132 D.L.R. (3d) 14, 3 C.H.R.R. D/781, McIntyre J.

BONA FIDE OCCUPATIONAL REQUIREMENT. Equivalent to bona fide occupational qualification. *Central Alberta Dairy Pool v. Alberta (Human Rights Commission)* (1990), 33 C.C.E.L. 1 at 14-15, 21, [1990] 2 S.C.R. 489, [1990] 6 W.W.R. 193, 72 D.L.R. (4th) 417, 76 Alta. L.R. (2d) 97, 90 C.L.L.C. 17,025, 113 N.R. 161, 12 C.H.R.R. D/417, 111 A.R. 241, Wilson J. (Dickson C.J.C., L'Heureux-Dubé and Cory JJ. concurring).

BONA FIDE PURCHASER. 1. A purchaser for value in good faith and without notice of any adverse claim who takes delivery of a security in bearer form or of a security in registered form issued to her or him, endorsed to her or him or endorsed in blank. 2. A purchaser for value, in good faith and without notice of any adverse claim, (i) who takes delivery of a security certificate in bearer form or order form or of a security certificate in registered form issued to him or endorsed to him or endorsed in blank, (ii) in whose name an uncertificated security is registered or recorded in records maintained by or on behalf of the issuer as a result of the issue or transfer of the security to him, or (iii) who is a transferee or pledgee as provided in section 85. *Business Corporations Amendment Act*, S.O. 1986, c. 57, s. 7.

BONA FIDES. [L.] Good faith.

BONA VACANTIA. [L.] 1. Things found which have no apparent owner and which belong to the Crown. W.B. Rayner & R.H. McLaren, *Falconbridge on Mortgages*, 4th ed. (Toronto: Canada Law Book, 1977) at 337. 2. ". . . [T]he ultimate surplus of assets of the defunct company remaining after all obligations of the company

are satisfied . . . the residue after all obligations were discharged . . . the residue only . . . being the bona vacantia." *Embree v. Millar* (1917), 33 D.L.R. 331 at 334, [1917] 1 W.W.R. 1200, 11 Alta. L.R. 127 (C.A.), the court per Beck J.A.

BOND. *n.* 1. ". . . [A] written instrument under seal whereby the person executing it makes a promise or incurs a personal liability to another." *Grimmer v. Gloucester (County)* (1902), 32 S.C.R. 305 at 310, the court per Sedgewick J. 2. Government obligations which are ordinarily unsecured and obligations of large public corporations. H. Sutherland, D.B. Horsley & J.M. Edmiston, eds., *Fraser's Handbook on Canadian Company Law*, 7th ed. (Toronto: Carswell, 1985) at 310. See BACK-~; BAIL-~; BID ~; BOTTOMRY ~; CONTRACT ~; COUPON ~; MORTGAGE ~; PEACE ~; PERFORMANCE ~.

BONDED GOODS. Dutiable goods for which a bond was given for payment of the duty.

BONDEE. *n.* A person named in a bond upon whose default in paying a debt or a debt of a class of debts specified in the bond the guarantor undertakes to pay a sum of money or to pay the debt. *Guarantors' Liability Act*, R.S.M. 1987, c. G120, s. 1.

BONDHOLDER'S TRUST. Assets pledged by a company which is borrowing from a bondholder are vested in a trustee as legal owner. The trustee's duties and powers arise traditionally only when the issuer or guarantor of the bonds defaults. D.M.W. Waters, *The Law of Trusts in Canada*, 2d ed. (Toronto: Carswell, 1984) at 449.

BONDSMAN. *n.* A surety.

BONUS. *n.* 1. Gratuity; premium. 2. ". . . [M]ay be a mere gift or gratuity as a gesture of goodwill, and not enforceable. Or it may be something which an employee is entitled to on the happening of a condition precedent and is enforceable when the condition is fulfilled. But in both cases it is something in addition to or in excess of that which is ordinarily received." *Minister of National Revenue v. Great Western Garment Co.* (1947), [1948] 1 D.L.R. 225 at 233, [1947] C.T.C. 343, [1947] Ex. C.R. 458, O'Connor J. 3. A benefit which a council supplies to a person, over and above the benefits other residents or ratepayers receive, and which consists of an expenditure of funds of the municipality or the giving up of a right or claim of the municipality to collect taxes or other payments from the person. The giving of aid to induce an undertaking to set up and continue itself in the municipality. I.M. Rogers, *The Law of Canadian Municipal Corporations*, 2d ed. (Toronto: Carswell, 1971-) at 864.

BOOK. *n.* 1. Includes every volume, part or division of a volume, pamphlet, sheet of letter-press, sheet of music, map, chart or plan separately published. *Copyright Act*, R.S.C. 1985, c. C-42, s. 2. 2. Library matter of every kind, nature and description and includes any document, paper, record, tape or other thing published by a publisher, on or in which information is written, recorded, stored or reproduced. *National Library Act*, R.S.C. 1985, c. N-12, s. 2. See ABSTRACT ~; CASH ~.

BOOK ACCOUNTS. All the accounts and debts current and future as in the ordinary course of business would be entered in the books, whether entered or not, and includes all books, documents and papers relating to the accounts and debts. *Book Accounts Assignment Act*, R.S.B.C. 1979, c. 32, s. 1.

BOOK DEBTS. All existing or future debts that in the ordinary course of business would be entered in books, whether actually entered or not, and includes any part or class thereof. *Assignment of Book Debts acts*.

BOOKMAKER. *n.* ". . . [A] person who engages in the occupation of taking bets (or even in negotiating bets) and the keeping of accounts, . . ." *R. v. Decome* (1991), 63 C.C.C. (3d) 460 at 472, [1991] R.J.Q. 618, 40 Q.A.C. 92, Proulx J.A. (Gendreau J.A. concur-

ring).

BOOK VALUE. ". . . [V]alue at which property is recorded in the financial accounts of its owner. Usually, property is recorded at historical cost less, in the case of depreciable property, the amount of accumulated depreciation. . . ." *Domglas Inc. v. Jarislowsky, Fraser & Co.* (1980), 13 B.L.R. 135 at 199, [1980] C.S. 925 (Que.), Greenberg J.

BORROWER. *n.* 1. A person to whom a loan has been made. 2. A person who receives credit.

BOTTOMRY BOND. 1. The hypothecation or mortgage of a ship in which her bottom or keel is pledged. 2. An agreement entered into by a ship's owner in which the borrower undertakes to repay money advanced for the use of the ship with interest if the ship ends her voyage successfully.

BOUNDARY. *n.* 1. Limit of territory; an imaginary line which divides two pieces of land. 2. The international boundary between Canada and the United States as determined and marked by the Commission. *International Boundary Commission Act*, R.S.C. 1985, c. I-16, s. 2.

BOUNDARY WATERS. The waters from main shore to main shore of the lakes and rivers and connecting waterways, or the portions thereof, along which the international boundary between the United States and Canada passes, including all bays, arms, and inlets thereof, but not including tributary waters which in their natural channels would flow into such lakes, rivers and waterways, or waters flowing from such lakes, rivers, and waterways, or the waters of rivers flowing across the boundary. *Canada Water Act*, R.S.C. 1985, c. C-11, s. 2.

BOUND OVER. See BIND OVER.

BOUNDS. See METES AND ~.

BOUNTY. *n.* Money or premium paid for the fulfilment of a particular service.

BOYCOTT. *v.* To take part in a boycott.

BOYCOTT. *n.* An organized refusal to deal with a particular person or business.

B.R. *abbr.* 1. Cour du Banc de la Reine/du Roi. 2. Recueils de jurisprudence de la Cour de banc de la Reine (du Roi) de Québec. 3. Rapports judiciaires du Québec, Cour du Banc de la Reine (ou du Roi) (Quebec Official Reports, Queen's (or King's) Bench, 1892-1941).

[ ] B.R. *abbr.* 1. Rapports judiciaires du Québec, Cour du Banc de la Reine (ou du Roi), 1942-1966. 2. Recueils de jurisprudence du Québec, Cour du Banc de la Reine, 1967-1969.

BRANCH. *n.* 1. An agency, the head office and any other office of a bank. *Bank Act*, R.S.C. 1985, c. B-1, s. 2. 2. "... [I]ncludes a local and subordinate office ... it also includes a component portion of an organization or system or a section, division, subdivision or department of a business." *Minister of National Revenue v. Panther Oil & Grease Manufacturing Co.*, [1961] C.T.C. 363 at 377, 61 D.T.C. 1222 (Ex. Ct.), Thorson P.

BRANDEIS BRIEF. A social science brief in which empirical data is appended to or included in a factum. P.W. Hogg, *Constitutional Law of Canada*, 2d ed. (Toronto: Carswell, 1985) at 182.

BRAWL. *v.* To create a disturbance.

BREACH. *n.* 1. Encroachment of a right. 2. Disregard of a duty. 3. Non-execution of a contract. G.H.L. Fridman, *The Law of Contract in Canada*, 2d ed. (Toronto: Carswell, 1986) at 523. See ANTICIPATORY ~; FUNDAMENTAL ~; PRISON ~.

BREACH OF CLOSE. Unjustified entry on another person's land.

BREACH OF CONFIDENCE. "... [C]onsists in establishing three elements: that the information conveyed was confidential, that it was communicated in confidence, and that it was misused by the party to whom it was communicated." *International Corona Resources Ltd. v. Lac Minerals Ltd.* (1989), 44 B.L.R. 1 at 16, [1989] 2 S.C.R. 574, 26 C.P.R. (3d) 97, 69 O.R. (2d) 287, 61 D.L.R. (4th) 14, 6 R.P.R. (2d) 1, 35 E.T.R. 1, 101 N.R. 239, 36 O.A.C. 57, La Forest J. (Wilson and Lamer JJ. concurring).

BREACH OF CONTRACT. See INTENTIONAL INDUCEMENT OF ~.

BREACH OF PRISON. Escape from a prison.

BREACH OF PRIVILEGE. Contempt of Parliament.

BREACH OF PROMISE TO MARRY. Conduct which permitted a common law action for damages.

BREACH OF THE PEACE. The violation of the peace, quiet, and security to which one is legally entitled.

BREACH OF TRUST. The violation of duty by an executor, public officer, trustee or other person who acts in a fiduciary capacity.

BREAK. *v.* (a) To break any part, internal or external, or (b) to open any thing that is used or intended to be used to close or to cover an internal or external opening. *Criminal Code*, R.S.C. 1985, c. C-46, s. 321.

BREAK AND ENTER. Obtain entrance by a threat or artifice or by collusion with a person within, or enter without lawful justification or excuse by a permanent or temporary opening. *Criminal Code*, R.S.C. 1985, c. C-46, s. 350(b). See ENTER.

BREAKDOWN OF MARRIAGE. A court may grant a divorce on the ground that there has been a breakdown of marriage which is established if the spouses have lived separate and apart for at least one year or the spouse against whom the divorce proceeding is brought has committed adultery ,or treated the other spouse with physical or mental cruelty of such kind as to render intolerable the continued cohabitation of the spouses. *Divorce Act*, R.S.C. 1985 (2d Supp.), c. 3, s. 8.

BREAKING AND ENTERING. See BREAK AND ENTER.

BREATHALYZER. *n.* An instrument to measure alcohol content in the blood by analysis of a breath sample.

B.R.E.F. *abbr.* 1. Bureau de révision de l'évaluation foncière. 2. Décisions du Bureau de révision de l'évaluation foncière du Québec.

BRIBE. *n.* 1. A gift to any person holding a position of trust or in public or judicial office intended to induce that person to betray trust or disregard official duty for the giver's benefit. 2. "... For the purposes of the civil law a bribe means the payment of a secret commission, which only means (i) that the person making the payment makes it to the agent of the other person with whom he is dealing; (ii) that he makes it to that person knowing that that person is acting as the agent of the other person with whom he is dealing; and (iii) that he fails to disclose to the other person with whom he is dealing that he made that payment to the person whom he knows to be the other person's agent. Those three are the only elements necessary to constitute the payment of a secret commission or bribe for civil purposes." *Indust. & Gen. Mtge. Co. v. Lewis*, [1949] 2 All E.R. 573 at 575, Slade J.

BRIBERY OF JUDICIAL OFFICER. Occurs when the holder of a judicial office, or a member of Parliament or a legislature corruptly accepts or obtains, agrees to accept or attempts to obtain any money, valuable consideration, office, place or employment for himself or another person in respect of anything done or omitted or to be done or omitted by him in his official capacity or, when another person gives or offers corruptly to a person who holds a judicial office or is a member of Parliament or a legislature any money, valuable consideration, office, place or employment in respect of anything done or omitted or to be done or omitted by him in his official capacity for himself or another person. *Criminal Code*, R.S.C. 1985, c. C-46, s. 119.

BRIBERY OF OFFICERS. Occurs when (a) a justice, police commissioner, peace officer, public officer, or officer of a juvenile court, or being employed in the administration of criminal law, corruptly (i) accepts or obtains, (ii) agrees to accept, or (iii) attempts to obtain, for himself or any other person any money, valuable consideration, office, place or employment with intent (iv) to interfere with the administration of justice, (v) to procure or facilitate the commission of an offence, or (vi) to protect from detection or punishment a person who has committed or who intends to commit an offence, or (b) anyone gives or offers, corruptly, to a person mentioned in paragraph (a) any money, valuable consideration, office, place or employment with intent that the person should do anything mentioned in subparagraph (a)(iv), (v) or (vi). *Criminal Code*, R.S.C. 1985, c. C-46, s. 120.

BRIDGE FINANCING. Construction of a building using a borrower's own funds or interim loans. D.J. Donahue & P.D. Quinn, *Real Estate Practice in Ontario*, 4th ed. (Toronto: Butterworths, 1990) at 225.

BRIEF. *n.* A file of all pleadings, documents and memoranda which serves as the basis for argument by the lawyer in the matter in court. See BRANDEIS ~; CHAMBERS ~; SOCIAL SCIENCE ~.

BRITISH NORTH AMERICA ACT, 1867. Renamed the Constitution Act, 1867 in 1982, this Act gave effect to the confederation scheme by uniting the provinces of Canada, Nova Scotia and New Brunswick. P.W. Hogg, *Constitutional Law of Canada*, 3d ed. (Toronto: Carswell, 1992) at 4, 36 and 37.

BROKER. *n.* 1. One who negotiates or makes contracts for the sale of property. 2. A person who is engaged for full or part time in the business of buying and selling securities and who, in the transaction concerned, acts for, or buys a security from, or sells a security to a customer. 3. A person who, for another or others, for compensation, gain or reward or hope or promise thereof, either alone or through one or more officials or salespersons, trades in real estate, or a person who claims to be such a person. 4. A person who, for compensation, acts or aids in any manner in negotiating contracts of insurance or placing risks or effecting insurance, or in negotiating the continuance or renewal of insurance contracts for another person. *Insurance acts.* 5. A person licensed to transact business as a custom-house broker. *Custom-House Brokers Licensing Regulations*, C.R.C., c. 456, s. 2. See CUSTOMS ~; MONEY ~; SPECIAL ~.

BROKERAGE. *n.* The commission which one pays to a broker.

BROKER-DEALER. *var.* **BROKER DEALER.** Any person or company that is recognized as a broker-dealer that engaged either for full or part time in the business of trading in securities in the capacity of an agent or principal.

BROTHEL. *n.* ". . . [T]he same thing as a 'bawdy-house', . . . applies to a place resorted to by persons of both sexes for the purpose of prostitution. . . ." *Singleton v. Ellison*, [1895] 1 Q.B. 607 at 608, Wills J.

BROUGHT. *v.* 1. ". . . '[I]nitiate[d]' . . ." *R. v. Henderson*, [1929] 2 W.W.R. 209 at 214, [1929] 4 D.L.R. 984, 52 C.C.C. 82, 41 B.C.R. 242 (C.A.), Macdonald J.A. 2. ". . . '[C]ommenced' . . ." *Krueger v. Raccah* (1981), 24 C.P.C. 14 at 16, 12 Sask. R. 130, 128 D.L.R. (3d) 177 (Q.B.), Cameron J.

BRUTUM FULMEN. [L. an empty noise] An empty threat.

BUDGET. *n.* A statement of the amounts of estimated revenues and expenditures. See CASH ~.

BUGGERY. *n.* Sodomy, anal intercourse.

BUILDERS' LIEN. ". . . [P]rovides at least a security or charge upon the land and the purpose of registering it is to protect the claim being made for services and work carried out in the improvement of land . . ." *Western International Contractors Ltd. v. Sarcee Developments Ltd.*, [1979] 2 C.N.L.R. 107 at 123-24, [1979] 3 W.W.R. 631

(Alta. C.A.), Morrow J.A. (Haddad J.A. concurring).

BUILDING. *n.* 1. A structure consisting of foundations, walls or roof, with or without other parts. 2. A structure that is used or intended to be used for the purpose of supporting or sheltering persons or animals or storing property. See ACCESSORY ~; PUBLIC ~.

BUILDING CODE. Detailed specifications for the design and construction of buildings which ensure structural safety, fire safety and the occupants' health. D. Robertson, *Ontario Health and Safety Guide* (Toronto: De Boo, 1988) at 5-35.

BUILDING CONSTRUCTION CODE. A code of building construction standards.

BUILDING CONSTRUCTION STANDARD. A standard for (a) construction materials, or plumbing or electrical materials or installations, or equipment or appliances, or any combination thereof, to be used or installed in any building or part of a building, or (b)the method to be used in the construction or demolition of any building or part of a building. *Buildings and Mobile Homes Act*, R.S.M. 1987, c. B93, s. 1.

BUILDING CONTRACT. A contract to build anything.

BUILDING INSPECTOR. An inspector appointed by a municipality to administer and enforce the building code.

BUILDING LEASE. 1. A lease of a vacant piece of land on which the lessee covenants to erect a building or to pull down an old building and erect a new one on the site. 2. The lease of land for a rent called ground rent.

BUILDING PERMIT. A permit, issued under a building bylaw of a municipality, authorizing the construction of all or part of any structure.

BULK. See STOCK IN ~.

BULK SALE. Sale of stock or part of stock which is out of the vendor's usual course of business or trade. G.H.L. Fridman, *Sale of Goods in Canada*, 3d ed. (Toronto: Carswell, 1986) at 489. See SALE IN BULK.

BULK SALES ACT. An act to protect creditors of a vendor who (a) sells stock, or a part of it, out of the usual course of business or trade or (b) sells what is substantially the vendor's stock or interest in the business. G.H.L. Fridman, *Sale of Goods in Canada*, 3d ed. (Toronto: Carswell, 1986) at 489.

BULL. *n.* One who buys shares expecting prices on the stock exchange to rise. See PURE-BRED ~; SCRUB ~.

BULL. ACBD. *abbr.* Bulletin ACBD (CALL Newsletter).

BULL. AVOCATS. *abbr.* Le Bulletin des avocats (Solicitor's Journal).

BULL. CCDJ. *abbr.* Bulletin d'information juridique du CCDJ (CLIC's Legal Materials Letter).

BULLION. *n.* Uncoined silver and gold.

"BULLOCK" ORDER. Named after the case of Bullock v. London General Omnibus Co., [1907] 1 K.B. 264 (C.A.). ". . . [O]rder under which the plaintiff paid the costs of the successful defendant and recovered them together with his own from the unsuccessful defendant . . ." *Rowe v. Investors Syndicate Ltd.* (1984), 46 C.P.C. 209 at 215 (Ont. H.C.), Henry J.

BURDEN. *n.* The duty to perform an obligation. See EVIDENTIAL ~; EVIDENTIARY ~; LEGAL ~ OF PROOF; MAJOR ~; PERSUASIVE ~; PRIMARY ~.

BURDEN OF PROOF. ". . . [M]ay be applied to cases like this in two distinct senses: . . . The first is in the sense of establishing a case. This is a matter of substantive law, . . . The other sense in which the term may be applied is that of introducing evidence. This is a matter of procedure, . . ." *R. v. Primak* (1930), 24 Sask. L.R. 417 at 419, [1930] 1 W.W.R. 755, [1930] 3 D.L.R. 345, 53 C.C.C. 203 (C.A.), the court per Mackenzie J.A.

BURGLARY. *n.* The common law offence of breaking and entering a dwelling-house at night with intent to commit a crime there.

BUS. *n.* Any vehicle adapted to carry more than six to twelve adult passengers in addition to the driver.

BUS. & L. *abbr.* Business & the Law.

BUSINESS. *n.* 1. Includes a profession, calling, trade, manufacture or undertaking of any kind whatsoever and includes an adventure or concern in the nature of trade but does not include an office or employment. 2. An undertaking carried on for the purpose of gain or profit, and includes an interest in any such undertaking. *Real Estate and Business Brokers acts.* 3. Any business, profession, trade, calling, manufacture or undertaking of any kind carried on in Canada or elsewhere whether for profit or otherwise, including any activity or operation carried on or performed in Canada or elsewhere by any government, by any department, branch, board, commission or agency of any government, by any court or other tribunal or by any other body or authority performing a function of government. *Canada Evidence Act*, R.S.C. 1985, c. C-5, s. 30(12). 4. The business of (a) manufacturing, producing, transporting, acquiring, supplying, storing and otherwise dealing in articles, and (b) acquiring, supplying and otherwise dealing in services. *Competition Act*, R.S.C. 1985, c. C-34, s. 2. 5. Those lawful objects and purposes for which a company is established. 6. The land and buildings used for a commercial enterprise. See BANKING ~; CARRY ON ~; FEDERAL ~ DEVELOPMENT BANK; FEDERAL WORK, UNDERTAKING OR ~; NON-CONTENTIOUS ~.

BUSINESS ASSET. 1. ". . . [A]ssets which have as their purpose the generation of income in an entrepreneurial sense. . . ." *Clarke v. Clarke* (1990), 28 R.F.L. (3d) 113 at 134, 73 D.L.R. (4th) 1, 113 N.R. 321, [1990] 2 S.C.R. 795, the court per Wilson J. 2. Property owned by one spouse and used principally in the course of a business carried on by that spouse, either alone or jointly with others, and includes shares that the spouse owns in a corporation through which he or she carries on a business.

BUSINESS COMBINATION. An acquisition of all or substantially all of the property of one body corporate by another or an amalgamation of two or more bodies corporate.

BUSINESS NAME. The name under which a business is carried on or is to be carried on and includes a firm name.

BUSINESS OCCUPANCY. Occupancy for the transaction of business.

BUSINESS OCCUPANCY TAX. A tax levied on occupants in respect of their use or occupation of real property for the purpose of or in connection with a business. *Municipal Grants Act*, R.S.C. 1985, c. M-13, s. 2.

BUSINESS OF SUPPLY. Considering estimates for interim supply, passing all stages of any bill based on them, and considering opposition motions. A. Fraser, W.A. Dawson & J. Holtby, eds., *Beauchesne's Rules and Forms of the House of Commons of Canada*, 6th ed. (Toronto: Carswell, 1989) at 255.

BUSINESS OR TRADE ASSOCIATION. An organization of persons that by an enactment, agreement or custom has power to admit, suspend, expel or direct persons in relation to any business or trade. *Human Rights codes*.

BUSINESS, PROFESSIONAL OR TRADE ASSOCIATION. Includes an organization of persons which by an enactment, agreement or custom has power to admit, suspend, expel or direct persons in relation to any business or trade or in the practice of any occupation or calling. *Human Rights Act*, R.S.P.E.I. 1988, c. H-12, s. 1(1)(a).

BUSINESS RECORDS. ". . . [T]hree prerequisites to their reception as admissible evidence of what they record – (1) if they are made in the usual and ordinary course of such business; (2) if it was in the usual and ordinary course of such business to make such a writing or record; (3) the record or writing was made at the time of the act, transaction,

occurrence or event or a reasonable time thereafter." *Tobias v. Nolan* (1985), 71 N.S.R. (2d) 92 at 102, 171 A.P.R. 92 (T.D.), MacIntosh J.

BUSINESS TAX. ". . . [O]ne imposed upon, and proportioned to, either the volume of business done in, or the volume of profits derived from, some business – though the latter would perhaps be rather in the nature of an income tax. . . ." *Dominion Express Co. v. Brandon (City)* (1910), 20 Man. R. 304 at 306, 17 W.L.R. 71 (C.A.), Richards J.A.

BUY. *v.* To purchase; to acquire by payment of money or equivalent.

BUYER. *n.* 1. A purchaser. 2. A person who buys or agrees to buy goods. 3. A person who buys or hires goods by a conditional sale. 4. A person who acquires stock in bulk. *Bulk Sales acts*. 5. A person who purchases goods or services on credit and includes that person's agent. 6. An individual who leases or purchases goods or services under an executory contract, and includes his agent. *Consumer Protection acts*.

BUY IN. For the original owner or person with interest in a property to purchase it at a mortgage, tax or other forced sale.

BUY ON MARGIN. To purchase securities partly on credit extended by a broker.

BY-ELECTION. *n.* 1. An election other than a general election. 2. An election held in a constituency on a date on which there is no general election. 3. An election held to fill a vacancy in the office of mayor, councillor or trustee at a time other than a general election.

BY-LAW. *var.* BYLAW. *n.* 1. ". . . [N]ot an agreement, but a law binding on all persons to whom it applies, whether they agree to be bound by it or not. All regulations made by a corporate body, and intended to bind not only themselves and their officers and servants, but members of the public who come within the sphere of their operation, may be properly called 'by-laws'." *London Association of Shipowners and Brokers v. London and India Docks Joint Committee* (1892), 3 Ch. 242 at 252, Lindley L.J. 2. A law which a municipality makes. 3. "... [A] local law, ..." *White v. Morely* (1899), 2 Q.B. 34 at 39, Channell J. 4. Includes a resolution on which the opinion of the electors is to be obtained. *Municipal Election acts*. 5. Includes a resolution and a question upon which the opinion of the electors is to be obtained. 6. Includes an order or resolution. See MONEY ~; ZONING ~.

C

C. *abbr.* 1. Court. 2. Chapter. 3. Chancellor.

C.A. *abbr.* 1. Court of Appeal. 2. Cour d'appel. 3. Recueils de jurisprudence de la Cour d'appel de Québec (Quebec Court of Appeals Reports).

[ ] C.A. *abbr.* Recueils de jurisprudence du Québec, Cour d'appel, 1970-.

CABINET. *n.* A body composed of the Prime Minister or Premier and Ministers of the Crown or a committee of Privy Council (federal) or Executive Council (provincial) which determines the direction of and makes policy decisions for the government. It is usually composed of members of the Prime Minister's or Premier's political party who have been elected as members of the House of Commons or the Legislature and is often referred to as "the government".

CABINET GOVERNMENT. Government in which Prime Minister or Premier selects members of her or his own party elected to Parliament and perhaps others to be Ministers of the Crown. This group collectively form the Cabinet, the policy-making arm of government. The Ministers and Cabinet are responsible to Parliament for the conduct of the government. The government remains in power so long as it has the confidence of a majority of the House of Commons or the Legislature. In theory, the Privy Council or Executive Council advises the formal head of state (the Governor General or Lieutenant Governor) though, in fact, the Committee of Council, known as the Cabinet, carries out this function in most situations.

CABINET MINISTER. A member of Cabinet who is responsible for a portfolio, usually a ministry or department of government. This person acts as political head of the ministry or department and is responsible to Parliament for the affairs of that ministry or department or the conduct of that portfolio.

C.A.C.F.P. *abbr.* Comité d'appel de la commission de la Fonction publique.

CAHIERS PROP. INTEL. *abbr.* Les Cahiers de propriété intellectuelle.

C.A.I. *abbr.* 1. Commission d'appel de l'immigration. 2. Décisions de la Commission d'accès à l'information.

CALCULATE. *v.* "... [P]lan deliberately ..." *Belmont v. Millhaven Institution* (1984), 41 C.R. (3d) 91 at 95, 9 Admin. L.R. 181 (Fed. T.C.), Dubé J.

CALCULATED. *adj.* "... [F]itted, suited, apt ..." *R. v. Hill* (1976), 33 C.C.C. (2d) 60 at 68 (B.C.C.A.), McIntyre J.A.

CALDERBANK LETTER. "... [A letter written] on a 'without prejudice' basis not only setting out an offer of settlement but expressly reserving the right, if the settlement offer was not accepted, to bring this letter to the attention of the trial Judge, after judgment, on the issue of costs ..." *Goodman v. Goodman* (1992), 2 C.P.C. (3d) 316 at 319 (B.C. S.C.), Sinclair

---

Prowse J.

CALL. *v.* 1. To make a request or demand. 2. To demand shareholders pay amount remaining on unpaid shares.

CALL. *n.* 1. Includes instalment, assessment and any other amount paid, payable or agreed to be paid in respect of a share. H. Sutherland, D.B. Horsley & J.M. Edmiston, eds., *Fraser's Handbook on Canadian Company Law*, 7th ed. (Toronto: Carswell, 1985) at 136. 2. "... [A] contract purchased for an agreed premium entitling the holder, at his option, to buy from the vendor on or before a fixed date a specified number of shares at a pre-determined price...." *Posluns v. Toronto Stock Exchange*, [1964] 2 O.R. 547 at 553, 46 D.L.R. (2d) 210 (H.C.), Gale J. 3. A request or command to come or assemble. 4. A demand for payment.

CALLABLE. *adj.* Describes an option to pay on call before maturity.

CALLING. *n.* A business; occupation; profession; trade; vocation.

CALL NEWSL. *abbr.* CALL Newsletter (Bulletin ACBD).

CALL TO THE BAR. 1. Admission to the Law Society of a province or to membership in the legal profession of a province. 2. The conferral on students of the degree of barrister-at-law.

CAM. *abbr.* Cameron's Privy Council Decisions, 1832-1929.

CA MAG. *abbr.* CA Magazine.

CAM. DIG. *abbr.* Cameron's Digest.

CAMERA. *n.* 1. A judge's chambers. 2. A room. See IN ~.

CAMPBELL'S (LORD) ACT. The name by which the Fatal Accidents Act, 1846, U.K. is known.

CAM. S.C. *abbr.* Reports Hitherto Unpublished, Supreme Court of Canada, Cameron, 1880-1900.

CAN. *abbr.* Canada.

CANADA. *n.* 1. The geographic unit. 2. The juristic federal unit. *Reference re Legislative Authority of Parliament of Canada* (1979), (sub nom. *Refer-*

ence re Legislative Authority of Parliament to Alter or Replace Senate) 102 D.L.R. (3d) 1 at 12, [1980] 1 S.C.R. 56, 30 N.R. 271, Laskin C.J.C., Martland, Ritchie, Pigeon, Dickson, Estey, Pratte and McIntyre JJ. See AUDITOR GENERAL OF ~; BANK OF ~; COASTAL WATERS OF ~; COASTING TRADE OF ~; COAST OF ~; CONSTITUTION OF ~; GOVERNOR OF ~; INFORMATION COMMISSIONER OF ~; LAW OF ~; LOWER ~; QUEEN'S PRIVY COUNCIL FOR ~; WORKS FOR THE GENERAL ADVANTAGE OF ~.

CANADA ACT, 1982. The statute of the Parliament of the United Kingdom which gave effect to the Constitution Act, 1982 proclaimed in force April 17, 1982. This statute patriated the Constitution and terminated the power of the U.K. Parliament to legislate for Canada.

CANADA ASSISTANCE PLAN. A group of income-support programmes and social services which began in the 1940s and 1950s. P.W. Hogg, *Constitutional Law of Canada*, 3d ed. (Toronto: Carswell, 1992) at 145.

CANADA CORPORATION. A body corporate incorporated by or under an Act of the Parliament of Canada.

CANADA DEPOSIT INSURANCE CORPORATION. A federal body with power to insure qualified Canadian currency deposits which member institutions hold and which makes loans to those institutions and to co-operative credit societies, finance corporations and other related organizations.

CANADA MORTGAGE AND HOUSING CORPORATION. The federal corporation which administers the National Housing Act, insures the mortgage loans which approved lenders make for new and existing homeowner and rental housing or for dwellings which non-profit and co-operative associations build.

CANADA PENSION PLAN. A contributory federal social insurance program which provides income protection, disability and survivor benefits at retirement. K.D. Cooper-Stephenson & I.B. Saunders, *Personal Injury Damages in Canada* (Toronto: Carswell, 1981) at 2.

CANADA POST CORPORATION. The body which gathers, sorts and delivers mail in Canada.

CANADIAN. *n.* 1. A Canadian citizen. 2. A permanent resident within the meaning of the Immigration Act, 1976. 3. A Canadian government, whether federal, provincial or local, or an agency thereof. 4. An entity that is Canadian-controlled.

CANADIAN BILL OF RIGHTS. This bill, enacted by 8-9 Elizabeth II, c. 44 (R.S.C. 1985, Appendix III), was the first attempt in Canada to give statutory recognition and protection to certain human rights, fundamental freedoms of religion, speech, assembly and association and the press and procedural rights. See BILL OF RIGHTS.

CANADIAN CHARTER OF RIGHTS AND FREEDOMS. Part 1 of the Constitution Act, 1982 which guarantees rights and freedoms. See CHARTER.

CANADIAN COMPANY. A company formed or incorporated by or under any Act of Parliament of Canada or of the Legislature of any province.

CANADIAN FORCES. The armed forces of Her Majesty raised by Canada.

CANADIAN HUMAN RIGHTS COMMISSION. The federal commission which administers the Canadian Human Rights Act.

CANADIAN JUDICIAL COUNCIL. A body constituted to encourage better, uniform, and efficient judicial service in county and superior courts.

CANADIAN MARITIME LAW. 1. "... [I]ncludes all that body of law which was administered in England by the High Court on its Admiralty side in 1934 as such law may, from time to time, have been amended by the federal Parliament, and as it has developed through judicial precedent to date. ... a body of federal law dealing with all claims in respect of maritime and admiralty matters ... the words 'maritime' and 'admiralty' should be interpreted within the modern context of commerce and shipping. In reality, the ambit of Canadian maritime law is limited only by the constitutional division of powers in the Constitution Act 1867 (30 & 31 Vict.), c. 3. ... a body of federal law encompassing the common law principles of tort, contract and bailment." *Miida Electronics Inc. v. Mitsui O.S.K. Lines Ltd.* (1986), (*sub nom. ITO – International Terminal Operators Ltd. v. Miida Electronics Inc.*) 28 D.L.R. (4th) 641 at 654, 656, 660, [1986] 1 S.C.R. 752, 68 N.R. 241, 34 B.L.R. 251, McIntyre J. (Dickson C.J.C., Estey and Wilson JJ. concurring). 2. Administered by the Exchequer Court of Canada on its Admiralty side by virtue of the Admiralty Act, chapter A-1 of the Revised Statutes of Canada, 1970, or any other statute, or that would have been so administered if that Court had had, on its Admiralty side, unlimited jurisdiction in relation to maritime and admiralty matters, as that law has been altered by this Act or any other Act of Parliament. *Federal Court Act*, R.S.C. 1985, c. F-7, s. 2.

CANADIAN PAYMENTS ASSOCIATION. A corporation whose members are: (a) The Bank of Canada; (b) any bank under the Bank Act, and any savings bank under the Quebec Savings Bank Act; (c) any trust company, loan company, central cooperative credit society, some credit unions, and any other party who "accepts deposits transferable by order to a third party", if that party meets certain requirements. I.F.G. Baxter, *The Law of Banking*, 3d ed. (Toronto: Carswell, 1981) at 174.

CANADIAN RADIO-TELEVISION AND TELECOMMUNICATIONS COMMISSION. The federal body which supervises and regulates every aspect of Canadian broadcasting (television, radio, cable and pay television and specialty services) and regulates federal telecommunications carriers.

CANADIAN STANDARDS AS-SOCIATION. A national standard-setting organization which certifies products covered by its standards. D. Robertson, *Ontario Health and Safety Guide* (Toronto: De Boo, 1988) at 5-42.

CANADIAN TRANSPORT COM-MISSION. The federal body which regulates transportation which is under federal jurisdiction in Canada (i.e. by air, water, rail and commodity pipeline) and certain kinds of interprovincial commercial motor transport.

CANADIAN WATERS. The territorial sea of Canada and all internal waters of Canada.

CANADIAN WHEAT BOARD. The federal body, established under the Canadian Wheat Board Act, which supervises export sales of barley, oats and wheat produced in Western Canada and domestic sales of these grains intended for human consumption. It controls the delivery of all major grains, coordinating grain movement to terminal elevators.

CAN-AM L.J. *abbr.* Canadian-American Law Journal.

CAN. BAR J. *abbr.* Canadian Bar Journal.

CAN. BAR REV. *abbr.* The Canadian Bar Review (La Revue du Barreau canadien).

CAN. BUS. L.J. *abbr.* Canadian Business Law Journal (Revue canadienne du droit de commerce).

CANCEL. *v.* 1. To revoke a will. *Bishop Estate v. Reesor* (1990), 39 E.T.R. 36 at 38 (Ont. H.C.), Kurisko L.J.S.C. 2. In the case of an instrument, to draw lines across it intending to indicate it is no longer in force.

CANCELLATION. *n.* ". . . [U]sed in relation to an insurance policy implies the bringing to an end of the policy during its term, i.e. for some reason rendering invalid what would otherwise be valid." *Bank of Nova Scotia v. Commercial Union Assurance of Canada* (1991), 104 N.S.R. (2d) 313 at 319, 283 A.P.R. 313, 6 C.C.L.I. (2d) 178 (T.D.), Tidman J.

CANCELLATION CLAUSE. A clause in an agreement that permits the parties to cancel and terminate their agreement.

CANCELLED CHEQUE. A cheque which bears the indication that it has been honoured by the bank upon which it was drawn.

CAN. C.L.G. *abbr.* Canadian Commercial Law Guide.

CAN. COMMUNIC. L. REV. *abbr.* Canadian Communications Law Review.

CAN. COMMUNITY L.J. *abbr.* Canadian Community Law Journal (Revue canadienne de droit communautaire).

CAN. COMPET. POLICY REC. *abbr.* Canadian Competition Policy Record.

CAN. COMP. POL. REC. *abbr.* Canadian Competition Policy Record.

CAN. COMPUTER L.R. *abbr.* Canadian Computer Law Reporter

CAN. COM. R. *abbr.* Canadian Commercial Reports, 1901-1905.

CAN. COUNCIL INT. L. *abbr.* Canadian Council on International Law. Conference. Proceedings. (Conseil canadien de droit international. Congrès. Travaux).

CAN. COUNCIL INT'L L. PROC. *abbr.* Canadian Council on International Law, Proceedings.

CAN. CRIM. FORUM. *abbr.* Canadian Criminology Forum (Le Forum canadien de criminologie).

CAN. CURR. TAX. *abbr.* Canadian Current Tax.

CAN. CURRENT TAX. *abbr.* Canadian Current Tax.

C. & F. *abbr.* Cost and freight. In a sales contract, means that the price includes cost and freight and the buyer must arrange insurance.

C & S. *abbr.* Clarke & Scully's Drainage Cases (Ont.), 1898-1903.

CAN. ENV. L.N.. *abbr.* Canadian Environmental Law News.

CAN. F.L.G. *abbr.* Canadian Family Law Guide.

CAN. H.R. ADVOC. *abbr.* Canadian Human Rights Advocate.

CAN. HUM. RTS. Y.B. *abbr.* Canadian Human Rights Yearbook (Annuaire canadien des droits de le personne).

CAN. IND. REL. ASSOC. *abbr.* Canadian Industrial Relations Association. Annual Meeting. Proceedings (Association canadienne des relations industrielles. Congrès. Travaux).

CAN. INTELL. PROP. REV. *abbr.* Canadian Intellectual Property Review.

CAN. I.T.G.R. *abbr.* Canada Income Tax Guide Report.

CAN. J. CRIM. *abbr.* Canadian Journal of Criminology (Revue canadienne de criminologie).

CAN. J. CRIM. & CORR. *abbr.* Canadian Journal of Criminology and Corrections.

CAN. J. FAM. L. *abbr.* Canadian Journal of Family Law (Revue canadienne de droit familial).

CAN. J. INS. L. *abbr.* Canadian Journal of Insurance Law.

CAN. J.L. & JURIS. *abbr.* The Canadian Journal of Law and Jurisprudence.

CAN. J.L. & SOCIETY. *abbr.* Canadian Journal of Law and Society (Revue canadienne de droit et société).

CAN. J. WOMEN & LAW. *abbr.* Canadian Journal of Women and the Law (Revue juridique "La femme et le droit").

CAN. LAW. *abbr.* Canadian Lawyer.

CAN. LAWYER. *abbr.* Canadian Lawyer.

CAN. LEGAL STUD. *abbr.* Canadian Legal Studies.

CAN. L.J. *abbr.* Canada Law Journal.

CAN. L.R.B.R. *abbr.* Canadian Labour Relations Board Reports, 1974-.

[ ] CAN. L.R.B.R. *abbr.* Canadian Labour Relations Board Reports.

CAN. L. REV. *abbr.* Canadian Law Review (1901-1907).

CAN. L.T. (1881-1922). *abbr.* Canadian Law Times.

CAN. MUN. J. *abbr.* Canadian Municipal Journal.

CANON. *n.* 1. A rule of law. 2. A church dignitary.

CAN. PETRO. TAX J. *abbr.* Canadian Petroleum Tax Journal.

CAN. PUB. POL. *abbr.* Canadian Public Policy.

CAN. S.L.R. *abbr.* Canadian Securities Law Reports.

CAN. S.T.R. *abbr.* Canadian Sales Tax Reports.

CAN. TAX FOUND. *abbr.* Canadian Tax Foundation (Conference Report).

CAN. TAX J. *abbr.* Canadian Tax Journal (Revue fiscale canadienne).

CAN. TAX N. *abbr.* Canadian Tax News.

CAN. TAX'N: J. TAX POL'Y. *abbr.* Canadian Taxation: A Journal of Tax Policy.

CAN.-U.S. L.J. *abbr.* Canada-United States Law Journal.

CANVASS. *v.* To personally solicit votes or donations.

CAN. Y.B. INT. L. *abbr.* Canadian Year Book of International Law (Annuaire canadien de droit international).

CAN. Y.B. INT'L. L. *abbr.* Canadian Year Book of International Law.

CAP. *abbr.* Chapter.

C.A.P.A.C. *abbr.* Composers, Authors and Publishers Association of Canada Limited.

CAPACITY. *n.* The capacity to understand and appreciate the nature of a consent or agreement and the consequences of giving, withholding, or revoking the consent or making, not making or terminating the agreement. *Child and Family Services Act,* R.S.O.

1990, c. C.11, s. 4. See CONTRAC-TUAL ~; TESTAMENTARY ~.

CAPIAS. [L. that you take] The name of writs which direct the sheriff to arrest the person named in the writs.

CAPITAL. *n.* 1. The means with which a business is carried on. 2. In estates, used in contradistinction to income. "... [W]hen applied to estate problems would clearly mean the value of the assets of the estate as of the date of the testator's death." *Thomson v. Morrison* (1980), 6 E.T.R. 257 at 266, 28 O.R. (2d) 403, 111 D.L.R. (3d) 390 (H.C.), Holland J. 3. Money raised through issuing shares, certificates, bonds, debentures, long-term notes or any other long-term obligation, contributed or earned surplus and reserves. See AUTHORIZED ~; CIRCULATING ~; EQUITY ~; FIXED ~; FLOATING ~; ISSUED ~; LIQUID ~; NATIONAL ~ COMMISSION; NATIONAL ~ REGION; NOMINAL ~.

CAPITAL ACCOUNT. The amount by which the assets of a person employed in the business exceed the liabilities arising from the business and all money advanced or loaned to the person for capital account.

CAPITAL ASSETS. Things used in a business to earn the income – land, buildings, plant, machinery, motor vehicles, ships. *Canada Steamship Lines Ltd. v. M.N.R.*, [1966] C.T.C. 255, 66 D.T.C. 5305 (Exch. Ct.).

CAPITAL COST. The cost involved in acquiring, constructing, designing, equipping, adding to, replacing or altering a capital work.

CAPITAL COST ALLOWANCE. "... [A] tax term signifying the writing-off of the capital cost of an asset in an amount allowed by income tax regulations." *Canning v. C.F.M. Fuels (Ontario) Ltd.*, [1977] 2 S.C.R. 207 at 214, 12 N.R. 541, 71 D.L.R. (3d) 321, the court per Dickson J.

CAPITAL EXPENDITURE. An outlay or the incurrence of a liability for the construction or acquisition or, for the addition to, a tangible asset.

CAPITAL GAIN. The profit earned when property is sold for more than was paid for it.

CAPITAL GAIN OR LOSS. The difference between the proceeds of disposition and the combination of the adjusted cost base and any expenses incurred when making the disposition. W. Grover & F. Iacobucci, *Materials on Canadian Income Tax*, 4th ed. (Toronto: De Boo, 1980) at 485.

CAPITALISATION. *var.*
CAPITALIZATION. *n.* 1. The total amount of shares and other securities issued by a corporation. 2. "... [U]nless the earnings as such actually or constructively pass from the company to the shareholder there is, for all purposes, capitalization.... When earnings are 'capitalized', they cease at that moment to be 'earnings'; they become part of the capital assets; ..." *Waters, Re (sub nom. Waters v. Toronto General Trusts Corp.)* [1956] C.T.C. 217 at 222, [1956] S.C.R. 889, 56 D.T.C. 1113, 4 D.L.R. (2d) 673, Rand J. 3. An estimate of yearly revenue in terms of the amount of capital which it is necessary to invest at a given rate of interest in order to receive that revenue.

CAPITAL LOSS. See CAPITAL GAIN OR LOSS; CARRY-OVER OF ~ES.

CAPITAL MURDER. A classification formerly used under the Criminal Code where a person personally caused or assisted in causing the death of (a) a police officer, police constable, constable, sheriff, deputy sheriff, sheriff's officer or other person employed for the preservation and maintenance of the public peace, acting in the course of that officer's duties, or (b) the warden, deputy warden, instructor, keeper, gaoler, guard or other officer or permanent employee of a prison, acting in the course of that officer's duties, or counselled or procured another person to do any act causing or assisting in causing the death.

CAPITAL PROPERTY. (i) Any depreciable property of the taxpayer, and (ii) any property (other than depreciable property), any gain or loss from the disposition of which would, if the property were disposed of, be a capital gain or a capital loss, as the case may be, of the taxpayer. *Income Tax Act*, R.S.C. 1952, c. 148 (as am. S.C. 1970-71-72, c. 63), s. 54(b).

CAPITAL PUNISHMENT. Punishment by death.

CAPITAL SECURITY. Any share of any class of shares of a company or any bond, debenture, note or other obligation of a company, whether secured or unsecured.

CAPITAL TRANSACTION. The general concept is that a transaction whereby an enduring asset or advantage is acquired for the business is a capital transaction. *Associated Investors v. M.N.R.*, [1967] C.T.C. 138, 67 D.T.C. 5096.

CAPITAL WORKS. Any building or other structure built on or into the land, and machinery, equipment, and apparatus that are affixed to or incorporated into such building or structure for the purpose of improving the serviceability or utility of the building.

CAPTION. *n.* The formal heading of an affidavit, deposition, indictment, information or recognisance which states before whom it was taken, found or made.

CAPTURE. *v.* To take; arrest; seize.

CARD. See CREDIT ~.

CARE. *n.* 1. Safekeeping. 2. "... [I]ncludes such things as feeding, clothing, cleaning, transporting, helping and protecting another person. ..." *Thornborrow v. MacKinnon* (1981), *(sub nom. Schmidt, Re)* 16 C.C.L.T. 198 at 207, 32 O.R. (2d) 740, 123 D.L.R. (3d) 124 (H.C.), Linden J. 3. "... [I]mplies at least physical possession of the motor vehicle with an element of 'control' and carries the sense of responsibility and includes a sense of charge, possession and management." *R. v. Young* (1979), 4 M.V.R. 38 at 43, 21 Nfld. & P.E.I.R. 77, 56 A.P.R. 77 (P.E.I. C.A.), M.J. McQuaid J.A. (Peake J.A. concurring).

See COMMUNITY ~ FACILITY; DAY ~.

CARE AND CUSTODY. All parental rights, duties and responsibilities toward a child.

CARELESS. *adj.* 1. "... [I]nfers an element of negligence or recklessness. It describes a state of conscious in difference [sic] or oblivion to the potential consequences of an act or a course of action." *R. v. Pawlivsky* (1981), 8 Sask. R. 356 at 359 (Div. Ct.), affirmed (1981), 10 Sask L.R. 179 (C.A.). 2. "... [N]ot caring ..." *R. v. King* (1984), 37 Sask. R. 29 at 32 (Q.B.), Hrabinsky J.

CAREY. *abbr.* Manitoba Reports, temp. Wood, 1875.

CARNAL KNOWLEDGE. Coitus, copulation, sexual intercourse.

CARRIER. *n.* 1. Any person engaged for hire or reward in transport of persons or commodities by railway, water, aircraft, motor vehicle undertaking or commodity pipeline. 2. An insurer. 3. A person who, without apparent symptoms of a communicable disease, harbours and may disseminate an infectious agent. *Public Health Act*, S.A. 1984, c. P-27.1, s. 1. See COMMON ~; MOTOR ~; PRIVATE ~.

CARRY. *v.* 1. Includes to store or have in possession. 2. In connection with insurance, to possess or hold.

CARRYING CHARGE. A charge made by creditor in addition to interest.

CARRY ON. To carry on, perform, operate, keep, hold, occupy, deal in or use, for gain, whether as principal or as agent.

CARRY ON BUSINESS. 1. Any action for the promotion or execution of any purpose of business. 2. Transaction of business.

CARRY-OVER OF CAPITAL LOSSES. Capital losses may be deducted from capital gains or income of other years. W. Grover & F. Iacobucci, *Materials on Canadian Income Tax*, 4th ed. (Toronto: De Boo, 1980) at 525.

CART. B.N.A. *abbr.* Cartwright's Constitutional Cases (Can.), 1868-1896.

CARTE BLANCHE. [Fr. white card] 1. Unlimited authority. 2. A blank card signed at the bottom which gives another person power to write anything above the signature.

CARTEL. *n.* An agreement between producers of raw materials or goods.

CARTER. See MARY ~ AGREEMENT.

C.A.S. *abbr.* 1. Children's Aid Societ(y)(ies). 2. Décisions de la Commission des affaires sociales.

CASE. *v.* For a potential thief or burglar to inspect a premises.

CASE. *n.* 1. "... '[S]uit' or 'appeal' and that ... it also included 'decision, question or matter'." *Iantsis (Papatheodorou) v. Papatheodorou* (1971), 3 R.F.L. 158 at 164, [1971] 1 O.R. 245, 15 D.L.R. (3d) 53 (C.A.), the court per Schroeder J.A. 2. Instance. *Lovibond v. Grand Trunk Railway*, [1934] O.R. 729 at 743, 43 C.R.C. 38, [1935] 1 D.L.R. 179 (C.A.), Macdonnell J.A. (Fisher J.A. concurring). 3. A sealed package, carton or container. See ACTION ON THE ~; LEADING ~; MCNAGHTEN'S ~; PRIMA FACIE ~; SPECIAL ~; STATED ~; TEST ~.

CASE LAW. The decisions of judges relating to particular matters in contrast to statute law; case law is a source of law and forms legal precedents.

CASE STATED. A written statement requesting an opinion on a question of law.

CASH. *v.* To convert a negotiable instrument to money.

CASH. *n.* Currency. *Irving Oil Co. Assessment, Re* (1948), 22 M.P.R. 63 at 72, [1948] 2 D.L.R. 774 (N.S. C.A.), Doull J.A. (Chisholm C.J., Graham and MacQuarrie JJ.A. concurring).

CASH ACCOUNT. 1. In bookkeeping, a record of cash transactions. 2. A brokerage firm account which is settled on a cash basis.

CASH BASIS. An accounting method which recognizes income when actually received and expenses when actually paid out.

CASH BOOK. An accounting record that combines cash receipts and disbursements.

CASH BUDGET. The estimated cash receipts and disbursements for a future period.

CASH DIVIDEND. The portion of profits and surplus paid to shareholders by a corporation in cash, in contrast with a stock dividend.

CASHIER. *v.* To dismiss from command or a position of authority.

CASHIER. *n.* A person who collects and records payments at a business.

CASH ON DELIVERY. A sale of goods on condition that cash be paid on delivery.

CASH PRICE. The price that would be charged by the seller for the goods or services to a buyer who paid cash for them at the time of purchase or hiring.

CASH SURRENDER VALUE. The amount an insurer will return to a policyholder upon cancellation of the policy.

CASS. PRAC. CAS. *abbr.* Cassels' Practice Cases (Can.).

CASS. S.C. *abbr.* Cassels' Supreme Court Decisions.

CAST. *v.* To deposit formally, as to cast a ballot.

CASTING VOTE. The deciding vote to break equality of votes, cast by the chair or presiding officer. Whether the chair has a casting vote depends on provisions of the relevant statute, by-laws, standing orders, regulations or articles.

CASUAL. *adj.* "... [T]he antonym of 'regular' and means occasional or coming at uncertain times without regularity in distinction from stated or regular...." *R. v. C.U.P.E.* (1981), 125 D.L.R. (3d) 220 at 224 (N.B. C.A.), the court per Stratton J.A.

CASUS BELLI. [L.] An incident which causes or justifies war.

CASUS OMISSUS. [L.] Something which should have been, but was not, provided for.

CATALOGUE. *n.* A bound, stitched, sewed or stapled book or pamphlet containing a list and description of goods, wares, merchandise or services, with specific information, with or without price.

CATCHING BARGAIN. An agreement to loan or pay money made on unfavourable terms to a person having property in reversion or expectancy.

C.A.T. (QUÉ.). *abbr.* Commission des accidents du travail (Québec).

CATV. *abbr.* 1. Community Antenna Television. 2. ". . . [I]t provides a well-located antenna with an efficient connection to the viewer's television set. . . ." *Fortnightly Corp. v. United Artists Television Inc.* (1968), 392 U.S. 390 at 399, Stewart J., cited with approval in *Capital Cities Communications Inc. v. Canada (Canadian Radio-Television & Telecommunications Commission)* (1977), 36 C.P.R. (2d) 1 at 13, [1978] 2 S.C.R. 141, 81 D.L.R. (3d) 609, 18 N.R. 181, Laskin C.J. (Martland, Judson, Ritchie, Spence and Dickson JJ. concurring).

CAUCUS. *n.* A group of members who are elected to the Assembly and who belong to the same political party.

CAUSA. [L.] Cause.

CAUSA CAUSANS. [L.] The immediate cause; the last of a chain of causes.

CAUSA MORTIS. [L.] Because of death; in case of death.

CAUSA PROXIMA. [L.] The immediate cause.

CAUSA PROXIMA NON REMOTA SPECTATUR. [L.] The immediate, not the remote, cause should be considered.

CAUSA SINE QUA NON. [L.] The cause without which the event would not have occurred.

CAUSATION. *n.* ". . . [A]n expression of the relationship that must be found to exist between the tortious act of the wrongdoer and the injury to the victim in order to justify compensation of the latter out of the pocket of the former." *Snell v. Farrell* (1990), 4 C.C.L.T. (2d) 229 at 243, 110 N.R. 200, [1990] 2 S.C.R. 311, the court per Sopinka J. See FACTUAL ~; LEGAL ~.

CAUSATION IN FACT. Factual causation. K.D. Cooper-Stephenson & I.B. Saunders, *Personal Injury Damages in Canada* (Toronto: Carswell, 1981) at 637.

CAUSE. *v.* ". . . [A] transitive verb which in its ordinary usage contemplates that someone or something brings about an effect." *Astro Tire & Rubber Co. v. Western Assurance Co.*, [1979] I.L.R. 1-1098 at 188, 24 O.R. (2d) 268, 97 D.L.R. (3d) 515 (C.A.), Blair J.A.

CAUSE. *n.* 1. A suit or action. *Hampton Lumber Mills v. Joy Logging Ltd.* (1977), 2 C.P.C. 312 at 317, [1977] 2 W.W.R. 289 (B.C. S.C.), Ruttan J. 2. That which produces an effect and includes any action, suit or other original proceeding between a plaintiff and a defendant and any criminal proceeding by the Crown. 3. In negligence cases, the defendant's fault is a cause of the damage if the damage would not have occurred but for the defendant's fault and the fault is not a cause if the damage would have happened with or without the defendant's fault. J.G. Fleming, *The Law of Torts*, 8th ed. (Sydney: Law Book, 1992) at 194. 4. "[In the context of dismissal for cause] . . . relates to the acts or the omissions of the employee, not the acts or the omissions of the employer." *Alberta v. A.U.P.E.* (1987), 53 Alta. L.R. (2d) 275 at 278, 82 A.R. 19 (Q.B.), Dea J. See CHALLENGE FOR ~; COSTS IN THE ~; DISMISSAL FOR ~; GOOD ~; MATRIMONIAL ~; NECESSARY ~; NO MAN SHALL BE JUDGE IN HIS OWN ~; PROBABLE ~; REASONABLE AND PROBABLE ~; SHOW ~ ORDER.

CAUSE CÉLÈBRE. [Fr.] A matter of great interest or importance.

CAUSE OF ACTION. "The classic

definition of a cause of action as stated by Diplock L.J. in Letang v. Cooper, [1965] 1 Q.B. 232 ... (H.L.) is as follows: 'A cause of action is simply a factual situation the existence of which entitles one person to obtain from the court a remedy against another person.' ..." *Consumers Glass Co. v. Foundation Co. of Canada/Cie fondation du Canada* (1985), 1 C.P.R. (2d) 208 at 215, 51 O.R. (2d) 385, 33 C.C.L.T. 104, 30 B.L.R. 87, 13 C.L.R. 149, 9 O.A.C. 193, 20 D.L.R. (4th) 126 (C.A.), the court per Dubin J.A.

CAUSE OF ACTION ESTOPPEL.
"... [P]recludes a person from bringing an action against another when the same cause of action has been determined in earlier proceedings by a court of competent jurisdicion ..." *Angle v. M.N.R.*, [1975] 2 S.C.R. 248 at 253-55, Dickson J.

CAUTION. *n.* 1. A warning. 2. A warning given to an accused concerning possibly incriminating statements. 3. "... [N]otice of adverse claim equivalent to a lis pendens and expires by lapse of time or otherwise as may be directed by the Court in an action: ..." *Ontario (Attorney General) v. Hargrave*, [1906] 11 O.L.R. 530 at 536 (H.C.), Master.

C.A.V. *abbr.* Curia advisari vult.

CAVEAT. *n.* [L. let one take heed] 1. "A caveat [under the Land Titles Act, R.S.A. 1980, c. L-5] is a warning, a notice and a prohibition. It creates no new rights, but prevents new ones arising other than subject to the claim of which it gives notice after registration. It is intended strictly to preserve the status quo ..." *Royal Bank v. Donsdale Developments Ltd.* (1986), 43 R.P.R. 59 at 75, 48 Alta. L.R. (2d) 289, [1987] 2 W.W.R. 14, 74 A.R. 161 (Q.B.), Andrekson J. 2. A document filed by an inventor before filing an application. H.G. Fox, *The Canadian Law and Practice Relating to Letters Patent for Inventions*, 4th ed. (Toronto: Carswell, 1969) at 242. 3. "[In the context of estates] ... 'a formal notice or caution given by a person interested, to a Court, Judge, or public officer,

against the performance of certain judicial or ministerial acts.' A caution, or caveat, while in force, may stop probate or administration from being granted without notice to or knowledge of the person who enters it. ..." *McDevitt, Re* (1913), 5 O.W.N. 333 at 335, 25 O.W.R. 309 (H.C.), Britton J.

CAVEAT ACTOR. [L.] Let the doer beware.

CAVEAT EMPTOR. [L. let the buyer beware] "The rule ... [means] that a buyer gets only what he bargains for." *Moretta v. Western Computer Investment Corp.* (1983), 26 B.L.R. 68 at 84, [1984] 2 W.W.R. 409, 29 Alta. L.R. (2d) 193 (C.A.), Kerans J.A.

CAVEAT EMPTOR; QUI IGNORARE NON DEBUIT QUOD JUS ALIENUM EMIT. [L.] A purchaser must be on guard; for the purchaser has no right to ignore the fact that what was bought belongs to someone else besides the vendor.

CAVEAT VENDITOR. [L.] Let the seller beware.

C.B.A. PAPERS. *abbr.* Canadian Bar Association Papers.

C.B.A. Y.B. *abbr.* Canadian Bar Year Book.

CBC. *abbr.* Canadian Broadcasting Corporation.

C.B.E.S. *abbr.* Cour du Bien-être social.

C.B.R. *abbr.* Canadian Bankruptcy Reports, 1920-1960.

C.B.R. (N.S.). *abbr.* Canadian Bankruptcy Reports, New Series, 1960-.

C.C.A.S. *abbr.* Catholic Children's Aid Societ(y)(ies).

C.C.C. *abbr.* Canadian Criminal Cases, 1893-1962.

[ ] C.C.C. *abbr.* Canadian Criminal Cases, 1963-1970.

C.C.C. (2d). *abbr.* Canadian Criminal Cases (Second Series), 1971-1983.

C.C.C. (3d). *abbr.* Canadian Criminal Cases (Third Series), 1983-.

C.C.D.P. *abbr.* Commission canadienne des droits de la personne.

C.C.E.A. *abbr.* Commission de contrôle de l'énergie atomique.

C.C.E.L. *abbr.* Canadian Cases on Employment Law, 1983-.

C. CIRC. *abbr.* Cour de circuit.

CCL. *abbr.* Canadian Congress of Labour, which is now part of the Canadian Labour Congress.

[ ] C.C.L. *abbr.* Canadian Current Law.

C.C.L.I. *abbr.* Canadian Cases on the Law of Insurance, 1983-.

C.C.L.R. *abbr.* Canada Corporations Law Reports.

C.C.L.T. *abbr.* Canadian Cases of the Law of Torts, 1976-.

C.C.P. *abbr.* Commission canadienne des pensions.

C.C.R.T. *abbr.* Conseil canadien des relations de travail.

C. DE D. *abbr.* Les Cahiers de droit.

C. DE L'É. *abbr.* Cour de l'Échiquier.

C. DE L'I.Q.A.J. *abbr.* Cahiers de l'institut québécois d'administration judiciaire.

CDIC. *abbr.* Canada Deposit Insurance Corporation.

C. DIST. *abbr.* Cour de district.

C. DIV. *abbr.* Cour divisionnaire.

CDN. *abbr.* Canadian.

CEASE. *v.* To stop; to suspend activity.

C.E.B. & P.G.R. *abbr.* Canadian Employment Benefits and Pension Guide Reports.

CEDE. *v.* 1. To give up or yield. 2. To transfer. 3. To surrender.

C.E.G.S.B. *abbr.* Crown Employees Grievance Settlement Board.

CELEBRATION OF MARRIAGE. The formal act by which two persons become husband and wife.

C.E.L.R. *abbr.* Canadian Environmental Law Reports.

C.E.L.R. (N.S.). *abbr.* Canadian Environmental Law Reports (New Series).

CENSOR. *n.* A person who regulates or prohibits distribution, production or exhibition of films or publication of books, plays, etc.

CENSORSHIP. *n.* The prohibition or regulation of publication, distribution or production of books, plays, films.

CENSURE. *n.* An official reprimand; condemnation.

CENSUS. *n.* A count or enumeration of the people.

CENT. *n.* 1. A coin. 2. One hundredth part of a dollar.

CENTRAL COOPERATIVE CREDIT SOCIETY. A cooperative organization incorporated or organized by or pursuant to an Act of Parliament or of the legislature of a province, the membership or shareholders of which consist wholly or substantially of local cooperative credit societies and the principal purpose of which is to provide services to its members. *Bank Act*, R.S.C. 1985, c. B-1, s. 2.

CENTRALIST. *adj.* Describes a form of federal government in which greater power is given to the central or federal government.

CENTRE. *n.* See COMMUNITY ~; CORRECTIONAL ~.

CENTURY. *n.* 1. One hundred. 2. One hundred years.

C.E.P.A.R. *abbr.* Canadian Estate Planning and Administration Reporter.

C.E.P.R. *abbr.* Canadian Estate Planning and Administration Reporter.

C.E.R. *abbr.* Canadian Customs and Excise reports, 1980-.

CEREMONY. See CIVIL ~.

CERTAIN. *adj.* 1. Definitive. 2. Free from doubt.

CERTAINTY. *n.* 1. Accuracy; absence of doubt. 2. Precision. See THREE CERTAINTIES.

CERTIFICATE. *n.* 1. An official assurance or representation concerning a matter within the knowledge or authority of the person making the certificate. 2. A document issued to identify those who have passed the required examinations or are members of a professional organization. See ARCHITECT'S ~; SHARE ~.

CERTIFICATE OF ASSESSMENT. A document given by an assessment officer to signify the completion of an assessment of party-and-party costs. M.M. Orkin, *The Law of Costs*, 2d ed. (Aurora: Canada Law Book, 1987) at 6-23.

CERTIFICATE OF COMPLETION. A certificate given by an architect under whose supervision a building contract has been carried out; contractor is generally not entitled to payment until the certificate is given.

CERTIFICATE OF CONTINUANCE. A certificate which permits a body corporate incorporated in one province or federally to be continued in a second jurisdiction if such continuance is authorized by the laws of the jurisdiction where it is incorporated. H. Sutherland, D.B. Horsley & J.M. Edmiston, eds., *Fraser's Handbook on Canadian Company Law*, 7th ed. (Toronto: Carswell, 1985) at 481.

CERTIFICATE OF CONVICTION. A certificate stating that an accused was convicted of an indictable offence, drawn up by a judge or magistrate when requested to do so by the prosecutor, the accused or a peace officer.

CERTIFICATE OF INCORPORATION. Documentary evidence, including letters patent, a special act or any other instrument, by which a corporation is incorporated stating that a corporation exists and was duly incorporated under the appropriate statute.

CERTIFICATE OF LIS PENDENS. A former term for a certificate of pending litigation. See CERTIFICATE OF PENDING LITIGATION; LIS PENDENS.

CERTIFICATE OF PENDING LITIGATION. A notice of a proceeding to a person who is not a party,

issued by a court and registered in the proper land registry office, of the commencement of a proceeding in which an interest in land is at issue (Courts of Justice Act, R.S.O. 1990, c. C.43, s. 103(1)). G.D. Watson & C. Perkins, eds., *Holmested & Watson: Ontario Civil Procedure* (Toronto: Carswell, 1984) at CJA-137.

CERTIFICATE OF READINESS. A former term for the document which a party in an action filed to indicate that the party is ready for trial. See now NOTICE OF READINESS FOR TRIAL.

CERTIFICATE OF TAXATION. A certificate signed and inscribed by a taxing officer when a bill of costs has been taxed. M.M. Orkin, *The Law of Costs*, 2d ed. (Aurora: Canada Law Book, 1987) at 12-9. See also CERTIFICATE OF ASSESSMENT.

CERTIFICATE OF TITLE. A certificate of title granted pursuant to a Land Titles Act.

CERTIFICATION. *n.* 1. "... [A] mechanism whereby an association which counts among its members an absolute majority of all an employer's employees, or of a separate group of an employer's employees, is recognized as the sole representative of those employees to this employer for collective bargaining purposes...." *Union des employés de service, local 298 v. Bibeault* (1988), 35 Admin L.R. 153 at 204, 95 N.R. 161, [1988] 2 S.C.R. 1048, the court per Beetz J. 2. "... [T]he name given to the marking of a cheque by the drawee bank to show that it is drawn by the person purporting to draw it, that it is drawn upon an existing account with the drawee, and that there are funds sufficient to meet it. Certification is demonstrated by some physical marking on the cheque, normally stamping on its face 'certified' ..." *A.E. LePage Real Estate Services Ltd. v. Rattray Publications* (1991), 84 D.L.R. (4th) 766 at 767, 5 O.R. (3d) 216 (Div. Ct.), Montgomery J. 3. A written attestation of a training organization as to the level of achievement attained by a student in an occupational training program. 4. The entry of the name of a person in the register.

CERTIFICATION MARK. A mark that is used for the purpose of distinguishing or so as to distinguish wares or services that are of a defined standard with respect to (a) the character or quality of the wares or services, (b) the working conditions under which the wares have been produced or the services performed, (c) the class of persons by whom the wares have been produced or the services performed, or (d) the area within which the wares have been produced or the services performed, from wares or services that are not of that defined standard. *Trade-marks Act*, R.S.C. 1985, c. T-13, s. 2.

CERTIFICATION OF LABOUR UNION. Official recognition by a labour relations board of a union as bargaining representative for employees in a particular bargaining unit.

CERTIFIED CHEQUE. When a cheque is certified at the holder's request, this amounts to payment in due course and discharge of the cheque according to the Bills of Exchange Act. But a cheque certified at the drawer's request clearly does not discharge the instrument. I.F.G. Baxter, *The Law of Banking*, 3d ed. (Toronto: Carswell, 1981) at 6-7.

CERTIFIED COPY. A copy certified to be a true copy.

CERTIFIED UNION. A union recognized by a labour relations board as bargaining agent of a group of workers.

CERTIFY. *v.* 1. "... [H]as the connotation that the person so doing formally vouches for the statement or guarantees its certainty ..." *First Investors Corp., Re*, Doc. No. Edmonton Appeal 8803-0942-AC (Alta C.A.), the court per Laycraft J.A. 2. "... [A] word of wide import which may also refer merely to a formal or legal certificate." *R. v. Lines* (1986), 27 C.C.C. (3d) 377 at 380 (N.W.T. C.A.), the court per Laycraft C.J.N.W.T.

CERTIORARI. *n.* 1. An order to "bring up" to a court on the basis of lack of jurisdiction the record of a statutory tribunal or lower court to be quashed. S.A. DeSmith, *Judicial Review of Administrative Action*, 4th ed. by J.M. Evans (London: Stevens, 1980) at 25. 2. "... [T]he prerogative writ adopted to quash a decision based upon an error of law which is apparent from the record...." *Minister of National Revenue v. Parsons* (1983), 4 Admin. L.R. 64 at 72, [1983] C.T.C. 321, 83 D.T.C. 5329 (Fed. T.D.), Cattanach J.

CERTIORARI IN AID. Certiorari ordered in connection with habeas corpus. *Perepolkin v. Superintendent of Child Welfare for British Columbia (No. 2)* (1958), 27 C.R. 95 at 97, 23 W.W.R. 592, 120 C.C.C. 67, 11 D.L.R. (2d) 417 (B.C. C.A.), Smith J.A.

CERTUM EST QUOD CERTUM REDDI POTEST. [L.] What is capable of being made certain is to be treated as certain.

C.E.S.H.G. *abbr.* Canadian Employment, Safety and Health Guide.

CESSATION OF CHARGE. An instrument which acknowledges that the claim against real property contained in a charge has been discharged.

CESTUI QUE TRUST. *pl.* **CESTUIS QUE TRUST.** A beneficiary; beneficial owner of trust property.

CESTUI QUE USE. A grantee to whom property was conveyed to use. R. Megarry & H.W.R. Wade, *The Law of Real Property*, 5th ed. (London: Stevens, 1984) at cxxiii.

CESTUI QUE VIE. One for whose life someone else holds an estate or interest in property. See TENANT PUR AUTRE VIE.

CETERIS PARIBUS. [L.] Other things being equal.

CF. *abbr.* Compare.

C.F. *abbr.* 1. Cour fédérale. 2. In sales contract, means price included cost and freight. 2. Recueils de jurisprudence de la Cour fédérale du Canada.

C.F. & I. See C.I.F.

C.F. (APPEL). *abbr*. Cour fédérale du Canada – Cour d'appel.

C.F.I. See C.I.F.

C.F.L.Q. *abbr*. Canadian Family Law Quarterly.

C.F. (1^(RE) INST.). *abbr*. Cour fédérale du Canada – Division de première instance.

CH. *abbr*. 1. Chapter. 2. Chancery.

[ ] CH. *abbr*. Law Reports, Chancery, 1891-.

CHAIN OF TITLE. Tracking successive transfers or other conveyances of a particular parcel of land.

CHAIRMAN. *n*. 1. A person who presides at meetings of the board of directors of a corporation. 2. A person appointed or elected head of a board, committee, commission or foundation.

CHALLENGE. *v*. 1. To object. 2. To take exception against a juror. See PEREMPTORY ~.

CHALLENGE FOR CAUSE. The suitability of a juror is objected to on basis of knowledge of the case or lack of qualifications or impartiality.

CHAMBER. *n*. The place where legislative assemblies are held; the assemblies themselves.

CHAMBER OF COMMERCE. 1. A corporation incorporated or continued under this Act as a membership corporation to carry on the activities of promoting and improving trade and commerce and thereby promoting and improving the economic, civic and social welfare of a district. *Non-profit Corporations Act*, S.S. 1979, c. N-41, s. 176.

CHAMBERS. *n*. Judge's office; a room in which motions or applications or other business not required to be carried out in court is transacted.

CHAMBERS BRIEF. "... [A]ssist[s] in clarifying the issues and so reduce[s] the length of time for hearing a motion or trial.... it should contain the following: (a) Description of the motion. (b) Authority for the motion. (c) State-

ment of facts. (d) Authorities. (e) Relief asked. (f) Form of Order." *Eileen's Quality Catering Ltd. v. Depaoli* (1985), 1 C.P.C. (2d) 152 at 154, 158 (B.C. S.C.), Bouck J.

CHAMPERTOR. *n*. A person who brings suits in order to have part of the gain or proceeds.

CHAMPERTY. *n*. 1. "... [A] bargain by which A, a stranger to B, having no interest recognized by law in a given property, agrees to help B to recover such property in a Court of Justice in consideration of getting a portion of the fruits of the suit, ..." *Hopper v. Dunsmuir* (1906), 3 W.L.R. 18 at 33 (C.A.), Martin J.A. 2. "... [T]o bargain with a plaintiff to pay the expenses of a suit wholly or in part on condition that the plaintiff will divide with the party who so shares in the expenses the land or other matter sued for, if successful in such suit, is undeniably champerty." *Meloche v. Deguire* (1903), 34 S.C.R. 24 at 37, Taschereau C.J. (Sedgewick, Nesbitt and Killam JJ. concurring). 3. A form of maintenance. *Pioneer Machinery (Rentals) Ltd. v. Aggregate Machine Ltd.* (1978), 8 C.P.C. 168 at 170, 15 A.R. 588, [1978] 6 W.W.R. 484, 93 D.L.R. (3d) 726 (T.D.), Laycraft J.

CHANCE. *n*. An accident; absence of explainable causation; risk. See GAME OF ~; LOSS OF ~.

CHANCELLOR. *n*. 1. The highest official of a university. 2. The presiding judge of a court of chancery.

CHANCERY. *n*. Originally an office where writs were issued. See COURT OF ~.

CHANGE. *v*. To alter; substitute; modify; exchange.

CHANGE. *n*. 1. Alteration, replacement, modification. *Simplex Floor Finishing Appliance Co. v. Duranceau*, [1941] 4 D.L.R. 260 at 264 (S.C.C.), Taschereau J. 2. Any change by way of alteration, substitution, modification, addition or adandonment. *Change of Name acts*. 3. Exchange of money for money of another denomination.

CHANGE OF NAME. Any change in the name of a physical person by alteration, substitution, addition or abandonment. *Change of Name Act*, R.S.Q. 1977, c. C-10, s. 1.

CHANGE OF PARTIES. Occurs where parties to litigation are added or substituted.

CHANGE OF POSSESSION. Such change of possession as is open and reasonably sufficient to afford public notice thereof. *Bills of Sale Acts*.

CHANGE OF SOLICITOR. The change of lawyer representing a client in an action effected by filing notice in court.

CHARACTER. *n.* The inclination of a person to act in a particular way relating to integrity, peaceableness, lawfulness, honesty and ultimately veracity. P.K. McWilliams, *Canadian Criminal Evidence*, 3d ed. (Aurora: Canada Law Book, 1988) at 39-1.

CHARGE. *v.* 1. To give instructions to a jury. 2. "... [E]xists only when a formal written complaint has been made against the accused and a prosecution initiated. ..." *R. v. Chabot*, [1980] 2 S.C.R. 985 at 1005, Dickson J. 3. To lay a duty upon a person. 4. To impose a tax. 5. To purchase on credit.

CHARGE. *n.* 1. An instrument creating security against property for payment of a debt or obligation. 2. The amount required, as the price of a thing or service sold or supplied. 3. A judge's instruction to a jury. 4. A price or rate. See CARRYING ~; CESSATION OF ~; CHARGES; EQUITABLE ~; FIXED ~; FLOATING ~; PREFER A ~; RENT ~; SPECIFIC ~.

CHARGEABLE. *adj.* Capable of or subject to being charged with a duty or obligation.

CHARGE ACCOUNT. An arrangement with a store or financial institution permitting purchase of goods and services on credit under which purchaser agrees to pay within specified time or periodically.

CHARGED. *adj.* 1. "The word 'charged' or 'charge' is not one of fixed or unvarying meaning at law. It may be and is used in a variety of ways to describe a variety of events. A person is clearly charged with an offence when a charge is read out to him in court and he is called upon to plead. ..." *R. v. Kalanj* (1989), 48 C.C.C. (3d) 459 at 465, 70 C.R. (3d) 260, [1989] 6 W.W.R. 577, [1989] 1 S.C.R. 1594, 96 N.R. 191, McIntyre J. (La Forest and L'Heureux-Dubé JJ. concurring). 2. "... [A] person is 'charged with an offence' within the meaning of s. 11 of the Charter when an information is sworn alleging an offence against him, or where a direct indictment is laid against him, when no information is sworn. ..." *R. v. Kalanj* (1989), 48 C.C.C. (3d) 459 at 469, 70 C.R. (3d) 260, [1989] 6 W.W.R. 577, [1989] 1 S.C.R. 1594, 96 N.R. 191, McIntyre J. (La Forest and L'Heureux-Dubé JJ. concurring).

CHARGES. *n.* Expenses; costs.

CHARGE THE JURY. A judge gives instructions to a jury before it deliberates with regard to the law as it applies to the case heard by them.

CHARGE TO THE JURY. See CHARGE THE JURY.

CHARGING ORDER. 1. A creditor can apply to a judge to order that shares of or in any public company stand charged with the payment of the judgment debt. 2. An order made for the benefit of a solicitor against funds in court or property realized through the endeavours of the solicitor.

CHARITABLE. *adj.* Having purposes of a charity.

CHARITABLE CORPORATION. A body constituted exclusively for charitable purposes no part of the income of which is payable to, or is otherwise available for the personal benefit of, any proprietor, member or shareholder thereof.

CHARITABLE FOUNDATION. A corporation or trust, other than a charitable organization, constituted and operated exclusively for charitable purposes.

CHARITABLE PURPOSE. "The starting point for a discussion of what may or may not constitute a good charitable purpose is the decision of the House of Lords in the case of Commrs. for Special Purposes of Income Tax v. Pemsel, [1891] A.C. 531 [(U.K.)] and, in particular, the legal meaning of the word 'charity' given by Lord Macnaghten at p. 583 of the report: 'How far then, it may be asked, does the popular meaning of the word "charity" correspond with its legal meaning? "Charity" in its legal sense comprises four principal divisions: trusts for the relief of poverty; trusts for the advancement of education; trusts for the advancement of religion; and trusts for other purposes beneficial to the community, not falling under any of the preceding heads.' That definition has been applied time after time in this country and has been approved by the Supreme Court of Canada (see Guaranty Trust Co. (Towle Estate) v. M.N.R., [1967] S.C.R. 133 at p. 141) . . ." *Native Communications Society of British Columbia v. Minister of National Revenue* (1986), 23 E.T.R. 210 at 218, 86 D.T.C. 6353, 67 N.R. 146, [1986] 2 C.T.C. 170, [1986] 4 C.N.L.R. 79, [1986] 3 F.C. 471 (C.A.), Stone J.A. (Heald and Mahoney JJ.A. concurring).

CHARITABLE TRUST. A trust for purposes which the law treats as charitable. R.H. Maudsley and J.E. Martin, *Hanbury and Maudsley Modern Equity*, 11th ed. (London: Stevens, 1981) at 423.

CHARITY. *n.* (a) Trusts for the relief of poverty, (b) trusts for the advancement of education, (c) trusts for the advancement of religion, (d) trusts for other purposes beneficial to the community not falling under any of the preceding heads. *Commrs. of Income Tax v. Pemsel*, [1891] A.C. 531 at 583, Lord Macnaghten.

CHARTER. *v.* ". . . [I]s not synonymous with 'hire'. It has such a meaning only when it is used in relation to a means of transportation." *Seaway Forwarding Ltd. v. Western*

Assurance Co., [1981] I.L.R. 1-1400 at 351 (Ont. H.C.), Galligan J.

CHARTER. *n.* 1. The Canadian Charter of Rights and Freedoms, Part I of the Constitution Act, 1982. 2. Includes any act, statute, or ordinance by or under which a corporation has been incorporated and any letters patent, supplementary letters patent, certificate of incorporation, memorandum of association, and any other document evidencing corporate existence. 3. An agreement to supply a vessel or aircraft for a voyage for a period of time. See TIME ~.

CHARTERED BANK. A bank to which the *Bank Act* (Canada) applies, and includes a branch, agency, and office of a bank.

CHARTERED COMPANY. A company incorporated by Royal Charter such as the Hudson's Bay Company.

CHARTERED SHIP. A ship hired; a ship subject to charter party.

CHARTERER. *n.* One who hires a ship or aircraft for a certain period or for a voyage.

CHARTER PARTY. *vars.* **CHARTERPARTY**, **CHARTER-PARTY**. An agreement to use or hire a ship or to convey goods for a specified period or on a specified voyage.

CHASE. *v.* To pursue rapidly with intent to overtake or send away.

CHATTEL. *n.* Colloquially used to refer to chattel mortgage. See CHATTELS; INCORPOREAL ~.

CHATTEL MORTGAGE. "To constitute a chattel mortgage, the contract between the parties must import a transfer of the property in the chattels from the mortgagor to the mortgagee, as security for a debt, defeasible on payment of the debt; . . ." *Dealers Finance Corp. v. Masterson Motors Ltd.*, [1931] 4 D.L.R. 730 at 735, [1931] 2 W.W.R. 214 (C.A.), Martin J.A.

CHATTEL PAPER. One or more than one writing that expresses both a monetary obligation and a security interest in or lease of specific goods and accessions.

CHATTELS. *n.* 1. "... [I]nclude[s] all personal property...." *Ontario (Attorney General) v. Royal Bank,* [1970] 2 O.R. 467 at 472, 11 D.L.R. (3d) 257 (C.A.), the court per Brooke J.A. 2. "... [T]he principles as summarized in [Stack v. Eaton Co. (1902), 4 O.L.R. 335 (C.A.) by Meredith C.J.] ... at p. 338, [are] as follows: 'I take it to be settled law: (1) That articles not otherwise attached to the land than by their own weight are not to be considered as part of the land, unless the circumstances are such as shew that they were intended to be part of the land. (2) That articles affixed to the land even slightly are to be considered part of the land unless the circumstances are such as to shew that they were intended to continue chattels. (3) That the circumstances necessary to be shewn to alter the prima facie character of the articles are circumstances which shew the degree of annexation and degree of such annexation, which are present to all to see. (4) That the intention of the person affixing the article to the soil is material only so far as it can be presumed from the degree and object of the annexation.' " *Dolan v. Bank of Montreal* (1985), 5 P.P.S.A.C. 196 at 201-2, 42 Sask. R. 202 (C.A.), Matheson J.A.

CHATTELS PERSONAL. "Pure personalty", either in action or in possession. E.L.G. Tyler & N.E. Palmer, eds., *Crossley Vaines' Personal Property,* 5th ed. (London: Butterworths, 1973) at 11.

CHATTELS REAL. Leaseholds.

CHAUFFEUR. *n.* A person who drives motor vehicles as a means of livelihood.

CH. D. *abbr.* Law Reports, Chancery Division, 1875-1890.

CHECKERBOARD. *v.* To divide land in the manner of a checkerboard so that one person owns the "red squares" and another owns the "black squares". The owners on title may be nominees or trustees for the actual landowner, or the actual landowner might retain "one set of squares" and transfer the "other set" to a nominee. B.J. Reiter, B.N. McLellan & P.M. Perell, *Real Estate Law,* 4th ed. (Toronto: Emond Montgomery, 1992) at 340.

CHEQUE. *n.* 1. Includes a bill of exchange drawn on any institution that makes it a business practice to honour bills of exchange or any particular kind thereof drawn on it by depositors. *Criminal Code,* R.S.C. 1985, c. C-46, s. 362(5) and 364(3). 2. "... [A] direction to some one, who may or may not have in his possession funds of the drawer, authorising him to pay to the payee a certain sum of money...." *Re Bernard,* (1911), 2 O.W.N. 716 at 717, Chief Justice of Exchequer Division. See CROSSED ~; STALE ~.

C.H.F.L.G. *abbr.* Canadian Health Facilities Law Guide.

CHIEF. See IN ~.

CHIEF GOVERNMENT WHIP. See CHIEF WHIP.

CHIEF JUDGE. 1. The person having authority to assign duties to the judge. *Courts of Justice Act,* R.S.O. 1990, c. C.43, s. 123(1). 2. The chief justice, chief judge or other person recognized by law as having rank or status senior to all other members of, or having the supervision of, that court, but where that court is a superior court constituted with divisions, then the person having such rank or status in relation to all other members of the division of which the particular judge is a member. *Judges Act,* R.S.C. 1985, c. J-1, s. 41(4).

CHIEF JUSTICE. The chief justice, chief judge or other person recognized by law as having rank or status senior to all other members of, or having the supervision of, that court, but where that court is a superior court constituted with divisions, then the person having such rank or status in relation to all other members of the division of which the particular judge is a member. *Judges Act,* R.S.C. 1985, c. J-1, s. 41(4).

CHIEF OPPOSITION WHIP. See

CHIEF WHIP.

CHIEF WHIP. Each party in Parliament has a person who keeps members of that party informed about the business of the House, ensures these members attend, determines pairing arrangements so that the votes of members who cannot attend divisions will be neutralized and not lost, and supplies lists of members to serve on the various House committees. A. Fraser, W.A. Dawson, & J. Holtby, eds., *Beauchesne's Rules and Forms of the House of Commons of Canada*, 6th ed. (Toronto: Carswell, 1989) at 57.

CHILD. *n.* "... [H]as two primary meanings. One refers to chronological age and is the converse of the term 'adult'; the other refers to lineage and is the reciprocal of the term 'parent'. A child in the first sense was defined at common law as a person under the age of 14. This definition may be modified by statutory provision ... No statutory modification, however, fixed an age higher than the age of majority which, in Ontario, pursuant to the Age of Majority and Accountability Act, R.S.O. 1980, c. 7, s. 1(1) is 18 years. A child in the second sense was defined at common law as the legitimate offspring of a parent, but in most jurisdictions this definition has been amended by statute to constitute all offspring, whether legitimate or not, as the 'children' of their natural or adoptive parents ..." *R. v. Ogg-Moss* (1984), [1985] 11 D.L.R. (4th) 549 at 558, [1984] 2 S.C.R. 173, 54 N.R. 81, 14 C.C.C. (3d) 116, 5 O.A.C. 81, 6 C.H.R.R. D/2498, 41 C.R. (3d) 297, the court per Dickson J. See BEST INTERESTS OF THE ~; FOSTER ~; ILLEGITIMATE ~; NATURAL ~; NEGLECTED ~.

CHILD ABDUCTION. The kidnapping of a child by the parent not awarded custody.

CHILD ABUSE. Physical, mental, sexual, emotional mistreatment of a child.

CHILD OF THE MARRIAGE. A child of two spouses or former spouses who, at the material time, (a) is under the age of sixteen years, or (b) is sixteen years of age or over and under their charge but unable, by reason of illness, disability or other cause, to withdraw from their charge or to obtain the necessaries of life. *Divorce Act, 1985*, S.C. 1986, c. 4, s. 2(1).

CHILDREN. *n.* "... Prima facie, the word 'children', in such context [using the words 'to her children in equal shares per stirpes'], denotes persons of the first degree of descent, and therefore is a word of designation." *Simpson, Re*, [1928] S.C.R. 329 at 331, [1928] 3 D.L.R. 773, the court per Duff J. See CHILD.

CHILDREN'S AID SOCIETY. An organized or incorporated society having among its objects the promotion of family and child welfare.

CHILD SUPPORT. Financial support, care and upbringing to which a child is entitled from his or her parent. *Nielsen v. Nielsen* (1980), 16 R.F.L. (2d) 203 at 205 (Ont. Co. Ct.), Macnab Co. Ct. J.

CHILD WELFARE AUTHORITY. Any provincially approved agency that has been designated by or under the provincial law or by the provincial authority for the purpose of administering or assisting in the administration of any law of the province relating to the protection and care of children. *Canada Assistance Plan*, R.S.C. 1985, c. C-1, s. 2.

CHILD WELFARE SERVICE. A residential or non-residential service, child protection service, adoption service, individual or family counselling.

CHINESE WALL. 1. A method in which a law firm may represent more than one client in the same transaction by having the lawyer who represents one side keep everything confidential from the lawyer who represents the other. 2. "... If the attorney practices in a firm, there is a presumption that lawyers who work together share each other's confidences. Knowledge of confidential matters is therefore imputed to other members of the firm. This latter presumption can, however, in some circumstances, be rebutted. The usual methods used to rebut the presumption are the setting up of a 'Chinese Wall' . . . at the time that the possibility of the unauthorized communication of confidential information arises. A 'Chinese Wall' involves effective 'screening' to prevent communication between the tainted lawyer and other members of the firm." *MacDonald Estate v. Martin* (1990), 48 C.P.C. (2d) 113 at 126, [1991] 1 W.W.R. 705, 121 N.R. 1, 77 D.L.R. (4th) 249, 70 Man. R. (2d) 241, [1990] 3 S.C.R. 1235, Sopinka J. (Dickson C.J., La Forest and Gonthier JJ. concurring). 3. "These two subsections [of the Securities Act, R.S.O. 1980, c. 466, s. 75(1) and (3)] provide for what is commonly referred to as a 'Chinese Wall' defence. That means the establishment within an organization of informational barriers to prevent the improper transmission of information within the organization concerning a material fact or material change that has not been generally disclosed. Chinese Walls are designed to insulate and to keep to a minimum persons in an organization who make investment decisions from persons in that organization who have confidential information which could affect those decisions." *R. v. Saliga* (1991), 14 O.S.C.B. 4777 at 4783 (Prov. Div.), Masse J. See CONE OF SILENCE.

CHITTY'S L.J. *abbr.* Chitty's Law Journal, 1953-.

CHOICE OF LAW. ". . . [R]efers to the conflicts rules which have developed, through legislation or jurisprudence, in order to determine which system of substantive law the forum court will apply in respect of a legal matter having connection with other jurisdictions. There are difference choice of law rules for different areas of law." *Tolofson v. Jensen* (1992), 4 C.P.C. (3d) 113 at 118, 65 B.C.L.R. (2d) 114, 9 C.C.L.T. (2d) 289, [1992] 3 W.W.R. 743, 89 D.L.R. (4th) 129, 11 B.C.A.L. 94, 22 W.A.C. 94, the court per Cumming J.A.

CHOSE. *n.* [Fr.] A chattel personal, either in action or in possession. See CHATTEL.

CHOSE IN ACTION. 1. "In Torkington v. Magee, [1902] 2 K.B. 427 at p. 430, Channel J. said: ' "Chose in action" is a known legal expression used to describe all personal rights of property which can only be claimed or enforced by action, and not by taking physical possession'. The term covers multifarious rights, many diverse in their essential nature, such as debts, company shares, negotiable instruments and rights of action founded on tort or breach of contract." *Di Guilo v. Boland* (1958), 13 D.L.R. (2d) 510 at 513, [1958] O.R. 384 (C.A.), the court per Morden J.A. 2. ". . . [A]n incorporeal right to something not in one's possession and, accordingly, it is not possible for the debtor to have possession of it. . . ." *Ontario (Attorney General) v. Royal Bank*, [1970] 2 O.R. 467 at 472, 11 D.L.R. (3d) 257 (C.A.), the court per Brooke J.A.

CHOSE IN POSSESSION. 1. A tangible. E.L.G. Tyler & N.E. Palmer, eds., *Crossley Vaines' Personal Property*, 5th ed. (London: Butterworths, 1973) at 14. 2. A corporeal thing, movable, tangible and visible, always in someone's possession. E.L.G. Tyler & N.E. Palmer, eds., *Crossley Vaines' Personal Property*, 5th ed. (London: Butterworths, 1973) at 11.

CH. R. *abbr.* Upper Canada Chambers Reports, 1857-1872.

C.H.R.C. *abbr.* Canadian Human Rights Commission.

C.H.R.R. *abbr.* Canadian Human Rights Reporter, 1980-.

CHY. CHRS. *abbr.* Upper Canada Chancery Chambers Reports.

CIDA. *abbr.* Canadian International Development Agency.

CIE. *abbr.* [Fr. compagnie] Company.

C.I.F. *abbr.* Cost insurance and freight.

C.I.F. CONTRACT. A contract in which price includes cost of the goods, insurance while in transit and freight charges incurred. G.H.L. Fridman, *Sale of Goods in Canada*, 3d ed. (Toronto: Carswell, 1986) at 480.

C.I.L.R. *abbr.* 1. Canadian Insurance Law Reports. 2. Canadian Insurance Law Review.

C.I.P.R. *abbr.* Canadian Intellectual Property Reports, 1984-.

CIRCA. [L.] About; around.

CIRC. CT. *abbr.* Circuit Court.

CIRCULATING CAPITAL. A part of the subscribed capital of a company intended to be temporarily circulated in business in the form of goods, money or other assets, which capital, or its proceeds, is intended to return to the company increased so that it can be used repeatedly, always to return with some increase. W. Grover & F. Iacobucci, *Materials on Canadian Income Tax*, 4th ed. (Toronto: De Boo, 1980) at 298.

CIRCUMSTANCE. *n.* An attendant or auxiliary fact.

CIRCUMSTANTIAL EVIDENCE. 1. Evidence (facts) from which a fact in issue or a fact relevant to an issue may be inferred. P.K. McWilliams, *Canadian Criminal Evidence*, 3d ed. (Aurora: Canada Law Book, 1988) at 5-1. 2. Evidence tending to establish the existence or non-existence of a fact that is not one of the elements of the offence charged, where the existence or non-existence of that fact reasonably leads to an inference concerning the existence or non-existence of a fact that is one of the elements of the offence charged. *Military Rules of Evidence*, C.R.C., c. 1049, s. 2.

CIT. *abbr.* 1. Citizen. 2. Citizenship.

C.I.T. *abbr.* Canadian Import Tribunal.

CITATION. *n.* 1. Calling on a person who is not a party to a proceeding or an action to appear in court. 2. In probate matters, notice of proceedings given to anyone whose interests are or may be affected.

CITATION OF AUTHORITIES. A reference to case or statute law to es-

tablish or support propositions of law advanced.

CITATOR. *n.* A set of books which provides historical information regarding statutes, cumulates amendments to statutes since the last revision or consolidation of the statutes and traces judicial consideration of sections of statutes.

CITE. *v.* 1. To refer to legal authorities. 2. To name in citation.

CITIZEN. *n.* A Canadian citizen. *Citizenship Act*, R.S.C. 1985, c. C-29, s. 2.

CITIZENSHIP. *n.* Canadian citizenship. *Citizenship Act*, R.S.C. 1985, c. C-29, s. 2. See OATH OR AFFIRMATION OF ~.

CITIZENSHIP COURT. An office of the Department of the Secretary of State or other place where a citizenship judge performs his duties under the Act. *Citizenship Regulations*, C.R.C, c. 400, s. 2.

CITIZENSHIP JUDGE. A citizenship judge appointed under the Citizenship Act. *Citizenship Act*, R.S.C. 1985, c. C-29, s. 2.

CIVIL. *adj.* Of legal matters, private as opposed to criminal.

CIVIL ACTION. Any type of action except criminal proceedings.

CIVIL CEREMONY. A marriage performed by a judge or justice of the peace, distinguished from a religious ceremony.

CIVIL CODE. The Civil Code of Lower Canada. *Interpretation Act*, R.S.Q. 1977, c. I-16, s. 61.

CIVIL CONSPIRACY. "... [W]hereas the law of tort does not permit an action against an individual defendant who has caused injury to the plaintiff, the law of torts does recognize a claim against them in combination as the tort of conspiracy if: (1) whether the means used by the defendants are lawful or unlawful, the predominant purpose of the defendants' conduct is to cause injury to the plaintiff; or, (2) where the conduct is directed towards the plaintiff (alone or together with others), and the defendants should know in the circumstances that injury to the plaintiff is likely to and does result." *Canada Cement LaFarge Ltd. v. British Columbia Lightweight Aggregate Ltd.*, [1983] 1 S.C.R. 452 at 471-2, Estey J.

CIVIL CONTEMPT. 1. "... [T]he purpose ... is to secure compliance with the process of a tribunal including, but not limited to, the process of a court ... initiated by a party or person affected by the order sought to be enforced. In order to secure compliance in a proceeding for civil contempt, a court may impose a fine or other penalty which will be exacted in the absence of compliance. However, the object is always compliance and not punishment." *U.N.A. v. Alberta (Attorney General)* (1992), 13 C.R. (4th) 1 at 22, [1992] 3 W.W.R. 481, 89 D.L.R. (4th) 609, 71 C.C.C. (3d) 225, 135 N.R. 321, 92 C.L.L.C. 14,023, 1 Alta. L.R. (3d) 129, 125 A.R. 241, 14 W.A.C. 241, [1992] 1 S.C.R. 901, 9 C.R.R. (2d) 29, Sopinka J. (dissenting). 2. "... [A] private wrong. The intervention of the court is called upon primarily to assist the position of one of the litigants to enforce an order favourable to that party...." *R. v.* Clement (1980), 17 R.F.L. (2d) 349 at 362, [1980] 6 W.W.R. 695, 4 Man. R. (2d) 18, 54 C.C.C. (2d) 252, 114 D.L.R. (3d) 656 (C.A.), Matas J.A. (Freedman C.J.M. concurring).

CIVIL LAW. 1. The legal system of Quebec based on the Civil Code and ultimately Roman law. 2. "... [A] body of private law, consists largely, although not exclusively, of the law enunciated in the Civil Code of Lower Canada and the Civil Code of Quebec, L.R.Q. 1977, c. C-25." *Laurentide Motels Ltd. c. Beauport (Ville)* (1989), 45 M.P.L.R. 1 at 11, 94 N.R. 1, [1989] 1 S.C.R. 705, 23 Q.A.C. 1, Beetz J. (McIntyre, Lamer, Wilson and La Forest JJ. concurring).

CIVIL LIBERTIES. 1. That which is not prohibited. Civil liberties exist when there is a lack of legal rules. P.W.

Hogg, *Constitutional Law of Canada*, 3d ed. (Toronto: Carswell, 1992) at 540. 2. Rights protected by the Charter of Rights and Freedoms: freedom of assembly, association, religion and expression (s. 2), voting rights (s. 3), mobility rights (s. 6), procedural and legal rights (ss. 7-14), the right to equal protection under the law (ss. 15, 28) and language rights (ss. 16-23). P.W. Hogg, *Constitutional Law of Canada*, 3d ed. (Toronto: Carswell, 1992) at 304. See EGALITARIAN ~; LEGAL ~; POLITICAL ~.

CIVIL MARRIAGE CEREMONY. A marriage performed by a judge or justice of the peace, distinguished from a religious ceremony.

CIVIL MATTER. A cause, issue or matter, other than a criminal matter, that involves or might involve a jury and includes an assessment of damages. *Juries Act*, R.S.N.S. 1989, c. 242, s. 2.

CIVIL ONUS. The standard of proof for the party bearing the onus is on a balance of probabilities. J. Sopinka & S.N. Lederman, *The Law of Evidence in Civil Cases* (Toronto: Butterworths, 1974) at 384-85.

CIVIL PRISON. Any prison, jail or other place in Canada in which offenders sentenced by a civil court in Canada to imprisonment for less than two years can be confined, and, if sentenced outside Canada, any prison, jail or other place in which a person, sentenced to that term of imprisonment by a civil court having jurisdiction in the place where the sentence was passed, can for the time being be confined. *National Defence Act*, R.S.C. 1985, c. N-5, s. 2.

CIVIL PROCEDURE. The law governing the process and practice of civil litigation.

CIVIL RIGHTS. 1. Those rights referred to in the list of provincial powers in the Constitution Act, 1867 are primarily proprietary, contractual or tortious rights. P.W. Hogg, *Constitutional Law of Canada*, 3d ed. (Toronto: Carswell, 1992) at 540. 2.

Procedural rights of an individual. See CIVIL LIBERTIES; PROPERTY AND ~.

CIVIL RIGHTS IN THE PROVINCE. Proprietary, contractual or tortious rights referred to in the Constitution Act, 1867. P.W. Hogg, *Constitutional Law of Canada*, 3d ed. (Toronto: Carswell, 1992) at 540.

CIVIL SERVANT. 1. A person appointed to the service of the Crown. 2. A member of the civil service. 3. A member of the staff of a department or Ministry of Government.

CIVIL SERVICE. The employees of the government.

CIVIL STATUS. ". . . [U]nder s. 10 [of the Quebec Charter of Rights and Freedoms, R.S.Q. 1977, c. C-12] includes a range of facts (and not necessarily recorded facts) relating to the three classical elements of civil status – birth, marriage, and death – to which arts. 39 et seq. C.C.L.C. refer. These facts are sometimes recorded in a person's own acts of civil status, sometimes recorded in the acts of another person, and sometimes not recorded in any act at all . . . Other facts, such as interdiction or emancipation, which do not relate to birth, marriage or death but instead to legal capacity may also be included in civil status under s. 10 . . . family relationships [are included in] 'civil status'. Like filiation, fraternity and sorority fall within the parameters which I have ascribed to civil status under s. 10 in this respect as well . . ." *Brossard (Ville) v. Québec (Commission des droits de la personne)* (1989), 10 C.H.R.R. D/5515 at D/5520, D/5522, 88 C.L.L.C. 17,031, [1989] 2 S.C.R. 279, 88 N.R. 321, 18 Q.A.C. 164, 53 D.L.R. (4th) 609, Beetz J. (McIntyre, Lamer and La Forest JJ. concurring).

CIVIL SUIT. See CIVIL ACTION; SUIT.

C.J. *abbr.* Chief Justice.

C.J.A.L.P. *abbr.* Canadian Journal of Admininstrative Law & Practice.

C.J.W.L. *abbr.* Canadian Journal of Women and the Law (Revue juridique "La femme et le droit").

CLAIM. *n.* 1. The demand or the subject matter for which any action, suit, or proceeding is brought. 2. A right, title, interest, encumbrance or demand of any kind affecting land. See COUNTER~; CROSS~; QUIT ~; STATEMENT OF ~.

CLAIMANT. *n.* 1. One who makes a claim. 2. A person who has or is alleged to have a right to maintenance or support. 3. Any person who claims or asserts or seeks to realize a lien. 4. A person who applies or has applied for benefit or compensation.

CLAIM PROVABLE. Any claim or liability provable in proceedings under this Act by a creditor. *Bankruptcy Act*, R.S.C. 1985, c. B-3, s. 2.

CLAIM PROVABLE IN BANKRUPTCY. Any claim or liability provable in proceedings under this Act by a creditor. *Bankruptcy Act*, R.S.C. 1985, c. B-3, s. 2.

CLAIMS ADJUSTER. Every person who, in insurance matters, on behalf of another and for remuneration or on behalf of an employer, investigates a loss, assesses damage arising from it or negotiates settlement of the claim.

CLASS. *n.* 1. A group of persons or things having common attributes. 2. Includes, in relation to securities, a series of a class of securities. 3. A group of positions involving duties and responsibilities so similar that the same or like qualifications may reasonably be required for, and the same schedule or range of pay can be reasonably applied to, all positions in the group. *Pay Equity Act*, R.S.P.E.I. 1988, c. P-2, s. 1. See SHARE ~.

CLASS ACTION. 1. A representative proceeding. 2. "It is necessary to consider the difference between a class action which is derivative in nature, and a representative action by persons having the same interest in the subject of the litigation. Derivative type class actions are those in which a wrong is done to the entity to which the members belong. Such an action may be brought by a member or members, but it is brought on behalf of the entity. A representative action can be brought by persons asserting a common right, and even where persons may have been wronged in their individual capacity." *Pasco v. Canadian National Railway* (1989), (*sub nom. Oregon Jack Creek Indian Band v. Canadian National Railway*) [1990] 2 C.N.L.R. 85 at 87, 34 B.C.L.R. (2d) 344, 56 D.L.R. (4th) 404 (C.A.), MacFarlane J.A.

CLASS GIFT. A gift to a number of persons who are united or connected by some common tie... the testator was looking to the body as a whole rather than to the members constituting the body as individuals ... if one or more of that body died in his lifetime the survivors should take the gift between them. *Kingsbury v. Walter*, [1901] A.C. 187 at 191, per Lord Macnaghten.

CLAUSE. *n.* 1. A paragraph or division of a contract. 2. A sentence or part of a sentence. 3. A numbered portion of a bill called a section once the bill becomes law. A. Fraser, W.A. Dawson, & J. Holtby, eds., *Beauchesne's Rules and Forms of the House of Commons of Canada*, 6th ed. (Toronto: Carswell, 1989) at 193-4. See ACCELERATION ~; ACT OF GOD ~; AMENDING ~; ARBITRATION ~; ATTESTATION ~; BASKET ~; CANCELLATION ~; COLA ~; DEEMING ~; DEFEASANCE ~; DEROGATORY ~; DISCLAIMER ~; ENACTING ~; ENTRENCHMENT ~; ESCALATION ~; EXCEPTIONS ~; EXCLUSION ~; EXCLUSIVE JURISDICTION ~; EXEMPTION ~; FINALITY ~; FORCE MAJEURE ~; GRANDFATHER ~; INTERPRETATION ~; PRIVATIVE ~; REMEDY ~.

CLEAN HANDS DOCTRINE. 1. "... [E]quity will refuse relief to any party who, in the matter of his claim, is himself tainted with fraud, misrepresentation, illegality or impropriety by reason of which his opponent has suffered a detriment of a kind rendering it unjust that the order sought should be made." *Miller v. F. Mendel Holdings Ltd.* (1984), 26 B.L.R. 85 at 100,

[1984] 2 W.W.R. 683, 30 Sask. R. 298 (Q.B.), Wimmer J. 2. "... [T]he theory of the doctrine is that a shareholder cannot invoke an equitable remedy when he himself is a principal source of the conflict and controversy which threaten the future of the corporation. ..." *Journet v. Superchef Food Industries Ltd.* (1984), 29 B.L.R. 206 at 224, [1984] C.S. 916 (Que.), Gomery J. See HE WHO COMES INTO EQUITY MUST COME WITH CLEAN HANDS; NO MAN CAN TAKE ADVANTAGE OF HIS OWN WRONG; NO ONE CAN BE ALLOWED TO DEROGATE FROM HIS OWN GRANT.

CLEAR. *adj.* 1. Free from doubt. 2. Free from encumbrance, lien or charge. 3. Free from deductions.

CLEARANCE. *n.* A certificate issued to indicate compliance with law or regulations.

CLEAR DAYS. Complete days in counting time for items such as notice; both first and last days are omitted.

CLEARING. *n.* 1. In banking, making exchanges and settling balances among banks. 2. In transport, departing having complied with customs regulations.

CLEARING AGENCY. (a) A person that (i) in connection with trades in securities, acts as an intermediary in paying funds, in delivering securities or in doing both of those things, and (ii) provides centralized facilities for the clearing of trades in securities, or (b) a person that provides centralized facilities as a depository in connection with trades in securities. *Securities acts.*

CLEARING HOUSE. An association or organization, whether incorporated or unincorporated, or part of a commodity futures exchange, through which trades in commodity contracts entered into on that exchange are cleared.

CLEARING SYSTEM. A mechanism by which debit and credit positions between banks are ascertained and cheques are sorted. The balances are settled by making transfers in the Chartered Banks' accounts with the Bank of Canada. I.F.G. Baxter, *The Law of Banking*, 3d ed. (Toronto: Carswell, 1981) at 173.

CLEAR TITLE. Good title; title free from encumbrances.

CLERICAL. *adj.* Relating to the office of clerk.

CLERICAL ERROR. 1. "... In Re Robert Sist Dev. Corpn. Ltd. (1977), 17 O.R. (2d) 305 ... (S.C.), Henry J. dealt with the meaning of 'clerical error' and adopted the definition given in [John Burke, ed.] Jowitt's Dictionary of English Law, 2nd ed. ([London: Sweet and Maxwell,] 1977), that a 'clerical error' is 'an error in a document which can only be explained by considering it to be a slip or mistake of the party preparing or copying it'. We believe that this furnishes an adequate definition of 'clerical error'...." *Ovens, Re* (1979), 32 C.B.R. (N.S.) 42 at 47, 26 O.R. (2d) 468, 1 P.P.S.A.C. 131, 8 B.L.R. 186, 103 D.L.R. (3d) 352 (C.A.), the court per Houlden J.A. 2. "[In the Patent Act, R.S.C. 1970, c. P-4, s. 8] ... errors caused by a clerk or stenographer." *Novopharm Ltd. v. Upjohn Co.* (1983), (sub nom. *Upjohn Co. v. Pat. Commr.*) 74 C.P.R. (2d) 228 at 232 (Fed. T.D.), Muldoon J.

CLERK. *n.* 1. The officer of a court who accepts filings, issues process, keeps records. 2. An officer of a municipality. 3. An officer of the Legislative Assembly or House of Commons. 4. A research assistant to a judge or judges. See ARTICLED ~; COURT ~; LAW ~ AND PARLIAMENTARY COUNSEL.

CLERK ASSISTANT. A person appointed by Letters Patent under the Great Seal to assist the Clerk of the House. A. Fraser, W.A. Dawson & J. Holtby, eds., *Beauchesne's Rules and Forms of the House of Commons of Canada*, 6th ed. (Toronto: Carswell, 1989) at 60.

CLERK OF THE COURT. The officer of a court who accepts filings, issues process, keeps records.

CLERK OF THE HOUSE OF COMMONS. The chief procedural advisor to the House, its members and the Speaker, who provides procedural services, directs and controls all officers and clerks employed by the House. A. Fraser, W.A. Dawson & J. Holtby, eds., *Beauchesne's Rules and Forms of the House of Commons of Canada*, 6th ed. (Toronto: Carswell, 1989) at 59-60.

CLERK OF THE PEACE. The person who assists justices of the peace to draw indictments, enter judgments, issue process and administer the courts.

CLERK OF THE QUEEN'S PRIVY COUNCIL. Clerk of the Privy Council and Secretary to the Cabinet. *Interpretation Act*, R.S.C. 1985, c. I-21, s. 35.

CLIC LETTER. *abbr.* CLIC's Legal Materials Letter (Bulletin d'information juridique du CCDJ).

CLIENT. *n.* 1. A person who receives services. 2. A person or body of persons on whose behalf a lawyer receives money for services. See SOLICITOR AND HIS OWN ~ COSTS.

CLIPPING. *n.* Impairing, diminishing or lightening a current gold or silver coin with intent that it should pass for a current gold or silver coin. *Criminal Code*, R.S.C. 1985, c. C-46, s. 413.

C.L.L.C. *abbr.* Canadian Labour Law Cases.

C.L.L.R. *abbr.* Canadian Labour Law Reports, 1973-.

CLOG ON EQUITY OF REDEMPTION. 1. A provision, repugnant to either a contractual or an equitable right to redeem, which is void. W.B. Rayner & R.H. McLaren, *Falconbridge on Mortgages*, 4th ed. (Toronto: Canada Law Book, 1977) at 54. 2. A device which prevents a mortgagor from getting property back after the obligations under the mortgage are discharged. D.J. Donahue & P.D. Quinn, *Real Estate Practice in Ontario*, 4th ed. (Toronto: Butterworths, 1990) at 232-233.

CLOSE. *n.* Conclusion. See BREACH OF ~.

CLOSE COMPANY. A company in

which shares are held by one shareholder or a very small number of shareholders.

CLOSE CORPORATION. A corporation in which shares are held by one shareholder or a very small number of shareholders.

CLOSED COMPANY. A company whose constituting documents provide for restrictions on the free transfer of shares, prohibit any distribution of securities to the public and limit the number of its shareholders to 50, exclusive of present or former employees of the company or of a subsidiary.

CLOSED SHOP. ". . . [O]ne in which membership in a particular union is a condition of employment. Its effect is not only to exclude non-union labour from jobs but also prevents the employer from hiring or retaining in his employment any one but members of a particular union." *B.S.O.I.W., Local No. 97 v. Canadian Ironworkers Union No. 1* (1970), 5 C.L.L.C. 236 at 252, 73 W.W.R. 172, 13 D.L.R. (3d) 559 (B.C. C.A.), Nemetz J.A. (dissenting).

CLOSED SHOP CONTRACT. ". . . [T]he effect of a 'closed shop' provision is to preclude a person from obtaining employment unless he is a member of the union certified as the bargaining agent for the bargaining unit." *Bhindi v. British Columbia Projectionists, Local 340, International Alliance of Picture Machine Operators of United States & Canada* (1986), 24 C.R.R. 302 at 321, 4 B.C.L.R. (2d) 145, [1986] 5 W.W.R. 303, 86 C.L.L.C. 14,052, 29 D.L.R. (4th) 47 (C.A.), Anderson J.A. (dissenting).

CLOSELY HELD CORPORATION. A private corporation the shares of which are not listed on a stock exchange.

CLOSE OF PLEADINGS. When either the plaintiff delivers a reply to every defence in the action or the time to deliver a reply has expired; and it has been noted that every defendant who is in default in delivering a defence in the action is in default (Ontario, Rules of Civil Procedure, r.

25.05). G.D. Watson & C. Perkins, eds., *Holmested & Watson: Ontario Civil Procedure* (Toronto: Carswell, 1984) at 25-4.

CLOSE THE DEAL. To complete a transaction by exchanging documents and funds.

CLOSING ADDRESS. A statement made by counsel at conclusion of a trial before a jury.

CLOSING ARGUMENT. A statement made by counsel at conclusion of a trial before a judge.

CLOSING A TRANSACTION. A meeting between the lawyers or agents representing the parties to complete the transaction by exchanging documents and funds.

CLOSURE. *n.* A procedure to conclude debate to force the House of Commons to decide a subject. A. Fraser, G.A. Birch & W.A. Dawson, eds., *Beauchesne's Rules and Forms of the House of Commons of Canada*, 5th ed. (Toronto: Carswell, 1978) at 117.

C.L.R. *abbr.* Construction Law Reports, 1983-.

C.L.R.B. *abbr.* Canada Labour Relations Board.

C.L.R.B.R. (N.S.). *abbr.* Canadian Labour Relations Board Reports (New Series).

C.L.S. *abbr.* Canada Labour Service.

C.L.T. *abbr.* Canadian Law Times, 1881-1922.

C.L.T. (OCC. N.). *abbr.* Canadian Law Times, Occasional Notes.

CLUB. *n.* 1. "Clubs are associations of a peculiar nature. They are societies the members of which are perpetually changing. They are not partnerships; they are not associations for gain; and the feature which distinguishes them from other societies is that no member as such becomes liable to pay to the funds of the society or to any one else any money beyond the subscriptions required by the rules of the club to be paid so long as he remains a member. . . ." *Taylor v. Peoples' Loan & Savings Corp.* (1928), 62 O.L.R. 564

at 568-69, [1928] 4 D.L.R. 598 (H.C.), Raney J. 2. An association of individuals for purposes of mutual entertainment and convenience. 3. A social, sporting, community, benevolent or fraternal order or society, or any branch thereof.

CLUB MEMBER. A person who, whether as a charter member or admitted in accordance with the by-laws or rules of a club, has become a member thereof, who maintains membership by the payment of regular periodic dues in the manner provided by the rules or by-laws, and whose name and address are entered on the list of members.

C. MAG. *abbr.* Cour de magistrat.

C.M.A.R. *abbr.* Canadian Court Martial Appeal Reports, 1957-.

CMHC. *abbr.* 1. Canada Mortgage and Housing Corporation. 2. Central Mortgage and Housing Corporation.

C.M.M. *abbr.* Cour municipale de Montréal.

CMND. *abbr.* Command papers.

C.M.P.R. *abbr.* Canadian Mortgage Practice Reports.

C.M.Q. *abbr.* Cour municipale de Québec.

C. MUN. *abbr.* Cour municipale.

C.N.L.C. *abbr.* Commission nationale de libérations conditionnelles.

C.N.L.R. *abbr.* Canadian Native Law Reporter.

CO. *abbr.* Company.

C/O. *symbol* In care of. *McLennan, Re* [1940] 1 W.W.R. 465 at 472 (Sask. Surr. Ct.), Bryant Surr. Ct. J.

COAST. *n.* The edge of land bordered by a sea.

COASTAL WATERS OF CANADA. 1. Includes all of Queen Charlotte Sound, all the Strait of Georgia and the Canadian waters of the Strait of Juan de Fuca. *Criminal Code*, R.S.C. 1985, c. C-46, s. 339(6). 2. All Canadian fisheries waters not within the geographical limits of any province. *Fisheries Act*, R.S.C. 1985, c. F-14, s. 47.

COASTING. *n.* The carrying by water transportation of goods and materials of every description to or from ports in the province. *Fishing and Coasting Vessels Bounties Act*, R.S.Nfld. 1990, c. F-17, s. 2.

COASTING TRADE. The employment of ships in the transportation of goods for hire or reward by water or land and water from one port or place in Canada to another port or place in Canada either directly or by way of a foreign port or in the transportation of passengers from one port or place in Canada to another port or place in Canada either directly or by way of a foreign port. *Coastwise and Foreign Shipping (Customs) Regulations*, C.R.C., c. 454, s. 2.

COASTING TRADE OF CANADA. The carriage by water of goods or passengers from one port or place in Canada to another port or place in Canada. *Canada Shipping Act*, R.S.C. 1985, c. S-9, s. 2.

COAST OF CANADA. The sea-coast of Canada and the salt water bays, gulfs and harbours on the sea-coast of Canada. *Canada Shipping Act*, R.S.C. 1985, c. S-9, s. 2.

CO. CT. *abbr.* County Court.

C.O.D. *abbr.* See CASH ON DELIVERY.

CODE. *n.* 1. A collection or system of laws, i.e. Code Napoléon or Civil Code. 2. A consolidation of existing statute and common law, i.e. Criminal Code. 3. Guidelines for a process or use of equipment to ensure safety, efficiency, or a level of quality established and published by a competent authority, i.e. building code, safety code. See BUILDING ~; BUILDING CONSTRUCTION ~; CIVIL ~; CRIMINAL ~.

CODE CIVIL. The civil law of Quebec.

CODICIL. *n.* An addition or change made to a will by a testator.

CODIFICATION. *n.* The collection of all the principles of any system or subject of law into one body of statutes or single statute.

CODIFYING STATUTE. A single statute which aims to state all the law on a particular subject by combining pre-existing statutory provisions with common law rules relating to the subject. P. St. J. Langan, ed., *Maxwell on The Interpretation of Statutes*, 12th ed. (Bombay: N.M. Tripathi, 1976) at 25.

COERCION. *n.* 1. ". . . [I]ncludes not only such blatant forms of compulsion as direct commands to act or refrain from acting on pain of sanction, coercion includes indirect forms of control which determine or limit alternative courses of conduct available to others." *R. v. Big M Drug Mart Ltd.* (1985), 13 C.R.R. 64 at 97-8 (S.C.C.), Dickson C.J.C. 2. Compelling by force or threats.

COGNISANCE. *n.* 1. Knowledge. 2. To take cognisance means to take judicial notice.

COHABIT. *v.* 1. To live together in a conjugal relationship, whether within or outside marriage. 2. To live together in a family relationship. *Child and Family Services and Family Relations Act*, S.N.B. 1980, c. C-2.1, s. 1.

COHABITATION AGREEMENT. (1) A man and a woman who are cohabiting and not married to one another may enter into an agreement in which they agree on their respective rights and obligations during cohabitation, or upon ceasing to cohabit or death, including, (a) ownership in or division of property; (b) support obligations; (c) the right to direct the education and moral training of their children, but not the right to custody of or access to their children; and (d) any other matter in the settlement of their affairs. *Family Law Reform Act*, R.S.O. 1980, c. 152, s. 50.

CO-HEIR. *n.* One of several people among whom an inheritance is divided.

CO-HEIRESS. *n.* A woman who shared an inheritance equally with another woman.

COIN. *v.* To stamp pieces of metal into a set shape and size and place marks on them under the aegis of a government.

COIN. *n.* A piece of metal stamped with certain marks and put into circulation as money of a certain value by a government.

CO-INSURANCE. *n.* Requires the insured to bear the proportion of the loss equivalent to the value of the property at risk, in excess of the insurance thereon, bears to the interest of the insured in the property or to the amount of insurance thereon. *Eckardt v. Lancashire Insurance Co.* (1900), 27 O.A.R. 373 at 382 (C.A.), Osler J.A.

COLA. *abbr.* Cost-of-living adjustment.

COLA CLAUSE. An agreement to provide employees with an increase in wages tied to an index such as the Consumer Price Index prepared by Statistics Canada.

COLLATERAL. *n.* 1. Property used to secure the payment of a debt or performance of an obligation. 2. A blood relation who is neither a descendant nor an ancestor. R. Megarry & H.W.R. Wade, *The Law of Real Property*, 5th ed. (London: Stevens, 1984) at cxxiii.

COLLATERAL. *adj.* ". . . '[P]arallel' or 'additional' or 'side by side with'." *Manitoba Development Corp. v. Berkowits* (1979), 9 R.P.R. 310 at 313, [1979] 5 W.W.R. 138, 101 D.L.R. (3d) 421 (Man. C.A.), the court per O'Sullivan J.A.

COLLATERAL ATTACK DOCTRINE. ". . . [A] court order may not be attacked collaterally – and a collateral attack may be described as an attack made in proceedings other than those whose specific object is the reversal, variation, or nullification of the order or judgment." *R. v. Wilson*, [1983] 2 S.C.R. 595 at 599, [1984] 1 W.W.R. 481, 37 C.R. (3d) 97, 26 Man. R. (2d) 194, 9 C.C.C. (3d) 97, 4 D.L.R. (4th) 577, 51 N.R. 321, McIntyre J. (Laskin C.J.C. and Estey J. concurring).

COLLATERAL CONTRACT. 1.

". . . [A]n oral agreement ancillary to a written agreement. . . ." *Ahone v.* Holloway (1988), 30 B.C.L.R. (2d) 368 at 373 (C.A.), the court per McLachlin J.A. 2. A statement, on the strength of which a person enters into a contract, may give rise to an entirely separate contract "collateral" to the main contract made between the maker of the statement and the person to whom the statement was made.

COLLATERAL QUESTION. A question connected to the merits or the heart of an inquiry but which is not the major question to be decided. S.A. DeSmith, *Judicial Review of Administrative Action*, 4th ed. by J.M. Evans (London: Stevens, 1980) at 114.

COLLATERAL RELATIVE. A person whose relationship to a second person is not in the direct line of descent from the second person, i.e. a brother's child.

COLLATERAL SECURITY. ". . . [A]ny property which is assigned or pledged to secure the performance of an obligation and as additional thereto, and which upon the performance of the obligation is to be surrendered or discharged: . . ." *Royal Bank of Canada v. Slack* (1958), 11 D.L.R. (2d) 737 at 746 (Ont. C.A.), Schroeder J.A., cited in *MacLaren, Re* (1978), 88 D.L.R. (3d) 222 at 231, 30 N.S.R. (2d) 694, 49 A.P.R. 694, 4 B.L.R. 191, 28 C.B.R. (N.S.) 56 (S.C.), Cowan C.J.T.D.

COLLATERAL TERM. Outside or distinct from the terms of the main contract.

COLLATION. *n.* Comparing a copy with its original to ensure its accuracy and completeness.

COLLECTION. *n.* A bank's handling of commercial and financial documents according to instructions received. I.F.G. Baxter, *The Law of Banking*, 3d ed. (Toronto: Carswell, 1981) at 141.

COLLECTIVE AGREEMENT. An agreement in writing between an employer or an employer's organization acting on behalf of employers, and a bargaining agent of employees acting on behalf of a unit of employees containing provisions respecting terms and conditions of employment and related matters.

COLLECTIVE BARGAINING. Negotiating with a view to the conclusion of a collective agreement or the renewal or revision thereof.

COLLECTIVE BARGAINING AGREEMENT. An agreement in writing between an employer or an employer's organization acting on behalf of an employer, on the one hand, and a bargaining agent of employees acting on behalf of the employees, on the other hand, containing terms or conditions of employment of employees.

COLLECTOR. *n.* A person authorized or required by or pursuant to a revenue act or by agreement to collect a tax.

COLLEGE. *n.* 1. A corporation, company, or society having certain privileges, i.e., College of Physicians and Surgeons. 2. A community college. 3. A regional college. 4. A college of applied arts and technology.

COLLEGE OF PHYSICIANS AND SURGEONS. The licensing and governing body of the medical profession in a province.

COLLISION. *n.* ". . . [I]mplies an impact, the sudden contact of a moving body with an obstruction in its line of motion. Both bodies may be in motion, or one in motion and the other stationary." *Aberdeen Paving Ltd. v. Guildhall Insurance Co.* (1966), 52 M.P.R. 349 at 362, 60 D.L.R. (2d) 45 (N.S. C.A.), Cowan J.A.

COLLOQUIUM. *n.* In pleading in a libel or slander action, the plaintiff must show that the statement complained of was "published of and concerning the plaintiff." R.E. Brown, *The Law of Defamation in Canada* (Toronto: Carswell, 1987) at 218.

COLLUSION. *n.* 1. Agreement to deceive. *Edison General Electric Co. v. Vancouver & New Westminster Tramway Co.* (1896), 4 B.C.R. 460 at 483 (C.A.), Drake J.A. 2. An agreement or conspiracy to which an applicant for a divorce is either directly or indirectly a party for the purpose of subverting the administration of justice, and includes any agreement, understanding or arrangement to fabricate or suppress evidence or to deceive the court, but does not include an agreement to the extent that it provides for separation between the parties, financial support, division of property or the custody of any child of the marriage. *Divorce Act*, R.S.C. 1985 (2d Supp.), c. 3, s. 11(4).

COLONIAL LAW. In a colony discovered and occupied, the laws of England; in a conquered colony or one ceded to England, its own laws until England changed them.

COLONIAL LAWS VALIDITY ACT, 1865. The British Act confirming the capacity of legislatures in the colonies to enact laws inconsistent with English laws. P.W. Hogg, *Constitutional Law of Canada*, 3d ed. (Toronto: Carswell, 1992) at 48.

COLONY. *n.* 1. A place settled by people from an older city or country. 2. A number of persons who hold land or any interest therein as communal property, whether as owners, lessees or otherwise, and whether in the name of trustees or as a corporation or otherwise, and includes a number of persons who propose to acquire land to be held in such manner.

COLORE OFFICII. [L.] Colour of office. See DURESS ~.

COLOUR. *n.* Appearance, pretext or pretence, apparent or prima facie.

COLOURABILITY. *n.* A doctrine invoked when a statute is addressed to a matter outside jurisdiction though it bears the formal trappings of a matter within the jurisdiction of the enacting legislature. P.W. Hogg, *Constitutional Law of Canada*, 3d ed. (Toronto: Carswell, 1992) at 387.

COLOURABLE. *adj.* In appearance but not in substance what it claims to be.

COLOUR OF OFFICE. Pretense of authority to carry out an act for which the actor has no authority.

COLOUR OF RIGHT. "... [G]enerally, although not exclusively, refers to a situation where there is an assertion of a proprietary or possessory right to the thing which is the subject-matter of the alleged theft.... The term ... is also used to denote an honest belief in a state of facts which, if it actually existed would at law justify or excuse the act done; ..." *R. v. DeMarco* (1973), 13 C.C.C. (2d) 369 at 372, 22 C.R.N.S. 258 (Ont. C.A.), Martin J.A.

COMBINATION. *n.* An association of persons for a particular purpose. See BUSINESS ~.

COMITY. *n.* 1. "... [T]he informing principle of private international law, which has been stated to be the defence [sic] and respect due by other states to the actions of a state legitimately taken within its territory.... For my part, I much prefer the more complete formulation of the idea of comity adopted by the Supreme Court of the United States in Hilton v. Guyot, 159 U.S. 113 ... (1895) at p. 163-4 in a passage cited by Estey J. in Spencer v. R., [1985] 2 S.C.R. 278 at p. 283 ... as follows: ' "Comity" in the legal sense, is neither a matter of absolute obligation, on the one hand, nor of mere courtesy and good will, upon the other. But it is the recognition which one nation allows within its territory to the legislative, executive or judicial acts of another nation, having due regard both to international duty and convenience, and to the rights of its own citizens or of other persons who are under the protection of its laws.' " *Morguard Investments Ltd. v. De Savoye* (1990), 46 C.P.C. (2d) 1 at 17, 19, 15 R.P.R. (2d) 1, 16, 52 B.C.L.R. (2d) 160, [1991] 2 W.W.R. 217, 76 D.L.R. (4th) 256, 122 N.R. 81, [1990] 3 S.C.R. 1077, the court per La Forest J.

COMITY OF NATIONS. A code of behaviour towards one another which nations observe from mutual convenience or courtesy.

COMM. *abbr.* Commission.

COMMAND PAPERS. In Britain, papers presented to Parliament at the Crown's command.

COMMENCEMENT. *n.* When used with reference to an enactment, means the time at which the enactment comes into force.

COMMERCE. *n.* Trade; exchange of goods or property. See CHAMBER OF ~; TRADE AND ~.

COMMERCIAL. *adj.* 1. Connected with trade and commerce in general. 2. Of real property, principally used for the sale of goods or services.

COMMERCIAL ARBITRATION. An adjudicative process, either voluntary or ad hoc, involving the application and interpretation of agreements. D.J.M. Brown & D.M. Beatty, *Canadian Labour Arbitration*, 3d ed. (Aurora: Canada Law Book, 1988) at 1-1 and 1-2.

COMMERCIAL ENTERPRISE. A sole proprietorship, partnership, co-operative or corporation having for its object the acquisition of gain.

COMMERCIAL ESTABLISH-MENT. Any establishment or other place where commodities are, or merchandise is, sold or offered for sale at retail.

COMMERCIAL LAW. The law of contracts, bankruptcy, intellectual property, corporations and partnerships and any other subjects dealing with rights and relations of persons engaged in commerce or trade.

COMMERCIAL LETTER OF CREDIT. 1. An irrevocable document issued by a buyer's bank in favour of a seller. The issuing bank will accept drafts drawn upon it for the price of the goods when the seller tenders shipping documents. G.H.L. Fridman, *Sale of Goods in Canada*, 3d ed. (Toronto: Carswell, 1986) at 260. 2. A document issued by a bank on an importer's application in which the bank undertakes to pay an exporter when the exporter complies with certain terms. I.F.G. Baxter, *The Law of Banking*, 3d ed. (Toronto: Carswell, 1981) at 141.

COMMERCIAL PAPER. A bill of exchange, cheque, promissory note, negotiable instrument, conditional sale agreement, lien note, hire purchase agreement, chattel mortgage, bill of lading, bill of sale, warehouse receipt, guarantee, instrument of assignment, things in action and, in addition, any document of title that passes ownership or possession and on which credit can be raised. *Interpretation Act*, R.S.B.C. 1979, c. 206, s. 29.

COMMERCIAL REALTY. Real property owned by the Crown or any person, used for or occupied by any industry, trade, business, profession, vocation or government business.

COMMERCIAL SPEECH. "[In considering s. 2(b) of the Charter] ... whatever else may be subsumed within the rubric 'commercial speech', (a) speech which does no more than propose a commercial transaction; (b) expression related solely to the economic interests of the speaker and audience, and (c) speech which advertises a product or service for profit or a business purpose may fairly be regarded as included ..." *R. v. Smith* (1988), 44 C.C.C. (3d) 385 at 424 (Ont. H.C.), Watt J. See FREEDOM OF EXPRESSION; HATRED.

COMMERCIAL TREATY. An international treaty concerning financial or economic relations.

COMMERCIAL UNIT. In human rights legislation, any building or other structure or part thereof that is used or occupied or is intended, arranged or designed to be used or occupied for the manufacture, sale, resale, processing, reprocessing, displaying, storing, handling, garaging or distribution of personal property, or any space that is used or occupied or is intended, arranged or designed to be used or occupied as a separate business or professional unit or office in any building or other structure or a part thereof.

COMMERCIAL USE. 1. A use in connection with a trade, business, profession, manufacture or other venture for profit. 2. Any use other than for residential or agricultural purposes.

COMMERCIAL VEHICLE. 1. A motor vehicle designed or adapted for the carrying of freight, goods, wares or merchandise. 2. A motor vehicle or trailer operated on a highway for the transportation of livestock or livestock products for gain or compensation, or by or on behalf of a person dealing in livestock or livestock products.

COMMINGLE. *v.* 1. To mass together. 2. Of funds, to mix into one larger fund.

COMMISSION. *n.* 1. The authority or order to act. 2. Remuneration paid to an agent or employee based on price. 3. ". . . [I]n the section [s. 207(3) of the Criminal Code, R.S.C. 1927, c. 36] is not restricted to the actual instantaneous act constituting the crime but includes the preparations for same and all factors which naturally arise in connection with such crime." *R. v. Roher* (1953), 10 W.W.R. (N.S.) 309 at 312, 17 C.R. 307, 61 Man. R. 311, 107 C.C.C. 103 (C.A.), McPherson C.J.M. (Coyne J.A. concurring). 4. An authority given to a person or persons to administer a program or statute, manage a fund or a public utility, investigate a matter or perform some other public function. 5. The name of a body which carries out the functions listed in definition 14. See CANADIAN HUMAN RIGHTS ~; CANADIAN TRANSPORT ~; DEL CREDERE ~; FEDERAL BOARD, ~ OR OTHER TRIBUNAL; ROYAL ~.

COMMISSION AGENT. 1. A person who receives goods for a principal and is employed to sell them for remuneration or commission.

COMMISSIONER. *n.* 1. A person authorised by letters patent, statute or other lawful warrant to examine any matters or execute a public office. 2. A member of a commission. 3. A person authorized to take the evidence of another person. 4. The Commissioner of the Royal Canadian Mounted Police. *Criminal Code*, R.S.C. 1985, c. C-46, s. 84. 5. The Commissioner of the Northwest Territories. *Northwest Territories Act*, R.S.C. 1985, c. N-27, s. 2. 6. The Commissioner of the Yukon

Territory. *Yukon Act*, R.S.C. 1985, c. Y-2, s. 2. See FAMILY LAW ~; INFORMATION ~ OF CANADA.

COMMISSIONER FOR TAKING AFFIDAVITS. One authorized to administer affirmations or oaths.

COMMISSIONER IN COUNCIL. The Commissioner of the Northwest Territories or Yukon acting by and with the advice and consent of the Council.

COMMISSIONER OF OFFICIAL LANGUAGES. The federal official empowered to see that both Canada's official languages, French and English, have equal status, rights and privileges in federal institutions.

COMMISSION EVIDENCE. A way to preserve or secure evidence when a witness is, because of (i) physical disability caused by illness, or (ii) any other good and sufficient reason, not able to attend a trial at the time it is held. P.K. McWilliams, *Canadian Criminal Evidence*, 3d ed. (Aurora: Canada Law Book, 1988) at 8-82. See COMMISSION ROGATORY; LETTERS ROGATORY; PERPETUATE TESTIMONY; ROGATORY LETTERS.

COMMISSION OF THE PEACE. A commission by which a number of persons are appointed as justices of the peace.

COMMISSION ROGATORY. A means of collecting evidence for courts of one country through the courts of another country. See COMMISSION EVIDENCE; LETTERS ROGATORY; PERPETUATE TESTIMONY; ROGATORY LETTERS.

COMMIT. *v.* 1. To send to prison by reason of lawful authority. 2. To send to trial, i.e. a provincial court judge commits a person to trial before another court. 3. To refer a bill to a committee in which the bill is considered and reported. A. Fraser, W.A. Dawson & J. Holtby, eds., *Beauchesne's Rules and Forms of the House of Commons of Canada*, 6th ed. (Toronto: Carswell, 1989) at 203. 4. To direct that a person be confined in a psychiatric facility.

COMMITMENT. *n.* 1. An agreement or promise to do something. 2. Sending a person to prison. 3. Directing that a person be confined in a psychiatric facility. See LOAN ~; MORTGAGE ~.

COMMITMENT LETTER. A letter prepared by a lender, setting out the conditions and terms upon which the lender is willing to advance money to a borrower. B.J. Reiter, B.N. McLellan & P.M. Perell, *Real Estate Law*, 4th ed. (Toronto: Emond Montgomery, 1992) at 836.

COMMITTAL ORDER. A court order for the committal of a person to a correctional facility or a federal penitentiary.

COMMITTED. . *adj.*". . . [An] offence is committed when the offender has completed the unlawful act or acts . . ." *R. v. MacDonald* (1989), 51 C.C.C. (3d) 191 at 192, 18 M.V.R. (2d) 276, 98 A.R. 308 (C.A.), Stevenson, Foisy and Irving JJ.A.

COMMITTEE. *n.* 1. A group of persons elected or appointed to whom any matter is referred by a legislative body, corporation or other institution. 2. A person appointed by the court to look after a person or the affairs of a person or a mentally incompetent person. See ADVISORY ~; AUDIT ~; DISCIPLINE ~; JUDICIAL ~; LEGISLATIVE ~; PARLIAMENTARY ~; SELECT ~; SPECIAL ~; STANDING ~.

COMMITTEE OF THE WHOLE HOUSE. The membership of the House when a chairman instead of the Speaker presides. This committee may deliberate any questions which, in the opinion of the House, it may more fitly discuss, including provisions of public bills. After second reading bills founded on a supply motion are referred to this committee. A. Fraser, W.A. Dawson & J. Holtby, eds., *Beauchesne's Rules and Forms of the House of Commons of Canada*, 6th ed. (Toronto: Carswell, 1989) at 249.

COMMODITY. *n.* 1. ". . . [A]nything that is usable for a purpose." *R. v. Robert Simpson Co.* (1964), 43 C.R.

366 at 371, [1964] O.R. 227, [1964] 3 C.C.C. 318 (H.C.), Landreville J. 2. Any agricultural product, forest product, product of the sea, mineral, metal, hydrocarbon fuel, currency or precious stone or other gem in the original or a processed state.

COMMODITY CONTRACT. A commodity futures contract or commodity futures option. *Commodity Contract Act*, R.S.B.C. 1979, c. 56, s. 1.

COMMODITY EXCHANGE. An association or organization, whether incorporated or unincorporated, operated to provide the facilities necessary for the trading of commodity contracts by open auction. *Commodity Contract Amendment Act*, S.B.C. 1985, c. 2, s. 1.

COMMODITY FUTURES CONTRACT. A contract to make or take delivery of a specified quantity and quality, grade or size of a commodity during a designated future month at a price agreed upon when the contract is entered into on a commodity futures exchange pursuant to standardized terms and conditions set forth in such exchange's by-laws, rules or regulations.

COMMODITY FUTURES EXCHANGE. An association or organization, whether incorporated or unincorporated, operated for the purpose of providing the physical facilities necessary for the trading of contracts by open auction.

COMMODITY FUTURES OPTION. A right, acquired for a consideration, to assume a long or short position in relation to a commodity futures contract at a specified price and within a specified period of time and any other option of which the subject is a commodity futures contract.

COMMODITY OPTION. A right, acquired for a consideration, to assume a long or short position in relation to a commodity at a specified price and within a specified period of time and any other option of which the subject is a commodity. *Commodity Contract*

Amendment Act, S.B.C. 1985, c. 2, s. 1.

COMMON. *n.* An interest one person can enjoy in the land of another, i.e. common of pasture is the right to pasture cattle on another person's land. See TENANCY IN ~.

COMMON. *adj.* Usual, ordinary; shared.

COMMON AREAS. Areas controlled by a landlord and used for access to residential premises or for the service or enjoyment of a tenant.

COMMON ASSAULT. "[At common law] ... any act in which one person intentionally caused another to apprehend immediate and unlawful violence.... The traditional common law definition always assumed that the absence of consent was a required element of that offence." *R. v. Jobidon* (1991), 7 C.R. (4th) 233 at 245, 66 C.C.C. (3d) 454, 128 N.R. 321, 49 O.A.C. 83, [1991] 2 S.C.R. 714, Gonthier J. (La Forest, L'Heureux-Dubé, Cory and Iacobucci JJ. concurring).

COMMON BAWDY-HOUSE. A place that is (a) kept or occupied, or (b) resorted to by one or more persons for the purpose of prostitution or the practice of acts of indecency. *Criminal Code*, R.S.C. 1985, c. C-46, c. 197.

COMMON BETTING HOUSE. A place that is opened, kept or used for the purpose of (a) enabling, encouraging or assisting persons who resort thereto to bet between themselves or with the keeper, or (b) enabling any person to receive, record, register, transmit or pay bets or to announce the results of betting. *Criminal Code*, R.S.C. 1985, c. C-46, s. 197.

COMMON CARRIER. "... [O]ne who holds himself out to the public to carry the goods of such persons as may choose to employ him." *Engel Canada Inc. v. Bingo's Transport Drivers* (1990), 23 M.V.R. (2d) 193 at 197 (Ont. H.C.), Austin J.

COMMON ELEMENTS. All property, except the condominium units, owned in common by all of the owners of units. B.J. Reiter, B.N.

McLellan & P.M. Perell, *Real Estate Law*, 4th ed. (Toronto: Emond Montgomery, 1992) at 549.

COMMON EXPENSES. The expenses of the performance of the objects and duties of a condominium corporation and any expenses specified as common expenses in a declaration.

COMMON FACILITY. An improvement in the common property that is available for the use of all the owners of a condominium.

COMMON GAMING HOUSE. A place that is (a) kept for gain to which persons resort for the purpose of playing games, or (b) kept or used for the purpose of playing games (i) in which a bank is kept by one or more but not all of the players, (ii) in which all or any portion of the bets on or proceeds from a game is paid, directly or indirectly, to the keeper of the place, (iii) in which, directly or indirectly, a fee is charged to or paid by the players for the privilege of playing or participating in a game or using gaming equipment, or (iv) in which the chances of winning are not equally favourable to all persons who play the game, including the person, if any, who conducts the game. *Criminal Code*, R.S.C. 1985, c. C-46, s. 197.

COMMON INTEREST. 1. "[In the context of a representative action refers to the fact that] ... the plaintiff and all those whom he claims to represent will gain some relief by his success, though possibly in different proportions and perhaps in different degrees." *A.E. Osler and Co. v. Solman* (1926), 59 O.L.R. 368 at 372 (H.C.), Orde J.A. 2. In condominium law, the interest in the common elements appurtenant to a unit. 3. In occupier's liability, a mutuality of interest or advantage to invitor and invitee. J.V. DiCastri, *Occupiers' Liability* (Vancouver: Burroughs/Carswell, 1980) at 35.

COMMON JAIL. Any place other than a penitentiary in which persons charged with offences are usually kept and detained in custody.

COMMON KNOWLEDGE. 1. "...

[K]nowledge of a general nature which has been acquired in common with other members of the general public...." *Maslej v. Canada (Minister of Manpower & Immigration)*, [1977] 1 F.C. 194 at 198 (C.A.), the court per Urie J. 2. "... [T]he common knowledge possessed by every man on the street, of which courts of justice cannot divest themselves ..." *In re Price Bros. Etc.* (1920), 60 S.C.R. 265 at 279, Anglin J.

COMMON LAW. 1. In contrast to statute law, law which relies for its authority on the decisions of the courts and is recorded in the law reports as decisions of judges along with the reasons for their decisions. 2. In contrast to canon (or ecclesiastical) and the civil (or Roman) law, the system of law in provinces other than Quebec.

COMMON LAW MARRIAGE. *var.* **COMMON-LAW MARRIAGE.** "... [A] voluntary union of a man and woman during their joint lives to the exclusion of all others which, for historical reasons, was treated as being just as valid as a regular marriage." *Louis v. Esslinger* (1981), 15 C.C.L.T. 137 at 161, [1981] 3 W.W.R. 350, 22 C.P.C. 68, 29 B.C.L.R. 41, 121 D.L.R. (3d) 17 (S.C.), McEachern C.J.S.C.

COMMON-LAW RELATIONSHIP . "... [S]ome sort of a stable relationship which involves not only sexual activity but a commitment between the parties. It would normally necessitate living together under the same roof with shared household duties and responsibilities as well as financial support ... such a couple would present themselves to society as a couple who were living together as man and wife. All or none of these elements may be necessary depending upon the intent of the parties." *Soper v. Soper* (1985), 44 R.F.L. (2d) 308 at 314, 67 N.S.R. (2d) 49, 155 A.P.R. 49 (C.A.), the court per Morrison J.A.

COMMON LAW SPOUSE. *var.* **COMMON-LAW SPOUSE.** Includes any man or woman who although not legally married to a person lives and cohabits with that person as the spouse of that person and is known as such in the community in which they have lived.

COMMON LAW UNION. Cohabitation by a man and a woman who publicly present themselves as spouses.

COMMON MISTAKE. "Where agreement has been reached but both parties in reaching that agreement have been under a common misapprehension." *Stepps Investments Ltd. v. Security Capital Corp.* (1976), 14 O.R. (2d) 259 at 269, 73 D.L.R. (3d) 351 (H.C.), Grange J. See MISTAKE.

COMMON NUISANCE. The offence of committing a common nuisance consists of doing an unlawful act or failing to discharge a legal duty and thereby (a) endangering the lives, safety, health, property or comfort or the public, or (b) obstructing the public in the exercise or enjoyment or any right that is common to all the subjects of Her Majesty in Canada. *Criminal Code*, R.S.C. 1985, c. C-46, s. 180(2).

COMMON PROPERTY. The part of the land included in a condominium plan that is not included in any unit shown in the condominium plan.

COMMONS. See HOUSE OF ~.

COMMON SHARE. 1. A share to which no special rights or privileges attach. 2. A share of a corporation (i) the holder of which is not precluded upon the reduction or redemption of the capital stock from participating in the assets of the corporation beyond the amount paid up on the share plus a fixed premium and a defined rate of dividend, and (ii) that carries a number of voting rights in the issuing corporation, in all circumstances and regardless of the number of shares held, that is not less than the number attached to any other share of the capital stock of that corporation.

COMMONWEALTH. *n.* 1. The association of countries named in the schedule. *Interpretation Act*, R.S.C. 1985, c. I-21, s. 35. 2. The social state of a country. 3. A republic. 4. The Australian federation called the Commonwealth of Australia. 5. The British government from 1649 to 1660.

COMMONWEALTH AND DEPENDENT TERRITORIES. The several Commonwealth countries and their colonies, possessions, dependencies, protectorates, protected states, condominiums and trust territories. *Interpretation Act*, R.S.C. 1985, c. I-21, s. 35.

COMMORIENTES. *n.* [L.] People who die in the same accident or on the same occasion.

COMMR. *abbr.* Commissioner.

COMMUNE. *n.* A small community of people who share common interests and who own property together.

COMMUNICATION. *n.* "... [I]nvolves the passing of thoughts, ideas, words or information from one person to another...." *R. v. Goldman*, 108 D.L.R. (3d) 17 at 32, [1980] 1 S.C.R. 976, 30 N.R. 453, 51 C.C.C. (2d) 1, 13 C.R. (3d) 228 (Eng.), 16 C.R. (3d) 330 (Fr.), McIntyre J. (Martland, Ritchie, Pigeon, Dickson, Beetz, Estey and Pratte JJ. concurring). See PRIVILEGED ~.

COMMUNICATIONS. *n.* 1. A method, manner or means by which information is transmitted, imparted or exchanged and includes the transmission and reception of sound, pictures, signs, signals, data or messages by means of wire, cable, waves or an electrical, electronic, magnetic, electromagnetic or optical means. 2. The business of radio and television broadcasting and the furnishing of community antenna services, telephone services and other electrical or electronic communication services. *Small Business Loans Regulations*, C.R.C., c. 1501, s. 3.

COMMUNITY. *n.* 1. "[In s. 24 of the Taxation Act, R.S.B.C. 1960, c. 376] ... must be interpreted in the sense that it means the public in general and not a community in the sense of an isolated or identifiable area or group." *Piers Island Assn. v. Saanich & Islands Area Assessor* (1976), 71 D.L.R. (3d) 270 at 275, 1 B.C.L.R. 279 (S.C.), Fulton J. 2. A city, town or village. *The Community*

Planning Profession Act, R.S.S. 1978, c. C-21, c. 2. 3. A geographic unit or group of persons sharing common interests within a geographic unit who provide or receive services on a collective basis. 4. A group of persons living together and observing common rules under the direction of a superior. 5. "[In the context of selecting a jury] ... a reasonably distinct, distinguishable group by language and culture. It should occupy, as well, a unique geographic area. If those conditions are met, then, it seems that those people living in that area should qualify as a community...." *R. v. Fatt* (1986), 54 C.R. (3d) 281 at 291, [1986] N.W.T.R. 388, 30 C.C.C. (3d) 69, 24 C.R.R. 259, [1987] 1 C.N.L.R. 74 (S.C.), Marshall J. See FULL ~.

COMMUNITY ANTENNA TELEVISION. A system by which television signals are received from distant stations on large antennae and transmitted by cable to individual consumers.

COMMUNITY CARE FACILITY. A facility that provides personal care, supervision, social or educational training, physical or mental rehabilitative therapy, with or without charge to persons not related by blood or marriage to an operator of the facility.

COMMUNITY CENTRE. Any public land improved, or buildings erected and equipped to provide recreational, sporting, cultural, or adult educational facilities for the public use of the community.

COMMUNITY DEVELOPMENT SERVICES. Services designed to encourage and assist residents of a community to participate in or continue to participate in improving the social and economic conditions of the community for the purpose of preventing, lessening or removing the causes and effects of poverty, child neglect or dependence on public assistance in the community.

COMMUNITY OF PROPERTY. See COMMUNITY PROPERTY REGIME; DEFERRED ~.

COMMUNITY PLAN. See OFFICIAL ~.

COMMUNITY PROPERTY REGIME. An arrangement whereby spouses share all property which one or both may own. A. Bissett-Johnson & W.M. Holland, eds., *Matrimonial Property Law in Canada* (Toronto: Carswell, 1980) at A-5.

COMMUNITY SANCTIONS. "... [R]efers to sanctions other than custody. It includes community programs or resources (e.g. supervised probation) or compensation to the community (e.g. fines or service). The sanctions are to be served or performed in the community with the community taking an active role in the rehabilitation, responsibility for, and treatment of the offender...." *R. v. P. (J.A.)* (1991), 6 C.R. (4th) 126 at 135, [1991] N.W.T.R. 301 (Y.T. Terr. Ct.), Lilles C.J.T.C.

COMMUNITY SERVICE. "... [A]n alternative to a custodial sentence in those cases where the public interest does not demand that the offender should be imprisoned. It allows the offender to continue to live in the community with his wife and family, supporting them by his normal work. It demonstrates to the offender that society is involved in his delinquency and that he has incurred a debt which can be repaid in some measure by work or service in the community...." *R. v. Jones* (1975), 25 C.C.C. (2d) 256 at 259 (Ont. G.S.P.), Stortini Co. Ct. J.

COMMUNITY SERVICE ORDER. An order requiring an offender to perform unpaid work in the community under supervision.

COMMUNITY STANDARD. 1. "... [C]oncerned not with what Canadians would not tolerate being exposed to themselves, but what they would not tolerate other Canadians being exposed to." *R. v. Butler* (1992), 70 C.C.C. (3d) 129 at 145, [1992] 2 W.W.R. 577, [1992] 1 S.C.R. 452, 11 C.R. (4th) 137, 134 N.R. 81, 8 C.R.R. (2d) 1, 89 D.L.R. (4th) 449, 78 Man. R. (2d) 1, 16 W.A.C. 1, Sopinka J. (Lamer C.J.C., La Forest, Cory, McLachlin, Stevenson and Iacobucci JJ. concurring). 2. "... [A]re not set by those of lowest taste or interest. Nor are they set exclusively by those of rigid, austere, conservative, or puritan taste and habit of mind. Something approaching a general average of community thinking and feeling has to be discovered.... Community standards must be contemporary...." *R. v. Dominion News & Gifts Ltd.* (1963), 40 C.R. 109 at 126, 42 W.W.R. 65, [1963] 2 C.C.C. 103 (Man. C.A.), Freedman J.A. (dissenting).

COMMUTATION. *n.* 1. Conversion. 2. Reduction of a punishment or penalty. 3. Change to the right to receive a gross or fixed payment from the right to receive a periodic or variable payment.

COMMUTED. *adj.* Of a sentence or penalty, changed from greater to lesser.

COMMUTED VALUE. In relation to benefits that a person has a present or future entitlement to receive, the actuarial present value of those benefits determined, as of the time in question, on the basis of actuarial assumptions and methods that are adequate and appropriate and in accordance with generally accepted actuarial principles.

COMPANION. *n.* The title granted certain members of honorary orders.

COMPANY. *n.* 1. An association of people formed to carry on some business or undertaking in the association's name. 2. Any body corporate. 3. A body corporate with share capital. 4. An entity distinct and separate in law from its individual shareholders or members. H. Sutherland, D.B. Horsley & J.M. Edmiston, eds., *Fraser's Handbook on Canadian Company Law*, 7th ed. (Toronto: Carswell, 1985) at 1. See AMALGAMATED ~; CANADIAN ~; CHARTERED ~; CLOSE ~; CLOSED ~; CONSTRAINED-SHARE ~; DOMINION ~; EXTRA-PROVINCIAL ~; FEDERAL ~; FOREIGN ~; GUARANTEE ~; HOLDING ~; INVESTMENT ~; JOINT STOCK ~; PARENT ~.

COMPANY-DOMINATED UNION. A union created with employer support or controlled by the employer.

COMPANY LIMITED BY GUARANTEE. A company having the liability of its members limited by the memorandum to the amount that the members may respectively thereby undertake to contribute to the assets of the company in the event of its being wound up. *Companies Act*, R.S.A. 1980, c. C-20, s. 1.

COMPANY LIMITED BY SHARES. A company having the liability of its members limited to the amount, if any, unpaid on the shares respectively held by them. *Companies Act*, R.S.A. 1980, c. C-20, s. 1.

COMPANY UNION. 1. A union the membership of which is limited to one company. 2. A union dominated by an employer.

COMPELLABILITY. *n.* Any person can be called upon and must give evidence unless an exception can be shown. P.K. McWilliams, *Canadian Criminal Evidence*, 3d ed. (Aurora: Canada Law Book, 1988) at 34-22.

COMPELLABLE. *adj.* Required by law to give evidence. S. Mitchell, P.J. Richardson & D.A. Thomas, eds., *Archbold Pleading, Evidence and Practice in Criminal Cases*, 43d ed. (London: Sweet & Maxwell, 1988) at 461.

COMPELLED. *adj.* "[In s. 11(c) of the Charter] . . . indicates to me that the section is referring to a legal compulsion forcing an accused to give evidence in proceedings brought against him or her. The tactical obligation felt by the accused will no doubt increase with the strength of the Crown's case, but it remains a tactical and not a legal compulsion. The decision whether or not to testify remains with the accused free of any legal compulsion." *R. v. Boss* (1988), 42 C.R.R. 166 at 182, 30 O.A.C. 184, 68 C.R. (3d) 123, 46 C.C.C. (3d) 523 (C.A.), the court per Cory J.A.

COMPELLING PRESUMPTION. Facts sufficient to require that a given conclusion be drawn from them. J.G. Fleming, *The Law of Torts*, 8th ed. (Sydney: Law Book, 1992) at 323.

COMPENSATION. *n.* 1. ". . . [A]n equitable monetary remedy which is available when the equitable remedies of restitution and account are not appropriate. By analogy with restitution, it attempts to restore to the plaintiff what has been lost as a result of the breach, . . ." *Canson Enterprises Ltd. v. Boughton & Co.* (1991), 9 C.C.L.T. (2d) 1 at 41, [1991] 1 W.W.R. 245, 61 B.C.L.R. (2d) 1, 85 D.L.R. (4th) 129, 131 N.R. 321, 43 E.T.R. 201, 39 C.P.R. (3d) 449, [1991] 3 S.C.R. 534, 6 B.C.A.C. 1, 3 W.A.C. 1, McLachlin J. (Lamer C.J.C. and L'Heureux-Dubé J. concurring). 2. A rate, remuneration, reimbursement or consideration of any kind paid, payable, promised, demanded or received, directly or indirectly. 3. The total amount of money or value that is required to be paid in respect of land expropriated. 4. ". . . [T]he owner [of land taken] is made 'economically whole'. . . ." *British Columbia (Minister of Highways) v. Richland Estates Ltd.* (1973), 4 L.C.R. 85 at 86 (B.C. C.A.), Farris C.J.B.C. 5. ". . . [T]he indemnity which the statute [Exchequer Court Act, R.S.C. 1906, c. 140] provides to the owners of lands which are compulsorily taken in, or injuriously affected by, the exercise of statutory powers." *John Pigott & Son v. R.* (1916), 53 S.C.R. 626 at 627, 32 D.L.R. 461, Fitzpatrick C.J. See CRIMINAL INJURIES ~; WORKERS' ~.

COMPENSATION OF VICTIMS OF CRIME. Benefits provided by the government to victims of crime in the form of ex gratia payments. J.G. Fleming, *The Law of Torts*, 8th ed. (Sydney: Law Book, 1992) at 36.

COMPENSATION ORDER. A court by which a person is convicted or discharged may make an order requiring that person to pay compensation for any loss or damage to property resulting from the offence.

COMPENSATION PLAN. The provisions, however established, for the determination and administration and implementation of compensation, and includes such provisions contained in a

COMPLIANCE ORDER

collective agreement or established bilaterally between an employer and an employee, unilaterally by an employer of an employee, established by an arbitrator or an arbitration board or by or pursuant to an enactment.

COMPETENCY. *n.* Ability to understand the nature of an oath is the basic test of a person's competency to testify. P.K. McWilliams, *Canadian Criminal Evidence*, 3d ed. (Aurora: Canada Law Book, 1988) at 34-15.

COMPETENT. *adj.* 1. Legally allowed to give evidence during a trial. 2. Having adequate skill and knowledge. 3. ". . . '[O]f sound mind, memory and understanding' . . ." *McHugh v. Dooley* (1903), 10 B.C.R. 537 at 546 (S.C.), Martin J. See MENTALLY ~.

COMPETENT AUTHORITY. A person or body authorized by statute to perform the act or carry out the function in question.

COMPETENT JURISDICTION. See COURT OF ~.

COMPETITION. *n.* A situation when two or more businesses seek customers in the same marketplace. See FREE ~.

COMPLAINANT. *n.* 1. The victim of an alleged offence. *Criminal Code*, R.S.C. 1985, c. C-46, s. 2. 2. A person who lodges or files a formal complaint.

COMPLAINT. *n.* 1. "In a rape case, . . . any statement made by the alleged victim which, given circumstances of the case, will, if believed, be of some probative value in negating the adverse conclusions the trier of fact could draw as regards her credibility had she been silent." *R. v. Timm* (1981), 21 C.R. (3d) 209 at 229, [1981] 2 S.C.R. 315, 28 C.R. (3d) 133, [1981] 5 W.W.R. 577, 37 N.R. 204, 29 A.R. 509, 59 C.C.C. (2d) 396, 124 D.L.R. (3d) 582, the court per Lamer J. 2. An allegation or allegations, made orally or in writing by a member of the public, concerning misconduct of a public officer or of a contravention or violation of a statute.

COMPLETE. *v.* To finish.

COMPLETE. *adj.* Finished; entire.

COMPLETED. *adj.* Whenever used with reference to a contract for an improvement, means substantial performance, not necessarily total performance. *Builders Lien Act*, R.S.B.C. 1979, c. 40, s. 1.

COMPLETED CONTRACT METHOD. "The completed contract or substantially completed contract method [of accounting] recognizes profit only when the contract has been completed or substantially completed. The completed or substantially completed contract method has the advantage that costs are known or virtually known at the time the profit is taken." *Toromont Industrial Holdings Ltd. v. Thorne, Gunn, Helliwell & Christenson* (1975), 23 C.P.R. (2d) 59 at 77, 10 O.R. (2d) 65, 62 D.L.R. (3d) 225 (H.C.), Holland J.

COMPLETION. *n.* Full performance of a contract. *Lambton (County) v. Canadian Comstock Co.* (1959), 21 D.L.R. (2d) 689 at 695, [1960] S.C.R. 86, the court per Judson J. See CERTIFICATE OF ~.

COMPLETION BOND. See PERFORMANCE BOND.

COMPLETION LOAN. The advance of the whole amount, minus costs, of a mortgage loan by a lender to a borrower when construction of the borrower's new building is completed, the lender has inspected the building and is satisfied. D.J. Donahue & P.D. Quinn, *Real Estate Practice in Ontario*, 4th ed. (Toronto: Butterworths, 1990) at 224.

COMPLETION OF THE CONTRACT. Substantial performance, not necessarily total performance, of the contract. *Mechanics' Lien acts*.

COMPLIANCE. See SUBSTANTIAL ~.

COMPLIANCE ORDER. Either an order, like a quia timet order or order for specific performance, that someone take positive action, or an order, like an injunction, that certain conduct be stopped. D.J.M. Brown & D.M. Beatty, *Canadian Labour Arbitration*, 3d ed. (Aurora: Canada Law Book, 1988-) at 2-34.

COMPLICITY. *n.* Being an accomplice; being involved in crime or conspiracy.

COMPLY. *v.* To conform; yield; accept.

COMPOSITION. *n.* 1. An arrangement for the payment of debts. 2. Refers to the total number of judges of a court and number of judges who must be drawn from each different region. P.W. Hogg, *Constitutional Law of Canada*, 3d ed. (Toronto: Carswell, 1992) at 82.

COMPOS MENTIS. [L.] Sound mind.

COMPOUND. *v.* 1. To compromise; to effect a composition with a creditor. 2. To combine; to unite.

COMPOUNDING AN INDICTABLE OFFENCE. Prohibited by s. 141 of the Criminal Code, R.S.C. 1985, c. C-46, it consists of, in return for valuable consideration, the concealment of criminal activity. It also includes the agreement to obtain or receive valuable consideration in return for compounding or concealing an indictable offence. Watt & Fuerst, *The Annotated 1995 Tremeear's Criminal Code* (Toronto: Carswell, 1994) at 230.

COMPOUND INTEREST. 1. Interest charged on interest. 2. "... [A]t periodic intervals unpaid interest is added to unpaid principal, and interest then begins to accrue on the aggregate sum ... To compound, the first overdue instalment is added to the principal, and the new amount ... commences to bear interest." *Elman v. Conto* (1978), 82 D.L.R. (3d) 742 at 747, 18 O.R. (2d) 449 (C.A.), the court per Arnup J.A.

COMPREHENSIVE COVERAGE. "... [A] form of automobile insurance that pays for loss or damage to the insured vehicle caused otherwise than by collision...." *Turner v. Co-operative Fire & Casualty Co.* (1983), 1 C.C.L.I. 1 at 7, [1983] I.L.R. 1-1678, 147 D.L.R. (3d) 342, 58 N.S.R. (2d) 1, 123 A.P.R. 1 (C.A.), Macdonald J.A. (Morrison J.A. concurring).

COMPROMISE. *n.* 1. A prospective litigant refrains from taking an action in return for the intended defendant's promise; or an action already commenced that is settled by such an agreement. G.H.L. Fridman, *The Law of Contract in Canada*, 2d ed. (Toronto: Carswell, 1986) at 85. 2. An arrangement between a company and its members or creditors with any class of shareholders affecting their rights. H. Sutherland, D.B. Horsley & J.M. Edmiston, eds., *Fraser's Handbook on Canadian Company Law*, 7th ed. (Toronto: Carswell, 1985) at 497.

COMP. TRIB. *abbr.* Competition Tribunal.

COMPTROLLER. *n.* One who examines the accounts of collectors of public money. See CONTROLLER.

COMPULSION. *n.* 1. Duress; force. 2. An integral part of duress. Anything which makes one person agree to another's demand because the other person's statements or conduct are so overbearing that the first person has no choice but to pay. G.H.L. Fridman, *Restitution*, 2d ed. (Toronto: Carswell, 1992) at 112.

COMPULSORY. *adj.* Forced; coerced.

COMPULSORY ARBITRATION. Arbitration that is required by law.

COMPULSORY PURCHASE. To acquire land for public purposes.

COMPULSORY UNIONISM. Employment conditional on union membership.

COMPUTER L. *abbr.* Computer Law.

COMPUTER PROGRAM. 1. Data representing instructions or statements that, when executed in a computer system, causes the computer system to perform a function. *Criminal Code*, R.S.C. 1985, c. C-46, s. 342.1(2), as added by *Criminal Law Amendment Act*, R.S.C. 1985 (1st Supp.), c. 27, s. 45. 2. A set of instructions or statements, expressed, fixed, embodied or stored in any manner, that is to be used directly or indirectly in a computer in order to bring about a specific result. *Copyright Act*, R.S.C. 1985 (4th Supp.), c. 10, s. 1(3).

COMPUTER SERVICE. Includes data processing and the storage or retrieval of data. *Criminal Code*, R.S.C. 1985, c. C-46, s. 342.1(2) as added by *Criminal Law Amendment Act*, R.S.C. 1985 (1st Supp.), c. 27, s. 45.

COMPUTER SYSTEM. A device that, or a group of interconnected or related devices one or more of which, (a) contains computer programs or other data, and (b) pursuant to computer programs, (i) performs logic and control, and (ii) may perform any other function. *Criminal Code*, R.S.C. 1985, c. C-46, s. 342.1(2) as added by *Criminal Law Amendment Act*, R.S.C. 1985 (1st Supp.), c. 27, s. 45.

CON. *adj.* Short form for confidence, as a "con game".

CON. *prep.* [L.] With.

CON. *pref.* Together.

CONCEAL. *v.* To hide, cover, keep from view; to prevent discovery.

CONCEALED. *adj.* 1. "[In R. v. Lemire (1980), 18 C.R. (3d) 166 at 170 (B.C. Co. Ct.)] Melvin Co. Ct. J. (as he was then) ... reviewed the authorities and dictionary definitions of the word 'concealed' [as used in s. 87 of the Criminal Code, R.S.C. 1970, c. C-34]: 'In my view, the definition of the word "conceal" clearly demonstrates that some purpose is required in addition to the object being merely not capable of being seen. To conceal, in a sense of keeping from the knowledge or observation of others or hide, imports into this offence regarding the act of concealment a mental element on the part of the accused. ...' ... The mens rea articulated by Mr. Justice Cavanaugh [in R. v. Coughlan (1974), 27 C.R.N.S. 195 at 195 (Alta. Q.B.)] for a proper interpretation of the word 'concealed' was[:] 'In my view, these definitions clearly impart the idea of an intentional putting out of sight for the purpose of being out of sight.' " *R. v. Felawka* (1991), 9 C.R. (4th) 291 at 297, 303, 68 C.C.C. (3d) 481, 3 B.C.A.C. 241, 7

W.A.C. 241, Toy J.A. (McEachern C.J.B.C., Wallace and Proudfoot JJ.A. concurring). 2. Rendered permanently inaccessible by the structure or finish of a building. *Power Corporation Act*, R.R.O. 1980, Reg. 794, s. 0.

CONCEALED DANGER. A deceptively safe appearance which hides a potential cause of injury. J.V. DiCastri, *Occupiers' Liability* (Vancouver: Burroughs/Carswell, 1980) at 97.

CONCEALING BODY OF CHILD. It is an offence to dispose of the dead body of a child with intent to conceal the fact that its mother has been delivered of it whether it died before, during or after birth. *Criminal Code*, R.S.C. 1985, c. C-46, s. 243.

CONCEALMENT. *n.* In insurance law describes the situation when an applicant for insurance fails to inform the insurer of a material fact which is known to the applicant. M.G. Baer & J.A. Rendall, eds., *Cases on the Canadian Law of Insurance*, 4th ed. (Toronto: Carswell, 1988) at 343.

CONCEALMENT OF BIRTH. See CONCEALING BODY OF CHILD.

CONCEALS. *v.* "... [A]s used in s. 350(a)(ii) [of the Criminal Code, R.S.C. 1970, c. C-34] contemplates some positive conduct on the part of the debtor [to conceal assets] as opposed to a mere failure to disclose the existence of the property, even though under a duty to do so [under the Bankruptcy Act, R.S.C. 1970, c. B-3, ss. 129 and 132]." *R. v. Goulis* (1981), 125 D.L.R. (3d) 137 at 142, 33 O.R. (2d) 55, 20 C.R. (3d) 360, 37 C.B.R. (N.S.) 290, 60 C.C.C. (2d) 347 (C.A.), the court per Martin J.A. See CONCEAL.

CONCEPTION. *n.* The beginning of pregnancy; fertilization of the ovum by spermatozoon.

CONCERN. *v.* To relate, be of interest or importance to.

CONCERNING. *adj.* Relating to; affecting.

CONCERT. *n.* To act in concert is to act together to bring about a planned result.

CONCILIATION. *n.* The process by which a third party attempts to assist an employer and a trade union to achieve a collective agreement.

CONCILIATION BOARD. A board established under labour legislation for the investigation and conciliation of a dispute.

CONCILIATION OFFICER. A person whose duties include the conciliation of disputes and who is under the control and direction of the Minister of Labour or other Minister.

CONCILIATOR. *n.* A person appointed to assist the parties to collective bargaining in reaching agreement.

CONCLUDE. *v.* To finish; to bar or estop.

CONCLUDED CONTRACT. ". . . [O]ne which settles everything that is necessary to be settled, and leaves nothing still to be settled by agreement between the parties. Of course, it may leave something which still has to be determined, but then that determination must be a determination which does not depend on the agreement between the parties." *May & Butcher Ltd. v. R.,* [1929] All E.R. Rep. 679 at 683-84 (U.K. H.L.), Viscount Dunedin.

CONCLUSION. *n.* 1. The finish, end, summation. 2. A rule of law or an irrefutable presumption.

CONCLUSION OF FACT. An inference or result drawn from evidence.

CONCLUSION OF LAW. A finding of law; a statement of law applicable to a matter.

CONCLUSIVE. *adj.* Final, decisive, clear.

CONCLUSIVE PRESUMPTION. A presumption which cannot be overcome by evidence or argument. May be indicated by the word "deemed" in a statute. *Gray v. Kerslake* (1957), 11 D.L.R. (2d) 225 at 239, [1958] S.C.R. 3, Cartwright J.; *R. v. Johnson* (1976), 37 C.R.N.S. 370 at 373 (B.C. C.A.), McFarlane J.A. (Seaton and McIntyre JJ.A. concurring).

CONCORD. *n.* An agreement to settle or refrain from bringing an action.

CONCUR. *v.* 1. To agree, consent. 2. ". . . [A]s used in [s. 4 of the Trade-unions Act, R.S.B.C. 1960, c. 384] means 'to combine in action' or to 'co-operate with' . . ." *Perini Pacific Ltd. v. I.U.O.E., Local 115* (1961), 36 W.W.R. 49 at 66, 28 D.L.R. (2d) 727 (B.C. S.C.), Monroe J.

CONCURRENCE. *n.* Agreement, consent.

CONCURRENT. *adj.* Contemporaneous.

CONCURRENT CONDITION. Describes promises made by both parties to a contract where each party's responsibility depends on the readiness and willingness of the other to perform. The Sale of Goods acts provide that delivery of the goods and payment of the price are concurrent conditions. The buyer must be ready and willing to pay the price in exchange for the goods and the seller must be ready and willing to give possession of the goods in exchange for the price.

CONCURRENT JURISDICTION. Two or more courts or tribunals having authority to try or hear the same subject matter.

CONCURRENTLY. *adv.* At the same time, contemporaneously.

CONCURRENT SENTENCE. Two or more terms of imprisonment served simultaneously.

CONCURRENT WRIT. A duplicate of an original writ. See ALIAS WRIT.

CONCURRING OPINION. The decision of a judge agreeing in the decision though not necessarily the reasons of another judge or judges.

CONDEMN. *v.* 1. To find guilty. 2. To sentence. 3. In admiralty law, to find that a vessel is a prize. 4. To expropriate. 5. To declare a building unfit for use or occupation.

CONDEMNATION. *n.* 1. An order that a building is unfit for use or occupation. 2. Expropriation. 3. A judgment that a prize or captured vessel has been lawfully captured.

CONDITION. *n.* 1. A provision or declaration in which an event must happen before a right may exist. 2. "... [A] contractual term which the parties intended to be fundamental to its performance." *Jorian Properties Ltd. v. Zellenrath* (1984), 26 B.L.R. 276 at 285, 4 O.A.C. 107, 46 O.R. (2d) 775, 26 B.C.L.R. 276, 10 D.L.R. (4th) 458 (C.A.), Blair J.A. (dissenting). 3. "... [O]f the parties [in s. 11(1) of the Divorce Act, R.S.C. 1970, c. D-8] includes their ages; their states of health, both physical and mental; their backgrounds; their education; their attitude toward family; their motives for seeking custody; their comparative abilities to provide psycological [sic], spiritual and emotional needs of the children; their respective modes of living; and so on." *Burgmaier v. Burgmaier* (1986), 50 R.F.L. (2d) 1 at 11, 46 Sask. R. 1 (C.A.), the court per Cameron J.A. See CONCURRENT ~; EXPRESS ~; IMPLIED ~; PRECEDENT ~; WORKING ~S.

CONDITIONAL. *adj.* Dependent upon, subject to.

CONDITIONAL ACCEPTANCE. The acceptor pays only when a condition stated in the bill is fulfilled. E.L.G. Tyler & N.E. Palmer, eds., *Crossley Vaines' Personal Property*, 5th ed. (London: Butterworths, 1973) at 236.

CONDITIONAL ADMISSIBILITY. See DE BENE ESSE.

CONDITIONAL APPEARANCE. 1. "Middleton J. in Wolsely Tool & Motor Car v. Jackson Potts & Co. (1914), 6 O.W.N. 109 (H.C.), described the conditional appearance as follows: 'A conditional appearance is not intended to be a provisional appearance, as in England, but a form of appearance to be used where for some reason it is not convenient to determine the question whether the case can be brought within Rule 25 until the hearing of the action.'" *Sea Electronics Aids Inc. v. Kaytronics Ltd.* (1979), 11 C.P.C. 275 at 277, 24 O.R. (2d) 38 (H.C.), Grange J. 2. A motion filed by a defendant,

with leave of the Court, to object to an irregularity in the commencement of the proceeding or the court's jurisdiction. D. Sgayias *et al.*, *Federal Court Practice 1988* (Toronto: Carswell, 1987) at 372.

CONDITIONAL BENEFIT. A benefit which may be received only if the potential recipient is not awarded damages for the same loss which the benefit is supposed to compensate. K.D. Cooper-Stephenson & I.B. Saunders, *Personal Injury Damages in Canada* (Toronto: Carswell, 1981) at 488.

CONDITIONAL DISCHARGE. 1. Disposition of a criminal matter by which a person is deemed not to be convicted after serving a period of probation. 2. "... [P]uts the accused conditionally at liberty, ..." *Ahluwalia, Re* (1989), 25 F.T.R. 208 at 217, [1989] 3 F.C. 209, Muldoon J.

CONDITIONAL LICENCE. A licence authorizing an activity prior to the issue of a final licence.

CONDITIONAL OFFER. 1. An offer which is not final until a condition is fulfilled. 2. A proposal to settle a strike with reservations.

CONDITIONAL SALE. 1. A contract for the sale of goods under which possession is to be delivered to a buyer and the property in the goods is to vest in her or him at a subsequent time on payment of the whole or part of the price or on the performance of any other condition. 2. A contract for the hiring of goods under which it is agreed that the hirer will become or have the option of becoming the owner of the goods on compliance with the terms of the contract.

CONDITIONAL WILL. A will which takes effect only in the event of the testator's death in a certain way, such as by accident, or during a certain period, such as on a trip; the will does not take effect unless the specified condition is met. T. Sheard, R. Hull & M.M.K. Fitzpatrick, *Canadian Forms of Wills*, 4th ed. (Toronto: Carswell, 1982) at 139.

CONDITION OF EMPLOYMENT.
1. A qualification or circumstance required for employment. 2. All matters and circumstances in any way affecting employers and employees in respect of the employment relationship. *Employment Standards Act*, S.B.C. 1980, c. 10, s. 1.

CONDITION OF SALE. A term upon which an interest is to be sold by auction or tender.

CONDITION PRECEDENT. ". . . [A]n external condition upon which the existence of the obligation depends. . . . a future uncertain event, the happening of which depends entirely upon the will of a third party . . ." *Turney v. Zhilka*, [1959] S.C.R. 578 at 583, Judson J. See TRUE ~.

CONDITION SUBSEQUENT. 1. A term of an agreement requiring that the agreement be valid and binding unless and until a specified event or occurrence happens. G.H.L. Fridman, *Sale of Goods in Canada*, 3d ed. (Toronto: Carswell, 1986) at 28. 2. After a gift is made, a condition subsequent may operate to defeat the gift. R. Megarry & H.W.R. Wade, *The Law of Real Property*, 5th ed. (London: Stevens, 1984) at cxxiv.

CONDO. *abbr.* Condominium.

CONDOMINIUM. *n.* A system of property ownership of multi-unit housing or commercial projects in which each unit owner is a tenant-in-common of the common elements and each unit is owned separately in fee simple. B.J. Reiter, B.N. McLellan & P.M. Perell, *Real Estate Law*, 4th ed. (Toronto: Emond Montgomery, 1992) at 549-50.

CONDOMINIUM UNIT. A bounded space in a building designated or described as a separate unit on a registered condominium or strata lot plan or description, or a similar plan or description registered pursuant to the laws of a province, and intended for human habitation and includes any interest in land appertaining to ownership of the unit. *National Housing Act*, R.S.C. 1985, c. N-11, s. 2.

CONDONATION. *n.* 1. Acquiescence, forgiveness. 2. ". . . [T]he reinstatement in his or her former marital position of a spouse who has committed a matrimonial wrong of which all material facts are known to the other spouse, with the intention of forgiving and remitting the wrong, on condition that the spouse whose wrong is so condoned does not thenceforward commit any further matrimonial offence." *MacDougall v. MacDougall*, [1970] 3 R.F.L. 175 at 176 (Ont. C.A.). 3. "In McIntyre v. Hockin (1889), 16 O.A.R. 498 [(C.A.)], Maclennan J.A., speaking for the Court, said at pp. 501-502: 'If [the employer] retains the servant in his employment for any considerable time after discovering his fault, that is condonation, and he cannot afterwards dismiss for that fault without anything new. No doubt the employer ought to have a reasonable time to determine what to do, to consider whether he will dismiss or not, or to look for another servant. So, also, he must have knowledge of the nature and extent of the fault, for he cannot forgive or condone matters of which he is not fully informed. Further, condonation is subject to an implied condition of future good conduct, and whenever any new misconduct occurs, the old offences may be invoked and may be put on the scale against the offender as cause for dismissal.' " *Nossal v. Better Business Bureau of Metropolitan Toronto* (1985), 12 C.C.E.L. 85 at 89, 51 O.R. (2d) 279, 19 D.L.R. (4th) 547, 9 O.A.C. 184 (C.A.), the court per Zuber J.A.

CONDUCT. *v.* 1. To manage or operate. *Saskatchewan Telecommunications v. Central Asphalt Ltd.* (1988), 70 Sask. R. 235 at 239, [1988] 6 W.W.R. 459 (Q.B.), Wright J. 2. To lead or guide. *R. v. Mackenzie* (1982), 135 D.L.R. (3d) 374 at 379, 36 O.R. (2d) 562, 66 C.C.C. (2d) 528 (C.A.), the court per Cory J.A.

CONDUCT. *n.* 1. Any act or omission. 2. Personal behaviour. 3. ". . . [I]ncludes the role of the parties in the break-up of the home; their behaviour in relation to one another, the children, and the family, both before and after the break-up; such agreements, if any, as they may have arrived at; and such other conduct tending to demonstrate their characters, personalities and temperaments, and other matters bearing upon their abilities to rear the children." *Burgmaier v. Burgmaier* (1986), 50 R.F.L. (2d) 1 at 10, 46 Sask. R. 1 (C.A.), the court per Cameron J.A. See EXCUSABLE ~; MIS~.

CONDUCT MONEY. 1. Fees payable to witnesses to defray expenses of coming to testify. 2. Attendance money.

CONE OF SILENCE. ". . . Knowledge of confidential matters is therefore imputed to other members of the firm. This latter presumption can, however, in some circumstances, be rebutted. The usual methods used to rebut the presumptions are the setting up of a . . . 'cone of silence' . . . at the time that the possibility of the unauthorized communication of confidential information arises . . . A 'cone of silence' is achieved by means of a solemn undertaking not to disclose by the tainted solicitor." *MacDonald Estate v. Martin* (1990), 48 C.P.C. (2d) 113 at 126, [1991] 1 W.W.R. 705, 121 N.R. 1, 77 D.L.R. (4th) 249, 70 Man. R. (2d) 241, [1990] 3 S.C.R. 1235, Sopinka J. (Dickson C.J.C., La Forest and Gonthier JJ. concurring). See CHINESE WALL.

CONF. COMMEM. MEREDITH. *abbr.* Conférences commémoratives Meredith (Meredith Memorial Lectures).

CONFEDERATION. *n.* 1. A loose association of states in which the state governments take precedence over the central government. P.W. Hogg, *Constitutional Law of Canada*, 3d ed. (Toronto: Carswell, 1992) at 101. 2. A league of nations or states.

CONFER. *v.* Grant or bestow. *Minister of National Revenue v. Pillsbury Holdings Ltd.*, [1964] C.T.C. 294 at 300, [1965] 1 Ex. C.R. 676, 64 D.T.C. 5184, Cattanach J.

CONFERENCE. *n.* A meeting of persons for consideration of matters, exchange of opinions. See FIRST MINISTERS' ~; PRE-TRIAL ~.

CONFESS. *v.* To admit; to concede.

CONFESSION. *n.* 1. An admission of guilt. 2. In civil procedure, a formal admission. 3. Formerly, a plea of guilty. F. Kaufman, *The Admissibility of Confessions*, 3d ed. (Toronto: Carswell, 1980) at 1. 4. ". . . [S]tatements made by an accused to a person in authority; . . ." *R. v. Rothman* (1981), 20 C.R. (3d) 97 at 122, [1981] 1 S.C.R. 640, 59 C.C.C. (2d) 30, 121 D.L.R. (3d) 578, 35 N.R. 485, Estey J. (dissenting) (Laskin C.J.C. concurring). 5. A statement made by an accused person, whether before or after he is accused of an offence, that is completely or partially self-incriminating with respect to the offence of which he is accused. *Military Rules of Evidence*, C.R.C., c. 1049, s. 2. See EXCULPATORY ~; INCULPATORY ~.

CONFESSION AND AVOIDANCE. 1. A pleading in which, though the defendant admits the plaintiff's allegation, the defendant then sets out other facts which deprive the allegation of the legal consequences for which the plaintiff argued. G.D. Watson & C. Perkins, eds., *Holmested & Watson: Ontario Civil Procedure* (Toronto: Carswell, 1984) at 25-28. 2. ". . . [A] submission [by the defendant] that if the plaintiff's allegations are true there are facts which provide a legal justification for the defendant's conduct . . ." *Royal Bank v. Rizkalla* (1984), 50 C.P.C. 292 at 295, 59 B.C.L.R. 324 (S.C.), McLachlin J.

CONFIDENCE. *n.* 1. Trust, reliance. 2. A communication made in reliance on another's discretion. See BREACH OF ~.

CONFIDENCE GAME. Obtaining money or property by a trick or device.

CONFIDENTIAL. *adj.* Intended to be kept secret.

CONFIDENTIAL INFORMATION. ". . . [T]he statement of Lord Greene in Saltman Engineering Co. v. Campbell Engineering Coy. (1948), 65 R.P.C.

R.P.C. 203 ... at 215 ... (C.A.) is apposite: 'The information, to be confidential, must, I apprehend, apart from contract, have the necessary quality of confidence about it, namely, it must not be something which is public property and public knowledge. On the other hand, it is perfectly possible to have a confidential document, be it a formula, a plan, a sketch, or something of that kind, which is the result of work done by the maker upon materials which may be available for the use of anybody; but what makes it confidential is the fact that the maker of the document has used his brain and thus produced a result which can only be produced by somebody who goes through the same process.'" *International Corona Resources Ltd. v. Lac Minerals Ltd.* (1989), 44 B.L.R. 1 at 77, [1989] 2 S.C.R. 574, 26 C.P.R. (3d) 97, 69 O.R. (2d) 287, 61 D.L.R. (4th) 14, 6 R.P.R. (2d) 1, 35 E.T.R. 12, 101 N.R. 239, 36 O.A.C. 57, Sopinka J. (dissenting) (McIntyre and Wilson JJ. concurring in part).

CONFIDENTIALITY. *n.* "... There are four fundamental conditions: (1) The communications must originate in a confidence that they will not be disclosed. (2) The element of confidentiality must be essential to the full and satisfactory maintenance of the relation between the parties. (3) The relation must be one which in the opinion of the community ought to be sedulously fostered. (4) The injury that would inure to the relation by the disclosure of the communications must be greater than the benefit thereby gained for the correct disposal of the litigation." *United Services Funds (Trustees of) v. Richardson Greenshields of Canada Ltd.* (1988), 24 B.C.L.R. (2d) 41 at 43 (S.C.), MacKinnon J.

CONFIDENTIAL RELATION. A relation of trust which gives rise to an expectation that communications will be held in confidence; fiduciary relation.

CONFINEMENT. *n.* "The essential ingredients of the offence may then be taken to be: (a) physical restraint; (b) contrary to the wishes of the person restrained; (c) to which the victim submits unwillingly; (d) depriving him of his liberty to move from one place to another." *R. v. Moore* (1989), 51 C.C.C. (3d) 566 at 572, 73 C.R. (3d) 120, 78 Nfld. & P.E.I.R. 284, 244 A.P.R. 284 (P.E.I. T.D.), McQuaid J.

CONFIRM. *v.* 1. To ratify; to make firm or certain; to give approval. 2. Approve. *R. v. Briardale Investments Ltd.* (1964), 50 W.W.R. 517 at 530, 45 C.R. 358, [1965] 2 C.C.C. 273, 48 D.L.R. (2d) 315 (Man. Q.B.), Smith J. 3. "... '[R]evive' ... By confirming the will of 1909, the testator revived it and made it a new will of the date of the codicil – the last will of the testator." *Findlay v. Pae* (1916), 37 O.L.R. 318 at 325, 31 D.L.R. 281 (H.C.), Latchford J.

CONFIRMATION. *n.* 1. Formal approval. 2. Ratification; a document which validates an agreement.

CONFIRMATION ORDER. 1. A confirmation order made under the Reciprocal Enforcement of Maintenance Orders Act or under the corresponding enactment of a reciprocating state. 2. An order of a court confirming the order of another court.

CONFISCATE. *v.* To seize property; to forfeit property.

CONFISCATION. *n.* 1. Seizure or forfeiture of property. 2. "... [T]he bringing of something into the treasury of a Government, ..." *R. v. Lane,* [1937] 1 D.L.R. 212 at 214, 67 C.C.C. 273, 11 M.P.R. 232 (N.B. C.A.), Baxter C.J. (Grimmer C.J. concurring).

CONFLICT OF INTEREST. 1. "... [T]he test must be such that the public represented by the reasonably informed person would be satisfied that no use of confidential information would occur.... Typically, these cases require two questions to be answered: (1) Did the lawyer receive confidential information attributable to a solicitor-and-client relationship relevant to the matter at hand? (2) Is there a risk that it will be used to the prejudice of the client?" *MacDonald Estate v. Martin*

(1990), 48 C.P.C. (2d) 113 at 137, [1991] 1 W.W.R. 705, 121 N.R. 1, 77 D.L.R. (4th) 249, 70 Man. R. (2d) 241, [1990] 3 S.C.R. 1235, Sopinka J. (Dickson C.J.C., La Forest and Gonthier JJ. concurring). 2. "It is not part of the job description that municipal councillors be personally interested in matters that come before them beyond the interest that they have in common with the other citizens in the municipality. Where such an interest is found, both at common law and by statute, a member of council is disqualified if the interest is so related to the exercise of public duty that a reasonably well-informed person would conclude that the interest might influence the exercise of that duty. This is commonly referred to as a conflict of interest . . ." *Old St. Boniface Residents Assn. v. Winnipeg (City)* (1990), 75 D.L.R. (4th) 385 at 408, 46 Admin. L.R. 161, 2 M.P.L.R. (2d) 217, [1991] 2 W.W.R. 145, 116 N.R. 46, 69 Man. R. (2d) 134, [1990] 3 S.C.R. 1170, Sopinka J. (Wilson, Gonthier and McLachlin JJ. concurring). 3. ". . . [A] situation in which an employee engages in activities which are external and parallel to those he performs as part of his job, and which conflict or compete with the latter." *Canadian Imperial Bank of Commerce v. Boisvert* (1986), 13 C.C.E.L. 264 at 292, [1986] 2 F.C. 431, 68 N.R. 355 (C.A.), Marceau J.A. (Lacombe and MacGuigan JJ.A. concurring). 4. ". . . [P]ersonal interest sufficiently connected with his professional duties that there is a reasonable apprehension that the personal interest may influence the actual exercise of the professional responsibilities." *Cox v. College of Optometrists (Ontario)* (1988), 33 Admin. L.R. 287 at 298, 28 O.A.C. 337, 65 O.R. (2d) 461, 52 D.L.R. (4th) 298 (Div. Ct.), the court per Campbell J.

CONFLICT OF LAWS. 1. Private international law, the branch of law concerned with private relations which contain a foreign element. 2. The body of laws which each province has in common law and in statute to govern issues concerning extraterritoriality.

These issues are: (a) the provincial court's jurisdiction in cases in which facts or parties are outside the province, (b) the provincial court's recognition of judgments obtained in other jurisdictions, and (c) the choice of law in any case involving extraterritorial elements and over which the court has jurisidiction. P.W. Hogg, *Constitutional Law of Canada*, 3d ed. (Toronto: Carswell, 1992) at 327.

CONFORM. *v.* Comply. *Bourk v. Temple* (1990), 50 M.P.L.R. 125 at 132, 73 Alta. L.R. (2d) 302, 105 A.R. 61, [1990] 5 W.W.R. 87 (Q.B.), Conrad J.

CONFORMING USE. In zoning or planning, use of property which complies with restrictions of use in effect in respect of the property.

CONFORMITY. *n.* Correspondence in some respect; agreement.

CONFUSION. *n.* "If goods of different persons are so mingled that they cannot be separated, there is what in law is denominated confusion of property. . . ." *Lawrie v. Rathbun* (1876), 38 U.C.Q.B. 255 at 263 (C.A.), Harrison C.J. (Morrison and Wilson JJ.A. concurring).

CON GAME. See CONFIDENCE GAME.

CONJECTURE. *n.* "The dividing line between conjecture and inference is often a very difficult one to draw. A conjecture may be plausible but of no legal value, for its essence is that it is a mere guess. An inference in the legal sense, on the other hand, is a deduction from the evidence, and if it is a reasonable deduction it may have the validity of legal proof. The attribution of an occurrence to a cause is, I take it, always a matter of inference. . . ." *Jones v. Great Western Rwy. Co.* (1930), 47 T.L.R. 39 at 45 (U.K. H.L.), Lord Macmillan.

CONJOINTS. *n.* People married to one another.

CONJUGAL. *adj.* Related to the married or marriage-like state.

CONJUGAL RIGHTS. Each

spouse's right to the society, comfort and affection of the other spouse.

CONJUNCTIVE. *adj.* Joining two concepts.

CONNIVANCE. *n.* Culpable agreement to do wrong.

CONSANGUINITY. *n.* Relationship by descent: either collaterally, i.e. from a common ancestor or lineally, i.e. mother and daughter.

CONSCIENCE. *n.* "... [S]elf-judgement [sic] on the moral quality of one's conduct or the lack of it...." *MacKay v. Manitoba* (1985), 23 C.R.R. 8 at 11, [1986] 2 W.W.R. 367, 24 D.L.R. (4th) 587, 39 Man. R. (2d) 274 (C.A.), Twaddle J.A. (Philp J.A. concurring). See FREEDOM OF ~ AND RELIGION.

CONSCIENTIOUS OBJECTOR. A person who, on moral or religious grounds, thinks it wrong to resist force with force and to kill.

CONSCRIPTION. *n.* Compulsory enrolment in the military service.

CONSCRIPTIVE EVIDENCE. "... [R]efers to evidence which emanates from the accused following a violation of s. 10(b) of the [Charter]...." *R. v. Wise* (1992), 11 C.R. (4th) 253 at 265, [1992] 1 S.C.R. 527, 70 C.C.C. (3d) 193, 133 N.R. 161, 8 C.R.R. (2d) 53, 51 O.A.C. 351, Cory J. (Lamer C.J.C., Gonthier, Stevenson JJ. concurring).

CONSECUTIVE. *adj.* One after the other; following.

CONSECUTIVELY. *adv.* Following immediately upon. *R. v. Cadeddu* (1980), 19 C.R. (3d) 93 at 96, 57 C.C.C. (2d) 264 (Ont. C.A.), the court per Morden J.A.

CONSECUTIVE SENTENCES. One sentence follows another in time.

CONSEIL CAN. D. INT. *abbr.* Conseil canadien de droit international. Congrès. Travaux (Canadian Council of International Law. Conference. Proceedings).

CONSENSUS AD IDEM. [L. agreement to the same thing] The consent required for a contract to be binding.

CONSENT. *n.* Freely given agreement. See AGE OF ~; INFORMED ~.

CONSENT JUDGMENT. A judgment the terms of which are agreed to by the parties.

CONSEQUENTIAL DAMAGES. The loss which occurs indirectly from the act complained of.

CONSEQUENTLY. *adv.* "... [C]an, in the one instance, import an inevitable sequence of events, one necessarily flowing from, and as a direct result of, the other ... On the other hand, it may also import something which follows by logical inference." *Campbell v. Blackett* (1978), 80 D.L.R. (3d) 252 at 257, 13 Nfld. & P.E.I.R. 64, 29 A.P.R. 64 (P.E.I. C.A.), the court per McQuaid J.A.

CONSERVATION. *n.* 1. Includes the prevention of waste, improvident or uneconomic production or disposition of natural resources. 2. Rehabilitation or development.

CONSERVATOR. *n.* One who protects, preserves, or maintains.

CONSERVE. *v.* To keep; to save.

CONSIDER. *v.* To examine, inspect; to turn one's mind to.

CONSIDERATION. *n.* 1. In a contract, an interest, right, profit or benefit accrues to the one party while some detriment, forebearance, loss or responsibility is suffered or undertaken by the other party. G.H.L. Fridman, *The Law of Contract in Canada*, 2d ed. (Toronto: Carswell, 1986) at 75. 2. In a contract for the sale of goods, it is called the price and must be in money. G.H.L. Fridman, *Sale of Goods in Canada*, 3d ed. (Toronto: Carswell, 1986) at 42. 3. "... [U]sed to describe that which is given or promised in order to bring a binding contract into existence. It is also used, however, to describe the performance of the promise ..." *Kiss v. Palachik* (1983), 146 D.L.R. (3d) 385 at 393, [1983] 1 S.C.R. 623, 47 N.R. 148, 22 R.F.L. (2d) 225, 15 E.T.R. 129, the court per Wilson J. See ADEQUATE ~; EXECUTED ~; EXECUTORY ~; FU-

TURE ~; GOOD ~; PAST ~; PRESENT ~; VALUABLE ~.

CONSIDERED. *adj.* Determined; regarded.

CONSIGNEE. *n.* A person to whom the goods are sent.

CONSIGNMENT. *n.* 1. "In its simplest terms, ... the sending of goods to another. An arrangement whereby an owner sends goods to another on the understanding that such other will sell the goods to a third party and remit the proceeds to the owner after deducting his compensation for effecting the sale is an example of a consignment agreement." *Stephanian's Persian Carpets Ltd., Re* (1980), 34 C.B.R. (N.S.) 35 at 37, 1 P.P.S.A.C. 119 (Ont. S.C.), Saunders J. 2. The goods themselves.

CONSIGNOR. *n.* A person who consigns goods.

CONSIST. *v.* To be made up of.

CONSISTENT. *adj.* Harmonious; in agreement with.

CONSOL. *abbr.* Consolidated.

CONSOLIDATE. *v.* To combine, unite.

CONSOLIDATED FUND. The aggregate of all public money that is on hand and on deposit to the credit of a province.

CONSOLIDATED LOAN. A loan acquired for the purpose of consolidating liabilities.

CONSOLIDATED REVENUE FUND. 1. Aggregate of all public moneys that are on deposit at the credit of the Receiver General. *Financial Administration Act*, R.S.C. 1985, c. F-11, s. 2. 2. The aggregate of all public moneys that are on deposit at the credit of the Treasurer or in the name of any agency of the Crown approved by the Lieutenant Governor in Council. *Ministry of Treasury and Economics Act*, R.S.O. 1990, c. M.37, s. 1.

CONSOLIDATING STATUTE. A statute which draws together, with only minor amendments and improvements, all statutory provisions related to a par-

ticular topic into a single act. P.St.J. Langan, ed., *Maxwell on The Interpretation of Statutes*, 12th ed. (Bombay: N.M. Tripathi, 1976) at 20 and 21.

CONSOLIDATION. *n.* 1. In statute law, the uniting of many acts of Parliament into one. 2. When two or more mortgages are vested in one person, that person may not allow one mortgage to be redeemed unless the other or others are redeemed also. R. Megarry & H.W.R. Wade, *The Law of Real Property*, 5th ed. (London: Stevens, 1984) at 955.

CONSOLIDATION ACT. An act, usually with amendments, which repeals a number of earlier acts and includes, sometimes, some rules of the common law.

CONSOLIDATION OF ACTIONS. The combination of proceedings involving the same parties or issues.

CONSORTIUM. *n.* "The term 'consortium' is not susceptible of precise or complete definition but broadly speaking, companionship, love, affection, comfort, mutual services, sexual intercourse – all belonging to the marriage state – taken together make up what we refer to as consortium." *Kungl v. Schiefer*, [1961] O.R. 1 at 7 (C.A.), Schroeder J.A.

CONSPIRACY. *n.* 1. "A conspiracy consists not merely in the intention of two or more, but in the agreement of two or more to do an unlawful act, or to do a lawful act by unlawful means. So long as such a decision rests in intention only, it is not indictable. When two agree to carry it into effect, the very plot is an act in itself, and the act of each of the parties, promise against promise, actus contra actum, capable of being enforced if lawful, punishable if for a criminal object or for the use of criminal means." *Mulcahy v. R.* (1868), L.R. 3 H.L. 306 at 317, Willes J. 2. " ... [W]hereas the law of tort does not permit an action against an individual defendant who has caused injury to the plaintiff, the law of torts does recognize a claim against them in combination as the tort of conspiracy if: (1) whether the means used by the defendants are lawful or unlawful, the predominant purpose of the defendants' conduct is to cause injury to the plaintiff; or (2) where the conduct of the defendants is unlawful, the conduct is directed toward the plaintiff . . . and the defendants should know in the circumstances that injury to the plaintiff is likely to and does result. In situation (2) it is not necessary that the predominant purpose of the defendants' conduct be to cause injury to the plaintiff but, in the prevailing circumstances, it must be a constructive intent derived from the fact that the defendants should have known that injury to the plaintiff would ensue. In both situations, however, there must be actual damage suffered by the plaintiff." *Canada Cement LaFarge Ltd. v. British Columbia Lightweight Aggregate Ltd.* (1983), 21 B.L.R. 254 at 274, [1983] 1 S.C.R. 452, [1983] 6 W.W.R. 385, 24 C.C.L.T. 111, 72 C.P.R. (2d) 1, 145 D.L.R. (3d) 385, 47 N.R. 191, the court per Estey J. See CIVIL ~; CRIMINAL ~; SEDITIOUS ~.

CONSPIRATOR. *n.* A person who takes part in a conspiracy.

CONSPIRE. *v.* "The word 'conspire' derives from two Latin words, 'con' and 'spirare', meaning 'to breathe together'. To conspire is to agree. . . ." *Cotroni v. R.*, [1979] 2 S.C.R. 256 at 276-77, Dickson J.

CONSTABLE. *n.* ". . . '[T]he holder of a police office' . . . exercising, so far as his police duties are concerned, an original authority . . . a member of a civilian force, and I take his assimilation to a soldier . . . to be an assimilation related only to whether an action per quod lies against a tortfeasor at common law for the loss of his services, and not to assimilation for other purposes, such as liability to peremptory discharge, if that be the case with a soldier." *Nicholson v. Haldimand-Norfolk (Regional Municipality) Commissioners of Police* (1978), 9 C.L.L.C. 249 at 253, [1979] 1 S.C.R. 311, 88 D.L.R. (3d) 671, 78 C.L.L.C. 14, 181, 23 N.R. 410, Laskin C.J.C.

CONSTITUENCY. *n.* A place or territorial area entitled to return a member to serve in a legislative assembly or in Parliament. See URBAN ~.

CONSTITUENCY ASSOCIATION. In an electoral district, means the association or organization endorsed by a registered party as the official association of that party in the electoral district.

CONSTITUENT. *n.* One entitled to vote in a constituency.

CONSTITUTION. *n.* 1. The body of law which establishes the framework of government for a nation or an organization. 2. The supreme law of Canada. *Constitution Act, 1982*, s. 52(1), being Schedule B of the *Canada Act, 1982* (U.K.), 1982, c. 11. 3. ". . . [I]s drafted with an eye to the future. Its function is to provide continuing framework for the legitimate exercise of governmental power and, when joined by a Bill or a Charter of Rights, for the unremitting protection of individual rights and liberties. Once enacted, its provisions cannot easily be repealed or amended. It must, therefore, be capable of growth and development over time to meet new social, political and historical realities often unimagined by its framers. *Canada (Director of Investigation & Research) v. Southam Inc.* (1984), 27 B.L.R. 297 at 307, [1984] 2 S.C.R. 145, 33 Alta. L.R. (2d) 193, 41 C.R. (3d) 97, [1984] 6 W.W.R. 577, 14 C.C.C. (3d) 97, 55 A.R. 291, 55 N.R. 241, 2 C.P.R. (3d) 1, 9 C.R.R. 355, 11 D.L.R. (4th) 641, 84 D.T.C. 6467, the court per Dickson J.

CONSTITUTION ACT, 1867. The act originally called the British North America Act (BNA Act).

CONSTITUTIONAL CONVENTION. "We respectfully adopt the definition given by the learned Chief Justice of Manitoba, Freedman C.J.M. in the Manitoba Reference [Reference re Amendment of the Constitution of Canada (No. 3) (1981), 120 D.L.R. (3d) 385] . . . : ' . . . a convention occupies a position somewhere in between a usage or custom on one hand and constitutional law on the other. There is a general agreement that if one sought to fix that position with greater precision he would place convention nearer to law than to usage or custom. There is also a general agreement that "a convention is a rule which is regarded as obligatory by the officials to whom it applies": Hogg, Constitutional Law of Canada (1977), p. 9.' . . . The existence of a definite convention is always unclear and a matter of debate. Furthermore conventions are flexible, somewhat imprecise and unsuitable for judicial determination." *Reference re Questions Concerning Amendment of the Constitution of Canada as set out in O.C. 1020/80* (1981), (*sub nom. Resolution to Amend the Constitution of Canada, Re*) 1 C.R.R. 59 at 137-38, [1981] 1 S.C.R. 753, [1981] 6 W.W.R. 1, 11 Man. R. (2d) 1, 39 N.R. 1, 34 Nfld. & P.E.I.R. 1, 95 A.P.R. 1, Martland, Ritchie, Dickson, Beetz, Chouinard and Lamer JJ. See CONVENTION.

CONSTITUTIONAL LAW. The body of law which deals with the distribution or exercise of the powers of government.

CONSTITUTION OF CANADA. 1. Includes (a) The Canada Act 1982, including this Act; (b) the Acts and orders referred to in the schedule; and (c) any amendment to any Act or order referred to in paragraph (a) or (b). *Constitution Act, 1982*, s. 52(2), being Schedule B of the *Canada Act, 1982* (U.K.), 1982, c. 11. 2. ". . . [T]he phrases 'Constitution of Canada' and 'Canadian Constitution' do not refer to matters of interest only to the federal government or federal juristic unit. They are clearly meant in a broader sense and embrace the global system of rules and principles which govern the exercise of constitutional authority in the whole and in every part of the Canadian state." *Reference re Questions Concerning Amendment of the Constitution of Canada as set out in O.C. 1020/80* (1981), (*sub nom. Resolution to Amend the Constitution of Canada, Re*) 1 C.R.R. 59 at 131, [1981] 1 S.C.R. 753, [1981] 6 W.W.R. 1, 11 Man. R. (2d) 1, 39 N.R. 1, 34 Nfld. & P.E.I.R. 1, 95 A.P.R. 1, Martland, Ritchie, Dickson, Beetz, Chouinard and Lamer JJ. 3. ". . . [M]eans the constitution of the federal Government, as distinct from the provincial Governments. . . ." *Reference re Legislative Authority of Parliament of Canada* (1979), (*sub nom. Reference re Legislative Authority of Parliament to Alter or Replace Senate*) 102 D.L.R. (3d) 1 at 12, [1980] 1 S.C.R. 56, 30 N.R. 271, Laskin C.J.C., Martland, Ritchie, Pigeon, Dickson, Estey, Pratte and McIntyre JJ.

CONSTRAINED-SHARE COMPANY. A category of company permitted to restrict the transfer of its shares in order to comply with requirements contained in legislation regarding Canadian ownership or control. S.M. Beck *et al.*, *Cases and Materials on Partnerships and Canadian Business Corporations* (Toronto: Carswell, 1983) at 157.

CONSTRUCTION. *n.* "[In Chatenay v. Brazilian Submarine Telegraph Co., [1891] 1 Q.B. 79] . . . Lindley L.J. at p. 85 said the following: 'The expression "construction" as applied to a document, at all events as used by English lawyers, includes two things: first, the meaning of the words; and secondly, their legal effect, or the effect which is to be given to them. The meaning of the words I take to be a question of fact in all cases, whether we are dealing with a poem or a legal document. The effect of the words is a question of law.' " *Wald v. Greater York Developments Ltd.* (1978), 8 C.P.C. 12 at 15 (Ont. H.C.), Sandler (Master).

CONSTRUCTION LIEN. A claim secured against real property made to ensure payment for materials furnished or work performed for construction.

CONSTRUCTIVE. *adj.* 1. Implied or inferred. R. Megarry & H.W.R. Wade, *The Law of Real Property*, 5th ed. (London: Stevens, 1984) at cxxiv. 2. Arising out of law without reference to any party's intention.

CONSTRUCTIVE DESERTION. One spouse by misconduct forces the other spouse to leave the home.

CONSTRUCTIVE DISCHARGE. Actions by the employer which cause an employee to resign.

CONSTRUCTIVE DISCRIMINATION. The imposition of requirements that are designed to assist a particular group.

CONSTRUCTIVE DISMISSAL. "... [O]ccurs when the employer commits either a present breach or an anticipatory breach of a fundamental term of a contract of employment, thereby giving the employee a right, but not an obligation, to treat the employment contract as being at an end ..." *Farquhar v. Butler Brothers Supplies Ltd.* (1988), 23 B.C.L.R. (2d) 89 at 92 (C.A.), Lambert J.A.

CONSTRUCTIVE EVICTION. Acts by the landlord which deprive a tenant of enjoyment of the property so that it is untenantable.

CONSTRUCTIVE FRAUD. 1. "... [E]quivalent of breach of fiduciary duty...." *Proprietary Mines Ltd. v. MacKay*, [1939] 3 D.L.R. 215 at 246, [1939] O.R. 461 (C.A.), Masten J.A. (Middleton J.A. concurring). 2. "It is a mistake to suppose that an actual intention to cheat must always be proved. A man may misconceive the extent of the obligation which a Court of Equity imposes on him. His fault is that he has violated, however innocently because of his ignorance, an obligation which he must be taken by the Court to have known, and his conduct has in that sense always been called fraudulent, even in such a case as a technical fraud on a power. It was thus that the expression 'constructive fraud' came into existence...." *Nocton v. Lord Ashburton*, [1914] A.C. 932 at 954.

CONSTRUCTIVE NOTICE. 1. "... [K]nowledge of other facts [other than the very fact required to be established] which put a person on inquiry to discover the fact required to be established. The classic distinction, ..., is that of Strong J. in Rose v. Peterkin

(1885), 13 S.C.R. 677 at 694: 'What such actual and direct notice is may well be ascertained very shortly by defining constructive notice, and then taking actual notice to be knowledge, not presumed as in the case of constructive notice, but shown to be actually brought home to the party to be charged with it, either by proof of his own admission or by the evidence of witnesses who are able to establish that the very fact, of which notice is to be established, not something which would have led to the discovery of the fact if an inquiry had been pursued, was brought to his knowledge.' " *Stoimenov v. Stoimenov* (1985), 35 R.P.R. 150 at 158, 44 R.F.L. (2d) 14, 7 O.A.C. 220 (C.A.), the court per Tarnopolsky J.A. 2. Knowledge attributed to someone who fails to make proper inquiries into the title of property purchased, who fails to investigate a fact, brought to notice, which suggests that a claim exists, or who deliberately does not inquire in order to avoid notice. See EQUITABLE DOCTRINE OF ~.

CONSTRUCTIVE POSSESSION. "... The doctrine [of constructive possession] is described in Harris v. Mudie (1882), 7 O.A.R. 414 (C.A.) at p. 427, as follows: ' ... when a party having colour of title enters in good faith upon the land professed to be conveyed, he is presumed to enter according to his title, and thereby gains a constructive possession of the whole land embraced in his deed.' ... The party must establish visible and exclusive possession of part of the property described in the deed, but occupation of a portion of the property will be extended by construction to all of the land within the boundary of the deed: Wood v. LeBlanc (1903), 36 N.B.R. 47 affirmed 34 S.C.R. 627." *Port Franks Properties Ltd. v. R.* (1979), [1981] 3 C.N.L.R. 86 at 99, 99 D.L.R. (3d) 28 (Fed. R.C.), Lieff D.J.

CONSTRUCTIVE TRUST. "... [A] remedy against unjust enrichment and that before unjust enrichment may ... exist, three elements must be shown – an enrichment, a corresponding deprivation and the absence of any 'juristic reason' for the enrichment (per Dickson J. in Becker v. Pettkus, [1980] 2 S.C.R. 834 ...)." *Hyette v. Pfenniger* (1991), 39 R.F.L. (3d) 30 at 41 (B.C. S.C.), Newbury J. See REMEDIAL ~.

CONSTRUE. *v.* To interpret; to ascertain the meaning of.

CONSUL. *n.* The agent of a foreign state who assists nationals of the state and protects the state's commercial interests. J.G. McLeod, *The Conflict of Laws* (Calgary: Carswell, 1983) at 77.

CONSULATE. *n.* The residence or office of a consul.

CONSUMER CREDIT. Loans to individuals to facilitate purchase of goods or services.

CONSUMER DEBT. Debt incurred by an individual for personal or household goods and services.

CONSUMER GOODS. Goods that are used or acquired for use primarily for personal, family or household purposes.

CONSUMER PRICE INDEX. 1. The consumer price index for Canada as published by Statistics Canada under the authority of the Statistics Act (Canada). 2. "... [T]he phrase, 'cost of living index', is used in Canada commonly and interchangeably for the phrase, 'consumer price index', and especially for the index published by ... Statistics Canada." *Collins Cartage & Storage Co. v. McDonald* (1980), 30 O.R. (2d) 234 at 236, 16 R.P.R. 71, 116 D.L.R. (3d) 570 (C.A.), the court per Goodman J.A. See COST OF LIVING INDEX.

CONSUMER PROTECTION LEGISLATION. Legislation regulating business practices of those dealing with consumers.

CONSUMER REPORT. A written, oral or other communication by a consumer reporting agency of credit information or personal information, or both, pertaining to a consumer.

CONSUMER REPORTING AGENCY. A person who, for gain or profit, or on a regular co-operative non-

profit basis, furnishes consumer reports.

CONSUMER'S COOPERATIVE. A cooperative which purchases consumer goods for resale to its members.

CONSUMMATE. *v.* 1. To finish. 2. "A marriage is consummated once sexual intercourse has taken place...." *Sau v. Sau* (1970), 1 R.F.L. 250 at 251 (Ont. H.C.), Parker J.

CONSUMMATE. *adj.* Completed; possessing extra skill or ability; excellent.

CONSUMMATION. *n.* Completion; act of sexual intercourse after marriage which completes the marriage.

CONTEMPLATE. *v.* To view, consider, study, ponder.

CONTEMPLATION. *n.* Consideration of a matter.

CONTEMPORANEA EXPOSITIO EST FORTISSIMA IN LEGE. [L.] The meaning openly given by current or long professional use should be taken as the true one. P.St.J. Langan, ed., *Maxwell on The Interpretation of Statutes*, 12th ed. (Bombay: N.M. Tripathi, 1976) at 264.

CONTEMPORANEA EXPOSITIO EST OPTIMA ET FORTISSIMA IN LEGE. [L.] The current meaning is the best and most compelling in law.

CONTEMPT. *n.* 1. "... [I]nterfering with the administration of the law and ... impeding and perverting the course of justice." *R. v. Kopyto* (1987), 61 C.R. (3d) 209 at 222, 24 O.A.C. 8, 62 O.R. 449, 39 C.C.C. (3d) 1, 47 D.L.R. (4th) 213 (C.A.), Dubin J.A. 2. Disobeying an order of the court. 3. "Acts which interfere with persons having duties to discharge in a Court of Justice, including parties, witnesses, jurors and officers of the Court, ..." *B.C.G.E.U., Re* (1988), 30 C.P.C. (2d) 221 at 242, [1988] 6 W.W.R. 577, 71 Nfld. & P.E.I.R. 93, 220 A.P.R. 93, 87 N.R. 241, [1988] 2 S.C.R. 214, 88 C.L.L.C. 14,047, 53 D.L.R. (4th) 1, 31 B.C.L.R. (2d) 273, 44 C.C.C. (3d) 289, the court per Dickson C.J.C. 4. A person who was required by law to attend or remain in attendance for the purpose of giving evidence, who fails, without lawful excuse, to attend or remain in attendance, is guilty of contempt of court. *Criminal Code*, R.S.C. 1985, c. C-46, s. 708(1). See CIVIL ~; CRIMINAL ~; SCANDALIZE THE COURT.

CONTEMPT IN THE FACE OF THE COURT. "... [A]ny word spoken or act done in or in the precinct of the court which obstructs or interferes with the due administration of justice or is calculated to do so." *R. v. Kopyto* (1987), 39 C.C.C. (3d) 1 at 9, 24 O.A.C. 8, 61 C.R. (3d) 209, 62 O.R. (2d) 449, 47 D.L.R. (4th) 213 (C.A.), Cory J.A.

CONTEMPT NOT IN THE FACE OF THE COURT. "... [I]ncludes words spoken or published or acts done which are intended to interfere or are likely to interfere with the fair administration of justice." *R. v. Kopyto* (1987), 39 C.C.C. (3d) 1 at 9, 24 O.A.C. 8, 61 C.R. (3d) 209, 62 O.R. (2d) 449, 47 D.L.R. (4th) 213 (C.A.), Cory J.A.

CONTEMPT OF PARLIAMENT. To obstruct the due course of proceedings in either House of Parliament.

CONTEMPT OUTSIDE THE COURT. "... [W]ords spoken or otherwise published, or acts done, outside court which are intended or likely to interfere with or obstruct the fair administration of justice...." *R. v. Cohn* (1984), 42 C.R. (2d) 1 at 10, 48 O.R. (2d) 65, 70 C.R.R. 142, 15 C.C.C. (3d) 150, 13 D.L.R. (4th) 680, 4 O.A.C. 293 (C.A.), the court per Goodman J.A.

CONTEMPTUOUS DAMAGES. Small damages awarded to a plaintiff who sustained no loss, but whose legal rights were technically infringed though in the court's opinion the action should not have been brought. K.D. Cooper-Stephenson & I.B. Saunders, *Personal Injury Damages in Canada* (Toronto: Carswell, 1981) at 69.

CONTENTIOUS. *adj.* Contested.

CONTEST. *v.* To oppose, resist, dispute.

CONTESTATION. *n.* A controversy; a disputed issue.

CONTESTED DIVORCE. A divorce action in which a respondent delivers an answer.

CONTEXT. *n.* Parts of text surrounding the portion under consideration.

CONTIGUOUS. *adj.* "One area is contiguous to another where both have a common boundary or even a common point of contact." *R. v. Alegria* (1992), 96 Nfld. & P.E.I.R. 128 at 140, 305 A.P.R. 128 (Nfld. C.A.), the court per Goodridge C.J.N.

CONTINENTAL SHELF. 1. The shallow area of the ocean which adjoins each continent. P.W. Hogg, *Constitutional Law of Canada*, 3d ed. (Toronto: Carswell, 1992) at 716. 2. The seabed and subsoil of those submarine areas that extend beyond the territorial sea throughout the natural prolongation of the land territory of Canada to the outer edge of the continental margin or to a distance of two hundred nautical miles from the inner limits of the territorial sea, whichever is the greater, or that extend to such other limits as are prescribed. *Customs and Excise Offshore Application Act*, R.S.C. 1985, c. C-53, s. 2.

CONTINGENCY. *n.* 1. An uncertain event on which an estate, interest, liability, right or obligation depends for its existence. 2. Accident, sickness, strikes and unemployment. K.D. Cooper-Stephenson & I.B. Saunders, *Personal Injury Damages in Canada Supplement to June 30, 1987* (Toronto: Carswell, 1987) at 244. See MITIGATION ~.

CONTINGENCY INSURANCE. An agreement by an insurer to pay when an event occurs regardless of the loss suffered. Examples are life or accident insurance. R. Colinvaux, *The Law of Insurance*, 5th ed. (London: Sweet & Maxwell, 1984) at 9.

CONTINGENT. *adj.* Conditional upon the occurrence of some future uncertain event.

CONTINGENT LEGACY. A legacy bequeathed payable on happening of a contingency.

CONTINGENT LIABILITY. "... [A] liability to make a payment is contingent if the terms of its creation include uncertainty in respect of any of these three things: (1) whether the payment will be made; (2) the amount payable; or (3) the time by which payment shall be made...." *Samuel F. Investments Limited v. M.N.R.* (1988), 88 D.T.C. 1106 at 1108 (T.C.C.).

CONTINGENT REMAINDER. A remainder which depends on an uncertain condition or event that may never be performed or happen, or which may not be performed or happen until after a preceding estate is determined.

CONTINGENT RIGHT. Includes a contingent or executory interest, a possibility coupled with an interest, whether the object of the gift or limitation of the interest or possibility is or is not ascertained, also a right of entry, whether immediate or future, and whether vested or contingent.

CONTINUANCE. See CERTIFICATE OF ~.

CONTINUATION. *n.* Statutes governing corporations may permit a corporation to continue its corporate existence under the law of another jurisdiction. S.M. Beck *et al.*, *Cases and Materials on Partnerships and Canadian Business Corporations* (Toronto: Carswell, 1983) at 153.

CONTINUE. See ORDER TO ~.

CONTINUED. *adj.* A company incorporated under one act may in certain circumstances be "continued" under the laws of some other jurisdiction so that its existence is maintained subject to the laws of the second jurisdiction.

CONTINUING. *adj.* Ongoing; enduring.

CONTINUING GARNISHMENT. Capturing all present and future income payments above those exempted by statute until a debt is paid. C.R.B. Dunlop, *Creditor-Debtor Law in Canada* (Toronto: Carswell, 1981) at 262.

CONTINUING OFFENCE. "... [N]ot simply an offence which takes or may take a long time to commit. It may be described as an offence where the conjunction of the actus reus and the mens rea, which makes the offence complete, does not, as well, terminate the offence. The conjunction of the two essential elements for the commission of the offence continues and the accused remains in what might be described as a state of criminality while the offence coninues.... Conspiracy to commit murder could be a continuing offence. The actus reus and the mens rea are present when the unlawful agreement is made and continue until the killing occurs or the conspiracy is abandoned. Whatever the length of time involved, the conspirators remain in the act of commission of a truly continuing offence...." *R. v. Bell* (1983), 8 C.C.C. (3d) 97 at 110, 36 C.R. (3d) 289, 3 D.L.R. (4th) 385, 50 N.R. 172, [1983] 2 S.C.R. 471, McIntyre J. (Beetz, Estey and Chouinard JJ. concurring).

CONTINUOUS. *adj.* Uninterrupted. *New Brunswick v. C.U.P.E.* (1981), 125 D.L.R. (3d) 220 at 224 (N.B. C.A.), the court per Stratton J.A.

CONTINUOUSLY. *adv.* Without ceasing; without break.

CONTRA. [L.] Against.

CONTRABAND. *n.* 1. Goods not permitted to be exported or imported, bought or sold. 2. Anything that is in a prisoner's possession in circumstances in which possession thereof is forbidden by any act or regulation, or by an order of general or specific application within the prison or penitentiary in which the prisoner is confined.

CONTRA BONOS MORES. [L.] Contrary to good morals.

CONTRACT. *n.* 1. An agreement between two or more persons, recognized by law, which gives rise to obligations that the courts may enforce. G.H.L. Fridman, *The Law of Contract in Canada*, 2d ed. (Toronto: Carswell, 1986) at 3. 2. A promise, or set of promises, which one person gives in exchange for the promise, or set of promises, of another person. G.H.L. Fridman, *The Law of Contract in Canada*, 2d ed. (Toronto: Carswell, 1986) at 1. See ACTION OF ~; ADOPTION OF ~; ALEATORY ~; ANNUITY ~; BILATERAL ~; BUILDING ~; C.I.F. ~; CLOSED SHOP ~; COLLATERAL ~; COMMODITY ~; COMMODITY FUTURES ~; COMPLETED ~ METHOD; COMPLETION OF THE ~; CONCLUDED ~; COST-PLUS ~; DOMESTIC ~; EMPLOYMENT ~; ESSENCE OF THE ~; EXECUTED ~; EXECUTORY ~; FIXED PRICE ~; F.O.R. ~; FORMAL ~; FREEDOM OF ~; ILLEGAL ~; IMMORAL ~; IMPLIED ~; INFORMAL ~; INVESTMENT ~; LAW OF ~; MARRIAGE ~; MATERIAL ~; NAKED ~; ORAL ~; PAROL ~; PRE-INCORPORATION ~; QUASI-~; SIMPLE ~; SPECIALTY ~; UNILATERAL ~; WAGERING ~.

CONTRACT BOND. ". . . [C]ontract of suretyship and guarantee. . . ." *Johns-Manville Canada Inc. v. John Carlo Ltd.* (1980), (*sub nom. Canadian Johns-Manville Co. v. John Carlo Ltd.*) 12 B.L.R. 80 at 87, 29 O.R. (2d) 592, 113 D.L.R. (3d) 686 (H.C.), R.E. Holland J. See PERFORMANCE BOND.

CONTRACT DATE. The date on which a contract is signed by both parties.

CONTRACT EMPLOYEE. An employee engaged by means of a contract for temporary employment for a fixed term.

CONTRACT FOR FUTURE SERVICES. An executory contract that includes a provision for services of a prescribed type or class to be rendered in the future on a continuing basis.

CONTRACT FOR SALE. A sale in which the thing sold is exchanged for a consideration in money or money's worth.

CONTRACTING STATE. Any state that has ratified or adhered to a convention and whose denunciation thereof

has not become effective.

CONTRACT IN RESTRAINT OF TRADE. ". . . Lord Hodson, [in Esso Petroleum Co. v. Harper's Garage (Stourport) Ltd., [1968] A.C. 269] at p. 317, adopted the dicta of Diplock, L.J., in Petrofina (Great Britain) Ltd. v. Martin, [1966] Ch. 146 at p. 180: 'A contract in restraint of trade is one in which a party (the covenantor) agrees with any other party (the convenantee) to restrict his liberty in the future to carry on trade with other persons not parties to the contract in such manner as he chooses.' " *Stephens v. Gulf Oil Canada Ltd.* (1975), 25 C.P.R. (2d) 64 at 77, 11 O.R. (2d) 129, 65 D.L.R. (3d) 193 (C.A.), the court per Howland J.A.

CONTRACT LAW. The branch of private law dealing with drafting, interpretation and enforcement of contracts between persons.

CONTRACT OF EMPLOYMENT. A contract by which an employee agrees to provide services to an employer.

CONTRACT OF INDEMNITY. ". . . [A] contract by which one party agrees to make good a loss suffered by the other and includes most contracts of insurance. . . ." *Callaghan Contracting Ltd. v. Royal Insurance Co. of Canada* (1989), [1990] 39 C.C.L.I. 65 at 70, 97 N.B.R. (2d) 381, 245 A.P.R. 381 (C.A.), the court per Stratton C.J.N.B.

CONTRACT OF INSURANCE. 1. "In . . . Re Bendix Automotive of Can. Ltd. and U.A.W., [1971] 3 O.R. 263 . . . (Ont. H.C.), [the court considered] the . . . definition of contract of insurance at p. 269: 'The basic elements which are common to all of these definitions may be stated as follows; i) an undertaking of one person; ii) to indemnify another person; iii) for an agreed consideration; iv) from loss or liability in respect of an event; v) the happening of which is uncertain.' " *Arklie v. Haskell* (1986), 25 C.C.L.I. 277 at 282, 284, 33 D.L.R. (4th) 458, [1987] I.L.R. 1-2176 (B.C.C.A.), McLachlin J.A. (Hutcheon and MacFarlane JJ.A. concurring). 2. An agreement by which an insurer, for a premium, agrees to indemnify the insured against loss. 3. A policy, certificate, interim receipt, renewal receipt, or writing evidencing the contract, whether sealed or not, and a binding oral agreement.

CONTRACT OF MARINE INSURANCE. A contract whereby the insurer undertakes to indemnify the assured, in manner and to the extent thereby agreed, against marine losses, that is to say, the losses incident to marine adventure. R. Colinvaux, *The Law of Insurance*, 5th ed. (London: Sweet & Maxwell, 1984) at 8.

CONTRACT OF SALE. Includes an agreement to sell as well as sale. *Sale of Goods acts.*

CONTRACT OF SERVICE. 1. "In Short v. J. and W. Henderson, Ltd. (1946), 174 L.T. 416, an appeal to the House of Lords from a decision of the Court of Session, Lord Thankerton . . . referred to four indicia of a contract of service which had been derived from the Lord Justice Clerk from the authorities referred to by him. They were, (a) the master's power of selection of his servant; (b) the payment of wages or other remuneration; (c) the master's right to control the method of doing work, and (d) the master's right of suspension or dismissal." *Marine Pipeline & Dredging Ltd. v. Canadian Fina Oil Ltd.* (1964), 46 D.L.R. (2d) 495 at 502 (Alta C.A.). 2. A contract, whether or not in writing, in which an employer, either expressly or by implication, in return for the payment of a wage to an employee, reserves the right of control and direction of the manner and method by which the employee carries out the duties to be performed under the contract, but does not include a contract entered into by an employee qualified in or training for qualification in and working for an employer in the practice of (i) accountancy, architecture, law, medicine, pharmacy, professional engineering, surveying, teaching, veterinary science, and (ii) such other professions and occupations that may be prescribed. *Labour Standards Act*, R.S. Nfld. 1990, c. L-2, s. 2.

CONTRACTOR. *n.* 1. Any person who, for another, carries out construction work or causes it to be carried out or makes or submits tenders, personally or through another person, to carry out such work for personal profit. 2. A person who enters into a pre-incorporation contract in the name of or on behalf of a corporation before its incorporation. See GENERAL ~; INDEPENDENT ~.

CONTRACTUAL CAPACITY. Ability in law to enter into a contract.

CONTRACTUAL PROMISE. An assurance made for, or supported by a consideration. G.H.L. Fridman, *The Law of Contract in Canada*, 2d ed. (Toronto: Carswell, 1986) at 9.

CONTRACT UNDER SEAL. A contract in writing which is signed and sealed by the parties; a specialty contract.

CONTRADICT. *v.* To disprove; to prove a fact conflicting with other evidence.

CONTRADICTION IN TERMS. A group of words the parts of which are expressly inconsistent.

CONTRADICTORY EVIDENCE. Evidence disproving earlier evidence.

CONTRA PACEM. [L.] Against the peace.

CONTRA PROFERENTEM. [L. against the party putting forward] "Estey J. . . . wrote in McClelland & Stewart Ltd. v. Mutual Life Assurance Co. of Canada, [1981] 2 S.C.R. 6[:] 'That principle of interpretation [the contra proferentem rule] applies to contracts and other documents on the simple theory that any ambiguity in a term of a contract must be resolved against the author if the choice is between him and the other party to the contract who did not participate in the drafting.'" *McKinlay Motors Ltd. v. Honda Canada Inc.* (1989), 46 B.L.R. 62 at 77 (Nfld. T.D.), Wells J.

CONTRARY. *adj.* Against; opposed to.

CONTRAVENE. *v.* ". . . [T]o prevent, to obstruct the operation of and to defeat or nullify." *Collins v. Ontario (Attorney General)* (1969), 6 C.R.N.S. 82 at 88-9, [1970] 1 O.R. 207, [1970] 1 C.C.C. 305 (H.C.), Addy J.

CONTRAVENTION. *n.* 1. Failure to comply. 2. Non-compliance.

CONTRIBUTION. *n.* 1. Indemnity. 2. "... [D]escribes a situation where the wrong-doer who has paid the plaintiff's damages, or more than his share of them, is entitled to receive a portion of this amount from the other wrong-doer ..." *Peter v. Anchor Transit Ltd.*, [1979] 4 W.W.R. 150 at 153, 100 D.L.R. (3d) 37 (B.C. C.A.), the court per Craig J.A. 3. The performance by all parties jointly liable, by contract or otherwise, of their shares of the liability. 4. An amount payable or sum paid under an agreement, usually a pension plan or agreement between governments.

CONTRIBUTORY NEGLIGENCE. "... [A] failure to take reasonable care for one's own safety in circumstances where one knows or reasonably ought to foresee danger to oneself...." *Reekie v. Messervey* (1989), 48 C.C.L.T. 217 at 277, 36 B.C.L.R. (2d) 316, 59 D.L.R. (4th) 481, 17 M.V.R. (2d) 94 (C.A.), Southin J.A. (dissenting in part).

CONTRIBUTORY PENSION PLAN. A plan for pension of employees to which employees themselves contribute as well as employer.

CONTROL. *n.* 1. Power to direct. 2. In respect of a body corporate, means (a) control in any manner that results in control in fact, whether directly through the ownership of shares, stocks, equities or securities or indirectly through a trust, a contract, the ownership of shares, stocks, equities or securities of another body corporate or otherwise, or (b) the ability to appoint, elect or cause the appointment or election of a majority of the directors of the body corporate, whether or not that ability is exercised. See DEVELOPMENT ~.

CONTROLLED. *adj.* "It has long been decided that for the purposes of this section [s. 39(4)(a) of the Income Tax Act, R.S.C. 1952, c. 148] '... the word "controlled" contemplates the right of control that rests in ownership of such a number of shares as carries with it the right to a majority of the votes in the election of the Board of Directors' ..." *Imperial General Properties Ltd. v. R.* (1985), 85 D.T.C. 5500 at 5502, [1985] 2 S.C.R. 288, [1985] 2 C.T.C. 299, 31 B.L.R. 77, 62 N.R. 137, 21 D.L.R. (4th) 741, Estey J. (Beetz, Chouinard and La Forest JJ. concurring).

CONTROLLER. *n.* An official who examines and verifies the accounts of other officials. See COMPTROLLER.

CONTROVERSY. *n.* A dispute between parties.

CONTUMACY. *n.* Failure or refusal to obey an order or to attend court as required.

CONVENIENCE. *n.* 1. "... [R]elates to the proper conduct and management of the entire trial including, of course, the decisional process." *Wipfli v. Britten* (1981), 24 C.P.C. 164 at 170, [1982] 1 W.W.R. 709, 32 B.C.L.R. 242 (S.C.), McEachern C.J.S.C. 2. "... [A]ccording to McBride J. in MacDonald v. Leduc Utilities Ltd. (1952), 7 W.W.R. (N.S.) 603 at 608 (Alta. T.D.), relates to 'the nature of the issues raised, technical or otherwise, and not to the personal convenience of individual jurymen'." *Przybylski v. Morcos* (1986), 14 C.P.C. (2d) 126 at 130, 49 Alta. L.R. (2d) 164, 75 A.R. 233 (Q.B.), Andrekson J. See FLAG OF ~.

CONVENTION. *n.* 1. An agreement between states which is intended to be binding in international law. P.W. Hogg, *Constitutional Law of Canada*, 3d ed. (Toronto: Carswell, 1992) at 281. 2. "We respectfully adopt the definition given by the learned Chief Justice of Manitoba, Freedman C.J.M. in the Manitoba Reference [Reference re Amendment of the Constitution of Canada (No. 3) (1981), 120 D.L.R. (3d) 385]...: '... a convention occupies a position somewhere in between a usage or custom on one hand and constitutional law on the other. There is a general agreement that if one sought to fix that position with greater precision he would place convention nearer to law than to usage or custom. There is also a general agreement that "a convention is a rule which is regarded as obligatory by the officials to whom it applies": Hogg, Constitutional Law of Canada (1977), p. 9.' . . . The existence of a definite convention is always unclear and a matter of debate. Furthermore conventions are flexible, somewhat imprecise and unsuitable for judicial determination." *Reference re Questions Concerning Amendment of the Constitution of Canada as set out in O.C. 1020/80* (1981), (*sub nom. Resolution to Amend the Constitution of Canada, Re*) 1 C.R.R. 59 at 137-38, [1981] 1 S.C.R. 753, [1981] 6 W.W.R. 1, 11 Man. R. (2d) 1, 39 N.R. 1, 34 Nfld. & P.E.I.R. 1, 95 A.P.R. 1, Martland, Ritchie, Dickson, Beetz, Chouinard and Lamer JJ. 3. A meeting, assembly. See CONSTITUTIONAL ~; GENEVA ~S; HAGUE ~S; SUB-JUDICE ~.

CONVENTIONAL. *adj.* Not found in the usual legal sources, i.e. statutes or decided cases. P.W. Hogg, *Constitutional Law of Canada*, 3d ed. (Toronto: Carswell, 1992) at 229.

CONVENTIONAL INTER-NATIONAL LAW. (a) Any convention, treaty or other international agreement that is in force and to which Canada is a party, or (b) any convention, treaty or other international agreement that is in force and the provisions of which Canada has agreed to accept and apply in an armed conflict in which it is involved. *Criminal Code*, S.C. 1987, c. 37, s. 1(1).

CONVERSATION. *n.* 1. ". . . [A]n interchange of a series of separate communications." *R. v. Cremascoli* (1979), (*sub nom. R. v. Goldman*) 108 D.L.R. (3d) 17 at 32, [1980] 1 S.C.R. 976, 30 N.R. 453, 51 C.C.C. (2d) 1, 13 C.R. (3d) 228, McIntyre J. (Martland, Ritchie, Pigeon, Dickson, Beetz, Estey and Pratte JJ. concurring). 2. Be-

haviour, conduct. See CRIMINAL ~.

CONVERSION. *n.* 1. ". . . [A] taking of chattels with an intent to deprive the Plaintiff of his property in them, or with an intent to destroy them or change their nature." *McLean v.* Bradley (1878), 2 S.C.R. 535 at 550, Strong J. (Taschereau and Fournier JJ. concurring). 2. ". . . [A]ct of wilful interference without justification with property, including money, in a manner inconsistent with the right of the owner whereby the owner is deprived of the use of possession of the property." *Austin v. Habitat Development Ltd.* (1992), 44 C.P.R. (3d) 215 at 220, 94 D.L.R. (4th) 359, 114 N.S.R. (2d) 379, 313 A.P.R. 379 (C.A.), Hallet J.A. See RE~.

CONVERT. *v.* To change shares into shares of another class, in the manner specified in the share provisions. H. Sutherland, D.B. Horsley & J.M. Edmiston, eds., *Fraser's Handbook on Canadian Company Law*, 7th ed. (Toronto: Carswell, 1985) at 76.

CONVERTIBLE MORTGAGE. A mortgage in which the lender has the option to purchase the property at a certain price, usually the market value of the property when the term of the mortgage began. D.J. Donahue & P.D. Quinn, *Real Estate Practice in Ontario*, 4th ed. (Toronto: Butterworths, 1990) at 232.

CONVERTIBLE SECURITY. A security that is convertible into or exchangeable for a security of another class or that carries the right or obligation to acquire a security of another class.

CONVEY. *v.* 1. To create a property right or change it between persons. 2. Applied to any person, means the execution by that person of every necessary or suitable assurance for conveying or disposing to another land of or in which the first person is seised or entitled to a contingent right, either for the first person's whole estate or for any less estate, together with the performance of all formalities required by law to validate the conveyance. *Trustee acts.*

CONVEYANCE. *n.* 1. Any instrument by which a freehold or leasehold estate, or other interest in real estate, may be transferred or affected. 2. Includes transfer, assignment, delivery over, appointment, lease, settlement, other assurance and covenant to surrender, payment, gift, grant, alienation, bargain, charge, incumbrance, limitation of use or uses of, in, to or out of real property or personal property by writing or otherwise. 3. Includes ships, vessels, aircraft, trains, and motor and other vehicles. See DEED OF ~; FRAUDULENT ~; RE~; VOLUNTARY ~.

CONVEYANCER. *n.* A paralegal or lawyer whose chief practice is conveyancing.

CONVEYANCING. *n.* Practice which deals with the creation and transferral of rights in real property. R. Megarry & H.W.R. Wade, *The Law of Real Property*, 5th ed. (London: Stevens, 1984) at 2.

CONVICT. *v.* To find guilty of offence.

CONVICT. *n.* A person against whom judgment of imprisonment has been pronounced or recorded by a court. See SERVICE ~.

CONVICTION. *n.* ". . . [A] word which has different meanings in different contexts. The different senses in which the word 'conviction' is used include: (i) the verdict or adjudication of guilt; (ii) the sentence; (iii) the verdict or adjudication of guilt plus the judgment of the court, that is, the sentence; (iv) the record of the conviction." *R. v. McInnis* (1973), 23 C.R.N.S. 152 at 156, 1 O.R. (2d) 1, 13 C.C.C. (2d) 471 (C.A.), the court per Martin J.A. See CERTIFICATE OF ~.

COOK ADM. *abbr.* Cook, Admiralty (Que.), 1873-1884.

COOLING-OFF PERIOD. *var.* **COOLING OFF PERIOD**. 1. An opportunity to resile from a contract and cancel it within a specified time period. G.H.L. Fridman, *Sale of Goods in Canada*, 3d ed. (Toronto: Carswell, 1986) at 492. 2. The time before which

a strike or lock-out may begin.

CO-OP. *abbr.* Cooperative.

COOPERATIVE. *var.* **CO-OPERATIVE.** *n.* 1. Corporation in which persons having economic and social needs in common unite for the prosecution of an enterprise according to the rules of cooperative action to meet those needs. *Cooperatives Act*, S.Q. 1982, c. 26, s. 3. 2. A rental residential property other than a condominium, that is (a) owned or leased or otherwise held by or on behalf of more than one person, where any owner or lessee has the right to present or future exclusive possession of a unit in the rental residential property, or (b) owned or leased or otherwise held by a corporation having more than one shareholder or member where any one of the shareholders or members, by reason of owning shares in or being a member of the corporation, has the right to present or future exclusive possession of a unit in the rental residential property. See CONSUMER'S ~.

COOPERATIVE ASSOCIATION. *var.* **CO-OPERATIVE ASSOCIATION.** 1. Any cooperative association or federation incorporated by or pursuant to an Act of Parliament or of the legislature of a province. *Canada Cooperative Associations Act*, R.S.C. 1985, c. C-40, s. 3. 2. A co-operative corporation of producers of farm products to which the Co-operative Corporations Act applies and which was incorporated for the purpose of grading, cleaning, packing, storing, drying, processing or marketing farm products.

COOPERATIVE BASIS. *var.* **CO-OPERATIVE BASIS.** The carrying on of an enterprise organized, operated and administered in accordance with the following principles and methods: (a) except in the case of an association the charter by-laws of which provide otherwise, each member or delegate has only one vote, (b) no member or delegate may vote by proxy except that a member of an association may vote by proxy for the election of directors if the charter by-laws of the association so provide, (c) interest or dividends on share or loan capital is limited to the percentage fixed in the articles of incorporation or application for continuation, or by-laws of the organization, (d) the enterprise is operated as nearly as possible at cost after providing for reasonable reserves and the payment or crediting of interest or dividends on share or loan capital, and (e) any surplus funds arising from the business of the organization, after providing for such reasonable reserves and interest or dividends, unless used to maintain or improve services of the organization for its members or donated for community welfare or the propagation of cooperative principles, are distributed in whole or in part among the members or the members and patrons of the organization in proportion to the volume of business they have done with or through the organization.

COOPERATIVE CREDIT SOCIETY. A cooperative organization the objects of which include the making of loans to, and the receiving of deposits from, its members. *Cooperative Credit Associations Act*, R.S.C. 1985, c. C-41, s. 2. See CENTRAL ~.

COOPERATIVE FEDERALISM. Relationships between the executives of the national and provincial governments to develop mechanisms to continuously redistribute powers and resources without resorting to the courts or the constitutional amending process. P.W. Hogg, *Constitutional Law of Canada*, 3d ed. (Toronto: Carswell, 1992) at 131.

COOPERATIVE PLAN. An agreement or arrangement for the marketing of agricultural products that provides for (a) equal returns for primary producers for agricultural products of the like grade and quality, (b) the return to primary producers of the proceeds of the sale of all agricultural products delivered under the agreement or arrangement and produced during the year, after deduction of processing, carrying and selling costs and reserves, if any, and (c) an initial payment to primary producers of the agricultural product to which the agreement relates of an amount fixed by regulations made by the Governor in Council on the recommendation of the Minister with respect to a reasonable amount that does not exceed the amount estimated by the Minister to be the amount by which the average wholesale price according to grade and quality of the agricultural product for the year in respect of which the initial payment will be made will exceed the processing, carrying and selling costs thereof for that year. *Agricultural Products Cooperative Marketing Act*, R.S.C. 1985, c. A-5, s. 2.

CO-ORDINATE JURISDICTION. See CONCURRENT JURISDICTION.

CO-OWNER. *n.* The person who owns property in common or jointly with one or more other persons. See JOINT TENANT; TENANCY IN COMMON.

COPARCENER. *n.* A person to whom an estate in common with one or more other persons has descended.

COPY. *n.* 1. A document written or taken from another document. 2. A reproduction of the original. 3. In relation to any record, includes a print, whether enlarged or not, from a photographic film of the record. *Canada Evidence Act*, R.S.C. 1985, c. C-5, s. 30(12). See CERTIFIED ~; TRUE ~.

COPYRIGHT. *n.* The sole right to produce or reproduce the work or any substantial part thereof in any material form whatever, to perform, or in the case of a lecture to deliver, the work or any substantial part thereof in public or, if the work is unpublished, to publish the work or any substantial part thereof, and includes the sole right (a) to produce, reproduce, perform or publish any translation of the work, (b) in the case of a dramatic work, to convert it into a novel or other non-dramatic work, (c) in the case of a novel or other non-dramatic work, or of an artistic work, to convert it into a dramatic work, by way of performance in public or otherwise, (d) in the case of a literary, dramatic or musical work, to make any record, perforated roll, cinematograph film or other contrivance by means of which the work may be mechanically performed or delivered, (e) subject to subsection (2), in the case of any literary, dramatic, musical or artistic work, to reproduce, adapt and publicly present the work by cinematograph, if the author has given the work an original character, and (f) in the case of any literary, dramatic, musical or artistic work, to communicate the work by radio communication, and to authorize any such acts. *Copyright Act*, R.S.C. 1985, c. C-42, s. 3.

COR. *abbr.* [L. coram] In the presence of.

CORAM JUDICE. [L.] In the presence of a judge; before an appropriate or properly constituted court.

CORAM NON JUDICE. [L.] Before a person who is not a judge.

CORAM PARIBUS. [L.] Before one's peers.

CO-RESPONDENT. *n.* A person identified in a divorce pleading as the party involved in a matrimonial offence with a spouse.

COR. JUD. *abbr.* Correspondances Judiciaires (Que.).

COROLLARY. *n.* A collateral or secondary consequence.

COROLLARY RELIEF. 1. Relief collateral to or secondary to the main relief granted in an action. 2. In divorce, custody or maintenance.

COROLLARY RELIEF PROCEEDING. A proceeding in a court in which either or both former spouses seek a support order or a custody order or both such orders. *Divorce Act*, R.S.C. 1985 (2d Supp.), c. 3, s. 2.

CORONER. *n.* The official who investigates the death of any person who was killed or died in suspicious circumstances.

CORP. *abbr.* Corporation.

CORP. MGMT. TAX CONF. *abbr.* Canadian Tax Foundation. Corporate Management Tax Conference. Proceedings.

CORPORAL. *adj.* Bodily; relating to the body.

CORPORAL OATH. Touching the Bible or other holy book with the hand while taking an oath.

CORPORAL PUNISHMENT. Punishment of the body such as flogging, lashing or whipping.

CORPORATE ACT. ". . . [T]he 'collective act' of . . . directors as expressed by resolution. . . ." *Hill v. Develcon Electronics Ltd.* (1991), 37 C.C.E.L. 19 at 32, 92 Sask. R. 241 (Q.B.), Baynton J.

CORPORATE NAME. A name given to a corporation.

CORPORATE SEAL. The impression of the company's name on important documents such as share certificates, bonds and debentures. H. Sutherland, D.B. Horsley & J.M. Edmiston, eds., *Fraser's Handbook on Canadian Company Law*, 7th ed. (Toronto: Carswell, 1985) at 339.

CORPORATE VEIL. See PIERCE ~.

CORPORATION. *n.* 1. A legal entity distinct from its shareholders or members with liability separate from its shareholders or members vested with the capacity of continuous succession. 2. A body corporate with or without share capital. See CANADA ~; CANADA DEPOSIT INSURANCE ~; CANADA MORTGAGE AND HOUSING ~; CANADA POST ~; CHARITABLE ~; CLOSELY HELD ~; CROWN ~; ELEEMOSYNARY ~; EXTRA-PROVINCIAL ~; FOREIGN ~; MEMBERSHIP ~; MUNICIPAL ~; MUTUAL FUND ~; NON-PROFIT ~; PARENT ~; STATUTORY ~.

CORPORATION AGGREGATE. A corporation with several members, created by the Crown through Royal Prerogative or by statute. G.H.L. Fridman, *The Law of Contract in Canada*, 2d ed. (Toronto: Carswell, 1986) at 151.

CORPORATION SOLE. 1. The corporate status granted an individual natural person by the law, which is distinct from that individual's natural personality. The main example is the Crown. G.H.L. Fridman, *The Law of Contract in Canada*, 2d ed. (Toronto: Carswell, 1986) at 151. 2. ". . . [O]ne single person being ex officio a corporate body, . . ." *Arnegard v. Barons Consolidated School District* (1917), 33 D.L.R. 735 at 739, [1917] 2 W.W.R. 303, 11 Alta. L.R. 460 (C.A.), the court per Stuart J.A.

CORPOREAL. *adj.* Describes that which is capable of physical possession. R. Megarry & H.W.R. Wade, *The Law of Real Property*, 5th ed. (London: Stevens, 1984) at cxxiv.

CORPOREAL HEREDITAMENT.
1. A material object in contrast to a right. It may include land, buildings, minerals, trees or fixtures. R. Megarry & H.W.R. Wade, *The Law of Real Property*, 5th ed. (London: Stevens, 1984) at 112. 2. Land. *Pegg v. Pegg* (1992), 38 R.F.L. (3d) 179 at 184, 21 R.P.R. (2d) 149, 1 Alta. L.R. (3d) 249, 128 A.R. 132 (Q.B.), Agrios J.

CORPOREAL PROPERTY. Property having a physical existence.

CORPSE. *n.* The dead body of a person.

CORPUS. *n.* [L.] The capital of a fund in contrast to income.

CORPUS DELICTI. [L. body of the offence] The ingredients of an offence: commonly, the dead body.

CORPUS JURIS. [L.] A body of law. A legal text.

CORRECTIONAL CENTRE. 1. A lawful place of confinement, jail, prison, lockup, place of imprisonment, camp, correctional institution. 2. ". . . [A] jail where full security is established for the confinement and rehabilitation of persons committed to it. . . ." *R. v. Degan* (1985), 20 C.C.C. (3d) 293 at 299, 38 Sask. R. 234 (C.A.), the court per Vancise J.A.

CORRECTIONAL FACILITY. 1. A jail, prison, correctional centre for the custody of offenders. 2. ". . . [I]ncludes a community-training residence, is a facility established for the confinement and rehabilitation of a person committed to it. . . ." *R. v. Degan* (1985), 20 C.C.C. (3d) 293 at 299, 38 Sask. R. 234 (C.A.), the court per Vancise J.A.

CORRECTIONAL INSTITUTION. Any building, correctional camp, rehabilitation camp, reformatory, forensic clinic, work site, gaol or place for the reception and lawful custody of inmates.

CORR. JUD. *abbr.* Correspondances judiciaires (1906).

CORROBORATE. *v.* ". . . As Lord Diplock observed in D.P.P. v. Hester [[1972] 3 All E.R. 1056 at 1071], the ordinary sense in which the verb 'corroborate' is used in the English language is the equivalent of 'confirmed' and (at p. 1073): 'What is looked for under the common law rule is confirmation from some other source that the suspect witness is telling the truth in some part of his story which goes to show that the accused committed the offence with which he is charged.' " *R. v. Vetrovec* (1982), 136 D.L.R. (3d) 89 at 104, [1982] 1 S.C.R. 811, 41 N.R. 606, 67 C.C.C. (2d) 1, 27 C.R. (3d) 304, [1983] 1 W.W.R. 193, the court per Dickson J.

CORROBORATION. *n.* Confirmation of a witness's evidence by independent testimony.

CORRUPT. *v.* To alter morals and behaviour from good to bad.

CORRUPT. *adj.* Spoiled; debased; depraved.

CORRUPTING MORALS. (1) The offence of (a) making, printing, publishing, distributing, circulating, or having in his possession for the purpose of publication, distribution or circulation any obscene written matter, picture, model, phonograph record or other thing whatever, or (b) making, printing, publishing, distributing, selling or having in his possession for the purpose of publication, distribution or circulation, a crime comic. (2) The offence of knowingly, without lawful justification or excuse, (a) selling, exposing to public view or having in his possession for such a purpose any obscene written matter, picture, model, phonograph record or other thing whatever, (b) publicly exhibiting a disgusting object or an indecent show, (c) offering to sell, advertising, or publishing an advertisement of, or having for sale or disposal, any means, instructions, medicine, drug or article intended or represented as a method of causing abortion or miscarriage, or (d) advertising or publishing an advertisement of any means, instructions, medicine, drug or article intended or represented as a method for restoring sexual virility or curing venereal diseases or diseases of the generative organs. *Criminal Code*, R.S.C. 1985, c. C-46, s. 163.

CORRUPTION. *n.* Granting of favours inconsistent with official duties.

CORRUPTION OF BLOOD. An effect of attainder, when a person attainted was considered corrupted by the crime, so that the person could no longer hold land, inherit it or leave it to any heirs.

CORRUPT PRACTICE. 1. "... [A] phrase, a term of art, created by statute for describing or dealing with a series of widely disparate acts and omissions.... There may be corrupt practices within the meaning of the defined term where there was no debased intent and there may be corrupt practices notwithstanding that there was no element of moral turpitude." *Johansen v. Dickerson* (1980), 117 D.L.R. (3d) 176 at 180, 30 O.R. (2d) 616 (Div. Ct.), the court per Anderson J. 2. "... By the 'Common law of Parliament' it included bribery, intimidation of electors and undue influence. Statutes have added treating, which is a form of bribery, hiring vehicles to convey voters to polls, personation and some other acts...." *Howley v. Campbell*, [1939] 1 D.L.R. 431 at 432, 71 C.C.C. 246, 13 M.P.R. 494 (N.S. C.A.), Doull J.A. (concurring in the result).

COST. *n.* "[In ss. 40(1)(c) and 54 of the Income Tax Act, S.C. 1970-71-72, c. 63] ... means the price that the taxpayer gave up in order to get the asset; it does not include any expense he may have incurred in order to put himself in a position to pay that price or to keep the property afterwards." *R. v. Stirling* (1985), 85 D.T.C. 5199, [1985] 1 F.C. 342, [1985] 1 C.T.C. 275 (C.A.), the court per Pratte J. See CAPITAL ~; ~S.

COST OF BORROWING. In relation to any loan or advance, (a) the interest or discount thereon, and (b) such charges in connection therewith as are payable by the borrower to a bank or to any person from whom a bank receives any charges directly or indirectly and as are prescribed to be included in the cost of borrowing. *Bank Act*, R.S.C. 1985, c. B-1, s. 202(2).

COST OF LIVING. The relationship between the cost of goods to the consumer and buying power of wages.

COST-OF-LIVING ADJUSTMENT. A change in wages or pension payments designed to offset changes in cost of living.

COST OF LIVING INDEX. "... [U]sed in Canada commonly and interchangeably for the phrase, 'consumer price index,' and especially for the index published by the Dominion Bureau of Statistics. Judicial notice may be taken of the fact that this government department is now known as Statistics Canada." *Collins Cartage & Storage Co. v. McDonald* (1980), 16 R.P.R. 71 at 74, 30 O.R. (2d) 234, 116 D.L.R. (3d) 570 (C.A.), the court per Goodman J.A. See CONSUMER PRICE INDEX.

COST-PLUS CONTRACT. A contract to sell a product or perform work for the selling price or contractor's costs plus a percentage or plus a fixed fee.

COSTS. *n.* 1. "... [I]ndemnity for the payment of legal fees and expenses...." *Dusome v. Maxwell* (1987), 11 R.F.L. (3d) 284 at 287, 62 O.R. (2d) 785 (Dist. Ct.), Corbett

D.C.J. 2. Money expended to prosecute or defend a suit which a party is entitled to recover. 3. "... [F]or the purpose of indemnification or compensation." *Bell Canada v. Consumers' Assn. of Canada* (1986), 17 Admin L.R. 205 at 228, [1986] 1 S.C.R. 190, 9 C.P.R. (2d) 145, 65 N.R. 1, 26 D.L.R. (4th) 573, the court per Le Dain J. See ASSESSED ~; ASSESSMENT OF ~; BILL OF ~; FIXED ~; FULL ~; OPERATING ~; PARTY-AND-PARTY ~; SECURITY FOR ~; SOLICITOR-AND-CLIENT ~; SOLICITOR AND HIS OWN CLIENT ~; SPECIAL ~; TAXATION OF ~; TAXED ~; WITH ~.

COSTS IF DEMANDED. An expression inserted in a judgment when either the successful party is a body like the Crown or the unsuccessful party faces financial ruin. M.M. Orkin, *The Law of Costs*, 2d ed. (Aurora: Canada Law Book, 1987) at 1-12.

COSTS IN ANY EVENT OF THE CAUSE. Order regarding costs of interlocutory proceedings which entitles party in whose favour the order is made to have the costs of the motion taken into account when the final taxation of the action occurs. *Otis Canada Inc. v. Condominium Plan 782-0751* (1992), 5 C.P.C. (3d) 91 at 101 and 102, 126 A.R. 303 (Q.B.), Veit J.

COSTS, INSURANCE AND FREIGHT. See C.I.F.; C.I.F. CONTRACT.

COSTS IN THE ACTION. See COSTS IN THE CAUSE.

COSTS IN THE CAUSE. "... [T]he costs of this motion are to be taken into account in the final taxation of the costs at the conclusion of the litigation between the parties." *Banke Electronics Ltd. v. Olvan Tool & Die Inc.* (1981), 32 O.R. (2d) 630 at 632-33 (H.C.), Cory J.

COSTS OF AND INCIDENTAL TO. Party-and-party costs. M.M. Orkin, *The Law of Costs*, 2d ed. (Aurora: Canada Law Book, 1987) at 1-13.

COSTS OF THE DAY. Costs awarded when adjournment of the trial was caused by one party's default. M.M. Orkin, *The Law of Costs*, 2d ed. (Aurora: Canada Law Book, 1987) at 2-73.

COSTS OF THIS HEARING. Costs which include both preparation for the hearing and the hearing itself. M.M. Orkin, *The Law of Costs*, 2d ed. (Aurora: Canada Law Book, 1987) at 1-12.

COSTS OF THIS PROCEEDING. Costs for all interlocutory motions and services, not only costs at trial. M.M. Orkin, *The Law of Costs*, 2d ed. (Aurora: Canada Law Book, 1987) at 1-12.

COSTS REASONABLY INCURRED. Party-and-party costs. M.M. Orkin, *The Law of Costs*, 2d ed. (Aurora: Canada Law Book, 1987) at 1-13.

COSTS SHALL ABIDE THE EVENT. Not the full costs of the proceedings but "such costs as under the statute and rules of court a plaintiff recovering the amount that he recovers by the event is entitled to." *Watson v. Garrett* (1860), 3 P.R. 70 at 74, Richards J.

COSTS SHALL FOLLOW THE EVENT. The event referred to is the outcome of the litigation. Event is to be read distributively so that neither party gets all the costs if success is divided on the various issues. *McLeod Engines Ltd. v. Canadian Atlas Diesel Engines Co. (No. 2)* (1951), 1 W.W.R. (N.S.) 803 at 814 (B.C. C.A.), Smith J.A.

COSTS TO THE SUCCESSFUL PARTY IN THE CAUSE. See COSTS IN THE CAUSE.

CO-SURETY. *n.* One who shares a surety's obligations.

COTENANCY. *n.* Includes tenancy in common and joint tenancy.

COUNCIL. *n.* 1. An assembly of people for governmental or municipal purposes. 2. The governing body of a city, village, summer village, municipal district, county or other municipality. 3. The Queen's Privy Council for Canada, committees of the Queen's Privy Council for Canada, Cabinet and committees of Cabinet. *Canada Evidence Act*, R.S.C. 1985, c. C-5, s. 39(3). 4. An advisory body to government. 5. Used to describe the governing body of an association, i.e. professional organizations. 6. Used in the title of administrative agencies. 7. An association of unions within an area. See BAND ~; COMMISSIONER IN ~; DISTRICT ~; EXECUTIVE ~; GOVERNOR GENERAL IN ~; GOVERNOR IN ~; HEAD OF ~; JUDICIAL ~; LIEUTENANT GOVERNOR IN ~; ORDER IN ~; PRIVY ~.

COUNCILLOR. *n.* A member of or a person serving on a council. See BAND ~.

COUNSEL. *v.* 1. To procure, solicit or incite. *Criminal Law Amendment Act*, R.S.C. 1985 (1st Supp.), c. 27, s. 7(3). 2. To advise or recommend.

COUNSEL. *n.* 1. A barrister or solicitor, in respect of the matters or things that barristers and solicitors, respectively, are authorized by the law of a province to do or perform in relation to legal proceedings. *Criminal Code*, R.S.C. 1985, c. C-46, s. 2. 2. When used in respect of proceedings in a provincial court (criminal division) includes an agent. *Provincial Offenses Act*, R.S.O. 1980, c. 400, s. 92. 3. ". . . [A]n adviser whether or not he is a lawyer, . . ." *Olavarria v. Canada (Minister of Manpower & Immigration)*, [1973] F.C. 1035 at 1037, 41 D.L.R. (3d) 472 (C.A.), Jackett, Thurlow and Hyde JJ.A. See DUTY ~; QUEEN'S ~; RIGHT TO ~.

COUNSELLING. *n.* ". . . [A]cts or words . . . such as to induce a person to commit the offences that one desires and passive communication does not constitute an offence even if its purpose is to have someone inflict those injuries." *R. v. Dionne* (1987), 38 C.C.C. (3d) 171 at 180, 58 C.R. (3d) 351, 79 N.B.R. (2d) 297, 201 A.P.R. 297 (C.A.), Ayles J.A.

COUNT. *n.* A charge in an information or indictment. *Criminal Code*, R.S.C. 1985, c. C-46, s. 2.

COUNTENANCE. *v.* To encourage; to aid and abet.

COUNTERCLAIM. *n.* ". . . [A]n independent action raised by a defendant, which because of the identity of the parties can conveniently be tried with the plaintiff's claim. While a counterclaim frequently (although not necessarily) arises from the same events as the plaintiff's claim, and while it may result in reduction of the plaintiff's claim, it is in principle an independent action." *Royal Bank v. Rizkalla* (1984), 50 C.P.C. 292 at 296, 59 B.C.L.R. 324 (S.C.), McLachlin J.

COUNTERFEIT. *n.* An unauthorized imitation intended to be used to defraud by passing off.

COUNTERFEIT COIN. See COUNTERFEIT MONEY.

COUNTERFEIT MONEY. Includes (a) a false coin or false paper money that resembles or is apparently intended to resemble or pass for a current coin or current paper money, (b) a forged bank-note or forged blank bank-note, whether complete or incomplete, (c) a genuine coin or genuine paper money that is prepared or altered to resemble or pass for a current coin or current paper money of a higher denomination, (d) a current coin from which the milling is removed by filing or cutting the edges and on which new milling is made to restore its appearance, (e) a coin cased with gold, silver or nickel, as the case may be, that is intended to resemble or pass for a current gold, silver or nickel coin, and (f) a coin or a piece of metal or mixed metals that is washed or coloured by any means with a wash or material capable of producing the appearance of gold, silver or nickel and that is intended to resemble or pass for a current gold, silver or nickel coin. *Criminal Code*, R.S.C. 1985, c. C-46, s. 448.

COUNTERFEIT TOKEN OF VALUE. A counterfeit excise stamp, postage stamp or other evidence of value, by whatever technical, trivial or deceptive designation it may be described, and includes genuine coin or paper money that has no value as money. *Criminal Code*, R.S.C. 1985, c. C-46, s. 448.

COUNTERFOIL. *n.* The complementary part of a cheque or receipt used to preserve a record of the contents.

COUNTERMAND. *v.* To revoke; to recall.

COUNTER OFFER. *var.* **COUNTER-OFFER.** A statement by the offeree rejecting the offer and creating a new offer.

COUNTERPART. *n.* A part which corresponds; a duplicate.

COUNTERPETITION. *n.* A claim for relief against the petitioner by respondent in a divorce proceeding.

COUNTER-PROPOSAL. *n.* An opposing offer made in collective bargaining following an offer or proposal by the other party.

COUNTER-SIGN. *var.* **COUNTERSIGN.** *v.* For a subordinate to sign to vouch for the authenticity of any writing by the superior.

COUNTERVAIL. *v.* To compensate; to balance.

COUNTRY. *n.* The total territory which is subject under a single sovereign to a single body of law. J.G. McLeod, *The Conflict of Laws* (Calgary: Carswell, 1983) at 5.

COUNTY. *n.* A territorial division for electoral, judicial or local government purposes.

COUNTY COURT. 1. A court with jurisdiction limited to a county by territory and limited by subject matter. P.W. Hogg, *Constitutional Law of Canada*, 3d ed. (Toronto: Carswell, 1992) at 162. 2. "... [A]n inferior statutory Court of record and its jurisdiction is to be found in its act of incorporation, namely the County Court Act, R.S.N.S. 1967, c. 64, and its antecedent enactments." *Whynot v. Giffin* (1984), 40 C.P.C. 344 at 346, 62 N.S.R. (2d) 112, 136 A.P.R. 112, 7 D.L.R. (4th) 68 (C.A.), the court per Macdonald J.A.

COUPON. *n.* Part of a commercial instrument designed to be cut off, which evidences something connected with the contract the instrument represents, usually interest.

COUPON BOND. A bond registrable as to principal only; interest is paid through coupons, payable to bearer, attached to the instrument. H. Sutherland, D.B. Horsley & J.M. Edmiston, eds., *Fraser's Handbook on Canadian Company Law*, 7th ed. (Toronto: Carswell, 1985) at 311.

COUPON DEBENTURE. A debenture registrable as to principal only; interest is paid through coupons, payable to bearer, attached to the instrument. H. Sutherland, D.B. Horsley & J.M. Edmiston, eds., *Fraser's Handbook on Canadian Company Law*, 7th ed. (Toronto: Carswell, 1985) at 311.

COURIER. *n.* An individual who, on personal account or as an employee of another person, provides to members of the public the service of carrying items of value in personal custody.

COURSE. *n.* "[As used in s. 2(f.1) of the Newfoundland Human Rights Code, R.S. Nfld. 1970, c. 262] ... imports the need for some series of events." *Aavik v. Ashbourne* (1990), 12 C.H.R.R. D/401 at D/407 (Nfld. Human Rights Comm.), Gallant (Member). See ORDER OF ~.

COURSE OF BUSINESS. The normal activities of business.

COURSE OF EMPLOYMENT. "... [W]ork- or job-related ..." *Robichaud v. Canada (Treasury Board)*, [1987] 2 S.C.R. 84 at 92, La Forest J., cited with approval in *Janzen v. Platy Enterprises Ltd.* (1989), 47 C.R.R. 274 at 305, [1989] 1 S.C.R. 1252, 25 C.C.E.L. 1, [1989] 4 W.W.R. 39, 59 D.L.R. (4th) 352, 10 C.H.R.R. D/6205, 58 Man. R. (2d) 1, the court per Dickson C.J.C.

COURT. *n.* 1. A place where justice is administered; a body or part of the judicial system. 2. A place where a sovereign resides. 3. The court or a judge of the court. 4. "... [A]ny judicial organism whatever its importance or jurisdiction. That is the usual meaning of the [word]. As well, [it has] a narrow meaning by which ... 'court' designates more specifically a judicial organism of superior jurisdiction ..." *Québec (Commission des droites de la personne) c. Canada (Procureur général)* (1978), (*sub nom. Human Rights Commission v. Solicitor-General of Canada*) 93 D.L.R. (3d) 562 at 570 (Que. C.A.), Mayrand J.A. (Bernier J.A. concurring). 5. Includes a judge, arbitrator, umpire, commissioner, provincial judge, justice of the peace or other office or person having by law or by the consent of the parties authority to hear, receive and examine evidence. *Evidence acts.* See ADMIRALTY ~; APPEAL ~; APPELLATE ~; CITIZENSHIP ~; CIVIL CONTEMPT; CONTEMPT; CONTEMPT IN THE FACE OF THE ~; CONTEMPT NOT IN THE FACE OF THE ~; CONTEMPT OUTSIDE ~; COUNTY ~; CRIMINAL CONTEMPT; DISTRICT ~; DIVIDED ~; DIVISIONAL ~; ECCLESIASTICAL ~; EXCHEQUER ~; FEDERAL ~; FOREIGN ~; FRIEND OF THE ~; FULL ~; INFERIOR ~; INTERNATIONAL ~ OF JUSTICE; NAVAL ~; OPEN ~; ORDINARY ~; ORIGINAL ~; PAYMENT INTO ~; POLICE ~; PROVINCIAL ~; RULES OF ~; SCANDALIZE THE ~; SMALL CLAIMS ~; STATUTORY ~; SUMMARY CONVICTION ~; SUPERIOR ~; SUPREME ~ OF CANADA; TERRITORIAL ~; TRIAL ~; YOUTH ~.

COURT CLERK. The chief administrator of a court who issues process, enters orders and performs other duties.

COURT MARTIAL. 1. A court which tries offences against naval, military or air force discipline, or offences committed by a member of the armed forces against the ordinary law. 2. Includes a General Court Martial, a Special General Court Martial, a Disciplinary Court Martial and a Standing Court Martial. *National Defence Act*, R.S.C. 1985, c. N-5, s. 2.

COURT MARTIAL APPEAL COURT. The Court Martial Appeal Court of Canada established by section 234. *National Defence Act*, R.S.C. 1985, c. N-5, s. 2.

COURT OF APPEAL. (a) In the Province of Ontario, the Court of Appeal, (b) in the Province of Quebec, the Court of Appeal, (c) in the Province of Nova Scotia, the Appeal Division of the Supreme Court, (d) in the Province of New Brunswick, the Court of Appeal, (e) in the Province of British Columbia, the Court of Appeal, (f) in the Province of Prince Edward Island, the Appeal Division of the Supreme Court, (g) in the Province of Manitoba, the Court of Appeal, (h) in the Province of Saskatchewan, the Court of Appeal, (i) in the Province of Alberta, the Court of Appeal, (j) in the Province of Newfoundland, the Court of Appeal, (k) in the Yukon Territory, the Court of Appeal, and (l) in the Northwest Territories, the Court of Appeal. *Criminal Code*, R.S.C. 1985, c. C-46, s. 2. See APPEAL; APPEAL COURT; APPELLATE COURT.

COURT OF CHANCERY. The main English court in which the part of law known as equity was enforced. The Lord Chancellor presided, assisted by the Master of the Rolls and judges called Vice-Chancellors.

COURT OF COMPETENT JURISDICTION. "... [A] court is competent if it has jurisdiction, conferred by statute, over the person and the subject-matter in question and, in addition, has authority to make the order sought." *R. v. Morgentaler* (1984), 48 O.R. (2d) 519 (C.A.), Brooke J.A., cited with approval in *R. v. Mills* (1986), 29 D.L.R. (4th) 161 at 177 (S.C.C.), McIntyre J. and *Cuddy Chicks Ltd. v. Ontario (Labour Relations Board)* (1989), 39 Admin. L.R. 48 at 68, 89 C.L.L.C. 14,051, 79 O.R. (2d) 179, 62 D.L.R. (4th) 125, [1989] O.L.R.B. Rep. 989, 35 O.A.C. 94, 44 C.R.R. 75 (C.A.), Finlayson J.A. (dissenting).

COURT OF CRIMINAL JURISDICTION. (a) A court of general or quarter sessions of the peace, when presided over by a superior court judge or a county or district court judge, or in the cities of Montreal and Quebec, by a municipal judge of the city, as the case may be, or a judge of the sessions of the peace, and (b) a magistrate or judge acting under Part XIX. *Criminal Code*, R.S.C. 1985, c. C-46, s. 2.

COURT OF EQUITY. Originally separate courts heard matters of equity but reforms of the late nineteenth century combined the jurisdiction of the courts of equity with the law courts so that courts now administer both law and equity, providing equitable remedies according to equitable principles where appropriate.

COURT OF FIRST INSTANCE. A court before which an action is first brought for trial.

COURT OF KING'S BENCH. See QUEEN'S BENCH.

COURT OF LAST RESORT. The court from which there is no further appeal.

COURT OF PROBATE. Any court having jurisdiction in matters of probate. *Probate Recognition Act*, R.S.B.C. 1979, c. 339, s. 1.

COURT OF QUEEN'S BENCH. See QUEEN'S BENCH.

COURT OF RECORD. 1. Any court which keeps a record of its judicial acts and proceedings. 2. "... [A] Court which has power to fine and imprison ..." *R. v. Fields* (1986), 28 C.C.C. (3d) 353 at 357-58, 16 O.A.C. 286, 53 C.R. (3d) 260, 56 O.R. (2d) 213 (C.A.), Dubin J.A.

COURT RECORD. The records of the office of any court and documents filed therein.

COURT REPORTER. 1. A person who records proceedings of a court and the evidence given in court. 2. "... [A]n officer of the court and enjoys an official status...." *R. v. Turner* (1981), 27 C.R. (3d) 73 at 79, [1982] 2 W.W.R. 142, 65 C.C.C. (2d) 335, 14 Sask. R. 321 (C.A.), Bayda C.J.S. (MacDonald J.A. concurring).

COUT. DIG. *abbr.* Coutlee's Digest.

COUT. S.C. *abbr.* Notes of Un-reported Cases, Supreme Court of Canada (Coutlee), 1875-1907.

COVENANT. *n.* 1. An agreement in writing signed and delivered and in the past under seal. 2. "... [R]efers to obligations of the landlord not only under any written agreement of lease between landlord and tenant, but also to any obligations imposed upon the landlord by reason of the Landlord and Tenant Act [R.S.O. 1980, c. 232]." *Kingsway v. Pooler* (1988), 4 T.L.L.R. 105 at 108 (Ont. Dist. Ct.), Davidson D.C.J. See CONTRACT IN RESTRAINT OF TRADE; DEED OF ~; QUIET ENJOYMENT; RESTRICTIVE ~; USUAL ~.

COVENANTEE. *n.* The party for whose benefit the covenant is made, the recipient of the covenant.

COVENANT FOR FURTHER ASSURANCE. A standard covenant which a vendor undertakes to protect the purchaser's interest in something purchased; the vendor agrees, at the purchaser's request and cost, to execute a further conveyance or other document to more perfectly assure the subject-matter conveyed.

COVENANT FOR PAYMENT. An agreement that the mortgagor will pay the mortgage money and interest.

COVENANTOR. *n.* The party who makes the covenant, who provides the covenant.

COVENANT RUNNING WITH THE LAND. See RUN WITH THE LAND; RUN WITH THE REVERSION.

COVENANT RUNNING WITH THE REVERSION. See RUN WITH THE LAND; RUN WITH THE REVERSION.

COVER. *v.* 1. To insure. 2. To buy back securities sold short.

COVERAGE. *n.* "... [C]an mean at least two things; a straight naming of the perils insured against, or on a larger view, a bundle of descriptions of the protection offered in the case of each individual peril contained in the one insurance policy. In British Columbia, I prefer the latter, more compendious understanding." *Dressew Supply Ltd. v. Laurentian Pacific Insurance Co.* (1991), [1992] 3 C.C.L.I. (2d) 286 at 310-11, 77 D.L.R. (4th) 317, 57 B.C.L.R. (2d) 198, [1991] 6 W.W.R. 174, [1991] I.L.R. 1-2755 (C.A.), the court per Locke J.A. See COMPREHENSIVE ~.

COVER NOTE. A document given to an insured to indicate insurance is in effect.

COVERT. *adj.* 1. Hidden. 2. Of a woman, under the protection of her husband.

COVERTURE. *n.* A woman's condition during marriage; the fact that she is married.

C.P. *abbr.* 1. Common Pleas. 2. Cour provinciale. 3. Recueils de jurisprudence, Cour provinciale.

CP. *abbr.* Compare.

C.P.C. *abbr.* 1. Carswell's Practice Cases, 1976-1985. 2. Canadian Pension Commission.

C.P.C. (2d). *abbr.* Carswell's Practice Cases (Second Series) 1985-.

C.P.D. *abbr.* Law Reports, Common Pleas Division.

C.P. DIV. CIV. *abbr.* Cour provinciale, Division civile.

C.P. DIV. CRIM. *abbr.* Cour provinciale, Division criminelle.

C.P. DIV. FAM. *abbr.* Cour provinciale, Division de la famille.

C.P. DU N. *abbr.* Cours de perfectionnement du Notariat.

C.P.R. *abbr.* Canadian Patent Reporter, 1942-1971.

C.P.R. (N.S.). *abbr.* Canadian Patent Reporter (New [Third] Series).

C. PROV. *abbr.* Cour provinciale.

C.P.R. (2d). *abbr.* Canadian Patent Reporter (Second Series), 1971-1984.

C.P.R. (3d). *abbr.* Canadian Patent Reporter (Third Series), 1985-.

C.R. *abbr.* Criminal Reports (Canada), 1946-1967.

C.R.A.C. *abbr.* Canadian Reports, Appeal Cases, 1828-1913.

CRAFT. *n.* 1. A skilled trade. 2. A small boat. 3. A guild.

CRAFT UNION. A union, membership in which is restricted to workers having a particular skill.

CRAFT UNIT. A collective bargaining unit consisting of employees having a particular skill.

C.R.C. *abbr.* Canadian Railway Cases.

CREATE. *v.* To bring into legal existence. *Manco Home Systems Ltd., Re* (1990), 78 C.B.R. (N.S.) 109 at 113 (B.C. C.A.), Southin J.A.

CREATION OF CURRENCY. To finance government expenditure by printing money. W. Grover & F. Iacobucci, *Materials on Canadian Income Tax*, 4th ed. (Toronto: De Boo, 1980) at 15.

CREATION OF LIEN. Mechanics', construction or builder's liens are created when work or services are performed or materials are placed or furnished. D.N. Macklem & D.I. Bristow, *Construction, Builders' and Mechanics' Liens in Canada*, 6th ed. (Toronto: Carswell, 1990-) at 1-10.

CREDIBILITY. *n.* ". . . [N]ot merely the appreciation of the witnesses' desire to be truthful but also of their opportunities of knowledge and powers of observation, judgment and memory – in a word, the trustworthiness of their testimony, . . ." *Raymond v. Bosanquet (Township)* (1919), 59 S.C.R. 452 at 460, 50 D.L.R. 560, Anglin J.

CREDIBLE. *adj.* Believable; worthy of belief.

CREDIT. *n.* 1. Belief in a person's trustworthiness. 2. An arrangement for obtaining loans or advances. *Bank Act*, R.S.C. 1985, c. B-1, s. 202(2). 3. The advancing of money, goods or services to or on behalf of another for repayment at a later time, whether or not there is cost of borrowing, and includes variable credit. *Consumer Protection acts.* See ANTICIPATORY ~; CONFIRMED ~; CONSUMER ~;

DOCUMENTARY ~; LETTER OF ~; SALE ON ~.

CREDIT BUREAU. An organization which collects information relating to the credit, responsibility and character of individuals and businesses for the purpose of providing the information to its members.

CREDIT CARD. Any card, plate, coupon book or other device issued or otherwise distributed for the purpose of being used (a) on presentation to obtain, on credit, money, goods, services or any other thing of value, or (b) in an automated teller machine, a remote service unit or a similar automated banking device to obtain any of the services offered through the machine, unit or device. *Criminal Law Amendment Act*, R.S.C. 1985 (1st Supp.), c. 27, s. 42.

CREDIT INFORMATION. Information about a consumer as to name, age, occupation, place of residence, previous places of residence, marital status, spouse's name and age, number of dependants, particulars of education or professional qualifications, places of employment, previous places of employment, estimated income, paying habits, outstanding debt obligations, cost of living obligations and assets. *Consumer Reporting acts.*

CREDIT INSTITUTION. A bank, treasury branch, credit union or a trust company.

CREDIT INSURANCE. Insurance against loss to the insured through insolvency or default of a person to whom credit is given in respect of goods, wares or merchandise. *Insurance acts.*

CREDIT LINE. The amount of money a lender agrees to supply to a person.

CREDIT NOTE. A note issued by a business indicating that a customer is entitled to be credited by the issuer with a certain amount.

CREDITOR. *n.* 1. A person to whom another person owes a debt. 2. "... [A] person entitled to the fulfilment of, an obligation." *Crown Lumber Co. v.*

Smythe, [1923] 3 D.L.R. 933 at 952, [1923] 2 W.W.R. 1019, 19 Alta. L.R. 558 (C.A.), Beck J.A. 3. A person having a claim, preferred, secured or unsecured, provable as a claim under this Act. *Bankruptcy Act*, R.S.C. 1985, c. B-3, s. 2. See JUDGMENT ~; PREFERRED ~; REGISTERED ~; SECURED ~; UNSECURED ~.

CREDITORS' MEETING. The first meeting of creditors of a bankrupt.

CREDITORS' RELIEF STATUTE. A statute which forces a judgment creditor to share pari passu any proceeds of execution with other unsecured creditors who filed writs of execution or certificates with the sheriff. C.R.B. Dunlop, *Creditor-Debtor Law in Canada* (Toronto: Carswell, 1981) at 416.

CREDIT RATE. The actual annual percentage of a credit charge.

CREDIT RATING. Evaluation of the credit worthiness of a business or individual based on ability to pay and past performance in paying debt.

CREDIT REPORT. A report of credit information or of a credit rating based on credit information, supplied by a credit reporting agency.

CREDIT REPORTING AGENCY. A person who is engaged in providing credit reports to any other person, whether for remuneration or otherwise.

CREDIT SOCIETY. See COOPERATIVE ~.

CREDIT UNION. A co-operative society, including caisses populaires, that provides its members with financial and other services.

CREED. *n.* "... [I]nvolve[s] a declaration of religious belief." *R. v. Ontario (Labour Relations Board)*, [1963] 2 O.R. 376 at 389, 39 D.L.R. (2d) 593, 63 C.L.L.C. 15,459 (H.C.), McRuer C.J.H.C.

CREMATION. *n.* Disposal of a dead body by incineration.

C. RÉV. *abbr.* Cour de révision.

CRIME. *n.* 1. "... [A]n act which the law, with appropriate penal sanctions, forbids; but as prohibitions are not enacted in a vacuum, we can properly look for some evil or injurious or undesirable effect upon the public against which the law is directed...." *Margarine Case* (1948), [1949] 1 D.L.R. 433 at 472, [1949] S.C.R. 1, Rand J. 2. An offence against the State, as the public's representative, for which the offender will be punished. J.G. Fleming, *The Law of Torts*, 8th ed. (Sydney: Law Book, 1992) at 1. 3. (a) An indictable offence under an Act of Canada, and (b) an offence, under an Act of Canada or of a province, that is punishable only on summary conviction. See WAR ~.

CRIME AGAINST HUMANITY. Murder, extermination, enslavement, deportation, persecution or any other inhumane act or omission that is committed against any civilian population or any identifiable group of persons, whether or not it constitutes a contravention of the law in force at the time and in the place of its commission, and that, at that time and in that place, constitutes a contravention of customary international law or conventional international law or is criminal according to the general principles of law recognized by the community of nations. *Criminal Code*, S.C. 1987, c. 36, s. 1(1).

CRIME COMIC. A magazine, periodical or book that exclusively or substantially comprises matter depicting pictorially (a) the commission of crimes, real or fictitious; or (b) events connected with the commission of crimes, real or fictitious, whether occurring before or after the commission of the crime. *Criminal Code*, R.S.C. 1985, c. C-46, s. 163(7).

CRIMEN FALSI. [L.] Forgery; perjury; suppression of evidence.

CRIMEN FURTI. [L.] Theft.

CRIMEN INCENDII. [L.] Arson.

CRIMEN RAPTUS. [L.] Rape.

CRIMEN ROBERIAE. [L.] Robbery.

CRIMINAL. *n.* A person found guilty of an offence. See HABITUAL ~.

CRIMINAL. *adj.* Relating to crimes or to the administration of the law in respect of crimes.

CRIMINAL CODE. The Criminal Code, R.S.C. 1985, c. C-46 as amended from time to time.

CRIMINAL CONSPIRACY. "... [An] agreement of two or more to do an unlawful act, or to do a lawful act by unlawful means." *R. v. O'Brien*, [1954] S.C.R. 666 at 669, 672 and 674.

CRIMINAL CONTEMPT. "... [W]hen the element of public defiance of the court's process in a way calculated to lessen societal respect for the courts is added to the breach [of a court order], it [the contempt] becomes criminal.... The gravamen of the offence is rather open, continuous and flagrant violation of a Court order without regard for the effect that [such actions] may have on the respect accorded to edicts of the Court.... To establish criminal contempt the Crown must prove that the accused defied or disobeyed a court order in a public way (the actus reus), with intent, knowledge or recklessness as to the fact that the public disobedience will tend to depreciate the authority of the court (the mens rea)...." *U.N.A. v. Alberta (Attorney General)* (1992), 13 C.R. (4th) 1 at 13-14, [1992] 3 W.W.R. 481, 89 D.L.R. (4th) 609, 71 C.C.C. (3d) 225, 135 N.R. 321, 92 C.L.L.C. 14,023, 1 Alta. L.R. (3d) 129, 125 A.R. 241, 14 W.A.C. 241, [1992] 1 S.C.R. 901, 9 C.R.R. (2d) 29, McLachlin J. (La Forest, Gonthier and Iacobucci JJ. concurring).

CRIMINAL CONVERSATION. A husband's claim for damages for adultery.

CRIMINAL INJURIES COMPENSATION. A statutory plan to compensate victims of specified crimes, or anyone injured while attempting to arrest a person, assist a peace officer or preserve the peace. K.D. Cooper-Stephenson & I.B. Saunders, *Personal Injury Damages in Canada* (Toronto: Carswell, 1981) at 3.

CRIMINALIZATION. *n.* Rendering an act criminal and therefore punishable.

CRIMINAL LAW. 1. A law which declares acts to be crimes and prescribes punishment for those crimes. 2. "... [L]egislation creating offences which have a national aspect or dimension may properly be characterized as criminal law ..." *R. v. Hoffman-La Roche Ltd.* (1981), 15 B.L.R. 217 at 265, 33 O.R. (2d) 694, 24 C.R. (3d) 193, 58 C.P.R. (2d) 1, 62 C.C.C. (2d) 118, 125 D.L.R. (3d) 607 (C.A.), the court per Martin J.A.

CRIMINAL MATTER. A prosecution or trial for an offence triable by a judge or jury in accordance with the Criminal Code of Canada.

CRIMINAL NEGLIGENCE. 1. Every one is criminally negligent who (a) in doing anything, or (b) in omitting to do anything that it is his duty to do shows wanton or reckless disregard for the lives or safety of other persons. *Criminal Code*, R.S.C. 1985, c. C-46, s. 219. 2. "In criminal cases, generally, the act coupled with the mental state or intent is punished. In criminal negligence, the act which exhibits the requisite degree of negligence is punished. . . ." *R. v. Tutton* (1989), 48 C.C.C. (3d) 129 at 140, 13 M.V.R. (2d) 161, 69 C.R. (3d) 289, 98 N.R. 19, [1989] 1 S.C.R. 1392, 35 O.A.C. 1, McIntyre J. 3. "... [T]he well-recognized tort of civil negligence: the sins of omission and commission that cause injury to one's neighbour, elevated to a crime by their magnitude of wanton and reckless disregard for the lives and safety of others." *R. v. Gingrich* (1991), 6 C.R. (4th) 197 at 209, 28 M.V.R. (2d) 161, 44 O.A.C. 290, 65 C.C.C. (3d) 188 (C.A.), Finlayson J.A. (Krever J.A. concurring).

CRIMINAL OFFENCE. "... Where the offence is criminal, the Crown must establish a mental element, namely, that the accused who committed the prohibited act did so intentionally or recklessly, with knowledge of the facts constituting the offence, or with wilful blindness toward them. Mere negligence is excluded from the concept of the mental element required for conviction. Within the context of a criminal prosecution a person who fails to make such inquiries as a reasonable and prudent person would make, or who fails to know facts he should have known, is innocent in the eyes of the law." *R. v. Sault Ste. Marie (City)* (1978), 3 C.R. (3d) 30 at 40, [1978] 2 S.C.R. 1299, 21 N.R. 295, 7 C.E.L.R. 53, 40 C.C.C. (2d) 353, 85 D.L.R. (3d) 161, the court per Dickson J.

CRIMINAL ONUS. The standard of proof required is that the case or issue be proved beyond a reasonable doubt. J. Sopinka & S.N. Lederman, *The Law of Evidence in Civil Cases* (Toronto: Butterworths, 1974) at 384-85.

CRIMINAL PROCEDURE. "... In one sense, it is concerned with proceedings in the criminal Courts and such matters as conduct within the courtroom, the competency of witnesses, oaths and affirmations, and the presentation of evidence. Some cases have defined procedure even more narrowly in finding that it embraces the three technical terms – pleading, evidence and practice. In a broad sense, it encompasses such things as the rules by which, according to the Criminal Code, police powers are exercised, the right to counsel, search warrants, interim release, procuring attendance of witnesses." *Di Iorio v. Montreal Jail* (1977), 73 D.L.R. (3d) 491 at 530, [1978] 1 S.C.R. 152, 35 C.R.N.S. 57, 8 N.R. 361, Dickson J. (Martland, Judson, Ritchie and Spence JJ. concurring).

CRIMINAL RATE. An effective annual rate of interest calculated in accordance with generally accepted actuarial practices and principles that exceeds sixty per cent on the credit advanced under an agreement or arrangement. *Criminal Code*, R.S.C. 1985, c. C-46, s. 347(2).

CRIMINAL RESPONSIBILITY. See AGE OF ~.

CRIMINAL SANCTIONS. Fines, imprisonment and probation.

CRIMINATE. *v.* To implicate.

CRIMINATION. See SELF-INCRIMINATION.

CRIMINOLOGIE. *abbr.* Journal published by Presses de l'Université de Montréal.

CRIMINOLOGY. *n.* The study of the nature, causes, treatment or punishment of criminal behaviour. D. Stuart, *Canadian Criminal Law: a Treatise*, 2d ed. (Toronto: Carswell, 1987) at 47.

CRIM. L.Q. *abbr.* Criminal Law Quarterly.

CRITICISM. *n.* The opinion of any person about a book, play or visual image.

C.R.N.S. *abbr.* Criminal Reports, New Series, 1967-1978.

C.R.O. *abbr.* Commission des relations ouvrières.

CROSS-ACTION. *n.* An action brought by a defendant against the plaintiff in the original action.

CROSS-APPEAL. *var.* **CROSS APPEAL.** An appeal by the respondent to an appeal.

CROSSCLAIM. *n.* A claim by one defendant against a co-defendant.

CROSSED CHEQUE. Two parallel lines drawn across the cheque to indicate it cannot be endorsed.

CROSS-EXAMINATION. *n.* The opposite side's examination of a witness which usually follows examination in chief. It is used to weaken the effect of the witness's testimony, to discredit the witness and to elicit evidence in favour of the cross-examining party. P.K. McWilliams, *Canadian Criminal Evidence*, 3d ed. (Aurora: Canada Law Book, 1988) at 37-3 and 37-4.

CROSS-EXAMINATION ON AFFIDAVIT. The opposite party's examination of an affiant on the contents of the affiant's affidavit.

CROWN. *n.* 1. In Canada, the federal government and each of the provincial governments. 2. Depending on the context, Her Majesty the Queen in right of a Province, Canada or both a province and Canada. 3. Used when speaking of the rights, duties or prerogatives of the sovereign. 4. Any of the Commonwealth governments which represent the head, which is Her Majesty. 5. The Sovereign of the United Kingdom, Canada and Her other Realms and Territories, and Head of the Commonwealth. 6. "Although at one time it was correct to describe the Crown as one and indivisible, with the development of the Commonwealth this is no longer so. Although there is only one person who is the Sovereign within the British Commonwealth, it is now a truism that in matters of law and government the Queen of the United Kingdom, for example, is entirely independent and distinct from the Queen of Canada. Further, the Crown is a constitutional monarchy, and thus when one speaks today, and as was frequently done in the course of the argument on this application, of the Crown 'in right of Canada', or of some other territory within the Commonwealth, this is only a short way of referring to the Crown acting through, and on the advice of her ministers in Canada or in that other territory within the Commonwealth." *R. v. Foreign & Commonwealth Affairs (Secretary .of State)* (1982), 1 C.R.R. 254 at 277, [1982] 2 All E.R. 118 (U.K. C.A.), May L.J. 7. "In Gauthier v. The King (1918), 56 S.C.R. 176 at p. 194 Mr. Justice Anglin said: ' . . . a reference to the Crown in a provincial statute shall be taken to be to the Crown in right of the Province only, unless the statute in express terms or by necessary intendment makes it clear that the reference is to the Crown in some other sense. . . .' It has been said that the Crown is one and indivisible. That is the ideal conception of the Crown, but in this country we have under our Federal system, a distribution of powers amongst the Dominion Parliament and the Provincial Legislatures, 'the Crown in right of the Dominion,' and 'the Crown in right of the Province,' are expressions which may therefore mean different things. . . ." *Montreal Trust Co. v. South Shore Lumber Co.* (1924), 33 B.C.R. 280 at

284, [1924] 1 W.W.R. 657, [1924] 1 D.L.R. 1030 (C.A.), Macdonald C.J.A. See DEMISE OF THE ~; FEDERAL ~; LAW OFFICER OF THE ~; MINISTER OF THE ~; PREROGATIVE RIGHTS OF THE ~.

CROWN AGENT. The determination as to whether a particular body is an agent of the Crown depends on the "nature and degree of control" exercised over that body by the Crown. *Westeel-Rosco Ltd. v. Bd. of Gov. of South Sask. Hosp. Centre* (1976), 69 D.L.R. (3d) 334 at 342 (S.C.C.), Ritchie J.

CROWN ATTORNEY. An agent of the Attorney General; prosecutor in criminal matters on behalf of the Crown.

CROWN CORPORATION. 1. A corporation that is accountable, through a Minister, to the Legislative Assembly or Parliament for the conduct of its affairs. 2. A corporation of which not less than 90 per cent of the shares ordinarily entitled to vote in an election for directors are owned by the government of the Province or of Canada. 3. A corporation of which all the directors or members of the governing body are appointed by the Lieutenant Governor in Council or the Governor General in Council. 4. A corporation which under any Act of the Province or of Canada is designated as such.

CROWN COUN. REV. *abbr.* Crown Counsel's Review.

CROWN GRANT. A transfer of Crown lands to a private person.

CROWN IMMUNITY. 1. The common law rule that the Crown is not bound by a statute, unless by express words or necessary implication. *R. v. Eldorado Nuclear Ltd.* (1983), 77 C.P.R. (2d) 1 at 8, 50 N.R. 120, 4 D.L.R. (4th) 193, 1 O.A.C. 243, 8 C.C.C. (3d) 449, [1983] 2 S.C.R. 551, 7 Admin. L.R. 195, Dickson J. (Laskin C.J.C. and Ritchie J. concurring). Statutory provisions in the various Interpretation Acts to the effect that the Crown is not bound unless by express words.

CROWN LAND. Land, whether or not it is covered by water, or an interest in land, vested in the Crown.

CROWN PRIVILEGE. The rule of evidence which states that relevant evidence which is otherwise admissible must not be admitted if to do so would injure the public interest. P.W. Hogg, *Constitutional Law of Canada*, 3d ed. (Toronto: Carswell, 1992) at 264-5.

CROWN'S NEWSL. *abbr.* Crown's Newsletter.

CROWN TIMBER. Includes any trees, timber and products of the forest in respect whereof the Crown is enabled to demand and receive any stumpage, royalty, revenue or money.

CROWN WARDSHIP ORDER. An order of a court making the Crown the legal guardian of a child in need of protection.

C.R.P. *abbr.* Conseil de révision des pensions.

C.R.R. *abbr.* Canadian Rights Reporter.

C.R.T.C. *abbr.* 1. Canadian Railway and Transport Cases, 1902-1966. 2. Canadian Radio-television and Telecommunications Commission (Conseil de la radio-diffusion et des télécommunications canadiennes).

C.R.T.F.P. *abbr.* Commission des relations de travail dans la Fonction publique.

C.R. (3d). *abbr.* Criminal Reports (Third Series), 1978-.

C.R.T.Q. *abbr.* Commission des relations du travail (Québec).

CRUEL AND UNUSUAL PUNISHMENT. "The general standard for determining an infringement of s. 12 [of the Charter] was set out by Lamer J. ... in R. v. Smith, [1987] 1 S.C.R. 1045 ... [at p. 1072]: 'The criterion which must be applied in order to determine whether a punishment is cruel and unusual within the meaning of s. 12 of the Charter is ... "whether the punishment prescribed is so excessive as to outrage standards of decency". In other words, though the state may impose punishment, the effect of that punishment must not be grossly disproportionate to what would have been appropriate.' " *Chiarelli v. Canada (Minister of Employment & Immigration)* (1992), 16 I.L.R. (2d) 1 at 22, 2 Admin. L.R. (2d) 125, 135 N.R. 161, 90 D.L.R. (4th) 289, 8 C.R.R. (2d) 234, 72 C.C.C. (3d) 214, [1992] 1 S.C.R. 711, the court per Sopinka J.

CRUELTY. *n.* 1. "... As used in ordinary parlance 'cruelty' signifies a disposition to inflict suffering; to delight in or exhibit indifference to the pain or misery of others; mercilessness or hard-heartedness as exhibited in action. If in the marriage relationship one spouse by his conduct causes wanton, malicious or unnecessary infliction of pain or suffering upon the body, the feelings or emotions of the other, his conduct may well constitute cruelty which will entitle a petitioner to dissolution of the marriage if, in the court's opinion, it amounts to physical or mental cruelty 'of such a kind as to render intolerable the continued cohabitation of the spouses'. That is the standard which the courts are to apply, and in the context of s. 3(d) of the [Divorce Act, S.C. 1967-68, c. 24] ... Care must be exercised in applying the standard set forth in s. 3(d) that conduct relied upon to establish cruelty is not a trivial act, but one of a 'grave and weighty' nature, and not merely conduct which can be characterized as little more than a manifestation of incompatability of temperament between the spouses...." *Knoll v. Knoll* (1970), 1 R.F.L. 141 at 149, 10 D.L.R. (3d) 199 (Ont. C.A.), the court per Schroeder J.A. 2. Conduct that creates a danger to life, limb or health, and includes any course of conduct that in the opinion of the Court is grossly insulting and intolerable, or is of such a character that the person seeking a separation could not reasonably be expected to be willing to live with the other after he or she has been guilty of such conduct. *Domestic Relations acts.* See ACTS OF ~.

CRYSTALLIZATION. *n.* "... [O]f a floating charge means that upon the happening of some event or events the charge that had been floating over the assets becomes fixed." *Bayhold Financial Corp. v. Clarkson Co.* (1991), (*sub nom. Barhold Financial Corp. v. Community Hotel Co. (Receiver of)*) 86 D.L.R. (4th) 127 at 149, 10 C.B.R. (3d) 159, 108 N.S.R. (3d) 198, 294 A.P.R. 198 (C.A.), the court per Hallett J.A.

CRYSTALLIZE. *v.* To convert a floating charge into a fixed charge. F. Bennett, *Receiverships* (Toronto: Carswell, 1985) at 33.

C.S. *abbr.* 1. Cour supérieure. 2. Cour suprème (provinciale). 3. Recueils de jurisprudence de la Cour supérieure de Québec (Quebec Superior Court Reports). 4. Rapports judiciaires du Québec, Cour supérieure, 1892-1941 (Official Reports, Superior Court).

[ ] C.S. *abbr.* 1. Rapports judiciaires du Québec, Cour supérieure, 1942-1966. 2. Recueils de jurisprudence du Québec, Cour Supérieure, 1967-.

C.S.A. *abbr.* Canadian Standards Association.

C.S.C. *abbr.* Cour supr me du Canada.

C.S. CAN. *abbr.* Cour Supr me du Canada.

C.S.P. *abbr.* 1. Cour des Sessions de la paix. 2. Recueils de jurisprudence, Cour des Sessions de la Paix.

C.S.P. QUÉ. *abbr.* Cour des sessions de la paix (Québec) (Court of Sessions of the Peace (Quebec)).

C.S. QUÉ. *abbr.* Cour supérieure (Québec).

CT. *abbr.* Court.

C.T. *abbr.* Commission du tarif.

C.T.C. *abbr.* 1. Canadian Transport Cases, 1966-. 2. Canadian Transport Commission (Commission canadienne des transports). 3. Centralized Traffic Control.

[ ] C.T.C. *abbr.* Canada Tax Cases, 1917-1971.

CTC(A). The Air Transport Committee of the Canadian Transport Commission. Canada regulations.

[ ] C.T.C. (N.S.). *abbr.* Canada Tax Cases, 1971-.

C.T.C. REGULATIONS. Regulations for the Transportation of Dangerous Commodities by Rail. Canada regulations.

CT. CRIM. APP. *abbr.* Court of Criminal Appeals.

CTEE. *abbr.* Committee.

C.T.M. *abbr.* Canada Tax Manual.

CT. MARTIAL APP. CT. *abbr.* Court Martial Appeal Court.

C.T.Q. *abbr.* Commission des transports du Québec.

C. TRANS. C. *abbr.* Canadian Transport Cases.

CT. REV. *abbr.* Court of Review.

CT. SESS. P. *abbr.* Court of Sessions of the Peace.

C.T./T.T. *abbr.* Décisions du Commissaire du travail et du Tribunal du travail.

CULPA. *n.* [L.] Fault; neglect.

CULPABILITY. *n.* Blame.

CULPABLE. *adj.* That which is to be blamed.

CULPABLE HOMICIDE. 1. Murder or manslaughter or infanticide. *Criminal Code*, R.S.C. 1985, c. C-46, s. 222(4). 2. A person commits culpable homicide when he causes the death of a human being, (a) by means of an unlawful act, (b) by criminal negligence, (c) by causing that human being, by threats or fear of violence or by deception, to do anything that causes his death, or (d) by wilfully frightening that human being, in the case of a child or sick person. *Criminal Code*, R.S.C. 1985, c. C-46, s. 222(5).

CULPRIT. *n.* A person accused of an offence; a person found guilty of an offence.

CUM DIV. *abbr.* Cum dividend.

CUM DIVIDEND. With dividend; when a share is sold cum div. the purchaser receives any declared and not yet paid dividend.

CUM RIGHTS. A purchaser of shares cum rights has the right to claim the rights to new shares or warrants which are about to be issued.

CUM TESTAMENTO ANNEXO. [L. with the will annexed] Administration with the will annexed is granted when a testator has not named an executor or the executor named is not willing to act.

CUMULATIVE. *adj.* Additional, to be added together, to be taken in succession.

CUMULATIVE DIVIDEND. A dividend which, if not paid in one year, continues to accumulate until paid in full.

CUMULATIVE LEGACY. A legacy given in addition to a prior legacy in the same will.

CUMULATIVE PREFERENCE SHARE. A share the dividend of which cumulates from year to year.

CUMULATIVE REMEDY. A mode of procedure available in addition to another possible remedy; opposite to alternative remedy.

CUMULATIVE VOTING. A voting method which permits all votes attached to all a shareholder's shares to be cast for one candidate for board of directors of a corporation.

CURATIVE. *adj.* Intended to remedy.

CURATIVE SECTION. A provision that if one substantially complies with provisions, such as registration of the claim for lien, no lien will be invalidated because one failed to comply with the requirements of such a section unless the Court judges that some person was prejudiced thereby (and then the award is only to the extent of that prejudice). D.N. Macklem & D.I. Bristow, *Construction, Builders' and Mechanics' Liens in Canada*, 6th ed. (Toronto: Carswell, 1990-) at 1-9.

CURATIVE STATUTE. A statute designed to operate on past events, acts or transactions so that irregularities and errors are corrected and acts which would otherwise be ineffective for the intended purpose are rendered valid. B.J. Reiter, R.C.B. Risk & B.N. McLellan, *Real Estate Law*, 3d ed. (Toronto: Emond Montgomery, 1986) at 527.

CURATOR. *n.* A protector of property.

CURE TITLE. To remove encumbrances or claims in order to create good or clear title.

CURFEW. *n.* A law requiring persons to remove themselves from the streets at a certain time of night.

CURIA. *n.* [L.] A court of justice.

CURIA ADVISARI VULT. [L.] The court will consider the matter.

CURIA REGIS. [L.] The monarch's court.

CURRENCY. *n.* 1. A period during which something is in force. 2. The medium of exchange which circulates in a country. 3. Money. See CREATION OF ~.

CURRENT. *adj.* Lawfully current in Canada or elsewhere by virtue of law, proclamation or regulation in force in Canada or elsewhere as the case may be. *Criminal Code*, R.S.C. 1985, c. C-46, s. 448.

CURRENT ASSETS. Cash, accounts receivable, inventory and assets which could be converted to cash in the near future.

CURRENT LIABILITY. A debt due within a short period of time.

CURRENT VALUE ACCOUNTING. One approximates changes in the value of tangible assets by estimating the values of specific items. W. Grover & F. Iacobucci, *Materials on Canadian Income Tax*, 4th ed. (Toronto: De Boo, 1980) at 602.

CURR. LEGAL PROBS. *abbr.* Current Legal Problems.

CURSE. *v.* To swear.

CURTESY. *n.* The interest in a wife's fee simple which a husband will have after her death until his own.

CURTILAGE. *n.* A courtyard, field

or land including any buildings on it lying near and belonging to a dwelling. C.R.B. Dunlop, *Creditor-Debtor Law in Canada* (Toronto: Carswell, 1981) at 390.

CUSTODIA LEGIS. [L.] The custody of the law.

CUSTODY. *n.* 1. "[As used in the Extra-Provincial Enforcement of Custody Orders Act, 1977 (Alta.), c. 20, s. 1(c)] . . . is not a word that has a narrow single meaning. It may mean only the care and control of the child, or it may mean all of the rights of guardianship." *Read v. Read*, [1982] 2 W.W.R. 25 at 29, 17 Alta. L.R. (2d) 273 (C.A.), Moir, Laycraft and McClung JJ.A. 2. ". . . Its meaning can range from immediate effective possession and control of the person, as where a jailer has custody of his prisoner, to control by a parent of a child in the widest possible sense, that is, not only physical but also intellectual, educational, spiritual, moral and financial . . . Thus the concept of custody under the Divorce Act [S.C. 1986, c. 4, s. 2] is for all practical purposes, co-extensive with guardianship of the person under the provincial Family Relations Act [R.S.B.C. 1979, c. 121, ss. 1, 25] . . ." *Clarke v. Clarke* (1987), 7 R.F.L. (3d) 176 at 178, 180, 12 B.C.L.R. (2d) 290 (S.C.), Gow L.J.S.C. 3. Personal guardianship of a child and includes care, upbringing and any other incident of custody having regard to the child's age and maturity. *The Children's Law Act*, S.S. 1990-91, c. C-8.1, s. 2(1). 4. Includes care, upbringing and any other incident of custody. *Divorce Act 1985*, S.C. 1986, c. 4, s. 2(1). See CARE AND ~; DIVIDED ~; JOINT ~; LEGAL ~; SOLE ~.

CUSTODY AGREEMENT. Any agreement with respect to the custody, care or control of a child.

CUSTODY ORDER. 1. The order of any court with respect to the custody, care or control of a child. 2. An order, or that part of an order, of an extra-provincial tribunal that grants custody of a child to any person and includes provisions, if any, granting another person a right of access or visitation to the child. *Extra-provincial Custody Orders Enforcement acts.* 3. An order made under subsection 16(1). *Divorce Act,* R.S.C. 1985 (2d Supp.), c. 3, s. 2.

CUSTODY PROVISION. A provision of an order or agreement awarding custody of a child. *Family Orders and Agreements Enforcement Assistance Act,* R.S.C. 1985 (2d supp.), c. 4, s. 2.

CUSTOM. *n.* 1. An unwritten law or right, established through long use. 2. ". . . [I]n the sense of a rule having the force of law and existing since time immemorial is not in issue in this case. Indeed, Canadian law being largely of imported origin will rarely, if ever, evince that sort of custom. Custom in Canadian law must be given a broader definition. In any event, both courts below were not using the term in such a technical sense, as is clear from the fact that both substituted the term 'practice' as a synonym." *International Corona Resources Ltd. v. Lac Minerals Ltd.* (1989), 26 C.P.R. (3d) 97 at 121, [1989] 2 S.C.R. 574, 69 O.R. (2d) 287, 61 D.L.R. (4th) 14, 6 R.P.R. (2d) 1, 44 B.L.R. 1, 35 E.T.R. 1, 101 N.R. 239, 36 Q.A.C. 57, La Forest J. (Wilson and Lamer JJ. concurring).

CUSTOMARY. *adj.* According to custom; usual.

CUSTOMARY AUTHORITY. An agent who is authorized to act for a principal in a particular business, market or locale has implied authority to act in accordance with the usages and customs of that business, market or locale. G.H.L. Fridman, *The Law of Agency,* 6th ed. (London: Butterworths, 1990) at 66. See USUAL OR ~.

CUSTOMARY INTERNATIONAL LAW. A national practice accepted as international law.

CUSTOM DUTY. The fee payable when importing goods.

CUSTOM-HOUSE. *n.* The office where any duty payable or receivable upon import or export is paid or received.

CUSTOM OF THE TRADE. Any practice usually observed by people dealing in a particular product.

CUSTOMS. *n.* Duties charged when goods are imported into, or exported out of, a country.

CUSTOMS BROKER. A person who acts as agent to clear goods through customs.

CUSTOMS DUTY. The tax when goods are imported.

CUSTOMS OFFICER. The collector or chief officer of customs at a port.

CUSTOMS UNION. An agreement between countries for the unification of territories for purposes of customs.

CY-PRES. [Fr. near to it] ". . . [I]f the settlor or testator specifies an object but that object is or afterwards becomes impossible or impracticable of performance, the gift will not fail, but the property will be used for some similar purpose as much resembling the specified object as possible, providing the settlor has expressed, or the Court is able to gather . . . from a trust instrument, the paramount instrument of charity. . . ." *Weatherby v. Weatherby* (1927), 53 N.B.R. 403 at 417 (S.C.), Hazen C.J.

D

DALHOUSIE L.J. *abbr*. Dalhousie Law Journal.

DAMAGE. *n*. 1. Harm; loss. 2. "... [U]sually used to refer to a particular head of loss for which compensation is awarded. The word 'damages' is generally used to identify the amount of money that is paid by a tortfeasor for inflicting the various items of damage.... certainly includes injury but it also includes more than that. It includes all of the different heads of damage and various expenses that may be suffered as a result of tortious conduct." *Vile v. Von Wendt* (1979), 14 C.P.C. 121 at 125-6, 26 O.R. (2d) 513, 103 D.L.R. (3d) 356 (Div. Ct.), the court per Linden J. See NEGATIVE ~; SPECIAL ~; STIPULATED ~.

DAMAGES. *n*. "... [A] monetary payment awarded for the invasion of a right at common law." *Canson Enterprises Ltd. v. Boughton & Co.* (1991), 9 C.C.L.T. (2d) 1 at 23, [1991] 1 W.W.R. 245, 61 B.C.L.R. (2d) 1, 85 D.L.R. (4th) 129, 131 N.R. 321, 43 E.T.R. 201, 39 C.P.R. (3d) 449, [1991] 3 S.C.R. 534, 6 B.C.A.C. 1, 3 W.A.C. 1, La Forest J. (Sopinka, Gonthier and Cory JJ. concurring). See AGGRAVATED ~; CONSEQUENTIAL ~; CONTEMPTUOUS ~; DAMAGE; DERISORY ~; EXEMPLARY ~; GENERAL ~; LIQUIDATED ~; MEASURE OF ~; MITIGATION OF ~; NOMINAL ~; PUNITIVE ~; UNLIQUIDATED ~; VINDICTIVE ~.

DAMAGES AT LARGE. "Damages other than for material loss ... These have been variously defined but appear generally to mean general damages consisting of non-economic loss and exemplary damages in appropriate cases. ... Because they include compensation for loss of reputation, damages at large probably encompasses economic loss that can be foreseen but not readily quantified." *Farrell v. Canadian Broadcasting Corp.* (1987), (*sub nom. Farrell v. Canadian Broadcasting Corp. (No. 1)*) 43 D.L.R. (4th) 667 at 667, 669, 66 Nfld. & P.E.I.R. 145, 204 A.P.R. 145 (Nfld. C.A.), Goodridge C.J.N.

DAMNA. *n*. [L.] Damages.

DAMNUM. *n*. [L.] 1. Damage. 2. Harm. 3. Loss.

DAMNUM ABSQUE INJURIA. [L.] Loss without an injury. Compare INJURIA ABSQUE DAMNO.

DANGER. *n*. Any hazard or condition that could reasonably be expected to cause injury or illness to a person exposed thereto before the hazard or condition can be corrected. *Canada Labour Code*, R.S.C. 1985 (1st Supp.), c. 9, s. 122. See CONCEALED ~.

DANGEROUS. *adj*. 1. "... [L]ikely or probable to cause injury ..." *Burns v. R.* (1945), 19 M.P.R. 178 at 185 (P.E.I. C.A.), Campbell C.J. 2. With reference to any person, means dangerous to himself or any other person. *Health and Public Welfare Act*, R.S. Nfld. 1970, c. 151, s. 97.

DANGEROUS ANIMAL. Animals ferae naturae which are normally dangerous and animals mansuetae naturae which are normally harmless but individuals may be dangerous. J.G. Fleming, *The Law of Torts*, 8th ed. (Sydney: Law Book, 1992) at 388.

DANGEROUS DRIVING. See DANGEROUS OPERATION OF MOTOR VEHICLES.

DANGEROUS OFFENDER. A court, acting under s. 753 of the Criminal Code, R.S.C. 1985, c. C-46, may find an offender to be a dangerous offender where the offender has been convicted of a "serious personal injury offence" and the offender constitutes a threat to the life, safety or physical or mental well-being of other persons on the basis of certain evidence defined in s. 753. Also, a person may be found to be a dangerous offender if he has been convicted of one of the forms of sexual assault listed in s. 752(b) and the offender by his conduct in any sexual matter has shown a failure to control his sexual impulses and a likelihood of his causing injury, pain or other evil to other persons through failure in the future to control his sexual impulses.

DANGEROUS OPERATION OF AIRCRAFT. Operating an aircraft in a manner that is dangerous to the public, having regard to all the circumstances, including the nature and condition of that aircraft or the place or air space in or through which the aircraft is operated. *Criminal Code*, R.S.C. 1985, c. C-46, s. 249(1)(c).

DANGEROUS OPERATION OF MOTOR VEHICLES. Operating a motor vehicle on a street, road, highway or other public place in a manner that is dangerous to the public, having regard to all the circumstances, including the nature, condition and use of such place and the amount of traffic that at the time is or might reasonably be expected to be on that place. *Criminal Code*, R.S.C. 1985, c. C-46, s. 249(1)(a).

DANGEROUS OPERATION OF VESSELS. Operating a vessel or any water skis, surf board, water sled or other towed object on or over any of the internal waters of Canada or the territorial sea of Canada, in a manner that is dangerous to the public, having regard to all the circumstances, including the nature and condition of such waters or sea and the use that at the time is or might reasonably be expected to be made of such waters or sea. *Criminal Code*, R.S.C. 1985, c. C-46, s. 249(1)(b).

DATA. *n.* 1. Facts. 2. Representations of information or of concepts that are being prepared or have been prepared in a form suitable for use in a computer system. *Criminal Code*, R.S.C. 1985, c. C-46 (as am. by *Criminal Law Amendment Act*, R.S.C. 1985 (1st Supp.), c. 27), s. 342.1(2).

DATE. *n.* 1. ". . . [T]ime 'given' or specified, time in some way ascertained and fixed; . . ." *Bement v. Trenton Locomotive Co.* (1866), 32 N.J.L. 513 at 515-6. 2. The year and the day of the month. See CONTRACT ~; ENUMERATION ~; PROCLAMATION ~.

DAY. *n.* 1. A calendar day. 2. ". . . [C]ommences at midnight and ends the following midnight: . . ." *Thornbury (Town) v. Grey (County)* (1893), 15 P.R. 192 at 194 (Ont. C.A.), the court per Armour C.J. 3. Any period of 24 consecutive hours. See APPOINTED ~; COSTS OF THE ~; JURIDICAL ~; ORDER OF THE ~.

DAY CARE. A service that provides daytime care of or services to children outside their own homes by an authorized person, with or without charge.

DAY PAROLE. Parole the terms and conditions of which require the inmate to whom it is granted to return to prison or correctional centre from time to time during the duration of the parole or to return to prison or correctional centre after a specified period. *Parole acts*.

DAYS OF GRACE. Time allowed to make a payment or do some other act when the time originally allowed has expired.

D.C.A. *abbr.* Dorion, Décisions de la Cour d'Appel (Queen's Bench Reports).

D.D.C.P. *abbr.* Décisions disciplinaires concernant les Corporations professionnelles.

DE. *prep.* [L.] Of; from; concerning.

DEALER. *n.* 1. ". . . [O]ne who trades in, buys or sells goods on his own account. It does not necessarily follow he must be the owner of the goods he sells; he may be a broker . . . so long as he is in the business for himself. . . ." *Harmon v. Russell* (1927), 21 Sask. L.R. 686 at 699, [1927] 2 W.W.R. 505, [1927] 3 D.L.R. 626 (C.A.), Mackenzie J.A. 2. Person whose business is to buy items and sell them to other persons. 3. A person who trades in securities as principal or agent. *Securities acts.* See BROKER–~.

DEATH BENEFIT. The amount received by a survivor or the deceased's estate upon or after the death of an employee in recognition of the employee's service in office or employment.

DEBASEMENT. *n.* A reduction of standard of fineness of coinage.

DEBATES. See OFFICIAL REPORT OF ~.

DE BENE ESSE. [L.] 1. To consider something well done for the moment, but when it is examined or tried more fully, it must stand or fall on its own merit. 2. "To do a thing de bene esse signifies allowing or accepting certain evidence for the present until more fully examined, valeat quantum valere potest. It is regarded as an additional examination to be utilized if necessary only in the event that witnesses cannot be examined later in the action in the regular way. This evidence therefore was taken 'for what it is was worth.' . . . *C.T. Gogstad & Co. v. "Camosun" (The)* (1941), 56 B.C.R. 156 at 157 (Ex. Ct.), MacDonald D.J.A.

DEBENTURE. *n.* 1. Any corporate obligation unsecured or frequently secured by a floating charge. H. Sutherland, D.B. Horsley & J.M. Edmiston, eds., *Fraser's Handbook on Canadian Company Law*, 7th ed. (Toronto: Carswell, 1985) at 310. 2. ". . . [A] document in which a debt is acknowledged and in which the debtor covenants to repay . . ." *Acmetrack Ltd. v. Bank Canadian National* (1984), 4 P.P.S.A.C. 199 at 206, 48 O.R. (2d) 49, 27 B.L.R. 319, 52 C.B.R. (N.S.) 235, 12 D.L.R. (4th) 428, 5 O.A.C. 321 (C.A.), the court per Zuber J.A. 3. ". . . [I]n municipal financing [a debenture] is, ordinarily . . . a promise under seal to pay the bearer a principal sum and interest at certain times, and is an instrument transferable on the markets by delivery." *Toronto (City) v. Canada Permanent Mortgage Corp.*, [1954] S.C.R. 576 at 582, [1954] 4 D.L.R. 529, Rand J. See BANK ~S; COUPON ~; MORTGAGE ~.

DEBIT. *n.* A sum due or owing.

DEBIT NOTE. A note which states that the account of the person to whom it is sent will be debited.

DE BONIS ASPORTATIS. [L.] For goods taken away. See TRESPASS ~.

DE BONIS NON ADMINISTRATIS. [L.] A grant made when an administrator dies without having fully administered an estate or an executor dies intestate.

DEBT. *n.* 1. ". . . [I]ncludes any claim, legal or equitable, on contract, express or implied, or under a statute on which a certain sum of money, not being unliquidated damages, is due and payable, though an enquiry be necessary to ascertain the exact amount due." *Boldrick v. Salz*, [1952] O.W.N. 487 at 488 (C.A.), Hope J.A. 2. ". . . [A] sum payable in respect of a liquidated money demand recoverable by action. . . ." *Walsh v. British Columbia (Minister of Finance)* (1979), 5 E.T.R. 179 at 191, [1979] 4 W.W.R. 161, [1979] C.T.C. 251, 13 B.C.L.R. 255 (S.C.), Anderson J. See ATTACHMENT OF ~S; BAD ~; BOOK ~S; CONSUMER ~; FAMILY ~; JUDGMENT ~; NATIONAL ~; SPECIALTY ~.

DEBTOR. *n.* 1. One who owes a debt. 2. A person to whom or on whose account money lent is advanced and includes every surety and endorser or other person liable for the repayment of money lent or upon agreement or collateral or other security given in respect thereof. *Unconscionable Transactions Relief acts.* R.S.C. 1985, c. B-3, s. 2. 3. An insolvent person and any person who, at any time an act of bankruptcy was committed by him, resided or carried on business in Canada and, where the context requires, includes a bankrupt. *Bankruptcy Act,* R.S.C. 1985, c. B-3, s. 2. See ABSCONDING ~; JUDGMENT ~.

DEBT SECURITY. Any bond, debenture, note or similar instrument representing indebtedness, whether secured or unsecured. *Securities Act,* R.R.O. 1980, Reg. 910, s. 1.

DÉC. B.-C. *abbr.* Décisions des Tribunaux du Bas-Canada (1851-1867).

DECEASED. *n.* 1. A dead person. 2. A testator or a person dying intestate. *Dependants Relief acts.*

DECEIT. *n.* ". . . [A] false representation of fact by words or conduct . . . made . . . with the knowledge of its falsity; . . . [and] with the intention that it be acted upon . . . [and that it was in fact acted upon] in reliance upon the representation and that . . . damage [was sustained in so doing]." *Bell v. Source Data Control Ltd.* (1988), 40 B.L.R. 10 at 17, 29 O.A.C. 134, 66 O.R. (2d) 78, 53 D.L.R. (4th) 580 (C.A.), Cory J.A. (dissenting).

DECEIVE. *v.* To induce a person to believe that something which is false is true.

DECERTIFICATION. *n.* Removal of a union's right to represent a group of employees for collective bargaining purposes.

DECISION. *n.* 1. A judgment, ruling, order, finding, or determination of a court. 2. ". . . [O]f a Court or Judge means the judicial opinion, oral or written, pronounced or delivered, upon which the 'judgment or order' is founded and the 'judgment or order' is the embodiment in legal procedure of the result of such decision . . ." *Fermini v. McGuire* (1984), 42 C.P.C. 189 at 191, 64 N.S.R. (2d) 421, 143 A.P.R. 421 (C.A.), Macdonald J.A. See

STATUTORY POWER OF ~.

DECLARATION. *n.* 1. A formal statement of the opinion or decision of a court on the rights of interested parties or the construction of a will, deed or other written instrument. 2. ". . . [D]iffers from other judicial orders in that it declares what the law is without pronouncing any sanction against the defendant, but the issue which is determined by a declaration clearly becomes res judicata between the parties and the judgment a binding precedent." *LeBar v. Canada* (1988), 46 C.C.C. (3d) 103 at 108, 33 Admin. L.R. 107, 22 F.T.R. 160n, 90 N.R. 5 (C.A.), the court per MacGuigan J.A. See DYING ~; SOLEMN ~; STATUTORY ~.

DECLARATION OF TRUST. Creation of a trust when the trust property is already held by the intended trustee by execution of a deed declaring that the trustee holds the property in trust for the executor of the deed.

DECLARATORY JUDGMENT. Declaring the parties' rights or expressing the court's opinion on a question of law, without ordering that anything be done.

DECLARATORY ORDER. A binding declaration of right, made by the Ontario Court (General Division), the Unified Family Court or the Court of Appeal, whether or not any consequential relief could be or is claimed (Courts of Justice Act, R.S.O. 1990, c. C.43, s. 97). G.D. Watson & C. Perkins, eds., *Holmested & Watson: Ontario Civil Procedure* (Toronto: Carswell, 1984-) at CJA-127.

DECLARATORY POWER. The power of the federal Parliament under s. 92(10)(C) of the Constitution Act, 1867 to bring a local work into federal jurisdiction by declaring that it is "for the general advantage of Canada". P.W. Hogg, *Constitutional Law of Canada,* 3d ed. (Toronto: Carswell, 1992) at 115. See WORKS FOR THE GENERAL ADVANTAGE OF CANADA.

DECLARATORY RELIEF. ". . . [A] remedy neither constrained by form nor bounded by substantive content, which avails persons sharing a legal relationship, in respect of which a 'real issue' concerning the relative interests of each has been raised and falls to be determined." *Solosky v. Canada* (1980), 105 D.L.R. (3d) 745 at 753, [1980] 1 S.C.R. 821, 30 N.R. 380, 50 C.C.C. (2d) 495, 16 C.R. (3d) 294, Dickson J. (Laskin C.J.C., Martland, Ritchie and Pigeon JJ. concurring).

DECLARATORY STATUTE. A declaration or formal statement of existing law.

DECREE. *n.* Judgment.

DECREE ABSOLUTE. 1. A final decree. 2. The final court order in a divorce action.

DECREE NISI. 1. A provisional decree which will become final or absolute unless there is reason shown not to do so. 2. A provisional court order which terminates marriage.

DECREE OF FORECLOSURE. This document states that a mortgagor will be finally foreclosed or deprived of the equitable right to redeem, unless, within a specified time, that mortgagor does redeem. W.B. Rayner & R.H. McLaren, *Falconbridge on Mortgages*, 4th ed. (Toronto: Canada Law Book, 1977) at 447.

DEDICATE. *v.* To make public a private road.

DEDICATION. *n.* The express or tacit opening of a road for public use.

DEDUCTION. *n.* 1. An amount deducted, taken away. 2. An amount withheld by an employer from an employee's wages for union dues, taxes, pension, insurance. 3. An amount permitted by tax laws to be subtracted from income before computing tax.

DEED. *n.* A document signed, sealed and delivered, through which an interest, property or right passes. See DISENTAILING ~; EXECUTION OF ~; PREMISES OF A ~; QUIT-CLAIM ~; REGISTRAR OF ~S; SUPPLEMENTAL ~; TRUST ~.

DEED OF CONVEYANCE. ". . . [A]

mere transfer of title, . . ." *Fraser-Reid v. Droumtskeas* (1979), 9 R.P.R. 121 at 139, [1980] 1 S.C.R. 720, 103 D.L.R. (3d) 385, Dickson J.

DEED OF COVENANT. A deed in which one party formally agrees to do certain things with another.

DEED OF GIFT. A deed which transfers property as a gift.

DEED OF GRANT. A deed which grants property.

DEED-POLL. *var.* **DEED POLL.** *n.* 1. A declaration of the act and intention of a grantor of property, so named because it was formerly polled (shaved even) at the top, whereas an indenture was indented (cut in acute angles). 2. A deed with one party only. R. Megarry & H.W.R. Wade, *The Law of Real Property*, 5th ed. (London: Stevens, 1984) at cxxiv. See INDENTURE.

DEED TO USES. A deed purporting to grant or convey land to such uses as the grantee may appoint, regardless of the method of appointment specified in the deed, and, until appointment or in default of appointment, purporting to grant or convey the land in the use of the grantee absolutely, and includes every such deed containing words of like import, but does not include a mortgage. *Registry Act*, R.S.O. 1980, c. 445, s. 59.

DEEM. *v.* 1. ". . . . [W]hen used in a statute . . . to bring in something which would otherwise be excluded. . . ." *Hillis v. Minister of National Revenue*, [1983] 6 W.W.R. 577 at 588, 15 E.T.R. 156, [1983] C.T.C. 348, 49 N.R. 1, 83 D.T.C. 5365 (Fed. C.A.), Heald J.A. (dissenting). 2. ". . . [T]o adjudge or decide . . . to decide judicially. . . ." *Hunt v. College of Physicians & Surgeons (Saskatchewan)*, [1925] 4 D.L.R. 834 at 839, [1925] 3 W.W.R. 758, 45 C.C.C. 39, 20 Sask. L.R. 305 (K.B.), MacKenzie J.

DEEMED. *adj.* ". . . [M]ay mean 'deemed conclusively' or 'deemed until the contrary is proved'. *Gray v. Kerslake* (1957), 11 D.L.R. (2d) 225 at 239, [1958] S.C.R. 3, [1957] I.L.R. 1-279, Cartwright J.

DEEMED TRUST. A trust created by statute which is designed to protect certain classes of creditors or to insure the recovery of certain taxes. F. Bennett, *Receiverships* (Toronto: Carswell, 1985) at 242.

DEEMING CLAUSE. ". . . [P]urpose of any 'deeming' clause is to impose a meaning, to cause something to be taken to be different from that which it might have been in the absence of the clause." *R. v. Sutherland* (1980), 113 D.L.R. (3d) 374 at 379, [1980] 2 S.C.R. 451, 35 N.R. 161, [1980] 5 W.W.R. 456, 53 C.C.C. (2d) 289, 7 Man. R. (2d) 359, [1980] 3 C.N.L.R. 71, the court per DicksonJ.

DE FACTO. [L.] In fact.

DE FACTO POSSESSION. Physical control.

DEFALCATION. *n.* ". . . [D]oes not necessarily entail a dishonest or wrongful act. It is sufficient if there is a failure to meet an obligation by a fiduciary. A breach of trust arises whenever a trustee fails to carry out his obligations under the terms of the trust. . . ." *Smith v. Henderson* (1992), 64 B.C.L.R. (2d) 144 at 149, 10 C.B.R. (3d) 153, 10 B.C.A.C. 249, 16 W.A.C. 249 (C.A.), the court per Legg J.A.

DEFAMATION. *n.* Libel or slander. *Defamation acts.*

DEFAMATORY. *adj.* Tending to lower the reputation of someone in the opinion of right thinking members of society. R.E. Brown, *The Law of Defamation in Canada* (Toronto: Carswell, 1987) at 9.

DEFAMATORY LIBEL. Matter published without lawful justification or excuse, that is likely to injure the reputation of any person by exposing him to hatred, contempt or ridicule, or that is designed to insult the person of or concerning whom it is published. A defamatory libel may be expressed directly or by insinuation or irony (a) in words legibly marked upon any substance, or (b) by any object signifying a defamatory libel otherwise than by words. *Criminal Code*, R.S.C. 1985, c. C-46, s. 298.

DEFAULT. *n.* 1. The failure to pay or otherwise perform the obligation secured when due or the occurrence of any event whereupon under the terms of the security agreement the security becomes enforceable. *Personal Property Security acts.* 2. The omission of something one should do; neglect. 3. Non-attendance in court.

DEFAULT JUDGMENT. The final judgment awarded to the plaintiff when the defendant fails to file an appearance or statement of defence.

DEFEASANCE. *n.* 1. A condition appended to an estate which defeats the estate when performed or a deed which defeats an estate. 2. A condition on an obligation which defeats it when performed.

DEFEASANCE CLAUSE. A proviso that a mortgage will become void on payment of the mortgage money. Thus, if one pays strictly according to the proviso, the estate without release or reconveyance becomes revested in the mortgagor or becomes vested in any other person entitled to it by subsequent mortgage or assignment from the mortgagor. W.B. Rayner & R.H. McLaren, *Falconbridge on Mortgages*, 4th ed. (Toronto: Canada Law Book, 1977) at 366.

DEFEASIBLE. *adj.* 1. Able to be abrogated or annulled. 2. "A gift that is subject to being defeated or terminated on an event such as re-marriage . . ." *Dontigny v. R.*, [1974] 1 F.C. 418 at 421, [1974] C.T.C. 532, 74 D.T.C. 6437 (C.A.), Jackett and St.-Germain JJ.A.

DEFEAT. *v.* To frustrate, prevent.

DEFECT. *n.* Absence of an essential. See INHERENT ~; LATENT ~; PATENT ~.

DEFECTIVE. *adj.* Wanting in an essential ingredient.

DEFECTIVE TITLE. In respect of real property, title in respect of which there is a question as to title and not just a question as to conveyancing. To be contrasted with marketable or good title. V. Di Castri, *Law of Vendor and*

Purchaser (Toronto: Carswell, 1988), para. 340.

DEFENCE. *n*. 1. ". . . [A] contention that the plaintiff's claim is not established. It adopts one or more of the following positions: (i) an objection on ground of jurisdiction; (ii) a denial of the plaintiff's allegations (traverse); (iii) a submission that if the plaintiff's allegations are true they disclose no cause of action (demurrer); and (iv) a submission that if the plaintiff's allegations are true there are facts which provide a legal justification for the defendant's conduct (confession and avoidance)." *Royal Bank v. Rizkalla* (1984), 50 C.P.C. 292 at 295, 59 B.C.L.R. 324 (S.C.), McLachlin J. 2. In criminal law, an assertion of innocence and denial of guilt. *R. v. Schwartz* (1988), 55 D.L.R. (4th) 1, [1989] 1 W.W.R. 289, 66 C.R. (3d) 251, 88 N.R. 90, [1988] 2 S.C.R. 443, 45 C.C.C. (3d) 97, 56 Man. R. (2d) 92. 3. In criminal law, generally a response to a criminal charge which would defeat the charge or an assertion which, if accepted, would require an acquittal. *R. v. Chaulk* (1990), 1 C.R.R. (2d) 1, 2 C.R. (4th) 1, 119 N.R. 161, [1991] 2 W.W.R. 385, 69 Man. R. (2d) 161, 62 C.C.C. (3d) 193, [1990] 3 S.C.R. 1303. See EXTRANEOUS ~; FULL ANSWER AND ~; INHERENT ~; STATEMENT OF ~.

DEFEND. *v*. To deny. See NOTICE OF INTENT TO ~.

DEFENDANT. *n*. 1. Includes every person served with any writ of summons or process, or served with notice of, or entitled to attend, any proceedings. 2. A person against whom an action is commenced. 3. A person to whom a summons is issued. 4. Includes a plaintiff against whom a counterclaim is brought.

DEFERRED ANNUITY. An annuity that becomes payable to the contributor at the time he reaches sixty years of age or another age specified by the governing statute.

DEFERRED COMMUNITY OF PROPERTY. Each spouse retains separate property during marriage, but when the marriage dissolves, each spouse is entitled to one-half of all property which forms the community. J.G. McLeod, *The Conflict of Laws* (Calgary: Carswell, 1983) at 372.

DEFERRED PENSION. A pension benefit, payment of which is deferred until the person entitled to the pension benefit reaches the normal retirement date under the pension plan.

DEFERRED PROFIT SHARING PLAN. A plan which allows an employer to share company profits with employees. W. Grover & F. Iacobucci, *Materials on Canadian Income Tax*, 4th ed. (Toronto: De Boo, 1980) at 444.

DEFERRED SHARING SCHEME. The sharing of matrimonial property is deferred until the happening of an event such as marriage breakdown. A. Bissett-Johnson & W.M. Holland, eds., *Matrimonial Property Law in Canada* (Toronto: Carswell, 1980) at A-5.

DEFERRED STOCK. A stock entitling holders to all the remaining net earnings after dividends have been paid to the preferred stock and ordinary stockholders.

DEFICIT. *n*. Loss; an amount by which expenditures exceed revenue.

DEFINE. *v*. To explain the meaning; to limit; to clarify.

DEFINED BENEFIT PLAN. A pension plan where the pension benefits under the plan are determined in accordance with a formula set forth in the plan and where the employer contributions under the plan are not so determined. *Pension Benefits Standards Regulations*, C.R.C., c. 1252, s. 2.

DEFINED CONTRIBUTION PLAN. A pension plan that consists of defined contribution provisions and does not contain defined benefit provisions, other than (a) a defined benefit provision relating to pension benefits accrued in respect of employment before the effective date of the pension plan, or (b) a defined benefit provision that provides for a minimum pension benefit whose additional value is not significant in the Superintendent's opinion. *Pension Benefit Standards Act*, R.S.C. 1985 (2d Supp.), c. 32, s. 2.

DEFINITION SECTION. A statutory provision which states that particular words and phrases, when used in the statute, will bear certain meanings. P.St.J. Langan, ed., *Maxwell on The Interpretation of Statutes*, 12th ed. (Bombay: N.M. Tripathi, 1976) at 270.

DEFRAUD. *v.* "... [T]wo elements are essential, 'dishonesty' and 'deprivation'.... The element of deprivation is satisfied on proof of detriment, prejudice or risk of prejudice to the economic interests of the victim...." *R. v. Olan* (1978), 5 C.R. (3d) 1 at 7, [1978] 2 S.C.R. 1175, 86 D.L.R. (3d) 212, 41 C.C.C. (2d) 145, 21 N.R. 504, Dickson J.

DEFUNCT. *adj.* No longer in operation; no longer carrying on business.

DEGREE. *n.* 1. A difference in relative importance between members of the same species. 2. One step in the line of consanguinity or descent. 3. Any recognition in writing of academic achievement which is called a degree; and includes the degrees of bachelor, master and doctor.

DE JURE. [L.] By right; lawful.

DELAY. *v.* To postpone, to put off.

DELAY. *n.* See INSTITUTIONAL ~.

DELAY DEFEATS EQUITIES. "[A court of equity] ... has always refused its aid to stale demands, where a party has slept upon his right and acquiesced for a great length of time. Nothing can call forth this court into activity, but conscience, good faith, and reasonable diligence; where these are wanting, the Court is passive, and does nothing." *Smith v. Clay* (1767), 3 Bro.C.C. 639n at 640n, Lord Camden L.C.

DEL CREDERE. Guarantee; warranty.

DEL CREDERE AGENT. A mercantile agent who will indemnify the principal if the third party fails to pay as contracted in respect of goods.

G.H.L. Fridman, *The Law of Agency*, 6th ed. (London: Butterworths, 1990) at 38-9.

DEL CREDERE COMMISSION. An extra commission paid to a del credere agent. G.H.L. Fridman, *The Law of Agency*, 6th ed. (London: Butterworths, 1990) at 38.

DELEGATED LEGISLATION. 1. Subordinate legislation made by authorities other than Parliament or a legislature. P.W. Hogg, *Constitutional Law of Canada*, 3d ed. (Toronto: Carswell, 1992) at 340. 2. A statutory instrument. S.A. DeSmith, *Judicial Review of Administrative Action*, 4th ed. by J.M. Evans (London: Stevens, 1980) at 147.

DELEGATION. *n.* 1. Entrusting someone else to act in one's place. 2. The assignment of a debt to someone else.

DELEGATUS NON POTEST DELEGARE. [L.] 1. One who already is a delegate cannot delegate. 2. "... Unless rebutted, it stands for the proposition that there is no authority to redelegate a delegated power...." *Hanson v. Ontario Universities Athletic Assn.* (1975), 25 C.P.R. (2d) 239 at 248, 11 O.R. (2d) 193, 65 D.L.R. (3d) 385 (H.C.), Lieff J.

DELIBERATE. *v.* To consider.

DELIBERATE. *adj.* "... [C]onsidered, not impulsive." *R. v. Nygaard* (1989), 51 C.C.C. (3d) 417 at 432, [1989] 2 S.C.R. 1074, [1990] 1 W.W.R. 1, 70 Alta. L.R. (2d) 1, 72 C.R. (3d) 257, 101 N.R. 108, 102 A.R. 186, Cory. J.

DELIBERATE ACT. "... [O]ne proceeding from an intention and an intelligence which knows the nature and quality of the criminal act...." *R. v. Pilon* (1965), 46 C.R. 272 at 294, [1968] 2 C.C.C. 53 (Qué. C.A.), Rivard J.A.

DELICT. *n.* A tort; a crime.

DELICTUM. *n.* [L.] A tort. See IN PARI DELICTO.

DELINQUENCY. *n.* 1. Failure; omission. 2. "... [T]wo categories of acts;

the first category includes acts that are in violation of 'any provision of the Criminal Code or of any federal or provincial statute, or of any by-law or ordinance of any municipality' (Juvenile Delinquents Act, R.S.C. 1970, c. J-9, s. 2(1)), or, as Fauteux J. put it in A.G.B.C. v. Smith (S.), [1967] S.C.R. 702 at 710 ... that are 'punishable breaches of the public law, whether defined by Parliament or the Legislature'; the second category includes sexual immorality or other similar forms of vice which, while not illegal in the case of adults, should be repressed in the case of juveniles." *R. v. Morris* (1979), 6 C.R. (3d) 36 at 48, 43 C.C.C. (2d) 129, [1979] 1 S.C.R. 405, 91 D.L.R. (3d) 161, 23 N.R. 109, Pratte J. (Martland, Ritchie, Pigeon and Beetz JJ. concurring).

DELINQUENT. *n.* 1. In respect of payments or other obligations, late or not carried out in accordance with the agreement. 2. For use in respect of the former Juvenile Delinquents Act. See DELINQUENCY; YOUNG PERSON.

DELIST. *v.* To remove a security from its trading on the stock exchange.

DELIVER. *v.* 1. With reference to a notice or other document, includes mail to or leave with a person, or deposit in a person's mail box or receptacle at the person's residence or place of business. 2. "... [T]urning over the custody of the person ..." *R. v. Dean* (1991), 5 C.R. (4th) 176 at 183 (Ont. Gen. Div.), Haley J.

DELIVERABLE STATE. Goods in such a state that the buyer would, under contract, be bound to take delivery of them. *Sale of Goods acts.*

DELIVERED. *adj.* "... [T]he party whose deed the document is expressed to be, having first sealed it, must by words or conduct expressly or impliedly acknowledge his intention to be immediately and unconditionally bound by the expressions contained therein: ..." *Metropolitan Theatres Ltd., Re* (1917), 40 O.L.R. 345 at 347 (H.C.), Rose J.

DELIVERY. *n.* 1. The voluntary

transfer of possession from one person to another. *Sale of Goods acts.* 2. Transfer of possession, actual or constructive, from one person to another. See CASH ON ~; WRIT OF ~.

DEMAND. *n.* 1. A claim that a person offer something due. 2. A request that a person do something which she or he is legally bound to do once the request is made. See LIQUIDATED ~; STALE ~.

DEMAND LETTER. A letter requesting immediate payment of debt.

DEMAND NOTE. A promissory note payable on demand.

DE MINIMIS NON CURAT LEX. [L.] The law does not bother itself about trifles.

DEMISE. *n.* 1. Includes any and every agreement or transaction whether in writing or by deed or parol whereby one person may become the tenant of another. 2. "... [C]reates an implied covenant for quiet enjoyment [pursuant to The Short Form of Leases Act, R.S.O. 1937, s. 159, Schedule B., clause 13] ..." *Bowra v. Henderson*, [1942] O.R. 734 at 739, [1943] 1 D.L.R. 672 (H.C.), Roach J. 3. "... [A]n effective word to convey an estate of freehold, and that it is of like import with and equivalent to the word 'grant.' ..." *Spears v. Miller* (1882), 32 U.C.C.P. 661 at 663 (Ont.), Armour J. See RE~.

DEMISE OF THE CROWN. The death, deposition or abdication of the sovereign.

DEMOCRATIC. *adj.* "... [R]efer[s] to a system in which the governors are chosen by elections in which all adult citizens have the right to vote ..." *Griffin v. College of Dental Surgeons (British Columbia)* (1989), 64 D.L.R. (4th) 652 at 677, 40 B.C.L.R. (2d) 188, [1990] 1 W.W.R. 503 (C.A.), Southin J.A. See FREE AND ~ SOCIETY.

DEMONSTRATIVE EVIDENCE. Real things as opposed to testimony, i.e., weapons, models, maps, photographs.

DEMONSTRATIVE LEGACY. 1. "... [T]o be paid not out of the general assets of the testator but out of the segregated bonds." *Lasham, Re* (1924-25), 56 O.L.R. 137 at 139 (Div. Ct.), Middleton J.A. 2. A legacy, general in nature, which is supposed to be satisfied out of part of a testator's property or a specified fund. T. Sheard, R. Hull & M.M.K. Fitzpatrick, *Canadian Forms of Wills*, 4th ed. (Toronto: Carswell, 1982) at 158.

DEMUR. *v.* To object by demurrer.

DEMURRAGE. *n.* 1. A charge payable on goods in transit remaining on Board property after the expiration of free time. *Wharfage Charges By-law*, C.R.C., c. 1066, s. 2. 2. An allowance made to a shipowner for detaining a ship in port after the agreed-on sailing time. 3. ". . . [A] penalty imposed for detention of [railway] cars; its enforcement tends to keep them moving and aids in transportation." *Toronto, Hamilton & Buffalo Railway v. Steel Co. of Canada* (1923), 55 O.L.R. 63 at 65 (H.C.), Kelly J.

DEMURRER. *n.* 1. ". . . [A] submission [by the defendant] that if the plantiff's allegations are true they disclose no cause of action . . ." *Royal Bank v. Rizkalla* (1984), 50 C.P.C. 292 at 295, 59 B.C.L.R. 324 (S.C.), McLachlin J. 2. ". . . [T]o admit all the facts that the plaintiff's pleadings alleged and to assert that these facts were not sufficient in law to sustain the plaintiff's case." *Hunt v. T & N plc.* (1990), (*sub nom. Hunt v. Carey Canada Inc.*), 74 D.L.R. (4th) 321 at 328, 4 C.C.L.T. (2d) 1, 43 C.P.C. (2d) 105, 117 N.R. 321, [1990] 6 W.W.R. 385, 49 B.C.L.R. (2d) 273, [1990] 2 S.C.R. 959, Wilson J.

DENIAL. *n.* Disputing the allegations of the opposite party. G.D. Watson & C. Perkins, eds., *Holmested & Watson: Ontario Civil Procedure* (Toronto: Carswell, 1984) at 25-28.

DENOMINATION. *n.* 1. A value or size of currency. 2. A religious organization and members bearing a particular name. 3. The act of naming.

DE NOVO. [L.] Fresh; new. See HEARING ~; TRIAL ~.

DE NOVO HEARING. A rehearing.

DEP. *abbr.* Deputy.

DEPARTMENT. *n.* 1. A branch of the civil service over which a minister presides. 2. ". . . [I]nvolves the idea of something which forms part of a larger thing, . . ." *Carlyle v. Oxford (County)* (1914), 18 D.L.R. 759 at 764, 5 O.W.N. 728, 30 O.L.R. 413 (C.A.), the court per Meredith C.J.O. 3. A department, secretariat, ministry, office or other similar agency of the executive government. 4. An academic unit administered by a head.

DEPARTMENT HEAD. 1. A member of the Executive Council charged with the administration of a department or agency. 2. The non-elected head of a department.

DEPARTURE TAX. A capital gains tax imposed on taxpayers who cease to be residents of Canada. W. Grover & F. Iacobucci, *Materials on Canadian Income Tax*, 4th ed. (Toronto: De Boo, 1980) at 115.

DEPENDANT. *n.* 1. A person who depends upon another for maintenance. 2. A person to whom another has an obligation to provide support. See DEPENDENT.

DEPENDENT. *n.* 1. The father, mother, grandfather, grandmother, brother, sister, uncle, aunt, niece or nephew, or child or grandchild of any age, who at the date of the death of the employee or pensioner is, by reason of mental or physical infirmity, dependent upon that person for support. 2. A child or other relative of a deceased victim who was, in whole or in part, dependent upon the income of the victim at the time of the victim's death. See DEPENDENTS.

DEPENDENT RELATIVE REVOCATION. Where a will is revoked by a codicil it is a question whether it was the intention of the testator that the provisions of the will are to be effective if those contained in the codicil are declared to be invalid. *Murray v. Murray*, [1956] 1 W.L.R. 605.

DEPENDENTS. *n.* 1. Those members of the victim's family and any stranger who stood in loco parentis to the victim, or to whom the victim stood in loco parentis, and who were wholly or partly dependent upon the victim's income or work for support at the time of death. *Crime Victims Compensation acts.* 2. The members of the family of a worker who were wholly or partly dependent upon that person's earnings at the time of the worker's death. *Workers' Compensation acts.* 3. Such person as a person, against whom a maintenance order is made, is liable to maintain according to the law in force in the place where the maintenance order is made. *Maintenance Orders Enforcement acts.* See DEPENDANT; DEPENDENT.

DEPONENT. *n.* 1. A person who testifies that certain facts are true. 2. One who makes an affidavit.

DEPORTATION. *n.* The removal under this Act of a person from any place in Canada to the place whence he came to Canada or to the country of his nationality or citizenship or to the country of his birth or to such country as may be approved by the Minister under this Act, as the case may be. *Immigration Act*, R.S.C. 1970, c. I-2, s. 2.

DEPOSE. *v.* 1. To remove from high office or a throne. 2. To affirm by making a deposition.

DEPOSIT. *v.* ". . . [F]iling, handing over, forwarding. . . ." *Sacchetti v. Lockheimer*, [1988] 1 S.C.R. 1049 at 1057, 86 N.R. 4, 49 R.P.R. 101, 15 Q.A.C. 89, the court per Lamer J.

DEPOSIT. *n.* 1. ". . . [A] contract by which a customer lends money to a bank. The terms of the loan may vary as agreed upon by the banker and the customer. In the absence of such expressly agreed upon terms, the common law dictates that what is intended is a loan that is payable on demand." *Saskatchewan Co-operative Credit Society Ltd. v. Canada (Minister of Finance)* (1990), 47 B.L.R. 85 at 92, 65 D.L.R. (4th) 437, 32 F.T.R. 91, [1990] 2 F.C. 115, Collier J. 2. The unpaid balance of the aggregate of moneys received or held by a federal or provincial institution, from or on behalf of a person in the usual course of business, for which the institution (a) has given or is obligated to give credit to that person's account or has issued or is obligated to issue a receipt, certificate, debenture (other than a debenture issued by a bank to which the Bank Act applies), transferable instrument, draft, certified draft or cheque, traveller's cheque, prepaid letter of credit, money order or other instrument in respect of which the institution is primarily liable, and (b) is obligated to repay the moneys on a fixed day, on demand by that person or within a specified period of time following demand by that person, including any interest accrued or payable to that person. *Canada Deposit Insurance Corporation Act*, R.S.C. 1985, c. C-3, s. 2. 3. Money paid as an earnest or security for a person to perform a contract. See BANK ~; SECURITY ~.

DEPOSITION. *n.* Every affidavit, affirmation or statement made under oath.

DEPOSITOR. *n.* A person whose account has been or is to be credited in respect of moneys constituting a deposit or part of a deposit or a person to whom a member institution is liable in respect of an instrument issued for moneys constituting a deposit or part of a deposit. *Canada Deposit Insurance Corporation Act*, R.S.C. 1985, c. C-3, s. 52(1).

DEPRECIATION. *n.* ". . . [A]n accounting term. It signifies . . . the writing-off of the cost of an asset over its useful life." *Canning v. C.F.M. Fuels (Ontario) Ltd.*, [1977] 2 S.C.R. 207 at 214, 12 N.R. 541, 71 D.L.R. (3d) 321, the court per Dickson J.

DEPT. *abbr.* Department.

DEPUTY. *n.* One who acts instead of another, or who exercises an office in another person's name.

DEPUTY HEAD. *var.* **DEPUTY-HEAD.** 1. The deputy of the member of the Executive Council presiding over a department and all others whom the Governor in Council designates as having the status of deputy. 2. The deputy minister of a department or the chief executive officer of an agency.

DEPUTY MARSHAL. In the Federal Court, each deputy sheriff is ex officio a deputy marshal. D. Sgayias *et al.*, *Federal Court Practice 1988* (Toronto: Carswell, 1987) at 56.

DEPUTY MINISTER. 1. The senior civil servant in a department who advises the minister and is the senior administrator of that department. P.W. Hogg, *Constitutional Law of Canada*, 3d ed. (Toronto: Carswell, 1992) at 236. 2. (a) The deputy of a minister, (b) an officer who, by an Act, is declared to have the status of a deputy minister, or (c) a person designated as a deputy minister.

DERELICT. *adj.* Abandoned.

DERELICTION. *n.* Abandoning something.

DERISORY DAMAGES. Small damages awarded to a plaintiff who sustained no loss, but whose legal rights were technically infringed though in the court's opinion the action should not have been brought. K.D. Cooper-Stephenson & 1.B. Saunders, *Personal Injury Damages in Canada* (Toronto: Carswell, 1981) at 69.

DERIVATIVE ACTION. "[Arises when] . . . a wrong is done to the entity to which the members belong. Such an action may be brought by a member or members, but it is brought on behalf of the entity . . ." *Pasco v. Canadian National Railway* (1989), (*sub nom. Oregon Jack Creek Indian Band v. Canadian National Railway*) 34 B.C.L.R. (2d) 344 at 348, 56 D.L.R. (4th) 404, [1990] 2 C.N.L.R. 85 (C.A.), the court per MacFarlane J.A.

DERIVATIVE EVIDENCE. " . . . [I]nclude all facts, events or objects whose existence is discovered as a result of a statement made to the authorities." *Thomson Newspapers Ltd. v. Canada (Director of Investigation & Research, Combines Investigation Branch)* (1990), 54 C.C.C. (3d) 417 at 528, 76 C.R. (3d) 129, 72 O.R. (2d) 415n, 67 D.L.R. (4th) 161, 29 C.P.R. (3d) 97, [1990] 1 S.C.R. 425, 39 O.A.C. 161, 106 N.R. 161, L'Heureux-Dubé J.

DEROGATE. *v.* To destroy; to evade; to prejudice. See NO ONE CAN BE ALLOWED TO ~ FROM HIS OWN GRANT.

DEROGATION. *n.* Evading an act passed or a rule made in the interest of the public, not for the actors' benefit.

DEROGATORY CLAUSE. "Constitutional provisions like s. 1 [of the Charter] . . . they permit some derogation from (in the sense of limitation of and not in any pejorative sense) the very human rights which are, in the words of the section, 'guaranteed' . . ." *Black v. Law Society (Alberta)* (1986), 20 C.R.R. 117 at 139, [1986] 3 W.W.R. 590, 44 Alta. L.R. (2d) 1, 20 Admin. L.R. 140, 27 D.L.R. (4th) 527, 68 A.R. 259 (C.A.), Kerans J.A.

DESCENDANT. *n.* Lineal progeny; child; grandchild.

DESCENT. *n.* The title to inherit real property by reason of consanguinity, as well when the heir is an ancestor or collateral relation as where he is a child or other issue. *Probate Act*, R.S.P.E.I. 1988, c. P-21, s. 1. See LINEAL ~.

DESCRIPTION. *n.* Identification of goods or other attributes which apply to identified, defined goods. G.H.L. Fridman, *Sale of Goods in Canada*, 3d ed. (Toronto: Carswell, 1986) at 175. See LEGAL ~; MIS~; SALE BY ~.

DESERTION. *n.* " . . . [A] forsaking and an abandonment of the conjugal relationship of husband and wife and requires the intention to desert against the wishes of the other spouse. It is not necessarily a withdrawal from a place, but from a state of things." *Reid v. Reid* (1970), 5 R.F.L. 37 at 42 (Ont. Prov. Ct.), Creighton Prov. Ct. J. See CONSTRUCTIVE ~.

DESIGN. *n.* 1. A plan, sketch, drawing, graphic representation or specification intended to govern the construction, enlargement or alteration of a building or part of a building and related site development. 2. ". . . [A] pattern or representation which the eye can see and which can be applied to a manufactured article. . . ." *Clatworthy & Son Ltd.* v. *Dale Display Fixtures Ltd.*, [1929] 3 D.L.R. 11 at 12, [1929] S.C.R. 429, the court per Lamont J. See INDUSTRIAL ~.

DESIGNATE. *n.* A person appointed.

DE SON TORT. See EXECUTOR ~; TRUSTEE ~.

DETAIN. See DETENTION.

DETAINED. See ARBITRARILY ~.

DETAINER. *n.* Wrongful retention. See FORCIBLE ~.

DETENTION. *n.* ". . . [M]ay be effected without the application or threat of application of physical restraint if the person concerned submits or acquiesces in the deprivation of liberty and reasonably believes that the choice to do otherwise does not exist. . . . Le Dain J.'s extension of 'detention' to instances of 'psychological' restraint or compulsion is predicated on two requirements: (1) a 'demand or direction', in responce to which (2) 'the person concerned submits or acquiesces in the deprivation of liberty and reasonably believes that the choice to do otherwise does not exist'." *R.* v. *Elshaw*, [1991] 3 S.C.R. 24 at 52, 55, 7 C.R. (4th) 333, 59 B.C.L.R. (2d) 143, 67 C.C.C. (3d) 97, 128 N.R. 241, 6 C.R.R. (2d) 1, 3 B.C.A.C. 81, 7 W.A.C. 81, L'Heureux-Dubé J. (dissenting). See PREVENTIVE ~.

DETENTION ORDER. An order that the accused be denied bail until trial.

DETERMINABLE. *adj.* Coming to an end.

DETERMINABLE FEE. A species of fee simple which terminates automatically on the happening of a specified event which may not occur. R. Megarry & H.W.R. Wade, *The Law of Real Property*, 5th ed. (London: Stevens, 1984) at 67.

DETERMINATE SENTENCE. A

sentence of imprisonment for a limited period of time.

DETERMINATION. *n.* ". . . [I]mplies an ending or finality, the ending of a controversy. . . ." *R.* v. *Appleby* (1974), 18 C.P.R. (2d) 194 at 200, 10 N.B.R. (2d) 162, 21 C.C.C. (2d) 282 (C.A.), Hughes C.J.N.B. (Ryan J.A. concurring).

DETERMINE. *v.* To come to an end.

DETERMINED. *adj.* Decided; fixed; delimited.

DETERRENCE. *n.* ". . . [T]he achieving of control by fear." *R.* v. *McGinn* (1989), 49 C.C.C. (3d) 137 at 155, 75 Sask. R. 161 (C.A.), VanciseJ.A. (dissenting).

DETERRENT. *n.* A penalty imposed with view to preventing others from committing same act.

DETERRENT. *adj.* Preventative.

DETINUE. *n.* ". . . [W]here there is a wrongful taking [of goods] the victim may have the alternative of claiming in detinue, where the unsuccessful defendant must replace the goods or pay the value at the time of the trial. . . ." *Steiman* v. *Steiman* (1982), 23 C.C.L.T. 182 at 187, 18 Man. R. (2d) 203, 143 D.L.R. (3d) 396 (C.A.), O'Sullivan J.A. (Hall J.A. concurring). See ACTION FOR ~.

DEVALUATION. *n.* An official reduction in the amount of gold relating to the paper value of currency.

DEVASTAVIT. [L.] One has wasted. Refers to loss to a deceased's estate caused by waste by the deceased's personal representative.

DEVELOPMENT. *n.* (a) The carrying out of any construction or excavation or other operations in, on, over or under land, or (b) the making of a change in the use or the intensity of use of land, buildings or premises. See COMMUNITY ~ SERVICES; FEDERAL BUSINESS ~ BANK.

DEVELOPMENT CONTROL. A type of land use control carried out by administrative means in contrast with zoning, which is accomplished through legislative means. It is used in Manitoba, Newfoundland and the Niagara Escarpment Region of Ontario. I.M. Rogers, *The Law of Canadian Municipal Corporations*, 2d ed. (Toronto: Carswell, 1971-) at 813.

DEVELOPMENT PLAN. A plan, policy and program, or any part thereof, approved under this act covering a development planning area or a portion thereof, as defined therein, designed to promote the optimum economic, social, environmental and physical condition of the area, and consisting of the texts and maps describing the program and policy. *Planning acts.*

DEVIATION. *n.* A major change in the method of performance agreed on in a contract. E.L.G. Tyler & N.E. Palmer, eds., *Crossley Vaines' Personal Property*, 5th ed. (London: Butterworths, 1973) at 103.

DEVISE. *n.* A disposition or gift by will. See EXECUTORY ~; SPECIFIC ~.

DEVISED. *adj.* Left in a will. E.L.G. Tyler & N.E. Palmer, eds., *Crossley Vaines' Personal Property*, 5th ed. (London: Butterworths, 1973) at 7.

DEVISEE. *n.* Includes the heir of a devisee and the devisee of an heir, and any person who claims right by devolution of title of a similar description. *Trustees acts.* See RESIDUARY ~.

DEVISOR. *n.* A testator.

DEVOLUTION. *n.* The transfer of an interest in property from one person to another through the operation of law, e.g., on bankruptcy or death.

DEVOLVE. *v.* To be transferred from one to another.

DICTA. *n.* Plural of DICTUM. See OBITER ~.

DICTUM. *n.* 1. "Some authorities distinguish between obiter dicta and judicial dicta. The former are mere passing remarks of the judge, whereas the latter consist of considered enunciations of the judge's opinions of the law on some point which does not arise for decision on the facts of the case before him, and so is not part of the ratio

decidendi. But there is . . . a third type of dictum, so far innominate. If instead of merely stating his own view of the point in question the judge supports it by stating what has been done in other cases, not reported, then his statement is one which rests not only on his own unsupported view of the law but also on the decisions of those other judges whose authority he has invoked. . . . Such a statement of the settled law or accustomed practice carries with it the authority not merely of the judge who makes it but also of an unseen cloud of his judicial brethren. A dictum of this type offers . . the highest authority that any dictum can bear . . ." *Richard West & Partners (Inverness) Ltd. v. Dick* (1968), [1969] 1 All E.R. 289 at 292 (U.K. Ch.), Megarry J. 2. ". . . Sometimes they may be called almost casual expressions of opinion upon a point which has not been raised in the case, and is not really present to the judge's mind . . . Some dicta however are of a different kind; they are, although not necessary for the decision of the case, deliberate expressions of opinion given after consideration upon a point clearly brought and argued before the Court . . . much greater weight attaches to them than to the former class." *Slack v. Leeds Industrial Co-operative Society Ltd.*, [1923] 1 Ch. 431 at 451 (U.K. C.A.), Lord Sterndale M.R.

DIE WITHOUT ISSUE. A want or failure of issue in the lifetime or at the time of the death of that person and not an indefinite failure of issue, subject to any contrary intention appearing by the will or to any requirements as to age or otherwise therein contained for obtaining a vested estate. *Wills acts.*

DIE WITHOUT LEAVING ISSUE. A want or failure of issue in the lifetime or at the time of death of that person, and does not mean an indefinite failure of issue unless a contrary intention appears by the will. *Wills acts.*

DIGEST. *n.* 1. A gathering of rules of law based on particular cases, in contrast to a code. 2. An arrangement of the summarized decisions of courts made either alphabetically or systematically. 3. A private author's collection of abstract rules or principles of law.

DILATORY. *adj.* Tending to cause delay in decision making.

DILATORY MOTION. A proposal that the original question be disposed of either permanently or for the time being. A. Fraser, W.A. Dawson & J. Holtby, eds., *Beauchesne's Rules and Forms of the House of Commons of Canada*, 6th ed. (Toronto: Carswell, 1989) at 173.

DILIGENCE. *n.* Care.

DIPLOMATIC PRIVILEGE. Not an absolute privilege; it is displaced when a member of the diplomatic corps has contravened the law with the intention of imperilling the safety of the State. P.K. McWilliams, *Canadian Criminal Evidence*, 3d ed. (Aurora: Canada Law Book, 1988) at 35-74.

DIPLOMATIC PROTECTION. Assistance which nations grant to their citizens against other nations.

DIR. *abbr.* Director.

DIRECT. *v.* To order; to instruct; to lead.

DIRECT. *adj.* Immediate; by the shortest route.

DIRECT DISCRIMINATION. "... [O]ccurs ... where an employer adopts a practice or rule which on its face discriminates on a prohibited ground." *Ontario (Human Rights Commission) v. Simpsons-Sears Ltd.*, [1985] 2 S.C.R. 536 at 551, 9 C.C.E.L. 185, 17 Admin L.R. 89, 86 C.L.L.C. 17,002, 64 N.R. 161, 7 C.H.R.R. D/3102, 23 D.L.R. (4th) 321, 12 O.A.C. 241, the court per McIntyre J.

DIRECTED VERDICT. See MOTION FOR ~.

DIRECT EVIDENCE. 1. A witness' testimony as to what was observed through the senses. P.K. McWilliams, *Canadian Criminal Evidence*, 3d ed. (Aurora: Canada Law Book, 1988) at 1-11. 2. "... [A] necessary connection between the facts proven and the principal fact or factum probandum

[exists]. ..." *R. v. Mitchell* (1963), 42 C.R. 12 at 26, 45 W.W.R. 199 (B.C. C.A.), Sheppard J.A.

DIRECT EXAMINATION. Questioning of a witness by the party which called that witness.

DIRECTION. *n.* 1. "... [A]uthoritative command ..." *R. v. Bazinet* (1986), 25 C.C.C. (3d) 273 at 284, 54 O.R. (2d) 129, 14 O.A.C. 15, 51 C.R. (3d) 139 (C.A.), the court per Tarnopolsky J.A. 2. The judge's instructions to the jury as to what the law is. See MIS~.

DIRECTIVE. *n.* An order.

DIRECTOR. *n.* "... [T]hose persons acting collectively to whom the duty of managing the general affairs of the company is delegated by the shareholders. Their duty is to conduct the business of the company for the greatest benefit of the shareholders...." *Minister of National Revenue v. Parsons* (1983), 4 Admin. L.R. 64 at 79, [1983] C.T.C. 321, 83 D.T.C. 5329 (Fed. T.D.), Cattanach J. See MANAGING ~.

DIRECTORY. *n.* A provision from which no invalidating consequence will follow if it is disregarded, unlike a mandatory provision, which must be followed.

DIRECT SALE. 1. A sale which involves a consumer and takes place at the buyer's dwelling. G.H.L. Fridman, *Sale of Goods in Canada*, 3d ed. (Toronto: Carswell, 1986) at 492. 2. A sale by a direct seller acting in the course of business as such. *Direct Sellers acts.*

DIRECT SELLER. A person who: (i) goes from house to house selling or offering for sale, or soliciting orders for the future delivery of goods or services; or (ii) by telephone offers for sale or solicits orders for the future delivery of goods or services.

DIRECT SELLING. Selling, offering for sale or soliciting of orders for the sale of goods or services by (i) going from house to house, (ii) telephone communication, or (iii) mail.

DIRECT TAX. 1. "... [O]ne that is demanded from the very person who it is intended or desired should pay it." *Reference re Grain Futures Taxation Act (Manitoba)* (1925), (*sub nom. Manitoba (Attorney General) v. Canada (Attorney General)*) [1925] 2 D.L.R. 691 at 694, [1925] 2 W.W.R. 60, [1925] A.C. 561 (Can. P.C.), the board per Viscount Haldane. 2. "... [O]ne that is imposed on the consumer...." *Chehalis Indian Band v. British Columbia* (1988), [1989] 1 C.N.L.R. 62 at 67, 31 B.C.L.R. (2d) 333, 53 D.L.R. (4th) 761 (C.A.), Marfarlane, Wallace and Locke JJ.A.

DISABILITY. *n.* 1. The absence of legal ability to do certain acts or enjoy certain benefits. 2. The incapacity of a minor or of a person who is mentally incompetent. 3. Any previous or existing mental or physical disability and includes disfigurement and previous or existing dependence on alcohol or a drug. *Canadian Human Rights Act*, R.S.C. 1985, c. H-6, s. 25. 4. The loss or lessening of the power to will and to do any normal mental or physical act. *Pension Act*, R.S.C. 1985, c. P-6, s. 2. 5. "... [P]hysical or mental incapacity, usually arising from injury or disease, although it might arise from other causes...." *Penner v. Danbrook* (1992), 10 C.R.R. (2d) 379 at 382, [1992] 4 W.W.R. 385, 39 R.F.L. (3d) 286, 100 Sask. R. 125, 18 W.A.C. 125 (C.A.), the court per Sherstobitoff J.A. See MENTAL ~; PARTY UNDER ~.

DISALLOWANCE. *n.* 1. The Queen's power to annul any statute enacted by the Parliament of Canada. P.W. Hogg, *Constitutional Law of Canada*, 3d ed. (Toronto: Carswell, 1992) at 230. 2. The federal power vested in the Governor General in Council to annul provincial statutes. P.W. Hogg, *Constitutional Law of Canada*, 3d ed. (Toronto: Carswell, 1992) at 231.

DISBAR. *v.* To expel a lawyer from membership in a law society.

DISBURSEMENT. *n.* 1. An expenditure or any other payment or transfer of public money. 2. Money expended

or paid out on behalf of the client, such as a fee paid to a court officer or court reporter or witness fees, for which a lawyer is entitled to a credit when an account is submitted. 3. "... [I]ndicative of an immediate outlay or payment and signifies an expenditure...." *R. v. McKee*, [1977] C.T.C. 491 at 494, 77 D.T.C. 5345 (Fed. T.D.), Addy J.

DISCHARGE. *v.* 1. To release a person from an obligation. *R. v. Simmons* (1984), 11 C.C.C. (3d) 193 at 214, 45 O.R. (2d) 609, 39 C.R. (3d) 223, 26 M.V.R. 168, 3 O.A.C. 1, 7 D.L.R. (4th) 719, 8 C.R.R. 333, 7 C.E.R. 159 (C.A.), Howland C.J.O. (Martin, Lacourcière and Houlden JJ.A. concurring). 2. To deprive a right or obligation of its binding force. 3. "... [T]o revoke or to rescind." *Lamontagne v. Lamontagne* (1964), 47 W.W.R. 321 at 331, 44 D.L.R. (2d) 228 (Man. C.A.), Freedman J.A. (Schultz J.A. concurring). 4. When used as a verb, includes add, deposit, leak or emit. *Environmental Protection Act*, R.S.O. 1990, c. E.19, s. 1(1).

DISCHARGE. *n.* 1. Section 662.1 of the Code gives judges discretion to release an accused after guilt is determined absolutely or on conditions a probation order prescribes. D. Stuart, *Canadian Criminal Law: a Treatise*, 2d ed. (Toronto: Carswell, 1987) at 494. 2. An instrument by which one terminates an obligation under contract. 3. Termination of employment by an employer other than a lay-off. See ABSOLUTE ~; CONDITIONAL ~; CONSTRUCTIVE ~.

DISCHARGED. *adj.* 1. Relieved from further performance of the contract. *Frustrated Contracts acts*. 2. Of a payment, made or paid. 3. "... '[N]ot committed on the charge laid' ..." *Myers v. R.* (1991), 65 C.C.C. (3d) 135 at 140, 91 Nfld. & P.E.I.R. 37, 286 A.P.R. 37 (Nfld. C.A.), Goodridge C.J.N. (Steele J.A. concurring). 4. "... [R]ecognizance is 'discharged' (that is, the debtor is released from his or her obligations), if the conditions of the contract are fulfilled." *Purves v.*

DISCIPLINARY ACTION

Canada (Attorney General) (1990), 54 C.C.C. (3d) 355 at 363 (B.C. C.A.), the court per Legg J.A.

DISCIPLINARY ACTION. ". . . The reason for disciplinary action is misconduct and the purpose is to punish." *Canada v. Evans* (1983), 49 N.R. 189 at 194 (Fed. C.A.), Le Dain J.A. (Urie J.A. concurring).

DISCIPLINARY COMMITTEE. See DISCIPLINE COMMITTEE.

DISCIPLINARY MATTER. Any matter involving an allegation of professional misconduct or fitness to practise on the part of a member, student or professional corporation.

DISCIPLINE. *n*. Correction; punishment.

DISCIPLINE COMMITTEE. A committee established under a statute regulating one of the self-governing professions.

DISCLAIM. *v*. To repudiate; to refuse to recognize.

DISCLAIMER. *n*. The act of renouncing generally substantiated by a deed.

DISCLAIMER CLAUSE. A clause in a contract denying that guarantees or other representations have been made.

DISCLOSED PRINCIPAL. A person whose existence the agent has revealed to the third party, but whose exact identity is still unknown. G.H.L. Fridman, *The Law of Agency*, 6th ed. (London: Butterworths, 1990) at 193.

DISCLOSURE. *n*. 1. A revelation. 2. "In its simplest form, disclosure will consist of simply displaying what must be disclosed to defence counsel for examination. In its absolute form, disclosure will consist of providing copies of the materials to be disclosed where copies are available and copies of notes, copies and 'will says'." *R. v. Vokey* (1992), 10 C.R.R. (2d) 360 at 370, 14 C.R. (4th) 311, 102 Nfld. & P.E.I.R. 275, 323 A.P.R. 275 (Nfld. C.A.), the court per Goodridge C.J.N.

DISCONTINUANCE. *n*. 1. Breaking off; interruption. 2. "Discontinuance

before judgment, . . . amounts to the abandonment of the exercise of a right. . . ." *Quebec (Expropriation Tribunal)* v. *Quebec (Attorney General)* (1983), 29 L.C.R. 6 at 8, [1983] R.D.J. 432 (Qué. C.A.), the court per Jacques J.A.

DISCOUNT. *v*. 1. Lessen, diminish. 2. "To discount a negotiable security is therefore to buy it at a discount; or it may mean, using another sense of the word, to lend money on the security, deducting the interest in advance . . ." *Jones v. Imperial* (1876), 23 Gr. 262 at 270 (Ont. Ch.), Proudfoot V.C.

DISCOUNT. *n*. 1. Lessening, diminishing. 2. The excess of the par or stated value of any security issued or resold over the value of the consideration received for the security. Canada regulations. 3. ". . . [I]n commerce a discount on the sale of an article of trade is an abatement or deduction from the nominal value or price of that article." *Consolboard Inc. v. MacMillan Bloedel (Saskatchewan) Ltd.* (1982), 63 C.P.R. (2d) 1 at 22 (Fed. T.D.), Cattanach J.

DISCOUNT RATE. ". . . [T]he difference between the interest rate that can be earned on the lump sum invested and the rate of inflation . . ." *McDermid v. Ontario* (1985), 5 C.P.C. (2d) 299 at 303, 53 O.R. (2d) 495 (H.C.), Rosenberg J.

DISCOVERY. *n*. 1. Disclosure by the parties before trial of information and documents. 2. ". . . [F]ollows upon the issues having been previously defined by the pleadings and the purpose of such discovery is to prove or disprove the issues so defined, by a cross-examination on the facts relevant to such issues." *Anglo-Cdn. Timber Products Ltd. v. B.C. Electric Co.* (1960), 31 W.W.R. 604 at 605, 23 D.L.R. (2d) 656 (B.C. C.A.), Sheppard J.A. See EXAMINATION FOR ~.

DISCREDIT. *v*. To throw doubt on the testimony of a witness.

DISCRETION. *n*. 1. ". . . [W]hen it is said that something is to be done within the discretion of the authorities . . . [it]

is to be done according to the rules of reason and justice, not according to private opinion . . . according to law, and not humour. It is to be, not arbitrary, vague, and fanciful, but legal and regular." *Sharp v. Wakefield*, [1891] A.C. 173 at 179 Lord Halsbury, cited by Kellock J. in *Wrights Canadian Ropes Ltd. v. Minister of National Revenue*, [1946] S.C.R. 139 at 166. 2. A person's own judgment of what is best in a given situation. See ADMINISTRATIVE ~; JUDICIAL ~.

DISCRETIONARY. *adj.* At the discretion of someone; not available as of right.

DISCRETIONARY DUTY. Something required of a trustee, such as allocating trust property, choosing how much a beneficiary should have, or choosing who should have a benefit from among a class of beneficiaries, and then how much that particular beneficiary should have. D.M.W. Waters, *The Law of Trusts in Canada*, 2d ed. (Toronto: Carswell, 1984) at 28-29.

DISCRETIONARY REMEDY. Given at a court's discretion, not available as of right.

DISCRETIONARY TRUST. A trust in which trustees are given absolute discretion concerning the allocation of the capital and income of the trust fund to beneficiaries.

DISCRIMINATION. *n.* ". . . [A] distinction, whether intentional or not but based on grounds relating to personal characteristics of the individual or group, which has the effect of imposing burdens, obligations, or disadvantages on such individual or group not imposed on others, or which withholds or limits access to opportunities, benefits, and advantages, available to other members of society. . . ." *Andrews v. Law Society (British Columbia)* (1989), 56 D.L.R. (4th) 1 at 18, 36 C.R.R. 193, [1989] 2 W.W.R. 289, 25 C.C.E.L. 255, 91 N.R. 255, 34 B.C.L.R. (2d) 273, 10 C.H.R.R. D/5719, [1989] 1 S.C.R. 143, McIntyre J. (Dickson C.J.C., Lamer, Wilson and L'Heureux-Dubé JJ. concurring). See ADVERSE

EFFECT ~; CONSTRUCTIVE ~; DIRECT ~; RACIAL ~; REVERSE ~; SEX ~.

DISEASE. *n.* ". . . [A]n ailment that disorders one or more of the vital functions or organs of the body, causing a morbid physical condition." *Tomlinson v. Prudential Insurance Co. of America*, [1954] O.R. 508 at 516, [1954] I.L.R. 1-144 (C.A.), the court per Laidlaw J.A. See OCCUPATIONAL ~; VENEREAL ~.

DISEASE OF THE MIND. 1. ". . . Any malfunctioning of the mind or mental disorder having its source primarily in some subjective condition or weakness internal to the accused (whether fully understood or not) may be a 'disease of the mind' if it prevents the accused from knowing what he is doing, but transient disturbances of consciousness due to certain specific external factors do not fall within the concept of disease of the mind. . . ." *R. v. Rabey* (1977), 40 C.R.N.S. 46 at 62-63, 17 O.R. (2d) 1, 1 L. Med. Q. 280, 37 C.C.C. (2d) 461, 79 D.L.R. (3d) 414 (C.A.), Martin J.A., adopted in *R. v. Rabey* (1980), 15 C.R. (3d) 225 (Eng.), [1980] 2 S.C.R. 513, 54 C.C.C. (2d) 1, 32 N.R. 451, 20 C.R. (3d) 1 (Fr.). 2. ". . . [I]n a legal sense, . . . embraces any illness, disorder or abnormal condition which impairs the human mind and its functioning, excluding, however, self-induced states caused by alcohol or drugs, as well as transitory mental states such as hysteria or concussion. . . ." *R. v. Cooper* (1979), 13 C.R. (3d) 97 at 117 (Eng.), [1980] 1 S.C.R. 1149, 18 C.R. (3d) 138 (Fr.), 51 C.C.C. (2d) 129, 31 N.R. 234, 4 Led. Med. Q. 227, 110 D.L.R. (3d) 46, Dickson J. (Laskin C.J.C., Beetz, Estey and McIntyre JJ. concurring). See INSANITY.

DISENTAIL. *v.* To bring an entail to an end. R. Megarry & H.W.R. Wade, *The Law of Real Property*, 5th ed. (London: Stevens, 1984) at cxxiv.

DISENTAILING DEED. An assurance through which a tenant in tail blocks the entail in order to convert it into a fee simple.

DISENTITLED. *adj.* Not entitled.

DISHONEST. *adj.* ". . . [N]ormally used to describe an act where there has been some intent to deceive or cheat. . . ." *Lynch & Co. v. United States Fidelity & Guaranty Co.*, [1971] 1 O.R. 28 at 37, 14 D.L.R. (3d) 294 (H.C.), Fraser J.

DISHONOUR. *v.* To neglect or refuse to accept or pay a bill of exchange when it is duly presented for payment. See NOTICE OF ~.

DISINHERIT. *v.* To end a right to inherit.

DISINTERMENT. *n.* 1. Exhumation. 2. Removal of human remains, along with the casket or container or any of the remaining casket or container holding the human remains, from the lot in which the human remains had been interred. *Cemetery and Funeral Services Act*, S.B.C. 1989, c. 21, s. 1.

DISJUNCTIVE TERM. Usually expressed by the word "or" which indicates alternative conditions or matters.

DISMISS. *v.* 1. In employment, to fire, let go, terminate. 2. In proceedings, to refuse the remedy requested.

DISMISSAL. *n.* 1. ". . . [O]f an employee may be effected either by words or conduct. The conduct [must] be such as to amount to a refusal by the employer to continue to be bound by the contract. . . ." *Gilson v. Fort Vermilion School Division No. 52* (1985), 12 C.C.E.L. 72 at 74, 61 A.R. 225 (Bd. of Reference), McFayden J. 2. ". . . [I]f made by a court of competent jurisdiction, a final disposition of the case against the accused sufficient to support the plea of autrefois acquit: . . ." *R. v. Dubois* (1986), 25 C.C.C. (3d) 221 at 232, [1986] 1 S.C.R. 366, [1986] 3 W.W.R. 577, 26 D.L.R. (4th) 481, 66 N.R. 289, 18 Admin. L.R. 146, 51 C.R. (3d) 193, 41 Man. R. (2d) 1, the court per Estey J. See CONSTRUCTIVE ~; JUST ~; WRONGFUL ~.

DISMISSAL FOR CAUSE. "[The employer] . . . is entitled to refuse to perform his future obligations because of the prior fundamental breach of the employee. . . ." *Carr v. Fama Holdings Ltd.* (1989), 28 C.C.E.L. 30 at 39, 41, 40 B.C.L.R. (2d) 125, 45 B.L.R. 42, [1990] 1 W.W.R. 264, 63 D.L.R. (4th) 25 (C.A.), Wallace J.A. (Hutcheon and Cumming JJ.A. concurring).

DISORDER. See MENTAL ~; PSYCHOPATHIC ~.

DISORDERLY HOUSE. A common bawdy-house, a common betting house or a common gaming house. *Criminal Code*, R.S.C. 1985, c. C-46, s. 197.

DISPARAGEMENT. *n.* A statement which casts doubt on ownership of property or on quality of goods.

DISPOSE. *v.* 1. ". . . [O]f property . . . to make the property over to another so that no interest therein remains . . ." *Harman v. Gray-Campbell Ltd.*, [1925] 2 D.L.R. 904 at 908, [1925] 1 W.W.R. 1134, 19 Sask. L.R. 526 (C.A.), Lamont. J.A. 2. To transfer by any method and includes assign, give, sell, grant, charge, convey, bequeath, devise, lease, divest, release and agree to do any of those things. *Interpretation Act*, R.S.B.C. 1979, c. 206, s. 29. 3. To destroy. *R. v. Cie Immobilière BCN*, [1979] 1 S.C.R. 865, [1979] C.T.C. 71, 79 D.T.C. 5068, 25 N.R. 361, 97 D.L.R. (3d) 238, the court per Pratte J. 4. ". . . '[T]o part with', 'to pass over the control of the thing to someone else' so that the person disposing no longer has the use of the property." *Victory Hotels Ltd. v. Minister of National Revenue*, [1962] C.T.C. 614 at 626, [1963] Ex. C.R. 123, 62 D.T.C. 1378, Noel J.

DISPOSITION. *n.* 1. Final settlement or sentencing of a criminal case. 2. "[In the context of the transfer of business from one employer to another] . . . something must be relinquished from the first business and obtained by the second." *W.W. Lester (1978) Ltd. v. U.A., Local 740* (1990), 48 Admin. L.R. 1 at 23, 76 D.L.R. (4th) 389, 91 C.L.L.C. 14,002, 123 N.R. 241, 88 Nfld. & P.E.I.R. 15, 274 A.P.R. 15, [1990] 2 S.C.R. 644, McLachlin J. (Lamer C.J.C., La Forest, Sopinka and Gonthier JJ. concurring). 3. The act of disposal or an instrument by which that act is affected or evidenced, and includes a Crown grant, order in council, transfer, assurance, lease, licence, permit, contract or agreement and every other instrument whereby lands or any right, interest or estate in land may be transferred, disposed of or affected, or by which the Crown divests itself of or creates any right, interest or estate in land. See PRE-~ REPORT.

DISPOSITIVE POWER. 1. The authority to distribute trust property, either capital or income or both, to a beneficiary or among several beneficiaries. D.M.W. Waters, *The Law of Trusts in Canada*, 2d ed. (Toronto: Carswell, 1984) at 691. 2. The authority of a trustee to draw on capital or income to maintain a beneficiary during infancy, or to give capital to a widow who takes an income interest under a testamentary trust when her husband dies. D.M.W. Waters, *The Law of Trusts in Canada*, 2d ed. (Toronto: Carswell, 1984) at 72.

DISPOSSESSION. *n.* Ouster; removal from possession.

DISPROOF. *n.* Proof that not the accused but a third party committed the crime. P.K. McWilliams, *Canadian Criminal Evidence*, 3d ed. (Aurora: Canada Law Book, 1988) at 18-27.

DISPROVE. *v.* To refute; to prove to be false.

DISPUTE. *n.* 1. A difference or apprehended difference arising in connection with the entering into, renewing or revision of a collective agreement. 2. Any dispute or difference or apprehended dispute or difference between an employer and one or more employees or a bargaining agent acting on behalf of the employees, as to matters or things affecting or relating to terms or conditions of employment or work done or to be done by the employee or employees or as to privileges, rights and duties of the employer or the employee or employees. See ALTERNATIVE ~ RESOLUTION; INDUSTRIAL ~; LABOUR ~.

DISQUALIFIED. *adj.* 1. Not eligible. 2. In which some condition precedent was not fulfilled.

DISS. *abbr.* Dissentiente.

DISSENT. *n.* 1. Disagreement. 2. The decision of a judge who does not agree with the majority of the members of the court. See RIGHT OF ~.

DISSENTIENTE. *adj.* Used in reports of judgments where one or more judges do not agree with the majority of the members of the court.

DISSENTING OPINION. The individual opinion of a judge who does not agree with the majority of the members of the court. Compare MAJORITY OPINION.

DISSOLUTION. *n.* 1. Putting an end to a legal entity or relation. 2. Of marriage, divorce. A. Bissett-Johnson & W.M. Holland, eds, *Matrimonial Property Law in Canada* (Toronto: Carswell, 1980) at BC-7. 3. Of Parliament, dissolution either by the expiration of five years or by proclamation. A. Fraser, W.A. Dawson & J. Holtby, eds., *Beauchesne's Rules and Forms of the House of Commons of Canada*, 6th ed. (Toronto: Carswell, 1989) at 66. 4. Of a corporation, ending of corporate existence. *Computerized Meetings & Hotel Systems Ltd. v. Moore* (1982), 20 B.L.R. 97, 40 O.R. (2d) 88, 141 D.L.R. (3d) 306 (Div. Ct.), Callaghan J.

DISSOLUTION OF MARRIAGE. "[Refers to] ... the decree absolute." *Pearce, Re* (1974), 18 R.F.L. 302 at 305, [1975] 2 W.W.R. 678, 52 D.L.R. (3d) 544 (B.C. S.C.), MacFarlane J.

DISSOLVE. *v.* To annul; to cancel; to put an end to.

DIST. *abbr.* District.

DIST. CT. *abbr.* District Court.

DISTINGUISH. *v.* To clarify an essential difference.

DISTRAIN. *v.* To seize goods using distress.

DISTRAINT. *n.* 1. Seizing. 2. Satisfying the wrong committed by taking a personal chattel from the wrongdoer and delivering to the party injured.

E.L.G. Tyler & N.E. Palmer, eds., *Crossley Vaines' Personal Property*, 5th ed. (London: Butterworths, 1973) at 493.

DISTRESS. *n.* 1. Lawfully seizing chattels extrajudicially in order to enforce a right such as payment of rent. R. Megarry & H.W.R. Wade, *The Law of Real Property*, 5th ed. (London: Stevens, 1984) at cxxiv. 2. Property which was distrained.

DISTRIBUTE. *v.* To deliver, handle, keep for sale or sell.

DISTRIBUTION. *n.* 1. Where used in relation to trading in securities, (a) a trade in a security of an issuer that has not been previously issued, (b) a trade by or on behalf of an issuer in a previously issued security of that issuer that has been redeemed or purchased by or donated to that issuer, (c) a trade in a previously issued security of an issuer from the holdings of a control person, (d) a trade by or on behalf of an underwriter in a security which was acquired by that underwriter, acting as underwriter, before the coming into force of this section, if that security continues, on the day this section comes into force, to be owned by or on behalf of that underwriter so acting, (e) a transaction or series of transactions involving further purchases and sales in the course of or incidental to a distribution. *Securities acts.* 2. (a) A trade by or on behalf of a bank in securities of the bank that have not previously been issued, (b) a trade by or on behalf of a bank in previously issued securities of the bank that have been redeemed or purchased by the bank, or (c) a trade in previously issued securities of a bank from the holdings of any person or group of persons who act in concert and who hold in excess of ten per cent of the shares of any class of voting shares of the bank. *Bank Act*, R.S.C. 1985, c. B-1, s. 145. 3. Division of property of an estate after debts and expenses of administration are paid.

DISTRIBUTION OF POWERS. The division of legislative powers between regional authorities (provincial legislatures) and a central authority (the federal Parliament) which is the essence of a federal constitution, binds the regional and central authorities, and cannot be altered by the unilateral action of any one of them. P.W. Hogg, *Constitutional Law of Canada*, 3d ed. (Toronto: Carswell, 1992) at 371-2.

DISTRICT. *n.* 1. A regional administrative unit. 2. A judicial district. 3. A local improvement district. 4. A school district. See ELECTORAL ~.

DISTRICT COUNCIL. An organization of union locals in a particular geographical area.

DISTRICT COURT. A court limited in territorial jurisdiction and by subject matter. P.W. Hogg, *Constitutional Law of Canada*, 3d ed. (Toronto: Carswell, 1992) at 162.

DISTURBANCE. *n.* 1. Infringement of an easement, franchise, profit à prendre or similar right. 2. Causing a tenant to leave through force, menace, persuasion or otherwise. 3. In section 175(a) of the Criminal Code, "[P]ublicly exhibited disorder . . . violent noise or confusion disrupting the tranquillity of those in the area in question. *R. v. Lohnes* (1991), 10 C.R. (4th) 125 at 133, [1992] 1 S.C.R. 167, 69 C.C.C. (3d) 289, 109 N.S.R. (2d) 145, 297 A.P.R. 145, 132 N.R. 297, the court per McLachlin J.

DIV. *abbr.* Divisional.

DIV. & MATR. CAUSES CT. *abbr.* Divorce and Matrimonial Causes Court.

DIV. CT. *abbr.* Divisional Court.

DIVERS. *adj.* [Fr.] Various, sundry.

DIVEST. *v.* 1. To take away; to deprive. 2. To remove an estate or interest which was already vested in a person.

DIVIDED COURT. Applied to a court consisting of more than one judge when the decision or opinion of the court is not unanimous.

DIVIDED CUSTODY. ". . . [T]he children to divide their time between the two homes, living in each temporarily, on some type of rotating basis...." *Colwell v. Colwell* (1992), 38 R.F.L. (3d) 345 at 349, 128 A.R. 4 (Q.B.), Bielby J.

DIVIDEND. *n.* 1. The division of profits of a corporation or trust. 2. "A payment from profits, whether in cash, specie or the shares of another company, is in essence a dividend." *Canadian Pacific Ltd., Re* (1990), 47 B.L.R. 1 at 30, 72 O.R. (2d) 545, 68 D.L.R. (4th) 9 (H.C.), Austin J. 3. Includes bonus or any distribution to shareholders as such. See ACCRUED ~; ACCUMULATED ~; ACCUMULATIVE ~; CASH ~; CUM ~; CUMULATIVE ~; INTERIM ~; NON-CUMULATIVE ~; PREFERRED ~; STOCK ~.

DIVISIBLE. *adj.* "... [T]hat may be taken apart...." *R. v. Ciesielski* (1958), 26 W.W.R. 695 at 701, 29 C.R. 312, 122 C.C.C. 247 (Alta. C.A.), Porter J.A.

DIVISION. *n.* 1. In the House of Commons, a recorded vote. A. Fraser, W.A. Dawson, & J. Holtby, eds., *Beauchesne's Rules and Forms of the House of Commons of Canada*, 6th ed. (Toronto: Carswell, 1989) at 91. 2. An administrative unit. See ELECTORAL ~.

DIVISIONAL COURT. The branch of the General Division called the Divisional Court is continued under that name (Courts of Justice Act, R.S.O. 1990, c. C.43, s. 18(1)). G.D. Watson & C. Perkins, eds., *Holmested & Watson: Ontario Civil Procedure* (Toronto: Carswell, 1984-) at CJA-41.

DIVORCE. *n.* 1. "... [D]issolution of marriage ..." *Hurson v. Hurson* (1970), 73 W.W.R. 765 at 767, 1 R.F.L. 19, 11 D.L.R. (3d) 759 (B.C. C.A.), the court per McFarlane J.A. 2. Dissolution and annulment of marriage and includes nullity of marriage. *Vital Statistics Act*, R.S.O. 1990, c. V.4, s. 1. See CONTESTED ~; NO-FAULT ~; UNCONTESTED ~.

DIVORCE PROCEEDING. A proceeding in a court in which either or both spouses seek a divorce alone or together with a support order or a custody order or both such orders. *Divorce Act 1985*, S.C. 1986, c. 4, s. 2(1).

D.L.Q. *abbr.* Droits et libertés au Québec.

D.L.R. *abbr.* Dominion Law Reports, 1912-1922.

[ ] D.L.R. *abbr.* Dominion Law Reports, 1923-1955.

D.L.R. (4th). *abbr.* Dominion Law Reports (Fourth Series), 1984-.

D.L.R. (2d). *abbr.* Dominion Law Reports (Second Series), 1956-1968.

D.L.R. (3d). *abbr.* Dominion Law Reports (Third Series), 1969-1984.

D.O.A. *abbr.* Dead on arrival.

DOCK. *n.* The physical location in which a prisoner is placed during trial in a criminal court.

DOCKET. *v.* To make a list of entries; to keep track of time spent on matters.

DOCKET. *n.* 1. A record of the time and disbursements a lawyer spent on a particular matter. 2. A list of cases to be heard.

DOCTRINE. See CLEAN HANDS ~; DOUBLE ASPECT ~; EQUITABLE ~ OF CONSTRUCTIVE NOTICE.

DOCTRINE OF ACQUIESCENCE. "In the first place the plaintiff must have made a mistake as to his legal rights. Secondly, the plaintiff must have expended some money or must have done some act (not necessarily upon the defendant's land) on the faith of his mistaken belief. Thirdly, the defendant, the possessor of the legal right, must know of the existence of his own right which is inconsistent with the right claimed by the plaintiff. If he does not know of it he is in the same position as the plaintiff and the doctrine of acquiescence is founded upon conduct with a knowledge of your legal rights. Fourthly, the defendant, the possessor of the legal right, must know of the plaintiff's mistaken belief of his rights. If he does not, there is nothing which calls upon him to assert his own rights. Lastly, the defendant, the possessor of the legal rights must have encouraged the plaintiff in his expenditure of money or in the other acts which he has done, either directly or by abstaining from asserting his legal right. Where all of these elements exist, there is a fraud of such a nature as will entitle the court to restrain the possessor of the legal right from exercising it, but, in my judgment, nothing short of this will do." *Wilomot v. Barber* (1880), 15 Ch. D. 96 at 105-106, Fry J. See ACQUIESCENCE.

DOCTRINE OF SHELTERING. Anyone who buys with notice from another person who bought without notice can be sheltered under the first buyer. W.B. Rayner & R.H. McLaren, *Falconbridge on Mortgages*, 4th ed. (Toronto: Canada Law Book, 1977) at 149.

DOCTRINE OF SUBROGATION. If a mortgagee or unpaid vendor insures an interest in property and receives insurance money when a loss occurs, and if that mortgagee or vendor afterwards receives the mortgage money or the purchase price with no deduction on account of the insurance, that mortgagee or vendor is liable to the insurer for a sum equal to the insurance money received, because one is not entitled to more than full indemnification. W.B. Rayner & R.H. McLaren, *Falconbridge on Mortgages*, 4th ed. (Toronto: Canada Law Book, 1977) at 792.

DOCTRINE OF THE TABULA IN NAUFRAGIO. An equitable mortgagee who takes with no notice of an earlier equitable mortgage may get in the legal estate and in some cases obtain priority over the earlier mortgagee. W.B. Rayner & R.H. McLaren, *Falconbridge on Mortgages*, 4th ed. (Toronto: Canada Law Book, 1977) at 126.

DOCUMENT. *n.* 1. ". . . [S]omething which gives you information. . . . something which makes evident what would otherwise not be evident. . . . the form which the so-called document takes is perfectly immaterial so long as it is information conveyed by some-thing or other; it may be anything, upon which there is written or inscribed information." *R. v. Hill*, [1945] 1 All E.R. 414 at 417 (U.K. K.B.), Humphreys J. 2. Any paper, parchment or other material on which is recorded or marked anything that is capable of being read or understood by a person, computer system or other device, and includes a credit card, but does not include trade-marks on articles of commerce or inscriptions on stone or metal or other like material. *Criminal Law Amendment Act*, R.S.C. 1985 (1st Supp.), c. 27, s. 42. See FALSE ~; ORIGINATING ~; PRIVILEGED ~; PUBLIC ~.

DOCUMENTARY CREDIT. A conditional letter of credit providing that any draft drawn under it may be negotiated only if bills of lading, invoices and insurance policies valued at least equally to the draft accompany the draft.

DOCUMENTARY EVIDENCE. A document or paper adduced to prove its contents. P.K. McWilliams, *Canadian Criminal Evidence*, 3d ed. (Aurora: Canada Law Book, 1988) at 1-12.

DOG. *n.* Any of the species Canis familiaris Linnaeus. See GUIDE ~; HEARING ~.

DOG GUIDE. A dog trained to guide a visually handicapped person.

DOLI CAPAX. [L.] Capable of a criminal act.

DOLI INCAPAX. [L.] Not capable of a criminal act.

DOM. *abbr.* Dominion.

DOMESTIC AMENDING FORMULA. A procedure to amend the Constitution in Canada without the need to involve the British Parliament.

DOMESTIC ANIMAL. 1. A horse, a dog or any other animal that is kept under human control or by habit or training lives in association with humans. 2. Cattle, horses, swine, sheep, goats and poultry.

DOMESTIC CONTRACT. 1. A cohabitation agreement, marriage contract, separation agreement or agreement between a deceased spouse's administrator or executor and the surviving spouse. A. Bissett-Johnson & W.M. Holland, eds, *Matrimonial Property Law in Canada* (Toronto: Carswell, 1980) at N-93. 2. A marriage contract, separation agreement, cohabitation agreement or paternity agreement. *Family Law Act*, R.S. Nfld. 1990, c. F-2, s. 2(1).

DOMESTIC TRIBUNAL. ". . . [N]ot created or empowered by statute and is not part of an incorporated entity." *Rees v. U.A., Local 527* (1983), 4 Admin. L.R. 179 at 183, 43 O.R. (2d) 97, 83 C.L.L.C. 14,067, 150 D.L.R. (3d) 493 (Div. Ct.), Henry J.

DOMICILE. *n.* A person's permanent home or principal establishment to which that person intends to return after every absence.

DOMINANT TENEMENT. A subject or tenement to the benefit of which an easement or servitude is constituted.

DOMINION. *n.* 1. Any of the following Dominions, that is to say, the Dominion of Canada, the Commonwealth of Australia, the Dominion of New Zealand, the Union of South Africa, the Irish Free State and Newfoundland. *Statute of Westminster, 1931*, (U.K.), 22 Geo. 5, c. 4, s. 1, reprinted in R.S.C. 1985, App. Doc. No. 27. 2. Dominion of Canada. *Interpretation Act*, R.S.Q. 1977, c. I-16, s. 61.

DOMINION COMPANY. A company incorporated by or under an Act of the Parliament of Canada.

DOMINUS LITIS. [L. master of the suit] One who has control over a judicial proceeding or an action.

DONATIO. *n.* [L.] Gift.

DONATIO INTER VIVOS. [L.] A gift between persons still living.

DONATIO MORTIS CAUSA. [L.] ". . . [T]hree essential conditions, . . . first, the gift must have been made in contemplation, though not necessarily in expectation, of death; second, there must have been delivery to the donee of the subject-matter of the gift; third,

the gift must be made under such circumstances as to show that the thing is to revert to the donor in case he should recover." *Szczepkowski v. Eppler*, [1945] 4 D.L.R. 104 at 110, [1945] O.R. 540 (C.A.), the court per Roach J.A. See GIFT MORTIS CAUSA.

DONATION. *n.* 1. Includes any gift, testamentary disposition, deed, trust or other form of contribution. 2. "To constitute a valid donation there must be sufficient words of gift, and an act. . . ." *Blain v. Terryberry* (1862), 9 Gr. 286 at 295 (Ont. H.C.), Spragge V.C.

DONATIVE INTENT. The intention of making a gift.

DONATIVE PROMISE. A promise to confer a benefit by gift. G.H.L. Fridman, *The Law of Contract in Canada*, 2d ed. (Toronto: Carswell, 1986) at 73.

DONEE. *n.* 1. One to whom a gift is made. 2. A person to whom a power of appointment is given is sometimes called the donee of the power.

DONOR. *n.* One who gives.

DOUBLE ASPECT DOCTRINE. ". . . [S]ubjects which in one aspect and for one purpose fall within sect. 92 [of the Constitution Act, 1867 (30 & 31 Vict.), c.3], may in another aspect and for another purpose fall within sect. 91." *Hodge v. The Queen* (1883), 9 App. Cas. 117 at 130 (P.C.).

DOUBLE ENTRY. Describing books of account kept by posting each entry as a debit and credit.

DOUBLE JEOPARDY. A second prosecution for the same offence. See RULE AGAINST ~.

DOWER. *n.* A life interest in one-third of any freehold estate of inheritance of which the husband died solely seised in possession either through a tenant or by himself and which he either brought with him into the marriage or acquired afterwards. A. Bissett-Johnson & W.M. Holland, eds., *Matrimonial Property Law in Canada* (Toronto: Carswell, 1980) at I-10. See BAR OF ~.

DOWN PAYMENT. A sum of money, the value of a negotiable instrument payable on demand, or the agreed value of goods, given on account at the time of the contract. *Consumer Protection acts.*

D.P.P. *abbr.* Director of Public Prosecutions.

DRAFT. *n.* 1. An order drawn by one person on another for the payment of money, i.e. a bill of exchange or cheque. 2. An order for the payment of money drawn by one banker on another. See RE-~.

DRAFTSMAN. *n.* Any person who drafts a legal document.

DRAPER. *abbr.* Draper (Ont.), 1828-1831.

DRAUGHT. *n.* 1. An order drawn by one person on another for the payment of money, i.e. a bill of exchange or cheque. 2. An order for the payment of money drawn by one banker on another.

DRAW. *v.* To write a bill of exchange and sign it.

DRAWEE. *n.* The person to whom a bill of exchange is addressed.

DRAWER. *n.* The person who signs or makes a bill of exchange.

DRIVER. *n.* 1. A person who drives or is in actual physical control of a vehicle or who is exercising control over or steering a vehicle being towed or pushed by another vehicle. 2. Includes a person who has the care or control of a motor vehicle whether it is in motion or not.

DRIVER'S LICENCE. 1. A licence which has been issued authorizing the person to whom it is issued to drive a motor vehicle and which has not expired, been suspended or cancelled. 2. A licence or a permit to drive a motor vehicle on a public highway.

DRIVER'S POLICY. A motor vehicle liability policy insuring a person named therein in respect of the operation or use by him of any automobile other than an automobile owned by him or registered in his name. *Insurance acts.*

DROIT. *n.* [Fr.] Equity; justice; right.

D.R.S. *abbr.* Dominion Report Service.

DRUG. *n.* 1. Any substance or mixture of substances manufactured, sold or represented for use in (a) the diagnosis, treatment, mitigation or prevention of a disease, disorder, abnormal physical state, or the symptoms thereof, in man or animal, (b) restoring, correcting or modifying organic functions in man or animal, or (c) disinfection in premises in which food is manufactured, prepared or kept. 2. Any substance that is capable of producing a state of euphoria, depression, hallucination or intoxication in a human being. 3. "... [A]ny substance or chemical agent the consumption of which will bring about impairment as contemplated by s. 234 [of the Criminal Code, R.S.C. 1970, c. C-34]." *R. v. Marionchuk* (1978), 1 M.V.R. 158 at 162, 4 C.R. (3d) 178, [1978] 6 W.W.R. 120, 42 C.C.C. (2d) 573 (Sask. C.A.), the court per Culliton C.J.S. See HALLUCINOGENIC ~.

DRUG ABUSE. (a) Addiction to a substance other than alcohol; or (b) the use, whether habitual or not, of a substance other than alcohol that is capable of inducing euphoria, hallucinations or intoxication in a person.

DRUNKENNESS. *n.* Intoxication.

D.T.C. *abbr.* Dominion Tax Cases.

DUBITANTE. *adj.* [L. doubting] Used in a law report to describe a judge's doubt that a proposition is correct without a decision that it is wrong.

DUCES TECUM. See SUBPOENA ~.

DUE. *adj.* 1. Payable; owing. *Mail Printing Co. v. Clarkson* (1895), 25 O.A.R. 1 (C.A.), Moss J.A. 2. "... [I]n relation to moneys in respect of which there is a legal obligation to pay them may mean either that the facts making the obligation operative have come into existence with the exception that the day of payment has not yet arrived, or it may mean that the obligation has not only been completely constituted but is also presently exigible...." *Ontario Hydro-Electric Power Commission v.*

Albright (1922), 64 S.C.R. 306 at 312, [1923] 2 D.L.R. 578, Duff J.

DUE COURSE. See HOLDER IN ~.

DUELLING. *n.* Challenging or attempting by any means to provoke another person to fight a duel, attempting to provoke a person to challenge another person to fight a duel, or accepting a challenge to fight a duel is an offence. *Criminal Code*, R.S.C. 1985, c. C-46, s. 71.

DUE PROCESS OF LAW. "... [T]he phrase 'due process of law' as used in s. 1(a) [of the Canadian Bill of Rights, R.S.C. 1970, App. III] is to be construed as meaning 'according to the legal processes recognized by Parliament and the Courts in Canada.' " *Curr v. R.*, [1972] S.C.R. 889 at 916, 18 C.R.N.S. 281, 7 C.C.C. (2d) 181, 26 D.L.R. (3d) 603, Ritchie J.

DUES. *n.* Fees, rates, charges or other moneys payable by any person to the Crown under and by virtue of a lease, licence or permit.

DULY. *adv.* In the proper manner; regularly.

DUM CASTA VIXERIT. [L.] As long as she lives chastely.

DUM SOLA. [L.] As long as she remains single or unmarried.

DUM SOLA ET CASTA. [L.] As long as she remains unmarried and lives chastely.

DUPLICATE. *v.* To copy.

DUPLICATE. *n.* A copy.

DUPLICITY. *n.* 1. "... [I]f the information in one count charges more than one offence, it is bad for duplicity ..." *R. v. Sault Ste. Marie (City)* (1978), 7 C.E.L.R. 53 at 57, [1978] 2 S.C.R. 1299, 3 C.R. (3d) 30, 21 N.R. 295, 40 C.C.C. (2d) 353, 85 D.L.R. (3d) 161, the court per Dickson J. 2. "... [T]he practice of including more than one claim in a pleading." *Flexi-Coil Ltd. v. Rite Way Manufacturing Ltd.* (1989), 28 C.P.R. (3d) 256 at 259, 31 F.T.R. 73, [1990] 1 F.C. 108, Giles (Associate Senior Prothonotary).

DURANTE. [L.] During.

DURANTE ABSENTIA. [L.] During absence.

DURESS. *n.* 1. "... [A] threat of death or serious physical injury is necessary to constitute duress at common law: ... Mere fear does not constitute duress in the absence of a threat, either express or implied." *R. v. Mena* (1987), 34 C.C.C. (3d) 304 at 320, 322, 57 C.R. (3d) 172, 20 O.A.C. 50 (C.A.), the court per Martin J.A. 2. "... [T]hreats must be made to a person who is a party and with the intention of inducing that person to enter into the agreement sought to be avoided; ... duress makes a contract voidable at the initiative of the innocent party, but there cannot be duress unless the acts complained of constitute a coercion of the complaining party's will so as to vitiate the consent of that party: ..." *Byle v. Byle* (1990), 46 B.L.R. 292 at 304, 65 D.L.R. (4th) 641 (B.C. C.A.), the court per Macdonald J.A. 3. "Economic pressure does not amount to duress unless there is a coercion of will to the point that the payment or contract was not a voluntary act." *Century 21 Campbell Munro Ltd. v. S & G Estates Ltd.* (1992), 89 D.L.R. (4th) 413 at 417, 54 O.A.C. 315 (Div. Ct.), the court per Campbell J. See ECONOMIC ~.

DURESS COLORE OFFICII. [L.] Abuse of an official or governmental position in which the offical requires a person to pay in order to obtain some authority, licence, permission or power to act or proceed in a particular way. G.H.L. Fridman, *Restitution*, 2d ed. (Toronto: Carswell, 1992) at 124.

DURESS OF PROPERTY. Wrongful seizure or detention of a plaintiff's goods. G.H.L. Fridman, *Restitution*, 2d ed. (Toronto: Carswell, 1992) at 122.

DURESS OF THE PERSON. Actual or threatened physical violence to a person, or violence or threatened violence to the physical safety of others, such as members of a payer's family. The concept now extends to threats of criminal process which might lead to imprisonment. G.H.L. Fridman, *Restitution*, 2d ed. (Toronto: Carswell,

1992) at 118-9.

DUTIES. *n.* Any duties or taxes levied on imported goods under the Customs Tariff, the Excise Tax Act, the Excise Act, the Special Import Measures Act or any other law relating to customs. See CUSTOM DUTY; CUSTOMS DUTY.

DUTY. *n.* 1. A requirement which the law recognizes to avoid conduct characterized by unreasonable risk of danger to other persons. J.G. Fleming, *The Law of Torts*, 8th ed. (Sydney: Law Book, 1992) at 135. 2. A duty imposed by law. *Criminal Code*, R.S.C. 1985, c. C-46, s. 219(2). See ACTIVE ~; CUSTOM ~; CUSTOMS ~; DISCRETIONARY ~; ESTATE ~; EXCISE ~; MINISTERIAL ~; PROBATE ~; STAMP ~; SUCCESSION ~.

DUTY COUNSEL. A lawyer appointed to assist any person appearing in court without having retained a lawyer.

DUTY OF CARE. "... [A] device which the courts have developed to control the extent to which defendants would otherwise be liable in negligence. In its modern manifestation as a basic principle of negligence, it owes its origin to the following words of Lord Atkins in *M'Alister (Donoghue) v. Stevenson*, [1932] A.C. 562 ... at pp. 580-581: 'Who, then, in law is my neighbour? The answer seems to be – persons who are so closely and directly affected by my act that I ought reasonably to have them in contemplation as being so affected when I am directing my mind to the acts or omissions which are called in question.' " *Layden v. Canada (Attorney General)* (1991), (*sub nom. Brewer Brothers v. Canada (Attorney General)*) 8 C.C.L.T. (2d) 45 at 68, 129 N.R. 1, [1992] 1 F.C. 25, 45 F.T.R. 325n (C.A.), the court per Stone J.A. See NEIGHBOUR TEST.

DUTY OF FAIRNESS. See DUTY TO ACT FAIRLY.

DUTY TO ACCOUNT. The duty of a trustee to have his accounts always ready, to afford all reasonable facilities for inspection and examination, and to give full information whenever required. *Sandford v. Porter* (1889), 16 O.A.R. 565 at 571.

DUTY TO ACT FAIRLY. 1. "Fairness involves compliance with only some of the principles of natural justice. Professor de Smith, Judicial Review of Administrative Action (1973), 3rd ed. p. 208, expressed lucidly the concept of a duty to act fairly: 'In general it means a duty to observe the rudiments of natural justice for a limited purpose in the exercise of functions that are not analytically judicial but administrative.' " *Martineau v. Matsqui Institution* (1979), 106 D.L.R. (3d) 385 at 411-12, [1980] 1 S.C.R. 602, 12 C.R. (3d) 1, 15 C.R. (3d) 315, 50 C.C.C. (2d) 353, 30 N.R. 119, Dickson J. 2. "... The basic objective of the duty to act fairly is to ensure that an individual is provided with a sufficient degree of participation necessary to bring to the attention of the decision-maker any fact or argument of which a fair-minded decision-maker would need to be informed in order to reach a rational conclusion." *Kindler v. Canada (Minister of Justice)* (1987), 1 Imm. L.R. (2d) 30 at 37, 8 F.T.R. 222, [1987] 2 F.C. 145, 34 C.C.C. (3d) 78, Rouleau J. See ECONOMIC DURESS; FAIRNESS.

DUTY TO MITIGATE. The requirement that the plaintiff take all reasonable steps to minimize a loss which follows a breach of contract or injury.

DWELLING. *n.* 1. "... [P]lace of residence, a place in which to live, a habitation." *Read v. Read*, [1950] 2 W.W.R. 812 at 813, [1950] 4 D.L.R. 676 (B.C. C.A.), the court per Sloan C.J.B.C. 2. A premises or any part thereof occupied as living accommodation.

DWELLING-HOUSE. *var.* **DWELLING HOUSE.** The whole or any part of a building or structure that is kept or occupied as a permanent or temporary residence, and includes (a) a building within the curtilage of a dwelling-house that is connected to it by a doorway or by a covered and enclosed passage-way, and (b) a unit that is designed to be mobile and to be used as a permanent or temporary residence and that is being used as such a residence.

DWELLING UNIT. A room or suite of rooms used or intended to be used as a domicile by one or more persons and usually containing cooking, eating, living, sleeping and sanitary facilities.

D.W.I. *abbr*. Died without issue.

DYING DECLARATION. "... [S]tatement made under a sense of impending death ..." *R. v. Davidson* (1898), 30 N.S.R. 349 at 359 (C.A.), Henry J.A.

DYING WITHOUT ISSUE. Dying without any child being born before or after death.

E

E. & A. *abbr.* Error and Appeal Reports (Grant) (Ont.), 1846-1866.

E. & O.E. *abbr.* Errors and omissions excepted.

EARNEST. *n.* Something given by the buyer and accepted by the seller at the time of the contract which indicates the contract is completed. G.H.L. Fridman, *Sale of Goods in Canada*, 3d ed. (Toronto: Carswell, 1986) at 45.

EARNINGS. *n.* 1. The pay received or receivable by an employee for work done for an employer. 2. "[As used in the Unemployment Insurance Act, S.C. 1970-71-72, c. 48, s. 58(q)] . . . in the broad sense are everything the worker derives in the form of pecuniary benefits from his work present or past, and in this sense a pension is still undoubtedly earnings, . . ." *Côté v. Canada (Employment & Immigration Commission)* (1986), 13 C.C.E.L. 255 at 262, 86 C.L.L.C. 14,050, 69 N.R. 126 (Fed. C.A.), Marceau J.A. (Pratte J. concurring).

EASEMENT. *n.* ". . . [A] right annexed to land which permits the owner of a dominant tenement to require the owner of a servient tenement to suffer something on such land. There are four characteristics of an easement: (1) There must be a dominant and a servient tenement. (2) An easement must accommodate the dominant tenement. (3) Dominant and servient owners must be different persons. (4) A right over land cannot amount to an easement unless it is capable of forming the subject-matter of a grant." *Vannini v.*

Sault Ste. Marie Public Utilities Commission (1972), [1973] 2 O.R. 11 at 16, 32 D.L.R. (3d) 661 (H.C.), Holland J.

EASEMENT IN GROSS. An easement created by private grant or statute, e.g. a power line or pipeline. J.V. DiCastri, *Occupiers' Liability* (Vancouver: Burroughs/Carswell, 1980) at 212.

E.C.B. *abbr.* Expropriations Compensation Board.

ECCLESIASTICAL. *adj.* Set apart for or belonging to the church.

ECCLESIASTICAL COURT. A court with jurisdiction in ecclesiastical matters only.

ECCLESIASTICAL LAW. Law which relates to the government, obligations and rights of a church.

ECONOMIC DURESS. ". . . [A]s used in recent cases . . . is not more than a recognition that in our modern life the individual is subject to societal pressures which can be every bit as effective, if improperly used, as those flowing from threats of physical abuse. . . . It must be a pressure which the law does not regard as legitimate and it must be applied to such a degree as to amount to 'a coercion of the will', . . . or it must place the party to whom the pressure is directed in a position where he has no 'realistic alternative' but to submit to it, . . ." *Stott v. Merit Investment Corp.* (1988), 19 C.C.E.L. 68 at 92, 25 O.A.C. 174, 63 O.R. (2d) 545, 48 D.L.R. (4th) 288 (C.A.), Finlayson J.A. (Krever J.A. concurring).

EDUC. & L.J. *abbr.* Education and Law Journal.

EFFECT. *v.* ". . . '[T]o bring about an event or result' . . ." *Gladstone v. Catena*, [1948] 2 D.L.R. 483 at 486-7, [1948] O.R. 182 (C.A.), Laidlaw J.A.

E.G. *abbr.* [L. exempli gratia] For instance.

EGALITARIAN CIVIL LIBERTIES. Include equal access to accommodation, employment, education, other benefits without illegitimate criteria of discrimination such as race or sex. Also include the right to the use of either of the official languages, French or English, and the rights of denominational or separate schools. P.W. Hogg, *Constitutional Law of Canada*, 3d ed. (Toronto: Carswell, 1992) at 765.

EGALITY. *n.* Equality.

EGRESS. Leaving, departing.

EJECTMENT. *n.* ". . . [A]n action for the recovery of land; . . ." *Point v. Dibblee Construction Co.*, [1934] O.R. 142 at 153, [1934] 2 D.L.R. 785 (H.C.), Armour J.

EJUSDEM GENERIS. [L. of the same kind] "Where there are general words following particular and specific words, the general words must be confined to things of the same kind as those specified. The principle applies only where the special words are of the same nature and can be grouped together in the same genus; where there are different genera the meaning of the general words is unaffected by their collocation with the special words and must be given their full and ordinary meaning." *Reg. v. Edmundson* (1859), 28 L.J.M.C. 213 at 215, Lord Campbell C.J.

ELECTION. *n.* 1. Making a choice. 2. Deciding on a representative. 3. "[When a party] . . . not only determined to follow one of his remedies but has communicated it to the other side in such a way as to lead the opposite party to believe that he has made that choice, he has completed his election . . ." *Scarf v. Jardine* (1882), 7

App. Cas. 345 at 360 (U.K.), Lord Blackburn. See BY-~; GENERAL ~.

ELECTOR. *n.* 1. Person eligible to vote at an election. 2. A person entitled to vote at an election. 3. A person qualified to vote at an election. 4. Any person who is or who claims to be registered as an elector in the list of voters for any electoral district; or who is, or claims to be, entitled to vote in any election.

ELECTORAL DISTRICT. 1. An area entitled to elect a member to serve in a legislature. 2. The area from which a school board member is to be elected.

ELECTORAL DIVISION. Any territorial division or district entitled to return a member.

ELECTRONIC SURVEILLANCE. Wiretapping or use of other electronic means to monitor a person's conversations and whereabouts.

ELEEMOSYNARY CORPORATION. A body corporate established to perpetually distribute free alms or its founder's gift.

ELEGIT. *n.* [L. one has chosen] A writ of execution by which a judgment creditor is awarded the debtor's land to hold until the debt is satisfied.

ELEMENTS. See COMMON ~.

ELIGIBILITY. *n.* Qualification.

E.L.J. *abbr.* Education & Law Journal.

E.L.R. *abbr.* Eastern Law Reporter, 1906-1914.

EMANATION. *n.* That which issues or proceeds from some source. *International Railway v. Niagara Parks Commission*, [1941] 3 D.L.R. 385 at 393, [1941] A.C. 328, [1941] 2 All E.R. 456, 53 C.R.T.C. 1 (Ont. P.C.), the board per Luxmoore L.J. Use in the expression "emanation of the Crown" was disapproved.

EMBARRASSING. *adj.* 1. ". . . [P]leadings framed in such a confused or ambiguous manner as to cause real and undue embarrassment or prejudice." *Rogers v. Clark* (1900), 13 Man. R. 189 at 196 (K.B.), Killam C.J.

2. ". . . [B]ringing forward a defence which the defendant is not entitled to make use of: . . ." *Stratford Gas Co. v. Gordon* (1892), 14 P.R. 407 at 414 (Ont. H.C.), Armour C.J. 3. ". . . [T]he allegations are so irrelevant that to allow them to stand would involve useless expenses and would also prejudice the trial of the action by involving the parties in a dispute that is wholly apart from the issues." *London (Mayor) v. Horner* (1914), 3 L.T.R. 512 at 514 (U.K.), Pickford L.J., cited in *Meyers v. Freeholders Oil Co.* (1956), 19 W.W.R. 546 at 549 (Sask. C.A.).

EMBASSY. *n.* 1. An ambassador's establishment. 2. The commission given by a nation to an ambassador, to deal with another nation.

EMBEZZLEMENT. *n.* Conversion to personal use of any chattel, money or valuable security received or taken into possession by an employee for, in the name or on account of the employer.

EMBLEMENTS. *n.* ". . . [T]he growing crops of those vegetable productions of the soil which are annually produced by the labour of the cultivator. They are a species of *fructus industriales,* but do not exhaust the genus." *Cochlin v. The Massey-Harris Co.* (1915), 8 Alta. L.R. 392 at 396, 8 W.W.R. 286, 23 D.L.R. 397 (C.A.), Beck J.A. (dissenting).

EMBRACERY. *n.* A common law offence of attempting to instruct or influence any jury member or giving a reward to a jury member for something done by that member.

EMIGRATION. *n.* The act of moving from one country to another with no intention of returning.

EMINENT DOMAIN. A government's right to take private property for public purposes, a doctrine which is American in origin. See EXPROPRIATION.

EMISSARY. *n.* One person sent on a mission as agent of another person.

EMOLUMENTS. *n.* 1. ". . . '[T]he profit arising from office or employ-ment,' and not merely the gross amount of salary, fees or perquisites, but the balance remaining after deduction of the necessary expenses paid out in earning the salary, fees or perquisites." *Lawless v. Sullivan* (1879), 3 S.C.R. 117 at 146, Henry J. 2. Includes fees, percentages and other payments made or consideration given, directly or indirectly, to a director as such, and the money value of any allowances or perquisites belonging to his office. *Companies Act,* R.S.N.S. 1989, c. 81, s. 100(4).

EMPANEL. *v.* "[S]electing a new jury from the . . . jurors already summoned, . . ." *R. v. Gaffin* (1904), 8 C.C.C. 194 at 196 (N.S. C.A.), the court per Graham E.J. See IMPANEL; JURY.

EMPHYTEUSIS. *n.* 1. "[As defined in Art. 567-571 of the Quebec Civil Code] . . . 'carries with it' ownership full and complete of land and buildings in contradistinction to the common law . . ." *Reitman v. Minister of National Revenue,* [1967] C.T.C. 368 at 375, [1968] 1 Ex. C.R. 120, 67 D.T.C. 5253, Dumoulin J. 2. The right to enjoy all the fruits, and dispose at pleasure of another's property on condition a yearly rent is paid.

EMPLEAD. *v.* To accuse; to indict; to bring a charge against.

EMPLOY. *v.* ". . . [C]an be used in the sense of the common law master/servant relationship in which control is a principle factor in determining the existence of the relationship . . . common, and grammatically correct, . . . to use the word[s] in the sense of 'utilize'." *Pannu, Re* (1986), (*sub nom. Pannu v. Prestige Cab Ltd.*) 87 C.L.L.C. 17,003 at 16,010, 47 Alta. L.R. (2d) 56, [1986] 6 W.W.R. 617, 73 A.R. 166, 31 D.L.R. (4th) 338, 8 C.H.R.R. D/3911 (C.A.), the court per Laycraft J.A.

EMPLOY. *n.* ". . . '[E]mployment' . . . 'service;' . . ." *Hirshman v. Beal* (1916), 38 O.L.R. 40 at 47, 28 C.C.C. 319, 32 D.L.R. 680 (C.A.), Meredith C.J.C.P.

EMPLOYED. *adj.* 1. Performing the duties of an office or employment. 2. ". . . '[O]ccupied or engaged'." *Might v. Minister of National Revenue*, [1948] Ex. C.R. 382 at 389, [1948] C.T.C. 144, [1949] 1 D.L.R. 250, O'Connor J.

EMPLOYEE. *n.* 1. Any person employed by an employer and includes a dependent contractor and a private constable, but does not include a person who performs management functions or is employed in a confidential capacity in matters relating to industrial relations. *Canada Labour Code*, R.S.C. 1985, c. L-2, s. 3. 2. Includes an officer. 3. Any person who is in receipt of or entitled to any compensation for labour or services performed for another. 4. Any person who performs duties and functions that entitle that person to compensation on a regular basis. 5. A person who is in receipt of or entitled to wages. See CONTRACT ~.

EMPLOYEE BARGAINING AGENCY. An organization of affiliated bargaining agents that are subordinate or directly related to the same provincial, national or international trade union, and that may include the parent or related provincial, national or international trade union, formed for purposes that include the representation of affiliated bargaining agents in bargaining and which may be a single provincial, national or international trade union. *Labour Relations Act*, R.S.O. 1980, c. 228, s. 137.

EMPLOYEE BENEFIT PLAN. A system to provide increased security to workers through schemes such as group insurance and cash benefits.

EMPLOYEE ORGANIZATION. Any organization of employees the purposes of which include the regulation of relations between the employer and its employees and includes, unless the context otherwise requires, a council of employee organizations.

EMPLOYEES' MUTUAL BENEFIT SOCIETY. *var.* **EMPLOYEES MUTUAL BENEFIT SOCIETY.** A society incorporated by the officers or officers and employees of a corporation for the purpose of providing support and pensions to such of the officers or employees as become incapacitated or as cease to be employed by the corporation or for the purpose of paying pensions, annuities or gratuities to or for dependants of such officers or employees or funeral benefits upon the death of such officers or employees. *Insurance acts.*

EMPLOYER. *n.* 1. Any person who employs one or more employees. 2. In relation to an officer, means the person from whom the officer receives remuneration. 3. Includes every person responsible for the payment of the wages of an employee under any act or law. 4. (a) Any person who employs one or more employees, and (b) in respect of a dependent contractor, such person as, in the opinion of the Board, has a relationship with the dependent contractor to such extent that the arrangement that governs the performance of services by the dependent contractor for that person can be the subject of collective bargaining. *Canada Labour Code*, R.S.C. 1985, c. L-2, s. 3.

EMPLOYER BARGAINING AGENCY. An employers' organization or group of employers' organizations formed for purposes that include the representation of employers in bargaining. *Labour Relations Act*, R.S.O. 1980, c. 228, s. 137.

EMPLOYER RIGHTS. Rights, such as hiring and price fixing, which management generally argues are not proper subjects of collective bargaining.

EMPLOYERS' ASSOCIATION. A group organization of employers having as its objects the study and safeguarding of the economic interests of its members, and particularly assistance in the negotiation and application of collective agreements. *Labour Code*, R.S.Q. 1977, c. C-27, s. 1.

EMPLOYERS' ORGANIZATION. Organization of employers formed for purposes that include the regulation of relations between employers and employees.

EMPLOYMENT. *n.* 1. The performance of services under an express or implied contract of service or apprenticeship, and includes the tenure of an office. 2. ". . . [T]he meaning is, in effect, what the U.K. Race Relations Act [1976 (Eng.), c. 74] [provides:] 'any contract in which one person agrees to execute any work or labour for another.' " *Cormier v. Alberta (Human Rights Commission)* (1984), 33 Alta. L.R. (2d) 359 at 366, 6 C.C.E.L. 60, 14 D.L.R. (4th) 55, 5 C.H.R.R. D/2441, 56 A.R. 351, 85 C.L.L.C. 17,003 (Q.B.), McDonald J. 3. Any activity for which a person receives or might reasonably be expected to receive valuable consideration. 4. The position of an individual in the service of some other person, including Her Majesty or a foreign state or sovereign. 5. The act of employing or the state of being employed. 6. ". . . '[A]ctivity' or 'occupation'." *Canada (Attorney General) v. Skyline Cabs (1982) Ltd.* (1986), 11 C.C.E.L. 292 at 295, 45 Alta. L.R. (2d) 296, [1986] 5 W.W.R. 16, 86 C.L.L.C. 14,047, 70 N.R. 210 (Fed. C.A.), the court per MacGuigan J.A. See ACT WITHIN SCOPE OF ~; CONDITION OF ~; CONTRACT OF ~; COURSE OF ~; FAIR ~ PRACTICE.

EMPLOYMENT AGENCY. Includes a person who undertakes, with or without compensation, to procure employees for employers and a person who undertakes, with or without compensation, to procure employment for persons. *Human Rights codes.*

EMPLOYMENT CONTRACT. ". . . [A] contract whereby a person agrees to provide sales services in consideration of payment of salary and a commission on sales, . . ." *Prozak v. Bell Telephone Co. of Canada* (1984), 4 C.C.E.L. 202 at 219, 46 O.R. (2d) 385, 4 O.A.C. 12, 10 D.L.R. (4th) 382 (C.A.), the court per Goodman J.A.

EMPLOYMENT INJURY. Personal injury, including disablement, caused by an industrial accident, occupational disease or employment hazard. *Canada Labour Code*, R.S.C. 1985, c. L-2, s. 122.

EMPTOR. *n.* A buyer.

ENABLING STATUTE. A statute which gives power or authority.

ENACT. *v.* 1. To decree; to establish by law. 2. Includes to issue, make, establish or prescribe.

ENACTING CLAUSE. 1. In federal statutes, "Her Majesty, by and with the advice and consent of the Senate and House of Commons of Canada, enacts as follows:" A. Fraser, W.A. Dawson & J. Holtby, eds., *Beauchesne's Rules and Forms of the House of Commons of Canada*, 6th ed. (Toronto: Carswell, 1989) at 193. 2. The formal portion of a by-law which describes the act or thing required to be done or forbidden. I.M. Rogers, *The Law of Canadian Municipal Corporations*, 2d ed. (Toronto: Carswell, 1971) at 417.

ENACTMENT. *n.* 1. An act or a regulation or any portion of an act or regulation, and as applied to a territory of Canada, includes an ordinance of the territory. 2. An act of the legislature of a province or a regulation, bylaw or other instrument having the force of law made under the authority of an act.

EN BANC. [Fr.] By the full court. Refers to a hearing before all the justices of a particular court.

ENCROACHMENT. *n.* An attempt to extend a right a person already possesses.

ENCUMBRANCE. *n.* 1. Any charge on land, created or effected for any purpose whatever, including mortgages, the hypothecation of a mortgage, a trust for securing money, mechanics' liens when authorized by statute or ordinance, and executions against lands, unless expressly distinguished. 2. ". . . [A] charge or liability to which land is subject. . . ." *Seltor Holdings Ltd. v. Kettles* (1983), 29 R.P.R. 214 at 221, 43 O.R. (2d) 659, 3 C.L.R. 259, 2 D.L.R. (4th) 373 (Div. Ct.), Saunders J. See INCUMBRANCE.

ENCUMBRANCEE. *n.* The owner of an encumbrance.

ENCUMBRANCER. *n.* The owner of any land or of any estate or interest in land subject to any encumbrance and includes a person entitled to the benefit of an encumbrance, or to require payment or discharge of an encumbrance.

ENCYCLOPEDIA. *n.* A collective work containing a series of articles by many contributors.

ENDORSE. *v.* 1. To place a signature on a negotiable bill of exchange. 2. Imprinting a stamp on the face of articles or other document sent to the Director. *Business Corporations Act*, R.S.O. 1990, c. B.16, s. 1. 3. To enter a record of a transaction or document. *Delgamuukw (Uukw) v. British* Columbia (1986), 41 R.P.R. 240 at 280, 28 D.L.R. (4th) 504, 5 B.C.L.R. (2d) 76, [1986] 4 C.N.L.R. 111 (S.C.), Finch J.

ENDORSED. *adj.* Written on any instrument or on any paper attached thereto by the registrar.

ENDORSEMENT. *n.* 1. Anything written by the registrar upon an instrument or upon a paper attached thereto. 2. An endorsement completed by delivery. *Bills of Exchange Act*, R.S.C. 1985, c. B-4, s. 2. 3. Includes entry, memorandum and notation. 4. An ordinary signature. I.F.G. Baxter, *The Law of Banking*, 3d ed. (Toronto: Carswell, 1981) at 96. 5. "... [I]n its literal sense means writing one's name of the back of the bill, ..." *Gorrie Co. v. Whitfield* (1920), 58 D.L.R. 326 at 329, 19 O.W.N. 336, 48 O.L.R. 605 (C.A.), Meredith C.J.O. (Magee and Hodgins JJ.A. concurring). See BLANK ~; INDORSEMENT.

ENDOWMENT. *n.* Any kind of property belonging permanently to a charity.

ENFEOFF. *v.* To give possession of lands or tenements.

ENFEOFFMENT. *n.* 1. Investing with a dignity or possession. 2. The deed or instrument by which one invests another with possessions.

ENFORCEABLE. *adj.* 1. "Refer[s] ... to ... [a] process ... to enable measures to be taken to secure compliance ..." *U.N.A. v. Alberta (Attorney General)* (1992), 71 C.C.C. (3d) 225 at 234, [1992] 3 W.W.R. 481, 1 Alta. L.R. (3d) 129, 13 C.R. (4th) 1, 89 D.L.R. (4th) 609, 135 N.R. 321, 92 C.L.L.C. 14,023, 9 C.R.R. (2d) 29, [1992] 1 S.C.R. 901, 125 A.R. 241, 14 W.A.C. 241, Sopinka J. (dissenting). 2. Refers to providing a penalty to induce obedience. *U.N.A. v. Alberta (Attorney General)* (1992), 71 C.C.C. (3d) 225 at 234, [1992] 3 W.W.R. 481, 1 Alta. L.R. (3d) 129, 13 C.R. (4th) 1, 89 D.L.R. (4th) 609, 135 N.R. 321, 92 C.L.L.C. 14,023, 9 C.R.R. (2d) 29, [1992] 1 S.C.R. 901, 125 A.R. 241, 14 W.A.C. 241, Sopinka J. (dissenting).

ENFORCEMENT. See LAW ~.

ENFRANCHISE. *v.* 1. To bestow a liberty; to make free. 2. To give someone the liberty to vote at an election.

ENGLISH REPORTS. The reprinted reports of English cases from 1220 to 1865.

ENGROSS. *v.* 1. To type or write an agreement, deed or like document from a draft with all amounts, dates and words set out at length, and with the formal attestation and testatum clauses, so that the document is ready to be executed. 2. Formerly, to write in a particular script derived from the courthand in which records were written in ancient times.

ENJOIN. *v.* To prohibit by court order, the effect of an injunction.

ENJOYMENT. *n.* 1. The use or application of a right. 2. "Ordinarily ... denotes the derivation of pleasure." *R. v. Phoenix* (1991), 64 C.C.C. (3d) 252 at 255 (B.C. Prov. Ct.), de Villiers Prov. J. 3. "... [A] different sense ... in reference to [real] property ... 'possession' ..." *R. v. Phoenix* (1991), 64 C.C.C. (3d) 252 at 255 (B.C. Prov. Ct.), de Villiers Prov. J. See QUIET ~.

ENLARGE. *v.* To lengthen time.

ENQUIRY. See INQUIRY.

ENRG. *abbr.* Enregistré.

ENRICHMENT. See UNJUST ~.

ENROL. *v.* To enter or copy a document into an official record.

ENTAIL. *n.* An estate or interest in land which descends only to the grantee's issue. R. Megarry & H.W.R. Wade, *The Law of Real Property*, 5th ed. (London: Stevens, 1984) at cxxiv.

ENTER. *v.* 1. To come onto land. 2. To note, in a record or book, a transcript of a document or a transaction. See BREAK AND ~.

ENTER JUDGMENT. To deliver to the Registrar an order embodying a judgment or to cause the Registrar to make a formal record of a judgment. *Rules of the Supreme Court*, S.Nfld. 1986, r. 1, s. 1.03.

ENTICEMENT. *n.* The deliberate inducement of a wife to leave her husband. The inducement must be made with knowledge of her marital status and with intent to interfere with the wife's duty to give consortium to her husband. J.G. Fleming, *The Law of Torts*, 8th ed. (Sydney: Law Book, 1992) at 653-54.

ENTIRETY. See TENANCY BY THE ~.

ENTITLE. *v.* To bestow a right.

ENTRAPMENT. *n.* "[Occurs] . . . when (a) the authorities provide a person with an opportunity to commit an offence without acting on a reasonable suspicion that this person is already engaged in criminal activity or pursuant to a bona fide inquiry; (b) although having such a reasonable suspicion or acting in the course of a bona fide inquiry, they go beyond providing an opportunity and induce the commission of an offence." *R. v. Mack* (1988), 37 C.R.R. 277 at 324, [1989] 1 W.W.R. 577, [1988] 2 S.C.R. 903, 67 C.R. (3d) 1, 90 N.R. 173, 44 C.C.C. (3d) 513, the court per Lamer J.

ENTRENCHED. *adj.* Able to be altered solely through a constitutional amendment. P.W. Hogg, *Constitutional Law of Canada*, 3d ed. (Toronto: Carswell, 1992) at 7.

ENTRENCHMENT CLAUSE. Section 52(3) of the Constitution Act, 1982: "Amendments to the Constitu-

tion of Canada shall be made only in accordance with the authority contained in the Constitution of Canada."

ENTRY. *n.* 1. Going onto land. 2. Setting down a record in a book. 3. Lawful permission to come into Canada as a visitor. *Immigration Act*, R.S.C. 1985, c. I-2, s. 2. 4. "[In the Canada Evidence Act, R.S.C. 1970, c. E-10, s. 29(1)] . . . an ordinary financial or bookkeeping entry, that is, the figures and the required explanation for such figures, in a ledger, book, card system or computer card system. . . ." *Minister of National Revenue v. Furnasman Ltd.*, [1973] F.C. 1327 at 1333, [1973] C.T.C. 830, 73 D.T.C. 5599 (T.D.), Addy J. See DOUBLE ~; FORCIBLE ~; RE-~; RIGHT OF ~.

ENUMERATED GROUNDS. Those grounds of discrimination listed in s. 15(1) of the Charter: race, national or ethnic origin, colour, religion, sex, age, mental or physical disability. D. Gibson, *The Law of the Charter: Equality Rights* (Toronto: Carswell, 1990) at 143.

ENUMERATION. *n.* A general residence to residence visitation to obtain or verify information respecting residence of voters and, where necessary, to obtain applications for registration for the purpose of updating or compiling new lists of voters. *Election Amendment Act, 1987*, S.B.C. 1988, c. 2, s. 1.

ENUMERATION DATE. In respect of an election in an electoral district, the date for the commencement of the preparation of the preliminary lists of electors for that election.

ENUMERATOR. *n.* 1. A person appointed to compile or revise a list of electors. 2. A person who takes a census.

ENURE. *v.* To take effect; to operate.

EN VENTRE SA MERE. [Fr. in the mother's womb] Describes an unborn child.

ENVIRONMENT. *n.* 1. The air, water, ice, snow and land and all animal and plant life therein. 2. Includes (i) air, land or water, (ii) plant and animal life, including human life, (iii) the social, economic, recreational, cultural and aesthetic conditions and factors that influence the life of humans or a community, (iv) any building, structure, machine or other device or thing made by humans, (v) any solid, liquid, gas, odour, heat, sound, vibration or radiation resulting directly or indirectly from the activities of humans, or (vi) any part or combination of the foregoing and the interrelationships between any two or more of them.

ENVIRONMENTAL ASSESSMENT. A process by which the environmental impact of an undertaking is predicted and evaluated before the undertaking has begun or occurred. *Environmental Assessment acts.*

ENVIRONMENTAL IMPACT. Any change in the present or future environment that would result from an undertaking. *Environmental Assessment acts.*

ENVOY. *n.* A diplomatic agent sent to one nation from another.

E.O.E. *abbr.* Errors and omissions excepted.

EQUALITY. See PROCEDURAL ~.

EQUALITY BEFORE AND UNDER THE LAW. "... [A] comparative concept, the condition of which may only be attained or discerned by comparison with the condition of others in the social and political setting in which the question arises. ... admittedly unattainable ideal should be that a law expressed to bind all should not because of irrelevant personal differences have a more burdensome or less beneficial impact on one than another." *Andrews v. Law Society (British Columbia),* 56 D.L.R. (4th) 1 at 10-11, 10 C.H.R.R. D/5719, [1989] 2 W.W.R. 289, 25 C.C.E.L. 255, 91 N.R. 255, 34 B.C.L.R. (2d) 273, 36 C.R.R. 193, 56 D.L.R. (4th) 1, [1989] 1 S.C.R. 143, McIntyre J.

EQUALITY BEFORE THE LAW. "The guarantee ... is designed to advance the value that all persons be subject to the equal demands and burdens of the law and not suffer any greater disability in the substance and application of the law than others. ..." *R. v. Turpin* (1989), 39 C.R.R. 306 at 333, 69 C.R. (3d) 97, 48 C.C.C. (3d) 8, 96 N.R. 115, [1989] 1 S.C.R. 1296, 34 O.A.C. 115, the court per Wilson J.

EQUALITY IS EQUITY. When there is property to be divided among persons, the persons are entitled to equal shares unless there is sufficient reason to use another basis for division. P.V. Baker & P. St. J. Langan, eds., *Snell's Equity,* 29th ed. (London: Sweet & Maxwell, 1990) at 36.

EQUALIZATION PAYMENT. Payment to a province to bring its share of tax rental payments up to the same per capita amount as the average per capita yield in the two provinces with the highest yield. P.W. Hogg, *Constitutional Law of Canada,* 3d ed. (Toronto: Carswell, 1992) at 138.

EQUAL PAY FOR EQUAL WORK. The same wage rate applied to jobs with no consideration of sex, race or other factors not related to ability to perform the work.

EQUIPMENT TRUST. A means for a company to raise funds on the security of equipment, established by setting up a certificate or indenture. D.M.W. Waters, *The Law of Trusts in Canada,* 2d ed. (Toronto: Carswell, 1984) at 452.

EQUITABLE. *adj.* Fair; according to the rules of equity.

EQUITABLE CHARGE. A security for a debt which does not provide the lender with a legal estate in the charged property.

EQUITABLE DOCTRINE OF CONSTRUCTIVE NOTICE. Any equitable claim is good against a mortgagee who should have known of it by acting prudently, i.e., if the mortgagee had made the usual title search. Mortgagees are obliged to be both honest and diligent. W.B. Rayner & R.H. McLaren, *Falconbridge on Mortgages,* 4th ed. (Toronto: Canada Law Book, 1977) at 115.

EQUITABLE ESTATE. A right relating to property which another person or the equitable owner in another capacity legally owns.

EQUITABLE ESTOPPEL. "... [W]here a representation is made by one party and relied upon by another to that person's detriment, the party making the representation will be estopped from following a contrary course of action. This concept has been modified to mean a basic sense of fairness and equity. One should not be able to say one thing, have it acted upon, and then behave differently than first represented." *Marchischuk v. Dominion Industrial Supplies Ltd.* (1989), 34 C.P.C. (2d) 181 at 182, [1989] 3 W.W.R. 74, 58 Man. R. (2d) 56 (Q.B.), Kennedy J.

EQUITABLE EXECUTION. "... [T]he practice of granting an equitable substitute for execution at common law in respect of equitable property of the debtor by the appointment of a receiver...." *Fox v. Peterson Livestock Ltd.*, [1982] 2 C.N.L.R. 58 at 60, [1982] 2 W.W.R. 204, 17 Alta. L.R. (2d) 311, 35 A.R. 471, 131 D.L.R. (3d) 716 (C.A.), the court per Belzil J.A.

EQUITABLE FRAUD. "... [C]onduct which, having regard to some special relationship between the two parties concerned, is an unconscionable thing for the one to do towards the other." *Kitchen v. Royal Air Force Ass'n. et al.*, [1958] 1 W.L.R. 563 at 573 (U.K.), Lord Evershed M.R.

EQUITABLE INTEREST. A right relating to property which another person or the equitable owner in another capacity legally owns.

EQUITABLE LEASEHOLD MORTGAGE. A mortgage created when one agrees to make a lease or sub-lease, to assign a lease, to deposit title deeds or to do any other thing which creates an equitable charge of freehold. W.B. Rayner & R.H. McLaren, *Falconbridge on Mortgages*, 4th ed. (Toronto: Canada Law Book, 1977) at 97.

EQUITABLE LIEN. 1. A lien not tied to possession. 2. "... [B]ased on the principle that if a person has acquired possession of property under a contract whereby he is obligated to pay for it, he will not be allowed to retain the property unless he does pay for it. It arises by operation of law and is an incident to the contract between the vendor and purchaser...." *Ahone v. Holloway* (1988), 30 B.C.L.R. (2d) 368 at 376 (C.A.), the court per McLachlin J.A. 3. An equitable right, such as an unpaid vendor's lien or a purchaser's lien, which the law confers on one person in the form of a charge on the real property of another person until particular claims are satisfied. W.B. Rayner & R.H. McLaren, *Falconbridge on Mortgages*, 4th ed. (Toronto: Canada Law Book, 1977) at 9-10.

EQUITABLE MAXIM. See MAXIMS OF EQUITY.

EQUITABLE MORTGAGE. 1. Commonly, a charge or mortgage other than a statutory or registered mortgage. W.B. Rayner & R.H. McLaren, *Falconbridge on Mortgages*, 4th ed. (Toronto: Canada Law Book, 1977) at 236. 2. A mortgage may be equitable either (1) because the interest mortgaged is future or equitable, or (2) because the mortgagor did not execute an instrument adequate to transfer the legal estate, e.g. a mortgage of the equity of redemption. Such a mortgage may also be created by depositing title deeds. W.B. Rayner & R.H. McLaren, *Falconbridge on Mortgages*, 4th ed. (Toronto: Canada Law Book, 1977) at 81.

EQUITABLE SET-OFF. "... [I]s available where there is a claim for a money sum whether liquidated or unliquidated: ... it is available where there has been an assignment. There is no requirement of mutuality." *Telford v. Holt* (1987), 37 B.L.R. 241 at 253, 21 C.P.C. (2d) 1, 78 N.R. 321, 54 Alta. L.R. (2d) 193, [1987] 6 W.W.R. 385, [1987] 2 S.C.R. 193, 46 R.P.R. 234, 81 A.R. 385, 41 D.L.R. (4th) 385, the court per Wilson J.

EQUITY. *n.* 1. Fairness. 2. That part

of the general law which provides remedies not available at common law in many cases. 3. Equity of redemption. 4. In business, the excess of assets over liabilities. 5. ". . . [S]uch interest as the seller has in property." *Bednarsky v. Weleschuk* (1961), 29 D.L.R. (2d) 270 at 272 (Alta. C.A.), the court per Johnson J.A. See BETTER ~; CLEAN HANDS DOCTRINE; DELAY DEFEATS EQUITIES; EQUALITY IS ~; FORMAL ~; HE WHO COMES INTO ~ MUST COME WITH CLEAN HANDS; HE WHO SEEKS ~ MUST DO ~; MAXIMS OF ~; NO MAN CAN TAKE ADVANTAGE OF HIS OWN WRONG; PAY ~.

EQUITY ACTS IN PERSONAM. Describes the procedure in equity but is now of less significance than previously. P.V. Baker & P. St. J. Langan, eds., *Snell's Equity*, 29th ed. (London: Sweet & Maxwell, 1990) at 41.

EQUITY AIDS THE VIGILANT AND NOT THE INDOLENT. "[A court of equity] . . . has always refused its aid to stale demands, where a party has slept upon his right and acquiesced for a great length of time. Nothing can call forth this court into activity, but conscience, good faith, and reasonable diligence; where these are wanting, the Court is passive, and does nothing." *Smith v. Clay* (1767), 3 Bro. C.C. 639n at 640n, Lord Camden L.C.

EQUITY CAPITAL. Of a corporation, the amount of consideration paid in money for which the outstanding equity shares of the corporation have been issued.

EQUITY FOLLOWS THE LAW. Equity will interfere only in a case when an important aspect is ignored by the common law. P.V. Baker & P. St. J. Langan, eds., *Snell's Equity*, 29th ed. (London: Sweet & Maxwell, 1990) at 29.

EQUITY IMPUTES AN INTENTION TO FULFIL AN OBLIGATION. An act other than that originally intended or required will be accepted as fulfillment of an obligation if the act is capable of being regarded as fulfillment of the obligation. P.V. Baker & P. St. J. Langan, eds., *Snell's Equity*, 29th ed. (London: Sweet & Maxwell, 1990) at 40.

EQUITY LOOKS ON THAT AS DONE WHICH OUGHT TO BE DONE. A contract will be treated as completed in favour of persons who have a right to enforce that contract. P.V. Baker & P. St. J. Langan, eds., *Snell's Equity*, 29th ed. (London: Sweet & Maxwell, 1990) at 40.

EQUITY LOOKS TO THE INTENT RATHER THAN TO THE FORM. "Courts of Equity make a distinction in all cases between that which is matter of substance and that which is matter of form; and if it find that by insisting on the form, the substance will be defeated, it holds it to be inequitable to allow a person to insist on such form, and thereby defeat the substance." *Parkin v. Thorold* (1852), 16 Beav. 59 at 466, Romilly M.R.

EQUITY OF A STATUTE. When a fact situation falls within a statute's spirit and intent, though apparently not its letter, it is within the equity of that statute.

EQUITY OF REDEMPTION. 1. A mortgagor's right to redeem a mortgage. 2. The interest remaining in a mortgagor after the execution of one or more mortgages upon any lands. 3. The amount by which a property's value exceeds the total charges, liens or mortgages against it. See CLOG ON ~.

EQUITY SECURITY. Any security of an issuer that carries a residual right to participate in the earnings of the issuer and, upon the liquidation or winding up of the issuer, in its assets. *Securities acts*.

EQUITY SHARE. A share of a class of shares of a corporation carrying voting rights under all circumstances and a share of a class of shares carrying voting rights by reason of the occurrence of a contingency that has occurred and is continuing.

EQUITY WILL NOT SUFFER A WRONG TO BE WITHOUT A REMEDY. The maxim upon which the enforcement of uses and trusts was founded by the Court of Chancery. A wrong will not go unredressed if the courts are able to remedy it. P.V. Baker & P. St. J. Langan, eds., *Snell's Equity*, 29th ed. (London: Sweet & Maxwell, 1990) at 28.

ERRATA. *n.* [L.] Errors.

ERRATUM. *n.* [L.] Error.

ERRED IN LAW. ". . . [C]apable of several different meanings. . . . [for example] the trial judge offended against case authority binding on him . . . the trial judge's conclusion is not in accord with the evidence." *Mallen v. Mallen* (1992), 40 R.F.L. (3d) 114 at 133, 65 B.C.L.R. (2d) 241, 11 B.C.A.C. 262, 22 W.A.C. 262 (C.A.), Gibbs J.A.

ERROR. *n.* 1. Incorrect information, and includes omission of information. *Vital Statistics acts.* 2. In old common law practice, a mistake in the proceeding which either the court in which it occurred or a superior court must correct. See CLERICAL ~; OFFICIALLY INDUCED ~; REVIEWABLE ~.

ERROR OF LAW. ". . . [A]n error committed by an administrative tribunal in good faith in interpreting or applying a provision of its enabling Act, of another Act, or of an agreement or other document which it has to interpret and apply within the limits of its jurisdiction." *C.A.W. v. Nova Scotia (Labour Relations Board)* (1988), 89 C.L.L.C. 14,003 at 12,017, 87 N.S.R. (2d) 61, 222 A.P.R. 61 (T.D.), Grant J.

ERRORS EXCEPTED. A phrase intended to excuse a small mistake or oversight in a stated account.

ESCALATION CLAUSE. 1. Clause in lease providing for increases in rent based on some factor such as tax increases. 2. Clause in wage contract or collective agreement providing for a raise in rate of pay based on a factor such as the Consumer Price Index.

ESCALATOR CLAUSE. See ESCALATION CLAUSE.

ESCAPE. *v.* Breaking prison, escaping from lawful custody or, without lawful excuse, being at large before the expiration of a term of imprisonment to which a person has been sentenced. *Criminal Code*, R.S.C. 1985, c. C-46, s. 149(3).

ESCHEAT. *n.* 1. The reversion of land or other property to the Crown when a company is dissolved or a person dies intestate without heirs. 2. ". . . [A]n incident of tenure by which for the failure of heirs the feud falls back into the lord's hand by a termination of the tenure, . . ." *Ontario (Attorney General) v. Mercer* (1879), 5 S.C.R. 538 at 625, Ritchie C.J.

ESCROW. *n.* 1. Holding something in trust until a contingency happens or a condition is performed. 2. ". . . [T]he delivery of a document in escrow is to render that document inoperative pending the conditions of the escrow being met. It is common ground that a delivery in escrow is not now confined to deeds, and it is also equally well established that the delivery need not be to a stranger . . ." *Draft Masonry (York) Co. v. PA Restoration Inc.* (1988), 48 R.P.R. 231 at 240, 29 C.L.R. 256 (Ont. Dist. Ct.), Hoilett D.C.J.

ESPIONAGE. *n.* Spying.

ESQ. *abbr.* Esquire.

ESSENCE OF THE CONTRACT. Describes a provision in a contract which both parties agreed at the time they entered into the contract was so important that performance of the contract without strict compliance with that provision would be pointless.

ESSENTIAL SERVICES. 1. ". . . [O]ne the interruption of which would threaten serious harm to the general public or to a part of the population." *Reference re Public Service Employee Relations Act (Alberta)* (1987), (*sub nom. A.U.P.E. v. Alberta (Attorney General)*) 28 C.R.R. 305 at 348, 87 C.L.L.C. 14,021, 38 D.L.R. (4th) 161, [1987] 1 S.C.R. 313, 51 Alta. L.R. (2d) 97, [1987] 3 W.W.R. 577, 74 N.R. 99, 78 A.R. 1, [1987] D.L.Q. 225, Dickson C.J.C. (dissenting) (Wilson J. concurring). 2. A class of services designated to be maintained during strikes; employees employed in such jobs have limited or no right to strike.

ESTABLISH. *v.* 1. "... [P]lace[s] a burden on an accused to prove the ... elements delineated thereafter on a balance of probabilities ..." *R. v. Wholesale Travel Group Inc.* (1991), 67 C.C.C. (3d) 193 at 222, 4 O.R. (3d) 799n, 8 C.R. (4th) 145, 84 D.L.R. (4th) 161, 130 N.R. 1, 38 C.P.R. (3d) 451, 49 O.A.C. 161, [1991] 3 S.C.R. 154, 7 C.R.R. (2d) 36, Lamer C.J.C. (Sopinka, Gonthier, McLachlin, Stevenson and Iacobucci JJ. concurring). 2. "... '[T]o prove'...." *R. v. Oakes* (1986), 24 C.C.C. (3d) 321 at 332, [1986] 1 S.C.R. 103, 53 O.R. (2d) 719n, 50 C.R. (3d) 1, 14 O.A.C. 335, 19 C.R.R. 308, 26 D.L.R. (4th) 200, 665 N.R. 87, Dickson C.J.C. (Chouinard, Lamer, Wilson and Le Dain JJ. concurring). 3. "... [I]n the educational statutes of Ontario ... 'set up'." *Crawford v. Ottawa (City) Board of Education*, [1971] 2 O.R. 179 at 188, 17 D.L.R. (3d) 271 (C.A.), the court per Kelly J.A.

EST. & TR. J. *abbr.* Estates & Trusts Journal.

EST. & TR. Q. *abbr.* Estates & Trusts Quarterly.

ESTATE. *n.* 1. "... [I]n regard to its uses in conveyances, is properly defined to mean a property which one possesses, especially property in land. It is also understood as defining the nature and quantity of interests in lands, &c." *Macdonald v. Georgian Bay Lumber Co.* (1878), 2 S.C.R. 364 at 392, Henry J. 2. "... [A]s applied to interests in land has a well recognized meaning due to the fact that under our law a person is not deemed to be the absolute owner of land but only of something which has for a long time been designated as an 'estate' in it." *Coleman (Town) v. Head Syndicate* (1917), 11 Alta. L.R. 314 at 317, [1917] 1 W.W.R. 1074 (C.A.), Harvey C.J. 3. All the property of which a testator or an intestate had power to dispose by will, otherwise than by virtue of a special power of appointment, less the amount of funeral, testamentary and administration expenses, debts and liabilities, and succession duties payable out of the estate on death. 4. Includes both real and personal property. *Intestate Succession acts.* See EQUITABLE ~; EXECUTORY ~; EXPECTANT ~; FREEHOLD ~; FUTURE ~; LEASEHOLD ~; LIFE ~; REAL ~.

ESTATE DUTY. A tax generally imposed on "property passing" when someone dies; its rate is based on the size of the estate. D.M.W. Waters, *The Law of Trusts in Canada*, 2d ed. (Toronto: Carswell, 1984) at 477.

ESTATE FREEZE. A transaction which replaces growth assets, i.e. common shares of an operating business corporation, with assets of limited growth potential, i.e. preferred shares, so that a ceiling approximately equal to the value at the date of the freeze is placed on the value of those assets for capital gain and succession duty purposes. Thus any future growth in the value of the assets usually benefits subsequent generations, who become common shareholders. W. Grover & F. Iacobucci, *Materials on Canadian Income Tax*, 4th ed. (Toronto: De Boo, 1980) at 793.

ESTATE PLANNING. Arranging business and property interests to pass to heirs and successors in such a way as to receive maximum benefit of laws relating to wills, income tax, estate tax, succession duty, property, insurance, securities, and so on.

ESTATE PUR AUTRE VIE. [Fr.] A grant to one person for the life of another. E.L.G. Tyler & N.E. Palmer, eds., *Crossley Vaines' Personal Property*, 5th ed. (London: Butterworths, 1973) at 5.

ESTATE TAX. A tax levied on all a deceased person's property, irrespective of its location or who may inherit it. P.W. Hogg, *Constitutional Law of Canada*, 3d ed. (Toronto: Carswell, 1992) at 746.

ESTIMATE. *n.* 1. A representation as to the future price of a consumer transaction. *Trade Practice Act*, R.S.B.C.

1979, c. 406, s. 1. 2. An estimate of the total cost of work on and repairs for a vehicle. *Motor Vehicle Repair Act*, R.S.O. 1990, c. M.43, s. 1. See ~S; FINAL ~.

ESTIMATES. *n.* Spending estimates of the Crown transmitted to the legislature and divided into classes, each one corresponding to a separate programme and each class divided into votes, on which the House committees may make separate decisions. A. Fraser, W.A. Dawson & J. Holtby, eds., *Beauchesne's Rules and Forms of the House of Commons of Canada*, 6th ed. (Toronto: Carswell, 1989) at 259. See ESTIMATE.

ESTOPPEL. *n.* 1. "The essential factors giving rise to an estoppel are . . . : (1) A representation or conduct amounting to a representation intended to induce a course of conduct on the part of the person to whom the representation is made. (2) An act or omission resulting from the representation, whether actual or by conduct, by the person to whom the representation is made. (3) Detriment to such person as a consequence of the act or omission." *Greenwood v. Martin's Bank Ltd.*, [1933] A.C. 51 at 57 (U.K. H.L.), Lord Tomlin. 2. ". . . [W]here one party has, by his words or conduct, made to the other a promise or assurance which was intended to affect the legal relations between them and to be acted on accordingly, then, once the other party has taken him at his word and acted on it, the one who gave the promise or assurance cannot afterwards be allowed to revert to the previous legal relations . . . subject to the qualification which he himself has so introduced, even though it is not supported in point of law by any consideration, but only by his word." *Coombe v. Coombe*, [1951] 1 All E.R. 767 at 770 (U.K.), Denning L.J. 3. ". . . [A]n evidentiary rule." *Royal Bank v. McArthur* (1985), 3 C.P.C. (2d) 141 at 146, 51 O.R. (2d) 86, 10 O.A.C. 394, 19 D.L.R. (4th) 762 (Div. Ct.), the court per Montgomery J. 4. ". . . [H]as been sought to be limited by a series of maxims: estoppel is only a rule of

evidence; estoppel cannot give rise to a cause of action; estoppel cannot do away with the need for consideration, and so forth. All these can now be seen to merge into one general principle shorn of limitations. When the parties to a transaction proceed on the basis of an underlying assumption (either of fact or law, and whether due to misrepresentation or mistake, makes no difference), on which they have conducted the dealings between them, neither of them will be allowed to go back on the assumption when it would be unfair or unjust to allow him to do so. If one of them does seek to go back on it, the courts will give the other such remedy as the equity of the case demands." *Amalgamated Investment & Property Co. Ltd. v. Texas Commerce Int'l. Bank Ltd.*, [1981] 3 All E.R. 577 at 584 (U.K. C.A.), Lord Denning M.R. See CAUSE OF ACTION ~; EQUITABLE ~; ISSUE ~; PROMISSORY ~; PROPRIETARY ~; QUASI-~.

ESTOPPEL PER REM JUDICATAM. 1. ". . . [D]irected to the capacity of the parties to an action and, where it is properly applicable, it prevents those parties from relitigating either a cause of action or an issue that has previously been decided. . . ." *Masunda v. Downing* (1986), 7 R.F.L. (3d) 26 at 37, 5 B.C.L.R. (2d) 113, 27 D.L.R. (4th) 268 (S.C.), Wood J. 2. ". . . [A] generic term which in modern law includes two species. The first species . . . 'cause of action estoppel', . . . prevents a party to an action from asserting or denying, as against the other party, the existence of a particular cause of action, the non-existence or existence of which has been determined by a court of competent jurisdiction in previous litigation between the same parties. . . . The second species . . . 'issue estoppel', . . . If in litigation upon one such cause of action any of such separate issues as to whether a particular condition has been fulfilled is determined by a court of competent jurisdiction, either upon evidence or upon admission by a party to the litigation, neither party can, in subsequent litigation between one another upon any cause of action which depends upon the fulfillment of the identical condition, assert that the condition was fulfilled if the court has in the first litigation determined that it was not, or deny that it was fulfilled if the court in the first litigation determined that it was." *Thoday v. Thoday*, [1964] P. 181 at 197-8 (U.K. C.A.), Diplock L.J.

ESTRAY. *n.* 1. An animal that is running at large. 2. An animal found on the premises of a person other than its owner.

ESTREAT. *n.* 1. Now used only in connection with forfeitures, fines and recognizances; if the condition of a recognizance is broken, the recognizance is forfeited, and, when it is estreated, the cognisors become the Crown's debtors. 2. Formerly, a copy of a court record. A recognizance was estreated or extracted when a copy was made from the original and sent for the proper authority to enforce. *R. v. Creelman* (1893), 25 N.S.R. 404 at 418 (C.A.), Meagher J.A.

ET AL. *abbr.* 1. Et alii. 2. Et alius.

ET ALII. [L.] And others.

ET ALIUS. [L.] And another.

E.T.R. *abbr.* Estates & Trusts Reports, 1977-.

ET SEQ. *abbr.* 1. Et sequentes. 2. Et sequentia.

ET SEQUENTES. [L.] And those following.

ET SEQUENTIA. [L.] And the following.

ET UX. *abbr.* Et uxor.

ET UXOR. [L.] And wife.

EUTHANASIA. *n.* The deliberate infliction of an intended death upon an animal other than death that arises directly as an immediate result of an experimental or testing procedure. *Animals for Research Act*, R.R.O. 1980, Reg. 18, s. 1.

EVADE. *v.* "... [I]mplies something of an underhanded or deceitful nature. In other words a deliberate attempt to escape the requirement of paying tax on income that has been earned." *R. v. Branch*, [1976] C.T.C. 193 at 196, [1976] W.W.D. 78, 76 D.T.C. 6112 (Alta. Dist. Ct.), Medhurst J. See TAX EVASION.

EVASION. *n.* The act of escaping by the use of artifice. See TAX ~.

EVASIVE. *adj.* Describes a pleading which answers the other party's pleading by a half-denial or a half-admission or fails to answer a substantial point.

EVERY ONE *var.* **EVERYONE.** 1. "[In s. 7 of the Charter] ... must be read in light of the rest of the section and defined to exclude corporations and other artificial entities incapable of enjoying life, liberty or security of the person, and include only human beings." *Irwin Toy Ltd. c. Québec (Procureur général)*, [1989] 1 S.C.R. 927 at 1004, 25 C.P.R. (3d) 417, 94 N.R. 167, 58 D.L.R. (4th) 577, 24 Q.A.C. 2, 39 C.R.R. 193, Dickson C.J.C., Lamer and Wilson JJ. 2. "... [I]ncludes every human being who is physically present in Canada and by virtue of such presence amenable to Canadian law." *Singh v. Canada (Minister of Employment & Immigration)* (1985), 14 C.R.R. 13 at 44, [1985] 1 S.C.R. 177, 12 Admin. L.R. 137, 17 D.L.R. (4th) 422, 58 N.R. 1, Wilson J. (Dickson C.J.C. and Lamer J. concurring). 3. "... [I]s an expression of the same kind as 'person' and therefore includes bodies corporate unless the context requires otherwise." *R. v. Union Colliery Co.* (1900), 31 S.C.R. 81 at 88, 21 C.L.T. 153, 4 C.C.C. 400, Sedgewick J. 4. Includes Her Majesty and public bodies, bodies corporate, societies, companies and inhabitants of counties, parishes, municipalities or other districts in relation to the acts and things that they are capable of doing and owning respectively. *Criminal Code*, R.S.C. 1985, c. C-46, s. 2.

EVICTION. *n.* The act of dispossessing; recovering land through legal action. See CONSTRUCTIVE ~.

EVIDENCE. *n.* 1. "One of the hallmarks of the common law of evidence is that it relies on witnesses as the means by which evidence is produced in court. As a general rule, nothing can be admitted as evidence before the court unless it is vouched for viva voce by a witness. Even real evidence, which exists independently of any statement by any witness, cannot be considered by the court unless a witness identifies it and establishes its connection to the events under consideration. Unlike other legal systems, the common law does not usually provide for self-authenticating documentary evidence." *R. v. Schwartz* (1988), 55 D.L.R. (4th) 1 at 26, [1989] 1 W.W.R. 289, 66 C.R. (3d) 251, 88 N.R. 90, [1988] 2 S.C.R. 443, 45 C.C.C. (3d) 97, 56 Man. R. (2d) 92, 39 C.R.R. 260, Dickson C.J.C. (dissenting). 2. "... [P]art of the procedure which signifies those rules of law whereby, it is determined what testimony is to be admitted, and what rejected in each case, and what weight is to be given to the testimony admitted...." *Belisle v. Moreau* (1968), 5 C.R.N.S. 68 at 70, [1968] 4 C.C.C. 229, 69 D.L.R. (2d) 530, (N.B. C.A.), the court per Hughes J.A. 3. An assertion of fact, opinion, belief or knowledge, whether material or not and whether admissible or not. *Criminal Code*, R.S.C. 1985, c. C-46, s. 118 as am. by *Criminal Law Amendment Act*, R.S.C. 1985 (1st Supp.), c. 27, s. 15. See ADMISSIBLE ~; CIRCUMSTANTIAL ~; COMMISSION ~; CONSCRIPTIVE ~; CONTRADICTORY ~; DEMONSTRATIVE ~; DERIVATIVE ~; DIRECT ~; DOCUMENTARY ~; EXPERT ~; EXTRINSIC ~; HEARSAY ~; INDIRECT ~; MINUTES OF PROCEEDINGS AND ~; ORAL ~; ORIGINAL ~; PAROL ~; PAROL ~ RULE; PRESUMPTIVE ~; PRIMA FACIE ~; PRIMARY ~; REAL ~; REBUTTAL ~; REPLY ~; SECONDARY ~; SIMILAR FACT ~; TESTIMONIAL ~; WEIGHT OF ~.

EVIDENTIAL BURDEN. "... [T]he requirement of putting an issue into play by reference to evidence before the court ... The party with an evidential burden is not required to convince the trier of fact of anything, only to

point out evidence which suggests that certain facts existed." *R. v. Schwartz* (1988), 39 C.R.R. 260 at 288, [1989] 1 W.W.R. 289, 66 C.R. (3d) 251, 88 N.R. 90, [1988] 2 S.C.R. 443, 45 C.C.C. (3d) 97, 56 Man. R. (2d) 92, 55 D.L.R. (4th) 1, Dickson C.J.C. (dissenting).

EVIDENTIARY BURDEN. Used, in contrast to persuasive burden, to describe the effect of a statutory presumption which relieves the prosecution from leading evidence to prove a material fact and used to describe the burden imposed on the defence by a mandatory rebuttable presumption that they lead evidence to avoid certain conviction. P.K. McWilliams, *Canadian Criminal Evidence*, 3d ed. (Aurora: Canada Law Book, 1988) at 25-2 and 25-3.

EX ABUNDANTI CAUTELA. [L.] Out of abundant caution.

EX AEQUO ET BONO. [L. out of what is equal and good] In equity and good conscience.

EXAMINATION. *n.* 1. The questioning of a person under oath. 2. An interview, conducted by an immigration officer, of a person seeking to come into Canada at a port of entry. *Immigration Act*, R.S.C. 1985, c. 1-2, s. 2. See CROSS-~; DIRECT ~.

EXAMINATION FOR DISCOVERY. 1. "... [E]mbraces two main elements: discovery of facts in the hands of an adversary and, the obtaining of admission for use in evidence...." *Minute Muffler Installations Ltd. v. Alberta* (1981), 23 C.P.C. 52 at 54, 16 Alta. L.R. (2d) 35, 23 L.C.R. 128, 30 A.R. 447 (C.A.), the court per Stevenson J.A. 2. "... [A]n examination of the opposite party or an opposite party.... [and] is in the nature of a cross-examination ..." *Stoikopoulous v. Remenda* (1985), 3 C.P.C. (2d) 303 at 305, 39 Sask. R. 58 (Q.B.), Estey J.

EXAMINATION IN AID OF EXECUTION. A creditor examining the judgment debtor or other people to determine the debtor's ability to settle the judgment. C.R.B. Dunlop,

Creditor-Debtor Law in Canada (Toronto: Carswell, 1981) at 109.

EXAMINATION-IN-CHIEF. *n.* Questioning of a witness by the counsel for the party who called that witness to adduce evidence which supports the case of that party.

EXAMINER. *n.* A person whom a court appoints to examine witnesses in an action. See OFFICIAL ~; SPECIAL ~.

EXAMINER. *abbr.* Examiner (L'Observateur) (Que.).

EXAMINER (L'OBSERVATEUR). *abbr.* Examiner (L'Observateur) (1861).

EXCELLENCY. *n.* The title of the Governor General.

EXCEPTIONS CLAUSE. A clause in a contract which excludes liability.

EXCHANGE. *n.* 1. When the consideration is giving other goods, it is a contract of barter or exchange. G.H.L. Fridman, *Sale of Goods in Canada*, 3d ed. (Toronto: Carswell, 1986) at 22. 2. "... [T]he act of giving or taking one thing for another ..." *Deyell v. Deyell* (1991), 90 Sask. R. 81 at 87 (C.A.), Cameron J.A. 3. A building or location where agents, merchants, brokers, bankers and others meet at certain times to trade. 4. A group of persons formed for the purpose of exchanging reciprocal contracts of indemnity or inter-insurance with each other through the same attorney. See BILL OF ~; COMMODITY ~; COMMODITY FUTURES ~; STOCK ~.

EXCHEQUER BILL. A bank-note, bond, note, debenture or security that is issued or guaranteed by Her Majesty under the authority of Parliament or the legislature of a province. *Criminal Code*, R.S.C. 1985, c. C-46, s. 321.

EXCHEQUER BILL PAPER. Paper that is used to manufacture exchequer bills. *Criminal Code*, R.S.C. 1985, c. C-46, s. 321.

EXCHEQUER COURT. The Exchequer Court of Canada, replaced by The Federal Court in 1971.

EXCISE DUTY. A tax on the distribution or manufacture of goods. P.W. Hogg, *Constitutional Law of Canada*, 3d ed. (Toronto: Carswell, 1992) at 742.

EXCISE TAXES. 1. The taxes imposed under the Excise Tax Act. *Duties Relief Act*, R.S.C. 1985 (2d Supp.), c. 21, s. 2. 2. Taxes on the quantity of goods manufactured. W. Grover & F. Iacobucci, *Materials of Canadian Income Tax*, 4th ed. (Toronto: De Boo, 1980) at 25.

EXCLUSION. *n.* 1. Of a witness is at the discretion of the trial judge who may, at any party's request, order that the witness stay out of the courtroom until called to give evidence (Ontario Rules of Civil Procedure, r. 52.06(1) and (2)). G.D. Watson & C. Perkins, eds., *Holmested & Watson: Ontario Civil Procedure* (Toronto: Carswell, 1984) at 52-4. 2. "... [A] term or provision of an insurance policy ..." *Ben's Ltd. v. Royal Insurance Co.*, [1985] I.L.R. 1-1969 at 7574, 7 C.C.E.L. 57, 68 N.S.R. (2d) 379, 159 A.P.R. 379 (T.D.), MacIntosh J.

EXCLUSIONARY RULE. A rule prohibiting the introduction of certain evidence.

EXCLUSION CLAUSE. A clause that removes certain obligations from consideration or limits a party's liabilities for not performing or misperforming the contract. G.H.L. Fridman, *Sale of Goods in Canada*, 3d ed. (Toronto: Carswell, 1986) at 282.

EXCLUSIVE AGENT. An agent with the sole right to act on the principal's behalf in regard of a particular transaction, type of transaction or property.

EXCLUSIVE BARGAINING RIGHT. The right of the union, which is designated as bargaining representative, to bargain collectively for all employees in the unit which it represents.

EXCLUSIVE JURISDICTION CLAUSE. A clause which states that a tribunal has exclusive and unreviewable jurisdiction to decide issues before it. P.W. Hogg, *Constitutional Law of Canada*, 3d ed. (Toronto: Carswell, 1992) at 197.

EXCLUSIVE LISTING. When a vendor names one broker to act as agent in the sale of property, that agent has the sole, exclusive and irrevocable right to sell that property during a defined time period. B.J. Reiter, R.C.B. Risk & B.N. McLellan, *Real Estate Law*, 3d ed. (Toronto: Emond Montgomery, 1986) at 75.

EXCLUSIVE POSSESSION. The right to occupy premises without any interference by another person.

EX. C.R. *abbr.* 1. Exchequer Court of Canada Reports. 2. Exchequer Court Reports of Canada, 1875-1922.

[ ] EX. C.R. *abbr.* Canada Law Reports Exchequer Court, 1923-1971.

EX. CT. *abbr.* Exchequer Court.

EXCULPATORY. *adj.* Relieving of guilt or responsibility.

EXCULPATORY CONFESSION. A statement which relieves the person giving it of guilt or responsibility.

EX CURIA. [L.] Out of court.

EXCUSABLE CONDUCT. Conduct which is acceptable, carries no legal consequences.

EXCUSE. *n.* "[In criminal theory] . . . concedes the wrongfulness of the action but asserts that the circumstances under which it was done are such that it ought not to be attributed to the actor. The perpetrator who is incapable, owing to a disease of the mind, of appreciating the nature and consequences of his acts, the person who labours under a mistake of fact, the drunkard, the sleepwalker: these are all actors of whose 'criminal' actions we disapprove intensely, but whom, in appropriate circumstances, our law will not punish." *R. v. Perka* (1984), 13 D.L.R. (4th) 1 at 12, [1984] 2 S.C.R. 232, [1984] 6 W.W.R. 289, 42 C.R. (3d) 113, 55 N.R. 1, 14 C.C.C. (3d) 385, Dickson J. See JUSTIFICATION; LAWFUL ~.

EX. D. *abbr.* Law Reports, Exchequer

Division, 1875-1890.

EX DEBITO JUSTITIAE. [L.] 1. The remedy to which an applicant is rightfully entitled. 2. ". . . To say in a case that the writ should issue ex debito justitiae simply means that the circumstances militate strongly in favour of the issuance of the writ rather than for refusal. . . ." *Harelkin v. University of Regina* (1979), 96 D.L.R. (3d) 14 at 41, [1979] 2 S.C.R. 561, 16 N.R. 364, [1979] 3 W.W.R. 676, Beetz J. (Martland, Pigeon and Pratte JJ. concurring).

EX DIV. *abbr.* Ex dividend.

EX DIVIDEND. [L. without dividend] When selling stocks and shares on which a dividend was declared or is anticipated, ex div., the buyer may not claim the dividend.

EXECUTE. *v.* 1. To carry into effect; to complete. 2. Of a deed, to sign, seal and deliver it. 3. Of a judgment or court order, to enforce or carry it into effect. 4. Of a writ, to obey the instructions within it.

EXECUTED. *adj.* Completed, done.

EXECUTED CONSIDERATION. Something done in exchange for a promise.

EXECUTED CONTRACT. When nothing remains for either party to do, and the transaction is complete.

EXECUTED TRUST. A trust after the estate is conveyed to trustees for particular beneficiaries.

EXECUTION. *n.* 1. The process of enforcing or carrying out a judgment. 2. A writ of fieri facias, and every subsequent writ for giving effect to a writ of fieri facias. 3. ". . . [I]n some situations means 'signed' and in other situations means 'signed, sealed and delivered'. . . ." *Johnston, Re* (1982), 43 C.B.R. (N.S.) 39 at 40, 2 P.P.S.A.C. 150 (Ont. S.C.), Saunders J. See EQUITABLE ~; EXAMINATION IN AID OF ~; LEGAL ~; WRIT OF ~.

EXECUTION OF DEEDS. The signing, sealing, and delivery of documents.

EXECUTIVE. *n.* The Crown in its administrative role; the government. This includes government officials and departments directed by ministers of the Crown and the principal executive body, the Cabinet, headed by the Prime Minister. See CHIEF ~ OFFICER; SENIOR ~.

EXECUTIVE COUNCIL. 1. The premier and members of cabinet of a province. 2. The Executive Council of the Government of the Northwest Territories composed of the Commissioner and the Executive Members. *Interpretation Act*, S.N.W.T. 1983 (2d Sess.), c. 4, s. 1.

EXECUTIVE GOVERNMENT. The Lieutenant-Governor and the Conseil exécutif du Québec. *Interpretation Act*, R.S.Q. 1977, c. I-16, s. 61.

EXECUTOR. *n.* 1. A person appointed in a testator's will to carry out directions and requests set out there and to distribute property according to the will's provisions. 2. Where used in referring to the executor of a deceased includes an executor of the will of the deceased, an administrator of the estate of the deceased, and an executor de son tort of any property of the deceased. *Succession Duty Tax* acts. See LIMITED ~.

EXECUTOR DE SON TORT. ". . . [A] stranger [who] takes upon himself to act as executor or administrator without any just authority (as by intermeddling with the goods of the deceased), . . ." *Raiz v. Vaserbakh* (1986), 9 C.P.C. (2d) 141 at 144 (Ont. Dist. Ct.), Trotter D.C.J.

EXECUTOR'S YEAR. ". . . [A] year within which to gather in the estate before a legal entitlement to demand payment arises." *Cassidy, Re* (1985), 24 E.T.R. 299 at 303, 60 A.R. 92 (Surr. Ct.), Dea J.

EXECUTORY. *adj.* Still to be effected, in contrast to executed.

EXECUTORY CONSIDERATION. ". . . [A] promise to do or forbear from doing some act in the future." *Butt v. Humber* (1976), 6 R.P.R. 207 at 216, 17 Nfld. & P.E.I.R. 92, 46 A.P.R. 92

(Nfld. T.D.), Goodridge J.

EXECUTORY CONTRACT. A contract between a buyer and a seller for the purchase and sale of goods or services in respect of which delivery of the goods or performance of the services or payment in full of the consideration is not made at the time the contract is entered into.

EXECUTORY DEVISE. Legal limitation of a future interest in lands by a will.

EXECUTORY ESTATE. An interest dependant on some subsequent contingency or event for its enjoyment.

EXECUTORY INTEREST. A legal interest in the future. E.L.G. Tyler & N.E. Palmer, eds., *Crossley Vaines' Personal Property*, 5th ed. (London: Butterworths, 1973) at 42.

EXECUTORY LIMITATION. A limitation, by will or deed, of a future interest.

EXECUTORY TRUST. An imperfect trust which requires some act to perfect it.

EXECUTRIX. *n.* A woman appointed by a testator to carry out the instructions in the will.

EXEMPLARY DAMAGES. ". . . [O]r punitive damages may be awarded where the defendant's conduct is such as to merit punishment. This may be exemplified by malice, fraud or cruelty as well as other abusive and insolent acts toward the victim. The purpose of the award is to vindicate the strength of the law and to demonstrate to the offender that the law will not tolerate conduct which wilfully disregards the rights of others." *Warner v. Arsenault* (1982), 27 C.P.C. 200 at 205, 53 N.S.R. (2d) 146, 109 A.P.R. 146 (C.A.), the court per Pace J.A.

EXEMPLIFICATION. *n.* The official copy of a document made under a court's or public functionary's seal.

EXEMPLI GRATIA. [L. for example] For instance.

EXEMPTION. *n.* Immunity; being free from duty or tax. "[May arise] . . .

by virtue of having never been made liable to a law or by having been made liable and then excluded from its application." *Crown Forest Industries Ltd. v. British Columbia* (1991), 4 M.P.L.R. (2d) 267 at 274, 55 B.C.L.R. (2d) 250 (C.A.), the court per Hollinrake J.A.

EXEMPTION CLAUSE. "... [G]enerally [has] the effect of excluding or limiting the liability of one party to a contract and ... generally, but not always, appear[s] in standard form contracts widely used in commercial matters...." *Bauer v. Bank of Montreal* (1980), 10 B.L.R. 209 at 217, 33 C.B.R. (N.S.) 291, [1980] 2 S.C.R. 102, 110 D.L.R. (3d) 424, 32 N.R. 191, the court per McIntyre J.

EXERCISE. *v.* To use.

EX GRATIA. [L.] 1. Voluntary. K.D. Cooper-Stephenson & I.B. Saunders, *Personal Injury Damages in Canada* (Toronto: Carswell, 1981) at 501. 2. "... [U]sed simply to indicate ... that the party agreeing to pay does not admit any pre-existing liability on his part; but he is certainly not seeking to preclude the legal enforceability of the settlement itself by describing the contemplated payment as 'ex gratia'." *Edwards v. Skyways Ltd.*, [1964] 1 All E.R. 494 at 500, [1964] 1 W.L.R. 349 (U.K. Q.B.), Megaw J.

EXHIBIT. *n.* A document or object admitted as evidence in court. F.A. Jaffe, *A Guide to Pathological Evidence*, 3d ed. (Toronto: Carswell, 1991) at 219.

EXHUMATION. *n.* Disinterring a body from a grave in a burial ground or cemetery. F.A. Jaffe, *A Guide to Pathological Evidence*, 3d ed. (Toronto: Carswell, 1991) at 25.

EXIGENCY. *n.* Need; want; demand.

EXIGIBLE. *adj.* 1. Subject to execution. 2. Able to be demanded or required.

EXISTING USE. The use to which land has already been put.

EX MERO MOTU. [L.] Of one's own accord.

EX NUDO PACTO NON ORITUR ACTIO. [L.] An action does not arise from an agreement with no consideration.

EX OFFICIO. [L.] By virtue of one's office.

EXONERATION. *n.* Relief from liability when that liability is thrown on another person.

EXOR. *abbr.* Executor.

EX PARTE. [L. on behalf of] 1. "[Refers to] ... an order made at the instance of one party without the opposite party having had notice of the application." *Anderson v. Toronto-Dominion Bank* (1986), 9 C.P.C. (2d) 179 at 183, 70 B.C.L.R. (2d) 267 (C.A.), the court per Hutcheon J.A. 2. "[Used in British Columbia Supreme Court Rules, R. 52] ... the absence of a party on the hearing of the application and not in the usual sense of an order made in the absence of service upon an interested person." *Dasmesh Holdings Ltd. v. McDonald* (1985), 49 C.P.C. 187 at 191, 60 B.C.L.R. 80 (C.A.), the court per Hutcheon J.A.

EXPECTANCY. *n.* Refers to an estate dependent on a contingency, a remainder or reversion. See IN ~.

EXPECTANT. *adj.* Relating to; depending on.

EXPECTANT ESTATE. An interest one will possess and enjoy at some future time, i.e. a reversion or remainder.

EXPECTANT HEIR. "... [P]hrase used in England in reference to a person who expects from a person then living and who is not allowed, under the circumstances, to encumber the future estate by improvident bargains." *Hall v. Marshall*, [1938] 3 D.L.R. 419 at 423, 13 M.P.R. 112 (N.S. S.C.), Doull J.

EXPECTATION OF LIFE. The number of years which someone of a certain age may, given equal chances, expect to live. See LOSS OF ~.

EXPEND. *v.* 1. To pay out. *Richer, Re* (1919), 46 O.L.R. 367 at 371, 50 D.L.R. 614, 17 O.W.N. 195 (C.A.),

Meredith C.J.C.P. 2. "[Implies] ... a recurring act of consumption ..." *McFarland, Re*, [1963] 1 O.R. 273 at 275 (H.C.), Grant J.

EXPENDITURE. *n.* (i) Payment authorized by a supply vote, (ii) a reimbursement under the authority of one supply vote, of a payment charged against another supply vote, (iii) a payment authorized by a statutory appropriation, other than a statutory appropriation authorizing a payment to a revolving fund, or (iv) a payment from a revolving fund. See CAPITAL ~; TAX ~.

EXPENSE. *n.* 1. Money laid out. 2. "... [W]ithin the meaning of paragraph s. 18(1)(a) of the Income Tax Act [R.S.C. 1952, c. 148 (as am. S.C. 1970-71-72, c. 63, s. 1)], is an obligation to pay a sum of money. ..." *R. v. Burnco Industries Ltd.*, [1984] 2 F.C. 218 at 218, 53 N.R. 393, [1984] C.T.C. 337, 84 D.T.C. 6348 (C.A.), the court per Pratte J.A. See COMMON ~S; FUNERAL ~S; LIVING ~; OPERATING ~.

EXPENSE ACCOUNT. A list of obligations incurred while working on behalf of one's employer.

EXPERT. *n.* "... [G]enerally called to testify to provide information to enable the Court or a jury to understand technical and scientific issues raised in the litigation. They are also called upon to provide opinions and conclusions in areas where the Courts or jury are unable to make the necessary inferences from the technical facts presented. The role of the expert is circumscribed by his area of expertise. It is essential that the witness be shown to possess the necessary qualifications and skill in the area or field in which his opinion is sought. Those qualifications and skill can be based on or derived from academic study or practical experience." *Rieger v. Burgess* (1988), 45 C.C.L.T. 56 at 95, [1988] 4 W.W.R. 577, 66 Sask. R. 1 (C.A.), Tallis, Cameron and Vancise JJ.A.

EXPERT EVIDENCE. The admissible opinion of someone whose competency to form an opinion on some

subject before the court was acquired by a special course of study or experience, e.g., in engineering, foreign law or medicine.

EXPERT WITNESS. "[F]unction ... is to provide for the jury or other trier of fact an expert's opinion as to the significance of, or the inference which may be drawn from, proved facts in a field in which the expert witness possesses special knowledge and experience going beyond that of the trier of fact. The expert witness is permitted to give such opinions for the assistance of the jury. ..." *R. v. Béland* (1987), 36 C.C.C. (3d) 481 at 493, 79 N.R. 263, 9 Q.A.C. 293, [1987] 2 S.C.R. 398, 60 C.R. (3d) 1, 43 D.L.R. (4th) 641, McIntyre J. (Dickson C.J.C., Beetz and Le Dain JJ. concurring).

EXPLANATORY NOTE. Technically not part of a bill and printed on the page across from the relevant clause. A. Fraser, W.A. Dawson & J. Holtby, eds., *Beauchesne's Rules and Forms of the House of Commons of Canada*, 6th ed. (Toronto: Carswell, 1989) at 194.

EXPORT. *v.* 1. "... [I]nvolves the idea of a severance of goods from the mass of things belonging to this country with the intention of uniting them with the mass of things belonging to some foreign country. It also involves the idea of transporting the thing exported beyond the boundaries of this country with the intention of effecting that. ..." *R. v. Carling Export Brewing & Malting Co.*, [1930] 2 D.L.R. 725 at 733, [1930] S.C.R. 351, Duff J. 2. Ship from Canada to any other country or from any province to any other province. *Fish Inspection Regulations*, C.R.C., c. 802, s. 2.

EXPORT TAX. A tax on goods to be exported. P.W. Hogg, *Constitutional Law of Canada*, 3d ed. (Toronto: Carswell, 1992) at 742.

EXPOSE. *v.* Includes (a) a wilful omission to take charge of a child by a person who is under a legal duty to do so, and (b) dealing with a child in a manner that is likely to leave that child exposed to risk without protection.

Criminal Code, R.S.C. 1985, c. C-46, s. 214.

EX POST FACTO. [L. by something done after] Describes a statute which, after the fact, either makes an act punishable which was not punishable when it was done, or which imposes punishment for an act which is different from what would have been inflicted when the act was done.

EXPRESS. *adj.* Of some act showing intention, means done to communicate the intention directly, as opposed to by implication.

EXPRESS AGENCY. Agency deliberately created and limited by the agreement or contract terms. G.H.L. Fridman, *The Law of Agency*, 6th ed. (London: Butterworths, 1990) at 54.

EXPRESS CONDITION. A term specified in the agreement.

EXPRESSION. *n.* "All activities which convey or attempt to convey meaning prima facie fall within the scope of the guarantee [of freedom of expression in s. 2(b) of the Charter]: . . ." *R. v. Keegstra* (1990), 61 C.C.C. (3d) 1 at 95, 1 C.R. (4th) 129, 77 Alta. L.R. (2d) 193, [1991] 2 W.W.R. 1, 117 N.R. 1, 114 A.R. 81, 3 C.R.R. (2d) 193, [1990] 3 S.C.R. 697, McLachlin J. (dissenting) (La Forest and Sopinka JJ. concurring). See *Irwin Toy Ltd. v. Québec (Procureur général)* (1989), 58 D.L.R. (4th) 577 at 607, [1989] 1 S.C.R. 927, 25 C.P.R. (3d) 417, 94 N.R. 167, 24 Q.A.C. 2, 39 C.R.R. 193, Dickson C.J.C., Lamer and Wilson JJ. See COMMERCIAL SPEECH; FREEDOM OF ~; HATRED.

EXPRESSIO UNIUS EST EXCLUSIO ALTERIUS. [L.] 1. To express one thing is to exclude another. 2. "Often, . . . invoked to compare two provisions of the same statute. If section A prohibits certain individuals from participating in a decision while section B concerns decision-making but has no parallel prohibitions, it may be concluded that the law was intentionally silent, and that the individuals referred to in section A may participate in the decision provided for in section

B." *Leblanc Estate v. Bank of Montreal* (1988), [1989] 1 W.W.R. 49 at 63, 69 Sask. R. 81, 54 D.L.R. (4th) 89 (C.A.), Sherstobitoff J.A.

EXPRESS TERM. A term particularly mentioned, agreed on by the parties, and its character, content and form expressed in any exchange between them when the contract was made. G.H.L. Fridman, *The Law of Contract in Canada*, 2d ed. (Toronto: Carswell, 1986) at 427.

EXPRESS TRUST. A trust which comes into existence because the settlor has expressed the intention to accomplish that effect. D.M.W. Waters, *The Law of Trusts in Canada*, 2d ed. (Toronto: Carswell, 1984) at 299.

EXPROPRIATE. *v.* For an expropriating authority to take land without the consent of the owner in the exercise of its statutory powers.

EXPROPRIATING AUTHORITY. The Crown or an association or person empowered to acquire land by expropriation.

EXPROPRIATION. *n.* 1. The acquisition of title to land without the consent of the owner. 2. Taking without the consent of the owner. 3. ". . . [E]xtinction of an interest in land must . . . be included . . ." *British Columbia v. Tener* (1985), 36 R.P.R. 291 at 301, [1985] 1 S.C.R. 533, [1985] 3 W.W.R. 673, 32 L.C.R. 340, 17 D.L.R. (4th) 1, 59 N.R. 82, 28 B.C.L.R. (2d) 241, Estey J. (Beetz, McIntyre, Chouinard and Le Dain JJ. concurring). 4. Derogation by Crown from its grant of a profit à prendre can amount to expropriation. *British Columbia v. Tener* (1985), 36 R.P.R. 291 at 319, [1985] 1 S.C.R. 533, [1985] 3 W.W.R. 673, 32 L.C.R. 340, 17 D.L.R. (4th) 1, 59 N.R. 82, 28 B.C.L.R. (2d) 241, Wilson J. (Dickson C.J.C. concurring).

EX PROPRIO MOTU. [L.] Of one's own accord.

EXPUNGE. *v.* To strike out all or part of a document or pleading (Ontario, Rules of Civil Procedure, r. 25.11). G.D. Watson & C. Perkins, eds., *Holmested & Watson: Ontario Civil*

Procedure (Toronto: Carswell, 1984) at 25-7.

EX REL. *abbr.* Ex relatione.

EX RELATIONE. [L. from information or a narrative] On the information of a citizen called the relator.

EX RIGHTS. Without any right to the new issue of shares which will be made to shareholders.

EXTANT. *adj.* Existing.

EXTENSION. *n.* 1. An indulgence by giving time to pay a debt or perform an obligation. 2. [In the expression extension of credit] . . . according or granting or indeed opening of credit . . ." *R. v. Cohen* (1984), 15 C.C.C. (3d) 231 at 236, [1984] C.A. 408 (Que.), the court per Tyndale J.A.

EXTENT. *n.* The special writ to recover debts owed to the Crown which at one time differed from an ordinary writ of execution because a debtor's land and goods could be taken all at once in order to force payment of the debt. See WRIT OF ~.

EXTINGUISHED. *adj.* Of a right or obligation, no longer existing.

EXTORTION. *n.* Every one commits extortion who, without reasonable justification or excuse and with intent to obtain anything, by threats, accusation, menaces or violence induces or attempts to induce any person, whether or not he is the person threatened, accused or menaced or to whom violence is shown, to do anything or cause anything to be done. *Criminal Code,* R.S.C. 1985, c. C-46, s. 346(1).

EXTRA BILLING. The billing for an insured health service rendered to an insured person by a medical practitioner or a dentist in an amount in addition to any amount paid or to be paid for that service by the health care insurance plan of a province. *Canada Health Act,* R.S.C. 1985, c. C-6, s. 2.

EXTRADITION. *n.* ". . . [T]he surrender by one state to another, on request, of persons accused or convicted of committing a crime in the state seeking the surrender." *R. v. Schmidt* (1987), 28 C.R.R. 280 at 289, 76 N.R.

12, [1987] 1 S.C.R. 500, 58 C.R. (3d) 1, 20 O.A.C. 161, 39 D.L.R. (4th) 18, 33 C.C.C. (3d) 193, 61 O.R. (2d) 530, La Forest J. (Dickson C.J.C., Beetz, McIntyre and Le Dain JJ. concurring).

EXTRAJUDICIAL. *var.* **EXTRA-JUDICIAL.** *adj.* Out of the usual conduct of legal procedure.

EXTRANEOUS DEFENCE. One which raises a new issue which oversteps the Crown's case. P.K. McWilliams, *Canadian Criminal Evidence,* 3d ed. (Aurora: Canada Law Book, 1988) at 25-8.

EXTRAORDINARY REMEDY. A writ of mandamus, quo warranto or habeas corpus.

EXTRA-PROVINCIAL. *adj.* Incorporated in another province.

EXTRA-PROVINCIAL COMPANY. *var.* **EXTRAPROVINCIAL COMPANY.** A company incorporated outside the province to which reference is made.

EXTRA-PROVINCIAL CORPORATION. 1. A body corporate incorporated otherwise than by or under the act of a legislature. 2. A company or certain class of companies incorporated in another jurisdiction which must become licensed or registered if they carry on business in a province. H. Sutherland, D.B. Horsley & J.M. Edmiston, eds., *Fraser's Handbook on Canadian Company Law,* 7th ed. (Toronto: Carswell, 1985) at 573.

EXTRA-TERRITORIAL. *adj.* Outside the territory of the jurisdiction which enacted the law in question.

EXTRINSIC EVIDENCE. ". . . [E]vidence which is not contained in the body of the document, agreement or contract which forms the, or a subject matter of the, issue under consideration and requiring determination. . . ." *Saskatoon Market Mall Ltd. v. Macleod-Stedman Inc.* (1989), 78 Sask. R. 179 at 194 (Q.B.), Grotsky J.

EX TURPI CAUSA NON ORITUR ACTIO. [L.] ". . . [R]ule means . . . that the courts will not enforce a right which would otherwise be enforceable if the right arises out of an act committed by the person asserting the right (or by someone who is regarded in law as his successor) which is regarded by the court as sufficiently anti-social to justify the court's refusal to enforce that right." *Hardy v. Motor Insurers' Bureau*, [1964] 2 All E.R. 742 at 750-51 (U.K.), Lord Diplock.

EYE-WITNESS. *n.* One who testifies about facts she or he has seen.

F

FACE VALUE. The nominal value printed or written on the face of a bond, debenture, note, share certificate or other document indicating its par value.

FACIAS. [L. that you cause] See FIERI FACIAS.

FACSIMILE. *n.* An accurate reproduction of a book, instrument, document or record and includes a print from microfilm and a printed copy generated by or produced from a computer record. *Land Titles Act*, R.S.O. 1990, c. L.5, s. 1.

FACT. *n.* ". . . [S]tatement, tale or news is an expression which, taken as a whole and understood in context, conveys an assertion of fact or facts and not merely the expression of opinion. . . . Expression which makes a statement susceptible of proof and disproof is an assertion of fact; expression which merely offers an interpretation of fact which may be embraced or rejected depending on its cogency or normative appeal, is opinion." *R. v. Zundel* (1992), 75 C.C.C. (3d) 449 at 492, 95 D.L.R. (4th) 202, [1992] 2 S.C.R. 731, 140 N.R. 1, 56 O.A.C. 161, 16 C.R. (4th) 1, 10 C.R.R. (2d) 193, Cory and Iacobucci JJ. (dissenting) (Gonthier J. concurring). See ACCESSORY AFTER THE ~; ACCESSORY BEFORE THE ~; ADJUDICATIVE ~S; CAUSATION IN ~; CONCLUSION OF ~; LEGISLATIVE ~S; MATERIAL ~; MISTAKE OF ~; MIXED QUESTION OF LAW AND ~; PRESUMPTIONS OF ~; PRIMARY ~S; QUESTION OF ~;

SIMILAR ~ EVIDENCE.

FACTA PROBANDA. [L.] Facts which must be proved; facts in issue.

FACTA PROBANTIA. [L.] Facts given in evidence to prove facta probanda; evidentiary facts.

FACT FINDER. See TRIER OF FACT.

FACTO. [L.] In fact.

FACTOR. *n.* 1. One who loans money on security of accounts receivable or merchandise and inventory or both, but who is in no way connected with selling them. I.F.G. Baxter, *The Law of Banking*, 3d ed. (Toronto: Carswell, 1981) at 190. 2. An agent who disposes of or sells products in the agent's control or possession. G.H.L. Fridman, *Sale of Goods in Canada*, 3d ed. (Toronto: Carswell, 1986) at 493.

FACTORAGE. *n.* The commission which a factor receives.

FACTORING OF RECEIVABLES. Purchasing and discounting short-term business accounts receivable. I.F.G. Baxter, *The Law of Banking*, 3d ed. (Toronto: Carswell, 1981) at 191.

FACTUAL CAUSATION. A causal link between any facts which constitute the breach of contract or tortious conduct and the loss or injury for which the plaintiff claims compensation. K.D. Cooper-Stephenson & I.B. Saunders, *Personal Injury Damages in Canada* (Toronto: Carswell, 1981) at 637.

FACTUM. *n.* [L.] 1. A deed; an act. 2. A statement of facts and law which each party files in an application, appeal or motion.

FAILURE OF ISSUE. Death without issue.

FAIR. *adj.* ". . . [R]easonable . . ." *Vanguard Coatings & Chemicals Ltd. v. R.* (1988), 30 Admin. L.R. 121 at 148, 88 D.T.C. 6374, Can. S.T.R. 80-020, [1988] 2 C.T.C. 178, 17 C.E.R. 71, 88 N.R. 241, 22 F.T.R. 80n, [1988] 3 F.C. 560, [1989] 1 T.S.T. 2025 (C.A.), MacGuigan J.A. (Urie J.A. concurring).

FAIR COMMENT. 1. ". . . An essential ingredient of that defence is that the comment was made on a matter of public interest and the customary form of pleading in this regard is to state that the words complained of 'were fair comment made in good faith and without malice upon a matter of public interest'. . . . This defence is one which is available to every member of the public and relates exclusively to comments or opinions made upon facts which are shown to have been true. . . ." *McLoughlin v. Kutasy* (1979), 8 C.C.L.T. 105 at 109, 26 N.R. 242, [1979] 2 S.C.R. 311, 97 D.L.R. (3d) 620, Ritchie J. (Martland, Pigeon, Beetz, Estey and Pratte JJ. concurring). 2. "As honesty of belief is an essential component of the defence of fair comment, that defence involves at least some evidence that the material complained of was published in a spirit of fairness." *Cherneskey v. Armadale Publishers Ltd.* (1978), 7 C.C.L.T. 69 at 87, [1979] 1 S.C.R. 1067, 24 N.R. 271, [1978] 6 W.W.R. 618, 90 D.L.R. (3d) 321, Ritchie J. (Laskin C.J.C., Pigeon and Pratte JJ. concurring).

FAIR EMPLOYMENT PRACTICE. Practice of offering equal employment opportunities to persons regardless of race, national origin, colour, religion, age, sex, marital status, physical handicap or conviction for which a pardon has been granted.

FAIR HEARING. ". . . [T]he tribunal which adjudicates upon his rights must act fairly, in good faith, without bias and in judicial temper, and must give to him the opportunity adequately to state his case." *Duke v. R.*, [1972] S.C.R. 917 at 923, 18 C.R.N.S. 302, 7 C.C.C. (2d) 474, 28 D.L.R. (3d) 129, the court per Fauteux C.J.C.

FAIRLY. See ACT ~; DUTY TO ACT ~.

FAIR MARKET VALUE. ". . . [T]he highest price available estimated in terms of money which a willing seller may obtain for the property in an open and unrestricted market from a willing knowledgeable purchaser acting at arm's length." *Minister of National Revenue v. Northwood Country Club* (1989), 89 D.T.C. 173 at 176, [1989] 1 C.T.C. 2230 (T.C.C.), Kempo T.C.J.

FAIRNESS. *n.* The duty of an administrator to act fairly regarding procedure. Any administrator must, minimally, let the party affected by her or his decision understand the case against that party and provide the party with a fair chance to answer it or to be heard. See ACT FAIRLY; DUTY TO ACT FAIRLY; PROCEDURAL ~.

FAIR OPPORTUNITY. Refers to the chance for accused persons to present their cases and to know the relevant evidence.

FAIR TRIAL. ". . . [M]ust be fair to the accused, to the jurors, and to everyone directly or indirectly involved. . . ." *R. v. Makow* (1974), 28 C.R.N.S. 87 at 93, [1975] 1 W.W.R. 299, 20 C.C.C. (2d) 513 (B.C. C.A.), Seaton J.A.

FAIR VALUE. 1. Value which is equitable and just in the circumstances; fair market value, intrinsic value or value to owner. A. Bissett-Johnson & W.M. Holland, eds., *Matrimonial Property Law in Canada* (Toronto: Carswell, 1980) at V-2. 2. ". . . [F]air value and fair market value (or market value), are not necessarily synonymous . . ." *Whitehorse Copper Mines Ltd., Re* (1980), 10 B.L.R. 113 at 142 (B.C. S.C.), McEachern C.J.S.C.

FAIR WAGES. Such wages as are generally accepted as current for competent workers in the district in which the work is being performed for the character or class of work in which those workers are respectively engaged, but shall in all cases be such wages as are fair and reasonable.

FALSE. *adj.* ". . . [S]hould be distinguished from the word inaccurate as the word 'false' implies an intention to mislead or deceive . . ." *Kingsdale Securities Co. v. Minister of National Revenue* (1974), [1975] C.T.C. 10 at 34, [1974] 2 F.C. 760, 74 D.T.C. 6674, 6 N.R. 240 (C.A.), Bastin D.J.A. (dissenting).

FALSE ARREST. "A necessary element of false arrest . . . is that the arrest, . . . is made without foundation or probable cause." *Nicely v. Waterloo Regional Police Force* (1991), 7 C.C.L.T. (2d) 61 at 69, 47 C.P.C. (2d) 105, 2 O.R. (3d) 612, 79 D.L.R. (4th) 14, 44 O.A.C. 147 (Div. Ct.), the court per Rosenberg J.

FALSE DOCUMENT. 1. A document (a) the whole or a material part of which purports to be made by or on behalf of a person (i) who did not make it or authorize it to be made, or (ii) who did not in fact exist, (b) that is made by or on behalf of the person who purports to make it but is false in some material particular, (c) that is made in the name of an existing person, by him or under his authority, with a fraudulent intention that it should pass as being made by a person, real or fictitious, other than the person who makes it or under whose authority it is made. *Criminal Code*, R.S.C. 1985, c. C-46, s. 321. 2. ". . . [A]ny document that is false in some material particular . . . a document which is false in reference to the very purpose for which the document was created . . ." *R. v. Gaysek* (1971), 15 C.R.N.S. 345 at 348, 352, [1971] S.C.R. 888, 2 C.C.C. (2d) 545, 18 D.L.R. (3d) 306, Ritchie J. (Judson and Spence JJ. concurring).

FALSEHOOD. See INJURIOUS ~.

FALSE IMPRISONMENT. Intentional restraint of a person's liberty without lawful authority by preventing the person from leaving a place or actively confining them. J.G. Fleming, *The Law of Torts*, 8th ed. (Sydney: Law Book, 1992) at 27.

FALSE NEWS. See SPREADING ~.

FALSE PRETENCE. A representation of a matter of fact either present or past, made by words or otherwise, that is known by the person who makes it to be false and that is made with a fraudulent intent to induce the person to whom it is made to act upon it. *Criminal Code*, R.S.C. 1985, c. C-46, s. 361.

FALSE REPRESENTATION. See DECEIT; FALSE PRETENCE; MISREPRESENTATION; REPRESENTATION.

FALSI CRIMEN. [L.] Fraudulently concealing or suborning in order to hide the truth, committed in words when a witness swears falsely; in writing when someone antedates a contract; or in doing something when a person sells using false weights and measures.

[ ] FAM. *abbr.* Law Reports, Family Division, 1972-.

FAM. CT. *abbr.* 1. Family Court. 2. Provincial Court (Family Division).

FAMILY. *n.* 1. The husband, wife, child, step-child, parent, step-parent, brother, sister, half-brother, half-sister, step-brother, step-sister, in each case whether legitimate or illegitimate, of a person. 2. Includes a man and woman living together as husband and wife, whether or not married in a permanent relationship, or the survivor of either, and includes the children of both or either, natural or adopted or to whom either stands in loco parentis, and any person lawfully related to any of the aforementioned persons. 3. The parents and any children wholly or substantially maintained by those parents. *Family Allowance Act*, R.S.C. 1985, c. F-1, s. 2.

FAMILY ASSET. A matrimonial home and property owned by one spouse or both spouses and ordinarily used or enjoyed by both spouses or one or more of their children while the spouses are residing together for shelter or transportation or for household, educational, recreational, social or aesthetic purposes, and includes, (i) money in an account with a chartered bank, savings office, credit union or trust company where the account is ordinarily used for shelter or transportation or for household, educational, recreational, social or aesthetic purposes, (ii) where property owned by a corporation, partnership or trustee would, if it were owned by a spouse, be a family asset, shares in the corporation or an interest in the partnership or trust owned by the spouse having a market value equal to the value of the benefit the spouse has in respect of the property, (iii) property over which a spouse has, either alone or in conjunction with another person, a power of appointment exercisable in favour of himself or herself, if the property would be a family asset if it were owned by the spouse, and (iv) property disposed of by a spouse but over which the spouse has, either alone or in conjunction with another person, a power to revoke the disposition or a power to consume, invoke or dispose of the property, if the property would be a family asset if it were owned by the spouse, but does not include property that the spouses have agreed by a domestic contract is not to be included in the family assets.

FAMILY DEBT. "... [A] convenient term to designate a liability of either or both of the spouses which has been incurred during the marriage for a family purpose." *Mallen v. Mallen* (1992), 40 R.F.L. (3d) 114 at 121, 65 B.C.L.R. (2d) 241, 11 B.C.A.C. 262, 22 W.A.C. 262 (C.A.), Wood J.A. (dissenting).

FAMILY LAW COMMISSIONER. One whom a judge directs to investigate and report on an issue relating to access, custody or maintenance.

FAMILY NAME. 1. A surname that does not contain more than one word which may occur alone as a surname. 2. A family name which is a single unhyphenated word.

FAMILY ORDER. A custody and access order; a money order for support; a property order. C.R.B. Dunlop, *Creditor-Debtor Law in Canada*, Second Cumulative Supplement

(Toronto: Carswell, 1986) at 208.

FAMILY PROVISION. A support provision, a custody provision or an access right. *Family Orders and Agreements Enforcement Assistance Act*, R.S.C. 1985 (2d Supp.), c. 4, s. 2.

FAMILY STATUS. 1. The status of being in a parent and child relationship.. *Human Rights acts*. 2. The status of an unmarried person or parent, a widow or widower or that of a person who is divorced or separated or the status of the children, dependants, or members of the family of a person. *Human Rights Act*, R.S.M. 1987, c. H175, s. 1.

FAM. L. REV. *abbr.* Family Law Review, 1978.

F.A.S. *abbr.* Free alongside ship. A seller undertakes to deliver goods alongside a ship at the seller's own expense. G.H.L. Fridman, *Sale of Goods in Canada*, 3d ed. (Toronto: Carswell, 1986) at 484-485.

FATAL ACCIDENT. An accident causing the death of a worker under circumstances that entitle that worker's dependents, if any, to compensation under this Act. *Workers' Compensation acts*.

FAULT. *n.* 1. "... [I]ncludes negligence, but it is much broader than that. Fault incorporates all intentional wrongdoing, as well as other types of substandard conduct." *Bell Canada v. Cope (Sarnia) Ltd.* (1980), 11 C.C.L.T. 170 at 180 (Ont. H.C.), Linden J. 2. Wrongful act or default. *Sale of Goods acts*.

FBDB. *abbr.* Federal Business Development Bank.

F.C. *abbr.* 1. Federal Court. 2. Federal Court of Canada Reports.

[ ] F.C. *abbr.* Canada Federal Court Reports, 1971- (Recueil des arrêts de la Cour fédérale du Canada).

F.C.A.D. *abbr.* Federal Court Appellate Division.

F.C.T.D. *abbr.* Federal Court Trial Division.

FEALTY. *n.* 1. A mutual bond of

obligation or special oath of fidelity between a lord and a tenant. 2. The general oath of allegiance of a subject to a sovereign.

FEASANCE. *n.* Executing or doing something. See MIS~; NON~.

FED. *abbr.* Federal.

FED. C.A. *abbr.* Federal Court of Canada – Appeal Division.

FEDERAL. *adj.* As applied to state documents, means of or pertaining to Canada. *Evidence acts*.

FEDERAL ACT. A law passed by the Parliament of Canada.

FEDERAL BOARD, COMMISSION OR OTHER TRIBUNAL. Any body or any person or persons having, exercising or purporting to exercise jurisdiction or powers conferred by or under an Act of Parliament, other than any such body constituted or established by or under a law of a province or any such person or persons appointed under or in accordance with a law of a province or under section 96 of the Constitution Act, 1867. *Federal Court Act*, R.S.C. 1985, c. F-7, s. 2.

FEDERAL BUSINESS DEVELOPMENT BANK. The bank, incorporated under the Federal Business Development Bank Act (Canada), which offers financial and management services to help businesses establish and develop themselves in Canada.

FEDERAL COMPANY. A corporation incorporated or continued by or under an Act of Canada.

FEDERAL COURT. 1. The Federal Court of Canada. *Interpretation Act*, R.S.C. 1985, c. I-21, s. 35. 2. "... [A] statutory court and its jurisdiction must be found in the Federal Court Act [R.S.C. 1970, (2d Supp.), c. 10] ..." *Piche v. Cold Lake Transmission Ltd.* (1979), [1981] 3 C.N.L.R. 78 at 85, [1980] 2 F.C. 369 (T.D.), Primrose D.J. 3. The federal court has jurisdiction in suits against the Crown in right of Canada. It also has jurisdiction over appeals from or judicial review of decisions of federal tribunals, maritime law and certain matters concerning intel-

lectual property. It was created in 1971 as the successor to the Exchequer Court of Canada.

FEDERAL COURT – APPEAL DIVISION. That division of the Federal Court of Canada called the Federal Court – Appeal Division or referred to as the Court of Appeal or Federal Court of Appeal by the Federal Court Act. *Interpretation Act*, R.S.C. 1985, c. I-21, s. 35.

FEDERAL COURT OF APPEAL. That division of the Federal Court of Canada called the Federal Court – Appeal Division or referred to as the Court of Appeal or Federal Court of Appeal by the Federal Court Act. *Interpretation Act*, R.S.C. 1985, c. I-21, s. 35.

FEDERAL COURT – TRIAL DIVISION. That division of the Federal Court of Canada so named by the Federal Court Act. *Interpretation Act*, R.S.C. 1985, c. I-21, s. 35.

FEDERAL CROWN. Her Majesty in right of Canada.

FEDERAL GOVERNMENT. 1. A person or body which exercises power delegated to it by two or more independent states which have mutually agreed not to exercise certain sovereign powers but to delegate the exercise of those powers to the person or body they have chosen jointly. 2. The Governor General in Council.

FEDERALISM. The system of government in Canada. Jurisdiction over legislative matters is divided between the Parliament of Canada and the legislatures of the provinces. This division of jurisdiction is prescribed by sections 91 and 92 of the Constitution Act, 1867. The powers of the provinces and the Parliament of Canada are coordinate, not subordinate to one another. P.W. Hogg, *Constitutional Law of Canada*, 3d ed. (Toronto: Carswell, 1992). See COOPERATIVE ~.

FEDERAL JURISDICTION. The legislative jurisdiction of the Parliament of Canada.

FEDERAL PARAMOUNTCY. The rule that the federal law prevails, which applies when there is a provincial law and a federal law which are each valid but inconsistent or conflicting. P.W. Hogg, *Constitutional Law of Canada*, 3d ed. (Toronto: Carswell, 1992) at 418-19.

FEDERAL PARLIAMENT. The parliament of Canada.

FEDERAL REFERENCE. A function of the Supreme Court, imposed by the Supreme Court Act, to give advisory opinions on questions which the federal government refers to the Court. P.W. Hogg, *Constitutional Law of Canada*, 3d ed. (Toronto: Carswell, 1992) at 214. See PROVINCIAL REFERENCE.

FEDERAL STATE. Distribution of government power between one central, federal or national authority and several regional, state or provincial authorities with the result that every individual is subject to the laws of two authorities. P.W. Hogg, *Constitutional Law of Canada*, 3d ed. (Toronto: Carswell, 1992) at 98.

FEDERAL STATUTE. A law passed by the Parliament of Canada.

FEDERAL TERRITORY. By a procedure established under the Constitution Act, 1867 (U.K.), 30 & 31 Vict., c. 3, s. 146, the areas of Rupert's Land and the North-western Territory were admitted to Canada as areas under the authority of the federal Parliament. P.W. Hogg, *Constitutional Law of Canada*, 3d ed. (Toronto: Carswell, 1992) at 38-9.

FEDERAL WATERS. Waters under the exclusive legislative jurisdiction of Parliament. *Canada Water Act*, R.S.C. 1985, c. C-11, s. 2.

FEDERAL WORK, UNDERTAKING OR BUSINESS. Any work, undertaking or business that is within the legislative authority of Parliament, including, without restricting the generality of the foregoing, (a) a work, undertaking or business operated or carried on for or in connection with navigation and shipping, whether inland or maritime, including the operation of ships and transportation by ship anywhere in Canada, (b) a railway, canal, telegraph or other work or undertaking connecting any province with any other province, or extending beyond the limits of a province, (c) a line of ships connecting a province with any other province, or extending beyond the limits of a province, (d) a ferry between any province and any other province or between any province and any country other than Canada, (e) aerodromes, aircraft or a line of air transportation, (f) a radio broadcasting station, (g) a bank, (h) a work or undertaking that, although wholly situated within a province, is before or after its execution declared by Parliament to be for the general advantage of Canada and for the advantage of two or more of the provinces, and (i) a work, undertaking or business outside the exclusive legislative authority of the legislatures of the provinces. *Canada Labour Code*, R.S.C. 1985, c. L-2, s. 2.

FEDERATION. *n.* A composite state whose constitution distributes certain functions to a central authority and others to member states.

FED. T.D. *abbr.* Federal Court of Canada – Trial Division.

FEE. *n.* 1. "... [I]ts technical common law meaning, i.e., an estate in land unrestricted as to time and capable of descending to the heir...." *Ameri-Cana Motel Ltd. v. Miller* (1983), 27 R.P.R. 75 at 79, [1983] S.C.R. 229, 46 N.R. 451, 143 D.L.R. (3d) 1, the court per Wilson J. 2. "... [I]n the context of s. 26 (now s. 29) of the Planning Act [R.S.O. 1970, c. 349] it was to be equated with the kind of interest in land which carries with it disposing power...." *Ameri-Cana Motel Ltd. v. Miller* (1983), 27 R.P.R. 75 at 79, [1983] S.C.R. 229, 46 N.R. 451, 143 D.L.R. (3d) 1, the court per Wilson J. 3. Recompense or reward for services. 4. An amount to be paid when filing documents. See DETERMINABLE ~; ~ SIMPLE; ~ TAIL.

FEED. *v.* To offer additional support; to strengthen after the fact, i.e. a subsequently acquired interest feeds an estoppel.

FEE SIMPLE. "... [T]he largest estate in land in both time and status with a right of alienation and inheritability." *Saint John (City) v. McKenna* (1987), 45 R.P.R. 61 at 64, 78 N.B.R. (2d) 393, 198 A.P.R. 393, 37 D.L.R. (4th) 160 (C.A.), Hoyt J.A. (Ryan J.A. concurring).

FEE TAIL. A lesser (lesser than fee simple) freehold estate which arises from a grant to a person and heirs, limited to the grantee's own issue. E.L.G. Tyler & N.E. Palmer, eds., *Crossley Vaines' Personal Property*, 5th ed. (London: Butterworths, 1973) at 5.

FELON. *n.* A person who was convicted of felony.

FELONY. *n.* Originally the condition of having forfeited goods and lands to the Crown when convicted of a certain offence; later the offence which caused such forfeiture, distinguished from misdemeanour, after conviction for which forfeiture did not follow. See MISPRISION OF ~.

FEME. *n.* A woman; a wife.

FEME COVERT. A woman who is married.

FEME SOLE. A woman who is unmarried: spinster, widow or divorcee.

FENERATION. *n.* 1. Usury. 2. Interest on loaned money.

FEOFFMENT. *n.* Formerly, the transfer of freehold land by livery of seisin and word of mouth.

FERAE NATURAE. [L.] Having a wild nature. See ANIMALS ~.

FEUDAL SYSTEM. A peculiar system in which absolute or nominal ownership of land was in one feudal superior or lord while the occupation, use and benefit was in the feudal inferior or tenant who rendered the lord certain services.

FIAT. *n.* [L. let it be done] A decree; order or warrant made by a judge or public officer to allow certain processes.

FIAT JUSTITIA. [L.] Let justice be done.

FICTION. *n.* A rule of law which assumes something which is false is true, and will not allow it to be disproved.

FIDUCIARY. *n.* 1. "... [W]here by statute, agreement, or perhaps by unilateral undertaking, one party has an obligation to act for the benefit of another, and that obligation carries with it a discretionary power, the party thus empowered becomes a fiduciary...." *Guerin v. R.* (1984), [1985] 1 C.N.L.R. 120 at 137, [1984] 2 S.C.R. 335, 36 R.P.R. 1, 210 E.T.R. ‑6, [1984] 6 W.W.R. 481, 59 B.C.L.R. 301, 13 D.L.R. (4th) 321, 55 N.R. 161, Dickson J. (Beetz, Chouinard and Lamer JJ. concurring). 2. "... [U]se[d] in at least three distinct ways.... [(a)] The focus is on the identification of relationships in which, because of their inherent purpose or their presumed factual or legal incidents, the Courts will impose a fiduciary obligation on one party to act or refrain from acting in a certain way. The obligation imposed may vary in its specific substance depending on the relationship, though compendiously it can be described as the fiduciary duty of loyalty and will most often include the avoidance of a conflict of duty and interest and a duty not to profit at the expense of the beneficiary.... [(b)] a fiduciary obligation can arise as a matter of fact out of the specific circumstances of a relationship. As such it can arise between parties in a relationship in which fiduciary obligations would not normally be expected.... [(c)] third usage of 'fiduciary' stems, it seems, from a perception of remedial inflexibility in equity. Courts have resorted to fiduciary language because of the view that certain remedies, deemed appropriate in the circumstances, would not be available unless a fiduciary relationship was present. In this sense, the label fiduciary imposes no obligations, but rather is merely instrumental or facilitative in achieving what appears to be the appropriate result." *International Corona Resources Ltd. v.*

LAC Minerals Ltd. (1989), 35 E.T.R. 1 at 20, 21-2, 26 C.P.R. (3d) 97, 69 O.R. (2d) 287, 61 D.L.R. (4th) 14, [1989] 2 S.C.R. 574, 6 R.P.R. (2d) 1, 44 B.L.R. 1, 101 N.R. 239, 36 O.A.C. 57, La Forest J. (Lamer J. concurring). 3. "Relationships in which a fiduciary obligation have been imposed seem to possess three general characteristics: (1) The fiduciary has scope for the exercise of some discretion or power. (2) The fiduciary can unilaterally exercise that power or discretion so as to affect the beneficiary's legal or practical interests. (3) The beneficiary is peculiarly vulnerable to or at the mercy of the fiduciary holding the discretion or power." *Frame v. Smith* (1987), [1988] 1 C.N.L.R. 152 at 155, 78 N.R. 40, 9 R.F.L. (3d) 225, 42 C.C.L.T. 1, [1987] 2 S.C.R. 99, 23 O.A.C. 84, 42 D.L.R. (4th) 81, Wilson J. (dissenting).

FIERI FACIAS. [L. that you cause to be made] A writ of execution used to levy a judgment debt. See WRIT OF ~.

FIERI FECI. [L. I have caused to be made] A return made by the sheriff who executed a writ of execution.

FI. FA. *abbr.* Fieri facias.

FILE. *v.* To leave with the appropriate office for keeping.

FILIBUSTER. *n.* A tactic used to delay legislative action.

FINAL. *adj.* 1. Last; conclusive; terminated. 2. ". . . [N]ot subject to further appeal. . . ." *Hi-Rise Structures Inc. v. Scarborough (City)* (1992), 12 M.P.L.R. (2d) 1 at 11, 94 D.L.R. (4th) 385, 10 O.R. (3d) 299, 27 O.M.B.R. 443, 57 O.A.C. 287 (C.A.), the court per Carthy J.A. 3. ". . . [A] judgment or order is . . . final . . . [if] it finally disposes of the rights of the parties. . . ." *Kampus v. Bridgeford* (1982), 25 C.P.C. 169 at 171, 131 D.L.R. (3d) 612 (Ont. C.A.), the court per Brooke J.A.

FINALITY CLAUSE. A statement in a statute that decisions of a tribunal shall not be subject to review. P.W. Hogg, *Constitutional Law of Canada*, 3d ed. (Toronto: Carswell, 1992) at 197. See PRIVATIVE CLAUSE.

FINAL JUDGMENT. 1. Any judgment, rule, order or decision that determines in whole or in part any substantive right of any of the parties in controversy in any judicial proceeding. *Supreme Court Act*, R.S.C. 1985, c. S-26, s. 2. 2. ". . . [A] judgment obtained in an action by which a previously existing liability of the defendant to the plaintiff is ascertained or established . . ." *Ex Parte Chinery* (1884), 12 Q.B.D. 342 at 345 (U.K.), Cotten L.J.

FINAL ORDER. ". . . [F]inally disposes of the rights of the parties, . . ." *Hendrickson v. Kallio*, [1932] 4 D.L.R. 580 at 585, [1932] O.R. 675 (C.A.), Middleton J.A.

FINANCIAL LEASE. A credit device which permits the lessee to have rights and obligations of ownership, while the lessor continues to be the technical owner. I.F.G. Baxter, *The Law of Banking*, 3d ed. (Toronto: Carswell, 1981) at 187.

FINANCIAL STATEMENT. A summary of financial condition of a business or organization, usually a balance sheet and statement of profit and loss.

FINANCIAL SUPPORT ORDER. An order or judgment for maintenance, alimony or support, including an order or judgment for arrears of payments, made pursuant to the Divorce Act, or pursuant to the law of a province relating to family financial support.

FINANCIAL YEAR. The year in respect of which the accounts of the company or of the business are made up.

FINANCING. *n.* See BRIDGE ~.

FINDING. *n.* The conclusion drawn after an inquiry of fact.

FINDING OF GUILT. The plea of guilty by a defendant to an offence or the finding that a defendant is guilty of an offence made before or by a court that makes an order directing that the defendant be discharged for the offence either absolutely or on the conditions prescribed in a probation order, where (a) the order directing the discharge is not subject to further appeal; or (b) no appeal is taken in respect of the order directing the discharge. *Evidence acts.*

FINE. *n.* 1. A pecuniary penalty or other sum of money. *Criminal Code*, R.S.C. 1985, c. C-46. 2. A sum of money ordered to be paid to the Crown by an offender, as a punishment for the offence.

FINGERPRINT. *n.* The pattern in the skin on the finger tips, used to identify people.

FIRE. *n.* Combustion together with a visible glow or flame. C. Brown & J. Menezes, *Insurance Law in Canada*, 2d ed. (Toronto: Carswell, 1991) at 182.

FIREARM. *var.* **FIRE-ARM.** *n.* 1. Any barrelled weapon from which any shot, bullet or other projectile can be discharged and that is capable of causing serious bodily injury or death to a person, and includes any frame or receiver of such a barrelled weapon and anything that can be adapted for use as a firearm. *Criminal Code*, S.C. 1991, c. 40, s. 2(1). 2. Includes a device that propels a projectile by means of an explosion, compressed gas or spring and includes a rifle, shotgun, air gun, pistol, revolver, handgun or spring gun. 3. Crossbow or longbow.

FIRM. *n.* (i) A person who is sole proprietor of a business carried on under a registered business name, or (ii) the persons who are associated as partners in a business carried on by the partnership under a registered business name.

FIRM NAME. The name under which a business is carried on.

FIRST DEGREE MURDER. 1. Murder when it is planned and deliberate. *Criminal Code*, R.S.C. 1985, c. C-46, s. 231. 2. Irrespective of whether it is planned and deliberate (a) when the victim is a police officer or one of other named officials. *Criminal Code*, R.S.C. 1985, c. C-46, s. 231. 3. When death is caused while committing or attempting to commit hijacking an aircraft, sexual assault, sexual assault with a weapon, threats to a third party or causing bodily harm, aggravated sexual assault, kidnapping and forcible confinement, or hostage taking. *Criminal Code*, R.S.C. 1985, c. C-46, s. 231.

FIRST IMPRESSION. Describes a case which presents a new question of law for which there is no precedent.

FIRST INSTANCE. See COURT OF ~.

FIRST MINISTERS' CONFERENCE. A federal-provincial conference of the federal Prime Minister and the provincial Premiers. P.W. Hogg, *Constitutional Law of Canada*, 3d ed. (Toronto: Carswell, 1992) at 131-2.

FIRST MORTGAGE. A mortgage which has priority over all other similar mortgages against the same land.

FIRST OFFENDER. One who was convicted for the first time.

FIRST READING. A purely formal stage of parliamentary deliberation decided without amendment or debate, coupled with an order to print the bill. A. Fraser, W.A. Dawson & J. Holtby, eds., *Beauchesne's Rules and Forms of the House of Commons of Canada*, 6th ed. (Toronto: Carswell, 1989) at 195.

FISCAL. *adj.* Relating to revenue.

FISCAL PERIOD. The period for which the accounts of the business of the taxpayer have been ordinarily made up and accepted for purposes of assessment under the Income Tax Act.

FISCAL YEAR. 1. When used to mean the fiscal year of the government means the period from April 1 in one year to March 31 in the next year. 2. The period for which the business accounts of a corporation or a business of a taxpayer are made up and accepted for the purposes of the Income Tax Act.

FISHERIES. *n.* The business of catching, harvesting, raising, cultivating and handling of fish directly or indirectly by a fisherman. See FISHERY.

FISHERY. *n.* "... [T]he right of

catching fish in the sea, or in a particular stream of water; ... also ... used to denote the locality where such right is exercised." *R. v. Fowler* (1980), 9 C.E.L.R. 115 at 121, [1980] 2 S.C.R. 213, [1980] 5 W.W.R. 511, 113 D.L.R. (3d) 513, 53 C.C.C. (2d) 97, 32 N.R. 230, the court per Martland J. See FISHERIES.

FISHING. *n.* "... [A] continuous process beginning from the time when the preliminary preparations are being made for the taking of the fish and extending down to the moment when they are finally reduced to actual and certain possession...." *"Frederick Gerring Jr." (The) v. R.* (1897), 27 S.C.R. 271 at 280, Sedgewick J.

FITNESS. *n.* The physical and mental condition of an individual that enables that person to function at their best in society.

FITNESS FOR THE PURPOSE. "Section 17(2) of the [Sale of Goods Act, R.S.A. 1980, c. S-2] is primarily designed to cover the aspect of the function of specific goods from an operating point of view.... The implied condition of goods being reasonably fit for the purpose for which they are required includes not only operational fitness but also fitness to be transported and to be hoisted into position in an appropriate fashion so as to enable those goods to become operational." *Prolite Plastics Ltd. v. International Cooling Tower Inc.* (1987), 51 Alta. L.R. (2d) 299 at 306, 79 A.R. 110 (Q.B.), Gallant J.

FIXED ASSET. Property used in a business which will not be used or converted into cash during the current fiscal year.

FIXED CAPITAL. That which a company retains, in the shape of assets upon which the subscribed capital has been expended, and which assets either themselves produce income, independent of any further action of the company, or being retained by the company are made use of to produce income or gain profits. *Ammonia Soda Company, Ltd. v. Chamberlain*, [1918] 1 Ch. 266.

FIXED CHARGE. A security interest similar to the charge which a typical real property mortgage creates. It is a charge on specific property, contrasted to a floating charge.

FIXED COSTS. Costs set as a lump sum without being constrained by tariffs. M.M. Orkin, *The Law of Costs*, 2d ed. (Aurora: Canada Law Book, 1987) at 2-5.

FIXED PRICE CONTRACT. Contract in which the price is preset regardless of actual cost.

FIXTURE. *n.* An object or thing which by its degree of attachment to the land has come in law to form part of the land. R. Megarry & H.W.R. Wade, *The Law of Real Property*, 5th ed. (London: Stevens, 1984) at 731.

FIXTURES. *n.* Personal chattels connected with or fastened to land. See TRADE ~.

FLAG. *n.* A banner; ensign; standard. See LAW OF ~.

FLAGRANT. *adj.* 1. "... [G]laring, scandalous or conspicuously wrongful: ..." *R. v. Harris* (1987), 35 C.C.C. (3d) 1 at 25, 20 O.A.C. 26, 57 C.R. (3d) 356 (C.A.), the court per Martin J.A. 2. "... [C]lear or obvious ... scandalous ..." *R. v. Nelson* (1987), 35 C.C.C. (3d) 347 at 350, [1987] 3 W.W.R. 144, 46 M.V.R. 145, 45 Man. R. (2d) 68, 29 C.R.R. 80 (C.A.), Huband J.A. (Hall J.A. concurring).

FLAGRANTE DELICTO. [L. while the crime is glaring] While committing the offence charged.

FLIGHT. *n.* 1. The act of flying or moving through the air. *Criminal Code*, R.S.C. 1985, c. C-46, s. 7(8). 2. "... '[A]ction of running away from danger,' ..." *Rowe v. R.* (1951), 100 C.C.C. 97 at 103, [1951] S.C.R. 713, 12 C.R. 148, [1951] 4 D.L.R. 238, Kellock J.

FLOATING CAPITAL. Capital available to meet current expenditure.

FLOATING CHARGE. 1. "... [A]n equitable charge on the assets for the time being of a going concern. It does not specifically affect any particular assets until some event occurs or some act is done on the part of the mortgagee which causes the security to crystallize into a fixed security. Until the security is crystallized the charge is an equitable one and the legal title to the goods remains in the mortgagor." *Meen v. Realty Development Co.* (1953), [1954] O.W.N. 193 at 194, [1954] 1 D.L.R. 649 (C.A.), the court per MacKay J.A. 2. "A floating security is not a future security; it is a present security, which presently affects all the assets of the company expressed to be included in it. On the other hand, it is not a specific security; the holder cannot affirm that the assets are specifically mortgaged to him. The assets are mortgaged in such a way that the mortgagor can deal with them without the concurrence of the mortgagee. A floating security is not a specific mortgage of the assets, plus a licence to the mortgagor to dispose of them in the course of his business, but a floating mortgage applying to every item comprised in the security, but not specifically affecting any item until some event occurs or some act on the part of the mortgagee is done which causes it to crystallize into a fixed security." *Evans v. Rival Granite Quarries Ltd.*, [1910] 2 K.B. 979 at 999 (U.K. C.A.), Buckley L.J.

F.L.R.A.C. *abbr.* Family Law Reform Act Cases, 1980-.

F.O.B. *abbr.* 1. Free on board. 2. "... [T]he seller is obliged to put the goods on the truck but thereafter the goods are at the risk of the buyer and the buyer alone is responsible for the freight and insurance ..." *George Smith Trucking Co. v. Golden Seven Enterprises Inc.* (1989), 55 D.L.R. (4th) 161 at 174, 34 B.C.L.R. (2d) 43, [1989] 3 W.W.R. 544 (C.A.), Hutcheon J.A. (dissenting).

F.O.R. *abbr.* Free on rail.

FOR. *prep.* 1. "... [W]ith the intention of ..." *R. v. Chow*, [1938] 2 D.L.R. 332 at 333, [1938] 1 W.W.R. 458, 70 C.C.C. 150, 52 B.C.R. 467 (C.A.), the court per Sloan J.A. 2. "... '[W]ith the object or purpose of ...'" *Blackstock v. Insurance Corp. of British Columbia*, [1983] I.L.R. 1-1630 at 6264, [1983] 3 W.W.R. 282, 20 M.V.R. 293, 143 D.L.R. (3d) 743 (B.C. S.C.), Macdonell J.

FORBID. *v.* "... '[P]rohibit' ..." *Krautt v. Paine* (1980), 17 R.P.R. 1 at 21, [1980] 6 W.W.R. 717, 118 D.L.R. (3d) 625, 25 A.R. 390 (C.A.), the court per Laycraft J.A.

FORCE MAJEURE. [Fr.] Irresistible urge.

FORCE MAJEURE CLAUSE. "... [G]enerally operates to discharge a contracting party when a supervening, sometimes supernatural, event, beyond the control of either party, makes performance impossible. The common thread is that of the unexpected, something beyond reasonable human foresight and skill." *Atlantic Paper Stock Ltd. v. St. Anne-Nackawic Pulp & Paper Co.* (1975), 10 N.B.R. (2d) 513 at 516, [1976] 1 S.C.R. 580, 4 N.R. 539, 56 D.L.R. (3d) 409, the court per Dickson J. See ACT OF GOD.

FORCIBLE DETAINER. 1. Refusal to restore goods to another though sufficient means were tendered. 2. Detaining any lands or tenements with threats or violence after entering them peaceably.

FORCIBLE ENTRY. Of a dwelling house occurs when entry is made with such threats and show of force as would, if resisted, cause a breach of the peace, even though no actual force was used. *R. v. Walker* (1906), 12 C.C.C. 197 at 199-200, 4 W.L.R. 288, 6 Terr. L.R. 276 (N.W.T. C.A.), Scott J. (Sifton C.J., Wetmore, Prendergast and Newlands JJ. concurring).

F.O.R. CONTRACT. A seller undertakes to deliver goods into railway cars at the station at personal expense. G.H.L. Fridman, *Sale of Goods in Canada*, 3d ed. (Toronto: Carswell, 1986) at 485.

FORECLOSE DOWN. See REDEEM UP, FORECLOSE DOWN.

FORECLOSURE. *n.* 1. An action brought by a mortgagee when a mortgagor is in default asking that a day be fixed on which the mortgagor is to pay off the debt, and that in default of payment the mortgagor may be foreclosed of, that is deprived of her or his right to redeem, the equity of redemption. 2. A proceeding, commenced by a vendor under an agreement for sale, in which the relief claimed is an order for one or more of the following: (a) specific performance of the agreement, (b) cancellation of the agreement, or (c) determination of the agreement. *Law Reform Act*, S.B.C. 1985, c. 10, s. 16.1. See DECREE OF ~.

FORECLOSURE ORDER. "... [N]ot a final order disposing of a proceeding; it merely fixes the amount due on a mortgage and forecloses the right of a mortgagor to redeem the property, unless the amount due on the mortgage plus costs is paid ..." *Golden Forest Holdings Ltd. v. Bank of Nova Scotia* (1990), 43 C.P.C. (2d) 16 at 19, 98 N.S.R. (2d) 429, 263 A.P.R. 429 (C.A.), the court per Hallett J.A.

FOREIGN. *adj.* 1. Out of a certain nation's jurisdiction. 2. "... [I]n a private international law (conflicts) sense, namely, a territory which does not share precisely the same law ..." *Canadian Commercial Bank v. McLaughlan* (1990), 73 D.L.R. (4th) 678 at 685, 39 E.T.R. 54, 75 Alta. L.R. (2d) 40, 107 A.R. 232 (C.A.), Bracco and Stevenson JJ.A. and Forsyth J. (ad hoc).

FOREIGN BILL. A bill that is neither drawn in Canada upon a person resident in Canada nor drawn and payable in Canada. I.F.G. Baxter, *The Law of Banking*, 3d ed. (Toronto: Carswell, 1981) at 117.

FOREIGN COMPANY. 1. A company formed or incorporated by or under the laws of any country other than Canada. 2. A company incorporated otherwise than by or under the act of a legislature and includes a dominion company.

FOREIGN CORPORATION. A corporation incorporated otherwise than under a law of Canada or a province.

FOREIGN COURT. "In Canada, the courts of one province are, with respect to the courts of the other provinces, foreign courts." *Brand v. National Life Assurance Co.* (1918), 44 D.L.R. 412 at 420, [1918] 3 W.W.R. 858 (Man. K.B.), Mathers C.J.K.B.

FOREIGN JUDGMENT. "... [J]udgments from another country." *Morguard Investments Ltd. v. De Savoye* (1988), 29 C.P.C. (2d) 52 at 59, 27 B.C.L.R. (2d) 155, [1988] 5 W.W.R. 650 (C.A.), the court per Seaton J.A.

FOREIGN JURISDICTION. A province, state, country or other jurisdiction outside the province enacting the legislation.

FOREIGN LAW. See FOREIGN.

FOREMAN. *n.* 1. The member of a jury who speaks for that body. 2. A supervisory employee.

FORENSIC. *adj.* Applied to the law; belonging to law courts.

FORENSIC MEDICINE. 1. Legal medicine. 2. Medical skills and knowledge which may be used to solve legal problems. F.A. Jaffe, *A Guide to Pathological Evidence*, 3d ed. (Toronto: Carswell, 1991) at 1. 3. Jurisprudence of medicine.

FORESEEABILITY. *n.* A reasonable person's ability to anticipate the consequences of his or her action.

FORESEEABLE. *adj.* A risk is foreseeable when a reasonable person would consider it real and not fanciful or far-fetched. J.G. Fleming, *The Law of Torts*, 8th ed. (Sydney: Law Book, 1992) at 115.

FORFEIT. *v.* "... '[T]o lose by some breach of condition; to lose by some offence.' ..." *R. v. Premier Cutlery Ltd.* (1980), 55 C.P.R. (2d) 134 at 154 (Ont. Prov. Ct.), Bernard Prov. J.

FORFEITURE. *n.* The surrender of goods or chattels to punish someone for a crime, for failure to comply with terms of a recognizance or pay duty or fulfil some obligation and to compensate the person to whom they were forfeited for any injury. See RELIEF

AGAINST ~.

FORGED PASSPORT. See UTTERING ~.

FORGERY. *n*. Making a false document, knowing it to be false, with intent (a) that it should in any way be used or acted upon as genuine, to the prejudice of any one whether within Canada or not, or (b) that some person should be induced, by the belief that it is genuine, to do or to refrain from doing anything, whether within Canada or not. *Criminal Code*, R.S.C. 1985, c. C-46, s. 366.

FORGERY OF PASSPORT. Everyone who, while in or out of Canada, (a) forges a passport, or (b) knowing that a passport is forged (i) uses, deals with or acts upon it, or (ii) causes or attempts to cause any person to use, deal with, or act upon it, as if the passport were genuine, is guilty of an offence. *Criminal Code*, R.S.C. 1985, c. C-46, s. 57.

FORM. *n*. The contents or structure of a document distinguished from its substance. See BEARER ~; EQUITY LOOKS TO THE INTENT RATHER THAN TO THE ~.

FORMAL ADMISSION. An admission which is made in order to dispense with the need for proof at trial. It is conclusive as to the matter(s) admitted. J. Sopinka and S.N. Lederman, *The Law of Evidence in Civil Cases* (Toronto: Butterworths, 1974) at 355-56.

FORMAL CONTRACT. A deed; a contract under seal. G.H.L. Fridman, *The Law of Contract in Canada*, 2d ed. (Toronto: Carswell, 1986) at 10.

FORMA PAUPERIS. See IN ~.

FORMS OF ACTION. The common law procedural devices compliance with which was necessary to seek a remedy before the courts, ex. assumpsit, trespass on the case.

FORNICATION. *n*. Voluntary sexual intercourse between two people not married to each other.

FORTHWITH. *adv.* Within a reasonable time, considering the circumstances and the object.

FORUM. *n*. [L. a place] The place where legal remedies can be sought, a court.

FORUM CAN. CRIM. *abbr.* Le Forum canadien de criminologie (Canadian Criminology Forum).

FORUM CONVENIENS. [L.] " '. . . [F]orum which is the more suitable for the ends of justice'." *United Oilseed Products Ltd. v. Royal Bank* (1988), 29 C.P.C. (2d) 28 at 38, 60 Alta. L.R. (2d) 73, [1988] 5 W.W.R. 181, 87 A.R. 337 (C.A.), the court per Stevenson J.A.

FORUM NON CONVENIENS. [L.] 1. Refers to a court's discretionary power to decline jurisdiction over a proceeding which may be more properly tried elsewhere. J.G. McLeod, *The Conflict of Laws* (Calgary: Carswell, 1983) at 779. 2. ". . . [T]wo conditions must be satisfied: (a) . . . (the defendant) must satisfy the court that there is another forum to whose jurisdiction he was amenable and in which justice can be done between the parties at substantially less inconvenience and expense; (b) if the first condition is met, the plaintiff may still prevent a stay being granted if he can show that a stay would deprive him of a legitimate personal or juridical advantage which would be available to him if he invoked the jurisdiction of the court where the stay is sought." *Avenue Properties Ltd. v. First City Development Corp.* (1986), 7 B.C.L.R. (2d) 45 at 51-52, [1987] 1 W.W.R. 249, 32 D.L.R. (4th) 40 (C.A.), McLachlin J.A.

FORUM REI. [L.] The court of the place where the subject thing or person is situated.

FOSTER CHILD. A child whose parents are unable, in the opinion of the provincial authority, to support him and who is cared for (by a person or persons standing in loco parentis to him) in a private home approved as a suitable place of care by a child welfare authority or by a person designated for that purpose by the provincial authority. *Canada Assistance Plan Regulations*, C.R.C., c. 382, s. 2.

FOSTER HOME. 1. A home, other than the home of the child's parent, in which a child is placed for care and supervision but not for the purposes of adoption. 2. With respect to a child who lacks normal parental relations, means a home other than that of parents or relatives, in which such child may be placed to be treated as a member of the family.

F.O.T. *abbr.* Free on truck. Describing a seller's responsibility to have the goods placed on a truck. I.F.G. Baxter, *The Law of Banking*, 3d ed. (Toronto: Carswell, 1981) at 136.

FOUNDATION. *n.* A corporation established to receive, hold, administer and apply any property or the income from it for purposes or objects in connection with a hospital, other public or charitable purpose.

FOUR UNITIES. Refers to the four conditions of a joint tenancy. See UNITY OF INTEREST; UNITY OF POSSESSION; UNITY OF TIME; UNITY OF TITLE.

FOX PAT. C. *abbr.* Fox's Patent, Trade Mark, Design and Copyright Cases, 1940-1971.

FRAME. *v.* To fabricate false evidence so it appears someone else committed an offence.

FRANCHISE. *n.* 1. At common law, a royal privilege. 2. An agreement whereby the right to supply electricity, natural gas or natural gas liquids to the residents of a defined area is given. 3. A contract, agreement or arrangement, either expressed or implied, whether oral or written, between 2 or more persons by which a franchisee is required to pay directly or indirectly a franchise fee in consideration for any of the following: (i) the right to engage in the business of offering, selling or distributing the goods manufactured, processed or distributed or the services organized and directed by the franchisor, (ii) the right to engage in the business of offering, selling or distributing any goods or services under a marketing plan or system prescribed or controlled by the franchisor, (iii) the

right to engage in a business which is associated with the franchisor's trademark, service mark, trade name, logotype, advertising or any business symbol designating the franchisor or its associate, (iv) the right to engage in a business in which the franchisee is reliant on the franchisor for the continued supply of goods or services, or (v) the right to recruit additional franchisees or subfranchisors, but excluding contracts, agreements or arrangements between manufacturers or if the franchisor is the Crown, a Crown agency or a municipal corporation.

FRANCHISEE. *n.* A person to whom a franchise is granted.

FRANCHISOR. *n.* A person who grants a franchise.

FRATERNAL BENEFIT SOCIETY. A corporation having a representative form of government and incorporated for fraternal, benevolent or religious purposes among which purposes is the insuring of the members, or the spouses or children of the members thereof, exclusively, against accident, sickness, disability or death, and includes a corporation incorporated for those purposes on the mutual plan for the purpose of so insuring the members, or the spouses or children of the members, thereof, exclusively.

FRATERNAL SOCIETY. A society, order or association incorporated for the purpose of making with its members only, and not for profit, contracts of life, accident or sickness insurance in accordance with its constitution, by-laws and rules and the governing statute.

FRAUD. *n.* 1. "... [T]wo essential elements of fraud are 'dishonesty' and 'deprivation', the latter element being satisfied ' ... on proof of detriment, prejudice, or risk of prejudice to the economic interests of the victim': ..." *R. v. Kirkwood* (1983), 73 C.P.R. (2d) 114 at 119, 42 O.R. (2d) 65, 35 C.R. (3d) 97, 148 D.L.R. (3d) 323, 5 C.C.C. (3d) 393 (C.A.), the court per Lacourcière J.A. 2. "Fraud is false representation of fact, made with a knowledge of its falsehood, or recklessly, without belief in its truth, with the intention that it should be acted upon by the complaining party, and actually inducing him to act upon it." *Parna v. G. & S. Properties Ltd.*, [1971] S.C.R. 306 at 316, 15 D.L.R. (3d) 336, the court per Spence J., adopting a quotation from Anson on Contract. 3. (1) Every one who, by deceit, falsehood or other fraudulent means, whether or not it is a false pretence within the meaning of this Act defrauds the public or any person whether ascertained or not, of any property, money or valuable security, is guilty of an offence. (2) Every one who, by deceit, falsehood or other fraudulent means, whether or not it is a false pretence within the meaning of this Act, with intent to defraud, affects the public market price of stocks, shares, merchandise or anything that is offered for sale to the public, is guilty of an offence. *Criminal Code*, R.S.C. 1985, c. C-46, s. 380 in part. See BADGES OF ~; CONSTRUCTIVE ~; EQUITABLE ~; STATUTE OF ~S.

FRAUDULENT CONVEYANCE. A conveyance which defrauds, delays or hinders creditors and others. *Toronto Dominion Bank v. Miller* (1990), (*sub nom. Miller, Re*) 3 C.B.R. (3d) 285 at 288, 1 O.R. (3d) 528 (Gen. Div.), Steele J.

FRAUDULENT MISREPRESEN-TATION. "... [O]ne (1) which is untrue in fact; (2) which defendant knows to be untrue or is indifferent as to its truth; (3) which was intended or calculated to induce the plaintiff to act upon it; and (4) which the plaintiff acts upon and suffers damage. . . ." *Francis v. Dingman* (1983), 23 B.L.R. 234 at 253, 43 O.R. (2d) 641, 2 D.L.R. (4th) 244 (C.A.), Goodman J.A. (Zuber J.A. concurring).

FRAUDULENT PREFERENCE. "... [A]n act by which one creditor obtained an advantage over the others when two things concurred: first, that the act was voluntary on the part of the debtor; and secondly, that it was done in contemplation of bankruptcy. . . ." *Stephens v. McArthur* (1891), 19

S.C.R. 446 at 462, 6 Man. R. 496, Patterson J.

FREE ALONGSIDE SHIP. A seller undertakes to deliver goods alongside a ship at the seller's own expense. G.H.L. Fridman, *Sale of Goods in Canada*, 3d ed. (Toronto: Carswell, 1986) at 484-485.

FREE AND CLEAR. Unencumbered.

FREE AND DEMOCRATIC SOCIETY. "... [T]he values and principles essential to a free and democratic society ... embody, to name but a few, respect for the inherent dignity of the human person, commitment to social justice and equality, accommodation of a wide variety of beliefs, respect for cultural and group identity, and faith in social and political institutions which enhance the participation of individuals and groups in society. . . ." *R. v. Oakes* (1986), 19 C.R.R. 308 at 334, [1986] 1 S.C.R. 103, 50 C.R. (3d) 1, 14 O.A.C. 335, 24 C.C.C. (3d) 321, 26 D.L.R. (4th) 200, 65 N.R. 98, Dickson C.J.C. (Chouinard, Lamer, Wilson and Le Dain JJ. concurring).

FREE COMPETITION. "... [A]s judicially understood, affirmatively may be stated, as a situation in which the freedom of any individual or firm to engage in legitimate economic activity is not restrained by (1) agreements or conspiracies between competitors, or (2) by predatory practices of a rival, contrary to The Combines Investigation Act. And 'free competition' thus understood is quite compatible with the presence of monopoly elements as understood by economists, in the economic sense of the word monopoly, for the antithesis of the economic conception of monopoly is not 'free competition', as understood by the courts, but 'pure competition'." *R. v. Canadian Coat & Apron Supply Ltd.* (1967), 2 C.R.N.S. 62 at 77 (Ex. Ct.), Gibson J.

FREEDOM. *n.* 1. "... [I]n a broad sense embraces both the absence of coercion and constraint, and the right to manifest beliefs and practices. Freedom means that, subject to such limitations as are necessary to protect public safety, order, health, or morals or the fundamental rights and freedoms of others, no one is to be forced to act in a way contrary to his beliefs or his conscience." *R. v. Big M Drug Mart* (1985), 13 C.R.R. 64 at 97, [1985] 1 S.C.R. 295, [1985] 3 W.W.R. 481, 37 Alta. L.R. (2d) 97, 58 N.R. 81, 18 C.C.C. (3d) 385, 60 A.R. 161, 18 D.L.R. (4th) 321, 85 C.L.L.C. 14,023, Dickson C.J.C. (Beetz, McIntyre, Chouinard and Lamer JJ. concurring). 2. ". . . [I]s defined by determining first the area which is regulated. The freedom is then what exists in the unregulated area – a sphere of activity within which all acts are permissible. It is a residual area in which all acts are free of specific legal regulation and the individual is free to choose. . . ." *R. v. Zundel* (1987), 56 C.R. (3d) 1 at 23, 18 O.A.C. 161, 58 O.R. (2d) 129, 31 C.C.C. (3d) 97, 35 D.L.R. (4th) 338, 29 C.R.R. 349 (C.A.), Howland C.J.O., Brooke, Martin, Lacourcière, and Houlden JJ.A. See FUNDAMENTAL ~; LIBERTY; RIGHT.

FREEDOM OF ASSEMBLY. The right to gather together in one another's physical presence. *Fraser v. Nova Scotia (Attorney General)* (1986), 74 N.S.R. (2d) 91 at 99, 180 A.P.R. 91, 30 D.L.R. (4th) 340, 24 C.R.R. 193 (T.D.), Grant J.

FREEDOM OF ASSOCIATION. 1. ". . . [T]he freedom to combine together for the pursuit of common purposes or the advancement of common causes. It is one of the fundamental freedoms guaranteed by the Charter, a sine qua non of any free and democratic society, protecting individuals from the vulnerability of isolation and ensuring the potential of effective participation in society. . . ." *Reference re Public Service Employee Relations Act (Alberta)* (1987), 38 D.L.R. (4th) 161 at 173, [1987] 1 S.C.R. 313, 87 C.L.L.C. 14,021, 51 Alta. L.R. (2d) 97, [1987] 3 W.W.R. 577, 74 N.R. 99, 28 C.R.R. 305, 78 A.R. 1, [1987] D.L.Q. 225, Dickson C.J.C. 2. ". . . [T]he freedom to work

for the establishment of an association, to belong to an association, to maintain it, and to participate in its lawful activity without penalty or reprisal is not to be taken for granted. . . ." *Reference re Public Service Employee Relations Act (Alberta)*, [1987] 1 S.C.R. 313 at 391, 87 C.L.L.C. 14,021, 38 D.L.R. (4th) 161, 51 Alta. L.R. (2d) 97, [1987] 3 W.W.R. 577, 74 N.R. 99, 28 C.R.R. 305, 78 A.R. 1, [1987] D.L.Q. 225, Le Dain J. (Beetz and La Forest JJ. concurring). 3. ". . . [I]nclude[s] freedom from forced association . . ." *Lavigne v. O.P.S.E.U.* (1991), 4 C.R.R. (2d) 193 at 212, 91 C.L.L.C. 14,029, 3 O.R. (3d) 511n, 81 D.L.R. (4th) 545, 126 N.R. 161, 40 O.A.C. 241, [1991] 2 S.C.R. 211, La Forest J. (Sopinka and Gonthier JJ. concurring).

FREEDOM OF CONSCIENCE AND RELIGION. 1. ". . . [B]roadly construed to extend to conscientiously-held beliefs, whether grounded in religion or in a secular morality. . . ." *R. v. Morgentaler* (1988), 37 C.C.C. (3d) 449 at 560, 82 N.R. 1, [1988] 1 S.C.R. 30, 63 O.R. (2d) 281n, 62 C.R. (3d) 1, 26 O.A.C. 1, 44 D.L.R. (4th) 385, 31 C.R.R. 1, Wilson J. 2. ". . . [W]hatever else freedom of conscience and religion [in s. 2(a) of the Charter] may mean, it must at the very least mean this: government may not coerce individuals to affirm a specific religious belief or to manifest a specific religious practice for a sectarian purpose. . . . freedom from compulsory religious observance . . ." *R. v. Big M Drug Mart* (1985), 18 C.C.C. (3d) 385 at 426-7, 85 C.L.L.C. 14,023, [1985] 1 S.C.R. 295, [1985] 3 W.W.R. 481, 37 Alta. L.R. (2d) 97, 58 N.R. 81, 13 C.R.R. 64, 60 A.R. 161, 18 D.L.R. (4th) 321, Dickson C.J.C. (Beetz, McIntyre, Chouinard and Lamer JJ. concurring).

FREEDOM OF CONTRACT. The parties to a contract are left by the court to use their own discretion and to make their own agreement. G.H.L. Fridman, *The Law of Contract in Canada*, 2d ed. (Toronto: Carswell, 1986) at 82.

FREEDOM OF EXPRESSION. 1. ". . . [P]urpose of the guarantee is to permit free expression to the end of promoting truth, political or social participation, and self-fulfilment. That purpose extends to the protection of minority beliefs which the majority regard as wrong or false: ..." *R. v. Zundel* (1992), 75 C.C.C. (3d) 449 at 506, 95 D.L.R. (4th) 202, [1992] 2 S.C.R. 731, 140 N.R. 1, 56 O.A.C. 161, 16 C.R. (4th) 1, 10 C.R.R. (2d) 193, McLachlin J. (La Forest, L'Heureux-Dubé and Sopinka JJ. concurring). 2. "... [I]ncludes the freedom to express oneself in the language of one's choice. ..." *Devine v. Quebec (Attorney General)* (1989), 10 C.H.R.R. D/5610 at D/5624, 90 N.R. 48, 19 Q.A.C. 33, [1988] 2 S.C.R. 790, 36 C.R.R. 64, 55 D.L.R. (4th) 641, Dickson C.J.C., Beetz, McIntyre, Lamer and Wilson JJ.

FREEDOM OF RELIGION. "... The essence of the concept of freedom of religion is the right to entertain such religious beliefs as a person chooses, the right to declare religious beliefs openly and without fear of hindrance or reprisal, and the right to manifest religious belief by worship and practice or by teaching and dissemination. But the concept means more than that. ... Freedom means that, subject to such limitations as are necessary to protect public safety, order, health, or morals or the fundamental rights and freedoms of others, no one is to be forced to act in a way contrary to his beliefs or his conscience." *R. v. Big M Drug Mart* (1985), 13 C.R.R. 64 at 97, [1985] 1 S.C.R. 295, [1985] 3 W.W.R. 481, 37 Alta. L.R. (2d) 97, 58 N.R. 81, 18 C.C.C. (3d) 385, 60 A.R. 161, 18 D.L.R. (4th) 321, 85 C.L.L.C. 14,023, Dickson C.J.C. (Beetz, McIntyre, Chouinard and Lamer JJ. concurring).

FREEDOM OF SPEECH. A privilege and fundamental right of any member of Parliament on the House floor and in committee. A. Fraser, W.A. Dawson, & J. Holtby, eds., *Beauchesne's Rules and Forms of the House of Commons of Canada*, 6th ed. (Toronto: Carswell, 1989) at 22. See FREEDOM OF EXPRESSION.

FREEDOM OF THE PRESS. 1. "... [R]efers to the dissemination of expression of thought, belief or opinion through the medium of the press." *Reference re s. 12(1) of the Juvenile Delinquents Act (Canada)* (1983), 6 C.R.R. 1 at 9, 146 D.L.R. (3d) 408, 3 C.C.C. (3d) 515, 41 O.R. (2d) 113, 33 R.F.L. (2d) 279, 34 C.R. (3d) 27 (C.A.), the court per MacKinnon A.C.J.O. 2. Includes free access to the court. *Reference re s. 12(1) of the Juvenile Delinquents Act (Canada)* (1983), 6 C.R.R. 1, 146 D.L.R. (3d) 408, 3 C.C.C. (3d) 515, 41 O.R. (2d) 113, 33 R.F.L. (2d) 279, 34 C.R. (3d) 27 (C.A.).

FREEHOLD. *n.* 1. Free tenure. R. Megarry & H.W.R. Wade, *The Law of Real Property*, 5th ed. (London: Stevens, 1984) at cxxv. 2. An estate the maximum duration of which is unknown. R. Megarry & H.W.R. Wade, *The Law of Real Property*, 5th ed. (London: Stevens, 1984) at cxxv.

FREEHOLDER. *n.* One who possesses a freehold estate.

FREEHOLD ESTATE. An interest in land by which the freeholder is entitled to hold the land for an unfixed and uncertain period of time.

FREEHOLD LANDS. All lands in a province, and all rights thereto and interests therein, that are not Crown lands, and, for greater certainty, includes all Crown-acquired lands.

FREE ON BOARD. 1. "... [T]he seller, and not the shipper, shall pay the cost of loading the cargo on board, where it is stipulated that the price shall be for a stipulated sum f.o.b. ..." *Johnson v. Logan* (1899), 32 N.S.R. 28 at 42 (C.A.), McDonald C.J. 2. "If, upon an order for undetermined goods to be shipped f.o.b., the seller delivers to the designated common carrier, goods which answer the order, without more, the property passes forthwith to the purchaser – and this is the case also if a bill of lading is taken, and taken in the name of the purchaser. If, however, the bill of lading is taken in the name of the seller, prima facie he retains the disposing power over and property in the goods. He may, indeed, endorse it over to the purchaser forthwith, and send it forward for delivery to the purchaser; in that case the taking of the bill of lading to his own order is a mere form, and the transaction is equivalent to taking the bill of lading in the name of the purchaser. The seller may endorse in blank and send forward to his agent, bank, etc., for delivery to the purchaser upon payment for the goods, acceptance of a draft, or performance of some other condition – in that case, the goods remain in the control and are the property of the seller, at least until the condition is fulfilled or the purchaser offers to fulfil it and demands the bill of lading . . ." *Vipond v. Sisco* (1913), 20 O.L.R. 200 at 203, 14 D.L.R. 129 (C.A.), Riddell J.A. (Sutherland, Leitch and Clute JJ.A. concurring).

FREE ON TRUCK. Describing a seller's responsibility to have the goods placed on a truck. I.F.G. Baxter, *The Law of Banking*, 3d ed. (Toronto: Carswell, 1981) at 136.

FREE SOCIETY. ". . . [O]ne which can accommodate a wide variety of beliefs, diversity of tastes and pursuits, customs and codes of conduct. A free society is one which aims at equality with respect to the enjoyment of fundamental freedoms and I say this without any reliance upon s. 15 of the Charter. Freedom must surely be founded in respect for the inherent dignity and the inviolable rights of the human person." *R. v. Big M Drug Mart* (1985), 13 C.R.R. 64 at 97, [1985] 1 S.C.R. 295, [1985] 3 W.W.R. 481, 37 Alta. L.R. (2d) 97, 58 N.R. 81, 18 C.C.C. (3d) 385, 60 A.R. 161, 18 D.L.R. (4th) 321, 85 C.L.L.C. 14,023, Dickson C.J.C. (Beetz, McIntyre, Chouinard and Lamer JJ. concurring).

FREE VOTE. A parliamentary division on a question for which party lines are ignored. A. Fraser, W.A. Dawson, & J. Holtby, eds., *Beauchesne's Rules and Forms of the House of Commons of Canada*, 6th ed. (Toronto: Carswell, 1989) at 93.

FREIGHT. *n.* 1. Includes the profit derivable by ship owners from the employment of their ships to carry their own goods or movables, as well as freight payable by a third party, but does not include passage-money. *Insurance acts.* 2. Any substance, article or thing. *Elevators and Lifts acts.* 3. Includes personal property of every description that may be conveyed on a motor vehicle or trailer, except a passenger's personal baggage. *Motor Carrier acts.* 4. ". . . [T]he reward which the law entitles a person to recover for bringing goods lawfully on a lawful voyage. It is the price to be paid for the actual carriage of the goods. . . ." *Edmonstone v. Young* (1862), 12 U.C.C.P. 437 at 442, Draper J.

FRESH PURSUIT. Used in s. 494 of the Criminal Code, R.S.C. 1985, in regard to the right to arrest without warrant. To be contrasted with a person who has lost his pursuers or was not immediately pursued at all. *R. v. Dean* (1966), 47 C.R. 311 at 321, [1966] 1 O.R. 592, [1966] 3 C.C.C. 228 (C.A.), Laskin J.A.

FRIEND. See NEXT ~.

FRIENDLY SOCIETY. A society, order, association or company formed or incorporated and operated for the purpose of making with its members only, and not for profit, contracts under which (i) sickness, accident and disability benefits, or any one or more of them, not exceeding five dollars per week, or (ii) funeral benefits not exceeding one hundred and fifty dollars, or all of those benefits may be paid only to its members or their beneficiaries in accordance with its charter and this Act. *Insurance acts.*

FRIENDLY SUIT. A suit brought which parties mutually arrange to bring to obtain a decision on a point which interests both.

FRIEND OF THE COURT. Any person who, with leave of a judge or at the invitation of a presiding judge or master, and without becoming a party to the proceeding, intervenes to render assistance to the court by way of argument (Ontario, Rules of Civil Procedure, r. 13.02). G.D. Watson & C. Perkins, eds., *Holmested & Watson: Ontario Civil Procedure* (Toronto: Carswell, 1984) at 13-2.

FRIVOLOUS. *adj.* ". . . '[L]acking in substance' . . ." *Halliday v. Gouge* (1919), 14 Alta. L.R. 296 at 303, [1919] 1 W.W.R. 359 (C.A.), Walsh J.A.

FRIVOLOUS OR VEXATIOUS ACTION. See VEXATIOUS ACTION.

FROM. *conj.* Depending on the context, may include or exclude the date referred to in a phrase beginning with this word. *Independent Order of Foresters, Lethbridge Local 2 v. Afaganis*, [1949] 1 W.W.R. 314 at 319, [1949] 2 D.L.R. 209 (Alta. Dist. Ct.), Sissons J.

FRONTAGE. *n.* When used in reference to a lot abutting directly on a work, means that side or limit of the lot that abuts directly on the work.

FROZEN. *adj.* Refers to a trust in which the trustee is required only to hold the original assets and return them to the settlor when the trust ends. D.M.W. Waters, *The Law of Trusts in Canada*, 2d ed. (Toronto: Carswell, 1984) at 438.

FROZEN TRUST. A trust for an office holder in which the trustee retains original assets and simply transfers them back to the settlor when the trust ends. D.M.W. Waters, *The Law of Trusts in Canada*, 2d ed. (Toronto: Carswell, 1984) at 438.

FRUSTRATION. *n.* ". . . [O]f a contract takes place when there supervenes an event (without default of either party and for which the contract makes no sufficient provision) which so significantly changes the nature (not merely the expense or onerousness) of the outstanding contractual rights and/or obligations from what the parties could reasonably have contemplated at the time of its execution that it would be unjust to hold them to the literal sense of its stipulations in the new circumstances; in such case the law declares both parties to be discharged from further performance."

National Carriers Ltd. v. Panalpina (Northern) Ltd., [1981] A.C. 675 at 700 (U.K. H.L.), Lord Simon.

F.T.R. *abbr.* Federal Trial Reports.

FUGITIVE. *n.* 1. A person accused of having committed an offence to which this Act applies in any part of Her Majesty's Realms and Territories, except Canada, and who has left that part. *Fugitive Offenders Act*, R.S.C. 1985, c. F-32, s. 2. 2. A person being or suspected of being in Canada, who is accused or convicted of an extradition crime committed within the jurisdiction of a foreign state. *Extradition Act*, R.S.C. 1985, c. E-23, s. 2.

FULL AGE. Age of majority.

FULL ANSWER AND DEFENCE. "[In the Charter] . . . entitle[s] the accused to put forward all defences, regardless of whether they are based on a technicality or not. Indeed, the adjective 'full' permits no other conclusion. The right to make a full answer and defence cannot be diminished to the right to make non-technical answer and defence." *R. v. Garofoli* (1990), 60 C.C.C. (3d) 161 at 210, 80 C.R. (3d) 317, 116 N.R. 241, 43 O.A.C. 1, [1990] 2 S.C.R. 1421, 50 C.R.R. 206, 36 Q.A.C. 161, McLachlin J. (dissenting) (L'Heureux-Dubé J. concurring).

FULL COMMUNITY. All immovables and movables acquired during marriage over which the husband has wide powers of administration. J.G. McLeod, *The Conflict of Laws* (Calgary: Carswell, 1983) at 371.

FULL COSTS. Party-and-party costs. *Williams v. Crow* (1884), 10 O.A.R. 301 at 306 (C.A.), Hagarty C.J.O.

FULL COURT. A court with all judges present.

FUNCTION. *n.* 1. An object, power or duty or group of them. 2. ". . . [T]he act of performing and is defined as the kind of action belonging to the holder of an office, hence the function is the performance of the duties of that office. By the performance of the duties of an office the holder thereof can be said to fulfil his function. Functions are therefore the powers and duties of an office." *Mudarth v. Canada (Minister of Public Works)* (1988), 27 C.C.E.L. 310 at 314-15, 22 F.T.R. 312, [1989] 3 F.C. 371 (T.D.), Addy J.

FUNCTUS OFFICIO. [L. having discharged one's duty] 1. ". . . [B]ased . . . on the policy ground which favours finality of proceedings rather than the rule which was developed with respect to formal judgments of a Court whose decision was subject to a full appeal. . . . its application must be more flexible and less formalistic in respect to the decisions of administrative tribunals which are subject to appeal only on a point of law. Justice may require the reopening of administrative proceedings in order to provide relief which would otherwise be available on appeal." *Chandler v. Assn. of Architects (Alberta)* (1989), 36 C.L.R. 1 at 14, [1989] 6 W.W.R. 521, [1989] 2 S.C.R. 848, 70 Alta. L.R. (2d) 193, 40 Admin. L.R. 128, 62 D.L.R. (4th) 577, 99 N.R. 277, 101 A.R. 321, Sopinka J. (Dickson C.J.C. and Wilson J. concurring). 2. ". . . [A]n adjudicator, be it an arbitrator, an administrative tribunal or a court, once it has reached its decision cannot afterwards alter its award except to correct clerical mistakes or errors arising from an accidental slip or omission . . ." *Chandler v. Assn. of Architects (Alberta),* [1989] 2 S.C.R. 848 at 867, 70 Alta. L.R. (2d) 193, 40 Admin. L.R. 128, 36 C.L.R. 1, 62 D.L.R. (4th) 577, 99 N.R. 277, 101 A.R. 321, [1989] 6 W.W.R. 521, L'Heureux-Dubé J. (dissenting) (La Forest J. concurring). 3. ". . . [A] trial judge sitting without a jury is not functus officio until he has finally disposed of the case. Where the accused is acquitted the trial judge will have exhausted his jurisdiction when the accused is discharged and the trial judge cannot then reopen the case. Following a finding of guilt, however, the judge's duties are not spent until after a sentence is imposed. . . . The state of the case-law until now is as follows. [In a case heard by judge and jury, even] after discharge, a jury can be reconvened to correct an improper or incom-

plete transmission or registration of a verdict, but cannot reconsider a verdict or complete its deliberations with a view to handing down additional verdicts on counts or on included offences it has not finally determined prior to that discharge; nor can anyone go behind the verdict or make inquiries as regards the nature of the deliberations." *R. v. Head* (1986), 30 C.C.C. (3d) 481 at 491, 495, [1987] 1 W.W.R. 673, 70 N.R. 364, [1986] 2 S.C.R. 684, 55 C.R. (3d) 1, 53 Sask. R. 1, 35 D.L.R. (4th) 231, Lamer J.

FUND. *n.* 1, A sum of money available to pay or discharge liabilities. 2. Capital, as opposed to income or interest. See ASSURANCE ~; BLENDED ~; CONSOLIDATED ~; LIEN ~; MUTUAL ~; NO-LOAD ~; SINKING ~; TRUST ~.

FUNDAMENTAL BREACH. "[Occurs] . . . where the event resulting from the failure by one party to perform a primary obligation has the effect of depriving the other party of substantially the whole benefit which it was the intention of the parties that he should obtain from the contract." *Syncrude Canada Ltd. v. Hunter Engineering Co.* (1989), 57 D.L.R. (4th) 321 at 369, [1989] 1 S.C.R. 426, [1989] 3 W.W.R. 385, 35 B.C.L.R. (2d) 145, 92 N.R. 1, Wilson J.

FUNDAMENTAL FREEDOM. ". . . [T]he freedom of the individual to take action to do something, to manifest and express himself, to make what he wants of his own individual skills, talents and abilities, to seek self-realization." *Reference re Public Service Employee Relations Act (Alberta)* (1985), 85 C.L.L.C. 14,027 at 12,163, 35 Alta. L.R. (2d) 124, [1985] 2 W.W.R. 289, 16 D.L.R. (4th) 359, 57 A.R. 268 (C.A.), Belzil J.A.

FUNDAMENTAL JUSTICE. 1. Not synonymous with natural justice. *Reference re s. 94(2) of the Motor Vehicle Act (British Columbia)* (1985), 23 C.C.C. (3d) 289 at 301-3, 310, [1985] 2 S.C.R. 486, 36 M.V.R. 240, 69 B.C.L.R. 145, 48 C.R. (3d) 289, 63 N.R. 266, 24 D.L.R. (4th) 536, 18

C.R.R. 30, [1986] 1 W.W.R. 481, Lamer J. (Dickson C.J.C., Beetz, Chouinard and Le Dain JJ. concurring). 2. "... [N]ot a right, but a qualifier of the right not to be deprived of life, liberty and security of the person; its function is to set the parameters of that right. Sections 8 to 14 [of the Charter] address specific deprivations of the 'right' to life, liberty and security of the person in breach of the principles of fundamental justice, and as such, violations of s. 7. They are therefore illustrative of the meaning, in criminal or penal law, of 'principles of fundamental justice'; they represent principles which have been recognized by the common law, the international conventions and by the very fact of entrenchment in the Charter, as essential elements of a system for the administration of justice which is founded upon a belief in the dignity and worth of the human person and the rule of law. Consequently, the principles of fundamental justice are to be found in the basic tenets and principles, not only of our judicial process, but also of the other components of our legal system.... those words cannot be given any exhaustive content or simple enumerative definition, but will take on concrete meaning as the courts address alleged violations of s. 7." *Reference re s. 94(2) of the Motor Vehicle Act (British Columbia)* (1985), 23 C.C.C. (3d) 289 at 301-3, 310, [1985] 2 S.C.R. 486, 36 M.V.R. 240, 69 B.C.L.R. 145, 48 C.R. (3d) 289, 63 N.R. 266, 24 D.L.R. (4th) 536, 18 C.R.R. 30, [1986] 1 W.W.R. 481, Lamer J. (Dickson C.J.C., Beetz, Chouinard and Le Dain JJ. concurring). See PRINCIPLES OF ~.

FUNDAMENTAL TERM. 1. Something which must be performed, regardless of any clause in the contract which relieves a party from performing other terms or from being liable for breaching those terms. G.H.L. Fridman, *Sale of Goods in Canada*, 3d ed. (Toronto: Carswell, 1986) at 284-285. 2. "...

'[S]omething which underlies the whole contract so that, if it is not complied with, the performance becomes something totally different from that which the contract contemplates' ..." *Murray v. Sperry Rand Corp.* (1979), 5 B.L.R. 284 at 295, 23 O.R. (2d) 456, 96 D.L.R. (3d) 113 (H.C.), Reid J.

FUNERAL EXPENSES. Expenses permitted before all other debts and charges against an estate.

FURTHER ASSURANCE. See COVENANT FOR ~.

FUTURE CONSIDERATION. A promise to something later.

FUTURE ESTATE. An expectancy; a reversion; a remainder.

FUTURE GOODS. Goods to be manufactured or acquired by the seller, after the making of the contract of sale. *Sale of Goods acts*.

FUTURE INTEREST. An interest, in existing property, which will come into existence in the future upon the happening of some event. See EXPECTANCY; EXPECTANT ESTATE; FUTURE ESTATE; REMAINDER; REVERSION.

FUTURE RIGHT. "... [I]s inchoate in that while it does not now exist, it may arise in the future...." *Elias v. Hutchison* (1981), 14 Alta. L.R. (2d) 268 at 275, 37 C.B.R. (N.S.) 149, 27 A.R. 1, 121 D.L.R. (3d) 95 (C.A.), the court per McGillivray C.J.A.

FUTURES. *n.* "... [S]peculative transactions, in which there is a nominal contract of sale for future delivery, but where in fact none is ever intended or executed.... a mere speculative contract, in which the parties speculate in the rise or fall of prices, and imply a contract in relation to the prices of the article, and not the article itself." *Betcherman v. E.A. Pierce & Co.*, [1933] 3 D.L.R. 99 at 111, [1933] O.R. 505 (C.A.), the court per Latchford C.J. See COMMODITY ~ CONTRACT.

G

GAAP. *abbr.* Generally accepted accounting principles.

GAAR. *abbr.* General anti-avoidance rule.

GAAS. *abbr.* Generally accepted auditing standards.

GAIN. *n.* ". . . [A] benefit, profit, or advantage, . . ." *R. v. James* (1903), 6 O.L.R. 35 at 38, 7 C.C.C. 196 (C.A.), Osler J.A. See CAPITAL ~.

GALLERY. *n.* Of the parliamentary chamber, consists of a press gallery, visitors galleries called the public gallery, galleries for the diplomatic corps and departmental officials and private galleries. A. Fraser, W.A. Dawson & J. Holtby, eds., *Beauchesne's Rules and Forms of the House of Commons of Canada*, 6th ed. (Toronto: Carswell, 1989) at 37.

GAMBLE. *v.* ". . . [A]nother form of the word 'game', . . ." *R. v. Shaw* (1891), 7 Man. R. 518 at 530 (C.A.), Bain J.A.

GAMBLING. See GAMING.

GAME. *n.* 1. A game of chance or mixed chance and skill. *Criminal Code*, R.S.C. 1985, c. C-46, s. 197. 2. Fur bearing animals, game animals and game birds, and also includes all species of animals and birds that are wild by nature. See CONFIDENCE ~.

GAME OF CHANCE. ". . . [W]ithin the definition of the criminal law, is one in which hazard entirely predominates; . . ." *R. v. Fortier* (1903), 13 Que. K.B. 308 at 313, 7

C.C.C. 417, the court per Wurtele J.

GAMING. *n.* ". . . [I]nvolves wagering or betting. . . . takes place where there is the chance not only of winning but of losing; in other words where some stake has been hazarded." *R. v. Di Pietro* (1986), 14 O.A.C. 387 at 398-9, [1986] 1 S.C.R. 250, 50 C.R. (3d) 266, 25 C.C.C. (3d) 100, 26 D.L.R. (4th) 412, 65 N.R. 245, the court per Lamer J. quoting from *Ellesmere (Earl) v. Wallace*, [1929] 2 Ch. 1 at 28 (U.K. C.A.) and *McCollom v. Wrightson*, [1968] A.C. 522 at 528 (U.K. H.L.).

GAMING HOUSE. See COMMON ~.

GAOL. *n.* 1. Prison; place to confine offenders. 2. A provincial institution where lesser offences are punished.

GARAGEMAN. *n.* A person who keeps a place of business for the housing, storage or repair of a motor vehicle and who receives compensation for such housing, storage or repair.

GARNISH. *v.* 1. To attach a debt. 2. To warn.

GARNISHEE. *n.* The person who owes a judgment debtor money and against whom the court issues garnishment process.

GARNISHEE ORDER. ". . . [G]ives to the garnishor certain statutory rights enabling him to prevent the garnishee paying money to the original creditor and also to give a valid discharge of that original creditor's claim. It does not confer any right by way of equitable assignment or otherwise in the original debt." *MacKay & Hughes (1973) Ltd. v. Martin Potatoes Inc.* (1984), 4 P.P.S.A.C. 107 at 113, 46 O.R. (2d) 304, 51 C.B.R. (N.S.) 1, 4 O.A.C. 1, 9 D.L.R. (4th) 439 (C.A.), the court per Blair J.A.

GARNISHMENT. *n.* A way to enforce a judgment by which money owed by the garnishee to the judgment debtor is attached to pay off the judgment debtor's debt to a judgment creditor.

GAZETTE. *n.* 1. A government's official newspaper. 2. Journal published by the Law Society of Upper Canada. See OFFICIAL ~.

GEN. *abbr.* General.

GENERAL ADVANTAGE OF CANADA. See WORKS FOR THE ~.

GENERAL AGENT. 1. One who has authority to do something on behalf of a principal, or to act for a principal in any matter or in every matter regarding a particular business or trade or of a certain nature. G.H.L. Fridman, *The Law of Agency*, 6th ed. (London: Butterworths, 1990) at 33. 2. A person acting under authority from an insurer to supervise and appoint agents, inspect risks and otherwise transact business for, or as a representative of, such insurer. *The Saskatchewan Insurance Act*, R.S.S. 1978, c. S-26, s. 2.

GENERAL CONTRACTOR. A contractor whose principal activity consists of organizing or coordinating construction work entrusted to persons under his orders or to contractors to execute. *Building Contractors Vocational Qualifications Act*, R.S.Q. 1977, c. Q-1, s. 53.

GENERAL DAMAGES. 1. "... [T]hose which, upon the breach of a legal duty, the law itself presumes to arise, and they can be shown by general evidence of matters which are accepted as affected by such a breach. . . ." *Rowlett v. Karas*, [1944] S.C.R. 1 at 10, [1944] 1 D.L.R. 241, Rand J. (Duff C.J. concurring). 2. ". . . [S]uch as the law will presume to be the direct, natural, or probable consequence of the

act complained of; . . ." *Graham v. Saville*, [1945] 2 D.L.R. 489 at 492, [1945] O.R. 301 (C.A.), Laidlaw J.A. (dissenting in part).

GENERAL ELECTION. 1. An election in respect of which election writs are issued for all electoral districts. 2. An election that is held in respect of each constituency on the same day.

GENERALIA SPECIALIBUS NON DEROGANT. [L.] 1. The general does not detract from the specific. 2. ". . . [W]here there are general words in a later Act capable of reasonable and sensible application without extending them to subjects specially dealt with by earlier legislation, you are not to hold that earlier and special legislation indirectly repealed, altered or derogated from merely by force of such general words, without any indication of a particular intention to do so." *Seward v. The Vera Cruz* (1884), 10 App. Cas. 59 at 68 (U.K. H.L.), Lord Selborne.

GENERALIBUS SPECIALIA DEROGANT. [L.] The special derogates from the general.

GENERAL INTENT. ". . . [O]ne in which the only intent involved relates solely to the performance of the act in question with no further ulterior intent or purpose . . ." *R. v. Bernard*, [1988] 2 S.C.R. 833 at 863, 67 C.R. (3d) 113, 90 N.R. 321, 45 C.C.C. (3d) 1, 32 O.A.C. 161, 38 C.R.R. 82, McIntyre J.

GENERAL JURISDICTION. Unrestricted and unlimited authority in any matter of substantive law, criminal or civil. S.A. Cohen, *Due Process of Law* (Toronto: Carswell, 1977) at 344.

GENERAL LEGACY. Describes a legacy which does not bequeath a specified item. P.V. Baker & P. St. J. Langan, eds., *Snells' Equity*, 29th ed. (London: Sweet and Maxwell, 1990) at 360.

GENERAL LIEN. A lien on personal property for an account due or general debt to the one who claims it, which operates as a form of floating charge on any of the debtor's personal property in the lien claimant's hands. D.N. Macklem & D.I. Bristow, *Construction and*

GENERALLY ACCEPTED ACCOUNTING PRINCIPLES

Mechanics' Liens in Canada, 5th ed. (Toronto: Carswell, 1985) at 579.

GENERALLY ACCEPTED ACCOUNTING PRINCIPLES. Conventions, rules and procedures that set out accepted accounting practice, usually the principles established by the Canadian Institute of Chartered Accountants.

GENERALLY ACCEPTED AUDITING STANDARDS. Standards concerning an auditor's conduct in carrying out examinations.

GENERAL MEETING. Any annual, regular, special or class meeting of the members.

GENERAL PARTNER. Person associated with one or more other persons in an enterprise and assuming personal liability. See LIMITED PARTNERSHIP.

GENERAL POWER. 1. Includes any power or authority enabling the donee or other holder thereof either alone or jointly with or, with the consent, of any other person to appoint, appropriate or dispose of property as she or he sees fit, whether exercisable by instrument inter vivos or by will, or both, but does not include (i) any power exercisable in a fiduciary capacity under a disposition not made by the donee except to the extent that having regard to the fiduciary restrictions imposed upon the donee under the disposition it is reasonable to regard the donee or holder of the power as capable of conferring the property or any part thereof upon herself or himself for her or his own benefit, or (ii) any power exercisable as a mortgagee, or (iii) any power exercisable jointly with, or with the consent of, any other person (A) who has a substantial interest in the property to which the power relates, and (B) whose interest in that property would be adversely affected by the exercise of the power in favour of the donee or holder. 2. The power of a donee to appoint property to anyone, including her or himself. D.M.W. Waters, *The Law of Trusts in Canada*, 2d ed. (Toronto: Carswell, 1984) at 72.

GENERAL VERDICT. A jury's decision for either the defendant or the plaintiff generally.

GENERAL WORDS. In a conveyance, mortgage or assurance of corporeal hereditament, words which describe every kind of appurtenance, easement or privilege, portions of the soil, fixtures or produce of the land and were added to the parcel or description of the property.

GENERIC. *adj.* 1. Relating to a group or class. 2. Chemical name of a drug.

GENEVA CONVENTIONS. Agreements to ameliorate the condition of wounded and sick members of the armed forces in the field, to ameliorate the condition of sick, wounded and ship-wrecked members of the armed forces at sea, to treat prisoners of war and civilian persons in time of war in particular ways.

GENOCIDE. *n.* Any of the following acts committed with intent to destroy in whole or in part any identifiable group, namely, (a) killing members of the group, or (b) deliberately inflicting on the group conditions of life calculated to bring about its physical destruction. *Criminal Code*, R.S.C. 1985, c. C-46, s. 318(2).

GIFT. *n.* 1. ". . . [T]o constitute a 'gift', it must appear that the property transferred was transferred voluntarily and not as the result of a contractual obligation to transfer it and that no advantage of a material character was received by the transferor by way of return." *Commissioner of Taxation of the Commonwealth v. McPhail* (1967), 41 A.L.J.R. 346 at 348, Owen J., cited with approval in *R. v. McBurney*, [1985] 2 C.T.C. 214 at 218, 85 D.T.C. 5433, 20 E.T.R. 283, 62 N.R. 104 (Fed. C.A.), Heald, Urie and Stone JJ.A. 2. ". . . [C]onstituted by two things – the words giving (not merely expressing a promise or intention) and possession in the donee. . . ." *Standard Trust Co. v. Hill* (1922), 68 D.L.R. 722 at 723, [1922] 2 W.W.R. 1003, 18 Alta. L.R. 137 (C.A.), Beck J.A. (Stuart and Hyndman JJ.A. concurring). See CLASS ~; DEED OF ~; INTER

VIVOS ~.

GIFT INTER VIVOS. A gift made by a living person to another living person.

GIFT MORTIS CAUSA. "... [A] gift conditioned upon the death of the donor...." *McIntyre v. Royal Trust Co.*, [1945] 3 D.L.R. 71 at 75, [1945] 2 W.W.R. 364, 53 Man. R. 353 (K.B.), Dysart J. See DONATIO MORTIS CAUSA.

GIFT OVER. A provision in a will which enables an interest in property to come into existence when a prior interest terminates or fails.

GIFT TAX. Tax imposed on the transfer of property by gift.

GIVE. *v.* To transfer property without compensation.

GIVEN NAME. "... [A] name given at birth to distinguish it from the surname, family or ancestral name." *Wilson, Re* (1984), 51 C.B.R.(N.S.) 85 at 87, 46 O.R. (2d) 28, 8 D.L.R. (4th) 271, 4 P.P.S.A.C. 69, 26 B.L.R. 271 (S.C.), Saunders J.

GLOSS. *n.* Interpretation consisting of an annotation, explanation or comment on any passage in a text. See SPECULAR ~.

GOD. See ACT OF ~ CLAUSE.

GODSON. *abbr.* Godson, Mining Commissioner's Cases (Ont.), 1911-1917.

GOLDEN RULE. When construing a statute, the ordinary meaning of the words and the ordinary rules of grammatical construction should be used unless that produces a result contrary to the intent of the legislators or leading to obvious repugnance or absurdity. P.St.J. Langan, ed., *Maxwell on The Interpretation of Statutes*, 12th ed. (Bombay: N.M. Tripathi, 1976) at 43.

GOOD. *adj.* When describing pleading, sound or valid.

GOOD CAUSE. 1. "... [F]air and just ..." *Vernon (City) v. British Columbia Public Utilities Commission* (1953), 9 W.W.R. (N.S.) 384 at 384 (B.C. C.A.), the court per O'Halloran

J.A. 2. "[In s. 73 of the County Courts Act, R.S.B.C. 1924, c. 53] ... means something that would bring the case out of the ordinary, ..." *Goldie v. Colquhoun* (1930), 42 B.C.R. 356 at 357, [1930] 1 W.W.R. 624, [1930] 2 D.L.R. 1002 (C.A.), Martin J.A. 3. "[In Saskatchewan King's Bench Rule of Court 672(3)] ... includes not only misconduct or oppression on the part of the successful party, but anything, which would make it just and reasonable, that there should be a departure from the rule that costs should follow the event. Forster v. Farquhar, [1893] 1 Q.B. 564 [(U.K.)] ..." *Dominion Fire Insurance Co. v. Thomson* (1923), 17 Sask. L.R. 527 at 531, [1923] 3 W.W.R. 1265, [1923] 4 D.L.R. 903 (C.A.), Lamont J.A. (Haultain C.J.S. and McKay J.A. concurring).

GOOD CONSIDERATION. 1. "... '[V]aluable [consideration]' ..." *China Software Corp. v. Leimbigler* (1990), 49 B.L.R. 173 at 177 (B.C. S.C.), Drake J. 2. "... [T]here must be a real and honest bargain, and not one which is so made that it is manifest that the form which it took was in reality a sham, or was intended to be and was a fraud. There may be overvaluation and yet an honest bargain. The test is honesty, and if that is present the Court will not inquire into the adequacy or inadequacy of the consideration...." *Hood v. Caldwell* (1921), 64 D.L.R. 442 at 456, 20 O.W.N. 251, 50 O.L.R. 397 (C.A.), Hodgins J.A.

GOOD FAITH. 1. "... [A] bona fide belief in the existence of a state of facts which, had they existed, would have justified him in acting as he did.... The contrast is with an act of such a nature that it is wholly wide of any statutory or public duty, i.e., wholly unauthorized and where there exists no colour for supposing that it could have been an authorized one. In such case there can be no question of good faith or honest motive." *Chaput v. Romain* (1955), 1 D.L.R. (2d) 241 at 261, [1955] S.C.R. 834, 114 C.C.C. 170, Kellock J. (Rand J. concurring). 2. "... In the context of s. 8 of the Charter, good faith has come to mean that state of mind which relies upon express statutory authority to support the lawfulness of a search...." *R. v. Klimchuk* (1991), 67 C.C.C. (3d) 385 at 419, 8 C.R. (4th) 327, 32 M.V.R. (2d) 202, 4 B.C.A.C. 26, 9 W.A.C. 26, 9 C.R.R. (2d) 153 (C.A.), Wood J.A.

GOODS. *n.* 1. Chattels personal other than things in action or money, and includes emblements, industrial growing crops and things attached to or forming part of the land that are agreed to be severed before sale or under the contract of sale. 2. Anything that is the subject of trade or commerce. *Criminal Code*, R.S.C. 1985, c. C-46, s. 379. 3. Any article that is or may be the subject of trade or commerce, but does not include land or any interest therein. *Bills of Exchange Act*, R.S.C. 1985, c. B-4, s. 188. 4. "[In the Customs Act, R.S.C. 1970, c. C-40] ... must ... be taken to include all movable effects of any kind.... In the Customs Tariff ... the word 'goods' is given a general meaning to include all personal effects, and not merely to include strictly items of commerce...." *Ladakis v. R.* (1985), 10 C.E.R. 95 at 102 (Fed. T.D.), Collier J. See ASCERTAINED ~; BONDED ~; CONSUMER ~; FUTURE ~; SALE OF ~; SLANDER OF ~; SPECIFIC ~; TRESPASS TO ~; UNASCERTAINED ~.

GOOD SAMARITAN LAW. A statute which protects those who render assistance in emergencies from liability where their assistance increases the injury to the one they seek to rescue or assist.

GOOD TITLE. Title which an unwilling purchaser can be forced to take. It is free from pending legislation or other potentially harmful defects. It will provide peaceful possession of the property. V. DiCastri, *Law of Vendor and Purchaser* (Toronto: Carswell, 1988) at 339.

GOODWILL. *n.* "... [T]he benefit and advantage of the good name, reputation and connection of a business. It is the attractive force which brings in custom." *Inland Revenue Commissioners v. Muller & Co.'s Margarine Ltd.*, [1901] A.C. 217 at 223-4, Lord Macnaghten.

GOVERNMENT. *n.* 1. "... [I]n its generic sense – meaning the whole of the governmental apparatus of the state ..." *Dolphin Delivery Ltd. v. R.W.D.S.U., Local 580* (1986), [1987] 1 W.W.R. 577 at 597, 38 C.C.L.T. 184, 71 N.R. 83, [1986] 2 S.C.R. 573, 9 B.C.L.R. (2d) 273, 87 C.L.L.C. 14,002, 33 D.L.R. (4th) 174, 25 C.R.R. 321, [1987] D.L.Q. 69, McIntyre J. (Dickson C.J.C., Estey, Chouinard and Le Dain JJ. concurring). 2. "... [T]he executive or administrative branch of a government. This is the sense in which one generally speaks of the Government of Canada or of a province...." *Dolphin Delivery Ltd. v. R.W.D.S.U., Local 580* (1986), [1987] 1 W.W.R. 577 at 597, 38 C.C.L.T. 184, 71 N.R. 83, [1986] 2 S.C.R. 573, 9 B.C.L.R. (2d) 273, 87 C.L.L.C. 14,002, 33 D.L.R. (4th) 174, 25 C.R.R. 321, [1987] D.L.Q. 69, McIntyre J. (Dickson C.J.C., Estey, Chouinard and Le Dain JJ. concurring). See CABINET ~; EXECUTIVE ~; FEDERAL ~; LOCAL ~; MUNICIPAL ~; PARLIAMENTARY ~.

GOVERNMENT BILL. A bill approved by cabinet and introduced into a legislature by a minister. P.W. Hogg, *Constitutional Law of Canada*, 3d ed. (Toronto: Carswell, 1992) at 244.

GOVERNMENT HOUSE LEADER. The member of the government, responsible to the Prime Minister, who arranges government business in the House of Commons. A. Fraser, W.A. Dawson & J. Holtby, eds., *Beauchesne's Rules and Forms of the House of Commons of Canada*, 6th ed. (Toronto: Carswell, 1989) at 56.

GOVERNOR GENERAL. *var.* **GOVERNOR-GENERAL.** The Governor General of Canada or other chief executive officer or administrator carrying on the government of Canada on behalf and in the name of the Sovereign, by whatever title that person is designated.

GOVERNOR GENERAL IN COUNCIL. *var.* **GOVERNOR-GENERAL IN COUNCIL.** The Governor General or person administrating the government of Canada, acting by and with the advice or, or by and with the advice and consent of, or in conjunction with the Queen's Privy Council for Canada.

GOVERNOR IN COUNCIL. 1. The Governor General of Canada acting by and with the advice of, or by and with the advice and consent of, or in conjunction with the Queen's Privy Council for Canada. 2. The Lieutenant Governor acting by and with the advice of the Executive Council of the Province. *Interpretation Act*, R.S.N.S. 1967, c. 151, s. 6. See LIEUTENANT ~.

GOVERNOR OF CANADA. The Governor General of Canada or other chief executive officer or administrator carrying on the Government of Canada on behalf of and in the name of the Sovereign, by whatever title that officer is designated. *Interpretation Act*, R.S.C. 1985, c. I-21, s. 35.

GOVT. *abbr.* Government.

GR. *abbr.* Upper Canada Chancery (Grant), 1849-1922.

GRACE. *n.* Dispensation; licence. See DAYS OF ~.

GRACE PERIOD. See DAYS OF GRACE.

GRANDFATHER CLAUSE. A provision allowing a period of time to comply with requirements of a statute or other requirements or permitting persons or situations to continue under new legislation although not technically qualified.

GRAND JURY. An inquisition which sits, receives indictments and hears evidence from the prosecution; any finding is only an accusation, to be tried afterwards. Compare PETIT JURY.

GRANT. *n.* 1. ". . . [T]he strongest and widest word of gift and conveyance known to the law. . . ." *Toronto (City) Board of Education v. Doughty* (1934), [1935] 1 D.L.R. 290

at 294, [1935] O.R. 85 (H.C.), Middleton J.A. 2. Any grant of Crown land, whether by letters patent under the Great Seal, a notification or any other instrument whether in fee or for years, and whether direct from Her Majesty or by or pursuant to any statute. 3. A right created or transferred by the Crown, for example the grant of a charter, franchise, patent or pension. 4. Public money devoted to a special purpose. 5. (i) A grant of probate, (ii) a resealed grant of probate or administration, (iii) a grant of administration, or (iv) a grant of letters of guardianship of the person or estate, or both, of a minor. See CROWN ~; DEED OF ~; NO ONE CAN BE ALLOWED TO DEROGATE FROM HIS OWN ~; RE-~.

GRANTEE. *n.* 1. A person to whom one makes a grant. 2. The person to whom real property is transferred by deed for value or otherwise. 3. Includes the bargainee, assignee, transferee, mortgagee or other person to whom a bill of sale is made.

GRANT OF ADMINISTRATION. The grant made when the proper court issues administration. See DE BONIS NON ADMINISTRATIS.

GRANT OF ADMINISTRATION WITH WILL ANNEXED. The grant made if the deceased leaves a will naming no executor or if the named executor declines to act. J.G. McLeod, *The Conflict of Laws* (Calgary: Carswell, 1983) at 400.

GRANT OF PROBATE. The grant made when the proper court issues probate.

GRANTOR. *n.* 1. A person who makes a grant. 2. Includes the bargainor, assignor, transferor, mortgagor, or other person by whom a bill of sale is made. *Bills of Sale acts*. See CREDIT ~.

GRATIS. *adj.* [L.] Without reward or recompense.

GRATIS DICTUM. [L.] A mere assertion; a voluntary statement.

GRATUITOUS. *adj.* Without reward

or recompense.

GRATUITOUS BAILMENT. Bailee takes charge of bailor's property without remuneration. *Sigstad v. Kirmac Collision Repairs Ltd.* (1989), 1 C.C.L.T. (2d) 295 at 307 (B.C. Co. Ct.), Perry Co. Ct. J.

GRATUITOUS PROMISE. 1. Promise made without consideration. 2. A promise to confer a benefit as a gift. G.H.L. Fridman, *The Law of Contract in Canada*, 2d ed. (Toronto: Carswell, 1986) at 73.

GRATUITY. *n.* A tip. *Canada (Attorney General) v. Canadian Pacific Ltd.* (1986), 86 C.L.L.C. 14,032 at 12,158, [1986] 1 S.C.R. 678, 11 C.C.E.L. 1, 66 N.R. 321, 27 D.L.R. (4th) 1, La Forest J. (Dickson C.J.C., Lamer and Le Dain JJ. concurring). 2. A reward for services rendered. *C. v. Minister of National Revenue* (1950), 2 Tax A.B.C. 6 at 10 (Can. App. Bd.), Graham (Chair) (Monet K.C. concurring).

GRAVAMEN. *n.* The essence of the complaint or grievance.

GREEN PAPER. A paper setting out matters of concern to the government for discussion purposes. Compare WHITE PAPER.

GRIEVANCE. *n.* Includes any disagreement between the parties to a collective bargaining agreement with respect to the meaning or application of a collective agreement or any violation of a collective bargaining agreement.

GRIEVANCE ARBITRATION. An adjudicative process by which disputes over the application or operation of a collective agreement are resolved. D.J.M. Brown & D.M. Beatty, *Canadian Labour Arbitration*, 3d ed. (Aurora: Canada Law Book, 1988) at 11.

GRIEVANCE SETTLEMENT PROVISION. A provision for final settlement without stoppage of work, by arbitration or otherwise, of all differences between the parties to or persons bound by a collective agreement or on whose behalf it was entered into, concerning its meaning or violation.

Canada Labour Code Act, R.S.C. 1970, c. L-1, s. 25.

GRIEVOR. *n.* A person who has a grievance. *Public Service Act*, R.R.O. 1980, Reg. 881, s. 36.

GRIEVOUS BODILY HARM. The injury need not be "either permanent or dangerous, if it be such as seriously to interfere with the comfort or health, it is sufficient . . ." *R. v. Ashman* (1858), 175 E.R. 638, Willes J., cited with approval in *R. v. Martineau* (1990), 79 C.R. (3d) 129 at 151, [1990] 6 W.W.R. 97, 58 C.C.C. (3d) 353, 112 N.R. 83, 76 Alta. L.R. (2d) 1, [1990] 2 S.C.R. 633, 109 A.R. 321, 50 C.P.R. 110, L'Heureux-Dubé J. (dissenting).

GROSS. *n.* See IN ~.

GROSS. *adj.* Entire; absolute.

GROSS NEGLIGENCE. 1. "[Implies] . . . conduct in which, if there is not conscious wrong doing, there is a very marked departure from the standards by which responsible and competent people in charge of motor cars habitually govern themselves. . . ." *McCulloch v. Murray*, [1942] 2 D.L.R. 179 at 180, [1942] S.C.R. 141, Duff C.J.C. 2. "[In the Municipal Act, R.S.O. 1914, s. 192] . . . The circumstances giving rise to the duty to remove a dangerous condition, including notice, actual or imputable, of its existence, and the extent of the risk which it creates – the character and the duration of the neglect to fulfil that duty, including the comparative ease or difficulty of discharging it – these elements must vary in infinite degree; and they seem to be important, if not vital, factors in determining whether the fault (if any) attributable to the municipal corporation is so much more than merely ordinary neglect that it should be held to be very great, or gross negligence . . ." *Holland v. Toronto (City)*, [1927] 1 D.L.R. 99 at 102, [1927] S.C.R. 242, 59 O.L.R. 628, the court per Anglin C.J.C. 3. ". . . [A] high or serious degree of negligence." *British Columbia Telephone Co. v. Quality Industries Ltd.* (1984), 49 C.P.C. 224 at 227, 59 B.C.L.R. 68 (C.A.), the court per Esson J.A. 4. Very great negligence. *Kingston (City) v. Drennan* (1897), 27 S.C.R. 46, Sedgewick J.

GROUND LEASE. Lease of bare land or land exclusive of any building on it.

GROUND-RENT. *n.* Rent, usually for many years, generally rent payable for land on which the lessee erects buildings under a building lease.

GROUNDS. *n.* Reasons. See ENUMERATED ~.

G.S.P. *abbr.* General Sessions of the Peace.

GUARANTEE. *n.* 1. ". . . [A] contract between a guarantor and a lender. The subject of the guarantee is a debt owed to the lender by a debtor. In the contract of guarantee, the guarantor agrees to repay the lender if the debtor defaults. The exact nature of the obligation owed by the guarantor to the lender depends on the construction of the contract of guarantee, but the liability of the guarantor is usually made coterminous with that of the principal debtor. . . ." *Communities Economic Development Fund v. Canadian Pickles Corp.* (1991), 8 C.B.R. (3d) 121 at 143, [1992] 1 W.W.R. 193, 85 D.L.R. (4th) 88, 121 N.R. 81, [1991] 3 S.C.R. 388, 76 Man. R. (2d) 1, 10 W.A.C. 1, the court per Iacobucci J. 2. A promise to answer for another's obligation. *Schell v. McCallum & Vannatter* (1918), 42 D.L.R. 563 at 571-2, 57 S.C.R. 15, [1918] 2 W.W.R. 735, Brodeur J. (dissenting).

GUARANTEE COMPANY. An incorporated company empowered to grant guarantees, bonds, policies or contracts for the integrity and fidelity of employed persons, or in respect of any legal proceedings, or for other like purposes.

GUARANTEE OF SIGNATURE. A guarantee signed by or on behalf of a person reasonably believed by the issuer to be responsible.

GUARANTOR. *n.* A surety, a person who is bound by a guarantee.

GUARANTY. *n.* A promise to pay another's debt or to perform another's obligation.

GUARD. *n.* ". . . [I]ndividual must exercise monitoring functions of a quasi-supervisory character with respect to other employees in the bargaining unit . . . they must perform duties . . . which clearly place them in a conflict of interest with those employees. . . ." *Therrian v. S.E.I.U., Local 204*, [1986] O.L.R.B. Rep. 152 at 153, MacDowell (Vice-Chair), Stamp and Ballentine (Members).

GUARDIAN. *n.* 1. Includes any person who has in law or in fact the custody or control of another person. *Criminal Code*, R.S.C. 1985, c. C-46, s. 150. 2. Includes a person who has in law or in fact custody or control of a child. *Criminal Code*, R.S.C. 1985, c. C-46, s. 214. See LITIGATION ~; OFFICIAL ~.

GUARDIAN AD LITEM. A litigation guardian.

GUARDIANSHIP. *n.* ". . . [T]he full bundle of rights and duties voluntarily assumed by an adult regarding an infant akin to those naturally arising from parenthood . . . Guardianship implies the voluntary assumption of a duty to maintain, protect and educate the ward. It includes the power to correct, to grant or withhold consent to marriages and, if the guardian is also the parent, to delegate parental authority. . . . the full bundle of parental personal rights, including necessarily the entitlement to physical possession of the child. . . ." *Anson v. Anson* (1987), 10 B.C.L.R. (2d) 357 at 361-2 (Co. Ct.), Huddart Co. Ct. J.

GUARDIANSHIP ORDER. 1. An order which transfers the guardianship of the child, including the custody, care and control of, and all parental rights and responsibilities with respect to, the child. 2. Any order of a court appointing a person as a guardian.

GUEST. *n.* 1. "To be a guest one must be willingly in the vehicle . . ." *King v. Hommy* (1962), 39 W.W.R. 209 at 213, 34 D.L.R. (2d) 770 (Alta. C.A.), the court per Johnson J.A. 2. A person who contracts for sleeping accommodation in a hotel and includes each member of that person's party.

GUEST STATUTE. A statute which imposes liability in respect of any gratuitous passenger on the driver of a car solely in a case of misconduct or gross negligence which is wanton, wilful or reckless. J.G. Fleming, *The Law of Torts*, 8th ed. (Sydney: Law Book, 1992) at 23.

GUIDE. *n.* "... [O]ne who accompanies another over unfamiliar terrain being ready to point the way, being ready to give advice, ..." *R. v. Kurth* (1990), 72 Alta. L.R. (2d) 300 at 303, 103 A.R. 75 (Q.B.), Veit J. See DOG

~.

GUIDE DOG. A dog that is trained as a guide for a blind person by a recognized school.

GUILT. See FINDING OF ~.

GUILTY. *adj.* 1. Having committed a tort or crime. 2. The word used by a prisoner entering a plea and by a convicting jury. 3. "With respect to an accused who has pleaded guilty, such a plea is ordinarily regarded as an admission that the matters alleged in the information are true." *R. v. Rapien* (1954), 18 C.R. 168 at 170, 11 W.W.R. 529, 108 C.C.C. 198 (Alta. C.A.), the court per MacDonald J.A. See NOT ~.

H

HABEAS CORPUS. [L. that you have the body] "... [T]he writ of habeas corpus is available to any subject detained or imprisoned, not to hear and determine the case upon the evidence, but to immediately and in a summary way test the validity of his detention or imprisonment. It matters not whether the basis for the detention or imprisonment be criminal or civil law ..." *Storgoff, Re (sub nom. R. v. Storgoff)* [1945] 3 D.L.R. 673 at 733, [1945] S.C.R. 526, 84 C.C.C. 1, Estey J.

HABENDUM. *n.* [L. having] 1. The first word of a clause which follows a legal description of land which is being granted. 2. "[Part of a deed which] ... is intended to include the designation of the estate or interest to be conveyed in the property described in the premises of the deed such as a term of years, a term for life, a fee simple or the interest in remainder." *Wheeler v. Wheeler (No. 2)* (1979), 25 N.B.R. (2d) 376 at 378, 51 A.P.R. 376 (C.A.), Limerick, Bugold and Ryan JJ.A.

HABITUAL CRIMINAL. See now DANGEROUS OFFENDER.

HABITUAL RESIDENCE. 1. "... [R]efers to the quality of residence. Duration may be a factor depending on the circumstances. It requires an animus less than that required for domicile; it is a midpoint between domicile and residence ..." *Adderson v. Adderson* (1987), 51 Alta. L.R. (2d) 193 at 198, 7 R.F.L. (3d) 185, 77 A.R. 256, 36 D.L.R. (4th) 361 (C.A.), the court per Laycraft J.A. 2. A regular, lasting physical presence. A. Bissett-Johnson & W.M. Holland, eds., *Matrimonial Property Law in Canada* (Toronto: Carswell, 1980) at A-9.

HAD AND RECEIVED. See MONEY ~.

HAGUE CONVENTIONS. Agreements on rules of international law relating to matters such as the peaceful settlement of international disputes and the conduct of war.

HALF-SECRET TRUST. The deceased's will on its face makes the devisee or legatee a trustee, but does not state the objects of the trust. D.M.W. Waters, *The Law of Trusts in Canada*, 2d ed. (Toronto: Carswell, 1984) at 223.

HALLUCINATION. *n.* An illusory sensory perception. F.A. Jaffe, *A Guide to Pathological Evidence*, 3d ed. (Toronto: Carswell, 1991) at 220.

HALLUCINOGENIC DRUG. A drug producing hallucination such as lysergic acid diethylamide (L.S.D.) or mescaline.

HANDICAP. See BECAUSE OF ~.

HANSARD. *n.* A record of speeches made in the House of Commons and verbatim answers to written questions from the Order Paper. A. Fraser, W.A. Dawson & J. Holtby, eds., *Beauchesne's Rules and Forms of the House of Commons of Canada*, 6th ed. (Toronto: Carswell, 1989) at 300.

HARASS. v. 1. "... '[A]nnoy'." *R. v. Sabine* (1990), 57 C.C.C. (3d) 209 at 212, 78 C.R. (3d) 34, 107 N.B.R. (2d) 73, 267 A.P.R. 73 (Q.B.), Stevenson J. 2. Includes worry, exhaust, fatigue, annoy, plague, pester, tease or torment, but does not include the lawful hunting, trapping or capturing of wildlife. *Wildlife Act*, S.B.C. 1982, c. 57, s. 1. 3. To engage in a course of vexatious comment or conduct that is known or ought reasonably to be known to be unwelcome. *Human Rights Code*, R.S. Nfld. 1990, c. H-14, s. 1.

HARASSMENT. n. Engaging in a course of vexatious comment or conduct that is known or ought reasonably to be known to be unwelcome. *Human Rights Code*, R.S.O. 1990, c. H.19, s. 10(1). See SEXUAL ~.

HARBOUR. v. To give refuge to, to shelter.

HARD CASE. A case in which the court feels compelled to stretch the existing law to accommodate the hardship produced by the actual fact situation on one of the litigants before them. Such decisions are said to make bad law because their logic may be unsupportable in subsequent fact situations where the element of hardship for one of the parties is missing.

HARM. See BODILY ~; IRREPARABLE ~; SERIOUS BODILY ~.

HARR. & HODG. *abbr.* Harrison & Hodgins' Municipal Reports (Ont.), 1845-1851.

HASH. n. "... [A] colloquial term for hashish." *R. v. O'Brien* (1987), 41 C.C.C. (3d) 86 at 88, 10 Q.A.C. 135, the court per McCarthy J.A.

HASHISH. n. A resinous juice found in the upper leaves and the flowering tops of the plant Cannabis sativa. F.A. Jaffe, *A Guide to Pathological Evidence*, 3d ed. (Toronto: Carswell, 1991) at 221.

HATE PROPAGANDA. 1. Any writing, sign or visible representation that advocates or promotes genocide or the communication of which by any person would constitute an offence under section 319. *Criminal Code*, R.S.C. 1985, c. C-46, s. 320(8) as am. 2. "... [E]xpression intended or likely to create extreme feelings of opprobrium and enmity against a racial or religious group, ..." *R. v. Keegstra* (1990), 61 C.C.C. (3d) 1 at 18, 1 C.R. (4th) 129, 77 Alta. L.R. (2d) 193, [1991] 2 W.W.R. 1, 117 N.R. 1, 114 A.R. 81, 3 C.R.R. (2d) 193, [1990] 3 S.C.R. 697, Dickson C.J.C. (Wilson, L'Heureux-Dubé and Gonthier JJ. concurring).

HATRED. n. "[In s. 319(2) of the Criminal Code, R.S.C. 1985, c. C-46] ... connotes emotion of an intense and extreme nature that is clearly associated with vilification and detestation.... a most extreme emotion that belies reason; an emotion, that, if exercised against members of an identifiable group, implies that those individuals are to be despised, scorned, denied respect and made subject to ill-treatment on the basis of group affiliation." *R. v. Keegstra* (1990), 3 C.R.R. (2d) 193 at 249, 1 C.R. (4th) 129, 77 Alta. L.R. (2d) 193, [1991] 2 W.W.R. 1, 61 C.C.C. (3d) 1, 117 N.R. 1, 114 A.R. 81, [1990] 3 S.C.R. 697, Dickson C.J.C. (Wilson, L'Heureux-Dubé and Gonthier JJ. concurring). See COMMERCIAL SPEECH; FREEDOM OF EXPRESSION.

HAVE. v. "... '[P]ossess'." *R. v. Theriault* (1951), 28 M.P.R. 412 at 417, 101 C.C.C. 233 (N.B. C.A.), Harrison J.A. See TO ~ AND TO HOLD.

HAVE NO ISSUE. A want or failure of issue in the lifetime or at the time of death of that person, and not an indefinite failure of issue unless a contrary intention appears by the will. *Wills acts*.

H.C. *abbr.* 1. High Court of Justice. 2. Haute Cour.

HEAD. n. In respect of a government institution, means (a) in the case of a department or ministry of state, the member of the Queen's Privy Council for Canada presiding over that institution, or (b) in any other case, the person designated by order in council to be the head of that institution. Canada statutes. See DEPARTMENT ~; DEPUTY ~.

HEADING. *n.* A text prefixed to a section or group of sections in a modern statute. P.St.J. Langan, ed., *Maxwell on The Interpretation of Statutes*, 12th ed. (Bombay: N.M. Tripathi, 1976) at 11.

HEADNOTE. *n.* The summary of a reported case preceding the full report of the case.

HEAD OFFICE. The principal office or place of business of a corporation.

HEALTH. *n.* ". . . [N]ot merely . . . the absence of disease and infirmity, but . . . a state of physical, mental and social well-being." *R. v. Morgentaler* (1988), 62 C.R. (3d) 1 at 29-30, 82 N.R. 1, [1988] 1 S.C.R. 30, 63 O.R. (2d) 281n, 26 O.A.C. 1, 44 D.L.R. (4th) 385, 31 C.R.R. 1, 37 C.C.C. (3d) 449, Dickson C.J.C. (Lamer J. concurring).

HEALTH L. CAN. *abbr.* Health Law in Canada.

HEARING. *n.* 1. ". . . [N]ormally . . . an oral hearing. But . . . a statutory board, acting in an administrative capacity, may . . . [hear applications] on written evidence and arguments, . . ." *Knight v. Indian Head School Division No. 19* (1990), 43 Admin. L.R. 157 at 189, 30 C.C.E.L. 237, [1990] 3 W.W.R. 289, [1990] 1 S.C.R. 653, 106 N.R. 17, 83 Sask. R. 81, 69 D.L.R. (4th) 489, 90 C.L.L.C. 14,010, L'Heureux-Dubé J. (Dickson C.J.C., La Forest and Cory JJ. concurring) quoting and agreeing with H.W.R. Wade, *Admninistrative Law*, 5th ed. (Oxford: Clarendon Press, 1982) at 482-3. 2. Includes a trial. See COSTS OF THIS ~; DE NOVO ~; FAIR ~; PRELIMINARY ~; PUBLIC ~; RE-~.

HEARING DE NOVO. ". . . [I]s . . . an altogether fresh or new hearing and not limited to an inquiry to determine if the tribunal acted properly and correctly on the evidence and material before it. . . ." *Newterm Ltd., Re* (1988), 38 M.P.L.R. 17 at 19, 70 Nfld. & P.E.I.R. 216, 215 A.P.R. 216 (Nfld. T.D.), Steele J.

HEARING DOG. A dog trained as a guide for a deaf person and having the qualifications prescribed by the regulations. *Blind Persons' Rights Amendment Act, 1983*, S.A. 1983, c. 19, s. 3.

HEARSAY. See RULE AGAINST ~.

HEARSAY EVIDENCE. "Evidence of a statement made to a witness by a person who is not himself called as a witness may or may not be hearsay. It is hearsay and inadmissible when the object is to establish the truth of what is contained in the statement. It is not hearsay and is admissible when it is proposed to establish by the evidence, not the truth of the statement, but the fact it was made. The fact that the statement was made, quite apart from its truth, is frequently relevant in considering the mental state and conduct thereafter of the witness or of some other person in whose presence the statement was made." *Subramaniam v. Public Prosecutor*, [1956] 1 W.L.R. 965 at 970 (Malaya P.C.).

HEIR. *n.* 1. ". . . [T]he party to which by the operation of law alone or by the will of man, the estate, rights and liabilities of the deceased are transmitted." *Levesque v. Turcotte* (1931), 12 C.B.R. 290 at 297, 69 Que. S.C. 148, Lemieux J. 2. Includes a person beneficially entitled to property of an intestate. See EXPECTANT ~; JOINT ~.

HEIR APPARENT. One whose right of inheritance is indisputable provided the ancestor dies first; the eldest son of the sovereign.

HEIRESS. *n.* A female heir.

HEIRLOOM. *n.* Originally personal chattels like evidences of title, deeds and charters which went to an heir along with the inheritance.

HEIR PRESUMPTIVE. A person likely to be heir if the ancestor dies immediately but who could be displaced if a nearer heir is born.

HEIRS. *n.* ". . . [T]he person or persons to whom the land of another person descends by operation of law, when that other person dies intestate."

Sparks v. Wolff (1898), 25 O.A.R. 326 at 334, (C.A.), MacLennan J.A.

HEIRSHIP. *n.* The condition or quality of being an heir; the relation between an heir and an ancestor.

HELD. *adj.* Decided.

HEREDITAMENT. *n.* Any kind of property which may be inherited. *Tomkins v. Jones* (1889), 22 Q.B.D. 599 at 602 (U.K. C.A.), Bowen L.J. See CORPOREAL ~; INCORPOREAL ~; LANDS, TENEMENTS AND ~S.

HER MAJESTY. 1. Her Majesty in right of Canada or of a province. 2. The Sovereign of the United Kingdom, Canada and Her other Realms and Territories, and Head of the Commonwealth.

HEROIN. *n.* Diacetyl morphine, a partly-synthetic narcotic analgesic derived from morphine. F.A. Jaffe, *A Guide to Pathological Evidence*, 3d ed. (Toronto: Carswell, 1991) at 185.

HE WHO COMES INTO EQUITY MUST COME WITH CLEAN HANDS. When a plaintiff seeks the assistance of a a court of equity, that plaintiff must be prepared to act fairly and properly and must be able to show that past behaviour regarding the transaction is beyond reproach. P.V. Baker & P. St. J. Langan, eds., *Snell's Equity*, 29th ed. (London: Sweet & Maxwell, 1990) at 31-2. See CLEAN HANDS DOCTRINE.

HE WHO SEEKS EQUITY MUST DO EQUITY. ". . . In many instances this contains a pun on the word 'equity' and means nothing more than that, 'he who seeks the assistance of a Court of Equity must in the matter in which he so asks assistance do what is just as a term of receiving such assistance.' 'Equity' means 'Chancery' in one instance and 'right' or 'fair dealing' in the other." *Richards v. Collins* (1912), 27 O.L.R. 3909 at 398, 9 D.L.R. 249 (Div. Ct.), Riddell J. (Falconbridge C.J. and Lennox J. concurring).

HIGH SEAS. The area of the ocean beyond territorial waters.

HIGH TREASON. Anyone commits high treason in Canada who kills or attempts to kill Her Majesty, or does her any bodily harm tending to death or destruction, maims or wounds her or imprisons or restrains her; levies war against Canada or does any act preparatory thereto; or assists an enemy at war with Canada, or any armed forces against whom Canadian Forces are engaged in hostilities whether or not a state of war exists between Canada and the country whose forces they are, and a Canadian citizen or person who owes allegiance to Her Majesty in right of Canada commits high treason who does any of these acts while in or out of Canada. *Criminal Code*, R.S.C. 1985, c. C-46, s. 46(1) and (3).

HIGHWAY. *n.* 1. ". . . [A] public road or way open equally to everyone for travel, and includes the public streets of an urban district equally with connecting roads between urban districts." *Consumers' Gas Co. v. Toronto (City)*, [1940] 4 D.L.R. 670 at 672, [1941] O.R. 175, 52 C.R.T.C. 98 (C.A.), Robertson C.J.O. 2. A road to which the public has the right of access, and includes bridges over which or tunnels through which a road passes. *Criminal Code*, R.S.C. 1985, c. C-46, s. 2. See PUBLIC ~.

HIJACKING. *n.* Unlawfully, by force or threat thereof, or by any form of intimidation, seizing or exercising control of an aircraft with intent (a) to cause any person on board the aircraft to be confined or imprisoned against his will, (b) to cause any person on board the aircraft to be transported against his will to any place other than the next scheduled place of landing of the aircraft, (c) to hold any person on board the aircraft for ransom or to service against his will, or (d) to cause the aircraft to deviate in a material respect from its flight plan. *Criminal Code*, R.S.C. 1985, c. C-46, s. 76.

HIRE. *n.* A bailment for compensation or a reward; hiring something to use; labour and work, services and care to be bestowed or performed on the thing delivered, or the carriage of goods from one place to another.

HIRE-PURCHASE AGREEMENT. An agreement by which the hirer of goods may either terminate the agreement or purchase the goods. I.H. Jacob, ed., *Bullen and Leake and Jacob's Precedents of Pleadings*, 12th ed. (London: Sweet and Maxwell, 1975) at 480.

HIS MAJESTY. The Sovereign of the United Kingdom, Canada and His other Realms and Territories, and Head of the Commonwealth.

HIT AND RUN. "[A case] . . . where, with the intent to escape civil or criminal liability, the driver of a motor vehicle involved in a motor vehicle accident fails to stop and give his name and address and where necessary to offer assistance." *Leggett v. Insurance Corp. of British Columbia* (1991), 50 C.C.L.I. 246 at 254 (B.C. S.C.), Harvey J.

H.L. *abbr.* House of Lords.

HODG. *abbr.* Hodgins, Elections (Ont.), 1871-1879.

HODGES'S CASE. See RULE IN ~.

HOLD. *v.* Of a judge, to pronounce a legal opinion.

HOLDBACK. *var.* **HOLD BACK.** Amount required under a builders or construction lien act to be deducted from payments made under a contract or a sub-contract and retained for a period prescribed.

HOLDER. *n.* 1. A person in possession of a security issued or endorsed to that person, to bearer or in blank. 2. The payee or endorsee of a bill or note who is in possession of it, or the bearer thereof. *Bills of Exchange Act*, R.S.C. 1985, c. B-4, s. 2.

HOLDER FOR VALUE. Someone who gives valuable consideration for a bill, who has a lien on it, or who claims through another holder for value. E.L.G. Tyler & N.E. Palmer, eds., *Crossley Vaines' Personal Property*, 5th ed. (London: Butterworths, 1973) at 232.

HOLDER IN DUE COURSE. A holder who takes a bill of exchange seemingly complete and regular, on condition (a) that the transfer is made before the bill is overdue, and without notice that it had been dishonoured previously if it was, and (b) that the bill, cheque or note is accepted for value and in good faith, and that at the time of the arrangement no notice of any defect in the title of the person giving the bill is offered. ". . . A 'holder in due course' is, in effect, a 'bona fide holder for value without notice.' . . ." *Standard Bank v.* Wettlaufer (1915), 33 O.L.R. 441 at 443, 23 D.L.R. 507 (H.C.), Clute J.

HOLD HARMLESS. To assume liability in a situation and relieve the other party of responsibility.

HOLDING. *n.* Land rented to a tenant.

HOLDING COMPANY. 1. A company the primary purpose of which is owning shares of one or more other companies. 2. A company is the holding company of another if, but only if, the other is its subsidiary. *Companies acts*.

HOLDING TRUST. The trustee retains assets until required under an independent agreement to transfer the assets to specific persons. D.M.W. Waters, *The Law of Trusts in Canada*, 2d ed. (Toronto: Carswell, 1984) at p. 101.

HOLD OVER. For a lessee to keep possession of land after the lease has expired.

HOLDS OUT. ". . . [P]resents himself . . ." *British Columbia (Attorney General) v. Cowen*, [1939] 1 D.L.R. 288 at 290, [1939] S.C.R. 20, Kerwin J.

HOLOGRAPH. *n.* A deed or writing written completely by the grantor.

HOLOGRAPH WILL. A will written entirely in the testator's own hand.

HOMESTEAD. *n.* 1. ". . . [T]he home place, the house and the adjacent land occupied as a home, the actual residence of the debtor and his family." *Re Hetherington* (1910), 14 W.L.R.

529 at 532, Lamont J. 2. A parcel of land (i) on which the dwelling house occupied by the owner of the parcel as his residence is situated, and (ii) that consists of (A) not more than 4 adjoining lots in one block in a city, town or village as shown on a plan registered in the proper land titles office, or (B) not more than one quarter section of land other than land in a city, town or village. *Dower Act*, R.S.A. 1980, c. D-38, s. 1. 3. Land, whether leasehold or freehold, together with erections or buildings, with their rights, members and appurtenances, registered as a homestead; and an erection or building on a homestead, whether or not affixed to the soil, shall be taken to be land and part of the homestead. *Homestead Act*, R.S.B.C. 1979, c. 173, s. 1.

HOMESTEAD LAW. Legislation to protect a home against execution creditors. A. Bissett-Johnson & W.M. Holland, eds., *Matrimonial Property Law in Canada* (Toronto: Carswell, 1980) at I-47.

HOMICIDE. *n.* Directly or indirectly, by any means, causing the death of a human being. *Criminal Code*, R.S.C. 1985, c. C-46, s. 222(1). See CULPABLE ~; JUSTIFIABLE ~; NON CULPABLE ~.

HONORARIUM. *n.* 1. "... (... [W]hich really means a gift on assuming an office, is now often used as equivalent to 'salary' by those who do not like to think they receive wages)." *Lavere v. Smith's Falls Public Hospital* (1915), 26 D.L.R. 346 at 347, 35 O.L.R. 98 (C.A.), Riddell J.A. 2. "... [A] compensation for services rendered, it is nevertheless not a payment for which the recipient, if not paid, could sue in a Court of law. It is thus in the nature of an ex gratia or gratuitous payment, unlike a salary or wage or other contracted remuneration. ..." *Vladicka v. Calgary Board of* Education (1974), 45 D.L.R. (3d) 442 at 453, [1974] 4 W.W.R. 149 (Alta. T.D.), McDonald J.

HONOUR. *v.* 1. For a drawee to accept a bill of exchange. 2. For the maker of a note or the acceptor of a bill

to pay it.

HONOUR. *n.* A title applied to judges and other officials.

HONOURABLE. *adj.* A title applied to judges and ministers of the Crown.

HORS DE LA LOI. [Fr.] Outlawed.

HOSTAGE. *n.* A person held in exchange for certain behaviour.

HOSTILE. *adj.* "... [N]ot giving her evidence fairly and with a desire to tell the truth because of a hostile animus toward the [party who called the witness] ..." *R. v. Coffin*, [1956] S.C.R. 191 at 213, 23 C.R. 1, 114 C.C.C. 1, Kellock J. (Rand and Fauteux JJ. concurring).

HOSTILE POSSESSION. See ADVERSE POSSESSION.

HOSTILE WITNESS. A witness whose demeanour, general attitude and evidence are such while under examination that the side which called that witness may, with the judge's leave, cross-examine.

HOTCHPOT. *n.* A blend or mix of chattels and lands.

HOT PURSUIT. A coastal state may pursue a foreign merchant ship which committed an offence against its local law within that state's territorial or national waters into the high seas.

HOUSEBREAKING. See BREAK AND ENTER.

HOUSE LEADER. See GOVERNMENT ~; OPPOSITION ~.

HOUSE OF COMMONS. The support of the majority of members of this body, elected by universal adult suffrage, is required for a Prime Minister and cabinet to govern. P.W. Hogg, *Constitutional Law of Canada*, 3d ed. (Toronto: Carswell, 1992) at 238-9. See CLERK OF THE ~.

HOUSE OF LORDS. The body of lords spiritual and temporal who constitute the second branch of the British Parliament and act as a supreme court of appeal from the British Court of Appeal.

HUMANITY. See CRIME AGAINST

~.

HUMAN RIGHTS. See CANADIAN ~ COMMISSION.

HUNG JURY. A jury unable to reach a unanimous decision in a criminal case.

HUNT. *abbr.* Hunter's Torrens Cases (Can.).

HYPOTHECATION. *n.* Pledging something as security for a demand or debt without giving up that thing.

HYPOTHETICAL. *adj.* Depending on an assumption of fact which may or may not be provable or true. R.J. Sharpe, ed., *Charter Litigation* (Toronto: Butterworths 1987) at 335.

I

I.A.B. *abbr.* Immigration Appeal Board.

I.A.C. *abbr.* Immigration Appeal Cases, 1970-1976.

IBID. *abbr.* Ibidem.

IBIDEM. *adv.* [L.] In the same place.

ID. *abbr.* Idem.

ID CERTUM EST QUOD CERTUM REDDI POTEST. [L.] What is certain is what can be made certain.

IDEM. [L.] The same.

IDENTIFICATION. *n.* Showing that some person or thing is the person or thing in question. See VALID ~.

IDENTITY. *n.* 1. ". . . [C]an be established not only by the name but also by a physical description of the person and other more sophisticated forensic methods such as fingerprints or voiceprints. . . ." *R. v. Khela* (1991), 68 C.C.C. (3d) 81 at 85, 9 C.R. (4th) 380 (Que. C.A.), Proulx J.A. (Tourigny J.A. concurring). 2. ". . . [I]nvolves all the ingredients by which a person purports to identify himself." *Francey v. Wawanesa Mutual Insurance Co.* (1990), 46 C.C.L.I. 240 at 254, 75 Alta. L.R. (2d) 257, [1990] 6 W.W.R. 329, 108 A.R. 82, 72 D.L.R. (4th) 544, [1990] I.L.R. 1-2652 (Q.B.), Fraser J. 3. ". . . [S]omething different from 'name and address', though name and address are sufficient to establish identity, . . ." *R. v. Lloyd* (1980), 16 C.R. (3d) 221 at 240, 53 C.C.C. (2d) 121 (B.C. C.A.), Hinkson J.A.

ID EST. [L. that is] That is to say.

I.E. *abbr.* Id est.

IGNORANTIA FACTI EXCUSAT; IGNORANTIA JURIS NON EXCUSAT. [L.] Ignorance of fact is excusable; ignorance of the law is no excuse.

IJC. *abbr.* International Joint Commission.

ILLEGAL. *adj.* Opposed to law. G.H.L. Fridman, *The Law of Contract in Canada*, 2d ed. (Toronto: Carswell, 1986) at 100. See UNLAWFUL.

ILLEGAL CONTRACT. An agreement to do anything forbidden either by statute or by the common law.

ILLEGALITY. *n.* ". . . [A] generic term covering any act not in accordance with the law. . . ." *Immeubles Port Louis Ltée c. Lafontaine (Village)* (1991), 5 M.P.L.R. (2d) 1 at 55, [1991] 1 S.C.R. 326, 78 D.L.R. (4th) 15, 121 N.R. 323, 38 Q.A.C. 253, the court per Gonthier J.

ILLEGITIMATE CHILD. In respect of the estate of his father, an illegitimate child who was born out of wedlock and has not been legitimized by operation of law, and who was under the care, control, maintenance or protection, either physically or financially, of his father for a period of not less than one year immediately preceding his father's death. *Estate Administration Act*, R.S.B.C. 1979, c. 114, s. 85.

ILLICIT. *adj.* 1. ". . . '[U]nlawful' . . ." *R. v. Deutsch* (1986), 18 O.A.C. 1 at 14, 52 C.R. (3d) 305, [1986] 2

228

S.C.R. 2, 68 N.R. 321, 27 C.C.C. (3d) 385, 30 D.L.R. (4th) 435, Le Dain J. (Beetz, McIntyre and Wilson JJ. concurring). 2. "... [R]eferring to sexual intercourse not authorized or sanctioned by lawful marriage." *R. v. Deutsch* (1986), 18 O.A.C. 1 at 14, 52 C.R. (3d) 305, [1986] 2 S.C.R. 2, 68 N.R. 321, 27 C.C.C. (3d) 385, 30 D.L.R. (4th) 435, Le Dain J. (Beetz, McIntyre and Wilson JJ. concurring).

I.L.R. *abbr.* 1. Canadian Insurance Law Reports. 2. Insurance Law Reporter (Can.).

IMMIGRATION. *n.* Entering a country for the purpose of establishing permanent residence in it.

IMM. L.R. (2d). *abbr.* Immigration Law Reporter (Second Series) 1987-.

IMMORAL CONTRACT. A contract based on consideration contra bonos mores and considered void.

IMMOVABLE. *n.* 1. Includes all interests in land and land. J.G. McLeod, *The Conflict of Laws* (Calgary: Carswell, 1983) at 317. 2. "... [C]omprises everything which could be regarded as real estate for the purposes of the taxation by-laws and resolutions ... and while it may not be so clear that such immovables as the pipes, poles, wires and transformers in question are real estate and real property, the weight of authority certainly favours that view ... the real property of English law is not entirely co-extensive with the immovables of the civil law.... *Montreal Light, Heat & Power Consolidated v. Westmount (Town)*, [1926] S.C.R. 515 at 523, [1926] 3 D.L.R. 466, Anglin C.J.C. (Duff, Mignault, Newcombe and Rinfret JJ. concurring).

IMMOVABLE BY NATURE. "... [T]he structures ... must participate in the fixity or immobility of the land, which is the ultimate measure of whether a thing is immovable by nature. This principle is observed as long as a structure participates in the immovable nature of the land, by adhering directly to it or to another structure, which in turn adheres to the land. In

either case the structure is immovable by nature because it is naturally immobile." *Cablevision (Montreal) Inc. v. Quebec.* [1978] 2 S.C.R. 64 at 73, 19 N.R. 121, the court per Beetz J.

IMMUNITY. *n.* The state of being free or exempt. See CROWN ~; JUDICIAL ~; SOVEREIGN ~.

IMPANEL. *v.* "... [S]ometimes means to enroll upon a panel or list for jury duty, and sometimes to draw from that panel and select a jury for a particular case." *R. v. Gaffin* (1904), 8 C.C.C. 194 at 196 (N.S. S.C.), the court per Graham E.J. See EMPANEL; JURY.

IMPARTIAL. *adj.* "... [C]onnotes absence of bias, actual or perceived." *R. v. Valente (No. 2)* (1985), 23 C.C.C. (3d) 193 at 201, [1985] 2 S.C.R. 673, 52 O.R. (2d) 779, 37 M.V.R. 9, 49 C.R. (3d) 97, 24 D.L.R. (4th) 161, 64 N.R. 1, 14 O.A.C. 79, 19 C.R.R. 354, [1985] D.L.Q. 85n, the court per Le Dain J.

IMPARTIALITY. See INSTITUTIONAL ~.

IMPEACH. *v.* "... [T]o call into question the veracity of evidence given by a witness by calling evidence to contradict, challenge or impugn the witness's prior testimony." *Machado v. Berlet* (1986), 15 C.P.C. (2d) 207 at 217, 57 O.R. (2d) 207, 32 D.L.R. (4th) 634 (H.C.), Ewaschuk J.

IMPEACHMENT. *n.* Attack on a patent by striking at its validity. H.G. Fox, *The Canadian Law and Practice Relating to Letters Patent for Inventions*, 4th ed. (Toronto: Carswell, 1969) at 515.

IMPERFECT OBLIGATION. A moral duty which the law cannot enforce.

IMPERFECT TRUST. An executory trust which is not sufficiently constituted or declared.

IMPERIAL. *adj.* As applied to state documents, means of or pertaining to the United Kingdom of Great Britain and Northern Ireland and includes any kingdom that included England, whether known as the United Kingdom of Great Britain and Ireland or otherwise. *Evidence acts.*

IMPERIAL PARLIAMENT. The parliament of the United Kingdom of Great Britain and Northern Ireland, as at present constituted, or any former kingdom that included England, whether known as the United Kingdom of Great Britain and Ireland or otherwise. *Evidence acts.*

IMPERSONATION. *n.* The act of representing that one is someone else, whether dead or living, fictitious or real.

IMPLEAD. *v.* 1. "... [A]sserting jurisdiction against the opposition of the parties sought to be sued." *Canadian Commercial Bank v. McLaughlan* (1990), 73 D.L.R. (4th) 678 at 685, 39 E.T.R. 54, 75 Alta. L.R. (2d) 40 (C.A.), Bracco and Stevenson JJ.A. and Forsyth J. 2. To institute legal proceedings against a person.

IMPLICATION. *n.* An inference which is necessary or may be presumed and arises out of words or acts in evidence.

IMPLIED. *adj.* Used in contradistinction to express. *R. v. Clement* (1981), 23 C.R. (3d) 193 at 200, [1981] 2 S.C.R. 468, [1981] 6 W.W.R. 735, 23 R.F.L. (2d) 255, 10 Man. R. (2d) 92, 38 N.R. 302, the court per Estey J.

IMPLIED AUTHORITY. A certain authority which may be read into an agent's express authority. G.H.L. Fridman, *The Law of Agency*, 6th ed. (London: Butterworths, 1990) at 59.

IMPLIED CONDITION. In some circumstances a court has a right to conclude that everything the parties agreed is not contained in their oral statements or in the written documents which appear to constitute the contract. The additional term is said to exist in the agreement though unspecified; a statute may imply it. G.H.L. Fridman, *The Law of Contract in Canada*, 2d ed. (Toronto: Carswell, 1986) at 448.

IMPLIED CONTRACT. A contract which law concludes does exist from an act, circumstance or relationship.

IMPLIED MALICE. One presumes that the malice needed to support a cause of action exists when someone publishes a defamatory remark. R.E. Brown, *The Law of Defamation in Canada* (Toronto: Carswell, 1987) at 730.

IMPLIED TERM. 1. "... [T]here may be cases where obviously some term must be implied if the intention of the parties is not to be defeated, some term of which it can be predicated that 'it goes without saying,' some term not expressed but necessary to give the transaction such business efficacy as the parties must have intended." *Luxor (Eastbourne) Ltd. v. Cooper*, [1941] A.C. 108 at 137 (U.K. H.L.), Lord Wright. 2. "... [S]ometimes ... denotes some term which does not depend on the actual intention of the parties but on a rule of law, such as the terms, warranties or conditions which, if not expressly excluded, the law imports, as for instance under the Sale of Goods Act, ..." *Luxor (Eastbourne) Ltd. v. Cooper*, [1941] A.C. 108 at 137 (U.K. H.L.), Lord Wright.

IMPLIED TRUST. A trust which comes about when an equitable interpretation is put on the conduct of the parties, for example where one person voluntarily transfers property to another person or pays for property and has that property put into another person's name.

IMPLIED WARRANTY. See IMPLIED CONDITION.

IMPOSSIBILITY. *n.* Something either physical, legal or logical: physical when it is unnatural, legal when a rule of law makes it not possible to do and logical when it goes against the essential qualities of the transaction.

IMPOUND. *v.* To place in legal custody.

IMPRISONED. See ARBITRARILY ~.

IMPRISONMENT. *n.* "... [C]arries with it a complete lack of choice. There must be an involuntary element to the confinement before it can be said to be a restraint on the personal liberty or freedom ..." *R. v. Degan* (1985), 20 C.C.C. (3d) 293 at 299, 38 Sask. R. 234 (C.A.), the court per Vancise J.A. See FALSE ~.

IMPROVEMENT. *n.* "... [O]rdinary meaning ... includes buildings, structures and all things which become attached to the land, but does not include buildings, structures or fixtures which merely rested on the land and which could be removed at will without changing the character of the land itself, ..." *Beloit Sorel Walmsley Ltd. v. New Brunswick* (1976), 10 L.C.R. 373 at 376, 71 D.L.R. (3d) 240 (N.B. C.A.), the court per Limerick J.A. See LOCAL ~.

IMPUTE. *v.* 1. To attribute responsibility to another. 2. To ascribe.

INADVERTENCE. *n.* 1. "... [A]ccidental or unintentional." *Guimond v. Sornberger* (1980), 13 Alta. L.R. (2d) 228 at 242, 13 M.P.L.R. 134, 25 A.R. 18, 115 D.L.R. (3d) 321 (C.A.), Clement J.A. 2. "... [I]nvolves oversight, inattention, carelessness and the like." *Campbell v. Dowdall* (1992), 12 M.P.L.R. (2d) 27 at 37 (Ont. Gen. Div.), Rutherford J.

INALIENABLE. *adj.* Not able to be transferred.

INAUGURATION. *n.* Solemn induction into office.

IN AUTRE DROIT. [Fr.] In the right of another.

IN BANC. See BANC.

IN BANCO. See BANCO.

IN BANK. See BANC; BANCO.

IN BEING. 1. Living or en ventre sa mere. *Perpetuities acts.* 2. Living or conceived but unborn. *Perpetuities Act*, R.S.A. 1980, c. P-4, s. 1.

INC. *abbr.* 1. Incorporated. 2. Incorporé.

IN CAMERA. [L.] "... '[W]ithout publicity, privately and, if possible, in the private office of the judge or a private room'...." *R. v. B. (C.)* (1981), 23 C.R. (3d) 289 at 294, 62 C.C.C. (2d) 107, 38 N.R. 451, [1981] 6 W.W.R. 701, 24 R.F.L. (2d) 225, 12 Man.

R. (2d) 361, [1981] 2 S.C.R. 480, 127 D.L.R. (3d) 482, the court per Chouinard J.

INCAPABLE. *adj.* Unable because of death, illness, absence from the province or otherwise. *Vital Statistics acts.*

INCAPACITY. *n.* In criminal law, a quality attributed to people with severe mental disorders and young children and, not as widely, to those who are intoxicated. D. Stuart, *Canadian Criminal Law: A Treatise*, 2d ed. (Toronto: Carswell, 1987) at 311. See LEGAL ~.

INCARCERATE. *v.* To imprison.

INCARCERATION. *n.* Imprisonment.

INCENDIARISM. See ARSON.

INCEST. *n.* Knowing that another person is by blood relationship his or her parent, child, brother, sister, grandparent or grandchild, as the case may be, having sexual intercourse with that person. *Criminal Code*, R.S.C. 1985, c. C-46, s. 155.

IN CHIEF. Describes the examination of a witness by the person who called that witness.

INCHOATE. *adj.* Commenced but not finished.

INCIDENT. *n.* Something which follows or appertains to another thing. See NUCLEAR ~.

INCITE. *v.* To arouse, provoke, encourage.

INCLOSURE. *n.* Fencing in property in order to cultivate it.

INCLUDE. *v.* 1. "... [G]enerally used in interpretation clauses in order to enlarge the meaning of words or phrases occurring in the body of a statute ..." *Dilworth v. New Zealand Commissioner of Stamps*, [1899] A.C. 99 at 105 (New Zealand P.C.), Lord Watson. 2. "... It may be equivalent to 'mean and include', and in that case it may afford an exhaustive explanation of the meaning ..." *Dilworth v. New Zealand Commissioner of Stamps*, [1899] A.C. 99 at 105-6 (New Zealand P.C.), Lord

Watson.

INCLUDED OFFENCE. 1. An offence which has the same basic elements as the principal offence with which a person is charged. 2. ". . . [P]art of the main offence. The offence charged, either as described in the enactment creating the offence or as charged in the count, must contain the essential elements of the offence said to be included . . . the offence charged, either as described in the enactment creating the offence or as charged in the count, must be sufficient to inform the accused of the included offences which he must meet." *R. v. Simpson* (1981), 20 C.R. (3d) 36 at 49, 50, 58 C.C.C. (2d) 308 (Ont. C.A.), the court per Martin J.A.

INCLUSIO UNIUS EST EXCLUSIO ALTERIUS. [L.] To include one is to exclude another.

INCOME. *n.* The net receipts over disbursements in the taxation year in the totality of the taxpayer's business as an ongoing concern other than capital expenditures, gifts and the like. *Premium Iron Ores Ltd. v. M.N.R.,* [1966] S.C.R. 685, [1966] C.T.C. 311, 66 D.T.C. 5280. See NET ~.

INCOME TAX. 1. Tax on net income, i.e., income after deducting expenses incurred in order to earn the income. P.W. Hogg, *Constitutional Law of Canada,* 3d ed. (Toronto: Carswell, 1992) at 743. 2. ". . . [A] charge upon the profits; the thing which is taxed is the profit that is made, . . ." *Ashton Gas Co. v. Attorney-General* (1905), [1906] A.C. 10 at 12 (U.K. H.L.), Earl of Halsbury L.C.

INCOMPETENCE. *n.* Acts or omissions of the part of a member of a professional body, in that member's occupation, that demonstrate a lack of knowledge, skill or judgment, or disregard for the interests of the recipient of the services of such a nature and to such an extent as to render that member unfit to carry on the occupation.

INCOMPETENCY. See MENTAL.

INCOMPETENT. See MENTAL ~.

INCONSISTENT. *adj.* 1. "[In the context of constitutional law] . . . refers to a situation where two legislative enactments cannot stand together . . ." *Friends of the Oldman River Society v. Canada (Minister of Transport)* (1992), 3 Admin. L.R.(2d) 1 at 37, [1992] 2 W.W.R. 193, [1992] 1 S.C.R. 3, 84 Alta. L.R. (2d) 129, 7 C.E.L.R. (N.S.), 1, 132 N.R. 321, 88 D.L.R. (4th) 1, 48 F.T.R. 160n, La Forest J. (Lamer C.J.C., L'Heureux-Dubé, Sopinka, Gonthier, Cory, McLachlin and Iacobucci JJ. concurring). 2. "Two laws are deemed to be inconsistent when 'compliance with one law involves breach of the other', see Smith v. R., [1960] S.C.R. 776 at 800 . . . per Martland J., or if resort to one statute from a practical point of view precludes the other from having any application: see Multiple Access Ltd. v. McCutcheon (1978), 19 O.R. (2d) 516 . . . (C.A.). . . ." *James v. Lockhart* (1981), 24 R.F.L. (2d) 333 at 335-6 (Ont. Co. Ct.), Flanigan Co. Ct. J.

INCORPORATION. *n.* 1. The formation of a group of people into a corporation or body politic. 2. Merger of one thing with another so that the two constitute one whole. See ARTICLES OF ~; CERTIFICATE OF ~; PRE-~ CONTRACT.

INCORPORATOR. *n.* A person who signs articles of incorporation.

INCORPOREAL. *adj.* Not capable of being possessed physically. R. Megarry & H.W.R. Wade, *The Law of Real Property,* 5th ed. (London: Stevens, 1984) at cxxv.

INCORPOREAL CHATTEL. An incorporeal right attached to chattels.

INCORPOREAL HEREDITAMENT. 1. "[A right] . . . in land, which [includes] such things as rent charges, annuities, easements, profits à prendre, and so on." *Pegg v. Pegg* (1992), 38 R.F.L. (3d) 179 at 184, 21 R.P.R. (2d) 149, 1 Alta. L.R. (3d) 249, 128 A.R. 132 (Q.B.), Agrios J. 2. Property which is not tangible but can be inherited. See PROFIT.

INCORRIGIBLE. *adj.* Uncorrectable.

INCREMENT. *n.* 1. The difference between two rates of pay, one for a higher position and one for a lower. 2. The difference between two levels of benefits paid under a statute or scheme. See EXPERIENTIAL ~.

INCRIMINATE. *v.* ". . . '[M]ay tend to bring him into the peril and possibility of being convicted as a criminal'. . . . [and may be extended] to any proceedings where an individual is exposed to a criminal charge, penalty or forfeiture as a result of having testified in earlier proceedings. . . ." *Grineage v. Coopman* (1988), 27 C.P.C. (2d) 187 at 189-90 (Ont. H.C.), O'Brien J.

INCULPATORY CONFESSION. A statement which incriminates the maker.

INCUMBRANCE. *n.* "By generally accepted definition . . . it comprehends 'every right to or interest in land which may subsist in third persons to the diminution of the value of land, but consistent with the passing of the fee by the conveyance' . . ." *Wotherspoon v. Canadian Pacific Ltd.* (1987), (*sub nom. Eaton Retirement Annuity Plan v. Canadian Pacific Ltd.*) 45 R.P.R. 138 at 192, 76 N.R. 241, 21 O.A.C. 79, [1987] 1 S.C.R. 952, 39 D.L.R. (4th) 169, the court per Estey J. See ENCUMBRANCE.

IN CURIA. [L.] In an open court.

IN CUSTODIA LEGIS. [L.] In legal custody.

INDECENT. *adj.* ". . . [S]uch as would shock or disgust the average member of the Canadian contemporary community." *Priape Enrg. c. Sous-Ministre du Revenu national* (1979), (*sub nom. Priape Enrg. v. Deputy Minister of National Revenue (Customs & Excise)*) 24 C.R. (3d) 66 at 71, [1980] C.S. 86, 52 C.C.C. (2d) 44, 2 C.E.R. 169 (Qué. S.C.), Hugessen A.C.J.S.C.

INDECENT ASSAULT. ". . . [A]n assault that is committed in circumstances of indecency, or, as sometimes described, an assault with acts of indecency. . . ." *R. v. Swietlinski* (1980), 18 C.R. (3d) 231 at 243, 34 N.R. 569, 55 C.C.C. (2d) 481, 117 D.L.R. (3d) 285, [1980] 2 S.C.R. 956, the court per McIntyre J.

INDEFEASIBLE. *adj.* Not able to be voided.

INDEMNIFICATION. *n.* Making good.

INDEMNIFY. *v.* To make good the loss which someone suffered through another's act or default; to grant an indemnity; to agree to indemnify.

INDEMNITY. *n.* ". . . [T]he concept of indemnity has central to it the idea of compensation, of making good, or paying moneys to a person, to reimburse them for losses sustained. . . ." *Arklie v. Haskell* (1986), 25 C.C.L.I. 277 at 284, 33 D.L.R. (4th) 458, [1987] I.L.R. 1-2176 (B.C. C.A.), McLachlin J.A. (Hutcheon and MacFarlane JJ.A. concurring). See CONTRACT OF ~.

INDENTURE. *n.* A deed which two or more parties made. See DEED-POLL; TRUST ~.

INDEPENDENCE. See INSTITUTIONAL ~; JUDICIAL ~.

INDEPENDENT. *adj.* "[In s. 11(d) of the Charter] . . . reflects or embodies the traditional constitutional value of judicial independence. As such, it connotes not merely a state of mind or attitude in the actual exercise of judicial functions, but a status or relationship to others, particularly to the Executive Branch of government, that rests on objective conditions or guarantees." *R. v. Valente (No. 2)* (1985), 23 C.C.C. (3d) 193 at 201, [1985] 2 S.C.R. 673, 52 O.R. (2d) 779, 37 M.V.R. 9, 49 C.R. (3d) 97, 24 D.L.R. (4th) 161, 64 N.R. 1, 14 O.A.C. 79, 19 C.R.R. 354, [1985] D.L.Q. 85n, the court per Le Dain J.

INDEPENDENT CONTRACTOR. A person who undertakes with another person to produce a given result but so that, in the actual execution of the work, he is not under the orders or control of the person for whom he does it, and may use his own discretion in things not specified beforehand. *Employment Standards Act*, R.S.M. 1987, c. E110, s. 1.

INDEPENDENT MEMBER. A member of a legislature who does not belong to a caucus.

INDETERMINATE SENTENCE. Imprisonment of undetermined length. P.W. Hogg, *Constitutional Law of Canada*, 3d ed. (Toronto: Carswell, 1992) at 1135.

INDEX. *n.* [L.] An alphabetical list of separate subjects or items contained in a book, writing or similar thing. See CONSUMER PRICE ~; COST OF LIVING ~.

INDIAN. *n.* 1. "... '[A]borigines.' ..." *Reference re whether the Term "Indians" in s. 91(24) of the Constitution Act 1867, includes Eskimo Inhabitants of Quebec*, [1939] S.C.R. 104 at 111, [1939] 2 D.L.R. 417, Duff C.J. 2. A person who pursuant to this Act is registered as an Indian or is entitled to be registered as an Indian. *Indian Act*, R.S.C. 1985, c. I-5, s. 2.

INDICIA. *n.* [L.] 1. Marks; signs. 2. Facts which cause inferences to be made.

INDICTABLE OFFENCE. A criminal offence which is triable by way of indictment.

INDICTABLE ONLY OFFENCE. A criminal offence which can only be tried by way of indictment.

INDICTED. *adj.* Charged with a criminal offence in an indictment.

INDICTMENT. *n.* 1. Includes (a) information or a count therein, (b) a plea, replication or other pleading, and (c) any record. *Criminal Code*, R.S.C. 1985, c. C-46, s. 2. 2. Includes an information or charge in respect of which a person has been tried for an indictable offence under Part XIX. *Criminal Code*, R.S.C. 1985, c. C-46, s. 673. See BILL OF ~; PREFERRED ~.

INDIFFERENT. *adj.* Not having any interest which may prevent impartial judgment.

INDIGENT. *n.* "... [A] person possessed of some means but such scanty means that he is needy and poor." *National Sanitarium Association v. Mattawa (Town)* (1925), 56 O.L.R. 474 at 477, [1925] 2 D.L.R. 491 (C.A.), the court per Mulock C.J.O.

INDIRECT EVIDENCE. Proof of related circumstances from which a controversial fact, not directly proved by documents or witnesses, may be inferred. See CIRCUMSTANTIAL EVIDENCE.

INDIRECTLY. See YOU CANNOT DO ~ WHAT YOU CANNOT DO DIRECTLY.

INDIVIDUAL. *n.* A natural person. *Rudolf Wolff & Co. v. Canada* (1990), 46 C.R.R. 263 at 269, 43 Admin. L.R. 1, 41 C.P.C. (2d) 1, [1990] 1 S.C.R. 695, 106 N.R. 1, 69 D.L.R. (4th) 392, 39 O.A.C. 1, the court per Cory J. See RELATED ~.

INDOLENT. See EQUITY AIDS THE VIGILANT AND NOT THE ~.

INDORSEE. *n.* The individual to whom a bill of exchange, bill of lading or promissory note, for example, is assigned by indorsing it.

INDORSEMENT. *n.* Anything printed or written on the back of a document or deed. See ENDORSEMENT; RESTRICTIVE ~.

INDORSER. *n.* The person who indorses the holder or payee by writing her or his name on the back of a bill of exchange.

INDUST. L.J. *abbr.* Industrial Law Journal.

INDUSTRIAL ACCIDENT. A sudden and unforeseen event, attributable to any cause, which happens to a person, arising out of or in the course of his work and resulting in an employment injury to him. *An Act Respecting Industrial Accidents and Occupational Diseases*, S.Q. 1985, c. 6, s. 2.

INDUSTRIAL ACTION. (a) A strike, (b) picketing. *Labour Code Amendment Act*, S.B.C. 1984, c. 24, s. 3. See UNLAWFUL ~.

INFANTICIDE

INDUSTRIAL AND INTELLECTUAL PROPERTY. The law which relates to industrial designs, patents and trade marks. H.G. Fox, *The Canadian Law of Copyright and Industrial Designs*, 2d ed. (Toronto: Carswell, 1967) at 3.

INDUSTRIAL DESIGN. "... [A] design to be 'applied' to 'the ornamenting' of an article ... something that determines the appearance of an article, or some part of an article, because ornamenting relates to appearance. And it must have as its objective making the appearance of an article more attractive because that is the purpose of ornamenting...." *Cimon Ltd. v. Bench Made Furniture Corp.* (1964), 48 C.P.R. 31 at 49, [1965] Ex. C.R. 811, 30 Fox Pat. C. 77 (Ex. Ct.), Jackett P.

INDUSTRIAL DISPUTE. Any dispute or difference or apprehended dispute or difference between an employer and one or more employees or a bargaining agent acting on behalf of the employees, as to matters or things affecting or relating to terms or conditions of employment or work done or to be done by the employee or employees or as to privileges, rights and duties of the employer, the employee or employees.

INDUSTRIAL PROPERTY. 1. Copyright, industrial design, patent and trade mark matters. D. Sgayias *et al.*, *Federal Court Practice 1988* (Toronto: Carswell, 1987) at 516. 2. All patents of invention, copyrights, industrial designs, and any other intellectual or industrial property rights in every country where the same exist from time to time, all applications therefor arising from or acquired in connection therewith and all right to make such applications. *IDEA Corporation Act, 1981*, S.O. 1981, c. 34, s. 1. 3. Land that is constructed to be used for the assembling, processing or manufacturing of finished or partially finished products from raw materials or fabricated parts. *Commercial Concentration Tax Act*, R.S.O. 1990, c. C.16, s. 1.

INDUSTRIAL RELATIONS. The interactions among unions, management, government, employees, and employers.

IN ESSE. [L.] Which actually exists.

INEVITABLE. *adj.* "... Damage is said to be 'inevitable' when the body responsible for it establishes to the satisfaction of the Court that it was demonstrably impossible to avoid the damage inasmuch as it had carried out its operations with a degree of skill and care commensurate with current scientific and technical knowledge, but with due allowance for practical considerations bearing on time and expense." *Tock v. St. John's (City) Metropolitan Area Board* (1989), 47 M.P.L.R. 113 at 145, [1989] 2 S.C.R. 1181, 1 C.C.L.T. (2d) 113, 64 D.L.R. (4th) 620, 104 N.R. 241, 82 Nfld. & P.E.I.R. 181, 257 A.P.R. 181, La Forest J. (Dickson C.J.C. concurring).

INEVITABLE ACCIDENT. An accident which cannot be avoided by exercising ordinary caution, care and skill.

IN EXPECTANCY. Executory, relating to some future thing. See INTEREST ~.

IN EXTREMIS. [L.] At the very last.

INFANT. *n.* 1. A person under the age of eighteen years. 2. Any person under the age of 19 years. *Public Trustee Act*, R.S.B.C. 1979, c. 348, s. 1. 3. Person who is unmarried and under the age of nineteen years, and includes a child who is unborn at the death of its father. *Guardianship Act*, R.S.N.S. 1989, c. 189, s. 2.

INFANTICIDE. *n.* 1. The murder of a child by its mother. F.A. Jaffe, *A Guide to Pathological Evidence*, 3d ed. (Toronto: Carswell, 1991) at 221. 2. A female person commits infanticide when by a wilful act or omission she causes the death of her newly-born child, if at the time of the act or omission she is not fully recovered from the effects of giving birth to the child and by reason thereof or of the effect of lactation consequent on the birth of the child her mind is then disturbed. *Criminal Code*, R.S.C. 1985, c. C-46, s. 233.

INFERENCE. *n.* 1. "... [I]n the legal sense ... is a deduction from the evidence, and if it is a reasonable deduction it may have the validity of legal proof. The attribution of an occurrence to a cause is, I take it, always a matter of inference...." *Jones v. Great Western Rwy. Co.* (1930), 47 T.L.R. 39 at 45, Lord Macmillan, cited with approval in *Gwyllt, Re*, [1944] O.W.N. 212 at 213 (C.A.), Henderson J.A. 2. Facts sufficient that a particular conclusion may be drawn from them. J.G. Fleming, *The Law of Torts*, 8th ed. (Sydney: Law Book, 1992) at 323.

INFERIOR COURT. 1. A court which is subject to the control of a higher court. 2. "[A court] ... in which provincially appointed judges sat ..." *Reference re s. 6 of Family Relations Act, 1978 (British Columbia)* (1982), 26 R.F.L. (2d) 113 at 141, [1982] 1 S.C.R. 62, [1982] 3 W.W.R. 1, 36 B.C.L.R. 1, 131 D.L.R. (3d) 257, 40 N.R. 206, Estey J. 3. A court staffed by justices of the peace or magistrates which has jurisdiction over minor criminal offences and small civil claims. P.W. Hogg, *Constitutional Law of Canada*, 3d ed. (Toronto: Carswell, 1992) at 162.

IN FIERI. [L.] While something was being accomplished.

INFIRMITY. *n.* "... [P]hysical weakness, debility, frailty or feebleness of body resulting from constitutional defect." *Tomlinson v. Prudential Insurance Co.*, [1954] O.R. 508 at 516, [1954] I.L.R. 1-144 (C.A.), the court per Laidlaw J.A.

IN FLAGRANTE DELICTO. [L.] In the actual act.

INFLUENCE. See UNDUE ~.

IN FORCE. "... [E]ffectively enacted ..." *Lord's Day Alliance of Canada v. Manitoba (Attorney General)* (1924), [1925] 1 D.L.R. 561 at 565, [1925] 1 W.W.R. 296, [1925] A.C. 384, 43 C.C.C. 185 (Man. P.C.), the board per Lord Blanesburgh.

INFORMAL. *adj.* Lacking proper legal form.

INFORMAL CONTRACT. A parol or simple contract. G.H.L. Fridman, *The Law of Contract in Canada*, 2d ed. (Toronto: Carswell, 1986) at 10.

INFORMANT. *n.* A person who lays an information. *Criminal Code*, R.S.C. 1985, c. C-46, s. 785.

IN FORMA PAUPERIS. [L. in the form of a poor person] A litigant allowed to proceed in this way is not liable to pay court costs.

INFORMATION. *n.* Includes (a) a count in an information, and (b) a complaint in respect of which a justice is authorized by an Act of Parliament or an enactment made thereunder to make an order. *Criminal Code*, R.S.C. 1985, c. C-46, s. 785. See CONFIDENTIAL ~; CREDIT ~.

INFORMATION AND BELIEF. Used in relation to the contents of affidavits. "Equivalent to 'belief' simply." *Adams v. Adams* (1921), 62 D.L.R. 721 at 724, [1922] 1 W.W.R. 47 (C.A.), the court per Beck J.A.

INFORMATION COMMISSIONER OF CANADA. A federal official appointed to hear complaints of government failure to comply with the rights provided by the Access to Information Act.

INFORMED CONSENT. An agreement a medical patient gives to a procedure after the risks involved are disclosed.

INFORMER. *n.* The one who commences an action or takes some other steps to recover a penalty. See POLICE ~ PRIVILEGE.

INFORMER PRIVILEGE. The privilege attached to the identity of a person who provided information to police leading to an investigation.

INFRA. [L. under, underneath, below] In a document, reference to a later part or page of the document.

INFRINGEMENT. *n.* 1. Interference with the right of another. 2. A complaint that the defendant has directly used and taken the plaintiff's trade mark totally, a colourable imitation or a substantial part of it. H.G. Fox, *The*

Canadian Law of Trade Marks and Unfair Competition, 3d ed. (Toronto: Carswell, 1972) at 323. 3. Something which, if done by the actual copyright owner, would exercise the statutory right conferred on the owner. H.G. Fox, *The Canadian Law of Copyright and Industrial Designs*, 2d ed. (Toronto: Carswell, 1967) at 326. 4. Any act which interferes with full enjoyment of the patentee's monopoly by making, using or putting into practice the invention or any aspect of it that is included in the claims. H.G. Fox, *The Canadian Law and Practice Relating to Letters Patent for Inventions*, 4th ed. (Toronto: Carswell, 1969) at 349-350.

IN FUTURO. [L.] In future.

INGRESS. *n.* Entry.

IN GROSS. Not appendant, appurtenant, or otherwise annexed to land. See EASEMENT ~.

INGROSS. *v.* To write a fair copy of an instrument or deed so that parties may formally execute it.

INHERENT DEFECT. An intrinsic fault or problem.

INHERENT DEFENCE. A defence such as lawful purpose, innocent intent or mistake of fact which simply denies the mens rea which must be proved by the prosecution. P.K. McWilliams, *Canadian Criminal Evidence*, 3d ed. (Aurora: Canada Law Book, 1988) at 25-8.

INHERENT JURISDICTION. "... The inherent jurisdiction of a superior court is derived not from any statute or rule of law but from the very nature of the court as a superior court: ... Utilizing this power, superior courts, to maintain their authority and to prevent their processes from being obstructed or abused, have amongst other things punished for contempt of court, stayed matters that are frivolous and vexatious and regulated their own processes. . . ." *R. v. Unnamed Person* (1985), 20 C.R.R. 188 at 190-91, 10 O.A.C. 305, 22 C.C.C. (3d) 284 (C.A.), the court per Zuber J.A.

INHERENT POWER. 1. A power vested in a court that is not derived from statutory authority. 2. Authority, possessed by a corporation, not obtained from statute or a charter, e.g. the power to own land the right of perpetual succession. I.M. Rogers, *The Law of Canadian Municipal Corporations*, 2d ed. (Toronto: Carswell, 1971-) at 361.

INHERIT. *v.* 1. To acquire by descent. 2. To acquire under a will.

INHERITABLE. *adj.* Able to inherit.

INHERITANCE. *n.* What descended to the heir of the owner who died intestate, formerly a hereditament.

INHERITANCE TAX. Succession duty calculated upon the inheritance received by any beneficiary. P.W. Hogg, *Constitutional Law of Canada*, 3d ed. (Toronto: Carswell, 1992) at 746.

IN JEOPARDY. At risk of being convicted of a criminal offence.

INJUNCTION. *n.* An equitable remedy pursuant to which one party must perform some act or refrain from some action harmful to the party who seeks relief. G.H.L. Fridman, *Sale of Goods in Canada*, 3d ed. (Toronto: Carswell, 1986) at 427. See INTERIM ~; INTERLOCUTORY ~; MANDATORY ~; MAREVA ~; PERMANENT ~; PERPETUAL ~; PROHIBITORY ~.

INJUNCTION QUIA TIMET. The injunction which a court awards to prevent an act which is threatened or feared. S.A. DeSmith, *Judicial Review of Administrative Action*, 4th ed. by J.M. Evans (London: Stevens, 1980) at 435.

INJURED. *adj.* 1. Bodily harm, and includes mental or nervous shock and pregnancy. *Criminal Injury Compensation acts*. 2. In respect of live stock or poultry means injured by wounding, worrying or pursuing.

INJURIA. *n.* [L.] An act which encroaches on some right.

INJURIA ABSQUE DAMNO. [L.] Wrong without damage. Compare DAMNUM ABSQUE INJURIA.

INJURIA NON EXCUSAT INJURIUM. [L.] Wrong does not justify wrong.

INJURIA NON PRAESUMITUR. [L.] One should not presume wrongdoing.

INJURIOUS AFFECTION. "The conditions required to give rise to a claim for compensation for injurious affection to a property, when no land is taken are now well established ... These conditions are: (1) the damage must result from an act rendered lawful by statutory powers of the person performing such act; (2) the damage must be such as would have been actionable under the common law, but for the statutory powers; (3) the damage must be an injury to the land itself and not a personal injury or an injury to business or trade; (4) the damage must be occasioned by the construction of the public work, not by its user." *R. v. Loiselle* (1962), 35 D.L.R. (2d) 274 at 275, [1962] S.C.R. 624, the court per Abbott J.

INJURIOUS FALSEHOOD. If an oral or written falsehood, neither defamatory nor actionable per se, is maliciously published and is calculated in the ordinary course of things to produce and does produce actual damage, it is possible to bring an action. I.H. Jacob, ed., *Bullen and Leake and Jacob's Precedents of Pleadings,* 12th ed. (London: Sweet and Maxwell, 1975) at 544.

INJURY. *n.* 1. "... The broadest acceptable sense of the word 'injury' is 'interference with a right'...." *Guest v. Bonderove & Co.* (1988), 59 Alta. L.R. (2d) 86 at 87, 28 C.P.C. (2d) 202, 88 A.R. 277 (C.A.), the court per Kerans J.A. 2. "... [B]odily injury." *Guest v. Bonderove & Co.* (1988), 59 Alta. L.R. (2d) 86 at 88, 28 C.P.C. (2d) 202, 88 A.R. 277 (C.A.), the court per Kerans J.A. 3. Actual bodily harm and includes pregnancy and mental or nervous shock. *Criminal Injuries Compensation acts.* 4. Disrupting tissue by violence. F.A. Jaffe, *A Guide to Pathological Evidence,* 3d ed. (Toronto: Carswell, 1991) at 221. See

EMPLOYMENT ~; PERSONAL ~.

IN KIND. 1. Of the same category. 2. In the same manner.

INLAND BILL. A bill that is, or on the face of it purports to be, (a) both drawn and payable within Canada; or (b) drawn within Canada upon some person resident therein. *Bills of Exchange Act,* R.S.C. 1970, c. B-5, s. 25.

INLAND NOTE. A note that is, or on the face of it purports to be, both made and payable within Canada. *Bills of Exchange Act,* R.S.C. 1970, c. B-5, s. 177.

IN LIMINE. [L.] At the beginning; preliminary.

IN LOCO PARENTIS. [L.] 1. In the place of the parent. 2. "A person in loco parentis to a child is one who has acted so as to evidence his intention of placing himself towards the child in the situation which is ordinarily occupied by the father for the provision of the child's pecuniary wants." *Shtitz v. Canadian National Railway* (1926), [1927] 1 D.L.R. 951 at 959, [1927] 1 W.W.R. 193, 21 Sask. L.R. 345 (C.A.), Turgeon J.A.

INMATE. *n.* 1. A person who, having been sentenced or committed to penitentiary, has been received and accepted at a penitentiary pursuant to the sentence or committal and has not been lawfully discharged therefrom or from any other place pursuant to section 23.1. *Penitentiary Act,* R.S.C. 1985 (2d Supp.), c. 35, s. 15. 2. A person admitted to a correctional facility pursuant to a committal order. 3. A person sentenced to a term of imprisonment in or detained in a correctional institution. 4. "[Of a common bawdy-house is] ... the prostitute who works on the premises with some regularity but is not responsible for any of the organizational duties involved in running the business as a business ..." *R. c.* Corbeil (1991), 64 C.C.C. (3d) 272 at 292, 5 C.R. (4th) 62, 124 N.R. 241, [1991] 1 S.C.R. 830, 40 Q.A.C. 283, L'Heureux-Dubé J. (dissenting). See PAROLED ~.

IN MEDIAS RES. [L. in the heart of

the subject] Without any introduction or preface.

INNOCENCE. See PRESUMPTION OF ~.

INNOCENT. *adj.* Negligently or in a circumstance which does not justify negligence being alleged. G.H.L. Fridman, *The Law of Contract in Canada*, 2d ed. (Toronto: Carswell, 1986) at 283 and 284. See RIGHT TO BE PRESUMED ~.

INNOCENT MISREPRESENTATION. A misstatement which the party making it did not know was such. G.H.L. Fridman, *Sale of Goods in Canada*, 3d ed. (Toronto: Carswell, 1986) at 153.

INNUENDO. *n.* Words not defamatory in their ordinary and plain meaning, but by virtue of circumstances or facts related to their publication. R.E. Brown, *The Law of Defamation in Canada* (Toronto: Carswell, 1987) at 154.

IN OMNIBUS QUIDEM, MAXIME TAMEN IN JURE, AEQUITAS SPECTANDA SIT. [L.] In all things, but particularly in law, equity should be regarded.

IN PAIS. Describes a legal transaction which took place without legal proceedings.

IN PARI DELICTO. [L.] Equally to blame; equally at fault. G.H.L. Fridman, *Restitution*, 2d ed. (Toronto: Carswell, 1992) at 98.

IN PARI DELICTO, POTIOR EST CONDITIO DEFENDENTIS. [L.] Where each party is equally at fault the defendant's position is superior. G.H.L. Fridman, *The Law of Contract in Canada*, 2d ed. (Toronto: Carswell, 1986) at 396.

IN PARI DELICTO, POTIOR EST CONDITIO POSSIDENTIS. [L.] Unless the parties are unequal, the one in possession has the advantage. G.H.L. Fridman, *Restitution*, 2d ed. (Toronto: Carswell, 1992) at 186.

IN PARI MATERIA. [L.] 1. In an analogous situation. 2. Describes statutes which deal with the same class,

person or thing. P. St. J. Langan, ed., *Maxwell on The Interpretation of Statutes*, 12th ed. (Bombay: N.M. Tripathi, 1976) at 66.

IN PERPETUITY. Forever.

IN PERSONAM. [L. in person] Describes an action the only purpose of which is to affect the rights of any parties to that action inter se. J.G. McLeod, *The Conflict of Laws* (Calgary: Carswell, 1983) at 60. See ACTION ~; EQUITY ACTS ~; JUS ~.

IN POSSE. Describes something which does not actually exist, but which may come to exist.

IN PRAESENTI. [L.] For the present time.

INQUEST. *n.* An inquiry held before a coroner by a jury regarding the death of a person who was killed or died under suspicious circumstances or suddenly.

INQUIRY. *n.* An investigation; a hearing.

IN RE. [L.] In the matter of, regarding.

IN REM. [L.] 1. Something done or directed with reference to no person in particular, and therefore with reference to or against anyone it might concern or the whole world. 2. Describes an action to determine the rights or interests of everyone with respect to a particular res, even though the action may involve only two people. J.G. McLeod, *The Conflict of Laws* (Calgary: Carswell, 1983) at 60. See ACTION ~; JUDGMENT ~.

INSANITY. *n.* 1. "The definition of 'legal insanity', or insanity which will preclude a criminal conviction, is found in subss. 16(2) and 16(3) of the [Criminal Code, R.S.C. 1985, c. C-46]." *R. v. Chaulk* (1990), 2 C.R. (4th) 1 at 18, 119 N.R. 116, [1991] 2 W.W.R. 385, 69 Man. R. (2d) 161, 62 C.C.C. (3d) 193, 1 C.R.R. (2d) 1, [1990] 3 S.C.R. 1303, Lamer C.J.C. (Dickson C.J.C., La Forest and Cory JJ. concurring). Criminal Code: S. 16(2) For the purposes of this section, a person is insane when the person is in a state of natural imbecility or has disease of the mind to an extent that renders the person incapable of appreciating the nature and quality of an act or omission or of knowing that an act or omission is wrong. 16(3) A person who has specific delusions, but is in other respects sane, shall not be acquitted on the ground of insanity unless the delusions caused that person to believe in the existence of a state of things that, if it existed, would have justified or excused the act or omission of that person. S. 16 now amended by S.C. 1991, c. 43, s. 2 to read in part: S. 16(1) No person is criminally responsible for an act committed or an omission made while suffering from a mental disorder that rendered the person incapable of appreciating the nature and quality of the act or omission or of knowing that it was wrong . . . 2. ". . . Under s. 615 [of the Criminal Code, R.S.C. 1985, c. C-46], insanity includes any 'illness, disorder or abnormal condition which impairs the human mind or its functioning'." *R. v. Steele* (1991), 63 C.C.C. (3d) 149 at 181, 4 C.R. (4th) 53, 36 Q.A.C. 47, the court per Fish J.A. See DISEASE OF THE MIND.

INSCRIBE. *v.* To enter; to record.

IN SE. [L.] In and of itself.

INSIDER. *n.* With respect to a corporation, (i) the corporation, (ii) an affiliate of the corporation, (iii) a director or officer of the corporation, (iv) a person who beneficially owns, directly or indirectly, more than 10 per cent of the voting securities of the corporation or who exercises control or direction over more than 10 per cent of the votes attached to the voting securities of the corporation, (v) a person employed or retained by the corporation, or (vi) a person who receives specific confidential information from a person described in this clause or elsewhere, including a person described in this subclause, and who has knowledge that the person giving the information is a person described in this clause or elsewhere, including a person described in this subclause, (vii) every director or

senior officer of a company that is itself an insider or subsidiary of an issuer, (viii) an issuer where it has purchased, redeemed or otherwise acquired any of its securities, for so long as it holds any of its securities.

INSIDER TRADING. ". . . [T]he purchase or sale of the securities of a company by a person who, by reason of his position in the company, has access to confidential information not known to other shareholders or the general public. . . ." *Multiple Access Ltd. v. McCutcheon* (1982), 18 B.L.R. 138 at 142, [1982] 2 S.C.R. 161, 138 D.L.R. 93d) 1, 44 N.R. 181, Dickson J. (Laskin C.J.C., Martland, Ritchie, McIntyre and Lamer JJ. concurring).

IN SIMILI MATERIA. [L.] Dealing with similar or related subject-matter.

IN SITU. [L.] In place; in the position originally held.

INSOLVENCY. *n.* "In a general sense, . . . inability to meet one's debts or obligations; in a technical sense, it means the condition or standard of inability to meet debts or obligations, upon the occurrence of which the statutory law enables a creditor to intervene, with the assistance of a Court, to stop individual action by creditors and to secure administration of the debtor's assets in the general interest of creditors; the law also generally allows the debtor to apply for the same administration." *British Columbia (Attorney General) v. Canada (Attorney General)*, [1937] A.C. 391 at 402, 18 C.B.R. 217, [1937] 1 W.W.R. 320, [1937] 1 D.L.R. 695 (B.C. P.C.), the board per Lord Thankerton. See BANKRUPTCY AND ~.

INSOLVENT. *adj.* 1. Unable to meet obligations as they come due in the ordinary course of business. 2. Either ceasing to pay one's debts in the ordinary course of business or unable to pay one's debts as they become due.

INSOLVENT PERSON. A person who is not bankrupt and who resides or carries on business in Canada, whose liabilities to creditors provable as claims under this Act amount to one thousand dollars, and (a) who is for any reason unable to meet his obligations as they generally become due, (b) who has ceased paying his current obligations in the ordinary course of business as they generally become due, or (c) the aggregate of whose property is not, at a fair valuation, sufficient, or, if disposed of at a fairly conducted sale under legal process, would not be sufficient to enable payment of all his obligations, due and accruing due. *Bankruptcy Act*, R.S.C. 1985, c. B-3, s. 2.

IN SPECIE. [L. in its own form] In money or coin.

INSPECTION. *n.* An examination of real or personal property ordered by a court when an examination is necessary to determine an issue in a proceeding. (Ontario, Rules of Civil Procedure, r. 32.01). G.D. Watson & C. Perkins, eds., *Holmested & Watson: Ontario Civil Procedure* (Toronto: Carswell, 1984-) at 32-3.

INSPECTION OF DOCUMENTS. See DISCOVERY.

INSPECTOR. *n.* 1. One who examines and reports. 2. A person appointed or designated under an act to carry out inspections or other duties prescribed. See BUILDING ~.

INSTALMENT. *n.* One part of a debt.

INSTANTER. *adv.* [L.] At once, immediately.

IN STATU QUO. [L.] In its former condition.

INSTITUTE. *v.* To commence.

INSTITUTE. *n.* 1. An organization, body. 2. A treatise; a commentary. See RESEARCH ~.

INSTITUTION. *n.* 1. A bank, credit union, trust company, treasury branch or other similar person, a public school, college, hospital, gaol, penitentiary, correctional institution. 2. "... [B]ears ... the concept of it having a public object ..." *Ontario (Attorney General) v. Tufford Rest Home* (1980), 30 O.R. (2d) 636 at 640 (Co. Ct.), Kovacs Co. Ct. J. 3. A law, rite or ceremony imposed by authority, as a permanent rule

of government or conduct. See CORRECTIONAL ~; CREDIT ~; PENAL ~.

INSTITUTIONAL DELAY. Delay in handling criminal cases expeditiously caused by lack of judges, courtrooms or adequate case management methods. P.W. Hogg, *Constitutional Law of Canada*, 3d ed. (Toronto: Carswell, 1992) at 1125.

INSTITUTIONAL IMPARTIALITY. "The test for institutional impartiality is the same as the test adopted in [R. v. Valente (1985), 24 D.L.R. (4th) 161] with respect to the issue of judicial independence, that is the apprehension of an informed person, viewing the matter realistically and practically, and having thought the matter through. . . ." *Alex Couture Inc. c. Canada (Procureur général)* (1991), (*sub nom. Alex Couture Inc. v. Canada (Attorney General)*) 38 C.P.R. (3d) 293 at 388, 83 D.L.R. (4th) 577, 41 Q.A.C. 1, [1991] R.J.Q. 2534, the court per Rousseau-Houle J.A. See IMPARTIAL.

INSTITUTIONAL INDEPENDENCE. "Judicial control over ... assignment of judges, sittings of the court, and court lists ... as well as the related matters of allocation of courtrooms and direction of the administrative staff engaged in carrying out these functions, has generally been considered the essential and minimum requirement ..." *R. v. Valente (No. 2)* (1985), 19 C.R.R. 354 at 368, 372, 376, 379-80, [1985] 2 S.C.R. 673, 52 O.R. (2d) 779, 37 M.V.R. 9, 49 C.R. (3d) 97, 23 C.C.C. (3d) 193, 24 D.L.R. (4th) 161, 64 N.R. 1, 14 O.A.C. 79, [1985] D.L.Q. 85n, the court per Le Dain J.

INSTRUCT. *v.* 1. For a client to convey information to a solicitor. 2. For a client to authorize a solicitor to appear on their behalf.

INSTRUCTION. *n.* A motion which gives a committee power to do something otherwise impossible, or to direct it to do something otherwise impossible. A. Fraser, W.A. Dawson & J. Holtby, eds., *Beauchesne's Rules and Forms of the House of Commons* *of Canada*, 6th ed. (Toronto: Carswell, 1989) at 203.

INSTRUMENT. *n.* 1. "... [A] word of very wide signification in our language and embraces, inter alia, such objects as implements or tools, a contrivance which produces sounds, as a musical instrument, or even a legal document." *R. v. Hayes* (1958), 29 C.R. 235 at 238, [1958] O.W.N. 449 (C.A.), the court per Schroeder J.A. 2. A formal legal document. 3. "... '[W]ritten document,' ..." *R. v. Evans* (1962), 37 W.W.R. 610 at 611, 37 C.R. 341, 132 C.C.C. 271 (B.C. C.A.), the court per Tysoe J.A. 4. Any grant, certificate of title, conveyance, assurance, deed, map, plan, will, probate or exemplification of probate of will, letters of administration or an exemplification thereof, mortgage or encumbrance, or any other document in writing relating to or affecting the transfer of or other dealing with land or evidencing title thereto. *Land Titles Act*, R.S.C. 1985, c. L-5, s. 2. See NEGOTIABLE ~; STATUTORY ~; TESTAMENTARY ~.

INSTRUMENTALITY. *n.* "... An agent ..." *Medicine Hat (City) v. Canada (Attorney General)* (1985), 29 M.P.L.R. 165 at 175, 37 Alta. L.R. (2d) 208, [1985] 4 W.W.R. 367, 85 D.T.C. 5365, 18 D.L.R. (4th) 428, 59 A.R. 355 (C.A.), the court per Prowse J.A.

INSURABLE INTEREST. 1. "... [I]f an insured can demonstrate ... 'some relation to, or concern in the subject of the insurance, which relation or concern by the happening of the perils insured against may be so affected as to produce a damage, detriment, or prejudice to the person insuring', ... To 'have a moral certainty of advantage or benefit, but for those risk[s] or dangers', or 'to be so circumstanced with respect to [the subject matter of the insurance] as to have benefit from its existence, prejudice from its destruction' ..." *Kosmopoulos v. Constitution Insurance Co. of Canada* (1987), (sub nom. *Constitution Insurance Co. of Canada v. Kosmopoulos*) 36 B.L.R. 233 at 255,

[1987] 1 S.C.R. 2, 22 C.C.L.I. 296, [1987] I.L.R. 1-2147, 74 N.R. 360, 21 O.A.C. 4, 34 C.L.R. (4th) 208, Wilson J. (Beetz, Lamer, Le Dain and La Forest JJ. concurring). 2. A person has an insurable interest in his own life and well-being and in the life and well-being of, (a) his child or grandchild; (b) his spouse; (c) any person upon whom he is wholly or in part dependent for, or from whom he is receiving, support or education; (d) his officer or employee; and (e) any person in whom he has a pecuniary interest. *Insurance acts.*

INSURANCE. *n.* The undertaking by one person to indemnify another person against loss or liability for loss in respect of a certain risk or peril to which the object of the insurance may be exposed, or to pay a sum of money or other thing of value upon the happening of a certain event. *Insurance acts.* See AUTOMOBILE ~; CONTINGENCY ~; CONTRACT OF ~; CONTRACT OF MARINE ~; CREDIT ~; MARINE ~; MORTGAGE ~; RE~; UNEMPLOYMENT ~.

INSURED. *n.* See NAMED ~.

INSURED PERSON. A person who enters into a subsisting contract of insurance with an insurer and includes (a) a person insured by a contract whether named or not; and (b) a person to whom or for whose benefit all or part of the proceeds of a contract of insurance is payable; and (c) a person entitled to have insurance money applied toward satisfaction of his judgment in accordance with the Insurance Act. *Insurance acts.*

INSURER. *n.* The person, corporation, underwriter, partnership, fraternal or other society, association, or syndicate who undertakes or agrees or offers to undertake a contract. *Insurance acts.*

INTANGIBLE. *n.* All personal property, including choses in action, that is not goods, chattel paper, documents of title, instruments or securities. *Personal Property Security acts.*

INTELLECTUAL PROPERTY. See INDUSTRIAL PROPERTY.

INTENT. *n.* Aim, actual desire, design, end, objective or purpose. D. Stuart, *Canadian Criminal Law: A Treatise*, 2d ed. (Toronto: Carswell, 1987) at 128. See EQUITY LOOKS TO THE ~ RATHER THAN TO THE FORM; GENERAL ~; LETTER OF ~; SPECIFIC ~; TRANSFERRED ~.

INTENTION. See EQUITY IMPUTES AN ~ TO FULFIL AN OBLIGATION.

INTENTIONAL INDUCEMENT OF BREACH OF CONTRACT. Liability arises where, knowing of the contract and with intent to prevent or hinder its performance, the defendant induces one party not to perform his part of the contract or the defendant commits a wrongful act to prevent the performance of the contract. J.G. Fleming, *The Law of Torts*, 8th ed. (Sydney: Law Book, 1992) at 690.

INTENTIONAL INFLICTION OF NERVOUS SHOCK. Conduct, including words, which causes severe emotional distress. J.G. Fleming, *The Law of Torts*, 8th ed. (Sydney: Law Book, 1992) at 31.

INTENTIONAL TORT. A tort in which the wrongdoer either wishes to accomplish the result or believes the result will follow from his act and the result is an injury to the plaintiff. J.G. Fleming, *The Law of Torts*, 8th ed. (Sydney: Law Book, 1992) at 77.

INTER ALIA. [L.] Among other things.

INTER-DELEGATION. *n.* The delegation of provincial power to the federal level or of federal power to the provinces. P.W. Hogg, *Constitutional Law of Canada*, 3d ed. (Toronto: Carswell, 1992) at 353.

INTERESSE TERMINI. [L.] An executory interest which is a right of entry that a lessee acquires in land through a demise.

INTEREST. *n.* 1. Something which a person has in a thing when that person has advantages, duties, liabilities, losses or rights connected with it, whether ascertained or potential,

present or future. 2. In the law of insurance, something which a person has in the life of a person or in property when the death of the person or destruction or damage to the property would expose that person to pecuniary liability or loss. 3. ". . . [I]s, in general terms, the return or consideration or compensation for the use or retention by one person of a sum of money, belonging to, in a colloquial sense, or owed to, another. . . ." *Saskatchewan (Attorney General) v. Canada (Attorney General)*, [1947] S.C.R. 394 at 411, [1947] 3 D.L.R. 689, Rand J. See ADVERSE IN ~; AGAINST ~; BENEFICIAL ~; BEST ~S OF THE CHILD; COMMON ~; COMPOUND ~; CONFLICT OF ~; EQUITABLE ~; EXECUTORY ~; INSURABLE ~; LIFE ~; MEMBERSHIP ~; MINERAL ~; PERFECTED SECURITY ~; POST-JUDGMENT ~; PRE-JUDGMENT ~; PUBLIC ~; REVERSIONARY ~; SECURITY ~; TIME SHARE ~; UNDIVIDED ~.

INTEREST IN EXPECTANCY. Includes an estate or interest in remainder or reversion and any other future interest whether vested or contingent, but does not include a reversion expectant on the determination of a lease.

INTERFERENCE. See UNLAWFUL ~ WITH CONTRACTUAL RELATIONS.

INTERIM. *adj.* ". . . '[I]n the meantime', . . . 'for the time being' . . ." *Bell Canada v. Canada (Canadian Radio-Television & Telecommunications Commission)* (1987), 43 D.L.R. (4th) 30 at 46, 79 N.R. 58, [1988] 1 F.C. 296 (C.A.) Marceau J.A.

INTERIM DIVIDEND. A dividend paid during a company's financial year.

INTERIM INJUNCTION. 1. A species of interlocutory injunction granted for a very brief period until application for an interlocutory injunction is made. G.H.L. Fridman, *The Law of Contract in Canada*, 2d ed. (Toronto: Carswell, 1986) at 727. 2. Includes an interlocutory injunction. *Trade Practice Act*, R.S.B.C. 1979, c. 406, s. 1.

INTERIM ORDER. 1. "... [I]nterim decisions may be reviewed and modified in a retrospective manner by a final decision. It is inherent in the nature of interim orders that their effect, as well as any discrepancy between the interim order and the final order, may be reviewed and remedied by the final order ..." *Bell Canada v. Canada (Canadian Radio-Television & Telecomunications Commission)* (1989), 38 Admin. L.R. 1 at 30, [1989] 1 S.C.R. 1722, 60 D.L.R. (4th) 682, 97 N.R. 15, the court per Gonthier J. 2. "... [A] temporary decision that does not finally dispose of the case before the tribunal." *Bell Canada v. Canada (Canadian Radio-Television & Telecommunications Commission)* (1987), 43 D.L.R. (4th) 30 at 33, 79 N.R. 58, [1988] 1 F.C. 296 (C.A.) Pratte J.A.

INTERIM RECEIVER. A person appointed under The Bankruptcy Act between filing a petition and making an order judging that the debtor is bankrupt. F. Bennett, *Receiverships* (Toronto: Carswell, 1985) at 3.

INTERIM RELEASE. See JUDICIAL ~.

INTERIM RELIEF. 1. "... [T]emporary relief which is granted pending determination of the application for final or permanent relief. An interim order terminates upon an order being made at trial." *St. Cyr v. Lechkoon* (1991), 36 R.F.L. (3d) 203 at 206 (Ont. Gen. Div.), Kozak J. 2. Interim custody, interim support and interim support pending confirmation or provisional variation. *Divorce Act, 1985*, S.C. 1986, c.4, ss. 15-19.

INTERIM SUPPLY. A measure to provide a government with money to meet any obligations before its main estimates are approved. A. Fraser, W.A. Dawson & J. Holtby, eds., *Beauchesne's Rules and Forms of the House of Commons of Canada*, 6th ed. (Toronto: Carswell, 1989) at 260.

INTERLINEATION. *n.* Inserting anything into a document after it has been executed.

INTERLOCUTORY. *adj.* 1. Incidental to the major intent of an action. 2. Temporary, provisional, not final. 3. "... [E]mployed to designate steps in an action intermediate between the initial and final proceeding, and merely leading towards the proceeding which finally terminates the litigation, ..." *Whiting v. Hovey* (1885), 12 O.A.R. 119 at 125 (C.A.), Patterson J.A.

INTERLOCUTORY INJUNCTION. 1. A measure intended to ensure that certain specified acts do not take place until the rights of the parties are finally determined by the court. G.H.L. Fridman, *The Law of Contract in Canada*, 2d ed. (Toronto: Carswell, 1986) at 727. 2. "... [A]n extraordinary and discretionary remedy and one which will not be granted unless the court is satisfied that it is a proper case in which to exercise its discretion. A tripartite test has evolved through the jurisprudence to assist the court in making a decision: (1) has the applicant shown a prima facie/serious issue to be tried; (2) is there a danger of irreparable harm to the applicant, and; (3) does the balance of convenience lie with the applicant." *Imperial Chemical Industries PLC v. Apotex Inc.* (1989), 23 C.P.R. (3d) 1 at 15, 22 C.I.P.R. 201, [1989] 2 F.C. 608, Rouleau J.

INTERLOCUTORY ORDER. "[An order which does not] ... finally dispose of the rights of the parties ..." *Hockin v. Bank of British Columbia* (1989), 35 C.P.C. (2d) 250 at 253, 37 B.C.L.R. (2d) 139 (C.A.), Wallace J.A.

INTERNATIONAL COURT OF JUSTICE. A judicial body created by the Charter of the United Nations.

INTERNATIONAL LAW. Of two kinds: public international law, a code of rules which controls the conduct of independent nations in their relations with one another and private international law, a branch of municipal law which determines before what nation's courts a certain action or suit ought to be brought and by what nation's law it should be settled. See CONVENTIONAL ~; CUSTOMARY ~; PRIVATE ~.

INTER PARES. [L.] Between or among equals.

INTER PARTES. [L.] Between or among parties.

INTERPLEADER. *n.* The process by which a person who expects to be or is sued by two or more parties with adverse claims to goods or a debt in the first person's hands, but in which the first person has no interest, obtains relief by arranging that the other parties try their rights between themselves. See STAKEHOLDER.

INTERPOLATE. *v.* To insert words in a finished document.

INTERPOLATION. *n.* The act of interpolating; the words which are inserted.

INTERPRETATION. *n.* 1. Construction of a document or statute. 2. Oral translation.

INTERPRETATION CLAUSE. A clause which sets out the meanings of particular words used in that statute.

INTERPRETATION SECTION. A section which sets out the meanings of particular words used in that statute.

INTERPRETER. *n.* At a trial, someone sworn to interpret the evidence of someone else who speaks a language which is not that of the proceedings, a mute or a hearing impaired person.

INTERPROVINCIAL. *adj.* Between provinces.

INTERREGNUM. *n.* [L.] A time when a throne is vacant.

INTERROGATION. *n.* The conduct of an inquiry; the asking of questions. S.A. Cohen, *Due Process of Law* (Toronto: Carswell, 1977) at 71. See MODE A ~.

INTERROGATORY. *n.* A written question addressed to one party on behalf of the other party to a cause.

IN TERROREM. [L.] Terrifying.

INTER SE. [L.] Between themselves.

INTERSECTION. *n.* The area embraced within the prolongation or connection of the lateral curb lines or, if none, then of the lateral boundary lines of two or more highways which join one another at an angle, whether or not one highway crosses the other.

INTERVENANT. *n.* Someone who intervenes in a suit in which he or she was not originally involved.

INTERVENE. *v.* A person who is not a party to a proceeding ... claims (a) an interest in the subject matter of the proceeding; (b) that the person may be adversely affected by a judgment in the proceeding; or (c) that there exists between the person and one or more of the parties to the proceeding a question of law or fact in common with one or more of the questions in issue in the proceeding ... (Ontario, Rules of Civil Procedure, r. 13.01).

INTERVENER. *n.* A person who files an intervention or who intervenes. See INTERVENOR.

INTERVENING CAUSE. An act occurring after the negligence of the defendant which actively functions to produce harm. J.G. Fleming, *The Law of Torts*, 8th ed. (Sydney: Law Book, 1992) at 216. See NOVUS ACTUS INTERVENIENS.

INTERVENOR. *n.* 1. "... [D]escribe persons or associations that are permitted to participate in proceedings to promote their own views, though the proceedings will not determine their legal rights." *Canada (Attorney General) v. Aluminum Co. of Canada* (1987), 35 D.L.R. (4th) 495 at 505, 26 Admin. L.R. 18, 15 C.P.C. (2d) 289, 10 B.C.L.R. (2d) 371, [1987] 3 W.W.R. 193 (C.A.), Seaton J.A. (Hinkson J.A. concurring). 2. A newsletter of the Canadian Environmental Law Association. See INTERVENER.

INTER VIVOS. [L.] Between living people. See GIFT ~.

INTER VIVOS GIFT. A gift made while the donor is living.

INTER VIVOS TRUST. Created by writing, a deed or oral declaration, a trust which is to take effect during the lifetime of the trust's creator. D.M.W. Waters, *The Law of Trusts in Canada*, 2d ed. (Toronto: Carswell, 1984) at 29.

INTESTACY. *n.* The condition or state of dying without a valid will.

INTESTATE. *n.* A person owning property who dies without a will.

INTIMIDATION. *n.* "The essential ingredients of the tort [of intimidation] are: 1. A threat by one person to use unlawful means (such as violence, or a tort or a breach of contract) so as to compel another to obey his wishes. 2. The person so threatened must comply with the demand rather than risk the threat being carried into execution." *Roth v. Roth* (1991), 9 C.C.L.T. (2d) 141 at 152, 4 O.R. (3d) 740, 34 M.V.R. (2d) 228 (Gen. Div.), Mandel J.

IN TOTO. [L.] Completely, entirely, wholly.

INTOXICANT. *n.* Includes alcohol, alcoholic, spirituous, vinous, fermently malt or other intoxicating liquor or combination of liquors and mixed liquor a part of which is spiritous, vinous, fermented or otherwise intoxicating and all drinks, drinkable liquids, preparations or mixtures capable of human consumption that are intoxicating.

INTOXICATED. *adj.* Under the influence of alcohol to the extent that a person's physical and mental functioning is substantially impaired. *Treatment of Intoxicated Persons Act*, R.S.N.B. 1973, c. T-11.1, s. 1.

INTOXICATION. See INVOLUNTARY ~.

INTRA VIRES. [L.] 1. Within the range of authority or power. 2. Said of a law found to be valid because it was enacted under powers allocated to the legislative body which enacted it, by the Constitution. P.W. Hogg, *Constitutional Law of Canada*, 3d ed. (Toronto: Carswell, 1992) at 372.

INTRODUCED. *adj.* ". . . '[P]resented, tendered or offered'." *Maritime Construction Ltd. v. R.* (1988), [1989] 1 C.T.C. 306 at 307, 93 N.B.R. (2d) 438, 238 A.P.R. 438 (Q.B.), McLellan J.

INURE. *v.* To take effect.

INVALID. *adj.* 1. Void, having no effect. 2. Physically or mentally incapable of earning financial remuneration.

INVENTION. *n.* Any new and useful art, process, machine, manufacture or composition of matter, or any new and useful improvement in any art, process, machine, manufacture or composition of matter.

INVENTOR. *n.* The person who applies for a patent and who invented the thing alone, not because another suggested it or because the person read about it. H.G. Fox, *The Canadian Law and Practice Relating to Letters Patent for Inventions*, 4th ed. (Toronto: Carswell, 1969) at 225.

INVENTORY. *n.* 1. Goods that are held by a person for sale or lease, or that are to be furnished or have been furnished under a contract of service, or that are raw materials, work in process or materials used or consumed in a business or profession. *Personal Property Security acts.* 2. A schedule or list which accurately describes goods and chattels.

INVEST. *v.* 1. To transfer possession. 2. To contribute money.

INVESTITURE. *n.* 1. The free transfer of possession or seisin. 2. The formal bestowal of office or honour.

INVESTMENT. *n.* 1. A purchase of a security of an issuer or a loan or advance to a person, but does not include a loan or advance, whether secured or unsecured, that is (a) made by mutual fund, its mutual fund manager or its mutual fund distributor, and (b) merely ancillary to the main business of the mutual fund, its manager or its distributor. 2. (a) An investment in a corporation by way of purchase of bonds, debentures, notes or other evidences of indebtedness thereof or shares thereof, or (b) a loan to a person or persons. See AUTHORIZED ~.

INVESTMENT COMPANY. A company (a) incorporated after January 1, 1972 primarily for the purpose of carrying on the business of investment, or (b) that carries on the business of investment, but does not include a company to which the Bank Act, the Quebec Savings Banks Act, chapter B-4 of the Revised Statutes of Canada, 1970, the Canadian and British Insurance Companies Act or the Cooperative Credit Associations Act applies or a loan company within the meaning of the Loan Companies Act. *Investment Companies Act*, R.S.C. 1985, c. I-22, s. 2.

INVESTMENT CONTRACT. A contract, agreement, certificate, instrument or writing containing an undertaking by an issuer to pay the holder thereof, or the holder's assignee or personal representative or other person, a stated or determinable maturity value in cash or its equivalent on a fixed or determinable date and containing optional settlement, cash surrender or loan values prior to or after maturity, the consideration for which consists of payments made or to be made to the issuer in instalments or periodically, or of a single sum, according to a plan fixed by the contract, whether or not the holder is or may be entitled to share in the profits or earnings of, or to receive additional credits or sums from, the issuer, but does not include a contract within the meaning of the Insurance Act.

INVESTMENT TRUST. A trust which collects, retains and invests funds for multiple purposes. D.M.W. Waters, *The Law of Trusts in Canada*, 2d ed. (Toronto: Carswell, 1984) at 101.

INVITATION TO TREAT. A statement which indicates general commercial intent, the wish of that party to contract with another party if they can make suitable arrangements. G.H.L. Fridman, *The Law of Contract in Canada*, 2d ed. (Toronto: Carswell, 1986) at 30.

INVITEE. *n.* One who is either impliedly or expressly invited to an occupier's premises for some purpose connected indirectly or directly with the occupier's business. In law, a guest is a licensee, not an invitee. J.V. DiCastri, *Occupiers' Liability* (Vancouver: Burroughs/Carswell, 1980) at 33.

INVITOR. *n.* A person who invites another to her or his premises for business purposes.

IN VITRO. [L. in glass] In a test tube. F.A. Jaffe, *A Guide to Pathological Evidence*, 3d ed. (Toronto: Carswell, 1991) at 221.

IN VIVO. [L.] In a living body. F.A. Jaffe, *A Guide to Pathological Evidence*, 3d ed. (Toronto: Carswell, 1991) at 221.

INVOICE. *n.* A written account of the particulars of goods shipped or sent to a purchaser.

INVOLUNTARY INTOXICATION. Intoxication which is not self-induced. D. Stuart, *Canadian Criminal Law: A Treatise*, 2d ed. (Toronto: Carswell, 1987) at 364.

IOTA. *n.* The smallest possible quantity.

IOU. *abbr.* I owe you. The written admission or expression of a debt.

I.P.J. *abbr.* Intellectual Property Journal.

IPSE DIXIT. [L. one said it oneself] A simple assertion.

IPSISSIMA VERBA. [L.] The very same words.

IPSO FACTO. [L.] By the very same act.

IPSO JURE. [L.] By the very law.

I.R.B. *abbr.* Industrial Relations Board.

IRREBUTTABLE. *adj.* Not rebuttable; not capable of disproof.

IRREGULARITY. *n.* A condition resulting when a judicial or extra-judicial proceeding is done wrongly or without proper formalities.

IRRELEVANT. *adj.* Not relevant.

IRREPARABLE HARM. "[The injury] ... must be material and one which cannot be adequately remedied by damages...." *Spooner Oils Ltd. v. Turner Valley Gas Conservation Board*, [1932] 2 W.W.R. 641 at 646, [1932] 4 D.L.R. 681 (Alta. C.A.),

McGillivary J.A.

IRREPLEVIABLE. *adj.* Unable to be replevied.

IRREPLEVISABLE. *adj.* Unable to be replevied.

IRREVOCABLE. *adj.* Not able to be revoked.

IRREVOCABLE BENEFICIARY. A designation by an insured of a beneficiary. The designation may not be altered or revoked without the consent of the beneficiary during his or her lifetime. M.G. Baer & J.A. Rendall, eds., *Cases on the Canadian Law of Insurance*, 4th ed. (Toronto: Carswell, 1988) at 774.

ISSUE. *v.* 1. In respect of an award, means make and publish to the parties to the arbitration. *Labour Code*, R.S.B.C. 1979, c. 212, s. 92. 2. With reference to a disposition that is required to be executed by the holder, means to mail or deliver 2 or more copies of the disposition to the intended holder for execution by him. *Public Lands Act*, R.S.A. 1980, c. P-30, s. 1.

ISSUE. *n.* 1. A matter in dispute. 2. The first delivery of a bill or note, complete in form, to a person who takes it as a holder. *Bills of Exchange Act*, R.S.C. 1985, c. B-4, s. 2. 3. "... [T]echnical meaning [is] 'descendants' ..." *Davidson, Re* (1926), 59 O.L.R. 643 at 644 (C.A.), the court per Latchford C.J. See DIE WITHOUT ~; DIE WITHOUT LEAVING ~; DYING WITHOUT ~; FAILURE OF ~; HAVE NO ~; JOINDER OF ~; MALE ~.

ISSUED. *adj.* Describes an originating process which a registrar dates, signs, seals with the seal of the court and to which a court file number is assigned (Ontario Rules of Civil Procedure, r. 14.07(1)). G.D. Watson & C. Perkins, eds., *Holmested & Watson: Ontario Civil Procedure* (Toronto: Carswell, 1984) at 14-5.

ISSUED CAPITAL. The quantity of shares allotted and issued. H. Sutherland, D.B. Horsley & J.M. Edmiston, eds., *Fraser's Handbook on Canadian Company Law*, 7th ed.

(Toronto: Carswell, 1985) at 41.

ISSUE ESTOPPEL. 1. "... [P]revents [the prosecution] from raising again any of the separate issues of fact which the jury have decided, or are presumed to have decided, in reaching their verdict in the accused's favour...." *R. v. Greeno* (1983), 6 C.C.C. (3d) 325 at 328, 58 N.S.R. (2d) 261, 123 A.P.R. 261 (C.A.), the court per Macdonald J.A. 2. "The requirements of issue estoppel still remain (1) that the same question has been decided; (2) that the judicial decision which is said to create the estoppel was final; and, (3) that the parties to the judicial decision or their privies were the same persons as the parties to the proceedings in which the estoppel is raised or their privies." *Carl-Zeiss-Stiftung v. Rayner & Keeler Ltd. (No. 2)*, [1967] 1 A.C. 853 at 935. [1966] 2 All E.R. 536 (U.K. H.L.), Lord Guest.

ISSUER. *n.* A person or company who has outstanding, issues or proposes to issue, a security or a body corporate, (i) that is required to maintain a securities register, (ii) that directly or indirectly creates fractional interests in its rights or property and issues security certificates or uncertified securities as evidence of the fractional interests, (iii) that places or authorizes the placing of its name on a security certificate, otherwise than as an authenticating trustee, registrar or transfer agent, or that otherwise authorizes the issue of a security certificate or an uncertificated security evidencing a share, participation or other interest in its property or in an enterprise or evidencing its duty to perform an obligation, or (iv) that becomes responsible for or in place of any other person described as an issuer.

ISSUER BID. An offer made by the issuer to acquire or an offer to redeem securities of an issuer, other than debt securities that are not convertible into equity securities.

ITEM. *n.* 1. That portion of a vote used for a specific program purpose. *Financial Administration acts.* 2. "...

[A]ny separate fact or statement...." *Goddard v. Barker* (1951), 4 W.W.R. (N.S.) 433 at 437 (B.C. C.A.), O'Halloran J.A. 3. "... [A] paragraph or a short article...." *Goddard v. Barker* (1951), 4 W.W.R. (N.S.) 433 at 437 (B.C. C.A.), O'Halloran J.A.

J

J. *abbr*. Justice.

J.A. *abbr*. Justice of appeal.

JACTITATION. *n*. A false pretension to marry.

JAIL. *n*. A prison or gaol. See COMMON ~; GAOL.

J. BUS. L. *abbr*. Journal of Business Law.

J. CAN. STUDIES. *abbr*. Journal of Canadian Studies (Revue d'études canadiennes).

J.E. *abbr*. Jurisprudence Express.

JEOPARDY. See DOUBLE ~; IN ~.

J. JUGES PROV. *abbr*. Journal des juges provinciaux (Provincial Judges Journal).

J.L. & SOCIAL POL'Y. *abbr*. Journal of Law and Social Policy (Revue des lois et des politiques sociales).

J.M.V.L. *abbr*. Journal of Motor Vehicle Law.

JOB. *n*. A specific assignment of work; a full-time work position.

JOBBER. *n*. Someone who buys and sells goods wholesale and handles goods on commission. G.H.L. Fridman, *Sale of Goods in Canada*, 3d ed. (Toronto: Carswell, 1986) at 493.

JOHN DOE. A made-up name used in legal proceedings for an imagined or unnamed plaintiff.

JOINDER. *n*. Coupling of matters, proceeding together. See MIS~; NON-~.

JOINDER OF CAUSES OF ACTION. The coupling of several matters in one proceeding or suit.

JOINDER OF ISSUE. Occurs when, at their time to plead, a party denies one particular part or every part of the previous pleading and does not allege any new facts to support their case so that the pleadings end completely or to some extent.

JOINDER OF PARTIES. The coupling of people as plaintiffs or defendants.

JOINT. *adj*. Combined; shared between many; possessed by the same party.

JOINT AND SEVERAL. Describes the obligation of two or more persons when all are liable jointly and each is liable severally.

JOINT BANK ACCOUNT. A common account in which associated people have funds and which all or some may draw upon on occasion. I.F.G. Baxter, *The Law of Banking*, 3d ed. (Toronto: Carswell, 1981) at 43.

JOINT COMMITTEE. A group consisting of members of both houses of Parliament, usually with an investigative or administrative purpose. A. Fraser, W.A. Dawson & J. Holtby, eds., *Beauchesne's Rules and Forms of the House of Commons of Canada*, 6th ed. (Toronto: Carswell, 1989) at 222.

JOINT CUSTODY. ". . . [S]hared parental responsibility. A joint custody award gives legal custody to both parents, with care and control to one and liberal access to the other." *Baker v. Baker* (1978), 3 R.F.L. (2d) 193 at 196, 95 D.L.R. (3d) 529, 1 Fam. L. Rev. 266 (Ont. H.C.), Boland J.

JOINT DEPOSIT. See JOINT BANK ACCOUNT.

JOINT HEIR. A co-heir.

JOINTLY. *adv.* ". . . '[T]ogether with' . . ." *Grieve McClory Ltd. v. Dome Lumber Co.*, [1923] 2 D.L.R. 154 at 156, [1923] 1 W.W.R. 989 (S.C.C.), Davies C.J.

JOINTLY AND SEVERALLY. Describes parties who are liable separately or all together.

JOINT STOCK COMPANY. In English law, an unincorporated company or large partnership with transferable shares formed in the nineteenth century.

JOINT TENANCY. 1. Describes ownership when the four unities of possession, time, interest and title are present and there are no words of severance. A. Bissett-Johnson & W.M. Holland, eds., *Matrimonial Property Law in Canada* (Toronto: Carswell, 1980) at 1-11. 2. ". . . [C]reated where the same interest in real or personal property is passed by the same conveyance to two or more persons in the same right or by construction or operation of law jointly, with a right of survivorship, ie. the right of the survivor or survivors to the whole property." *R. v. Uniacke*, [1944] 4 D.L.R. 297 at 301, 3 W.W.R. 232, 82 C.C.C. 247 (Sask. C.A.), the court per Martin C.J.S.

JOINT TENANT. One who holds an undivided equal interest in the entire property; after death, the survivor acquires the deceased's interest.

JOINT TORT. ". . . [A] common wrongful act by several persons, in which there is but one injuria, giving rise to a joint and several liability by all, and in which each is liable for the whole damage. . . ." *Lambert v. Roberts Drug Stores Ltd. (No. 1)*, [1933] 4 D.L.R. 193 at 194-5, [1933] 2 W.W.R. 508, 41 Man. R. 322 (C.A.), the court

per Trueman J.A.

JOINT TORTFEASORS. Persons who have acted in common and whose action is the cause of the tort and who as a consequence are responsible for the same tort. J.G. Fleming, *The Law of Torts*, 8th ed. (Sydney: Law Book, 1992) at 255.

JOINTURE. *n.* A provision a husband makes to support his wife after he dies.

JOINT VENTURE. An association of two or more person or entities, where the relationship among those associated persons or entities does not, under the laws in force in Canada, constitute a corporation, a partnership or a trust and where, in the case of an investment to which this Act applies, all the undivided ownership interests in the assets of the Canadian business or in the voting interests of the entity that is the subject of the investment are or will be owned by all the persons or entities that are so associated. *Investment Canada Act*, R.S.C. 1985 (1st Supp.), c. 28, s. 3.

JOINT WILL. ". . . [A] will made by two or more testators contained in the same document duly executed by testator and testatrix disposing either of their separate properties or their joint property. It operates on the death of each testator as his will disposing of his separate property and is in, effect, two or more wills . . ." *Ohorodnyk, Re* (1979), 4 E.T.R. 233 at 244, 24 O.R. (2d) 228, 97 D.L.R. (3d) 502 (H.C.), Hollingworth J. See MUTUAL WILLS.

JOURNALS. *n.* The official and permanent record of proceedings in the House of Commons. A. Fraser, W.A. Dawson & J. Holtby, eds., *Beauchesne's Rules and Forms of the House of Commons of Canada*, 6th ed. (Toronto: Carswell, 1989) at 299.

JOYRIDE. *v.* ". . . [T]he unauthorized taking of a motor vehicle with the intent to drive or use it temporarily . . ." *Lafrance v. R.* (1973), 23 C.R.N.S. 100 at 115, 13 C.C.C. (2d) 289, 39 D.L.R. (3d) 693, [1975] 2 S.C.R. 201, Laskin J. (dissenting) (Hall and Spence JJ. concurring).

J.P. *abbr.* Justice of the peace.

J. PLAN. & ENV. L. *abbr.* Journal of Planning and Environmental Law.

J.S.D. *abbr.* Doctor of Juristic Science; Doctor of Juridical Science.

J. SOCIAL WELFARE L. *abbr.* Journal of Social Welfare Law.

JUDGE. *n.* 1. The person authorized to determine any question or cause in a court. 2. Includes any person lawfully presiding in a court. See CHIEF ~; CITIZENSHIP ~; NO MAN SHALL BE ~ IN HIS OWN CAUSE.

JUDGE-MADE LAW. See JUDICIAL LEGISLATION.

JUDGE'S NOTES. Notes usually taken by a judge when evidence is given viva voce.

JUDGMENT. *n.* 1. A judicial decision; the determination of a court; a court's sentence or decision on the major question in a proceeding. 2. Includes orders. *Muzak Corp. v. C.A.P.A.C.*, [1953] 2 S.C.R. 182 at 196-7, 13 Fox Pat. C. 168, 19 C.P.R. 1, Cartwright J. 3. The reasons a court gives for a decision. See CONSENT ~; DECLARATORY ~; DEFAULT ~; ENTER ~; FINAL ~; FOREIGN ~; MERGER INTO ~; SUMMARY ~.

JUDGMENT CREDITOR. 1. The person by whom the judgment was obtained, and includes the executors, administrators, successors and assigns of that person. 2. The person in whose favour the judgment was given, and includes that person's executors, administrators, successors and assigns.

JUDGMENT DEBT. A sum of money or any costs, charges or expenses made payable by or under a judgment in a civil proceeding.

JUDGMENT DEBTOR. 1. Includes a party required to make a payment of money and costs, or either, under an order, and any executor, administrator or assignee of a judgment debtor. 2. The person against whom the judgment was given and includes any person against whom the judgment is enforceable under the law of the territory of origin. 3. The person liable for the payment of money payable under a judgment or order.

JUDGMENT IN REM. "... [A]n adjudication pronounced upon the status of some particular subject matter by a tribunal having competent authority for that purpose. Such an adjudication being a solemn declaration from the proper and accredited quarter that the status of the thing adjudicated upon is as declared, concludes all persons from saying that the status of the thing adjudicated upon was not such as declared by the adjudication." *Sleeth v. Hurlbert* (1896), 25 S.C.R. 620 at 630, 3 C.C.C. 197, Sedgewick J. (Gwynne, King and Girouard JJ. concurring). See IN REM.

JUDGMENT SUMMONS. A summons which requires a judgment debtor to appear so that a court officer or judge may examine the debtor's income and assets. C.R.B. Dunlop, *Creditor-Debtor Law in Canada* (Toronto: Carswell, 1981) at 105.

JUDICIAL. *adj.* "... [T]he question of whether any particular function is 'judicial' is not to be determined simply on the basis of procedural trappings. The primary issue is the nature of the question which the tribunal is called upon to decide. Where the tribunal is faced with a private dispute between parties, and is called upon to adjudicate through the application of a recognized body of rules in a manner consistent with fairness and impartiality, then, normally, it is acting in a 'judicial capacity' ... the judicial task involves questions of 'principle', that is consideration of the competing rights of individuals or groups. This can be contrasted with questions of 'policy' involving competing views of the collective good of the community as a whole ..." *Reference re Residential Tenancies Act* (1981), (*sub nom. Residential Tenancies Act of Ontario, Re*) 123 D.L.R. (3d) 554 at 571, [1981] 1 S.C.R. 714, 37 N.R. 158, Dickson J.

JUDICIAL ACT. "... [A]n act done by competent authority upon consideration of acts and circumstances, and imposing liability or affecting the rights of others." *The Queen v. Corporation of Dublin* (1878), 2 L.R. Ir. 371 at 377, May C.J.

JUDICIAL COMMITTEE. A committee of the Privy Council made up of Privy Councillors who are judges. They advise the Queen how to dispose of each appeal, and their advice is considered to be a binding judgment. P.W. Hogg, *Constitutional Law of Canada*, 3d ed. (Toronto: Carswell, 1992) at 202-3.

JUDICIAL COMMITTEE OF THE PRIVY COUNCIL. In the days of the British empire, the final appeal court from every colonial court. It continues as a Commonwealth court for Commonwealth nations which haved retained that appeal. P.W. Hogg, *Constitutional Law of Canada*, 3d ed. (Toronto: Carswell, 1992) at 202.

JUDICIAL COUNCIL. See CANADIAN ~.

JUDICIAL DISCRETION. During a trial, the freedom of a judge to summarily decide certain matters which cannot afterwards be questioned.

JUDICIAL IMMUNITY. ". . . [A] judge of a superior court is protected when he is acting in the bona fide exercise of his office and under the belief that he has jurisdiction, though he may be mistaken in that belief and may not in truth have any jurisdiction. . . ." *Sirros v. Moore*, [1974] 3 All E.R. 776 at 784 (U.K.), Lord Denning M.R.

JUDICIAL INDEPENDENCE. ". . . [T]he generally accepted core of the principle of judicial independence has been the complete liberty of individual judges to hear and decide the cases that come before them: no outsider - be it government, pressure group, individual or even another judge - should interfere in fact, or attempt to interfere, with the way in which a judge conducts his or her case and makes his or her decision." *R. v. Beauregard* (*sub nom. Beauregard v. Canada*), [1986] 2 S.C.R. 56 at 69, 73, 70 N.R. 1, 30 D.L.R. (4th) 481, 26 C.R.R. 59, Dickson C.J. (Estey J. and Laskin JJ. con-

curring). See INSTITUTIONAL INDEPENDENCE.

JUDICIAL INTERIM RELEASE. The judge's setting free the accused between committal for trial and the trial's completion.

JUDICIAL LEGISLATION. Growth or advancement of law through a judicial decision.

JUDICIAL NOTICE. ". . . [T]he acceptance by a Court or judicial tribunal, without the requirement of proof, of the truth of a particular fact or state of affairs that is of such general or common knowledge in the community that proof of it can be dispensed with. . . ." *R. v. Potts* (1982), 134 D.L.R. (3d) 227 at 233, 36 O.R. (2d) 195, 14 M.V.R. 72, 26 C.R. (3d) 252, 66 C.C.C. (2d) 219 (C.A.), the court per Thorson J.A.

JUDICIAL OFFICER. See BRIBERY OF ~.

JUDICIAL OR QUASI-JUDICIAL PROCEEDING. "It is possible . . . to formulate several criteria for determining whether a decision or order is one required by law to be made on a judicial or quasi-judicial basis. The list is not intended to be exhaustive. (1) Is there anything in the language in which the function is conferred or in the general context in which it is exercised which suggests that a hearing is contemplated before a decision is reached? (2) Does the decision or order directly or indirectly affect the rights and obligations of persons? (3) Is the adversary process involved? (4) Is there an obligation to apply substantive rules to many individual cases rather than . . . in a broad sense?" *Minister of National Revenue v. Coopers & Lybrand*, [1979] 1 S.C.R. 495 at 504, 92 D.L.R. (3d) 1, [1978] C.T.C. 829, 78 D.T.C. 6258, the court per Dickson J.

JUDICIAL PROCEEDING. 1. A proceeding (a) in or under the authority of a court of justice, (b) before the Senate or House of Commons or a committee of the Senate or House of Commons, or before a legislative council, legislative assembly or house of assembly or a committee thereof that is authorized by law to administer an oath, (c) before a court, judge, justice, provincial court judge or coroner, (d) before an arbitrator or umpire, or a person or body of persons authorized by law to make an inquiry and take evidence therein under oath, or (e) before a tribunal by which a legal right or legal liability may be established, whether or not the proceeding is invalid for want of jurisdiction or for any other reason. *Criminal Code*, R.S.C. 1985, c. C-46, s. 118 as am. by R.S.C. 1985 (1st Supp.), c. 27, s. 15. 2. Includes any action, suit, cause, matter or other proceeding in disposing of which the court appealed from has not exercised merely a regulative, administrative or executive jurisdiction. *Supreme Court Act*, R.S.C. 1985, c. S-26, s. 2.

JUDICIAL REVIEW. 1. The right of a court to investigate and question the validity of any legislation enacted by a Canadian legislative body, notably as to whether that statute transgresses some constitutional prohibition. P.W. Hogg, *Constitutional Law of Canada*, 3d ed. (Toronto: Carswell, 1992) at 117 and 119. 2. The investigation and determination by a court of the legal validity of an act, decision, instrument or transaction, of a question of vires, jurisdiction, concerning an obligation to observe the rules of natural justice or "act fairly", or concerning principles which should be observed when statutory discretion is exercised. S.A. DeSmith, *Judicial Review of Administrative Action*, 4th ed. by J.M. Evans (London: Stevens, 1980) at 26.

JUDICIAL SEPARATION. A decree which does not affect status of a married couple but simply acknowledges the deterioration of a union. J.G. McLeod, *The Conflict of Laws* (Calgary: Carswell, 1983) at 702.

JUDICIAL TRUSTEE. In the Yukon Territory and the Northwest Territories, British Columbia, Alberta and Saskatchewan, there is provision in the territorial or provincial Trustee ordinance or act for the appointment of any "fit and proper person" to this role. D.M.W. Waters, *The Law of Trusts in Canada*, 2d ed. (Toronto: Carswell, 1984) at 103.

JUDICIARY. *n.* The bench, the judges collectively.

JUNIOR. *adj.* Younger; of lower rank.

JURAT. *n.* [L.] A clause at the bottom of an affidavit which states where, when and before whom that affidavit was sworn.

JURIDICAL. *adj.* Relating to the administration of justice.

JURIDICAL DAY. A day on which one may transact legal business.

JURISDICTION. *n.* 1. "... [R]efers to the power of the court to hear a particular matter...." *Tolofson v.* Jensen (1992), 9 C.C.L.T. (2d) 289 at 293, 4 C.P.C. (3d) 113, 65 B.C.L.R. (2d) 114, [1992] 3 W.W.R. 743, 89 D.L.R. (4th) 129, 11 B.C.A.C. 94, 22 W.A.C. 94, the court per Cumming J.A. 2. A province or territory of Canada or a state outside Canada having sovereign power. See APPELLATE ~; CONCURRENT ~; COURT OF COMPETENT ~; EXCLUSIVE ~ CLAUSE; FEDERAL ~; FOREIGN ~; GENERAL ~; INHERENT ~; STATUTORY ~; SUMMARY ~.

JURIS ET DE JURE. [L. of law and from law] Describes a presumption which is a conclusive presumption.

JURISPRUDENCE. *n.* 1. The philosophy or science of law which ascertains the principles which are the basis of legal rules. 2. A body of law. See MEDICAL ~.

JURIST. *n.* A civil lawyer; an eminent legal theorist; a civilian.

JURISTIC PERSON. See LEGAL PERSON.

JUROR. *n.* [L.] A person who serves on a jury.

JURORS' PRIVILEGE. Jurors are privileged against disclosing deliberations in a jury room. Section 649 of the Criminal Code, R.S.C. 1985, c. C-46 makes disclosing such information an offence. P.K. McWilliams, *Canadian Criminal Evidence*, 3d ed. (Aurora:

Canada Law Book, 1988) at 35-74.

JURY. *n.* A group of people sworn to deliver a verdict after considering evidence delivered to them concerning the issue. See CHARGE THE ~; EM-PANEL; GRAND ~; HUNG ~; IM-PANEL.

JURY PANEL. Those persons summoned from amongst whom a jury will be selected.

JUS. *n.* [L.] Law; right; equity; rule; authority. See IGNORANTIA JURIS HAUD EXCUSAT.

JUS ACCRESCENDI. [L.] The right of survivorship which is essential to joint tenancy. E.L.G. Tyler & N.E. Palmer, eds., *Crossley Vaines' Personal Property*, 5th ed. (London: Butterworths, 1973) at 56.

JUS CIVILE. [L.] Local law.

JUS COMMUNE. [L.] Common law.

JUS DISPONENDI. [L.] The right to dispose.

JUS GENTIUM. [L.] Customary law.

JUS HABENDI. [L.] The right to actually possess property.

JUS HAEREDITATIS. [L.] The right to inherit.

JUS IN PERSONAM. [L.] A right which gives the one holding it power to help another person to do or not to do, to gain or give anything.

JUS IN RE. [L.] A full and complete right; a real right or a right to have something to the exclusion of everyone else.

JUS NATURALE. [L.] Natural law.

JUS POSSESSIONIS. [L.] The right to possess.

JUS PRIVATUM. [L.] The municipal or civil law.

JUS PUBLICUM. [L.] The law concerning public affairs.

JUST. *adj.* ". . . [A] just remedy in the context of the criminal law is one which, while furthering the object of the right guaranteed by the [Charter] that has been infringed, nevertheless does that, as far as possible, in a way that does not offend the reasonable expectations of the community for the enforcement of the criminal law." *R. v. Germain* (1984), (*sub nom. Germain v. R.*) 10 C.R.R. 232 at 341, 53 A.R. 264 (Q.B.), McDonald J.

JUST CAUSE. 1. "If an employee has been guilty of serious misconduct, habitual neglect of duty, incompetence, or conduct imcompatible with his duties, or prejudicial to the employer's business, or if he has been guilty of wilful disobedience to the employer's orders in a matter of substance, the law recognizes the employer's right summarily to dismiss the delinquent employee." *Port Arthur Shipbuilding Co. v. Arthurs*, [1967] 2 O.R. 49 at 55, 62 D.L.R. (2d) 342, 67 C.L.L.C. 14,024 (C.A.), Schroeder J.A. (dissenting), approved on appeal [1969] S.C.R. 85. 2. Journal published by Canadian Legal Advocacy, Information and Research Association of the Disabled.

JUST DISMISSAL. ". . . [D]ismissal based on an objective, real and substantial cause, independent of caprice, convenience or purely personal disputes, entailing action taken exclusively to ensure the effective operation of the business . . ." *Canadian Imperial Bank of Commerce v. Boisvert* (1986), 13 C.C.E.L. 264 at 291, [1986] 2 F.C. 431, 68 N.R. 355 (C.A.), Marceau J.A. (MacGuigan and Lacombe JJ.A. concurring).

JUS TERTII. [L.] Third party right.

JUSTICE. *n.* 1. The principle of giving every person her or his due. 2. A judge of certain courts. 3. A justice of appeal. 4. A justice of the peace. See ADMINISTRATION OF ~; CHIEF ~; FUNDAMENTAL ~; INTER-NATIONAL COURT OF ~; NATURAL ~; OBSTRUCTING ~.

JUSTICE OF THE PEACE. A judicial official with jurisdiction over matters which relate to the initiation of a legal process and minor criminal offences.

JUSTICE REP. *abbr.* Justice Report.

JUSTICE SHOULD NOT ONLY BE DONE BUT SHOULD

MANIFESTLY AND UN-DOUBTEDLY BE SEEN TO BE DONE. A rule enunciated in *R. v. Sussex Justices, Ex parte McCarthy*, [1924] 1 K.B. 256 at 259 (U.K. Div. Ct.), Lord Hewart C.J.

JUSTICIABLE. *adj.* Proper to be examined in a court of justice, triable.

JUSTIFIABLE HOMICIDE. Homicide which is not culpable, the killing of a human being when no legal guilt is incurred.

JUSTIFICATION. *n.* 1. "[In criminal theory, in contrast to excuse] . . . challenges the wrongfulness of an action which technically constitutes a crime. The police officer who shoots the hostage-taker, the innocent object of an assault who uses force to defend himself against his assailant, the good Samaritan who commandeers a car and breaks the speed laws to rush an ac-cident victim to the hospital, these are all actors whose actions we consider rightful, not wrongful. . . ." *R. v. Perka* (1984), 13 D.L.R. (4th) 1 at 12, [1984] 2 S.C.R. 232, [1984] 6 W.W.R. 289, 42 C.R. (3d) 113, 55 N.R. 1, 14 C.C.C. (3d) 385, Dickson J. (Ritchie J. concurring). 2. Truth, a complete defence to a defamation action. R.E. Brown, *The Law of Defamation in Canada* (Toronto: Carswell, 1987) at 361.

JUSTIFY BAIL. To prove the suf-ficiency of sureties or bail.

JUV. CT. *abbr.* Juvenile Court.

JUVENILE COURT. See YOUTH COURT.

JUVENILE DELINQUENT. See YOUNG PERSON.

JUXTA FORMAM STATUTI. [L.] According to the statute's form.

K

K.B. *abbr.* 1. King's Bench. 2. Court of King's Bench. See QUEEN'S BENCH.

K.C. *abbr.* King's Counsel. See QUEEN'S COUNSEL.

KEEPER. *n.* 1. A person who (a) is an owner or occupier of a place, (b) assists or acts on behalf of an owner or occupier of a place, (c) appears to be, or to assist or act on behalf of an owner or occupier of a place, (d) has the care or management of a place, or (e) uses a place permanently or temporarily, with or without the consent of the owner or occupier thereof. *Criminal Code*, R.S.C. 1985, c. C-46, s. 197. 2. "In terms of what it means to be a 'keeper' of a common bawdy-house, an element of participation in the wrongful use of the place is a minimum requirement: R. v. Kerim, [1963] S.C.R. 124 ..." *Reference re ss. 193 & 195.1(1)(c) of the Criminal Code (Canada)*, [1990] 4 W.W.R. 481 at 510, 77 C.R. (3d) 1, 56 C.C.C. (3d) 65, [1990] 1 S.C.R. 1123, 109 N.R. 81, 68 Man. R. (2d) 1, 48 C.R.R. 1, Lamer J.

KEEP THE PEACE. To prevent or avoid breaches of the peace.

KICKBACK. *n.* Payment back to a seller or employer of a portion of purchase price or wages of an employee.

KIDNAP. *v.* "... The crime is complete when the person is picked up and then transported by fraud to his place of confinement...." *R. v. Metcalfe* (1983), 10 C.C.C. (3d) 114 at 118 (B.C. C.A.), the court per Nemetz

C.J.B.C.

KIENAPPLE PRINCIPLE. "Multiple convictions are only precluded under the Kienapple principle [named after Kienapple v. R., [1975] 1 S.C.R. 729] if they arise from the same 'cause', 'matter', or 'delict', and if there is sufficient proximity between the offences charged. This requirement of sufficient proximity between offences will only be satisfied if there is no additional and distinguishing element contained in the offence for which a conviction is sought to be precluded by the Kienapple principle." *R. v. Wigman* (1987), 33 C.C.C. (3d) 97 at 103, [1987] 4 W.W.R. 1, 56 C.R. (3d) 289, [1987] 1 S.C.R. 246, 75 N.R. 51, 38 D.L.R. (4th) 530, Dickson C.J.C., Beetz, McIntyre, Chouinard, Lamer, Le Dain and La Forest JJ.

KIN. *n.* Relatives by blood. See NEXT OF ~.

KINDRED. *n.* Relations by blood.

KING. *n.* A male sovereign of the United Kingdom, Canada and other Realms and Territories, and Head of the Commonwealth.

KING'S BENCH. See QUEEN'S BENCH.

KING'S COUNSEL. See QUEEN'S COUNSEL.

KING'S PRINTER. See QUEEN'S PRINTER.

KING'S PROCTOR. See QUEEN'S PROCTOR.

KINSFOLK. *n.* Relatives; members

of the same family.

KINSMAN. *n.* A man of the same family or race.

KINSWOMAN. *n.* A woman of the same family or race.

KITING. *n.* "... [A] term used with regard to obtaining money by cheques passed through banks without value being deposited against the cheque – that is, kiting is an effort to obtain the use of money during the process of a cheque passing through one bank or through a clearing house to another, and perhaps through many more." *Corp. Agencies Ltd. v. Home Bank of Canada*, [1927] 2 D.L.R. 1 at 2, [1927] 1 W.W.R. 1004, [1927] A.C. 318 (Can. P.C.), the board per Lord Wrenbury.

KLEPTOMANIA. *n.* An uncontrollable inclination to steal.

KNOW. *v.* "... [H]as a positive connotation requirng a bare awareness, the act of receiving information without more...." *R. v. Barnier*, [1980] 1 S.C.R. 1124 at 1137, 109 D.L.R. (3d) 257, 13 C.R. (3d) 129 (Eng.), 19 C.R. (3d) 371 (Fr.), [1980] 2 W.W.R. 659, 31 N.R. 273, 51 C.C.C. (3d) 193, the court per Estey J.

KNOWINGLY. *adv.* "The general principle of criminal law is that accompanying a prohibited act there must be an intent in respect of every element of the act, and that is ordinarily conveyed in statutory offences by the word 'knowingly'." *R. v. Rees* (1956), 24 C.R. 1 at 8, [1956] S.C.R. 640, 115 C.C.C. 1, 4 D.L.R. (2d) 406, Rand J. (Locke J. concurring).

KNOWLEDGE. See COMMON ~.

KN. P.C. *abbr.* Knapp, Privy Council, 1829-1836.

L

LABOUR ARBITRATION. A general term which includes grievance arbitration and interest arbitration, two different processes. D.J.M. Brown & D.M. Beatty, *Canadian Labour Arbitration*, 3d ed. (Aurora: Canada Law Book, 1988-) at 1-1.

LABOUR DISPUTE. Any dispute between employers and employees, or between employees and employees, that is connected with the employment or non-employment, or the terms or conditions of employment, of any persons. *Unemployment Insurance Act*, R.S.C. 1985, c. U-1, s. 2.

LABOURER. *n.* A person employed for wages in any kind of labour whether employed under a contract of service or not.

LABOUR RELATIONS. All matters concerning the worker-employer relationship.

LABOUR UNION. Any organization of employees that has as one of its purposes the regulation of relations between employers and employees and that has a constitution setting out its objectives and its conditions for membership. *Corporations and Labour Unions Returns Act*, R.S.C. 1985, c. C-43, s. 2. See CERTIFICATION OF ~.

L.A.C. *abbr.* Labour Arbitration Cases.

L.A.C. (4th). *abbr.* Labour Arbitration Cases (Fourth Series), 1989-.

LACHES. *n.* [Fr.] "Unreasonable delay simpliciter is not sufficient to allow a party to succeed in the defence of laches. The defendants must establish that the consequences flowing from the unreasonable delay are such that, having regard to the relative positions of the parties presently, granting injunctive relief would lead to inequitable results." *Institut national des appellations d'origine des vins & eaux-de-vie v. Andres Wines Ltd.* (1987), 16 C.P.R. (3d) 385 at 446, 41 C.C.L.T. 94, 60 O.R. (2d) 316, 14 C.I.P.R. 138, 40 D.L.R. (4th) 239 (H.C.), Dupont J.

L.A.C. (2d). *abbr.* Labour Arbitration Cases (Second Series), 1973-1981.

L.A.C. (3d). *abbr.* Labour Arbitration Cases (Third Series), 1982-1989.

LADING. See BILL OF ~.

L.A.N. *abbr.* Labour Arbitration News.

LAND. *n.* 1. "... [I]n the great majority of cases, where the context does not require a special and technical meaning, ... it means something quite concrete and tangible, something distinguished from water as a rule, or it may be from movable property ..." *Murphy Estate, Re* (1955), 37 M.P.R. 107 at 111, [1955] 5 D.L.R. 768 (Nfld. C.A.), Winter J.A. 2. "... [I]s not, in law, the soil we touch, but the rights attached to it. Such rights include the right to work the soil, to mine beneath the surface and build in the airspace above it and the incorporeal rights to light, support and the use of water flowing across land." *Trizec Manitoba Ltd. v. Winnipeg City Assessor* (1986),

34 M.P.L.R. 9 at 12, 41 R.P.R. 176, [1986] 5 W.W.R. 97, 42 Man. R. (2d) 98 (C.A.), Twaddle J.A. (Huband J.A. concurring). 3. "... [I]n its primary meaning refers to corporeal hereditaments: ..." *Wiener v. Elgin (County)*, [1947] 2 D.L.R. 346 at 348, [1947] O.W.N. 360 (H.C.), Urquhart J. 4. Lands, messuages, tenements and hereditaments, corporeal and incorporeal, of every nature and description, and every estate or interest therein, whether the estate or interest is legal or equitable, together with all paths, passages, ways, watercourses, liberties, privileges, easements, mines, minerals and quarries appertaining thereto, and all trees and timber thereon and thereunder lying or being, unless specially excepted. 5. The solid part of the earth's surface and includes the foreshore and land covered by water. See ALLODIAL ~S; ARABLE ~; CROWN ~; FREEHOLD ~S; PARCEL OF ~; PRIVATE ~; PROVINCIAL ~; RUN WITH THE ~; TRESPASS TO ~.

L. & C. *abbr.* Lefroy & Cassels' Practice Cases (Ont.), 1881-1883.

LANDING. *n.* Lawful permission to come into Canada to establish permanent residence. *Immigration Act*, R.S.C. 1985, c. I-2, s. 2.

LANDLORD. *n.* Includes lessor, owner or the person giving or permitting the occupation of the residential premises in question and the heirs, assigns and legal representatives thereof.

LANDMARK. *n.* An object which fixes the boundary of property or an estate.

LANDS, TENEMENTS AND HEREDITAMENTS. A traditional description of real property, considered the most comprehensive.

LAND TITLES SYSTEM. The government makes a brief, simple statement concerning the ownership of land and all outstanding interests or claims so that the purchaser need not be concerned, as in a registry system, with the history of the transactions which affected that land. B.J. Reiter,

B.N. McLellan & P.M. Perell, *Real Estate Law*, 4th ed. (Toronto: Emond Montgomery, 1992) at 388.

LAPSE. *v.* To fail, said of a bequest or devise of property which goes into residue as if the gift had not been made when the person to whom the property was bequeathed or devised dies before the testator.

LAPSE. *n.* Error; failure in duty.

LAST ANTECEDENT DOCTRINE. A rule of statutory interpretation which provides that a modifier will apply only to the word immediately preceding it.

LAST CLEAR CHANCE DOCTRINE. A doctrine which permits full recovery by a plaintiff even if that plaintiff was contributorily negligent if the defendant had the last chance to avoid an accident but negligently did not take advantage of that chance. J.G. Fleming, *The Law of Torts*, 8th ed. (Sydney: Law Book, 1992) at 270.

LAST RESORT. Describes a court from which there is no further appeal. See COURT OF ~.

LATENT. *adj.* Concealed, hidden; secret.

LATENT AMBIGUITY. "... [W]here the language is equivocal, or if unequivocal but its application to the facts is uncertain or difficult, a latent ambiguity is said to be present. The term 'latent ambiguity' seems now to be applied generally to all cases of doubtful meaning or application." *Leitch Gold Mines Ltd. v. Texas Gulf Sulphur Co.* (1968), 3 D.L.R. (3d) 161 at 216, [1969] 1 O.R. 469 (H.C.), Gale C.J.O.

LATENT DEFECT. 1. Some fault which one would not expect an ordinary purchaser to discover during a routine inspection. B.J. Reiter, B.N. McLellan & P.M. Perell, *Real Estate Law*, 4th ed. (Toronto: Emond Montgomery, 1992) at 247. 2. "... 'Not discernible by adequate inspection' ..." *Scottish Metropolitan Assurance Co. v. Canada Steamship Lines Ltd.*, [1930] S.C.R. 262 at 279,

Lines Ltd., [1930] S.C.R. 262 at 279, [1930] 1 D.L.R. 201, Anglin C.J.C. (Rinfret and Lamont JJ. concurring).

LAW. *n.* 1. A rule to govern action. 2. An enactment. See ADJECTIVE ~; ADMINISTRATIVE ~; ADMIRALTY ~; ANTITRUST ~; BLUE-SKY ~; BY~; CASE ~; CHOICE OF ~; CIVIL ~; COLONIAL ~; COMMERCIAL ~; COMMON ~; CONCLUSION OF ~; CONSTITUTIONAL ~; CONTRACT ~; CRIMINAL ~; ECCLESIASTICAL ~; EQUALITY BEFORE AND UNDER THE ~; EQUALITY BEFORE THE ~; EQUITY FOLLOWS THE ~; ERRED IN ~; ~; ERROR OF ~; FAMILY ~ COMMISSIONER; HOMESTEAD ~; INTERNATIONAL ~; MARITIME ~; MARTIAL ~; MERCANTILE ~; MERE ERROR OF ~; MILITARY ~; MISTAKE OF ~; MIXED QUESTION OF ~ AND FACT; MUNICIPAL ~; NATURAL ~; PENAL ~; POSITIVE ~; PRESCRIBED BY ~; PRESUMPTION OF ~; PRIVATE ~; PROPER ~; PROPERTY ~; PUBLIC ~; QUESTION OF ~; RULE OF ~; SUBSTANTIVE ~.

LAW CLERK AND PARLIAMENTARY COUNSEL. An official appointed by Letters Patent under the Great Seal whose principal duty is to provide comprehensive legal advice to the Speaker, officers of the House of Commons and Board of Internal Economy and who helps members of Parliament draft legislation. A. Fraser, W.A. Dawson, & J. Holtby, eds., *Beauchesne's Rules and Forms of the House of Commons of Canada*, 6th ed. (Toronto: Carswell, 1989) at 61.

LAW ENFORCEMENT. (a) Policing, (b) investigations or inspections that lead or could lead to proceedings in a court or tribunal if a penalty or sanction could be imposed in those proceedings, and (c) the conduct of proceedings referred to in clause (b). Ontario statutes.

LAWFUL. *adj.* Authorized by law. *R. v. Robinson* (1948), 6 C.R. 343 at 346, [1948] O.R. 857, 92 C.C.C. 223 (C.A.), Laidlaw J.A.

LAWFUL EXCUSE. 1. "... [N]ormally includes all of the defences which the common law considers sufficient reason to excuse a person from criminal liability. It can also include excuses specific to particular offences...." *R. v. Holmes* (1988), 34 C.R.R. 193 at 200, 85 N.R. 21, 27 O.A.C. 321, [1988] 1 S.C.R. 914, 64 C.R. (3d) 97, 41 C.C.C. (3d) 497, Dickson C.J.C. (Lamer J. concurring). 2. "... [I]ncludes any honest and reasonable belief in a state of facts which if they had been as the accused believed them to be would have made his act innocent...." *R. v. Ireco Canada II Inc.* (1988), 17 C.E.R. 245 at 258, 65 C.R. (3d) 160, 43 C.C.C. (3d) 482, 29 O.A.C. 161 (C.A.), Martin, Cory and Finlayson JJ.A.

LAW LIST. A listing of all persons who are practicing as barristers or solicitors and any other lawyers.

LAW LORDS. In England, the Lord Chancellor, the Lords of Appeal in Ordinary, former Lord Chancellors and other peers who held high judicial offices.

LAW MERCHANT. The law which governs any mercantile transaction.

LAW OF AGENCY. The law to govern relationships which come into existence when one person uses another person to perform certain tasks on her or his behalf. G.H.L. Fridman, *The Law of Agency*, 6th ed. (London: Butterworths, 1990) at 3.

LAW OF CANADA. In s. 101 of the Constitution Act, 1867 (30 & 31 Vict.), c. 3 includes federal common law. *Wewayakum Indian Band v. Canada* (1989), 3 R.P.R. (2d) 1 at 8, 13, 16, 92 N.R. 241, 25 F.T.R. 161, [1989] 3 W.W.R. 117, 35 B.C.L.R. (2d) 1, 57 D.L.R. (4th) 197, [1979] 1 S.C.R. 322, [1989] 2 C.N.L.R. 146, the court per Wilson J.

LAW OF CONTRACT. Law for the purpose of ensuring that the promises of persons are performed. J.G. Fleming, *The Law of Torts*, 8th ed. (Sydney: Law Book, 1992) at 2.

LAW OFFICER OF THE CROWN.

General. 2. The Minister of Justice of Québec. *Interpretation Act*, R.S.Q. 1977, c. I-16, s. 61.

LAW OF FLAG. The law of the country the flag of which a ship is flying.

LAW OF NATIONS. Public international law.

LAW REPORT. 1. The published account of any legal proceeding. 2. The report of a judgment of a court on points of law, published so that it may be used as a precedent.

LAW REPR. *abbr.* The Law Reporter (Ramsay & Morin) (Que.), 1854.

LAW SCHOOL ADMISSION TEST. An aptitude test which law schools in Canada and the United States require first year applicants to take.

LAW SUIT. Litigation; an action.

LAWYER. *n.* In the Province of Quebec, an advocate, lawyer or notary and, in any other province, a barrister or solicitor.

LAY. *adj.* Not professional, belonging to the general population in contrast to a certain profession.

LAYING AN INFORMATION. Any person may present a statement of facts in writing and under oath upon which a criminal charge in respect of an indictable offence is to be based to a Justice. Upon hearing the evidence of the informant, and perhaps witnesses, the Justice may confirm the appearance notice, promise to appear or recognizance and endorse the information accordingly or take a variety of other possible steps.

LAY OFF. *v.* To terminate.

LAY-OFF. *var.* **LAYOFF.** *n.* 1. "... [A] period during which a workman is temporarily discharged ..." *Air-Care Ltd. v. U.S.W.A.*, [1976] 1 S.C.R. 2 at 6, 3 N.R. 267, 49 D.L.R. (3d) 467, Dickson J. 2. Temporary or indefinite termination of employment because of lack of work. See TEMPORARY ~; WEEK OF ~.

L.C.B. *abbr.* Land Compensation Board.

L.C.J. *abbr.* Lord Chief Justice.

L.C. JUR. *abbr.* Lower Canada Jurist, 1857-1891.

L.C. JURIST. *abbr.* Lower Canada Jurist (1848-1891).

L.C.L.J. *abbr.* Lower Canada Law Journal (1865-1868).

L.C.R. *abbr.* 1. Land Compensation Reports, 1971-. 2. Lower Canada Reports, 1851-1867 (Décisions des Tribunaux du Bas-Canada).

L.C. REP. *abbr.* Lower Canada Reports.

LEAD. *v.* To call or adduce evidence.

LEADER OF THE OPPOSITION. 1. A member of Parliament or a legislature recognized by the Speaker as the leader of Her Majesty's loyal opposition. 2. The member of the House of Commons who is presently leader of the party opposing the Government and who has certain special rights regarding the questioning of Ministers. A. Fraser, W.A. Dawson & J. Holtby, eds., *Beauchesne's Rules and Forms of the House of Commons of Canada*, 6th ed. (Toronto: Carswell, 1989) at 55-6.

LEADING CASE. A judicial precedent or decision which settled the principles in a certain branch of law.

LEADING QUESTION. 1. A question which suggests the answer required of that witness. 2. A question which assumes a fact or set of facts which is the subject of dispute. J. Sopinka & S.N. Lederman, *The Law of Evidence in Civil Cases* (Toronto: Butterworths, 1974) at 481.

LEASE. *n.* 1. "... [U]sed in various senses: it is sometimes applied to term or estate created, and sometimes to the conveyance creating the estate. To constitute a lease, however, the possession of the lessee must be exclusive ... under a lease the lessee's right to possession is exclusive until the expiration of the term agreed upon ..." *Johnston v. British Canadian Insurance Co.*, [1932] 4 D.L.R. 281 at 284, [1932] S.C.R. 680, Lamont J. 2. Every agreement in writing, and every parol agreement whereby one person as landlord confers upon another person as tenant the right to occupy land, and every sublease and every agreement for a sublease and every assurance whereby any rent is secured by condition. 3. ". . . [M]ay be a security agreement; it becomes so when it in substance is intended to have and has the effect of permitting the lessee to acquire title to the chattel leased by a series of time payments expressed as rental which will, over the term, discharge the purchase debt and give him title, or will do so on a final optional payment that is nominal and cannot reasonably be refused. . . ." *Corporate Leasing Inc. v. William Day Construction Ltd.* (1986), 6 P.P.S.A.C. 188 at 200 (Ont. H.C.), Henry J. See BUILDING ~; FINANCIAL ~; GROUND ~; MINING ~; NET ~; NET NET ~; REVERSIONARY ~; UNDER ~.

LEASEBACK. *var.* **LEASE BACK.** An arrangement in which land or property is sold and then leased back to the vendor. See SALE-~.

LEASEHOLD. *n.* 1. The area demised by a lease. 2. An area distinguished from a freehold because its duration is certain and both its beginning and its end are defined. E.L.G. Tyler & N.E. Palmer, eds., *Crossley Vaines' Personal Property*, 5th ed. (London: Butterworths, 1973) at 5. See EQUITABLE ~ MORTGAGE; LEGAL ~ MORTGAGE.

LEASEHOLD ESTATE. In contrast to a freehold estate, an estate of fixed duration.

LEAVE. *n.* Permission.

LEAVE AND LICENCE. A defence to a trespass action in which the defendant claims that plaintiff consented to the act complained of.

LEAVE OF ABSENCE. A period of time during which an employee is permitted to be absent from work, usually without pay.

LEGACY. *n.* 1. The means by which personal property is disposed of by will. 2. A personal gift as opposed to a

"bequest" to charity. *Smith v. Chatham (City) Home of the Friendless*, [1932] 4 D.L.R. 173 at 174, [1932] S.C.R. 713, Duff J. See CONTINGENT ~; CUMULATIVE ~; DEMONSTRATIVE ~; GENERAL ~; SPECIFIC ~.

LEGAL. *adj.* According to law, lawful. See MEDICO-~.

LEGAL AGE. The age of majority.

LEGAL AID. Legal advice and services available or furnished under a legal aid act.

LEGAL BURDEN OF PROOF. 1. ". . . [T]he burden of establishing a case . . ." *R. v. Schwartz* (1988), 45 C.C.C. (3d) 97 at 115, [1989] 1 W.W.R. 289, 66 C.R. (3d) 351, 88 N.R. 90, [1988] 2 S.C.R. 443, 56 Man. R. (2d) 92, 55 D.L.R. (4th) 1, Dickson C.J.C. (dissenting). 2. In general, the burden of proof is on the person who asserts, but in a criminal trial the prosecution bears that burden. P.K. McWilliams, *Canadian Criminal Evidence*, 3d ed. (Aurora: Canada Law Book, 1988) at 25-1.

LEGAL CAUSATION. A concept which subsumes the notions of proximity, remoteness and novus actus interveniens. K.D. Cooper-Stephenson & I.B. Saunders, *Personal Injury Damages in Canada* (Toronto: Carswell, 1981) at 638.

LEGAL CIVIL LIBERTIES. Includes freedom from seizure, search, imprisonment, arrest, cruel and unusual punishment and unfair procedures at trial. P.W. Hogg, *Constitutional Law of Canada*, 3d ed. (Toronto: Carswell, 1992) at 765.

LEGAL CUSTODY. Any restraint of a person that is authorized by law.

LEGAL DESCRIPTION. 1. "Normally . . . used to indicate the exact boundaries of a piece of land. . . ." *Edkar Construction Ltd. v. Thompson (City) Board of Revision*, [1992] 6 W.W.R. 563 at 568, 8 Admin. L.R. (2d) 278, 82 Man. R. (2d) 118 (Q.B.), Morse J. 2. A description sufficient to describe a property for the purpose of its registration in a land title office.

Taxation (Rural Area) Act, R.S.B.C. 1979, c. 400, s. 1.

LEGAL EXECUTION. An execution obtained by a common law writ like fieri facias or elegit. C.R.B. Dunlop, *Creditor-Debtor Law in Canada* (Toronto: Carswell, 1981) at 139.

LEGAL FICTION. See FICTION.

LEGAL INCAPACITY. 1. Mental infirmity of such a nature as would, but for this Act, invalidate or terminate a power of attorney. *Powers of Attorney Act*, R.S.O. 1990, c. P.20, s. 1. 2. Mental disability of a nature (i) such that were a person to engage in an action he or she would be unable to understand its nature and effect, and (ii) that would, but for this Act, invalidate or terminate a power of attorney. *Enduring Powers of Attorney Act*, R.S. Nfld. 1990, c. E-11, s. 2(1).

LEGALISATION. *var.* **LEGALIZATION.** *n.* The transformation of a prima facie illegal act into a legal act.

LEGALISE. *var.* **LEGALIZE.** *v.* To transform a prima facie illegal act into a legal act.

LEGAL LEASEHOLD MORTGAGE. Created by granting a lease as a mortgage; a tenant may legally mortgage the term of the mortgage of that leasehold by making a sub-lease or by assigning the unexpired portion of the term. W.B. Rayner & R.H. McLaren, *Falconbridge on Mortgages*, 4th ed. (Toronto: Canada Law Book, 1977) at 97.

LEGAL MEDICINE. See FORENSIC MEDICINE.

LEGAL MED. Q. *abbr.* Legal Medical Quarterly.

LEGAL MONUMENT. A device planted by a surveyor.

LEGAL MORTGAGE. A mortgage under which the legal estate is transferred. P.V. Baker & P. St. J. Langan, eds., *Snell's Equity*, 29th ed. (London: Sweet and Maxwell, 1990) at 389.

LEGAL N. *abbr.* Legal News (1878-1897).

LEGAL PERSON. Any entity having juridical personality.

LEGAL POSSESSION. The condition of a person who has both physical control of and title to a chattel or a person who has physical control of and a clear intention to keep control of a chattel. E.L.G. Tyler & N.E. Palmer, eds., *Crossley Vaines' Personal Property*, 5th ed. (London: Butterworths, 1973) at 49.

LEGAL POWER. Enables its holder to perform tasks such as conveying an estate. D.M.W. Waters, *The Law of Trusts in Canada*, 2d ed. (Toronto: Carswell, 1984) at 71.

LEGAL PROCEEDING. Any civil or criminal proceeding or inquiry in which evidence is or may be given, and includes an arbitration. *Evidence acts.*

LEGAL PROFESSIONAL PRIVILEGE. ". . . Waugh v. British Railways Board, [1979] 2 All E.R. 1169. Under that authority a party need not produce a document otherwise subject to production if the dominant purpose for which the document was prepared was submission to a legal advisor for advice and use in litigation (whether in progress or as contemplated). Such documents are shielded from production by what is usually described as legal professional privilege. . . . the legal professional privilege should only be applied when there is a significant connection between the preparation of the document and the anticipation of litigation. This leads to the introduction of the 'dominant purpose' test." *Nova, An Alberta Corporation v. Guelph Engineering Co.* (1984), 80 C.P.R. (2d) 93 at 95, 97, [1984] 3 W.W.R. 314, 42 C.P.C. 194, 30 Alta. L.R. (2d) 183, 5 D.L.R. (4th) 755, 50 A.R. 199 (C.A.), the court per Stevenson J.A. See SOLICITOR-CLIENT PRIVILEGE.

LEGAL PROCESS. ". . . [D]oes not mean 'by lawful means'. It means 'by a process available through the operation of law', such as by seizure under a writ of execution. . . ." *Rogerson Lumber Co. v. Four Seasons Chalet Ltd.* (1980), 12 B.L.R. 93 at 102, 29 O.R.

(2d) 193, 36 C.B.R. (N.S.) 141, 1
P.P.S.A.C. 160, 113 D.L.R. (3d) 671
(C.A.), Arnup J.A.

LEGAL REPRESENTATIVE. An
executor, an administrator, a judicial
trustee of the estate of a deceased person or a guardian of the person or
estate, or both, of a minor.

LEGAL RIGHT. "[In s. 215(3) of the
Criminal Code, R.S.C. 1970, c. C-34]
... a right which is sanctioned by law,
for example, the right to use lawful
force in self-defence, as distinct from
something that a person may do without incurring any legal liability...." *R.
v. Haight* (1976), 30 C.C.C. (2d) 168 at
175 (Ont. C.A.), the court per Martin
J.A.

LEGAL RIGHTS. Refers to ss. 7 to
14 of the Charter but does not have a
precise meaning. Refers to the rights of
persons in the criminal justice system
and the limits on government powers of
search, seizure, arrest, detention, trial
and punishment. P.W. Hogg,
Constitutional Law of Canada, 3d ed.
(Toronto: Carswell, 1992) at 1021.

LEGAL SET-OFF. "... '[R]equires
the fulfilment of two conditions. The
first is that both obligations must be
debts. The second is that both debts
must be mutual cross obligations. Both
conditions must be fulfilled at the same
time': ..." *Canadian Commercial
Bank (Liquidator of) v. Parlee McLaws*
(1989), 72 C.B.R. (N.S.) 39 at 43, 64
Alta. L.R. (2d) 218 (Q.B.), Wachowich
J.

LEGAL TENDER. The tender of
payment of money provided by the
Currency and Exchange Act as long as
it is made in notes issued by the Bank
of Canada or in gold or subsidiary
coins issued by the Government of
Canada. C.R.B. Dunlop,
Creditor-Debtor Law in Canada
(Toronto: Carswell, 1981) at 22.

LEGATEE. *n.* 1. One to whom a
legacy is left. *Smith v. Chatham (City)
Home of the Friendless*, [1931] 4
D.L.R. 173 at 174, [1932] S.C.R. 713,
Duff J. 2. Includes a devisee. *Probate
Courts Act*, R.S.N.B. 1973, c. P-17, s.

1. See RESIDUARY ~.

LEGISLATION. *n.* The creation of
law; a collection of statutes, regulations, by-laws. See CONSUMER
PROTECTION ~; JUDICIAL ~; SUB-
ORDINATE ~.

LEGISLATIVE ACT. The establishment and promulgation of some
general rule of conduct which does not
refer to particular cases. S.A. DeSmith,
*Judicial Review of Administrative
Action*, 4th ed. by J.M. Evans (London:
Stevens, 1980) at 71.

LEGISLATIVE ASSEMBLY. The
legislative assembly of a province.

**LEGISLATIVE ASSEMBLY OF-
FICE.** The office of the clerk of a
legislative assembly.

LEGISLATIVE COMMITTEE. Appointed by the House to consider a
specific bill and amendments; its existence ends when the bill is reported
back to the House. A. Fraser, W.A.
Dawson & J. Holtby, eds.,
*Beauchesne's Rules and Forms of the
House of Commons of Canada*, 6th ed.
(Toronto: Carswell, 1989) at 222.

LEGISLATIVE FACTS. "... [T]wo
categories of facts in constitutional
litigation: 'adjudicative facts' and
'legislative facts'.... Legislative facts
are those that establish the purpose and
background of legislation, including its
social, economic and cultural context.
Such facts are of a more general nature
and are subject to less stringent admissibility requirements ..." *Danson v.
Ontario (Attorney General)* (1990), 50
C.R.R. 59 at 69, 43 C.P.C. (2d) 165, 73
D.L.R. (4th) 686, [1990] 2 S.C.R.
1086, 41 O.A.C. 250, 74 O.R. (2d)
763n, 112 N.R. 362, the court per
Sopinka J.

LEGISLATIVE HISTORY. The history of a statute from its conception
through enactment.

LEGISLATOR. *n.* A member of a
legislature; a lawmaker.

LEGISLATURE. *n.* 1. A provincial
parliament. P.W. Hogg, *Constitutional
Law of Canada*, 3d ed. (Toronto:
Carswell, 1992) at 105. 2. Includes any

legislative body or authority competent to make laws for a dominion. *Evidence acts*. 3. The Lieutenant Governor acting by and with the advice and consent of the legislative assembly of a province. See PROVINCIAL ~.

LEGITIMATE. *adj.* Lawful; describing children who were born in wedlock.

LEGITIMATION. *n.* The act by which one makes a person born illegitimate legitimate.

LESSEE. *n.* 1. The person to whom one makes or gives a lease. 2. The holder of a lease.

LESSER OFFENCE. "... [A] 'part of the offence' which is charged, and it must necessarily include some element of the 'major offence', but be lacking in some of the essentials, without which the major offence would be incomplete." *Fergusson v. R.* (1961), [1962] S.C.R. 229 at 233, 36 C.R. 271, 132 C.C.C. 112, the court per Taschereau J.

LESSOR. *n.* The person who makes or gives anything to someone else by lease.

LET. *v.* 1. To lease. 2. To permit. 3. To award a contract.

LETTER. *n.* See CALDERBANK ~; COMMITMENT ~; DEMAND ~; POST ~; ROGATORY ~S.

LETTER OF CREDIT. 1. "... [A] proposal or request to the person named therein, or, in the case of an open letter, to persons generally, to advance money on the faith of it, and the advance constitutes an acceptance of the proposal, thus making a contract between the giver of the letter of credit and the person cashing or negotiating the draft, by which the former is bound to honour the draft." *Kingsway Electric Co. v. 330604 Ontario Ltd.* (1979), 9 B.L.R. 316 at 322, 27 O.R. (2d) 541, 11 R.P.R. 96, 33 C.B.R. (N.S.) 137, 107 D.L.R. (3d) 172 (H.C.), Lovekin L.J.S.C. 2. "... [I]n effect, a guarantee by the bank that upon presentation of predetermined documentation, the bank will pay the beneficiary named in the

letter. ..." *Canadian Pioneer Petroleums Inc. v. Federal Deposit Insurance Corp.* (1984), 25 B.L.R. 1 at 3, [1984] 2 W.W.R. 563, 30 Sask. R. 315 (Q.B.), Halvorson J. See COMMERCIAL ~.

LETTER OF INTENT. 1. "... [U]sed by businessmen and contractors as an initial means of establishing a contractual relationship and at the same time, not committing themselves to legally binding commitments until details are negotiated to conclusion." *Marathon Realty Co. v. Toulon Construction Corp.* (1987), 45 R.P.R. 233 at 255, 80 N.S.R. (2d) 390, 200 A.P.R. 390 (T.D.), Davison J. 2. "[In labour law] ... documents that clarify the meaning of provisions in the main document containing the collective agreement ... documents which create obligations not contained in the main agreement. ..." *Hiram Walker & Sons Ltd. v. Canadian Union of Distillery Workers, Local 1* (1976), 13 L.A.C. (2d) 417 at 421 (Ont.), Beck.

LETTER OF REQUEST. See LETTERS ROGATORY.

LETTERS OF ADMINISTRATION. An instrument, granted by a Surrogate Court, giving authority to an administrator to manage and distribute the estate of a person who died without making a will.

LETTERS OF ADMINISTRATION WITH WILL ANNEXED. Special letters of administration used when the executor named in the will is unwilling or unable to serve, or when no executor was named in the will.

LETTERS PATENT. 1. A document sealed with the Great Seal by which a company or person may do something or enjoy privileges not otherwise possible. The document is so called because it is open, with seal affixed, ready to be exhibited to confirm the grant. 2. When used with respect to public lands, includes any instrument by which such lands or any interest therein may be granted or conveyed. *Exchequer Court Act*, R.S.C. 1970, c. E-11, s. 2. 3. A method of incorporation by the grant of a charter of incorporation. H. Sutherland, D.B. Horsley & J.M. Edmiston, eds., *Fraser's Handbook on Canadian Company Law*, 7th ed. (Toronto: Carswell, 1985) at 17. See SUPPLEMENTARY ~.

LETTERS PROBATE. An instrument, granted by a Surrogate Court, giving authority to an executor to carry out the provisions of a person's will.

LETTERS ROGATORY. "... [S]ometimes known as letters of request. They constitute a request from one Judge to another asking for the examination of a witness by commission in the jurisdiction which is foreign to the requesting Court ..." *A-Dec Inc. v. Dentech Products Ltd.* (1988), 32 C.P.C. (2d) 290 at 294, 31 B.C.L.R. (2d) 320 (S.C.), Bouck J. See COMMISSION EVIDENCE; COMMISSION ROGATORY; PERPETUATE TESTIMONY; ROGATORY; ROGATORY LETTERS.

LEVY. *v.* 1. "... [T]o take all the necessary steps to enforce payment, that is, such steps as under the particular circumstances of the case would be reasonable and proper." *Bayview Estates Ltd., Re* (1980), 28 Nfld. & P.E.I.R. 225 at 243, 79 A.P.R. 225 (Nfld. T.D.), Mahoney J. 2. "... [S]ignifies the execution of legislative power which charges on person or property the obligation of or liability for a tax." *Vancouver (City) v. British Columbia Telephone Co.*, [1951] S.C.R. 3 at 6, [1950] 4 D.L.R. 289, Rand J. (Rinfret C.J.C. concurring).

LEVY. *n.* 1. A payment which results directly or indirectly from a seizure under execution. C.R.B. Dunlop, *Creditor-Debtor Law in Canada* (Toronto: Carswell, 1981) at 424. 2. A tax or duty. See SEIZURE.

LEX. *n.* [L.] Law.

LEX CAUSAE. [L.] "... [T]he system of law found to be applicable under the conflict of laws rule of the forum ..." *243930 Alberta Ltd. v. Wickham* (1990), 14 R.P.R. (2d) 95 at 98, 73 D.L.R. (4th) 474, 75 O.R. (2d) 289, 40 O.A.C. 367 (C.A.), Lacourcière J.A.

LEX CONVENTIONALIS. [L. conventional law] The law which the parties agreed will govern their contract. J.G. McLeod, *The Conflict of Laws* (Calgary: Carswell, 1983) at 779.

LEX DOMICILII. [L.] The law of the country where someone is domiciled. J.G. McLeod, *The Conflict of Laws* (Calgary: Carswell, 1983) at 779.

LEX FORI. [L. law of the forum] The law of the jurisdiction where a legal proceeding is commenced and heard. *243930 Alberta Ltd. v. Wickham* (1990), 14 R.P.R. (2d) 95 at 98, 73 D.L.R. (4th) 474, 75 O.R. (2d) 289, 40 O.A.C. 367 (C.A.), Lacourcière J.A.

LEX LOCI. [L.] The law of a place.

LEX LOCI ACTUS. [L.] The law of the jurisdiction where an act took place. J.G. McLeod, *The Conflict of Laws* (Calgary: Carswell, 1983) at 779.

LEX LOCI CELEBRATIONIS. [L.] The law of the jurisdiction in which a marriage was celebrated. J.G. McLeod, *The Conflict of Laws* (Calgary: Carswell, 1983) at 779.

LEX LOCI CONTRACTUS. [L.] 1. The law of the jurisdiction in which the contract was made. J.G. McLeod, *The Conflict of Laws* (Calgary: Carswell, 1983) at 779. 2. The law of the jurisdiction where the last necessary act to make a contract took place. J.G. McLeod, *The Conflict of Laws* (Calgary: Carswell, 1983) at 196.

LEX LOCI DELICTI. [L.] The law of the jurisdiction where the tort or wrong is considered, legally, to have occurred. J.G. McLeod, *The Conflict of Laws* (Calgary: Carswell, 1983) at 194.

LEX LOCI DOMICILII. [L.] The law of the jurisdiction in which the party is domiciled.

LEX LOCI REI SITAE. [L.] The law of the jurisdiction where the thing is located.

LEX LOCI SOLUTIONIS. [L.] The law of the jurisdiction in which a debt will be paid, a contract be performed or another obligation met. J.G. McLeod,

The Conflict of Laws (Calgary: Carswell, 1983) at 779.

LEX PATRIAE. [L.] The law of the country to which one owes allegiance. J.G. McLeod, *The Conflict of Laws* (Calgary: Carswell, 1983) at 779.

LEX PERSONALIS. [L. personal law] An inclusive term of which lex patriae and lex domicilii are examples. J.G. McLeod, *The Conflict of Laws* (Calgary: Carswell, 1983) at 779.

LEX SITUS. [L.] The law of the jurisdiction where a thing is located. J.G. McLeod, *The Conflict of Laws* (Calgary: Carswell, 1983) at 779.

LIABILITY. *n.* The situation in which one is potentially or actually subject to some obligation. See ALTERNATIVE ~; CONTINGENT ~; CURRENT ~; OCCUPIERS' ~; OUTLET ~; PRODUCTS ~; STRICT ~; STRICT ~ OFFENCE; VICARIOUS ~.

LIABLE. *adv.* 1. Exposed to. *R. v. Robinson* (1951), 12 C.R. 101 at 113, [1951] S.C.R. 522, Cartwright J. 2. Used to create a legal obligation. *Canada Trust Co. v. British Columbia (Attorney General)* (1980), 7 E.T.R. 93 at 113, [1980] 2 S.C.R 466, 23 B.C.L.R. 86, [1980] 5 W.W.R. 591, [1980] C.T.C. 338, 7 F.T.R. 93, 112 D.L.R. (3d) 592, 52 N.R. 326, the court per Dickson J. 3. Likely or probably. *Mermuys v. Delodder* (1990), 86 Nfld. & P.E.I.R. 326 at 330, 268 A.P.R. 326, 35 C.P.R. (3d) 146 (P.E.I. T.D.), McQuaid J.

LIBEL. *n.* The more permanent or written form of a defamatory statement. R.E. Brown, *The Law of Defamation in Canada* (Toronto: Carswell, 1987) at 9. See DEFAMATORY ~; SEDITIOUS ~.

LIBERTIES. See CIVIL ~.

LIBERTY. *n.* 1. "... [T]he right of liberty contained in s. 7 [of the Charter] guarantees to every individual a degree of personal autonomy over important decisions intimately affecting their private lives...." *R. v. Morgentaler* (1988), 62 C.R. (3d) 1 at 107, 82 N.R.

1, [1988] 1 S.C.R. 30, 63 O.R. (2d) 281n, 26 O.A.C. 1, 44 D.L.R. (4th) 385, 31 C.R.R. 1, 37 C.C.C. (3d) 449, Wilson J. 2. "... [N]ot confined to mere freedom from bodily restraint. It does not, however, extend to protect property or pure economic rights. It may embrace individual freedom of movement, including the right to choose one's occupation and where to pursue it, subject to the right of the state to impose, in accordance with the principles of fundamental justice, legitimate and reasonable restrictions on the activities of individuals...." *Wilson v. British Columbia (Medical Services Commission)* (1988), 41 C.R.R. 276 at 295, 30 B.C.L.R. (2d) 1, 34 Admin. L.R. 235, [1989] 2 W.W.R. 1, 53 D.L.R. (4th) 171 (C.A.), Nemetz C.J.B.C., Carrothers, Hinkson, Macfarlane and Wallace JJ.A. See FREEDOM; RIGHT.

LICENCE. *n.* 1. The permission given to do something which would otherwise be unlawful. 2. A permit, certificate, approval, registration or similar form of permission required by law. 3. An instrument issued conferring upon the holder the privilege of doing the things set forth in it, subject to the conditions, limitations and restrictions contained in it. 4. "... [U]nder a licence the licensee has no exclusive possession, and his right both to the possession and the use may be revoked at any time by the licensor, unless the licence is coupled with an interest or the circumstances raise equitable considerations to which the court will give effect." *Johnson v. British Canadian Insurance Co.*, [1932] 4 D.L.R. 281 at 284, [1932] S.C.R. 680, Lamont J. See CONDITIONAL ~; DRIVER'S ~; LEAVE AND ~.

LICENSED PREMISES. The premises in respect of which a licence has been issued and is in force. *Liquor Control acts.*

LICENSEE. *n.* 1. A person who holds a subsisting licence. 2. "... [A] person who is neither a passenger, servant nor trespasser, and not standing in any contractual relation with the owner of the premises, and is permitted to come upon the premises for his own interest, convenience, or gratification." *Smiles v. Edmonton (Board of Education)* (1918), (*sub nom. Smiles v. Edmonton School District*) 43 D.L.R. 171 at 180, [1918] 3 W.W.R. 673, 14 Alta. L.R. 351 (C.A.), Hyndman J.A. 3. A person who, in furtherance of the sole pursuit of her or his own business, convenience or pleasure goes on another's property, either by that other person's express license or leave, or by that person's implied acquiescence. J.V. DiCastri, *Occupiers' Liability* (Vancouver: Burroughs/Carswell, 1980) at 71. See BARE ~.

LICENSING AUTHORITY. A body which may grant or refuse to grant a licence.

LIE. *v.* Of an action, to be, on the facts of the case, able to be properly begun or continued.

LIE DETECTOR TEST. An analysis, examination, interrogation or test taken or performed by means of or in conjunction with a device, instrument or machine, whether mechanical, electrical, electromagnetic, electronic or otherwise, and that is taken or performed for the purpose of assessing or purporting to assess the credibility of a person.

LIEN. *n.* 1. "In law, a lien is a right to retain possession of property until a debt due to the person detaining the property is satisfied. . . ." *Montreal Lithographing Ltd. v. Deputy Minister of National Revenue (Customs & Excise)* (1984), 12 C.E.R. 1 at 3, [1984] 2 F.C. 22, 8 C.R.R. 299 (T.D.), Cattanach J. 2. "Originally a lien was a possessory interest, but a lien was later recognized under some circumstances in equity, notwithstanding that the holder of it had surrendered possession. Sometimes a lien was an interest in specific property, whilst at other times it was an interest in all of the debtor's property. The one characteristic which each lien had in common was that it was an interest which a person had in property belonging to another." *John Deere Ltd. v. Firdale Farms Ltd.*

(Receiver of) (1987), 8 P.P.S.A.C. 52 at 82, [1988] 2 W.W.R. 406, 45 D.L.R. (4th) 641, 50 Man. R. (2d) 45 (C.A.), Twaddle J.A. (Hall J.A. concurring). 3. A charge, similar to a mortgage, against property. B.J. Reiter, B.N. McLellan & P.M. Perell, *Real Estate Law*, 4th ed. (Toronto: Emond Montgomery, 1992) at 777. 4. A right created by common law or generally by statute when a worker or artisan repairs, adds to or otherwise improves a moveable object or chattel so that the worker or artisan has the right to hold that object or chattel until the owner pays the account. D.N. Macklem & D.I. Bristow, *Construction and Mechanics' Liens in Canada*, 5th ed. (Toronto: Carswell, 1985) at 579. See BUILDERS' ~; CONSTRUCTION ~; CREATION OF ~; EQUITABLE ~; GENERAL ~; MECHANICS' ~; PARTICULAR ~; POSSESSORY ~; PURCHASER'S ~; STATUTORY ~; UNPAID SELLER'S ~; VENDOR'S ~.

LIEN FUND. The percentage retained by an owner to be holdback along with any amount the owner should pay under the contract which was not paid in good faith before the lien was registered. D.N. Macklem & D.I. Bristow, *Construction and Mechanics' Liens in Canada*, 5th ed. (Toronto: Carswell, 1985) at 173.

LIENHOLDER. *n.* Any person having a lien.

LIEUTENANT GOVERNOR. *var.* **LIEUTENANT-GOVERNOR.** The lieutenant governor or other chief executive officer or administrator carrying on the government of the province indicated by the enactment, by whatever title that officer is designated, and, in relation to the Yukon Territory or the Northwest Territories, means the Commissioner thereof.

LIEUTENANT GOVERNOR IN COUNCIL. *var.* **LIEUTENANT-GOVERNOR IN COUNCIL.** The lieutenant governor acting by and with the advice of, or by and with the advice and consent of, or in conjunction with the executive council of the province indicated by the enactment and, in relation to the Yukon Territory or the Northwest Territories, means the Commissioner thereof.

LIEUT. GOV. *abbr.* Lieutenant Governor.

LIFE ANNUITY. A yearly payment while any particular life or lives continues.

LIFE ESTATE. A grant to a person for her or his life. E.L.G. Tyler & N.E. Palmer, eds., *Crossley Vaines' Personal Property*, 5th ed. (London: Butterworths, 1973) at 5.

LIFE INSURANCE. 1. "... [I]n its characteristic forms involves, as its essence, a risk in a specified payment of money absolute from the moment the contract takes effect. That constitutes the security sought by the insured, the premiums for which in turn furnish the consideration to the insurer." *Gray v. Kerslake* (1957), 11 D.L.R. (2d) 225 at 227, [1957] I.L.R. 1-279, [1958] S.C.R. 3, Rand J. 2. Insurance whereby an insurer undertakes to pay insurance money: (i) on death; (ii) on the happening of an event or contingency dependent on human life; (iii) at a fixed or determinable future time; or (iv) for a term dependent on human life; and, without limiting the generality of the foregoing, includes: (v) accidental death insurance; (vi) disability insurance; and (vii) an undertaking given by an insurer to provide an annuity or what would be an annuity except that the periodic payments may be unequal in amount; but does not include accident insurance.

LIFE INTEREST. An interest for another's life (pur autre vie) or one's own life.

LIFE TENANT. One who beneficially holds property as long as she or he lives.

LIMIT. See REASONABLE ~S.

LIMITATION. *n.* 1. Of an interest or estate, the designation of the greatest period during which it will continue. 2. Includes any provision whereby property or any interest is disposed of,

created or conferred. *Perpetuities acts.* See EXECUTORY ~; STATUTE OF ~S; WORDS OF ~.

LIMITATION OF ACTION. A fixed period within which, following the maxim "interest reipublicae ut sit finis litium", proceedings must be taken or an action brought.

LIMITATIONS PERIOD. The time period specified by a statute and within which an action must be brought or a complaint filed.

LIMITED ADMINISTRATION. The temporary and special administration of a testator's or intestate's designated particular effects.

LIMITED EXECUTOR. An executor with an appointment which is limited in time or place or subject-matter.

LIMITED OWNER. A tenant for life, by the curtesy or in tail, or any person who does not have a fee simple absolutely.

LIMITED PARTNERSHIP. Partnership in which the liability of some partners is limited to their capital contribution and in which these limited partners do not exercise management functions with respect to the business of the partnership. See PARTNERSHIP.

LINE. *n.* 1. An ordered series of relatives. 2. A boundary. See CREDIT ~; PICKET ~.

LINEAGE. *n.* A family, progeny or race in either ascending or descending order.

LINEAL DESCENT. The proper bequest of an estate from an ancestor to an heir.

LIQUID ASSETS. Cash or property which can be easily realized.

LIQUIDATE. *v.* To change assets into cash.

LIQUIDATED. *adj.* Ascertained, fixed.

LIQUIDATED DAMAGES. "The essence of liquidated damages is a genuine covenanted pre-estimate of damage ..." *Canadian General Electric Co. v. Canadian Rubber Co.* (1915), 27 D.L.R. 294 at 295, 52 S.C.R. 349, Fitzpatrick C.J.

LIQUIDATED DEMAND. "[A demand] ... the amount of which had been ascertained or settled by agreement of the parties...." *Logistique & Transport Internationaux Ltée v. Armada Lines Ltd.* (1991), 50 F.T.R. 21 at 23, Dubé J.

LIQUIDATION. *n.* "... [A] winding up of the affairs of the company by getting in all its assets and distributing the proceeds to those entitled...." *Linder v. Rutland Moving & Storage Ltd.*, [1991] 4 W.W.R. 355 at 362, 54 B.C.L.R. (2d) 98, 78 D.L.R. (4th) 755, [1991] 1 C.T.C. 517 (C.A.), the court per Hollinrake J.A.

LIQUIDATOR. *n.* "... [A] person appointed to carry out the winding up of a company whose duty is to get in and realize the property of the company, to pay its debts and to distribute the surplus (if any) among the shareholders." *Minister of National Revenue v. Parsons* (1983), 4 Admin. L.R. 64 at 79, [1983] C.T.C. 321, 83 D.T.C. 5329 (Fed. T.D.), Cattanach J.

LIQUID CAPITAL. The amount by which active assets exceed the sum of total liabilities.

LIS. *n.* [L.] An action or suit; a controversy or dispute.

LIS ALIBI PENDENS. [L. a suit pending somewhere else] 1. A plea that an action in one forum should be postponed until litigation begun elsewhere is concluded. C.R.B. Dunlop, *Creditor-Debtor Law in Canada* (Toronto: Carswell, 1981) at 484. 2. "... [U]sed to describe a situation in which the defendant may have instituted his own action against the plaintiffs in a foreign jurisdiction ... the applicant must establish that the foreign jurisdiction is the more appropriate natural forum to try the actions in the sense that the foreign jurisdiction has the most real and substantial connection with the lawsuit." *Galatco Redlaw Castings Corp. v.*

Brunswick Industrial Supply Co. (1989), 69 O.R. (2d) 478 at 482, 36 C.P.C. (2d) 225 (H.C.), Gray J.

LIS MOTA. [L.] Anticipated or existing litigation.

LIS PENDENS. [L. a pending suit] To register a lis pendens is to give intending mortgagees or purchasers notice of the litigation.

LIST. *n.* 1. A calendar of cases to be heard in a particular court on a particular day or during a particular session. See BLACK ~; LAW ~; VOTERS ~.

LISTED STOCK. A security admitted for trading on a stock exchange.

LISTING. See EXCLUSIVE ~; MULTIPLE ~; OPEN ~.

LISTING AGREEMENT. A contract during which a vendor agrees to pay a broker commission on any exchange or sale no matter how it took place. B.J. Reiter, B.N. McLellan & P.M. Perell, *Real Estate Law*, 4th ed. (Toronto: Emond Montgomery, 1992) at 72.

LITERAL PROOF. Evidence in writing.

LITIGANT. *n.* A person who engages in a law-suit.

LITIGATION. *n.* A law-suit.

LITIGATION ADMINISTRATOR. Formerly known as an administrator ad litem.

LITIGATION GUARDIAN. Formerly known as next friend or guardian ad litem, a person who acts on behalf of an absentee, minor or mentally incompetent person. M.M. Orkin, *The Law of Costs*, 2d ed. (Aurora: Canada Law Book, 1987) at 2-34.1.

LITIGATION PRIVILEGE. Attaches to correspondence and other material prepared in anticipation of litigation.

LITIGIOUS. *adj.* 1. Said of a person who frequently commences law suits. 2. Said of a matter which is subject to an action or other proceeding.

LIVERY. *n.* Delivery; giving possession or seisin.

LIVERY OF SEISIN. In times past, the public act needed to transfer an immediate freehold estate in tenements or lands.

LIVING EXPENSES. Expenses of a continuing nature including expenses for food, clothing, shelter, utilities, household sundries, household maintenance, medical and dental services and life insurance premiums.

L.J. *abbr.* 1. Law Journal Reports. 2. Lord Justice of Appeal.

LL.B. *abbr.* Bachelor of Laws.

LL.D. *abbr.* Doctor of Laws.

L. LIB. *abbr.* Law Librarian.

LL.M. *abbr.* Master of Laws.

LLOYD'S ASSOCIATION. An association of individuals formed on the plan known as Lloyd's, whereby each associate underwriter becomes liable for a stated, limited or proportionate part of the whole amount insured by a contract. *Insurance acts.*

LOAN. *n.* 1. Anything given or lent to someone on condition that it be repayed or returned. 2. ". . . [T]he lending of money with the expectation that the money will be repaid. . . ." *Canada Deposit Insurance Corp. v. Canadian Commercial Bank* (1990), 73 Alta. L.R. (2d) 230 at 244, [1990] 4 W.W.R. 445, 105 A.R. 368 (Q.B.), Wachowich J. See COMPLETION ~; CONSOLIDATED ~.

LOAN AGREEMENT. A document or memorandum in writing (i) evidencing a loan, (ii) made or given as security for a loan, or (iii) made or given as security for a past indebtedness arising under a previous loan agreement or time sale agreement, and made or given in substitution for the previous agreement, and includes a mortgage of real property.

LOAN COMMITMENT. A document executed by a lender and borrower when the lender agrees to provide the loan requested which sets out any terms and conditions for that loan. B.J. Reiter, B.N. McLellan & P.M. Perell, *Real Estate Law*, 4th ed. (Toronto: Emond Montgomery, 1992) at 836.

LOBBYIST. *n.* A person engaged to represent the interests of a certain group in dealings with the government.

LOC. *abbr.* Local.

LOCAL ACT. An act which deals with a matter relating to a particular area, usually a municipality.

LOCAL AUTHORITY. 1. Any public organization created by an act of a legislature and exercising jurisdiction or powers of a local nature. 2. The council of a municipality.

LOCAL BOARD. Any board, commission, committee, body or local authority of any kind established to exercise or exercising any power or authority under any general or special act with respect to any of the affairs or purposes of a municipality or parts thereof or of two or more municipalities or parts thereof, or to which a municipality or municipalities are required to provide funds.

LOCAL CTS. & MUN. GAZ. *abbr.* Local Courts' and Municipal Gazette (1865-1872).

LOCAL GOVERNMENT. 1. A system of government by which administration of local affairs is entrusted to local authority. 2. A body with legislative power over a local area but which national authority may overrule. P.W. Hogg, *Constitutional Law of Canada*, 3d ed. (Toronto: Carswell, 1992) at 98.

LOCAL IMPROVEMENT. A work or service intended to be paid for or maintained wholly or partly by special assessments against the land benefitted thereby.

LOCAL STATUTE. See LOCAL ACT.

LOC. CIT. *abbr.* Loco citato.

LOC. CT. GAZ. *abbr.* Local Courts & Municipal Gazette (Ont.), 1865-1872.

LOCKOUT. *var.* **LOCK-OUT.** *n.* Includes the closing of a place of employment, a suspension of work by an employer or a refusal by an employer to continue to employ some employees, done to compel the employees, or to aid another employer to compel those employees, to agree to certain terms or conditions of employment.

LOCO CITATO. [L.] At the quoted passage.

LOCO PARENTIS. See IN LOCO PARENTIS.

LOCUM TENENS. [L.] A person who lawfully executes another person's office, a deputy.

LOCUS. [L.] Place.

LOCUS IN QUO. [L. a place in which] A place where.

LOCUS SIGILLI. [L. the place of the seal] The place at the bottom of a document which requires a seal.

LOCUS STANDI. [L. a place to stand] The right to be heard or appear during a proceeding.

LODGER. *n.* A person who occupies rooms in a house.

LODGING HOUSE. *var.* **LODGING-HOUSE.** A house in which sleeping accommodation is let to transient lodgers.

LOITER. *v.* "... '[H]anging around' ..." *R. v. Andsten* (1960), 32 W.W.R. 329 at 331, 33 C.R. 213 (B.C. C.A.), the court per Davey J.A.

LOITERER. *n.* "... [A]n individual who is wandering about, apparently without precise destination, who does not have, in his manner of moving, a purpose or reason to do so other than to pass the time, who is not looking for anything identifiable and who often is merely motivated by the whim of the moment...." *R. v. Cloutier* (1991), 66 C.C.C. (3d) 149 at 154, 51 Q.A.C. 143, the court per Chevalier J.A.

L.O.M.J. *abbr.* Law Office Management Journal.

LONG TITLE. A description which sets out the purposes of a bill or statute in general terms. A. Fraser, W.A. Dawson, & J. Holtby, eds., *Beauchesne's Rules and Forms of the House of Commons of Canada*, 6th ed. (Toronto: Carswell, 1989) at 192.

LONG VACATION. The months July and August when the courts traditionally did not sit. D. Sgayias *et al.*, *Federal Court Practice 1988* (Toronto: Carswell, 1987) at 253.

LORD. *n.* See HOUSE OF ~S; MESNE ~.

LOSS. *n.* 1. Includes the happening of an event or contingency by reason of which a person becomes entitled to a payment under a contract of insurance of money other than a refund of unearned premiums. *Insurance acts.* 2. "... [T]he inverse of profit ..." *Mountain Park Coals Ltd. v. Minister of National Revenue*, [1952] Ex. C.R. 560 at 568, [1952] C.T.C. 392, [1952] D.T.C. 1221, Thorson P. See NON-PECUNIARY ~; PARTIAL ~; PECUNIARY ~; TOTAL ~.

LOSS OF AMENITIES. A physical disability the victim sustained in an accident, and the effect that disability has on all the victim's activities. K.D. Cooper-Stephenson & I.B. Saunders, *Personal Injury Damages in Canada* (Toronto: Carswell, 1981) at 354.

LOSS OF CHANCE. "... [T]he damage which results from the loss of an opportunity either to realize a benefit or to avoid an injury.... the damage is future or hypothetical and clearly not certain. It is distinguished by the fact that it is contingent, or dependent on an element of chance which must be evaluated in terms of probabilities. This contingent or probabilistic aspect provides the potential for ascertainment of damages in the present...." *Laferrière v. Lawson* (1991), 6 C.C.L.T. (2d) 119 at 196, 123 N.R. 325, 38 Q.A.C. 161, [1991] R.R.A. 320, [1991] 1 S.C.R. 541, 78 D.L.R. (4th) 609, Gonthier J. (Lamer, L'Heureux-Dubé, Sopinka, Cory and McLachlin JJ. concurring).

LOSS OF EXPECTATION OF LIFE. Shortening of the length of the victim's life. K.D. Cooper-Stephenson & I.B. Saunders, *Personal Injury Damages in Canada* (Toronto:

Carswell, 1981) at 358.

LOSS OF SERVICES. A claim by a husband against a person who injured his wife wrongfully or a claim by a parent for loss occasioned by the wrongful injury of his or her child or a claim by a master in respect of an injury to her or his servant. J.G. Fleming, *The Law of Torts*, 8th ed. (Sydney: Law Book, 1992) at 658, 660, 684.

LOST. *adj.* ". . . [T]he location of the person or thing is unknown or uncertain. In other usages, 'lost' may mean mislaid and not found after reasonably diligent search." *Gagnon v. Northwest Territories (Registrar of Vehicles)*, [1983] N.W.T.R. 289 at 292 (C.A.), the court per Laycraft J.A.

LOST CORNER. A corner established during an original survey or during a survey of a plan of subdivision where the original post no longer exists or never existed and which cannot be re-established from the field notes of either of such surveys or by evidence under oath.

LOST MONUMENT. A monument which has disappeared entirely and the position of which cannot be established by evidence. *Surveys acts*.

LOT. *n.* 1. A lot or any other area defined and designated by an original survey or by a registered plan. 2. The method of determining the candidate to be excluded or the candidate to fill the vacancy, as the case may be, by placing the names of the candidates on equal size pieces of paper placed in a box and one name being drawn by a person chosen by the clerk. *Municipal Act*, R.S.O. 1990, c. M.45, s. 45(6). 3. A parcel of land containing or which may contain one or more graves and includes a space within a building or structure which contains or may contain one or more places for the permanent placement of human remains.

LOTTERY. *n.* A game of chance; a division and sharing of prizes by chance or lot.

LOW. CAN. R. *abbr.* Lower Canada Reports, 1851-1867.

LOWER CANADA. That part of Canada which heretofore constituted the Province of Lower Canada, and means now the province of Québec. *Interpretation Act*, R.S.Q. 1977, c. I-16, s. 61.

L.Q. REV. *abbr.* Law Quarterly Review.

L.R. *abbr.* Law Reports.

L.R.B. *abbr.* Labour Relations Board.

L.R. 1 A. & E. *abbr.* Law Reports, Admiralty and Ecclesiastical Cases, 1865-1875.

L.R. 1 C.C.R. *abbr.* Law Reports, Crown Cases Reserved, 1865-1875.

L.R. 1 CH. *abbr.* Law Reports, Chancery Appeals, 1865-1875.

L.R. 1 C.P. *abbr.* Law Reports, Common Pleas, 1865-1875.

L.R. 1 EQ. *abbr.* Law Reports, Equity Cases, 1865-1875.

L.R. 1 EX. *abbr.* Law Reports, Exchequer, 1865-1875.

L.R. 1 H.L. *abbr.* Law Reports, House of Lords Cases, 1865-1875.

L.R. 1 P. & D. *abbr.* Law Reports, Probate and Divorce, 1865-1875.

L.R. 1 P.C. *abbr.* Law Reports, Privy Council Cases, 1865-1875.

L.R. 1 Q.B. *abbr.* Law Reports, Queen's Bench, 1865-1875.

L.R. 1 SC. & DIV. *abbr.* Law Reports, Scottish and Divorce.

L.R.P.C. *abbr.* Law Reports Privy Council Appeals.

L.S. *abbr.* Locus sigilli. The place for the seal.

LSAT. *abbr.* Law School Admission Test.

L. SOC. GAZ. *abbr.* Law Society Gazette (Law Society of Upper Canada).

L.S.U.C. *abbr.* Law Society of Upper Canada.

L.T. *abbr.* Law Times Reports.

L.V.A.C. *abbr.* Land Value Appraisal Commission.

M

MACNAUGHTON'S CASE. See MCNAGHTEN'S CASE.

MADE. *adj.* 1. ". . . [R]efers to pronouncement, not entry: . . ." *Levesque v. Levesque* (1992), 41 R.F.L. (3d) 96 at 98, 3 Alta. L.R. (3d) 193, 131 A.R. 106, 25 W.A.C. 106 (C.A.), Côté J.A. 2. ". . . [P]ronouncement [or] . . . signed or entered in court . . ." *Harvey v. Harvey* (1989), 23 R.F.L. (3d) 53 at 55, 60 Man. R. (2d) 302 (C.A.), Helper J.A.

MAG. *abbr.* Magistrate(s).

MAG. CT. *abbr.* Magistrate's Court.

MAGISTRATE. *n.* 1. A magistrate, a police magistrate, a stipendiary magistrate, a district magistrate, a provincial magistrate, a judge of the sessions of the peace, a recorder or any person having the power and authority of two or more justices of the peace, and includes (a) with respect to the provinces of Ontario, Quebec, New Brunswick and British Columbia, a judge of the provincial court, (b) with respect to the province of Nova Scotia, a judge of the Provincial Magistrate's Court, (c) with respect to the Provinces of Prince Edward Island, Manitoba and Alberta, a provincial judge, (d) with respect to the province of Saskatchewan, a judge of the Magistrates' Courts, and (e) with respect to the Yukon Territory and the Northwest Territories, a judge of the Supreme Court, and the lawful deputy of each of them. *Criminal Code*, R.S.C. 1985, c. C-46, s. 2. 2. (a) A person appointed under the law of a province, by whatever title he may be designated, who is specially authorized by the terms of his appointment to exercise the jurisdiction conferred on a magistrate by this Part, but does not include two or more justices of the peace sitting together, (b) with respect to the Yukon Territory, a judge of the Supreme Court or a magistrate or deputy magistrate appointed under an Ordinance of the Territory, and (c) with respect to the Northwest Territories, a judge of the Supreme Court or a magistrate or deputy magistrate appointed under an Ordinance of the Territories. *Criminal Code*, R.S.C. 1985, c. C-46, s. 552. 3. Any justice of the peace or any person having authority to issue a warrant for the apprehension of persons accused of offences and to commit those persons for trial. *Fugitive Offenders Act*, R.S.C. 1985, c. F-32, s. 2.

MAGNA CARTA. A charter or collection of statutes based largely on Saxon common law granted by the British King John in 1215 to confirm certain liberties.

MAIL. *v.* Refers to the deposit of the matter to which the context applies in the Canada Post Office at any place in Canada, postage prepaid, for transmission by post, and includes delivery. *Interpretation Act*, R.S.B.C. 1979, c. 206, s. 29.

MAIL. *n.* Mailable matter from the time it is posted to the time it is delivered to the addressee thereof. *Canada Post Corporation Act*, R.S.C.

1985, c. C-10, s. 2.

MAILABLE MATTER. Any message, information, funds or goods that may be transmitted by post. *Canada Post Corporation Act*, R.S.C. 1985, c. C-10, s. 2.

MAINTAIN. *v.* 1. "[To provide] . . ; financial or other material support . . ," *Desjarlais v. Macdonell Estate* (1988), 31 E.T.R. 18 at 24, [1988] 3 W.W.R. 534, 23 B.C.L.R. (2d) 195 (C.A.), Anderson J.A. (Esson and McLachlin JJ.A. concurring). 2. ". . . [M]ay mean either to bring or institute an action or proceeding or to continue or further prosecute an action already commenced. . . ." *Komnick System Sandstone Brick Machinery Co. v. B.C. Pressed Brick Co.* (1918), 56 S.C.R. 539 at 549, 41 D.L.R. 423, [1918] 2 W.W.R. 564, Anglin J. 3. ". . . [T]o keep in being, to keep up and to repair. . . ." *Red Lake (Township) v. Drawson*, [1964] 1 O.R. 324 at 328, 42 D.L.R. (2d) 121 (H.C.), Ferguson J.

MAINTENANCE. *n.* 1. ". . . [I]n the ordinary sense, mean[s] 'keep in repair'; . . ." *Canadian Pacific Railway v. Grand Trunk Railway* (1914), 20 D.L.R. 56 at 63, 49 S.C.R. 525, 17 C.R.C. 300, Brodeur J. 2. Pecuniary support including support or alimony to be paid to someone who is not a spouse. C.R.B. Dunlop, *Creditor-Debtor Law in Canada*, Second Cumulative Supplement (Toronto: Carswell, 1986) at 209. 3. "The law of maintenance as I understand it upon the modern constructions, is confined to cases where a man improperly and for the purpose of stirring up litigation and strife, encourages others either to bring actions or to make defences which they have no right to make." *Findon (Finden) v. Parker* (1843), 152 E.R. 976 at 979 (U.K. Ex.), Lord Abinger, C.B.

MAINTENANCE ORDER. An order for the periodical payment of money as alimony or as maintenance for a wife or former wife or reputed wife or a child or any other dependant of the person against whom the order was made.

MAJOR BURDEN. ". . . [T]he burden of establishing a case . . ." *R. v. Schwartz* (1988), 45 C.C.C. (3d) 97 at 115, [1989] 1 W.W.R. 289, 66 C.R. (3d) 251, 88 N.R. 90, [1988] 2 S.C.R. 443, 56 Man. R. (2d) 92, 55 D.L.R. (4th) 1, Dickson C.J.C. (dissenting).

MAJORITY. *n.* 1. Age of maturity. 2. The largest number.

MAJORITY OPINION. 1. The opinion agreed upon by the greater number of the members of a hearing panel or court consisting of three or more members or judges. 2. The opinion of the greater number of a group. Compare DISSENTING OPINION.

MAL. *pref.* Wrong; bad; fraudulent.

MALA FIDE. [L.] In bad faith.

MALA FIDES. [L.] Bad faith, contrasted to bona fides, good faith.

MALA IN SE. [L.] "[At] common law . . . truly criminal conduct . . . [was designated] mala in se . . . today [such] prohibited acts are . . . classified as . . . crimes . . ." *R. v. Wholesale Travel Group Inc.* (1991), 8 C.R. (4th) 145 at 159, 67 C.C.C. (3d) 193, 4 O.R. (3d) 799n, 84 D.L.R. (4th) 161, 130 N.R. 1, 38 C.P.R. (3d) 451, 49 O.A.C. 161, [1991] 3 S.C.R. 154, 7 C.R.R. (2d) 36, Cory J. (L'Heureux-Dubé J. concurring).

MALA PROHIBITA. [L.] "[At] common law . . . conduct, otherwise lawful, which is prohibited in the public interest . . . today . . . [such] prohibited acts are . . . classified as . . . regulatory offences." *R. v. Wholesale Travel Group Inc.* (1991), 8 C.R. (4th) 145 at 159, 67 C.C.C. (3d) 193, 4 O.R. (3d) 799n, 84 D.L.R. (4th) 161, 130 N.R. 1, 38 C.P.R. (3d) 451, 49 O.A.C. 161, [1991] 3 S.C.R. 154, 7 C.R.R. (2d) 36, Cory J. (L'Heureux-Dubé J. concurring).

MALE. See ~ ISSUE.

MALE ISSUE. Descendants in the male line. T. Sheard, R. Hull & M.M.K. Fitzpatrick, *Canadian Forms of Wills*, 4th ed. (Toronto: Carswell, 1982) at 191.

MALFEASANCE. *n.* The commission of an unlawful act. See MISFEASANCE.

MALICE. *n.* "[In defamation] ... not limited to spite or ill will, although these are its most obvious instances. Malice includes any indirect motive or ulterior purpose, and will be established if the plaintiff can prove that the defendant was not acting honestly when he published the comment. ...", *Cherneskey v. Armadale Publishers Ltd.,* [1979] 1 S.C.R. 1067 at 1099, 24 N.R. 271, [1978] 6 W.W.R. 618, 7 C.C.L.T. 69, 90 D.L.R. (3d) 321, Dickson J. (dissenting) (Spence and Estey JJ. concurring). See IMPLIED ~.

MALICE AFORETHOUGHT. 1. "... [W]as ... adopted to distinguish murder from manslaughter, which denoted all culpable homicides other than murder. ... was not limited to its natural and obvious sense of premeditation, but would be implied whenever the killing was intentional or reckless. In these instances, the malice was present and it is the premeditation which was implied by law." *R. v. Vaillancourt* (1987), 60 C.R. (3d) 289 at 321, 81 N.R. 115, [1987] 2 S.C.R. 636, 68 Nfld. & P.E.I.R. 281, 209 A.P.R. 281, 10 Q.A.C. 161, 39 C.C.C. (3d) 118, 47 D.L.R. (4th) 399, 32 C.R.R. 18, Lamer J. (Dickson C.J.C. and Wilson J. concurring). 2. "... [A]t least in modern usage, is misleading, but it has come to be a comprehensive term to describe the various forms of mens rea or the various mental elements which must be present to justify a conviction for murder ... has been greatly broadened in modern times. ...", *R. v. Switelinski* (1980), 18 C.R. (3d) 231 at 246, 248, 34 N.R. 569, 55 C.C.C. (2d) 481, 117 D.L.R. (3d) 285, [1980] 2 S.C.R. 956, the court per McIntyre J.

MALICIOUSLY. *adv.* With an intent to cause harm or while being reckless about whether that harm will occur. S. Mitchell, P.J. Richardson & D.A. Thomas, eds., *Archbold On Pleading, Evidence and Practice in Criminal Cases,* 43d ed. (London: Sweet & Maxwell, 1988) at 1343.

MALICIOUS PROSECUTION. "... [F]our necessary elements which must be proved for a plaintiff to succeed in an action for malicious prosecution: (a) the proceedings must have been initiated by the defendant; (b) the proceedings must have terminated in favour of the plaintiff; (c) the absence of reasonable and probable cause; (d) malice, or a primary purpose other than that of carrying the law into effect." *Nelles v. Ontario* (1989), 37 C.P.C. (2d) 1 at 21, 49 C.C.L.T. 217, [1989] 2 S.C.R. 170, 71 C.R. (3d) 358, 60 D.L.R. (4th) 609, 98 N.R. 321, 69 O.R.(2d) 448n, 35 O.A.C. 161, 42 C.R.R. 1, 41 Admin. L.R. 1, Lamer J. (Dickson C.J.C. and Wilson J. concurring).

MALPRACTICE. *n.* "... [B]ad or unskilful practice by a physician or surgeon, whereby the health of the patient is injured. ...", *Town v. Archer* (1902), 4 O.L.R. 383 at 387, 1 O.W.R. 391 (H.C.), Falconbridge C.J.

MALUM IN SE. [L.] See MALA IN SE.

MALUM PROHIBITUM. [L.] See MALA PROHIBITA.

MAN. *n.* See DRAFTS~.

MANAGEMENT RIGHTS. Rights which an employer retains such as hiring, contracting and price fixing.

MANAGER. *n.* When a receiver is appointed and it is necessary to continue the debtor's business, the person appointed by the court to continue the business. F. Bennett, *Receiverships* (Toronto: Carswell, 1985) at 1. See MUTUAL FUND ~; RECEIVER AND ~.

MANAGING DIRECTOR. 1. "... [A] director having the management of affairs." *Claudet v. Golden Giant Mines Ltd.* (1910), 13 W.L.R. 348 at 350, 15 B.C.R. 13 (C.A.), Galliher J.A. (Macdonald C.J.A. concurring). 2. "... [A]n ordinary director entrusted with some special powers: ..." *Standard Construction Co. v. Crabb* (1914), 7 W.W.R. 719 at 721, 30 W.L.R. 151, 7 Sask. L.R. 365 (C.A.), the court per Lamont J.A.

MAN. & SASK. TAX R. *abbr.* Manitoba & Saskatchewan Tax Reports.

MAN. BAR N. *abbr.* Manitoba Bar News.

MANDAMUS. *n.* [L. we command] "[An extraordinary remedy which] ... lies to secure the performance of a public duty in the performance of which the applicant has sufficient legal interest. The applicant must show that he demanded the performance of the duty and that performance of it has been refused by the authority obliged to discharge it ... Another pricinple is that a mandamus will not be issued to order a body as to how to exercise its jurisdiction or discretion." *Turmel v. Canada (Canadian Radio-Television & Telecommunications Commission)* (1980), 60 C.P.R. (2d) 37 at 38, 117 D.L.R. (3d) 697, [1981] 2 F.C. 411 (T.D.), Walsh J.

MANDATE. *n.* 1. A request; a directive. 2. A bailment of goods, without recompense, to have something done in connection with them or to be transported from one place to another.

MANDATORY. *adj.* Imperative.

MANDATORY INJUNCTION. A requirement that a defendant do something. G.H.L. Fridman, *The Law of Contract in Canada*, 2d ed. (Toronto: Carswell, 1986) at 722.

MANDATORY PRESUMPTION. 1. "... [R]equires that the inference be made." *R. v. Oakes* (1986), 24 C.C.C. (3d) 321 at 330, [1986] 1 S.C.R. 103, 53 O.R. (2d) 719, 50 C.R. (3d) 1, 14 O.A.C. 335, 19 C.R.R. 308, 26 D.L.R. (4th) 200, 65 N.R. 87, Dickson C.J.C. (Chouinard, Wilson and Le Dain JJ. concurring). 2. "... [R]equires the trier of fact to find the presumed fact upon proof of the fact giving rise to the presumption, in the absence of some countering evidence." *R. v. Oakes* (1983), 3 C.R.R. 289 at 308, 40 O.R. (2d) 660, 2 C.C.C. (3d) 339, 32 C.R. (3d) 193, 145 D.L.R. (3d) 123 (C.A.), the court per Martin J.A.

MAN. L.J. *abbr.* Manitoba Law Journal.

MAN. L.R. *abbr.* Manitoba Law Reports (First Series).

MANSLAUGHTER. *n.* 1. Culpable homicide that is not murder or infanticide. *Criminal Code*, R.S.C. 1985, c. C-46, s. 234. 2. Culpable homicide that otherwise would be murder may be reduced to manslaughter if the person who committed it did so in the heat of passion caused by sudden provocation. *Criminal Code*, R.S.C. 1985, c. C-46, s. 232(1). 3. "... [A]n unlawful killing without proof of the existence of the required specific intent has always been characterized as manslaughter." *R. v. Switelinski* (1980), 18 C.R. (3d) 231 at 248, 34 N.R. 569, 55 C.C.C. (2d) 481, 117 D.L.R. (3d) 285, [1980] 2 S.C.R. 950, the court per McIntyre J.

MANSUETAE NATURAE. [L.] Harmless animals. J.G. Fleming, *The Law of Torts*, 8th ed. (Sydney: Law Book, 1992) at 358. See ANIMALS ~; DANGEROUS ANIMALS.

MAREVA INJUNCTION. 1. Originally a prejudgment remedy intended to freeze assets until judgment was obtained and a writ of execution issued which was named after the case *Mareva Compania Naviera S.A. v. Int. Bulkcarriers S.A.*, [1980] 1 All E.R. 213 (U.K. C.A.). C.R.B. Dunlop, *Creditor-Debtor Law in Canada*, Second Cumulative Supplement (Toronto: Carswell, 1986) at 88. 2. "The gist of the Mareva action is the right to freeze exigible assets when found within the jurisdiction, wherever the defendant may reside, providing, of course, there is a cause between the plaintiff and the defendant which is justiciable in the Courts of England. However, unless there is a genuine risk of disappearance of assets, either inside or outside the jurisdiction, the injunction will not issue. This generally summarizes the position in this country ..." *Aetna Financial Services Ltd. v. Feigelman* (1985), 29 B.L.R. 5 at 25, [1985] 1 S.C.R. 2, [1985] 2 W.W.R. 97, 55 C.B.R. (N.S.) 1, 56 N.R. 241, 15 D.L.R. (4th) 161, 4 C.P.R. (3d) 145, 32 Man. R (2d) 241, the court per Estey J. 3. A remedy designed to (1) obtain something like security, at least by ensuring that there are funds available to meet any judgment, and (2) put pressure on a defendant to provide proper security for any claim. However, it has been held that such an injunction does not create a proprietary right in the enjoined property; it merely prevents dealing with that property in particular ways. C.R.B. Dunlop, *Creditor-Debtor Law in Canada* (Toronto: Carswell, 1981) at 190.

MARGINAL NOTE. Something printed beside the section of an act which summarizes the effect of that section. P. St. J. Langan, ed., *Maxwell on The Interpretation of Statutes*, 12th ed. (Bombay: N.M. Tripathi, 1976) at 9.

MARINE INSURANCE. 1. Insurance against marine losses; that is to say, the losses incident to marine adventures, and may by the express terms of a contract or by usage of trade extend so as to protect the insured against losses on inland waters or by land or air which are incidental to any sea voyage. 2. Insurance against, (i) liability arising out of, (A) bodily injury to or death of a person, or (B) the loss of or damage to properties; or (ii) the loss of or damage to property, occurring during a voyage or marine adventure at sea or on an inland waterway or during delay incidental thereto, or during transit otherwise than by water incidental to such a voyage or marine adventure. See CONTRACT OF ~.

MARITAL. *adj.* Pertaining to the state of marriage; relating to a husband.

MARITAL HOME. Property in which one or both spouses have an interest and that is or has been occupied as their family residence, and where property that includes a marital home is used for a purpose in addition to a family residence, that marital home is that portion of the property that may reasonably be regarded as necessary to the use and enjoyment of the family residence.

MARITAL PROPERTY. (a) Family assets; (b) property owned by one spouse or by both spouses that is not a

family asset and that was acquired while the spouses cohabited, or in contemplation of marriage, except (i) a business asset, (ii) property that was a gift from one spouse to the other, including income from that property, (iii) property that was a gift, devise, or bequest from any other person to one spouse only, including income from that property, (iv) property that represents the proceeds of disposition of property that was not a family asset and was not acquired while the spouses cohabited or in contemplation of marriage, or that was acquired in exchange for or was purchased with the proceeds of disposition of such property or that represents insurance proceeds with respect to loss of or damage to such property; and (v) property that represents the proceeds of disposition of property referred to in subparagraphs (ii) and (iii) or that was acquired in exchange for or was purchased with the proceeds of disposition of such property or that represents insurance proceeds with respect to loss of or damage to such property; and (c) property that was acquired by one spouse after the cessation of cohabitation and that was acquired through the disposition of property that would have been marital property had the disposition not occurred; but does not include property that the spouses have agreed by a domestic contract is not to be included in marital property.

MARITAL STATUS. 1. The status of being single, engaged to be married, married, separated, divorced, widowed or a man and woman living in the same household as if they were married. *Human Rights Act*, S.N.S. 1991, c. 12, s. 3. 2. "... [I]n the Canadian Human Rights Act, S.C. 1976-77, c. 33 does not mean the status of a married person but, rather, the status of a person in relation to marriage, namely, whether that person is single, married, divorced or widowed." *Schaap v. Canada (Canadian Armed Forces)* (1988), 27 C.C.E.L. 1 at 8, 56 D.L.R. (4th) 105 (Fed. C.A.), Pratte J.A. (concurring).

MARITIME LAW. The law relating to ships, harbours and mariners. See

CANADIAN ~.

MARITIME PERILS. The perils consequent on or incidental to the navigation of the sea, that is to say, perils of the seas, fire, war perils, pirates, rovers, thieves, captures, seizures, restraints, and detainments of princes and peoples, jettisons, barratry, and any other perils, either of the like kind or which may be designated by the policy. *Insurance acts.*

MARK. *n.* See CERTIFICATION ~; TRADE- ~.

MARKET. *n.* 1. A place where a person may go to buy or sell whatever she or he wants. G.H.L. Fridman, *Sale of Goods in Canada*, 3d ed. (Toronto: Carswell, 1986) at 358-359. 2. ". . . [T]he action or business of buying and selling commodities." *Schecter v. Bluestein* (1981), 23 C.R. (3d) 39 at 45, [1981] C.S. 477, 121 D.L.R. (3d) 345, 58 C.C.C. (2d) 208 (Que. S.C.), Malouf J. 3. ". . . [D]efined by a certain number of properties which establish equivalence of price, of goods and of availability. It is often in relation to a geographic place which may be local, regional, national or international, depending upon the clientele. Often, and more and more frequently, a market will depend on a network such as in the case of currency or electronics . . ." *Alex Couture Inc. c. Canada (Procureur général)* (1990), (*sub nom. Alex Couture Inc. v. Canada (Attorney General)*) 30 C.P.R. (3d) 486 at 514, 69 D.L.R. (4th) 635 (Qué. C.S.), Philippon J. See AFTER-~; AVAILABLE ~.

MARKETABLE TITLE. See GOOD TITLE.

MARKETING. *n.* Buying, selling, shipping for sale or offering for sale. See BLACK ~.

MARKET OVERT. Open market.

MARKET PRICE. 1. The highest price for which an owner can sell property under conditions prevalent in that market. A. Bissett-Johnson & W.M. Holland, eds., *Matrimonial Property Law in Canada* (Toronto: Carswell, 1980) at V-11. 2. As to securities to which there is a published market, the price at any particular date determined in accordance with regulations. See MARKET VALUE.

MARKET VALUE. 1. ". . . '[R]ealizable money value'. . . ." *R. v. Thomas Lawson & Sons Ltd.*, [1948] Ex. C.R. 44 at 82, [1948] 3 D.L.R. 334, 62 C.R.T.C. 277, Thorson P. 2. The amount in terms of cash that would probably be realized for property in an arm's length sale in an open market under conditions requisite to a fair sale, the buyer and seller each acting knowledgeably and willingly. *Loan and Trust Companies acts.* 3. The amount of money a willing and informed buyer would pay to a willing and informed seller on usual terms and conditions in a competitive market where neither party was acting under abnormal pressure. *Farm Credit Regulations*, C.R.C., c. 644, s. 2. 4. The most probable sale price indicated by consideration of the cost of reproduction, the sale price of comparable properties and the value indicated by rentals or anticipated net income. *Real Property Assessment Act*, R.S.P.E.I. 1988, c. R-4, s. 1. 5. Market price. A. Bissett-Johnson & W.M. Holland, eds., *Matrimonial Property Law in Canada* (Toronto: Carswell, 1980) at V-11. See FAIR ~.

MARRIAGE. *n.* 1. ". . . [T]he classic definition of marriage is provided by Lord Penzance in Hyde v. Hyde (1866), L.R. 1 P. & D. 130, as [at p. 133]: 'the voluntary union for life of one man and one woman, to the exclusion of all others.' " *Keddie v. Currie* (1991), 44 E.T.R. 61 at 76 (B.C. C.A.), Cumming J.A. (Legg J.A,. concurring). 2. "While marriage is a civil status of a man and woman capable of entering into a valid contract uniting them by mutual consent for life for the discharge of duties legally incumbent on a husband [sic] a wife to each other and to the community, it is essentially a civil contract and capacity and consent are indispensable requisites to its creation." *Capon v. McLay*, [1965] 2 O.R. 83 at 89, 49 D.L.R. (2d) 675 (C.A.), the court per Schroeder J.A.

See BREAKDOWN OF ~; CELEBRA-
TION OF ~; CHILD OF THE ~;
COMMON LAW ~; NULLITY OF ~;
RESTRAINT OF ~; SOLEMNIZA-
TION OF ~.

MARRIAGE CONTRACT. An
agreement two people enter into before
their marriage, during their marriage or
while cohabiting which may deal with
almost any marital right or obligation,
whether it arises during marriage, on
separation, when a marriage is dissolved or annulled or upon death.
A. Bissett-Johnson & W.M. Holland,
eds., *Matrimonial Property Law in
Canada* (Toronto: Carswell, 1980) at
NB-38.

MARRIAGE SETTLEMENT. Any
indenture, contract, agreement,
covenant or settlement entered into in
consideration of marriage whereby one
of the parties agrees to pay a sum or
sums of money to or for the benefit of
self or the other party or any other
person or the issue of the marriage, and
whereby that party settles, grants, conveys, transfers, mortgages, or charges,
or agrees to settle, grant, convey, transfer, mortgage or charge, real or personal property of any description upon
or to or in favour of any person for the
benefit of self or the other party or any
other person or the issue of the marriage.

**MARRIED WOMEN'S PROPERTY
ACT.** An act most provinces passed to
give a wife the right to acquire and
hold property in her own name.
A. Bissett-Johnson & W.M. Holland,
eds., *Matrimonial Property Law in
Canada* (Toronto: Carswell, 1980) at
I-16.

MARSHAL. *v.* "The doctrine of mar-
shalling, in its application to mortgages
or charges upon two estates or funds,
may be stated as follows: If the owner
of two estates mortgages them both to
one person, and then one of them to
another, either with or without notice,
the second mortgagee may insist that
the debt of the first mortgagee shall be
satisfied out of the estate not
mortgaged to the second, so far as that
will extend. This right is always subject

to two important qualifications: first,
that nothing will be done to interfere
with the paramount right of the first
mortgagee to pursue his remedy against
either of the two estates; and, second,
that the doctrine will not be applied to
the prejudice of third parties: ..."
*Ernst Brothers Co. v. Canada Per-
manent Mortgage Corp.* (1920), 47
O.L.R. 362 at 367 (H.C.), Orde J.

MARSHAL. *n.* An ex officio court
officer; every sheriff of the Federal
Court. D. Sgayias *et al.*, *Federal Court
Practice 1988* (Toronto: Carswell,
1987) at 56. See DEPUTY ~.

MARTIAL LAW. 1. Military law. 2.
The replacement of ordinary law and
the temporary government of a nation
or area by a military council if this is
done following a government
proclamation or notice by military authorities.

MARY CARTER AGREEMENT.
An agreement between a plaintiff and
one of two co-defendants. The defendant advances funds to the plaintiff in
settlement of the claim and the plaintiff
agrees to return the money to the
defendant who takes part in the trial if
any recovery is made against the other
defendant. G.D. Watson & C. Perkins,
eds., *Holmested & Watson: Ontario
Civil Procedure* (Toronto: Carswell,
1984-) at 49-14.

MASTER. *n.* Formerly a judicial officer of the Supreme Court who may
decide certain matters before or after
trial. There will be no new masters
appointed and their judicial duties will
eventually be performed by General
Division judges. G.D. Watson &
C. Perkins, eds., *Holmested & Watson:
Ontario Civil Procedure* (Toronto:
Carswell, 1984) at CJA-113-14.

MASTER AND SERVANT. "...
[T]he relationship imports the existence
of power in the employer not only to
direct what work the servant is to do,
but also the manner in which it is to be
done ..." *Atlas Industries Ltd. v.
Goertz* (1985), 4 C.P.C. (2d) 187 at
193, [1985] 4 W.W.R. 598, 38 Sask.
R. 294 (Q.B.), Grotsky J.

MATERIAL. *adj.* 1. Important; essential. 2. "... [T]hat which goes to the foundation of the decision or which goes to the crux of a central issue before the court. ..." *International Corona Resources Ltd. v. Lac Minerals Ltd.* (1988), 54 D.L.R. (4th) 647 at 658, 66 O.R. (2d) 610 (H.C.), Osborne J.

MATERIAL FACT. Where used in relation to securities issued or proposed to be issued, a fact that significantly affects, or would reasonably be expected to have a significant effect on, the market price or value of those securities.

MATERIAL WITNESS. A person whose evidence is important in the prosecution or defence of a case.

MATERNITY. *n.* The state of motherhood.

MATERNITY LEAVE. A leave of absence allowed to a worker who is pregnant or who has given birth.

MATRIMONIAL CAUSE. A proceeding by petition under the Divorce Act (Canada) and a proceeding by petition for a decree of nullity of marriage, or of judicial separation, or of restitution of conjugal rights or jactitation of marriage or any other matrimonial cause within the jurisdiction of the court. *Queen's Bench Act*, S.M. 1973, c. 15, s. 1.

MATTER. *n.* 1. Includes every proceeding in the court not in a cause. 2. Includes every proceeding in the court not in an action. *Judicature Act*, R.S.P.E.I. 1974, c. J-3, s. 1. 3. "The content or subject matter" of the law. *Reference re Anti-Inflation Act, 1975 (Canada)*, [1976] 2 S.C.R. 373 at 450, 9 N.R. 541, 68 D.L.R. (3d) 452, Beetz J. 4. The subject matter or content, pith and substance or true character and nature of a law. P.W. Hogg, *Constitutional Law of Canada*, 2d ed. (Toronto: Carswell, 1985) at 313. See CIVIL ~; CRIMINAL ~; DISCIPLINARY ~; MAILABLE ~.

MATTER OF FACT. See QUESTION OF FACT.

MATTER OF LAW. See QUESTION OF LAW.

MATURITY. *n.* The date on which a note, loan or obligation becomes due.

MAXIM. *n.* A general principle; an axiom.

MAXIMS OF EQUITY. These include: equity will not allow a wrong to exist without a remedy; equity looks to intent rather than to form; equity considers what ought to be done as having been done; an equitable remedy is discretionary; delay defeats equity; one who comes to equity must come with clean hands; one who seeks equity must do equity; equity never lacks a trustee. See CLEAN HANDS DOCTRINE; EQUALITY IS EQUITY; DELAY DEFEATS EQUITIES; EQUITY ACTS IN PERSONAM; EQUITY AIDS THE VIGILANT AND NOT THE INDOLENT; EQUITY FOLLOWS THE LAW; EQUITY IMPUTES AN INTENTION TO FULFIL AN OBLIGATION; EQUITY LOOKS ON THAT AS DONE WHICH OUGHT TO BE DONE; EQUITY LOOKS TO THE INTENT RATHER THAN TO THE FORM; EQUITY WILL NOT SUFFER A WRONG TO BE WITHOUT A REMEDY; HE WHO COMES INTO EQUITY MUST COME WITH CLEAN HANDS; HE WHO SEEKS EQUITY MUST DO EQUITY; NO MAN CAN TAKE ADVANTAGE OF HIS OWN WRONG; NO ONE CAN BE ALLOWED TO DEROGATE FROM HIS OWN GRANT.

MAY. *v.* 1. "... [C]ommonly used to denote a discretion ..." *R. c. Potvin*, [1989] 1 S.C.R. 525 at 547, 93 N.R. 42, 68 C.R. (3d) 193, 47 C.C.C. (3d) 289, 21 Q.A.C. 258, La Forest J. and Dickson C.J. 2. "... [P]ermissive and empowering and confers an 'area of discretion'." *Charles v. Insurance Corp. of British Columbia* (1989), 34 B.C.L.R. (2d) 331 at 337 (C.A.), the court per Lambert J.A. 3. "... [S]hould not be construed as imperative unless the intention that it should be so construed is clear from the context....." *Heare v. Insurance Corp. of British Columbia* (1989), 34 B.C.L.R. (2d) 324 at 327 (C.A.), the court per Lambert J.A.

M.C. *abbr.* Master's Chambers.

MCGILL L.J. *abbr.* McGill Law Journal (Revue de droit de McGill).

MCNAGHTEN'S CASE. R. v. McNaghten or M'Naghten or Macnaughton (1843) 4 St.Tr. (N.S.) 847, a British case which established the law relating to insanity with special reference to criminal responsibility.

M.C.R. *abbr.* Montreal Condensed Reports, 18541884.

MEAN. *v.* 1. Where a definition uses the word "means" and not "includes" ". . . the definition is to be construed as being exhaustive." *Yellow Cab Ltd. v. Alberta (Industrial Relations Board)*, [1980] 2 S.C.R. 761 at 768, 14 Alta. L.R. (2d) 39, 24 A.R. 275, 80 C.L.L.C. 14,066, 33 N.R. 585, 114 D.L.R. (3d) 427, the court per Ritchie J. 2. ". . . [N]ormally construed as comprehending that which is specifically described or defined . . ." *R. v. Hauser* (1979), 98 D.L.R. (3d) 193 at 213, [1979] 1 S.C.R. 984, 26 N.R. 541, [1979] 5 W.W.R. 1, 46 C.C.C. (2d) 481, 16 A.R. 91, 8 C.R. (3d) 89 (Eng.), 8 C.R. (3d) 281 (Fr.), Dickson J. (dissenting) (Pratte J. concurring).

MEANS. *n.* ". . . [T]he historical interpretation of the term as including all pecuniary resources, capital assets, income from employment or earning capacity, and other sources from which the person receives gains or benefits." *Strang v. Strang* (1992), 3 Alta. L.R. (3d) 1 at 7, 137 N.R. 203, 39 R.F.L. (3d) 233, 125 A.R. 331, 14 W.A.C. 331, 92 D.L.R. (4th) 762, [1992] 2 S.C.R. 112, the court per Cory J.

MEASURE OF DAMAGES. A test to determine the amount of damages which should be given.

MECHANICS' LIEN. 1. A lien which favours a mechanic or other person who conferred skill, money and materials on a chattel. D.N. Macklem & D.I. Bristow, *Construction, Builders' and Mechanics' Liens in Canada*, 6th ed. (Toronto: Carswell, 1990-) at 1-13.

2. Protection of a lien against land given to a supplier of the labour and material which benefitted that land. D.N. Macklem & D.I. Bristow, *Construction, Builders' and Mechanics' Liens in Canada*, 6th ed. (Toronto: Carswell, 1990-) at 1-1. 3. A right in the nature of a lien on any money paid by the owner of land to a contractor given to a worker or supplier of materials. D.N. Macklem & D.I. Bristow, *Construction, Builders' and Mechanics' Liens in Canada*, 6th ed. (Toronto: Carswell, 1990-) at 1-3.

MEDIATION. *n.* The reconciliation of a dispute by a third party.

MEDIATOR. *n.* 1. One who resolves disputes by mediation. 2. "The status of a mediator allows its holder to decide on the basis of equity, without being bound by substantive or procedural rules of law, except of course for rules of public order such as those of natural justice which provide for impartiality, opportunity for the parties to be heard, reasons to be given for the award, and so on. Mediation is not, as such, a legal concept distinct from that of arbitration. Rather, the mediator is an arbitrator who is exempted from compliance with the rules of law as provided in art. 948 [of the Code of Civil Procedure, R.S.Q. 1977, c. C-25] . . . The mediator is in fact only the 'bon père de famille' of the Civil Code transposed to arbitration matters. Mediation is a departure from the law of arbitration. Like any exception it must, if it is not expressly provided for, at least result from a clear and unambiguous intent . . ." *Zittrer c. Sport Maska Inc.* (1988), 38 B.L.R. 221 at 310, 83 N.R. 322, [1988] 1 S.C.R. 564, 13 Q.A.C. 241, L'Heureux-Dubé J. (Lamer, Wilson and Le Dain JJ. concurring).

MEDICAL JURISPRUDENCE. The part of the law related to the practice of medicine. F.A. Jaffe, *A Guide to Pathological Evidence*, 3d ed. (Toronto: Carswell, 1991) at 1.

MEDICARE. *n.* A medical care programme which makes doctors' services universally available. P.W. Hogg,

Constitutional Law of Canada, 3d ed. (Toronto: Carswell, 1992) at 145.

MEDICO-LEGAL. *adj.* Concerning the law relating to medical issues.

MEETING. *n.* A gathering of people to decide, by proper voting procedure, whether something should be done. See CREDITORS' ~; GENERAL ~.

MEMBER. *n.* 1. A subscriber of the memorandum of a company, and includes every other person who agrees to become a member of a company and whose name is entered in its register of members or a branch register of members. 2. In relation to a pension plan that has not been terminated, an employee or, in the case of a multi-employer plan, a former employee, who has made contributions to the plan or on whose behalf the employer was required by the plan to make contributions to it and who has not terminated membership or commenced the pension. 3. A member of the House of Commons. 4. A member of the Legislative Assembly. See CLUB ~; INDEPENDENT ~; PUBLIC ~.

MEMBERSHIP. *n.* 1. Includes a share of a credit union. 2. Includes a share of a corporation.

MEMBERSHIP CORPORATION. A corporation incorporated or continued to carry on activities that are primarily for the benefit of its members.

MEMBERSHIP INTEREST. The rights, privileges, restrictions and conditions conferred or imposed on a member or each class of members of a corporation in accordance with the provisions of its articles or bylaws. *Non-profit Corporations Act*, S.S. 1979, c. N-4.1, s. 2.

MEMORANDUM. *n.* 1. The memorandum of association of a company, as originally framed or as altered in pursuance of this Act. *Companies Act*, R.S.N.S. 1989, c. 81, s. 2. 2. The memorandum of association for incorporation of a society incorporated under this Act. *Societies Act*, R.S.N.S. 1989, c. 435, s. 2. 3. The endorsement on the certificate of title and on the

duplicate copy thereof of the particulars of any instrument presented for registration. *Land Titles acts.*

MEMORANDUM OF AGREEMENT. A written, ratified and signed document which frequently precedes a formal collective agreement. Usually when the collective agreement is executed, the memorandum is merged. D.J.M. Brown & D.M. Beatty, *Canadian Labour Arbitration*, 3d ed. (Aurora: Canada Law Book, 1988-) at 4-2.

MEMORANDUM OF ASSOCIATION. An incorporating document in some jurisdictions. It contains the name, capital structure and proposed business of the company. S.M. Beck *et al.*, *Cases and Materials on Partnerships and Canadian Business* Corporations (Toronto: Carswell, 1983) at 159.

MENSA ET THORO. [L.] From bed and board.

MENS REA. [L.] 1. ". . . [A] basis for the imposition of liability. Mens rea focuses on the mental state of the accused and requires proof of a positive state of mind such as intent, recklessness or wilful blindness." *R. v. Wholesale Travel Group Inc.* (1991), 8 C.R. (4th) 145 at 176, 67 C.C.C. (3d) 193, 4 O.R. (3d) 799n, 84 D.L.R. (4th) 161, 130 N.R. 1, 38 C.P.R. (3d) 451, 49 O.A.C. 161, [1991] 3 S.C.R. 154, 7 C.R.R. (2d) 36, Cory J. (L'Heureux-Dubé J. concurring). 2. ". . . [A] complex concept having different meanings in different contexts, but is most frequently used to describe the minimum necessary mental element required for criminal liability where a particular mental element is not expressly made a constituent element of the offence. The minimum mental element required for criminal liability for most crimes is knowledge of the circumstances which make up the actus reus of the crime and foresight or intention with respect to any consequence required to constitute the actus reus of the crime. *R. v. Metro News Ltd.* (1986), 23 C.R.R. 77 at 95, 16 O.A.C. 319, 56 O.R. (2d) 321, 53 C.R. (3d) 289, 29 C.C.C. (3d) 35, 32 D.L.R. (4th)

321 (C.A.), the court per Martin J.A.

MENTAL DISABILITY. (i) A condition of mental retardation or impairment, (ii) a learning disability, or a dysfunction in one or more of the processes involved in understanding or using symbols or spoken language, or (iii) a mental disorder.

MENTAL DISORDER. 1. A disease of the mind. *Criminal Code*, S.C. 1991, c. 43, s. 1. 2. A substantial disorder of thought, mood, perception, orientation or memory, any of which grossly impairs judgment, behaviour, capacity to recognize reality or ability to meet the ordinary demands of life but mental retardation or a learning disability does not of itself constitute a mental disorder.

MENTAL ILLNESS. A disorder of mind, other than psychoneurosis and psychopathic disorder, that results in such a change in the behaviour and judgment of a person as to require medical treatment, or in respect of which disorder of mind, treatment, care, and supervision, of the person are necessary for the protection or welfare of the person and others.

MENTAL INCOMPETENCY. The condition of mind of a mentally incompetent person.

MENTAL INCOMPETENT. A person, (i) in whom there is such a condition of arrested or incomplete development of mind, whether arising from inherent causes or induced by disease or injury, or (ii) who is suffering from such a disorder of the mind, that that person requires care, supervision and control for self protection and the protection of that person's property.

MENTALLY COMPETENT. Having the ability to understand the subject matter in respect of which consent is requested and the ability to appreciate the consequences of giving or withholding consent.

MENTALLY DISORDERED PERSON. A person who is suffering from mental illness, mental retardation or any other disorder or disability of the mind.

MENTALLY INCOMPETENT PERSON. 1. A person (a) in whom there is such a condition of arrested or incomplete development of mind, whether arising from inherent causes or induced by disease or injury, or (b) who is suffering from such a disorder of the mind, that that person requires care, supervision and control for self protection or welfare or for the protection of others or for the protection of that person's property. 2. A person, (i) in whom there is such a condition of arrested or incomplete development of mind, whether arising from inherent causes or induced by disease or injury, or (ii) who is suffering from such a disorder of the mind, that that person requires care, supervision and control for self protection and the protection of that person's property.

MERCANTILE AGENT. A person having, in the customary course of business as an agent, authority either to sell goods or to consign goods for the purpose of sale, or to buy goods or to raise money on the security of goods.

MERCANTILE LAW. The law concerning matters like bills of exchange, marine insurance and contracts of affreightment.

MERCHANTABLE. *adj.* "... [W]hatever else merchantable may mean, it does mean that the article sold, if only meant for one particular use in ordinary course, is fit for that use; ..." *Grant v. Australian Knitting Mills Ltd.* (1935), [1936] A.C. 85 at 99, [1936] 1 W.W.R. 145, 105 L.J.P.C. 6, [1932] All E.R. 209 (Australia P.C.), the board per Lord Wright.

MERCY. See PARDON; RECOMMENDATION TO ~.

MEREDITH MEM. LECT. *abbr.* Meredith Memorial Lectures (Conférences commémoratives Meredith).

MERE ERROR OF LAW. "... [A]n error committed by an administrative tribunal in good faith in interpreting or applying a provision of its enabling Act, of another Act, or of an agreement or other document which it has to interpret and apply within the limits of its jurisdiction. A mere error of law is to be distinguished from one resulting from a patently unreasonable interpretation of a provision which an administrative tribunal is required to apply within the limits of its jurisidiction. . . . A mere error of law should also be distinguished from a jurisdictional error." *Syndicat des employés de production du Québec et de l'Acadie v. Canada (Labour Relations Board)*, [1984] 2 S.C.R. 412 at 420, 14 Admin. L.R. 72, 84 C.L.L.C. 14,069, 55 N.R. 321, 14 D.L.R. (4th) 457, Beetz J.

MERGE. *v.* Of original cause of action, to include in the judgment of a domestic court of record if the plaintiff succeeds. J.G. McLeod, *The Conflict of Laws* (Calgary: Carswell, 1983) at 606.

MERGED. *adj.* 1. Of the rights and duties created by a contract for the sale of land, subsumed by a deed and discharged when the deed of conveyance is delivered and accepted. B.J. Reiter, R.C.B. Risk & B.N. McLellan, *Real Estate Law*, 3d ed. (Toronto: Emond Montgomery, 1986) at 920. 2. Of original remedies for a debt subsumed in a higher security, when that security is taken or obtained for the debt. I.H. Jacob, ed., *Bullen and Leake and Jacob's Precedents of Pleadings*, 12th ed. (London: Sweet and Maxwell, 1975) at 1213.

MERGER. *n.* 1. ". . . [I]n real estate law merger occurs when two estates coalesce through a vesting in the same person at the same time in the same right. . . ." *Fraser-Reid v. Droumtsekas* (1979), 9 R.P.R. 121 at 139, [1980] 1 S.C.R. 720, 103 D.L.R. (3d) 385, 29 N.R. 424, Dickson J. (Martland, Estey and McIntyre JJ. concurring). 2. The acquisition by one or more persons, whether by purchase or lease of shares or assets or otherwise, of any control over or interest in the whole or part of the business of a competitor, supplier, customer or any other person, whereby competition (a) in a trade, industry or profession, (b) among the sources of supply of a trade, industry or profes-

sion, (c) among the outlets for sales of a trade, industry or profession, or (d) otherwise than in paragraphs (a) to (c), is or is likely to be lessened to the detriment or against the interest of the public, whether consumers, producers or others. *Competition Act*, R.S.C. 1985, c. C-34, s. 2. 3. The acquisition or establishment, direct or indirect, by one or more persons, whether by purchase or lease of shares or assets, by amalgamation or by combination or otherwise, of control over or significant interest in the whole or a part of the business of a competitor, supplier, customer or other person. *Competition Act*, R.S.C. 1985 (2d Supp.), c. 19, s. 91. 4. ". . . [T]hat branch of res judicata which is known as merger: [is described as follows] all claims which the plaintiff might have had against the defendants . . . have merged in the judgment . . . and the maxim nemo debet bis vexari pro una et eadem causa applies." *Thornton v. Tittley* (1985), 4 C.P.C. (2d) 13 at 19, 51 O.R. (2d) 315 (H.C.), Scott L.J.S.C.

MERGER INTO JUDGMENT. A theory that once a creditor begins an action against a debtor which is carried to judgment, the original obligation is transformed into a judgment debt. C.R.B. Dunlop, *Creditor-Debtor Law in Canada* (Toronto: Carswell, 1981) at 51.

MERITS. *n.* Used to describe a good cause of action or defence when it is based, not on technical grounds, but on the real issues in question. *R. v. Cronin* (1875), 36 U.C.Q.B. 342 at 345 (C.A.), the court per Richards C.J. See AFFIDAVIT OF ~.

MERO MOTU. See EX ~.

MESNE. *adj.* Intermediate. E.L.G. Tyler & N.E. Palmer, eds., *Crossley Vaines' Personal Property*, 5th ed. (London: Butterworths, 1973) at 4.

MESNE LORD. A lord who holds something on behalf of a higher lord, and on whose behalf an inferior lord or tenant holds something.

MESNE PROCESS. 1. Pre-judgment. C.R.B. Dunlop, *Creditor-Debtor Law* *in Canada* (Toronto: Carswell, 1981) at 198. 2. In an action or suit, writs which come between the beginning and end.

MESNE PROFIT. An action for damages suffered when possession of land has been withheld improperly. *Mortimer v. Shaw* (1922), 66 D.L.R. 311 at 312, [1922] 2 W.W.R. 562, 15 Sask. L.R. 476 (C.A.), Lamont J.A. (McKay J.A. concurring).

MESSUAGE. *n.* A dwelling-house including any out-buildings, adjacent land and curtilage assigned to its use.

METES AND BOUNDS. The description of land's boundaries beginning at a fixed point and then outlining the borders in north, south, west and east directions and in degrees, minutes and seconds.

METHOD. See COMPLETED CONTRACT ~.

METIS. *n.* A person of aboriginal ancestry who identifies with Metis history and culture. *Metis Settlement Act*, S.A. 1990, c. M-14.3, s. 1.

MILITARY. *adj.* Relating to all or any part of the Canadian Forces.

MILITARY LAW. 1. "[In s. 11(f) of the Charter means] ... a system of law administered by the military itself and the most important institution of which has always been the General Court Martial." *R. v. Genereux* (1990), 60 C.C.C. (3d) 536 at 543, 70 D.L.R. (4th) 207, 114 N.R. 321, 4 C.R.R.(2d) 307, (Can. Ct. Martial Appeal Ct.), Pratte J. 2. Includes all laws, regulations or orders relating to the Canadian Forces. *Criminal Code*, R.S.C. 1985, c. C-46, s. 2.

MILITARY OFFENCE. An offence recognized by a military court, e.g. insubordination.

MIN. *abbr.* 1. Minister. 2. Ministry. 3. Minute.

MIND. See DISEASE OF THE ~; INSANITY.

MINERAL. *n.* 1. Any natural, solid, inorganic or fossilized organic substance. 2. Any nonliving substance formed by the processes of nature which occurs in, on or under land, of any chemical or physical state, but does not include oil, earth, surface water and ground water. 3. "... [M]ineral substances and ... petroleum and natural gas ..." *Crows Nest Pass Coal Co. v. R.*, [1961] S.C.R. 750 at 761, 36 W.W.R. 513, 82 C.R.T.C. 10, 30 D.L.R. (2d) 93, the court per Locke J. 4. "... '[M]ining rights' ..." *Tisdale (Township) v. Cavana*, [1942] 4 D.L.R. 65 at 68, [1942] S.C.R. 384, the court per Kerwin J.

MINERAL INTEREST. (i) The ownership of, title to, or an interest in, or (ii) a right, a licence other than a licence issued by the Crown, or an option, to drill for, take, win, or gain, and remove from land, oil or gas, whether acquired by way of instrument commonly called a lease or otherwise, and includes a grant or assignment of a profit à prendre in respect of any oil or gas; but does not include the ownership of, title to, or an interest in oil or gas purchased or otherwise acquired by any person as a result of that person's purchase or other acquisition of land or interest in land the title to which includes the mines and minerals in, under, or upon the land.

MINERAL RIGHT. An estate in fee simple in a mineral located in a tract.

MINERAL RIGHTS. 1. The right to enter upon or use lands for the sole purpose of exploring, drilling for, winning, taking, removing or raising the minerals situate therein and includes such easements, rights of way or other similar rights of access as are incidental to winning, taking, removing or raising the minerals situate therein. *Land Transfer Tax Act*, R.R.O. 1980, Reg. 571, s. 1. 2. The right to explore for, work and use natural mineral substances situated within the volume formed by the vertical projection of the perimeter of a parcel of land, including the right to explore for underground reservoirs or to develop or use them for the storage or permanent disposal of any mineral substance or of any industrial product or residue. *Mining Act*, R.S.Q. 1977, c. M-13, s. 1.

MINERAL TITLE. A claim or a lease. *Mineral Tenure Act*, S.B.C. 1988, c. 5, s. 1.

MINIMUM WAGE. The lowest compensation established by statute.

MINING CONCESSION. A mining property sold out of the public domain for the purpose of operating mining rights. *Mining Act*, R.S.Q. 1977, c. M-13, s. 1.

MINING LEASE. A lease, grant or licence for mining purposes, including the searching for, working, getting, making merchantable, smelting or otherwise converting or working for the purposes of any manufacture, carrying away or disposing of mines or minerals, and substances in, on or under the land, obtainable by underground or by surface working or purposes connected therewith.

MINING PROPERTY. A right to prospect, explore or mine for minerals or a property the principal value of which depends upon its mineral content. *Income Tax Act*, R.S.C. 1952, c. 148 (as am. S.C. 1970-71-72, c. 63), s. 35(2)(a).

MINING RIGHT. A mining or mineral claim, a mining licence or lease.

MINING RIGHTS. 1. "... '[M]inerals' ..." *Banner Coal Co. v. Gervais (No. 1)* (1922), 18 Alta. L.R. 535 at 541, 70 D.L.R. 206, [1922] 3 W.W.R. 564 (C.A.), the court per Beck J.A. 2. Includes the right to the minerals and mines upon or under the surface of the land. 3. In respect of any land are granted or reserved, the grant or reservation shall be construed to convey or reserve the ores, mines and minerals on or under the land, together with such right of access for the purpose of winning the ores, mines and minerals as is incidental to a grant of ores, mines and minerals. *Conveyancing and Law of Property Act*, R.S.O. 1980, c. 90, s. 16. 4. The ores, mines and minerals on or under any land where they are or have been dealt with separately from the surface. *Mining Act*, R.S.O. 1980, c. 268, s. 1.

5. The right to explore for, work and use natural mineral substances situated within the volume formed by the vertical projection of the perimeter of a parcel of land, including the right to explore for underground reservoirs or to develop or use them for the storage or permanent disposal of any mineral substance or of any industrial product or residue. *Mining Act*, R.S.Q. 1977, c. M-13, s. 1.

MINISTER. *n.* 1. A member of the Cabinet. 2. A member of the Queen's Privy Council for Canada as is designated by the Governor in Council. 3. A member of the Executive Council appointed as a Minister who is responsible for the enactment or its subject matter or the department to which its context refers. See CABINET ~; DEPUTY ~.

MINISTERIAL. *adj.* Describes the discharge of a duty without discretion or independent judgment or the issue of a formal instruction determined beforehand. S.A. DeSmith, *Judicial Review of Administrative Action*, 4th ed. by J.M. Evans (London: Stevens, 1980) at 70.

MINISTERIAL DUTY. A duty involved in operating a trust, i.e., keeping of accounts or hiring an agent like a solicitor or valuer. D.M.W. Waters, *The Law of Trusts in Canada*, 2d ed. (Toronto: Carswell, 1984) at 28.

MINISTERIAL RESPONSIBILITY. The traditional responsibility of a minister of government for all the activities of his department.

MINISTER OF THE CROWN. A member of the Queen's Privy Council for Canada in that member's capacity of managing and directing or having responsibility for a department. *Municipal Grants Act*, R.S.C. 1985, c. M-13, s. 2.

MINISTER WITHOUT PORTFOLIO. A member of the cabinet not in charge of a department. P.W. Hogg, *Constitutional Law of Canada*, 3d ed. (Toronto: Carswell, 1992) at 236.

MINISTRY. *n.* A department of

government.

MINOR. *n.* A person who has not attained the age of majority.

MINORITY. *n.* The situation of being under the age of majority.

MINORITY LANGUAGE EDUCATION RIGHTS. The rights, set out and limited by section 23 of the Canadian Charter of Human Rights and Freedoms, of persons to receive education in French or English when they are part of the French or English linguistic minority in the province in which they reside.

MINORITY OPINION. The decision and reasons of the minority of three or more judges who heard and decided a case.

MINUTE. *n.* A record or note of a transaction.

MINUTES OF PROCEEDINGS AND EVIDENCE. Of legislative and standing committees, a record of the proceedings of a committee prepared and signed by the clerk of that committee. A. Fraser, W.A. Dawson & J. Holtby, eds., *Beauchesne's Rules and Forms of the House of Commons of Canada*, 6th ed. (Toronto: Carswell, 1989) at 233.

MINUTES OF SETTLEMENT. A document filed with a court which sets out terms by which the parties have agreed to settle the dispute.

MISAPPROPRIATION. *n.* "... [Dishonest or fraudulent appropriation of] money or other property entrusted to or received by [a person] whether to his own use or to the use of a third party." *Poy v. Law Society (British Columbia)* (1987), 36 D.L.R. (4th) 313 at 318, [1987] 3 W.W.R. 659, 11 B.C.L.R. (2d) 246 (C.A.), the court per Hinkson J.A.

MISBEHAVIOUR. *n.* "[In relation to an office] ... improper exercise of the functions appertaining to the office, or non-attendance or neglect of or refusal to perform the duties of the office." *Chesley v. Lunenburg (Town)* (1916), 28 D.L.R. 571 at 572, 50 N.S.R. 85 (C.A.), Harris J.A. (Graham C.J. concurring).

MISC. *abbr.* Miscellaneous.

MISCARRIAGE. *n.* 1. "... [S]uch departure from the rules which permeate all judicial procedure as to make that which happened not in the proper use of the word judicial procedure at all." *Robins v. National Trust Co.*, [1927] 1 W.W.R. 692 at 695, [1927] A.C. 515, [1927] 2 D.L.R. 97, [1927] All E.R. Rep. 73 (Ont. P.C.), Viscount Dunedin. 2. "... Proof of actual prejudice resulting from an error of law is not requisite to a finding that a 'miscarriage of justice' has occurred. It may be enough that an appearance of unfairness exists: ..." *R. v. Duke* (1985), 39 Alta. L.R. (2d) 313 at 319, [1985] 6 W.W.R. 386, 62 A.R. 204, 22 C.C.C. (3d) 217 (C.A.), the court per McClung J.A. 3. The expulsion of a fetus, usually in the second third of a pregnancy. F.A. Jaffe, *A Guide to Pathological Evidence*, 3d ed. (Toronto: Carswell, 1991) at 223.

MISCHIEF. *n.* 1. Wilfully destroying or damaging property; rendering property dangerous, useless, inoperative or ineffective; obstructing, interrupting or interfering with the lawful use, enjoyment or operation of property; or obstructing, interrupting or interfering with any person in the lawful use, enjoyment or operation of property. *Criminal Code*, R.S.C. 1985, c. C-46, s. 430(1). 2. Wilfully destroying or altering data, rendering data meaningless, useless or ineffective, obstructing, interrupting or interfering with the lawful use of data; or obstructing, interrupting or interfering with any person in the lawful use of data or denying access to data to any person who is entitled to access thereto. *Criminal Code*, R.S.C. 1985, c. C-46, s. 430(1.1) as added by R.S.C. 1985, c. 27 (1st Supp.), s. 57. 3. "... [R]efers to the misuse of confidential information by a lawyer against a former client." *MacDonald Estate v. Martin* (1990), 48 C.P.C. (2d) 113 at 125, [1991] 1 W.W.R. 705, 121 N.R. 1, 77 D.L.R. (4th) 249, 70 Man. R. (2d) 241, [1990] 3 S.C.R. 1235, Sopinka J. (Dickson

C.J.C., La Forest and Gonthier JJ. concurring). See PUBLIC ~.

MISCHIEF RULE. 1. It is the duty of every judge to always construe a situation to suppress mischief and advance the remedy. *Heydon's Case* (1584), 3 Co. Rep. 7a at 7b, 76 E.R. 637 (U.K.). 2. A test of the purpose or object of a statute. "... [R]equires the court to consider the evil or defect the law was meant to remedy and to see that the decision reached reinforces the remedy and does not compound the mischief." *Vijendren v. Hopkins* (1987), 11 R.F.L. (3d) 132 at 135 (Ont. Prov. Ct.), Campbell Prov. J.

MISCONDUCT. *n.* "[A servant] ... not being able to perform, in a due manner, his duties [to his master], or ... not being able to perform his duty in a faithful manner, ..." *Pearce v. Foster* (1885), 17 Q.B. 536 at 539 (U.K. C.A.), Lord Esher M.R. See PROFESSIONAL ~.

MISDEMEANOUR. *n.* A lesser offence than a felony.

MISDESCRIPTION. *n.* An incorrect description.

MISDIRECTION. *n.* An error in law made when a judge charges a jury or when a judge sitting alone puts the wrong questions forward to answer.

MISFEASANCE. *n.* The improper execution of a lawful act, e.g. to be guilty of negligence in fulfilling a contract.

MISJOINDER. *n.* The erroneous involvement of someone as a plaintiff or defendant in an action.

MISLEAD. *v.* "To withhold truthful, relevant and pertinent information may very well have the effect of 'misleading' just as much as to provide, positively, incorrect information." *Hilario v. Canada (Minister of Manpower & Immigration)* (1978), 18 N.R. 529 at 530, [1978] 1 F.C. 697 (C.A.), the court per Heald J.A.

MISNOMER. *n.* Naming wrongly.

MISPLEADING. *n.* Omission of anything essential to a defence or action.

MISPRISION. *n.* Used to describe an offence which is not given a specific name.

MISPRISION OF FELONY. For someone who knows that another person committed a felony to conceal or bring about the concealment of that knowledge.

MISREPRESENT. *v.* "... [A]lways connotes a positive act. One cannot misrepresent without positively representing, either by words or conduct, a material circumstance, which circumstance does not truly accord with the representation. ..." *Taylor v. London Assurance Corp.*, [1934] O.R. 273 at 279, [1934] O.W.N. 199, [1934] 2 D.L.R. 657 (C.A.), Masten J.A. (dissenting).

MISREPRESENTATION. *n.* 1. "... [M]ay consist just as well in the concealment of that which should be disclosed as in the statement of that which is false for misrepresentation unquestionably may be made by concealment. If the non-disclosure of a material fact which the representor is bound to communicate is deliberate the misrepresenation is a fraudulent one; if it is unintentional it is none the less a misrepresentation though an innocent one." *Stearns v. Stearns* (1921), 56 D.L.R. 700 at 708, [1921] 1 W.W.R. 40 (Alta. T.D.), Walsh J. 2. "... [M]ay be made by silence when either the representee or a third person in his presence, or to his knowledge, states something false which indicates to the representor that the representee either is being, or will be, misled unless the necessary correction is made. Silence under the circumstances is either a tacit adoption by the party of another's misrepresentation as his own or a tacit confirmation of another's error as true." *Toronto Dominion Bank v. Leigh Instruments Ltd. (Trustee of)* (1991), 40 C.C.E.L. 262 at 289, 51 D.A.C. 321, 4 B.L.R. (2d) 220 (Div. Ct.), the court per Rosenberg J. 3. "... [A]s used in the relevant sections [of the Income Tax Act (Canada)] must be construed to mean any representation which was false in substance and in fact at the material date and it includes both innocent and fraudulent representations." *Hawrish v. Minister of National Revenue*, [1975] C.T.C. 446 at 453, 75 D.T.C. 5314 (Fed. T.D.), Heald J. 4. (a) An untrue statement of a material fact, or (b) an omission to state a material fact that is (i) required to be stated, or (ii) necessary to prevent a statement that is made from being false or misleading in the circumstances in which it was made. *Securities acts.* See FRAUDULENT ~; INNOCENT ~; NEGLIGENT ~.

MISTAKE. *n.* 1. Misunderstanding about the existence of something which arises either from a false belief or ignorance. 2. "... [A] written instrument does not accord with the true intention of the party who prepared it...." *Farbwerke Hoechst A.G. Vormals Meister Lucius & Bruning v. Canada (Commissioner of Patents)* (1966), 33 Fox Pat. C. 99 at 108, [1966] S.C.R. 604, 50 C.P.R. 220, the court per Martland J. See COMMON ~; MUTUAL ~; NON EST FACTUM; UNILATERAL ~.

MISTAKE OF FACT. 1. "... [A] defence, ... where it prevents an accused from having the mens rea which the law requires for the very crime with which he is charged. Mistake of fact is more accurately seen as a negation of guilty intention than as the affirmation of a positive defence. It avails an accused who acts innocently, pursuant to a flawed perception of the facts, ..." *R. v. Pappajohn (sub nom. Pappajohn v. R.)* (1980), 52 C.C.C. (2d) 481 at 494, [1980] 2 S.C.R. 120, 14 C.R. (3d) 243, 19 C.R. (3d) 97, [1980] 4 W.W.R. 387, 111 D.L.R. (3d) 1, 32 N.R. 104, Dickson J. 2. A misunderstanding about the existence of some fact or about the existence of a right which depends on questions of mixed fact and law.

MISTAKE OF LAW. 1. An error, not in the actual facts, but relating as to their legal consequence, relevance or significance. D. Stuart, *Canadian Criminal Law: A Treatise*, 2d ed. (Toronto: Carswell, 1987) at 299. 2. An error regarding some general rule of

law. 3. Examples of mistakes of law which a statutory decision maker may make include "... addressing his or her mind to the wrong question, applying the wrong principle, failing to apply a principle he or she should have applied, or incorrectly applying a legal principle." *Fraser v. Canada (Treasury Board, Department of National Revenue)* (1985), (*sub nom. Fraser v. Public Service Staff Relations Board*) 9 C.C.E.L. 233 at 242, [1985] 2 S.C.R. 455, 18 Admin. L.R. 72, 86 C.L.L.C. 14,003, 63 N.R. 161, 23 D.L.R. (4th) 122, 19 C.R.R. 152, [1986] D.L.Q. 84n, the court per Dickson C.J.C.

MISTAKE OF TITLE. "... '[T]he belief that the land is his own.' If the land turns out not to be the property of the person occupying it, and that belief is bona fide, then that is a mistake of title." *Robertson v. Saunders* (1977), 75 D.L.R. (3d) 507 at 512 (Man. Q.B.), Hamilton J.

MISTRIAL. *n.* An incorrect trial. The trial is of no effect and reaches no conclusion.

MITIGATE. See DUTY TO ~.

MITIGATION. *n.* Reduction.

MITIGATION CONTINGENCY. An event which may still have an impact on the seriousness of loss resulting from a death, the two major being remarriage and adoption. K.D. Cooper-Stephenson & I.B. Saunders, *Personal Injury Damages in Canada* (Toronto: Carswell, 1981) at 452.

MITIGATION OF DAMAGES. "... [T]he defendant cannot be called upon to pay for avoidable losses which would result in an increase in the quantum of damages payable to the plaintiff.... the extent of those losses [a plaintiff may recover] depend on whether he has taken reasonable steps to avoid their unreasonable accumulation." *Michaels v. Red Deer College*, [1976] 2 S.C.R. 324 at 330-1, [1975] 5 W.W.R. 575, 5 N.R. 99, 75 C.L.L.C. 14,280, 57 D.L.R. (3d) 386, Laskin C.J.C.

MIXED ACTION. An action involving both a claim to real property and a claim for damages.

MIXED PROPERTY. A combination of personalty and realty.

MIXED QUESTION. A question which arises when foreign and domestic laws conflict. See ~ OF LAW AND FACT.

MIXED QUESTION OF LAW AND FACT. A case in which a jury finds the particular facts, and the court must decide on the legal quality of those facts using established rules of law, without general inferences or conclusions drawn by the jury.

M.L. DIG. & R. *abbr.* Monthly Law Digest and Reporter (Que.), 1892-1893.

M.L.R. (Q.B.). *abbr.* Montreal Law Reports (Queen's Bench), 1885-1891.

M.L.R. (S.C.). *abbr.* Montreal Law Reports (Superior Court), 1885-1891.

M.M.C. *abbr.* Martin's Mining Cases (B.C.), 1853-1908.

M'NAGHTEN'S CASE. See MCNAGHTEN'S CASE.

M'NAUGHTEN'S CASE. See MCNAGHTEN'S CASE.

M.N.R. *abbr.* Minister of National Revenue.

MOBILITY RIGHTS. 1. "[In s. 6 of the Charter] . . . [R]ights of the person to move about, within and outside the national boundaries." *Skapinker v. Law Society of Upper Canada*, [1984] 1 S.C.R. 357 at 377, 9 D.L.R. (4th) 161, 8 C.R.R. 193, 53 N.R. 169, 3 O.A.C. 321, 11 C.C.C. (3d) 481, 20 Admin. L.R. 1, the court per Estey J. 2. ". . . Section 6(2) [of the Charter] touches only (a) the right to move freely from one province to another; (b) the right to take up residence in the province of one's choice; and (c) the right to work in any province, whether resident there or not." *Reference re Lands Protection Act (Prince Edward Island)* (1987), 48 R.P.R. 92 at 110, 64 Nfld. & P.E.I.R. 249, 197 A.P.R. 249, 40 D.L.R. (4th) 1 (P.E.I. C.A.), McQuaid J.A. (Carruthers C.J.P.E.I. concurring).

MOD. L. REV. *abbr.* Modern Law Review.

MODUS. *n.* [L.] Manner; method.

MODUS OPERANDI. [L.] Method of operating.

MODUS TENENDI. [L.] Manner of holding.

MODUS TRANSFERRENDI. [L.] Manner of transferring.

MODUS VACANDI. [L.] Manner of vacating.

MOIETY. *n.* A half; any fraction.

MONARCHY. *n.* A government in which a single person holds supreme power.

MONEY. *n.* 1. ". . . [A]s commonly understood is not necessarily legal tender. Any medium which by practice fulfils the function of money and which everybody will accept in payment of a debt is money in the ordinary sense of the words even though it may not be legal tender . . ." *Reference re Alberta Legislation*, [1938] 2 D.L.R. 81 at 92, [1938] S.C.R. 100, Duff C.J.C. (Davis J. concurring). 2. ". . . [W]hen used in a will means money in its strict sense unless there is a context which is sufficient to show that the testator used it in a more extended sense . . ." *Lubeck, Re*, [1927] 1 W.W.R. 980 at 981 (Alta. C.A.), Clarke J.A. 3. ". . . [I]n the strict sense includes cash in hand and in the bank and any money for which at the time of his death the testator might have claimed immediate payment: . . ." *Couperthwaite v. Couperthwaite*, [1950] 2 W.W.R. 58 at 63, [1950] 3 D.L.R. 229 (Sask. C.A.), the court per Martin C.J.S. See ATTENDANCE ~; CONDUCT ~; COUNTERFEIT ~; MORTGAGE ~; PUBLIC ~.

MONEY BILL. 1. A bill to impose, repeal, remit, alter or regulate taxation, to impose charges on a consolidated fund to pay debt or for other financial purposes or to supply government requirements. 2. A bill introduced in the House of Commons only after recommendation by the Governor General. P.W. Hogg, *Constitutional Law of Canada*, 3d ed. (Toronto: Carswell, 1992) at 244.

MONEY BROKER. A person who raises or lends money for or to other people.

MONEY BY-LAW. 1. A by-law for contracting a debt or obligation or for borrowing money. 2. A by-law which must be advertised and may be required to be submitted to a vote of the proprietary electors. Alberta statutes.

MONEY HAD AND RECEIVED. Money a defendant has received and which for reasons of equity the defendant should not retain. See ACTION FOR ~.

MONEY-LENDER. *var.* **MONEY LENDER.** A person who carries on the business of money lending or advertises or claims in any way to carry on that business, but does not include a registered pawn broker as such.

MONEY ORDER. An order to pay money which may be purchased at a bank or post office.

MONOGAMY. *n.* The marriage of one wife to one husband.

MONOPOLY. *n.* A situation where one or more persons either substantially or completely control throughout Canada or any area thereof the class or species of business in which they are engaged and have operated that business or are likely to operate it to the detriment or against the interest of the public, whether consumers, producers or others, but a situation shall not be deemed a monopoly within the meaning of this definition by reason only of the exercise of any right or enjoyment of any interest derived under the Patent Act or any other Act of Parliament. *Competition Act*, R.S.C. 1985, c. C-34, s. 2.

MONTH. *n.* 1. A calendar month. 2. A period calculated from a day in one month to a day numerically corresponding to that day in the following month.

MONUMENT. *n.* An iron post, wooden post, mound, pit or trench, or anything else used to mark a boundary corner or line by a qualified surveyor. See LEGAL ~; LOST ~.

MOO. P.C. *abbr.* Moore, Privy Council.

MOO. P.C. (N.S.). *abbr.* Moore (N.S.) Privy Council.

MOOT. *n.* An exercise in which students plead and argue doubtful questions and cases.

MOOT. *adj.* Describing the situation in which an issue used to exist between parties, but the issue exists no longer when the case comes before a tribunal. R.J. Sharpe, ed., *Charter Litigation* (Toronto: Butterworths, 1987) at 331.

MOOTNESS. *n.* ". . . [A]n aspect of a general policy or practice that a court may decline to decide a case which raises merely a hypothetical or abstract question. The general principle applies when the decision of the court will not have the effect of resolving some controversy which affects or may affect the rights of the parties. If the decision of the court will have no practical effect on such rights, the court will decline to decide the case. This essential ingredient must be present not only when the action or proceeding is commenced but at the time when the court is called upon to reach a decision. Accordingly if, subsequent to the initiation of the action or the proceeding, events occur which affect the relationship of the parties so that no present live controversy exists which affects the rights of the parties, the case is said to be moot." *Borowski v. Canada (Attorney General)* (1989), 38 C.R.R. 232 at 239, [1989] 3 W.W.R. 97, 33 C.P.C. (2d) 105, 47 C.C.C. (3d) 1, 57 D.L.R. (4th) 231, 92 N.R. 110, [1989] 1 S.C.R. 342, 75 Sask. R. 82, the court per Sopinka J.

MORAL OBLIGATION. "[Considering oneself] . . . compelled to [do something] by what [one] thought was the right thing to do." *Norman v. Norman* (1972), 11 R.F.L. 105 at 106, 32 D.L.R. (3d) 262 (N.S. T.D.), Bissett J.

MORALS. See CORRUPTING ~.

MORATORIUM. *n.* The authorized delay in paying a debt.

MORE OR LESS. 1. A phrase used

to compensate for slight inaccuracies in description in a contract for the sale of land or conveyance. 2. "... '[A]bout' ... words of general import and the excess or deficiency, as the case may be, which they cover bears a very small proportion to the amount named...." *Canada Law Book Co. v. Boston Book Co.* (1922), 64 S.C.R. 182 at 200-201, 66 D.L.R. 209, Anglin J. (Mignault J. concurring).

MORTGAGE. *v.* To convey as security for a debt.

MORTGAGE. *n.* The conveyance of land as a security for the discharge of an obligation or the payment of a debt, a security which may be redeemed when the obligation or debt is discharged or paid. B.J. Reiter, B.N. McLellan & P.M. Perell, *Real Estate Law*, 4th ed. (Toronto: Emond Montgomery, 1992) at 813. See BANK ~ SUBSIDIARY; BLANKET ~; CANADA ~ AND HOUSING COR-PORATION; CHATTEL ~; CON-VERTIBLE ~; EQUITABLE LEASEHOLD ~; EQUITABLE ~; FIRST ~; LEGAL LEASEHOLD ~; LEGAL ~; SECOND ~; WRAP-AROUND ~.

MORTGAGE BACK. The vendor receives a mortgage on property in exchange for loaning part of the purchase price. B.J. Reiter, B.N. McLellan & P.M. Perell, *Real Estate Law*, 4th ed. (Toronto: Emond Montgomery, 1992) at 832.

MORTGAGE BOND. A type of corporate debt security in which the indenture is a mortgage on property of the corporation and the indenture trustee is mortgagee on behalf of the bondholders. S.M. Beck *et al.*, *Cases and Materials on Partnerships and Canadian Business Corporations* (Toronto: Carswell, 1983) at 799. See FIRST ~.

MORTGAGE BROKER. A person who, (i) directly or indirectly, carries on the business of lending money on the security of real estate, whether the money is personal or that of another person; (ii) carries on the business of dealing in mortgages; or (ii) represents or, by an advertisement, notice or sign, claims to be a mortgage broker or a person who carries on the business of dealing in mortgages.

MORTGAGE COMMITMENT. A document issued by a lender to a borrower when, based on a credit report and property appraisal, the lender decides to go ahead with the loan. D.J. Donahue & P.D. Quinn, *Real Estate Practice in Ontario*, 4th ed. (Toronto: Butterworths, 1990) at 224.

MORTGAGE DEBENTURE. "... [F]orm of security, a debenture which is both an obligation for the payment of the money which is payable by the terms of it, and a mortgage on the property of the company by which it is issued, or some part of it, or secured by such a mortgage, ..." *Farmers' Loan & Savings Co., Re* (1898), 20 O.R. 337 at 354 (C.A.), Meredith J.A.

MORTGAGEE. *n.* 1. The owner of a mortgage. 2. The person who assumes a mortgage to secure a loan.

MORTGAGE INSURANCE. Insurance against loss caused by default on the part of a borrower under a loan secured by a mortgage upon real property, a hypothec upon immovable property or an interest in real or immovable property.

MORTGAGE MONEY. Money or money's worth secured by a mortgage. *Casson v. Westmorland Investment Ltd.* (1961), 27 D.L.R. (2d) 674 at 677, 33 W.W.R. 28 (B.C. C.A.), the court per Tysoe J.A.

MORTGAGE TRUST. A trustee holds mortgaged assets on behalf of multiple lenders on the same mortgage security. D.M.W. Waters, *The Law of Trusts in Canada*, 2d ed. (Toronto: Carswell, 1984) at 450.

MORTGAGOR. *n.* 1. One who borrows. B.J. Reiter, B.N. McLellan & P.M. Perell, *Real Estate Law*, 4th ed. (Toronto: Emond Montgomery, 1992) at 811. 2. A person who gives a mortgage to secure a loan. 3. The owner or transferee of land or of any estate or interest in land pledged as security for a debt or loan. 4. Includes chargor.

MORTIS CAUSA. See DONATIO ~; GIFT ~.

MORTIS CAUSA DONATIO. See DONATIO MORTIS CAUSA.

MORTMAIN. *n.* [Fr. dead hand] 1. The state of possession of land which makes it inalienable. 2. Refers to a corporation's owning of real property. R. Megarry & H.W.R. Wade, *The Law of Real Property*, 5th ed. (London: Stevens, 1984) at cxxvi.

MORTMAIN ACT. An act which forbade the conveyance of land into the "dead hand" of the church or another corporation because a lord might thus be deprived of the benefits of tenure which arose in the lord's favour when the tenant died, because such conveyance prevented free alienation. Under these acts, the Crown always had the power to regulate the holding of land and there were significant statutory exceptions to these rules. E.L.G. Tyler & N.E. Palmer, eds., *Crossley Vaines' Personal Property*, 5th ed. (London: Butterworths, 1973) at 16.

MOTION. *n.* An oral or written application that the court rule or make an order before, during or after a trial. See DILATORY ~; NOTICE OF ~; WAYS AND MEANS ~.

MOTIVE. *n.* 1. "... [T]hat which precedes and induces the exercise of the will. ... in criminal law sense [means] 'ulterior intention' ..." *R. v. Lewis* (1979), 98 D.L.R. (3d) 111 at 120-1, [1979] 2 S.C.R. 821, 27 N.R. 451, 10 C.R. (3d) 299 (Eng.), 12 C.R. (3d) 315 (Fr.), 47 C.C.C. (3d) 24, the court per Dickson J. 2. "... [R]efers to an emotion or inner feeling such as hate or greed which is likely to lead to the doing of an act. The word 'motive' is also used, however, to refer to external events, for example, a previous quarrel, which is likely to excite the relevant feeling." *R. v. Malone* (1984), 11 C.C.C. (3d) 34 at 43, 2 O.A.C. 321 (C.A.), Martin J.A. (Lacourcière and Goodman JJ.A. concurring).

MOTOR CARRIER. A person operating, whether alone or with another, a motor vehicle with or without trailer attached, as a public passenger vehicle or as a freight vehicle.

MOTOR VEHICLE. "... [A] vehicle which is capable of being and is ordinarily self propelled by power generated within itself, as distinct, for example, from a horse drawn vehicle, or from one that is propelled by the application of externally generated power." *R. v. Thornton* (1950), 25 M.P.R. 140 at 148, 96 C.C.C. 323 (N.S. C.A.), Parker J.A. (Hall, MacQuarrie and Ilsley JJ.A. concurring). See DANGEROUS OPERATION OF ~S; REGISTRAR OF ~S.

MOVABLES. *n.* Any movable tangible property, other than the ship, and includes money, valuable securities, and other documents. *Insurance acts.*

MOVE. *v.* To bring a motion or an application before a court or tribunal.

M.P.L.R. *abbr.* Municipal and Planning Law Reports, 1976-.

M.P.R. *abbr.* Maritime Provinces Reports, 1929-1968.

M.R. *abbr.* Master of the Rolls.

M.R.N. *abbr.* Ministre du Revenu national.

M.T.R. *abbr.* Maritime Tax Reports.

MUGGING. *n.* Strangling by throwing the arm around a victim's neck from behind. F.A. Jaffe, *A Guide to Pathological Evidence*, 3d ed. (Toronto: Carswell, 1991) at 223.

MULTIFARIOUS. *adj.* Refers to the inappropriate joinder of causes of action.

MULTILATERAL. *adj.* Concerning more than two nations. P.W. Hogg, *Constitutional Law of Canada*. 3d ed. (Toronto: Carswell, 1992) at 281.

MULTIPARTITE. *adj.* Divided into many parts.

MULTIPLE LISTING. 1. An agreement between a vendor and one broker authorizing other brokers to sell the property for a portion of the commission agreed. 2. Property listed through a real estate board's multiple listing service.

MULTIPLE SUFFICIENT CAUSATION. Two legally relevant causes, each alone sufficient to cause an injury or loss and each required (in a but for sense) if the other were absent, combine to originate an injury or loss. K.D. Cooper-Stephenson & I.B. Saunders, *Personal Injury Damages in Canada* (Toronto: Carswell, 1981) at 653.

MULTIPLICITY. *n.* Excessive division or fracture of one cause or suit.

MUN. *abbr.* 1. Municipal. 2. Municipality.

MUN. CT. *abbr.* Municipal Court.

MUNICIPAL. *adj.* Related to a municipal corporation.

MUNICIPAL CORPORATION. 1. The legal entity established under legislation which is distinct from residents, ratepayers or members of municipal council and which transacts the business of a municipality. 2. ". . . [A] public corporation created by the government for political purposes and having subordinate and local powers of legislation. It can exercise its corporate powers only within its defined limits. It does not own its defined territorial area, but is limited thereto as to its jurisdiction." *Hatch v. Rathwell* (1909), 12 W.L.R. 376 at 377, 19 Man. R. 465 (C.A.), the court per Cameron J.A.

MUNICIPAL COURT. An inferior court created under provincial legislation (*Municipal Courts Act*, R.S.Q. 1977, c. C-72, for example). It has limited civil jurisdiction and jurisdiction over violations of the act governing the municipality, the municipal charter and by-laws.

MUNICIPAL GOVERNMENT. A body subordinate to national authority with legislative power over a local territory. P.W. Hogg, *Constitutional Law of Canada*, 3d ed. (Toronto: Carswell, 1992) at 98.

MUNICIPALITY. *n.* A locality the inhabitants of which are incorporated.

MUNICIPAL LAW. 1. Law relating to municipal corporations and their government. 2. Law relating exclusively to the citizens and inhabitants of a country, differing thus from the law of nations and political law.

MUNICIPAL SERVICE. The water, sewer, police, fire protection, recreation, cultural activities, roads, garbage removal and disposal, lighting, snow removal or septic tank cleaning service supplied by a municipality or a municipal corporation.

MUNICIPAL TAX. ". . . [T]axes imposed by the governing body of a municipality for the purposes of the municipality., . . ." *Canadian Pacific Railway v. Winnipeg (City)* (1900), 30 S.C.R. 558 at 564, the court per Sedgewick J.

MUNIMENT. *n.* A record; defence; a written document upon which one establishes a right or claim and depends; evidence.

MUNITIONS OF WAR. Arms, ammunition, implements or munitions of war, military stores or any articles deemed capable of being converted thereunto or made useful in the production thereof. *Official Secrets Act,* R.S.C. 1985, c. O-5, s. 2.

M.U.R.B. *abbr.* Multi-unit residential building.

MURDER. *n.* 1. "The classic definition of murder is that of Sir Edward (Chief Justice) Coke . . . 'Murder is when a man . . . unlawfully killeth . . . any reasonable creature in rerum natura under the king's peace, with malice aforethought, either expressed by the party, or implied by law, so as the party wounded, or hurt, etc., die of the wound, or hurt, etc. within a year and a day after the same.' . . . Murder requires, positively, the mental element traditionally known as 'malice aforethought', and, negatively, the absence of certain mitigating circumstances that would turn the case into one of manslaughter. . . . the law has consistently required that murder be an offence of specific intent. The specific intents have generally been clearly described in Canada in statutory form, and an unlawful killing without proof of the existence of the required specific intent has always been characterized as manslaughter. On all the authorities, the mental element – the 'malice aforethought' of ancient usage – must always be demonstrated in order to procure a conviction of murder." *R. v. Swietlinski* (1980), 18 C.R. (3d) 231 at 247-9, 34 N.R. 569, 55 C.C.C. (2d) 481, 117 D.L.R. (3d) 285, [1980] 2 S.C.R. 956, the court per McIntyre J. 2. Culpable homicide is murder (a) where the person who causes the death of a human being (i) means to cause his death, or (ii) means to cause him bodily harm that he knows is likely to cause his death, and is reckless whether death ensues or not; (b) where a person, meaning to cause death to a human being or meaning to cause him bodily harm that he knows is likely to cause his death, and being reckless whether death ensues or not, by accident or mistake causes death to another human being, notwithstanding that he does not mean to cause death or bodily harm to that human being; or (c) where a person, for an unlawful object, does anything that he knows or ought to know is likely to cause death, and thereby causes death to a human being, notwithstanding that he desires to effect his object without causing death or bodily harm to any human being. *Criminal Code*, R.S.C. 1985, c. C-46, s. 229. 3. Culpable homicide is murder when committed while committing or attempting to commit certain offences if certain conditions are met. *Criminal Code*, R.S.C. 1985, c. C-46, s. 230. See CAPITAL ~; FIRST DEGREE ~; NON-CAPITAL ~; SECOND DEGREE ~.

MURDER IN COMMISSION OF OFFENCES. Culpable homicide is murder where a person causes the death of a human being while committing or attempting to commit high treason or treason or sabotage, piracy, hijacking an aircraft, escape or rescue from prison or lawful custody, assaulting a peace officer, resisting lawful arrest, sexual assault, kidnapping, forcible confinement, hostage taking, breaking and entering, robbery, or arson whether or not the person means to cause death to any human being and whether or not he knows that death is likely to be caused to any human being, if (a) he means to cause bodily harm for the purpose of (i) facilitating the commission of the offence, or (ii) facilitating his flight after committing or attempting to commit the offence, and the death ensues from the bodily harm; (b) he administers a stupefying or overpowering thing for a purpose mentioned in paragraph (a), and the death ensues therefrom; (c) he wilfully stops, by any means, the breath of a human being for a purpose mentioned in paragraph (a), and the death ensues therefrom; or (d) he uses a weapon or has it upon his person (i) during or at the time he commits or attempts to commit the offence, or (ii) during or at the time of his flight after committing or attempting to commit the offence, and the death ensues as a consequence. *Criminal Code*, R.S.C. 1985, c. C-46, s. 230.

MUTATIS MUTANDIS. [L.] With needed changes in the details. *R. v. Century 21 Ramos Realty Inc.* (1987), 56 C.R. (3d) 150 at 181-2, 87 D.T.C. 5158, 19 O.A.C. 25, 32 C.C.C. (3d) 353, 37 D.L.R. (4th) 649, 29 C.R.R. 320, [1987] 1 C.T.C. 340, 58 O.R. (2d) 737 (C.A.), Martin, Houlden and Tarnopolsky JJ.A.

MUTILATION. *n.* Depriving of any necessary part or limb.

MUTINY. *n.* Collective insubordination or a combination of two or more persons in the resistance of lawful authority in any of Her Majesty's Forces or in any forces cooperating therewith. *National Defence Act*, R.S.C. 1985, c. N-5, s. 2.

MUTUAL BENEFIT SOCIETY. A mutual company formed for the purpose of providing sick and funeral benefits for its members or for this and any other purposes necessary or incidental thereto except life insurance. See EMPLOYEES' ~.

MUTUAL FUND. Includes an issuer of a security that entitles the holder to receive on demand, or within a specified period after demand, an amount computed by reference to the value of a proportionate interest in the whole or in a part of the net assets, including a separate fund or trust account, of the issuer of the security.

MUTUAL FUND CORPORATION. A company that offers public participation in an investment portfolio through the issue of one or more classes of mutual fund shares.

MUTUAL FUND SHARE. A share having conditions attached thereto that include conditions requiring the company issuing the share to accept, at the demand of the holder thereof and at prices determined and payable in accordance with the conditions, the surrender of the share, or fractions or parts thereof, that are fully paid.

MUTUALITY OF ASSENT. Regarding the main or necessary part of any agreement, for each party to intend the same thing and to know what the other will do.

MUTUALITY OF OBLIGATION. For each party to an agreement to be bound to do something.

MUTUALITY OF REMEDY. For each party to an agreement to be able to enforce that agreement against the other.

MUTUAL MISTAKE. Mistake which is suffered by both parties to an agreement. Each party is mistaken as to the intention of the other party, but neither pary realizes that their respective promises have been misunderstood. *Stepps Investments Ltd. v. Security Capital Corp.* (1976), 14 O.R. (2d) 259 at 269, 73 D.L.R. (3d) 351 (H.C.), Grange J.

MUTUAL PROMISES. Simultaneous considerations which support each other.

MUTUAL WILLS. "... [T]hey confer mutual benefits upon two or more testators and there must be something in the nature of a contract, that is one contracting party agrees to confer certain benefits by will, the other contracting party will confer reciprocal benefits by his will. The situation should be one in which one party would not make his will unless the other one also made a will conferring similar benefits...." *Ohorodnyk, Re* (1979), 4 E.T.R. 233 at 244, 97 D.L.R. (3d) 502, 24 O.R. (2d) 228 (H.C.), Hollingworth J.

M.V.R. *abbr.* Motor Vehicle Reports, 1979-1988.

M.V.R. (2d). *abbr.* Motor Vehicle Reports (Second Series), 1988-.

N

NAKED CONTRACT. A contract which lacks consideration.

NAKED TRUST. See BARE TRUST.

NAME. *n.* A given name and surname. See BUSINESS ~; CHANGE OF ~; CORPORATE ~; FAMILY ~; FIRM ~; GIVEN ~; TRADE-~.

NAMED INSURED. A person specified in a contract of insurance as the one protected by the contract.

NAMED PRINCIPAL. A party whose name was revealed by the agent to the third party. G.H.L. Fridman, *The Law of Agency*, 6th ed. (London: Butterworths, 1990) at 193.

NAT. BANKING L. REV. *abbr.* National Banking Law Review.

NAT. CREDITOR/DEBTOR REV. *abbr.* National Creditor/Debtor Review.

NAT. INSOLVENCY REV. *abbr.* National Insolvency Review.

NATION. *n.* People distinct from other people, usually because of language or government. See INTERNATIONAL LAW; LAW OF ~S.

NATIONAL. *n.* 1. An individual possessing the nationality of a state. 2. Any legal person, partnership and association deriving its status as such from the law in force in a state.

NATIONAL CAPITAL REGION. The seat of the Government of Canada and its surrounding area, more particularly described in the schedule.

National Capital Act, R.S.C. 1985, c. N-4, s. 2.

NATIONAL DEBT. Money which a national government owes and on which interest is paid.

NATIONALITY. *n.* The character or quality which originates in a person belonging to a particular nation and which determines that individual's political status.

NATIONALIZATION. *n.* The acquisition of a business by government.

NATIONAL PAROLE BOARD. A federal body with exclusive authority and final discretion to grant a temporary absence with no escort or parole under the Penitentiary Act, to terminate or revoke day parole for inmates in federal institutions and inmates in provincial institutions in the Atlantic and Prairie provinces.

NAT. LABOUR REV. *abbr.* National Labour Review.

NAT'L BANKING L. REV. *abbr.* National Banking Law Review.

NAT'L INSOLV. REV. *abbr.* National Insolvency Review.

NAT. PROPERTY REV. *abbr.* National Property Review.

NATURAL AFFECTION. The love which someone has for kin, held to be not a valuable but a good consideration in certain circumstances.

NATURAL CHILD. A child of one's body; a child in fact.

NATURALIZATION. *var.*

NATURALISATION. *n*. 1. The act of becoming the subject of a nation. 2. "... [S]eems prima facie to include the power of enacting what shall be the consequences of naturalization, or, in other words, what shall be the rights and privileges pertaining to residents in Canada after they have been naturalized...." *Union Colliery Co. of British Columbia v. Bryden*, [1899] A.C. 580 at 586, 15 T.L.R. 598, 1 M.M.C. 337 (B.C. P.C.), the board per Lord Watson.

NATURAL JUSTICE. 1. "... [T]wo main components, the right to be heard and the right to a hearing from an unbiased tribunal, ..." *Wark v. Green* (1985), (*sub nom. Wark v. C.U.P.E.*) 66 N.B.R. (2d) 77 at 83, 169 A.P.R. 77, 86 C.L.L.C. 14,020, 23 D.L.R. (4th) 594 (C.A.), Hoyt J.A. 2. "The concept of natural justice is an elastic one, that can and should defy precise definition. The application of the principle must vary with the circumstances. How much or how little is encompassed by the term will depend on many factors; to name a few, the nature of the hearing, the nature of the tribunal presiding, the scope and effect of the ruling made." *Tandy Electronics Ltd. v. U.S.W.A.* (1979), 79 C.L.L.C. 14,216 at 170, 26 O.R. (2d) 68, 102 D.L.R. (3d) 126 (Div. Ct.), the court per Cory J.

NATURAL LAW. The code of rules which originates with the divine, nature or reason in contrast to laws people make.

NATURAL OBLIGATION. A duty with a definite purpose which is not necessarily governed by legal obligation.

NATURAL PERSON. A human being.

NAVAL COURT. Any officer who commands a ship belonging to Her Majesty on any foreign station or any consular officer may hold such a court when a complaint which requires immediate investigation arises, when the owner's interest in any Canadian ship or cargo seems to require it or when a Canadian ship is abandoned, wrecked or lost. R.M. Fernandes & C. Burke,

The Annotated Canada Shipping Act (Toronto: Butterworths, 1988) at 213.

N.B. *abbr*. 1. New Brunswick. 2. Nota bene.

N.B. EQ. *abbr*. New Brunswick Equity Reports, 1894-1912.

N.B.L.L.C. *abbr*. New Brunswick Labour Law Cases.

N.B.R. *abbr*. New Brunswick Reports, 1825-1929.

N.B.R. (2d). *abbr*. New Brunswick Reports (Second Series), 1969-.

N.E.B. *abbr*. National Energy Board.

NECESSARIES OF LIFE. "... In order to establish that the articles are necessaries, it must be shown that they are necessary to maintain the person in the station in life in which he finds himself." *Consumers Gas Co. v. Stewart* (1980), 31 O.R. (2d) 559 at 561, 36 C.B.R. (N.S.) 136, 119 D.L.R. (3d) 286 (Div. Ct.), Southey J.

NECESSARY CAUSE. A cause without which the loss or injury would not have happened. K.D. Cooper-Stephenson & I.B. Saunders, *Personal Injury Damages in Canada* (Toronto: Carswell, 1981) at 641.

NECESSARY INFERENCE. The only possible deduction which can be made from a proposition.

NECESSARY PARTY. A party whose participation in an action is required in order to satisfactorily resolve the issues before the court.

NECESSITY. *n*. 1. "The [defence of necessity] doctrine exists as an excusing defence, operating in very limited cirucmstances, when conduct that would otherwise be illegal and sanctionable is excused and made unsanctionable because it is properly seen as the result of a 'morally involuntary' decision ..." *R. v. Goltz*, [1991] 3 S.C.R. 485 at 519, 8 C.R. (4th) 82, 31 M.V.R. (2d) 137, 61 B.C.L.R. (2d) 145, 67 C.C.C. (3d) 481, 131 N.R. 1, 7 C.R.R. (2d) 1, 5 B.C.A.C. 161, 11 W.A.C. 161, Gonthier J. (La Forest, L'Heureux-Dubé, Sopinka, Cory and Iacobucci JJ. concurring). 2. "...

[R]efers to the necessity of the hearsay evidence to prove a fact in issue. . . . the criterion of necessity must be given a flexible definition, capable of encompassing diverse situations. What these situations will have in common is that the relevant direct evidence is not, for a variety of reasons, available." *R. v. Smith* (1992), 75 C.C.C. (3d) 257 at 271, 15 C.R. (4th) 133, 139 N.R. 323, 94 D.L.R. (4th) 590, 55 O.A.C. 321, [1992] 2 S.C.R. 915, the court per Lamer C.J.C. See BASIC NECESSITIES.

NEGATIVE. *v.* To deny or contradict.

NEGATIVE. *n.* Denial.

NEGATIVE. *adj.* Describes that which denies or contradicts.

NEGATIVE DAMAGE. The removal of desirable things: amenities, earnings, enjoyment and expectation of life. K.D. Cooper-Stephenson & I.B. Saunders, *Personal Injury Damages in Canada* (Toronto: Carswell, 1981) at 52.

NEGATIVE PREGNANT. In pleading, an evasive answer to something alleged, a literal answer but not an answer to substance.

NEGLECT. *n.* A lack or failure to provide necessary care, aid, guidance or attention which causes or is reasonably likely to cause the victim severe physical or psychological harm or significant material loss to his estate. *Adult Protection Act*, R.S.P.E.I. 1988, c. A-5, s. 1(k).

NEGLECTED CHILD. A child in need of protection and without restricting the generality of the foregoing includes any child who is within one or more of the following descriptions: (i) a child who is not being properly cared for; (ii) a child who is abandoned or deserted by the person in whose charge that child is or who is an orphan who is not being properly cared for; (iii) a child when the person in whose charge that child is cannot, by reason of disease, infirmity, misfortune, incompetence or imprisonment, or any combination thereof, care properly for the child; (iv) a child who is living in an unfit or improper place; (v) a child found associating with an unfit or improper person; (vi) a child found begging in a public place; (vii) a child who, with the consent or connivance of the person in whose charge the child is, commits any act that renders the child liable to a penalty under an Act of Canada or of the Legislature, or under a municipal by-law; (viii) a child who is misdemeanant by reason of inadequacy of the control exercised by the person in whose charge the child is, or who is being allowed to grow up without salutory parental control or under circumstances tending to make the child idle or dissolute; (ix) a child who, without sufficient cause, habitually is away from home or school; (x) a child where the person in whose charge the child is neglects or refuses to provide or obtain proper medical, surgical or other medical care or treatment necessary for the child's health and well-being, or refuses to permit that care or treatment to be supplied to the child when it is recommended by a physician; (xi) a child whose emotional or mental development is endangered because of emotional rejection or deprivation of affection by the person in whose charge the child is; (xii) a child whose life, health or morals may be endangered by the conduct of the person in whose charge the child is; (xiii) a child who is being cared for by and at the expense of someone other than the child's parents and in circumstances which indicate that the child's parents are not performing their parental duties; (xiv) a child who is not under proper guardianship or who has no parent (A) capable of exercising, (B) willing to exercise, or (C) capable of exercising and willing to exercise, proper parental control over the child; (xv) a child whose parent wishes to be rid of parental responsibilities toward the child.

NEGLIGENCE. *n.* 1. An independent tort which consists of breach of a legal duty to take care which results in damage, undesired by the defendant, to the plaintiff. 2. ". . . [C]onduct which falls below the standard required in particular circumstances in order to protect others against unreasonable risk of harm, as opposed to some risk of harm." *Funk v. Clapp* (1986), 68 D.L.R. (4th) 229 at 244, 35 B.C.L.R. 266 (C.A.), Craig J.A. (dissenting). 3. ". . . [M]easures the conduct of the accused on the basis of an objective standard, irrespective of the accused's subjective mental state. Where negligence is the basis of liability, the question is not what the accused intended, but rather whether the accused exercised reasonable care." *R. v. Wholesale Travel Group Inc.* (1991), 8 C.R. (4th) 145 at 176, 67 C.C.C. (3d) 193, 4 O.R. (3d) 799n, 84 D.L.R. (4th) 161, 130 N.R. 1, 38 C.P.R. (3d) 451, 49 O.A.C. 161, [1991] 3 S.C.R. 154, 7 C.R.R. (2d) 36, Cory J. (L'Heureux-Dubé J. concurring). See CONTRIBUTORY ~; CRIMINAL ~; GROSS ~.

NEGLIGENT MISREPRESENTA-TION. "An action for negligent misrepresentation is made out where there is: (a) a negligent misrepresentation; (b) made carelessly and in breach of a duty owed by the representor to the representee to take reasonable care to ensure that the representation is adqueate; which (c) causes loss which was the foreseeable consequence of the misrepresentation at the time it was made to the representee." *Rainbow Industrial Caterers Ltd. v. Canadian National Railway* (1991), 8 C.C.L.T. (2d) 225 at 238, 59 B.C.L.R. (2d) 129, [1991] 6 W.W.R. 385, 84 D.L.R. (4th) 291, 126 N.R. 354, 3 B.C.A.C. 1, 7 W.A.C. 1, [1991] 3 S.C.R. 3, McLachlin J. (dissenting).

NEGOTIABILITY. *n.* Having in law the characteristics of current coin, except that coinage is the only legal tender. E.L.G. Tyler & N.E. Palmer, eds., *Crossley Vaines' Personal Property*, 5th ed. (London: Butterworths, 1973) at 208.

NEGOTIABLE INSTRUMENT. 1. Something which: (i) if payable to bearer, is transferable by delivery alone, or if payable to order, by delivery together with indorsement; (ii) presumes the giving of consideration; (iii) permits a transferee to take in good faith and for value to acquire good title despite lack of or defects in the transferor's title. E.L.G. Tyler & N.E. Palmer, eds., *Crossley Vaines' Personal Property*, 5th ed. (London: Butterworths, 1973) at 208. 2. Includes any cheque, draft, traveller's cheque, bill of exchange, postal note, money order, postal remittance and any other similar instrument.

NEGOTIABLE RECEIPT. A receipt in which it is stated that the goods therein specified will be delivered to bearer or to the order of a named person. *Warehouse Receipts acts.*

NEGOTIATE. *v.* 1. To transfer for value, by indorsement or delivery, a bill of exchange or other negotiable instrument. 2. To bargain in good faith with a view to the conclusion of an agreement or the revision or the renewal of an existing agreement.

NEGOTIATION. *n.* 1. Transference of a bill from one person to another so that the transferee becomes the holder of the bill. E.L.G. Tyler & N.E. Palmer, eds., *Crossley Vaines' Personal Property*, 5th ed. (London: Butterworths, 1973) at 222. 2. Deliberation and discussion upon the terms of a proposed agreement, and includes conciliation and arbitration. See PLEA ~.

NEIGHBOUR TEST. The test of proximity between defendant and plaintiff in a negligence suit per Lord Atkin in *Donoghue v. Stevenson*, [1932] A.C. 562, 580: "You must take reasonable care to avoid acts or omissions which you can reasonably foresee would be likely to injure your neighbour. Who, then, in law is my neighbour? The answer seems to be – persons who are so closely and directly affected by my act that I ought reasonably to have them in contemplation as being so affected when I am directing my mind to the acts or omissions which are called in question."

NEM. CON. *abbr.* [L. nemine contradicente] Without anyone saying otherwise.

NEM. DIS. *abbr.* [L. nemine dissentiente] Without dissent.

NEMO DAT QUOD NON HABET. [L.] No one gives what one does not possess.

NEMO DEBET BIS VEXARI, SI CONSTAT CURIAE QUOD SIT PRO UNA ET EADEM CAUSA. [L.] Non one should be harassed twice, if the court agrees that it is for one and the same cause.

NEMO DEBET ESSE JUDEX IN PROPRIA CAUSA. [L.] No one should judge one's own cause.

NEMO EST HAERES VIVENTIS. [L.] No one is the heir of a living person.

NEMO EST SUPRA LEGIS. [L.] No one is above the law.

NEMO JUDEX IN CAUSA SUA DEBET ESSE. [L.] "... [N]o one ought to be a Judge in his own cause...." *Barry v. Alberta Securities Commission* (1989), 35 Admin. L.R. 1 at 10, 93 N.R. 1, 65 Alta. L.R. (2d) 97, [1989] 3 W.W.R. 456, 57 D.L.R. (4th) 458, [1989] 1 S.C.R. 301, 96 A.R. 241, the court per L'Heureux-Dubé J.

NEMO POTEST ESSE SIMUL ACTOR ET JUDEX. [L.] No one can be suitor and judge at the same time.

NEMO TENETUR SEIPSUM ACCUSARE. [L.] "... [T]he privilege of a witness not to answer a question which may incriminate him. That is all that is meant by the Latin maxim, nemo tenetur seipsum accusare, often incorrectly advanced in support of a much broader proposition...." *Marcoux v. R.* (1975), 60 D.L.R. (3d) 119 at 122, [1976] 1 S.C.R. 763, 29 C.R.N.S. 211, 4 N.R. 64, 24 C.C.C. (2d) 1, Dickson J. See PRIVILEGE AGAINST SELF-INCRIMINATION.

NERVOUS SHOCK. "... [T]he claimant [must] show through the application of the relevant principles of negligence law that the negligent conduct of the defendant caused injuries to others whose suffering was seen and heard by the plaintiff, who was shocked by the experience and, as a result, developed a recognizable psychiatric or emotional illness. The plaintiff must show he suffers from some medically recognizable psychiatric or emotional illness, but damages will only be awarded if he shows the negligent conduct of the defendant caused the illness." *Beecham v. Hughes* (1988), 45 C.C.L.T. 1 at 18-19, 27 B.C.L.R. (2d) 1, [1988] 6 W.W.R. 33, 52 D.L.R. (4th) 635 (C.A.), Taggart J.A. (Carrothers J.A. concurring).

NET. *n.* In accounting, an amount of money after all specified expenditures or deductions are deducted.

NET INCOME. Income less expenses.

NET LEASE. "... [T]ype of lease, wherein the lessor undertakes to pay certain expenses ..." *Boots Drug Stores (Canada) Ltd. v. Ritt* (1980), 12 R.P.R. 114 at 116 (Ont. H.C.), Callaghan J.

NET NET LEASE. "... [L]ease under which a tenant pays all such costs and the landlord rents the premises in an 'as is' state without covenanting to pay any costs attendant upon the maintenance or operation of the leasehold premises...." *Boots Drug Stores (Canada) Ltd. v. Ritt* (1980), 12 R.P.R. 114 at 116 (Ont. H.C.), Callaghan J.

NET PROFIT. Clear profit after every deduction.

NET VALUE. The value of the estate, wherever situate, both within and without the province, after payment of the charges thereon and the debts, funeral expenses, expenses of administration, succession duty and estate tax. *Intestate Succession acts.*

NEUTRALISATION. *n.* By treaty, exclusion of some territory from a region at war so that the territory has neutral status.

NEUTRALITY. *n.* A situation in which a territory is allied to neither side of a war.

NEW TRIAL. Application to the court for this is the only remedy when there is any defect in judgment through entirely extrinsic causes or something outside the record.

NEXT FRIEND. The person who intervenes to bring an action on behalf of an infant. See LITIGATION GUARDIAN.

NEXT OF KIN. *var.* **NEXT-OF-KIN.** The mother, father, children, brothers, sisters, spouse and common law spouse of a deceased person, or any of them.

NFLD. & P.E.I.R. *abbr.* Newfoundland and Prince Edward Island Reports, 1971-.

NFLD. R. *abbr.* Newfoundland Reports, 1817-1949.

NFLD. SEL. CAS. *abbr.* Tucker's Select Cases (Nfld.), 1817-1828.

NIHIL. [L.] Nothing.

NIHIL DAT QUI NON HABET. [L.] One who has nothing gives nothing.

NIL. *n.* [L.] Nothing.

NIL DEBET. [L.] One owes nothing.

NISI. [L.] Describes an order effective only when the affected party fails to respond to it by a certain time. See DECREE ~; RULE ~.

NISI PRIUS. [L.] Unless before.

N.L. *abbr.* [L.] Non liquet. It is not evident.

NO. *abbr.* Number.

NO-FAULT DIVORCE. Divorce based on grounds other than a matrimonial offence.

NOLLE PROSEQUI. [L.] 1. To be not willing to prosecute. 2. A stay of proceedings.

NO-LOAD FUND. A mutual fund which charges little or no fee in the sale of its shares.

NO MAN CAN TAKE ADVANTAGE OF HIS OWN WRONG. "... [M]axim ... recognized by Courts of law and of equity, ..." *Houghton v. May* (1910), 22 O.L.R. 434 at 439 (H.C.), Clute J. See CLEAN HANDS DOCTRINE.

NO MAN SHALL BE JUDGE IN HIS OWN CAUSE. See *House Repair & Service Co. v. Miller* (1921), 49 O.L.R. 205 at 212-13, 64 D.L.R.

115 (C.A.), the court per Hodgins J.A.

NOM DE PLUME. [Fr.] Pen name.

NOMINAL CAPITAL. The quantity of shares or the aggregate par value of shares which a company is authorized to issue, fixed in the company's memorandum or articles of incorporation or letters patent. H. Sutherland, D.B. Horsley & J.M. Edmiston, eds., *Fraser's Handbook on Canadian Company Law*, 7th ed. (Toronto: Carswell, 1985) at 41.

NOMINAL DAMAGES. "... [A] technical phrase which means that you have negatived anything like real damage, but that you are affirming by your nominal damages that there is an infraction of a legal right which, though it gives you no right to any real damages at all, yet gives you a right to the verdict or judgment because your legal right has been infringed ..." *Mediana (The)*, [1900] A.C. 113 at 116 (U.K. H.L.), Lord Halsbury L.C.

NOMINAL PARTNER. A person who does not have any actual interest in a business, trade or its profits but appears to have an interest because her or his name is used in the trade or business.

NOMINAL PLAINTIFF. 1. "... [O]ne who merely represents others ..." *U.F.C.W. Local 1252, Fishermen's Union v. Cashin* (1987), 6 Nfld. & P.E.I.R. 181 at 185, 204 A.P.R. 181 (Nfld. T.D.), Cameron J. 2. "... [A] plaintiff is only a nominal plaintiff within the meaning of [Ontario Rules of Practice] R. 373(f) if he has no interest whatever in the result of the action." *Lincoln Terrace Restaurant Ltd. v. Bray* (1980), 19 C.P.C. 290 at 292 (Ont. Master), Garfield (Master).

NOMINATION. *n.* A mention by name.

NON-AGE. *n.* The state of being a minor.

NON ASSUMPSIT. [L.] One did not promise.

NON-CAPITAL MURDER. All murder other than capital murder. *Criminal Code*, R.S.C. 1970, c. C-34,

s. 214. See now SECOND DEGREE MURDER.

NON COMPOS MENTIS. [L.] Not sound in mind.

NON-CONFORMING USE. Use of land or buildings in a manner or for a purpose "lawful when it commenced and lawful prior to a change in a government land use by-law...." *Mehta v. Truro (Town)* (1991), 5 M.P.L.R. (2d) 216 at 218, 104 N.S.R. (2d) 440, 283 A.P.R. 440 (C.A.), Hallett J.A.

NON CONSTAT. [L.] It does not follow; it is not clear.

NON-CONTENTIOUS BUSINESS. A proceeding or matter pertaining to probate, administration or guardianship, but does not include contentious business. *Administration of Estates Act*, R.S.A. 1980, c. A-1, s. 1.

NON CULPABLE HOMICIDE. Homicide that is not culpable is not an offence. *Criminal Code*, R.S.C. 1985, c. C-46, s. 222(3).

NONCUMULATIVE DIVIDEND. A dividend which need not be paid in a subsequent year if it was not paid in an earlier year.

NON DAT QUI NON HABET. [L.] One who does not have cannot give.

NON-DELIVERY. *n.* Neglect or failure to deliver goods on the part of a bailee, carrier, or other expected to deliver.

NON EST FACTUM. [L.] 1. It is not that person's deed. 2. "... [A] form of mistake, where the mistake goes to the very nature of the document which is being signed. Where such a mistake is established, it is invariably a fundamental mistake causing the contract to be void." *Granville Savings & Mortgage Corp. v. Slevin* (1992), 12 C.C.L.T. (2d) 275 at 297, [1992] 5 W.W.R. 1, 24 R.P.R. (2d) 185, 93 D.L.R. (4th) 268, 6 B.L.R. (2d) 192, 78 Man. R. (2d) 241, 16 W.A.C. 241 (C.A.), O'Sullivan J.A. (dissenting in part).

NONFEASANCE. *n.* The failure or neglect to do something which a person

ought to do.

NON-JOINDER. *n.* The omission of someone from an action who should be made party.

NON LIQUET. [L.] It is not evident.

NON OBSTANTE. [L.] Notwithstanding.

NON OBSTANTE VEREDICTO. [L.] The verdict notwithstanding.

NON-PECUNIARY LOSS. 1. Compensation for suffering and pain, for loss of enjoyment of life and amenities, and for shortened expectation of life. *Reekie v. Messervey* (1989), 48 C.C.L.T. 217 at 235, 36 B.C.L.R. (2d) 316, 59 D.L.R. (4th) 481, 17 M.V.R. (2d) 94 (C.A.), Lambert J.A. 2. Includes loss of care and guidance from a parent or loss generally of guidance, care and companionship. K.D. Cooper-Stephenson & I.B. Saunders, *Personal Injury Damages in Canada Supplement to June 30, 1987* (Toronto: Carswell, 1987) at 29 and 30.

NON-PERFORMANCE. *n.* The failure to complete a contract.

NON-PROFIT CORPORATION. A corporation, no part of the income of which is payable to or is otherwise available for the personal benefit of any proprietor, member or shareholder thereof.

NON-PROFIT ORGANIZATION. An organization (i) wholly owned by the Government, by a municipality or by any agency of either of them; or (ii) constituted exclusively for charitable or benevolent purposes where no part of the income is payable to or otherwise available for the personal benefit of any proprietor, member or shareholder.

NON PROS. *abbr.* Non prosequitur.

NON PROSEQUITUR. [L.] One does not follow up.

NON-RESIDENT. *var.* **NON RESIDENT.** *var.* **NONRESIDENT.** 1. (a) An individual who is not ordinarily resident in Canada; (b) a corporation incorporated, formed or otherwise organized elsewhere than in Canada; (c) a corporation that is controlled directly or indirectly by nonresidents as defined in paragraph (a) or (b); (d) a trust established by a nonresident as defined in paragraph (a), (b) or (c), or a trust in which non-residents as so defined have more than 50 per cent of the beneficial interest, or (e) a corporation that is controlled directly or indirectly by a trust mentioned in paragraph (d). 2. A person who is not a resident of the province.

NON SEQUITUR. [L.] It does not follow.

NON SUI JURIS. [L.] Not able to manage one's own affairs; with no legal capacity.

NONSUIT. *n.* The judgment ordered when a plaintiff cannot establish any legal cause of action or cannot support pleadings with any evidence.

NO ONE CAN BE ALLOWED TO DEROGATE FROM HIS OWN GRANT. See *Keewatin Power Co. v. Keewatin Flour Mills Ltd.*, [1928] 1 D.L.R. 32 at 53, 61 O.L.R. 363 (H.C.), Grant J. See CLEAN HANDS DOCTRINE.

NOSCITUR A SOCIIS. [L.] 1. One is known by one's associates. 2. ". . . [W]here general words are closely associated with preceding specific words the meaning of the general words must be limited by reference to the specific words." *Insurance Corp. of British Columbia v. Canada (Registrar of Trade Marks)* (1978), 44 C.P.R. (2d) 1 at 11, [1980] 1 F.C. 669 (T.D.), Cattanach J.

NOSCITUR EX SOCIO, QUI NON COGNOSCITUR EX SE. [L.] One who cannot be known from the self is known from an associate.

NOSCUNTUR A SOCIIS. [L.] When one joins words which could have analogous meaning, one is using them in their cognate sense. P. St. J. Langan, ed., *Maxwell on The Interpretation of Statutes*, 12th ed. (Bombay: N.M. Tripathi, 1976) at 289. See NOSCITUR A SOCIIS.

NOTA BENE. [L.] Note well.

NOTARIAL ACT. 1. A notary's written authentication or certification, under official seal or signature, of any entry or document. 2. Any attestation, certificate or instrument which a notary executes.

NOTARIAL CERTIFICATE. An instrument which certifies the authenticity of the document to which it is attached.

NOTARY. *n.* One who attests a deed or document to make it authentic in another jurisdiction.

NOTARY PUBLIC. One who attests a deed or document to make it authentic in another jurisdiction and is empowered to take affidavits and declarations and to perform various other acts relating to legal matters.

NOTE. *v.* Of a dishonoured foreign bill, for a notary public to record her or his initials, the day, month, year and reason, if given, for non-payment.

NOTE. *n.* 1. A promissory note. *Bills of Exchange Act*, R.S.C. 1985, c. B-4, s. 2. 2. Any corporate obligation, unsecured or secured. H. Sutherland, D.B. Horsley & J.M. Edmiston, eds., *Fraser's Handbook on Canadian Company Law*, 7th ed. (Toronto: Carswell, 1985) at 310. See BANK-~; COVER ~; CREDIT ~; DEBIT ~; DEMAND ~; INLAND ~; MARGINAL ~; PROMISSORY ~.

NOTES. *n.* See JUDGE'S ~.

NOT GUILTY. The plea appropriate to an indictment when the accused chooses to raise a general issue, *i.e.*, to deny everything and let the prosecution prove whatever they can.

NOTICE. *n.* 1. Cognisance; knowledge. 2. Judicial notice. 3. To give someone notice of a fact is to bring that fact to the person's attention. 4. A document which informs or advises someone that that person's interests are involved in a proceeding or which informs the person of something which that person has a right to know. 5. ". . . [S]omething which is in a form calculated to attract attention." *Montreal Trust v. Canadian Pacific Airlines Ltd.*, [1977] 2 S.C.R. 793 at

802, 12 N.R. 408, 72 D.L.R. (3d) 257, Ritchie J. (Laskin C.J.C., Spence and Dickson JJ. concurring). See ACTUAL ~; ADEQUATE ~; APPEARANCE ~; CONSTRUCTIVE ~; JUDICIAL ~; OFFICIAL ~.

NOTICE OF ACTION. A document containing a short statement about the nature of the claim which may commence any action other than a divorce action when there is not enough time to prepare a full statement of claim (Ontario, Rules of Civil Procedure, r. 14.03(2)).

NOTICE OF APPEAL. A document by which an appeal is commenced.

NOTICE OF DISHONOUR. A formal notice concerning a bill of exchange. I.F.G. Baxter, *The Law of Banking*, 3d ed. (Toronto: Carswell, 1981) at 117.

NOTICE OF INTENT TO DEFEND. In Ontario practice, the document which a defendant who intends to defend an action delivers and which gives that defendant 10 more days to file a statement of defence.

NOTICE OF MOTION. In Ontario practice, the document which initiates a motion and notifies other parties of the motion, used unless the circumstances or the nature of the motion make it unnecessary.

NOTICE OF READINESS FOR TRIAL. In Ontario practice, the document, formerly called a certificate of readiness, which the party who is ready for trial and who wishes to set the action down for trial serves on every other party to the action.

NOTICE PAPER. A document by which members of Parliament give notice that they intend to introduce bills, seek answers to written questions or move a motion as Private Members' business. A. Fraser, W.A. Dawson & J. Holtby, eds., *Beauchesne's Rules and Forms of the House of Commons of Canada*, 6th ed. (Toronto: Carswell, 1989) at 300.

NOTICE TO QUIT. The notice required for either a landlord or a tenant to terminate a tenancy without the other's consent when that tenancy runs from year to year or for some other indefinite period.

NOTIFY. *v.* "... [M]eans, in its everyday sense, 'to inform expressly', and in law: ... 'to make known, to give notice, to inform'." *Brière v. Canada (Employment & Immigration* Commission) (1988), 89 C.L.L.C. 14,025 at 12,203, 93 N.R. 115, 25 F.T.R. 80n, 57 D.L.R. (4th) 402 (C.A.), Lacombe J.A.

NOTING. *n.* A notary's record on a bill at the time it is dishonoured. I.F.G. Baxter, *The Law of Banking*, 3d ed. (Toronto: Carswell, 1981) at 117.

NOTORIOUS. *adj.* In evidence, describes a matter which need not be proved.

N.O.V. *abbr.* Non obstante veredicto.

NOVA CAUSA INTERVENIENS. [L.] A new cause intervenes. *Emerson v. Skinner* (1906), 12 B.C.R. 154 at 155, 4 W.L.R. 255 (C.A.), Hunter C.J.A.

NOVATION. *n.* "... [A] trilateral agreement by which an existing contract is extinguished and a new contract brought into being in its place. Indeed, for an agreement to effect a valid novation the appropriate consideration is the discharge of the original debt in return for a promise to perform some obligation. The assent of the beneficiary (the creditor or mortgagee) of those obligations to the discharge and substitution is crucial. The Courts have established a three part test for determining if novation has occurred. It is set out in Polson v. Wulffsohn (1890), 2 B.C.R. 39 at 43 (S.C.) as follows: ' ... first, the new debtor must assume the complete liability; second, the creditor must accept the new debtor as a principal debtor, and not merely as an agent or guarantor; and third, the creditor must accept the new contract in full satisfaction and substitution for the old contract ...' " *National Trust Co. v. Mead* (1990), 12 R.P.R. (2d) 165 at 180, [1990] 2 S.C.R. 410, [1990] 5 W.W.R. 459, 71 D.L.R. (4th) 488, 112 N.R. 1, Wilson J. (Lamer C.J.C., La Forest,

L'Heureux-Dubé, Gonthier and Cory JJ. concurring).

NOVUS ACTUS INTERVENIENS. [L.] 1. A new act intervenes. 2. "... [A] '... conscious act of human origin intervening between a negligent act or omission of a defendant and the occurrence by which the plaintiff suffers damage ... ' ... The important element in the defence 'novus actus interveniens' is that the intervening act must be one which the party defending could not reasonably [sic] forsee...." *Mercantile Bank of Canada v. Carl B. Potter Ltd.* (1979), 7 B.L.R. 54 at 77-8, 31 N.S.R. (2d) 402, 52 A.P.R. 402 (C.A.), Coffin J.A. 3. "... One such case is where, although an act of the accused constitutes a cause sine qua non of (or necessary condition for) the death of the victim, nevertheless the intervention of a third person may be regarded as the sole cause of the victim's death, thereby relieving the accused of criminal responsibility. Such intervention, if it has such an effect, has often been described by lawyers as a novus actus interveniens." *R. v. Pagett* (1983), 76 Cr. App. R. 279 at 288 (U.K. C.A.), the court per Lord Goff.

N.P.B. *abbr.* National Parole Board.

N.R. *abbr.* National Reporter, 1974-.

N.S.F. *abbr.* Not sufficient funds.

N.S. L. NEWS. *abbr.* Nova Scotia Law News.

N.S.R. *abbr.* Nova Scotia Reports, 1834-1929.

N.S.R. (2d). *abbr.* Nova Scotia Reports (Second Series), 1970-.

NUDA PACTIO OBLIGATIONEM NON PARIT. [L.] A simple promise does not create an obligation.

NUDUM PACTUM. [L. a bare agreement] An agreement made with no consideration.

NUISANCE. *n.* 1. An activity or physical condition which causes harm or annoyance or the harm resulting from the activity or condition. J.G. Fleming, *The Law of Torts*, 8th ed. (Sydney: Law Book, 1992) at 410. 2.

A condition that is or that might become injurious or dangerous to the public health, or that might hinder in any manner the prevention or suppression of disease. 3. Anything which is injurious to the health, or indecent, or offensive to the senses, or an obstruction to the free use of property so as to interfere with the comfortable enjoyment of life or property. See ABATEMENT OF ~; COMMON ~; PRIVATE ~; PUBLIC ~.

NULLA BONA. [L. no goods] The proper return of a writ when the judgment debtor has no goods in the sheriff's bailiwick or there are no proceeds available to satisfy the writ. C.R.B. Dunlop, *CreditorDebtor Law in Canada* (Toronto: Carswell, 1981) at 399.

NULLA POENA SINE LEGE. [L.] There should be no punishment except according to predetermined, fixed law. D. Stuart, *Canadian Criminal Law: A Treatise*, 2d ed. (Toronto: Carswell, 1987) at 15.

NULLITY. *n.* Something which has no legal effect.

NULLITY OF MARRIAGE. The total invalidity of an attempted, pretended or supposed marriage which was void from the beginning because the parties lacked consent or capacity to marry or which was voidable or liable to annulment later because one spouse was unable to consummate the marriage.

NULLUM CRIMEN SINE LEGE. [L.] There should be no crime except according to predetermined, fixed law. D. Stuart, *Canadian Criminal Law: A Treatise*, 2d ed. (Toronto: Carswell, 1987) at 15.

NUNC PRO TUNC. [L. now for then] 1. The order of a court that a proceeding be dated with an earlier date than the date it actually took place, or that the same effect be produced as if the proceeding had happened at an earlier date. 2. "... [U]sed to refer to the common law power of the Court to permit that to be done now which ought to have been done before...."

Krueger v. Raccah (1981), 24 C.P.C. 14 at 17, 12 Sask. R. 130, 128 D.L.R. (3d) 177 (Q.B.), Cameron J.

NUNCUPATIVE WILL. "... [A] will made by a soldier under circumstances in which it is presumed he would not be able to have a proper will drawn and properly witnessed." *Smith*

v. Hubbard, [1917] 1 W.W.R. 1237 at 1238 (B.C. S.C.), Macdonald J.

N.W.T. *abbr.* 1. Northwest Territories. 2. North West Territories Reports, 1887-1898.

[ ] N.W.T.R. *abbr.* Northwest Territories Reports, 1983-.

O

O.A.C. *abbr.* Ontario Appeal Cases.

OAKES TEST. The test applied to determine whether a restriction of rights under the Charter is salvaged by s. 1 of the Charter involves the application of the decision of the Supreme Court of Canada in R. v. Oakes, [1986] 1 S.C.R. 103, 50 C.R. (3d) 1, 26 D.L.R. (4th) 200, 24 C.C.C. (3d) 321, 14 O.A.C. 335, 19 C.R.R. 308. *R. v. Penno* (1990), 29 M.V.R. (2d) 161 at 176, [1990] 2 S.C.R. 865, 80 C.R. (3d) 97, 59 C.C.C. (3d) 344, 49 C.R.R. 50, 115 N.R. 249, 42 O.A.C. 271, Lamer C.J.C. See PROPORTIONALITY TEST; REASONABLE LIMITS.

O.A.R. *abbr.* Ontario Appeal Reports, 1876-1900.

OATH. *n.* 1. "... [A]n appeal to a Supreme Being in whose existence the person taking the oath believes to be a rewarder of truth and an avenger of falsehood: ... The purpose of the oath is to bind the conscience of the witness ..." *R. v. Defillipi*, [1932] 1 W.W.R. 545 at 546, 57 C.C.C. 401, 26 Alta. L.R. 134 (C.A.), the court per McGillivray J.A. 2. ".... Canada's emerging multi-cultural society requires an acknowledgement in the courts that the Judaic-Christian form of oath is not necessarily the only form of religious oath to be administered, and that persons of other religious persuasions should not automatically be given affirmation as the only alternative." *R. v. Kalevar* (1991), 4 C.R. (4th) 114 at 117 (Ont. Gen. Div.), Haley J.

OATH OF ALLEGIANCE. The words of the oath are: I, _____ , do swear that I will be faithful and bear true allegiance to Her Majesty Queen Elizabeth the Second, Queen of Canada, Her Heirs and Successors. So help me God. *Oaths of Allegiance Act*, R.S.C. 1985, c. O-1, s. 2(1).

OATH OR AFFIRMATION OF CITIZENSHIP. The words of the oath are: I swear (or affirm) that I will be faithful and bear true allegiance to Her Majesty Queen Elizabeth the Second, Queen of Canada, Her Heirs and Successors, and that I will faithfully observe the laws of Canada and fulfill my duties as a Canadian citizen. *Citizenship Act*, R.S.C. 1985, c. C-29, Schedule.

OBITER DICTA. [L.] "... [M]ere passing remarks of the judge, ..." *Richard West & Partners (Inverness) Ltd. v. Dick* (1968), [1969] 1 All E.R. 289 at 292 (U.K. Ch.), Megarry J.

OBITER DICTUM. [L. a remark in passing] 1. An opinion not required in a judgment and so not a binding precedent. 2. "... [T]he time is past ... when the language of a conclusion is minutely scrutinized regardless of the underlying reasons and the conclusions sought in the action, and everything not echoed in the conclusion [is] necessarily regarded as an obiter dictum." *Celliers du Monde Inc. c. Dumont Vins & Spiriteux Inc.* (1992), 42 C.P.R. (3d) 197 at 204, 139 N.R. 357, [1992] 2 F.C. 634 (C.A.), the court per Decary J.A.

OBJECT OF A POWER. A person

310

in whose favour one may exercise a power of appointment.

OBJECTS CLAUSE. The clause in an incorporating document which sets out the purposes for which the corporation is established.

OBLIGATION. *n.* 1. "... [R]efers to something in the nature of a contract, such as a covenant, bond or agreement...." *Stokes v. Leavens* (1918), 40 D.L.R. 23 at 24, [1918] 2 W.W.R. 188, 28 Man. R. 479 (C.A.), Perdue J.A. 2. "[Not restricted] to a duty arising out of contract [but] ... also includes a duty or liability arising from an actionable tort." *Smith v. Canadian Broadcasting Corp.*, [1953] O.W.N. 212 at 214, [1953] 1 D.L.R. 510 (H.C.), Judson J. 3. "... [T]hat which constitutes legal duty and which renders one liable to coercion for neglecting it – an act which binds a person to some performance." *Ging, Re* (1890), 20 O.R. 1 at 5 (H.C.), Robertson J. 4. "[In the definition of property in the Bankruptcy Act, R.S.C. 1970, c. B-3, s. 2] ... an asset owing to the bankrupt as an obligee ..." *Targa Holdings Ltd. v. Whyte* (1974), 21 C.B.R. (N.S.) 54 at 71, [1974] 3 W.W.R. 632, 44 D.L.R. (3d) 208 (Alta. C.A.), Clement J.A. See EQUITY IMPUTES AN INTENTION TO FULFIL AN ~; IMPERFECT ~; MORAL ~; MUTUALITY OF ~; NATURAL ~.

OBSCENE. *adj.* Any publication whose dominant characteristic is the undue exploitation of sex, or of sex and any one or more of the following subjects, namely: crime, horror, cruelty and violence, shall be deemed to be obscene. *Criminal Code*, R.S.C. 1985, c. C-46, s. 163(8).

OBSTRUCTING JUSTICE. 1. Every one who wilfully attempts in any manner to obstruct, pervert or defeat the course of justice in a judicial proceeding, (a) by indemnifying or agreeing to indemnify a surety, in any way and either in whole or in part; or (b) where he is a surety, by accepting or agreeing to accept a fee or any form of indemnity whether in whole or in part from or in respect of a person who is released or is to be released from custody. *Criminal Code*, R.S.C. 1985, c. C-46, s. 139(1). 2. Every one shall be deemed wilfully to attempt to obstruct, pervert or defeat the course of justice who in a judicial proceeding, existing or proposed, (a) dissuades or attempts to dissuade a person by threats, bribes or other corrupt means from giving evidence; (b) influences or attempts to influence by threats, bribes or other corrupt means a person in his conduct as a juror; or (c) accepts or obtains, agrees to accept or attempts to obtain a bribe or other corrupt consideration to abstain from giving evidence, or to do or to refrain from doing anything as a juror. *Criminal Code*, R.S.C. 1985, c. C-46, s. 139(3).

OBSTRUCTION. *n.* 1. "... [A]ny act, not necessarily an unlawful act, including a concealment, which frustrates or makes more difficult the execution of a peace officer's duty...." *R. v. Moore* (1977), 40 C.R.N.S. 93 at 105, [1977] 5 W.W.R. 241, 36 C.C.C. (2d) 481 (B.C. C.A.), Carrothers J.A. 2. Any slide, dam or other obstruction impeding the free passage of fish. *Fisheries Act*, R.S.C. 1985, c. F-14, s. 2.

O.C. *abbr.* Order in Council.

OCCUPANCY. *n.* Mere use or possession either through an agreement or some other way, so that there is no other claim to the enjoyment or ownership of property. See BUSINESS ~.

OCCUPANCY PERMIT. A permit, certificate or other document issued by a municipality or an official thereof in respect of a building indicating that the building or a part thereof may be occupied.

OCCUPANT. *n.* 1. The owner, lessee, or other person having possession of or control over lands. 2. "To be an 'occupant' of premises, as that word is understood in law, a person must have control of them." *Stinson v. Middleton (Township)*, [1949] O.R. 237 at 252, [1949] 2 D.L.R. 328 (C.A.), Robertson C.J.O. 3. "... [I]n a wide sense means 'one who occupies, resides in or is at the time in a place'." *Stinson v. Middleton (Township)*, [1949] 2 D.L.R. 328 at 333, [1949] O.R. 237 (C.A.), Laidlaw J.A.

OCCUPATION. *n.* 1. An employment, business, calling, pursuit, trade, vocation or profession. 2. The act of possessing. 3. "... [T]hat which engages the time and attention...." *Northern Trusts Co. v. Eckert*, [1942] 3 D.L.R. 121 at 124, 23 C.B.R. 387, [1942] 2 W.W.R. 382 (Alta. C.A.), Ewing J.A. (Hawsen J.A. concurring). See USE AND ~.

OCCUPATIONAL DISEASE. 1. Any disease or illness or departure from normal health arising out of, or in the course of, employment in a workplace and includes an industrial disease. 2. A disease contracted out of or in the course of work and characteristic of that work or directly related to the risks peculiar to that work.

OCCUPATIONAL ILLNESS. A condition that results from exposure in a workplace to a physical, chemical or biological agent to the extent that the normal physiological mechanisms are affected and the health of the worker is impaired thereby and includes an industrial disease as defined in the Worker's Compensation Act. *Occupational Health and Safety Act*, R.S.O. 1990, c. 0.1, s. 1(1).

OCCUPATIONAL QUALIFICATION. See BONA FIDE ~.

OCCUPATIONAL REQUIREMENT. "... [A] requirement for the occupation, not a requirement limited to an individual. It must apply to all members of the employee group concerned because it is a requirement of general application concerning the safety of employees. The employee must meet the requirement in order to hold the employment. It is, by its nature, not susceptible to individual application." *Bhinder v. Canadian National Railway*, [1985] 2 S.C.R. 561 at 558-9, 9 C.C.E.L. 135, 17 Admin. L.R. 111, 86 C.L.L.C. 17,003, 7 C.H.R.R. D/3093, 23 D.L.R. (4th) 481, 63 N.R. 185, McIntyre J. See BONA FIDE ~.

OCCUPIER. *n.* 1. The person occupying any dwelling, and includes the person having the management or charge of any public or private institution where persons are cared for or confined and the proprietor, manager, keeper or other person in charge of a hotel, inn, apartment, lodging house or other dwelling or accommodation. *Vital Statistics acts*. 2. Includes: (i) a person who is in physical possession of the land; or (ii) a person who has responsibility for and control over the condition of land or the activities there carried on, or control over persons allowed to enter the land, notwithstanding that there is more than one occupier of the same land. 3. Includes a licensee, permittee or tenant of the owner. 4. A person who is qualified to maintain an action for trespass.

OCCUPIERS' LIABILITY. An area of the law of negligence concerning the duty owed to an intruder or a visitor by one who owns or occupies land. J.V. DiCastri, *Occupiers' Liability* (Vancouver: Burroughs/Carswell, 1980) at 1.

O.C.M. *abbr.* Ontario Corporation Manual.

OF COURSE. Describes a step in a proceeding or action which a court or its officers may not refuse provided that the proper formalities were observed.

OFFENCE. *n.* 1. "... The rights guaranteed by s. 11 of the Charter are available to persons prosecuted by the state for public offences involving punitive sanctions, i.e., criminal, quasi-criminal and regulatory offences, either federally or provincially enacted.... a true penal consequence which would attract the application of s. 11 is imprisonment or a fine which by its magnitude would appear to be imposed for the purpose of redressing the wrong done to society at large rather than to the maintenance of internal discipline within the limited sphere of activity." *R. v. Wigglesworth* (1987), 37 C.C.C. (3d) 385 at 397, 401, [1988] 1 W.W.R. 193, 61 Sask. R. 105, 60 C.R. (3d) 193, 81 N.R. 161, 28 Admin. L.R. 294,

[1987] 2 S.C.R. 541, 24 O.A.C. 321, 45 D.L.R. (4th) 235, 32 C.R.R. 219, Wilson J. (Dickson C.J.C., Beetz, McIntyre, Lamer and La Forest JJ. concurring). 2. "... [T]hree categories of offences ... 1. Offences in which mens rea, consisting of some positive state of mind such as intent, knowledge, or recklessness, must be proved by the prosecution either as an inference from the nature of the act committed, or by additional evidence. 2. Offences in which there is no necessity for the prosecution to prove the existence of mens rea; the doing of the prohibited act prima facie imports the offence, leaving it open to the accused to avoid liability by proving that he took all reasonable care. This involves consideration of what a reasonable man would have done in the circumstances. The defence will be available if the accused reasonably believed in a mistaken set of facts which, if true, would render the act or omission innocent, or if he took all reasonable steps to avoid the particular event. These offences may properly be called offences of strict liability. 3. Offences of absolute liability where it is not open to the accused to exculpate himself by showing that he was free of fault. Offences which are criminal in the true sense fall in the first categroy. Public welfare offences would prima facie be in the second category. They are not subject to the presumption of full mens rea. An offence of this type would fall in the first category only if such words as 'wilfully', 'with intent', 'knowingly' or 'intentionally' are contained in the statutory provision creating the offence. On the other hand, the principle that punishment should in general not be inflicted on those without fault applies. Offences of absolute liability would be those in respect of which the Legislature had made it clear that guilt would follow proof merely of the proscribed act. The overall regulatory pattern adopted by the Legislature, the subject matter of the legislation, the importance of the penalty, and the precision of the language used will be primary considerations in determining whether the offence falls into the third category." *R. v. Sault Ste. Marie (City)* (1978), 7 C.E.L.R. 53 at 70, [1978] 2 S.C.R. 1299, 3 C.R. (3d) 30, 21 N.R. 295, 40 C.C.C. (2d) 353, 85 D.L.R. (3d) 161, the court per Dickson J. 3. An offence created by an act or by any regulation or by-law made under an act or a municipal by-law. 4. The contravention of an enactment. See CRIMINAL ~; INCLUDED ~; INDICTABLE ~; INDICTABLE ONLY ~; LESSER ~; MILITARY ~; PARTIES TO AN ~; REGULATORY ~; SERIOUS PERSONAL INJURY ~; STRICT LIABILITY ~.

OFFENDER. *n.* A person who has been determined by a court to be guilty of an offence, whether on acceptance of a plea of guilty or on a finding of guilt. *Criminal Code*, R.S.C. 1985, c. C-46, s. 2 as amended by *Criminal Law Amendment Act*, R.S.C. 1985 (1st Supp.), c. 27, s. 2. See DANGEROUS ~; FIRST ~.

OFFENSIVE WEAPON. Has the same meaning as "weapon". *Criminal Code*, R.S.C. 1985, c. C-46, s. 2 as amended by *Criminal Law Amendment Act*, R.S.C. 1985 (1st Supp.), c. 27, s. 2.

OFFER. *n.* 1. One person's indication to another that she or he is willing to enter into a contract with that person on certain terms. G.H.L. Fridman, *The Law of Contract in Canada*, 2d ed. (Toronto: Carswell, 1986) at 24. 2. "... [A]n offer to sell or deliver a narcotic is complete once the offer is put forward by the accused in a serious manner intending to induce [the offeree] to act upon it and accept it as an offer." *R. v. Sherman*, [1977] 5 W.W.R. 283 at 283, 39 C.R.N.S. 255, 36 C.C.C. (2d) 207 (B.C. C.A.), the court per McFarlane J.A. 3. Includes an invitation to make an offer. 4. An invitation to treat. *Saskatchewan Human Rights Code*, S.S. 1979, v. S-24.1, s. 2. See CONDITIONAL ~; COUNTER ~.

OFFEREE. *n.* 1. A person to whom an offer is made. Acceptance will result in the formation of a contract. 2. A person to whom a take-over bid is made.

OFFEROR. *n.* 1. A person who

makes an offer. Acceptance of the offer by the other party will create a contract. 2. A person, other than an agent, who makes a take-over bid, and includes two or more persons who, directly or indirectly, (a) make take-over bids jointly or in concert; or (b) intend to exercise jointly or in concert voting rights attached to shares for which a take-over bid is made. 3. A person who makes an offer to acquire or an issuer bid. 4. (i) A person or company, other than an agent, who makes a take-over bid or an issuer bid; or (ii) an issuer who accepts from a security holder an offer to sell securities of the issuer other than debt securities that are not convertible into voting securities.

OFFICE. *n.* ". . . [A] position of duty, trust or authority in the public service or is a service under constituted authority. . . ." *R. v. Sheets* (1971), 15 C.R.N.S. 232 at 236, [1971] S.C.R. 614, [1971] 1 W.W.R. 672, 1 C.C.C. (2d) 508, 16 D.L.R. (3d) 221, the court per Fauteux C.J.C. See HEAD ~; LEGISLATIVE ASSEMBLY ~; POST ~; REGISTERED ~.

OFFICER. *n.* 1. A person holding the position entitling that person to a fixed or ascertainable stipend or remuneration and includes a judicial office, the office of a minister of the Crown, the office of a lieutenant governor, the office of a member of the Senate or House of Commons, a member of a legislative assembly or a member of a legislative or executive council and any other office the incumbent of which is elected by popular vote or is elected or appointed in a representative capacity, and also includes the position of a corporation director. 2. In relation to the Crown, includes a minister of the Crown and any servant of the Crown. 3. Includes a trustee, director, manager, treasurer, secretary or member of the board or committee of management of an insurer and a person appointed by the insurer to sue and be sued in its behalf. 4. A person employed in connection with the administration and management of a department. 5. The chairman and any vice-chairman of the board of directors, the president, any

vice-president, the secretary, any assistant secretary, the treasurer, any assistant treasurer, the general manager and any other person designated an officer by by-law or by resolution of the directors, and any other individual who performs functions for a company similar to those normally performed by an individual occupying any of those offices. 6. A commissioned or subordinate officer of the regular force. See ASSESSMENT ~; BRIBERY OF ~S; ~; CONCILIATION ~; CUSTOMS ~; PEACE ~; PROBATION ~; PUBLIC ~; RETURNING ~.

OFFICIAL. *n.* 1. Includes president, vice-president, secretary, treasurer, managing director, general manager, department manager, branch office manager and every person acting in a similar capacity whether so designated or not. 2. Any person employed in, or occupying a position of responsibility in, the service of Her Majesty and includes any person formerly so employed or formerly occupying such a position.

OFFICIAL. *adj.* Authorized; formal.

OFFICIAL COMMUNITY PLAN. A master plan of community development and land utilization prepared by a local planning authority and legally adopted by or on behalf of a municipality. *National Housing Act*, R.S.C. 1985, c. N-11, s. 2.

OFFICIAL EXAMINER. 1. The officer of a court who presides over examinations for discovery, cross-examinations on affidavits and other examinations. 2. A special examiner. G.D. Watson & C. Perkins, eds., *Holmested & Watson: Ontario Civil Procedure* (Toronto: Carswell, 1984) at CJA-122-23.

OFFICIAL GUARDIAN. One who acts as litigation guardian of minors or other people as required or authorized by acts, rules or court order and who superintends minors' interests, including their property when appointed under s. 89 of the Ontario Court of Justice Act. G.D. Watson & C. Perkins, eds., *Holmested & Watson: Ontario Civil Procedure* (Toronto: Carswell, 1984-)

at CJA-119 and 7-23.

OFFICIAL LANGUAGE. The English language or the French language. See COMMISSIONER OF ~S.

OFFICIALLY INDUCED ERROR. "The defence of 'officially induced error', exists where the accused, having adverted to the possibility of illegality, is led to believe, by the erroneous advice of an official, that he is not acting illegally." *R. v. Cancoil Thermal Corp.* (1986), 23 C.R.R. 257 at 265, 11 C.C.E.L. 219, 14 O.A.C. 225, 52 C.R. (3d) 188, 27 C.C.C. (3d) 295 (C.A.), the court per Lacourcière J.A.

OFFICIAL NOTICE. In proceedings before administrative tribunals, the equivalent of judicial notice. S.A. DeSmith, *Judicial Review of Administrative Action*, 4th ed. by J.M. Evans (London: Stevens, 1980) at 204.

OFFICIAL OPPOSITION. The largest minority political party which is prepared, in the event the government resigns, to assume office. A. Fraser, W.A. Dawson, & J. Holtby, eds., *Beauchesne's Rules and Forms of the House of Commons of Canada*, 6th ed. (Toronto: Carswell, 1989) at 55.

OFFICIAL PLAN. See OFFICAL COMMUNITY PLAN.

OFFICIAL RECEIVER. A person delegated by the Superintendent to accept debtors' assignments in bankruptcy and generally supervise trustees' administration of bankrupt estates. F. Bennett, *Receiverships* (Toronto: Carswell, 1985) at 3.

OFFICIAL REPORT. The publication of reports of cases directed by statute or a court itself.

OFFICIAL REPORT OF DEBATES. Hansard, a record of speeches made in the House of Commons and verbatim answers to written questions from the Order Paper. A. Fraser, W.A. Dawson & J. Holtby, eds., *Beauchesne's Rules and Forms of the House of Commons of Canada*, 6th ed. (Toronto: Carswell, 1989) at 300.

OFFICIAL TRUSTEE. The title for the public trustee in some provinces.

OFFICIO. See EX ~.

O.L.R. *abbr.* Ontario Law Reports, 1901-1931.

O.L.R.B. *abbr.* Ontario Labour Relations Board.

O.L.R.B. REP. *abbr.* Ontario Labour Relations Board Reports, 1974-.

O.M.B. *abbr.* Ontario Municipal Board.

O.M.B.R. *abbr.* Ontario Municipal Board Reports, 1973-.

OMBUDSMAN. *n.* A person appointed to consider and investigate complaints of members of the public concerning the administration of the government.

OMISSION. *n.* ". . . [M]eans the failure to do something which it is one's duty to do, or which a reasoanble man would do." *Greenlaw v. Canadian Northern Railway* (1913), 12 D.L.R. 402 at 405, [1913] 4 W.W.R. 847, 15 C.R.C. 329, 23 Man. R. 410, 24 W.L.R. 509 (C.A.), Perdue J.A. (Howell C.J.M., Cameron and Haggart JJ.A. concurring).

OMNIA PRAESUMUNTUR RITE ACTA ESSE. [L.] ". . . [W]here acts are of an official nature or require the concurrence of official persons a presumption arises in favour of their due execution." *Kane v. University of British Columbia* (1980), 31 N.R. 214 at 229, [1980] 2 S.C.R. 1105, 18 B.C.L.R. 124, [1980] 3 W.W.R. 125, 110 D.L.R. (3d) 311, Ritchie J. (dissenting).

OMNIA PRAESUMUNTUR RITE ET SOLEMNITER ESSE ACTA. [L.] All things are presumed to be done correctly and solemnly. See *Davidson v. Garrett* (1899), 30 O.R. 653 at 660, 5 C.C.C. 200 (C.A.), Rose J.A.

OMNIA PRAESUMUNTUR RITE ET SOLEMNITER ESSE DONEC PROBETUR IN CONTRARIUM. [L.] "[The] . . . presumption of the proper and due performance of administrative acts, until the contrary is proved . . ." *Ettershank v. Owen* (1981), 26 C.P.C. 228 at 233 (Ont.

ONE

Prov. Ct.), Vogelsang Prov. J.

ONE. See EVERY ~.

O.N.E. *abbr.* Office national de l'énergie.

ONT. CASE LAW DIG. *abbr.* Ontario Case Law Digest.

ONT. CORPS. LAW GUIDE *abbr.* Ontario Corporations Law Guide.

ONT. DIV. CT. *abbr.* Supreme Court of Ontario, High Court of Justice (Divisional Court).

ONT. ELEC. *abbr.* Ontario Election Cases, 1884-1900.

ONT. H.C. *abbr.* Supreme Court of Ontario, High Court of Justice (including Family Law Division).

ONT. PROV. CT. (CIV. DIV.). *abbr.* Ontario Provincial Court, Civil Division.

ONT. R.E.L.G. *abbr.* Ontario Real Estate Law Guide.

ONT. S.C. *abbr.* Supreme Court of Ontario (in Bankruptcy).

ONT. TAX R. *abbr.* Ontario Tax Reports.

ONUS. *n.* [L.] Burden. See CIVIL ~; CRIMINAL ~.

ONUS OF PROOF. ". . . [S]hould be restricted to the persuasive burden, since an issue can be put into play without being proven." *R. v. Schwartz* (1988), 45 C.C.C. (3d) 97 at 115, [1989] 1 W.W.R. 289, 66 C.R. (3d) 251, 99 N.R. 90, [1988] 2 S.C.R. 443, 56 Man. R. (2d) 92, 55 D.L.R. (4th) 1, Dickson C.J.C.

ONUS PROBANDI. [L. the burden of proving] "The strict meaning of the term onus probandi is this, that if no evidence is given by the party on whom the burden is cast, the issue must be found against him." *Barry v. Butlin* (1838), 2 Moo. P.C. 480 at 484, Parke B.

OP. CIT. *abbr.* [L.] Opere citato.

OPEN COURT. ". . . [T]he Court must be open to any who may present themselves for admission. The remoteness of the possibility of any public

attendance must never by judicial action be reduced to the certainty that there will be none." *McPherson v. McPherson*, [1936] 1 D.L.R. 321 at 327 (Alta. P.C.), Lord Blanesborough.

OPEN LISTING. Authority, given to a single or multiple agents, which usually implies or states that a commission will be paid only when a sale is consummated and in which the vendor usually retains a right to sell the property without reference to any agent. B.J. Reiter, R.C.B. Risk & B.N. McLellan, *Real Estate Law*, 3d ed. (Toronto: Emond Montgomery, 1986) at 74 and 75.

OPEN MARKET. A market of willing sellers and willing buyers.

OPERATE. *v.* 1. ". . . '[U]se' . . ." *Hudson v. Insurance Corp. of British Columbia* (1991), 2 C.C.L.I. (2d) 157 at 163, 57 B.C.L.R. (2d) 183, 83 D.L.R. (4th) 377, [1992] I.L.R. 1-2792, 8 B.C.A.C. 13, 17 W.A.C. 13 (C.A.), the court per Locke J.A. 2. ". . . [T]o superintend, or conduct, or manage, or direct." *O'Reilly v. Canada Accident & Fire Assurance Co.*, [1928] 4 D.L.R. 415 at 417, 62 O.L.R. 654 (H.C.), Kelly J. 3. To have the management and control.

OPERATING EXPENSE. An expenditure for administration or management.

OPERATION. *n.* ". . . [M]ay be given two distinct meanings – a wider meaning when used figuratively (as where a person 'operates' a fleet of vehicles by organizing a system of activity, without necessarily driving any of the vehicles himself), and a more narrow meaning restricted to the physical acts or omissions of the operator of a vehicle while it is being driven." *R. v. Twoyoungmen* (1979), 48 C.C.C. (2d) 550 at 559, 16 A.R. 413, [1979] 5 W.W.R. 712, 3 M.V.R. 186, 101 D.L.R. (3d) 598 (C.A.), the court per Prowse J.A. See DANGEROUS ~ OF AIRCRAFT.

OPERATIONAL. *adj.* Describes a ". . . function of government [which] . . . involves the use of governmental powers for the purpose of implementing, giving effect to or enforcing compliance with the general or specific goals of a policy decision." *Just v. British Columbia* (1985), 33 C.C.L.T. 49 at 52, 34 M.V.R. 124, 64 B.C.L.R. 349, [1985] 5 W.W.R. 570 (S.C.), McLachlin J.

OPERATIVE PART. In a mortgage, lease, conveyance or other formal instrument, the part which expresses the main object of that instrument.

OPERATIVE WORD. A word which contributes to the origin or transfer of an estate.

OPERATOR. *n.* 1. In relation to any work, undertaking or business, means the person having the charge, management or control of the work, undertaking or business, whether on that person's own account or as the agent of any other person. 2. A person who drives a motor vehicle on a public highway.

OPERE CITATO. [L.] In the work just cited.

OPINION. *n.* 1. The advice a counsel gives on the facts of a case. 2. A statement which may be admissible as evidence. The opinion of an expert witness is called expert evidence. 3. "... [S]tatement, tale or news is an expression which, taken as a whole and understood in context, conveys an assertion of fact or facts and not merely the expression of opinion.... Expression which makes a statement susceptible of proof and disproof is an assertion of fact; expression which merely offers an interpretation of fact which may be embraced or rejected depending on its cogency or normative appeal, is opinion." *R. v. Zundel* (1992), 75 C.C.C. (3d) 449 at 492, 95 D.L.R. (4th) 202, [1992] 2 S.C.R. 731, 140 N.R. 1, 56 O.A.C. 161, 16 C.R. (4th) 1, 10 C.R.R. (2d) 193, Cory and Iacobucci JJ. (dissenting) (Gonthier J. concurring). 4. "In section 742 [of the Criminal Code, S.C. 1892, c. 29] the word 'opinion' must be construed as meaning the decision or judgment of the court ..." *R. v. Viau* (1898), 2 C.C.C. 540 at 544, 29 S.C.R. 90, the court per Strong C.J. See CONCUR-

RING ~; DICTUM; DISSENTING ~; EXPERT EVIDENCE; MINORITY ~; OBITER DICTUM.

OPPOSITE PARTY. "... [A] party on the other side of the record to the applicant, or a party on the same side between whom and the applicant there is some right to be adjusted in the action...." *Rose & Laflamme Ltd. v. Campbell, Wilson & Strathdee Ltd.*, [1923] 2 W.W.R. 1067 at 1068-9, [1923] 4 D.L.R. 92, 17 Sask. L.R. 332 (C.A.), the court per Lamont J.A.

OPPOSITION. *n.* See LEADER OF THE ~; OFFICIAL ~.

OPPOSITION HOUSE LEADER. A member of the Official Opposition designated by its Leader to discuss with the Government Hosue Leader business arrangements for the House and to reach compromise on the length of debate on each item. A. Fraser, W.A. Dawson & J. Holtby, eds., *beauchesne's Rules and Forms of the House of Commons of Canada*, 6th ed. (Toronto: Carswell, 1989) at 56.

OPPRESSION. *n.* 1. The state from which a minority shareholder may claim relief. A majority exercises "... [I]ts authority in a manner 'burdensome, harsh, wrongful' ..." *Scottish Co-operative Wholesale Society v. Meyer*, [1959] A.C. 324 at 342, [1958] 3 All E.R. 66 (U.K. H.L.), Viscount Simonds. Suggests "... [A] lack of probity and fair dealing in the affairs of a company to the prejudice of some portion of its members." *Scottish Co-operative Wholesale Society v. Meyer*, [1959] A.C. 324 at 364, [1958] 3 All E.R. 66 (U.K. H.L.), Lord Keith. 2. "... [S]omething which tends to sap, and has sapped, that free will, which must exist before a confession is voluntary ..." *R. v. Priestly* (1965), 50 Cr. App. R. 183 in a note reported at 51 Cr. App. R. 1 (U.K.), Sachs J.

OPPRESSIVE. *adj.* "... [B]urdensome, harsh and wrongful ..." *Scottish Co-operative Wholesale Society v. Meyer*, [1959] A.C. 324 at 342, [1958] 3 All E.R. 66 (U.K. H.L.), Viscount Simonds.

OPTING OUT. This occurs when the legislative assembly of a province passes, by constitutional formula, a resolution dissenting from an amendment to the constitution so that the amendment has no effect in that province. P.W. Hogg, *Constitutional Law of Canada*, 3d ed. (Toronto: Carswell, 1992) at 75.

OPTION. *n.* 1. ". . . [A] right acquired by contract to accept or reject a present offer within a limited, or, it may be, a reasonable time in the future." *Paterson v. Houghton* (1909), 19 Man. R. 168 at 175 (C.A.), Cameron J.A. 2. A privilege, acquired by consideration, to call or to make delivery or both, within a certain time, of some specified article or stock at a certain price. 3. "The obligation to hold an offer open for acceptance, until the expiration of a specified time, . . ." *Day v. M.N.R.*, [1971] Tax A.B.C. 1050 at 1054, 71 D.T.C. 723. See COMMODITY FUTURES ~; COMMODITY ~; STOCK ~.

O.R. *abbr.* Ontario Reports, 1882-1900.

[ ] O.R. *abbr.* Ontario Reports, 1931-1973.

ORAL. *adj.* Conveyed by mouth; not in writing.

ORAL ARGUMENT. The presentation of an argument before a court.

ORAL CONTRACT. A contract whose terms are not written down.

ORAL EVIDENCE. Evidence given by a witness by spoken word.

ORAL QUESTION. A method of dealing with urgent matters recognized by the Standing Orders of Parliament. A. Fraser, W.A. Dawson & J. Holtby, eds., *Beauchesne's Rules and Forms of the House of Commons of Canada*, 6th ed. (Toronto: Carswell, 1989) at 119.

ORDER. *n.* 1. The direction of a court or judge which commands a party to do or not to do something in particular. 2. ". . . [A] proposal in the nature of an offer which invites, without more, some form of acceptance intended to lead to an obligation; that acceptance, according to the nature of the order, may be by promise or by some act as, say, the delivery of goods to a carrier." *Canadian Atlas Diesel Engines Co. v. McLeod Engines Co.*, [1952] 2 S.C.R. 122 at 129, [1952] 3 D.L.R. 513, Rand J. (dissenting) (Cartwright J. concurring). 3. ". . . [A] proper term for describing an act of the Governor-in-council by which he exercises a law-making power, whether the power exist as part of the prerogative or devolve upon him by statute." *Gray, Re* (1918), 57 S.C.R. 150 at 167, [1918] 3 W.W.R. 111, 42 D.L.R. 1, Duff J. 4. ". . . [A] ruling which a tribunal is specifically authorized to make by statute and which takes immediate effect to force the doing or not doing of something by somebody. . . ." *Canadian Pacific Air Lines Ltd. v. C.A.L.P.A.* (1988), 30 Admin. L.R. 277 at 281, 84 N.R. 81 (Fed. C.A.), the court per Hugessen J.A. See AFFILIATION ~; ANTON PILLER ~; "BULLOCK" ~; CHARGING ~; COMMITTAL ~; COMMUNITY SERVICE ~; COMPENSATION ~; COMPLIANCE ~; CONFIRMATION ~; CUSTODY ~; DECLARATORY ~; DETENTION ~; EXCLUSION ~; FAMILY ~; FINAL ~; FORECLOSURE ~; GARNISHEE ~; GUARDIANSHIP ~; HOLD ~; INTERIM ~; INTERLOCUTORY ~; MAINTENANCE ~; MONEY ~; PAYABLE TO ~; PREROGATIVE ~; RECEIVING ~; REGISTERED ~; SANDERSON ~; SHOW CAUSE ~; STANDING ~; STANDING, SESSIONAL AND SPECIAL ~; STOP ~; SUPPORT ~; VESTING ~; WINDING-UP ~.

ORDER FOR THE RECOVERY OF PERSONAL PROPERTY. See REPLEVIN.

ORDER IN COUNCIL. *var.* **ORDER-IN-COUNCIL.** An order made by the Lieutenant Governor or Governor General by and with the advice of the Executive or Privy Council, sometimes under statutory authority or sometimes by virtue of royal prerogative.

ORDER OF COURSE. An order,

made on an ex parte application, which a party is rightfully entitled to on that party's own statement and at that party's own risk.

ORDER OF THE DAY. A proceeding which may be considered only as the result of a previous order made in the House itself, except for a measure requiring immediate consideration such as the successive stages of a bill. A. Fraser, W.A. Dawson, & J. Holtby, eds., *Beauchesne's Rules and Forms of the House of Commons of Canada*, 6th ed. (Toronto: Carswell, 1989) at 110-11.

ORDER PAPER. The official agenda which lists every item which may be brought forward during that day's sitting. A. Fraser, W.A. Dawson & J. Holtby, eds., *Beauchesne's Rules and Forms of the House of Commons of Canada*, 6th ed. (Toronto: Carswell, 1989) at 300.

ORDER TO CONTINUE. An order obtained by someone entitled to carry on the proceedings or someone not already a party on whom the interest devolved, *e.g.*, the personal representative of a plaintiff who is deceased. G.D. Watson & C. Perkins, eds., *Holmested & Watson: Ontario Civil Procedure* (Toronto: Carswell, 1984) at 11-15.

ORDINANCE. *n.* 1. A municipal enactment. 2. The enactment of a territorial council. 3. Includes a proclamation bringing a statute into effect. *R. v. Markin* (1969), 2 D.L.R. (3d) 606 at 607, 5 C.R.N.S. 265, 67 W.W.R. 14, [1969] 3 C.C.C. 191 (B.C. S.C.), Seaton J.

ORDINARY RESOLUTION. A resolution passed by a majority of the votes cast by or on behalf of the shareholders who voted in respect of that resolution.

ORGANIZATION. *n.* See EMPLOYEE ~; EMPLOYERS' ~; NON-PROFIT ~; RE~.

ORIENTATION. See SEXUAL ~.

ORIGINAL. *n.* The document actually prepared, not a copy.

ORIGINAL COURT. In relation to any judgment means the court by which the judgment was given.

ORIGINAL DOCUMENT RULE. See BEST EVIDENCE RULE.

ORIGINAL EVIDENCE. Evidence offered to prove that a statement was made, either in a document or orally, not that the statement is true. P.K. McWilliams, *Canadian Criminal Evidence*, 3d ed. (Aurora: Canada Law Book, 1988) at 1-13.

ORIGINATING DOCUMENT. A writ of summons, counter-claim, petition for divorce, counter-petition for divorce or originating notice that initiates an application, an originating application or a statement of claim that commences a proceeding.

O.R. (2d). *abbr.* Ontario Reports (Second Series), 1974-1991.

O.R. (3d). *abbr.* Ontario Reports (Third Series), 1991-.

O.S. *abbr.* 1. Old Series. 2. Upper Canada, Queen's Bench Old Series, 1831-1844.

O.S.C.B. *abbr.* Ontario Securities Commission Bulletin.

OSGOODE HALL L.J. *abbr.* Osgoode Hall Law Journal.

OSTENSIBLE. *adj.* Apparent; professed.

OSTENSIBLE AUTHORITY. "... [A] legal relationship between the principal and the contractor created by a representation, made by the principal to the contractor, intended to be and in fact acted upon by the contractor, that the agent has authority to enter on behalf of the principal into a contract of a kind within the scope of the 'apparent' authority, so as to render the principal liable to perform any obligations imposed upon him by such contract. To the relationship so created the agent is a stranger. He need not be (although he generally is) aware of the existence of the representation but he must not purport to make the agreement as principal himself." *Freeman & Lockyer v. Buckhurst Park Properties (Magnal) Ltd.*, [1964] 2 Q.B. 480 at 503 (U.K. C.A.),

Diplock L.J.

OTTAWA L. REV. *abbr*. Ottawa Law Review (Revue de droit d'Ottawa).

OUST. *v*. To put out of possession.

OUSTER. *n*. Being put out of possession.

OUTER BAR. The area outside the bar where junior barristers plead in contrast to Queen's Counsel, who plead within the bar.

OVERDRAFT. *n*. "... [A]ny adverse balance in the customer's general account, whether this balance was created by charging up cheques of the customer or debiting past due bills and notes to that account. The resulting debit balance against the customer would be an 'overdraft,' ..." *Cox v. Canadian Bank of Commerce* (1911), 18 W.L.R. 568 at 574, 21 Man. R. 1 (C.A.), Perdue J.A.

OVERDUE. *adj*. Past the time a payment should be made.

OVERHOLDING TENANT. A person who was a tenant of premises and who does not vacate the premises after the tenancy has expired or been terminated. *Landlord and Tenant Amendment Act, 1991*, S.A. 1991, c. 18, s. 3.

OVERRIDE. *v*. Under section 33, for Parliament or a legislature to disregard a provision of the Charter included in section 2 or sections 7 to 15. This is accomplished by having the statute expressly declare that this statute will operate notwithstanding that provision. P.W. Hogg, *Constitutional Law of Canada*, 3d ed. (Toronto: Carswell, 1992) at 304-5.

OVERRULE. *v*. To set aside an earlier decision's authority.

OVERT. *adj*. Open. See MARKET ~.

OVERT ACT. An act done in the open.

OWE. *v*. Of a sum of money, to be under the obligation to pay it.

OWING. *adj*. 1. Due. *Smith v. McIntosh* (1893), 3 B.C.R. 26 at 28 (S.C.), Crease J. 2. Required to be paid by

obligation. C.R.B. Dunlop, *Creditor-Debtor Law in Canada* (Toronto: Carswell, 1981) at 245.

O.W.N. *abbr*. Ontario Weekly Notes, 1909-1932.

[ ] O.W.N. *abbr*. Ontario Weekly Notes, 1933-1962.

OWNED. *adj*. 1. Having an interest in. 2. Beneficially owned.

OWNER. *n*. 1. "... [H]as no definite meaning. It may refer to owners having either the whole or partial interests. It is not a legal term but must be understood from its ordinary use. It may be taken to mean any parties who have any interest. ..." *Royal Bank v. Port Royal Pulp & Paper Co.*, [1937] 4 D.L.R. 254 at 257, 12 M.P.R. 219 (N.B. C.A.), the court per Baxter C.J. 2. "Ordinarily the word 'owner' of land means the person who holds it in fee simple, though it may be used to include one who is not the actual owner or who has an interest less than a fee simple. In the latter cases the subject matter dealt with, and the context in connection with which it is used, extend its ordinary meaning to cover other situations in particular instances; but it does not (unless possibly in special connection) mean a person without any interest in the land who is neither occupant nor in possession." *Springhill (Town) v. McLeod* (1929), 60 N.S.R. 272 at 277, [1929] 1 D.L.R. 882 (C.A.), Graham J.A. (Harris C.J., Chisholm, Jenks and Paton JJ.A. concurring). See BENEFICIAL ~; LIMITED ~; PART-~; REGISTERED ~.

OWNERSHIP. *n*. The most far-ranging right in rem the law allows to a person: to deal with something to the exclusion of everyone else or of everyone except one or more designated people. See BENEFICIAL ~.

O.W.R. *abbr*. Ontario Weekly Reporter, 1902-1916.

OYER. [Fr.] To hear.

OYER AND TERMINER. [Fr.] To hear and decide.

OYEZ. [Fr. hear ye] Pay attention.

P

P. *abbr.* President, chief judge or chief justice of a court (Exchequer Court in Canada).

[ ] P. *abbr.* Law Reports, Probate, 1891-1971.

PACT. *n.* Bargain; contract; covenant.

PACTA SUNT SERVANDA. [L.] Contracts should be kept.

PACTUM. See NUDUM ~.

PACTUM DE CONTRAHENDO. [L.] An agreement to negotiate or complete a contract.

PAID UP. *var.* **PAID-UP.** When applied to the capital of a company, means capital stock or shares on which there remains no liability, actual or contingent, to the issuing company.

PAIN AND SUFFERING. Every kind of emotional distress which a victim feels and which was caused by a personal injury. K.D. Cooper-Stephenson & I.B. Saunders, *Personal Injury Damages in Canada* (Toronto: Carswell, 1981) at 351.

PANEL. *n.* 1. A page or schedule which contains the names of jurors called to serve. 2. A list of consultants or authoritative people from whom one might seek a decision or advice. See JURY ~.

PAPER. See CHATTEL ~; COMMAND ~S; COMMERCIAL ~; EXCHEQUER BILL ~; NOTICE ~; ORDER ~; WHITE ~.

PAR. *n.* State of equality; equal value. See ABOVE ~; BELOW ~.

PARAGRAPH. *n.* A section or part of an affidavit, contract, pleading, statute or will.

PARAMOUNT. *adj.* Superior; of the highest jurisdiction.

PARAMOUNTCY. *n.* "There can be a domain in which provincial and Dominion legislation may overlap in which case neither legislation will be ultra vires if the field is clear, but if the field is not clear and the two legislations meet the Dominion legislation must prevail ..." *Reference re Fisheries Act, 1914 (Canada)*, (*sub nom. Canada (Attorney General) v. British Columbia (Attorney General)*) [1930] A.C. 111 at 118, [1929] 3 W.W.R. 449, [1930] 1 D.L.R. 194 (P.C.), Lord Tomlin. See FEDERAL ~.

PARCEL. *n.* Any lot, block or other area in which land is held or into which land is divided or subdivided.

PARCEL OF LAND. 1. A lot or block within a registered plan of subdivision. 2. A quarter section of land or any smaller area owned by one person. 3. Area owned by one person, or by more persons than one as tenants in common or as joint tenants.

PARCENER. *n.* A person who, with one or more others, equally shares an estate inherited from a common ancestor.

PARDON. *v.* For the Crown to release a person from the punishment that person incurred for some offence.

PARDON. *n.* A pardon granted by the Governor-in-Council under subsection

4(8). *Criminal Records Act*, R.S.C. 1985, c. C-47, s. 2.

PARENS PATRIAE. [L.] The role of the Crown as superintendent of charities, children and mentally incompetent persons. S.A. DeSmith, *Judicial Review of Administrative Action*, 4th ed. by J.M. Evans (London: Stevens, 1980) at 432.

PARENT. *n.* 1. The father or mother of a child, whether or not the child is born in wedlock, and includes an adoptive parent. *Citizenship Regulations*, C.R.C., c. 400, s. 2. 2. "... [T]he word 'parent' has no precise meaning in the law of companies. One can readily understand if one company is a wholly owned subsidiary of another company that the latter could be said to be the parent company. But that does not necessarily mean that the parent company controls the activities of the subsidiary.... Before the parent is liable in law for the acts and omissions of the subsidiary, one must show that control existed and was exercised." *Hunt v. T & N plc* (1989), 38 C.P.C. (2d) 1 at 3-4, 41 B.C.L.R. (2d) 269 (C.A.), the court per Hutcheon J.A. See CHILD; DEPENDENT ~.

PARENT COMPANY. A company is deemed to be another's parent company if, but only if, that other is its subsidiary.

PARENT CORPORATION. A corporation that controls another corporation.

PARENTIS. See IN LOCO ~.

PARI DELICTO. See IN PARI DELICTO.

PARI PASSU. [L.] Equally; with no preference.

PARLIAMENT. *n.* 1. The Queen, the House of Commons and the Senate. *Constitution Act, 1867* (U.K.), 30 & 31 Vict., c. 3, s. 17. 2. The Parliament of Canada. *Interpretation Act*, R.S.C. 1985, c. I-21, s. 35. 3. In Canada, this title is limited to the federal parliament. P.W. Hogg, *Constitutional Law of Canada*, 3d ed. (Toronto: Carswell, 1992) at 105. 4. A period between the Governor General's summons after a general election and dissolution by the Crown before a general election which does not exceed 5 years. A. Fraser, W.A. Dawson & J. Holtby, eds., *Beauchesne's Rules and Forms of the House of Commons of Canada*, 6th ed. (Toronto: Carswell, 1989) at 65. See ACT OF ~; CONTEMPT OF ~; FEDERAL ~; IMPERIAL ~.

PARLIAMENTARY AGENT. A person who promotes private bills and conducts proceedings upon petitions against such bills. A. Fraser, W.A. Dawson & J. Holtby, eds., *Beauchesne's Rules and Forms of the House of Commons of Canada*, 6th ed. (Toronto: Carswell, 1989) at 296.

PARLIAMENTARY COMMITTEE. A committee of the whole House, a standing or joint committee.

PARLIAMENTARY COUNSEL. See LAW CLERK AND ~.

PARLIAMENTARY GOVERNMENT. Government in which Prime Minister or Premier selects members of her or his own party elected to Parliament and perhaps others to be Ministers of the Crown. This group collectively form the Cabinet, the policy-making arm of government. The Ministers and Cabinet are responsible to Parliament for the conduct of the government. The government remains in power so long as it has the confidence of a majority of the House of Commons or the Legislature. In theory, the Privy Council or Executive Council advises the formal head of state (the Governor General or Lieutenant Governor) though, in fact, the Committee of Council, known as the Cabinet, carries out this function in most situations.

PARLIAMENTARY PRIVILEGE. Rights required to discharge their functions which exceed rights possessed by other individuals or bodies enjoyed by each House collectively as a representative part of the High Court of Parliament and by each member of each House. A. Fraser, W.A. Dawson & J. Holtby, eds., *Beauchesne's Rules and Forms of the House of Commons of Canada*, 6th ed. (Toronto: Carswell,

1989) at 11.

PAROL. *adj.* Verbal, oral.

PAROL AGREEMENT. An oral agreement.

PAROL CONTRACT. An oral contract.

PAROLE. *n.* Authority granted to an inmate to be at large during the inmate's term of imprisonment.

PAROLE. *adj.* [Fr.] Oral.

PAROLE BOARD. See NATIONAL ~; PROVINCIAL ~.

PAROLED INMATE. A person to whom parole has been granted.

PAROLEE. *n.* An inmate who has been granted parole.

PAROL EVIDENCE. Oral testimony by a witness.

PAROL EVIDENCE RULE. "... [I]f there be contract which has been reduced into writing, verbal evidence is not allowed to be given of what passed between the parties, either before the written instrument was made, or during the time that it was in the state of preparation, so as to add to or subtract from, or in any manner to vary or qualify the written contract; but after the agreement has been reduced into writing, it is competent to the parties, at any time before breach of it, by a new contract not in writing, either altogether to waive, dissolve, or annul the former agreements, or in any manner to add to, or subtract from, or vary or qualify the terms of it, and thus to make a new contract; which is to be proved, partly by the written agreement, and partly by the subsequent verbal terms engrafted upon what will be thus left of the written agreement...." *Goss v. Lord Nugent* (1833), 5 B. & Ad. 58 at 64-5, 110 E.R. 713 at 716 (U.K.), Denman C.J.

PART. *n.* A class into which parties to a formal instrument are divided according to their interests or estates in the subject-matter. See COUNTER~; OPERATIVE ~.

PARTIAL LOSS. "... [O]ne in which the insurers are liable to pay an amount less than that insured for damage happening to the subject, or expense incurred and occasioned by the perils insured against." *Mowat v. Boston Marine Insurance Co.* (1895), 33 N.B.R. 108 at 121 (C.A.), Tuck J.A.

PARTICEPS CRIMINIS. [L.] "... [O]ne who shares or co-operates in a criminal offence...." *R. v. Morris*, (1979) 10 C.R. (3d) 259 at 281, [1979] 2 S.C.R. 1041, 26 N.B.R. (2d) 273, 55 A.P.R. 273, 27 N.R. 313, 47 C.C.C. (2d) 257, 99 D.L.R. (3d) 420, Spence J. (dissenting) (Laskin C.J.C., Dickson and Estey JJ. concurring).

PARTICIPATE. *v.* "... [T]o take part or share ..." *Graham, Re*, [1945] 3 W.W.R. 713 at 717, [1946] 1 D.L.R. 357 (Alta.C.A.), the court per Harvey C.J.A.

PARTICULAR LIEN. A lien which only attaches to the debtor's actual property on which materials and labour have been expended and attaches only as long as the article stays in the lien claimant's possession. D.N. Macklem & D.I. Bristow, *Construction and Mechanics' Liens in Canada*, 5th ed. (Toronto: Carswell, 1985) at 579.

PARTICULARS. *n.* 1. In a pleading, the details of an allegation which are ordered (1) to define any issues; (2) to prevent surprise; (3) to enable the parties to get ready for trial and (4) to facilitate a hearing. *Fairbairn v. Sage* (1925), 56 O.L.R. 462 at 470 (C.A.), Ferguson J.A. 2. " The function of particulars in a criminal trial is twofold. Primarily their function is to give such exact and reasonable information to the accused respecting the charge against him as will enable him to establish fully his defence. The second purpose is to facilitate the adminstration of justice: ..." *R. v. Canadian General Electric Co.* (1974), 16 C.P.R. (2d) 175 at 184, 17 C.C.C. (2d) 433 (Ont. H.C.), Pennell J. 3. "... [G]iven to supplement paragraphs of a statement of claim or a defense as the case may be and should stand by themselves in connection with the paragraphs which they particularize without any reference to the evidence supporting them." *Cercast*

PARTIES

Inc. v. Shellcast Foundaries Inc. (No. 3) (1973), 9 C.P.R. (2d) 18 at 29, [1973] F.C. 28 (T.D.), Walsh J.

PARTIES. *n.* 1. In any act or deed, the people concerned; litigants. 2. (a) In relation to collective bargaining or arbitration of a dispute, the employer and a bargaining agent, and (b) in relation to a grievance, the employer and the employee who presented the grievance. 3. (a) In relation to the entering into, renewing or revising of a collective agreement and in relation to a dispute, the employer and the bargaining agent that acts on behalf of his employees; (b) in relation to a difference relating to the interpretation, application, administration or alleged contravention of a collective agreement, the employer and the bargaining agent; and (c) in relation to a complaint to the Board under this Part, the complainant and any person or organization against whom or which a complaint is made. *Canada Labour Code*, R.S.C. 1985, c. L-2, s. 3. See CHANGE OF ~; JOINDER OF ~; PARTY.

PARTIES TO AN OFFENCE. 1. Every one is a party to an offence who actually commits it, does or omits to do anything for the purpose of aiding any person to commit it, or abets any person in committing it. *Criminal Code*, R.S.C. 1985, c. C-46, s. 21. 2. Each person who is one of two or more persons who formed an intention in common to carry out an unlawful purpose when an offence is committed by any one of them in carrying out the unlawful purpose and the person knew or ought to have known that the commission of the offence would be a probable consequence of carrying out the common purpose is a party to any offence. *Criminal Code*, R.S.C. 1985, c. C-46, s. 21.

PARTITION. *n.* 1. Division. 2. A proceeding involving dividing real property, previously owned by tenants in common or joint tenants, into different parts.

PARTITION OR SALE. The name of a proceeding concerning division of land.

PARTNER. *n.* A member of a partnership. See GENERAL ~; NOMINAL ~; SILENT ~.

PARTNERSHIP. *n.* " ... [T]here should be some common profit or gain to be derived from it. Whether or not the element of division or distribution of the common profit or gain among the members is an essential, need not be discussed; but there must be ... a community of interest in the benefits accruing from the joint activity of the partners. If that community of interest is lacking, there is no partnership...." *Ottawa Lumbermen's Credit Bureau v. Swan*, [1923] 4 D.L.R. 1157 at 1163, 53 O.L.R. 135 (C.A.), Orde J.A. See LIMITED ~.

PART-OWNER. *n.* A person entitled to property in common, jointly or in coparcenary.

PART PAYMENT. " ... [P]ayment ... made on account of a greater debt, ..." *Stark v. Sommerville* (1918), 41 D.L.R. 496 at 496, 41 O.L.R. 591 (C.A.), the court per Meredith C.J.C.P.

PART PERFORMANCE. In relation to a contract, partial completion.

PARTY. *n.* 1. Every person served with notice of, or entitled to attend any proceeding, even if that person is not named in the record. 2. A political party registered under an Election Act. 3. A person whose rights will be varied or affected by the exercise of a statutory power or by an act or thing done pursuant to that power. 4. A person bound by a collective agreement, or involved in a dispute. See ACCOMMODATION ~; ADVERSE ~; OPPOSITE ~; PARTIES; POLITICAL ~; SECURED ~.

PARTY-AND-PARTY COSTS. *var.* **PARTY AND PARTY COSTS.** 1. "The fundamental principle of party and party costs has always been that they are given as an indemnity to the party entitled to them." *Kendall v. Hunt (No. 2)* (1979), 12 C.P.C. 264 at 267, 16 B.C.L.R. 295, 106 D.L.R. (3d) 277 (C.A.), Craig J.A. 2. Costs in keeping with the tariffs and practice of a court which one litigant pays to another.

They are meant to reimburse the party who receives them for the costs that party must pay a solicitor. M.M. Orkin, *The Law of Costs*, 2d ed. (Aurora: Canada Law Book, 1987) at 1-2 and 2-1.

PARTY UNDER DISABILITY. A general term which includes those declared by a court incapable of managing their affairs, minors, absentees and mental incompetents whether or not declared so by a court. G.D. Watson & C. Perkins, eds., *Holmested & Watson: Ontario Civil Procedure* (Toronto: Carswell, 1984) at 7-10.

PARTY WALL. 1. "... [M]ay ... be used in four different senses. First, a wall of which the two adjoining owners are tenants in common ... that is the most common and the primary meaning of the term. [Secondly,] a wall divided longitudinally into two strips, one belonging to each of the neighbouring owners ... thirdly, ... a wall which belongs entirely to one of the adjoining owners, but is subject to an easement or right in the other to have it maintained as a dividing wall between the two tenements; [and fourthly,] a wall divided longitudinally into two moieties, each moiety being subject to a cross easement in favour of the owner of the other moiety." *Watson v. Gray* (1880), 14 Ch. D. 192 at 195 (U.K.), Fry J. 2. A wall jointly owned and jointly used by 2 parties under easement agreement or by right in law, and erected at or upon a line separating 2 parcels of land each of which is, or is capable of being, a separate real-estate entity. *Building Code Act*, R.R.O. 1980, Reg. 87, s. 1.

PAR VALUE. 1. The face value of a share or security, as opposed to its market or selling price. 2. An arbitrary value placed on a share at the time of issue. S.M. Beck *et al.*, *Cases and Materials on Partnerships and Canadian Business Corporations* (Toronto: Carswell, 1983) at 784.

PASS. *v.* 1. To transfer or to be transferred. 2. To change hands. *Wagstaff, Re*, [1941] O.R. 71 at 77, [1941]

D.L.R. 108 (H.C.), Roach J. 3. For a legislature to give final approval to an act. 4. To bring into court an account for approval. 5. Of a by-law, to deliberate on the merits of a proposal framed as a draft by-law and finally to adopt it as the law of the municipal corporation. A by-law is considered passed when the enacting is finished and the presiding officer announces that the motion for final reading has been carried. I.M. Rogers, *The Law of Canadian Municipal Corporations*, 2d ed. (Toronto: Carswell, 1971-) at 458.

PASSAGE. *n.* 1. "... [C]oming into operation...." *Winnipeg (City) v. Brock* (1911), 20 Man. R. 669 at 683, 18 W.L.R. 28 (C.A.), Perdue J.A. (Cameron J.A. concurring). 2. The easement to pass over a body of water.

PASS AN ACCOUNT. For a court to approve an account.

PASS BOOK. See BANK ~.

PASS OFF. 1. "... [T]he gist of the action of 'passing off' is that the defendant is attempting to sell its wares, services or business under a description which would mislead customers of the plaintiff into thinking that they were buying the plaintiff's wares or doing business with the plaintiff." *Westfair Foods Ltd. v. Jim Pattison Industries Ltd.* (1990), 30 C.P.R. (3d) 174 at 179, 45 B.C.L.R. (2d) 253, 68 D.L.R. (4th) 481, [1990] 5 W.W.R. 484 (C.A.), the court per Wallace J.A. 2. "To succeed in a passing-off action, the plaintiff must first establish that there is a distinguishing feature to his goods and that his goods are known and have acquired a reputation by reason of that distinguishing feature. Secondly, the plaintiff must show that the defendant passed off his goods for those of the plaintiff: ..." *Ayerst, McKenna & Harrison Inc. v. Apotex Inc.* (1983), 72 C.P.R. (2d) 57 at 66, 41 O.R. (2d) 366, 146 D.L.R. (3d) 93 (C.A.), the court per Cory J.A.

PASSPORT. *n.* A document issued by or under the authority of the Secretary of State for External Affairs for the purpose of identifying the holder thereof. *Criminal Code*, R.S.C. 1985, c. C-46, s. 57(5). See FORGERY OF ~;

UTTERING FORGED ~.

PAST CONSIDERATION. Consideration for services already performed which do not support a promise or create a contract which may be enforced. G.H.L. Fridman, *The Law of Contract in Canada*, 2d ed. (Toronto: Carswell, 1986) at 96.

PAT. APP. BD. *abbr.* Patent Appeal Board.

PAT. COMMR. *abbr.* Commissioner of Patents.

PATENT. *n.* 1. During its term, an absolute monopoly which prohibits anyone other than the patentee using the new manufacture which the patentee invented. H.G. Fox, *The Canadian Law of Copyright and Industrial Designs*, 2d ed. (Toronto: Carswell, 1967) at 4. 2. Letters patent for an invention. *Patent Act*, R.S.C. 1985, c. P-4, s. 2. 3. A grant from the Crown in fee simple or for a less estate under the Great Seal. See LETTERS ~.

PATENT AGENT. Any person or firm whose name is entered on the Register. *Patent Rules*, C.R.C., c. 1250, s. 2.

PATENT AMBIGUITY. Something clearly doubtful in the text of an instrument.

PATENT DEFECT. Something which an unsophisticated purchaser can discover on cursory inspection. B.J. Reiter, B.N. McLellan & P.M. Perell, *Real Estate Law*, 4th ed. (Toronto: Emond Montgomery, 1992) at 247.

PATENTEE. *n.* 1. The person for the time being entitled to the benefit of a patent. *Patent Act*, R.S.C. 1985, c. P-4, s. 3. 2. Includes grantee. *Crown Lands Act*, R.S.M. 1970, c. C340, s. 2.

PATENTLY UNREASONABLE. "Refers to an error in interpretation of 'a provision which an administrative tribunal is required to apply within the limits of its jurisdiction.' This kind of error amounts to a fraud on the law or a deliberate refusal to comply with it. As Dickson J. (as he then was) described it, speaking for the whole court in *Canadian Union of Public Employees Local 963 v. New Brunswick Liquor Corporation*, [1979] 2 S.C.R. 227 at p. 237, it is '. . . so patently unreasonable that its construction cannot be rationally supported by the relevant legislation and demands intervention by the court upon review . . .' An error of this kind is treated as an act which is done arbitrarily or in bad faith and is contrary to the principles of natural justice." *Syndicat des Employés de production du Québec et de l'Acadie v. Canada (Labour Relations Board)*, [1984] 2 S.C.R. 412 at 420, 14 Admin. L.R. 72, 84 C.L.L.C. 14,069, 55 N.R. 321, 14 D.L.R. (4th) 457, the court per Beetz J.

PATERNITY. *n.* The relationship of a father.

PATERNITY AGREEMENT. Where a man and a woman who are not spouses enter into an agreement for: (a) the payment of the expenses of prenatal care and birth in respect of a child; (b) the support of a child; or (c) burial expenses of the child or mother, on the application of a party to the agreement or a children's aid society made to a provincial court (family division) or the Unified Family Court, the court may incorporate the agreement in an order, and Part II applies to the order in the same manner as if it were an order for support made under that Part. *Family Law Reform Act*, R.S.O. 1980, c. 152, s. 58.

PATR. ELEC. CAS. *abbr.* Patrick, Contested Elections (Ont.), 1824-1849.

PATRIATION. *n.* Terminating the United Kingdom Parliament's authority over Canada by adopting domestic amending procedures. P.W. Hogg, *Constitutional Law of Canada*, 3d ed. (Toronto: Carswell, 1992) at 58-9.

PATRICIDE. *n.* 1. Killing a father. 2. One who kills a father.

PAWN. *n.* A pledge, a kind of bailment in which a debtor delivers goods to the creditor for the creditor to keep until the debt is discharged. E.L.G. Tyler & N.E. Palmer, eds., *Crossley Vaines' Personal Property*, 5th ed. (London: Butterworths, 1973) at 459.

PAWNBROKER. *n.* A person whose business is taking any article as a pawn or pledge for the repayment of money lent against that article.

PAY. *v.* ". . . [M]eans primarily to discharge a debt by money." *McIntosh, Re*, [1923] 2 W.W.R. 605 at 607 (Man. K.B.), Dysart J.

PAY. *n.* 1. Remuneration in any form. 2. Wages due or paid to an employee and compensation paid or due to an employee but does not include deductions from wage that may lawfully be made by an employer. See EQUAL ~ FOR EQUAL WORK; TAKE-HOME ~.

PAYABLE. *adj.* Describes a sum of money when someone is obliged to pay it.

PAYABLE TO ORDER. Describes a cheque or bill of exchange payable to the person named on it or in any way directed by an endorsement.

PAY EQUITY. A compensation practice which is based primarily on the relative value of the work performed, irrespective of the gender of employees, and includes the requirement that no employer shall establish or maintain a difference between the wages paid to male and female employees, employed by that employer, who are performing work of equal or comparable value. *The Pay Equity Act*, S.M. 1985-86, c. 21, s. 1.

PAYMENT. *n.* 1. Remuneration in any form. 2. ". . . [A] sum expressly applicable in reduction of the particular demand on which it is made; that demand is therefore reduced by the extent of the payment. . . ." *Miron v. McCabe* (1867), 4 P.R. 171 at 174 (H.C.), Wilson J. 3. Includes the set-off of any amount against indebtedness incurred. See BALLOON ~; BLENDED ~; CANADIAN ~S ASSOCIATION; COVENANT FOR ~; DOWN ~; EQUALIZATION ~; PART ~.

PAYMENT INTO COURT. The deposit of money with a court official in connection with proceedings commenced in that court.

P.C. *abbr.* 1. Privy Council. 2. Privy Councillor. 3. Police constable.

P.D. *abbr.* Law Reports, Probate, Divorce and Admiralty Division, 1875-1890.

PEACE. *n.* 1. Quiet behaviour towards the sovereign and the sovereign's subjects. 2. The condition of international relations in which a nation does not bring military force against another. See BREACH OF THE ~; CLERK OF THE ~; JUSTICE OF THE ~; KEEP THE ~.

PEACE BOND. A written promise made to a court to keep the peace.

PEACE OFFICER. 1. Includes (a) a mayor, warden, reeve, sheriff, deputy sheriff, sheriff's officer and justice of the peace; (b) a warden, deputy warden, instructor, keeper, jailer, guard and any other officer or permanent employee of a prison; (c) a police officer, police constable, bailiff, constable, or other person employed for the preservation and maintenance of the public peace or for the service or execution of civil process; (d) an officer or a person having the powers of a customs or excise officer when performing any duty in the administration of the Customs Act, chapter C-40 of the Revised Statutes of Canada, 1970 or the Excise Act; (e) a person appointed or designated as a fishery officer under the Fisheries Act when performing any of his duties or functions pursuant to that Act; (f) the pilot in command of an aircraft (i) registered in Canada under regulations made under the Aeronautics Act; or (ii) leased without crew and operated by a person who is qualified under regulations made under the Aeronautics Act to be registered as owner of an aircraft registered in Canada under those regulations, while the aircraft is in flight; and (g) officers and men of the Canadian Forces who are (i) appointed for the purposes of section 156 of the National Defence Act; or (ii) employed on duties that the Governor in Council, in regulations made under the National Defence Act for the purposes of this paragraph, has prescribed to be of such a kind as to necessitate that the officers and men performing them have the powers of peace officers. *Criminal Code,* R.S.C. 1985, c. C-46, s. 2. 2. A police officer, police constable or other person employed for the preservation and maintenance of the public peace. 3. A member of the Royal Canadian Mounted Police or a member of a municipal police force.

PEACE, ORDER AND GOOD GOVERNMENT. 1. "[Under s. 91 of the Constitution Act, 1867 (30 & 31 Vict.), c. 3 includes] ... federal competence [based] on the existence of a national emergency; ... federal competence [may arise] because the subject-matter did not exist at the time of Confederation and clearly cannot be put into the class of matters of merely local or private nature; [or] ... Where the subject-matter 'goes beyond local or provincial concern or interests and must, from its inherent nature be the concern of the Dominion as a whole' ..." *Labatt Breweries of Canada Ltd. v. Canada (Attorney General)* (1979), 9 B.L.R. 181 at 208, [1980] 1 S.C.R. 914, 30 N.R. 496, Estey J. (Martland, Dickson, Beetz and Pratte JJ. concurring). 2. "... [T]he true test must be found in the real subject matter of the legislation; if it is such that it goes beyond local or provincial concern or interests and must from its inherent nature be the concern of the Dominion as a whole ... then it will fall within the competence of the Dominion Parliament as a matter affecting the peace, order and good government of Canada [contained in s. 91 of the Constitution Act, 1867 (30 & 31 Vict.), c. 3], though it may in another aspect touch on matters specially reserved to the provincial legislature." *Reference re Canada Temperance Act,* [1946] A.C. 193 at 205, 1 C.R. 229, [1946] 2 W.W.R. 1, 85 C.C.C. 225, [1946] 2 D.L.R. 1 (Ont. P.C.), the board per Viscount Simon. See RESIDUARY POWER.

PECUNIARY. *adj.* Concerning money.

PECUNIARY LOSS. 1. The loss of earnings, profit, future cost of care or other expenses. K.D. Cooper-Stephenson & I.B. Saunders, *Personal Injury Damages in Canada* (Toronto: Carswell, 1981) at 29. 2. "... As applied to a dependent's loss from death the term has been interpreted to mean 'the reasonable expectation of pecuniary benefit from the continued life of the deceased' ... In a later decision, Mason v. Peters (1982), 139 D.L.R. (3d) 104 ... Robins J.A. ... said at p. 109: 'Pecuniary loss may consist of the support, services or contributions which the claimant might reasonably have expected to receive from the deceased had he not been killed.' Thus, the courts have recognized that the child of a deceased mother may recover, as pecuniary loss, an amount to compensate for the loss of a mother's care and moral training ..." *Harris Estate v. Roy's Midway Transport Ltd.* (1989), 60 D.L.R. (4th) 99 at 103, 50 C.C.L.T. 67 (N.B. C.A.), the court per Stratton C.J.N.B. 3. Does not include loss arising from pain and suffering, physical inconvenience and discomfort, social discredit, injury to reputation, mental suffering, injury to feelings, loss of amenities and of expectation of life or loss of society of spouse or child.

PEDESTRIAN. *n.* A person afoot.

PEER. *n.* 1. An equal, a person of the same rank. 2. In England, a member of the House of Lords.

P.E.I. *abbr.* Haszard & Warburton's Reports, 1850-1872.

PENAL. *adj.* 1. "... [A]n accurate and convenient way of describing provincial 'criminal' proceedings." *Trumbley v. Metropolitan Toronto Police Force (sub nom. Trumbley v. Fleming)* (1986), 21 Admin. L.R. 232 at 254, 55 O.R. (2d) 570, 29 D.L.R. (4th) 557, 24 C.R.R. 333, 15 O.A.C. 279 (C.A.), the court per Morden J.A. 2. Inflicting punishment.

PENAL INSTITUTION. Includes jail, prison, lockup, or adult reformatory institution. *Court and Penal Institutions Act,* R.S.N.S. 1967, c. 67, s. 37.

PENAL LAW. Law imposing a penalty for breach of a public right. J.G. McLeod, *The Conflict of Laws* (Calgary: Carswell, 1983) at 207.

PENAL STATUTE. A law which imposes a penalty or punishment for the offence committed.

PENALTY. *n.* 1. "... [A] sum of money the purpose of which is not to compensate, but to discourage certain conduct." *Bank of Nova Scotia v. Dunphy Leasing Enterprises Ltd.* (1987), 51 Alta. L.R. (2d) 324 at 328, 77 A.R. 181, 38 D.L.R. (4th) 575 (C.A.), Prowse J.A. 2. (a) A fine; or (b) a term of imprisonment including a term of imprisonment in default of payment or satisfaction of a fine. 3. "... [T]he payment of a stipulated sum on breach of the contract, irrespective of the damage sustained." *Canadian General Electric Co. v. Canadian Rubber Co.* (1915), 27 D.L.R. 294 at 295, 52 S.C.R. 349, Fitzpatrick C.J.

PENDENTE LITE. [L.] During litigation.

PENITENTIARY. *n.* An institution or facility of any description, including all lands connected therewith, that is operated by the Service for the custody, treatment or training of persons sentenced or committed to penitentiary, and includes any place declared to be a penitentiary pursuant to subsection 3(1) or (2). *Penitentiary Act*, R.S.C. 1985, c. P-5, s. 2.

PENOLOGY. *n.* The study of prison management and rehabilitation of inmates.

PENSION. *n.* 1. "... [A] pension is the fruit, through insurance, of all the money which was set aside in the past in respect of his past work." *Parry v. Cleaver*, [1970] A.C. 1 at 16 (U.K. H.L.), Lord Reid. 2. "... [I]ncludes periodic money payments payable on involuntary retirement due to disability occasioned by illness or injury as well as retirement due to age...." *Webb v. Webb* (1985), 49 R.F.L. (2d) 279 at 285, 70 B.C.L.R. 15 (S.C.), Lysyk J. 3. An annual allowance made to a person, usually in consideration of past services. 4. A series of payments that continues for the life of a former member of a pension plan, whether or not it is thereafter continued to any other person. See DEFERRED ~.

PEPPERCORN RENT. A rent far below actual value.

PER ANNUM. [L.] By year.

PER AUTRE VIE. [Fr.] For the length of someone else's life.

PER CAPITA. [L. by heads] In equal shares, one a person. R. Megarry & H.W.R. Wade, *The Law of Real Property*, 5th ed. (London: Stevens, 1984) at cxxvi. See PER STIRPES.

PER CENT. *abbr.* [L.] 1. Per centum. By one hundred. 2. Per cent by weight unless otherwise stated. Canada regulations.

PER CENTUM. [L.] By one hundred.

PER CUR. *abbr.* [L.] Per curiam. By a court.

PER CURIAM. [L.] By a court.

PER DIEM. [L.] By day.

PEREMPTORY. *adj.* Determinate, final and, concerning statutes, obligatory in contrast to permissive.

PEREMPTORY CHALLENGE. "... [A]llows a party to dismiss a person from serving on [a] jury without providing a reason...." *R. v. Bain* (1992), 10 C.R. (4th) 257 at 274, [1992] 1 S.C.R. 91, 69 C.C.C. (3d) 481, 87 D.L.R. (4th) 449, 133 N.R. 1, 51 O.A.C. 161, 7 C.R.R. (2d) 193, Stevenson J.

PERFECT. *v.* To register.

PERFECTED SECURITY INTEREST. "... [A]n interest the protection of which against third parties has been accomplished by the doing of whatever was necessary to achieve such in the jurisdiction from which the debtor has moved." *Juckes (Trustee of) v. Holiday Chevrolet Oldsmobile (1983) Ltd.* (1990), 82 Sask. R. 303 at 307, 68 D.L.R. (4th) 142, 79 C.B.R. (N.S.) 143 (Q.B.), Armstrong J.

PERFECTION. *n.* "... [O]f a security interest deals with those steps legally required to give the secured party an interest in the property against the grantor's creditors. An instrument such as a debenture or mortgage is said to become perfected when it is recorded or registered in the appropriate registry as a matter of record, and that recording or registration renewed and kept current and subsisting so that notice to the grantor's debtors does not lapse." *First City Capital Ltd. v. Ampex Canada Inc.* (1989), 75 C.B.R. (N.S.) 109 at 140, 97 A.R. 256 (Q.B.), Yanosik J.

PERFORMANCE. *n.* "... [T]he equitable doctrine of performance [is] expressed in the maxim 'equity imputes an intention to fulfil an obligation'. According to this doctrine a man under an obligation, who does an act which is suitable to be the means of performing the obligation, will be presumed in equity to have done the act with that intention. ... The difference between performance and satisfaction is that whereas the former does not, the latter does, depend upon intention." *Northern Trust Co. v. Coldwell* (1914), 18 D.L.R. 512 at 514, 516, 6 W.W.R. 1165, 25 Man. R. 120, 28 W.L.R. 625 (K.B.), Mathers C.J. See PART ~; SPECIFIC ~; SUBSTANTIAL ~.

PERFORMANCE BOND. 1. A bond that is conditioned upon the completion by the principal of a contract in accordance with its terms. 2. "... [G]uarantee to the owner that the contractor will perform the terms of the contract." *Johns-Manville Canada Inc. v. John Carlo Ltd.* (1980), (*sub nom. Canadian Johns-Manville Co. v. John Carlo Ltd.*) 12 B.L.R. 80 at 87, 29 O.R. (2d) 592, 113 D.L.R. (3d) 686 (H.C.), R.E. Holland J. See CONTRACT BOND.

PERIL. *n.* 1. A risk of unavoidable misfortune. 2. Danger arising from failure to be duly circumspect. See MARITIME ~S.

PERILS OF THE SEAS. 1. "Where there is an accidental incursion of seawater into a vessel at a part of the vessel and in a manner where seawater is not expected to enter in the ordinary course of things and there is consequent damage to the thing insured, there is prima facie a loss by perils of the sea. ... It is the fortuitous entry of the seawater which is the peril of the sea in such cases. ..." *Canada Rice Mills v. Union Marine & General Insurance Co.* (1940), [1941] 1 D.L.R. 1 at 9, [1941] A.C. 55, [1941] 3 W.W.R. 401, [1940] 4 All E.R. 169, 8 I.L.R. 1 (P.C.), Lord Wright for their Lordships. 2. Refers only to fortuitous accidents or casualties of the seas. It does not include the ordinary action of the winds and waves. *Marine Insurance acts.*

PER INCURIAM. [L.] Through carelessness.

PERIOD. *n.* 1. An interval of time. 2. A space of time. 3. Any length of time. See ACCOUNTING ~; COOLING-OFF ~; LIMITATIONS ~; RENTAL ~.

PERIODIC TENANCY. Tenancy from week to week, month to month or year to year. R. Megarry & H.W.R. Wade, *The Law of Real Property*, 5th ed. (London: Stevens, 1984) at cxxvi.

PERJURY. *n.* With intent to mislead, making before a person who is authorized by law to permit it to be made before him a false statement under oath or solemn affirmation, by affidavit, solemn declaration or deposition or orally, knowing that the statement is false. *Criminal Code*, R.S.C. 1985, c. C-46, s. 131(1).

PERMANENT INJUNCTION. An injunction to finally settle and enforce the rights of disputing parties. G.H.L. Fridman, *The Law of Contract in Canada*, 2d ed. (Toronto: Carswell, 1986) at 727.

PERMISSIVE PRESUMPTION. "[Leaves] ... it optional as to whether the inference of the presumed fact is drawn following proof of the basic fact." *R. v. Oakes* (1986), 24 C.C.C. (3d) 321 at 330, [1986] 1 S.C.R. 103, 50 C.R. (3d) 1, 14 O.A.C. 335, 19 C.R.R. 308, 26 D.L.R. (4th) 200, 65 N.R. 87, Dickson C.J.C. (Chouinard, Lamer, Wilson and Le Dain JJ. concurring).

PERMISSIVE WASTE. 1. "...

[W]aste is either voluntary or permissive ... Permissive waste involves the failure or omission to take some precaution which results in damage to the property." *Prior v. Hanna* (1987), 55 Alta. L.R. (2d) 276 at 282, 82 A.R. 3, 43 D.L.R. (4th) 612 (Q.B.), Miller A.C.J.Q.B. 2. Neglect to make needed repairs. R. Megarry & H.W.R. Wade, *The Law of Real Property*, 5th ed. (London: Stevens, 1984) at 96-7.

PERMIT. *n.* An authorization, a written authority. See BUILDING ~; OCCUPANCY ~.

PERPETUAL INJUNCTION. An injunction to finally settle and enforce the rights of disputing parties. G.H.L. Fridman, *The Law of Contract in Canada*, 2d ed. (Toronto: Carswell, 1986) at 727.

PERPETUATE TESTIMONY. To preserve and perpetuate evidence which is likely to be lost because the witness is old, infirm or going away before the matter it relates to can be investigated judicially so that justice does not fail. See COMISSION EVIDENCE; COMMISSION ROGATORY; LETTERS ROGATORY; ROGATORY; ROGATORY LETTERS.

PERPETUITY. *n.* 1. Time without limit. 2. Tying up or preventing property from being disposed of freely. R. Megarry & H.W.R. Wade, *The Law of Real Property*, 5th ed. (London: Stevens, 1984) at cxxvi.

PERPETUITY RULE. Limits the time during which a grantor may withdraw property granted from commerce or effectively control the use of property by future generations, by making the property subject to a series of successive interests. D.M.W. Waters, *The Law of Trusts in Canada*, 2d ed. (Toronto: Carswell, 1984) at 282. See RULE AGAINST PERPETUITIES.

PER QUOD. [L.] Whereby.

PER QUOD CONSORTIUM AMISIT. [L.] Whereby one lost the benefit of the other's society.

PER QUOD SERVITIUM AMISIT. [L.] Whereby one lost the benefit of the other's service.

PER SE. [L. by itself] Alone.

PERSON. *n.* 1. "The scope of 'person' as set out in s. 2 of the [Criminal Code, R.S.C. 1985, c. C-46] extends somewhat beyond the individual, covering additionally public bodies, corporations, societies and companies, but groups having common characteristics such as race, religion, colour and ethnic origin are not included in the definition." *R. v. Keegstra* (1990), 61 C.C.C. (3d) 1 at 19, 1 C.R. (4th) 129, 77 Alta. L.R. (2d) 193, [1991] 2 W.W.R. 1, 117 N.R. 1, 114 A.R. 81, 3 C.R.R. (2d) 193, [1990] 3 S.C.R. 697, Dickson C.J.C. (Wilson, L'Heureux-Dubé and Gonthier JJ. concurring). 2. "... [T]he term, as used in s. 203 of the Criminal Code, R.S.C. 1970, c. C-34 is synonymous with the term 'human being' [as used in s. 206]." *R. v. Sullivan* (1991), 3 C.R. (4th) 277 at 288, 122 N.R. 166, 63 C.C.C. (3d) 97, 55 B.C.L.R. (2d) 1, [1991] 1 S.C.R. 489, Lamer C.J.C. (Wilson, La Forest, Sopinka, Gonthier, Cory, McLachlin and Stevenson JJ. concurring). 3. "... [I]n the context of s. 11(b) of the Charter includes corporations." *R. v. C.I.P. Inc.* (1992), 12 C.R. (4th) 237 at 250, 71 C.C.C. (3d) 129, 135 N.R. 90, 52 O.A.C. 366, [1992] 1 S.C.R. 843, 9 C.R.R. (2d) 62, 7 C.O.H.S.C. 1, the court per Stevenson J. 4. "... [A]ny being that is capable of having rights and duties, and is confined to that. Persons are of two classes only – natural persons and legal persons. A natural person is a human being that has the capacity for rights or duties. A legal person is anything to which the law gives a legal or fictional existence or personality, with capacity for rights and duties. The only legal person known to our law is the corporation – the body corporate." *Hague v. Cancer Relief & Research Institute*, [1939] 4 D.L.R. 191 at 193, [1939] 3 W.W.R. 160, 47 Man. R. 325 (K.B.), Dysart J. See ABORIGINAL ~; ARTIFICIAL ~; DURESS OF THE ~; INSOLVENT ~; INSURED ~; LEGAL ~; MEN-

TALLY DISORDERED ~; MENTALLY INCOMPETENT ~; NATURAL ~; REASONABLE ~; SECURITY OF THE ~; SELF-EMPLOYED ~; YOUNG ~.

PERSONAL. *adj.* Referring to an individual's person. See CHATTELS ~.

PERSONAL ACTION. "The general, indeed the invariable, rule is: that a personal action is one brought for the specific recovery of goods and chattels, or for damages or other redress for breach of contract, or other injuries, of whatever description, the specific recovery of lands, tenements, and hereditament only excepted . . ." *McConnell v. McGee* (1917), 39 O.L.R. 460 at 463, 37 D.L.R. 486 (C.A.), Meredith C.J.C.P. (Lennox J.A. concurring).

PERSONAL INJURY. Bodily or physical injury. K.D. Cooper-Stephenson & I.B. Saunders, *Personal Injury Damages in Canada* (Toronto: Carswell, 1981) at 5.

PERSONAL INJURY OFFENCE. See SERIOUS ~.

PERSONAL PROPERTY. ". . . [G]oods, wares, merchandise, or effects [but not land] . . ." *Merritt v. Toronto (City)* (1895), 22 O.A.R. 205 at 213 (C.A.), MacLennan J.A. (Hagarty C.J.O. and Burton J.A. concurring). See TANGIBLE ~.

PERSONAL REPRESENTATIVE. An executor, an administrator, and an administrator with the will annexed.

PERSONAL SERVICE. ". . . Hogg J.A. stated in Re Avery, [1952] 2 D.L.R. 413 at p. 415 . . . (C.A.): 'Personal service has been said to be service made by delivering the process into the defendant's hands or by seeing him and bringing the process to his notice.' Modern cases stress that the question of whether the purpose of giving notice to the person being served has been achieved is the relevant question [in satisfying the requirement of being 'served personally' within the meaning of the Federal Court Rules, C.R.C. 1978, c. 663, s. 355(4)]. In Re Consiglio, [1971] 3 O.R. 798 (Master's Ch.) . . . the court held that personal service was satisfied if it appeared that the document came to the knowledge or into possession of the person to be served either directly or indirectly from a third party. Then, in Rupertsland Mortgage Invsestment Ltd. v. City of Winnipeg (1981), 25 Man. R. (2d) 29 . . . (Co. Ct.) . . . It was held that . . . personal service will be effected if it can be shown that the person to be served actually received the document and was apprised of the contents whether directly or through an intermediary." *Polo Ralph Lauren Corp. v. Ashby* (1990), 31 C.P.R. (3d) 129 at 137, 36 F.T.R. 81, [1990] F.C. 541, Reed J.

PERSONALTY. *n.* Personal property.

PERSONATING POLICE OFFICER. Falsely representing oneself to be a peace officer or public officer, or using a badge or article of uniform or equipment in a manner that is likely to cause persons to believe that one is a peace officer or a public officer. *Criminal Code*, R.S.C. 1985, c. C-46, s. 130.

PERSONATION. *n.* The act of representing that one is someone else, whether dead or living, fictitious or real.

PER STIRPES. [L. according to stocks] ". . . [M]eans 'by roots' or 'by stocks'. When used in the context of a gift to issue, it indicates that the gift will be divided among a certain number of 'stirpes' on the date that the gift vests, and will be distributed within each stirpe according to generation. Children never take concurrently with their parents in a stirpital distribution. Instead, all generations of descendants represent their ancestors and take the share to which those ancestors have been entitled had they survived until the distribution date." *Fraser Estate, Re* (1986), 23 E.T.R. 57 at 66 (Ont. H.C.), White J. See PER CAPITA.

PERSUASIVE AUTHORITY. A judgment or other origin of law whose intrinsic value takes strength from something other than its being binding in character.

PERSUASIVE BURDEN. "[Refers] ... to the requirement of proving a case or disproving defences, ... The party who has the persuasive burden is required to persuade the trier of fact, to convince the trier of fact that a certain set of facts existed. Failure to persuade means that the party loses...." *R. v. Schwartz* (1988), 55 D.L.R. (4th) 1 at 19, [1989] 1 W.W.R. 289, 66 C.R. (3d) 251, 88 N.R. 90, [1988] 2 S.C.R. 443, 45 C.C.C. (3d) 97, 56 Man.R. (2d) 92, Dickson C.J.C. (dissenting).

PERVERSE VERDICT. 1. A verdict in which a jury refuses to follow the judge's direction on a point of law. 2. "... [O]ne, for instance, in which it appears that the jury have not confined themselves to the terms of the issue and to the evidence legitimately brought before them, but have allowed extraneous topics to be introduced into the jury box." *Evenden v. Merchants Casualty Insurance Co.*, [1935] 2 W.W.R. 484 at 490, 2 I.L.R. 288 (Sask. C.A.), Turgeon J.A.

PETERS. *abbr.* Peters' Reports (P.E.I.), 1850-1872.

PETITION. *n.* 1. The process which originates a divorce action. 2. A petition for a receiving order. *Bankruptcy Rules*, C.R.C., c. 368, s. 66. 3. A written document by which an ordinary citizen asks the Crown and Parliament for redress, presented through a member following conditions laid down in the Standing Orders of the House. A. Fraser, W.A. Dawson & J. Holtby, eds., *Beauchesne's Rules and Forms of the House of Commons of Canada*, 6th ed. (Toronto: Carswell, 1989) at 277. See COUNTER~; PRAYER.

PETITION OF RIGHT. A common law method to obtain possession or restitution of real or personal property from the Crown or damages to compensate for breach of a contract. Such a petition could proceed to hearing only if the monarch consented by endorsing it "fiat justitiae" (let right be done). P.W. Hogg, *Constitutional Law of Canada*, 3d ed. (Toronto: Carswell, 1992) at 263.

PETIT JURY. The jury which tries cases with a judge. Contrasted with the grand jury, which had an investigatory role. Consists of various numbers of jurors, from six to twelve, depending on the type of case tried and the jurisdiction.

P.G. *abbr.* Procureur général.

PHILANTHROP. *abbr.* The Philanthropist (Le Philanthrope).

PHILANTHROPIC. *adj.* "... '[B]enevolent' ..." *Brewer v. McCauley*, [1954] S.C.R. 645 at 647, [1955] 1 D.L.R. 415, Rand J.

PICKETING. *n.* Watching and besetting, or attending at or near a person's place of business, operations or employment for the purpose of persuading or attempting to persuade anyone not to (a) enter that place of business, operations or employment; (b) deal in or handle that person's products; or (c) do business with that person, and a similar act at such place that has an equivalent purpose. *Labour Code*, R.S.B.C. 1979, c. 212, s. 1.

PICKET LINE. An area in which picketing is carried on.

PIERCE CORPORATE VEIL. To find corporate officers or directors liable or responsible for acts where the existence of the corporation would ordinarily shield them from liability or responsibility.

PIRACY. *n.* Acts of violence and robbery at sea.

PIRATICAL ACTS. (a) Stealing a Canadian ship; (b) stealing or without lawful authority throwing overboard, damaging or destroying anything that is part of the cargo, supplies or fittings in a Canadian ship; (c) doing or attempting to do a mutinous act on a Canadian ship or (d) counselling a person to do anything mentioned in paragraph (a), (b) or (c). *Criminal Code*, R.S.C. 1985, c. C-46, s. 75 as am. by R.S.C. 1985 (1st Supp.), c. 27, s. 7(3)

PITH AND SUBSTANCE. 1. Variously described as the matter, a name for the content or subject matter, leading feature or true nature and character of a law. P.W. Hogg, *Constitutional Law of Canada*, 3d ed. (Toronto: Carswell, 1992) at 377. 2. "In determining the 'pith and substance' of the legislation, 'it is necessary to identify the dominant or most important characteristic of the challenged law': see Hogg, *Constitutional Law of Canada*, 2nd ed., p. 313 . . ." *R. v. Swain* (1991), 63 C.C.C. (3d) 481 at 525, 5 C.R. (4th) 253, 125 N.R. 1, 3 C.R.R. (2d) 1, 47 O.A.C. 81, [1991] 1 S.C.R. 933, Lamer C.J.C. (Sopinka and Cory JJ. concurring).

PL. *abbr.* [L.] Placitum. Any point decided in a judgment summarized by the reporter.

PLACE. *v.* To transfer a child from the care and control of one person or agency to another person or agency.

PLACE. *n.* "[In s. 10(1)(a) of the Narcotic Control Act, R.S.C. 1970, c. N-1] . . . includes places of fixed location such as offices or ships or gardens as well as vehicles, vessels and aircraft. It does not, however, include public streets, or other public places: . . . when found in a statute is usually associated with other words which control its meaning. . . ." *R. v. Rao* (1984), 12 C.C.C. (3d) 97 at 125, 46 O.R. (2d) 80, 40 C.R. (3d) 1, 4 O.A.C. 162, 9 D.L.R. (4th) 542, 10 C.R.R. 275 (C.A.), the court per Martin J.A. See PUBLIC ~.

PLACITUM. *n.* [L.] Any point decided in a judgment summarized by the reporter.

PLAGIARISM. *n.* The act of publishing the thought or writing of someone else as one's own.

PLAGIARIST. *n.* One who publishes the thought or writing of someone else as one's own.

PLAINTIFF. *n.* 1. A person who commences an action. 2. A person at whose instance a summons is issued. See NOMINAL ~.

PLAN. *n.* 1. The map of a piece of real property divided into lots and parcels. 2. ". . . [D]esign is the concept of the project when finally completed. A plan is a description of that design set

out graphically. . . ." *Bird Construction Co. v. United States Fire Insurance Co.* (1985), 45 Sask. R. 96 at 99, 18 C.L.R. 115, [1987] I.L.R. 1-2047, 24 D.L.R. (4th) 104, 18 C.C.L.I. 92 (Sask. C.A.), Vancise J.A. See CANADA ASSISTANCE ~; CANADA PENSION ~; COMPENSATION ~; COOPERATIVE ~; DEFINED CONTRIBUTION ~; DEVELOPMENT ~.

PLANNING. *n.* ". . . . [E]ssential to orderly development of a municipality. Generally, a plan is developed for the municipality, and zoning by-laws implement the plan. . . ." *Zive Estate v. Lynch* (1989), 47 M.P.L.R. 310 at 314, 7 R.P.R. (2d) 180, 94 N.S.R. (2d) 401, 247 A.P.R. 401 (C.A.), the court per Macdonald J.A. See ESTATE ~.

PLANNING SCHEME. A statement of policy with respect to the use and development of land and the use, erection, construction, relocation and enlargement of buildings within a defined area.

PLAN OF SUBDIVISION. A plan by which the owner of land divides the land into areas designated on the plan.

PLEA. *n.* 1. An action or suit. 2. A way to put forward a defence in certain proceedings. 3. A defendant's factual answer to a plaintiff's declaration. See ROLLED UP ~.

PLEA BARGAIN. For an accused person to agree to plead guilty, or to give material information or testimony in exchange for an apparent advantage which the prosecutor offers, acting within the scope of a prosecutor's seeming authority. S.A. Cohen, *Due Process of Law* (Toronto: Carswell, 1977) at 179.

PLEAD. *v.* 1. To allege something in a cause. 2. To argue a case in court.

PLEADING. *n.* 1. The process in which parties to an action alternately present written statements of their contentions, each one responding to the preceding statement, and each statement attempting to better define the controversial areas. 2. ". . . [A] statement in writing, in summary form, of material facts on which a party to a dispute relies in support of a claim or defence...." *Zavitz Technology Inc. v. 146732 Canada Inc.* (1991), 49 C.P.C. (2d) 26 at 38 (Ont. Gen. Div.), Isaac J. See CLOSE OF ~S; MIS~; RULES OF ~.

PLEAD OVER. To reply to an opponent's pleading but to overlook a defect to which one might have taken exception.

PLEA IN ABATEMENT. A common law plea which raises a matter like the inability of a party to sue or be sued, the non-joinder of parties or another action which is pending concerning the same subject matter. G.D. Watson & C. Perkins, eds., *Holmested & Watson: Ontario Civil Procedure* (Toronto: Carswell, 1984) at 25-30.

PLEA NEGOTIATION. For an accused person to agree to plead guilty, or to give material information or testimony in exchange for an apparent advantage which the prosecutor offers, acting within the scope of a prosecutor's seeming authority. S.A. Cohen, *Due Process of Law* (Toronto: Carswell, 1977) at 179.

PLEBISCITE. *n.* The referral of an issue to the population to decide by vote.

PLEDGE. *n.* "Delivery is necessary to constitute a pledge, and the pledgee's right or special property is to hold the goods as security for the debt, and on default to sell the goods as pledged...." *N.M. Patterson & Co. v. Carnduff*, [1931] 2 W.W.R.221 at 227 (Sask. C.A.), Martin J.A. See PAWN.

PLENARY. *adj.* 1. Complete, full. 2. Describes a proceeding with formal steps and gradations, in contrast to summary.

PLENE ADMINISTRAVIT. [L. one has fully administered] An executor's or administrator's defence that that person fully administered all the assets which that person received.

PLURAL. *adj.* Referring to more than one.

PLURALITY. *n.* A greater number.

P.M. *abbr.* 1. Prime Minister. 2. "...

Police Magistrate...." *R. v. Linder*, [1924] 3 D.L.R. 505 at 507, [1924] 2 W.W.R. 646, 42 C.C.C. 289, 20 Alta. L.R. 415 (C.A.), the court per Becker J.A.

P.O. *abbr.* Post office.

P.O.G.G. *abbr.* Peace, order and good government. See RESIDUARY POWER.

POLICE. *n.* A force of people charged with maintenance of public order, detection, and prevention of crime. See ROYAL CANADIAN MOUNTED ~.

POLICE COURT. The court of a magistrate.

POLICE FORCE. "... [A] body of police...." *R. v. Gendron* (1985), 22 C.C.C. (3d) 312 at 321, 10 O.A.C. 122 (C.A.), Grange J.A. (dissenting).

POLICY. *n.* 1. The instrument evidencing a contract. *Insurance acts*. 2. A government commitment to the public to follow an action or course of action in pursuit of approved objectives. *Public Service Act*, S.N.W.T. 1983 (1st Sess.), c. 12, s. 1. 3. "... [D]ecisions concerning budgetary allotments for departments or government agencies will be classified as policy decisions." *Just v. British Columbia* (1989), 1 C.C.L.T. (2d) 1 at 18, [1989] 2 S.C.R. 1228, 18 M.V.R. (2d) 1, [1990] 1 W.W.R. 385, 41 B.C.L.R. (2d) 350, 103 N.R. 1, 64 D.L.R. (4th) 689, 41 Admin. L.R. 161, [1990] R.R.A. 140n, Cory J. (Dickson C.J.C., Wilson, La Forest, L'Heureux-Dubé and Gonthier JJ. concurring) 4. "... [R]efers to a decision of a public body at the planning level involving the allocation of scarce resources or balancing such factors as efficiency and thrift ... One hallmark of a policy, as opposed to an operational, decision is that it involves planning.... A second characteristic of a policy decision as opposed to an operational function is that a policy decision involves allocating resources and balancing factors such as efficiency or thrift ... A third criterion is found in the suggestion that the greater the discretion conferred on the decision-making body, the more likely the resultant decision is to be a matter of policy rather than operational ... Fourthly, it has been suggested that where there are standards against which conduct can be evaluated, a decision may move into the operational area and immunity should not be granted: ... The setting of a standard is a policy function; its implementation is an operational function. ... the fact the person or body making the decision is working in the field does not prevent it from being a policy decision ..." *Just v. British Columbia* (1985), 33 C.C.L.T. 49 at 52-4, 34 M.V.R. 124, 64 B.C.L.R. 349, [1985] 5 W.W.R. 570 (S.C.), McLachlin J. See DRIVER'S ~; PUBLIC ~; VALUED ~.

POLICYHOLDER. *n.* A person who owns an insurance policy.

POLITICAL CIVIL LIBERTIES. Include freedom of assembly, association, religion and speech, the right to be a candidate for elected office and vote, the freedom to leave and enter Canada and move between provinces. P.W. Hogg, *Constitutional Law of Canada*, 3d ed. (Toronto: Carswell, 1992) at 765.

POLITICAL PARTY. An association, organization or affiliation of voters comprising a political organization whose prime purpose is the nomination and support of candidates at elections.

POLITICAL SUBDIVISION. A province, state or other like political subdivision of a foreign state that is a federal state. *State Immunity Act*, R.S.C. 1985, c. S-18, s. 2.

POLL. *v.* 1. At an election, to give a vote or to receive a vote. 2. To take the votes of everyone entitled to vote.

POLL-TAX. *n.* A tax on every person.

POLLUTION. *n.* 1. The presence in the environment of substances or contaminants that substantially alter or impair the usefulness of the environment. *Waste Management Act*, S.B.C. 1982, c. 41, s. 1. 2. Alteration of the physical, chemical, biological or aesthetic properties of the environment including the addition or removal of any contaminant that will render the environment harmful to the public health, that is unsafe or harmful for domestic, municipal, industrial, agricultural, recreational or other lawful uses or that is harmful to wild animals, birds or aquatic life.

POLYANDRY. *n.* Polygamy in which one woman has several husbands.

POLYGAMY. *n.* 1. The state of having many wives or husbands. 2. It is an offence (a) to practise or enter into or in any manner agree or consent to practise or enter into (i) any form of polygamy, or (ii) any kind of conjugal union with more than one person at the same time, whether or not it is by law recognized as a binding form of marriage; or (b) celebrate, assist or be a party to a rite, ceremony, contract or consent that purports to sanction a relationship mentioned in subparagraph (a)(i) or (ii). *Criminal Code*, R.S.C. 1985, c. C-46, s. 293(1).

POLYGRAPH. *n.* A lie detector; an apparatus which records physiological changes in the body.

PORNOGRAPHY. *n.* "... [C]an be usefully divided into three categories: (1) explicit sex with violence; (2) explicit sex without violence but which subjects people to treatment that is degrading or dehumanizing, and (3) explicit sex without violence that is neither degrading nor dehumanizing. Violence in this context includes both actual physical violence and threats of physical violence. ..." *R. v. Butler* (1992), 11 C.R. (4th) 137 at 163, [1992] 2 W.W.R. 577, [1992] 1 S.C.R. 452, 70 C.C.C. (3d) 129, 134 N.R. 81, 8 C.R.R. (2d) 1, 89 D.L.R. (4th) 449, 78 Man. R. (2d) 1, 16 W.A.C. 1, Sopinka J. (Lamer C.J.C., La Forest, Cory, McLachlin, Stevenson and Iacobucci JJ. concurring).

PORT. *n.* A place where vessels or vehicles may discharge or load cargo.

POSITIVE LAW. Rules of conduct set down and enforced with the sanction of authority.

POSSE. *n.* [L.] A possibility. Something in posse is something which possibly may be; something in esse is something which actually is.

POSSE COMITATUS. [L.] The sheriff of a county traditionally could summon it to defend that county against enemies of the Crown, to pursue felons, to keep the peace or to enforce a royal writ.

POSSESSION. *n.* 1. "... [O]f land ... means actual occupation." *Logan v. Brennand* (1921), 62 D.L.R. 644 at 644, [1921] 3 W.W.R. 896, 20 Alta.L.R. 119 (C.A.), the court per Beck J.A. 2. The right of control or disposal of any article, irrespective of the actual possession or location of such article. 3. "[In s. 282 of the Criminal Code, R.S.C. 1985, c. C-46 means] ... physical control over the child or physical custody of the child." *R. v. McDougall* (1990), 3 C.R. (4th) 112 at 124, 1 O.R. (3d) 247, 42 O.A.C. 223, 62 C.C.C. (3d) 174 (C.A.), the court per Doherty J.A. See ACTUAL ~; ADVERSE ~; CHANGE OF ~; CHOSE IN ~; CONSTRUCTIVE ~; DE FACTO ~; EXCLUSIVE ~; LEGAL ~; RECENT ~; VACANT ~; WRIT OF ~.

POSSESSORY. *adj.* Describes something arising out of or concerned with possession.

POSSESSORY LIEN. A common law lien which arises from an express or implied agreement and which can be extinguished when the amount due is tendered and can be lost by an express or implied waiver. It continues only as long as one retains actual possession.

POSSESSORY TITLE. The title of a squatter.

POSSIBILITY. *n.* 1. A future event, which may or may not happen. 2. In real property, an interest in land which depends on such an event happening.

POSSIBLE. *adj.* "... [C]ould in some circumstances be coloured by context to mean more likely than not. But in the case at bar it is coupled with words indicating that the prognosis is 'uncertain'." *Bola v. Canada (Minister of Employment & Immigration)* (1990), 107 N.R. 311 at 316 (Fed. C.A.), MacGuigan J.A.

POST. *adv.* [L.] After.

POSTDATE. *v.* To give a bill, note or cheque a later date in order to delay the payment date. I.F.G. Baxter, *The Law of Banking*, 3d ed. (Toronto: Carswell, 1981) at 84.

POST-JUDGMENT INTEREST. Interest payable on the amount awarded under a judgment including costs calculated from the date of the order calculated at the postjudgment interest rate. (*Courts of Justice Act*, R.S.O. 1990, c. C.43, s. 129(1)). G.D. Watson & C. Perkins, eds., *Holmested & Watson: Ontario Civil Procedure* (Toronto: Carswell, 1984-) at CJA-202.

POSTMORTEM. *n.* An autopsy. F.A. Jaffe, *A Guide to Pathological Evidence*, 3d ed. (Toronto: Carswell, 1991) at 1.

POST OFFICE. Includes any place, receptacle, device or mail conveyance authorized by the Corporation for the posting, receipt, sorting, handling, transmission or delivery of mail. *Canada Post Corporation Act*, R.S.C. 1985, c. C-10, s. 2.

POWER. *n.* 1. A right or privilege. 2. "... [T]he description of an authority in respect to property or an interest in property which does not itself belong to the person holding the power. Even when a power to dispose of property is wide enough to enable the holder of the power to exercise it in favour of himself the power itself, in the absence of any exercise of it is not regarded as equivalent to ownership of the property...." *Montreal Trust Co. v. Minister of National Revenue* (1960), 60 D.T.C. 1183 at 1185, [1960] C.T.C. 308, [1960] Ex. C.R. 543, Thurlow J. See DECLARATORY ~; DISTRIBUTION OF ~S; GENERAL ~; INHERENT ~; LEGAL ~; OBJECT OF A ~; RESIDUARY ~; SPENDING ~; STATUTORY ~ OF DECISION; TRUST ~.

POWER OF APPOINTMENT. The power of a donee or appointor to appoint by will the people who will succeed to property after the person to whom the power is given dies. This power is given by a donor using an instrument such as a trust inter vivos, marriage settlement or will. J.G. McLeod, *The Conflict of Laws* (Calgary: Carswell, 1983) at 428.

POWER OF ATTORNEY. Authority for a donee or donees to do on behalf on a donor or principal anything which that donor can lawfully do through an attorney. G.H.L. Fridman, *The Law of Agency*, 6th ed. (London: Butterworths, 1990) at 55-6.

POWER OF SALE. The power of a mortgagee to sell the property subject to his mortgage in order to realize on the mortgage debt.

P.P.S.A.C. *abbr.* Personal Property Security Act Cases, 1980-.

P.R. *abbr.* Practice Reports (Ont.), 1848-1900.

PRACTICABLE. *adj.* "... [W]hen it is capable of being done, having regard to all the circumstances 'feasible'." *R. v. Cambrin* (1982), 1 C.C.C. (3d) 59 at 61, [1983] 2 W.W.R. 250, 18 M.V.R. 160 (B.C. C.A.), Craig J.A.

PRACTICAL. *adj.* "... [C]apable of being done usefully or at not too great a cost ..." *Crédit foncier franco-canadien v. McGuire* (1979), 12 C.P.C. 103 at 105, 14 B.C.L.R. 281 (S.C.), van der Hoop L.J.S.C.

PRACTICE. *n.* 1. "... [T]hose legal rules which direct the course of proceedings to bring parties into court, and the course of the court after they are brought in ..." *Delisle v. Moreau* (1968), 5 C.R.N.S. 68 at 70, [1968] 4 C.C.C. 229, 69 D.L.R. (2d) 530, (N.B. C.A.), the court per Hughes J.A. 2. "'... [I]n its larger sense,' says Lord Justice Lush in Payser v. Minors, (1881); 7 Q.B.D. 329 at 333 (C.A.), 'denotes the mode of proceeding by which a legal right is enforced as distinguished from the law which gives or defines the right.' Where used in its ordinary and common sense, it denotes the rules that make or guide the cursus curiae and regulate procedure within

the walls or limits of the Court itself: Attorney-General v. Sillem, 33 L.J. Ex. 209." *Morris Provincial Election, Re* (1907), 6 W.L.R. 742 at 748 (Man. K.B.), Mathers J. 3. "... [T]he exercise of [a] profession or calling frequently, customarily or habitually:..." *R. v. Mills* (1963), [1964] 1 O.R. 74 at 76 (C.A.), the court per McLennan J.A. 4. "... [T]he accepted 'way of doing things'; [the parties' in collective bargaining] uniform and constant response to a recurring set of circumstances: ..." *Dominion-Consolidated Truck Lines Ltd. v. I.T.B., Local 141* (1980), 28 L.A.C. (2d) 45 at 49 (Ont.), Adams, McRae and Fosbery. See FAIR EMPLOYMENT ~.

PRAECIPE. *n.* [L.] 1. A requisition. 2. "... [I]nstructions to the Registrar to issue the writ. In old times it was the name given to the writ itself; now it is nothing more than instructions to the officer...." *Kimpton v. McKay* (1895), 4 B.C.R. 196 at 211 (C.A.), Drake J.A. (Walkem J.A. concurring). 3. A piece of paper on which one party to a proceeding specifies what document that party wishes to have prepared or issued and the particulars of the document.

PRAYER. *n.* The conclusion of a petition to Parliament which expresses the petitioners' particular object. A. Fraser, W.A. Dawson & J. Holtby, eds., *Beauchesne's Rules and Forms of the House of Commons of Canada*, 6th ed. (Toronto: Carswell, 1989) at 278. See PETITION.

PRAYER FOR RELIEF. The portion of a statement of claim requesting damages or an order of the court.

P.R.B. *abbr.* Pension Review Board.

PREAMBLE. *n.* A preface which states the reasons for and intended effects of legislation. A. Fraser, W.A. Dawson & J. Holtby, eds., *Beauchesne's Rules and Forms of the House of Commons of Canada*, 6th ed. (Toronto: Carswell, 1989) at 193.

PRECATORY WORDS. An expression in a will which indicates a wish, desire or request that something be done.

PRECEDENCE. *n*. The state or act of going first.

PRECEDENT. *n*. A decision or judgment of a court of law which is cited as the authority for deciding a similar situation in the same manner, on the same principle or by analogy.

PRECEDENT CONDITION. Something which must be performed or happen before an interest can vest or grow or an obligation be performed.

PRECEPT. *n*. Direction, order.

PRECINCT. *n*. 1. The immediate environs of a court. 2. The district of a constable.

PRECIPE. See PRAECIPE.

PREDECESSOR. *n*. One person who preceded another.

PRE-DISPOSITION REPORT. *var*.
PREDISPOSITION REPORT. A report on the personal and family history and present environment of a young person.

PREFER. *v*. 1. To move for, to apply. 2. For a prosecutor to make a bill of indictment in respect of a charge based on facts disclosed at a preliminary inquiry. S.A. Cohen, *Due Process of Law* (Toronto: Carswell, 1977) at 166. 3. " ... [T]o bear or carry before, or to give the object of the preference a place before some other.... conveys the idea of giving one creditor a position more advanced than the others, or precedence in relation to the payment of his debt...." *Stephens v. McArthur* (1891), 19 S.C.R. 446 at 464-5, 6 Man. R. 496, Patterson J.

PREFER A CHARGE. " ... [D]one by reading to him, as it appears from the information and complaint laid against him upon which he was committed for trial (as well as such additional charges as may by leave of the Judge be preferred by the prosecuting officer under sec. 834 [of the Criminal Code, S.C. 1892, c. 29]), and when this is done the preferring of the charge is complete and constitutes the first part of the arraignment ..." *R. v. Goon*

(1916), 25 C.C.C. 415 at 421, 28 D.L.R. 374, 10 W.W.R. 24, 22 B.C.R. 381 (C.A.), Martin J.A. (McPhillips J.A. concurring).

PREFERENCE. *n*. " ... [O]f one creditor over another ... consists ... in the voluntary disposition by an insolvent of some portion of his property so as to confer greater benefit upon one or more of his creditors than upon others, when unable to pay all in full. To constitute a preference it must have been given by the insolvent of his own mere motion, and as a favour or bounty proceeding voluntarily from himself." *Molsons Bank v. Halter* (1890), 18 S.C.R. 88 at 102, Gwynne J. See FRAUDULENT ~.

PREFERENCE SHARE. " ... [S]hares which carry a preference may properly be denominated preference shares, though in certain respects they may be shorn of rights which belong to common shares ..." *Rubas v. Parkinson* (1929), 64 O.L.R. 87 at 93, 56 O.W.N. 133, [1929] 3 D.L.R. 558 (C.A.), Masten J.A. (Latchford C.J., Orde, Fisher and Riddell JJ.A. concurring). See CUMULATIVE ~.

PREFERRED. *adj*. " ... [A]n indictment based upon a committal for trial without the intervention of a grand jury is not 'preferred' against an accused until it is lodged with the trial court at the opening of the accused's trial, with a court ready to proceed with the trial." *R. v. Chabot* (1980), 18 C.R. (3d) 258 at 271, [1980] 2 S.C.R. 985, 22 C.R. (3d) 350, 34 N.R. 361, 55 C.C.C. (2d) 385, 117 D.L.R. (3d) 527, the court per Dickson J.

PREFERRED CREDITOR. A creditor whom the common law or legislation gives some advantage over other claimants. C.R.B. Dunlop, *Creditor-Debtor Law in Canada* (Toronto: Carswell, 1981) at 434.

PREFERRED DIVIDEND. A dividend attached to a class of shares other than common shares. A preferred dividend must be paid in full before dividends may be distributed to common or other classes of shares.

PREFERRED INDICTMENT. "... [L]odged by the Attorney-General against an accused ..." *R. v. Biernacki* (1962), 37 C.R. 226 at 235 (Que. S.P.), Trottier J.S.P. See PREFERRED.

PREFERRED SHARE. 1. A share other than a common share. 2. A share in the capital stock of an association that is not a co-op share. *Canada Cooperative Associations Act*, R.S.C. 1985, c. C-40, s. 3. See PREFERENCE SHARE.

PREGNANCY. *n.* The state of having a child in utero.

PRE-INCORPORATION CONTRACT. *var.* **PREINCORPORATION CONTRACT.** A contract entered into by a contractor in the name of or on behalf of a corporation before its incorporation.

PRE-JUDGMENT INTEREST. Interest awarded on the principal sum owing under a judgment at the prejudgment interest rate calculated from the day the cause of action arose to order day (*Courts of Justice Act*, R.S.O. 1990, c. C.43, s. 128(1)). G.D. Watson & C. Perkins, eds., *Holmested & Watson: Ontario Civil Procedure* (Toronto: Carswell, 1984-) at CJA-193.

PREJUDICE. *n.* An injury. See WITHOUT ~.

PREJUDICED. *adj.* 1. "[In Mechanics' Lien Act, S.A. 1906, s. 21, s. 14] ... I think must be taken to mean 'unjustly made to suffer' ..." *Rendall, MacKay, Michie Ltd. v. Warren & Dyett* (1915), 8 W.W.R. 113 at 118, 21 D.L.R. 801 (Alta. T.D.), Beck J. 2. "... [S]uffered a pecuniary loss or damage ..." *Gray-Campbell v. Jamieson*, [1923] 3 D.L.R. 845 at 847, [1923] 3 W.W.R. 478, 17 Sask. L.R. 405 (K.B.), Maclean J.

PRELIMINARY HEARING. The hearing, held in accordance with procedure set out in Part XVIII of the Criminal Code, in which a justice determines whether there is sufficient evidence to commit an accused for trial.

PRELIMINARY QUESTION. 1. A question collateral to the merits or the heart of an inquiry but which is not the major question to be decided. S.A. DeSmith, *Judicial Review of Administrative Action*, 4th ed. by J.M. Evans (London: Stevens, 1980) at 114. 2. "The current tendency is ... to limit the concept of a 'preliminary question' as far as possible. Even those who favour retaining this concept limit it to questions concerning jurisdiction in the strict sense, of the initial power to proceed with an inquiry ... These questions are identified by the fact that they fall outside the limits of the enabling legislation itself, and are not usually within the area of expertise of the administrative tribunal ..." *Blanchard c. Control Data Canada Ltée* (1984), 14 Admin. L.R. 133 at 170, [1984] 2 S.C.R. 476, 84 C.L.L.C. 14,070, 55 N.R. 194, 14 D.L.R. (4th) 289, Lamer J. (McIntyre J. concurring).

PREMIER. *n.* 1. A minister of the Crown holding the recognized position of first Minister. 2. The Prime Minister.

PREMISES. *n.* 1. ".... [A]lthough in popular language it is applied to buildings, in legal language means 'a subject or thing previously expressed'; ..." *Beacon Life Assurance & Fire Co. v. Gibb* (1862), 7 L.C. Jur. 57 at 61, 15 E.R. 630, 1 Moo. P.C. (N.S.) 73, 8 R.U.R.Q. 476, 13 Low. Can. R. 81 (P.C.), their Lordships per Lord Chelmsford. 2. "... [I]n the ordinary acceptation of the term, means the grounds immediately surrounding a house." *Martin v. Martin* (1904), 8 O.L.R. 462 at 466 (C.A.), Falconbridge C.J. See LICENSED ~.

PREMISES OF A DEED. 1. "It is customary to include in the premises [of a deed] the effectual date of the transfer; the names of the parties to the transfer of title as grantor and grantees, the recitals, the words of grant and the description of the property transferred." *Wheeler v. Wheeler (No. 2)* (1979), 25 N.B.R. (2d) 376 at 378 (C.A.), Limerick, Bugold and Ryan JJ.A. 2. "... [A]ll the foreparts of a deed before the habendum, and the office of this part of the deed is rightly to name the grantor and grantee, and to comprehend the certainty of the thing granted, and herein is sometimes (though improperly) set down, the estate ..." *Jamieson v. London & Canadian Loan & Agency Co.* (1896), 23 O.A.R. 602 at 619 (C.A.), Burton J.A.

PREMIUM. *n.* A single or periodical payment.

PREPONDERANCE. *n.* "... [T]he most weight. ..." *Snider v. Harper* (1922), 66 D.L.R. 149 at 158, [1922] 2 W.W.R. 417, 18 Alta. L.R. 82 (C.A.), Hyndman J.A. (Beck J.A. concurring).

PREROGATIVE. *n.* An exceptional power, privilege or pre-eminence which the law grants to the Crown. See ROYAL ~.

PREROGATIVE ORDER. An act by which a superior court prevents a subordinate tribunal from exceeding jurisdiction, from making errors of law on the face of its judgments and from denying natural justice. Examples are writs of habeas corpus or prohibition. S. Mitchell, P.J. Richardson & D.A. Thomas, eds., *Archbold Pleading, Evidence and Practice in Criminal Cases*, 43d ed. (London: Sweet & Maxwell, 1988) at 171.

PREROGATIVE RIGHTS OF THE CROWN. The body of special common law rules which apply to Her Majesty. C.R.B. Dunlop, *Creditor-Debtor Law in Canada* (Toronto: Carswell, 1981) at 446.

PREROGATIVE WRIT. A writ of certiorari, habeas corpus, mandamus, prohibition or quo warranto. S.A. DeSmith, *Judicial Review of Administrative Action*, 4th ed. by J.M. Evans (London: Stevens, 1980) at 25.

PRESCRIBE. *v.* In a modern act of Parliament, to regulate the details after the general nature of the proceedings is indicated.

PRESCRIBED BY LAW. "The limit will be prescribed by law within the meaning of s. 1 [of the Charter] if it is expressly provided for by statute or regulation, or results by necessary implication from the terms of a statute or regulation or from its operating requirements. The limit may also result from the application of a common law rule." *R. v. Therens*, [1985] 1 S.C.R. 613 at 645, [1985] 4 W.W.R. 286, 32 M.V.R. 153, 45 C.R. (3d) 97, 38 Alta. L.R. (2d) 99, 18 C.C.C. (3d) 481, 13 C.R.R. 193, 40 Sask. R. 122, 18 D.L.R. (4th) 655, 59 N.R. 122, Le Dain J.

PRESCRIPTION. *n.* A common law doctrine extended by statute whereby profits and easements can be acquired over others' land. It is fundamentally a rule of evidnce which presumes that the owner granted the land so that title is derived from her or him. R. Megarry & H.W.R. Wade, *The Law of Real Property*, 5th ed. (London: Stevens, 1984) at 1030.

PRESENT. *v.* To offer; to tender.

PRESENT CONSIDERATION. A consideration exchanged at time of contract formation.

PRE-SENTENCE REPORT. A report prepared before sentencing containing information concerning the offender's history to be used in assisting the court in passing sentence.

PRESENTMENT. *n.* 1. Exhibiting a paper to the person from whom one seeks payment. I.F.G. Baxter, *The Law of Banking*, 3d ed. (Toronto: Carswell, 1981) at 106. 2. A species of report given by a jury. 3. "The public return of the bill [of indictment] in open court was termed the 'presentment' of the indictment." *R. v. Chabot* (1980), 18 C.R. (3d) 258 at 265, [1980] 2 S.C.R. 985, 22 C.R. (3d) 350, 34 N.R. 361, 55 C.C.C. (2d) 385, 117 D.L.R. (3d) 527, the court per Dickson J.

PRESENTS. *n.* In a deed, the term which refers to the deed itself.

PRESIDENT. *n.* 1. A person placed in authority over other people; a person in charge of others. 2. One who exercises chief executive functions. H. Sutherland, D.B. Horsley & J.M. Edmiston, eds., *Fraser's Handbook on Canadian Company Law*, 7th ed. (Toronto: Carswell, 1985) at 251. 3. A Chief Justice or Chief Judge.

PRESUMPTION. *n.* 1. ". . . [A]n evidentiary technique by which the elements of a cause of action may be established; it cannot itself stand as an element of a cause of action." *Machtinger v. HOJ Industries* (1992), 40 C.C.E.L. 1 at 20, 7 O.R. (3d) 480n, 92 C.L.L.C. 14,022, 91 D.L.R. (4th) 491, [1992] 1 S.C.R. 986, 136 N.R. 40, 53 O.A.C. 200, McLachlin J. 2. ". . . [E[]]ffect is to impose a duty on the party against whom they operate to adduce some evidence . . ." *Powell v. Cockburn* (1976), 22 R.F.L. 155 at 161, [1977] 2 S.C.R. 218, 8 N.R. 215, 68 D.L.R. (3d) 700, Dickson J. (Laskin C.J., Spence and Beetz JJ. concurring). See COMPELLING ~; CONCLUSIVE ~; MANDATORY ~; PERMISSIVE ~.

PRESUMPTION OF ADVANCEMENT. An exception to ordinary equitable rules relating to resulting trusts, in which property paid for by a husband and conveyed into the name of his wife or child is presumed to be a gift by the husband. A. Bissett-Johnson & W.M. Holland, eds., *Matrimonial Property Law in Canada* (Toronto: Carswell, 1980) at I-13.

PRESUMPTION OF INNOCENCE. The provision in section 11(d) of the Charter of Rights that any person charged with an offence has the right to be presumed innocent until proven guilty according to law in a fair and public hearing by an independent and impartial tribunal. P.W. Hogg, *Constitutional Law of Canada*, 3d ed. (Toronto: Carswell, 1992) at 1100.

PRESUMPTION OF LAW. 1. "[Their] . . . influence on the resolution of the issue is limited to the burden of proof. Text writers and courts are divided on whether presumptions of law affect only the evidential burden or both the evidential and the legal burden. This Court, in Circle Film Enterprises Inc. v. Canadian Broadcasting Corp., [1959] S.C.R. 602 . . . adopted the former or evidentiary burden view, . . ." *Goodman, Estate v. Geffen* (1991), 42 E.T.R. 97 at 136, [1991] 5 W.W.R. 389, 80 Alta. L.R. (2d) 293, 125 A.R. 81, 14 W.A.C. 81,

81 D.L.R. (4th) 211, [1991] 2 S.C.R. 353, Sopinka J. 2. ". . . [I]nvolves actual legal rules." *R. v. Oakes* (1986), 24 C.C.C. (3d) 321 at 331, [1986] 1 S.C.R. 103, 53 O.R. (2d) 719n, 50 C.R. (3d) 1, 14 O.A.C. 335, 19 C.R.R. 308, 26 D.L.R. (4th) 200, 65 N.R. 87, Dickson C.J.C. (Chouinard, Lamer, Wilson and Le Dain JJ. concurring). See REBUTTABLE ~.

PRESUMPTION OF RESULTING TRUST. ". . . [A] presumption of a (resulting) trust arises 'where a person transfers his property into another's name gratuitously', but that presumption is rebuttable by the transferee: Goodfriend v. Goodfriend, [1972] S.C.R. 640." *Fediuk v. Gluck* (1990), 26 R.F.L. (3d) 454 at 459 (Man. Q.B.), Wright J.

PRESUMPTION OF SURVIVORSHIP. Where two or more people die in the same accident it is presumed that the younger survived.

PRESUMPTIONS OF FACT. ". . . A natural inference which has become standardized and which may be drawn by the tribunal of fact, although it is not obliged to draw the inference." *R. v. Boyle* (1983), 5 C.C.C. (3d) 193 at 205, 41 O.R. (2d) 713, 35 C.R. (3d) 34, 148 D.L.R. (3d) 449, 5 C.R.R. 218 (C.A.), the court per Martin J.A.

PRESUMPTIVE EVIDENCE. Evidence which implies the large probability if not the certainty that the facts and the inference are related. P.K. McWilliams, *Canadian Criminal Evidence*, 3d ed. (Aurora: Canada Law Book, 1988) at 1-12 and 1-13. See now CIRCUMSTANTIAL EVIDENCE.

PRETENCE. See FALSE ~.

PRE-TRIAL CONFERENCE. A meeting to consider possibly settling any or all of the issues in a proceeding, simplifying the issues, possibly obtaining admissions which would facilitate the hearing, liability or any other matter that might assist in a just, efficient and inexpensive disposition of that proceeding (Ontario, Rules of Civil Procedure, r. 50.01). G.D. Watson & C. Perkins, eds., *Holmested & Watson:*

Ontario Civil Procedure (Toronto: Carswell, 1984) at 50-2.

PREVENTIVE DETENTION. Detention in a penitentiary for an indeterminate period. *Criminal Code*, R.S.C. 1970, c. C-34, s. 687.

PRICE. *n.* 1. A consideration in money. G.H.L. Fridman, *Sale of Goods in Canada*, 3d ed. (Toronto: Carswell, 1986) at 11. 2. Includes rate or charge for any service. See CASH ~; PURCHASE ~.

PRICE. *abbr.* Price's Mining Commissioner's Cases (Ont.), 1906-1910.

PRICE MAINTENANCE AGREEMENT. An agreement between a manufacturer and a retailer in which the retailer contracts not to sell the manufacturer's goods at less than a specified price.

PRIMA FACIE. [L.] At first glance; on the surface.

PRIMA FACIE CASE. ". . . [I]n this context [adverse effect discrimination] is one which covers the allegations made and which, if they are believed, is complete and sufficient to justify a verdict in the complainant's favour in the absence of an answer from the respondent-employer." *Ontario (Human Rights Commission) v. Simpsons-Sears Ltd.* (1985), 7 C.R.H.H. D/3102 at D/3108, 9 C.C.E.L. 185, 17 Admin. L.R. 89, 86 C.L.L.C. 17,002, 64 N.R. 161, 23 D.L.R. (4th) 321, 12 O.A.C. 241, [1985] 2 S.C.R. 536, the court per McIntyre J.

PRIMA FACIE EVIDENCE. ". . . [H]as two meanings as described by authors such as Dean Wigmore and Sir Rupert Cross, namely: 1. Where the Crown evidence is so strong that no reasonable man would fail to convict. (This is the mandatory sense in which the term is used and compels conviction if there is no evidence to displace the prima facie case). 2. Where the Crown evidence is sufficiently strong to entitle a reasonable man to find the accused guilty although as a matter of common sense he is not obliged to do

so. (This is the permissive and usual sense in which the term is used). . . ." *R. v. Pye* (1984), 11 C.C.C. (3d) 64 at 68, 38 C.R. (3d) 375, 62 N.S.R. (2d) 10, 136 A.P.R. 10, 7 D.L.R. (4th) 275 (C.A.), the court per Macdonald J.A.

PRIMARY BURDEN. "The burden of establishing a case . . ." *R. v. Schwartz* (1988), 45 C.C.C. (3d) 97 at 115, [1989] 1 W.W.R. 289, 66 C.R. (3d) 251, 88 N.R. 90, [1988] 2 S.C.R. 443, 56 Man. R. (2d) 92, 55 D.L.R. (4th) 1, Dickson C.J.C. (dissenting).

PRIMARY EVIDENCE. The best evidence, in contrast to secondary evidence.

PRIMARY FACTS. ". . . [F]acts which are observed by witnesses and proved by oral testimony or facts proved by the production of a thing itself, such as original documents. Their determination is essentially a question of fact for the tribunal of fact, and the only question of law that can arise on them is whether there was any evidence to support the finding." *British Launderers' Research Association v. Hendon Rating Authority*, [1949] 1 K.B. 462 at 471 (U.K. C.A.), Denning L.J.

PRIME MINISTER. The minister with power to select, promote, demote or dismiss other ministers, who is personally responsible for advising the Governor General about when Parliament should be dissolved for an election and when the elected parliament should be called into session and who enjoys special authority because she or he was selected as the leader of a political party which was victorious in the previous election. P.W. Hogg, *Constitutional Law of Canada*, 3d ed. (Toronto: Carswell, 1992) at 235. See PREMIER.

PRIME RATE. The lowest rate of interest quoted by a bank to its most credit-worthy borrowers for prime business loans.

PRIMOGENITURE. *n.* 1. Seniority; the status of being born first. 2. A rule of inheritance by which the oldest of two or more males of the same degree succeeds to an ancestor's land, excluding all the others.

PRINCIPAL. *n.* 1. A chief; a head. 2. A capital amount of money loaned at interest. See DISCLOSED ~; NAMED ~; UNDISCLOSED ~.

PRINCIPAL RESIDENCE. Residential premises that constitute a person's normal or permanent place of residence and to which, when that person is absent, that person has the intention of returning.

PRINCIPLE. *n.* Something which, unlike a rule, does not set out legal consequences which follow automatically if certain conditions are met. S.A. Cohen, *Due Process of Law* (Toronto: Carswell, 1977) at 203. See GENERALLY ACCEPTED ACCOUNTING ~S; KIENAPPLE ~.

PRINCIPLES OF FUNDAMENTAL JUSTICE. 1. "... [R]eflect the fundamental tenets on which our legal system is based. Those tenets include, but are not limited to, the rules of natural justice and the duty to act fairly that have been developed over the years in the administrative law context.... included in these fundamental principles is the concept of a procedurally fair hearing before an impartial decision-maker...." *Pearlman v. Law Society (Manitoba)* (1991), 6 C.R.R. (2d) 259 at 268, [1991] 6 W.W.R. 289, 2 Admin. L.R. (2d) 185, 84 D.L.R. (4th) 105, 130 N.R. 121, 75 Man. R. (2d) 81, 6 W.A.C. 81, [1991] 2 S.C.R. 869, the court per Iacobucci J. 2. "The term ... is not a right, but a qualifier of the right not to be deprived of life, liberty and security of the person; its function is to set the parameters of that right. Sections 8 to 14 [of the Charter] address specific deprivations of the 'right' to life, liberty and security of the person in breach of the principles of fundamental justice, and as such, violations of s. 7. They are therefore illustrative of the meaning, in criminal or penal law, of 'principles of fundamental justice'; they represent principles which have been recognized by the common law, the international conventions and by the very fact of

entrenchment in the Charter, as essential elements of a system for the administration of justice which is founded upon a belief in the dignity and worth of the human person and the rule of law. Consequently, the principles of fundamental justice are to be found in the basic tenets and principles, not only of our judicial process, but also of the other components of our legal system...." *Reference re Section 94(2) of Motor Vehicle Act (British Columbia)* (1985), 23 C.C.C. (3d) 289 at 309, 24 D.L.R. (4th) 536, [1985] 2 S.C.R. 486, 36 M.V.R. 240, 69 B.C.L.R. 145, 48 C.R. (3d) 289, 63 N.R. 266, 18 C.R.R. 30, [1986] 1 W.W.R. 481, Lamer J. (Dickson C.J.C., Beetz, Chouinard and Le Dain JJ. concurring). 3. "... [P]rinciples that govern the justice system. They determine the means by which one may be brought before or within the justice system, and govern how one may be brought within the system and, thereafter, the conduct of judges and other actors once the individual is brought within it. Therefore, the restrictions on liberty and security of the person that s. 7 [of the Charter] is concerned with are those that occur as a result of an individual's interaction with the justice system, and its administration...." *Reference re ss. 193 and 195(1)(c) of the Criminal Code (Canada)* (1990), 56 C.C.C. (3d) 65 at 102, 77 C.R. (3d) 1, [1990] 1 S.C.R. 1123, [1990] 4 W.W.R. 481, 109 N.R. 81, 68 Man. R. (2d) 1, 48 C.R.R. 1 , Lamer J.

PRIORITY. *n.* When two or more competing claims which arose at different times against the same parcel of land are asserted, the one who is entitled to exercise rights to the exclusion of the others is said to have priority. B.J. Reiter, B.N. McLellan & P.M. Perell, *Real Estate Law*, 4th ed. (Toronto: Emond Montgomery, 1992) at 403.

PRISON. *n.* 1. Includes a penitentiary, common jail, public or reformatory prison, lock-up, guard-room or other place in which persons who are charged with or convicted of offences are usually kept in custody. *Criminal*

Code, R.S.C. 1985, c. C-46, s. 2. 2. A prison other than a penitentiary, and includes a reformatory school or industrial school. *Criminal Code*, R.S.C. 1985, c. C-46, s. 618(5). 3. A place of confinement other than a penitentiary. See BREACH OF ~; CIVIL ~.

PRISON BREACH. Every one who (a) by force or violence breaks a prison with intent to set at liberty himself or any person confined therein; or (b) with intent to escape forcibly breaks out of, or makes any breach in, a cell or other place within a prison in which he is confined. *Criminal Code*, R.S.C. 1985, c. C-46, s. 144.

PRISONER. *n.* A person under arrest, remand or sentence who is confined in a correctional centre according to law. See REMAND ~.

PRIVACY. *n.* ". . . [M]ay be defined as the right of the individual to determine for himself when, how, and to what extent he will release personal information about himself, . . ." *R. v. Sanelli* (1990), (*sub nom. R. v. Duarte*) 45 C.R.R. 278 at 290, 74 C.R. (3d) 281, 103 N.R. 86, 37 O.A.C. 322, [1990] 1 S.C.R. 30, 53 C.C.C. (3d) 1, 65 D.L.R. (4th) 240, 71 O.R. (2d) 575, La Forest J. (Dickson C.J.C., L'Heureux-Dubé, Sopinka, Gonthier and McLachlin JJ. concurring).

PRIVATE BILL. 1. A bill relating to matters of particular interest or benefit to an individual or group. A. Fraser, W.A. Dawson & J. Holtby, eds., *Beauchesne's Rules and Forms of the House of Commons of Canada*, 6th ed. (Toronto: Carswell, 1989) at 192. 2. A bill relating to a particular person, institution or locality which is often introduced by a private member and enacted by a different and simpler procedure, not requiring government sponsorship. P.W. Hogg, *Constitutional Law of Canada*, 3d ed. (Toronto: Carswell, 1992) at 244.

PRIVATE CARRIER. ". . . [O]ne who undertakes to carry goods in a particular case, but is not engaged in the business of so carrying as a public employment and does not undertake to carry goods for persons generally."

Tri-City Drilling Co. Ltd. v. Velie (1960), 30 W.W.R. 61 at 64, 82 C.R.T.C. 69 (Alta. T.D.), Riley J.

PRIVATE INTERNATIONAL LAW. Or conflict of laws, the part of a country's law that is concerned with resolving legal disputes which involve one or more foreign elements. J.G. McLeod, *The Conflict of Laws* (Calgary: Carswell, 1983) at 3.

PRIVATE LAND. Land other than land vested in the Crown.

PRIVATE LAW. All law relating to persons; used in distinction to public law.

PRIVATE MEMBER'S BILL. A bill, either public or private, introduced by a private member. P.W. Hogg, *Constitutional Law of Canada*, 3d ed. (Toronto: Carswell, 1992) at 244.

PRIVATE NUISANCE. Substantial and unreasonable interference which damages the enjoyment by its occupier of land. *Pugliese v. Canada (National Capital Commission)* (1979), 8 C.E.L.R. 68 at 74, [1979] 2 S.C.R. 104, 8 C.C.L.T. 69, 25 N.R. 498, 97 D.L.R. (3d) 631, the court per Pigeon J.

PRIVATE RECEIVER. A receiver appointed by a letter or similar instrument by one who holds security over a debtor's assets according to the powers specified in the security instrument. F. Bennett, *Receiverships* (Toronto: Carswell, 1985) at 2.

PRIVATE RIGHT. A right at common law or created by statute the infringement of which gives rise to a cause of action for tort, breach of contract or trust or other cause. *Finlay v. Canada (Minister of Finance)* (1986), 17 C.P.C. (2d) 289 at 301, [1986] 1 W.W.R. 603, [1986] 2 S.C.R. 607, 71 N.R. 338, 23 Admin. L.R. 197, 33 D.L.R. (4th) 321, 8 C.H.R.R. D/3789, the court per Le Dain J.

PRIVATE CLAUSE. A provision which purports to exclude judicial review of a tribunal's decision. P.W. Hogg, *Constitutional Law of Canada*, 3d ed. (Toronto: Carswell, 1992) at 197. See FINALITY CLAUSE.

PRIVILEGE. *n.* 1. An exceptional advantage or right; an exemption to which certain people are entitled from an attendance, burden or duty. 2. "... [A]n exclusionary rule of evidence which is appropriately asserted in court...." *Thomson Newspapers Ltd. v. Canada (Director of Investigation & Research)* (1990), 47 C.R.R. 1 at 94, 76 C.R. (3d) 129, 72 O.R. (2d) 415n, 54 C.C.C. (3d) 417, 67 D.L.R. (4th) 161, 29 C.P.R. (3d) 97, [1990] 1 S.C.R. 425, 39 O.A.C. 161, 106 N.R. 161, Sopinka J. (dissenting in part). 3. In the law of evidence, the right of the State or some person or the duty of a witness to withhold otherwise admissible and relevant evidence from a court of law. P.K. McWilliams, *Canadian Criminal Evidence*, 3d ed. (Aurora: Canada Law Book, 1988) at 35-2. See ABSOLUTE ~; BREACH OF ~; COMMON INTEREST ~; INFORMER ~; JURORS' ~; LEGAL PROFESSIONAL ~; LITIGATION ~; PARLIAMENTARY ~; QUALIFIED ~; SOLICITOR-CLIENT ~.

PRIVILEGE AGAINST SELF-INCRIMINATION. 1. "... [O]ften used as a general term embracing aspects of the right to remain silent ... in modern usage, the privilege against self-incrimination is limited to the right of an individual to resist testimony as a witness in a legal proceeding. A privilege is an exclusionary rule of evidence which is appropriately asserted in court. A modern statement of the privilege emphasizing its application in juridicial proceedings is contained in the judgment of Goddard L.J. in Blunt v. Park Lane Hotel Ltd. ... [1942] 2 K.B. 253 [(U.K. C.A.)]. He stated, at p. 257: ' ... the rule is that no one is bound to answer any question if the answer thereto would, in the opinion of the judge, have a tendency to expose the deponent to any criminal charge, penalty or [in a criminal case] forfeiture which the judge regards as reasonably likely to be preferred or sued for.' " *Thomson Newspapers Ltd. v. Canada (Director of Investigation & Research)* (1990), 47 C.R.R. 1 at 94, 76 C.R. (3d) 129, 72 O.R. (2d) 415n, 54 C.C.C. (3d) 417, 67 D.L.R. (4th) 161, 29 C.P.R. (3d) 97, [1990] 1 S.C.R. 425, 39 O.A.C. 161, 106 N.R. 161, Sopinka J. (dissenting in part). 2. "... [T]he privilege of a witness not to answer a question which may incriminate him. That is all that is meant by the Latin maxim, nemo tenetur seipsum accusare, often incorrectly advanced in support of a much broader proposition.... As applied to witnesses generally, the privilege must be expressly claimed by the witness when the question is put to him in the witness box, Canada Evidence Act, R.S.O. 1970, c. E-10, s. 5. As applied to an accused the privilege is the right to stand mute. An accused cannot be asked, much less compelled, to enter the wintess-box or to answer incriminating questions. If he chooses to testify, the protective shield, of course, disappears. In short, the privilege extends to the accused qua witness and not qua accused, it is concerned with testimonial compulsion specifically and not with compulsion generally ..." *Marcoux v. R.* (1975), 60 D.L.R. (3d) 119 at 112-3, [1976] 1 S.C.R. 763, 29 C.R.N.S. 211, 4 N.R. 64, 24 C.C.C. (2d) 1, Dickson J.

PRIVILEGED COMMUNICATION. 1. A communication which one cannot compel a witness to divulge. 2. "In slander or libel the term 'privileged communication' comprehends all cases of communications made bona fide in pursuance of a duty, or with a fair and reasonable purpose of protecting the interest of the party uttering the defamatory matter: ... Privileged communications are of four kinds, viz.: (1). When the publisher of the alleged slander acted in good faith in the discharge of a public or private duty, legal or moral, or in prosecution of his own rights or interests. (2). Anything said or written by a master concerning the character of a servant who has been in his employment. (3). Words used in the course of a legal or judicial proceeding. (4). Publications duly made in the ordinary mode of parliament: Clarke v. Molyneux (1877), 3 Q.B.D. 237." *Trafton v. Deschene* (1917), 36 D.L.R.

433 at 435, 44 N.B.R. 552 (C.A.), Grimmer J.A.

PRIVILEGED DOCUMENT. "A document which was produced or brought into existence with either the dominant purpose of its author, or of the person or authority under whose direction, whether particular or general, it was produced or brought into existence, of using it or its contents in order to obtain legal advice or to conduct or aid in the conduct of litigation, at the time of its production in reasonable prospect, should both be privileged and excluded for inspection." *Voth Brothers Construction (1974) Ltd. v. North Vancouver School District No. 44*, [1981] 5 W.W.R. 91 at 94, 29 B.C.L.R. 114 (C.A.), Nemetz J.A. adopting the test of Barwick C.J. Aust. in *Grant v. Downs* (1976), 135 C.L.R. 674 at 677 (H.C.).

PRIVITY. *n.* 1. Being a participant in or a party to a contract. G.H.L. Fridman, *The Law of Contract in Canada*, 2d ed. (Toronto: Carswell, 1986) at 161. 2. The direct connection between the one to pay the money being sought in an action for recovery and the one to receive such money. G.H.L. Fridman, *Restitution*, 2d ed. (Toronto: Carswell, 1992) at 65.

PRIVY. *n.* 1. Someone who partakes or has an interest in some action or thing. 2. Someone related to another person.

PRIVY. *adj.* Participating in some act.

PRIVY COUNCIL. 1. In Canada, the Queen's Privy Council for Canada including cabinet ministers and other people as well. P.W. Hogg, *Constitutional Law of Canada*, 3d ed. (Toronto: Carswell, 1992) at 234. 2. In the United Kingdom, a large body which now exercises formal functions only. The Queen, on the advice of the Prime Minister, appoints its members. P.W. Hogg, *Constitutional Law of Canada*, 3d ed. (Toronto: Carswell, 1992) at 202. See JUDICIAL COMMITTEE OF THE ~; QUEEN'S ~ FOR CANADA.

PRO. *prep.* [L.] For, in respect of.

PROBABLE CAUSE. Grounds which are reasonable. *Archibald v. McLaren* (1892), 21 S.C.R. 588 at 594, Strong J. (Fournier J. concurring). See REASONABLE AND ~.

PROBATE. *n.* A process to prove the originality and validity of a will. See COURT OF ~; GRANT OF ~; LETTERS ~.

PROBATE DUTY. A tax on the gross value of a deceased testator's personal property.

PROBATION. *n.* 1. The disposition of a court authorizing a person to be at large subject to the conditions of a probation order or community service order. 2. Temporarily appointing a person to an office until that person has, by conduct, proved to be fit to fill it.

PROBATIONER. *n.* A convicted person who is placed on probation by a court or a person who is discharged conditionally by a probation order of a court.

PROBATION OFFICER. The person who supervises another person placed on probation.

PROBATIVE VALUE. "To have probative value the evidence must be susceptible of an inference relevant to the issues in the case other than the inference that the accused committed the offence because he or she has a disposition to the type of conduct charged . . . As in the case of relevance, evidence can be logically probative but not legally probative. When the term 'probative value' is employed in the cases, reference is made to legally probative value." *R. v. B. (C.R.)* (1990), 55 C.C.C. (3d) 1 at 7, [1990] 3 W.W.R. 385, 73 Alta. L.R. (2d) 1, [1990] 1 S.C.R. 717, 107 N.R. 241, 109 A.R. 81, Sopinka J.

PROB. CT. *abbr.* Probate Court.

PRO BONO PUBLICO. [L.] For the public good.

PROCEDURAL EQUALITY. Equality of application of the law without necessarily treating persons equally.

PROCEDURAL FAIRNESS. ". . .

[R]equires that the complainant be provided with an opportunity to make submissions, at least in writing, before any action is taken on the basis of the report; however, a hearing is not necessarily required. . . . in order to ensure that such submissions are made on an informed basis, it must, prior to its decision, disclose the substance of the case against the party." *Radulesco v. Canada (Canadian Human Rights Commission)* (1984), 9 C.C.E.L. 6 at 9, [1984] 2 S.C.R. 407, 9 Admin. L.R. 261, 84 C.L.L.C. 17,029, 14 D.L.R. (4th) 78, 55 N.R. 384, 6 C.H.R.R. D/2831, the court per Lamer J.

PROCEDURE. *n.* 1. "The concept of procedure, too, is . . . a comprehensive one, including process and evidence, methods of execution, rules of limitation affecting the remedy and the course of the Court with regard to the kind of relief that can be granted to a suitor. . . ." *Livesley v. E. Clemens Horst Co.* (1924), [1925] 1 D.L.R. 159 at 161, [1924] S.C.R. 605, the court per Duff J. 2. ". . . [P]roperly means neither the machinery nor the product, but rather the rules set forth by the managers of the machine, showing not who have the right to use it, but how those who have the right are to behave. If the machine exists for you, if there is a Court of Appeal in criminal matters, these shall be the rules by which you shall approach the machine to obtain your result. . . ." *R. v. Johnson* (1892), 2 B.C.R. 87 at 88 (C.A.), Begbie C.J.A. (Drake J.A. concurring). 3. ". . . [W]hen used in a statute such as the Bankruptcy Act [R.S.C. 1970, c. B-3] refers to the mode or method by which a litigant secures his rights. . . ." *Eisler, Re* (1984), 54 C.B.R. (N.S.) 235 at 239 (B.C. S.C.), Murray J. 4. " . . .; [P]leading, evidence and practice. . . ." *Delisle v. Moreau* (1968), 5 C.R.N.S. 68 at 70, [1968] 4 C.C.C. 229, 69 D.L.R. (2d) 530, (N.B. C.A.), the court per Hughes J.A. See CIVIL ~; CRIMINAL ~.

PROCEEDING. *n.* 1. ". . . [O]ne of those words of very wide import that must be interpreted according to the context in which it is used. . . ." *I.W.A.,*

Local 1-324 v. Wescana Inn Ltd. (1978), 27 C.B.R. (N.S.) 201 at 206, [1978] 1 W.W.R. 679, 82 D.L.R. (3d) 368 (Man. C.A.), O'Sullivan J.A. (Freedman C.J.M. concurring). 2. ". . . [C]apable of including every species of activity in matters legal, from an interlocutory application in Chambers to an appeal in a Court of last resort." *Ontario (Attorney General) v. Palmer* (1979), 108 D.L.R. (3d) 349 at 358-9, 28 O.R. (2d) 35, 15 C.P.C. 125, [1980] I.L.R. 1-1196 (C.A.), Anderson J.A. (dissenting). 3. ". . . [R]efers to the whole event, from the commencement of action by the issuance of a writ to the conclusion of the trial, no matter how many causes of action are raised by way of pleadings in either the statement of claim or in the counterclaim." *Hughes v. O'Sullivan* (1986), 12 C.P.C. (2d) 62 at 66 (B.C. S.C.), Toy J. 4. A matter, cause or action, whether civil or criminal, before the court. 5. "' . . . [A] step in an action.' " *Hannah v. Flagstaff*, [1926] 4 D.L.R. 470 at 473, [1926] 3 W.W.R. 301 (Alta. T.D.), Simmons C.J. See ADMIRALTY ~; AFFILIATION ~; COSTS OF THIS ~; DIVORCE ~; JUDICIAL OR QUASI-JUDICIAL ~; JUDICIAL ~; LEGAL ~; MINUTES OF ~S AND EVIDENCE ~; VEXATIOUS ~.

PROCESS. *n.* 1. ". . . [A]s a legal term is a word of comprehensive signification. In its broadest sense it is equivalent to 'proceedings' or 'procedure' and may be said to embrace all the steps and proceedings in a case from its commmencement to its conclusion. 'Process' may signify the means whereby a Court compels a compliance with its demands. Every writ is of course, a process, and in its narrowest sense the term 'process' is limited to writs or writings issued from or out of a Court under the seal of the Court and returnable to the Court. . . ." *Selkirk, Re* (1961), 27 D.L.R. (2d) 615 at 621, [1961] O.R. 391 (C.A.), Schroeder J.A. (McGillivray J.A. concurring). 2. ". . . [A] writ or other judicial order: . . ." *R. v. Landry* (1986), 50 C.R. (3d) 55 at 72, [1986] 1 S.C.R. 145, 54 O.R. (2d) 512n, 65 N.R. 161,

25 C.C.C. (3d) 1, 14 O.A.C. 241, 26 D.L.R. (4th) 368, La Forest J. (dissenting). See ABUSE OF ~; LEGAL ~; MESNE ~; SERVICE OF ~.

PROCLAMATION. *n.* 1. Authorized publication. 2. A proclamation under the Great Seal.

PROCLAMATION DATE. The date on which a statute is proclaimed in force when the statute provides that it will come into force when proclaimed.

PROCTOR. See QUEEN'S ~.

PROCURE. *v.* "... [I]n the context in which is used is s. 422 [of the Criminal Code, R.S.C. 1970, c. C-34] means to instigate, persuade or solicit." *R. v. Gonzague* (1983), 4 C.C.C. (3d) 505 at 508, 34 C.R. (3d) 169 (Ont. C.A.), the court per Martin J.A.

PRODUCTION. *n.* In court, the exhibition of a document.

PRODUCTS LIABILITY. Liability of manufacturers and sellers to buyers and others for damages suffered because of defects in the goods manufactured or sold.

PROFESSIONAL MISCONDUCT. 1. "... [C]onduct which would be reasonably regarded as disgraceful, dishonourable, or unbecoming of a member of the profession by his well respected brethren in the group – persons of integrity and good reputation amongst the membership." *Law Society (Manitoba) v. Savino* (1983), 6 C.R.R. 336 at 343, [1983] 6 W.W.R. 538, 23 Man. R. (2d) 293, 1 D.L.R. (4th) 285 (C.A.), Monnin C.J.M. 2. "... [S]omething improper, disgraceful, or professionally inappropriate." *Forster v. Saskatchewan Teachers' Federation* (1992), 89 D.L.R. (4th) 283 at 286, [1992] 2 W.W.R. 651, 97 Sask. R. 98, 12 W.A.C. 98 (C.A.), the court per Gerwing J.A.

PROFESSIONAL PRIVILEGE. See LEGAL ~.

PROFIT. *n.* 1. "... [T]he profit of a trade or business is the surplus by which the receipts from the trade or business exceed the expenditure necessary for the purpose of earning those receipts." *Russell v. Town & Country Bank* (1888), 13 App. Cas. 418 at 424 (U.K.), Lord Herschell. 2. Gain which results from using either labour or capital or a combination of both. W. Grover & F. Iacobucci, *Materials on Canadian Income Tax*, 4th ed. (Toronto: De Boo, 1980) at 261. See NET ~.

PROFIT À PRENDRE. [Fr.] 1. "... [A] right to take something off the land of another person. ... more fully defined as a right to enter on the land of another person and take some profit of the soil such as minerals, oil, stones, trees, turf, fish or game, for the use of the owner of the right. It is an incorporeal hereditament, and unlike an easement it is not necessarily appurtenant to a dominant tenement but may be held as a right in gross, and as such may be assigned and dealt with as a valuable interest according to the ordinary rules of property." *Cherry v. Petch*, [1948] O.W.N. 378 at 380 (H.C.), Wells J. 2. "... [I]t is the right of severance which results in the holder of the profit à prendre acquiring title to the thing severed. The holder of the profit does not own the minerals in situ. They form part of the fee. What he owns are mineral claims and the right to exploit them ..." *British Columbia v. Tener* (1985), 36 R.P.R. 291 at 309, [1985] 1 S.C.R. 533, [1985] 3 W.W.R. 673, 32 L.C.R. 340, 17 D.L.R. (4th) 1, 59 N.R. 82, 28 B.C.L.R. (2d) 241, Wilson J. (dissenting) (Dickson C.J. concurring).

PRO FORMA. [L.] In order to observe proper form.

PROHIBIT. *v.* "... '[F]orbid' ..." *Krautt v. Paine* (1980), 17 R.P.R. 1 at 21, [1980] 6 W.W.R. 717, 118 D.L.R. (3d) 625, 25 A.R. 390 (C.A.), the court per Laycraft J.A.

PROHIBITION. *n.* 1. An order which prevents an inferior tribunal from proceeding further with some matter before it. S.A. DeSmith, *Judicial Review of Administrative Action*, 4th ed. by J.M. Evans (London: Stevens, 1980) at 25 and 26. 2. An order to prevent a person from driving a motor vehicle.

PROHIBITORY INJUNCTION. An order which requires a defendant to refrain from doing something. G.H.L. Fridman, *The Law of Contract in Canada*, 2d ed. (Toronto: Carswell, 1986) at 722.

PROLIXITY. *n.* ". . . [A]pplied to pleadings . . . taken to imply length and wordiness; diffuseness, discussion at great length; tediousness. . . ." *Maclean v. Kingdon Printing Co.* (1908), 9 W.L.R. 370 at 371, Cameron J.

PROMISE. *n.* A party's undertaking about its future conduct. G.H.L. Fridman, *The Law of Contract in Canada*, 2d ed. (Toronto: Carswell, 1986) at 1. See BREACH OF ~ TO MARRY; CONTRACTUAL ~; DONATIVE ~; GRATUITOUS ~; MUTUAL ~S.

PROMISEE. *n.* One to whom one makes a promise.

PROMISOR. *n.* One who makes a promise.

PROMISSORY ESTOPPEL. ". . . The party relying on the doctrine must establish that the other party has, by words or conduct, made a promise or assurance which was intended to affect their legal relationship and to be acted on. Furthermore, the representee must establish that, in reliance on the representation, he acted on it or in some way changed his position. . . ." *Maracle v. Travellers Indemnity Co. of Canada* (1991), 50 C.P.C. (2d) 213 at 220, I.L.R. 1-2728, 125 N.R. 294, 3 O.R. (3d) 510n, 80 D.L.R. (4th) 652, 3 C.C.L.I. (2d) 186, 47 O.A.C. 333, [1991] 2 S.C.R. 50, the court per Sopinka J.

PROMISSORY NOTE. An unconditional promise in writing made by one person to another person, signed by the maker, engaging to pay, on demand or at a fixed or determinable future time, a sum certain in money to, or to the order of, a specified person or to bearer. *Bills of Exchange Act*, R.S.C. 1985, c. B-4, s. 176.

PROMULGATION. *n.* The act of publishing.

PROOF. *n.* 1. Testimony; evidence. 2. Of a will, obtaining probate of it. See BURDEN OF ~; LITERAL ~; ONUS OF ~; STANDARD OF ~.

PROOF OF SERVICE. Proof provided by the affidavit of the person who served it, by a certificate of service or by a solicitor's written admission or acceptance of the service or in accordance with rules regarding document exchanges (Ontario Rules of Civil Procedure, r.16.09). G.D. Watson & C. Perkins, eds., *Holmested & Watson: Ontario Civil Procedure* (Toronto: Carswell, 1984) at 16-10.

PROPAGANDA. See HATE ~.

PROP. COMP. BD. *abbr.* Property Compensation Board.

PROPER LAW. 1. The system of law which the parties intend to govern the contract, or, if their intention is not expressed or inferred from their circumstances, the system of law with which the transaction is most closely and really connected. G.H.L. Fridman, *Sale of Goods in Canada*, 3d ed. (Toronto: Carswell, 1986) at 473. 2. What determines the lex causae by referring to every fact in the individual case. J.G. McLeod, *The Conflict of Laws* (Calgary: Carswell, 1983) at 195.

PROPERTY. *n.* 1. ". . . [I]n its ordinary sense may include both personalty and realty. But in any partricular case its meaning must be gathered from the whole of the instrument." *London Guarantee & Accident Co. v. George* (1906), 3 W.L.R. 236 at 238, 16 Man. R. 132 (K.B.), Richards J. 2. ". . . [E]ven in its widest sense, is limited to things which are capable of ownership and which are transferable or assignable. It does not include purely personal rights such as the right to personal safety . . . the right to privacy or the right to be free from physical restraint. None of these are considered subject to ownership in the ordinary sense. . . ." *Marr v. Marr* Estate (1989), 71 Alta. L.R. (2d) 168 at 176, 63 D.L.R. (4th) 500, 101 A.R. 43, [1990] 2 W.W.R. 638 (Q.B.), O'Leary J. 3. ". . . [A] broad term which embraces choses in action. . . ."

Herchuk v. Herchuk (1983), 35 R.F.L. (2d) 327 at 336, [1983] 6 W.W.R. 474 (Alta. C.A.), the court per Stevenson J.A. 4. ". . . [I]mports the right to exclude others from the enjoyment of, interference with or appropriation of a specific legal right. . . ." *National Trust Co. v. Bouckhuyt* (1987), 38 B.L.R. 77 at 86, 46 R.P.R. 221, 21 C.P.C. (2d) 226, 7 P.P.S.A.C. 273, 23 O.A.C. 40, 61 O.R. (2d) 640, 43 D.L.R. (4th) 543 (C.A.), the court per Cory J.A. 5. ". . . [A] word of wide signification and certainly includes money." *R. v. Ruggles* (1973), 21 C.R.N.S. 359 at 360, 12 C.C.C. (2d) 65 (Ont. C.A.), the court per Schroeder J.A. See CAPITAL ~; COMMON ~; CORPOREAL ~; DURESS OF ~; INDUSTRIAL AND INTELLECTUAL ~; INDUSTRIAL ~; MARRIED WOMEN'S ~ ACT; MINING ~; MIXED ~; PERSONAL ~; PUBLIC ~; QUALIFIED ~; REAL ~; SPECIAL ~; TANGIBLE ~.

PROPERTY AND CIVIL RIGHTS. An area in relation to which provincial legislatures have power to make laws under section 92(13) of the Constitution Act, 1867. P.W. Hogg, *Constitutional Law of Canada*, 3d ed. (Toronto: Carswell, 1992) at 537.

PROPERTY LAW. Law which deals with ownership, rights and interests in property.

PROPERTY TAX. Tax levied on property. *Petrofina Canada Ltd. v. Markland Developments Ltd.* (1977), 3 R.P.R. 33 at 37, 29 N.S.R. (2d) 158, 45 A.P.R. 158 (T.D.), Hallett J.

PROPORTIONALITY TEST. "There are . . . three important components of a proportionality test. First, the measures adopted . . . must be rationally connected to the objective. Second, the means, even if rationally connected to the objective in this first sense, should impair 'as little as possible' the right or freedom in question . . . Third, there must be a proportionality between the effects of the measures which are responsible for limiting the Charter right or freedom, and the objective which has been identified as of 'sufficient importance'." *R.*

v. Oakes, [1986] 1 S.C.R. 103 at 139, 50 C.R. (3d) 1, 14 O.A.C. 335, 19 C.R.R. 308, 24 C.C.C. (3d) 321, 26 D.L.R. (4th) 200, 65 N.R. 87, Dickson C.J.C. (Chouinard, Lamer, Wilson and Le Dain JJ. concurring). See OAKES TEST; REASONABLE LIMITS.

PROPOSITUS. *n.* [L. the one proposed] The person from whom one traces descent.

PROPOUND. *v.* With respect to a will, to offer as authentic.

PROPRIETARY. *adj.* Owned by a private organization or an individual and operated for profit.

PROPRIETARY ESTOPPEL. An order permitting a party to retain a proprietary interest in land even though the owner asserts strict legal rights because the owner's conduct misled the party who alleges estoppel. G.H.L. Fridman, *The Law of Contract in Canada*, 2d ed. (Toronto: Carswell, 1986) at 112.

PROPRIETARY INTEREST. An interest as an owner. *Cooney v. Sheppard* (1895), 23 O.A.R. 4 at 6 (C.A.), Osler J.A.

PROPRIETOR. *n.* 1. The owner, lessee or other person in lawful possession of any property. 2. In relation to a business enterprise, means the person by whom the enterprise is carried on or is about to be carried on, whether as sole proprietor or in association or partnership with any other person having a proprietary interest therein, but does not include Her Majesty or an agent of Her Majesty in right of Canada or a province, a municipality or a municipal or other public body that performs a function of government. *Small Business Loans Act*, R.S.C. 1985, c. S-11, s. 2.

PROPRIETORSHIP. *n.* One who carries on business under a name other than one's own. See SOLE ~.

PRO RATA. [L.] In proportion, according to a certain percentage or rate.

PROROGATION. *n.* 1. Prolongation or postponement until another day. 2. The termination of a session of Parliament. A. Fraser, W.A. Dawson & J. Holtby, eds., *Beauchesne's Rules and Forms of the House of Commons of Canada*, 6th ed. (Toronto: Carswell, 1989) at 66.

PROROGUE. *v.* To terminate a session of Parliament.

PRO SE. [L.] For himself.

PROSECUTION. *n.* 1. ". . . [I]mplies 'suit', but that is only one meaning of the word in its legal sense because it is just as much attributable to a pressing of claims without suit. . . ." *Taylor v. Mackintosh*, [1924] 3 D.L.R. 926 at 932, [1924] 3 W.W.R. 97, 42 C.C.C. 327, 34 B.C.R. 56 (C.A.), Martin J.A. 2. The putting of an offender on trial. See MALICIOUS ~.

PROSECUTOR. *n.* 1. The Attorney General or, where the Attorney General does not intervene, means the person who institutes proceedings to which this Act applies, and includes counsel acting on behalf of either of them. *Criminal Code*, R.S.C. 1985, c. C-46, s. 2. 2. The Attorney General or, where the Attorney General does not intervene, the informant, and includes counsel or an agent acting on behalf of either of them. *Criminal Code*, R.S.C. 1985, c. C-46, s. 785 as am. by *Criminal Law Amendment Act*, R.S.C. 1985 (1st Supp.), c. 27, s. 170.

PROSPECTUS. *n.* Any prospectus, notice, circular or advertisement of any kind whatsoever, whether of the kind hereinbefore enumerated or not, whether in writing or otherwise offering to the public for purchase or subscription any shares or debentures of any company.

PROSTITUTE. *n.* A person of either sex who engages in prostitution.

PROSTITUTION. *n.* ". . . [T]he exchange of sexual services of one person in return for payment by another." *Reference re ss. 193 & 195.1(1)(c) of the Criminal Code (Canada)* (1990), 48 C.R.R. 1 at 30, 77 C.R. (3d) 1, 56 C.C.C. (3d) 65, [1990] 4 W.W.R. 481, [1990] 1 S.C.R. 1123, 109 N.R. 81, 68 Man. R. (2d) 1, Lamer J.

PRO TANTO. [L. for so much] To such an extent.

PRO TEM. *abbr.* Pro tempore.

PRO TEMPORE. [L. for the time being] Temporarily.

PROTEST. *n.* 1. The solemn declaration that a bill is dishonoured. I.F.G. Baxter, *The Law of Banking*, 3d ed. (Toronto: Carswell, 1981) at 117. 2. A serious declaration of opinion, usually dissent. 3. The express declaration by someone doing something that the act does not imply what it might.

PROTHONOTARY. *n.* 1. Of the Federal Court, a barrister or advocate from any province who is needed for the Court to work efficiently and whose powers are set out in Rule 336. D. Sgayias *et al.*, *Federal Court Practice 1988* (Toronto: Carswell, 1987) at 55. 2. Prothonotary of the Supreme Court at Halifax. *Barristers and Solicitors Act*, R.S.N.S. 1967, c. 18, s. 1. 3. Not only the prothonotary of the Superior Court, but also the clerk of any other court to which the provision is applicable. *Code of Civil Procedure*, R.S.Q. 1977, c. C-25, s. 4. 4. Includes clerk or registrar. *Reciprocal Enforcement of Judgments Act*, R.S.N.S. 1989, c. 388, s. 2(1).

PROTOCOL. *n.* 1. The rules concerning ceremony observed in the official relations between nations and their representatives. 2. The minutes of a deliberative gathering of representatives of different countries. 3. The original drafts or copy of any document.

PROV. *abbr.* 1. Provincial. 2. Province.

PROV. CT. *abbr.* 1. Provincial Court. 2. Provincial Court (Criminal Division).

PROV. CT. CIV. DIV. *abbr.* Provincial Court Civil Division.

PROV. CT. CRIM. DIV. *abbr.* Provincial Court Criminal Division.

PROV. CT. FAM. DIV. *abbr.* Provincial Court Family Division.

PROVE. *v.* 1. To establish. *R. v.*

Whyte (1988), 35 C.R.R. 1 at 9, 6 M.V.R. (2d) 138, [1988] 45 W.W.R. 26, 86 N.R. 328, 64 C.R. (3d) 123, 42 C.C.C. (3d) 97, [1988] 2 S.C.R. 8, 29 B.C.L.R. (2d) 273, 51 D.L.R. (4th) 481, the court per Dickson C.J.C. 2. ". . . [I]n criminal law [requires] . . . convincing proof, at least on the balance of probabilities." *R. v. Whyte* (1988), 35 C.R.R. 1 at 9, 6 M.V.R. (2d) 138, [1988] 45 W.W.R. 26, 86 N.R. 328, 64 C.R. (3d) 123, 42 C.C.C. (3d) 97, [1988] 2 S.C.R. 8, 29 B.C.L.R. (2d) 273, 51 D.L.R. (4th) 481, the court per Dickson C.J.C. 3. With respect to a will, to obtain probate.

PROVINCE. *n.* 1. A province of Canada. 2. A field of duty. 3. Her Majesty the Queen in right of the Province. See CIVIL RIGHTS IN THE ~.

PROVINCIAL AUDITOR. The officer charged by law with the audit of the accounts of the government of a province.

PROVINCIAL CORPORATION. A corporation that is incorporated by or under the act of a legislature.

PROVINCIAL COURT. 1. Under section 92(14) of the Constitution Act, 1867 the body which a provincial legislature constitutes, maintains, and organizes to administer justice in the province. P.W. Hogg, *Constitutional Law of Canada*, 3d ed. (Toronto: Carswell, 1992) at 660. 2. ". . . [C]ourts which, as to their jurisdiction are primarily subjects of provincial legislation and whose process in civil matters, save in certain exceptional cases which will be adverted to, does not run beyond the limits of the province." *Reference re Privy Council Appeals (1940),* (*sub nom. Reference re Supreme Court Act Amendment*) [1940] S.C.R. 49 at 56, [1940] 1 D.L.R. 289, Duff C.J.

PROVINCIAL LAND. Land vested in the Crown in right of a province.

PROVINCIAL LEGISLATURE. Any legislative body other than the Parliament of Canada.

PROVINCIAL PAROLE BOARD.

In relation to any province, a parole board appointed pursuant to section 12 and includes (a) the Board of Parole that Ontario may appoint pursuant to subsection 12(1) of the Prisons and Reformatories Act, if that board has been appointed to act as a parole board under this Act; and (b) the Board of Parole that British Columbia may appoint pursuant to subsection 13(1) of the Prisons and Reformatories Act, if that board has been appointed to act as a parole board under this Act. *Parole Act,* R.S.C. 1985, c. P-2, s. 2.

PROVINCIAL REFERENCE. Each province has enacted legislation which permits the provincial government to send a reference to its provincial court of appeal. P.W. Hogg, *Constitutional Law of Canada,* 3d ed. (Toronto: Carswell, 1992) at 215.

PROVINCIAL SUPERIOR COURT. 1. ". . . They are descendants of the Royal Courts of Justice as Courts of general jurisdiction. They cross the dividing line, as it were, in the federal-provincial scheme of division of jurisdiction, being organized by the provinces under s. 92(15) of the [Constitution Act, 1867 (30 & 31 Vict.), c. 3] and are presided over by Judges appointed and paid by the federal government (ss. 96 and 100 of the Constitution Act, 1867). . . ." *Canada (Attorney General) v. Law Society (British Columbia)* (1982), 19 B.L.R. 234 at 257, [1982] 2 S.C.R. 307, 37 B.C.L.R. 145, [1982] 5 W.W.R. 289, 43 N.R. 451, 137 D.L.R. (3d) 1, 66 C.P.R.(2d) 1, the court per Estey J. 2. "They are not mere local courts for the administration of the local laws passed by the Local Legislatures of the Provinces in which they are organized. They are the courts which were established courts of the respective Provinces before Confederation . . . They are the Queen's Courts, bound to take cognizance of and execute all laws, whether enacted by the Dominion Parliament or the Local Legislatures." *Valin v. Langlois* (1879), 3 S.C.R. 1 at 19-20, Ritchie C.J.C.

PROVISION. *n.* In a legal document,

a clause. See CUSTODY ~; FAMILY ~; SUPPORT ~.

PROVISO. *n.* [L.] 1. A clause in a document which sets a condition, limits, qualifies or covenants, as the case may be. 2. "[Something] ... which, according to the ordinary rules of construction, the effect must be to except out of the earlier part of the section something which, but for the proviso, would be within it." *Duncan v. Dixon* (1890), 38 W.R. 700 at 701 (U.K. Ch. D.), Kekewich J.

PROV. JUDGES J. *abbr.* Provincial Judges Journal (Journal des juges provinciaux).

PROVOCATION. *n.* 1. A wrongful act or insult that is of such a nature as to be sufficient to deprive an ordinary person of the power of self-control is provocation for the purposes of this section if the accused acted upon it on the sudden and before there was time for his passion to cool. *Criminal Code*, R.S.C. 1985, c. C-46, s. 232(2). 2. "... [T]wo key elements to a defence of provocation reducing what would otherwise be culpable murder to manslaughter [under s. 215 of the Criminal Code, R.S.C. 1970, c. C-34]. The person causing death must have done so (i) in the 'heat of passion', caused by (ii) 'sudden provocation'. Whether the accused was provoked to lose his self-control is a question of fact for the jury." *R. v. Faid* (1983), 33 C.R. (3d) 1 at 12, [1983] 1 S.C.R. 265, [1983] 3 W.W.R. 673, 25 Alta. L.R. (2d) 1, 2 C.C.C. (3d) 513, 145 D.L.R. (3d) 67, 46 N.R. 461, 42 A.R. 308, the court per Dickson J.

PROXIMATE CAUSE. 1. "... [A]n expression referring to the efficiency as an operating factor upon the result. Where various factors or causes are concurrent, and one has to be selected, the matter is determined as one of fact, and the choice falls upon the one to which may be variously ascribed the qualities of reality, predominance, efficiency. The true efficient cause never loses its hold. The result is produced, a result attributable in common language to the casualty as a cause, and this

result, proximate as well as continuous in its efficiency, properly meets, whether under contract or under the statute, the language of the expression 'proximately caused.' " *Leyland Shipping Co., Ltd. v. Norwich Union Fire Ins. Society, Ltd.,* [1918] A.C. 350 at 370-71 (U.K. H.L.), Lord Shaw of Dunfermline. 2. "... [E]ffective cause ..." *Boulay v. Rousselle* (1984), 30 C.C.L.T. 149 at 164, 57 N.B.R. (2d) 235, 148 A.P.R. 235 (Q.B.), Meldrum J. See CAUSA CAUSANS.

PROXIMITY. *n.* "... [B]efore the law will impose liability there must be a connection between the defendant's conduct and [the] plaintiff's loss which makes it just for the defendant to indemnify the plaintiff ... In tort, [this] notion is proximity. Proximity may consist of various forms of closeness – physical, circumstantial, causal or assumed – which serve to identify the categories of cases in which liability lies.... Proximity is the controlling factor which avoids the spectre of unlimited liability." *Canadian National Railway v. Norsk Pacific Steamship Co.* (1992), 11 C.C.L.T. (2d) 1 at 26, 137 N.R. 241, 91 D.L.R. (4th) 289, [1992] 1 S.C.R. 1021, 53 F.T.R. 79n, McLachlin J. (L'Heureux-Dubé and Cory JJ. concurring).

PROXY. *n.* "... [U]sed in two senses. It may be used to designate the person appointed by a shareholder (or a limited partner) to vote his shares in the company (or his interest in a limited partnership). It may also be used to designate the instrument by which a person is appointed to vote the shares (or interest) of another." *Beatty v. First Exploration Fund (1987) & Co.* (1988), 40 B.L.R. 90 at 95, 25 B.C.L.R. (2d) 377 (S.C.), Hinds J.

P.S. *abbr.* Post script.

P.S.A.B. *abbr.* Public Service Adjudication Board.

P.S.C.A.B. *abbr.* Public Service Commission Appeal Board.

PSEUDONYM. *n.* A nom de plume.

P.S.L.R. ADJUD. *abbr.* Public Service Labour Relations Act Adjudicator.

P.S.L.R.B. *abbr.* Public Service Labour Relations Board.

P.S.S.R.B. *abbr.* Public Service Staff Relations Board.

PSYCHOPATHIC DISORDER. A persistent disorder or disability of mind other than mental illness that results in abnormally aggressive or serious socially disruptive conduct on the part of a person.

PUBLIC ACCOUNTS. The accounts of a country's or province's expenditures.

PUBLIC ACT. See ACT OF PARLIAMENT.

PUBLICATION. *n.* 1. "... [A]ny act of communication from one to another: ..." *Peel Board of Education v. B. (W.)* (1987), 36 M.P.L.R. 95 at 103, 24 Admin. L.R. 164, 59 O.R. (2d) 654, 38 D.L.R. (4th) 566 (H.C.), Reid J. 2. In relation to any work, means the issue of copies of the work to the public, and does not include the performance in public of a dramatic or musical work, the delivery in public of a lecture, the exhibition in public of an artistic work or the construction of an architectural work of art, but for the purpose of this provision, the issue of photographs and engravings of works of sculpture and architectural works of art shall not be deemed to be publication of those works. *Copyright Act*, R.S.C. 1985, c. C-42, s. 4.

PUBLIC BILL. A bill relating to public policy matters. A. Fraser, W.A. Dawson & J. Holtby, eds., *Beauchesne's Rules and Forms of the House of Commons of Canada*, 6th ed. (Toronto: Carswell, 1989) at 192.

PUBLIC BUILDING. 1. Any building to which the public has a right of access. 2. A place of public resort or amusement.

PUBLIC DOCUMENT. Includes certificates under the Great Seal of a province, legal documents, vouchers, cheques, accounting records, correspondence, maps, photographs and all other documents created in the administration of public affairs.

PUBLIC FUNDS. Money from the treasury of the federal, provincial or municipal government. *Les Soeurs de la Visitation d'Ottawa v. Ottawa*, [1952] O.R. 61 at 71, 72.

PUBLIC HEARING. 1. "... [O]ne in open court which the public including representatives of the media are entitled to attend." *Canadian Newspapers Co. v. Canada (Attorney General)* (1985), 14 C.R.R. 276 at 302, 49 O.R. (2d) 557, 17 C.C.C. (3d) 385, 16 D.L.R. (4th) 642, 44 C.R. (3d) 97, 7 O.A.C. 161, the court per Howland C.J.O. 2. A hearing of which public notice is given, which is open to the public, and at which any person who has an interest in a matter may be heard.

PUBLIC HIGHWAY. Any part of a bridge, road, street, place, square or other ground open to public vehicular traffic.

PUBLIC INTEREST. 1. "In R. v. Collins, [(1987), 33 C.C.C. (3d) 1 (S.C.C.)], ... at p. 18 ... Lamer J. (now C.J.C.) writing for the Supreme Court of Canada, set out one of the criteria that a judge must take into consideration when dealing with public interest: 'It serves as a reminder to each individual judge that his discretion is grounded in community values and in particular long term community values.' " *R. v. Shah* (1991), 7 C.R. (4th) 102 at 115 (Ont. Gen. Div.), Caswell J. 2. "... [I]nvolves many considerations, not the least of which is the 'public image' of the Criminal Code, [R.S.C. 1970, c. C-34], the Bail Reform Act, [S.C. 1970-71-2, c. 37] amendments, the apprehension and conviction of the criminals, the attempts at deterrence of crime, and ultimately the protection of that overwhelming percentage of citizens of Canada who are not only socially conscious but law-abiding. ..." *R. v. Powers* (1972), 20 C.R.N.S. 23 at 36, 9 C.C.C. (2d) 533 (Ont. H.C.), Lerner J.

PUBLIC INTERNATIONAL LAW. See INTERNATIONAL LAW.

PUBLIC LAW. All law dealing with relations between an individual and the state or between states and the organization of government, i.e., criminal, administrative, constitutional and international law.

PUBLIC MEMBER. A person representing the public, the state, on an arbitration panel or board as opposed to a member representing a particular interest.

PUBLIC MISCHIEF. With intent to mislead, causes a peace officer to enter upon or continue an investigation by (a) making a false statement that accuses some other person of having committed an offence; (b) doing anything that is intended to cause some other person to be suspected of having committed an offence that the person has not committed, or to divert suspicion from himself; or (c) reporting that an offence has been committed when it has not been committed; or (d) reporting or in any other way making it known or causing it to be made known that he or some other person has died when he or that other person has not died. *Criminal Code*, R.S.C. 1985, c. C-46, s. 140.

PUBLIC MONEY. 1. All money belonging to Canada received or collected by the Receiver General or any other public officer in his official capacity or any person authorized to receive or collect such money, and includes (a) duties and revenues of Canada; (b) money borrowed by Canada or received through the issue or sale of securities; (c) money received or collected for or on behalf of Canada; and (d) all money that is paid to or received or collected by a public officer under or pursuant to any Act, trust, treaty, undertaking or contract, and is to be disbursed for a purpose specified in or pursuant to that Act, trust, treaty, undertaking or contract. *Financial Administration Act*, R.S.C. 1985, c. F-11, s. 2. 2. All money belonging to the province received or collected by a minister or any public officer in an official capacity or any person authorized to receive or collect such money, and includes (i) revenues of a province; (ii) money borrowed by the

province or received through the sale of securities; (iii) money received or collected for or on behalf of the province; and (iv) money paid to the province for a special purpose.

PUBLIC NUISANCE. 1. A cause of action for personal injury or other loss in which a private claimant must be able to show that she or he incurred a special loss beyond the inconvenience or annoyance suffered by the general public. No right relating to land need be involved. J.G. Fleming, *The Law of Torts*, 8th ed. (Sydney: Law Book, 1992) at 411. 2. "... [O]ne which affects citizens generally as opposed to a private nuisance which only affects particular individuals, but a normal and legitimate way of proving a public nuisance is to prove a sufficiently large collection of similar private nuisances: ..." *British Columbia (Attorney General) v. Couillard* (1984), 31 C.C.L.T. 26 at 32, 42 C.R. (3d) 273, 59 B.C.L.R. 102, 11 D.L.R. (4th) 567, 14 C.C.C. (3d) 169 (S.C.), McEachern C.J.

PUBLIC OFFICER. 1. "... [E]very one who is appointed to discharge a public duty, and receives a compensation in whatever shape, whether from the crown or otherwise, is constituted a public officer ..." *Henly v. Mayor and Burgesses of Lyme* (1828), 5 Bing. 91 at 107, 130 E.R. 995 at 1001, Best C.J. 2. Includes any person in the public service (i) who is authorized by or under an enactment to do or enforce the doing of an act or thing or to exercise a power; or (ii) upon whom a duty is imposed by or under an enactment. 3. Includes a minister of the Crown and any person employed in the public service. 4. Includes (a) an officer of customs and excise; (b) an officer of the Canadian Forces; (c) an officer of the Royal Canadian Mounted Police; and (d) any officer while the officer is engaged in enforcing the laws of Canada relating to revenue, customs, excise, trade or navigation. *Criminal Code*, R.S.C. 1985, c. C-46, s. 2.

PUBLIC PLACE. Includes any place to which the public have access as of right or by invitation, express or implied. *Criminal Code*, R.S.C. 1985, c. C-46, s. 150.

PUBLIC POLICY. 1. The notion that no person can lawfully do what tends to injure the public or go against the public good. G.H.L. Fridman, *The Law of Contract in Canada*, 2d ed. (Toronto: Carswell, 1986) at 350. 2. "... [A]n action [will be barred] on the ground of public policy only if we could say it was contrary to 'essential public or moral interest' or 'contrary to our conceptions of essential justice and morality.' " *Block Brothers Realty Ltd. v. Mollard* (1981), 122 D.L.R. (3d) 323 at 330, [1981] 4 W.W.R. 65, 27 B.C.L.R. 17 (C.A.), the court per Craig J.A. 3. "... [F]ederal and provincial statutes and public law may be resorted to as a guide to public policy ..." *Seneca College of Applied Arts & Technology v. Bhadauria* (1979), 9 B.L.R. 117 at 125, 27 O.R. (2d) 142, 11 C.C.L.T. 121, 105 D.L.R. (3d) 707, 80 C.L.L.C. 14,003 (C.A.), the court per Wilson J.A.

PUBLIC PROPERTY. Property, immovable or movable, real or personal, belonging to Her Majesty in right of a province or in right of Canada and includes property belonging to an agency of government.

PUBLIC SALE. A sale either by public auction or public tender.

PUBLIC SERVANT. 1. Any person employed in a department, and includes a member of the Canadian Forces or the Royal Canadian Mounted Police. *Public Servants Inventions Act*, R.S.C. 1985, c. P-32, s. 2. 2. A person appointed under this Act to the service of the Crown by the Lieutenant Governor in Council, by the Commission or by a minister. *Public Service Act*, R.S.O. 1990, c. P.47, s. 1.

PUBLIC SERVICE. 1. The several positions in or under any department or other portion of the public service of Canada specified in Schedule I. *Public Service Staff Relations Act*, R.S.C. 1985, c. P-35, s. 2. 2. All ministries or any part thereof. *Management Board of Cabinet Act*, R.S.O. 1990, c. M.1, s.

1(1).

PUBLIC TRUST. A trust established to benefit the public or a section of it. D.M.W. Waters, *The Law of Trusts in Canada*, 2d ed. (Toronto: Carswell, 1984) at 24.

PUBLIC TRUSTEE. One who attends to matters relating to persons who are mentally incompetent, especially to property. G.D. Watson & C. Perkins, eds., *Holmested & Watson: Ontario Civil Procedure* (Toronto: Carswell, 1984) at 7-23.

PUBLISH. *v.* With respect to a libel, when he (a) exhibits it in public; (b) causes it to be read or seen; or (c) shows or delivers it, or causes it to be shown or delivered, with intent that it should be read or seen by the person whom it defames or by any other person. *Criminal Code*, R.S.C. 1985, c. C-46, s. 299.

PUBLISHED. *adj.* Communicated to someone else.

PUFF. *n.* A statement which praises a seller's goods but which an ordinary, reasonable buyer does not usually regard as important. G.H.L. Fridman, *Sale of Goods in Canada*, 3d ed. (Toronto: Carswell, 1986) at 149-150.

PUISNE. *adj.* [Fr.] Junior, of lower rank.

PUNISHMENT. *n.* A penalty for breaking the law. *R. v. Johnson* (1972), 17 C.R.N.S. 254 at 256, [1972] 3 W.W.R. 145, 6 C.C.C. (2d) 380 (B.C. C.A.), the court per Bull J.A. See ARBITRARY ~; CAPITAL ~; CRUEL AND UNUSUAL ~.

PUNITIVE DAMAGES. 1. "... [A]warded to punish the defendant and to make an example of him or her in order to deter others from committing the same tort: ..." *Norberg v. Wynrib* (1992), 12 C.C.L.T. (2d) 1 at 29, [1992] 4 W.W.R. 577, 68 B.C.L.R. (2d) 29, 138 N.R. 81, 8 B.C.A.C. 1, 19 W.A.C. 1, 92 D.L.R. (4th) 449, [1992] 2 S.C.R. 226, La Forest J. (Gonthier and Cory JJ. concurring). 2. "... [M]ay only be employed in circumstances where the conduct giving the cause for complaint is of such nature that it merits punishment. . . . may only be awarded in respect of conduct which is of such nature as to be deserving of punishment because of its harsh, vindictive, reprehensible and malicious nature . . . in any case where such an award is made the conduct must be extreme in its nature and such that by any reasonable standard it is deserving of full condemnation and punishment . . ." *Vorvis v. Insurance Corp. of British Columbia* (1989), 58 D.L.R. (4th) 193 at 201-2, 205-9, [1989] 1 S.C.R. 1085, [1989] 4 W.W.R. 193, 25 C.C.E.L. 81, 90 C.L.L.C. 14,035, 36 B.C.L.R. (2d) 273, 94 N.R. 321, 42 B.L.R. 111, McIntyre J. (Beetz and Lamer JJ. concurring).

PUR AUTRE VIE. [Fr.] For or during the life of another. R. Megarry & H.W.R. Wade, *The Law of Real Property*, 5th ed. (London: Stevens, 1984) at cxxvii. See ESTATE ~.

PURCHASE. *n.* 1. Contract, conveyance or assignment under or by which any beneficial interest in any kind of property may be acquired. 2. Includes taking by sale, lease, negotiation, mortgage, pledge, gift or any other consensual transaction creating an interest in personal property. *Personal Property Security acts.* See COMPULSORY ~.

PURCHASE PRICE. "[In a contract for commission means] . . . the actual price or sum at which the property was sold . . ." *George v. Howard* (1913), 16 D.L.R. 468 at 469, 5 W.W.R. 1152, 49 S.C.R. 75, 27 W.L.R. 425, Davies J.

PURCHASER. *n.* 1. A person who buys or agrees to buy goods or services. 2. A person who takes by sale, mortgage, hypothec, pledge, issue, reissue, gift or any other voluntary transaction creating an interest in a security. See BONA FIDE ~.

PURCHASER FOR VALUE WITHOUT NOTICE. One who purchased property bona fide for a valuable, even if inadequate, consideration without notice of any prior title or right that, if upheld, would restrict or limit the title which the purchaser supposedly acquired.

PURCHASER'S LIEN. A lien which protects the deposit and any other money that a person who agreed to purchase land paid on account of the purchase price, as well as costs and interest. B.J. Reiter, B.N. McLellan & P.M. Perell, *Real Estate Law*, 4th ed. (Toronto: Emond Montgomery, 1992) at 777.

PURE ECONOMIC LOSS. "[Usually refers to] . . . a diminution of worth incurred without any physical injury to any asset of the plaintiff . . ." *Ontario (Attorney General) v. Fatehi* (1984), 31 M.V.R. 301 at 307, [1984] 2 S.C.R. 536, 31 C.C.L.T. 1, 56 N.R. 62, 6 O.A.C. 270, 15 D.L.R. (4th) 132, the court per Estey J.

PURGE. *v.* With respect to contempt, to make amends for or clear oneself of contempt of court.

PURPOSE. See BASE ~; CHARITABLE ~.

PURSUANT. *adv.* 1. ". . . '[W]ithin the limits of' or 'as circumscribed by' . . ." *R. v. Melford Developments Inc.*, [1981] 2 F.C. 627 at 634, 36 N.R. 9, [1981] C.T.C. 30, 81 D.T.C. 5020 (C.A.), Urie J.A. (Thurlow C.J. concurring). 2. ". . . '[B]y reason of' . . ." *Canada (Minister of National Revenue) v. Armstrong*, [1954] C.T.C. 236 at 240, [1954] Ex. C.R. 529, 54 D.T.C. 1104, Potter J.

PURSUE. *v.* Of an authority or warrant, to execute or carry it out.

PURVIEW. *n.* The policy or scope of a statute.

PUT. *v.* With respect to a question, to read a motion or amendment from the Chair, seeking the House's pleasure. A. Fraser, W.A. Dawson & J. Holtby, eds., *Beauchesne's Rules and Forms of the House of Commons of Canada*, 6th ed. (Toronto: Carswell, 1989) at 93.

PUTATIVE. *adj.* Supposed, reputed.

PUTATIVE FATHER. A person alleged to have caused the pregnancy whereby a woman has become a mother.

PYKE. *abbr.* Pyke's Reports, King's Bench (Que.), 1809-1810.

Q

Q.A.C. *abbr.* Causes en appel au Québec (Quebec Appeal Cases).

Q.B. *abbr.* 1. Queen's Bench. 2. Court of Queen's Bench. 3. Supreme Court, Queen's Bench Division.

[ ] Q.B. *abbr.* Law Reports, Queen's Bench, 1891-.

Q.B.D. *abbr.* 1. Queen's Bench Division. 2. Law Reports, Queen's Bench Division, 1875-1890.

Q.C. *abbr.* Queen's Counsel.

Q.L.R. *abbr.* Quebec Law Reports, 1875-1891 (Rapports judiciaires du Québec).

QUA. *adv.* [L.] As, in the aspect of.

QUAERE. [L.] Inquire. Used to indicate that the proposition which follows is not settled law.

QUALIFICATION. *n.* 1. What makes anyone fit to do a particular act. 2. Limitation; diminishing. 3. Of an expert witness, ability to be an expert established after hearing evidence for and against, and after cross-examination. P.K. McWilliams, *Canadian Criminal Evidence*, 3d ed. (Aurora: Canada Law Book, 1988) at 9-10. See BONA FIDE OCCUPATIONAL ~.

QUALIFIED ACCEPTANCE. An acceptance with some change in the effect of the bill as originally drawn.

QUALIFIED PRIVILEGE. "... [A]n occasion where the person who makes a communication has an interest or a duty, legal, social, or moral, to make it to the person to whom it is made, and the person to whom it is so made has a corresponding interest or duty to receive it." *Adam v. Ward*, [1916-17] All E.R.Rep. 157 at 170 (U.K. H.L.), Lord Atkinson, definition accepted in *McLoughlin v. Kutasy* (1979), 8 C.C.L.T. 105 at 110, 26 N.R. 242, [1979] 2 S.C.R. 311, 97 D.L.R. (3d) 620, Ritchie J. (Martland, Pigeon, Beetz, Estey and Pratte JJ. concurring).

QUALIFIED PROPERTY. Limited and special ownership.

QUALIFIED TITLE. A registered title which is subject to an excepted estate, interest or right arising under a particular instrument or before a particular date, or otherwise specifically described in the register.

QUALIFY. *v.* To become legally entitled.

QUANTUM. *n.* [L.] An amount.

QUANTUM MERUIT. [L. as much as one earned] "The remedy of quantum meruit exists in two distinct settings. In a contractual setting, remuneration is said to be paid on a quantum meruit basis when, although a valid contract is found to exist in fact and law, there is no clause spelling out in express terms the consideration for the contract. In such circumstances, the Courts award reasonable remuneration to the person who has rendered the services. In an unjust enrichment setting, an action for quantum meruit is based, in general, upon the rendering of services by one person to another who has requested such services be rendered or freely accepted them with the knowledge that they are not rendered gratuitously." *Gill v. Grant* (1988), 30 E.T.R. 255 at 271 (B.C.S.C.), Rowles J.

QUANTUM VALEBANT. [L. as much as they were worth] A claim for goods "sold" or provided another way. G.H.L. Fridman, *Restitution*, 2d ed. (Toronto: Carswell, 1992) at 13.

QUARANTINE. *n.* (i) In respect of a person or animals, the limitation of freedom of movement and contact with other persons or animals; and (ii) in respect of premises, the prohibition against or the limitation on entering or leaving the premises, during the incubation period of the communicable disease in respect of which the quarantine is imposed.

QUARE. [L.] Inquire.

QUARE CLAUSUM FREGIT. [L. why one broke the close] Trespass on the plaintiff's lands.

QUARREL. *n.* A contest; a dispute.

QUASH. *v.* 1. "[In s. 39 of the Supreme Court Act, R.S.C. 1906, s. 139] ... 'annul' or 'make void.'" *Shawinigan Hydro Electric Co. v. Shawinigan Water & Power Co.* (1910), 43 S.C.R. 650 at 653, Fitzpatrick C.J.C. 2. "... [A] discharging or setting aside [of a by-law] and any remedy would be the simple act of quashing in itself...." *Gray v. Ottawa (City)*, [1971] 3 O.R. 112 at 115, 19 D.L.R. (3d) 524 (H.C.), Henderson J.

QUASI. *adv.* [L.] As if; as it were.

QUASI. *pref.* [L.] Similar but not the same as.

QUASI-CONTRACT. *n.* 1. "A contract is in some cases said to be implied by law, which really is an obligation imposed by law independently of any actual agreement between the parties, and may even be imposed notwithstanding an expressed intention by one of the parties to the contrary; it is an obligation of the class known in the civil law as quasi-contracts." *Dominion Distillery Products Co. v. R.*, [1938] 1

D.L.R. 597 at 613, [1937] Ex. C.R. 145, Maclean J. 2. A liability which cannot be attributed to any other legal principle and which requires someone to pay money to another person because non-payment would confer an unjust benefit on the proposed payor. See RESTITUTION; UNJUST ENRICHMENT.

QUASI-CRIMINAL OFFENCE. An offence created by provincial law which carries a penalty similar to that for a crime.

QUASI-ESTOPPEL. *n.* Once one party makes a representation about a present or past fact and the other party relies on it detrimentally, the representor cannot repudiate the representation and put forward the true facts. G.H.L. Fridman, *The Law of Contract in Canada*, 2d ed. (Toronto: Carswell, 1986) at 110.

QUASI-JUDICIAL. *adj.* With respect to a function, one that is partly administrative and partly judicial such as investigating facts, ascertaining that facts exist, holding hearings and drawing conclusions to guide official action from them and exercising discretion in a judicial way. S.A. DeSmith, *Judicial Review of Administrative Action*, 4th ed. by J.M. Evans (London: Stevens, 1980) at 77. See JUDICIAL OR ~ PROCEEDING.

[ ] **QUE. C.A.** *abbr.* Quebec Official Reports (Court of Appeal), 1970-.

QUEEN. *n.* 1. A woman who is the monarch of a kingdom. 2. The Sovereign of the United Kingdom, Canada and Her other Realms and Territories, and Head of the Commonwealth.

QUEEN'S BENCH. 1. In some provinces, the name given to the superior court. 2. In England, a superior court of common law.

QUEEN'S COUNSEL. A barrister appointed counsel to the Crown who wears a silk gown, sits within the bar and in court takes precedence over ordinary barristers.

QUEEN'S L.J. *abbr.* Queen's Law

Journal.

QUEEN'S PRINTER. Includes government printer or other official printer. *Evidence acts*.

QUEEN'S PRIVY COUNCIL FOR CANADA. A group which aids and advises the government of Canada and whose members are appointed or removed by the Governor General. P.W. Hogg, *Constitutional Law of Canada*, 3d ed. (Toronto: Carswell, 1992) at 230. See CLERK OF THE QUEEN'S PRIVY COUNCIL; PRIVY COUNCIL.

QUEEN'S PROCTOR. A representative of the Crown who may intervene in a divorce proceeding.

QUE. K.B. *abbr.* Quebec Official Reports (King's Bench), 1892-1941.

[ ] QUE. K.B. *abbr.* Quebec Official Reports (King's Bench), 1942-1969.

QUE. LAB. CT. *abbr.* Quebec Labour Court (Tribunal du travail)

QUE. L.R.B. *abbr.* Quebec Labour Relations Board (Commission des relations de travail du Québec).

QUE. P.R. *abbr.* Quebec Practice Reports, 1897-1944 (Rapports de Pratique du Québec).

[ ] QUE. P.R. *abbr.* Quebec Practice Reports, 1945- (Rapports de Pratique du Québec).

QUE. Q.B. *abbr.* 1. Quebec Court of Queen's (King's) Bench Reports. 2. Quebec Official Reports (Queen's Bench), 1892-1941.

[ ] QUE. Q.B. *abbr.* Quebec Official Reports (Queen's Bench), 1942-1969.

QUE. S.C. *abbr.* Quebec Official Reports (Superior Court), 1892-1941 (Rapports Judiciaires du Québec, Cour Supérieure).

[ ] QUE. S.C. *abbr.* Quebec Official Reports (Superior Court), 1942- (Recueils de jurisprudence du Québec, Cour Supérieure).

QUESTION. *n.* 1. An interrogation. 2. "... '[I]ssue'." *Blackburn v. Kochs Trucking Inc.* (1988), 25 C.P.C. (2d) 113 at 121, 58 Alta. L.R. (2d) 358,

[1988] 34 W.W.R. 272, 86 A.R. 321 (Q.B.), McDonald J. 3. "[In s. 42(1) of the Marital Property Act, 1980, S.N.B. 1980, c. M-1.1] ... means a point on which the parties are not agreed, that is, it means 'dispute' and does not simply mean an interrogatory." *George v. George* (1987), 37 D.L.R. (4th) 466 at 467, 8 R.F.L. (3d) 368, 80 N.B.R. (2d) 357, 202 A.P.R. 357 (Q.B.), Montgomery J. See COLLATERAL ~; LEADING ~; MIXED ~; ORAL ~; PRELIMINARY ~.

QUESTION OF FACT. 1. "... Where the term is simple and ordinary, and, as it were, can be reduced no further in simplicity or definition, and which to define would require words that themselves need definition, the question is one of fact. The terms 'resident' and 'insulting' are good examples. Where the term gives rise to some complexity, or has acquired a special or technical meaning, the question is likely, but not always, one of law." *Peters v. University Hospital* (1983), 1 Admin. L.R. 221 at 234, [1983] 5 W.W.R. 193, 4 C.H.R.R. D/1464, 147 D.L.R. (3d) 385, 23 Sask. R. 123 (C.A.), Bayda C.J.S. 2. "The construction of a statutory enactment is a question of law, while the question of whether the particular matter or thing is of such a nature or kind as to fall within the legal definition of its term is a question of fact." *Hollinger Consolidated Gold Mines Ltd. v. Tisdale (Township)*, [1933] 3 D.L.R. 15 at 16, [1933] S.C.R. 321, the court per Cannon J.

QUESTION OF LAW. 1. "... [I]n construing a will, deed, contract, prospectus or other commercial document, the legal effect to be given to the language employed, is a question of law ..." *R. v. Alberta Giftwares Ltd.* (1973), 11 C.P.R. (2d) 233 at 237, [1974] S.C.R. 584, [1973] 5 W.W.R. 458, 11 C.C.C. (2d) 513, 36 D.L.R. (3d) 321, the court per Ritchie J. 2. "... [W]ould include (without attempting anything like an exhaustive definition which would be impossible) questions touching the scope, effect or application of a rule of law which the Courts apply in determining the rights of parties; and by long usage, the term 'question of law' has come to be applied to questions which, when arising at a trial by a Judge and jury, would fall exclusively to the Judge for determination; for example, questions touching the construction of documents and a great variety of others including questions whether, in respect of a particular issue of fact, there is any evidence upon which a jury could find the issue in favour of the party on whom rests the burden of proof. . . ." *Canadian National Railway v. Bell Telephone Co.*, [1939] 3 D.L.R. 8 at 15, [1939] S.C.R. 308, 50 C.R.C.10, the court per Duff C.J.C. 3. "The construction of a statutory enactment is a question of law, while the question of whether the particular matter or thing is of such a nature or kind as to fall within the legal definition of its term is a question of fact." *Hollinger Consolidated Gold Mines Ltd. v. Tisdale (Township)*, [1933] 3 D.L.R. 15 at 16, [1933] S.C.R. 321, the court per Cannon J. 4. ". . .[W]hether a person's constitutional right has been infringed is a question of law." *R. v. Dunnett* (1990), 26 M.V.R. (2d) 194 at 200, 62 C.C.C. (3d) 14, 111 N.B.R. (2d) 67, 277 A.P.R. 67 (C.A.), Hoyt J.A. (Ayles J.A. concurring).

QUE. TAX R. *abbr.* Quebec Tax Reports.

QUIA EMPTORES. See STATUTE OF ~.

QUIA TIMET INJUNCTION. [L. because one fears] ". . . [A]n interim injunction to protect against feared future harm." *Bradley Resources Corp. v. Kelvin Energy Ltd.* (1985), 18 D.L.R. (4th) 468 at 471, [1985] 5 W.W.R. 763, 39 Alta.L.R. (2d) 193, 61 A.R. 169 (C.A.), the court per Kerans J.A. See INJUNCTION ~.

QUICQUID PLANTATUR SOLO, SOLO CEDIT. [L.] Whatever is affixed to the soil goes with the soil. *Canadian Imperial Bank of Commerce v. Alberta (Assessment Appeal Board)* (1990), 73 D.L.R. (4th) 271 at 277, 75 Alta. L.R. (2d) 362, [1990] 6 W.W.R. 425, 109 A.R. 203 (Q.B.), Andrekson

J. and *Collis v. Carew Lumber Co.*, [1930] 4 D.L.R. 996 at 999, 65 O.L.R. 520, 38 O.W.N. 237 (C.A.), Middleton J.A.

QUID PRO QUO. [L. something for something] A consideration.

QUIET. *v.* To settle; to render unassailable.

QUIET. *adj.* Unmolested, free from interference.

QUIET ENJOYMENT. 1. A covenant that a lessor or anyone claiming through or under the lessor may not enter. 2. ". . . [N]o act of a lessor will constitute an actionable breach of a convenant for quiet enjoyment unless it involves some physical or direct interference with the enjoyment of demised premises." *Owen v. Gadd*, [1956] 2 All E.R. 28 at 32 (U.K. C.A.), Romer L.J.

QUIETING TITLE. The judicial investigation of title and the ascertainment and declaration of the validity of title to real property.

QUIT. *v.* 1. With respect to a job, to resign. 2. With respect to leased premises, to surrender possession. See NOTICE TO ~.

QUIT CLAIM. To relinquish or release any claim to real property.

QUIT-CLAIM DEED. The conveyance without promises or warranties only of an interest, if any, which the grantor has in the land. It is often used to release an interest in land, e.g. the purchaser's interest, under an agreement of purchase and sale, which was registered against the title. B.J. Reiter, B.N. McLellan & P.M. Perell, *Real Estate Law*, 4th ed. (Toronto: Emond Montgomery, 1992) at 805.

QUIT RENT. A rent by which a tenant quits and is free of any other service.

QUITTANCE. *n.* An acquittal, a release.

QUOD VIDE. [L.] See this.

QUORUM. *n.* [L. of whom] 1. The majority of the whole group. 2. The number of members of a group able to transact business when other members are absent.

QUO WARRANTO. [L. by what authority] 1. A prerogative writ which challenges the usurpation of a public office by the continued exercise of authority which is not conferred legally. S.A. DeSmith, *Judicial Review of Administrative Action*, 4th ed. by J.M. Evans (London: Stevens, 1980) at 463. 2. "... [C]ivil proceedings. They are instituted by the Attorney-General, or through the intervention of the Attorney-General, ..." *R. v. Quesnel* (1909), (*sub nom. Tuttle v. Quesnel*) 11 W.L.R. 96 at 98 (Man. C.A.), the court per Howell C.J.A. 3. "... [L]ies against persons who claim any office, franchise, or privilege of a public nature, and not merely ministerial and held at the will and pleasure of others ..." *R. v. Roberts* (1912), 26 O.L.R. 263 at 271, 22 O.W.R. 50, 4 D.L.R. 278 (H.C.), Riddell J.

Q.V. *abbr.* [L.] Quod vide. See this.

R

R. *abbr.* 1. [L. regina] Queen. 2. [Fr. reine] Queen. 3. [L. rex] King. 4. [Fr. roi] King. 5. Rule.

R.A.C. *abbr.* Ramsay's Appeal Cases (Que.), 1873-1886.

RACIAL DISCRIMINATION. "... [C]learly involves something more than merely burdening a particular individual or group under the law; it involves the imposition of some such burden in a manner which creates or involves some stigma, as where there is 'a denial of the essential worth and dignity of the class against whom the law is directed' or 'a denial based upon unwarranted stereotypes about the capacities and roles of members of that class.' " *R. v. Punch* (1985), [1986] 2 C.N.L.R. 114 at 124, [1985] N.W.T.R. 373, [1986] 1 W.W.R. 592, 48 C.R. (3d) 374, 22 C.C.C. (3d) 289, 18 C.R.R. 74 (S.C.), de Weerdt J.

RACK-RENT. *n.* Rent which is not less than two-thirds of the full annual net value of the property out of which the rent arises. *City of St. John's Act*, R.S.Nfld. 1970, c. 40, s. 2.

RAM. & MOR. *abbr.* Ramsay & Morin, The Law Reporter (Journal de jurisprudence).

RAPE. *n.* "... [N]on-consensual sexual intercourse...." *R. v. McCraw* (1991), 7 C.R. (4th) 314 at 325, 66 C.C.C. (3d) 517, 128 N.R. 299, 49 O.A.C. 47, [1991] 3 S.C.R. 72, the court per Cory J. See AGGRAVATED SEXUAL ASSAULT; SEXUAL ASSAULT; STATUTORY ~.

RATE. *n.* Includes a general, individual or joint rate, fare, toll, charge, rental or other compensation of a public utility, a rule, regulation, practice, measurement, classification or contract of a public utility or corporation relating to a rate and a schedule or tariff respecting a rate. See CREDIT ~; CRIMINAL ~; DISCOUNT ~; PRIME ~.

RATES. *n.* The charges set or made for the supply of a public utility. See RATE.

RATIFICATION. *n.* 1. The act of confirming. 2. "In order to find the parties, in whose name and behalf an unauthorized person has assumed to enter into a contract, by subsequent recognition and adoption it must be shown that either expressly, or impliedly by conduct, the parties whom it is sought to bind have, with a full knowledge of all the terms of the agreement come to by the person who assumed to bind them, assented to the same terms and agreed to abide by and be bound by the contract undertaken on their behalf." *Cameron v. Paxton, Tate & Co.* (1888), 15 S.C.R. 622 at 633, Strong J. 3. Agency is created by ratification when an agent does something on behalf of a principal when they are not yet in the relation of principal and agent. Later, however, the principal accepts and adopts the agent's act as if there had been prior authorisation to do what was done. G.H.L. Fridman, *The Law of Agency*, 6th ed. (London: Butterworths, 1990) at 74. 4. Formal approval given to terms negotiated in collective bargaining. 5. "... [I]n respect of treaties, the formal adoption by the high contracting party of a previous assent conveyed by the signature of so-called plenipotentiaries." *Canada (Attorney General) v. Ontario (Attorney General)*, [1937] 1 D.L.R. 673 at 677, [1937] A.C. 326, [1937] 1 W.W.R. 299, [1937] W.N. 53 (Can. P.C.), the court per Lord Atkin.

RATING. *n.* The process by which tax rates are fixed and imposed by local authorities. I.M. Rogers, *The Law of Canadian Municipal Corporations*, 2d ed. (Toronto: Carswell, 1971-) at 567. See CREDIT ~.

RATING BUREAU. Any association or body created or organized for the purpose of filing or promulgating rates of premium payable upon contracts of insurance or which assumes to file or promulgate such rates by agreement, among the members thereof or otherwise.

RATIO. *n.* [L. a reason] The grounds or reason for deciding.

RATIO DECIDENDI. [L.] The grounds or reason for deciding.

RATIO LEGIS EST ANIMA LEGIS. [L.] The reason for the law is the essence of the law.

R.C. DE L'É. *abbr.* Recueils de jurisprudence de la Cour de l'Échiquier.

R.C.L.J. *abbr.* Revue critique de législation et de jurisprudence du Canada.

RCMP. *abbr.* Royal Canadian Mounted Police.

R.C.P.I. *abbr.* Revue canadienne de propriété intellectuelle.

R.C.S. *abbr.* Recueils des arrêts de la Cour Suprême du Canada.

[ ] R.C.S. *abbr.* Rapports judiciaires du Canada, Cour Suprême du Canada, 1964-.

R. DE J. *abbr.* Revue de jurisprudence.

R. DE L. *abbr.* Revue de Législation (1845-1848).

R.D.F. *abbr.* Recueil de droit de la famille.

R.D.F.Q. *abbr.* Recueil de droit fiscal québécois.

[ ] R.D.F.Q. *abbr.* Recueil de droit fiscal Québécois, 1977-.

R.D.I. *abbr.* Recueil de droit immobilier.

R.D.J. *abbr.* Revue de droit judiciaire, 1983-.

R.D. MCGILL. *abbr.* Revue de droit de McGill (McGill Law Journal).

R.D.T. *abbr.* Revue de droit de travail.

R. DU B. *abbr.* La Revue du Barreau.

R. DU B. CAN. *abbr.* La Revue du Barreau canadien (The Canadian Bar Review).

R. DU D. *abbr.* Revue du droit (1922-1939).

R. DU N. *abbr.* La Revue du Notariat.

R.D. U.N.-B. *abbr.* Revue de droit de l'Université du Nouveau-Brunswick (University of New Brunswick Law Review).

R.D.U.S. *abbr.* Revue de droit, Université de Sherbrooke.

RE. *prep.* [L.] Concerning, in the matter of.

READING. See FIRST ~; SECOND ~; THIRD ~.

READING DOWN. A doctrine which requires that, as much as possible, a statute be interpreted as within power. When the language of a statute will bear both a valid, limited meaning and an invalid, extended meaning, the limited meaning should be selected. P.W. Hogg, *Constitutional Law of Canada*, 3d ed. (Toronto: Carswell, 1992) at 393.

REAL. See CHATTELS ~.

REAL ACTION. The common law proceeding by which a freeholder was able to recover land.

REAL ESTATE. 1. "... [A]ll hereditaments...." *Montreal Light, Heat & Power Consolidated v. Westmount (Town)*, [1926] S.C.R. 515

at 523, [1926] 3 D.L.R. 466, Anglin C.J.C. (Duff, Mignault, Newcombe and Rinfret JJ. concurring). 2. Includes messuages, lands, tenements and hereditaments, whether freehold or of any other tenure, and whether corporeal or incorporeal, and any undivided share thereof, and any estate, right or interest therein.

REAL EVIDENCE. 1. "Evidence has been found to be 'real' when it referred to tangible items...." *R. v. Wise* (1992), 11 C.R. (4th) 253 at 265, [1992] 1 S.C.R. 527, 70 C.C.C. (3d) 193, 133 N.R. 161, 8 C.R.R. (2d) 53, 51 O.A.C 351, Cory J. (Lamer C.J.C., Gonthier and Stevenson JJ. concurring). 2. "... [E]xists independently of any statement by any witness, ..." *R. v. Schwartz* (1988), 55 D.L.R. (4th) 1 at 26, [1989] 1 W.W.R. 289, 66 C.R. (3d) 251, 88 N.R. 90, [1988] 2 S.C.R. 443, 45 C.C.C. (3d) 97, 56 Man. R. (2d) 92, 39 C.R.R. 260, Dickson C.J.C. (dissenting).

REALIZE. *v.* "... [T]o sell, to convert into money, ..." *Bayne, Re*, [1946] 3 D.L.R. 49 at 50 (N.S. S.C.), Chisholm C.J. (Hall J. concurring).

REAL LIKELIHOOD OF BIAS. See REASONABLE APPREHENSION OF BIAS.

REALM. *n.* A country; a territory subject to a sovereign.

REAL PROPERTY. 1. "... [C]orporeal and incorporeal hereditaments ... land [and].... rights in land, ..." *Pegg v. Pegg* (1992), 38 R.F.L. (3d) 179 at 184, 21 R.P.R. (2d) 149, 1 Alta. L.R. (3d) 249, 128 A.R. 132 (Q.B.), Agrios J. 2. Includes messuages, lands, rents and hereditaments whether of freehold or any other tenure whatever and whether corporeal or incorporeal and any undivided share thereof and any estate, right or interest other than a chattel interest therein. 3. The ground or soil and everything annexed to it, and includes land covered by water, all quarries and substances in or under land other than mines or minerals and all buildings, fixtures, machinery, structures and things erected on or under or affixed to land.

4. Includes any estate, interest or right to or in land, but does not include a mortgage secured by real property.

REASONABLE. *adj.* 1. "... [I]mplies a reason related to the purpose of the regulation, a rational connection between purpose and action and, in my view, it also implies a qualification on the nature of the action taken, that it be reasonable in the circumstances...." *Jackson v. Joyceville Penitentiary* (1990), 55 C.C.C. (3d) 50 at 80, 75 C.R. (3d) 174, 32 F.T.R. 96, 1 C.R.R. (2d) 327 (T.D.), Mackay J. 2. "A search will be reasonable if it is authorized by law, if the law itself is reasonable and if the manner in which the search was carried out is reasonable." *R. v. Collins*, [1987] 3 W.W.R. 699 at 712, 56 C.R. (3d) 193, 74 N.R. 276, 13 B.C.L.R. (2d) 1, [1987] 1 S.C.R. 265, 33 C.C.C. (3d) 1, 28 D.L.R. (4th) 508, 28 C.R.R. 122, Lamer J. 3. "... [T]he term 'reasonable' when used in the context of an interpretation of a provision in a collective agreement means an interpretation that is not absurd, one that is not ridiculous, outrageous, patently unjustifiable, extreme or excessive, but one that is a product of a sensible analysis, which may or may not be flawed, and one that may generally be described as within the bounds of reason. The interpretation does not have to be correct to be reasonable...." *University Hospital v. S.E.I.U., Local 333 U.H.* (1986), 26 D.L.R. (4th) 248 at 250, 46 Sask. R. 19, 86 C.L.L.C. 14,064 (C.A.), Bayda C.J.S. (dissenting). 4. "... [A]s used in the law of nuisance must be distinguished from its use elsewhere in the law of tort and especially as it is used in negligence actions.... [In nuisance] 'reasonable' means something more than merely 'taking proper care'. It signifies what is legally right between the parties, taking into account all the circumstances of the case, ..." *Russell Transport Ltd. v. Ontario Malleable Iron Co.*, [1952] O.R. 621 at 629, [1952] 4 D.L.R. 719 (H.C.), McRuer C.J.H.C. 5. In negligence, to take reasonable care means to take proper care. *Russell Transport Ltd. v.*

Ontario Malleable Iron Co., [1952] O.R. 621 at 629, [1952] 4 D.L.R. 719 (H.C.), McRuer C.J.H.C.

REASONABLE AND PROBABLE CAUSE. "Reasonable and probable cause has been defined as (Hicks v. Faulkner (1878), 8 Q.B.D. 167, at p. 171, per Hawkins J.): '... an honest belief in the guilt of the accused based upon a full conviction, founded on reasonable grounds, of the existence of a state of circumstances which, assuming them to be true, would reasonably lead any ordinary prudent and cautious man, placed in the position of the accuser, to the conclusion that the person charged was probably guilty of the crime imputed.' This test contains both a subjective and objective element. There must be both actual belief on the part of the prosecutor and that belief must be reasonable in the circumstances. The existence of reasonable and probable cause is a matter for the judge to decide as opposed to the jury." *Nelles v. Ontario* (1989), 42 C.R.R. 1 at 20, 49 C.C.L.T. 217, [1989] 2 S.C.R. 170, 37 C.P.C. (2d) 1, 71 C.R. (3d) 358, 60 D.L.R. (4th) 609, 98 N.R. 321, 69 O.R. (2d) 448n, 35 O.A.C. 161, 41 Admin. L.R. 1, Lamer J. (Dickson C.J.C. and Wilson J. concurring).

REASONABLE APPREHENSION OF BIAS. "The proper test to be applied in a matter of this type was correctly expressed by the Court of Appeal ... the apprehension of bias must be a reasonable one, held by reasonable and right minded persons, applying themselves to the question and obtaining thereon the required information. In the words of the Court of Appeal, that test is 'what would an informed person, viewing the matter realistically and practically – and having thought the matter through – conclude' ... I can see no real difference between the expressions found in the decided cases, be they 'reasonable apprehension of bias', 'reasonable suspicion of bias' or 'real likelihood of bias'...." *Committee for Justice & Liberty v. Canada (National Energy Board)*, [1978] 1 S.C.R. 369 at 394-5, 9 N.R. 115, 68 D.L.R. (3d) 716, de Grandpré J. (dissenting).

REASONABLE DOUBT. See BEYOND A ~.

REASONABLE LIMITS. 1. In section 1 of the Charter, rights are subject to such legal limitation as one can demonstrate is justified in a free and democratic society. 2. "... [O]ne which having regard to the principles enunciated in [R. v. Oakes (1986), 26 D.L.R. (4th) 200 (S.C.C.)], it was reasonable for the Legislature to impose...." *R. v. Videoflicks Ltd.* (1986), (*sub nom. Edwards Books & Art Ltd. v. R.*) 35 D.L.R. (4th) 1 at 51, 87 C.L.L.C. 14,001, 28 C.R.R. 1, 55 C.R. (3d) 193, 19 O.A.C. 239, 71 N.R. 161, [1986] 2 S.C.R. 713, 30 C.C.C. (3d) 385, 58 O.R. (2d) 442n, Dickson C.J.C. (Chouinard and Le Dain JJ. concurring). 3. "Two requirements must be satisfied to establish that a limit is reasonable and demonstrably justified in a free and democratic society. First, the legislative objective which the limitation is designed to promote must be of sufficient importance to warrant overriding a constitutional right. It must bear on a 'pressing and substantial concern'. Secondly, the means chosen to attain those objectives must be proportional or appropriate to the ends. The proportionality requirement, in turn, normally has three aspects: the limiting measures must be carefully designed, or rationally connected, to the objective; they must impair the right as little as possible; and their effects must not so severely trench on individual or group rights that the legislative objective, albeit important, is, nevertheless, outweighed by the abridgment of rights. The court stated that the nature of the proportionality test would vary depending on the circumstances." *R. v. Videoflicks Ltd.* (1986), (*sub nom. Edwards Books & Art Ltd. v. R.*) 35 D.L.R. (4th) 1 at 41, 87 C.L.L.C. 14,001, 28 C.R.R. 1, 55 C.R. (3d) 193, 19 O.A.C. 239, 71 N.R. 161, [1986] 2 S.C.R. 713, 30 C.C.C. (3d) 385, 58 O.R. (2d) 442n, Dickson C.J.C. (Chouinard and Le Dain JJ. concurring).

REASONABLE PERSON. 1. "[In the context of provocation in criminal law] ... the ordinary or reasonable person has a normal temperament and level of self-control. It follows that the ordinary person is not exceptionally excitable, pugnacious or in a state of drunkenness. ... particular characteristics that are not peculiar or idiosyncratic can be ascribed to an ordinary person wihout subverting the logic of the objective test of provocation." *R. v. Hill* (1985), 51 C.R. (3d) 97 at 114, [1986] 1 S.C.R. 313, 27 D.L.R. (4th) 187, 68 N.R. 161, 25 C.C.C. (3d) 322, 17 O.A.C. 33, Dickson C.J.C. (Beetz, Chouinard and La Forest JJ. concurring). 2. "[In the context of determining the existence of bias] ... it obviously is neither the 'anti-establishment or complaisant' person (Tremblay v. Quebec (Commission des Affaires Sociales) [(1989), 25 Q.A.C. 169 (Que. C.A.)] ... or even someone who is narrow-minded. Nor a functionary in the justice system or a person who knows all the intricacies of the justice system. Rather, it is the average person in society who must serve as the model." *Lippé c. Charest* (1990), (*sub nom. R. v. Lippé*) 60 C.C.C. (3d) 34 at 71, 80 C.R. (3d) 1, [1990] R.J.Q. 2200, 31 Q.A.C. 161, Proulx J.A.

REASONABLE SEARCH. "A search will be reasonable if it is authorized by law, if the law itself is reasonable and if the manner in which the search was carried out is reasonable." *R. v. Collins* (1987), 28 C.R.R. 122 at 132, [1987] 3 W.W.R. 699, 56 C.R. (3d) 193, 74 N.R. 276, 13 B.C.L.R. (2d) 1, [1987] 1 S.C.R. 265, 33 C.C.C. (3d) 1, 28 D.L.R. (4th) 508, Lamer J.

REASONABLE SUSPICION OF BIAS. See REASONABLE APPREHENSION OF BIAS.

REBUT. *v.* To contradict; to reply.

REBUTTABLE PRESUMPTION OF LAW. "... [T]hree categories of rebuttable presumptions (s. 241(1)(c) [of the Criminal Code, R.S.C. 1970, c. C-34] ... First, a permissive presump-

tion may tactically require an accused merely to raise a reasonable doubt once the Crown establishes a proved fact giving rise to the presumed fact, failing which the trier of fact may infer the presumed fact. Second, a mandatory presumption legally requires an accused to raise reasonable doubt as to the presumed fact, failing which the trier of fact must infer the presumed fact. Third, a mandatory presumption legally requires an accused to disprove the presumed fact on a balance of probabilities, failing which the trier of fact must infer the presumed fact." *R. v. Hummel* (1987), 36 C.C.C. (3d) 8 at 13, 1 M.V.R. (2d) 4, 60 O.R. (2d) 545, 60 C.R. (3d) 78 (H.C.), Ewaschuk J.

REBUTTAL EVIDENCE. Evidence which rebuts or contradicts evidence which the defence adduced in the case. P.K. McWilliams, *Canadian Criminal Evidence*, 3d ed. (Aurora: Canada Law Book, 1988) at 31-1.

REBUTTER. *n.* In pleadings, the defendant's response to the surrejoinder.

REC. ANN. WINDSOR ACCÈS JUSTICE. *abbr.* Recueil annuel de Windsor d'accès à la justice (Windsor Yearbook of Access to Justice).

RECEIPT. *n.* An acknowledgement in writing that one received money or property. See NEGOTIABLE ~.

RECEIVABLE. *adj.* "... '[T]o be received' ..." *Wilson & Wilson Ltd. v. Minister of National Revenue*, [1960] C.T.C. 1 at 10, [1960] Ex. C.R. 205, 60 D.T.C. 1018, Cameron J. See FACTORING OF ~S.

RECEIVER. *n.* 1. A person who was appointed to take possession of property which belongs to a third party. F. Bennett, *Receiverships* (Toronto: Carswell, 1985) at 1. 2. A person appointed by a court to receive the rent and profit of real estate or to collect personal goods. When the appointment is by way of equitable execution, the receiver has the power to sell the personalty and to distribute the rents, proceeds and profits of the real estate to any judgment creditors. C.R.B.

Dunlop, *Creditor-Debtor Law in Canada* (Toronto: Carswell, 1981) at 281. 3. "... [C]an encompass a receiver-manager...." *Cook's Ferry Band v. Cook's Ferry Band Council* (1989), (*sub nom. Minnabarriet v. Cook's Ferry Band Council*) 75 C.B.R. (N.S.) 228 at 232, [1989] 4 C.N.L.R. 105 (Fed. T.D.), Reed J. See INTERIM ~; OFFICIAL ~; PRIVATE ~,

RECEIVER AND MANAGER. A person appointed to carry on or superintend a trade, business or undertaking in addition to receiving rents and profits, or to get in outstanding property.

RECEIVING ORDER. An order which declares a debtor to be bankrupt and which results in the trustee of the bankrupt estate being appointed rather than a receiver. F. Bennett, *Receiverships* (Toronto: Carswell, 1985) at 3.

RECENT POSSESSION. "... [T]he presumption ... resulting from the mere circumstances of recent possession of stolen goods, is that the initial possession was gained with the knowledge that the goods were stolen." *R. v. Suchard*, [1956] S.C.R. 425 at 427, 23 C.R. 207, 114 C.C.C. 257, 2 D.L.R. (2d) 609, Fauteux J. (Taschereau J. concurring).

RECESS. *n.* 1. The period between Parliament being prorogued and reassembling for a new session. A. Fraser, W.A. Dawson & J. Holtby, eds., *Beauchesne's Rules and Forms of the House of Commons of Canada*, 6th ed. (Toronto: Carswell, 1989) at 66. 2. A short pause in a sitting of a court.

RECIDIVIST. *n.* A person who repeatedly commits crimes.

RECIPROCITY. *n.* Refers to agreements to recognize orders or judgments of another state. Usually accomplished by the enactment of similar legislation in both states. See, for example, Reciprocal Enforcement of Maintenance acts and Reciprocal Enforcement of Judgments acts.

RECISSION. *n.* Commonly, the ending of a contract because a contract term classified as a condition was breached or a party repudiated or absolutely refused to perform its contractual obligations. B.J. Reiter, B.N. McLellan & P.M. Perell, *Real Estate Law*, 4th ed. (Toronto: Emond Montgomery, 1992) at 681. 2. Technically, an equitable remedy that restores parties to their position before the contract. B.J. Reiter, B.N. McLellan & P.M. Perell, *Real Estate Law*, 4th ed. (Toronto: Emond Montgomery, 1992) at 681.

RECITAL. *n.* A statement in an agreement, deed or other formal document intended to lead up to or explain the operative part of the document.

RECKLESS. *adj.* 1. "... [H]eedless of consequences, headlong or irresponsible...." *R. v. Barron* (1984), 39 C.R. (3d) 379 at 391 (Ont. H.C.), Ewaschuk J. 2. "[In s. 202 of the Criminal Code, R.S.C. 1970, c. C-34] ... reckless means a person shows carelessness for the consequence of his act so far as the lives or safety of other persons are concerned...." *R. v. Canadian Liquid Air Ltd.* (1972), 20 C.R.N.S. 208 at 210 (B.C. S.C.), McKay J.

RECKLESSLY. *adv.* "... [I]ntention will be attributed or imputed to an accused where he acts recklessly in the circumstances. In such a situation, 'The term "recklessly" is ... used to denote the subjective state of mind of a person who foresees that his conduct may cause the prohibited result but, nevertheless, takes a deliberate and unjustifiable risk of bringing it about ...': see R. v. Buzzanga (1979), 25 O.R. (2d) 705 ... (C.A.). Depending on the definitional elements of and terms employed in the crime, the accused may be sufficiently reckless to have imputed to him the necessary guilty intention where his foresight indicates to him that the unjustified risk will probably result in the prohibited harm, will be highly probable or, for certain crimes, substantially certain to occur ..." *R. v. Barron* (1984), 39 C.R. (3d) 379 at 390 (Ont. H.C.), Ewaschuk J.

RECOGNIZANCE. *n.* "The recognizance contemplated by a. 22 [of the Coroner's Act, R.S.S. 1978, c. C-38] is in the nature of a performance bond: an acknowledgement by the person from whom it is taken that he is indebted to the Crown in the amount fixed therein, provided always, that if he fulfills the condition of the undertaking and appears as required the debt ceases . . ." *McMillan v. Bassett* (1983), [1984] 1 W.W.R. 150 at 154, 29 Sask. R. 272, 9 C.C.C. (3d) 45 (C.A.), the court per Cameron J.A.

RECOMMENDATION TO MERCY. Before the death penalty was abolished, a jury who found an accused guilty of murder could accompany their verdict by recommending the prisoner to the Crown's mercy, on certain particular grounds.

RECONCILIATION. *n.* ". . . [D]oes not take place unless and until mutual trust and confidence are restored. It is not to be expected that the parties can ever recapture the mutual devotion which existed when they were first married, but their relationship must be restored, by mutual consent, to a settled rhythm in which the past offences, if not forgotten, at least no longer rankle and embitter their daily lives. Then, and not till then, are the offences condoned. Reconciliation being the test of condonation, nothing short of it will suffice." *Mackrell v. Mackrell*, [1948] 2 All E.R. 858 at 860-61 (U.K. C.A.), Denning L.J.

RECONSTRUCTION. *n.* Transferring the assets, or a major part of them, of one company to a new company formed for just that purpose in exchange for shares of the new company to be distributed among the old company's shareholders. H. Sutherland, D.B. Horsley & J.M. Edmiston, eds., *Fraser's Handbook on Canadian Company Law*, 7th ed. (Toronto: Carswell, 1985) at 349. See REORGANIZATION.

RECONVERSION. *n.* An imaginary process in which an earlier constructive conversion is annulled and the converted property is restored to its original condition in contemplation of law.

RECONVEYANCE. *n.* Conveying mortgaged property again, free from the mortgage debt, to the mortgagor or the mortgagor's representatives after the mortgage debt is paid off.

RECORD. *n.* 1. ". . . [M]ust contain at least the document which initiates the proceedings, the pleadings, if any, and the adjudication, but not the evidence, nor the reasons, unless the tribunal chooses to incorporate them." *R. v. Northumberland Comp. App. Trib.; Ex parte Shaw*, [1952] 1 All E.R. 122 at 131 (U.K. C.A.), Denning L.J. 2. "In *Farrell v. Workmen's Compensation Bd.* . . . 26 D.L.R. (2d) 177 . . . the British Columbia Court of Appeal held (. . . at p. 196 and . . . at p. 201) that the record consisted only of the initiating document, the pleadings, if any, and the adjudication (including the reasons if incorporated in the decision) but not the evidence or the supporting documents referred to in the adjudication. . . ." *Woodward Stores (Westmount) Ltd. v. Alberta (Assessment Appeal Board, Division No. 1)*, [1976] 5 W.W.R. 496 at 511, 69 D.L.R. (3d) 450 (Alta. T.D.), McDonald J. See COURT OF ~; COURT ~.

RECOUPMENT. *n.* Complete repayment in that the whole sum of money spent effectively discharges the debt for which, though both parties are liable, the defendant is largely liable. G.H.L. Fridman, *Restitution*, 2d ed. (Toronto: Carswell, 1992) at 242.

RECOURSE. *n.* The right to recover against a party secondarily liable. See WITHOUT ~ TO ME.

RECOVER. *v.* 1. ". . . The usual meaning in the context of the judicial process is that of 'gaining through a judgment or order'. . . ." *Centrac Industries Ltd. v. Vollan Enterprises Ltd.* (1989), 70 Alta. L.R. (2d) 396 at 398, 100 A.R. 301, 39 C.P.C. (2d) 136 (C.A.), Lieberman, Stevenson and Irving JJ.A. 2. ". . . [T]he taking of possession of some form of property . . ." *Prism Petroleum Ltd. v. Omega Hydrocarbons Ltd.* (1992), 4 Alta. L.R.

(3d) 332 at 348, [1993] 1 W.W.R. 204, 130 A.R. 114 (Q.B.), Egbert J.

RECOVERY. *n.* 1. Obtaining something which was wrongfully taken or withheld from someone, or to which that person is otherwise entitled. 2. That a person who is, or was, a patient is no longer infectious. *Public Health Act*, R.R.O. 1980, Reg. 836, s. 1.

RECTIFICATION. *n.* "... [O]perates in a proper case to reform the instruments in order to ensure that they express the agreement actually reached by the parties...." *Soni v. Malik* (1985), 1 C.P.C. (2d) 53 at 57, 61 B.C.L.R. 36 (S.C.), McEachern C.J.S.C.

RECTIFY. *v.* To alter the written words of an agreement so that they reflect what the parties really agreed. D.J.M. Brown & D.M. Beatty, *Canadian Labour Arbitration*, 3d ed. (Aurora: Canada Law Book, 1988-) at 2-33.

R.E.D. *abbr.* 1. Russell's Equity Decisions (N.S.), 1873-1882. 2. Ritchie's Equity Decisions (Can.) 3. Ritchie's Equity Decisions, by Russell (N.S.). 4. Ritchie's Equity Reports, by Russell (N.S.).

REDDENDUM. *n.* [L. that which is to be paid or rendered] The clause in a lease, usually using the words "yielding and paying", which states the amount of the rent and the time at which it should be paid.

REDEEM. *v.* To buy back. See ACTION TO ~.

REDEEMABLE SECURITY. A security which exists for a fixed term and is redeemable at the end of that term at a specified value.

REDEEMABLE SHARE. A share issued by a corporation (a) that the corporation may purchase or redeem on the demand of the corporation; or (b) that the corporation is required by its articles to purchase or redeem at a specified time or on the demand of a shareholder.

REDEEM UP, FORECLOSE DOWN. Expression which refers to the mortgagor's right to redeem the interest of all mortgagees and the right of a mortgagee to redeem the interest of all mortgagees prior to (above) him in title. A third mortgagee may redeem the interest of a first mortgagee. However, a second mortgagee may only foreclose the interest of subsequent (lower) mortgagees or encumbrancers and cannot foreclose the interest of the first mortgagee.

REDELIVERY. *n.* Yielding and delivering something back.

REDEMISE. *n.* Re-granting land.

REDEMPTION. *n.* 1. The payment of the amount owing under a mortgage to, in effect, buy back the title to the property. An equitable right of the mortgagor or those who claim under him. 2. In relation to mutual fund shares of the company, be deemed to be a reference to acceptance by the company of the surrender of those shares. *Companies Act*, R.S.N.W.T. 1974, c. C-7, s. 71. See EQUITY OF ~.

REDRESS. *n.* Relief in the form of damages or equitable relief.

REDUCTIO AD ABSURDUM. [L.] The way to disprove an argument by demonstrating that it leads to an unreasonable conclusion.

REDUNDANCY. *n.* Unneeded or extraneous material inserted in a pleading.

RE-ENTRY. *n.* In a lease, a proviso which empowers the lessor to re-enter the leased premises if the rent has not been paid for a certain period.

REF. *abbr.* Reference.

REFER. *v.* With respect to a question, to have it decided by someone nominated for that purpose.

REFEREE. *n.* A person to whom a court refers a pending cause so that that person may take testimony, hear the parties, and report back.

REFERENCE. *n.* 1. Sending a whole proceeding or a particular issue to the referring judge, a registrar or other court officer, a person the parties agree on or a family law commissioner. G.D.

Watson & C. Perkins, eds., *Holmested & Watson: Ontario Civil Procedure* (Toronto: Carswell, 1984) at 54-2. 2. A question which a government presents to a court for an opinion concerning the constitutionality of an enactment although there is no real dispute. Robert J. Sharpe, ed., *Charter Litigation* (Toronto: Butterworths, 1987) at 337. 3. In order to take accounts or make inquiries, to determine any question or issue of fact, the court may refer any matter to a judge whom the Associate Chief Justice nominates, a prothonotary, or any other person the court deems to be qualified for the purpose so that that person may inquire and report. D. Sgayias *et al., Federal Court Practice 1988* (Toronto: Carswell, 1987) at 499. See ADOPTION BY ~; FEDERAL ~; PROVINCIAL ~.

REFERENDUM. *n.* The direct vote of electors concerning a particular by-law or question affecting the municipality. I.M. Rogers, *The Law of Canadian Municipal Corporations*, 2d ed. (Toronto: Carswell, 1971-) at 111.

REFORM. *v.* With respect to an instrument, to rectify it.

REFORMATORY. *n.* An institution where offenders are sent to be reformed.

REFRESH. *v.* With respect to a witness' memory, to refer to a document which may not itself be admissible as evidence.

REFUGEE. *n.* A person who, by reason of a well-founded fear of persecution for reasons of race, religion, nationality, political opinion or membership in a particular social group, (a) has been lawfully admitted to Canada for permanent residence after leaving the country of his nationality and is unable or, by reason of that fear, is unwilling to avail himself of the protection of that country; or (b) has been lawfully admitted to Canada for permanent residence after leaving the country of his former habitual residence and is unable or, by reason of that fear, is unwilling to return to that country and includes, on designation by

the Lieutenant Governor in Council, any other person or class of persons admitted to Canada under section 6(2) of the Immigration Act, 1976 (Canada). *Refugee Settlement Program of British Columbia Act*, S.B.C. 1979, c. 27, s. 1.

REG. *abbr.* 1. [L. regina] Queen. 2. Regulation. 3. Registrar.

REGIME. See COMMUNITY PROPERTY ~.

REGISTER. *v.* To file or deposit.

REGISTER. *n.* 1. That part of the records where information respecting registered titles is stored. 2. The register of members and students of a professional body.

REGISTERED. *adj.* Filed, listed or holder of a particular status in accordance with an act.

REGISTERED CREDITOR. A creditor who is named in a consolidation order. *Bankruptcy Act*, R.S.C. 1985, c. B-3, s. 217.

REGISTERED OFFICE. A head office or chief place of business the address of which is provided to the provincial or federal authority governing the company and where notices and process may be served on the company and certain documents and books must be kept. H. Sutherland, D.B. Horsley & J.M. Edmiston, eds., *Fraser's Handbook on Canadian Company Law*, 7th ed. (Toronto: Carswell, 1985) at 429.

REGISTERED ORDER. (i) A final order made in a reciprocating state and filed under this Act or under an enactment repealed by this Act with a court in the Province; (ii) a final order deemed to be a registered order; or (iii) a confirmation order that is filed. *Maintenance Orders Enforcement acts.*

REGISTERED OWNER. 1. An owner of land whose interest in the land is defined and whose name is specified in an instrument in the registry office. 2. The person registered in a land titles office as owner of the fee simple in land unless it appears from the records of the land titles office that another person has purchased the land under an agreement for sale in which case it means that other person. 3. A person in whose name a vehicle is registered.

REGISTRAR. *n.* 1. The person responsible for the operation and management of a registration system. 2. With respect to a court, the administrative officer who is responsible for filing and issuing particular documents, retaining court files and occasionally for assessing costs. 3. The registrar or master of deeds or land titles or other officer with whom a title to land is registered or recorded.

REGISTRAR GENERAL. 1. The provincial officer who registers any birth, death and marriage. 2. The Registrar General as defined in the Vital Statistics Act.

REGISTRAR OF DEEDS. Includes the registrar of land titles or other officer with whom a title to the land is registered.

REGISTRAR OF LAND TITLES. A registrar of land titles appointed under a Land Titles Act.

REGISTRAR OF MOTOR VEHICLES. The person who from time to time performs the duties of superintending the registration of motor vehicles in a province.

REGISTRATION. *n.* 1. (i) Bringing lands under this Act; (ii) entering upon the certificate of title a memorandum authorized by this Act, of any document. *Land Titles acts.* 2. A valid and subsisting registration permit. 3. The admission of an individual to membership in a professional association and enrolment of that person's name in a register. 4. The entry of the name of a person in a register.

REGISTRY. *n.* The office of the Registrar.

REGISTRY ACT SYSTEM. 1. A person acquiring an interest in land registered in this system must examine the title as it is recorded in the Registry Office, and a vendor usually must show that she or he is lawfully entitled to own the land through a chain of title extending back for a period of years.

W.B. Rayner & R.H. McLaren, *Falconbridge on Mortgages*, 4th ed. (Toronto: Canada Law Book, 1977) at 127. 2. Under such a system, anyone who acquires interest in land may register a copy of the document which transfers that interest. The registered documents are organized so that any person may, for a small fee, examine those which affect a particular piece of land. In most cases, a claim which is not registered does not affect a later mortgagee or purchaser who acquired an interest for value and without actually being notified of the unregistered claim, but simple registration of a document does not assure its effectiveness. B.J. Reiter, B.N. McLellan & P.M. Perell, *Real Estate Law*, 4th ed. (Toronto: Emond Montgomery, 1992) at 388.

REGNAL YEAR. A year calculated from a sovereign's accession to the throne, thus 7 Eliz. 2 means the seventh year after the accession of Elizabeth II on February 6, 1952 (February 6, 1958, to February 5, 1959).

RE-GRANT. *v.* For a grantor to grant again granted property which came back.

REGULAR FORCE. 1. The regular force of the Canadian Forces and includes (a) the forces known before February 1, 1968 as the regular forces of the Canadian Forces; and (b) the forces known before February 1, 1968 as the Royal Canadian Navy, the Canadian Army Active Force, the Permanent Active Militia, the Permanent Militia Corps, the permanent staff of the Militia, the Royal Canadian Air Force (Regular) and the Permanent Active Air Force. *Canadian Forces Superannuation Act*, R.S.C. 1985, c. C-17, s. 2. 2. The component of the Canadian Forces that is referred to in the National Defence Act as the regular force. *Interpretation Act*, R.S.C. 1985, c. I-21, s. 35.

REGULATE. *v.* ". . . [T]he regulation and governance of a trade may involve the imposition of restrictions on its exercise both as to time and to a certain extent as to place where such restrictions are in the opinion of the public authority necessary to prevent a nuisance or for the maintenance of order. But ... there is a marked distinction to be drawn between the prohibition or prevention of a trade and the regulation or governance of it, indeed a power to regulate [as described in the Municipal Act, ...] and govern seems to imply the continued existence of that which is to be regulated or governed ... when the Legislature intended to give power to prevent or prohibit it did so by express words.... a municipal power of regulation ... without express words of prohibition, does not authorize the making it unlawful to carry on a lawful trade in a lawful manner." *Toronto (City) v. Virgo*, [1896] A.C. 88 at 93 (Can. P.C.), the board per Lord Davey.

REGULATION. *n.* 1. "That a power of regulation does not extend to restriction was well stated by MacMahon J., in Re Imperial Starch Co. [(1905), 10 O.L.R. 22 (H.C.) at 25], in language which was adopted in a later case, and which their Lordships would repeat: 'The statute gives the company power to pass by-laws "regulating the transfer" of stock; that is; how and in what manner and with what formalities it is to be transferred....' " *Canada National Fire Insurance Co. v.* Hutchings (1918), 39 D.L.R. 401 at 405, [1918] 3 W.W.R. 154, [1918] A.C. 451 (Man. P.C.), the board per Sir Walter Phillimore. 2. Includes an order, regulation, rule, rule of court, form, tariff of costs or fees, letters patent, commission, warrant, proclamation, by-law, resolution or other instrument issued, made or established (a) in the execution of a power conferred by or under the authority of an Act; or (b) by or under the authority of the Governor in Council. *Interpretation Act*, R.S.C. 1985, c. I-21, s. 2. 3. A regulation, order, rule, form, tariff of costs or fees, proclamation or by-law enacted (i) in the execution of a power conferred by or under the authority of an act; or (ii) by or under the authority of the Lieutenant Governor in Council, but does not include an order of a court or

an order made by a public officer or administrative tribunal in a dispute between two or more persons. 4. A statutory instrument (a) made in the exercise of a legislative power conferred by or under an Act of Parliament; or (b) for the contravention of which a penalty, fine or imprisonment is prescribed by or under an Act of Parliament, and includes a rule, order or regulation governing the practice or procedure in any proceedings before a judicial or quasi-judicial body established by or under an Act of Parliament, and any instrument described as a regulation in any other Act of Parliament. *Statutory Instruments Act*, R.S.C. 1985, c. S-22, s. 2. See C.T.C. ~S.

REGULATORY OFFENCE. "... '[A] wide category of offences created by statutes enacted for the regulation of individual conduct in the interests of health, convenience, safety and general welfare of the public' which are not subject to the common law presumption of mens rea as an essential element to be proven by the Crown." *R. v. Wholesale Travel Group Inc.* (1991), 8 C.R. (4th) 145 at 160, 67 C.C.C. (3d) 193, 4 O.R. (3d) 799n, 84 D.L.R. (4th) 161, 130 N.R. 1, 38 C.P.R. (3d) 451, 49 O.A.C. 161, [1991] 3 S.C.R. 154, 7 C.R.R. (2d) 36, Cory J. (L'Heureux-Dubé J. concurring).

REHABILITATE. *v.* 1. To restore to former rank, right or privilege. 2. To qualify again. 3. To restore a lost right.

REHABILITATION. *n.* The establishment or the restoration of a disabled person to a state of economic and social sufficiency.

RE-HEARING. *n.* Presentation of evidence and argument and the pronunciation of a second judgment in a cause or matter which was already decided.

REINSTATE. *v.* In an insurance policy, to restore buildings or chattels which have been damaged. R. Colinvaux, *The Law of Insurance*, 5th ed. (London: Sweet & Maxwell, 1984) at 181.

REINSTATEMENT. *n.* A remedy available when a labour board proves a claim of unfair dismissal against an employer. It requires that the employer act as though the employee had never been dismissed.

REINSURANCE. *n.* 1. An agreement whereby contracts made by a licensed insurer or any class or group thereof are undertaken or reinsured by another insurer either by novation, transfer, assignment or as a result of amalgamation of the insurers. 2. New insurance under a new policy upon the same risk, which may be in wider or narrower form and which was insured before, that indemnifies the insurer from previous liability. R. Colinvaux, *The Law of Insurance*, 5th ed. (London: Sweet & Maxwell, 1984) at 186.

REJOINDER. *n.* The defendant's answer to the plaintiff's reply.

RELATION BACK. A doctrine by which an act produces the same effect as it would have if it had happened at an earlier time.

RELATIVE. *n.* ". . . [C]ommonly understood to refer to a relation of consanguinity, close or distant, and to a legally recognized affinity created, for instance, by marriage or adoption." *Leroux v. Co-operators General Insurance Co.* (1990), 44 C.C.L.I. 253 at 259, [1990] I.L.R. 1-2566, 65 D.L.R. (4th) 702, 71 O.R. (2d) 641 (H.C.), Arbour J. See COLLATERAL ~; DEPENDENT ~ REVOCATION.

RELATOR ACTION. An action in which a relator tries by injunction to prevent any interfering with or infringing of a public right, to stop a public nuisance or to force a public duty to be performed or observed. The relator brings this action in the Attorney-General's name after obtaining leave to do so. I.H. Jacob, ed., *Bullen and Leake and Jacob's Precedents of Pleadings*, 12th ed. (London: Sweet and Maxwell, 1975) at 768.

RELEASE. *v.* 1. To surrender or relinquish a claim or interest in property. *Donnell, Re*, [1930] 4 D.L.R. 1037 at 1037 (Ont. Surr. Ct.), Widdifield Surr. Ct. J. 2. In relation to any information, document, recording or statement, means to communicate, disclose or make available the information, document, recording or statement. *Canadian Aviation Safety Board Act*, R.S.C. 1985, c. C-12, s. 2. 3. In respect of goods, means to authorize the removal of the goods from a customs office, sufferance warehouse, bonded warehouse or duty free shop for use in Canada.

RELEASE. *n.* 1. The document by which a claim or interest in property is surrendered or relinquished. 2. The termination of the service of an officer or non-commissioned member in any manner. *Defence Act*, R.S.C. 1985 (1st Supp.), c. 31, s. 1. 3. A document issued by the Court which releases property arrested by warrant. D. Sgayias *et al.*, *Federal Court Practice 1988* (Toronto: Carswell, 1987) at 540.

RELEVANCY. *n.* Relationship to that which is the subject of the action. P.K. McWilliams, *Canadian Criminal Evidence*, 3d ed. (Aurora: Canada Law Book, 1988) at 11-2.

RELEVANT. *adj.* Applying to the matter in issue.

RELICTION. *n.* The sudden receding of sea from the land.

RELIEF. *n.* Includes every species of relief, whether by way of damages, payment of money, injunction, declaration, restitution of an incorporeal right, return of land or chattels or otherwise. See ANCILLARY ~; COROLLARY ~; CREDITORS' ~ STATUTE; DECLARATORY ~; INTERIM ~; PRAYER FOR ~.

RELIEF AGAINST FORFEITURE. In an appropriate and limited case a court of equity will grant this relief for breach of a condition or covenant when the main object of the deal was to secure a certain result and provision for forfeiture was added to secure that result. F. Bennett, *Receiverships* (Toronto: Carswell, 1985) at 355.

RELIGION. See FREEDOM OF CONSCIENCE AND ~; FREEDOM OF ~.

REM. *abbr.* Remanet.

REMAINDER. *n.* That part of a grantor's interest in an estate which is disposed of, but which is postponed to some estate in possession created at the same time. R. Megarry & H.W.R. Wade, *The Law of Real Property*, 5th ed. (London: Stevens, 1984) at 236 and cxxvii. See VESTED ~.

REMAINDERMAN. *n.* A person with rightful claim to an expectant estate.

REMAIN SILENT. See RIGHT TO ~.

REMAND. *v.* To adjourn a hearing to a future date, ordering the defendant, unless permitted bail, to be kept in the meantime in custody.

REMAND PRISONER. A prisoner (i) remanded in custody by a judge or court; and (ii) awaiting trial, or the resumption or conclusion of a trial, for contravention of an Act of the Parliament of Canada or a legislature or of any regulations or order made pursuant to any such act.

REMANET. *n.* [L.] 1. Whatever remains. 2. An action, scheduled for trial in a certain session, which does not come on so that it stands over to the next session.

REMEDIAL CONSTRUCTIVE TRUST. ". . . [T]he acts of the parties are such that a wrong is done by one of them to another so that, while no substantive trust relationship is then and there brought into being by those acts, nonetheless a remedy is required in relation to property and the court grants that remedy in the form of a declaration which, when the order is made, creates a constructive trust by one of the parties in favour of another party. . . . A remedial constructive trust is a trust imposed by Court order as a remedy for a wrong . . . the trust itself [is created] by the order of the Court." *Atlas Cabinets & Furniture Ltd. v. National Trust Co.* (1990), 37 E.T.R. 16 at 27, 38 C.L.R. 106, 45 B.C.L.R. (2d) 99, 68 D.L.R. (4th) 161 (C.A.), Lambert J.A. (Hinkson, Toy and Cumming JJ.A. concurring).

REMEDIAL STATUTE. A statute drafted to remedy a defect in the law.

REMEDY. *n.* The means by which one prevents, redresses or compensates the violation of a right. See APPRAISAL ~; CUMULATIVE ~; DISCRETIONARY ~; EQUITY WILL NOT SUFFER A WRONG TO BE WITHOUT A ~; EXTRAORDINARY ~; MUTUALITY OF ~.

REMEDY CLAUSE. Section 24(1) of the Charter, which allows a remedy to be granted to enforce the rights or freedoms the Charter guarantees. P.W. Hogg, *Constitutional Law of Canada*, 3d ed. (Toronto: Carswell, 1992) at 915.

REMISSION. *n.* 1. A release; a pardon. 2. A decrease in the length of imprisonment.

REMIT. *v.* To send back.

REMITMENT. *n.* The act of sending back into custody.

REMITTANCE. *n.* Money which one person sends to another.

REMITTEE. *n.* The person to whom one sends a remittance.

REM JUDICATAM. See ESTOPPEL PER ~.

REMOTENESS. *n.* 1. Lack of close relation between a wrong and damages. 2. "In Koufos v. C. Czarnikow (The Heron II), [1969] 1 A.C. 350 . . . [(U.K.H.L.)] . . . it was determined that the proper test for remoteness [for recovery of damages for breach of contract] was not the 'reasonable foreseeability' of the head of damages claimed as in an action in tort, but whether the probability of the occurrence of the damage in the event of breach should have been within the reasonable contemplation of the contracting parties at the time of the entry into the contract. (Vide Brown & Root Ltd. v. Chimo Shipping Ltd., [1967] S.C.R. 642 per Ritchie J. at p. 648 . . ." *Baud Corp., N.V., v. Brook* (1978), (*sub nom. Asamera Oil Corp. v. Sea Oil & General Corp.*) 5 B.L.R. 225 at 237, [1979] 1 S.C.R 633, [19878] 6 W.W.R. 301, 23 N.R. 181, 12 A.R.

271, 89 D.L.R. (3d) 1, the court per Estey J.

REMOVER. *n.* The transfer of a cause or suit from one court to another.

REMUNERATION. *n.* Payment for services provided. *Sheridan v. Minister of National Revenue* (1985), 57 N.R. 69 at 74, 85 C.L.L.C. 14,048 (Fed. C.A.), the court per Heald J.A.

RENEWAL. *n.* ". . . [T]he more 'standard' meaning is the one that assumes the continued existence of the matter 'renewed'. If it is not in existence then the process is really one of re-creation rather than renewal. Further, in a general legal context concerned with the renewal of rights, privileges and other interests, conferred under instruments such as leases, contracts and licences, it is, I think, a general understanding that renewal involves the temporal extension of something that is in existence and not the revival of something that has ceased to exist." *R. v. Pleich* (1980), 55 C.C.C. (2d) 13 at 28, 16 C.R. (3d) 194 (Ont. C.A.), the court per Morden J.A. See AUTOMATIC ~.

RENOUNCE. *v.* 1. Of a right, to give up. 2. Of probate, for an executor to decline to take probate of a will.

RENT. *v.* To let. *Daugherty v. Armaly* (1921), 58 D.L.R. 380 at 382, 49 O.L.R. 310, 19 O.W.N. 573 (C.A.), the court per Meredith C.J.O.

RENT. *n.* ". . . [T]he compensation which a tenant of the land or other corporeal hereditament makes to the owner for the use thereof. It is frequently treated as a profit arising out of the demised land. . . ." *Johnson v. British Canadian Insurance Co.*, [1932] S.C.R. 680 at 684, [1932] 4 D.L.R. 281, Lamont J. See GROUND-~; PEPPERCORN ~; QUIT ~; RACK-~.

RENTAL PERIOD. The interval for which rent is paid. *Residential Tenancies Act*, R.S. Nfld. 1990, c. R-14, s. 2.

RENT CHARGE. Includes all annuities and periodical sums of money charged upon or payable out of land.

RENUNCIATION. ". . . [O]f a contract may be express or implied. A party to a contract may state before the time of performance that he will not, or cannot, perform his obligations. This is tantamount to an express renunciation. On the other hand, a renunciation will be implied if the conduct of a party is such as to lead a reasonable person to the conclusion that he will not perform, or will not be able to perform, when the time for performance arises." *McCallum v. Zivojinovic* (1977), 16 O.R. (2d) 721 at 723, 2 R.P.R. 164, 26 Chitty's L.J. 169, 79 D.L.R. (3d) 133 (C.A.), the court per Howland J.A.

RENVOI. *n.* When one determines, by the appropriate choice of law rule, that the questionable issue may be decided according to "the law" of a certain country, the court must decide whether the term "the law" refers to the internal domestic law of that country or to its conflict of laws rules as well. This concept is not firmly entrenched in Canadian law. J.G. McLeod, *The Conflict of Laws* (Calgary: Carswell, 1983) at 198 and 201.

REORGANIZATION. *n.* A court order made under (a) a Corporations Act; (b) the Bankruptcy Act approving a proposal; or (c) any other act that affects the rights among the corporation, its shareholders and creditors.

REPAIR. *v.* "[R]estoration to a previously designed or constructed state. . . ." *Fry v. Henry* (1985), 64 A.R. 304 at 305 (C.A.), the court per Laycraft C.J.A.

REPARATION. *n.* 1. Restitution. 2. "[In s. 663(2)(e) of the Criminal Code, R.S.C. 1970, c. C-34] . . . would have the additional meaning [to the meaning of restitution which refers to property only] of compensating a victim for loss or damage – both to property and person. . . ." *R. v. Groves* (1977), 39 C.R.N.S. 366 at 380, 17 O.R. (2d) 65, 37 C.C.C. (2d) 429, 79 D.L.R. (3d) 561 (H.C.), O'Driscoll J.

REPATRIATION. *n.* Recovering possession of the nationality which a person lost or abandoned.

REPEAL. *v.* To strike out, revoke, cancel or rescind.

REPLACE. *v.* In insurance, to restore buildings or chattels which have been destroyed. R. Colinvaux, *The Law of Insurance*, 5th ed. (London: Sweet & Maxwell, 1984) at 181.

REPLEVIN. *n.* "... [N]ow called an order for the recovery of possession of personal property, has remained what its new name suggests: a means of getting back the possession which an applicant for the remedy has lost." *Manitoba Agricultural Credit Corp. v. Heaman* (1990), 70 D.L.R. (4th) 518 at 523, [1990] 4 W.W.R. 269, 65 Man. R. (2d) 269 (C.A.), the court per Twaddle J.A. See ACTION FOR ~.

REPLEVY. *v.* To redeliver goods which were unlawfully taken or detained to their owner.

REPLY. *n.* The pleading of a petitioner, plaintiff or party, who institutes a proceeding, in answer to the defendant.

REPLY EVIDENCE. Rebuttal evidence which a plaintiff may present at the end of the defendant's case to contradict or qualify new facts or issues which the defendant raised in the course of presenting her or his case. J. Sopinka and S.N. Lederman, *The Law of Evidence in Civil Cases* (Toronto: Butterworths, 1974) at 517.

REPORT. *n.* See CONSUMER ~; CREDIT ~; LAW ~; OFFICIAL ~; OFFICIAL ~ OF DEBATES; PRE-DISPOSITION ~; PRE-SENTENCE ~.

REPRESENTATION. *n.* 1. A statement concerning a past or existing fact, not a promise concerning a future event or state of affairs. G.H.L. Fridman, *The Law of Contract in Canada*, 2d ed. (Toronto: Carswell, 1986) at 2. 2. Standing in someone else's place for a certain purpose. 3. "... The element of representation in s. 163 of the [Criminal Code, R.S.C. 1985, c. C-46] is therefore a suggestion, a depiction to the public...." *R. v. Butler* (1992), 11 C.R. (4th) 137 at 184, [1992] 2 W.W.R. 577, [1992] 1 S.C.R. 452, 70 C.C.C. (3d) 129, 134 N.R. 81, 8 C.R.R.

(2d) 1, 89 D.L.R. (4th) 449, 78 Man. R. (2d) 1, 16 W.A.C. 1, Gonthier J. (L'Heureux-Dubé J. concurring). See MIS~.

REPRESENTATIVE. *n.* The person who takes the place of or represents another person. A deceased person's executor or administrator is called a personal representative. See LEGAL ~; PERSONAL ~.

REPRESENTATIVE ACTION. 1. "... [F]or a proper representative action there must be a 'common interest' of the plaintiff with those he claims to represent, the exertion of a 'common right' or a 'common grievance', normally arising from a 'common origin', but once the alleged rights of the class are denied or ignored it is immaterial that the individuals have been wronged in their individual capacity, provided, of course, that their claims were not for personal damages. It appears to me that the many passages uttered by Judges of high authority over the years really boil down to a simple proposition that a class action is appropriate where if the plaintiff wins the other persons he purports to represent win too, and if he, because of that success, becomes entitled to relief whether or not in a fund or property, the others also become likewise entitled to that relief, having regard, always, for different quantitiative participations." *Shaw v. Vancouver Real Estate Board* (1973), 36 D.L.R. (3d) 250 at 253-4, [1973] 4 W.W.R. 391 (B.C. C.A.), Bull J.A. 2. "... [C]an be brought by persons asserting a common right, and even where persons may have been wronged in their individual capacity." *Pasco v. Canadian National Railway* (1989), 34 B.C.L.R. (2d) 344 at 348, [1990] 2 C.N.L.R. 85, 56 D.L.R. (4th) 404 (C.A.), the court per Macfarlane J.A. 3. "An action by members of a corporation challenging allegedly ultra vires acts thus should normally be taken in representative form so that all members or shareholders of the company will be bound by judgment and the company not harassed by a multiplicity of actions...." *Gordon v. N.S.T.U.* (1983), 36 C.P.C. 150 at 156, 59

N.S.R. (2d) 124, 125 A.P.R. 124, 1 D.L.R. (4th) 676 (C.A.), the court per MacKeigan C.J.N.S.

REPRIEVE. *n.* The temporary withdrawal of a sentence so that its execution is suspended.

REPRIMAND. *n.* The formal, public reproach of an offence.

REPRISAL. *n.* Recaption; taking one thing in place of another.

REPUBLICATION. *n.* Of a codicil or will, execution again by the testator.

REPUDIATION. *n.* ". . . [O]rdinarily means a refusal to carry out all one's obligations under a contract." *Park v. Parsons Brown & Co.* (1989), 27 C.C.E.L. 224 at 242, 39 B.C.L.R. (2d) 107, 62 D.L.R. (4th) 108 (B.C. C.A.), Southin J.A.

REPUGNANCY. *n.* ". . . [W]here one clear clause contradicts another clause equally clear. In a deed where there is a repugnancy the rule is the first shall prevail, but in a will the second: . . ." *Westholme Lumber Co. v. St. James Ltd.* (1915), 21 D.L.R. 549 at 555, 8 W.W.R. 122, 21 B.C.R. 100, 30 W.L.R. 781 (C.A.), Irving J.A. (Macdonald C.J.A. concurring).

REPUGNANT. *adj.* Inconsistent with; contrary to.

REPUTATION. *n.* 1. ". . . [M]erely hearsay, simply what the public says about a person, . . ." *R. v. Sands* (1915), 25 C.C.C. 120 at 123, 28 D.L.R. 375, 9 W.W.R. 496, 25 Man. R. 690 (C.A.), the court per Howell C.J.M. 2. Immediately before a defamatory publication, the long-range composite view which the general public had of the plaintiff's character, credit, honour or good name. R.E. Brown, *The Law of Defamation in Canada* (Toronto: Carswell, 1987) at 1030.

REQUISITION. *n.* 1. A praecipe. 2. A written instruction which requires a court registrar to do something.

REQUISITION ON TITLE. A written inquiry to the solicitor for a vendor of real estate requesting that defects and clouds in the title be removed.

RES. *n.* [L.] Any physical thing in which someone may claim a right.

RESALE. *n.* A right reserved by the vendor if the purchaser defaults in paying the purchase price.

RESCIND. *v.* 1. With respect to a contract, for one or more parties to end it. 2. ". . . [D]ischarging [an order] or setting it aside. . . ." *Stewart v. Braun*, [1924] 3 D.L.R. 941 at 942, [1924] 2 W.W.R. 1103 (Man. K.B.), Mathers C.J.K.B.

RESCISSION. *n.* 1. ". . . [W]ill only occur where the changes go to the very root of the original agreement such that there is patent the intention to completely extinguish the first contract, nor merely to alter it, however extensively, in terms which leave the original subsisting . . ." *Niagara Air Bus Inc. v. Camerman* (1989), 37 C.P.C. (2d) 267 at 285, 69 O.R. (2d) 717 (H.C.), Watt J. 2. Exercise of an option which ends the necessity to perform. B.J. Reiter, B.N. McLellan & P.M. Perell, *Real Estate Law*, 4th ed. (Toronto: Emond Montgomery, 1992) at 681.

RESCUE. *v.* To knowingly and forcibly free someone from an imprisonment or arrest.

RESCUER. *n.* A person who, having reasonable cause to believe another person to be in danger of his life or of bodily harm, benevolently comes to his assistance. *An Act to Promote Good Citizenship*, R.S.Q. 1977, c. C-20, s. 1.

RESEALING. *n.* Validation of a grant of representation originally issued by a court in a jurisdiction with similar laws and allegiance to the same sovereign, i.e. in the United Kingdom, any territory or province of Canada, the Commonwealth or any British possession. This has the same effect as if the validating court had made the original grant. J.G. McLeod, *The Conflict of Laws* (Calgary: Carswell, 1983) at 404 and 405.

RESERVATION. *n.* 1. A clause in a deed by which a donor, grantor or lessor claims or reserves something new out of whatever was granted by the same deed earlier. 2. Power of the

Lieutenant-Governor with regard to a bill passed by the Legislature. It is subject "... to the restriction that the discretion of the Lieutenant-Governor shall be exercised subject to the Governor General's Instructions." *Reference re Power of Disallowance & Power of Reservation (Canada)*, [1938] S.C.R. 71 at 79, [1938] 2 D.L.R. 81, Duff C.J. (Davis J. concurring).

RESERVE. *v.* For the Governor General to withhold the royal assent from a bill which both Houses of Parliament passed "for the signification of the Queen's Pleasure" or, similarly, for a Lieutenant Governor to withhold assent from a provincial bill for the Governor General's pleasure. P.W. Hogg, *Constitutional Law of Canada*, 3d ed. (Toronto: Carswell, 1992) at 230-31.

RESERVE. *n.* 1. A tract of land, the legal title to which is vested in Her Majesty, that has been set apart by Her Majesty for the use and benefit of a band. *Indian Act*, R.S.C. 1985, c. I-5, s. 2. 2. A parcel of land reserved for use as a park, recreation area or a school site. 3. "... [S]omething set aside that can be relied upon for future use; ..." *Crane Ltd. v. Minister of National Revenue*, [1960] C.T.C. 371 at 378, [1961] Ex. C.R. 147, 60 D.T.C. 1248, Kearney J.

RES GESTAE. [L. things done] 1. "One of the earliest definitions of res gestae was given by Cockburn C.J. in his commentary on R. v. Bedingfield (1879), 14 Cox C.C. 341.... 'Whatever acts or series of acts constitute or in point of time immediately accompany and terminate in the principal act charged as an offence against the accused from its inception to its consummation or final completion, or its prevention or abandonment, whether on the part of the agent or wrongdoer in order to its performance, or on that of the patient or party wronged in order to its prevention, and whatever may be said by either of the parties during the continuance of the transaction with reference to it ... form part of the principal transaction, and may be given in evidence as part of the res gestae or particulars of it ..." *R. v. Klippenstein* (1981), 19 C.R. (3d) 56 at 63, [1981] 3 W.W.R. 111, 57 C.C.C. (2d) 393, 26 A.R. 568 (C.A.), the court per Laycraft J.A. 2. As an exception to the hearsay rule includes (a) statements which accompany and explain a certain act; (b) statements simultaneous with and directly related to a fact at issue; (c) a person's statements concerning state of mind or emotions at a certain time; (d) a person's statements concerning physical sensations at a certain time. P.K. McWilliams, *Canadian Criminal Evidence*, 3d ed. (Aurora: Canada Law Book, 1988) at 21-2 and 21-3.

RESIDENCE. *n.* 1. "... [C]hiefly a matter of the degree to which a person in mind and fact settles into or maintains or centralizes his ordinary mode of living with its accessories in social relations, interests and conveniences at or in the place in question. It may be limited in time from the outset, or it may be indefinite, or so far as it is thought of, unlimited. ..." *Thomson v. Minister of National Revenue*, [1946] S.C.R. 209 at 225, [1946] C.T.C. 51, [1946] 1 D.L.R. 689, Rand J. 2. The chief or habitual place of abode of a person. 3. "... [T]he head office or other place designated in the incorporating instrument as being the chief place of business of the corporation." *Canada Life Assurance Co. v. Canadian Imperial Bank of Commerce* (1979), 8 B.L.R. 55 at 63, 27 N.R. 227, [1979] 2 S.C.R. 669, 98 D.L.R. (3d) 670, the court per Estey J. See ACTUAL ~; HABITUAL ~; PRINCIPAL ~.

RESIDUARY. *adj.* Relating to the part which remains.

RESIDUARY BEQUEST. A gift of any of the testator's personal property which the will did not otherwise give. T. Sheard, R. Hull & M.M.K. Fitzpatrick, *Canadian Forms of Wills*, 4th ed. (Toronto: Carswell, 1982) at 178.

RESIDUARY DEVISEE. The person designated in a will to take the real property which remains after the other devises.

RESIDUARY LEGATEE. The person to whom a testator leaves what remains of a personal estate after all debts and specific legacies are discharged.

RESIDUARY POWER. 1. With respect to the federal parliament, the power conferred by section 91 of the Constitution Act, 1867 to make laws for the "peace, order, and good government of Canada" which is residuary in relation to provincial governments because it is specifically limited to matters not assigned to the provincial legislatures. P.W. Hogg, *Constitutional Law of Canada*, 3d ed. (Toronto: Carswell, 1992) at 435-6. 2. With respect to a provincial parliament, the power conferred by section 92(16) over "all matters of a merely local or private nature in the province." P.W. Hogg, *Constitutional Law of Canada*, 3d ed. (Toronto: Carswell, 1992) at 540.

RESIDUE. *n.* 1. "[What remained of an estate] . . . after payment of debts, funeral and testamentary expenses." *Prout, Re*, [1943] 2 D.L.R. 125 at 128, [1943] O.W.N. 156 (C.A.), Robertson C.J.O., Fisher and Kellock JJ.A. 2. ". . . [T]he testator meant by the word 'residue' . . . that part of his estate which might remain after the death of his wife. . . . the run of this language shows that his mind was directed to what remained of his estate at the death of his wife, and not what remained at his own death." *Wilson v. Wilson*, [1944] 2 D.L.R. 729 at 732, [1944] 2 W.W.R. 412, 60 B.C.R. 287 (C.A.), Smith J.A. (O'Halloran and Roberson JJ.A. concurring).

RES IPSA LOQUITUR. [L. the thing speaks for itself] 1. ". . . [U]sed in connection with . . . class of cases where, by force of a specific rule of law, if certain facts are established then the defendant is liable unless he proves that the occurrence out of which the damage has arisen falls within the category of inevitable accident." *Hutson v. United Motor Service Ltd.*, [1937] 1 D.L.R. 737 at 739, [1937] S.C.R. 294, 4 I.L.R. 91, Duff C.J.C. 2. ". . .

[D]escribes the situation where the happening of the accident is sufficient in the absence of an explanation to justify the inference that most probably the defendant was negligent and that his negligence caused the injury even though the plaintiff may not be able to establish the precise cause of the accident. . . ." *Schanilec Estate v. Harris* (1987), (*sub nom. Rocha v. Harris*) 39 C.C.L.T. 279 at 291, 11 B.C.L.R. (2d) 233, 36 D.L.R. (4th) 410 (C.A.), the court per Craig J.A.

RES JUDICATA. [L.] 1. A final judicial decision. 2. "Three requirements for a finding of res judicata are confirmed by the Manitoba Court of Appeal in Solomon v. Smith, [1988] 1 W.W.R. 410 . . . They are: 1. That the same question has previously been decided. 2. That the judicial decision which is said to create the estoppel was final; and 3. That the parties to the judicial decision or their privies were the same persons as the parties to the proceedings in which the estoppel is raised or their privies." *Newman v. Newman* (1990), 26 R.F.L. (3d) 313 at 318, 65 Man. R. (2d) 294 (Q.B.), Davidson J. See ESTOPPEL PER REM JUDICATAM.

RESOLUTION. *n.* 1. A solemn decision or judgment. 2. A meeting's expression of intention or opinion. 3. The revocation of a contract. 4. Declares the intention of a municipal council regarding a matter of a temporary nature without prescribing a permanent rule. I.M. Rogers, *The Law of Canadian Municipal Corporations*, 2d ed. (Toronto: Carswell, 1971-) at 410. See ORDINARY ~.

RESPITE. *n.* An interruption, reprieve or suspension of sentence.

RESPONDEAT SUPERIOR. [L. let the principal answer] In certain circumstances when a servant acted in the course of employment, the master is liable for the servant's wrongful acts. *Lavere v. Smith's Falls Public Hospital* (1915), 26 D.L.R. 346 at 363, 35 O.L.R. 98 (C.A.), Latchford J.

RESPONDENT. *n.* 1. A person against whom one presents a petition,

issues a summons or brings an appeal.
2. A person in the Province or in a reciprocating state who has or is alleged to have an obligation to pay maintenance for the benefit of a claimant, or against whom a proceeding under this Act, or a corresponding enactment of a reciprocating state, is commenced. *Maintenance Orders Enforcement acts.* 3. A person or a department in respect of whom or which or in respect of whose activities any report or information is sought or provided. *Statistics acts.* See CO-~.

RESPONDENTIA. *n.* [L.] The hypothecation of the goods or cargo on a ship to secure repayment of a loan.

RESPONSIBLE GOVERNMENT. The formal head of state (monarch, Governor General or Lieutenant Governor) must always act under the direction of ministers who are members of the majority elected to the legislative branch. P.W. Hogg, *Constitutional Law of Canada*, 3d ed. (Toronto: Carswell, 1992) at 229.

RESTITUTIO IN INTEGRUM. [L.] 1. "... The injured person is to be restored to the position he would have been in had the accident not occurred, insofar as this can be done with money. This is the philosophical justification for damages for loss of earning capacity, cost of future care and special damages." *Milina v. Bartsch* (1985), 49 B.C.L.R. (2d) 33 at 78 (S.C.), McLachlin J. 2. In a case in which someone according to strict law lost a right and a court decision restores the original position on equitable principles. 3. Equitable relief given when a contract is rescinded because of fraud or in a similar case in which each party can be restored to its original position.

RESTITUTION. *n.* 1. "... [T]he function of the law of restitution 'is to ensure that where a plaintiff has been deprived of wealth that is either in his possession or would have accrued to his benefit, it is restored to him.' Restitution is a distinct body of law governed by its own developing system of rules. Breaches of fiduciary duties and breaches of confidence are both

wrongs for which restitutionary relief is often appropriate." *International Corona Resources Ltd. v. Lac Minerals Ltd.* (1989), 44 B.L.R. 1 at 45, [1989] 2 S.C.R. 574, 26 C.P.R. (3d) 97, 69 O.R. (2d) 287, 61 D.L.R. (4th) 14, 6 R.P.R. (2d) 1, 35 E.T.R. 1, 101 N.R. 239, 26 O.A.C. 57, La Forest J. (Wilson and Lamer JJ. concurring in part). 2. The law which relates to any claim, whether quasi-contractual in nature or not, which is based on unjust enrichment. 3. "An examination of the language of these sections [ss. 653 and 654 of the Criminal Code, R.S.C. 1970, c. C-34] indicates that Parliament viewed the term 'restitution' as dealing with the return of identical property obtained as a result of the commission of an offence to its owner, . . . a restoration of property." *R. v. Groves* (1977), 39 C.R.N.S. 366 at 380, 17 O.R. (2d) 65, 37 C.C.C. (2d) 429, 79 D.L.R. (3d) 561 (H.C.), O'Driscoll J.

RESTORE. *v.* In insurance, to reinstate or replace buildings or chattels which have been damaged or destroyed. R. Colinvaux, *The Law of Insurance*, 5th ed. (London: Sweet & Maxwell, 1984) at 181.

RESTRAINING ORDER. 1. In some provinces, the order of a court to prevent disposal or waste of family property. C.R.B. Dunlop, *Creditor-Debtor Law in Canada*, Second Cumulative Supplement (Toronto: Carswell, 1986) at 211. 2. "... [A] restrictive injunction ..." *Peterson v. MacPherson* (1991), 32 R.F.L. (3d) 333 at 338, [1991] N.W.T.R. 178 (S.C.), de Weerdt J.

RESTRAINT OF MARRIAGE. In general, any contract designed to prevent someone from marrying is void.

RESTRAINT OF TRADE. Refers to a contract otherwise freely entered into, that restricts a party's future use of skill, time and expertise. G.H.L. Fridman, *The Law of Contract in Canada*, 2d ed. (Toronto: Carswell, 1986) at 368. See CONTRACT IN ~.

RESTRAINT ON ALIENATION. A condition which restrains alienation of absolute interest in either real or personal property is generally considered void because it is repugnant.

RESTRICTED WEAPON. (a) Any firearm, not being a prohibited weapon, designed, altered or intended to be aimed and fired by the action of one hand; (b) any firearm that (i) is not a prohibited weapon, has a barrel that is less than 18 inches in length and is capable of discharging centre-fire ammunition in a semi-automatic manner; or (ii) is designed or adapted to be fired when reduced to a length of less than 26 inches by folding, telescoping or otherwise; or (c) any firearm that is designed, altered or intended to fire bullets in rapid succession during one pressure of the trigger and that, on January 1, 1978, was registered as a restricted weapon and formed part of a gun collection in Canada of a genuine gun collector; or (d) a weapon of any kind, not being a prohibited weapon or a shotgun or rifle of a kind that, in the opinion of the Governor in Council is reasonable for use in Canada for hunting or sporting purposes, that is declared by order of the Governor in Council to be a restricted weapon. *Criminal Code*, R.S.C. 1985, c. C-46, s. 84.

RESTRICTIVE COVENANT. "... [S]omething in the nature of a negative easement, requiring for its creation and continuance a dominant and a servient tenement..." *Hunt v. Bell* (1915), 34 O.L.R. 256 at 262, 24 D.L.R. 590 (C.A.), Garrow J.A. (Meredith C.J.O., MacLaren and Magee JJ.A. concurring).

RESTRICTIVE ENDORSEMENT. A notation which prohibits any further negotiation of a promissory note or bill of exchange.

RESULTING. *adj.* Describes the return of property to the grantor or the remaining in him of property as a result of the implication of law or equity. R. Megarry & H.W.R. Wade, *The Law of Real Property*, 5th ed. (London: Stevens, 1984) at cxxvii.

RESULTING TRUST. 1. "... [W]ill be presumed in favour of a person who

is proved to have paid the purchase-money for real property in the character of purchaser if the real property is conveyed to another." *Rathwell v. Rathwell* (1978), 1 R.F.L. (2d) 1 at 10, [1978] 2 S.C.R. 436, [1978] 2 W.W.R. 101, 19 N.R. 91, 1 E.T.R. 307, 83 D.L.R. (3d) 289, Dickson J. (Laskin C.J.C. and Spence J. concurring). 2. "... [A]rises when a court of equity presumes from the nature of the transaction, the relations of the parties and the requirement of good faith that a trust was intended." *Gerry v. Metz* (1979), 12 R.F.L. (2d) 346 at 351 (Sask. C.A.), the court per Hall J.A. See PRESUMPTION OF ~.

RESULTING USE. A use which is implied.

RETAIN. *v.* For a client to engage a solicitor or counsel to defend or take proceedings, to advise or act on one's behalf.

RETAINER. *n.* "... [T]he act of employing a solicitor or counsel, or ... the document by which such employment is evidenced [or] ... a preliminary fee given to secure the services of the solicitor and induce him to act for the client...." *Solicitor, Re* (1910), 22 O.L.R. 30 at 31 (C.A.), the court per Riddell J.A.

RETIRE. *v.* 1. To withdraw to consider a decision or verdict. 2. To cease employment.

RETIREMENT. *n.* "... [A] cessation of or withdrawal from work because of an age stipulation or because of some other condition agreed between employer and employee." *Specht v. R.*, [1975] C.T.C. 126 at 133, [1975] F.C. 150, 75 D.T.C. 5069 (T.D.), Collier J.

RETRACTATION. *n.* In probate practice, withdrawal of renunciation.

RETRIAL. *n.* A rehearing of a matter.

RETRIBUTION. *n.* Something given or demanded in payment; punishment based on the notion that every crime demands payment in the form of punishment.

RETROACTIVE STATUTE. 1. "... [O]ne that operates backwards, i.e., that is operative as of a time prior to its enactment, either by being deemed to have come into force at a time prior to its enactment (e.g., budgetary measures) or by being expressed to be operative with respect to past transactions as of a past time (e.g., acts of indemnity)...." *Royal Canadian Mounted Police Act (Canada), Re,* [1991] 1 F.C. 529 at 548 (C.A.), MacGuigan J.A. 2. "... [O]perates forward in time, starting from a point further back in time than the date of its enactment; so it changes the legal consequences of past events as if the law had been different than it really was at the time those events occurred." *Hornby Island Trust Commmittee v. Stormwell* (1988), 53 D.L.R. (4th) 435 at 441, 39 M.P.L.R. 300, 30 B.C.L.R. (2d) 383 (C.A.), Lambert J.A. (Hutcheon J.A. concurring).

RETROSPECTIVE STATUTE. 1. "... [C]hanges the law only for the future but looks backward by attaching new consequences to completed transactions. It thus opens up closed transactions ..." *Royal Canadian Mounted Police Act (Canada), Re,* [1991] 1 F.C. 529 at 548 (C.A.), MacGuigan J.A. 2. "... [O]perates forward in time, starting only from the date of its enactment, but from that time forward it changes the legal consequences of past events." *Hornby Island Trust Commmittee v. Stormwell* (1988), 39 M.P.L.R. 300 at 307-8, 53 D.L.R. (4th) 435, 30 B.C.L.R. (2d) 383 (C.A.), Lambert J.A. (Hutcheon J.A. concurring).

RETURN. *n.* 1. The report of an officer of a court, e.g. a sheriff, which shows how a duty imposed on that officer was performed. 2. The record of any report or information provided by a respondent. *Statistics acts.* 3. A return prescribed pursuant to any revenue act.

RETURNING OFFICER. A person responsible for conducting a municipal or parliamentary election.

REV. CAN. CRIM. *abbr.* Revue canadienne de criminologie (Canadian Journal of Criminology).

REV. CAN. D.A. *abbr.* Revue canadienne du droit d'auteur.

REV. CAN. D. COMM. *abbr.* Revue canadienne du droit de commerce (Canadian Business Law Journal).

REV. CAN. D. COMMU-NAUTAIRE. *abbr.* Revue canadienne du droit communautaire (Canadian Community Law Journal).

REV. CAN. D. & SOCIÉTÉ. *abbr.* Revue canadienne de droit et société (Canadian Journal of Law and Society).

REV. CAN. D. FAM. *abbr.* Revue canadienne de droit familial (Canadian Journal of Family Law).

REV. CRIT. *abbr.* Revue critique (1870-1875).

REV. D. OTTAWA. Revue de droit d'Ottawa (Ottawa Law Review).

REVENUE. *n.* 1. Annual profit; income. 2. All public money collected or due. See NET ~.

REVENUE ACT. A statute imposing a tax or fee.

REVERSAL. *n.* Making a judgment void because of error.

REVERSE. *v.* To make void, repeal or undo. A judgment is reversed when a court of appeal sets it aside.

REVERSE DISCRIMINATION. "... [D]iscriminates against [persons not belonging to one race, for example] because whenever there is a finite number of persons seeking some advantage (in this case employment), to prefer one because of his race is to the disadvantage of another because of the race of the first person." *Athabasca Tribal Council v. Amoco Canada Petroleum Co.,* [1981] 1 C.N.L.R. 35 at 48, [1980] 5 W.W.R. 165, 22 A.R. 541, 112 D.L.R. (3d) 200, 1 C.H.R.R. D/174 (C.A.), Laycraft J.A. (McGillivray C.J.A. concurring).

REVERSION. *n.* "... [A]n undisposed of estate in property, left in a grantor after he has parted with some particular interest less than the fee simple therein. In the second place, it is an estate which returns to the grantor after the determination of such particular estate ..." *Ferguson v. MacLean,* [1931] 1 D.L.R. 61 at 67,

[1930] S.C.R. 630, Anglin C.J.C. (Rinfret J. concurring). See RUN WITH THE ~.

REVERSIONARY INTEREST. ". . . [F]uture interests in real as well as personal property which are not by operation of law or otherwise interests reserved to the grantor or donor; but are merely interests which take effect at the expiration of a preceding estate or interest, or . . . interests which simply take effect in the future. . . ." *Ferguson v. MacLean*, [1931] 1 D.L.R. 61 at 79, [1930] S.C.R. 630, Duff J.

REVERSIONARY LEASE. A lease which takes effect in the future; a second lease which becomes effective after the first lease expires.

REVERSIONARY VALUE. ". . . [S]ome value to the landowner which will accrue to him once the 'taking' has served its use." *Dome Petroleum Ltd. v. Grekul* (1983), 28 Alta. L.R. (2d) 260 at 268, [1988] 1 W.W.R. 447, 29 C.L.R. 111, 5 Admin. L.R. 252, 49 A.R. 256 (Q.B.), Miller J.

REVERT. *v.* 1. To return; e.g., when the owner of land grants a small estate to another person and when that estate terminates, the land reverts to the grantor. 2. "[T]o . . . 'fall back into' his estate." *Carter v. Goldstein* (1921), 66 D.L.R. 34 at 35, 63 S.C.R. 207, Davies C.J.

REVERTER. *n.* Reversion.

REV. ÉTUDES CAN. *abbr.* Revue d'études canadiennes (Journal of Canadian Studies).

REV. FISCALE CAN. *abbr.* Revue fiscale canadienne (Canadian Tax Journal).

REVIEW. *n.* ". . . [I]s occasionally taken in popular use as meaning more than a first instance 'looking over' or 'examination'. In its legal sense . . . it usually means more than that, as implying a formal, second instance 're-examination' or 'reconsideration' with a view to revision or re-determination if something be found wrong or lacking." *Saskatoon (City) v. Plaxton* (1989), 33 C.P.C. (2d) 238 at 250,

[1989] 2 W.W.R. 577, 78 Sask. R. 215 (C.A.), Cameron J.A. (Gerwing J.A. concurring). See JUDICIAL ~.

REVIEWABLE ERROR. ". . . [A]n arbitrator in construing a statutory provision in the course of an arbitration proceeding commits reviewable error if his or her construction is wrong. . . ." *Cape Breton Development Corp. v. U.M.W., District No. 26, Local 4522* (1985), 85 C.L.L.C. 14,041 at 12,222, 68 N.S.R. (2d) 181, 159 A.P.R. 181 (T.D.), MacIntosh J.

REVIEWABLE TRANSACTION. In bankruptcy matters, a transaction which was not at arm's length or was made by people who are "related". F. Bennett, *Receiverships* (Toronto: Carswell, 1985) at 326.

REVISED STATUTES. 1. A consolidation and declaration of the law as contained in the acts which they supplant; they do not come into force as new or independent statutes. I.M. Rogers, *The Law of Canadian Municipal Corporations*, 2d ed. (Toronto: Carswell, 1971-) at 390. 2. The latest revised and consolidated statutes of a province or the federal government.

REVIVAL. *n.* 1. Re-execution of a will by a testator after it was revoked; execution of a will or codicil which shows the intention to revive it. 2. "[A corporation through] revival . . . acquires all the rights and privileges and is liable for all the obligations that it would have had if it had not been dissolved . . ." *Computerized Meetings & Hotel Systems Ltd. v. Moore* (1982), 20 B.L.R. 97 at 106, 40 O.R. (2d) 88, 141 D.L.R. (3d) 306 (Div. Ct.), Callaghan J.

REVIVOR. *n.* A motion needed to continue proceedings when the suit abated before final consummation because of death or some other reason.

REV. JUR. FEMME & D. *abbr.* Revue juridique "La Femme et le droit" (Canadian Journal of Women and the Law).

REV. LOIS & POL. SOCIALES. *abbr.* Revue des lois et des politiques sociales (Journal of Law and Social Policy).

REVOCATION. *n*. 1. Undoing something granted; destroying or voiding a deed which existed until revocation made it void; revoking. 2. Cancellation. *Motor Vehicle Act*, R.S.N.B. 1973, c. M-17, s. 2. 3. ". . . [C]ancellation . . ." *R. v. Whynacht*, [1942] 1 D.L.R. 238 at 240, 16 M.P.R. 267, 77 C.C.C. 1 (N.S. C.A.), Chisholm C.J. 4. With respect to a will, for a testator to render it inoperative or annul it by a later act. See DEPENDENT RELATIVE ~.

REWARD. *n*. Payment of financial consideration to a person who helped apprehend another charged with an offence.

REX. *n*. [L. king] Monarch.

R.F.L. *abbr*. Reports of Family Law, 1971-1977.

R.F.L. REP. *abbr*. Reports of Family Law, Reprint Series.

R.F.L. (2d). *abbr*. Reports of Family Law (Second Series), 1978-1986.

R.F.L. (3d). *abbr*. Reports of Family Law (Third Series), 1986-.

R.G.D. *abbr*. Revue générale de droit (Section de droit civil, Faculté de droit, Université d'Ottawa).

R.I.B.L. *abbr*. Review of International Business Law.

RIDER. *n*. A clause inserted later.

RIGHT. *n*. 1. ". . . [I]s defined positively as what one can do." *R. v. Zundel* (1987), 29 C.R.R. 349 at 365, 18 O.A.C. 161, 58 O.R. (2d) 129, 31 C.C.C. (3d) 97, 56 C.R. (3d) 1, 35 D.L.R. (4th) 338 (C.A.), Howland C.J.O., Brooke, Martin, Lacourcière and Houlden JJ.A. 2. ". . . [S]pecific, detailed and imposes a duty; . . ." *R.W.D.S.U., Locals 496, 544,635, 955 v. Saskatchewan* (1985), 85 C.L.L.C. 14,054 at 12,277, [1985] 5 W.W.R. 97, 39 Sask. R. 193, 21 C.R.R. 286 (C.A.), Bayda C.J.S. 3. Includes power, authority, privilege and licence. *Interpretation acts.* See ACCRUED ~; ACCRUING ~; BARGAINING ~; COLOUR OF ~; CONTINGENT ~;

FUTURE ~; LEGAL ~; LIBERTY; MINERAL ~; MINING ~; PETITION OF ~; PRIVATE ~.

RIGHT OF ACTION. 1. ". . . [T]he right to institute civil proceedings in court for the determination of a right or claim." *Reference re Sections 32 & 34 of the Workers' Compensation Act, 1983 (Newfoundland)* (1987), 36 C.R.R. 112 at 145, 67 Nfld. & P.E.I.R. 16, 206 A.P.R. 16, 44 D.L.R. (4th) 501 (Nfld. C.A.), Morgan J.A. 2. ". . . A bare 'right of action' is not a right in the ordinary use of the term. It is rather a mere claim to a right, and it only becomes an actual right when it has ripened into a judgment." *McGregor v. Campbell* (1909), 11 W.L.R. 153 at 161, 19 Man. R. 38 (C.A.), Richards J.A.

RIGHT OF APPEAL. ". . . [T]he right of appeal is a statutory right, and there is no such right unless it is expressly given." *Dale v. Commercial Union Assurance Co. of Canada* (1981), 22 C.P.C. 29 at 31, 32 O.R. (2d) 238, [1981] I.L.R. 1-1342, 121 D.L.R. (3d) 503 (C.A.), the court per Brooke J.A.

RIGHT OF ASSOCIATION. The right of workers to form unions or other trade associations.

RIGHT OF ENTRY. The right to take or resume possession of land by entering it peacefully.

RIGHT OF SURVIVORSHIP. The right of a surviving joint tenant to take the property of the other, deceased joint tenant.

RIGHT OF WAY. *var*. **RIGHT-OF-WAY.** 1. ". . . [S]impliciter, bears no precise legal incidence other than that which the name implies, a right to pass over the lands of another. It may be an easement which the owner of a dominant tenement has been granted over a servient tenement and running with the land, or it may be a simple licence to merely pass by foot over a person's land to reach another place." *Blue Haven Motel Ltd. v. Burnaby (District)* (1965), 52 W.W.R. 345 at 353-4 (B.C. C.A.),

Bull J.A. (Norris J.A. concurring). 2. "... [A] generally understood meaning as the land reserved for placement of a physical improvement such as a railway, transmission line or pipeline...." *British Columbia Assessment Commissioner v. Canadian National Railway Co.* (1989), 42 M.P.L.R. 71 at 79 (B.C.S.C.), McLachlin C.J.S.C. 3. The privilege of the immediate use of the highway. 4. Includes land or an interest in land required for the purpose of constructing, maintaining or operating a road, railway, aerial, electric or other tramway, surface or elevated cable, electric or telephone pole line, chute, flume, pipeline, drain or any right or easement of a similar nature.

RIGHTS. *n.* See ABORIGINAL ~; BILL OF ~; CIVIL ~; CONJUGAL ~; CUM ~; EMPLOYER ~; LEGAL ~; MANAGEMENT ~; MINERAL ~; MINING ~; MINORITY LANGUAGE EDUCATION ~; MOBILITY ~; OIL SANDS ~; PREROGATIVE ~ OF THE CROWN; RIGHT; RIPARIAN ~; SURFACE ~; VESTED ~.

RIGHT TO BEGIN. The right to be first to address a court or jury.

RIGHT TO BE PRESUMED INNOCENT. "... [I]s, in popular terms, a way of expressing the fact that the Crown has the ultimate burden of establishing guilt; if there is any reasonable doubt at the conclusion of the case on any element of the offence charged, an accused person must be acquitted. In a more refined sense, the presumption of innocence gives an accused the initial benefit of a right of silence and the ultimate benefit (after the Crown's evidence is in and as well as any evidence tendered on behalf of the accused) of any reasonable doubt: ..." *R. v. Appleby*, [1972] S.C.R. 303 at 317, 16 C.R.N.S. 35, [1971] 4 W.W.R. 601, 3 C.C.C. (2d) 354, 21 D.L.R. (3d) 325, Laskin J.

RIGHT TO COUNSEL. 1. Everyone has the right on arrest or detention to retain and instruct counsel without delay and to be informed of that right. *Canadian Charter of Rights and Freedoms*, Part I of the *Constitution Act, 1982*, being Schedule B of the *Canada Act 1982* (U.K.), 1982, c. 11, s. 10(b). 2. "... [T]he right to retain and instruct counsel [in s. 10(b) of the Charter], in modern Canadian society, has come to mean more than the right to retain a lawyer privately. It now also means the right to have access to counsel free of charge where the accused meets certain financial criteria set up by the provincial legal aid plan, and the right to have access to immediate, although temporary, advice from duty counsel irrespective of financial status...." *R. v. Brydges* (1990), 46 C.R.R. 236 at 256, [1990] 2 W.W.R. 220, [1990] 1 S.C.R. 190, 71 Alta. L.R. (2d) 145, 103 N.R. 282, 74 C.R. (3d) 129, 53 C.C.C. (3d) 330, 104 A.R. 124, Lamer J. (Wilson, Gonthier and Cory JJ. concurring).

RIGHT TO REMAIN SILENT. "... [T]he basis for the non-compellability of the accused as a witness at trial but it extends beyond the witness box. In R. v. Esposito (1985), 20 C.R.R. 102, at p. 108, Martin J.A. outlined its scope: 'The right of a suspect or an accused to remain silent ... operates both at the investigative stage of the criminal process and at the trial stage." ... it is a right not to be compelled to answer questions or otherwise communicate with police officers or others whose function it is to investigate the commission of criminal offences. As with the privilege against self-incrimination, the right to remain silent protects the individual against the affront to dignity and privacy which results if crime enforcement agencies are allowed to conscript the suspect against himself or herself...." *Thomson Newspapers Ltd. v. Canada (Director of Investigation & Research)* (1990), 47 C.R.R. 1 at 94, 97, 76 C.R. (3d) 129, 72 O.R. (2d) 415n, 54 C.C.C. (3d) 417, 67 D.L.R. (4th) 161, 29 C.P.R. (3d) 98, [1990] 1 S.C.R. 425, 39 O.A.C. 161, 106 N.R. 161, Sopinka J. (dissenting in part).

RIGHT TO SILENCE. "In R. v. Hebert [1990] 2 S.C.R. 151, this Court found that s. 7 of the Charter includes a right to silence which includes the right to choose whether or not to make a statement to the authorities. In Hebert, Justice McLachlin described the right as follows, at p. 186: 'The essence of the right to silence is that the suspect be given a choice; the right is quite simply the freedom to choose – the freedom to speak to the authorities on the one hand, and the right to refuse to make a statement to them on the other.' " *R. v. Broyles*, [1991] 3 S.C.R. 595 at 605, 9 C.R. (4th) 1, [1992] 1 W.W.R. 289, 68 C.C.C. (3d) 308, 84 Alta. L.R. (2d) 1, 131 N.R. 118, 120 A.R. 189, 8 W.A.C. 189, 8 C.R.R. (2d) 274, the court per Iacobucci J.

RIGHT TO VOTE. "[In s. 3 of the Charter] . . . should be defined as guaranteeing the right to effective representation. The concept of absolute voter parity does not accord with the development of the right to vote in the Canadian context and does not permit of sufficient flexibility to meet the practical difficulties inherent in representative government in a country such as Canada." *Reference re Provincial Electoral Boundaries*, [1991] 2 S.C.R. 158 at 188, [1991] 5 W.W.R. 1, 127 N.R. 1, 81 D.L.R. (4th) 16, McLachlin J. (La Forest, Gonthier, Stevenson and Iacobucci JJ. concurring).

RIGHT TO WORK. 1. The right of an employee to keep a job without being a union member. 2. "[Used to describe] . . . the right not to be regulated. It had little to do with the important personal right of otherwise qualified professional people to have an opportunity to attempt to build a practice in their province and in their chosen communities. One may be deprived of such a right in accordance with the principles of fundamental justice: . . ." *Wilson v. British Columbia (Medical Services Commission)* (1988), 34 Admin. L.R. 235 at 262, 30 B.C.L.R. (2d) 1, [1989] 2 W.W.R. 1, 53 D.L.R. (4th) 17 (C.A.), Nemetz C.J.B.C., Carrothers, Hinkson, Macfarlane and Wallace JJ.A.

RIGOR MORTIS. [L.] The stiffening and contracting of the voluntary and involuntary muscles in the body after death. F.A. Jaffe, *A Guide to Pathological Evidence*, 3d ed. (Toronto: Carswell, 1991) at 225.

RIOT. *n.* An unlawful assembly that has begun to disturb the peace tumultuously. *Criminal Code*, R.S.C. 1985, c. C-46, s. 64.

RIOT ACT. The name commonly given to the proclamation set out in section 67 of the Criminal Code, R.S.C. 1985, c. C-46 which is read at the time of a riot.

RIPARIAN. *adj.* ". . . [A]pplies to a river and flowing water. . . ." *Rickey v. Toronto (City)* (1914), 30 O.L.R. 523 at 524, 19 D.L.R. 146 (H.C.), Boyd C.

RIPARIAN RIGHTS. 1. ". . . [D]o not carry exclusive possession; they exist as incorporeal rights arising from ownership, in the nature of servitudes, among other things, over foreshore." *Canada (Attorney General) v. Higbie*, (*sub nom. Canada (Attorney General) v. Western Higbie*) [1945] 3 D.L.R. 1 at 44, [1945] S.C.R. 385, Rand J. 2. "The rights enjoyed by a riparian owner are classified as follows in [G.V. LaForest, Water Law in Canada: The Atlantic Provinces] ([Ottawa: Information Canada,] 1973), at p. 201: '(1) the right of access to water; (2) the right of drainage; (3) rights relating to the flow of water; (4) rights relating to the quality of water (pollution); (5) rights relating to the use of water; and (6) the right of accretion.' " *Welsh v. Marantette* (1983), 27 C.C.L.T. 113 at 125-6, 44 O.R. (2d) 137, 30 R.P.R. 111, 3 D.L.R. (4th) 401 (H.C.), Maloney J.

RISK. *n.* ". . . [I]n insurance contracts refer to the very object of the contract of insurance, the happening of which – the 'loss' – triggers the obligation of the insurer to indemnify the insured or his beneficiary." *Metropolitan Life Insurance Co. v. Frenette*, [1992] I.L.R. 1-2823 at 1784, 89 D.L.R. (4th) 653, [1992] 1 S.C.R. 647, 46 Q.A.C. 161, [1992] R.R.A. 466, L'Heureux-Dubé J. See VOLUNTARY ASSUMPTION OF ~; WAR ~S.

R.J.E.L. *abbr.* Revue juridique des étudiants de l'Université Laval.

R.J.F.D. *abbr.* Revue juridique "La Femme et le droit" (Canadian Journal of Women and the Law).

R.J.Q. *abbr.* 1. Rapports judiciaires du Québec, 1875-1891 (Quebec Law Reports). 2. Recueil de jurisprudence du Québec.

R.J.R.Q. *abbr.* Rapports judiciaires revisés de la province de Québec (Mathieu), 1726-1891 (Quebec Revised Reports).

R.J.T. *abbr.* La Revue juridique Thémis.

R.L. *abbr.* La Revue Légale (Qué.), 1980-.

[ ] R.L. *abbr.* La Revue Légale (Qué.), 1943-1979.

R.L.N.S. *abbr.* La Revue Légale (N.S.) (Qué.), 1895-1942.

R.L.O.S. *abbr.* La Revue Légale (Qué.), 1869-1891.

ROAD. *n.* Land used or intended for use for the passage of motor vehicles.

ROB. & JOS. DIG. *abbr.* Robinson & Joseph's Digest.

ROBBERY. *n.* (a) Stealing; and for the purpose of extorting whatever is stolen or to prevent or overcome resistance to the stealing, using violence or threats of violence to a person or property; (b) stealing from any person and, at the time he steals or immediately before or immediately thereafter, wounding, beating, striking or using any personal violence to that person; (c) assaulting any person with intent to steal from him; or (d) stealing from any person while armed with an offensive weapon or imitation thereof. *Criminal Code*, R.S.C. 1985, c. C-46, s. 343.

ROGATORY. See COMMISSION EVIDENCE; COMMISSION ~; LETTERS ~; PERPETUATE TESTIMONY; ~ LETTERS.

ROGATORY LETTERS. A commission in which one judge requests another to examine a witness. See COMMISSION EVIDENCE; COMMISSION ROGATORY; LETTERS ROGATORY; PERPETUATE TESTIMONY; ROGATORY.

ROLL. *n.* 1. The list of the members in good standing of a professional body. 2. A real estate assessment roll. See ASSESSMENT ~; STRIKE OFF THE ~.

ROLLED UP PLEA. "... [S]tates that the allegations of fact in the libel are true, that they are of public interest, and that the comments upon them contained in the libel were fair. The allegation of truth is confined to the facts averred, and the averment as to the comments is not that they are true but only that they were made in good faith, and that they are fair and do not exceed the proper standard of comment upon such matters." *Sutherland v. Stopes*, [1925] A.C. 47 at 62-3 (U.K. C.A.), Viscount Finlay.

ROOT OF TITLE. One traces ownership of property from the document which forms the root of title. R. Megarry & H.W.R. Wade, *The Law of Real Property*, 5th ed. (London: Stevens, 1984) at cxxvii.

ROY. *n.* [Fr. king] Monarch.

ROYAL ASSENT. Approval of a bill, public or private, which was agreed to by both the Senate and the House of Commons. This approval gives the bill the perfection and complement of law. It is rarely given personally by the Governor General but more often by a Deputy acting on the Governor General's behalf. A. Fraser, W.A. Dawson & J. Holtby, eds., *Beauchesne's Rules and Forms of the House of Commons of Canada*, 6th ed. (Toronto: Carswell, 1989) at 217-18.

ROYAL CANADIAN MOUNTED POLICE. A federal police force which prevents and detects offences against federal statutes and provides protective and investigative services for federal agencies and departments. The force acts as the local police force in provinces which enter into agreements with the force to provide this service. It is also the police force for the Territories.

ROYAL COMMISSION. A person or body appointed to inquire into and report on a matter of general public interest.

ROYAL PREROGATIVE. 1. Power and privilege which the common law accords to the Crown. P.W. Hogg, *Constitutional Law of Canada*, 3d ed. (Toronto: Carswell, 1992) at 13. 2. ". . . [W]hat has been left to the King from the wide discretionary powers he enjoyed at the time he governed as an absolute monarch . . ." *Operation Dismantle Inc. v. R.* (1983), 39 C.P.C. 120 at 156, [1983] 1 F.C. 429 (C.A.), Marceau J.A.

ROYAL STYLE AND TITLES. ELIZABETH THE SECOND, by the Grace of God of the United Kingdom, Canada and Her other Realms and Territories QUEEN, Head of the Commonwealth, Defender of the Faith. *Royal Style and Titles Act*, R.S.C. 1985, c. R-12, s. 2.

ROYALTIES. *n.* 1. "[In s. 3(1)(f) of the Income War Tax Act, R.S.C. 1927, c. 97] . . . does not bear the original meaning ascribed to it as rights belonging to the Crown jure coronae . . . it has a special sense when used in mining grants or licences signifying that part of the reddendum which is variable and depends upon the quantity of minerals gotten. It is a well-known term in connection with patents and copyrights." *Minister of National Revenue v. Wain-Town Gas & Oil Co.*, [1952] 2 S.C.R. 377 at 382, 13 Fox Pat. C. 5, [1952] C.T.C. 147, 16 C.P.R. 73, [1952] 4 D.L.R. 81, 52 D.T.C. 1138, Kerwin J. (Rinfret C.J.C. and Taschereau JJ. concurring). 2. ". . . [B]ona vacantia falls within the term 'royalties' . . ." *R. v. British Columbia (Attorney General)* (1922), 68 D.L.R. 106 at 115, 63 S.C.R. 622, [1922] 3 W.W.R. 269, Anglin J. 3. "Assuming then, though without deciding, that the term 'royalties' as used in s. 109 of the Constitution Act, 1867 (30 & 31 Vict.), c. 3 is apt to include fines imposed for infraction of the criminal law, . . ." *Toronto (City) v. R.*, [1932] 1 D.L.R. 161 at 165, 56 C.C.C. 273 (Ont. P.C.), the court per Lord Macmillan. See ROYALTY.

ROYALTY. *n.* 1. A financial consideration paid for the right to use a copyright or patent or to exercise a similar incorporeal right; payment made from the production from a property which the grantor still owns. H.G. Fox, *The Canadian Law of Trade Marks and Unfair Competition*, 3d ed. (Toronto: Carswell, 1972) at 696. 2. The amount payable to the Crown for timber harvested on Crown Lands as prescribed by regulation. *Crown Lands and Forests Act*, S.N.B. 1980, c. C-38.1, s. 1. See ROYALTIES.

R.P. *abbr.* Rapports de Pratique du Québec, 1898-1944 (Quebec Practice Reports).

[ ] R.P. *abbr.* Rapports de Pratique du Québec, 1945-1982 (Quebec Practice Reports).

R.P.C. *abbr.* Reports of Patent Cases.

R.P.F.S. *abbr.* Revue de planification fiscale et successorale.

R.P. QUÉ. *abbr.* Rapports de Pratique de Québec.

R.P.R. *abbr.* Real Property Reports, 1977-.

R.P.R. (2d). *abbr.* Real Property Reports, Second Series.

R.Q.D.I. *abbr.* Revue québécoise de droit international.

R.R.A. *abbr.* Recueil en responsabilité et assurance.

RRSP. *abbr.* A registered retirement savings plan within the meaning of the Income Tax Act (Canada).

R.S. *abbr.* Revised Statutes.

R.S.C. *abbr.* 1. Revised Statutes of Canada. 2. Rules of the Supreme Court.

R.T.P. COMM. *abbr.* Restrictive Trade Practices Commission.

RUBRIC. *n.* With respect to a statute, its title, which was formerly written in red.

RULE. *n.* A law which an administrative agency or court enacts to regulate its procedure. P.W. Hogg, *Constitutional Law of Canada*, 3d ed. (Toronto: Carswell, 1992) at 340. See BEST EVIDENCE ~; GOLDEN ~;

MISCHIEF ~; PAROL EVIDENCE ~; PERPETUITY ~; SLIP ~.

RULE ABSOLUTE. "... [O]ne that is operative forthwith and constitutes an adjudication upon some point at some stage in an action or a proceeding ..." *R. v. U.F.A.W.* (1967), [1968] 1 C.C.C. 194 at 197, 60 W.W.R. 370, 63 D.L.R. (2d) 356 (B.C. C.A.), Davey C.J.B.C. (Branca J.A. concurring).

RULE AGAINST DOUBLE JEOPARDY. After an accused is tried for an offence and finally convicted or acquitted, that person may not be placed in jeopardy a second time, i.e. be tried again, for the same offence. P.W. Hogg, *Constitutional Law of Canada*, 3d ed. (Toronto: Carswell, 1992) at 1112. See AUTREFOIS ACQUIT; AUTREFOIS CONVICT.

RULE AGAINST HEARSAY. Requires that evidence of a witness be restricted to what she or he perceived herself or himself (primary evidence) and excludes anything she or he gathered from other sources. J. Sopinka & S.N. Lederman, *The Law of Evidence in Civil Cases* (Toronto: Butterworths, 1974) at 39-40.

RULE AGAINST PERPETUAL DURATION. A rule with the same object as the rule against perpetuities, but which is applied to any trust with non-charitable purposes. D.M.W. Waters, *The Law of Trusts in Canada*, 2d ed. (Toronto: Carswell, 1984) at 282.

RULE AGAINST PERPETUITIES. For an interest in property to be good it must vest no later than 21 years after some life in being when the interest was created. T. Sheard, R. Hull & M.M.K. Fitzpatrick, *Canadian Forms of Wills*, 4th ed. (Toronto: Carswell, 1982) at 231. See PERPETUITY RULE.

RULE IN HODGES'S CASE. "... [I]n a criminal case, where proof of any issue of fact essential to the case of the Crown consists of circumstantial evidence it is the duty of the judge to instruct the jury that before they can find the accused guilty they must be satisfied not only that the circumstances are consistent with an affirmative finding on the issue so sought to be proved but that the circumstances are inconsistent with any other rational conclusion ... the rule is not one merely of prudent practice but of positive law." *R. v. Mitchell* (1964), 43 C.R. 391 at 401, [1964] S.C.R. 471, 47 W.W.R. 591, 46 D.L.R. (2d) 384, [1965] 1 C.C.C. 155, Cartwright J.

RULE IN PHILLIPS V. EYRE. "As a general rule, in order to found a suit in England for a wrong alleged to have been committed abroad, two conditions must be fulfilled. First, the wrong must be of such a character that it would have been actionable if committed in England ... Secondly, the act must not have been justifiable by the law of the place where it was done." *Phillips v. Eyre* (1870), L.R. 6 Q.B. 1 at 28-9 (U.K. Ex. Ct.), Willes J.

RULE IN RYLANDS V. FLETCHER. Anyone who, for their own reasons, brings on their land, collects and keeps there anything which may do harm if it escapes, must keep it in at their own peril. If they do not do so, they are prima facie answerable for any damages which result from its escape. I.H. Jacob, ed., *Bullen and Leake and Jacob's Precedents of Pleadings*, 12th ed. (London: Sweet and Maxwell, 1975) at 802.

RULE IN SAUNDERS V. VAUTIER. Narrowly it states that a court will not enforce a trust for accumulation, in which no one but the legatee has any interest when an absolute vested gift is made payable at a future event, with direction in the meantime to accumulate any income and pay it with the principal. More broadly it states that, if beneficiaries agree and they are not under a disability, the specific performance of a trust may be arrested, and they may extinguish or modify the trust without referring to the wishes of either the settlor or the trustees. D.M.W. Waters, *The Law of Trusts in Canada*, 2d ed. (Toronto: Carswell, 1984) at 963.

RULE IN SHELLEY'S CASE. If

one vests land in trustees in fee simple in trust for some person for life, placing the remainder in trust for that person's heirs or the heirs of that person's body, that person takes an estate tail or equitable fee simple. D.M.W. Waters, *The Law of Trusts in Canada*, 2d ed. (Toronto: Carswell, 1984) at 22.

RULE NISI. ". . . [I]ndicates that the Court is satisfied that a prima facie case has been made out to justify calling upon the other side to make answer at the time and place indicated to the contention upon which the rule was founded." *R. v. U.F.A.W.* (1967), [1968] 1 C.C.C. 194 at 197, 60 W.W.R. 370, 63 D.L.R. (2d) 356 (B.C. C.A.), Davey C.J.B.C. (Branca J.A. concurring).

RULE OF LAW. 1. ". . . [A] fundamental principle of our Constitution, must mean at least two things. First, that the law is supreme over officials of the government as well as private individuals, and thereby preclusive of the influence of arbitrary power. Second, the rule of law requires the creation and maintenance of an actual order of positive laws which preserves and embodies the more general principle of normative order. Law and order are indispensable elements of civilized life." *Reference re Language Rights Under s. 23 of Manitoba Act, 1870 and s. 133 of Constitution Act, 1867*, [1985] 1 S.C.R. 721 at 748-9, [1985] 4 W.W.R. 385, 35 Man. R. (2d) 83, 59 N.R. 321, 19 D.L.R. (4th) 1, Dickson C.J., Beetz, Estey, McIntyre, Lamer, Wilson and Le Dain JJ. 2. ". . . [A] highly textured expression, importing many things . . . but conveying, for example, a sense of orderliness, of subjection to known legal rules and of executive accountability to legal authority." *Reference re Questions Concerning Amendment of the Constitution of Canada as set out in O.C. 1020/80* (1981), (*sub nom. Resolution to Amend the Constitution of Canada, Re*) 1 C.R.R. 59 at 99, [1981] 1 S.C.R. 753, [1981] 6 W.W.R. 1, 11 Man. R. (2d) 1, 39 N.R. 1, 34 Nfld. & P.E.I.R. 1, 95 A.P.R. 1, Laskin C.J.C., Dickson, Beetz, Estey, McIntyre, Chouinard and Lamer JJ.

RULES OF COURT. Rules made by the authority having for the time being power to make rules or orders regulating the practice and procedure of that court.

RULES OF PLEADING. Rules governing the form that pleadings take which have three basic requirements: (a) to plead the material facts; (b) to deny material facts and (c) to plead an affirmative defence. One might add the right of a party to request, and the court to order, particulars. G.D. Watson & C. Perkins, eds., *Holmested & Watson: Ontario Civil Procedure* (Toronto: Carswell, 1984) at 25-13 and 14.

RULING. *n.* 1. Determination obtained by a motion to the court of the propriety of a question in an examination to which one objected without receiving an answer (Ontario, Rules of Civil Procedure, r. 34.12(3)). G.D. Watson & C. Perkins, eds., *Holmested & Watson: Ontario Civil Procedure* (Toronto: Carswell, 1984) at 34-7. 2. ". . . [A] disposition of a motion for non-suit made during the course of a trial is not an order . . . . [I]t is instead, in my judgment, what [is] more properly described as a ruling, or a ruling on evidence which is part of the trial process, and it is not appealable until after the trial has been completed." *Rahmatian v. HFH Video Biz, Inc.* (1991), 46 C.P.C. (2d) 312 at 315 (B.C. C.A.), MacEachern C.J.B.C.

RUN. *v.* To take effect at a certain place or time. See HIT AND ~.

RUN WITH THE LAND. Said of a covenant with land conveyed in fee when either the right to take advantage of it or the liability to perform it, passes to the person to whom that land is assigned.

RUN WITH THE REVERSION. Said of a covenant with leased land when either the right to take advantage of it or the liability to perform it, passes to the person to whom that reversion is assigned.

RUS. *abbr.* Russell's Election Cases (N.S.), 1874.

RYLANDS V. FLETCHER. See   RULE IN ~.

S

S. *abbr.* Section.

S.A. *abbr.* Société Anonyme.

SABOTAGE. *n.* Doing a prohibited act for a purpose prejudicial to (a) the safety, security or defence of Canada; or (b) the safety or security of the naval, army or air forces of any state other than Canada that are lawfully present in Canada. *Criminal Code*, R.S.C. 1985, c. C-46, s. 52.

SAFETY. *n.* 1. The prevention of physical injury to workers and the prevention of physical injury to other persons arising out of or in connection with activities in the workplace. *Workplace Safety and Health Act*, R.S.M. 1987, c. W210, s. 1. 2. Freedom from bodily injury or freedom from damage to health. *Construction Safety Act*, R.S.N.S. 1967, c. 52, s. 1.

S.A.G. *abbr.* Sentences arbitrales de griefs (Québec), 1970-.

SAID. *adj.* ". . . [G]rammatically applies to the last antecedent . . ." *Toronto General Trusts Co. v. Irwin* (1896), 27 O.R. 491 at 495 (H.C.), Meredith C.J.

SALARY. *n.* Compensation paid to an employee for labour or services.

SALE. *n.* 1. ". . . [T]he primary meaning of sale was the transfer of property to another for a price. . . ." *Leading Investments Ltd. v. New Forest Investments Ltd.* (1986), 38 R.P.R. 201 at 213, [1986] 1 S.C.R. 70, 65 N.R. 209, 14 O.A.C. 159, 25 D.L.R. (4th) 161, La Forest J. (Dickson C.J.C. and Lamer J. concurring). 2. ". . . [M]ay be inter-

preted to mean either a binding agreement for sale or a completed sale. . . ." *Leading Investments Ltd. v. New Forest Investments Ltd.* (1986), 38 R.P.R. 201 at 223, [1986] 1 S.C.R. 70, 65 N.R. 209, 14 O.A.C. 159, 25 D.L.R. (4th) 161, Estey J. (McIntyre and Chouinard JJ. concurring). See ACTION FOR ~; AGREEMENT FOR ~; BARGAIN AND ~; BILL OF ~; BULK ~; CONDITIONAL ~; CONDITION OF ~; CONTRACT FOR ~; CONTRACT OF ~; DIRECT ~; PARTITION OR ~; POWER OF ~; PUBLIC ~; TIME ~; TRUST FOR ~.

SALE BY DESCRIPTION. ". . . [T]here is a sale by description even though the buyer is buying something displayed before him on the counter: a thing is sold by description, though it is specific, so long as it is sold not merely as the specific thing but as a thing corresponding to a description . . ." *Grant v. Australian Knitting Mills Ltd.*, [1936] S.C. 85 at 100 (Australia P.C.), Lord Wright for their Lordships.

SALE BY SAMPLE. "To constitute a sale by sample, in the legal sense of that term, it must, . . . appear that the parties contracted with reference to a sample, and with a mutual understanding that the sample furnished a description (in this case) of the quality of the oats and that the bulk must conform with the sample." *Wawryk v. McKenzie Co.* (1921), 61 D.L.R. 25 at 26, [1921] 2 W.W.R. 951 (Sask. C.A.), the court per Lamont J.A.

SALE IN BULK. A sale of a stock, or

part thereof, out of the usual course of business or trade of the vendor or of substantially the entire stock of the vendor, or of an interest in the business of the vendor.

SALE-LEASEBACK. *n*. A way to raise money on land by which a vendor receives from the purchaser current full market value of both land and the buildings built on the land and becomes a tenant of the purchaser under a long term lease of the property. D.J. Donahue & P.D. Quinn, *Real Estate Practice in Ontario*, 4th ed. (Toronto: Butterworths, 1990) at 231.

SALE OF GOODS. A contract by which a seller agrees to transfer or transfers property in goods to a buyer for financial consideration, called the price. G.H.L. Fridman, *Sale of Goods in Canada*, 3d ed. (Toronto: Carswell, 1986) at 11.

SALE ON APPROVAL. The sale of goods with the right of the purchaser to return the goods if the purchaser is not satisfied with them within a specified time.

SALE ON CREDIT. A sale in which payment of the whole price is delayed, or the price is paid in instalments over a period to which the parties agree so that agreed-on interest is paid on the delayed part of the purchase price. G.H.L. Fridman, *Sale of Goods in Canada*, 3d ed. (Toronto: Carswell, 1986) at 260.

SALES TAX. A tax which, if a seller imposes it, is like an excise tax and is on occasion called an excise tax. P.W. Hogg, *Constitutional Law of Canada*, 3d ed. (Toronto: Carswell, 1992) at 742.

SALVAGE. *v*. 1. "... [R]escue from threatened loss or injury...." *Canadian Pacific Navigation Co. v. "C.F. Sargent" (The)* (1893), 3 B.C.R. 5 at 7 (Ex. Ct.), Begbie L.J.A. 2. "... [T]o rescue or save from wreckage, ..." *R. v. Greenspoon Brothers Ltd.*, [1965] 2 O.R. 528 at 529, [1965] 4 C.C.C. 53 (C.A.), the court per Roach J.A.

SALVAGE. *n*. 1. A reward, not for

services attempted without result, but for benefits conferred. A salvor must show that, when the services were rendered, the cargo or ship was in danger of being destroyed. G.H.L. Fridman, *Restitution*, 2d ed. (Toronto: Carswell, 1992) at 281. 2. "... [T]hat which is ... rescued or saved [from wreckage]...." *R. v. Greenspoon Brothers Ltd.*, [1965] 2 O.R. 528 at 529, [1965] 4 C.C.C. 53 (C.A.), the court per Roach J.A. 3. Includes second-hand, used, discarded or surplus metals, bottles or goods, unserviceable, discarded or junked motor vehicles, bodies, engines or other component parts of a motor vehicle, and articles of every description.

SAMPLE. *n*. A small amount of a commodity displayed as a specimen at a private or public sale. See SALE BY ~.

SANCTION. *n*. A punishment or penalty used to enforce obedience to law. See COMMUNITY ~S; CRIMINAL ~S; ECONOMIC ~.

SANDERSON ORDER. A simpler form of a Bullock order by which the unsuccessful defendant must pay the successful defendant's costs directly. The name comes from *Sanderson v. Blyth Theatre Co.*, [1903] 2 K.B. 644.

SASK. BAR REV. *abbr*. Saskatchewan Bar Review.

SASK. L.R. *abbr*. Saskatchewan Law Reports.

SASK. L. REV. *abbr*. Saskatchewan Law Review.

SASK. R. *abbr*. Saskatchewan Reports, 1979-.

SATISFACTION. *n*. 1. Compensation under law. 2. Payment for an injury or of money owed. 3. Completion of an obligation by performance or something equivalent to performance. See ACCORD AND ~.

SATISFACTION PIECE. 1. "... [A] specialized form of receipt ..." *Heitman Financial Services Ltd. v. Towncliff Properties Ltd.* (1981), 24 C.P.C. 116 at 120, 35 O.R. (2d) 189 (H.C.), Callaghan J. 2. A judgment creditor's formal written acknowledgement, filed in court, that the judgment debtor has fully paid.

SAUNDERS V. VAUTIER. See RULE IN ~.

SAVING CLAUSE. A provision in a contract stating that if any term is found invalid the rest of the contract will not be affected.

S.C. *abbr.* 1. Supreme Court. 2. Supreme Court (provincial) [of Judicature]. 3. Superior Court. 4. Same case. 5. Sessions Cases.

SC. *abbr.* [L.] Scilicet. That is to say.

S.C.A.D. *abbr.* Supreme Court (provincial) [of Judicature] Appellate Division.

SCANDALIZE THE COURT. ". . . [T]raditionally encompasses two forms of conduct: (a) scurrilous abuse of a court, or of a judge not in his personal capacity but as a judge: . . . and (b) attacks upon the integrity or impartiality of a judge or court: . . . there may be a third form, namely, 'publications that are thought to lower the repute of a judge or court.' " *R. v. Kopyto* (1987), 39 C.C.C. (3d) 1 at 36, 24 O.A.C. 8, 61 C.R. (3d) 209, 62 O.R. (2d) 449, 47 D.L.R. (4th) 213 (C.A.), Houlden J.A. See CONTEMPT.

S.C.C. *abbr.* Supreme Court of Canada.

SCHED. *abbr.* Schedule.

SCHEDULE. *n.* 1. An inventory. 2. Additional or appendant writing. 3. Detailed information attached to a statute or regulation.

SCHEME. *n.* 1. A plan for marketing or regulating any natural product. 2. A plan for distributing property among people with conflicting claims. 3. ". . . [I]n the commercial sense of that word, that is a plan, design, formula or programme of action devised in order to attain some end, usually unilaterally described or stated . . ." *Canadian Allied Property Investment Ltd., Re* (1979), (*sub nom. Gregory v. Canadian Allied Property Investment Ltd.*) 98 D.L.R. (3d) 358 at 364, [1979] 3 W.W.R. 609, 11 B.C.L.R. 253

(C.A.), the court per Carrothers J.A. See PLANNING ~.

SCIENS. *adj.* [L.] ". . . '[K]nowing' . . ." *Waldick v. Malcolm* (1991), 8 C.C.L.T. (2d) 1 at 17, 3 O.R. (3d) 471n, 125 N.R. 372, 47 O.A.C. 241, 83 D.L.R. (4th) 114, [1991] 2 S.C.R. 456, the court per Iacobucci J.

SCIENTER. *adv.* [L.] Knowingly.

SCIENTER ACTION. "At common law the principle of scienter governed the owner's liability for damage caused by his animals. For example, if a dog bit a person liability depended upon proof that the owner of the dog knew or ought to have known of the animal's dangerous character. . . . The common law also recognized that certain animals were, by their nature, so dangerous to man that the keeper of them could not be heard to say that he did not know of their character. Scienter, in such a case, was to be conclusively presumed. 'Strict liability' was imposed in such cases, with certain defences permitted. . . ." *Brewer v. Saunders* (1986), 37 C.C.L.T. 237 at 242 (N.S. C.A.), the court per Matthews J.A.

SCILICET. [L.] That is to say.

SCINTILLA JURIS. [L.] A fragment or spark of right.

SCOPE OF EMPLOYMENT. See ACT WITHIN ~.

S.C.R. *abbr.* Reports of the Supreme Court of Canada, 1876-1922.

[ ] S.C.R. *abbr.* 1. Canada Law Reports, Supreme Court of Canada, 1964- (Rapports judiciaires du Canada, Cour Suprême du Canada). 2. Canada Law Reports, Supreme Court of Canada, 1923-1963.

S.C.R.R. *abbr.* Securities and Corporate Regulation Review.

S.C.T.D. *abbr.* Supreme Court (provincial) [of Judicature] Trial Division.

SEAL. *v.* "[One seals] . . . a contract by placing paper seals opposite the signatures to it . . ." *R. v. Crane* (1985), 55 Nfld. & P.E.I.R. 340 at 342, 162 A.P.R.

340 (Nfld. Dist. Ct.), Barry D.C.J.

SEAL. *n.* A wafer or wax marked with an impression. See CORPORATE ~.

SEARCH. *v.* Of title, to search in public offices to be sure that the vendor can convey free of all competing claims. B.J. Reiter, B.N. McLellan & P.M. Perell, *Real Estate Law*, 4th ed. (Toronto: Emond Montgomery, 1992) at 6.

SEARCH. *n.* 1. "In determining whether the beeper monitoring . . . constitutes a search [within the meaning of Charter, s. 8], the initial question is whether there is a reasonable expectation of privacy in respect of the monitored activity. If the police activity invades a reasonable expectation of privacy, then the activity is a search." *R. v. Wise* (1992), 8 C.R.R. (2d) 53 at 57, 11 C.R. (4th) 253, [1992] 1 S.C.R. 527, 70 C.C.C. (3d) 193, 133 N.R. 161, 51 O.A.C. 351, Cory J. (Lamer C.J.C., Gonthier and Stevenson JJ. concurring). 2. ". . . [I]mplies an effort to find what is concealed, to get past the shield surrounding privacy, to defeat the efforts of an individual to keep hidden certain elements pertaining to his life or personality. . . ." *Weatherall v. Canada (Attorney General)* (1990), 78 C.R. (3d) 257 at 265, 58 C.C.C. (3d) 424, 73 D.L.R. (4th) 57, 49 C.R.R. 347, [1991] 1 F.C. 85, 112 N.R. 379, 37 F.T.R. 80n (C.A.), Marceau J.A. (dissenting in part). 3. Examination of original documents, official books and records while investigating a title to land. See REASONABLE ~; UNREASONABLE ~.

SEARCH OR SEIZURE. 1. ". . . [I]mply an intrusion into the citizen's home or place of business by a third person who looks for and removes documents or things. Searches and seizures are normally effected under a warrant or writ which is addressed to the officer conducting the search or seizure and permits him to enter the premises for those purposes. . . ." *Ziegler v. Canada (Director of Investigation & Research, Combines Investigation Branch)* (1983), (*sub nom. Ziegler v. Hunter*) 39 C.P.C. 234 at 259, 8 D.L.R. (4th) 648, [1984] 2 F.C. 608, 51 N.R.1, 8 C.R.R. 47 (C.A.), Hugessen J.A. 2. ". . . [E]lectronic surveillance constitutes a 'search or seizure' within the meaning of s. 8 of the [Charter] . . ." *R. v. Thompson* (1990), 59 C.C.C. (3d) 225 at 267, [1990] 6 W.W.R. 481, 49 B.C.L.R. (2d) 321, 80 C.R. (3d) 129, 73 D.L.R. (4th) 596, 114 N.R. 1, 50 C.R.R. 1, [1990] 2 S.C.R. 1111, Sopinka J. (Dickson C.J.C., Lamer C.J.C. and L'Heureux-Dubé J. concurring).

SEARCH WARRANT. ". . . [A]n order issued by a Justice under statutory powers, authorizing a named person to enter a specified place to search for and seize specified property which will afford evidence of the actual or intended commission of a crime." *MacIntyre v. Nova Scotia (Attorney General)* (1982), 132 D.L.R. (3d) 385 at 397, [1982] S.C.R. 175, 26 C.R. (3d) 193, 40 N.R. 181, 49 N.S.R. (2d) 609, 96 A.P.R. 609, 65 C.C.C. (2d) 129, Dickson J. (Laskin C.J.C., McIntyre, Chouinard and Lamer JJ. concurring).

SEAT BELT. Any strap, webbing, or similar device designed to secure the driver or a passenger in a motor vehicle.

SECK. *adj.* Barren; dry. See RENT ~.

SECONDARY EVIDENCE. Proof admitted when primary evidence is lost.

SECOND DEGREE MURDER. 1. All murder which is not first degree murder. *Criminal Code*, R.S.C. 1985, c. C-46, s. 231. 2. Murder other than planned or deliberate murder and other than murder of the type specified in s. 231 of the Criminal Code.

SECOND MORTGAGE. A charge or mortgage which ranks after a prior charge or mortgage.

SECOND READING. Parliamentary consideration of the principle of a measure at which time one may consider other methods of reaching its proposed objective. At this stage, the order is made to commit the bill. A. Fraser, W.A. Dawson & J. Holtby, eds., *Beauchesne's Rules and Forms of* the House of Commons of Canada, 6th ed. (Toronto: Carswell, 1989) at 195.

SECRET. See TRADE ~.

SECRETARY. *n.* The head of a government department. 2. The officer of an association, club or company. 3. The corporate officer who takes minutes of meetings of directors and shareholders, sends out notices of meetings and is in charge of the minute books and other books of the company. H. Sutherland, D.B. Horsley & J.M. Edmiston, eds., *Fraser's Handbook on Canadian Company Law*, 7th ed. (Toronto: Carswell, 1985) at 253.

SECRETARY OF STATE. 1. A title applied to some members of cabinet or heads of departments. 2. The federal ministry empowered to support multiculturalism and youth and to encourage the use of both official languages.

SECRET BALLOT. See VOTE BY ~.

SECRET PROFIT. A financial advantage, including a bribe, which an agent receives over and above what the agent is entitled to receive from the principal as remuneration. G.H.L. Fridman, *The Law of Agency*, 6th ed. (London: Butterworths, 1990) at 162.

SECRET TRUST. ". . . [T]he three necessary requirements to establish a secret trust are an intention on the part of the deceased to create a trust, notwithstanding the apparent benefit to a named legatee; communication of the intention to the intended recipient of the property; and acceptance of the trust by the intended recipient of the property." *Riffel Estate, Re* (1987), 28 E.T.R. 1 at 4, 64 Sask. R. 190 (Q.B.), Matheson J.

SECTION. *n.* 1. A numbered paragraph in a statute. 2. A division of land equalling one square mile or 640 acres. See DEFINITION ~; INTERPRETATION ~.

SECURED CREDITOR. 1. A person holding a mortgage, hypothec, pledge, charge, lien or privilege on or against the property of the debtor or any part

thereof as security for a debt due or accruing due to that person from the debtor. 2. A person whose claim is based on, or secured by, a negotiable instrument held as collateral security and on which the debtor is only indirectly or secondarily liable. *Bankruptcy Act*, R.S.C. 1985, c. B-3, s. 2 (part).

SECURED PARTY. A person who has a security interest.

SECURED TRANSACTION. A transaction with two main elements: that consideration flows from the creditor and creates a debt and that an interest in the debtor's property secures payment of the debt. F. Bennett, *Receiverships* (Toronto: Carswell, 1985) at 27.

SECURITIES. *n.* (a) Bonds, debentures and obligations of or guaranteed by governments, corporations or unincorporated bodies, whether such corporations and unincorporated bodies are governmental, municipal, school, ecclesiastical, commercial or other, secured on real or personal property or unsecured, and rights in respect of such bonds, debentures and obligations; (b) shares of capital stock of corporations and rights in respect of such shares; (c) equipment trust certificates or obligations; (d) all documents, instruments and writings commonly known as securities; and (e) mortgages and hypothecs. See SECURITY.

SECURITIES REGISTER. A record of securities which a company issues. H. Sutherland, D.B. Horsley & J.M. Edmiston, eds., *Fraser's Handbook on Canadian Company Law*, 7th ed. (Toronto: Carswell, 1985) at 394.

SECURITY. *n.* 1. A thing which makes the enforcement or enjoyment of a right more certain or secure. 2. "Security for a debt, in the ordinary meaning of the term, carries with it the idea of something or somebody to which, or to whom, the creditor can resort in order to aid him in realizing or recovering the debt, in case the debtor fails to pay; the word implies something in addition to the mere obligation of the debtor. . . ." *Child & Gower*

Piano Co. v. Gambrel, [1933] 2 W.W.R. 273 at 281 (Sask. C.A.), Martin J.A. (MacKenzie J.A. concurring). 3. A share of any class or series of shares of a corporation or a debt obligation of a corporation and includes a certificate evidencing any share or debt obligation. See CAPITAL ~; COLLATERAL ~; CONVERTIBLE ~; DEBT ~; EQUITY ~; REDEEMABLE ~; SECURITIES; UNION ~; VOTING ~.

SECURITY AGREEMENT. An agreement that creates or provides for a security interest.

SECURITY DEPOSIT. Any money, property or right paid or given by a tenant of residential premises to a landlord or to anyone on the landlord's behalf to be held by or for the landlord as security for the performance of an obligation or the payment of a liability by the tenant or to be returned to the tenant on the happening of a condition.

SECURITY FOR COSTS. Security which a plaintiff may be required to provide in a proceeding to ensure that the plaintiff will be able to pay any costs which may be awarded to the defendant.

SECURITY INTEREST. 1. An interest in collateral that secures payment or performance of an obligation. 2. An interest in or charge upon the property of a body corporate by way of mortgage, hypothec, pledge or otherwise, to secure payment of a debt or performance of any other obligation of the body corporate. See PERFECTED ~.

SECURITY OF TENURE. A tenant's right to remain in leased premises unless the tenancy is terminated by the landlord for a cause specified in the governing legislation.

SECURITY OF THE PERSON. 1. ". . . [T]he right to 'security of the person' under s. 7 of the Charter protects both the physical and psychological integrity of the individual . . ." *R. v. Morgentaler* (1988), 31 C.R.R. 1 at 87, 82 N.R. 1, [1988] 1 S.C.R. 30, 63 O.R. (2d) 281n, 63 C.R. (3d) 1, 26 O.A.C.

1, 44 D.L.R. (4th) 385, 37 C.C.C. (3d) 449, Wilson J. 2. ". . . The case law leads me to the conclusion that state interference with bodily integrity and serious state-imposed psychological stress at least in the Criminal law context constitute a breach of security of the person." *R. v. Morgentaler* (1988), 31 C.R.R. 1 at 20, 82 N.R. 1, [1988] 1 S.C.R. 30, 63 O.R. (2d) 281n, 63 C.R. (3d) 1, 26 O.A.C. 1, 44 D.L.R. (4th) 385, 37 C.C.C. (3d) 449, Dickson C.J.C. (Lamer J. concurring).

SEDITION. *n.* See SEDITIOUS CONSPIRACY; SEDITIOUS INTENTION; SEDITIOUS WORDS.

SEDITIOUS CONSPIRACY. An agreement between two or more persons to carry out a seditious intention. *Criminal Code*, R.S.C. 1985, c. C-46, s. 59(3).

SEDITIOUS INTENTION. Everyone who teaches, advocates, publishes or circulates any writing that advocates, without authority of law, the use of force as a means of accomplishing a governmental change within Canada is presumed to have a seditious intention. *Criminal Code*, R.S.C. 1985, c. C-46, s. 59(4) in part.

SEDITIOUS LIBEL. A libel that expresses a seditious intention. *Criminal Code*, R.S.C. 1985, c. C-46, s. 59(2).

SEDITIOUS WORDS. Words that express a seditious intention. *Criminal Code*, R.S.C. 1985, c. C-46, s. 59(1).

SEDUCTION. *n.* Inducing a person to have unlawful intercourse.

SEGREGATION. *n.* In a prison, solitary confinement.

SEIGN. QUESTIONS. *abbr.* Lower Canada Reports, Seignorial Questions, vols. A & B (Décisions des Tribunaux du Bas-Canada).

SEIGN. REP. *abbr.* Seignorial Reports (Que.).

SEISED. *adj.* Is applicable to any vested estate for life or of a greater description, and shall extend to estates at law and in equity, in possession or in futurity, in land. *Trustee acts.*

SEISIN. *n.* A freeholder's holding of land. R. Megarry & H.W.R. Wade, *The Law of Real Property*, 5th ed. (London: Stevens, 1984) at cxxvii. See LIVERY OF ~.

SEIZED. *adj.* See SEISED.

SEIZURE. *n.* 1. ". . . [T]he essence of seizure under s. 8 [of the Charter] is the taking of a thing from a person by a public authority without that person's consent. . . . If I were to draw the line between a seizure and a mere finding of evidence, I would draw it logically and purposefully at the point at which it can reasonably be said that the individual had ceased to have a privacy interest in the subject-matter allegedly seized." *R. v. Dyment* (1988), 38 C.R.R. 301 at 312, 316, 10 M.V.R. (2d) 1, 66 C.R. (3d) 348, 89 N.R. 249, [1988] 2 S.C.R. 417, 45 C.C.C. (3d) 244, 73 Nfld. & P.E.I.R. 13, 229 A.P.R. 13, 55 D.L.R. (4th) 503, La Forest J. (Dickson C.J.C. concurring). 2. A species of execution in which a sheriff executes a writ of fi. fa. by taking possession of the chattels of the debtor. 3. What takes place when goods are confiscated as a punishment for smuggling. See SEARCH OR ~.

SEIZURE AND SALE. See WRIT OF ~.

SELECT COMMITTEE. A committee of Parliament or a legislature set up to investigate a particular matter.

SELF-CRIMINATION. See SELF-INCRIMINATION.

SELF-DEFENCE. *n.* 1. Defence of one's person or property directly against another exerting unlawful force. D. Stuart, *Canadian Criminal Law: A Treatise*, 2d ed. (Toronto: Carswell, 1987) at 405. 2. ". . . [A] man who is attacked may defend himself. It is both good law and good sense that he may do, but only do, what is reasonably necessary. . . ." *Palmer v. R.*, [1971] 1 All E.R. 1077 at 1088, [1971] A.C. 814, 55 Cr. App. R. 223 (Jamaica P.C.), the board per Lord Morris of Borth-Y-Gest.

SELF-EMPLOYED PERSON. A person who is engaged in an occupa-

tion on his own behalf.

SELF-HELP. *n.* An action in which an injured party seeks redress without resorting to a court.

SELF-INCRIMINATION. *n.* Behaviour indicating one's guilt. See PRIVILEGE AGAINST ~.

SELF-SERVING STATEMENT. An exculpatory statement. S. Mitchell, P.J. Richardson & D.A. Thomas, eds., *Archbold Pleading, Evidence and Practice in Criminal Cases*, 43d ed. (London: Sweet & Maxwell, 1988) at 1278.

SEMBLE. *v.* [Fr. appears] A word used to introduce a legal proposition which one does not intend to state definitely.

SENATE. *n.* 1. The second federal legislative body whose members are appointed by the Governor General, which means, in fact, by the cabinet. P.W. Hogg, *Constitutional Law of Canada*, 3d ed. (Toronto: Carswell, 1992) at 240. 2. The governing body of a university or college.

SENATOR. *n.* A person who is a member of a senate.

SENTENCE. *n.* ". . . [U]sed in reference to the determination or pronouncement of punishment or like action following a finding of guilt; . . . utilized to define the fate or punishment of a person who has been adjudged guilty, . . ." *Morris v. R.* (1979), 91 D.L.R. (3d) 161 at 177, [1979] 1 S.C.R. 405, 23 N.R. 109, 6 C.R. (3d) 36, 43 C.C.C. (2d) 129, Pratte J. (Martland, Ritchie, Pigeon and Beetz JJ. concurring). See CONCURRENT ~; CONSECUTIVE ~S; DETERMINATE ~; INDETERMINATE ~; PRE-~ REPORT; SUSPENDED ~.

SEPARATION. *n.* 1. The decision by a husband and wife to live apart. 2. The termination of employment. See JUDICIAL ~.

SEPARATION AGREEMENT. An agreement in writing between spouses who are living or intend to live separate and apart. See WRITTEN ~.

SEQUESTER. *v.* To prevent the

owners from using by setting aside.

SEQUESTRATION. *n.* Property is temporarily placed by some judicial or quasi-judicial process in the hands of persons called sequestrators, who manage it and receive the rents and profits.

SERIATIM. *adv.* [L.] Separately and in order.

SERIES. *n.* In relation to shares, means a division of a class of shares.

SERIOUS BODILY HARM. "... [F]or the purposes of the section [s. 264.1 of the Criminal Code, R.S.C. 1985, c. C-46] is any hurt or injury, whether physical or psychological, that interferes in a substantial way with the physical or psychological integrity, health or well-being of the complainant." *R. v. McCraw* (1991), 66 C.C.C. (3d) 517 at 523, 7 C.R. (4th) 314, 128 N.R. 299, 49 O.A.C. 47, [1991] 3 S.C.R. 72, the court per Cory J.

SERIOUS PERSONAL INJURY OFFENCE. (a) An indictable offence, other than high treason, treason, first degree murder or second degree murder, involving (i) the use or attempted use of violence against another person; or (ii) conduct endangering or likely to endanger the life or safety of another person or inflicting or likely to inflict severe psychological damage on another person, and for which the offender may be sentenced to imprisonment for 10 years or more; or (b) an offence or attempt to commit an offence mentioned in section 271 (sexual assault), 272 (sexual assault with a weapon, threats to a third party or causing bodily harm) or 273 (aggravated sexual assault). *Criminal Code*, R.S.C. 1985, c. C-46, s. 752.

SERVANT. *n.* 1. "... [A] person subject to the command of his master as to the manner in which he shall do his work ..." *Tully v. Genbey*, [1939] 1 D.L.R. 559 at 565, [1939] 1 W.W.R. 161, 46 Man. R. 439 (C.A.), Trueman J.A. 2. "... '[E]mployee' ..." *Atherton v. Boycott* (1989), 36 C.P.C. (2d) 250 at 255 (Ont. H.C.), Cusinato

L.J.S.C. See CIVIL ~; MASTER AND ~; PUBLIC ~.

SERVE. *v.* Of a copy of a legal document, to deliver it to parties interested in a legal proceeding so that they know about the proceeding.

SERVED. *n.* Served personally on a person or on an adult residing at the residence of the person who is at the residence at the time of service, or sent by registered mail to the person at his latest known address, and where sent by registered mail service shall be deemed to have been effected on the fifth day after the day of mailing. *Expropriation Act*, R.S.N.B. 1973, c. E-14, s. 1.

SERVICE. *n.* 1. Service in the Canadian Forces or in the naval, army or air forces of Canada since the commencement of World War I. *Pension Act*, R.S.C. 1985, c. P-6, s. 2. 2. With respect to a document, the act of serving it. 3. "... [D]oes not necessarily means 'personal service' ... means bringing it to the attention of the person to be served." *Canada Trust Co. v. Kakar Properties Ltd.* (1983), 32 C.P.C. 280 at 289, 26 R.P.R. 202 (Ont. Master), Peppiatt (Master). See AFFIDAVIT OF ~; CIVIL ~; COMMUNITY ~; COMMUNITY ~ ORDER; COMPUTER ~; MUNICIPAL ~; PERSONAL ~; ~S; SUBSTITUTED ~.

SERVICE OF PROCESS. Bringing the effect or contents of a document to the attention of a person affected.

SERVICES. *n.* 1. "... [T]he product of the work supplying it." *Xerox of Canada Ltd. v. Ontario Regional Assessment Commissioner, Region No. 10* (1981), 13 O.M.B.R. 41 at 42, [1981] 2 S.C.R. 137, 127 D.L.R. (3d) 511, Martland, Dickson, Beetz, McIntyre and Chouinard JJ. 2. "... '[H]elp' or 'benefit' or 'advantage' conferred...." *R. v. Laphkas* (1942), 77 C.C.C. 142 at 145, [1942] S.C.R. 84, [1942] 2 D.L.R. 47, Taschereau J. 3. "[In s. 20 of the Charter] ... means, generally, the administration of public affairs as the same applies to the individual...." *Jenkins v. Prince Edward Island (Workers' Compensation Board)*

(1986), 15 C.C.E.L. 55 at 65-6, 21 C.C.L.I. 149, 31 D.L.R. (4th) 536, 61 Nfld. & P.E.I.R. 206, 185 A.P.R. 206, 9 C.H.R.R. D/5145 (P.E.I. C.A.), the court per McQuaid J.A. See COMMUNITY DEVELOPMENT ~; ESSENTIAL ~; LOSS OF ~; MUNICIPAL ~; PERSONAL ~; SERVICE.

SERVICE TRIBUNAL. A court martial or a person presiding at a summary trial. *National Defence Act*, R.S.C. 1985, c. N-5, s. 2.

SERVIENT TENEMENT. The land over which one exercises an easement.

SESSION. *n.* 1. The period of time between the first meeting of Parliament and a prorogation. One Parliament usually includes several sessions. A. Fraser, W.A. Dawson & J. Holtby, eds., *Beauchesne's Rules and Forms of the House of Commons of Canada*, 6th ed. (Toronto: Carswell, 1989) at 65. 2. "... [T]he period of time during which members of the Legislature are called together for the despatch of public business." *Sessional Allowances under the Ontario Legislative Assembly Act, Re*, [1945] 2 D.L.R. 631 at 636, [1945] O.R. 336 (C.A.), McRuer J.A. 3. The sitting of a court. 4. "The word 'term' would be more accurate than 'session' to describe the time prescribed by law for holding court, as a session of the Court is the time of its actual sitting and terminates each day with its rising. The distinction is not always observed, however, and the words are often used interchangeably." *MacDonald v. Dawson* (1955), 20 C.R. 357 at 358, 36 M.P.R. 34, 112 C.C.C. 44 (Nfld. C.A.), the court per Walsh C.J.

SET ASIDE. To negate or annul an order or judgment.

SET DOWN FOR TRIAL. With respect to a matter, to serve a trial record or filing a trial record in the case of an undefended action. G.D. Watson & C. Perkins, eds., *Holmested & Watson: Ontario Civil Procedure* (Toronto: Carswell, 1984-) at 48-3.

SET OFF. *var.* **SET-OFF**. 1. "A statutory set-off was available, before the fusion of law and equity, either in equity or at law. It is still available. It requires the fulfilment of two conditions. The first is that both obligations must be debts. The second is that both debts must be mutual cross obligations. Both conditions must be fulfilled at the same time: ..." *Canadian Imperial Bank of Commerce v. Tuckerr Industries Inc.* (1988), 48 C.B.R. (N.S.) 1 at 3, [1983] 5 W.W.R. 602, 46 B.C.L.R. 7, 149 D.L.R. (3d) 172 (C.A.), the court per Lambert J.A. 2. "Equitable set-off is available where there is a claim for a money sum whether liquidated or unliquidated: Abacus Cities Ltd. v. Aboussafy [1981] 4 W.W.R. 660 ... (Alta. C.A.) at p. 666 ... it is available where there has been an assignment. There is no requirement of mutuality.... The party relying on a set-off must show some equitable ground for being protected against his adversary's demands: ... The equitable ground must go to the very root of the plaintiff's claim before a set-off will be allowed: ... A cross-claim must be so clearly connected with the demand of the Plaintiff that it would be manifestly unjust to allow the plaintiff to enforce payment without taking into consideration the cross-claim: ... The plaintiff's claim and the cross-claim need not arise out of the same contract: ... Unliquidated claims are on the same footing as liquidated claims: ..." *Telford v. Holt* (1987), 21 C.P.C. (2d) 1 at 13, 18, 78 N.R. 321, 54 Alta. L.R. (2d) 193, [1987] 6 W.W.R. 385, [1987] 2 S.C.R. 193, 46 R.P.R. 234, 81 A.R. 385, 41 D.L.R. (4th) 385, 37 B.L.R. 241, the court per Wilson J. 3. "... [S]omething in the way of a defence: where claim and cross-claim are merged and the lesser is thereby extinguished. True set-off must be distinguished from procedural set-off, where two unrelated claims are balanced up and a net judgment given: ..." *Abacus Cities Ltd. v. Aboussafy* (1981), (*sub nom. Aboussafy v. Abacus Cities Ltd.*) 39 C.B.R. (N.S.) 1 at 10, [1981] 4 W.W.R. 660, 124 D.L.R. (3d) 150, 29 A.R. 607 (C.A.), the court per Kerans J.A. 4. "Where a customer has two accounts with the same bank and one is in credit and the other in debit the bank may set off one against the other and combine the two accounts: . . ." *Bank of Montreal v. R & R Entertainment Ltd.* (1984), 27 B.L.R. 159 at 166, 56 N.B.R. (2d) 154, 146 A.P.R. 154, 13 D.L.R. (4th) 726 (C.A.), the court per Hughes C.J.N.B. See EQUITABLE ~; LEGAL ~; STATUTORY ~.

SETTLE. *v.* 1. ". . . [T]o bring a dispute to an end by arrangement of the parties as opposed to by judgment of a court on the merits [and does not necessarily require a compromise]." *Data General (Canada) Ltd. v. Molnar Systems Group Inc.* (1991), 3 C.P.C. (3d) 180 at 187, 85 D.L.R. (4th) 392, 6 O.R. (3d) 409, 52 O.A.C. 212 (C.A.), the court per Morden J.A. 2. With respect to property, to limit it, or the income from it, to several people in succession, so that any person who possesses or enjoys it does not have power to deprive another of the right to enjoy it in future. 3. With respect to a document, to make it right in substance and in form.

SETTLED ESTATE. Land and all estates or interests in land that are the subject of a settlement.

SETTLEMENT. *n.* 1. An agreement by parties in dispute. 2. An unincorporated community of persons. 3. ". . . [A] disposition of property to be held, either in original form or in such form that it can be traced, for the enjoyment of some other person . . ." *Geraci, Re*, [1970] 3 O.R. 49 at 51, 14 C.B.R. (N.S.) 253, [1970] I.L.R. 1-343, 12 D.L.R. (3d) 314 (C.A.), the court per Jessup J.A. See MARRIAGE ~; MINUTES OF ~; STRUCTURED ~.

SETTLOR. *n.* 1. A person who creates a trust. 2. Any party named or described in a marriage settlement who agrees or is liable to pay any sum or sums of money mentioned therein, or who in any marriage settlement settles, grants, conveys, transfers, mortgages, or charges, or agrees to settle, grant, convey, transfer, mortgage, or charge, any real or personal property upon or to any person. *Marriage Settlement acts.*

SEVER. *v.* To divide.

SEVERABLE. *adj.* Able to be divided.

SEVERAL. *adj.* The opposite of "joint". See JOINT AND ~.

SEVERALLY. See JOINTLY AND ~.

SEVERAL TENANCY. A tenancy which is separate and not held jointly with another person.

SEVERAL TORTFEASORS. Those whose acts occur in the same sequence of events causing the damage but who have not acted in common. They are responsible for the same damage, but not for the same tort. J.G. Fleming, *The Law of Torts*, 8th ed. (Sydney: Law Book, 1992) at 255.

SEVERALTY. *n.* Property belongs to people "in severalty" when each person's share can be distinguished in contrast to joint ownership, coparcency or ownership in common in which owners hold undivided shares.

SEVERANCE. *n.* 1. Separation; severing. 2. A court order for the separate trials of two or more people jointly indicted, done in the interests of justice. S.A. Cohen, *Due Process of Law* (Toronto: Carswell, 1977) at 273. 3. Division of one statute into an invalid and a valid part regarding them as two laws concerning two different "matters" because one assumes that the legislature would have enacted the valid part even if it understood that it could not enact the other. P.W. Hogg, *Constitutional Law of Canada*, 3d ed. (Toronto: Carswell, 1992) at 391. 4. A court recognizes that valid and objectionable parts of a contract are separate and gives effect to the former though it refuses to enforce the latter. G.H.L. Fridman, *The Law of Contract in Canada*, 2d ed. (Toronto: Carswell, 1986) at 399. 5. ". . . [T]o put an end to the joint ownership relationship of property." *Laprise (Crow) v. Crow* (1991), 32 R.F.L. (3d) 82 at 93, 101 N.S.R. (2d) 194, 275 A.P.R. 194 (C.A.), the court per Hallett J.A. 6. ". . . [A] complete separation of the employment relationship. . . ." *Max Factor*

Canada v. U.S.W.A., Local 9050 (1988), 33 L.A.C. (3d) 274 at 276 (Ont.), Simmons. 7. "... Severance at law of a joint tenancy, therefore, occurs when one or more of the four unities (title, interest, possession and time) is destroyed, either as a result of the actions of one of the joint tenants or as a consequence of the common intention of the joint tenants." *Walker v. Dubord* (1991), 41 E.T.R. 307 at 313-14 (B.C. S.C.), Callaghan J.

SEVERANCE CLAUSE. The section of a statute which provides that, if any part of that statute is judged to be unconstitutional, the rest will continue to be effective. P.W. Hogg, *Constitutional Law of Canada*, 3d ed. (Toronto: Carswell, 1992) at 392.

SEVERANCE PAY. "... [T]he nature and purpose of severance pay is similar to the nature and purpose of common law damages for failure to give reasonable notice of termination of employment. The triggering event is the same, namely, termination of employment. Severance pay cushions economic hardship and provides some compensation for loss of employment ... this payment is made whether or not the employee gets another job ..." *Mattocks v. Smith & Stone (1982) Inc.* (1990), 34 C.C.E.L. 273 at 279 (Ont. Gen. Div.), Corbett J.

SEX. *n.* "Gender, ..." *Janzen v. Platy Enterprises Ltd.* (1986), 8 C.H.R.R. D/3831 at D/3845, [1987] 1 W.W.R. 385, 33 D.L.R. (4th) 32, 87 C.L.L.C. 17,014, 43 Man. R. (2d) 293 (C.A.), Twaddle J.A.

SEX DISCRIMINATION. 1. "... [P]ractices or attitudes which have the effect of limiting the conditions of employment of, or the employment opportunities available to, employees on the basis of a characteristic related to gender." *Janzen v. Platy Enterprises Ltd.* (1989), 47 C.R.R. 274 at 295, [1989] 1 S.C.R. 1252, 25 C.C.E.L. 1, [1989] 4 W.W.R. 39, 59 D.L.R. (4th) 352, 10 C.H.R.R. D/6205, 58 Man. R. (2d) 1, 89 C.L.L.C. 17,011, 95 N.R. 81, the court per Dickson C.J.C. 2. "... Discrimination on the basis of preg-

nancy is a form of sex discrimination because of the basic biological fact that only women have the capacity to become pregnant. ..." *Brooks v. Canada Safeway Ltd.* (1989), 10 C.H.R.R. D/6183 at D/6193, 26 C.C.E.L. 1, [1989] 4 W.W.R. 193, 89 C.L.L.C. 17,012, 94 N.R. 373, [1989] 1 S.C.R. 1219, 59 D.L.R. (4th) 321, 58 Man. R. (2d) 161, 45 C.R.R. 115, Dickson C.J.C. (Beetz, McIntyre, Wilson, La Forest and L'Heureux-Dubé JJ. concurring).

SEXUAL ASSAULT. "... [A]n assault within any one of the definitions of that concept in s. 244(1) of the Criminal Code ... which is committed in circumstances of a sexual nature, such that the sexual integrity of the victim is violated. The test to be applied in determining whether the impugned conduct has the requisite sexual nature is an objective one: 'Viewed in the light of all the circumstances, is the sexual or carnal context of the assault visible to a reasonable observer?' (R. v. Taylor (1985), 19 C.C.C. (3d) 156 ... per Laycraft C.J.A., at p. 162 C.C.C.). The part of the body touched, the nature of the contact, the situation in which it occurred, the words and gestures accompanying the act, and all other circumstances surrounding the conduct, including threats which may or may not be accompanied by force, will be relevant: ... The intent or purpose of the person committing the act, to the extent that this may appear from the evidence, may also be a factor in considering whether the conduct is sexual. ..." *R. v. Chase* (1987), 37 C.C.C. (3d) 97 at 103, 59 C.R. (3d) 193, [1987] 2 S.C.R. 293, 80 N.R. 247, 82 N.B.R. (2d) 229, 208 A.P.R. 229, 45 D.L.R. (4th) 98, the court per McIntyre J. See AGGRAVATED ~.

SEXUAL HARASSMENT. 1. Any conduct, comment, gesture or contact of a sexual nature (a) that is likely to cause offence or humiliation to any employee; or (b) that might, on reasonable grounds, be perceived by that employee as placing a condition of a sexual nature on employment or on any opportunity for training or promotion.

Canada Labour Code, R.S.C. 1985 (1st Supp.), c. 9, s. 247.1. 2. ". . . [I]n the workplace may be broadly defined as unwelcome conduct of a sexual nature that detrimentally affects the work environment or leads to adverse job-related consequences for the victims of the harassment. It is . . . an abuse of power." *Janzen v. Platy Enterprises Ltd.* (1989), 89 C.L.L.C. 17,011 at 16,072, 47 C.R.R. 274, [1989] 1 S.C.R. 1252, 25 C.C.E.L. 1, [1989] 4 W.W.R. 39, 59 D.L.R. (4th) 352, 10 C.H.R.R. D/6205, 58 Man. R. (2d) 1, 95 N.R. 81, the court per Dickson C.J.C. See QUID PRO QUO ~.

SEXUAL ORIENTATION. "[Denotes] . . . an individual's orientation or preference in terms of sexual relationship to others, whether homosexual or heterosexual or perhaps both . . ." *Leshner v. Ontario* (1992), (*sub nom. Leshner v. Ontario (No. 2)*) 16 C.H.R.R. D/184 at D/196, 92 C.L.L.C. 17,035, C.E.B. & P.R.G. 8133 (Ont. Bd. of Inquiry), Cumming, Dawson and Plaut.

SHALL. *v.* 1. Is to be construed as imperative. 2. ". . . Parliament when it used the word 'shall' in s. 23 of the Manitoba Act, 1870, and s. 133 of the Constitution Act, 1867 [(30 & 31 Vict.), c. 3] intended that those sections be construed as mandatory or imperative, in the sense that they must be obeyed, unless such an interpretation of the word 'shall' would be utterly inconsistent with the context in which it has been used and would render the sections irrational or meaningless. . . ." *Reference re Language Rights Under s. 23 of Manitoba Act, 1870 and s. 133 of Constitution Act, 1867*, [1985] 1 S.C.R. 721 at 737, [1985] 4 W.W.R. 385, 35 Man. R. (2d) 83, 59 N.R. 321, 19 D.L.R. (4th) 1, Dickson C.J., Beetz, Estey, McIntyre, Lamer, Wilson and Le Dain JJ.

SHAM. *n.* ". . . [A] transaction purporting to create apparent legal rights and obligations which are at variance with the legal relationships which in fact characterize the arrangement. . . ." *Jodrey v. Nova Scotia* (1980), (*sub nom. Covert v. Nova Scotia (Minister of Finance)*) 8 E.T.R. 69 at 118, [1980] 2 S.C.R. 774, 41 N.S.R.(2d) 181, 76 A.P.R. 181, [1980] C.T.C. 437, 32 N.R. 275, Dickson J. (dissenting) (Ritchie and McIntyre JJ. concurring).

SHAM TRANSACTION. ". . . [A] transaction conducted with an element of deceit so as to create an illusion calculated to lead the tax collector away from the taxpayer or the true nature of the transaction; or, simple deception whereby the taxpayer creates a facade of reality quite different from the disguised reality." *Stubart Investments Ltd. v. R.*, [1984] 1 S.C.R. 536 at 545, 53 N.R. 241, [1984] C.T.C. 294, 84 D.T.C. 6305, 10 D.L.R. (4th) 1, Estey J. (Beetz and McIntyre JJ. concurring).

SHARE. *n.* 1. An integral, separate part of a company's authorized capital. H. Sutherland, D.B. Horsley & J.M. Edmiston, eds., *Fraser's Handbook on Canadian Company Law*, 7th ed. (Toronto: Carswell, 1985) at 107. 2. ". . . [I]s not an isolated piece of property. It is rather, in the well-known phrase, a 'bundle' of interrelated rights and liabilities. A share is not an entity independent of the statutory provisions that govern its possession and exchange. Those provisions make up its constituent elements. They define the very rights and liabilities that constitute the share's existence. The Canada Business Corporations Act [S.C. 1974-75-76, c. 33] defines and governs the right to vote at shareholders' meetings, to receive dividends, to inspect the books and records of the company, and to receive a portion of the corporation's capital upon a winding up of the company, among many others. A 'share' and thus a 'shareholder' are concepts inseparable from the comprehensive bundle of rights and liabilities created by the Act." *Sparling v. Québec (Caisse de dépôt & de placement)* (1988), 41 B.L.R. 1 at 11, 55 D.L.R. (4th) 63, [1988] 2 S.C.R. 1015, 89 N.R. 120, 20 Q.A.C. 174, the court per La Forest J. 3. ". . . [I]ntangible, incorporeal property rights represented or evidenced by share certificates. They are not in themselves capable of individual identification and isolation from all other shares of the corporation of the same class." *Baud Corp., N.V. v. Brook* (1978), (*sub nom. Asamera Oil Corp. v. Sea Oil & General Corp.*) 5 B.L.R. 225 at 235, [1979] 1 S.C.R. 633, [1978] 6 W.W.R. 301, 23 N.R. 181, 12 A.R. 271, 89 D.L.R. (3d) 1, the court per Estey J. See COMMON ~; EQUITY ~; MUTUAL FUND ~; PREFERENCE ~; PREFERRED ~; REDEEMABLE ~; VOTING ~.

SHARE CERTIFICATE. 1. An instrument certifying that the person named in it (the shareholder) is entitled to a certain number of shares of the corporation. 2. ". . . [I]s not in itself a share or shares of the corporation but only evidence thereof, . . ." *Baud Corp., N.V. v. Brook* (1978), (*sub nom. Asamera Oil Corp. v. Sea Oil & General Corp.*) 5 B.L.R. 225 at 235, [1979] 1 S.C.R. 633, [1978] 6 W.W.R. 301, 23 N.R. 181, 12 A.R. 271, 89 D.L.R. (3d) 1, the court per Estey J. 3. ". . . [I]s in no sense a contractual document and even though it is required to be issued under the corporate seal it is not a deed. The holder's legal right depends not on the certificate but upon entry in the share register. A share certificate is not a negotiable instrument whereas a share warrant or a share purchase warrant is." *Henderson v. Minister of National Revenue*, [1973] C.T.C. 636 at 660, 73 D.T.C. 5471 (Fed. T.D.), Cattanach J.

SHARE CLASS. "The concept of share 'classes' is not technical in nature, but rather is simply the accepted means by which differential treatment of shares is recognized in the articles of incorporation of a company. As Professor Welling . . . succinctly explains, 'a class is simply a sub-group of shares with rights and conditions in common which distinguish them from other shares' . . ." *McClung v. Canada (Minister of National Revenue)* (1990), 50 B.L.R. 161 at 187, [1991] 1 C.T.C. 169, 119 N.R. 101, 91 D.T.C. 5001, [1991] 2 W.W.R. 244, 76 D.L.R. (4th) 217, 49 F.T.R. 80n, [1990] 3 S.C.R.

1020, Dickson C.J.C. (Sopinka, Gonthier and Cory JJ. concurring).

SHAREHOLDER. *n.* 1. Someone who holds shares in a company. 2. A subscriber to or holder of stock in a company. 3. A shareholder of a corporation and includes a member of a corporation or other person entitled to receive payment of a dividend or to a share in a distribution on the winding-up of the corporation. 4. ". . . [O]ne who has a proportionate interest in its [a corporation's] assets and is entitled to take part in its control and receive its dividends." *Kootenay Valley Fruit Lands Co., Re* (1911), 18 W.L.R. 145 at 147 (Man. K.B.), MacDonald J.

SHARE WARRANT. A document under a corporate seal which certifies that its bearer is entitled to shares specified in the document. H. Sutherland, D.B. Horsley & J.M. Edmiston, eds., *Fraser's Handbook on Canadian Company Law*, 7th ed. (Toronto: Carswell, 1985) at 103.

SHELLEY'S CASE. See RULE IN ~.

SHELTERING. See DOCTRINE OF ~.

SHERIFF. *n.* 1. An officer charged with the execution of a writ or other process. 2. A sheriff enforces any order of a court arising out of a civil proceeding which is enforceable in Ontario, unless an act provides otherwise (Courts of Justice Act, R.S.O. 1990, c. C.43, s. 141(1)). G.D. Watson & C. Perkins, eds., *Holmested & Watson: Ontario Civil Procedure* (Toronto: Carswell, 1984-) at CJA-249.

SHIFTING USE. An executory or secondary use, which, when executed, derogates from a preceding estate, e.g. land is conveyed to the use of one person provided that when a second person pays a designated sum of money, the estate will go to a third person.

SHOPLIFTING. *var.*
SHOP-LIFTING. *n.* Theft of merchandise.

SHOW CAUSE. 1. The presentation to a court of reasons why a certain order should not take effect. 2. "In s. 457.5(7)(e) of the Criminal Code [R.S.C. 1970, c. C-34] 'To show cause' means not merely to show that the justice made some error, but to show that the detention is wrong." *R. v. English* (1983), 8 C.C.C. (3d) 487 at 491 (Ont. Co. Ct.), Zaler Co. Ct. J.

SHOW CAUSE ORDER. ". . . [I]s simply the document which initiates the hearing under R. 355(4) [of the Federal Court Rules]. The show cause order is analogous to a summons . . . It is at the subsequent hearing, not in the application for the show cause order, that the contempt ultimately must be proved." *Cutter (Canada) Ltd. v. Baxter Travenol Laboratories of Canada Ltd.* (1984), 3 C.I.P.R. 143 at 152, 1 C.P.R. (3d) 289, 56 N.R. 282 (Fed. C.A.), the court per Urie J.A., quoting Dickson C.J.C. for the Court in *Baxter Travenol Laboratories of Canada Ltd. v. Cutter (Canada) Ltd.* (*sub nom. Baxter Laboratories of Canada Ltd. v. Cutter (Can.) Ltd.*) (1983), 1 C.I.P.R. 46 at 66, [1983] 2 S.C.R. 388, 36 C.P.C. 305, 75 C.P.R. (2d) 1, [1983] R.D.J. 481, 2 D.L.R. (4th) 621, 50 N.R. 1.

SHOW CAUSE SUMMONS. A document which requires a debtor to appear again in court and show why the debtor should not be jailed for contempt of a payment order. C.R.B. Dunlop, *Creditor-Debtor Law in Canada* (Toronto: Carswell, 1981) at 105-106.

S.I. *abbr.* Statutory instrument.

SIBLING. *n.* A person who has the same biological mother or biological father as another person. See BIRTH ~.

SIC. *adv.* [L. so, thus] This word is put in brackets in a quoted passage to show that any mistakes or apparent omissions in the quotation appear also in the original source.

SIC UTERE TUO UT ALIENUM NON LAEDAS. [L. use your own property so as not to injure your neighbour's] ". . . [T]he defendant [landowner] can protect himself in any way he pleases as long as in so doing he does not injure his neighbour who is

no party to the nuisance." *Canadian Pacific Railway v. McBryan* (1896), 5 B.C.R. 187 at 208 (C.A.), Drake J.A.

SIDENOTE. *n.* A marginal note.

SIGIL. *n.* [L.] A signature; a seal.

SIGNATURE. *n.* 1. ". . . [T]he name or special mark of a person written with his or her own hand as an authentication of some document or writing . . . It is not essential that a signature be in any particular form, as for example, that it include all the given names as well as the surname of the signatory, or that it be legible. Indeed, in some cases, it may amount to no more than a mark." *R. v. Kapoor* (1989), 52 C.C.C. (3d) 41 at 65, 19 M.V.R. (3d) 41 (Ont. H.C.), Watt J. 2. ". . . [S]tamped impressions have been recognized as valid in connection with certain legal documents. Today's business could not be conducted if stamped signatures were not recognized as legally binding. The affixing of a stamp conveys the intention to be bound by the document so executed just as effectively as the manual writing of a signature by hand . . ." *United Canso Oil & Gas Ltd., Re* (1980), 12 B.L.R. 130 at 136, 41 N.S.R. (2d) 282, 76 A.P.R. 282 (T.D.), Hallett J. 3. A mark or sign impressed on something. 4. The name which one writes oneself. See GUARANTEE OF ~.

SILENT PARTNER. A partner who puts money into a partnership without taking an active part in management.

SILK GOWN. The gown worn by Queen's Counsel; thus "to take silk" means to become a Queen's Counsel.

SIMILAR FACT EVIDENCE. Evidence admissible to show object or purpose, not to prove the principal act. It is admissible to rebut or prove a defence in cases such as accident, mistake, ignorance or an innocent intention or motive. J. Sopinka & S.N. Lederman, *The Law of Evidence in Civil Cases* (Toronto: Butterworths, 1974) at 21.

SIMPLE CONTRACT. A contract not under seal.

SIMPLE TRUST. A trust in which one person holds property in trust for another and, because the trust is not qualified by the settlor, the law determines its parameters. P.V. Baker & P. St. J. Langan, eds., *Snell's Equity*, 29th ed. (London: Sweet & Maxwell, 1990) at 103. See BARE TRUST.

SINE DIE. [L. without a day being fixed] Indefinitely.

SINE QUA NON. [L. without which not] An indispensible condition or necessity.

SINKING FUND. 1. An amount which is set aside annually with interest which if capitalized annually will be great enough at maturity to retire the principal with interest. I.M. Rogers, *The Law of Canadian Municipal Corporations*, 2d ed. (Toronto: Carswell, 1971-) at 654. 2. A special account to which is credited annually an actuarially determined amount for the purpose of providing a fund for future payments. *Financial Administration Act*, R.S.N.W.T. 1974, c. F-4, s. 2.

SITTING. *n.* "Generally speaking, a sitting of a court [as used in the Criminal Code, R.S.C. 1970, c. C-34, s. 645(4)(c)] is said to refer to time during which judicial business is transacted before the court; in that sense, it could mean a day or, again, different days within a given timespan for transacting that court's business." *R. v. Paul* (1982), 27 C.R. (3d) 193 at 203, [1982] 1 S.C.R. 621, 67 C.C.C. (2d) 97, 138 D.L.R. (3d) 455, 41 N.R. 1, the court per Lamer J.

SITTINGS. *n.* A term or session of court: the part of the year in which one transacts judicial business.

SITUS. *n.* [L.] A location; a situation.

SLANDER. *n.* Making a defamatory statement orally or in a more transitory form. R.E. Brown, *The Law of Defamation in Canada* (Toronto: Carswell, 1987) at 9.

SLANDER OF GOODS. "... [A]n action for slander of goods will lie whenever one maliciously publishes a false statement in disparagement of the goods of another and, thereby, causes the other special damage. The false statement may be in writing or by word of mouth. ..." *Rust Check Canada Inc. v. Young* (1988), 22 C.P.R. (3d) 512 at 529, 530 (Ont. H.C.), Watt J.

SLANDER OF TITLE. Writing, speaking or publishing words which impeach a plaintiff's title to any property, real or personal, which that plaintiff owns. I.H. Jacob, ed., *Bullen and Leake and Jacob's Precedents of Pleadings*, 12th ed. (London: Sweet and Maxwell, 1975) at 544.

SLIP RULE. "... [M]inor corrections to an order can be made. There is no doubt that a court can correct clerical or mathematical errors and other minor slips or omissions in an order so long as the alterations are confined to expounding its manifest intent ... and it is equally clear that a similar rule applies to orders of administrative bodies, ..." *Lodger's International Ltd. v. O'Brien* (1983), 4 C.H.R.R. D/1349 at D/1352, 45 N.B.R. (2d) 342, 118 A.P.R. 243, 83 C.L.L.C. 17,014, 145 D.L.R. (3d) 293 (C.A.), the court per La Forest J.A.

S.L.R. *abbr.* Statute Law Revision Act of England.

SMALL CLAIMS COURT. 1. An inferior court with a limited jurisdiction over civil matters. 2. The branch of the Ontario Court (General Division) continued as such (Courts of Justice Act, R.S.O. 1990, c. C-43, s. 22(1)). G.D. Watson & C. Perkins, eds., *Holmested & Watson: Ontario Civil Procedure* (Toronto: Carswell, 1984-) at CJA-46.

SM. & S. *abbr.* Smith & Sager's Drainage Cases (Ont.), 1904-1917.

SMUGGLING. *n.* The offence of exporting or importing forbidden or restricted goods, or of exporting or importing goods without paying any duties imposed on them.

SOC. *abbr.* Society.

SOCAGE. *n.* A kind of tenure with certain temporal services which originally were agricultural. Common free socage is equivalent to freehold tenure.

SOCIAL SCIENCE BRIEF. A brief in which empirical data is appended to or included in the factum. P.W. Hogg, *Constitutional Law of Canada*, 2d ed. (Toronto: Carswell, 1985) at 182.

SOCIETY. *n.* Includes a society or club that is incorporated by an act of a legislature and that has for its object the provision of facilities for the social intercourse and recreation of its members. See CHILDREN'S AID ~; FRATERNAL ~; FREE AND DEMOCRATIC ~; FREE ~; FRIENDLY ~; MUTUAL BENEFIT ~.

SODOMY. *n.* Anal intercourse.

SOLE. *adj.* Single; alone; not married. See CORPORATION ~; FEME ~.

SOLE CUSTODY. Custody of a child by one parent only under an agreement or order.

SOLEMN ADMISSION. A plea of guilty when one is arraigned in court. P.K. McWilliams, *Canadian Criminal Evidence*, 3d ed. (Aurora: Canada Law Book, 1988) at 14-7.

SOLEMN DECLARATION. A solemn declaration in the form and manner from time to time provided by the provincial evidence acts or by the Canada Evidence Act.

SOLEMNIZATION. *n.* Entering into marriage publicly before witnesses.

SOLEMNIZATION OF MARRIAGE. "... [N]ot confined to the ceremony itself. It legitimately includes the various steps or preliminaries leading to it." *Albert (Attorney General) v. Underwood*, [1934] S.C.R. 635 at 639, [1934] 4 D.L.R. 167, the court per Rinfret J.

SOLE PROPRIETORSHIP. A business organization having one owner who must and does make all major decisions concerning the business. S.M. Beck *et al.*, *Cases and Materials on Partnerships and Canadian Business Corporations* (Toronto: Carswell, 1983) at 1.

SOLICIT. *v.* 1. "... [T]o endeavour to obtain by asking. ..." *Burns v. Chiropractic Assn. (Alberta)* (1981), 31 A.R. 176 at 177, 16 Alta. L.R. (2d) 128, 125 D.L.R. (3d) 475 (C.A.), the court per Clement J.A. 2. In [s. 195.1 of the Criminal Code, R.S.C. 1970, c. C-34] includes an element of persistence or pressure. It was decided that the mere demonstration by a woman of her willingness and availability for prostitution would not suffice to ground a conviction. In addition, the Crown would be required to prove that her approach to a prospective customer was accompanied by pressure or persistent conduct. ..." *Hutt v. R.* (1978), 38 C.C.C. (2d) 418 at 422-3, [1978] 2 S.C.R. 476, 1 C.R. (3d) 164, [1978] 2 W.W.R. 247, 19 N.R. 330, 82 D.L.R. (3d) 95, Spence J. (Laskin C.J., Dickson, Martland and Estey JJ. concurring). See SOLICITATION.

SOLICITATION. *n.* (a) A request for a proxy whether or not it is accompanied by or included in a form of proxy; (b) a request to execute or not to execute a form of proxy or to revoke a proxy; (c) the sending of a form of proxy or other communication to a security holder under circumstances reasonably calculated to result in the procurement, withholding or revocation of a proxy of that security holder; or (d) the sending, along with a notice of a meeting, of a form of proxy to a security holder by management of a reporting issuer, but does not include (e) the sending of a form of proxy to a security holder in response to an unsolicited request made by the security holder or on that person's behalf; or (f) the performance by any person of ministerial acts or professional services on behalf of a person soliciting a proxy.

SOLICITOR. *n.* 1. In the Province of Quebec, an advocate or a notary and, in any other province, a barrister or solicitor. *Criminal Code*, R.S.C. 1985, c. C-46, s. 183. 2. A person who is, by virtue of section 11 of the Act, an officer of the Court. *Federal Court Rules*, C.R.C., c. 663, s. 2. 3. "In some jurisdictions there is a distinction between a barrister or counsel and a solicitor. The kind of work which may be undertaken or performed by each is clearly defined. The business of a barrister is advocacy, drafting pleadings and advising on questions of law, while the solicitor interviews clients, takes instructions and prepares the necessary material in the litigation, which is submitted to counsel who will appear at the trial. In those jurisdictions where the distinction exists solicitors do not appear in court." *Griffen v. Spanier*, [1947] 1 W.W.R. 489 at 491 (Sask. C.A.), McNiven J.A. See BARRISTER AND ~; CHANGE OF ~.

SOLICITOR-AND-CLIENT COSTS. 1. Costs which a client pays to a solicitor for services rendered. M.M. Orkin, *The Law of Costs*, 2d ed. (Aurora: Canada Law Book, 1987) at 2-1. 2. "The underlying purpose of an award of costs on the basis of those between solicitor and client is to provide complete indemnification for all costs, including fees and disbursements, reasonably incurred in the course of defending or prosecuting the action but excluding the costs for extra services not reasonably necessary." *Scott Paper Co. v. Minnesota Mining & Manufacturing Co.* (1982), 70 C.P.R. (2d) 68 at 79 (Fed. T.D.), Cattanach J.

SOLICITOR AND HIS OWN CLIENT COSTS. "[Allowing the costs which would] . . . provide complete indemnity to her [the client] as to the costs essential to, and . . . 'arising within, the four corners of litigation.' " *Seitz, Re* (1974), 6 O.R. (2d) 460 at 465, 53 D.L.R. (3d) 223 (H.C.), Lerner J.

SOLICITOR-CLIENT PRIVILEGE. 1. ". . . [A]n evidentiary rule, invented by Judges in pursuance of public policy, to protect a client against compulsory testimonial disclosure by himself or by his legal advisor in legal proceedings." *Herman v. Canada (Deputy Attorney General)* (1979), 13 C.P.C. 363 at 368, 26 O.R. (2d) 520, 103 D.L.R. (3d) 491, 79 D.T.C. 5372 (C.A.), Lacourcière J.A. (Weatherston J.A. concurring). 2. ". . . [T]he privilege belongs to the client alone. One consequence of this is that confidential communications between solicitor and client can only be divulged in certain circumscribed situations. The client may . . . herself choose to disclose the contents of her communications with her legal representative and thereby waive the privilege. Or, the client may authorize the solicitor to reveal those communications for her. So important is the privilege that the courts have also stipulated that the confidentiality of communications between solicitor and client survives the death of the client and enures to his or her next of kin, heirs or successors in title." *Goodman Estate v. Geffen* (1991), 42 E.T.R. 97 at 125-6, [1991] 5 W.W.R. 389, 80 Alta. L.R. (2d) 293, 125 A.R. 81, 14 W.A.C. 81, 81 D.L.R. (4th) 211, [1991] 2 S.C.R. 353, Wilson J. (Cory J. concurring). See LEGAL PROFESSIONAL PRIVILEGE.

SOLICITOR GENERAL CANADA. The federal ministry which controls penitentiaries, paroles and remissions and law enforcement and supervises the National Parole Board, the Correctional Service and the RCMP.

SOLICITOR'S J. *abbr.* Solicitor's Journal (Le Bulletin des avocats).

SOLICITOR'S LIEN. The lien to which a solicitor is entitled in respect to his or her fees. The lien may entitle a solicitor to retain papers or other property of the client which are in his or her possession. In other cases, it may entitle the solicitor to an order charging the proceeds, in court, of a successful action (otherwise belonging to the client) with the lien.

SOUND IN DAMAGES. To have the basic quality of damages, said of actions brought to recover damages.

SOVEREIGN. *n.* 1. Any supreme or chief person. 2. The Sovereign of the United Kingdom, Canada and Her or His other realms and territories and head of the Commonwealth. See ACCESSION OF THE ~.

SOVEREIGN IMMUNITY. 1. Canadian courts will not exercise jurisdiction over the property or person of an independent foreign state or sovereign without consent. Any such proceedings may be stayed if the state or sovereign moves to set the proceedings aside or remains passive. A foreign state includes any state which the forum recognizes, de facto or de jure. J.G. McLeod, *The Conflict of Laws* (Calgary: Carswell, 1983) at 68. 2. "... [T]he doctrine of absolute sovereign immunity .... [was] stated by Lord Denning M.R., in Trendtex Trading Corp. v. Central Bank of Nigeria [1977] 1 Q.B. 529 (C.A.) at page 559. Lord Denning said: 'The doctrine grants immunity to a foreign government or its department of state, or any body which can be regarded as an "alter ego or organ" of the government.'" *Ferranti-Packard Ltd. v. Cushman Rentals Ltd.* (1980), 19 C.P.C. 132 at 133, 30 O.R. (2d) 194, 115 D.L.R. (3d) 691 (Div. Ct.), the court per Reid J.

SOVEREIGNTY. *n*. The supreme authority within a state.

SOVEREIGNTY-ASSOCIATION. *n*. A compromise proposed in Quebec between outright separation and continuance as a province of Canada. Although it involved the secession of Quebec (sovereignty), it also involved economic association between Quebec and the rest of Canada (association). P.W. Hogg, *Constitutional Law of Canada*, 3d ed. (Toronto: Carswell, 1992) at 125.

S.P. *abbr.* Sessions of the Peace.

SPEAKER. *n*. With repect to the House of Commons, the representative of the House itself in power, proceedings and dignity; the representative of the House in relation to the Crown, the Senate and other people and authorities outside Parliament; the person who presides over debates and enforces observance of any rule for preserving order. This person is elected by the House itself and, on behalf of the House, controls the accommodation and services in the part of the Parliament Buildings and its precincts which the House of Commons occupies. A. Fraser, W.A. Dawson & J. Holtby, eds., *Beauchesne's Rules and Forms of the House of Commons of Canada*, 6th ed. (Toronto: Carswell, 1989) at 33 and 47.

SPECIAL ACT. A local, personal or private act; an act which applies to a certain kind of person or thing only.

SPECIAL AGENT. One authorized to transact only a particular business for the principal, as opposed to a general agent. G.H.L. Fridman, *The Law of Agency*, 6th ed. (London: Butterworths, 1990) at 34. Contrast GENERAL AGENT.

SPECIAL CASE. The statement of a question of law for the opinion of the court by all parties to a proceeding, and which any party moves that the judge determine (Ontario, Rules of Civil Procedure, r. 22.01 (1)). G.D. Watson & C. Perkins, eds., *Holmested & Watson: Ontario Civil Procedure* (Toronto: Carswell, 1984) at 22-3.

SPECIAL COMMITTEE. A body the House appoints to inquire into a specified subject. When its final report is presented, it ceases to exist. A. Fraser, W.A. Dawson & J. Holtby, eds., *Beauchesne's Rules and Forms of the House of Commons of Canada*, 6th ed. (Toronto: Carswell, 1989) at 222.

SPECIAL COSTS. "... [M]ore or less the old solicitor-and-client costs as described in the 1989 Rules [British Columbia Rules of Court]: ..." *Bradshaw Construction Ltd v. Bank of Nova Scotia* (1991), 48 C.P.C. (2d) 74 at 89, 54 B.C.L.R. (2d) 309 (S.C.), Bouck J.

SPECIAL DAMAGE. 1. Pecuniary loss before the trial. K.D. Cooper-Stephenson & I.B. Saunders, *Personal Injury Damages in Canada* (Toronto: Carswell, 1981) at 29 and 43. 2. Pecuniary loss which the plaintiff is able to prove occurred as a result of the facts which he alleges in his pleadings. *Chitty on Contracts*, 26th ed. (London: Sweet & Maxwell, 1989) at para. 1772.

SPECIAL EXAMINER. An official examiner.

SPECIALIA GENERALIBUS

DEROGANT. [L.] Special words restrict general ones.

SPECIAL PROPERTY. Limited or qualified property.

SPECIALTY. *n.* A contract under seal.

SPECIALTY CONTRACT. A contract under seal.

SPECIALTY DEBT. 1. A bond, mortgage or debt which one secures by writing under seal. 2. ". . . [S]ometimes used to denote any contract under seal, but it is more often used in the sense of meaning a specialty debt, that is, an obligation under seal securing a debt or a debt due from the Crown or under statute. . . ." *Williams v. R.*, [1942] 3 D.L.R. 1 at 1, [1942] 2 W.W.R. 321, [1942] A.C. 541, [1942] 2 All E.R. 951 (P.C.), the court per Viscount Maugham.

SPECIE. *n.* 1. Metallic money. 2. Something in its own true form, not a substitute, equivalent or compensation.

SPECIFIC BEQUEST. The gift of a certain item of personal estate in a will.

SPECIFIC CHARGE. "One that, without more, fastens on ascertained and definite property, or property capable of being ascertained and defined." *Illingworth v. Houldsworth*, [1904] A.C. 355 at 358, Lord Macnaghten.

SPECIFIC DEVISE. The gift of a certain item of real property in a will.

SPECIFIC GOODS. Goods identified and agreed upon at the time a contract of sale is made. *Sale of Goods acts.*

SPECIFIC INTENT. "[An offence] . . . which involves the performance of the actus reus, coupled with an intention or purpose going beyond the mere performance of the questioned act. Striking a blow or administering poison with intent to kill, or assault with intent to maim or wound, are examples of such offences." *R. v. Bernard* (1988), 38 C.R.R. 82 at 90, 67 C.R. (3d) 113, 90 N.R. 321, 45 C.C.C. (3d) 1, [1988] 2 S.C.R. 833, 32 O.A.C. 161, McIntyre J. (Beetz J. concurring).

SPECIFIC LEGACY. ". . . [A] gift of a particular thing . . ." *Rodd, Re* (1981), 10 E.T.R. 117 at 125, 40 Nfld. & P.E.I.R. 239, 115 A.P.R. 239 (P.E.I. S.C.), McQuaid J.

SPECIFIC PERFORMANCE. 1. A court order which compels a person to do something previously promised according to a contractual obligation. B.J. Reiter, B.N. McLellan & P.M. Perell, *Real Estate Law*, 4th ed. (Toronto: Emond Montgomery, 1992) at 697. 2. Considered to be a secondary remedy, an equitable remedy, available only where monetary compensation is not adequate, for example, when goods which are the subject of the contract are unique or when the subject of the contract is land. It is not usually available to enforce a contract of personal service. S.M. Waddams, *The Law of Contract*, 2d ed. (Toronto: Canada Law Book, 1984) at 508, 517, 535.

SPEC. LECT. L.S.U.C. *abbr.* Special Lectures of the Law Society of Upper Canada.

SPEECH. *n.* ". . . [A]udible oral communication." *Tadman v. Seaboard Life Insurance Co.* (1989), 64 Alta. L.R. (2d) 285 at 288, 93 A.R. 83, [1989] I.L.R. 1-2441, 36 C.C.L.I. 215 (C.A.), Belzil, Bracco and Foisy JJ.A. See COMMERCIAL ~; FREEDOM OF ~.

SPEECH FROM THE THRONE. The Governor General's speech which opens a session of Parliament and outlines the legislative programme for that session as planned by cabinet. This speech is written by the Prime Minister. P.W. Hogg, *Constitutional Law of Canada*, 3d ed. (Toronto: Carswell, 1992) at 244.

SPENDING POWER. A power, though not explicitly mentioned in the Constitution Act, 1867, which is inferred from the powers to legislate in relation to "public property" (section 91(1A)), to levy taxes (section 91(3)), and to appropriate federal funds (section 106). P.W. Hogg, *Constitutional Law of Canada*, 3d ed. (Toronto: Carswell, 1992) at 150.

SPES SUCCESSIONIS. [L.] Hope of succession, in contrast to a vested right.

SPLIT. *v.* With respect to a cause of action, to sue for only a part of a demand or claim, with intent to sue for the rest in another action.

SPREADING FALSE NEWS. A person who wilfully publishes a statement, tale or news that he knows is false and that causes or is likely to cause injury or mischief to a public interest is guilty of an offence. *Criminal Code*, R.S.C. 1985, c. C-46, s. 181.

SPRINGING USE. A use like an executory interest which directs property to vest at a future time which need not coincide with the common law termination of a legal estate.

SQUATTER. *n.* Someone who occupies land without consent or licence.

SQUATTER'S TITLE. Title acquired by someone who has occupied land without paying rent or in any other way acknowledging superior title for so long that that person acquires indefeasible title.

S.R. *abbr.* Saskatchewan Reports, 1979-.

S.R. & O. *abbr.* Statutory rules and orders in England.

STAKE. *n.* A deposit made in hopes a particular event takes place.

STAKEHOLDER. *n.* 1. A person who holds money pending the outcome of a wager or bet. 2. A person who holds property or money which rival claimants claim, but who claims no personal interest in that property or money. See INTERPLEADER.

STALE CHEQUE. A cheque which a bank may dishonour after a certain period, without breaching the banker-customer contract. I.F.G. Baxter, *The Law of Banking*, 3d ed. (Toronto: Carswell, 1981) at 85.

STALE DEMAND. A claim made so long ago that it is presumed that it was waived.

STAMP. *n.* An impressed or adhesive stamp used for the purpose of revenue by the government of Canada or a Canadian province or by the government of a foreign state. *Criminal Code*, R.S.C. 1985, c. C-46, s. 376(3).

STAMP DUTY. A tax raised by placing a stamp on a written instrument like a conveyance or lease pursuant to a Stamp Act.

STANDARD. *n.* See BUILDING CONSTRUCTION ~; COMMUNITY ~.

STANDARD OF PROOF. A standard which sets the degree of probability which the evidence must create in order to entitle the party who bears the burden of proof to succeed in proving her or his case or an issue in the case. J. Sopinka and S.N. Lederman, *The Law of Evidence in Civil Cases* (Toronto: Butterworths, 1974) at 384-85. See also BALANCE OF PROBABILITIES; CIVIL ONUS; CRIMINAL ONUS; BEYOND A REASONABLE DOUBT.

STANDING. *n.* 1. "... [T]o establish status as a plaintiff in a suit seeking a declaration that legislation is invalid, if there is a serious issue as to its invalidity, a person need only to show that he is affected by it directly or that he has a genuine interest as a citizen in the validity of the legislation and that there is no other reasonable and effective manner in which the issue may be brought before the Court." *Borowski v. Canada (Minister of Justice)*, (sub nom. *Canada (Minister of Justice) v. Borowski*) [1981] 2 S.C.R. 575 at 598, [1982] 1 W.W.R. 97, 24 C.P.C. 62, 24 C.R. (3d) 352, 12 Sask. R. 420, 64 C.C.C. (2d) 97, 130 D.L.R. (3d) 588, 39 N.R. 331, Martland J. (Ritchie, Dickson, Beetz, Estey, McIntyre and Chouinard JJ. concurring). 2. "... [I]n order to obtain standing as a person 'interested' in litigation between other parties, the applicant must have an interest in the actual lis between those parties." *Schofield v. Ontario (Minister of Consumer & Commercial Relations)* (1980), 19 C.P.C. 245 at 251, 28 O.R. (2d) 764, 112 D.L.R. (3d) 132 (C.A.), Wilson J.A. See LOCUS STANDI; PUBLIC INTEREST ~.

STANDING COMMITTEE. A body

appointed under a standing order to consider and report on estimates, to examine and report on government agencies and departments and, to conduct any investigation or inquiry which the House requires. Since 1985, they have been given permanent general orders of reference. A. Fraser, W.A. Dawson & J. Holtby, eds., *Beauchesne's Rules and Forms of the House of Commons of Canada*, 6th ed. (Toronto: Carswell, 1989) at 221-2.

STANDING, SESSIONAL AND SPECIAL ORDERS. The rules and regulations which the House of Commons uses to govern its proceedings. A. Fraser, W.A. Dawson & J. Holtby, eds., *Beauchesne's Rules and Forms of the House of Commons of Canada*, 6th ed. (Toronto: Carswell, 1989) at 5.

STARE DECISIS. [L.] 1. The principle by which a precedent or decision of one court binds courts lower in the judicial hierarchy. P.W. Hogg, *Constitutional Law of Canada*, 3d ed. (Toronto: Carswell, 1992) at 219. 2. "... [D]ecided cases which lay down a rule of law are authoritative and must be followed. The general statement is, of course, subject to qualifications, ... The decisions of our own Supreme Court of Canada until reversed are binding on all Canadian Courts, and the Supreme Court is bound by its own previous decisions ..." *Reference re Canada Temperance Act*, [1939] 4 D.L.R. 14 at 33, 72 C.C.C. 145, [1939] O.R. 570 (C.A.), McTague J.A.

STATE. *n.* 1. A group of people who occupy a certain territory and have an executive and legislative organization under their own, exclusive control. 2. Part of a larger state, i.e. the separate organizations which collectively make up Australia. 3. Includes a political subdivision of a state and an official agency of a state. 4. "... [T]he definition of the word 'state' [in s. 2 of the Reciprocal Enforcement of Maintenance Orders Act, R.S.N.B. 1973, c. R-4] is sufficiently broad to include the concept of 'law district' and in Canada it has long been recognized that each province is a separate and distinct law

district, ..." *Brewer (Mousseau) v. Brewer* (1981), 35 N.B.R. (2d) 329 at 340, 88 A.P.R. 329, 22 C.P.C. 143 (C.A.), the court per Richard J.A. 5. Any state or territory of the United States of America and includes the District of Columbia. See ACT OF ~; CONTRACTING ~; DELIVERABLE ~; FEDERAL ~; SECRETARY OF ~; UNITARY ~.

STATED CASE. A case tried on the basis of a statement of facts agreed on by the parties.

STATEMENT. *n.* 1. "... [A] written or oral communication. I have no doubt that a nod of the head to indicate yes or a shaking of the head to indicate no would also be considered a 'statement' within the meaning of s. 56 [of the Young Offenders Act, S.C. 1980-81-82-83, c. 110]...." *R. v. J. (J.T.)* (1988), 40 C.C.C. (3d) 97 at 123, [1988] 2 W.W.R. 509, 50 Man. R.(2d) 300 (C.A.), Huband J.A. 2. "[In s. 9(1) of the Evidence Act, R.S.C. 1970, c. E-10] ... there is a mention only of 'a statement'. That 'statement' has been held to include an oral statement: ..." *R. v. Carpenter* (1982), 1 C.C.C. (3d) 149 at 154, 31 C.R. (3d) 261, 142 D.L.R. (3d) 237 (Ont. C.A.), the court per Grange J.A. 3. An assertion of fact, opinion, belief or knowledge, whether material or not and whether admissible or not. *Criminal Code*, R.S.C. 1985, c. C-46, s. 118 as am. by *Criminal Law Amendment Act*, R.S.C. 1985 (1st Supp.), c. 27, s. 15. 4. The originating process which commences an action (Ontario, Rules of Civil Procedure, r. 14.03(1)). G.D. Watson & C. Perkins, eds., *Holmested & Watson: Ontario Civil Procedure* (Toronto: Carswell, 1984) at 14-3. 5. Any representation of fact whether made in words or otherwise. See FINANCIAL ~; SELF-SERVING ~.

STATEMENT OF CLAIM. 1. "[The function of a statement of claim] is not to cast the plaintiff's right of action into formal legal shape but to state the constitutive facts giving rise to the right upon which he relies and to formulate the relief he demands ..." *Smith v.*

STATEMENT OF DEFENCE

Upper Canada College (1920), 57 D.L.R. 648 at 661, 61 S.C.R. 413, [1921] 1 W.W.R. 1154, Duff J. 2. A printed or written statement by the plaintiff in an action which shows the facts relied on to support any claim against the defendant and the remedy or relief sought.

STATEMENT OF DEFENCE. A brief written statement by a defendant to respond to each allegation in a statement of claim: (a) by admission; (b) by denial; (c) by a statement that the defendant does not know; or (d) by a statement of the defendant's own version of the facts.

STATEMENT OF FACTS. See AGREED ~.

STATU QUO. See IN ~.

STATUS. *n.* "[In s. 9(1)(c)(ii) of the Canadian Human Rights Act, S.C. 1976-77, c. 33] ... a legal concept which refers to the particular position of a person with respect to his or her rights and limitations as a result of his or her being a member of some legally recognized and regulated group." *Canada (Attorney General) v. Mossop* (1990), 32 C.C.E.L. 276 at 291, 12 C.H.R.R. D/355, 114 N.R. 241, [1991] 1 F.C. 18 (C.A.), Marceau J.A. See FAMILY ~; MARITAL ~.

STATUS QUO. [L.] The state in which something is or was.

STATUTE. *n.* A law or act which expresses the will of a legislature or Parliament. See CODIFYING ~; CONSOLIDATING ~; CREDITORS' RELIEF ~; CURATIVE ~; DECLARATORY ~; ENABLING ~; EQUITY OF A ~; FEDERAL ~; GUEST ~; PENAL ~; REMEDIAL ~; RETROACTIVE ~; RETROSPECTIVE ~; REVISED ~S.

STATUTE BARRED. Said of a cause of action for which proceedings cannot be brought because the limitation period has expired.

STATUTE OF FRAUDS. The Statute of Frauds requires that certain contracts are in writing or are evidenced by an appropriate memoran-

dum. If one fails to conform to the statutory provisions, the contract is unenforceable. G.H.L. Fridman, *Restitution*, 2d ed. (Toronto: Carswell, 1992) at 161.

STATUTE OF LIMITATIONS. A statute which prescribes the specified period of time within which criminal charges must be laid or legal actions must be taken.

STATUTE OF QUIA EMPTORES. "The primary purpose of [the Statute of Quia Emptores 1290, 18 Edw. 1, St. 1] was to prevent the practice of the day of subinfeudation which resulted in the feudal landlords losing control of their property. As an incident of the abolition of subinfeudation, the right of unrestricted alienation of fee simple estates was pronounced without loss to the feudal landlords." *Laurin v. Iron Ore Co.* (1977), 7 R.P.R. 137 at 154, 19 Nfld. & P.E.I.R. 111, 50 A.P.R. 111, 82 D.L.R. (3d) 634 (Nfld. T.D.), Goodridge J.

STATUTE OF WESTMINSTER. The 1931 British statute which repealed the Colonial Laws Validity Act as it applied to the dominions. By section 2(2) it granted each dominion power to amend or repeal imperial statutes which were part of the law of that dominion and it stated that no dominion statute would be void on grounds of repugnancy to an existing or future imperial statute. Section 7(2) clarified that section 2 applied to Canada's provincial Legislatures in addition to Canada's federal Parliament, but that the Parliament and each legislature could only enact laws within their own jurisdiction under the B.N.A. Act. The power to amend or repeal extended to both future and existing imperial statutes. P.W. Hogg, *Constitutional Law of Canada*, 3d ed. (Toronto: Carswell, 1992) at 50.

STATUTORY. *adj.* Governed or introduced by statute law.

STATUTORY CORPORATION. A corporation the business of which is confined to the powers conferred in the statute which created the corporation. I.M. Rogers, *The Law of Canadian*

Municipal Corporations, 2d ed. (Toronto: Carswell, 1971-) at 11.

STATUTORY COURT. A court which derives its existence and powers from statute, e.g., The Federal Court of Canada. S.A. Cohen, *Due Process of Law* (Toronto: Carswell, 1977) at 395.

STATUTORY DECLARATION. A solemn declaration in the form and manner from time to time provided by the provincial evidence acts or by the Canada Evidence Act.

STATUTORY DUTY. A duty imposed, by statute, on a person or body.

STATUTORY INSTRUMENT. (a) Any rule, order, regulation, ordinance, direction, form, tariff of costs or fees, letters patent, commission, warrant, proclamation, by-law, resolution or other instrument issued, made or established (i) in the execution of a power conferred by or under an Act of Parliament, by or under which such instrument is expressly authorized to be issued, made or established otherwise than by the conferring on any person or body of powers or functions in relation to a matter to which such instrument relates; or (ii) by or under the authority of the Governor-in-Council, otherwise than in the execution of a power conferred by or under an Act of Parliament; but (b) does not include (i) any instrument referred to in paragraph (a) and issued, made or established by a corporation incorporated by or under an Act of Parliament unless (A) the instrument is a Regulation and the corporation by which it is made is one that is ultimately accountable, through a Minister, to Parliament for the conduct of its affairs; or (B) the instrument is one for the contravention of which a penalty, fine or imprisonment is prescribed by or under an Act of Parliament; (ii) any instrument referred to in paragraph (a) and issued, made or established by a judicial or quasi-judicial body, unless the instrument is a rule, order or regulation governing the practice or procedure in proceedings before a judicial or quasi-judicial body established by or under an Act of Parliament; (iii) any instrument referred to in paragraph (a) and in respect of which, or in respect of the production or disclosure of which, any privilege exists by law or whose contents are limited to advice or information intended only for use or assistance in the making of a decision or the determination of policy, or in the ascertainment of any matter necessarily incidental thereto; or (iv) an Ordinance of the Yukon Territory or the Northwest Territories or any instrument issued, made or established thereunder. *Statutory Instruments Act*, R.S.C. 1985, c. S-22, s. 2.

STATUTORY JURISDICTION. Jurisdiction whose source is a statute which defines the limits within which the jurisdiction must be exercised. S.A. Cohen, *Due Process of Law* (Toronto: Carswell, 1977) at 344.

STATUTORY LIEN. A lien on property which arises purely by statute; the lienholder's rights depend on the relevant statutory provisions. W.B. Rayner & R.H. McLaren, *Falconbridge on Mortgages*, 4th ed. (Toronto: Canada Law Book, 1977) at 11.

STATUTORY POWER. A power or right conferred by or under a statute, (i) to make any regulation, rule, by-law or order, or to give any other direction having force as subordinate legislation; (ii) to exercise a statutory power of decision; (iii) to require any person or party to do or to refrain from doing any act or thing that, but for such requirement, such person or party would not be required by law to do or to refrain from doing; (iv) to do any act or thing that would, but for such power or right, be a breach of the legal rights of any person or party.

STATUTORY POWER OF DECISION. A power or right conferred by or under a statute to make a decision deciding or prescribing, (i) the legal rights, powers, privileges, immunities, duties or liabilities of any person or party; or (ii) the eligibility of any person or party to receive, or to the continuation of, a benefit or licence, whether that person or party is legally entitled thereto or not, and includes the powers of an inferior court.

STATUTORY SET-OFF. "...
[R]equires the fulfilment of two conditions. The first is that both obligations must be debts. The second is that both debts must be mutual cross obligations." *Telford v. Holt* (1987), 37 B.L.R. 241 at 251, 21 C.P.C. (2d) 1, 78 N.R. 321, 54 Alta. L.R. (2d) 193, [1987] 6 W.W.R. 385, [1987] 2 S.C.R. 193, 46 R.P.R. 234, 81 A.R. 385, 41 D.L.R. (4th) 385, the court per Wilson J.

STAY. *n.* With respect to proceedings, an action to suspend them.

STAY OF PROCEEDINGS. "...
[A] stopping or arresting of a judicial proceedings by the direction or order of a court.... A stay may imply that the proceedings are suspended to await some action required to be taken by one of the parties, as, for example, when a non-resident has been ordered to give security for costs. In certain circumstances, however, a stay may mean the total discontinuance or permanent suspension of the proceedings." *R. v. Jewitt* (1985), 47 C.R. (3d) 193 at 203, [1985] 2 S.C.R. 128, [1985] 6 W.W.R. 127, 61 N.R. 159, 21 C.C.C. (3d) 7, 20 D.L.R. (4th) 651, the court per Dickson C.J.C.

STEAL. *v.* To commit theft. *Criminal Code*, R.S.C. 1985, c. C-46, s. 2.

STEPHENS' DIG. *abbr.* Stephens' Quebec Digest.

STET. [L.] Let it stand.

STEVENS' DIG. *abbr.* Stevens' New Brunswick Digest.

STEWART. *abbr.* Stewart's Vice-Admiralty Reports (N.S.), 1803-1813.

STIPEND. *n.* Salary.

STIPULATED DAMAGE. Liquidated damages.

STIPULATION. *n.* 1. A bargain. 2. In an agreement, a material term.

STIRPES. See PER ~.

STOCK. *n.* 1. (a) Stock of goods, wares, merchandise and chattels ordinarily the subject of trade and commerce; (b) the goods, wares, merchandise or chattels in which a person

trades, or that he produces or that are outputs of, or with which he carries on, any business, trade or occupation. *Bulk Sales acts*. 2. Includes a share, stock, fund, annuity or security transferable in books kept by a company or society established or to be established, or transferable by deed alone, or by deed accompanied by other formalities, and a share or interest in it. See DEFERRED ~; LISTED ~.

STOCKBROKER. *n.* ... [O]ne who buys and sells stock as an agent for others. The relationship between client and broker is that of principal and agent, fiduciary in its nature and one of the governing principles of law demands the fullest disclosure by agent to principal...." *R. v. Solloway*, [1930] 2 W.W.R. 516 at 519, 54 C.C.C. 129 (Alta. T.D.), Ives J.

STOCK DIVIDEND. 1. "... [S]tock distributed to those already holding stock, by way of dividend upon their holdings. It is not a new investment in any sense; it is a mode of distributing accumulated profits in the shape of new stock, which, pro tanto, reduces the value of the stock held." *Fulford, Re* (1913), 14 D.L.R. 844 at 846-7, 5 O.W.N. 125, 29 O.L.R. 375 (H.C.), Middleton J. 2. Includes any dividend paid by a corporation to the extent that it is paid by the issuance of shares of any class of its capital stock.

STOCK EXCHANGE. "The four essential elements appearing in each definition [of 'stock exchange', Criminal Code, R.S.C. 1970, c. C-34, s. 340(c)] are, namely, a reunion of persons, a particular place, buying and selling, and, finally buying and selling of a particular class of things, namely, securities." *Schecter c. Bluestein* (1981), (*sub nom. Bluestein c. Schecter*) 121 D.L.R. (3d) 345 at 349, 23 C.R. (3d) 39, [1981] C.S. 477, 58 C.C.C. (2d) 208 (Que. S.C.), Malouf J.

STOCK IN BULK. A stock or portion of a stock that is the subject of a sale in bulk. *Bulk Sales acts*.

STOCK IN TRADE. "... [G]oods which a merchant has in his possession, for sale or hire...." *R. v. North*

American Van Lines (Alberta) Ltd. (1986), 2 M.V.R. (2d) 176 at 187, 16 O.A.C. 230 (C.A.), the court per Blair J.A.

STOCK OPTION. "[Takes] ... the form of negotiable bearer contracts [which] are simply bought and sold like any other commodity for the trading of which there is no exchange. There are six types of stock options: a call; a put; a straddle; a strap; a strip; and a spread...." *Posluns v. Toronto Stock Exchange,* [1964] 2 O.R. 547 at 553, 46 D.L.R. (2d) 210 (H.C.), Gale J.

STOCKTON. *abbr.* Stockton's Vice-Admiralty Reports (N.B.), 1879-1891.

STOP ORDER. An order issued on application to the court by someone who claims to be entitled to securities or money held or to be held by the accountant for the benefit of someone else which directs that the securities or money shall not be handled without notifying the applicant or moving party (Ontario, Rules of Civil Procedure, r. 72.05(1)). G.D. Watson & C. Perkins, eds., *Holmested & Watson: Ontario Civil Procedure* (Toronto: Carswell, 1984) at 72-5.

STOPPAGE IN TRANSITU. The right of an unpaid seller to take back the possession of goods sold on credit and to retain them until the buyer, who became insolvent before possessing the goods, tenders the price.

STRICT CONSTRUCTION. Interpretation of a tax or penal statute strictly against the body imposing the tax or penalty where there is any ambiguity.

STRICTISSIMI JURIS. [L.] Of the strictest law. *Dragun v. Dragun* (1984), 47 C.P.C. 106 at 108, [1984] 6 W.W.R. 171, 30 Man. R. (2d) 126 (Q.B.), Helper J.

STRICT LIABILITY. 1. Criminal liability based on simple negligence. D. Stuart, *Canadian Criminal Law: A Treatise,* 2d ed. (Toronto: Carswell, 1987) at 157. 2. Imposed in tort law when a lawful activity exposes others to extraordinary risks even though no fault is involved on the part of the

"wrongdoer". J.G. Fleming, *The Law of Torts,* 8th ed. (Sydney: Law Book, 1992) at 329.

STRICT LIABILITY OFFENCE. "Offences in which there is no necessity for the prosecution to prove the existence of mens rea; the doing of the prohibited act prima facie imports the offence, leaving it open to the accused to avoid liability by proving that he took all reasonable care. This involves consideration of what a reasonable man would have done in the circumstances. The defence will be available if the accused reasonably believed in a mistaken set of facts which, if true, would render the act or omission innocent, or if he took all reasonable steps to avoid the particular event. These offences may be properly called offences of strict liability." *R. v. Sault Ste. Marie (City),* [1978] 2 S.C.R. 1299 at 1326, 3 C.R. (3d) 30, 21 N.R. 295, 7 C.E.L.R. 53, 40 C.C.C. (2d) 353, 85 D.L.R. (3d) 161, the court per Dickson J.

STRIKE. *n.* Includes a cessation of work or a refusal to work by employees, in combination, in concert or in accordance with a common understanding, and a slowdown of work or other concerted activity on the part of employees in relation to their work that is designed to restrict or limit output.

STRIKE OFF THE ROLL. To remove the name of a solicitor from the rolls of a court and thereby disentitle that person to practise.

STRIKE OUT. To expunge part or all of a document or pleading, with or without leave to amend (Ontario, Rules of Civil Procedure, r. 25.11). G.D. Watson & C. Perkins, eds., *Holmested & Watson: Ontario Civil Procedure* (Toronto: Carswell, 1984) at 25-7.

STRIKING OUT. See STRIKE OUT.

STRUCTURED SETTLEMENT. ... [A]n agreement to pay the plaintiff, as compensation for the damages suffered by him, a sum of money by periodic payments, rather than a lump sum payment." *Fuchs v. Brears* (1986), 44 Sask. R. 112 at 115, [1986] 3 W.W.R. 409 (Q.B.), Vancise J.

STUART. *abbr.* Stuart, Vice-Admiralty Reports (Que.), 1836-1874.

STUD. CANON. *abbr.* Studia Canonica.

STUDENT. *n.* See ARTICLED ~.

STUDENT-AT-LAW. *n.* A person serving articles of clerkship approved by the Society to a member. *Legal Profession Act*, S.N.W.T. 1976, c. 4, s. 2.

STUFF GOWN. The court robe worn by lawyers who are not Queen's Counsel.

STU. K.B. *abbr.* Stuart's Reports (Que.), 1810-1835.

STYLE. *v.* To name, call or entitle someone.

STYLE. *n.* A title; an appellation. See ROYAL ~ AND TITLES.

STYLE OF CAUSE. The name or title of a proceeding which sets out the names of all the parties and their capacity, if other than a personal capacity (Ontario, Rules of Civil Procedure, r. 14.06(1)). G.D. Watson & C. Perkins, eds., *Holmested & Watson: Ontario Civil Procedure* (Toronto: Carswell, 1984) at 14-5.

SUBCONTRACTOR. *var.* **SUB-CONTRACTOR.** *n.* 1. A person who has contracted with a prime contractor or with another subcontractor to perform a contract. 2. A person not contracting with or employed directly by an owner or the owner's agent for the doing of any work, rendering of any services or the furnishing of any material but contracting with or employed by a contractor or under the contractor by another subcontractor, but does not include a labourer.

SUBDIVIDE. *v.* To divide a parcel of land into two or more parcels.

SUBDIVISION. *var.* **SUB-DIVISION.** *n.* 1. "... [O]ccurs not only where lots or parcels are divided one from the other, but where interests in such lots or parcels are divided for the purpose of sale...." *J.C.D. Holdings Ltd. v. Buie* (1985), 61 B.C.L.R. 119 at 125, 17 D.L.R. (4th) 373 (S.C.), McLachlin J. 2. A division of a parcel by means of a plan of subdivision, plan of survey, agreement or any instrument, including a caveat, transferring or creating an estate or interest in part of the parcel. See PLAN OF ~.

SUBINFEUDATION. *n.* Division of land first granted to tenants in chief among their followers. E.L.G. Tyler & N.E. Palmer, eds., *Crossley Vaines' Personal Property*, 5th ed. (London: Butterworths, 1973) at 4.

SUBJECT TO. 1. "In a contract, 'subject to' a stipulated condition, ... means that the dominant but conditional obligation of the contract, namely, to purchase, is to become operative and effective only on fulfilment of the condition or occurrence of the event stipulated in the condition; unless there is such fulfilment or occurrence the conditional contract never becomes unconditional, operative or binding and the parties are in the same position as if no contract had been entered into...." *Kiernicki v. Jaworski* (1956), 18 W.W.R. 289 at 293 (Man. C.A.), Coyne J.A. 2. "The meaning of the expression 'subject to' in statutes was, in my opinion, correctly stated by the late Professor Elmer A. Driedger in The Composition of Legislation: Legislative Forms and Precedents, 2d ed. (Ottawa: Canadian Government Publishing Centre, Supply & Services Canada, 1976) at pp. 139-40 as follows: 'Subject to – Used to assign a subordinate position to an enactment, or to pave the way for qualifications. Where two sections conflict, and one is not merely an exception to the other, the subordinate one should be preceded by subject to; this reconciles the conflict and serves as a warning that there is more to come.' " *Murphy v. Welsh* (1991), 4 C.P.C. (3d) 301 at 309-10, 30 M.V.R. (2d) 163, 3 O.R. (3d) 182, 81 D.L.R. (4th) 475, 50 O.A.C. 246, the court per Blair J.A.

SUB JUDICE. [L.] In the course of a trial.

SUB-JUDICE CONVENTION. The expectation that members of Parliament will not discuss matters that are before

SUBROGATED

tribunals or the courts which are courts of record. A. Fraser, W.A. Dawson & J. Holtby, eds., *Beauchesne's Rules and Forms of the House of Commons of Canada*, 6th ed. (Toronto: Carswell, 1989) at 153.

SUBLEASE. *var.* **SUB-LEASE.** *n.* 1. A tenant's grant of interest in the leased premises which is less than that tenant's own. 2. Includes an agreement for a sublease where the sublessee has become entitled to have his sublease granted. *Landlord and Tenant acts.*

SUB-LET. *v.* For a tenant to lease the whole or part of the premises during a portion of the unexpired balance of the lease's term.

SUBMISSION. *n.* 1. Acquisition of jurisdiction which it would not otherwise possess by a court because the defendant, by conduct, cannot object to the jurisdiction. This may occur either impliedly or expressly, provided the person submitting is capable of doing so. C.R.B. Dunlop, *Creditor-Debtor Law in Canada* (Toronto: Carswell, 1981) at 470. 2. Definition of an arbitrator's jurisdiction over a particular case, i.e. a written grievance or a separate document. D.J.M. Brown & D.M. Beatty, *Canadian Labour Arbitration*, 3d ed. (Aurora: Canada Law Book, 1988-) at 2-14. 3. A written agreement to submit present or future differences to arbitration whether an arbitrator is named therein or not.

SUBMIT. *v.* To offer, as an advocate, a proposition to a court.

SUB MODO. [L.] Under restriction or condition.

SUBMORTGAGE. *n.* A mortgage of a mortgage. R. Megarry & H.W.R. Wade, *The Law of Real Property*, 5th ed. (London: Stevens, 1984) at cxxvii.

SUB NOM. *abbr.* Sub nomine.

SUB NOMINE. [L.] Under a name.

SUBORDINATE LEGISLATION. 1. Legislation of a subordinate body, i.e. one other than a legislature or Parliament, such as a statutory instrument, regulation or by-law. 2. Any regulation, proclamation, rule, order, by-law or in-

strument that is of a legislative nature and made or approved under the authority of an Act including those made by any board, commission or other body, whether incorporated or unincorporated, all the members of which, or all the members of the board of management or board of directors of which, are appointed by an Act or by the Lieutenant-Governor in Council, but does not include any regulation, proclamation, rule, order, by-law, resolution or other instrument made by a local authority or, except as otherwise provided in this paragraph, by a corporation incorporated by or under an Act or by the board of directors or board of management of such a corporation. *Statutes and Subordinate Legislation Act*, S.Nfld. 1977, c. 108, s. 10.

SUBORNATION. *n.* The crime of getting someone else to do something unlawful.

SUBPOENA. *n.* A document requiring a person to attend as a witness.

SUBPOENA DUCES TECUM. [L. subpoena you shall bring with you] . . . [A]n order in the nature of a subpoena duces tecum . . . would compel not the production of documents but rather would require the attendance before the inquiry of [a witness] with [her or his] relevant documents." *Canada Deposit Insurance Corp. v. Code* (1988), 49 D.L.R. (4th) 57 at 60 (Alta. C.A.), the court per Kerans J.A.

SUBROGATE. *v.* ". . . [T]o put one in the place of, or to substitute one for, another in respect of a right or a claim." *Big Wheels Transport & Leasing Ltd. v. Richard* (1987), 46 D.L.R. (4th) 108 at 110, 27 C.C.L.I. 243, 70 Nfld. & P.E.I.R. 104, 215 A.P.R. 104 (P.E.I. C.A.), the court per McQuaid J.A.

SUBROGATED. *adj.* Describes the rights acquired by a singly secured creditor in property in which she or he had no rights when a doubly secured creditor realized a claim out of the parcel on which the singly secured creditor had her or his security making it unavailable to the singly secured creditor. W.B. Rayner & R.H. McLaren, *Falconbridge on Mortgages*, 4th ed. (Toronto: Canada Law Book, 1977) at 314.

SUBROGATION. *n.* 1. The equitable principle which permits the person who pays a debt on behalf of someone else to seek restitution from that debtor. C.R.B. Dunlop, *Creditor-Debtor Law in Canada*, Second Cumulative Supplement (Toronto: Carswell, 1986) at 224. 2. "... [W]hen one person has been bound to indemnify another against a loss, he is entitled to any benefit in respect of the indemnified loss received by that person over and above the full amount of the loss. From this it follows that the right of subrogation does not arise until there has been recovery in full by the person suffering the loss ..." *Bigl v. Alberta* (1989), 37 C.C.L.I. 40 at 45, 67 Alta. L.R. (2d) 349, 60 D.L.R. (4th) 438 (C.A.), the court per Laycraft J.A. 3. "The most common [way of avoiding double recovery] is subrogation. Indemnity insurance is subject to the insurer's right to claim back payments to the extent the plaintiff recovers damages. Many statutory benefits, such as worker's compensation, are subject to legislative indemnity provisions." *Ratych v. Bloomer* (1990), 3 C.C.L.T. (2d) 1 at 23, 30 C.C.E.L. 161, 69 D.L.R. (4th) 25, [1990] 1 S.C.R. 940, 107 N.R. 335, 73 O.R. (2d) 448n, 39 O.A.C. 103, [1990] R.R.A. 651n, McLachlin J. (Lamer, La Forest, L'Heureux-Dubé and Sopinka JJ. concurring). 4. "To subrogate is to substitute. An insurer to recover a loss by way of subrogation must be able to place itself in the position of the insured. It follows, then, that the insurer is only entitled to make such claims, in the name of the insured, as could have been made by the insured...." *Bow Helicopters Ltd. v. Bell Helicopter Textron* (1981), 14 B.L.R. 133 at 142, 16 Alta. L.R. (2d) 149, 31 A.R. 49, 125 D.L.R. (3d) 386, [1981] I.L.R. 1-1415 (C.A.), the court per Haddad J.A. See DOCTRINE OF ~.

SUBSCRIBE. *v.* 1. To write under. 2. To sign.

SUBSIDIARY. *n.* A corporation which, in respect of another corporation, is controlled, either directly or indirectly, by that other corporation.

SUB SILENTIO. [L.] Silently.

SUBSTANTIAL COMPLIANCE. "When a statute requires substantial compliance ... it requires the doing of those things which are of real importance, of substance, having regard to the object and scheme of the Act ... I would therefore interpret 'substantial' as importing a measure of compliance – has the claimant made a reasonable effort to provide the information that the Act requires for its effective operation...." *Ed Miller Sales & Rental Ltd. v. Canadian Imperial Bank of Commerce* (1987), 51 Alta. L.R. (2d) 54 at 57, 37 D.L.R. (4th) 179, 7 P.P.S.A.C. 87, 79 A.R. 161 (C.A.), the court per Stevenson J.A.

SUBSTANTIAL PERFORMANCE. Exists where a contract has been carried out in all its essentials and only technical or unimportant omissions or defects have occurred.

SUBSTANTIVE LAW. ".... [C]reates rights and obligations and is concerned with the ends which the administration of justice seeks to attain, ... substantive law determines [the parties'] conduct and relations in respect of the matters litigated." *Sutt v. Sutt*, [1969] 1 O.R. 169 at 175, 2 D.L.R. (3d) 33 (C.A.), Schroeder J.A. (McGillivray J.A. concurring).

SUBSTITUTED SERVICE. Service of a document on a person representing the party to be served, instead of on the party personally or by some means not involving personal service.

SUBTENANCY. *n.* A tenancy created by sublease.

SUBTENANT. *var.* **SUB-TENANT.** *n.* 1. A person entering into a lease with a head tenant who reserves at least one day of her or his original term of tenancy. W.B. Rayner & R.H. McLaren, *Falconbridge on Mortgages*, 4th ed. (Toronto: Canada Law Book, 1977) at 101. 2. Includes any person deriving title under a sublease.

SUB VOCE. [L.] Under title.

SUCCESSION. *n.* As the case requires, (i) the property of the deceased to which a successor becomes beneficially entitled; or (ii) the acquisition by a successor of any property of the deceased by reason of the death of the deceased or a successor's becoming beneficially entitled to property of a deceased by reason of the death of the deceased.

SUCCESSION DUTY. Inheritance tax levied against each beneficiary on an inheritance. P.W. Hogg, *Constitutional Law of Canada*, 3d ed. (Toronto: Carswell, 1992) at 746.

SUCCESSOR. *n.* 1. One who takes another's place. 2. An heir, executor or administrator. *Land Registration Reform Act*, R.S.O. 1990, c. L.4, s. 1. 3. "When used in reference to corporations, ... generally denotes another corporation which, through merger, amalgamation or some other type of legal succession, assumes the burdens and becomes vested with the rights of the first corporation...." *National Trust Co. v. Mead* (1991), 12 R.P.R. (2d) 165 at 177, [1990] 2 S.C.R. 410, [1990] 5 W.W.R. 459, 71 D.L.R. (4th) 488, 112 N.R. 1, Wilson J. (Lamer C.J.C., La Forest, L'Heureux-Dubé, Gonthier and Cory JJ. concurring).

SUE. *v.* To bring a civil action against a person.

SUFFER. *v.* To permit; to allow.

SUFFERING. See PAIN AND ~.

SUFFICIENT CAUSATION. See MULTIPLE ~.

SUFFRAGE. *n.* Vote; electoral franchise.

SUICIDE. *n.* Killing oneself.

SUI GENERIS. [L.] Of one's own class or kind.

SUI JURIS. [L.] Of one's own right, without disability. R. Megarry & H.W.R. Wade, *The Law of Real Property*, 5th ed. (London: Stevens, 1984) at cxxvii.

SUIT. *n.* "... [W]as authoritatively defined by the Supreme Court of Canada in Lenoir v. Ritchie (1879), 3 S.C.R. 575. Fournier, J. said, at p. 601, 'The term (suit) is certainly a very comprehensive one, and is understood to apply to any proceeding in a Court of justice, by which an individual pursues that remedy in a Court of justice, which the law affords him. The modes of proceeding may be various, but if a right is litigated between parties in a Court of justice, the proceeding by which the decision of the Court is sought, is a suit.' This definition has been adopted by this court ..." *Canadian Workers' Union v. Frankel Structural Steel Ltd.*, (1976), 76 C.L.L.C. 14,010 at 51, 12 O.R. (2d) 560 (Div. Ct.), Reid J. See FRIENDLY ~; LAW ~; NON~.

SUMMARY. *n.* An abridgment.

SUMMARY APPLICATION. A request to a judge or court without a full and formal proceeding.

SUMMARY CONVICTION COURT. A person who has jurisdiction in the territorial division where the subject-matter of the proceedings is alleged to have arisen and who (a) is given jurisdiction over the proceedings by the enactment under which the proceedings are taken; (b) is a justice or provincial court judge, where the enactment under which the proceedings are taken does not expressly give jurisdiction to any person or class of persons; or (c) is a provincial court judge, where the enactment under which the proceedings are taken gives jurisdiction in respect thereof to two or more justices. *Criminal Code*, R.S.C. 1985, c. C-46, s. 785 as am. by *Criminal Law Amendment Act*, R.S.C. 1985 (1st Supp.), c. 27, s. 170.

SUMMARY CONVICTION OFFENCE. An offence which is tried summarily.

SUMMARY JUDGMENT. In Ontario, once the defendant has served a notice of motion or delivered a statement of defence, a plaintiff may apply for summary judgment in respect of part or all of the claim set out in the statement of claim (Ontario, Rules of Civil Procedure, r. 20.01(1)). G.D.

SUMMARY JURISDICTION

Watson & C. Perkins, eds., *Holmested & Watson: Ontario Civil Procedure* (Toronto: Carswell, 1984) at 20-2.

SUMMARY JURISDICTION. The ability of a court to make an order or give a judgment on its own initiative at once.

SUMMARY TRIAL. A trial conducted by or under the authority of a commanding officer pursuant to section 163 and a trial by a superior commander pursuant to section 164. *National Defence Act*, R.S.C. 1985, c. N-5, s. 2.

SUMMONS. *n.* A citation; a warning to appear in court. See JUDGMENT ~; SHOW CAUSE ~; WRIT OF ~.

SUMMONS TO WITNESS. Used instead of a subpoena, this document directs a witness to appear in court at a given time and place or to bring certain documents or things along.

SUM UP. For a judge to recapitulate evidence or parts of it for a jury, directing what form of verdict they should give. Each counsel has the right to sum up evidence adduced and the judge sums up everything.

SUP. CT. *abbr.* Superior Court.

SUP. CT. L. REV. *abbr.* The Supreme Court Law Review.

SUPERIOR COURT. 1. (a) In the Province of Ontario, Nova Scotia, Prince Edward Island or Newfoundland, the Supreme Court of the Province; (b) in the Province of Quebec, the Court of Appeal and the Superior Court in and for the Province; (c) in the Province of New Brunswick, Manitoba, Saskatchewan or Alberta, the Court of Appeal for the Province and the Court of Queen's Bench for the Province; (d) in the Province of British Columbia, the Court of Appeal and the Supreme Court of the Province; (e) in the Yukon Territory or the Northwest Territories, the Supreme Court thereof, and includes the Supreme Court of Canada and the Federal Court. *Interpretation Act*, R.S.C. 1985, c. I-21. s. 35. 2. A court not under the control of any other court except by appeal. 3.

". . . [D]escribed in s. 96 [of the Constitution Act, 1867 (30 & 31 Vict.), c. 3] were referred to as 'superior courts' . . ." *Reference re s.6 of the Family Relations Act (British Columbia)* (1982), 26 R.F.L. (2d) 113 at 131, [1982] 1 S.C.R. 62, [1982] 3 W.W.R. 1, 36 B.C.L.R. 1, 131 D.L.R. (3d) 257, 40 N.R. 206, Estey J. 4. A court with jurisdiction throughout a province, not limited to any subject matter. P.W. Hogg, *Constitutional Law of Canada*, 3d ed. (Toronto: Carswell, 1992) at 162. See PROVINCIAL ~.

SUPERSEDE. *v.* 1. ". . . [A] meaning that connotes superiority, priority or preference; . . ." *National Trust Co. v. Massey Combines Corp.* (1988), 39 B.L.R. 245 at 249, 69 C.B.R. (N.S.) 171 (Ont. H.C.), Saunders J. 2. ". . . [A] meaning that connotes removal, setting aside, annulment or alteration, followed by a replacement." *National Trust Co. v. Massey Combines Corp.* (1988), 39 B.L.R. 245 at 249, 69 C.B.R. (N.S.) 171 (Ont. H.C.), Saunders J.

SUPERSEDEAS. *n.* A writ which ordered, when good cause was shown, the stay of an ordinary proceeding which should otherwise proceed.

SUPPLEMENTARY LETTERS PATENT. Any letters patent granted to the company subsequent to the letters patent incorporating the company.

SUPPLY. *n.* See BUSINESS OF ~; INTERIM ~.

SUPPORT. *n.* 1. "[In Succession Law Reform Act, R.S.O. 1980, c. 488] . . . financial assistance to permit a dependant to provide for the necessities and amenities of life." *Mannion v. R.* (1982), 140 D.L.R. (3d) 189 at 190, 39 O.R. (2d) 609, 13 E.T.R. 49, 31 R.F.L. (2d) 133 (Div. Ct.), the court per Saunders J. 2. Includes maintenance or alimony. *Reciprocal Enforcement of Support Orders Act*, R.S. Nfld. 1990, c. R-5, s. 2.

SUPPORT ORDER. An order or judgment for maintenance, alimony or family financial support that is enforceable in any province. See FINANCIAL ~.

SUPPORT PROVISION. A provision of an order or agreement for maintenance, alimony or family financial support and includes any order for arrears of payments thereof. *Family Orders and Agreements Enforcement Assistance Act,* R.S.C. 1985 (2d Supp.), c. 4, s. 2.

SUPRA. *prep.* [L.] Above.

SUPRA PROTEST. After protesting.

SUPREMACY CLAUSE. Section 52(1) of the Constitution Act, 1982 which gives the Charter power to override other provisions. P.W. Hogg, *Constitutional Law of Canada,* 3d ed. (Toronto: Carswell, 1992) at 903-4.

SUPREME COURT OF CANADA. The general court of appeal for all of Canada, the final interpreter of all Canadian law whatever its source. P.W. Hogg, *Constitutional Law of Canada,* 3d ed. (Toronto: Carswell, 1992) at 208.

SUPT. *abbr.* Superintendent.

SURETY. *n.* ". . . [I]s one who contracts with a creditor that he will be answerable for the debt, default, or miscarriage or another who is the principal debtor and primarily liable." *Schmidt v. Gavriloff,* [1923] 2 W.W.R. 173 at 174, 17 Sask. L.R. 218 (C.A.), Lamont J.A. See CO-~.

SURNAME. *n.* Family name.

SURPRISE. *n.* Any event which causes a party to litigation to be put at a disadvantage. This may involve the introduction of evidence, a witness or an issue previously unknown to the party opposite.

SURR. CT. *abbr.* Surrogate Court.

SURREBUTTAL. *n.* The calling of evidence by the defence to meet the Crown's rebuttal evidence. P.K. McWilliams, *Canadian Criminal Evidence,* 3d ed. (Aurora: Canada Law Book, 1988) at 31-12.

SURREBUTTER. *n.* In pleadings, the plaintiff's response to the rebutter.

SURREJOINDER. *n.* In pleadings, the plaintiff's response to the rejoinder.

SURRENDER. *n.* "The doctrine of surrender is not limited to cases of landlord and tenant . . . As stated by Parke B. in Lyon v. Reed [(1844) 13 M. & W. 285 at 306]: 'This term is applied to cases where the owner of a particular estate has been a party to some act, the validity of which he is by law afterwards estopped from disputing, and which would not be valid if his particular estate had continued to exist. There the law treats the doing of such act as amounting to a surrender.' " *Saskatchewan (Attorney General) v. Whiteshore Salt & Chemical Co.,* [1955] S.C.R. 43 at 46, [1955] 1 D.L.R. 241, Kellock J. (Kerwin C.J.C. and Fauteux J. concurring).

SURROGATE. *n.* One who is appointed or substituted for another.

SURROGATE COURT. A court which deals with matters of probate and the administration of estates.

SURTAX. *n.* Tax payable in addition to tax at the standard rate.

SURVEILLANCE. *n.* Location of a person suspected of engaging in criminal activity, following that person, observing their activities and overhearing their conversations with other people. S.A. Cohen, *Due Process of Law* (Toronto: Carswell, 1977) at 64. See ELECTRONIC ~.

SURVIVORSHIP. *n.* 1. The living of one of several people after the death of one or all of the group. 2. The right of the joint tenant who outlives the other(s) to the whole land. R. Megarry & H.W.R. Wade, *The Law of Real Property,* 5th ed. (London: Stevens, 1984) at cxxvii. See PRESUMPTION OF ~; RIGHT OF ~.

SUSPECT. *n.* ". . . In ordinary parlance, whether someone is a 'suspect' refers to the existence of grounds to believe that the individual has engaged in forbidden activities." *Thomson Newspapers Ltd. v. Canada (Director of Investigation & Research)* (1990), 47 C.R.R. 1 at 67, 76 C.R. (3d) 129, 72 O.R. (2d) 415n, 54 C.C.C. (3d) 417, 67 D.L.R. (4th) 161, 29 C.P.R. (3d) 97, [1990] 1 S.C.R. 425, 39 O.A.C. 161,

106 N.R. 161, L'Heureux-Dubé J.

SUSPENDED SENTENCE. 1. "... [S]uspension of the imposition of a sentence ..." *R. v. Cruickshanks*, [1946] 3 W.W.R. 225 at 226, 63 B.C.R. 102, 2 C.R. 323, 86 C.C.C. 257, [1946] 4 D.L.R. 645 (C.A.), O'Halloran J.A. 2. "... [S]uspending the passing of the sentence." *R. v. Switzki*, [1930] 2 W.W.R. 479 at 480, 54 C.C.C. 332, 24 Sask. L.R. 587 (C.A.), the court per Haultain C.J.S.

S.V. *abbr.* Sub voce.

SWEAR. *v.* 1. To put under oath, to administer an oath to. 2. In the case of persons for the time being allowed by law to affirm or declare instead of swearing, includes affirm and declare.

SWEARING. *n.* 1. Declaration under oath. 2. "The essence of swearing [as found is s. 160(a) of the Criminal Code, S.C. 1953-54, c. 51] appears to be a reference to God and in the form of an oath. Often used in legal proceedings and in legal documents as an appeal to the truth by invoking the deity the word also includes the use of language which is contemptuous or irreverent of God or the deity." *R. v. Enns* (1968), 66 W.W.R. 318 at 320, 5 C.R.N.S. 115 (Sask. Dist. Ct.), Maher D.C.J.

SYNALLAGMATIC. *adj.* 1. Involving reciprocal and mutual duties and obligations. 2. Describing a situation in which one party undertakes to another party to do or not to do something, and, if that party fails to perform the undertaking, the law provides a remedy to the other party. G.H.L. Fridman, *The Law of Contract in Canada*, 2d ed. (Toronto: Carswell, 1986) at 10.

T

T.A. *abbr.* Décisions du Tribunal d'arbitrage.

T.A.B. *abbr.* Tax Appeal Board.

TACKING. *n.* 1. Extending a mortgagee's security to cover a subsequent loan. R. Megarry & H.W.R. Wade, *The Law of Real Property*, 5th ed. (London: Stevens, 1984) at cxxviii. 2. A doctrine concerning priorities between competing mortgages on the same property. If a third mortgage is taken without notice of a second and the third mortgagee purchases the first mortgage, the third mortgagee may "tack" the third mortgage to the first mortgage and so obtain priority. W.B. Rayner & R.H. McLaren, *Falconbridge on Mortgages*, 4th ed. (Toronto: Canada Law Book, 1977) at 195. 3. A doctrine by which a mortgagor's devisees or heirs may not redeem the mortgage without also paying a judgment debt or bond owing by the mortgagor because any equity of redemption in the hands of the devisees or heirs are assets for the payment of that debt. W.B. Rayner & R.H. McLaren, *Falconbridge on Mortgages*, 4th ed. (Toronto: Canada Law Book, 1977) at 196-197. 4. "A first or prior mortgagee may claim priority, up to the face amount of the mortgage, for moneys advanced under the first or prior mortgage subsequent to the registration and advancement of funds under a second or subsequent mortgage provided that such first or prior mortgagee did not have 'notice' of the second or subsequent mortgage at the time such subsequent advances were made. The 'notice' previously referred to is actual notice, not constructive notice." *I.W.A. Credit Union v. Johnson* (1978), 6 B.C.L.R. 271 at 280, 4 R.P.R. 181 (S.C.), Hinds L.J.S.C.

TAIL. See FEE ~.

TAKE-BACK. See VENDOR ~.

TAKE-HOME PAY. Net pay after withholding tax and other deductions.

TAKE OVER BID. *var.* **TAKE-OVER BID.** An offer made by an offeror to shareholders to acquire all of the shares of any class of shares of an offeree corporation not already owned by the offeror, and includes every take-over bid by a corporation to repurchase all of the shares of any class of its shares which leaves outstanding voting shares of the corporation.

TANGIBLE PERSONAL PROPERTY. (i) Means personal property that can be seen, weighed, measured, felt or touched or that is in any way perceptible to the senses, (ii) includes electricity, telecommunication and telephone services, (iii) includes transient accommodation, (iv) includes repair services. *Health Services Tax Act*, R.S.N.S. 1989, c. 198, s. 2.

TANGIBLE PROPERTY. Property having a physical existence.

TARIFF. *n.* 1. "[In the National Energy Board Act, R.S.C. 1970, c. N-6] . . . a list of tolls or rates. . . . It has been sometimes defined as 'a schedule of rates together with rules and regulations.'" *Saskatchewan Power Corp. v. Trans-Canada*

Pipelines Ltd. (1981), 130 D.L.R. (3d) 1 at 11, 39 N.R. 595, [1982] 1 W.W.R. 289, 14 Sask. R. 271, [1982] 2 S.C.R. 688, the court per Laskin C.J.C. 2. The schedule of fees to be charged for various legal services.

TAX. *n.* 1. ". . . [T]he . . . levies . . . are taxes. . . . Compulsion is an essential feature of taxation . . . the committee is a public authority, and . . . the imposition of these levies is for the public purposes. . . ." *British Columbia (Lower Mainland Dairy Products Sales Adjustment Committee) v. Crystal Dairy Ltd.*, [1933] 1 D.L.R. 82 at 85, [1933] 3 W.W.R. 639, [1933] A.C. 168 (P.C.), Lord Thankerton. 2. "Tax is a term of general import, including almost every species of imposition on persons or property for supplying the public treasury, as tolls, tributes, subsidies, excise, imposts, or customs . . ." *Lovitt v. Nova Scotia (Attorney General)* (1903), 33 S.C.R. 350 at 360, Mills J. 3. ". . . [E]very contribution to a public purpose imposed by superior authority is a 'tax' and nothing less." *Monette v. LeFebvre* (1889), 16 S.C.R. 387 at 403, Strong J. (Patterson J. concurring). See AREA ~; ARREARS OF ~; BUSINESS OCCUPANCY ~; DEPARTURE ~; ESTATE ~; EXCISE ~ES; EXPORT ~; GIFT ~; INCOME ~; INHERITANCE ~; MUNICIPAL ~; POLL-~; PROPERTY ~.

TAX A.B.C. *abbr.* Tax Appeal Board Cases, 1949-1971.

TAXATION OF COSTS. See ASSESSMENT OF COSTS.

TAXATION YEAR. 1. The fiscal year in relation to which the amount of tax is being computed. 2. In the case of a corporation, a fiscal period and in the case of an individual, a calendar year.

TAX AVOIDANCE. Attempts by a taxpayer to minimize or eliminate a tax obligation either by deliberately arranging income earning affairs to benefit from provisions of income tax legislation or by relying on reasonable and different interpretations of that legislation. W. Grover & F. Iacobucci, *Materials on Canadian Income Tax*, 4th ed. (Toronto: De Boo, 1980) at 993.

TAXED COSTS. Costs taxed in accordance with the rules of court.

TAX EVASION. In a case where the law clearly obliges one to report income and pay tax, a wilful attempt by the taxpayer not to disclose or to suppress income and thus not to pay tax on it. W. Grover & F. Iacobucci, *Materials on Canadian Income Tax*, 4th ed. (Toronto: De Boo, 1980) at 991.

TAX EXPENDITURE. A feature of the income tax system such as an exemption, exclusion, or deduction which is in fact a method of providing financial assistance and is not required for purposes of administering the income tax itself. W. Grover & F. Iacobucci, *Materials on Canadian Income Tax*, 4th ed. (Toronto: De Boo, 1980) at 163.

TAXING OFFICER. 1. The registrar or other officer appointed under the Act for the taxation or fixing of costs or the passing of accounts. *Bankruptcy Rules*, C.R.C., c. 368, s. 2. 2. A master of the Supreme Court, or a judge of the Trial Division or the Court of Appeal. *Rules of the Supreme Court*, S.Nfld. 1986, r. 1, s. 1.03. 3. An assessment officer.

TAX PAYER. *var.* **TAXPAYER**. A person required by a revenue Act to pay a tax.

TAYLOR. *abbr.* Taylor's King's Bench Reports (Ont.), 1823-1827.

T.B. *abbr.* Tariff Board.

TBA. *abbr.* To be agreed.

T. BD. *abbr.* Transport Board.

T.B.R. *abbr.* Tariff Board Reports, 1937-1962.

T.C.C. *abbr.* Tax Court of Canada.

T.C.I. *abbr.* Tribunal canadien des importations.

T.D. *abbr.* Supreme Court, Trial Division.

TENANCY. *n.* 1. The exclusive right to occupy residential premises granted to a tenant by a landlord, for which the tenant agrees to pay or provide rent for a term that may be terminated by the landlord or tenant. 2. The condition of being a tenant. 3. The relation of a tenant to the property the tenant holds. See JOINT ~; PERIODIC ~; SEVERAL ~; TERM OF ~.

TENANCY AGREEMENT. An agreement between a landlord and a tenant for possession or occupation of residential premises, whether written, oral or implied.

TENANCY AT WILL. An interest which permits a grantee to enter into possession of land at the pleasure of the grantor and her or himself.

TENANCY BY THE ENTIRETY. A condition like a joint tenancy, which cannot be severed, created through a conveyance to a husband and wife with no words of severance. A. Bissett-Johnson & W.M. Holland, eds., *Matrimonial Property Law in Canada* (Toronto: Carswell, 1980) at 1-11.

TENANCY IN COMMON. A condition created when there are words of severance or one of the four unities is lacking; unequal sharing may be created; each tenant may dispose of their share by will. A. Bissett-Johnson & W.M. Holland, eds., *Matrimonial Property Law in Canada* (Toronto: Carswell, 1980) at 1-12.

TENANT. *n.* 1. "... [T]he person who, by reason of his possession of occupancy or his rights thereto, whether by privity of contract or estate, for the time being holds the premises under title immediately or mediately from the landlord or his predecessor in title, and by reason of his so holding is the person liable for the time being to pay the rent...." *Calgary Brewing & Malting Co., Re* (1915), 9 W.W.R. 563 at 565, 25 D.L.R. 859 (Alta. T.D.), Beck J. 2. "... [O]ne of a class of persons ... who have a right to use the premises, not by license or invitation as occasion arises, but by a contract which gives a right to such use continuously during the currency of the contract without licence or invitation." *Watt v. Adams Brothers Harness Manufacturing Co.* (1927), 23 Alta. L.R. 94 at 97, [1927] 3 W.W.R. 580, [1928] 1 D.L.R.

59 (C.A.), Beck J.A. See JOINT ~; LIFE ~; OVERHOLDING ~.

TENANTS IN COMMON. Two or more people who have an equal, undivided interest in property; each of them may occupy all the land in common with the others. Each tenant may dispose of their interest by will or deed. There is no right of survivorship as in a joint tenancy.

TENDER. *n.* 1. A payment of the precise amount that is due. To offer a larger amount without asking for change is acceptable, but to offer less is not. If it was agreed that the debt be paid on a certain day, payment after or before that date is not proper, and for the payment to be proper it must be unconditional. C.R.B. Dunlop, *Creditor-Debtor Law in Canada* (Toronto: Carswell, 1981) at 21 and 22. 2. Legal currency. 3. A call for tender by written public advertisement. See LEGAL ~.

TENEMENT. *n.* Something which may be held; something which is subject to tenure. See DOMINANT ~; LANDS, ~S AND HEREDITAMENTS.

TENURE. *n.* 1. A way to hold or occupy. 2. The mode in which all land is theoretically owned and occupied. See SECURITY OF ~.

T.E. (QUÉ.). *abbr.* Tribunal de l'expropriation (Québec).

TERM. *n.* 1. A contract provision which explains an obligation or group of obligations imposed on one or more of the parties. G.H.L. Fridman, *The Law of Contract in Canada*, 2d ed. (Toronto: Carswell, 1986) at 427. 2. "[Used] ... to designate the length of time for which a person is elected to serve in political office or for which a person is incarcerated as a penalty for the commission of a crime." *R. v. Laycock* (1989), 51 C.C.C. (3d) 65 at 68, 17 M.V.R. (2d) 1 (Ont. C.A.), the court per Goodman J.A. 3. "The word 'term' would be more accurate than 'session' to describe the time prescribed by law for holding court, as a session of the Court is the time of its actual sitting and terminates each day with its rising. The distinction is not always observed, however, and the words are often used interchangeably." *MacDonald v. Dawson* (1955), 20 C.R. 357 at 358, 36 M.P.R. 34, 112 C.C.C. 44 (Nfld. C.A.), the court per Walsh C.J. See COLLATERAL ~; DISJUNCTIVE ~; EXPRESS ~; FUNDAMENTAL ~; IMPLIED ~.

TERMINATION. *n.* 1. "... [W]hen in the context of a breach of contract one speaks of 'termination' what is meant is no more than that the innocent party or, in some cases, both parties are excused from further performance." *Photo Production Ltd. v. Securicor Transport Ltd.*, [1980] 1 All E.R. 556 at 562 (U.K. H.L.), Lord Wilberforce. 2. "[Includes] ... an ending of the contract [of insurance] by time lapse." *Bank of Nova Scotia v. Commercial Union Assurance of Canada* (1991), 104 N.S.R. (2d) 313 at 319, 283 A.P.R. 313, 6 C.C.L.I. (2d) 178 (T.D.), Tidman J.

TERM OF TENANCY. The length of time over which a tenancy agreement is to run.

TERR. CT. *abbr.* Territorial Court.

TERRITORIAL COURT. A court established by Parliament for two federal territories, the Northwest Territories and the Yukon Territory. P.W. Hogg, *Constitutional Law of Canada*, 3d ed. (Toronto: Carswell, 1992) at 182.

TERRITORIAL SEA. "... [A]s defined by international law, i.e., the waters and submerged lands to a width of three miles seaward of the coast of the mainland but when the mainland coast is deeply indented or has a fringe of islands in its immediate vicinity, seaward from baselines enclosing these features." *Canada (Attorney General) v. British Columbia (Attorney General)*, [1984] 4 W.W.R. 289 at 299, [1984] 1 S.C.R. 388, 8 D.L.R. (4th) 161, 52 N.R. 335, 54 B.C.L.R. 97, Dickson J. (Beetz, Estey and Chouinard JJ. concurring).

TERR. L.R. *abbr.* Territories Law Reports (N.W.T.), 1885-1907.

TEST. *v.* 1. To determine veracity. 2. "... [T]o try out, experiment with, check out." *Murray v. Insurance Corp. of British Columbia* (1992), 10 C.C.L.I. (2d) 47 at 56 (B.C. S.C.), Gow J.

TEST. *n.* A standard by which one judges. See LIE DETECTOR ~; NEIGHBOUR ~; PROPORTIONALITY ~.

TESTAMENT. *n.* 1. A bequest of personal property. 2. A will.

TESTAMENTARY. *adj.* With respect to a document or gift, made to take effect only after the person making it dies. *Cock v. Cooke* (1866), L.R. 1 P. & P. 241 at 243, Wilde J.

TESTAMENTARY CAPACITY. Ability to make a valid will.

TESTAMENTARY INSTRUMENT. Includes any will, codicil or other testamentary writing or appointment, during the life of the testator whose testamentary disposition it purports to be and after his death, whether it relates to real or personal property or to both. *Criminal Code*, R.S.C. 1985, c. C-46, s. 2.

TESTAMENTARY TRUST. A trust that arises upon and in consequence of the death of an individual.

TESTATE. *adj.* Having executed a will.

TESTATOR. *n.* 1. The person making a will, whether the person be male or female. 2. A person who has died leaving a will.

TESTATRIX. *n.* A woman who has made a will.

TESTATUM. *n.* A part of an indenture, known as the witnessing clause, which begins with the words "now this indenture witnesseth".

TEST CASE. 1. An action whose result determines liability in other actions. 2. "[A case in which there is a] ... factual or legal relationship between [the case] ... and ... other actions depending on its result...." *Asbjorn Horgard A/S v. Gibbs/Nortac Industries Ltd.* (1987), 81 N.R. 1 at 2

(Fed. C.A.), Urie J.A.

TESTE. *n.* The final part of a writ which gives the date and place it was issued.

TESTIFY. *v.* ". . . [T]he giving of evidence by means of oral communication in a proceeding. . . ." *Thomson Newspapers Ltd. v. Canada (Director of Investigation & Research, Combines Investigation Branch)* (1990), (*sub nom. Thomson Newspapers v. Canada (Director of Investigation & Research, Restrictive Trade Practices Commission)*) 29 C.P.R. (3d) 97 at 218, 76 C.R. (3d) 129, 72 O.R. (2d) 415n, 54 C.C.C. (3d) 417, 67 D.L.R. (4th) 161, [1990] 1 S.C.R. 425, 39 O.A.C. 161, 106 N.R. 161, L'Heureux-Dubé J.

TESTIMONIAL EVIDENCE. In a broad sense, any evidence about which a competent witness testifies, even to simply identify an object. P.K. McWilliams, *Canadian Criminal Evidence*, 3d ed. (Aurora: Canada Law Book, 1988) at 1-11.

TESTIMONIUM. *n.* Of a deed, the concluding part which reads "In witness whereof . . ." and contains the signatures of the parties and witnesses.

TESTIMONY. *n.* 1. The evidence which a witness gives viva voce in a court or tribunal. 2. "[In s. 43 of the Canada Evidence Act, R.S.C. 1970, c. E-10] . . . includes both oral evidence and documentary evidence (Radio Corp. of Amer. v. Rauland Corp., [1956] 1 Q.B. 618 [(U.K.)] and Radio Corp. of Amer. v. Rauland Corp., (Can.) [[1956] O.R. 630 (H.C.)]." *United States District Court, Middle District of Florida v. Royal American Shows Inc.*, [1981] 4 W.W.R. 148 at 152, 58 C.C.C. (2d) 274, 120 D.L.R. (3d) 732, 26 A.R. 136 (C.A.), Lieberman J.A. See PERPETUATE ~.

TEXT BOOK. *var.* **TEXTBOOK.** A treatise which collects decisions or explains principles concerning some branch of the law.

THEFT. *n.* Fraudulently and without colour of right taking, or fraudulently and without colour of right converting to his use or to the use of another person, anything whether animate or inanimate, with intent, (a) to deprive, temporarily or absolutely, the owner of it or a person who has a special property or interest in it; (b) to pledge it or deposit it as security; (c) to part with it under a condition with respect to its return that the person who parts with it may be unable to perform; or (d) to deal with it in such a manner that it cannot be restored in the condition in which it was at the time it was taken or converted. *Criminal Code*, R.S.C. 1985, c. C-46, s. 322(1).

THING. *n.* A subject of dominion or property.

THING IN ACTION. ". . . [A]n anglicization of the more usual and well-known common law expression '[chose] in action'. . . ." *Deloitte, Haskins & Sells Ltd. v. Graham* (1983), 47 C.B.R. (N.S.) 172 at 177, [1983] 3 W.W.R. 687, 32 R.F.L. (2d) 356, 25 Alta. L.R. (2d) 84, 144 D.L.R. (3d) 539, 42 A.R. 76 (Q.B.), D.C. MacDonald J. See CHOSE IN ACTION.

THIRD PARTY. A person who is not a party to an action but from whom a defendant claims relief.

THIRD READING. Parliamentary review of a bill in its final form. A. Fraser, W.A. Dawson & J. Holtby, eds., *Beauchesne's Rules and Forms of the House of Commons of Canada*, 6th ed. (Toronto: Carswell, 1989) at 195.

THREAT. *n.* ". . . [A] 'tool of intimidation which is designed to instil a sense of fear in its recipient': R. v. McCraw . . . [(1991), 66 C.C.C. (3d) 517 (S.C.C.)]. . . . may be express or implicit and made by means of words, writings or actions. . . ." *R. v. Pelletier* (1992), 71 C.C.C. (3d) 438 at 441 (Que. C.A.), the court per Proulx J.A.

THREE CERTAINTIES. The three essential characteristics required to create a trust: (a) certain intention; (b) certain subject-matter; (c) certain objects. D.M.W. Waters, *The Law of Trusts in Canada*, 2d ed. (Toronto: Carswell, 1984) at 107.

TIMBER. *n.* ". . . [G]enerally treated as connoting growing trees which are a part of the realty and pass with a conveyance of land unless expressly reserved...." *Highway Sawmills Ltd. v. Minister of National Revenue*, [1966] C.T.C. 150 at 160 (S.C.C.), Ritchie J. (dissenting). See CROWN ~.

TIME CHARTER. A charterparty for a certain time.

TIME SALE. A sale or an agreement to sell under which the purchase price and credit charges in addition to the purchase price, if any, are to be paid by one or more future payments.

TIME SHARE INTEREST. The interest of a person in a time share plan.

TIME SHARE OWNERSHIP PLAN. Any plan by which a person participating in the plan acquires an ownership interest in real property and the right to use or occupy all or part of that property, including accommodations or facilities situated on all or part of that property, for specific or determinable periods of time.

TIME SHARE PLAN. Any time share ownership plan or time share use plan, whether in respect of land situated inside or outside a province, that provides for the use, occupation or possession of real property to circulate in any year among persons participating in the plan.

TIME SHARE USE PLAN. Any plan by which a person participating in the plan acquires a right to use or occupy real property, including accommodations or facilities situated on that property, for specific or determinable periods of time but does not acquire an ownership interest in that property.

TITLE. *n.* 1. "... [A] vested right or title, something to which the right is already acquired, though the enjoyment may be postponed." *O'Dell v. Gregory* (1895), 24 S.C.R. 661 at 663, the court per Strong C.J. 2. "... [M]ay simply describe the right (or entitlement) to an interest in property...." *Canadian Imperial Bank of Commerce v. 64576 Man. Ltd.* (1990), 1 P.P.S.A.C. (2d) 1 at 7 (Man. Q.B.), Jewers J. 3. A general heading which includes particulars, i.e. of a book. 4. An appellation of dignity

or honour. See ABSTRACT OF ~; BAD ~; CERTIFICATE OF ~; CHAIN OF ~; CLEAR ~; CURE ~; DEFECTIVE ~; DOCUMENT OF ~; FIRST ~; GOOD ~; LONG ~; MARKETABLE ~; MINERAL ~; MISTAKE OF ~; POSSESSORY ~; QUALIFIED ~; REQUISITION ON ~; ROOT OF ~; ROYAL STYLE AND ~S; SLANDER OF ~; SQUATTER'S ~.

TITLE OF PROCEEDING. The name which sets out the names of all the parties and their capacity, if other than a personal capacity (Ontario, Rules of Civil Procedure, r. 14.06 (1)). G.D. Watson & C. Perkins, eds., *Holmested & Watson: Ontario Civil Procedure* (Toronto: Carswell, 1984) at 14-5.

[ ] T.J. *abbr.* Recueils de Jurisprudence, Tribunal de la Jeunesse.

T.J. (QUÉ.). *abbr.* Tribunal de la jeunesse (Québec).

T.L.R. *abbr.* Times Law Reports.

T.M. *abbr.* Trade Marks.

T.O. *abbr.* 1. Taxing Officer. 2. Taxing Office.

TORT. *n.* 1. Wrong. 2. Generally, an injury other than a breach of contract for which recovery of damages is permitted by the law. J.G. Fleming, *The Law of Torts*, 8th ed. (Sydney: Law Book, 1992) at 1. 3. "... [I]ntended to restore the injured person to the position he enjoyed prior to the injury, rather than to punish the tortfeasor whose only wrong may have been a moment of inadvertence...." *Ratych v. Bloomer* (1990), 30 C.C.E.L. 161 at 171, 39 O.A.C. 103, [1990] 1 S.C.R. 940, 69 D.L.R. (4th) 25, 107 N.R. 335, 3 C.C.L.T. (2d) 1, McLachlin J. (Lamer, La Forest, L'Heureux-Dubé and Sopinka JJ. concurring). 4. "A fundamental proposition underlies the law of tort: that a person who by his or her fault causes damage to another may be held responsible." *Canadian National Railway v. Norsk Pacific Steamship Co.* (1992), 11 C.C.L.T. (2d) 1 at 16, 137 N.R. 241, 91 D.L.R. (4th) 289, [1992] 1 S.C.R. 1021, 53 F.T.R. 79n, McLachlin J. (L'Heureux-Dubé and

Cory JJ. concurring). See AD-MINISTRATOR DE SON ~; INTENTIONAL ~; JOINT ~.

TORTFEASOR. *var.* **TORT-FEASOR.** *n.* 1. A wrongdoer. 2. A party who commits a tort. See JOINT ~S; SEVERAL ~S.

TORTIOUS. *adj.* Wrongful.

TORTURE. *n.* Any act or omission by which severe pain or suffering, whether physical or mental, is intentionally inflicted on a person (a) for a purpose including (i) obtaining from the person or from a third person information or a statement, (ii) punishing the person for an act which that person or a third person has committed or is suspected of having committed, and (iii) intimidating or coercing the person or a third person, or (b) for any reason based on discrimination of any kind, but does not include an act or omission arising only from, inherent in or incidental to lawful sanctions. *Criminal Code*, S.C. 1987, c. 13, s. 245.4(2).

TOTAL LOSS. ". . . [I]n the case of a ship the subject of insurance must be either such an entire wreck as to be reduced, as it is said, to a mere 'congeries of planks', or if it still subsists in specie it must, as a result of perils insured against, be placed in such a situation that it is totally out of the power of the owner or the underwriter at any labor, and by means of any expenditure, to get it afloat and cause it to be repaired and used again as a ship." *McGhee v. Phoenix Insurance Co.* (1890), 18 S.C.R. 61 at 70, Strong J.

TO WIT. Namely.

TRACING. *n.* 1. ". . . [A] convenient term adopted by many matrimonial property cases to describe the effect of identifying property by a source. . . ." *Harrower v. Harrower* (1989), 21 R.F.L. (3d) 369 at 378, 68 Alta. L.R. (2d) 97, 97 A.R. 141 (C.A.), the court per Stevenson J.A. 2. The right to follow property into the hands of a defendant. A. Bissett-Johnson & W.M. Holland, eds., *Matrimonial Property Law in Canada* (Toronto: Carswell, 1980) at

O-25.

TRADE AND COMMERCE. 1. A power of the federal Parliament under section 91(2) of the Constitution Act, 1867. P.W. Hogg, *Constitutional Law of Canada*, 3d ed. (Toronto: Carswell, 1992) at 521. 2. ". . . [T]he power to regulate international and interprovincial trade and . . . 'the general regulation of trade affecting the whole of Canada' . . ." *Alex Couture Inc. c. Canada (Procureur général)* (1991), 38 C.P.R. (3d) 293 at 308, 83 D.L.R. (4th) 577, 41 Q.A.C. 1, [1991] R.J.Q. 2534, the court per Rousseau-Houle J.A.

TRADE FIXTURES. The fixtures, machinery, and other chattels, other than stock, with which a person carries on a business. *Bulk Sales Act*, R.S.Nfld. 1990, c. B-11, s. 2.

TRADE L. TOPICS. *abbr.* Trade Law Topics.

TRADE-MARK. *var.* **TRADE MARK.** (a) A mark that is used by a person for the purpose of distinguishing or so as to distinguish wares or services manufactured, sold, leased, hired or performed by him from those manufactured, sold, leased, hired or performed by others; (b) a certification mark; (c) a distinguishing guise; or (d) a proposed trade-mark. *Trade-Marks Act*, R.S.C. 1985, c. T-13, s. 2.

TRADE-NAME. *var.* **TRADE NAME.** The name under which any business is carried on, whether or not it is the name of a corporation, a partnership or an individual. *Trade-Marks Act*, R.S.C. 1985, c. T-13, s. 2.

TRADE SECRET. Something known only to an employer and those employees to whom it is necessary to confide it, which may be improperly used. H.G. Fox, *The Canadian Law of Trade Marks and Unfair Competition*, 3d ed. (Toronto: Carswell, 1972) at 654.

TRADE UNION. *var.* **TRADE-UNION.** 1. Any organization of employees, or any branch or local thereof, the purposes of which include the regulation of relations between employers and employees. 2. Such combination, whether temporary or permanent, for regulating the relations between workmen and masters, or for imposing restrictive conditions on the conduct of any trade or business, as would, but for this Act, have been deemed to be an unlawful combination by reason of some one or more of its purposes being in restraint of trade. *Trade Unions Act*, R.S.C. 1985, c. T-14, s. 2.

TRADING. See INSIDER ~.

TRANSCRIPT. *n.* 1. Something copied from an original. 2. In a court, an official copy of proceedings. 3. ". . . [A] direct, written copy of words used in a conversation. . . ," *R. v. Ouellet* (1976), 33 C.C.C. (2d) 417 at 422, [1977] 2 W.W.R. 295 (B.C. Prov. Ct.), Paradis J.

TRANSFER. *n.* 1. ". . . [T]o give or hand over property from one person to another." *Murphy v. R.* (1980), 8 E.T.R. 120 at 131 (Fed. T.D.), Cattanach J. 2. ". . . [N]ot a term of art and has not a technical meaning . . . All that is required is that [party A] should so deal with the property as to divest himself of it and vest it in [party B], that is to say, pass the property from [A] to [B]. The means by which he accomplishes this result, whether direct or circuitous, may properly be called a transfer." *Fasken v. Canada (Minister of National Revenue)* (1948), [1949] 1 D.L.R. 810 at 822, [1948] C.T.C. 265, [1948] Ex. C.R. 580, Thorson P. 3. The passing of any estate or interest in land under this Act, whether for valuable consideration or otherwise. *Land Titles acts.* 4. In relation to stock, includes the performance and execution of every deed, power of attorney, act, and thing on the part of the transferor to effect and complete the title in the transferee. *Trustee acts.* 5. Includes transmission by operation of law. *Corporations acts.*

TRANSFEREE. *n.* 1. A person in whose favour a transfer is given. 2. The person to whom any interest or estate in land is transferred whether for value or otherwise. *Land Titles acts.*

TRANSFEROR. *n.* 1. The person by

whom any interest or estate in land is transferred, whether for valuable consideration or otherwise. *Land Titles acts.* 2. A person who gives a transfer.

TRANSFERRED INTENT. "The literature on transferred intent distinguishes between two kinds of situations in which the 'wrong victim' suffers harm at the hands of the accused. The first, sometimes called error *in objecto* involves a mistake by the perpetrator as to the identity of the victim . . . It is the second 'wrong victim' situation, sometimes called aberratio ictus, or more poetically, 'a mistake of the bullet' that has led to the controversy surrounding the doctrine of transferred intent. In this second situation the perpetrator aims at X but by chance or lack of skill hits Y." *R. v. Droste* (1984), 10 C.C.C. (3d) 404 at 410, [1984] 1 S.C.R. 208, 39 C.R. (3d) 26, 6 D.L.R. (4th) 607, 52 N.R. 176, 3 O.A.C. 179, Dickson J. (Ritchie, Estey, McIntyre, Chouinard and Lamer JJ. concurring).

TRANSMISSION. *n.* 1. ". . . [I]n the ordinary sense of the language, connotes the delivery from an origination point to a reception point. It does not connote a conceptual transfer of something with neither sender nor receiver. . . ," *R. v. McLaughlin* (1980), 18 C.R. (3d) 339 at 348, [1980] 2 S.C.R. 331, [1981] 1 W.W.R. 298, 32 N.R. 350, 23 A.R. 530, 53 C.C.C. (2d) 417, 113 D.L.R. (3d) 386, Estey J. (concurring). 2. Applies to change of ownership consequent on death, lunacy, sale under execution, order of court or other act of law, or on a sale for arrears of taxes or on any settlement or any legal succession in case of intestacy. *Land Titles acts.* 3. "[With regard to shares] . . . used to express the legal result which follows on death, but not to express the actual step which is necessary to invest the new holder. That is done by transfer, and that transfer in such a case is effectuated by a change in the register where the shares are registered, . . ." *Brassard v. Smith* (1924), [1925] 1 D.L.R. 528 at 531, [1925] A.C. 371, [1925] 1 W.W.R. 311, 38 Que. K.B. 208 (Que. P.C.), the board per Lord Dunedin.

TRAP. *n.* ". . . [A]n intrinsically dangerous situation. The danger should not be apparent but hidden: . . . generally includes some connotation of abnormality and surprise, in view of the circumstances; . . ." *Rubis v. Gray Rocks Inn Ltd.*, [1982] 1 S.C.R. 452 at 466, 41 N.R. 108, 21 C.C.L.T. 64, Beetz J. (Chouinard and Lamer JJ. concurring).

TRAVERSE. *n.* ". . . [A] denial [by the defendant] of the plaintiff's allegations . . ." *Royal Bank v. Rizkalla* (1984), 50 C.P.C. 292 at 295, 59 B.C.L.R. 324 (S.C.), McLachlin J.

T.R.B. *abbr.* Tax Review Board.

TREASON. *n.* (a) Using force or violence for the purpose of overthrowing the government of Canada or a province; (b) without lawful authority, communicating or making available to an agent of a state other than Canada, military or scientific information or any sketch, plan, model, article, note or document of a military or scientific character that he knows or ought to know may be used by that state for a purpose prejudicial to the safety or defence of Canada; (c) conspiring with any person to commit high treason or to do anything mentioned in paragraph (a); (d) forming an intention to do anything that is high treason or that is mentioned in paragraph (a) and manifesting that intention by an overt act; or (e) conspiring with any person to do anything mentioned in paragraph (b) or forming an intention to do anything mentioned in paragraph (b) and manifesting that intention by an overt act. *Criminal Code*, R.S.C. 1985, c. C-46, s. 46(2). See HIGH ~.

TREASURE TROVE. Any coin, money, gold, silver, bullion or plate buried or hidden in a private place; because its owner is unknown it belongs to the Crown. E.L.G. Tyler & N.E. Palmer, eds., *Crossley Vaines' Personal Property*, 5th ed. (London: Butterworths, 1973) at 419.

TREASURY BILL. A bill issued by or on behalf of Her Majesty for the payment of a principal sum specified in the bill to a named recipient or to a bearer at a date not later than 12 months from the date of issue of the bill. *Financial Administration Act*, R.S.C. 1985, c. F-11, s. 2.

TREAT. See INVITATION TO ~.

TREATMENT. *n.* "[In s. 12 of the Charter] . . . connotes any conduct, action or behaviour towards another person. It is a word of more expansive or comprehensive import than is its disjunctive partner 'punishment', in that it extends, or potentially so, to all forms of disability or disadvantage and not merely to those imposed as a penalty to ensure the application and enforcement of a rule of law . . ." *R. v. Blakeman* (1988), 48 C.R.R. 222 at 239 (Ont. H.C.), Watt J.

TREATY. *n.* 1. In international law, a binding agreement between states. P.W. Hogg, *Constitutional Law of Canada*, 3d ed. (Toronto: Carswell, 1992) at 281. 2. ". . . [A] treaty with the Indians is unique, . . . it is an agreement sui generis which is neither created nor terminated according to the rules of international law. . . . it is clear that what characterizes a treaty is the intention to create obligations, the presence of mutually binding obligations and a certain measure of solemnity. . . ." *Sioui v. Quebec (Attorney General)* (1990), (sub nom. *R. v. Sioui*) 56 C.C.C. (3d) 225 at 239, [1990] 1 S.C.R. 1025, 109 N.R. 22, 70 D.L.R. (4th) 427, [1990] 3 C.N.L.R. 127, 30 O.A.C. 280, the court per Lamer J. 3. "[In s. 88 of the *Indian Act*, R.S.C. 1970, c. I-6] . . . is not a word of art and . . . it embraces all such engagements made by persons in authority as may be brought within the term 'the word of the white man' the sanctity of which was, at the time of British exploration and settlement, the most important means of obtaining the goodwill and co-operation of the native tribes . . . On such assurance the Indians relied." *R. v. White* (1964), 50 D.L.R. (2d) 613 at 648-9, 52 W.W.R. 193 (B.C. C.A.), Norris J.A. See COMMERCIAL ~.

TRESPASS. *n.* 1. ". . . [U]njustified invasion of another's possession. . . ."

Harrison v. Carswell (1975), 75 C.L.L.C. 14,286 at 614, [1976] 2 S.C.R. 200, [1975] 6 W.W.R. 673, 5 N.R. 523, 25 C.C.C. (2d) 186, 62 D.L.R. (3d) 68, the court per Dickson J. 2. All forcible, direct and immediate injury to the plaintiff's person, land or goods. May be committed by propelling a person or object onto the land or by refusing to leave land after a licence to enter has terminated. J.G. Fleming, *The Law of Torts*, 8th ed. (Sydney: Law Book, 1992) at 16, 41-2. 3. ". . . [A]n action for the wrong committed in respect of the plaintiff's land by entry on the same without lawful authority." *Point v. Dibblee Construction Co.* [1934] O.R. 142 at 153, [1934] 2 D.L.R. 785 (H.C.), Armour J.

TRESPASS AB INITIO. A person who lawfully entered another's land lost immunity from action for trespass if that person abused the privilege by committing a tort against the possessor or the possessor's property. J.G. Fleming, *The Law of Torts*, 6th ed. (Sydney: Law Book, 1983) at 95.

TRESPASS BY RELATION. A person who has a right to immediate possession of land may, upon entry, sue for any trespass committed after that right to entry accrued. J.G. Fleming, *The Law of Torts*, 8th ed. (Sydney: Law Book, 1992) at 44.

TRESPASS DE BONIS ASPORTATIS. A writ used as a remedy in a case in which something was totally carried away or destroyed. J.G. Fleming, *The Law of Torts*, 8th ed. (Sydney: Law Book, 1992) at 52.

TRESPASSER. *n.* Someone who goes on another's land without any lawful authority, right or express or implied licence or invitation, and whose presence is either unknown to the occupier or is objected to if known. J.V. DiCastri, *Occupiers' Liability* (Vancouver: Burroughs/Carswell, 1980) at 123.

TRESPASS TO GOODS. Intentional interference or use of a chattel in such a way as to violate the plaintiff's possessory rights. J.G. Fleming, *The Law of Torts*, 8th ed. (Sydney: Law Book, 1992) at 52-3.

TRESPASS TO LAND. Entry onto or any immediate and direct interference with the possession of land. I.H. Jacob, ed., *Bullen and Leake and Jacob's Precedents of Pleadings*, 12th ed. (London: Sweet and Maxwell, 1975) at 878.

TRIAL. *n.* 1. ". . . In its popular and general sense a trial by jury consists of arraignment and plea, calling and swearing the jury, the opening address of Crown counsel, the examination and cross-examination of witnesses for the Crown and for the defence, the closing addresses of counsel, the judge's charge and, last, the jury's verdict. The cases have, by and large, tended to give a rather more restricted meaning to the word 'trial'. . . ." *R. v. Basarabas* (1982), 31 C.R. (3d) 193 at 197, [1982] 2 S.C.R. 730, [1983] 4 W.W.R. 289, 144 D.L.R. (3d) 115, 2 C.C.C. (3d) 257, 46 N.R. 69, the court per Dickson J. 2. "[In the case of a trial by jury] . . . the trial proper does not start until the accused is given in charge to the jury which stage is, of course, not reached until after the plea has been taken and the adoption of this more restricted meaning of the word 'trial' has been widely accepted in our own courts for many years." *R. v. Dennis* (1960), 30 W.W.R. 545 at 550, [1960] S.C.R. 286, 32 C.R. 210, 125 C.C.C. 321, the court per Ritchie J. 3. ". . . [T]he investigation and determination of a matter in issue between parties before a competent tribunal, advancing through progressive stages from its submission to the court or jury to the pronouncement of judgment." *Catherwood v. Thompson*, [1958] O.R. 326 at 331, 13 D.L.R. (2d) 238 (C.A.), the court per Schroeder J.A. See FEDERAL COURT — DIVISION; FAIR ~; MIS~; NEW ~; NOTICE OF READINESS FOR ~; SET DOWN FOR ~; SUMMARY ~.

TRIAL COURT. The court by which an accused was tried and includes a judge or a provincial court judge acting under Part XIX. *Criminal Code*, R.S.C. 1985, c. C-46, s. 673 as amended by

Criminal Law Amendment Act, R.S.C. 1985 (1st Supp.), c. 27, s. 138.

TRIAL DE NOVO. A form of appeal in which the case is retried.

TRIB. *abbr.* Tribunal.

TRIB. CONC. *abbr.* Tribunal de la concurrence.

TRIBUNAL. *n.* 1. "... [A] generic word which includes courts in its scope. Thus, in this generic sense, all courts are tribunals, but all tribunals are not courts...." *Russell v. Radley* (1984), 11 C.C.C. (3d) 289 at 305, [1984] 1 F.C. 543, 5 Admin. L.R. 39 (T.D.), Muldoon J. 2. A court of justice. 3. A body or person which exercises a judicial or quasi-judicial function outside the regular court system. 4. One or more persons, whether or not incorporated and however described, on whom a statutory power of decision is conferred. See ADMINISTRATIVE ~; ARBITRAL ~; DOMESTIC ~; FEDERAL BOARD, COMMISSION OR OTHER ~; SERVICE ~.

TRIER OF FACT. The person or group who must make findings of fact in a hearing before a tribunal or court. The jury is the trier of fact in a jury trial. In a trial without a jury, the judge is the trier of fact as well as the decision maker with regard to matters of law.

TROVER. *n.* An action on the case, the remedy for a plaintiff who is deprived, by wrongful taking, detention or disposal, of goods. J.G. Fleming, *The Law of Torts*, 8th ed. (Sydney: Law Book, 1992) at 52 and 55.

TRU. *abbr.* Trueman's Equity Cases (N.B.), 1876-1903.

TRUE BILL. An indorsement made by a grand jury on a bill of indictment when after hearing the evidence they are satisfied that the accusation is probably true. *R. v. Chabot* (1980), 18 C.R. (3d) 258 at 264, [1980] 2 S.C.R. 985, 34 N.R. 361, 55 C.C.C. (2d) 385, 117 D.L.R. (3d) 527, the court per Dickson J.

TRUE CONDITION PRECEDENT. An external condition which the

obligation depends on to exist. G.H.L. Fridman, *The Law of Contract in Canada*, 2d ed. (Toronto: Carswell, 1986) at 415.

TRUE COPY. 1. "It has been said (per Kay J., Sharp v. McHenry, (1887) 38 Ch. D. 427), that a copy is true if it is true in all essential particulars, so that no one can be misled as to the effect of the instrument, but that if the true effect is mis-stated it is immaterial whether it is mis-stated in favour of one party or of the other." *Commercial Credit Co. v. Fulton Brothers*, [1923] 3 D.L.R. 611 at 618, [1923] A.C. 798 (Can. P.C.), the board per Lord Sumner. 2. A copy of a legal document exactly the same as the original with notations, court stamps, signatures of parties and the court registrar, insertions and corrections written in the copy within quotation marks.

TRUST. *n.* "... A trust arises ... whenever a person is compelled in equity to hold property over which he has control for the benefit of others (the beneficiaries) in such a way that the benefit of the property accrues not to the trustee, but to the beneficiaries." *Guerin v. R.* (1984), [1985] 1 C.N.L.R. 120 at 155, [1984] 2 S.C.R. 335, 36 R.P.R. 1, 20 E.T.R. 6, [1984] 6 W.W.R. 481, 59 B.C.L.R. 301, 13 D.L.R. (4th) 321, 55 N.R. 161, Dickson J. (Beetz, Chouinard and Lamer JJ. concurring). See ACCUMULATION ~; ACTIVE ~; BONDHOLDER'S ~; BREACH OF ~; CESTUI QUE ~; CHARITABLE ~; CONSTRUCTIVE ~; DECLARATION OF ~; DEEMED ~; DISCRETIONARY ~; EQUIPMENT ~; EXECUTED ~; EXECUTORY ~; EXPRESS ~; FROZEN ~; HOLDING ~; IMPERFECT ~; IMPLIED ~; INTER VIVOS ~; INVESTMENT ~; MORTGAGE ~; PUBLIC ~; RESULTING ~; SECRET ~; SIMPLE ~; TESTAMENTARY ~; UNIT ~; VARIATION OF ~; VOTING ~.

TRUST DEED. A separate document in favour of a trust company as trustee for the holders of the instruments which evidences an obligation, the usual way to issue a corporate obligation sold to the public, which may contain a specific charge or mortgage or a floating charge or both. H. Sutherland, D.B. Horsley & J.M. Edmiston, eds., *Fraser's Handbook on Canadian Company Law*, 7th ed. (Toronto: Carswell, 1985) at 310.

TRUSTEE. *n.* 1. Somone who holds property in trust. 2. Includes a liquidator, receiver, receiver-manager, trustee in bankruptcy, assignee, executor, administrator, sequestrator or any other person performing a function similar to that performed by any such person. 3. An authorized trustee under the Bankruptcy Act (Canada) appointed for the bankruptcy district or division in which the stock of the vendor, or some part of it, is located, or the vendor's business or trade, or some part of it, is carried on, at the time of the sale in bulk; a person who is appointed trustee; and a person named as trustee by the creditors of the vendor in their written consent to a sale in bulk. *Bulk Sales acts.* 4. A person who is declared by any Act to be a trustee or is, by the law of a province, a trustee, and, without restricting the generality of the foregoing, includes a trustee on an express trust created by deed, will or instrument in writing, or by parol. *Criminal Code*, R.S.C. 1985, c. C-46, s. 2. See JUDICIAL ~; OFFICIAL ~; PUBLIC ~.

TRUSTEE DE SON TORT. A person treated like a trustee even though not appointed as a trustee, who assumes responsibility to hold trust property for a beneficiary. D.M.W. Waters, *The Law of Trusts in Canada*, 2d ed. (Toronto: Carswell, 1984) at 399.

TRUSTEE IN BANKRUPTCY. The person in whom a bankrupt's property is vested in trust for creditors.

TRUST FOR SALE. Imposes an obligation on the trustee to sell when the testator or settlor transfers property to the trustee on trust to convert the assets into money, and to distribute or invest these proceeds as directed. D.M.W. Waters, *The Law of Trusts in Canada*, 2d ed. (Toronto: Carswell, 1984) at 887.

TRUST FUND. 1. Money or property held in trust. 2. Money paid to a contractor by an owner or to a subcontractor by a contractor for the benefit of workers and people who supplied material for a contract. D.N. Macklem & D.I. Bristow, *Construction, Builders' and Mechanics' Liens in Canada*, 6th ed. (Toronto: Carswell, 1990-) at 1-3.

TRUST INDENTURE. Any deed, indenture or other instrument, including any supplement or amendment thereto, made by a body corporate under which the body corporate issues or guarantees debt obligations and in which a person is appointed as trustee for the holders of the debt obligations issued or guaranteed thereunder.

TRUST POWER. Imposes an obligation on the donee to exercise the power. D.M.W. Waters, *The Law of Trusts in Canada*, 2d ed. (Toronto: Carswell, 1984) at 692.

T.T. *abbr.* Tribunal du Travail (Jurisprudence en droit du travail).

T.T. (QUÉ.). *abbr.* Tribunal du travail (Québec).

TURPIS CAUSA. [L.] A consideration so vile that no action can be founded on it. See EX TURPI CAUSA NON ORITUR ACTIO.

TWP. *abbr.* Township.

U

U.B.C. L. REV. *abbr.* University of British Columbia Law Review.

UBERRIMA FIDES. [L.] "... [A] longstanding tenet of insurance law which holds parties to an insurance contract to a standard of utmost good faith in their dealing. It places a heavy burden on those seeking insurance coverage to make full and complete disclosure of all relevant information when applying for a policy." *Coronation Insurance Co. v. Taku Air Transport Ltd.*, [1991] 3 S.C.R. 622 at 636, [1992] 1 W.W.R. 217, 61 B.C.L.R. (2d) 41, 4 C.C.L.I. (2d) 115, 85 D.L.R. (4th) 609, [1992] I.L.R. 1-2797, 131 N.R. 241, 6 B.C.A.C. 161, 13 W.A.C. 161, Cory J.

U.C. *abbr.* Upper Canada.

U.C. CH. *abbr.* Grant, Upper Canada Chambers Reports, 1846-1852.

U.C. CHAMB. *abbr.* Upper Canada Chambers Reports, 1846-1852.

U.C.C.P. *abbr.* Upper Canada Common Pleas Reports, 1850-1882.

U.C.E. & A. *abbr.* Upper Canada Error & Appeal Reports, 1846-1866.

U.C. JUR. *abbr.* Upper Canada Jurist, 1844.

U.C. JURIST. *abbr.* Upper Canada Jurist (1844-1848).

U.C.K.B. *abbr.* Upper Canada, King's Bench Reports (Old Series), 1831-1844.

U.C.L.J. *abbr.* Upper Canada Law Journal (1855-1864).

U.C.O.S. *abbr.* Upper Canada, King's Bench Reports (Old Series), 1831-1844.

U.C.Q.B. *abbr.* Upper Canada, Queen's Bench Reports, 1844-1882.

U.F.C. *abbr.* Unified Family Court.

U.K. *abbr.* United Kingdom.

ULTRA. *prep.* [L.] Beyond.

ULTRA VIRES. [L. beyond the powers] 1. Describes a statute judicially determined to be outside the powers conferred by the Constitution on the legislative body that enacted the statute; it is therefore invalid. P.W. Hogg, *Constitutional Law of Canada*, 3d ed. (Toronto: Carswell, 1992) at 119. 2. That a particular transaction is outside the capacity or power of a corporation. S.M. Beck *et al.*, *Cases and Materials on Partnerships and Canadian Business Corporations*, (Toronto: Carswell, 1983) at 192. 3. "... [I]s not a principle of the English common law and does not rest upon any theory as to the nature of corporations or as to the legal relationship subsisting between a corporation and its governing body ... It is a rule resting upon the interpretation of the legislative enactments through which the companies to which it applies derive their corporate existence and capacity." *Prevost v. Bedard* (1915), 24 D.L.R. 153 at 154, 51 S.C.R. 149, Duff J. 4. Describes an invalid enactment, order or decision made outside the jurisdiction of the body purporting to make it.

U.N. *abbr.* United Nations.

UNASCERTAINED GOODS. 1. Goods defined by referring to a genus. G.H.L. Fridman, *Sale of Goods in Canada*, 3d ed. (Toronto: Carswell, 1986) at 57. 2. Goods identified only by description. G.H.L. Fridman, *Sale of Goods in Canada*, 3d ed. (Toronto: Carswell, 1986) at 89.

U.N.B.L.J. *abbr.* University of New Brunswick Law Journal.

U.N.B. L. REV. *abbr.* University of New Brunswick Law Journal (Revue de droit de l'Université du Nouveau-Brunswick).

UNCERTAINTY. *n.* In interpreting a will, a general reason to consider some gift or provision void because it is impossible to ascertain what the testator's intention was.

UNCONSCIONABILITY. *n.* 1. "... [E]quity will grant relief where there is inequality combined with substantial unfairness, and that in its modern application poverty and ignorance combined with lack of independent advice on the part of the party seeking relief (plus, presumably, some evidence of unfairness) places an onus on the other party to show that the bargain was in fact fair. ..." *Smyth v. Szep* (1992), 8 C.C.L.I. (2d) 81 at 90, 63 B.C.L.R. (2d) 52, [1992] 2 W.W.R. 673, 10 B.C.A.C. 108, 21 W.A.C. 108 (C.A.), Taylor J.A. (Wood J.A. concurring). 2. "The test for setting aside an agreement on grounds of unconscionability was set out by McIntyre J.A. in Harry v. Kreutziger (1978), 9 B.C.L.R. 166 ... (C.A.) [at p. 173]: 'Where a claim is made that a bargain is unconscionable, it must be shown ... that there was inequality in the position of the parties due to the ignorance, need or distress of the weaker, which would leave him in the power of the stronger, coupled with proof of substantial unfairness in the bargain.' The essential idea of unconscionability is therefore that of fraud." *Ahone v. Holloway* (1988), 30 B.C.L.R. (2d) 368 at 374 (C.A.), the court per McLachlin J.A.

UNCONTESTED DIVORCE. A divorce proceeding in which a respondent does not file a counter-petition or answer.

UNDER LEASE. *var.* **UNDER-LEASE.** A lessee's grant to someone else (the under-lessee, undertenant, sub-lessee or sub-tenant) of part of the whole interest under the original lease which reserves a reversion to the lessee.

UNDER LESSEE. *var.* **UNDER-LESSEE.** Includes any person deriving title under or from a lessee or an under lessee. *Landlord and Tenant acts.*

UNDERTAKING. *n.* 1. An assurance. 2. Every kind of business that an association or company is authorized to carry on. 3. An enterprise or activity, or a proposal, plan or program in respect of an enterprise or activity. 4. An undertaking in Form 12 given to a justice or judge. *Criminal Code.* R.S.C. 1985, c. C-46, s. 493. 5. "... I adopt the definition of an undertaking proposed by Judge Lesage in ... Mode Amazone c. Comité conjoint de Montréal de l'Union internationale des ouvriers du vêtement pour dames, [1983] T.T. 227 at 231: '(Translation) The undertaking consists in an organization of resources that together suffice for the pursuit, in whole or in part, of specific activities. These resources may, according to the circumstances, be limited to legal, technical, physical, or abstract elements. Most often, particularly where there is no operation of the undertaking by a subcontractor, the undertaking may be said to be constituted when, because a sufficient number of those components that permit the specific activities to be conducted or carried out are present, one can conclude that the very foundations of the undertaking exist: in other words, when the undertaking may be described as a going concern. In [Barnes Security Service Ltd. c. A.I.M., Local 2235, [1972] T.T. 1], Judge René Beaudry, as he then was, expressed exactly the same idea when he stated that the undertaking consists of "everything used to implement the employer's ideas." ' " *Union des employés de service, local 298 v.*

Bibeault (1988), (*sub nom. Syndicat national des employés de la Commission scolaire régionale de l'Outaouais v. U.E.S.*) 35 Admin. L.R. 153 at 209, 95 N.R. 161, [1988] 2 S.C.R. 1048, the court per Beetz J. 6. "... [I]s not a physical thing, but is an arrangement under which ... physical things are used." *Regulation & Control of Radio Communication in Canada, Re*, [1932] A.C. 304 at 315, [1932] 1 W.W.R. 563, 39 C.R.C. 49, [1932] 2 D.L.R. 81 (P.C.), Viscount Dunedin for their Lordships. See FEDERAL WORK, ~ OR BUSINESS.

UNDERWRITER. *n.* 1. A person who, (a) as principal, agrees to purchase a security for the purpose of distribution; (b) as agent, offers for sale or sells a security in connection with a distribution; or (c) participates directly or indirectly in a distribution described in paragraph (a) or (b), but does not include (d) a person whose interest in the transaction is limited to receiving the usual and customary distributor's or seller's commission payable by an underwriter or issuer; (e) a mutual fund that accepts its securities for surrender and resells them; (f) a corporation that purchases shares of its own issue and resells them; or (g) a bank with respect to securities described in this Act and to prescribed banking transactions. *Securities acts.* 2. A person who, as principal, agrees to purchase securities of a bank with a view to distribution thereof, or who, as agent for a bank or another person, offers for sale or sells securities of the bank in connection with a distribution of such securities, and includes a person who participates directly or indirectly in such a distribution other than a person whose interest in the transaction is limited to receiving a distributor's or seller's commission payable by an underwriter. *Bank Act*, R.S.C. 1985, c. G-1, s. 145.

UNDERWRITING. *n.* With respect to a security, means the primary or secondary distribution of the security, in respect of which distribution (a) a prospectus is required to be filed, accepted or otherwise approved under or pursuant to a law enacted in Canada for the supervision or regulation of trade in securities; or (b) a prospectus would be required to be filed, accepted or otherwise approved but for an express exemption contained in or given pursuant to a law mentioned in paragraph (a). *Competition Act*, R.S.C. 1985, c. C-34, s. 5(2).

UNDISCLOSED PRINCIPAL. Neither the principal's identity nor the fact that the agent is acting on someone else's behalf, is revealed to a third party with whom the agent contracts. G.H.L. Fridman, *The Law of Agency*, 6th ed. (London: Butterworths, 1990) at 93.

UNDIVIDED INTEREST. Refers to the interest of a tenant in common in property. The percentage share of a tenant in common in property. The share is not divided from the shares of the other tenants in common. The interest is fixed for all time and is not affected by the death of one of the tenants in common, as is the case with the interest of a joint tenant in property. R. Megarry & M.P. Thompson, *Megarry's Manual of Real Property*, 7th ed. (London: Sweet & Maxwell, 1993) at 284.

UNDUE INFLUENCE. 1. "... '[U]nconscientious use by one person of power possessed by him over another in order to induce the other to' do something." *Berdette v. Berdette* (1991), 33 R.F.L. (3d) 113 at 125, 41 E.T.R. 126, 3 O.R. (3d) 513, 81 D.L.R. (4th) 194, 47 O.A.C. 345 (C.A.), the court per Galligan J.A. 2. "... [T]he ability of one person to dominate the will of another, whether through manipulation, coercion, or outright but subtle abuse of power ... To dominate the will of another simply means to exercise a persuasive influence over him or her. The ability to exercise such influence may arise from a relationship of trust or confidence, but it may arise from other relationships as well. The point is that there is nothing per se reprehensible about persons in a relationship of trust or confidence exerting influence, even undue influence, over their beneficiaries. It depends on their motivation and the objective they seek to achieve thereby." *Goodman Estate v. Geffen* (1991), 42 E.T.R. 97 at 119, [1991] 5 W.W.R. 389, 80 Alta. L.R. (2d) 293, 125 A.R. 81, 14 W.A.C. 81, 81 D.L.R. (4th) 211, [1991] 2 S.C.R. 353, Wilson J. (Cory J. concurring).

UNEMPLOYMENT INSURANCE. A contributory, federal social insurance program to provide earnings-related benefits to anyone who is off work or unable to accept or look for work because of injury or other cause. K.D. Cooper-Stephenson & I.B. Saunders, *Personal Injury Damages in Canada* (Toronto: Carswell, 1981) at 2.

UNENFORCEABLE. *adj.* Describes a contract which, although it is valid, cannot be sued upon, for example because the Statute of Frauds requires written evidence.

U.N.E.S.C.O. *abbr.* United Nations Educational, Scientific and Cultural Organisation.

UNEXECUTED. *adj.* Describes one party's promise and side of a contract when that party's undertaking is not yet completed. G.H.L. Fridman, *The Law of Contract in Canada*, 2d ed. (Toronto: Carswell, 1986) at 2.

UNFIT TO STAND TRIAL. Unable on account of mental disorder to conduct a defence at any stage of the proceedings before a verdict is rendered or to instruct counsel to do so, and, in particular, unable on account of mental disorder to (a) understand the nature or object of the proceedings, (b) understand the possible consequences of the proceedings, or (c) communicate with counsel. *Criminal Code*, S.C. 1991, c. 43, s. 1.

UNIF. FAM. CT. *abbr.* Unified Family Court.

UNIF. L. CONF. PROC. *abbr.* Uniform Law Conference of Canada, Proceedings.

UNILATERAL. *adj.* Having one side.

UNILATERAL CONTRACT. 1. Where a promisor agrees to do or not to do something if the promisee does or does not do something, but the promisee does not actually agree to do or not to do that thing. G.H.L. Fridman, *The Law of Contract in Canada*, 2d ed. (Toronto: Carswell, 1986) at 11. 2. An agreement between someone who auctions goods with no reserve and the highest bidder. G.H.L. Fridman, *Sale of Goods in Canada*, 3d ed. (Toronto: Carswell, 1986) at 460.

UNILATERAL MISTAKE. "To succeed on a plea of unilateral mistake the defendant must establish: (1) that a mistake occurred; (2) that there was fraud or the equivalent of fraud on the plantiff's part in that she knew or must be taken to have known when the agreement was executed that the defendant misunderstood its significance and that she did nothing to enlighten the defendant ..." *Alampi v. Swartz*, [1964] 1 O.R. 488 at 494, 43 D.L.R. (2d) 11 (C.A.), the court per McGillivray J.A.

UNINCORPORATED ASSOCIATION. "... [H]as no legal existence, apart from its members, and is not a legal entity capable of suing or being sued." *Tel-Ad Advisors Ontario Ltd. v. Tele-Direct (Publications) Inc.* (1986), 8 C.P.C. (2d) 217 at 218 (Ont. H.C.), Griffiths J.

UNION. *n.* 1. A trade union. 2. "... [A]n unincorporated group or association of workmen who have banded together to promote certain objectives for their mutual benefit and advantage ..." *Astgen v. Smith*, [1970] 1 O.R. 129 at 134, 7 D.L.R. (3d) 657 (C.A.), Evans J.A. 3. Any organization of employees, or any branch or local thereof, the purposes of which include the regulation of relations between employers and employees. See CERTIFIED ~; COMMON LAW ~; COMPANY-DOMINATED ~; COMPANY ~; CRAFT ~; CREDIT ~; CUSTOMS ~; LABOUR ~; TRADE ~.

UNION RIGHTS. Specific provisions which a union frequently attempts to include in the terms of an agreement and which benefit the union itself, its officers or officials. The overriding purpose of such clauses is usually to insure that the union may fully discharge its statutory and contractual function to supervise the terms of the agreement. D.J.M. Brown & D.M. Beatty, *Canadian Labour Arbitration*, 3d ed. (Aurora: Canada Law Book, 1988-) at 9-1.

UNION SECURITY. Provisions like voluntary check-off of union dues, union and closed shops which insure that any employees who are the beneficiaries of the agreement share any costs associated with the union's activities. D.J.M. Brown & D.M. Beatty, *Canadian Labour Arbitration*, 3d ed. (Aurora: Canada Law Book, 1988-) at 9-2.

UNITARY STATE. A nation in which supreme authority is in one centre.

UNIT TRUST. A trust under which the interest of each beneficiary is described by reference to units of the trust.

UNITY OF INTEREST. Said of a joint tenant who has no greater interest in a property than any other joint tenant.

UNITY OF POSSESSION. Said of joint tenants who have undivided possession.

UNITY OF SEISIN. A situation in which someone seised of land which is subject to a profit à prendre, easement or similar right also becomes seised of the land to which that profit or right is annexed.

UNITY OF TIME. Said of joint tenants whose interests must arise at the same time.

UNITY OF TITLE. Said of joint tenants who hold their property by one and the same title.

UNJUST ENRICHMENT. 1. "The determination that the enrichment is 'unjust' does not refer to abstract notions of morality and justice, but flows directly from the finding that there was a breach of a legally recognized duty for which the Courts will grant relief." *International Corona Resources Ltd. v.*

Lac Minerals Ltd. (1989), 44 B.L.R. 1 at 45, [1989] 2 S.C.R. 574, 26 C.P.R. (3d) 97, 69 O.R. (2d) 287, 61 D.L.R. (4th) 14, 6 R.P.R. (2d) 1, 25 E.T.R. 1, 101 N.R. 239, 36 O.A.C. 57, La Forest J. (Wilson and Lamer JJ. concurring). 2. ". . . [T]hree requirements that must be satisfied before it can be said that an unjust enrichment exists. These include: (a) an enrichment; (b) a corresponding deprivation; and (c) the absence of any juristic reason for the enrichment." *Sorochan v. Sorochan* (1986), 23 E.T.R. 143 at 149, 2 R.F.L. (3d) 225, 46 Alta. L.R. (2d) 97, [1986] 5 W.W.R. 289, 29 D.L.R. (4th) 1, 69 N.R. 81, [1986] 2 S.C.R. 38, [1986] R.D.I. 448, [1986] R.D.F. 501, 74 A.R. 67, the court per Dickson C.J.C. 3.

UNLAWFUL. *adj.* 1. Illegal. 2. ". . . There appear to be three categories of actions or events which are contrary to the law and which sometimes fall into the description 'unlawful' or 'illegal'. These are: (a) offences against statutes prohibiting defined conduct; (b) actions which are without legal consequence in the sense of creating enforceable rights, such as gaming contracts; and (c) actions taken by statutory bodies outside the limits of authority granted or established in the statute. . . ." *Nepean Hydro-Electric Commission v. Ontario Hydro*, [1982] 1 S.C.R. 347 at 406-7, 18 B.L.R. 215, 132 D.L.R. (3d) 193, 41 N.R. 1, Estey J. (Martland and Lamer JJ. concurring). See ILLEGAL.

UNLAWFUL ACT. ". . . [T]he concept of an unlawful act as it is used in that section [s. 269 of the Criminal Code, R.S.C. 1985, c. C-46] includes only federal and provincial offences. Excluded from this general category of offences are any offences which are based on absolute liabilty and which have constitutionally insufficient mental elements on their own. Additionally, the term 'unlawfully' . . . requires an act which is at least objectively dangerous." *R. v. DeSousa* (1992), 15 C.R. (4th) 66 at 81, 142 N.R. 1, 9 O.R. (3d) 544n, 76 C.C.C.(3d) 124, 95 D.L.R. (4th) 595, 56 O.A.C. 109, [1992] 2 S.C.R. 944, 11 C.R.R. (2d) 193, the court per Sopinka J.

UNLAWFUL ASSEMBLY. An assembly of three or more persons who, with intent to carry out any common purpose, assemble in such a manner or so conduct themselves when they are assembled as to cause persons in the neighbourhood of the assembly to fear, on reasonable grounds that they (a) will disturb the peace tumultuously; or (b) will by that assembly needlessly and without reasonable cause provoke other persons to disturb the peace tumultuously. *Criminal Code*, R.S.C. 1985, c. C-46, s. 63(1).

UNLAWFUL INTERFERENCE WITH CONTRACTUAL RELATIONS. "The tort of unlawful interference with contractual relations is established where the defendant, with knowledge of a contract and with intent to prevent or hinder its performance, (1) persuades, induces or procures a party to the contract not to perform its obligations, or (2) commits some act, wrongful, in itself, to prevent performance of the contract . . ." *Niedner Ltd. v. Lloyds Bank of Canada* (1990), 72 D.L.R. (4th) 147 at 153, 77 O.R. (2d) 574, 38 E.T.R. 306 (Ont. H.C.), Ewaschuk J.

UNLAWFULLY. *adv.* ". . . [W]ithout legal authority or justification. . . ." *R. v. Kapij* (1905), 1 W.L.R. 130 at 136, 15 Man. R. 110, 9 C.C.C. 186 (C.A.), the court per Perdue J.A.

UNLIQUIDATED. *adj.* Not ascertained.

UNLIQUIDATED DAMAGES. Damages whose amount depends on circumstances, and on the parties' conduct or is fixed by an estimate or opinion.

UNPAID SELLER'S LIEN. A possessory lien which entitles the creditor to keep the debtor's goods until the debt is paid. G.H.L. Fridman, *Sale of Goods in Canada*, 3d ed. (Toronto: Carswell, 1986) at 314.

UNREASONABLE. See PATENTLY ~; REASONABLE.

UNREASONABLE SEARCH. Prima facie, an illegal search. P.K. McWilliams, *Canadian Criminal Evidence*, 3d ed. (Aurora: Canada Law Book, 1988) at 4-24. See REASONABLE SEARCH.

UNSECURED CREDITOR. Any creditor of a company who is not a secured creditor.

UNUSUAL. See CRUEL AND ~ PUNISHMENT.

USAGE. *n.* 1. ". . . [A] course of conduct which is recognized as being normal in various types of occupations and contractual relationships. . . ." *Gainers Ltd. v. United Packinghouse, Food & Allied Workers, Local 319* (1964), 47 W.W.R. 544 at 552, 64 C.L.L.C. 14,030 (Alta. T.D.), Riley J. 2. A practice which a government ordinarily follows, though it is not obligatory. Such a practice may become a convention. P.W. Hogg, *Constitutional Law of Canada*, 3d ed. (Toronto: Carswell, 1992) at 21. See CONVENTION.

USE. *v.* 1. ". . . [U]tilization or employment of, with some aim or purpose. . . ." *Andison Estate, Re* (1986), 44 Man. R. (2d) 135 at 137 (Q.B.), Kennedy J. 2. ". . . [C]onnotation of the actual carrying into action, operation or effect . . ." *R. v. Chang* (1989), 50 C.C.C. (3d) 413 at 422 (B.C. C.A.), Carrothers J.A. 3. ". . . '[U]se' of property involves control or personal possession of the property by the insured and/or the insured putting the property to his own service. . . ." *Kenting Drilling Ltd. v. General Accident Assurance Co. of Canada* (1979), [1980] I.L.R. 1-1168 at 542, [1979] 5 W.W.R. 68, 26 A.R. 90, 102 D.L.R. (3d) 99 (T.D.), Moshansky J. 4. ". . . [T]he working, manipulation, operation, handling or employment of the vehicle, not just merely making use of it by riding in it. . . ." *Watts v. Centennial Insurance Co.* (1967), 62 W.W.R. 175 at 177, [1969] I.L.R. 1-220, 65 D.L.R. (2d) 529 (B.C. S.C.), Wilson C.J.S.C.

USE. *n.* See CESTUI QUE ~; COMMERCIAL ~; CONFORMING ~; NON-CONFORMING ~; RESULTING ~; SHIFTING ~; SPRINGING ~.

USE AND OCCUPATION. A person may claim for use and occupation when that person uses and occupies another's land with permission but without a lease or leasing agreement at a set rent.

USER. *n.* 1. A person who uses a thing. 2. Enjoyment or use, not the person who uses. R. Megarry & H.W.R. Wade, *The Law of Real Property*, 5th ed. (London: Stevens, 1984) at cxxviii.

USUAL COVENANT. One of the covenants ordinarily inserted in a deed.

USUAL OR CUSTOMARY AUTHORITY. The authority which an agent in that particular business, trade, profession or place would customarily or normally possess unless the principal expressly said something to contradict it. G.H.L. Fridman, *The Law of Agency*, 6th ed. (London: Butterworths, 1990) at 55.

USUFRUCT. *n.* The right to reap the fruits of something belonging to another, without wasting or destroying the subject over which one has that right.

USUFRUCTUARY. *n.* The person who enjoys a usufruct.

USURY. *n.* "In ancient times the lending of money at interest was described as the practice of usury. Today, usury is generally thought of as lending money at an excessive rate of interest." *Pioneer Envelopes Ltd. v. British Columbia (Minister of Finance)* (1980), 18 C.P.C. 119 at 121, 21 B.C.L.R. 175 (S.C.), Bouck J.

U.T. FAC. L. REV. *abbr.* University of Toronto Faculty of Law Review.

U.T.L.J. *abbr.* University of Toronto Law Journal.

U. TORONTO FACULTY L. REV. *abbr.* University of Toronto Faculty of Law Review.

U. TORONTO L.J. *abbr.* University of Toronto Law Journal.

UTTER. *v.* Includes sell, pay, tender and put off. *Criminal Code*, R.S.C. 1985, c. C-46, s. 448.

UTTERING FORGED PASSPORT. While in or out of Canada, (a) forges a passport; or (b) knowing that a passport is forged (i) uses, deals with or acts upon it; or (ii) causes or attempts to cause any person to use, deal with, or act upon it, as if the passport were genuine. *Criminal Code*, R.S.C. 1985, c. C-46, s. 57(1).

U.W.O. L. REV. *abbr.* University of Western Ontario Law Review.

V

V. *abbr.* 1. Versus. 2. Volume. 3. Victoria.

VACANT. *adj.* 1. "... [A]pplies to the absence of inanimate objects in a premises ..." *Mohammed v. Canadian Northern Shield Insurance Co.* (1992), 10 C.C.L.I. (2d) 118 at 124, [1992] B.C.W.L.D. 1776 (S.C.), Lamperson J. 2. "[In a fire insurance policy applies to] ... inanimate objects ..." *Miller v. Portage la Prairie Mutual Insurance Co.*, [1936] 2 D.L.R. 787 at 791, [1936] 2 W.W.R. 104, 3 I.L.R. 377 (Sask. C.A.), the court per Gordon J.A.

VACANTIA BONA. See BONA VACANTIA.

VACANT POSSESSION. "... [A] house free of household furniture and effects as well as animate occupancy." *Burke v. Campbell* (1978), 87 D.L.R. (3d) 427 at 432, 20 O.R. (2d) 300, [1979] I.L.R. 1-1148 (H.C.), Craig J.

VACATE. *v.* 1. To cancel; to make ineffective. 2. "[Used in Criminal Code, R.S.C. 1970, c. C-34] ... to indicate what has occurred is terminated but without impairing what has previously occurred." *Purves v. Canada (Attorney General)* (1990), 54 C.C.C. (3d) 355 at 364 (B.C. C.A.), the court per Legg J.A.

VAGRANCY. *n.* Every one commits vagrancy who (a) supports himself in whole or in part by gaming or crime and has no lawful profession or calling by which to maintain himself; or (b) having at any time been convicted of an offence under section 151, 152 or 153, subsection 160(3) or 173(2) or section 271, 272 or 273 or of an offence under a provision referred to in paragraph (b) of the definition "serious personal injury offence" in section 687 of the Criminal Code, chapter C-34 of the Revised Statutes of Canada, 1970, as it read before January 4, 1983, is found loitering or wandering in or near a school ground, playground, public park or bathing area. *Criminal Code*, R.S.C. 1985, c. C-46, s. 179(1).

VAGUENESS. *n.* "... [A] law will be found unconstitutionally vague if it so lacks in precision as not to give sufficient guidance for legal debate. This statement of the doctrine best conforms to the dictates of the rule of law in the modern state, and it reflects the prevailing argumentative, adversarial framework for the administration of justice." *R. v. Pharmaceutical Society (Nova Scotia)* (1992), (sub nom. *R. v. Nova Scotia Pharmaceutical Society*) 43 C.P.R. (3d) 1 at 26, 15 C.R. (4th) 1, 93 D.L.R. (4th) 36, 74 C.C.C. (3d) 289, 10 C.R.R. (2d) 34, [1992] 2 S.C.R. 606, 139 N.R. 241, 114 N.S.R. (2d) 91, 313 A.P.R. 91, the court per Gonthier J.

VALID. *adj.* 1. Having force legally. 2. Issued in accordance with the applicable law and the articles of the issuer or validated. *Business Corporations acts.*

VALIDATE. *v.* To render in force for a prescribed period of time.

VALUABLE CONSIDERATION. 1. Includes: (i) any consideration sufficient to support a simple contract; (ii) an antecedent debt or liability. *Assignment of Book Debts acts.* 2. "... [M]ay consist either in some right, interest, profit, or benefit accruing to the one party, or some forbearance, detriment, loss, or responsibility, given, suffered, or undertaken by the other ..." *Currie v. Misa* (1875), L.R. 10 Ex. 153 at 162 (U.K.), the court per Lusk J. See ADEQUATE ~; FULL AND ~; GOOD CONSIDERATION.

VALUATION. *n.* 1. "... [A]n expression of an opinion as to value." *Sanwa Bank California v. Quebec, North Shore & Labrador Railway* (1988), 48 D.L.R. (4th) 360 at 364, 69 Nfld. & P.E.I.R. 220, 211 A.P.R. 220 (Nfld. T.D.), Russell J. 2. The determination of the value of property for taxation purposes.

VALUE. *n.* 1. "... [I]n the case of Montreal Island Power Co. v. Laval des Rapides, [1936] 1 D.L.R. 621, [1935] S.C.R. 304. At pp. 621-2 D.L.R., p. 305 S.C.R. [Duff C.J.C.] quotes from a judgment of Lord MacLaren in Lord Advocate v. Earl of Home (1891), 28 Sc. L.R. 289 at p. 293: '... [W]hen it occurs in a contract ... means exchangeable value – the price which the subject will bring when exposed to the test of competition.' " Continuing, Duff C.J.C. says: 'When used for the purpose of defining the valuation of property for taxation purposes, the Courts have, in this country, and, generally speaking, on this continent, accepted this view of the term "value".' *Withycombe Estate, Re,* [1945] 2 D.L.R. 274 at 286, (sub nom. A.G. of Alta. v. Royal Trust Co.) [1945] S.C.R. 267, Hudson J. (Taschereau J. concurring). 2. Any consideration sufficient to support a simple contract. *Personal Property Security acts.* 3. Valuable consideration. *Bills of Exchange Act,* R.S.C. 1985, c. B-4, s. 2. See ACTUAL ~; AMORTIZED ~; ASSESSED ~; BOOK ~; COMMUTED ~; CURRENT ~ ACCOUNTING; FACE ~; FAIR ~; HOLDER FOR ~; MARKET ~; NET ~; PAR ~; PROBATIVE ~; REVERSIONARY ~.

VALUED POLICY. The policy of insurance is based on an agreement as to the value of the item insured. In the event of total loss, the insured can recover the total value and in the event of partial loss, a proportion of the agreed value. R. Colinvaux, *The Law of Insurance,* 5th ed. (London: Sweet & Maxwell, 1984) at 9.

VANDALISM. *n.* "... There must be a wrongful intention accompanying the destruction of property to warrant the term 'vandalism'...." *Reliable Distributors Ltd. v. Royal Insurance Co. of Canada* (1986), 5 B.C.L.R. (2d) 367 at 370, [1986] 6 W.W.R. 1, 18 C.C.L.I. 267, 30 D.L.R. (4th) 426, [1987] I.L.R. 1-2123 (C.A.), Seaton J.A.

VARIANCE. *n.* Permission to contravene a by-law to permit development of certain land which does not meet criteria prescribed in the by-law. I.M. Rogers, *The Law of Canadian Municipal Corporations,* 2d ed. (Toronto: Carswell, 1971) at 832.11. See MINOR ~.

VARIATION. *n.* An express or implied agreement by which parties agree on a new contract or a new contract term which is mutually convenient and beneficial. G.H.L. Fridman, *Sale of Goods in Canada,* 3d ed. (Toronto: Carswell, 1986) at 272.

VARIATION OF TRUST. The power of the court to change the terms of a trust or the powers of the trustees on behalf of a person entitled or who may become entitled to an interest under the trust. See, for example, *Variation of Trusts Act,* R.S.O. 1990, c. V.1.

V.C. *abbr.* Vice-chancellor.

VEHICLE. *n.* 1. "... [I]n its original sense conveys the meaning of a structure on wheels for carrying persons or goods. We have generally distinguished carriage from haulage, and mechanical units whose chief function is to haul other units, to do other kinds of work than carrying, are not usually looked upon as vehicles. But that meaning has ... been weakened by the multiplied forms in which wheeled bodies have appeared with the common features of self-propulsion by motor . . ." *Bennett & White (Calgary) Ltd. v. Sugar City (Municipality)*, [1950] S.C.R. 450 at 463, [1950] C.T.C. 410, [1950] 3 D.L.R. 81, Rand J. (Taschereau, Estey and Locke JJ. concurring). 2. Any conveyance that may be used for transportation by sea, land or air. See ARTICULATED ~; CANADIAN ~; CAR POOL ~; COMMERCIAL ~; MOTOR ~.

VENDEE. *n.* The person to whom one sells something.

VENDING. *n.* ". . . [S]elling . . ." *Domco Industries Ltd. v. Mannington Mills Inc.* (1990), 29 C.P.R. (3d) 481 at 490, 107 N.R. 198 (Fed. C.A.), the court per Iacobucci C.J.

VENDOR. *n.* A person who sells something.

VENDOR'S LIEN. 1. When a vendor sells property on credit, the vendor may be entitled to a lien on it to secure an obligation from the purchaser. B.J. Reiter, B.N. McLellan & P.M. Perell, *Real Estate Law*, 4th ed. (Toronto: Emond Montgomery, 1992) at 781. 2. ". . . [C]an only arise on the sale of land, or of an equitable interest in land, and the lien may exist in favour of an equitable owner. . . ." *Horn v. Sanford*, [1929] 3 D.L.R. 130 at 133, [1929] 2 W.W.R. 33, 23 Sask. L.R. 509 (C.A.), the court per Haultain C.J.S.

VENDOR TAKE-BACK. A vendor lends the purchaser part of the purchase price in exchange for a mortgage on the property. B.J. Reiter, B.N. McLellan & P.M. Perell, *Real Estate Law*, 4th ed. (Toronto: Emond Montgomery, 1992) at 832.

VENEREAL DISEASE. 1. Syphilis, gonorrhea or soft chancre. *Criminal Code*, R.S.C. 1985, c. C-46, s. 289(4). 2. Includes syphilis, gonorrhea, chancroid, granuloma inguinale and lymphogranuloma venereum.

VENUE. *n.* 1. ". . . [T]he place where the charges are laid and the place where the trial takes place: . . ." *R. v. Gagne* (1990), 59 C.C.C. (3d) 282 at 286, [1990] R.J.Q. 2165 (C.A.), Bernier J.A. 2. ". . . [T]he place where the crime is charged to have been committed. . . ." *Smitheman, Ex parte* (1904), 35 S.C.R. 490 at 493, 9 C.C.C. 17, the court per Killam J. 3. ". . . [O]riginally indicated the locality of the crime only, has come to indicate with equal propriety, and is more often used to signify, the locality of the trial: as when we speak of the change of venue, which cannot possibly mean a change of the locality of the crime." *R. v. Malott* (1886), 1 B.C.R. (Pt. II) 212 at 215 (C.A.), Begbie C.J.A.

VERDICT. *n.* 1. ". . . [T]he finding of a jury . . ." *R. v. Murray* (1912), 8 D.L.R. 208 at 210, 27 O.L.R. 382, 4 O.W.N. 368, 23 O.W.R. 492, 20 C.C.C. 197 (C.A.), Maclaren J.A. (Garrow, Meredith and Magee JJ.A. and Lennox J. concurring). 2. Includes the finding of a jury and the decision of a judge in an action. 3. In the case of an action being tried by a judge without a jury includes judgment. See GENERAL ~; PERVERSE ~.

VERSUS. *prep.* [L.] Against.

VEST. *v.* 1. With respect to a right or estate, to rest in some person. 2. Of a pension, to obtain or become entitled to an unalterable right to either transfer or withdraw that lump sum to another pension plan or R.R.S.P. or to receive, in the future, a deferred life annuity. A. Bissett-Johnson & W.M. Holland, eds., *Matrimonial Property Law in Canada* (Toronto: Carswell, 1980) at V-91.

VESTED. *adj.* ". . . [A] future estate or interest is vested when there is a person who has an immediate right to that interest upon the cessation of the present or previous interest. . . ." *Re Legh's Resettlement Trusts; Pub. Trustee v. Legh*, [1938] Ch. 39 at 52 (U.K. C.A.), MacKinnon L.J.

VESTED IN INTEREST. With respect to an existing fixed right of future enjoyment.

VESTED IN POSSESSION. With respect to a right of present enjoyment which actually exists.

VESTED REMAINDER. An expectant interest which is limited or transmitted to the one who is able to receive it.

VESTED RIGHT. 1. "... [O]ne which exists and produces effects. That does not include a right which could have been exercised but was not, and which is no longer available under the law...." *Quebec (Expropriation Tribunal) v. Quebec (Attorney General)* (1986), 35 L.C.R. 1 at 8, [1986] 1 S.C.R. 732, 66 N.R. 380, the court per Chouinard J. 2. A right which is not contingent or may not be defeated by a condition precedent.

VESTING. *adj.* "... [I]n relation to the rule against perpetuities has a special meaning as three conditions must be satisfied before an interest can be said to be vested: (1) the beneficiaries must be ascertained; (2) the interests they take must be determined; and (3) any conditions attached to the interests must be satsified...." *Ogilvy, Re,* [1966] 2 O.R. 755 at 763, 58 D.L.R. (2d) 385 (H.C.), Lieff J.

VESTING ORDER. A court order to give a person an interest in real or personal property which the court has authority to dispose of, encumber or convey.

VETO. *n.* 1. A prohibition; the right to forbid. 2. "... '[D]isallowance' ... [refers] to the provisions of secs. 55 and 56 [of the Constitution Act 1867] as applied to a province." *Reference re Initiative & Referendum Act (Manitoba)* (1916), 32 D.L.R. 148 at 170, 1 W.W.R. 1012, 27 Man. R. 1, (C.A.), Perdue J.A.

VEXATIOUS ACTION. "An action may be vexatious if it is obvious that it cannot succeed: ... or if no reasonable person can possibly expect to obtain relief in it: ... or if the Court has no power to grant the relief sought: ... or if the applicant has no status to pursue the remedy, or no proper authority to do so: ... or if the same relief might be sought in a subsisting action: ... or if the same purpose might have been effected in a previous action: ... In some cases the Courts have considered the lack of bona fides in classifying an action as vexatious, as where the plaintiff had no cause of action at all: ... A legal proceeding may be vexatious even though there were reasonable grounds for its institution if, for instance, the plaintiff is asking for relief in a way which necessarily involves injustice." *Foy v. Foy (No. 2)* (1979), 12 C.P.C. 188 at 197, 26 O.R. (2d) 220, 102 D.L.R. (3d) 342 (C.A.), Howland C.J.O. (Brooke J.A. concurring).

VEXATIOUS PROCEEDING. A proceeding in which the party bringing it wishes only to embarass or annoy the other party.

VICARIOUS LIABILITY. 1. Responsibility in law for the misconduct of another person. J.G. Fleming, *The Law of Torts,* 8th ed. (Sydney: Law Book, 1992) at 366. 2. "In the criminal law, a natural person is responsible only for those crimes in which he is the primary actor either actually or by express or implied authorization. There is no vicarious liability in the pure sense in the case of the natural person. That is to say that the doctrine of respondeat superior is unknown in the criminal law where the defendant is an individual.... where the defendant is corporate the common law has become pragmatic, as we have seen, and a modified and limited 'vicarious liability' through the identification doctrine has emerged...." *R. v. McNamara (No. 1),* (sub nom. *R. v. Canadian Dredge & Dock Co.*) [1985] 1 S.C.R. 662 at 692, 45 C.R. (3d) 289, 9 O.A.C. 321, 19 C.C.C. (3d) 1, 19 D.L.R. (4th) 314, 59 N.R. 241, the court per Estey J.

VICARIOUS RESPONSIBILITY. The automatic responsibility of one person for another's wrongdoing through prior relationship only, irrespective of the first person's fault or deed. It is clear common law doctrine in the law of torts that a master can be vicariously liable for a tort committed by a "servant" who acts in the course and scope of employment. D. Stuart, *Canadian Criminal Law: A Treatise,* 2d ed. (Toronto: Carswell, 1987) at 522.

VICE CHANCELLOR. *n.* The deputy chief judge of a court of chancery.

VICE VERSA. Conversely.

VICINAGE. *n.* Neighbourhood; places next to one another.

VICTIM IMPACT STATEMENT. In determining sentence or possible discharge of an offender under the Criminal Code, the court may consider a statement of a victim of the offence describing the harm done to, or loss suffered by, the victim arising from the commission of the offence. *Criminal Code*, R.S.C. 1985, c. C-46, s. 735.

VIDE. *v.* [L.] See.

VIDE ANTE. [L.] See an earlier passage in the text.

VIDE INFRA. [L.] See a later passage in the text.

VIDELICET. *adv.* [L.] Namely; that is to say.

VIDE POST. [L.] See a later passage in the text.

VIDE SUPRA. [L.] See an earlier passage in the text.

VI ET ARMIS. [L.] By force and arms.

VIEW. *n.* A jury's inspection of any controversial thing, place where a crime was committed or person which a judge may order in the interest of justice at any time between when the jury is sworn and when they give their verdict. P.K. McWilliams, *Canadian Criminal Evidence*, 3d ed. (Aurora: Canada Law Book, 1988) at 7-7.

VIGILANT. See EQUITY AIDS THE ~ AND NOT THE INDOLENT.

VINDICTIVE DAMAGES. Damages based on punishing the defendant, beyond compensating the plaintiff.

VIOLENCE. *n.* ". . . [C]onnotes actual or threatened physical interference with the activities of others." *R. v. Keegstra* (1990), 1 C.R. (4th) 129 at 236, 77 Alta. L.R. (2d) 193, [1991] 2 W.W.R. 1, 61 C.C.C. (3d) 1, 117 N.R. 1, 114 A.R. 81, 3 C.R.R. (2d) 193, [1990] 3 S.C.R. 697, McLachlin J. (dissenting) (Sopinka J. concurring).

VISITOR. *n.* 1. (i) An entrant as of right; (ii) a person who is lawfully present on premises by virtue of an express or implied term of a contract; (iii) any other person whose presence on premises is lawful; or (iv) a person whose presence on premises becomes unlawful after his entry on those premises and who is taking reasonable steps to leave those premises. *Occupiers' Liability Act*, R.S.A. 1980, c. O-3, s. 1. 2. A person who is lawfully in Canada, or seeks to come into Canada, for a temporary purpose, other than a person who is (a) a Canadian citizen; (b) a permanent resident; (c) a person in possession of a permit; or (d) an immigrant authorized to come into Canada pursuant to paragraph 14(2)(b), 23(1)(b) or 32(3)(b). *Immigration Act*, R.S.C. 1985, c. I-2, s. 2. 3. An inspector for an eleemosynary, ecclesiastical or other corporation or institution such as a university.

VIS MAJOR. The operation of natural forces and the malicious acts of strangers. J.G. Fleming, *The Law of Torts*, 8th ed. (Sydney: Law Book, 1992) at 345. See ACT OF GOD.

VITIATE. *v.* To render void.

VIVA VOCE. [L.] When describing the examination of witnesses, means orally.

VIZ. *abbr.* Videlicet.

VOID. *adj.* ". . . [L]acking validity and so without legal force." *British Columbia (Minister of Finance) v. Woodward Estate*, [1971] D.T.C. 341 at 348, [1971] 3 W.W.R. 645, 21 D.L.R. (3d) 681 (B.C. C.A.), Tysoe J.A.

VOIDABLE. *adj.* ". . . [D]oes not necessarily mean 'valid until rescinded.' It is sometimes used to mean 'invalid until validated'; . . ." *American-Abell Engine & Thresher Co. v. McMillan* (1909), 42 S.C.R. 377 at 396, Duff J.

VOIDANCE. *n.* Avoidance.

VOIR DIRE. [Fr.] 1. An initial examination to determine the competency of a juror or witness. 2. ". . . [A] 'trial within a trial'. It is merely a descriptive phrase to describe a procedure which takes place, namely. a procedure to determine the admissibility of certain evidence." *R. v. Brydon* (1983), 6 C.C.C. (3d) 68 at 70 (B.C. C.A.), Craig J.A.

VOLENTI NON FIT INJURIA. [L.] 1. Wrong is not done to someone who is willing. J.G. Fleming, *The Law of Torts*, 8th ed. (Sydney: Law Book, 1992) at 79. 2. ". . . [V]olenti will arise only where the circumstances are such that it is clear that the plaintiff, knowing of the virtually certain risk of harm, in essence bargained away his right to sue for injuries incurred as a result of any negligence on the defendant's part. The acceptance of risk may be express or may arise by necessary implication from the conduct of the parties, but it will arise, in cases such as the present, only where there can truly be said to be an understanding on the part of both parties that the defendant assumed no responsibility to take due care for the safety of the plaintiff, and that the plaintiff did not expect him to." *Dubé v. Labar* (1986), 36 C.C.L.T. 105 at 114-5, 2 B.C.L.R. (2d) 273, 27 D.L.R. (4th) 653, [1986] 3 W.W.R. 750, [1986] 1 S.C.R. 649, Estey J. (McIntyre, Chouinard and Le Dain JJ. concurring). 3. ". . . [I]nvolves not only knowledge of the risk, but also a consent to the legal risk, or, in other words, a waiver of legal rights that may arise from the harm or loss that is being risked. . . ." *Waldick v. Malcolm* (1991), 8 C.C.L.T. (2d) 1 at 17, 3 O.R. (3d) 471n, 125 N.R. 372, 47 O.A.C. 241, 83 D.L.R. (4th) 114, [1991] 2 S.C.R. 456, the court per Iacobucci J. See VOLUNTARY ASSUMPTION OF RISK.

VOLUNTARY. *adj.* ". . . '[W]ithout compulsion' . . ." *R. v. British Columbia (Workmen's Compensation Board)*, [1942] 2 W.W.R. 129 at 133, 57 B.C.R. 412, [1942] 2 D.L.R. 665 (C.A.), McDonald C.J.B.C. (dissenting) (McQuarrie, Sloan, O'Halloran and Fisher JJ.A. concurring).

VOLUNTARY ASSUMPTION OF RISK. "The defence of voluntary assumption of risk is based on the moral supposition that no wrong is done to one who consents. By agreeing to assume the risk the plaintiff absolves the defendant of all responsibility for it . . . Since the volenti defence is a complete bar to recovery and therefore anomalous in an age of apportionment, the Courts have tightly circumscribed its scope. It only applies in situations where the plaintiff has assumed both the physical and the legal risk involved in the activity . . ." *Crocker v. Sundance Northwest Resorts Ltd.* (1988), 44 C.C.L.T. 225 at 239, 86 N.R. 241, 64 O.R. (2d) 64n, [1988] 1 S.C.R. 1186, 29 O.A.C. 1, 51 D.L.R. (4th) 321, [1988] R.R.A. 444, the court per Wilson J. See VOLENTI NON FIT INJURIA.

VOLUNTARY CONVEYANCE. A conveyance by something like a gift with no valuable consideration.

VOLUNTARY WASTE. ". . . [W]aste is either voluntary or permissive . . . voluntary waste involves an act that is either wilful or negligent. Hence, damage to rented premises caused by a fire started by the negligence of the tenant constitutes voluntary waste and the tenant can be held liable: . . ." *Prior v. Hanna* (1987), 55 Alta. L.R. (2d) 276 at 282, 82 A.R. 3, 43 D.L.R. (4th) 612 (Q.B.), Miller A.C.J.Q.B.

VOTE. *v.* See RIGHT TO ~.

VOTE. *n.* 1. A ballot paper which has been detached from the counterfoil, and has been furnished to a voter, and has been marked and deposited as a vote by the voter. 2. Suffrage. See CASTING ~; FREE ~.

VOTE BY SECRET BALLOT. A vote by ballots cast in such a manner that a person expressing a choice cannot be identified with the choice expressed.

VOTER. *n.* 1. Any person entitled to vote. 2. Any person who votes at an election.

VOTERS LIST. *var.* **VOTERS' LIST.** 1. Includes any list made and revised of persons entitled to vote at an election. 2. A list of electors required to be prepared.

VOTES AND PROCEEDINGS. A record of proceedings of the House of Commons. A. Fraser, W.A. Dawson, & J. Holtby, eds., *Beauchesne's Rules and Forms of the House of Commons of Canada*, 6th ed. (Toronto: Carswell, 1989) at 299.

VOTING SECURITY. Any security other than a debt security of an issuer carrying a voting right either under all circumstances or under some circumstances that have occurred and are continuing.

VOTING SHARE. Any share that carries voting rights under all circumstances or by reason of an event that has occurred and is continuing.

VOTING TRUST. The rights to vote some or all shares of a corporation are settled upon trustees who under the terms of the trust have authority, with or without restriction, to exercise the voting rights. S.M. Beck *et al.*, *Cases and Materials on Partnerships and Canadian Business Corporations*, (Toronto: Carswell, 1983) at 650.

VOUCH. *v.* To call on; to rely on; to quote authoritatively.

VOUCHER. *n.* 1. A document which is evidence of a transaction, i.e. a receipt for money paid. 2. An instrument issued under this Act and the regulations that authorizes the supplying of specified goods or the rendering of specified services to the person named therein. *Social Welfare Act*, R.S.N.B. 1973, c. S-11, s. 1.

VS. *abbr*. Versus.

W

WAFER. *n.* A small circle of red paper used to seal a deed instead of sealing wax.

WAGE. *n.* 1. Any compensation measured by time, piece or otherwise. 2. Salary, pay, commission or remuneration for work. See BASIC ~; MINIMUM ~; ~S.

WAGER. *n.* "[A contract by which] ... two persons, professing to hold opposite views touching the issue of a future uncertain event, mutually agree that dependent upon the determination of that event one shall win from the other, and that the other shall pay or hand over to him a sum of money or other stake, neither of the contracting parties having any other interest in that contract than the sum or stake he will win or lose, there being no other real consideration for the making of such a contract by either of the parties. It is essential to a wagering contract that each party may under it either win or lose ..." *Carlill v. Carbolic Smoke Ball Co.*, [1892] 2 Q.B. 484 at 490-91 (U.K.), Hawkins J.

WAGERING CONTRACT. A mutual promise by which each party gains or loses by the outcome of an uncertain event. Each party's promise is her or his only interest in the transaction. G.H.L. Fridman, *The Law of Contract in Canada*, 2d ed. (Toronto: Carswell, 1986) at 334.

WAGES. *n.* "... [A]ny compensation for labour or services." *Davenport, Re* (1930), (*sub nom. Davenport v. McNiven*) [1930] 4 D.L.R. 386 at 387,

[1930] 2 W.W.R. 263, 42 B.C.R. 468 (C.A.), Macdonald C.J.B.C. See ATTACHMENT OF ~; FAIR ~; WAGE.

WAIVE. *v.* To surrender or renounce a right, privilege or claim.

WAIVER. *n.* 1. An act by which one party relieves the other from performing an obligation or from liability for not performing without actually ending the contract. G.H.L. Fridman, *Sale of Goods in Canada*, 3d ed. (Toronto: Carswell, 1986) at 274. 2. "[To forego] ... reliance upon some known right or defect. It is important that the right or defect, as the case may be, be known, since one should not be able to waive rights of which he was not fully aware or apprised. ... In determining whether waiver applies, the defendant must take steps in the proceedings knowingly and to its prejudice, which amount to foregoing a reliance upon some right or defect. In order to waive a right it must be a known right. ..." *Marchischuk v. Dominion Industrial Supplies Ltd.* (1991), 3 C.C.L.I. (2d) 173 at 176-7, 30 M.V.R. (2d) 102, [1991] 4 W.W.R. 673, [1991] I.L.R. 1-2729, 125 N.R. 306, 80 D.L.R. (4th) 670, 50 C.P.C. (2d) 231, [1991] 2 S.C.R. 61, 73 Man. R. (2d) 271, 3 W.A.C. 271, the court per Sopinka J. adopting the reasons of the trial judge. 3. "... [W]aiver does not confer rights, it repudiates them. If you waive your right to A, it does not mean that you are entitled to B. It means only that you are no longer entitled to A." *R. v. Turpin* (1989), 39 C.R.R. 306 at 329, 69 C.R. (3d) 97, 48 C.C.C. (3d) 8, 96 N.R. 115, [1989] 1

S.C.R. 1296, 34 O.A.C. 115, the court per Wilson J.

WANTONNESS. *n.* "[In Criminal Code, R.S.C. 1970, c. C-34, s. 202(1)] . . perhaps a subclass of recklessness. It is a wild, mad or arrogant kind of recklessness and thus closely related to 'wilfulness'." *R. v. Walker* (1974), 26 C.R.N.S. 268 at 273, 18 C.C.C. (2d) 179 (N.S. C.A.), MacKeigan C.J.N.S.

WAR CRIME. An act or omission that is committed during an international conflict, whether or not it constitutes a contravention of the law in force at the time and in the place of its commission, and that, at that time and in that place, constitutes a contravention of the customary international law or conventional international law applicable in international armed conflicts. *Criminal Code*, S.C. 1987, c. 37, s. 1(1).

WARD. *n.* 1. An electoral division. 2. A child committed to the care and custody of the Director or a Society. *Child Welfare acts*.

WARDSHIP. *n.* Guardianship.

WARDSHIP ORDER. See CROWN ~.

WARRANT. *n.* 1. The order of a judicial authority that a ministerial officer arrest, seize, search or execute some judicial sentence. 2. An option; an agreement by a corporation to sell to the holder a certain number of shares at a price specified in the agreement. S.M. Beck *et al.*, *Cases and Materials on Partnerships and Canadian Business Corporations* (Toronto: Carswell, 1983) at 788. See BACK A ~; BENCH ~; SEARCH ~; SHARE ~.

WARRANTEE. *n.* A person to whom one makes a warranty.

WARRANTOR. *n.* A party who warrants.

WARRANTY. *n.* ". . . [A] term in contract which does not go to the root of the agreement between the parties but simply expresses some lesser obligation, the failure to perform which can give rise to an action for damages but never to the right to rescind or repudiate the contract: . . ." *Fraser-Reid v. Droumtsekas* (1980), 103 D.L.R. (3d) 385 at 392, [1980] 1 S.C.R. 720, 29 N.R. 424, 9 R.P.R. 121, Dickson J. (Martland, Estey and McIntyre JJ. concurring).

WAR RISKS. The risks of loss or damage arising from hostilities, rebellion, revolution, civil war, piracy, action taken to repel an imagined attack or from civil strife consequent to their happening. *Marine and Aviation War Risks Act*, R.S.C. 1970, c. W-3, s. 2.

WASTE. *n.* 1. "Waste in law is destruction of a part of the inheritance by a limited owner, such as a tenant for life or years." *"Freiya" (The) v. "R.S." (The)* (1922), 65 D.L.R. 218 at 222, [1922] 1 W.W.R. 409, 21 Ex. C.R. 232, Audette J. 2. ". . . [W]aste is either voluntary or permissive . . . voluntary waste involves an act that is either wilful or negligent. Hence, damage to rented premises caused by a fire started by the negligence of the tenant constitutes voluntary waste and the tenant can be held liable: . . . Permissive waste involves the failure or omission to take some precaution which results in damage to the property." *Prior v. Hanna* (1987), 55 Alta. L.R. (2d) 276 at 282, 82 A.R. 3, 43 D.L.R. (4th) 612 (Q.B.), Miller A.C.J.Q.B. See AMELIORATING ~; PERMISSIVE ~; VOLUNTARY ~.

WASTING ASSET. Property which exists under restriction, such as a natural resource or leasehold.

WAYS AND MEANS MOTION. The first step needed before Parliament imposes a new tax, continues an expiring tax, increases the rate of an existing tax or extends a tax to include people not already paying. A. Fraser, W.A. Dawson, & J. Holtby, eds., *Beauchesne's Rules and Forms of the House of Commons of Canada*, 6th ed. (Toronto: Carswell, 1989) at 265.

W.C.A.T.R. *abbr.* Workers' Compensation Appeals Tribunal Reporter.

W.C.B. *abbr.* 1. Workers' Compensation Board. 2. Workmen's Compensation Board.

W.D.C.P. *abbr.* Weekly Digest of Civil Procedure.

WEAPON. *n.* 1. (a) Anything used, designed to be used or intended for use in causing death or injury to any person or (b) anything used, designed to be used or intended for use for the purpose of threatening or intimidating any person, and, without restricting the generality of the foregoing, includes any firearm as defined in subsection 84(1). *Criminal Code*, S.C. 1991, c. 40, s. 1. 2. A firearm or any other device that propels a projectile by means of an explosion, spring, air, gas, string, wire or elastic material or any combination of those things. *Wildlife Act*, S.A. 1984, c. W-9.1, s. 1. 3. Includes any thing by which a person may cause harm to himself or herself or to another person. *Provincial Offences Procedure Act*, S.N.B. 1987, c. P-22.1, s. 1. See AUTOMATIC ~; OFFENSIVE ~; RESTRICTED ~.

WEAR AND TEAR. The waste of any material by ordinary use.

WEIGHT OF EVIDENCE. For the evidence of one side to be so far superior to the other's that the verdict should go to the first.

WEST. L. REV. *abbr.* Western Law Review (1961-1966).

WESTMINSTER. See STATUTE OF ~.

WEST. ONT. L. REV. *abbr.* Western Ontario Law Review (1967-1976).

WHITE PAPER. An official government memorandum which sets out a problem and the issues related to it with the policy the government recommends.

WHOLE HOUSE. See COMMITTEE OF THE ~.

WHOLESALER. *n.* "... [T]o be one, the sale must not only be in large quantities but it must be to a person other than the end-user...." *Buchman & Son Lumber Co. v. Ontario Regional Assessment Commissioner, Region No., 9* (1982), 141 D.L.R. (3d) 95 at 97, 20 M.P.L.R. 78, 14 O.M.B.R. 166 (Div. Ct.), Steele J. (O'Leary J. concurring).

WILFULLY. *adv.* 1. "... [D]eliberately and purposefully ..." *R. v. Hafey* (1985), (*sub nom. R. v. Stoke-Graaham*) 44 C.R. (3d) 289 at 298, [1985] 1 S.C.R. 106, 67 N.S.R. (2d) 181, 155 A.P.R. 181, 17 C.C.C. (3d) 289, 16 D.L.R. (4th) 321, 57 N.R. 321, Dickson J. 2. "... [H]as not been uniformly interpreted and its meaning to some extent depends upon the context in which it is used. Its primary meaning is 'intentionally', but it is also used to mean 'recklessly' ... The word 'wilfully' has, however, also been held to mean no more than that the accused's act is done intentionally and not accidentally." *R. v. Buzzanga* (1979), 101 D.L.R. (3d) 488 at 498, 500, 25 O.R. (2d) 705, 49 C.C.C. (2d) 369 (C.A.), Martin J.A.

WILFULNESS. *n.* "... [M]ust imply both deliberation and knowledge ..." *R. v. Hafey* (1985), (*sub nom. R. v. Stoke-Graaham*) 44 C.R. (3d) 289 at 307, [1985] 1 S.C.R. 106, 67 N.S.R. (2d) 181, 155 A.P.R. 181, 17 C.C.C. (3d) 289, 16 D.L.R. (4th) 321, 57 N.R. 321, Wilson J.

WILL. *n.* The written statement by which a person instructs how her or his estate should be distributed after death. See ADMINISTRATOR WITH ~ ANNEXED; CONDITIONAL ~; GRANT OF ADMINISTRATION WITH ~ ANNEXED; HOLOGRAPH ~; LETTERS OF ADMINISTRATION WITH ~ ANNEXED; MUTUAL ~S; NUNCUPATIVE ~; TENANCY AT ~.

WINDING UP. *var.* WINDING-UP. 1. The process of ending the business of a corporation or partnership by settling accounts and liquidating assets. 2. In relation to a pension plan that has been terminated, the process of distributing the assets of the plan.

WINDING-UP ORDER. An order granted by a court under this Act to wind up the business of a company, and includes any order granted by the court to bring under this Act any company in liquidation or in process of being wound up. *Winding-up Act*, R.S.C. 1985, c. W-11, s. 2.

WINDSOR Y.B. ACCESS JUST.

abbr. The Windsor Yearbook of Access to Justice.

WINDSOR Y.B. ACCESS JUSTICE. *abbr.* The Windsor Yearbook of Access to Justice (Recueil annuel de Windsor d'accès à la justice).

WIT. See TO ~.

WITH COSTS. In the expression "motion dismissed with costs", means that costs will be assessed and paid only when the trial is over. M.M. Orkin, *The Law of Costs*, 2d ed. (Aurora: Canada Law Book, 1987) at 1-13.

WITHDRAWAL. *n.* 1. Unlike a stay of proceedings which has statutory basis in Canadian law, withdrawal of charge is based on English common law, in force through section 8(2) of the Criminal Code. S.A. Cohen, *Due Process of Law* (Toronto: Carswell, 1977) at 157. 2. "... When a charge has been withdrawn, there is no charge on record, and in order to continue the prosecution a new charge would have to be laid. Withdrawing a charge has the effect of ending the proceedings." *R. v. Leonard* (1962), (sub nom. *Crown Practice Rules, Re*) 38 W.W.R. 300 at 303, 37 C.R. 374, 133 C.C.C. 230 (Alta. T.D.), Kirby J. 3. For a defendant to retract a defence by filing and serving written notice. Formerly also meant discontinuance by a plaintiff of part, not the whole, action. G.D. Watson & C. Perkins, eds., *Holmested & Watson: Ontario Civil Procedure* (Toronto: Carswell, 1984) at 23-19.

WITHOUT PREJUDICE. 1. "The use of this expression ['without prejudice'] is commonly understood to mean that if there is no settlement, the party making the offer is free to assert all its rights, unaffected by anything stated or done in the negotiations." *Maracle v. Travellers Indemnity Co. of Canada* (1991), 50 C.P.C. (2d) 213 at 222, [1991] I.L.R. 1-2728, 125 N.R. 294, 3 O.R. (3d) 510n, 80 D.L.R. (4th) 652, 3 C.C.L.I. (2d) 186, 47 O.A.C. 333, [1991] 2 S.C.R. 50, the court per Sopinka J. 2. "... [A] party to a correspondence within the 'without prejudice' privilege is, generally speaking, protected from being required to disclose it on discovery or at trial in proceedings by or against a third party." *I. Waxman & Sons Ltd. v. Texaco Canada Ltd.*, [1968] 2 O.R. 452 at 453, 69 D.L.R. (2d) 543 (C.A.), the court per Aylesworth J.A. quoting the trial judge. 3. "... [T]he words 'without prejudice' [endorsing an order] do not operate to freeze time limitations or suspend any other application of the law, but simply prevent the respondent from raising the defence of res judicata and that the endorsement should be given its plain meaning ..." *Ternoey v. Goulding* (1982), 25 R.F.L. (2d) 113 at 120, 35 O.R. (2d) 29, 132 D.L.R. (3d) 44 (C.A.), Houlden J.A. (Howland C.J.O. concurring).

WITHOUT RECOURSE TO ME. A phrase used to protect the indorser of a note or bill from liability.

WITNESS. *n.* 1. "... [O]ne who, in the course of judicial processes, attests to matters of fact; ..." *Bell v. Klein (No. 1)*, [1955] S.C.R. 309 at 317, [1955] 2 D.L.R. 513, Rand J. 2. A person who gives evidence orally under oath or by affidavit in a judicial proceeding, whether or not he is competent to be a witness, and includes a child of tender years who gives evidence but does not give it under oath, because, in the opinion of the person presiding, the child does not understand the nature of the oath. *Criminal Code*, R.S.C. 1985, c. C-46, s. 118. See ADVERSE ~; ATTESTING ~; EXPERT ~; EYE-~; HOSTILE ~; MATERIAL ~.

WKRS. *abbr.* Workers(').

[ ] W.L.A.C. *abbr.* Western Labour Arbitration Cases, 1966-.

W.L.R. *abbr.* Western Law Reporter, 1905-1916.

[ ] W.L.R. *abbr.* Weekly Law Reports.

W.L.T. *abbr.* Western Law Times, 1890-1895.

WORDS. *n.* See APT ~; GENERAL ~; PRECATORY ~; SEDITIOUS ~.

WORDS OF ART. Words employed in a technical sense.

WORDS OF LIMITATION. Words which effectively restrict the continuation of an estate.

WORK. *n.* "... [M]ay mean action or exertion put forth to accomplish some end or it may mean the product of or the result of action or exertion." *Ruthenian Sisters of the Immaculate Conception v. Saskatoon (City)*, [1937] 2 W.W.R. 625 at 628 (Sask. C.A.), Martin J.A. (Mackenzie J.A. concurring). See BARGAINING UNIT ~; EQUAL PAY FOR EQUAL ~; RIGHT TO ~; ~S.

WORKER. *n.* 1. An employee. 2. A person who has entered into or works under a contract of service or apprenticeship, written or oral, express or implied, whether by way of manual labour or otherwise and includes a learner. 3. "The word 'worker' includes: (1) a person who enters into a contract of service, and (2) a person who works under a contract of service...." *British Airways Board v. British Columbia (Workers' Compensation Board)* (1985), 61 B.C.L.R. 1 at 16, 13 Admin. L.R. 78, 17 D.L.R. (4th) 36 (C.A.), Macfarlane J.A. (Seaton J.A. concurring). 4. "The definition of 'worker' [in s. 1 of the Occupational Health and Safety Act, R.S.O. 1980, c. 32] applies equally to employment or independent contactor relationships. It does not, for example, restrict the applicability of the statute to contracts of employment as it might have done if the word 'employee' and not the work 'worker' had been used as the correlative to the word 'employer'." *R. v. Wyssen* (1992), 10 O.R. (3d) 193 at 197, 58 O.A.C. 67 (C.A.), Blair J.A. (Dubin C.J.O. concurring).

WORKERS' COMPENSATION. 1. A program to provide financial, rehabilitation and medical assistance to any worker who is partially or totally disabled by an accident which arose "out of and in the course of employment". K.D. Cooper-Stephenson & I.B. Saunders, *Personal Injury Damages in Canada* (Toronto: Carswell, 1981) at 2 and 3. 2. "... [I]s paid to partially replace lost wages due to injury on the job. It is not ... insurance, nor is it damages, nor is it a settlement." *Dixon v. Dixon* (1981), 25 R.F.L. (2d) 266 at 269, 14 Man. R. (2d) 40 (Co. Ct.), Ferg Co. Ct. J. 3. "The primary object of the legislation, broadly speaking, is to provide a machanism whereby workmen, who fall within the ambit of the Act and who are injured in the workplace, receive compensation, presumably commensurate with their degree of injury, regardless of fault, and, with respect to any such workman who is killed in the workplace, that their dependants receive such compensation as the Act provides. The latter also applies regardless of where fault may lie. The Legislature has also provided that, in return for such benefits as are guaranteed to the workman, or his dependant, any right of action which might otherwise arise out of the incident which occasioned injury or death is forfeited. This is not a government or funded scheme, but rather it is funded by industrial levy. It is not available to all who find employment in the workplace, but only to those who are employed in industry subject to levy." *Jenkins v. Prince Edward Island (Workers' Compensation Board)* (1986), 21 C.C.L.I. 149 at 154, 31 D.L.R. (4th) 536, 61 Nfld. & P.E.I.R. 206, 185 A.P.R. 206, 15 C.C.E.L. 55, 9 C.H.R.R. D/5145 (P.E.I. S.C.), the court per McQuaid J.

WORKING CONDITIONS. "... [C]onditions under which a worker or workers, individually or collectively, provide their services, in accordance with the rights and obligations included in the contract of employment by the consent of the parties or by operation of law, and under which the employer receives those services.... a worker's obligation to provide his or her services and the employer's obligation to pay his or her wages. ... the right to refuse to work, the continuation of the right to wages and other benefits, availability, assignment to other duties and the right to return to employment at the end of the assignment or cessation or work ..." *Québec (Commission de la Santé*

& de la Sécurité du travail) v. Bell Canada, [1988] 1 S.C.R. 749 at 798, 801-2, 51 D.L.R. (4th) 161, 21 C.C.E.L. 1, 85 N.R. 295, 15 Q.A.C. 217, the court per Beetz J.

WORKS. *n.* "... '[P]hysical things, not services'." *Shur Gain Division, Canada Packers Inc., Re* (1991), 85 D.L.R. (4th) 317 at 336, 91 C.L.L.C. 14,046, [1992] 2 F.C. 3, 135 N.R. 6 (C.A.), Desjardins J.A. See CAPITAL ~; WORK.

WORKS FOR THE GENERAL ADVANTAGE OF CANADA. By virtue of section 92(10)(c) and section 91(29) of the Constitution Act, the federal Parliament has power to make laws relating to: "(c) Such works as, although wholly situate within the province, are before or after their execution declared by the Parliament of Canada to be for the general advantage of Canada or for the advantage of two or more of the provinces." P.W. Hogg, *Constitutional Law of Canada*, 3d ed. (Toronto: Carswell, 1992) at 579. See DECLARATORY POWER.

WORSHIP. *n.* The title of a magistrate or mayor.

WOUND. *n.* 1. "... [A] breaking of the skin, ..." *R. v. Hostetter* (1902), 7 C.C.C. 221 at 222 (N.W.T. C.A.), the court per Prendergast J.A. 2. The disrupting of tissue caused by violence. F.A. Jaffe, *A Guide to Pathological Evidence*, 3d ed. (Toronto: Carswell, 1991) at 229. 3. "... [A]n appropriate description of assault causing bodily harm...." *R. v. Lucas* (1987), 34 C.C.C. (3d) 28 at 33, 10 Q.A.C. 47, [1987] R.L. 212 (C.A.), the court per L'Heureux-Dubé J.A.

WRAP-AROUND MORTGAGE. A second mortgage, granted when the first mortgage is small and at a low interest rate, whose principal includes the whole principal of the first mortgage even though the whole amount is not immediately advanced. The second mortgagee must make payments under the first mortgage as long as the second mortgage is valid. If the first mortgage matures, the mortgagee must pay it off and obtain a discharge so that the second mortgage becomes a first mortgage. D.J. Donahue & P.D. Quinn, *Real Estate Practice in Ontario*, 4th ed. (Toronto: Butterworths, 1990) at 226.

WRECK. *n.* 1. (a) Jetsam, flotsam, lagan and derelict found in or on the shores of the sea or of any tidal water, or of any of the inland waters of Canada; (b) cargo, stores, tackle of any vessel and of all parts of the vessel separated therefrom; (c) the property of shipwrecked persons; and (d) any wrecked aircraft or any part thereof and cargo thereof. 2. Includes the cargo, stores and tackle of a vessel and all parts of a vessel separated from the vessel, and the property of persons who belong to, are on board or have quitted a vessel that is wrecked, stranded or in distress at any place in Canada. *Criminal Code*, R.S.C. 1985, c. C-46, s. 2.

WRIT. *n.* 1. The formal order or command of a court which directs or enjoins a person or persons to do or refrain from doing something in particular. 2. A document which originates certain legal proceedings. 3. "... [T]he initial process issuing out of the Court." *Fleishman v. T.A. Allan & Sons* (1932), 45 B.C.R. 553 at 560 (C.A.), Macdonald C.J.B.C. 4. The document addressed by the Chief Electoral Officer to a returning officer requiring an election to be held. See ALIAS ~; CONCURRENT ~; PREROGATIVE ~.

WRIT OF ASSISTANCE. 1. A writ which operates like a search warrant with respect to a crime under the Narcotic Control Act, the Food and Drugs Act, the Customs Act or the Excise Act. It is a general warrant, unlimited in time or place. S.A. Cohen, *Due Process of Law* (Toronto: Carswell, 1977) at 94. 2. "... [A] document issued out of the Federal Court which identifies the holder as a person entitled to exercise without a warrant the statutory powers of search and seizure under the relevant statute. It is like an identification card signifying that the holder is entitled to conduct warrantless searches and seizures pursuant to the search and seizure powers conferred by the relevant statute. Consequently, searches under a writ of assistance are warrantless searches by designated persons pursuant to statutory powers." *R. v. Noble* (1984), 16 C.C.C. (3d) 146 at 156, 48 O.R. (2d) 643, 42 C.R. (3d) 209, 6 O.A.C. 11, 14 D.L.R. (4th) 216, 12 C.R.R. 138 (C.A.), the court per Martin J.A.

WRIT OF DELIVERY. A writ of execution directing that goods be delivered by the defendant to the plaintiff.

WRIT OF EXECUTION. 1. By wide interpretation, most processes available to enforce a judgment; the five main writs are: capias, fi. fa., levari facias, elegit, and extent. C.R.B. Dunlop, *Creditor-Debtor Law in Canada* (Toronto: Carswell, 1981) at 140. 2. By narrower interpretation, the old writ of fi. fa. or its contemporary equivalent. C.R.B. Dunlop, *Creditor-Debtor Law in Canada* (Toronto: Carswell, 1981) at 141. 3. ". . . [C]ommands the sheriff to levy of the goods and lands of the debtor the amount of the judgment debt. Its authority is not limited to property of which the debtor is then presently the owner. It is a warrant to the sheriff to seize and sell any property of the debtor which is not exempt from seizure which he may at any time during its currency be able to find in his bailiwick." *Lee v. Armstrrong* (1917), 37 D.L.R. 738 at 749, [1917] 3 W.W.R. 889, 13 A.L.R. 160 (C.A.), Walsh J.A.

WRIT OF EXTENT. A writ by which a sheriff may seize the lands, goods and body of a debtor without having to choose between execution against the person and execution against property. C.R.B. Dunlop, *Creditor-Debtor Law in Canada* (Toronto: Carswell, 1981) at 449.

WRIT OF FIERI FACIAS. An order that someone, out of a party's goods and chattels, collect the sum recovered by the judgment along with any interest on that sum. C.R.B. Dunlop, *Creditor-Debtor Law in Canada*

(Toronto: Carswell, 1981) at 126.

WRIT OF FI. FA. See WRIT OF FIERI FACIAS.

WRIT OF POSSESSION. A writ to recover the possession of land.

WRIT OF SEIZURE AND SALE. The equivalent of a writ of fieri facias.

WRIT OF SUMMONS. The writ by which an action is commenced.

WRIT OF VENDITIONI EXPONAS. An order that a sheriff sell goods for the best possible price. C.R.B. Dunlop, *Creditor-Debtor Law in Canada* (Toronto: Carswell, 1981) at 400.

WRONG. *n.* 1. Deprivation of a right; an injury. 2. The consequence of the violation or infringement of a right. 3. "[In s. 16(2) of the Criminal Code, R.S.C. 1985, c. C-46] . . . '[M]orally wrong' . . ." *R. v. Ratti* (1991), 2 C.R. (4th) 293 at 301, 120 N.R. 91, 62 C.C.C. (3d) 105, 44 O.A.C. 161, [1991] 1 S.C.R. 68, Lamer C.J.C. (La Forest and Cory JJ. concurring). See EQUITY WILL NOT SUFFER A ~ TO BE WITHOUT A REMEDY; NO MAN CAN TAKE ADVANTAGE OF HIS OWN ~.

WRONGFUL ACT. A failure to exercise reasonable skill or care toward the deceased which causes or contributes to the death of the deceased. *Fatal Accidents Act*, R.S.P.E.I. 1988, c. F-5, s. 1(n).

WRONGFUL DISMISSAL. The unjustified dismissal of an employee from employment by the employer. 2. "In wrongful dismissal cases, the wrong suffered by the employee is the breach by the employer of the implied contractual term to give reasonable notice before terminating the contract of employment. Damages are awarded to place the employee in the same position as he/she would have been had reasonable notice been given." *Piazza v. Airport Taxi Cab (Malton) Assn.* (1989), 26 C.C.E.L. 191 at 194, 69 O.R. (2d) 281, 60 D.L.R. (4th) 759, 234 O.A.C. 349, 10 C.H.R.R. D/6347 (C.A.), Zuber J.A.

W.W.D. *abbr.* Western Weekly Digests, 1975-1976.

W.W.R. *abbr.* Western Weekly Reports, 1912-1916.

[ ] W.W.R. *abbr.* Western Weekly Reports, 1917-1950 and 1971-.

W.W.R. (N.S.). *abbr.* Western Weekly Reports (New Series), 1951-1970.

Y

Y.A.D. *abbr.* Young's Admiralty Decisions (N.S.), 1865-1880.

YEAR. *n.* 1. A calendar year. 2. Any period of 12 consecutive months. 3. Any period of 12 consecutive months, except that a reference (a) to a "calendar year" means a period of 12 consecutive months commencing on January 1; (b) to a "financial year" or "fiscal year" means, in relation to money provided by Parliament, or the Consolidated Revenue Fund, or the accounts, taxes or finances of Canada, the period beginning on April 1 in one calendar year and ending on March 31 in the next calendar year; and (c) by number to a Dominical year means the period of 12 consecutive months commencing on January 1 of that Dominical year. *Interpretation Act*, R.S.C. 1985, c. I-21, s. 37. 4. Three hundred and sixty-five days. See EXECUTOR'S ~; FINANCIAL ~; FISCAL ~; REGNAL ~; TAXATION ~.

YIELDING AND PAYING. In a lease, the first words used in a reddendum clause.

YOU CANNOT DO INDIRECTLY WHAT YOU CANNOT DO DIRECTLY. "The maxim 'you cannot do indirectly what you cannot do directly" is a much abused one. It was used to invalidate legislation ... It is a pithy way of describing colourable legislation: ... However, it does not preclude a limited legislature from achieving directly under one head of legislative power what it could not do

directly under another head." *Reference re Questions Concerning Amendment to the Constitution of Canada as set out in O.C. 1020/80* (1981), (*sub nom. Resolution to Amend the Constitution of Canada, Re*) 1 C.R.R. 59 at 94, [1981] 1 S.C.R. 753, [1981] 6 W.W.R. 1, 11 Man. R. (2d) 1, 39 N.R. 1, 34 Nfld. & P.E.I.R. 1, 95 A.P.R. 1, Laskin C.J.C., Dickson, Beetz, Estey, McIntyre, Chouinard and Lamer JJ.

YOUNG ADM. *abbr.* Young's Admiralty Decisions (N.S.).

YOUNG OFFENDER. See YOUNG PERSON.

YOUNG PERSON. 1. A person who is or, in the absence of evidence to the contrary, appears to be 12 years of age or more, but under 18 years of age and, where the context requires, includes any person who is charged under this Act with having committed an offence while he was a young person or is found guilty of an offence under this Act. *Young Offenders Act*, R.S.C. 1985, c. Y-1, s. 2. 2. A person fourteen years of age or more but under the age of eighteen years. *Criminal Code*, S.C. 1987, c. 24, s. 146(2).

YOUTH COURT. A court established or designated by or under an Act of the legislature of a province, or designated by the Governor in Council or the Lieutenant Governor in Council of a province, as a youth court for the purposes of this Act. *Young Offenders Act*, R.S.C. 1985, c. Y-1, s. 2.

Y.R. *abbr.* Yukon Reports.

Z

ZONING. *n.* 1. The control of the use of land. 2. "The objectives of modern zoning legislation are described in [I.M.] Rogers's Canadian Law of Planning and Zoning (Toronto: Carswell, 1973 (looseleaf)) at 115 where the author states: 'Zoning is a form of regulation of property by local governments. It is the division of a municipality into zones or areas and in each area either prohibiting certain uses and allowing all the others or permitting the uses which may be carried on to the exclusion of all others. . . . Zoning is the deprivation for the public good of certain uses by owners of property to which the property might otherwise be put. Underlying planning statutes is the principle that the interest of landowners in securing the maximum value of their land must be controlled by the community. . . . The objective of zoning must be considered from the standpoint of the public welfare and of all the property within any particular use district.' " *Zive Estate v. Lynch* (1989), 47 M.P.L.R. 310 at 314, 7 R.P.R. (2d) 180, 94 N.S.R. (2d) 401, 247 A.P.R. 401 (C.A.), the court per Macdonald J.A. See DEVELOPMENT CONTROL.

ZONING BYLAW. ". . . [R]emedial in character in that one of their objectives is to preserve existing property from depreciation. They are designed not only to protect residential neighbourhoods against intrusion of buildings to be used for commercial and manufacturing or trade purposes, but to confine commercial and industrial purposes to specific parts of the municipality to the exclusion of residential construction: . . ." *Zive Estate v. Lynch* (1989), 47 M.P.L.R. 310 at 315, 7 R.P.R. (2d) 180, 94 N.S.R. (2d) 401, 247 A.P.R. 401 (C.A.), the court per Macdonald J.A.